Comparative Politics

Comparative Politics

Edited by
Daniele Caramani

OXFORD
UNIVERSITY PRESS

OXFORD

UNIVERSITY PRESS

Great Clarendon Street, Oxford OX2 6DP

Oxford University Press is a department of the University of Oxford.
It furthers the University's objective of excellence in research, scholarship,
and education by publishing worldwide in

Oxford New York

Auckland Cape Town Dar es Salaam Hong Kong Karachi
Kuala Lumpur Madrid Melbourne Mexico City Nairobi
New Delhi Shanghai Taipei Toronto

With offices in

Argentina Austria Brazil Chile Czech Republic France Greece
Guatemala Hungary Italy Japan Poland Portugal Singapore
South Korea Switzerland Thailand Turkey Ukraine Vietnam

Oxford is a registered trade mark of Oxford University Press
in the UK and in certain other countries

Published in the United States
by Oxford University Press Inc., New York

British Library Cataloguing in Publication Data

Data available

Library of Congress Cataloging in Publication Data

Comparative politics / edited by Daniele Caramani.
       p. cm.
    ISBN 978–0–19–929841–9
    1. Political science—Study and teaching.   2. Comparative government.
I. Caramani, Daniele.
    JA86.C526 2008
       320.3—dc22

                                                    2007047245

Typeset by Laserwords Private Limited, Chennai, India
Printed in Italy
on acid-free paper by
Leqoprint S.p.A

ISBN 978–0–19–929841–9

10 9 8 7 6 5 4 3 2 1

Preface

About the book

In designing this new textbook on *Comparative Politics* the ambition has been to produce an exciting, authoritative, and up-to-date teaching instrument. We have tried to write chapters of the highest standards in terms of their contents with information presented comparatively and supported by cutting-edge theories and a rigorous methodology. We aimed at comprehensive chapters in their substantive coverage of the field, and a worldwide range of countries.

We hope that the book that resulted from these endeavours will speak to comparative politics students at all levels, as well as to teachers who will use it for their classes. Our goal was to produce an integrated text with a maximum of cross-references between chapters. On the other hand, the modular structure with self-contained chapters should maximize its appeal to lecturers and students, alongside an accessible language enhanced by a number of learning features and a similar format throughout. This structure does not require that it is read cover-to-cover. The book can thus be used in any order, and makes it possible to compose courses with a 'variable geometry'. For the same reason, more but shorter chapters have been preferred to fewer and longer ones.

Rationale for the book

First, the volume aims at a *comprehensive and wide-ranging coverage*, both the coverage of the *subject areas* of comparative politics and the *geographical* spread of cases. The range of countries includes not only advanced industrial nations but also developing regions and emerging economies (in post-communist countries, Latin America, Asia, the Middle East, and Africa).

The range of topics, too, is more comprehensive than most commonly taught courses in comparative politics. On the one hand, throughout the book attention is given to *theory and methodology*, and three chapters on the comparative approach deal specifically with these topics in Section 1 on 'Theories and methods'. As far as possible all chapters include the most important theoretical approaches in each field of the discipline and present the most recent advances and current debates. Deliberately no specific approach has been privileged. Methodologically, it is based on rigorous comparative analysis and up-to-date empirical data.

On the other hand, the range of *substantive topics* is reflected in a number of chapters that add to the usual core areas of comparative politics courses. The book devotes a great deal of attention to sub-national institutions and actors (Chapters 11 and 15) and to non-institutional actors such as interest groups, social movements, and media (in Section 4 on 'Actors and processes'). Most importantly, perhaps, the book includes an entire section on 'Public policies': not only how policies are made but also their impact on economies and societies (with a focus on the welfare state in Europe and its undergoing reform). This gives a better balance between the 'input' and 'output' sides of the political system. Finally, the book has an entire section (Section 6 on 'Beyond the nation-state') on, first, new types of political systems (such as the European

Union) and, second, on interactions between political systems and which take into account transnational and international factors that affect politics at the supra-national, national, and sub-national level. Theoretically this section deals with major challenges to comparative politics.

In spite of the wide coverage of topics, a number of them had to be omitted, namely a larger section on theories, a chapter on political ideologies, a chapter on comparative political economy, and a chapter on institutional engineering and reform. Most of the topics in these fields are dealt with in the chapters of the book as they stand now, as well as in the Online Resource Centre that accompanies this book: www.oxfordtextbooks.co.uk/orc/caramani/.

The second important feature is the *analytical and comparative* approach of the volume. Information and data are presented thematically rather than country-by-country and systematic comparison between countries is carried out on specific political, institutional, and socio-economic phenomena. For us, comparative politics should not be reduced to the one-by-one description of single countries. Case studies (see the various 'Country profiles') are theoretically useful only if inserted in a broader comparative framework. We understand comparative politics in analytical terms, as a combination of substance (the study of political systems, actors, and processes) and method, i.e. identifying and explaining differences and similarities between cases through the test of hypotheses about relationships—law-like generalizations—between concepts and variables applicable in more than one context.

This thematic, analytical, and comparative approach leads to the basic choice of organizing chapters by topics rather than by countries. The book is organized around major substantive themes, and the discussion of countries takes place in the context of these themes, rather than in a set of country studies.

Third, the book presents a large amount of *comparative empirical data*. The analytical approach of the book leads us to present information and data in tables and figures throughout the chapters (as well as in the 'World data' tables and 'Comparative tables'). Many of these data are previously unpublished and have been collected for this textbook.

Particular attention is given to historical trends, longitudinal data, and time series (see 'Trends' figures). The book is comparative and contemporary but, in addition, it includes a long-term perspective allowing a better appreciation of current changes. It thus combines *time and space dimensions*. There is a specific reason for this. The development of the modern nation-state and of mass democracies in the nineteenth century are a unique change that has no previous equivalent in history. This change involved a totally new political organization—based on principles of individual equality, civil liberties, voting rights—and social organization, in particular with industrialization and the following development of the welfare state towards the end of the century. The understanding of contemporary society can therefore not be complete without a long-term perspective highlighting the scope of these changes.

The empirical approach leads us also to provide students with the possibility of *analysing data* themselves. The Online Resource Centre includes a large amount of *comparative data*, making it not just a learning device but a truly research-oriented data depository. With files in different formats, students can analyse data and teachers prepare exercises. Furthermore, a web directory allows students to look for and collect more data in the internet archives of international and national organizations, official and academic data collections, websites specializing in elections, referenda, or survey data and opinion polls.

The Online Resource Centre is therefore not simply the electronic version of the printed book. Although it includes also additional substantial information that could not be fitted on paper—as well as learning devices such as review questions, PowerPoint presentations of each chapter, extra tables and figures, and exam questions—its most important feature is that it allows empirical data analysis. We believe that comparative politics is an empirical discipline and that theories and methods are of no use if they are not combined with data. The website makes this textbook an ongoing and cumulative project with information and material that will be placed on it over the years.

In attempting to reach these goals, we are aware that we have not produced an 'easy' book. We believe, however, that most students are much better, more motivated, and harder working than is often assumed. And we believe also that it is when confronted with challenge and unexplored fields that young people enjoy learning, perform best, and acquire self-confidence. Against what seems a trend towards scholarization of university teaching (either to increase numbers of students or degrees awarded), we are convinced that an effort on the part of students will be rewarding and that they will learn from this book and its website. Comparative politics is a broad and fascinating discipline dealing with important current world issues. Studying it will prove a life-time investment.

Acknowledgements

We very much appreciate that Oxford University Press—and our editor Ruth Anderson in particular—shared this approach with strong commitment and encouragement, and supported us substantially, technically, and logistically. As editor of the volume, I am very grateful that Ruth agreed to additional chapters not figuring in the initial plan. From the first steps of the project up to its conclusion, her input has been remarkable and crucial to the successful completion of this volume.

When defining the line-up of contributors the criteria were those of excellence. I am very happy that it has been possible to bring together an outstanding group of highly respected 'comparativists' coming from a spread of nationalities and academic traditions. All are currently engaged in research, and thus are 'research-minded' and in touch with the most recent advances in their fields of expertise. On a personal level, I am honoured that such a prestigious group of scholars has trusted a younger and less experienced colleague to edit this volume. To overcome geographical distance we have set up a website where all outlines and draft chapters could be accessed by all authors through the different stages. This has allowed us to produce a more integrated and coherent volume, increase 'cross-fertilization' between chapters, and reduce the risks of overlap. I am very thankful to the authors of this volume who have worked with high professionality and collaborative spirit.

Finally, I would like to thank my research assistants—Patrick Lengg, Matthias Meyer-Schwarzenberger, and Eszter Kiss-Déak—for the marvellous job they did in preparing the Online Resource Centre, the 'Country profiles', the data for the 'Trends' and 'Comparative tables', and, more generally, for supporting us throughout the project with extreme professionalism and dedication. Their substantial criticisms, too, allowed us to clarify obscure points in several chapters. I am deeply grateful to them for their engagement.

Daniele Caramani
July 2007

Guided tour of textbook features

This text is enriched with a range of learning tools to help you navigate the text material and reinforce your knowledge of Comparative Politics. This guided tour shows you how to get the most out of your textbook package.

Reader's guides

Reader's guides at the beginning of every chapter set the scene for upcoming themes and issues to be discussed, and indicate the scope of coverage within each chapter topic.

Boxes

A number of topics benefit from further explanation or exploration in a way that does not disrupt the flow of the main text. Throughout the book, boxes provide you with extra information on particular topics to complement your understanding of the main chapter text.

Country profiles and world trends

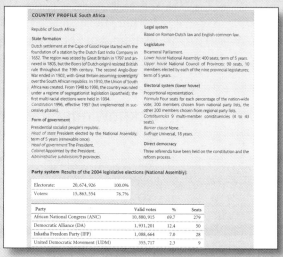

The book includes twenty country profiles with information on each country's state formation, form of government, legal system, legislature, and electoral system.

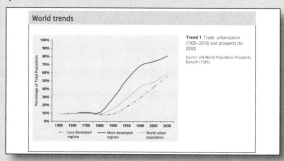

The book also includes eight graphs on world long-term trends such as military expenditures, number of democracies in the world, and urbanization.

Comparative tables

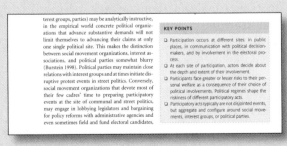

At the end of the book you will find twelve comparative tables which show how different countries compare in terms of topics such as demography and development.

World data

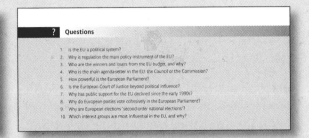

You can also find worldwide information on languages and religions in the world, as well as the most important socio-economic indicators in tables covering the whole world.

Key points

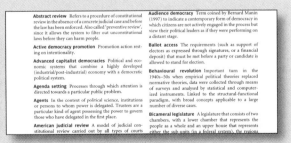

Each main chapter section ends with a set of key points that summarize the most important arguments developed within each chapter topic.

Questions

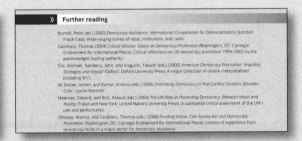

A set of carefully devised questions has been provided to help you assess your comprehension of core themes, and may also be used as the basis of seminar discussion and coursework.

Further reading

To take your learning further, reading lists have been provided as a guide to find out more about the issues raised within each chapter topic and to help you locate the key academic literature in the field.

Glossary terms

Key terms appear in colour in the text and are defined in a glossary at the end of the text, to aid you in exam revision.

Guided tour of the Online Resource Centre

The Online Resource Centre that accompanies this book provides students and instructors with a wealth of ready-to-use research, learning, and teaching materials.

www.oxfordtextbooks.co.uk/orc/caramani/

For research

Comparative data sets

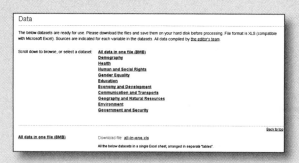

Comparative data is available in Excel format for about 200 countries. Files include more than 200 indicators on:

1. demography
2. health
3. human and social rights
4. gender equality
5. education
6. economy and development
7. communication and transports
8. geography and natural resources
9. environment
10. government and security.

Information is taken from official national sources and international organizations. These files can be used for empirical analysis, essay writing, and lab exercises with computer programmes for data analysis.

Web directory

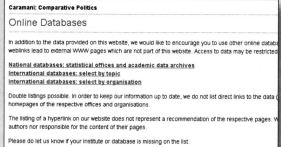

A web directory has been provided to point you in the direction of general statistics made available by international organizations; international academic data archives; national data archives; national statistical offices; national institutions; elections and direct democracy websites; and survey data.

For students

The 'Country Comparator'

This interactive tool allows students to select specific information on several countries and compare them on the screen.

Country profiles

An interactive world map is provided with 'hot spots' on a selection of countries. Simply click on the country you are interested in knowing more about, and a pop-up window will appear with information on its state formation, form of government, legal system, legislature, and electoral system.

Web links

Annotated web links from each chapter in the book.

Flashcard glossary

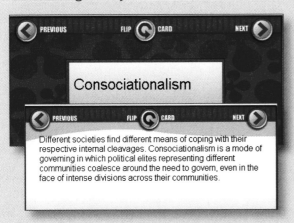

A series of interactive flashcards containing key terms and concepts have been provided to test your understanding of terminology.

Review questions and exercises

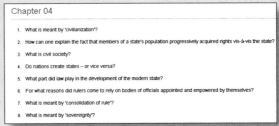

A suite of review questions and exercises to encourage class debate and reinforce understanding of key chapter themes.

For lecturers

PowerPoint slides

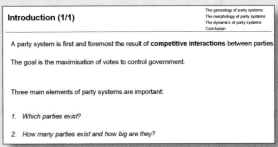

A suite of customizable PowerPoint slides has been included for use in lectures. Arranged by chapter, the slides may also be used as hand-outs in class.

Figures and tables from the textbook

Additional figures and tables plus those in the textbook are available to download electronically to assist lecturer preparation and help explain key concepts.

Contents in brief

Detailed contents

List of country profiles

List of world trends

List of comparative tables

List of figures

List of boxes

List of tables

Abbreviations

The list of abbreviations does not include the names of political parties, trade unions, social movements, interest groups, or other organizations.

2RS	Two-round (electoral) system
AV	Alternative vote (electoral system)
CAP	Common Agricultural Policy (European Union)
CDI	Centre for Democratic Institutions (Australia)
CFSP	Common Foreign and Security Policy (European Union)
CIS	Commonwealth of Independent States
CLRAE	Congress of Local and Regional Authorities of Europe
CMEs	Coordinated Market Economies
CMP	Comparative Manifesto Project
DG	Democracy and Governance
ECB	European Central Bank
ECJ	European Court of Justice
ECSC	European Coal and Steel Community
EEA	European Economic Area
EEC	European Economic Communities
EIDHR	European Initiative for Democracy and Human Rights (European Union)
EMU	Economic and Monetary Union
ENEP	Effective Number of Elective Parties
ENP	European Neighbourhood Policy (European Union)
ENPP	Effective Number of Parliamentary Parties
EP	European Parliament
ESDP	European Security and Defence Cooperation (European Union)
ESS	European Social Survey
EU	European Union
F	Fractionalisation index
FAO	United Nations Food and Agriculture Organization
FCO	Foreign and Commonwealth Office (UK)
FDI	Foreign Direct Investment
FPTP	First-past-the-post (electoral system)
GDP	Gross Domestic Product
GEM	Gender Empowerment Measure
GWP	Gross World Product
ICC	International Criminal Court
ICTs	Information and Communication Technologies
IGO	International Governmental Organizations
ILO	International Labour Organisation
INGO	International Non-Governmental Organizations
IRI	International Republican Institute (US)

ISO	International Organization for Standardization
LMEs	Liberal Market Economies
LSq	Least Square index
MDSD	Most Different Systems Design
MEP	Member of European Parliament
MMM	Mixed-member majoritarian (electoral system)
MMP	Mixed-member proportional (electoral system)
MP	Member of Parliament
MSSD	Most Similar Systems Design
NAFTA	North American Free Trade Agreement
NATO	North Atlantic Treaty Organisation
NDI	National Democratic Institute for International Affairs (US)
NED	National Endowment for Democracy (US)
NEPAD	New Partnership for Africa's Development
NIMD	Netherlands Institute for Multiparty Democracy
NPM	New Public Management
OAS	Organization of American States
OCA	Optimal Currency Area
ODA	Official Development Assistance
OECD	Organisation for Economic Co-operation and Development
OMC	Open Method of Coordination
OPEC	Organization of Petroleum Exporting Countries
OSCE	Organization for Security and Co-operation in Europe
PACs	Political Action Committees
PDA	Personal Digital Assisstant
PPP	Purchasing Power Parities
PR	Proportional representation (electoral system)
QMV	Qualified Majority Voting (European Union)
RoP	Rules of Procedure (legislatures)
RSS	Really Simple Syndication
SGP	Stability and Growth Pact
SIDA	Swedish International Development Cooperation Agency
SMEs	Social Market Economies
SMO	Social Movement Organisation
SMP	Single-member plurality (electoral system)
STV	Single transferable vote (electoral system)
TNC	Transnational companies
UFW	United Farm Workers
UN	United Nations
UNCTAD	United Nations Conference on Trade and Development
UNDP	United Nations Development Programme
USAID	United States Agency for International Development
USSR	Union of Soviet Socialist Republics
WEF	World Economic Forum
WFD	Westminster Foundation for Democracy (UK)
WHO	World Health Organization
WTO	World Trade Organization
WVS	World Value Survey

About the contributors

Klaus von Beyme is Emeritus Professor at the Institute of Political Science, University of Heidelberg, Germany. His research interests include the analysis of institutions and political regimes, political parties and trade unions, as well as political theories and the history of ideologies and political thought. His publications include *Political Parties in Western Democracies* (Gower, 1985), *Transitions to Democracy in Eastern Europe* (Macmillan, 1996), *Parliamentary Democracy* (Macmillan, 2000), *The Legislator: German Parliament as a Decision-Making Centre* (St Martin's Press, 1998), *Politische Theorien im Zeitalter der Ideologien: 1789–1945* (Westdeutscher Verlag, 2002).

James Bickerton is Professor of Political Science at St Francis Xavier University, Canada. He received his Ph.D. from Carleton University in 1988. His research interests include Canadian nationalism, federalism, regionalism, and regional development, as well as party and electoral politics in Canada. Recent publications include the 4th edition of *Canadian Politics* (Broadview Press, 2004), with Alain Gagnon, and *Freedom, Equality, Community: The Political Philosophy of Six Influential Canadians* (McGill-Queen's University Press, 2006), with Stephen Brooks and Alain Gagnon. He has been a Visiting Professor at Cornell University, Simon Fraser University, and the University of Victoria.

Paul Brooker is Senior Lecturer in Comparative Politics at Victoria University of Wellington, New Zealand. He belongs to the Political Science and International Relations Programme and teaches courses on insurgency and leadership in democracy. His recent publications include *Twentieth-Century Dictatorships: The Ideological One-Party States* (Macmillan, 1997), *Defiant Dictatorships: Communist and Middle-Eastern Dictatorships in a Democratic Age* (Macmillan, 1997), *Non-Democratic Regimes* (Palgrave, 2008, 2nd edn), *Leadership in Democracy: From Adaptive Response to Entrepreneurial Initiative* (Palgrave, 2005) and *Modern Stateless Warfare* (Palgrave, forthcoming).

Peter Burnell is Professor of Politics in the Department of Politics and International Studies, University of Warwick, UK. He is the author or editor of thirteen books, among which the most recent are *Globalizing Democracy: Party Politics in Emerging Democracies* (Routledge, 2006) and *Evaluating Democracy Support: Methods and Experiences* (International IDEA and SIDA, 2007). He has also authored over thirty-five articles and many book chapters on democratization, the political economy of foreign aid, and politics in Zambia. He is founding editor of the journal *Democratization* and co-editor of *Politics in the Developing World* (Oxford University Press).

Daniele Caramani is Professor of Comparative Politics at the University of St Gallen, Switzerland. He is the author of *The Nationalization of Politics* (Cambridge University Press, 2004)—awarded the Stein Rokkan Prize for Comparative Research in the Social Sciences—and *Introduction to the Comparative Method with Boolean Algebra* (Sage, 'Quantitative Applications in the Social Sciences', 2008), as well as of the handbook and CD-ROM *Elections in Western Europe since 1815* (Palgrave, 2000). He is the editor of the *Swiss Political Science Review*.

Svante Ersson is a Lecturer in Political Science at Umeå University, Sweden. His research interests include comparative politics, Swedish politics, the analysis of political institutions, and methodology. He has co-authored *European Politics: An Introduction*

(Sage, 1996), *Comparative Political Economy* (Pinter, 1997, 2nd edn), *Politics and Society in Western Europe* (Sage, 1999, 4th edn), *The New Institutional Politics: Performance and Outcomes* (Routledge, 2000), *Democracy: A Comparative Approach* (Routledge, 2003), and *Culture and Politics: A Comparative Approach* (Ashgate, 2005).

Alain G. Gagnon is Canada Research Chair in Quebec and Canadian Studies at the Université du Québec à Montréal, Canada. In 2007 he received the First Josep Maria Vilaseca i Marcet Award granted by the Institute of Autonomous Studies of Catalonia for his work entitled *Au-delà de la nation unificatrice: Plaidoyer pour le fédéralisme multinational.* He is the director of the Research Group on Multinational Societies (GRSP) as well as of the Centre de Recherche Interdisciplinaire sur la Diversité au Québec (CRIDAQ). Among other recent publications is *Federalism, Citizenship and Quebec: Debating Multinationalism* (University of Toronto Press, 2007).

Michael Gallagher is Professor of Comparative Politics at Trinity College, University of Dublin, Ireland. He has been a visiting professor at New York University, City University of Hong Kong, and Sciences Po Lille. He is co-editor or co-author of *How Ireland Voted 2007* (Palgrave, 2007), *Representative Government in Modern Europe* (McGraw Hill, 2006, 4th edn), *The Politics of Electoral Systems* (Oxford University Press, 2005), *Politics in the Republic of Ireland* (Routledge, 2005, 4th edn), *Days of Blue Loyalty* (PSAI Press, 2002), and *The Referendum Experience in Europe* (Macmillan, 1996).

Rachel Gibson is Professor of New Media Studies in the Department of Media and Communication at the University of Leicester, UK. She has worked extensively in the area of politics and new media, focusing particularly on parties' and candidates' uses of the new information and communication technologies in their election campaigns. She has co-edited *The Internet and Politics: Citizens, Voters and Activists* (Routledge, 2005) and *Electronic Democracy: Political Organisations, Mobilisation and Participation Online* (Routledge, 2004).

Jørgen Goul Andersen is Professor of Political Sociology and Director of the Centre for Comparative Welfare Studies (CCWS) at Aalborg University, Denmark. His main research areas are comparative welfare studies, electoral behaviour, and political participation. Among his recent publications in English are authored and co-authored volumes such as *The Changing Face of Welfare: Consequences and Outcomes from a Citizenship Perspective* (Policy Press, 2005), *Europe's New State of Welfare: Unemployment, Employment Policies and Citizenship* (Policy Press, 2002), and *Democracy and Citizenship in Scandinavia* (Palgrave, 2001).

Simon Hix is Professor of European and Comparative Politics at the London School of Economics and Political Science, UK. He is also Director of the Political Science and Political Economy group at the LSE, Director of the European Parliament Research Group and Associate Editor of *European Union Politics*. He is author of *The Political System of the European Union* (Palgrave, 2005, 2nd edn) and co-author of *Democratic Politics in the European Parliament* (Cambridge University Press, 2007). In 2005 he won the Longley Prize of the APSA for the best article on representation and electoral systems published in 2004. In 2004 he won a Distinguished Scholar Award from the US–UK Fulbright Commission.

Richard S. Katz is Professor of Political Science at the Johns Hopkins University, Baltimore, US. He has held faculty appointments at the City University of New York and the State University of New York at Buffalo. He is co-editor of the *European Journal of Political Research*, and from 1996 until 2006 was co-editor of the EJPR *Political Data Yearbook*. He has served on the editorial boards of numerous journals, as convenor of the ECPR Standing Group on Political Parties, and as chairman of the APSA Representation and Electoral Systems Organized Section and the Conference Group on Italian Politics and Society. On political parties he co-edited *Party Organizations: A Data Handbook* (Sage, 1992) and *How Parties Organize: Change and Adaptation in Party Organizations in Western Democracies* (Sage, 1994), as well as *Handbook of Party Politics* (Sage, 2006).

Hans Keman is Professor of Comparative Political Science at the Free University of Amsterdam, the Netherlands. His research interests include political parties and government coalitions, comparative research methodologies, labour markets and welfare statism, and parties' policy positions. He has published *Comparative Politics: New Directions in Theory and Method* (VU Press, 1993), *Party Government in 48 Democracies (1945–98): Composition, Duration, Personnel* (Kluwer Academic Publishers, 2000), *Doing Research in Political Science: An Introduction to Comparative Methods and Statistics* (Sage, 2006, 2nd edn). He is the editor of the international journal *Acta Politica*.

Kees van Kersbergen is Professor of Political Science at the Free University of Amsterdam, the Netherlands, where he also serves as Head of Department, and Director of the Centre for Comparative Social Studies. His research interests lie in the fields of comparative political sociology, comparative politics, political economy, and the welfare state. His publications include *Social Capitalism: A Study of Christian Democracy and the Welfare State* (Routledge, 1995), which was awarded the 'Stein Rokkan Prize', *Shifts in Governance: Problems of Legitimacy and Accountability* (NOW, 2001), as well as articles in numerous journals. Current projects focus on religion and the welfare state.

Herbert Kitschelt is George V. Allen Professor of International Relations in the Department of Political Science at Duke University, US. His research focuses on the role of political parties and party systems in democratic polities. He has written on social democratic party strategies, ecology/left-libertarian parties, and the new radical right in post-industrial democracies. He has also investigated the emerging party systems of post-communist Eastern Europe. He is currently working on party competition in Latin America, and on programmatic or clientelistic politics in over eighty democratic polities world wide. His publications include *The Transformation of European Social Democracy* (Cambridge University Press, 1994) and *The Radical Right in Western Europe: A Comparative Analysis* (University of Michigan Press, 1995).

Christoph Knill is Professor of Comparative Public Policy and Administration at the University of Konstanz, Germany. His main research interests lie in the areas of comparative policy analysis and public administration. His focus is on policy-making in the European Union, the analysis of processes of international policy convergence and policy diffusion as well as research on policy implementation. His recent publications include *The Europeanization of National Administrations: Patterns of Institutional Change and Persistence* (Cambridge University Press, 2001) and *Environmental Politics in the European Union: Policy-Making, Implementation and Patterns of Multilevel Governance* (Manchester University Press, 2007). In 2005 he edited a special issue on policy convergence of the *Journal of European Public Policy*.

Amie Kreppel is Jean Monnet Chair and serves as Director of the University of Florida's Center for European Studies (CES), US. She is an Associate Professor in the Department of Political Science and has written extensively on the political institutions of Europe in general and the European Union more specifically. Her publications include articles in a wide variety of journals including *Comparative Political Studies*, the *British Journal of Political Research, European Union Politics*, the *European Journal of*

Political Research, Political Research Quarterly, the *Journal of European Public Policy*, and the *Journal of Common Market Studies*. She is a founding member of the transatlantic European Parliament Research Group (EPRG) and was a Public Policy Scholar at the Woodrow Wilson International Center for Scholars in 2000.

Hanspeter Kriesi is Professor of Comparative Politics at the Institute of Political Science of the University of Zurich, Switzerland. Previously, he has taught at the universities of Amsterdam and Geneva. His research interests include the study of social movements, political parties and interest groups, public opinion, the public sphere and the media, as well as direct democracy. He has recently co-edited *The Blackwell Companion to Social Movements* (Blackwell, 2004). His recent books include *Direct Democratic Choice: The Swiss Experience* (Lexington, 2005). He is currently the director of a Swiss national research programme on the 'Challenges to Democracy in the Twenty-First Century'.

Jan-Erik Lane is Professor of Comparative Politics at the University of Geneva, Switzerland. He teaches also at the University of South Pacific, Fiji Islands. He has taught politics and economics at many universities around the world, and is a member of several editorial boards of political science journals. He has authored or co-authored *Culture and Politics* (Ashgate, 2002), *Democracy: A Comparative Approach* (Routledge, 2003), *Politics and Religion in the Muslim Civilization* (Gower Press, 2003), and *Comparative Politics: The Principal–Agent Perspective* (forthcoming).

John Loughlin is Professor of European Politics at Cardiff University, UK. He founded and edited *Regional and Federal Studies: An International Journal* and was joint convenor of the ECPR Standing Group on Regionalism. He has served as an expert on regional and local democracy for the Committee of the Regions, the United Nations, and the Council of Europe. His publications include authored and edited volumes such as *Subnational Government: The French Experience* (Palgrave, 2007), *Subnational Democracy in the European Union: Challenges and Opportunities* (Oxford University Press, 2001), *Culture, Institutions and Regional Development: A Comparative Analysis of Eight European Regions* (Edward Elgar, 2003) and *The Political Economy of Regionalism* (Frank Cass, 1997).

Peter Mair is Professor of Comparative Politics at the European University Institute, Florence, Italy, and at Leiden University, the Netherlands. He is co-editor of the journal *West European Politics*. He is author or co-author of *Identity, Competition and Electoral Availability* (Cambridge University Press, 1990), winner of the Stein Rokkan Prize for Comparative Research in the Social Sciences, and recently republished in the ECPR Classics series, *Party System Change* (Oxford University Press, 1997), and *Representative Government in Modern Europe* (McGraw Hill, 2005, 4th edn).

Philip Manow is Professor of Political Science at the University of Konstanz, Germany. His research interests include comparative welfare state research, comparative political economy, political corruption, European integration, and legislative turnover. He was a visiting scholar at the Center for European Studies, Harvard, and at the Centre d'Études Européennes, Paris. From 2002 to 2006 he was leader of the research group 'Economic Governance and Democratic Government' at the Max Planck Institute for the Study of Societies, Cologne. He has published in *Legislative Studies Quarterly, Comparative Political Studies, Journal of European Public Policy*, and *West European Politics* among others. He has co-edited *Comparing Welfare Capitalism: Social Policy and Political Economy in Europe, Japan and the USA* (Routledge, 2001).

Wolfgang C. Müller is Professor of Political Science at the University of Mannheim and currently Director of the Mannheim Centre for European Social Research (MZES),

Germany. Previously he taught at the Universities of Vienna, Humboldt University Berlin, University of California, San Diego, Institute d'Études Politiques de Lille, and was Academic Visitor, Nuffield College, University of Oxford, Research Fellow University of Bergen, and Joseph A. Schumpeter Fellow at Harvard University. His has recently co-authored or co-edited *Policy, Office, or Votes? How Political Parties in Western Europe Make Hard Decisions* (Cambridge University Press, 1999), *Coalition Governments in Western Europe* (Oxford University Press, 2000), *Delegation and Accountability in Parliamentary Democracies* (Oxford University Press, 2003), *Political Parties and Electoral Change* (Sage, 2004), and *Cabinets and Coalition Bargaining: The Democratic Life Cycle in Western Europe* (Oxford University Press, 2007).

B. Guy Peters is Maurice Falk Professor of American Government at the University of Pittsburgh, US. His research interests include political theory (with a focus on institutionalism), methodology, American public policy, and the study of bureaucracy. He is the author of numerous volumes including *Comparative Politics: Theory and Methods* (Macmillan, 1998), *Institutional Theory in Political Science: The New Institutionalism* (Continuum, 2005), *The Politics of Bureaucracy* (Longman, 1994, 4th edn), *Handbook of Public Administration* (Sage, 2003), and *American Public Policy: Promise and Performance* (Chatham House, 1996).

Gianfranco Poggi is Emeritus Professor of Sociology at the University of Virginia, US. He has held posts in sociology or political science in several universities (in the UK, Canada, Australia, Germany, and Italy). Lately, he held a chair of sociology at the University of Trento, Italy, and still resides in that town. He has been a Fellow at the Center for Advanced Behavioral Studies in Stanford and at the Wissenschaftskolleg in Berlin. His main research interests are the history of social theory and the analysis of political institutions and the state. His publications include *The Development of the Modern State* (Stanford University Press, 1978), *The State: Its Nature, Development and Prospects* (Polity Press, 1990), and *Forms of Power* (Polity Press, 2001).

Philipp Rehm is a Ph.D. candidate in Political Science at Duke University, US. Currently, he is a visiting student at the Institute for Quantitative Social Sciences (Harvard University) as well as research fellow at the Institute for International Integration Studies (Trinity College, Dublin). His research interests include political behaviour, political economy of advanced industrialized countries, and applied statistics. His dissertation explores the link between labour market dynamics and the formation of social policy preferences as well as the impact of public opinion on social policy outputs. Publications include articles in chapters in edited volumes and journal articles (listed in the Online Resource Centre).

Andrea Römmele is Professor of Communication Management at the International University in Bruchsal, Germany. She is the author or co-author of *Handbuch Politikberatung* (Verlag für Sozialwissenschaften, 2006), *Direkte Kommunikation Zwischen Parteien und Wählern* (Verlag für Sozialwissenschaften, 2005) and *Electronic Democracy: Participation, Organisation and Mobilization via new ICTs* (Routledge, 2004). She is also the organizer of the Summer Academy on Political Consulting and Strategic Campaign Communication (www.political-campaigns.net).

Georg Sørensen is Professor of Political Science at the University of Aarhus, Denmark. He is the author or co-author of *Introduction to International Relations: Theories and Approaches* (Oxford University Press, 2007, 3rd edn), *Changes in Statehood: The Transformation of International Relations* (Palgrave, 2001), *The Transformation of the State: Beyond the Myth of Retreat* (Palgrave, 2004), and *Democracy and Democratization: Processes and Prospects in a Changing World* (Westview Press, 2007, 3rd edn).

Alec Stone Sweet is Leitner Professor of Law, Politics, and International Studies at the Yale Law School and the Yale Department of Political Science, US. His research interests are in the fields of comparative law and politics, international law and politics, and European integration. Recent books include *The Judicial Construction of Europe* (Oxford University Press, 2004) and *On Law, Politics, and Judicialization* (Oxford University Press, 2002).

Jale Tosun is Junior Research Fellow in Comparative Public Policy and Administration at the University of Konstanz, Germany. Her research interests include in particular the determinants of policy change and termination. Her forthcoming publications (listed in the Online Resource Centre) include chapters and articles on multi-level governance in the EU, the Europeanization of environmental policies and party programmes, regulation policies in comparative perspective, labour policies, and conditional trade offers.

Timothy Werner is a Ph.D. candidate in Political Science at the University of Wisconsin, Madison. His dissertation examines the political motivations behind the self-regulatory behaviour of major American corporations and its implications for business' political power. His research on campaign finance has been published in *PS: Political Science and Politics* and in several edited volumes (listed in the Online Resource Centre).

Graham K. Wilson is Professor of Political Science at Boston University, US. His research focuses on public policy, interest groups, and business and government relations in the United States and Europe. His books include *Business and Politics: A Comparative Introduction* (Palgrave/Chatham, 2002, 3rd edn), *Interest Groups* (Blackwell, 1990), and *Interest Groups in the United States* (Oxford University Press, 1981). He has also published extensively in journals and edited volumes and is the former editor of *Governance* and the *British Journal of Political Science*.

Map of the world in 2007

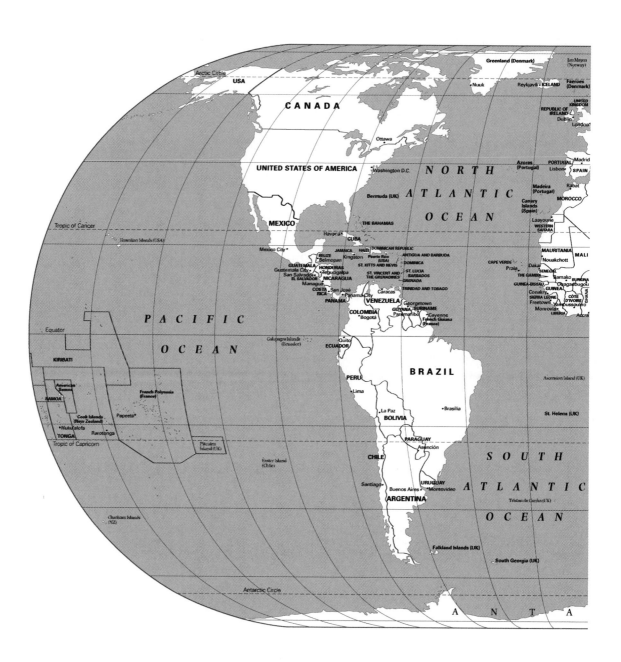

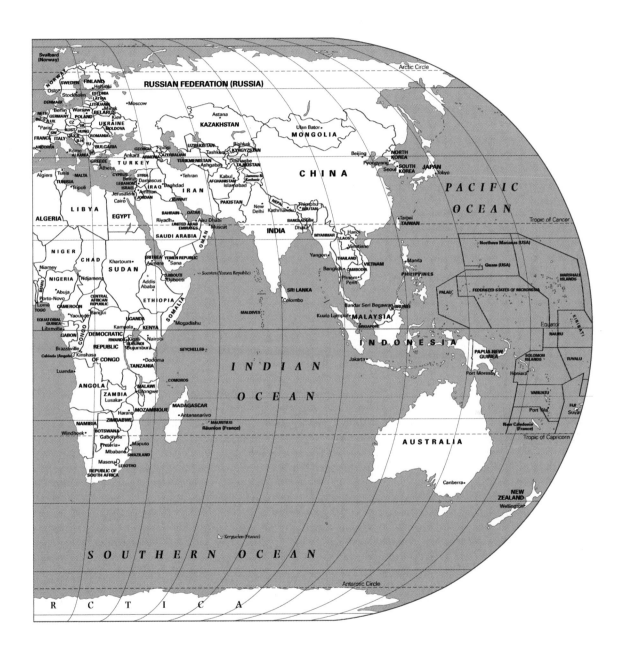

World data

World data 1 The most spoken languages

Languages	Absolute figures (million)	%	Geographical area
Mandarin	835	13.3	China
English	470	7.5	United Kingdom, US, Canada, New Zealand, Australia
Hindi	400	6.3	India
Spanish	392	6.2	Spain, Latin America
Russian	288	4.6	Russia
Bahasian	200	3.2	Indonesia
Portuguese	182	2.9	Portugal and overseas territories, Brazil, Angola
Bengali	180	2.9	Bangladesh
Urdu	150	2.4	India, Pakistan
Japanese	127	2.0	Japan
Arabic	150	2.4	Maghreb, Middle East
French	110	1.7	France and overseas territories, Switzerland, Belgium, Canada
Others	2,800	44.4	All remaining areas

Figures are approximate. The table includes only languages spoken by more than 100 million people. The remaining languages are classified under 'others'.

Sources: See comparative table 3.

World data 2 Religions in the world

Religions	Absolute figures (million)	%
Christianity	2,100	33.3
Islam	1,200	19.1
No religion	900	14.3
Hinduism	850	13.5
Buddhism	375	6.0
Chinese traditionalism	300	4.8
Animism	250	4.0
African traditionalism	90	1.4
Sikhism	24	0.4
Judaism	15	0.2
Spiritism	14	0.2
Confucianism	6	0.1
Jainism	5	0.1
Baha'i	7	0.1
Cao Dai	4	0.1
Shintoism	3	0.0
Zoroastrianism	2	0.0
Tenrikyo	2	0.0
Taoism	2	0.0
Others	150	2.4

Figures are approximate. Christianity includes Roman Catholicism (52.5%), Protestantism (17.6%), Orthodoxy (10.4%), and Anglicanism (3.8%), as well as Pentecostalism, Latter-Day Saints, Evangelicalism, Jehovah's Witnesses, Quakerism, etc. Islam includes Sunnis (83.0%) and Shiites (16.1%).

Sources: See comparative table 2.

World data 3 Socio-economic indicators

Indicators	Western Europe	Central and Eastern Europe	Latin America	North America	Middle East and Maghreb	Sub-Saharan Africa	Central and Northern Asia	South-East Asia	Oceania	Total
Population (million)	396	323	541	324	308	705	3,035	540	31	6,202
Life expectancy (years)	79	69	72	78	70	47	68	67	75	67
Aged 65 or above (%)	15.0	12.0	5.0	11.0	7.0	3.0	5.0	4.0	9.0	6.0
Richest to poorest 10%	9.1	7.1	47.4	15.2	11.2	24.2	6.5	12.4	12.7	10.6
GDP per capita 2003 (US$)	27,996	3,425	3,199	36,413	2,465	618	2,454	1,244	19,560	2,889
Literacy (%)	99.0	99.0	89.0	99.0	68.0	61.0	76.0	89.0	90.0	80.0
Carbon dioxide emissions (% share of world total)	13.5	10.6	5.4	26.7	5.6	2.0	30.7	3.8	1.7	100.0
Female activity rate (%)	46.0	57.0	2.7	59.7	37.7	61.1	57.0	61.2	58.9	53.6
Health expenditure per capita 2002 (PPP US$)	2,384	534	519	5,046	324	94	272	160	1,978	673
Unemployment (%)	8.5	9.0	8.7	5.3	14.2	18.7	6.8	7.6	5.4	8.2
Labour force (million)	192	156	238	166	111	224	1,615	261	17	2,980
agriculture (%)	3.8	14.8	19.9	2.0	29.6	68.0	50.0	48.4	5.0	41.9
industry (%)	27.1	26.1	18.0	23.0	19.7	10.9	20.0	17.7	21.7	20.0
services (%)	69.0	59.1	62.1	75.0	50.8	21.1	30.0	33.9	73.3	38.1

Figures are approximate and have been weighted by size of population. Central and Eastern Europe is inclusive of Russia. South-East Asia includes Thailand, Laos, Vietnam, Burma, Cambodia, Indonesia, Malaysia, Singapore, East Timor, Philippines, Brunei. Oceania includes Australia, New Zealand, Micronesia, Palau, Salomon Islands, Vanuatu, Fiji, Tonga, Kiribati, Marshall Islands, Papua New Guinea, Tuvalu. Middle East and Maghreb include Iraq, Jordan, Lebanon, Syria, Saudi Arabia, Bahrain, United Arab Emirates, Kuwait, Oman, Qatar, Yemen, Iran, Egypt, Libya, Tunisia, Algeria, Morocco, and West Sahara. Central and Northern Asia include Bangladesh, Bhutan, India, Maldives, Nepal, Sri Lanka, China, North and South Korea, Japan, Mongolia, Taiwan.
Sources: See various comparative tables.

Introduction to comparative politics

Daniele Caramani

Chapter contents

Reader's guide

Comparative politics is one of the three main disciplines of political science, alongside political theory and international relations. It deals with internal political structures (institutions like parliaments and executives), individual and collective actors (voters, parties, social movements, interest groups) and processes (policy-making, communication and socialization processes, and political cultures). The main goal of this empirical discipline is to describe, explain, and predict similarities and differences across political systems, be it countries, regions, cities, or supra-national political systems (such as empires or the European Union). This can be done through the intensive analysis of few cases (or one case) or with large-scale extensive analyses of many cases, and can be either synchronic or diachronic (including a temporal dimension). Comparative politics uses both quantitative and qualitative data. Increasingly, the analysis of domestic politics is challenged by the growing geographical scope and interdependence between regions and countries through globalization bringing comparative politics and international relations closer.

Introduction

This book is about politics. It is a book about all the most important dimensions of political life, not about one specific aspect of political life (such as elections or policies). Furthermore, it is a *comparative* book, meaning that we look at a variety of countries from all over the world. It is not a book about politics in one place only. Finally, it is not only about politics today, but rather about how politics changed over a period of time beginning with the transition to mass democracy in the nineteenth century. In sum, it is a book about the long-term comparative study of politics.

But what, precisely, is politics? Politics is the human activity of **making public and authoritative decisions**. First, they are public because they concern the whole of a society (not just inside groups, such as decisions in a family or university). Political decisions apply to everyone who is part of a given citizenship and/or living in a specific territory (a state). Second, they are authoritative because the government that makes such decisions is invested with the authority (and legitimacy) to make them binding and compulsory, meaning that they are supported by the possibility to sanction individuals who do not comply with them. 'Authorities' have the authority—as it were—to compel or force individuals to comply through coercive means. Politics is thus the activity of **acquiring** (and maintaining) the **power** of making such decisions and of **exercising** this power. It is the **conflict or competition** for power and its use. Who makes political decisions? How did they acquire the power of making political decisions? Where does the authority to make decision applying to all come from? What decisions have been taken, why, and how

do they affect societies' life? These are the questions that comparative politics seeks to answer.

It goes without saying that these are important questions. **What decisions are made** concerns our everyday life. The decision to increase taxation is a political decision. So are the decisions to cut welfare benefits such as maternity leave from the workplace, introduce military conscription or carry out military intervention in a neighbouring country, and invest in nuclear power as a source of energy. But also **how decisions are made** is important. The way in which public and authoritative decisions are made varies a great deal. In democracies we, as citizens, are directly involved through elections or referenda. If we are unhappy with them we can protest through demonstrations, petitions, letters, or vote differently at the next election and 'send the rascals home'. In other types of government individuals are excluded (as in authoritarian or totalitarian regimes). Under absolute rule the king or queen used to be invested with such a power. And, finally, **who makes or influences decisions** also counts. Many decisions on the maintenance of generous pension systems today are supported by elderly age cohorts in disagreement with younger ones who pay for them. Or, as another example, take the decision to introduce high taxation for polluting industries. Such a decision is heavily influenced by lobbies and pressure groups and by the protest of ecological activists. Configurations of power relationships can be very different but all point to the basic fact that political decisions are made by individuals or groups who acquired that power—against others—through either peaceful/democratic or violent means.

BOX I.1 Definition of 'comparative politics'

Comparative politics is one of the three main subfields of political science (alongside political theory and international relations) focusing on internal political structures, actors, and processes, and analysing them empirically by describing, explaining, and predicting their variety (similarities and differences) across political systems—be it national political systems, regional, municipal, or even supra-national political systems.

KEY POINTS

❑ Politics is the human activity of making public and authoritative decisions. It is the activity of acquiring the power of making such decisions and of exercising this power. It is the conflict or competition for power and its use.

❑ Who decides what, and how, is important for the life of societies.

What is comparative politics?

A science of politics

Even though the questions addressed above are very broad, they do not cover the whole spectrum of political science. Comparative politics is one of the three main subfields in political science:

- comparative politics;
- political theory;
- international relations.[1]

Whereas political theory deals with normative and theoretical questions (about equality, democracy, justice, etc.), comparative politics deals with empirical questions. The concern of comparative politics is not primarily whether participation is a good or a bad thing for democracy, but rather investigates which forms of participation people choose to use, why young people use more unconventional forms of participation than older age groups, and if there are differences in how much groups participate, say, in elections. Even though comparative political scientists are of course concerned also by normative questions, the discipline as such is empirical and **value-neutral**. It is a discipline that analyses political phenomena as they appear in the 'real world'.

On the other hand, whereas international relations deals with interactions between political systems (balance of power, war, trade), comparative politics deals with *interactions within political systems*. Comparative politics does not analyse wars between nations but rather investigates which party is in government and why it has voted in favour of military intervention, what kind of electoral constituency has supported this party, how strong has been the influence of the arms industry on foreign or trade policy, and so on. As a subject matter, it is concerned with power relationships between individuals, groups, and organizations, classes, institutions within political systems (either nation-states, empires, even sub-national systems such as federated states or regions). Comparative politics does not ignore external influences on internal structures, but its ultimate concern is power configurations within systems.

As subsequent chapters clarify, the distinction between these three disciplines is not so neat. Many

---

BOX 1.2 Important works in comparative politics: Aristotle

Aristotle (350 BC), *Ta Politika (Politics)*

The typologies of political systems presented in this work are based on a data compilation of the constitutions and practices in 158 Greek city-states carried out by Aristotle's students. This collection, unfortunately, is now lost (with the exception of *The Constitution of Athens*). This work represents the oldest attempt on record of a comparative empirical data collection and analysis of political institutions. Aristotle distinguished three types of Greek city-states: those ruled by one person, by few persons, and by all citizens. He further separates the corrupt from the non-corrupt ones.

---

argue that, because of globalization and increasing interdependence and diffusion processes between countries, comparative politics and international relations converge towards one single discipline. And, indeed, the greatest scholars bridge the two fields. What is important for the moment is to understand that comparative politics is a discipline that deals with the very essence of politics where sovereignty resides—i.e. in the *state*: questions of power between groups, the institutional organization of political systems, and authoritative decisions that affect the whole of a community. For this reason, over centuries of political thought the comparative analysis of the state has continuously been at the very heart of political science. For a long time thinkers have been concerned with the empirical investigation of politics. Scholars like Aristotle, Machiavelli, and Montesquieu—with many others, see the various boxes in this Introduction—were interested in the question of 'how does politics work?'

In spite of being a vast and variegated discipline, comparative politics constitutes a subdiscipline of political science in its own right and, as Peter Hall has recently asserted, '[n]o respectable department of political science would be without scholars of comparative politics' (Hall 2004: 1). Similarly, Chapter 1 in this book shows that the most influential political scientists have been 'comparativists', according to two surveys at different times and countries (see Box 1.1).

Types of comparative politics

The term 'comparative politics' originates from the way in which the empirical investigation of the question 'how does politics work?' is carried out. The discipline of comparative politics includes three different traditions (van Biezen and Caramani 2006).

1. The first tradition is oriented towards the **study of single countries.** This reflects the understanding of comparative politics in its formative years in the US, where it mainly meant the study of political systems outside the US, often in isolation from one another and involving little, if any, comparison. For long comparative politics—especially in the Anglo-Saxon world—has meant the study of foreign countries. Still today many courses on comparative politics include 'German politics', 'Spanish politics', and so on, and many textbooks are structured in 'country chapters'. As Chapter 3 discusses, case studies have a useful purpose for comparative analysis, but only when they are put in comparative perspective and generate hypotheses to be tested in analytical studies involving more than one case, such as implicit comparisons, the analysis of deviant cases (with respect to general laws), and proving ground for new techniques.

2. The second tradition is **methodological** and is principally concerned with establishing rules and standards of comparative analysis. This tradition addresses the question of how comparative analyses should be carried out in order to enhance their potential for the descriptive cumulation of comparative information, explanation (to provide causal explanations and associations between key variables), and prediction. This strand is concerned with rigorous conceptual, logical, and statistical techniques of analysis, involving also issues of measurement and case selection.

3. The third tradition of comparative politics is **analytical,** in that it combines empirical substance and method. The body of literature in this tradition is primarily concerned with the identification and explanation of differences and similarities between countries and their institutions, actors, and processes through systematic comparison using cases of a common phenomenon. Its principal goal is to be explanatory. It aims to go beyond merely ideographic descriptions and ultimately aspires to arrive at the identification of **law-like explanations.** Through comparison researchers control, test, verify, and falsify whether associations and causal relationships between variables hold true empirically across a number of cases. The comparative character of cases is derived from the identification of shared properties among the cases. Whether based on 'large N' or 'small N' research designs with mostly similar or different cases (with N indicating the number of cases considered), and using either qualitative or quantitative data and logical or statistical techniques for testing the empirical validity of hypotheses, this tradition ultimately aims at causal explanation.

This book takes this latter approach.

Thus, as all scientific disciplines, comparative politics is a combination of **substance** (the study of countries or regions, and their political systems, actors, and processes) and **method** (identifying and explaining differences and similarities between cases following established rules and standards of comparative analysis and using concepts that are applicable in more than one case). Comparative politics involves the *analysis of similarities and differences* between cases. Are there differences, how large are they, and how can we explain them? Like all sciences, it is only by looking at more than one case that we can say something general about the world, i.e. that generalizations can be reached. In comparative politics, as we are going to see, the cases are political systems—mostly nation-states (or countries) but also regions (sub-national or supra-national ones). We do not always compare the whole of political systems, but sometimes just elements such as institutions (parliaments) or actors (parties) or processes (policy-making).

What does comparative politics do in practice?

1. In the first place, to compare means that similarities and differences are **described.** Comparative politics describes the real world and, building on these descriptions, establishes **classifications** and **typologies.** For example, we classify different types of electoral systems.

2. Similarities and differences are **explained.** Why did social revolutions take place in France and Russia but not in Germany and Japan? Why is there no socialist party in the US whereas they

exist in all other Western democracies? Why is electoral turnout in the US and Switzerland so much lower than in any other democracy? As in all scientific disciplines, we formulate **hypotheses** trying to explain these differences (to control variation) and use empirical data to test them—to check whether or not hypotheses hold true in reality. It is through this method that causality can be inferred, generalizations produced, and theories developed and improved. For example, is it empirically true that proportional representation (PR) tends to produce more fragmented party systems?

3. Comparative politics aims at formulating **predictions.** If we know that PR electoral systems favour the proliferation of parties in the legislature, could we have predicted that the change of electoral law in New Zealand in 1998 from first-past-the-post to PR would lead to a more fragmented party system?

As a social science, comparative politics is not experimental. We cannot go to a laboratory and artificially change an electoral law in order to see if the number of parties shrinks or increases. Researchers cannot raise levels of literacy to see if political violence decreases, like a physicist increases heat to see if water boils faster. John Stuart Mill, Max Weber, and others all stressed long ago the impossibility of carrying out experiments in the social sciences (see Chapter 3). In the social sciences we need to look at different cases (countries or regions) with different levels of poverty to see if there is an *association* between poverty and violence.

'Comparative politics' as a label stresses the analytical, scientific, and 'quasi-experimental' character of the discipline. Traditionally, the analysis of politics was carried out through single-case descriptions: a country (politics in Nigeria), a specific party (the organization of the German SPD), a leader (the personality of Chairman Mao), and so on. As stressed above, comparative politics has for long meant studying foreign countries or cultures without comparison. There are plenty of books stressing the supposed 'uniqueness' and 'uncomparability' of this or that political system. It was in the 1950s–1960s that the awareness of the need to carry out systematic comparisons for more robust theories increased. The 'comparative' label before 'politics' was added to

> **BOX 1.3** Important works in comparative politics: Machiavelli
>
> Niccolò Machiavelli (written 1513, published posthumously 1532), *Il Principe* (*The Prince*; Florence: Bernardo di Giunta)
>
> This book was novel in its time because it told how principalities and republics are governed most successfully from a realist perspective and not how they should be governed in an ideal world. Machiavelli makes his argument through examples taken from empirical observations compared with each other. In *The Prince* he compares mainly different types of principalities (hereditary, new, mixed, and ecclesiastic ones), whereas in *The Discourses on Livy* (*Discorsi Sopra la Prima Deca di Tito Livio*) his comparison between princely and republican government is more systematic.

make a methodological point in a discipline that was not yet fully aware of the importance of explicit comparison.

In fact, however, single-case studies can be comparative, at least in an implicit way. Many famous case studies are carried out within a comparative framework, like Tocqueville's *Democracy in America* (1835). As John Stuart Mill noted in his review of the book in 1840, US specificities are constantly contrasted to France in a quasi-experimental manner. Similarly, books on single countries in the 1960s and early 1970s—on Belgium, Italy, Norway, Spain, Switzerland, etc.—did not only show that 'politics works differently over here' but also included systematic, if hidden, comparison with the better-known cases of the US, Britain, and France.

In practice the label 'comparative' was needed as a battlehorse. In an established discipline, in principle, this label could and should be dropped. Today it goes without saying that the analysis of political phenomena is comparative, i.e. entails more than one case. We should therefore conclude that—since comparative politics covers all aspects of domestic politics—if we forget the obvious term 'comparative', the discipline of comparative politics simply becomes 'synonymous with the scientific study of politics' (Schmitter 1993: 171). All the dimensions of the political system can be compared, so that all is potentially comparative politics. As Mair notes, '[i]n terms of its substantive concerns . . . the fields of comparative politics seem hardly separable from those of political science *tout court*, in that any focus of inquiry can be approached either comparatively (using cross-national data) or not (using data from just one country)' (Mair 1996: 311). All scientific analysis of politics is comparative by definition. The generality of the scope of coverage of comparative politics leads us now to talk about its substance in more depth.

KEY POINTS

❑ Comparative politics is one of the three main subfields of political science, alongside international relations and political theory.

❑ Comparative politics is an empirical science that studies chiefly domestic politics.

❑ The goals of comparative politics are: first, to describe differences and similarities between political systems and their features; second, to explain these differences; third, to predict which factors may cause similar or different effects.

The substance of comparative politics

What is compared?

'What' does comparative politics compare? Comparative politics compares mainly political systems and, mainly, at the national level. The classical cases of comparative politics are **national political systems.** These are (still) the most important political units in the contemporary world. However, national political systems are not the only cases that comparative politics analyses.

On the one hand, non-national political systems can be compared: **sub-national regional political systems** (state-level in the US, the German *Länder*, or city-states as Aristotele did with Greek constitutions) or **supra-national units** such as (1) regions (Western Europe, Central–Eastern Europe, North America, Latin America, and so on), (2) political systems of empires (Ottoman, Habsburg, Russian, Chinese, Roman, etc.), (3) international organizations (European Union, NAFTA, etc.), and finally (4) types of political systems rather than geographical units (a comparison between democratic and authoritarian regimes in terms of, say, economic performance).

On the other hand, comparative politics compares **single elements** or components of the political system rather than the whole system. Researchers compare the structure of parliaments of different countries or regional governments (or other institutions), they compare policies (e.g. welfare state or environmental policies), the finances of parties or trade unions, the presence or not of direct democracy institutions, electoral laws, and so on.

The various chapters of this book compare the most important features (the properties or components) of national political systems: regimes, institutions, actors, and processes. As can be seen in the Contents list at the beginning of the volume the variety of topics is very large and comparative politics covers—in principle—all aspects of the political system. It has been argued that precisely because comparative politics encompasses 'everything' from a substantial point of view, it has no substantial specificity, but rather only a methodological one resting on comparison, and its status as a discipline has been questioned, especially in recent literature (Verba 1985; Dalton 1991; Keman 1993*a*). Yet, there is a specificity, and this is the focus on internal or domestic political processes. There is a substantial specificity which resides in the empirical analysis of internal structures, actors, and processes. But it is also true that comparative politics is a broad discipline and, over the decades, it has had moments in which it focused on particular aspects. This evolution is what the next two sections describe.

From institutions to functions . . .

Comparative politics before the Second World War was mainly concerned with the analysis of the state and its institutions. Institutions were defined in a

---

BOX I.4 Important works in comparative politics: Montesquieu

Charles de Secondat, baron de Montesquieu (1748)
De l'Esprit des Loix (On the Spirit of the Laws;
Geneva: Barrillot et fils)

In this very influential book in which for the first time the idea of the separation of powers is presented systematically, Montesquieu distinguishes between republics, monarchies, and despotic regimes. He describes comparatively the working of each type of regime

through historical examples. Furthermore, Montesquieu was really a pioneer of 'political sociology' as, first, he analysed the influence of factors such as geography, location, and climate on a nation's culture and, indirectly, its social and political institutions and, second, did so by applying an innovative naturalistic and scientific method.

---

narrow sense overlapping with state powers (legislative, executive, and judiciary), civil administration, and the military bureaucracy. The type of analysis was formal (rather than substantial), using as main sources of information constitutional texts, legal documents, and jurisprudence. The traditional and narrow emphasis on the study of formal political institutions focused, naturally, on the geographical areas where they first developed, namely Western Europe and North America primarily.

While the study of state institutions and bureaucracy remains important, the reaction against what was perceived as the legalistic study of politics led to one of the major turns in the discipline which took place between the late 1920s and the 1960s—a period considered by many the 'Golden Age' of comparative politics (Dalton 1991). The behavioural revolution—imported from social anthropology, biology, and sociology—shifted the substance of comparative politics away from institutions. Pioneers of comparative politics such as Gabriel A. Almond—founder of the Committee on Comparative Politics in 1954 (an organization of the American Social Science Research Council)—started analysing other aspects of politics than formal institutions, to privilege concrete aspects rather than legal ones, and to observe politics in practice rather than as defined in official texts.

What triggered this revolution? Primarily, more attention was devoted to 'new' cases, that is, a rejection of the almost exclusive focus on the West and the developed world. Early comparativists like James Bryce, Charles Merriam, A. Lawrence Lowell, and Woodrow Wilson—all, as Philippe Schmitter has noted, 'Dead, White, European Men, but not Boring' (Schmitter 1993: 173)—assumed that the world would converge toward Western models of 'political order'. With this state of mind, obviously,

it makes sense to focus on major Western countries. However, the rise of communist regimes in Eastern Europe (and, later, in China and Central America), the breakdown of democracy in most of Europe where fascist dictatorships came to power before the Second World War—and in some cases lasted until the 1970s as in Portugal, Spain, and Latin America (Stepan 1971; Linz 1978; O'Donnell and Schmitter 1986), to some extent also in Greece—made it clear that other types of 'political order' could exist and needed to be understood and explained. After the Second World War patterns of de-colonization spurred analyses that would go beyond that of Anglo-Saxon-style liberal democratic institutions. New patrimonialist regimes emerged in Africa and the Middle East and populist ones in South America (Huntington 1968; O'Donnell 1973).

These divergent patterns could not be understood within the narrow categories of Western institutions. New categories and new concepts were required, as was more attention to other actors, such as parties in totalitarian single-party regimes and clans under patrimonialistic leadership. The mobilization of the masses that took place in communist and fascist regimes in Europe, as well as under populism in South America, turned attention away from institutions toward ideologies, belief systems, and communication. The breakdown of democracies in the 1930s motivated comparativists to ask which were the favourable conditions for democratic stability and, thus, to look into political cultures, social capital, and traditions of authority.[2]

Finally, even the closer analysis of Europe contributed to a shift away from the formal analysis of legal institutions. From the 1960s on, European comparative political scientists started to question the supposed 'supremacy'—in terms of stability and

Alexis Charles Henri Clérel de Tocqueville (1835) *De la Démocratie en Amérique* (*On Democracy in America*; Paris: C. Gosselin)

Although this book represents a 'case study'—an analysis of democracy in the United States—it is an example of comparison with an 'absent' case—i.e. France and, more generally, Europe. In his implicit comparison he analyses the uniqueness of conditions in American society and

geography that were particularly favourable to the development of democracy. Tocqueville follows Montesquieu in going beyond public institutions to include social and cultural aspects. For example, he speaks of aristocratic and democratic societies when comparing France with the US. More generally, Tocqueville was strongly influenced by the incipient application of the naturalistic methods to political matters by Montesquieu.

efficiency—of Anglo-Saxon democracies based on majoritarian institutions and homogeneous cultures. Other types of democracies were not necessarily the imperfect and unstable democracies of France, Germany, or Italy. The analyses of Norway by Stein Rokkan (1966), Austria by Gerhard Lehmbruch (1967), Switzerland by Jürg Steiner (1974), Belgium by Val Lorwin (1966*a* and 1966*b*), the Netherlands by Hans Daalder (1966), and Arend Lijphart (1968*a*)—most published in Robert Dahl's influential volume *Political Oppositions in Western Democracies* (1966)—as well as Canada, South Africa, Lebanon, India, all showed that politics worked differently from the Anglo-Saxon model.

Although ethnically, linguistically, and religiously divided, these societies were not only stable and peaceful but also wealthy and socially just (most remarkably in the case of the Scandinavian welfare states). On the one hand, these new cases showed that *other forms of democracies were viable*. Besides the 'Westminster' type of majoritarian democracy, these authors stressed the 'consociational' type with patterns of compromise between elites—rather than competition—'amicable agreements', and 'accommodation'; in short, **alternative practices of politics beyond formal institutions** and **alternative models of political order**. On the other hand, these new cases stimulated the investigation of the role of cleavage structures (overlapping vs. cross-cutting pluralism), specific policies as in the case of welfare economies, as well as to the role of elite collaboration in the political economy of small countries, which later led to important publications (see e.g. Esping-Andersen 1990; Katzenstein 1985).

What have been the consequences of the broadening of the geographical scope and historical experiences?

First, it increased the **variety of political systems**. Second, it pointed to the role of **agencies other than institutions**, in particular parties and interest groups, the role of civil-society organizations, public opinion, social movements, etc. (Almond 1979: 14). Third, it introduced a **new methodology** based on:

- the analysis of 'real' behaviour and roles (in practice rather than in principle) based on empirical observation;
- many cases ('large N'), i.e. extensive global large-scale comparisons;
- the development of statistical techniques for the analysis of large datasets;
- an extraordinary effort of systematic data collection across cases (mostly quantitative),[3] the creation of data archives, combined with the introduction of computerization and machine-readable datasets.

Fourth, a new 'language'—a new framework (Ostrom 2007)—namely, *systemic functionalism*, was imported in comparative politics. The challenge posed by the extension of the scope of comparison was to elaborate a conceptual body able to encompass the diversity of cases. Concepts, categories, operationalizations, indicators, and measurements that had been developed for a set of Western cases—revolving around formal institutions—did not fit the new cases. It also soon became evident that 'Western concepts' had a different meaning in other parts of the world. What Sartori has called the 'travelling problem' (1970: 1033) is closely related to the expansion of politics and appears when concepts and categories are applied to cases different from those around which they had originally been developed.

New cases led to the abandonment of the emphasis on institutions and the state because of the need for **more general and universal categories**. Since the behavioural revolution we do not talk any longer about the state but rather about the political system (Easton 1953, 1965*a*). Concepts were redefined to cover non-Western settings, pre-modern, societies and non-state polities. Most of these categories were taken, almost naturally, from the very abstract depiction of the social system by Talcott Parsons (1968). These more general categories could not be organizations or institutions that did not exist elsewhere but the functional equivalents or tasks needed for societies and political systems to exist.

Functions dealing with the survival of systems were seen as particularly important. From biology and cybernetics David Easton (1965*a*) and Karl Deutsch (1966) imported the idea of the *system*—ecological systems, body systems, and so on—and identified 'survival' as its most important function. What is the most important function of our body organs? To keep us alive. Similarly—still in the shadow of the dark memory of the breakdown of democratic systems between the two world wars through fascism and communism (and, incidentally, here one also sees how the concern of these scholars was an eminently practical and applied one)—in the 1950s the most important topic was to understand why some democracies survived while others collapsed. Almond and Verba's *The Civic Culture* (1963) is considered as a milestone precisely because it identified specific cultural conditions favourable or unfavourable to democratic stability.

...and back to institutions

It soon also became clear, however, that the price to be paid for encompassing transcultural and transportable concepts was an excessively high level of abstraction. This framework was not informative

Table I.1 Comparative politics before and after the 'behavioural revolution'

Dimensions of analysis	Before	After
Unit	State	Political system
Subject matter	Regimes and their formal institutions, leadership.	Expansion to all actors involved in the process of political decision-making.
Cases	Major democracies: US, Britain, France; analysis of democratic breakdown in Germany and Italy; authoritarianism in Spain.	Objective extension of cases (decolonization) and subjective extension with development of discipline in various countries: 'discovery' of small and welfare democracies.
Indicators/variables	West-centric, qualitative categories, typologies.	New abstract concepts, able to travel (functionalism); empirical universals and quantitative variables.
Method	Narrative accounts and juxtapositions between cases.	Development of machine-readable datasets and statistics; quasi-experimental comparative method.
Data	Constitutional and legal texts.	Individual survey data and aggregate data.
Theory	Normative: institutional elitism and pluralism; no elaborate conceptualization.	Empirical: structural functionalism, systems theory neo-institutionalism, rational choice theory.

enough, culturally biased (as in the case of rationally motivated individuals), remote with regard to the concrete historical context of specific polities, and unlikely to lead to empirically testable statements and measurable phenomena. Already European comparative political scientists like Rokkan, Lehmbruch, and others (and even more so area specialists from Eastern Europe, Latin America, Africa, Asia, the Middle East) had noted in the 1960s–1970s that the a-historical categories of systemic functionalism did not allow the understanding of concrete cases—which was precisely the original aim of the behavioural revolution. The chapter by Lipset and Rokkan on 'Cleavage Structures, Party Systems, and Voter Alignments' (1967) is the emblematic piece of research that puts history and context back in the equation.

The counter-reaction to systemic functionalism starts precisely in 1967 and involves (1) a shift of *substantial* focus, (2) a narrowing of *geographical* scope, (3) a change of *methodology*, and (4) a *theoretical turn* devoting greater attention to the rationality of actors and their strategies.

Bringing the state back in

The shift of substantial focus consists of a return to the primacy of the state and its main institutions (Skocpol 1985). In recent years there has been a re-establishment of the centrality of institutions more broadly defined as sets of rules, procedures, and social norms. In the new-institutionalism theory (March and Olson 1989; Hall and Taylor 1996; Thelen 1999; Pierson and Skocpol 2002; Przeworski 2004) institutions are seen as the most important actors rather than formalities, with autonomy and part of real politics. Institutions, furthermore, are seen as determining the opportunity structures and the limits within which individuals formulate preferences.[4]

Grounded theory

The excessive abstraction of concepts and categories in systemic functionalism was countered also by a return of attention to varying historical structures, cultural elements, and geographic location, and in which the specific socio-economic context plays a central role (Thelen and Steinmo 1992). Rather than general universalistic theories, middle-range or 'grounded' theories are privileged, stressing the advantages of case studies or in-depth analyses of a few countries.

Some authors argue that the reawakening of attention to the state and its institutions is in fact a consequence of this narrowing of geographical scope (Mair 1996). The general language introduced by systemic functionalism—and which nearly discarded the state and its institutions—was needed to encompass a greater variety of polities and political orders. Institutions have recently been reappreciated because of a closer focus. Systemic functionalism did not forget institutions; simply, they were 'absorbed upward into the more abstract notions of role, structure and function' (Mair 1996: 317). A regionally more restricted perspective giving up global comparisons does not require the same level of abstraction of concepts. The shift of substantial focus is therefore a consequence of less ambitious theoretical constructions of a discipline that contents itself with middle-range theories. The change of substantial focus has been favoured by the narrowing of the geographical focus.

Case-oriented analysis

This narrowing of scope entailed not only the 're-discovery' of the state and its institutions, but also a methodological change. From a methodological point of view the counter-reaction to large-scale comparisons based on universal concepts came from the development of methods based on few cases ('small N', see Ragin 1987). They revitalize today a type of comparative investigation that had long been criticized because few cases did not allow the testing of the impact of large numbers of factors—the problem that Lijphart (1971, 1975) named 'few cases, many variables'. This difficulty made the analysis of rare social phenomena, such as revolutions, impossible with statistical techniques. Hence the great importance of this 'new' comparative method. It provides the tool for analysing rigorously phenomena of which only few instances occur historically (see below for more details, and Chapter 3).

Rational choice theory

At the end of the 1980s another turn took place in comparative politics strengthening further the place of institutions. It was the turn given by the increasing influence of rational choice theory in comparative politics.

Whereas the behavioural revolution imported models and concepts from sociology primarily (the notions of functions and system in particular from the sociology of Talcott Parsons), the turn at the end of the 1980s was inspired by developments in economics. In addition, unlike the behavioural revolution, the rational choice turn does not revolve around a redefinition of the political, for it applies a more general theory of action—based on a number of assumptions—that applies equally well to all types of human behaviour, be it in the economic world, in the political system, in the media sphere, or elsewhere (Munck 2001; Tsebelis 1990).

This theory of action is based on the idea that actors (individuals but also organizations such as political parties) are rational and self-interested. They are able to order alternative options from most to least preferred and then, through their choice, seek the maximization of their preferences (utility). For example, voters are considered able to identify what their interest is and to distinguish the different alternatives that political parties offer in their programmes in regard to specific policies. Voters then maximize their utility by voting for the political party whose policy promises are closest to their interests. It is rational for political parties to offer programmes that appeal to a large segment of the electorate as this leads to the maximization of votes. It is clear from these premises that the place for 'sociological' factors on which the behavioural revolution insisted—such as socio-economic status and cultural traits—assumes a lower key in rational choice models. These models have been crucial to understanding the behaviour of a number of actors. In the field of party politics, examples include work by Downs (1957), Przeworski (Przeworksi and Sprague 1986), and Cox (1997). Other examples include the work of Popkin (1979) on peasants in Vietnam, Bates (1981) on markets in Africa,

Fearon and Laitin (1996) on ethnicity, Przeworski on democratization (1991), Gambetta (1993, 2005) on the mafia and suicide missions, and Acemoglou and Robinson (2006) on the origins of political regimes.

Rational choice theory in political science owes a lot to the work of William Riker. He is the founder of the 'Rochester School' (Riker 1990; see also Amadae and Bueno de Mesquita 1999). Today, rational choice theory comes in various forms and degrees of formalization. They range from 'hard' game theoretical versions, in which the degree of mathematical formalization is very high, to 'softer' versions in which the basic assumptions are maintained but in which there is no formal theorizing. What is important to note is that the rational choice turn did not lead to a redefinition of comparative politics as a subject matter precisely because it does not offer a meta-theory that is specific to politics—as did the general theory of Easton with its definition of politics as the authoritative allocation of values. The subject matter did not change under the impulse of rational choice theory. On the contrary, **it has reinforced the pre-eminence of institutions in comparative politics**. Rational choice institutionalism, in particular, sees institutions as constraints of actors' behaviour (Weingast 2002). An example of this approach is the concept of 'veto player' developed by Tsebelis (2002).

What is left?

As we have seen, there has been an almost cyclical process.[5] However, comparative politics did not simply return to its starting point.

1. In spite of the recent narrowing of scope and the tendency to concentrate on 'grounded theories',

---

BOX 1.6 Important works in comparative politics: Easton

David Easton (1953) *The Political System: An Inquiry into the State of Political Science* (New York: Alfred A. Knopf)

This volume is the first of a series of books by Easton on the political system. His work respresents the most systematic and encompassing effort on the 'theoretical side' of the behavioural revolution. Scholars like David Easton and Karl W. Deutsch imported the notion of system from other scientific disciplines (most notably, cybernetics).

This notion soon replaced the formal and legal concept of state and enlarged the field of comparative politics to non-institutional actors. The framework developed by Easton and his colleagues, and its conceptual components (input, output, feedback loop, black box, etc.) are today common language. Easton's work remains the last major attempt to develop a general empirical theory of politics.

the expansion that took place in the 1950s and 1960s left behind an extraordinary variety of topics covered by comparative politics. A glance at the list of Contents shows how many **features of the political system** comparative politics deals with: different types of political systems (of which the nation-state is only the most recent one), different types of regimes (democratic and authoritarian), diverse institutions and structures (from parliaments to electoral laws, from courts to local government), various actors and processes (parties, trade unions, social movements, the electorate and its values, culture and behaviour, the various forms of political communication), and finally different types of policies (how they are made in different systems, the main types of policies, and their impact).

2. Also the great contribution made by the systemic paradigm has not been lost. We continue to speak of a political system and use this descriptive tool to organize the various dimensions of domestic politics. In fact, the structure and coverage of the book has been designed accordingly and mirrors the political system as described by David Easton (see Figure I.1 and Box I.6).

There is a great paradox concerning Easton's work. It is a monumental theoretical construction of the structural-systemic paradigm, still unrivalled and probably the most important work of empirical theory including all actors and processes of political systems. However, recent work would hardly acknowledge its importance, citations of it are rare, and the place of this paradigm in courses on comparative politics is very limited. On the other hand, it is the last attempt to build a general empirical theory of politics. Why has such a central work not been pursued further and not been cited more often?

Easton's work has been a victim of its own success. His concepts have impregnated the minds of political scientists, as well as those of the wider public, so deeply that, in a way, it goes 'beyond citation'. His attempt has also been an extremely systematic one, with subsequent and cumulative books drafted towards one single end. His concept of **political system**, as a set of structures (institutions and agencies) whose decision-making function is to reach the collective and authoritative allocation of values (**output**, i.e. public policies) receiving support as well as demands (**inputs**) from the domestic as well as the international environment which it shapes through outputs in the **feedback loop**, includes all aspects of what is described in this book for example: from communication to culture, socialization and behaviour, interest articulation through parties, movements or pressure groups, institutions in democratic and authoritarian regimes, decision-making and policies, as well as the interaction with other systems—addressed in the last section of this book.

3. The substantive scope has not ceased to grow and this trend has continued over the most recent decades. As Chapter 1 discusses, there has been a change in focus from 'input' processes in the political system to 'output' processes, namely public policies, the processes of policy-making, as well as the outcome and impact of policies. This is the reason why a specific section of this book is devoted to these topics. In particular, recent trends of 'what' is compared include industrial, trade, and economic policies (aspects stressed in both Chapters 22 and 24), the reawakening of ethnic, religious, and nationalist movements, and trends towards regionalization (aspects stressed in Chapters 11, 15, and 17), the increasing role of pressure groups in corporatist decision-making negotiations (see Chapter 14).

New trends include also the increasing awareness of the interdependence between national political systems (which is discussed below more extensively). Chapter 23 analyses the integration between member-states of the European Union; Chapter 24 addresses the increasing blurring of national boundaries; and Chapter 25 shows how states increasingly influence others through institutional engineering and peace keeping.

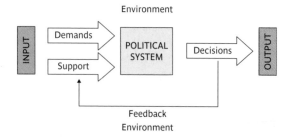

Fig. I.1 The political system

Source: Easton (1965).

KEY POINTS

❑ Comparative politics is not limited to the comparison of national political systems but includes other units such as sub-national and supra-national regions, international organization, single political actors, processes and policies.

❑ With the widening of the number of 'cases' (new states or other regions) the need for more general concepts that could 'travel' beyond Western countries led to a focus on functions rather than institutions. In the last two decades, however, a reaction against overly

abstract and general analysis led back to 'grounded theories' limited in space and time.

❑ As for the behavioural revolution, also rational choice aims at a general and unified theory of politics applicable in all times and places. This is an increasingly dominant paradigm imported into political science from economics that stresses the role of institutions.

❑ Comparative politics includes as a subject matter all features of political systems and, recently, has turned its attention increasingly towards the interaction between them, approaching international relations.

The method of comparative politics

Having briefly discussed the 'what' of comparison, we turn now to the 'how' of comparison. **How** does comparative politics compare?

A variety of methods

I should stress straight away that comparative politics does not rely on a specific method, for four reasons mainly.

1. Depending on the number of cases included in the analysis (say, two countries or 150), on the types of data the analysis deals with (quantitative electoral results or qualitative typologies of administrative systems), the time period covered (the most recent census or longitudinal trends since the mid-nineteenth century), the methods employed are different. The important point to note is, therefore, that **which research method is used depends**

on the research question. We first address the problem and formulate the research question; we then look for the most appropriate data and methods to analyse it. The choice of cases depends very often on the research question: there are political phenomena that occur rarely, sometimes only once. As Chapter 3 explains, comparative politics may analyse **one single case** (a case study). Research designs can be more or less **intensive or extensive** (depending on the balance between the number of cases and the number of features analysed), it can be **synchronic or diachronic**, and so on. What matters here is that the research method follows the research question.

2. Also the dimensions of comparison can be diverse. It is wrong to suppose that comparative politics is always cross-sectional, that is, that it involves a spatial comparison between countries, regions,

---

BOX 1.7 Important works in comparative politics: Lazarsfeld *et al.*

Paul Lazarsfeld, Bernard R. Berelson, and Hazel Gaudet (1944) *The People's Choice: How the Voter Makes up his Mind in a Presidential Campaign* (New York: Columbia University Press)

This book is a marvellous example of the use of modern statistical methods, and bivariate and multi-variate analysis of elections, public opinion, socialization processes, and communication through large datasets and the employment of rudimentary computing techniques. It is an

application of the positivist approach to politics and has paved the way for countless studies of the determinants of people's vote: the crucial questions of what categories of people (classes, professional groups, age cohorts, gender, and so on) tend to turn out more often and what categories of people tend to vote for which parties. A follow-up volume entitled *Voting* (1954) pursued this line of research. This book is an example of the 'empirical side' of the behavioural revolution.

areas, or groups of political systems. In fact, **spatial (cross-sectional) comparison** is only one of the possible dimensions of comparison (for example, the comparison of the size of national legislatures across countries). A second dimension of comparison is **the functional (cross-organizational or cross-process) comparison**. Take, as an example, the comparison of the liberal and the nationalist ideologies in Europe. Or the comparison of policy-making processes in the case of environmental and military expenditure policies in, say, the US. Or the comparison of leadership in social movements such as the civic right movement, the feminist movement, the environmental protection movement, and the pacifist movement. The dimension of comparison is, in these three examples, not territorial. A third dimension of comparison is the **longitudinal (cross-temporal) comparison**. We can compare institutions, actors, and processes across time rather than space as, for example, in the comparison of party organizations in the nineteenth century (cadre parties), after the First World War (mass parties), after the Second World War (catch-all parties), and since the 1980s (cartel parties).

3. **Units of analysis** can be diverse. As we have seen above, 'what' is compared can be either whole political systems or single actors, institutions, processes, or trends.

4. Comparative research designs can either focus on **similarities**, or focus on **differences**. Sometimes we ask questions about similar outcomes, such as 'why did social revolutions take place in France, Russia and China?' (Skocpol 1979) or 'why did democracy resist attacks from anti-system forces in some countries and not in others?' (Capoccia 2005). To explain similar outcomes we look for common factors (something that is present in all the cases in which the outcome occurred—either a revolution or a democratic breakdown) among cases otherwise very different from each other. As we will see in Chapter 3, this research design was called by John Stuart Mill the Method of Difference (Przeworksi and Teune 1970 called this the 'Most Similar Systems Design').

Sometimes, however, we use the Method of Agreement (or 'Most Different Systems Design'), in which we ask questions about different outcomes, such as 'why did Britain democratise early and Prussia/Germany late?' (Moore 1966). To explain different outcomes we look at factors that vary (something that is either present or absent in the case in which the outcome either occurred or did not—democracy) among otherwise similar cases. We also often combine these two methods, looking for common factors among cases in which the outcome occurred and for cases in which these factors are absent (and, indeed, the outcome did not take place).

From cases to variables...

Comparative politics prior to the behavioural revolution was typically a discipline that compared few cases. Today, we speak of **'small N' research designs**. As explained above, it was thought that the world would converge towards the Anglo-Saxon model of democracy and that, consequently, these were the cases that comparative political scientists should concentrate upon. The number of cases (the 'N') was therefore limited to the US, Britain, France, and a few other cases such as Canada, sometimes Australia and New Zealand, as well as the 'failed' democracies of Germany or Italy. Obviously, with such a limited number of cases the employment of statistical research methods was extremely problematic and, consequently, did not develop.

The behavioural revolution involved the widening of cases, that is, much greater numbers. On the one hand, this involved a much larger effort of **data collection**. Large datasets were created also with the help of the incipient development of computer technology. On the other hand, this involved the need for comparability of indicators and, as it turned out, the most general 'language' was that of **quantities**. It is very difficult to establish whether or not civic culture, honour, patriotism, justice, etc. have the same meaning in different cultures across the continents. It is possible, however, to measure in all countries of the world the number of cars, televisions, internet connections, or mobile telephones. Both factors—the increasing number of cases and the quantification of indicators—led to the development of more and more sophisticated **statistical techniques**, which became the dominant method. Research designs based on a 'large N' therefore typically employ techniques such as regression analysis, factor analysis, analysis of variance, based on numerical coefficients

---

BOX 1.8 Important works in comparative politics: Downs

Anthony Downs (1957) *An Economic Theory of Democracy* (New York: Harper & Collins)

This is a small book (Downs' Ph.D. dissertation) that had an enourmous impact, showing the great potential of rational choice theory for the study of politics. It introduced economic models for the analysis of actors' behaviour as well as the deductive analytical rigour in comparative politics. Today, rational choice models are one of the dominant approaches in comparative politics, especially in the US. Although this approach had an impact in all fields of comparative politics, in the field of electoral studies it still remains one of the most important works, alongside that of Maurice Duverger and Giovanni Sartori, inspiring pioneering research such as that of Gary Cox on voting behaviour, and the impact of electoral systems on politics.

---

allowing the causal association between social and political phenomena to be 'quantified'.

This trend turned attention away from cases and shifted it towards variables. **Intensive** research designs became **extensive**: many cases and few variables. Ragin (1987) defines the **large-N research design** as 'variable-oriented', implying that, with many cases, we finally know very little about the historical, cultural, and socio-economic context of the countries. Not only did concepts become increasingly abstract in the search for the most general, most comparable, and most equivalent concepts, but the analysis itself referred increasingly to abstract relationships between variables (political phenomena). For example, we would know that higher literacy levels are associated with higher turnout rates, but we would be ignorant about patterns in single countries.

… and back to cases

More recently there has been a return to 'small N' and case-oriented research designs and, today, *the* comparative method is in fact equated with the qualitative techniques based on John Stuart Mill's Methods of Agreement and Difference and on the search for sufficient and necessary conditions. Theda Skocpol (1984), David Collier (1991) and, most prominently, Charles Ragin with his pioneering *The Comparative Method* (1987), showed that rigorous empirical tests could be carried out also when the number of cases is small (for an overview see Caramani 2008).

This methodological shift stresses intrinsic advantages of the study of few cases. Case-oriented scholars stress that small-N comparisons allow for in-depth analyses in which configurations or combinations of factors are privileged in explanations. Cases are seen as 'wholes' rather than divided into isolated variables.

These authors focus on the complex constellations that factors build together rather than on the impact of each factor one-by-one.

Methodologically this is a reaction against early writings on the comparative method in the social sciences which made strong arguments precisely against configurative or combinatorial analyses in which a large number of potential explicative variables were listed (e.g. Przeworski and Teune 1970). On the contrary, the focus was on parsimonious explanatory designs, that is, a few key variables whose impact should be tested on as many cases as possible. In two famous articles, Arend Lijphart (1971, 1975) suggested increasing the number of cases (for example, by selecting several time points) and decreasing the number of variables by focusing on similar cases (thus reducing the number of factors that vary across them), looking at key explanatory factors, and combining them.

As we saw above, comparative methods developed in a period when social sciences were looking for a general language, that is, theoretical and operative concepts that could be used without substantial, temporal, or spatial limitations. Such a move implied 'replacing proper names with variables' (Przeworski and Teune 1970), defining concepts able to 'travel' (Sartori 1970), and using 'sets of universals' applicable to all political systems (Almond 1966; Lasswell 1968). In addition, because of the small number of cases for many research questions, a parsimonious use of variables was also invoked. This has led to 'a strong argument against … "configurative" or "contextual" analysis' (Lijphart 1971: 690) unable to give rise to generalizing statements. Thirty years later, a large part of the recent debates around methods in the social sciences focus on the opposite reaction, namely a swing away from the variable-oriented

BOX 1.9 Important works in comparative politics: Almond and Verba

Gabriel A. Almond and Sidney Verba (1963) *The Civic Culture: Political Attitudes and Democracy in Five Nations* (Princeton: Princeton University Press)

This book was the first seminal attempt to make systematic use of individual-level data collected comparatively through survey techniques. It is a phenomenal effort in individual data collection and analysis, in the US, the UK, Germany, Italy, and Mexico, at the dawn of the computer age. Within the behavioural paradigm, it analyses the function of political culture in political systems and, in particular, the central role that the 'civic culture' plays in the survival of democratic political systems. This book opened the way to studies on values, trust, and social capital pursued most prominently by Ronald Inglehart and Robert Putnam.

approach in which more properties are analysed in 'thicker' middle-range contexts.

The critique of case-oriented approaches denounces a return to the past. As John Goldthorpe notes, this represents a revival of holism against which Przeworski and Teune (1970) had directed their work, stressing variables replacing 'proper names'. In addition, even if one concentrates on 'whole' cases, one still refers to a number of their features or attributes. Comparison can take place only when one compares cases' values of shared properties or attributes, that is, variables (Goldthorpe 2000; see also Bartolini 1993: 137). The accusation is that we are going back to holism. And, again, we observe a cyclical pattern in the development of the **method** of comparative politics just as we did for the development of its **subject matter**.

From aggregate to individual data...

For a long time, the only available data were those collected as official statistics. The term 'statistics' itself goes back to the seventeenth century and the German School of Statistics. Etymologically, the term means 'science of the state' and its purpose is, as it were, to analyse **state** matters. Statistics started developing during the formation of the modern mercantilist European nation-states and flourished in the course of the nineteenth century when the great economic transformations (industrialization) and population movements (urbanization) strengthened the need for states to monitor increasingly complex societies.

The same period saw the development of the liberal nation-state, which, as discussed in Chapters 4 and 8, progressively increased its intervention in the society and economy, a tendency which was accentuated further with the welfare state. To act states needed to improve their knowledge of the society and the economy they were supposed to rule and govern. Democratization obviously gave a big push towards the development of statistics as governments became accountable through universal suffrage; they had to perform, which involved a systematic collection of information. To meet this need, that is, to increase their 'cybernetic capacity' (Flora 1977: 114), methods and techniques for gathering information have progressively improved.

Primarily, mass statistics were collected for practical and pragmatic reasons linked to the economic and military action of governments requiring information about their environment. The privileged contents of national statistics relate to the direct activity of the state: security and finance (military and criminal statistics, and statistics relating to income and expense items, taxation, and natural resources). With the growth of welfare states, the transformation of the population and health issues are monitored very closely: birth rates, mortality, health, and mental illness (often linked to crime statistics in the last century under the heading of 'moral' statistics or 'deviant' behaviour). As far as political statistics are concerned, they were usually included under the heading of juridical statistics. The presence of political statistics is, however, less common than that of other categories, in particular as electoral statistics are concerned which are very much linked to democratization processes and to attempts to legitimize regimes (see Caramani 2000: 1005–15).

The landmark of this development has been the organization of regular censuses—every five or ten years depending on the country—and the establishment of the annual publication of statistical yearbooks. These often include statistics of neighbouring countries requiring a certain degree of standardization of information to allow for comparisons.

These data are called **aggregate or ecological data** because they are available at some territorial level: provinces, regions, whole countries. Typical aggregate data are election results. We never know how individuals vote because voting is secret. However, we know aggregates: the number of voters in a specific constituency and the number of votes for parties and candidates in that constituency. These data can be aggregated into upper levels (entire regions or the whole country). Similarly, we often have data for unemployment rates, population density, employment in a given sector (for example, agriculture) at the level of territorial units.

With the behavioural revolution, however, the dominant approach to data collection changed radically.

1. Scientific researchers became more sceptical about official statistics which, especially in pre- or non-democratic states, may be subject to *manipulation*. This concerns data on elections and all aspects of civil rights, but also data on economic performance (unemployment, GDP, etc.). The creation of large datasets by university researchers independent from politics is therefore one of the most important aspects of the behavioural revolution.

2. Official statistics do not include all variables of interest to researchers. On the one hand, official statistics do not include information on political actors and—when they are included—the risk of manipulation remains strong. An example is data on political parties, their members, and their finances (very difficult to obtain and rarely reliable). On the other hand, and more importantly, official statistics do not include information on **individuals' values, opinions, attitudes and beliefs, competence and trust in political institutions, differences between elites and masses in political preferences.** Through official statistics we would not know whether an individual has authoritarian attitudes, post-material values, whether he or she is strongly religious, and so on. Census data are the closest type of data on this information, but, first, they concern primarily households rather than individuals and, second,

they do not include political data. We do not know, for example, what the party preference of a respondent is. The behavioural revolution introduced **surveys** as a systematic instrument to collect **individual data** as opposed to aggregate data. As Chapter 17 shows, political culture cannot be analysed without this type of data, which can be found throughout the world in surveys such as the World Value Survey, Eurobarometers, European Social Survey (certainly the highest quality data so far), Latinobarometers, etc.

3. The collection of individual data involved much larger datasets. Whereas institutional information or data about political parties involves a limited number of cases, there are thousands of individuals included in a survey. This amount of data can be dealt with only through the **computerization of the social sciences** which began in the 1950s. The behavioural revolution involved the analysis of individual data through a new electronic computing technology. Certainly, in the past there had been examples of extraordinary data analysis without computers. Durkheim's *Le Suicide* (1897) is a breathtaking example of comparative multivariate analysis of a huge amount of data presented in tables and figures on suicide in Europe without the auxiliary help of computers. Every social scientist should admire this effort. Another such example is Almond and Verba's *The Civic Culture* (1963) with individual-level data for five countries (see Box I.9). Yet, computerization put this type of analysis within the reach of all researchers, first through mainframe systems (usually in a university) and, in the late 1980s, through personal computers (PCs) and statistical software designed for them. Today every undergraduate student has Excel, SPSS, SAS, Stata, or other packages on his or her laptop.

4. The year 1950 proved to be devastating for analysis with aggregate data. This was the year when William S. Robinson published his famous article about 'ecological fallacy' (Robinson 1950). This article undermined the assumption that correlations observed at the level of aggregated units could be inferred at the individual level. Problems of ecological inference arise in the attempt to infer conclusions reached on the basis of analyses with territorial units down to the individual level. Put

---

Stein Rokkan (1970) *Citizens, Elections, Parties* (Oslo: Universitetsforlaget)

This book is a collection of previously published articles and chapters, complemented by unpublished bits and pieces, and conference papers by Stein Rokkan (who never wrote an authored monograph but rather preferred to work over and over again his writings). Nonetheless, Rokkan's work provides the most systematic comparative picture of a huge amount of empirical material on similarities and differences between countries in their patterns of state formation, nation-building, democratization, and the structuring of party systems and electoral alignments. In the great tradition of 'comparative historical sociology' (to which belong also Reinhart Bendix, Otto Hintze, Barrington Moore, and others), his work encompasses centuries of political development and has inspired generations of scholars. It led to the 'historical neo-institutionalism' in the work of Theda Skocpol and Charles Tilly.

---

simply, what is true on an aggregated level is not necessarily true at the individual level. Robinson showed that through aggregate data (based on counties and states in the US) there was a strong correlation between race and levels of literacy, but this correlation disappeared when individual data were used. The effect of this article was disruptive, the term 'ecological fallacy' became popular, and analyses based on ecological data were for long discredited.

… and back to aggregate data

The reaction to this 'shock' began almost immediately, with methodological work attempting to find solutions to 'ecological fallacy'. Crucial events for the recovery of ecological techniques and aggregate data were the International Social Science Consortium (ISSC) Symposium held at Yale in 1963 and the International Sociology Association (ISA) World Congress held in Evian in 1966. These important meetings led to collective publications devoted to comparing nations with aggregate data (see Merritt and Rokkan 1966; Dogan and Rokkan 1969; for recent discussions of ecological data analysis see Berglund and Thomsen 1990; King 1997; King *et al.* 2004).[6]

Furthermore, the reaction to Robinson's blow to ecological data involved the creation of international networks for the collection of comparable 'hard data' worldwide. International data archives were set up. The most important ones are today the Inter-University Consortium for Political and Social Research (ICPSR at the University of Michigan), the Data Archive (at the University of Essex), the Mannheim Centre for European Social Research (MZES,

at the University of Mannheim), and the Norwegian Data Archive (at the University of Bergen). Data archives developed in all countries are linked together in a global network (see the Online Resource Centre). Such efforts led to major publications of aggregate data collections with documentation, most notably the three editions of the *World Handbook of Political and Social Indicators* (Russett *et al.* 1964; Taylor and Hudson 1972; Taylor and Jodice 1983) but also other projects (see the 'Yale Political Data Program'; Deutsch *et al.* 1966). These publications are updated today through the internet resources of the ICPSR.

International organizations such as the United Nations, the World Trade Organization, the World Bank, the International Monetary Fund, the UN Food and Agriculture Organization (FAO), and World Health Organization (WHO), the Organization for Security and Co-operation in Europe (OSCE), and so forth, also contributed to the creation of large comparative datasets with aggregate data in their sectors of competence. The Online Resource Centre provides all the links to these datasets.

But perhaps the main reason for a 'recovery' of ecological data analysis resides in the intrinsic weaknesses of individual-level data. Data based on individuals' cultural traits, values, and *Weltanschauungen* are more exposed to the 'travelling problem', and do not apply as universally as first hoped. This problem of 'ethno-centrism' was already present in the landmark publication of *The Civic Culture* in 1963 in which it became clear that, for example, national pride had a different meaning in a civic, political nation like the US and in an ethnic, cultural nation like Germany. The Western concepts developed to guide

---

BOX I.11 Important works in comparative politics: Esping-Andersen

Gøsta Esping-Andersen (1990) *The Three Worlds of Welfare Capitalism* (Cambridge: Polity Press)

This is the book that best illustrates the shift in comparative politics from input processes to public policies. It presents a typology and an explanation of what can be considered the most encompassing of all public policies after the Second World War—the development of the welfare

state as the latest stage in the construction of the modern nation-state, where social rights complement political and civic rights (as distinguished by T. H. Marshall). This work has inspired large research programmes, namely on varieties of capitalism (e.g. Susan Strange's work), international political economy (e.g. Peter Hall), as well as on welfare states (e.g. Peter Flora).

---

data collection worldwide had a high degree of subjectivity and were not always useful 'data containers' (Sartori 1970). Concepts like trust and honour, for example, do not have the same meaning in all parts of the world.

In addition, it is more difficult to build long time series with individual data. Only aggregate data that we can collect from the beginning of the nineteenth century (for example, percentages about national languages or religious groups) allow us to understand topics that need a long-term perspective—such as state formation and democratization. This was particularly true during the 1960s and 1970s when 'developmental' and modernization approaches were used to understand newly decolonized countries. Panel studies—surveys carried out with the same group of respondents over protracted periods of time—are extremely costly (and, anyway, do not allow us to go 'back' in time). And the use of existing surveys for comparative purposes is not straightforward. Intelligence services, especially US ones, carried out a number of surveys in Europe after the Marshall Plan to investigate the public's attitudes, its propensity to favour democratic values, the potential of a communist menace or fascist return. These early studies, however, are fragmented, with different questions asked and different groups or respondents.

The 'hard' aggregate data have therefore not disappeared and, on the contrary, provide more solid bases than individual-level data for international long-term comparisons.

KEY POINTS

❏ Comparative politics employs statistical techniques when research designs include many cases and quantitative indicators (variable-oriented, large-N studies), or comparative methods when research designs include few cases and qualitative indicators (case-oriented, small-N studies). Case studies, too, can be carried out in a comparative perspective.

❏ The dimensions of comparison are multiple: spatial, temporal, and functional.

❏ The purpose of comparative politics is descriptive, explanatory, and predictory. To this end research designs can aim either at selecting similar cases and explain their different outcomes (Most Similar Systems Designs, the 'Method of Difference'), or at selecting different cases and explain similar outcomes (Most Different Systems Designs, the 'Method of Agreement').

❏ Comparative politics uses aggregate, individual, and text data.

Conclusion

The variety of comparative politics

The great variety of approaches, methods, and data of comparative politics matches the great variety of the world's societies, economies, cultures, and political systems. In this book we have inserted a number of

'Comparative tables' on various indicators at the end of the volume. We have also inserted a number of 'Trends', figures which show how societies and political systems have changed over the most recent decades. 'Trends' figures are scattered across the book, as are the various 'Country profiles', small files on the most diverse political systems around the world.

This book rests on the methodological principle that 'everything' is comparable. The large-scale comparisons through both space and time in this book are based on the idea that there are no limits to comparison. Everything—i.e. any case in the world at any point in time—is, in principle, comparable. Analytical comparison never compares cases as such (say, countries) but rather properties (for example, turnout levels) and their values for each case: whether turnout levels are high or low according to countries. Obviously, turnout applies only where there are democratic elections—so the level of generality and the spatial and temporal scope of the comparison of turnout is limited (there would be no point in analysing turnout in France under Louis XIV or in China today). The empirical material presented in all tables and figures throughout this book relies, therefore, on these methodological principles.

What does the world look like? In what kind of world do we live? Certainly, it is a world that has changed enormously over time and in which large differences persist.

The nineteenth century witnessed what is probably the greatest change in the political organization of human societies with the development of modern nation-states and democracies. There was no previous experience of mass democracy based on principles of fundamental equality between individuals, civic liberties, political rights, and open participation to the political process and to social welfare. The scope of this change was matched only by the Industrial Revolution during the same period. This is a unique period in our history and we should be aware of its exceptional character but also of its shortness. It is therefore crucial to cover the development of the nation-state and mass democracy over nearly 200 years. In spite of the many differences between countries, this change has affected the entire world.

This Introduction to comparative politics has stressed the great variety of what—after all—is a huge field of study that covers all aspects of domestic politics, with many areas of specialization and subdisciplines which are reflected in the large number of chapters in *Comparative Politics*. The great variety—and the consequent specialization and fragmentation of the field—is the main reason why it is difficult to single out the most important books (see the various boxes scattered through this Introduction). Each subdiscipline has its 'classic' work: in

the field of coalition formation, in that of the study of electoral systems, or in that of the formation of modern nations, and so forth.

It is not only the broadness of its substantial focus of the topics that gives comparative politics a character of great variety (what features of the political systems are compared, which units are compared, and how many cases). This variety appears also in the **research design** (what methodology is employed, which research strategies and dimensions of comparison, the type of data we use) and in the **theoretical frameworks** we apply (from institutionalism to rational choice theory; see the five 'I's distinguished in Chapter 2). Today, this variety becomes even larger as comparative politics increasingly 'invades' the discipline of international relations (and vice versa). The boundaries between the two become more and more blurred. Yet, in spite of fragmentation and current changes towards the overlap with other disciplines, the intent of comparative politics is that of a rigorous scientific and empirical field of study: description, explanation, and prediction.

From divergence to convergence…

Comparative politics was born out of diversity. There would be no comparative politics without the diversity of political systems and their features. The literature up to the 1950s assumed that there would be a **convergence** towards the model of the major Western liberal democracies. But it is on the contrary the fact that no convergence occurred, there has been **divergence** (in the form of alternative models of political order), that led to the actual development of comparative politics.

Is it still like that? Currently trends towards convergence are very strong. The end of the Cold War in 1989 and the disappearance of the leading superpower that embodied one of the major alternative political models, the 'Third Wave' of democratization in Central and Eastern Europe, the pressures towards market economy coming from the intensification of world trade and globalization in a country like China, the numerous initiatives to 'export' and 'promote' democracy in Africa and the Middle East, democratic consolidation in Latin America—these are all patterns of worldwide convergence.

The role of comparative politics is thus called into question in a world that is less and less diverse. What is the future of comparative politics in a globalized world? Comparative politics—like all 'quasi-experimental' methods—bases its explanations on the co-variation between phenomena which, quite naturally, leads to focus on **differences** between analytical cases. Yet, how does such a discipline deal with the existence of **commonalities**, patterns of **homogenization**, and **diffusion** effects? Furthermore, comparative politics was built on the methodological assumption that cases—i.e. national political systems—are independent of each other. Traditionally, it has been less concerned with the explanation of common aspects and interactions.[7]

As Sørensen notes at the beginning of Chapter 24, '[t]he standard image of the sovereign nation-state is that of an entity within well-defined territorial borders: a national polity, a national economy, and a national community of citizens', and on this premise comparative politics researchers thought that they could 'safely ignore what takes place outside of the borders of the countries they were studying'. Although comparative politics has also considered other types of states (city-states in Ancient Greece and Renaissance Italy, empires such as the Roman, the Chinese, and the Habsburg), and although the behavioural revolution replaced the concept of 'state' (limited in time and space) with that of 'political system' (allowing the comparison of sub-national and supra-national regional systems), its main concern has for long remained the study of the Westphalian territorial state.

It is, however, increasingly difficult to maintain such a position and, indeed, the literature has addressed these issues. In recent years there has been a resurgence of interest in the so-called 'Galton's problem', that is, the methodological issue raised at the end of the nineteenth century by the polymath and anthropologist Francis Galton concerning associations between phenomena that are, in fact, the result of diffusion effects between cases—ultimately, therefore, spurious associations. Contagion processes among cases violate the assumption of independence among units of analysis. Units of analysis—be it organizations or territorial units—are not isolated from one another. In temporal developments phenomena spread from one case to the other.

Most countries are today open systems increasingly subject to external influences: borrowing but also learning from the practices of others and imitation. For example, it is plausible to suppose that the development of welfare states in various countries is affected by diffusion processes (see Chapters 20 and 22, for examples of diffusion processes through policy transfers and policy learning between countries). There are factors of coordination when they belong to some overarching integrating organization (the European Union, for example, as shown in Chapter 23) as well as cases of imposition by conquest, colonialism, economic dependency (as discussed in Chapter 4, many current states were part of other states before secession). Finally, our current world, more than ever, experiences migrations (for data on migrations see Comparative table 14 at the end of this volume).

The risk for comparative politics is—methodologically speaking—of ending up with 'N=1'. Przeworski and Teune in their classic book on the comparative method ask: 'how many independent events can we observe? If the similarity within a group of systems is a result of diffusion, there is only one independent observation' (1970: 52). Our current methodology is not fit to analyse common developments, changes without variation between cases, and situations of dependence between them. The problem obviously increases with transnationalization processes, the amelioration of communication, spread of information, and acceleration of exchanges. In an increasingly interdependent world, comparative political scientists realize that social phenomena are not isolated and self-contained, but rather are affected by events occurring within other societies, not necessarily neighbouring countries but also more remote locations. And, with a 'shrinking world', the problem is stronger today than in the past.

... and back to divergence?

The last section of the book addresses precisely these questions with chapters on integration, globalization, and promotion of democracy in non-Western parts of the world. This is where comparative politics and international relations become contiguous and their efforts, in the future, will increasingly be common efforts.

Nonetheless, one should not forget that while there are processes of convergence and homogenization, there are signals pointing also in other, divergent directions. Examples include the renewed role that religion plays in some parts of the world, such as the Muslim areas, but also in the US; the emergence of alternative forms of neo-populist 'Bolivarian' democracies in Latin America, particularly in Bolivia and Venezuela; differentiation at the sub-national level that points to the resurgence—as a parallel process to the weakening of the Westphalian nation-state caused by supra-national integration—of new regionalist phenomena with ethno-linguistic support; also, supra-national integration, when and where it takes place, occurs to different degrees and at different paces; finally, cultural fault lines pull the world apart while it integrates economically.

All this is to say that it is difficult to detect linear, or cyclical, developments in world politics over short periods of time and by looking at few cases only. This is one of the reasons why this book adopts a long-term perspective from the beginning of modern politics—the formation of national states, mass democracies, and industrialization in the nineteenth century—as well as a broad cross-country perspective. The French expression *reculer pour mieux sauter* (to step backwards in order to jump further) was a favourite of Stein Rokkan's, one of the founding pioneers of the discipline of comparative politics. To have a firm ground for looking at the future fits very well with the philosophy of this book too. Basically, the mission of comparative politics could be simply summarized as 'one needs a little perspective'.

» Further reading

'Classics' of comparative politics are shown in the boxes in this Introduction. Those books should be on every comparative political scientist's shelves.

Overviews of the discipline

Blondel, Jean (1999) 'Then and Now: Comparative Politics', *Political Studies,* 47(1): 152–60.

Daalder, Hans (1993) 'The Development of the Study of Comparative Politics', in Keman (ed.), *Comparative Politics* (Amsterdam: Free University Press), 11–30.

Dalton, Russell J. (1991) 'Comparative Politics of the Industrial Democracies: From the Golden Age to Island Hopping', in William Crotty (ed.), *Political Science* (Evanston, Ill.: Northwestern University Press), 15–43.

Eckstein, Henry (1963) 'A Perspective on Comparative Politics, Past and Present', in Henry Eckstein and David E. Apter (eds.), *Comparative Politics: A Reader* (New York: Free Press), 3–32.

Mair, Peter (1996) 'Comparative Politics: An Overview', in Robert E. Goodin and Hans-Dieter Klingemann (eds.), *A New Handbook of Political Science* (Oxford: Oxford University Press), 309–35.

Rogowski, Ronald (1993) 'Comparative Politics', in Ada W. Finifter (ed.), *Political Science: The State of the Discipline* (Washington, DC: American Political Science Association), 431–50.

Schmitter, Philippe (1993) 'Comparative Politics', in Joel Krieger (ed.), *The Oxford Companion to Politics of the World* (Oxford: Oxford University Press), 171–7.

Verba, Sidney (1985) 'Comparative Politics: Where have we Been, Where are we Going?', in Howard J. Wiarda (ed.), *New Directions in Comparative Politics* (Boulder, Colo.: Westview Press), 26–38.

Recent treatments of comparative politics as a discipline

Almond, Gabriel A. (1990) *A Discipline Divided: Schools and Sects in Political Science* (Newbury Park, Calif.: Sage).

Chilcote, Ronald H. (1994) *Theories of Comparative Politics: The Search for a Paradigm Reconsidered* (Boulder, Colo.: Westview Press, 2nd edn).

——(2000) *Comparative Inquiry in Politics and Political Economy* (Boulder, Colo.: Westview Press).

Landman, Todd (2007) *Issues and Methods in Comparative Politics: An Introduction* (London: Routledge, 2nd edn).

Lichbach, Mark I., and Zuckerman, Alan S. (1997) *Comparative Politics: Rationality, Culture, and Structure* (Cambridge: Cambridge University Press).

Peters, B. Guy (1998) *Comparative Politics: Theory and Methods* (Basingstoke: Macmillan).

Wiarda, Howard J. (ed.) (2002) *New Directions in Comparative Politics* (Boulder, Colo.: Westview Press, 3rd edn).

Reference work

Boix, Carles, and Stokes, Susan C. (2007) *Oxford Handbook of Comparative Politics* (Oxford: Oxford University Press).

Other titles in the 'Oxford Handbooks of Political Science' series

Moran, Michael, Rein, Martin, and Goodin, Robert E. (2006) *Oxford Handbook of Public Policy* (Oxford: Oxford University Press).

Weingast, Barry R., and Wittman, Donald (2006) *Oxford Handbook of Political Economy* (Oxford: Oxford University Press).

Dryzek, John S., Honig, Bonnie, and Phillips, Anne (2006) *Oxford Handbook of Political Theory* (Oxford: Oxford University Press).

Rhodes, R. A. W., Binder, Sarah A., and Rockman, Bert A. (2006) *Oxford Handbook of Political Institutions* (Oxford: Oxford University Press).

Dalton, Russell, J., and Klingemann, Hans-Dieter (2007) *Oxford Handbook of Political Behaviour* (Oxford: Oxford University Press).

Whittington, Keith E., Kelemen, Daniel R., and Caldeira, Gregory A. (2008) *Oxford Handbook of Law and Politics* (Oxford: Oxford University Press).

Reus-Smit, Christian, and Snidal, Duncan (2008) *Oxford Handbook of International Relations* (Oxford: Oxford University Press).

Box-Steffensmeier, Janet M., Brady, Henry, and Collier, David (2008) *Oxford Handbook of Political Methodology* (Oxford: Oxford University Press).

For specific topics see the 'further reading' section at the end of each chapter.

Scientific comparative politics research publishes results in a number of specialized journals. The most important scientific journals with a focus on comparative politics are the following: *Comparative Politics, Comparative Political Studies, Comparative European Government, European Journal of Political Research, West European Politics*, among others.

In addition, most countries have political science journals that publish research in comparative politics. Examples include *American Political Science Review, British Journal of Political Science, Revue Française de Science Politique, Scandinavian Political Studies, Politische Vierteljahresschrift, Irish Political Studies, Australian Journal of Politics and History, Swiss Political Science Review*.

Finally, for each subject (elections, parties, communication, etc.) there are specialized journals which include comparative work. Examples are *Party Politics, Electoral Studies, European Journal of Public Policy, American Journal of Comparative Law, Local Government Studies, Publius: The Journal of Federalism, Journal of Common Market Studies, Journal of Democracy, Democratization, Journal of European Social Policy, Media, Culture and Society, Political Communication*.

 Visit the Online Resource Centre that accompanies this book for more information:
www.oxfordtextbooks.co.uk/orc/caramani/

SECTION 1

Theories and methods

1 The evolution of comparative politics

Klaus von Beyme

Chapter contents

Reader's guide

The history of comparative politics shows that the discipline as a scientific enterprise is fairly recent. Machiavelli in the pre-modern era came closest to a modern social science approach. In the nineteenth century the predominance of historicism was not favourable for comparisons. John Stuart Mill was the first to differentiate between Methods of Agreement and Difference. In the time of modern comparative politics there were two approaches to comparison: one, ranging from Durkheim to systems theory, thought that all social sciences are comparative; the other school, in the wake of Max Weber, developed a comparative method based on a hermeneutic approach of 'understanding'. The value-free approach to comparison was challenged when policies, the result of political decision-making, were analysed and considered as more important than the institutional setting which favoured certain decisions. The chapter also shows that comparative politics has been shaped by many influences from historical events.

Introduction

The evolution of comparative politics has been classified in stages, such as the 'pre-paradigmatic phase' which was not dominated by a single theoretical approach in the scientific community, and the 'paradigmatic phase', in which the scientific community adhered to a dominant theory. According to this classification (Chilcote 1994: 58) the paradigmatic phase is followed by as 'crisis phase' and finally ends up in a 'phase of scientific revolution' which occurs when the scientific community shifts to different paradigms.

Kuhn's frequently abused term paradigm, however, is hardly applicable in this context. Most phases in the evolution of political science have been 'pre-paradigmatic' in the sense that no single approach predominated completely. Chilcote is aware that his subdivision of 'traditional', 'behavioural', and 'post-behavioural' approaches do not precisely fit Kuhn's definition of paradigms. Only the dominance of the 'behavioural revolution' came close to the idea of a paradigm which conquered the community and tolerated deviant approaches only in marginal positions. But the typology is ethnocentric in so far as it generalizes the American development. In Europe there was never a dominance of the behavioural approach. In this chapter I prefer a threefold classification for the evolution of comparative politics, with stages such as 'pre-modern', 'modern', and 'post-modern'.

> **KEY POINTS**
>
> ❑ It is difficult to describe the evolution of comparative politics as a sequence of paradigms (even in the case of the behavioural revolution; see the Introduction to this volume).
> ❑ The evolution of comparative politics follows the pre-modern, modern, and post-modern sequence.

Comparative politics in pre-modern times

The pre-modern stage or the traditional approach to comparison since Aristotle was highly speculative and normative, mostly ethnocentric used comparison in an anecdotal way, but hardly ever attempted a systematic comparison over time. Political science is the youngest social science in terms of modern professional performance. Comparative political science owes a lot to other sciences: philosophy since Aristotle, legal constitutionalism from Bodin to Bryce, political economy from Smith, Ricardo, Bentham, Marx, and Mill. Mill was especially fruitful in methodology. In the nineteenth century 'sociology' was added—a term coined by Auguste Comte—and soon became important in helping political science liberate itself from jurisprudence and be transformed into a 'social science'.

During the Renaissance Machiavelli came close to a social science approach, minimizing the philosophical normativism of former times. Later comparisons were sometimes used to criticize one's regime, disguised under the description of distant systems, as in Montesquieu's *Lettres Persanes* (1721) or even utopian constructions of systems such as in the *Oceana* (1656) of James Harrington. One of the earliest and most complete comparisons was the work of a follower of Machiavelli's, Traiano Boccalini (1614: 1). In his *Ragguagli di Parnaso* a 'university of politicians' was summoned by Apollo on Mount Parnassus and had to give responsible answers concerning their various political systems. In spite of many insights, this work was distorted by a blind hatred of the 'imperialist power' of that time, the Spanish monarchy, which according to Boccalini interfered too much in Italian affairs.

Many historical comparisons in early modern times—from Machiavelli's *Discourses on the First Ten Books of Titus Livius* (1513) to Montesquieu's *Considérations sur les Causes de la Grandeur des Romains et de leur Décadence* (1734)—were rather ahistorical confrontations of Roman experiences and the life of modern states. Reasons for the decay of the Roman Empire were popular as a kind of normative warning for modern states. The diachronic comparisons treated various systems like contemporary societies. But they did not help to develop a critical methodology of comparison.

The evolutionist counter-reaction to the French Revolution was also not favourable for a scientific theory of comparison. History in the nineteenth century turned increasingly to historicism and the discipline developed more reservations to the comparative method than former political theories in the age of Enlightenment. Every historical event and development was declared 'unique'. Goethe indeed said 'only blockheads compare'—but he had only works of art and literature in mind. Goethe was afraid that mediocre connoisseurs might avoid a value judgement about works of art. This was indeed a permanent danger of the comparative sciences in many fields: relativism describing various historical solutions led neither to a conclusion nor even to a prediction about possible future historical developments.

Otto Hintze, with his comparative typologies, was an outsider in his discipline of German history. Troeltsch (1922, 1961: 191), another social science oriented historian, accepted comparisons only when they kept their 'methodological and heuristic character' at the level of building of hypotheses. This was consistent with older pioneers of the historical method such as Droysen (1858, 1960: 163) who knew already that without implied comparisons no meaningful hypothesis could be found in an ocean of facts and motivations among historical actors. American history in the twentieth century, with Barrington Moore, Charles Tilly, Theda Skocpol, and many others, led the anti-historicist counter-reaction and gave up the anti-comparative bias of historicist historiography.

Since Tocqueville (1961: 5, 12) there had been a widespread assumption that a new world under conditions of modernization needs a 'new political science', able to work on certain social developments which were likely to spread in all modern societies. The US were only a pretext to denounce the threats of equalization and democratization which were likely to spread also in Europe. Even a pioneer of comparative methods such as John Stuart Mill (1840, 1859: 62) in the *Edinburgh Review* resented that his friend Tocqueville in his seminal book 'has bound up in one abstract idea the whole of tendencies of modern commercial society, and given them one name—democracy'. This was an important precedent in the history of book reviews, criticizing the remains of a teleological approach to the evolution of comparative politics.

In pre-modern political theories certain features of the decision-making process in polities were mostly deduced as constant types, but hardly ever scientifically analysed as politics. The policies were still more rarely investigated. Some utopias, such as Harrington's *Oceana* (1656) represented a notable exception. The theory of the 'reason of state' of Machiavellians like Giovanni Botero (1589, 1948: 58 ff.)—which represented a kind of 'Jesuit welfare-Machiavellism'—went far beyond Machiavelli's obsession with foreign and military policies in so far as he developed the elements of domestic welfare policies in different states as the main criterion for political stability.

Pre-modern comparisons mostly aimed at classifications of whole political orders (**polity**). Only in modern times was **politics** compared when the techniques of ruling in theories of 'reason of the state' or 'sovereignty' were discussed after Machiavelli. Comparisons were rather simple typologies, such as those counting the number of rulers. Many of them contained normative assumptions. The characteristic features were not always logically consistent, such as Montesquieu's classification of monarchy, republic, and despotism. Voltaire mocked this typology which appeared to him as logical as the categories of a 'church registration of births', containing the elements: 'male', 'female', and 'illegitimate'.

Pre-modern approaches in the nineteenth century 'modernized' by turning away from static ontological classifications to historical theories of evolution. The most influential models were the evolutionary model of Darwin and the historical materialism of Marx with his historical stages. In comparative social science the two extremes were sometimes synthesized as in the evolutionary model of Herbert Spencer. The three authors presented approaches to theory-building: Darwin's was a kind of early 'functionalism', Marx adopted from Hegel the dialectical method, and Spencer established himself as a precursor of systems theory. Since John Stuart Mill (1959: 253) the logic of social science implied two methods, the Method of Agreement and the Method of Difference. The first method was a kind of 'artificial experiment' and the second method was to be applied in situations where experiments were unfeasible. Early comparisons in the pre-modern era were obsessed with finding similarities. Only in the twentieth century was the primacy of the Method of Difference increasingly developed.

KEY POINTS

❑ Pre-modern comparative politics was speculative, normative, and anecdotal. The boundaries with philosophy, jurisprudence, and history were not clearly defined.

❑ Machiavelli, Montesquieu, and Tocqueville come close to founding a modern comparative political science. This was acknowledged by John Stuart Mill when establishing his Methods of Agreement and Difference.

❑ Polities, rather than politics and policies, were described. The main goal of these analyses was to establish classifications and typologies. Very often these classifications concerned evolutionary models (derived from Darwinism), as in the case of Spencer and Marx.

Comparative politics in modern times

Scientific comparison as controlled experiment

There is no agreement when modernity starts. In art and literature it is often located earlier in the nineteenth century. In the social sciences modernity is scheduled later. The criteria of definition—a truly scientific theory which can be controlled empirically—offer a more precise proof for modernity than works of arts. In order to avoid quarrels of definition we should use the term **classical modernity** for the new social sciences in the twentieth century.

Classical modernity coincides largely with the establishment of separate disciplines in the social sciences, such as sociology and political science. The neighbouring social sciences, such as public law, political economy, or general history, in the nineteenth century still claimed to deal with politics in the evolution of modernization and specialization. In the twentieth century they withdrew from comparative politics. 'Comparative economics' continued to exist as a subfield, but it never played the dominant role of comparative politics in political science because of the mathematical character of the most influential economic models.

The German *Staatslehre* (theory of state), located in the law departments, had a certain influence among the founding fathers of American political science, such as Francis Lieber, a Prussian refugee who taught at Columbia University. But the second generation of American scholars, including Woodrow Wilson, already abhorred general theories of the state. A pioneer of group theory, such as Arthur F. Bentley (1908, 1949: xix), after studies in Berlin and Freiburg, turned away from the 'spooks in the grain fields' which he

discovered in the metaphysical-minded *Staatslehre*. On the basis of American pragmatism he developed in Chicago an extremely anti-state theory of politics. Groups—instead of states—were now the basic concept of comparative analysis. Former deductive elements of comparisons were substituted by inductive observations. In Europe British guild socialism and Harold Laski created an equivalent of an empirical political theory, directed against the 'statism' of continental political theory.

Spencer among the 'evolutionists' of the nineteenth century was the most influential thinker for empirical comparative politics. But in spite of his variation of a systems theory the founder of structural-functional systems theory, Talcott Parsons (1961: 3), opened his theory of action with an attack: 'Spencer is dead, but who killed him and how?' Spencer was not killed, but increasingly forgotten—as were most of the theories of historical stages in the nineteenth century, especially Auguste Comte. Parsons tried to smooth down his verdict in a footnote: 'Not, of course, that nothing in his thought will last. It is his social theory as a total structure that is dead.' Critical rationalism of the neo-positivist school of Karl Popper was later keen on 'hunting' what it called 'historicism'. Charles Merriam and other founders of political science in the US were more tolerant and recognized at least a certain progress because this kind of historicism was 'historical-comparative' and no longer normative and purely deductive like the traditional, mainly anecdotal, comparisons in the classical political literature.

The various approaches had some assumptions in common, even if Durkheim, Weber, and Pareto, for Parsons (1961) the champions of modern social science, differed in many ways. Oddly enough they did not relate to each other—though all the three were able to read the language of the two others. Historical factors, which Darwin (biological struggle for life) or Marx (class conflict grounded on the contradiction between the economic base and the political superstructure) saw as the driving force behind the evolution, were no longer accepted. But nevertheless a 'dominant variable' was behind the modern evolution: for Weber it was occidental rationalism and bureaucracy, for Durkheim it was the division of labour, leading to a kind of 'organic solidarity', and for Pareto it was the cycles of rise and decay of elites.

In spite of these differences there are four principles common to all thinkers of classical modernism:

1. **History is not identical with evolution.** There is no longer a *telos*, a final point where the evolution is aiming at. In so far as political theory has to give up the old normative idea, *historia magistra vitae*, history can no longer serve as a teacher for later generations.

2. **Theory and practice are divided.** The scholar is not obliged to take political action, as was still the case in the theories of Marx and Engels. This did not prevent Pareto and Weber from standing as candidates for parliamentary election. Fortunately for the progress of social science they failed. Anti-normative value-free science was discovered as a protection against the interferences of the state as well as against the demands of political groups which consider scholars close to their ideologies. There is no longer the hope for a 'philosopher king' who combines knowledge and political action.

3. **Subsystems are autonomous.** The spheres of life and sub-systems of the social system are separated and autonomous. There is no hope that the political system—as in the times of absolutism—will be able to steer the subsystems of the whole society. With totalitarian ideologies this kind of hope was renewed, until the dictatorships collapsed between 1949 and 1989. Carl Schmitt was probably the most influential political theoretician who tried, in a heroic turn back to 'revolutionary conservatism', to reinstall 'political decision' in its primordial rights in society. The driving force behind this was that Schmitt

was afraid of a lasting dominance of the economy in society. Especially after the failures of dictatorship, political theory reduced its claims and renounced of the primacy of the political subsystem.

4. **Science is guided by theory.** Value-free science should be comparative and theory-guided, not just an enumeration and typology of institutions, as in the works of some pioneers of 'comparative government'—as the new discipline was initially called by scholars from James Bryce to Carl J. Friedrich.

Typologies are the initial stage of theory-building in order to develop a hypothesis for empirical work. Some typologies claimed to be a theory. Theories contain generalizations about political reality, typologies are abstractions about political reality according to some formal criteria. Some theories were close to one approach, such as functionalism (see Chapter 2). In other cases a methodology such as the behaviouralist approach tried to gain the status of a monopolistic theory. In recent times rational choice showed similar tendencies. Some typologies were comparative only in an indirect way. Even Max Weber's typology of types of legitimate rule—traditional, charismatic, and rational or legal-bureaucratic rule—are not free of remainders of the old debate on 'uniqueness vs. comparability' because the ideal types contained elements of uniqueness as 'individual totalities'. The ideal types served to elaborate the special features of social institutions. Only in the time of classical modernity were typologies of dynamic processes offered. Historical research continued, however, to suspect such taxonomies as they were developed in Crane Brinton's *Anatomy of Revolutions* (1937).

We should not identify the modern breakthrough to scientific comparisons with behaviourism, as sometimes occurs in American literature. Even the broader and less rigid form of 'behaviouralism'—which dominated for a while the torchbearers of modern political science in the 1950s and 1960s—was soon combined with other approaches, such as functionalist system theories. Functional considerations were not completely compatible with the strictly individualistic assumptions of behaviourism.

This contradiction can be shown in the seminal research on *The Civic Culture* by Almond and Verba

(1963: 52, 68). The authors had some misgivings whether the uses of comparative survey studies would allow the 'uniformity of a psychological type' to be discovered in a whole country. In order not to distort the results a concentration was recommended on the behaviour or attitudes that are least determined by the structure of the situation. Behaviouralism started from a rather mechanistic stimulus–response model of behaviour, functionalism was closer to organic models. Systems theory is holistic and presupposes 'purposes' of a system which was speculative for many behaviouralists. But neither systems theory nor behaviouralism in practice stayed completely dogmatic, so that a cooperation of various methodological tenets was possible.

Beyond the general metatheoretical consensus of all empirical scholars in political science, behaviouralism developed major tenets, as David Easton classified them in his *Framework for Political Analysis* (1965: 7):

- Regularities or uniformities in political behaviour should be expressed in generalizations or theory.

- The validity of these generalizations has to be tested. Contrary to Popper's orthodoxy, which admitted only falsification, verification was possible.

- Techniques of seeking and interpreting data have to be developed.

- Quantification and measurement in the recording of data.

- Values as distinguished between propositions relating to ethical evaluation and those relating to empirical explanation.

- 'Pure science', or the seeking of understanding and explanation of behaviour before utilization of knowledge for solution of societal problems.

- Integration of political research with that of other social sciences.

Only once political science was well established in American universities did 'comparative politics' develop its dominant position, in theory-building of the discipline as well as in the evaluation of the ranks of individual scholars in the scientific community. American and German rankings since Somit and Tanenhaus (1964: 66) and Falter and Klingemann (1998) have shown that comparative scholars had the highest reputations among their colleagues. In American political science after 1945 seven scholars among the top ten were in comparative politics, two in theory, and one in international politics. In the German case there was only one scholar in the field of international relations among the top ten in political science. All the rest—mostly Americans, one Italian, one Dutch, one German—were scholars in comparative politics (see Table 1.1).

Thanks to a new world situation, the development of the 'Third World' and modernization theories which dealt with the transition from traditional societies to modern democracy, the main theoretical innovations in political science were developed by comparative scholars. Only political science has accommodated the comparative aspects in a special subfield. The existence of a subdiscipline 'comparative politics', however, was not uncontested in the organized discipline. There was never a dominant behavioural stage of comparative politics as postulated by Chilcote (1994: 56).

From *sociology*—in methodological questions far more sophisticated—political science inherited two traditions:

1. The historical-institutional tradition of Max Weber was comparative. Weber almost excessively looked in all the great cultures of the world for comparable elements, especially in his sociology of religions.

2. The opposite school was initiated by Herbert Spencer and led by Emile Durkheim (1950: 137) He opposed a subdiscipline of 'comparative sociology' because comparison for him was *la sociologie même* (sociology itself). Systems theory with various degrees of intensity joined this opinion, most vehemently the autopoietic variant of Niklas Luhmann (1970: 25, 46) who tried to go beyond Talcott Parsons's structural–functional theory.

From **economics**—in mathematical questions far more sophisticated—political science inherited formal modelling. In economics the former historical orientations were increasingly substituted by mathematical models. One branch of political science took over this kind of approach. Anthony Downs gave the prediction abilities of political theory priority over its capacity to describe the political reality: 'Theoretical models should be tested primarily by the accuracy of

Table 1.1 Ranking of influential political scientists

US ranking by Somit and Tanenhaus (1964)			German ranking by Falter and Klingemann (1998)		
Rank	Author	Discipline	Rank	Author	Discipline
1	Key	CP	1	Huntington	CP and IR
2	Truman	PT	2	Lipset	CP
3	Morgentau	IR	3	Lijphart	CP
4	Dahl	CP and PT	4	Keohane	IR
5	Lasswell	CP and PT	5	Dahl	CP and PT
6	Simon	CP	6	Almond	CP
7	Almond	CP	7	Schmitter	CP
8	Easton	CP and PT	8	Linz	CP and PT
9	Strauss	CP	9	Sartori	CP and PT
10	Friedrich	CP	10	Von Beyme	CP and PT

CP = comparative politics; IR = international relations; PT = political theory.

their predictions rather than by the reality of their assumptions' (1957: 21).

Comparative politics therefore has been particularly embarrassed by its failure to predict any major political events since 1945. The student rebellions of the 1960s, the oil crisis, the rise of new fundamentalism, the collapse of communism of 1989—all these events came as a surprise to comparative political scientists. Some forecasts were correct, such as the possible end of the Soviet Union, but the prediction was based on the wrong reasons, such as a Chinese–Soviet war in the bestseller of Amalrik (1970). Forecasting had to lower its ambitions. In forecasting short-term electoral results the discipline boasts of only 5 per cent margins of error. Many political scientists came to accept that macro-theoretical predictions are little more than informed guess-work. The evolution can only be reconstructed *ex post facto* (postdiction).

The 'most similar design' of comparison was still widespread, but some researchers preferred a 'most different system design' (Przeworski and Teune 1970: 31 ff.; see also Chapter 3 below). In historical perspective the similarities were mostly demonstrated by the diffusion of institutions, a method widely applied in anthropology. Systems theory on the contrary looked for dissimilarities which were able to serve as 'functional equivalents' in various systems with sometimes 'similar results'. Only the post-modernist Luhmann went as far as to claim the one-party state in Communist systems was a functional equivalent of the pluralist democratic party regimes in the West.

Typologies and classifications: the first step to comparison

There is a large consensus that the main purpose of comparative research is not comparing but explaining. Comparison is a tool for building empirically falsifiable explanatory theories. A first step is a rigid classification. 'Miscomparing' starts from 'misclassification', 'concept stretching', and what Sartori (1991: 248) called 'degreeism'. This neologism meant the replacement of dichotomous treatment by continuous notions. According to Sartori the classification by degrees leads to logical messiness. Pre-modern and some modern typologies do not live up to these rigid criteria. The predicaments of typological work as a base for comparison show that systems theories are frequently characterized by geometrical obsessions of order, while institutional typologies follow arithmetic intentions. Religious remainders invade typologies: trinities are discovered everywhere (see Table 1.2).

These trinities do not violate Sartori's verdict against 'degreeism', but logically we would prefer dual typologies, such as Spencer's (society of warriors/industrial society), Durkheim's (mechanical/organic solidarity), Tönnies's (community/society), Bagehot's (dignified/efficient parts of the constitution). If more than three elements are put into one taxonomy the danger cannot be excluded that the theoretical value is reduced to a kind of checklist. Remainders of a teleological typology are frequently found in trinitarian classifications. The third element is quite often hailed as the normatively desired type in the development.

The problem of different criteria in classifications of types of regimes was not always solved—not even in modern typologies. Probably the last scholar who tried to classify all the regimes in history—from anarchy and tribal rule to totalitarian dictatorships—was Carl J. Friedrich (1963: 188–9). He listed thirteen types of rule, but they lacked a common criterion of classification. Some regimes were characteristic of early societies, others were only minor institutional variations of representative government, such as presidential or parliamentary systems. Some regimes, such as the types of dictatorship, were classified not by their institutional characteristics, but by the extent of control over the citizens. In formal sociology there was for a while a tendency to classify outrageously, as in the treatises of Georges Gurvitch in France or of Leopold von Wiese in Germany. In political science this happened only occasionally in the classification of regimes. Classifications of regime types should not reinvent Greek notions as Küchenhoff (1967) did, but rather try and find a common-sense solution in terms which are accepted by scholars as well as by the public debate.

Excessive preoccupation with terminological clarity revealed a predicament: neologisms, mostly in Greek or Latin, reduced terminological ambiguities, but they had no chance of entering the public debate. Political science terminology is imbued with traditional perceptions of politics and can hardly proceed like chemistry or medicine in preserving purely scientific jargon. As an example of this predicament we might consider the type of a 'semi-presidential system' (see Chapter 5). The term is not quite correct, because a system with a popularly elected president remains a variation of a parliamentary system: parliament can topple the government by votes of non-confidence and the president can dissolve the chambers. But Duverger's expression (1988) was accepted in the scientific community. In popular debates, however, 'presidial' or even 'presidential government' still occurs for this type of representative government. A survey has shown that as many as 6 per cent of the German deputies wrongly classified the German parliamentary system.

The problem of miscomparing by misclassification has been overcome by the construction of fourfold matrices which allow at least two classificatory elements (close to a typology of Arend Lijphart 1984) to be put into relation to each other and to subsume various countries in four fields (Figure 1.1)

The more complex such a matrix, the more comparative scholars have to be aware that such instant pictures can change quickly. British devolution, for instance, since the institutionalization of parliaments for Scotland and Wales has developed in the direction of Spain—with the exception of the electoral law. If proportional electoral system—under the pressure from the European Union—is one day accepted even for British elections the whole type might shift to top quarter of the matrix. Russia with its mixed type of an electoral law and with different levels of equality of the rights of the federal units is somewhere in-between the four fields of the matrix.

From the comparisons of 'polities' and 'politics' to the comparisons of 'policies'

Comparative politics overcame the remainders of institutional typologies in the 1970s and 1980s when it turned from politics to policies. Input–output comparisons were clearly inspired by the economic sciences. The main question was: 'does politics matter?' (See, for a development of this question, Chapter 3.) Comparative politics, influenced by political economy, even suggested that the difference between capitalist and communist systems in the

Table 1.2 Typologies in comparative social sciences

Authors	Types
Historical types	
Compte	Theological era
	Metaphysical era
	Positive era
Morgan	Wildness
	Barbarianism
	Civilization
Engels	Communist original society
	Exploiting society (slavery, feudalism, capitalism)
	Communism
Theoretical types	
Weber	Traditional rule
	Charismatic rule
	Rational rule
Almond	Absolute value orientation
	Traditional style
	Pragmatic bargaining style
	Subject political culture
Almond and Verba	Parochial political culture
	Participant political culture
Duverger	Party cells and militia
	Traditional electoral committee of notables
	Mobilized party organised in sections

(continued)

Table 1.2 (*continued*)

Authors	Types
Apter	Mobilization developing regime
	Consociational developing regime
	Modernizing developing regime

light of modernization theory was exaggerated by the propaganda of both systems in a bipolar world of confrontation. Socio-economic determinism of Western theories of convergence of the systems since the 1970s had some traits in common with economy-centred Marxism which for reasons of methodology was not accepted.

By the early 1970s **comparative public policy** had emerged as a recognized subdiscipline within political science (see Chapter 20). The timing was not as a surprise. The worldwide intellectual unrest from Berkeley to Berlin had mobilized scholars to support an activist image of the state. Most of the scholars—except Huntington who wrote from a neo-conservative point of view—were liberal leftists. Though many of these comparativists had some 'social-democratic bias' and admired the Scandinavian welfare state, they were tired of ideological discussions. The grand debates between neo-Marxism and critical rationalism were abandoned. Scholars from different metatheoretical schools agreed to stop discussing abstract constructs and study instead the needs of groups in the society. 'The state is better described by its policies than by its principles and alleged norms of individual choice and preference' (Ashford 1977: 572) was a widely shared assumption, especially in American political science, though less so in Europe where the remains of ideological debates were still strong.

The behaviouralist approach in the 1950s and 1960s frequently started with survey studies of individuals. Therefore it was normally less open to transnational comparisons. The predicament of the small number of cases for comparison drove

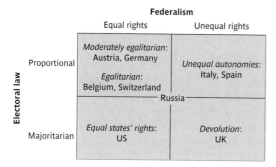

Federalism

	Equal rights	Unequal rights
Proportional	*Moderately egalitarian:* Austria, Germany / *Egalitarian:* Belgium, Switzerland	*Unequal autonomies:* Italy, Spain
	Russia	
Majoritarian	*Equal states' rights:* US	*Devolution:* UK

Electoral law

Fig. 1.1 Institutional mix for the mitigation of territorial conflicts

research into studies of cities or parts of cities in the Californian Bay area or in New York (Sharpe and Newton 1984: 218). Przeworski and Teune (1970) pleaded for concentration on the sub-units of a political system for comparison. But the result sometimes came close to a new parochialism which could be dubbed 'The Westside story' of comparative politics, because research concentrated on comparisons of hospitals or school districts in Westside New York.

One further result of this kind of evolution was the abandoning of theories in comparative research. The new policy orientation in the 1970s again concentrated on transnational comparisons. A model was created when Heidenheimer, Heclo, and Adams got an award for the best political science publication. Their definition was as follows: 'Comparative public policy is the cross-national study of how, why, and to what effect government policies are developed' (1975: v). The two schools which initiated comparative research continued to fight each other also in the subfield of 'comparative public policy'. The Heidenheimer-Heclo school was criticized for its descriptions without theories.

The 'Quasi-Eastonians' in the school of Dye (1966) and Hofferbert, on the other hand, overcame the lack of theory by adopting abundantly the terminology of structural–functional systems theory. On the ground of a modernization theory this approach had one assumption in common with the neo-Marxists: levels of economic development were more important than the political characteristics of individual states. In the US this assumption was mainly tested by comparisons among the policy performance of states. Harold Wilensky (1975: xiii) upheld the hypothesis about the centrality of economic development for the provision of social services: 'Economic growth and its

demographic and bureaucratic outcomes are the root causes of the general emergence of the welfare state'. Only European-born scholars, such as Anthony King (1973: 423), challenged this widespread consensus on the priority of economic development by asserting that ideas constitute a sufficient condition for explaining the variance in policy performance. Most scholars combined the importance of ideas with the focus on elite groups or answered positively the question 'Do parties matter?' The discovery of corporatism in the 1970s linked the elite approach with an emphasis on interest groups rather than on parties alone.

The Heidenheimer–Heclo school, based on historical and institutional studies, had the virtue of not neglecting 'politics' and the actors of decision, or reducing them to a kind of 'black box' for the production of a policy outcome which had little causal links to the decision-making process. Parties and interest groups were considered as analytically important. Increasingly, the role of the administrators was discovered. These were the main actors in an intermediary stage of decision. They operated between input and output of the political system and their contribution has been called **within-put**. The variance in the output of the compared systems was frequently explained in terms of rather vague special institutions, such as corporatism in Scandinavia or consensus democracy in Switzerland and the Benelux countries. Only the enlightened neo-institutionalism of the 1980s stopped to look for unilateral causal relationships between two variables in the polity system and the policy output. But the inclination of comparative public policy for historical determination of policy outputs was mostly preserved.

The concept of path dependence was introduced to explain why so many rising expectations for reform had failed in the 1970s. Restrictions, generated by historical developments and institutional barriers, left only 'narrow corridors' and windows of opportunity for policy action (on path dependence see Chapter 21). To avoid a new kind of historicism it was important that comparative research was growing in order to avoid 'culture-bound generalizations' as a danger of one-country studies. The hopes for reform proved to be dependent on the type of decision which has been classified. Different types of conflicts give rise to different types of legislative response and measures. **Policy determines politics** was an exaggerated slogan

COUNTRY PROFILE United Kingdom

United Kingdom of Great Britain and Northern Ireland

State formation

England has existed as a unified entity since the 10th century. The union with Wales was first formalized in 1536; in 1707, England and Scotland joined as Great Britain. The union of Great Britain and Ireland was implemented in 1801 (United Kingdom of Great Britain and Ireland). After the partition of Ireland in 1921, six northern Irish counties remained part of the United Kingdom.
Constitution Unwritten; partly statutes, common law, and practice.

Form of government

Constitutional monarchy.
Head of state The monarchy is hereditary.
Head of government Prime Minister, usually the leader of the majority party in the lower house.
Cabinet Cabinet of Ministers appointed by the Prime Minister.
Administrative subdivisions England: 47 boroughs, 36 counties, 29 London boroughs, 12 cities and boroughs, 10 districts, 12 cities, 3 royal boroughs. Northern Ireland: 24 districts, 2 cities, 6 counties (historic). Scotland: 32 council areas. Wales: 11 county boroughs, 9 counties, 2 cities and counties.

Legal system

Common law tradition with early Roman and modern continental influences; nonbinding judicial review of acts of Parliament.

Legislature

Bicameral parliament.
Lower house House of Commons: 646 seats; term of 5 years unless the House is dissolved earlier.
Upper house House of Lords: approximately 500 life peers, 92 hereditary peers and 26 clergy. No elections (but in 1999 elections were held to determine the 92 hereditary peers; elections are held only as vacancies in the hereditary peerage arise).

Electoral system (lower house)

Simple majority vote (plurality).
Constituencies 646 single-member constituencies.
Barrier clause Not applicable.
Suffrage Universal, 18 years.

Direct democracy

Every referendum needs a special ad hoc law.

Party system Results of the 2005 legislative elections (House of Commons):

Electorate	44,245,939	100.0%
Voters	27,148,510	61.4%

Party	Valid votes	%	Seats
Labour Party	9,552,436	35.2	355
Conservative Party	8,784,915	32.4	198
Liberal Democratic Party	5,985,454	22	62
UK Independence Party	605,973	2.2	0
Scottish National Party	412,267	1.5	6
Green Party	283,414	1	0
Democratic Unionist Party	241,856	0.9	9
Plaid Cymru	174,838	0.6	3
Sinn Féin	174,530	0.6	5
Ulster Unionist Party	127,414	0.5	1
Social Democratic and Labour Party	125,626	0.5	3
Independent	99,691	0.4	0
Respect	68,094	0.3	1

(*continued*)

COUNTRY PROFILE United Kingdom (*continued*)

Party	Valid votes	%	Seats
Health Concern	18,739	0.1	1
No label	22,725	0.1	1
Speaker	15,153	0.1	1
Others	417,602	1.6	0
Total	27,110,727	100.0	646

Notes: Category 'Others' includes parties with less than 1% nation-wide and no seats.
Source: The Electoral Commission.

by Theodore Lowi (1964) frequently tested in comparative politics. Lowi's typology initially showed a trinitarian design (regulative, distributive, and redistributive). Later he added a fourth type: constituent policy (see Chapter 20). The elements of the typology were, however, not all on the same logical level. If we differentiate between regulative (restrictive limitation of rights, regulative laws, neutral to the question of gain and loss, extensive measures aiming at an enlargement of rights) and distributive levels of decision (protective, distributive, and redistributive measures) we end up with a sixfold typology (Beyme, 1998: 5–6).

The typologies of policy fields and instruments of politics were soon connected by the network approach. A new slogan **network determines policy** was launched, but the differences between network theory and Lowi's assumptions were slight. Both predominantly saw a determination of the policy output by interest groups and other actors in the 'cosy triangles' of the decision-making process (deputies, interest groups, and administrators who prepare implementation) even if they start from policies as an 'independent variable'.

KEY POINTS

❑ In classical modernity separate disciplines are established: sociology and political science. Evolution theories are abandoned and theory and practice are separated (evaluative science). Also, politics is seen as following its own logic, different from that of other sciences.

❑ The behavioural revolution played a crucial role in establishing a modern comparative political science: regularities lead to generalizations to be tested empirically and measured quantitatively.

❑ Comparative politics was progressively established in US and then European universities with departments and chairs. Internationally, associations and consortia were created for the exchange of information and scientific collaboration.

❑ From typologies and classifications of polities, comparative politics moved to the analysis of politics and policies.

Comparative politics in post-modern times

Post-modernism in comparative political theory is not conceived as a completely new paradigm. Most reasonable post-modernists accept post-modernism only as a stage of modernity which implements its basic principles in a more consequential and systematic way than classical modernity. It cannot be equated with post-materialism or with certain processes of further differentiation and individualization which may lead to more decline of the old class social stratification and end up in theories of 'lifestyle'.

Post-modernity is a set of theoretical assumptions rather than a clearly discernible new structure of society. The hopes which were widespread in those European countries where ecological parties were strong, that a new 'society of movements' might develop, failed to materialize. The new social movements in most systems were strong in the phase of agenda setting (see Chapter 16). But decision and implementation was predominantly directed by traditional organizations.

Post-modernism strengthened thinking in terms of constructivism. Durkheim's assumption that sociology is by definition comparative was most eagerly adopted in post-modern autopoietic theories of systems. But Durkheim was still a realist and not yet a constructivist. 'Le fait social', the social fact, was his basic assumption but, in spite of his realistic way of thinking, it was a kind of 'construct'. Post-modernist theories sometimes referred to Durkheim's approach to comparative social science.

The comparative method was not a special approach for Luhmann, because he suspected that it aimed at a 'normative ontological framework'. He emphasized instead that comparative aspects had to be kept 'variable'. In autopoietic systems theory comparisons were not concerned with facts. In a society without a steering centre only the 'codes' which determined the development of the subsystems could be compared. But radically different codes (government–opposition in politics, true–false in science, legal–illegal in law, beautiful–ugly in the arts) can hardly be compared since they function according to radically different logics. Systems and subsystems which evolve according to different codes can only 'observe' but not 'influence' each other. Adaptations from one system in another are hardly feasible. Thus the main impetus for comparative politics was given up.

Post-modern theories, such as Foucault's *Archaeology of Knowledge* (1969), looked for variety. The 'summing up notions' in the 'archaeological comparisons' aimed at further pluralization of discourses. The critical approach to comparative politics in post-modern thinking was overdue. But 'thinking in fragments' finally leads 'ad absurdum' since a controlled comparison is no longer feasible. In autopoietic theories of systems comparisons are close to pathology in biology, where degenerated cells are compared with sound elements of an organism.

The evolution of comparative politics is not—as it has sometimes been presented in the literature—a clear evolution of subsequent paradigms. There is permanent change in the perception of the needs of scientific comparisons, but a dominant mainstream can hardly ever be traced which deserves Kuhn's mostly overstretched term of a 'paradigm'. There are, however, phases in the relationship of political theory toward comparisons. The eras of 'pre-modernity', 'classical modernity', and 'post-modernism' show differences in the application of comparative methods. Pre-modern scholars mostly used comparison in an anecdotal way or deducted characteristics from human nature or certain forms of rule (e.g. the Roman Empire vs. Greek states). From the nineteenth century a historicist approach, believing in a teleological development of the political systems, began to spread. Comparisons had to show the influence of a dominant factor such as demography or economy on the political systems. Comparison was predominantly applied to 'polities', rarely to 'politics', and seldom to the 'policies' in the respective systems.

The era of classical modernity for the first time developed rigorous criteria for scientific comparison, no longer confounding evolution and history, theory and practice, and accepting that the political subsystem was no longer steering a whole society. Post-modern theories aimed more strongly still at variety and doing away with the remains of 'reification' of phenomena in classical modernity. 'Communication' as a key concept and the assumption of constructed mutual perceptions changed the mood of comparative scholars. The authors of classical modernity also for the first time tried to develop logically consistent typologies as a tool for developing hypotheses.

Two traditions dominated comparative research which can be traced back to Max Weber's historical institutional comparisons or to Emile Durkheim's early systems approach, starting from the assumption that there is no special field of comparative social science. Sociology and political science were considered as comparative *per se*. The second line of development—under the impact of economic theory—was more interested in forecasting future developments than in realistic description of facts.

KEY POINTS

❑ Post-modernism contests the idea that there are 'social facts' and is rather based on the idea that social facts are social constructs. However, this does not represent a total rupture with the past but rather a different set of ontological assumptions.

Political influences on comparative politics

Theories and methodological approaches do not arise out of a blue sky. Methods of comparative politics proved to be influenced by political events. After 1945 American interest in foreign countries called for a new interest in foreign institutions. Soon, however, the behavioual revolution was distinguished from the old institutionalism in the tradition of Herman Finer or Carl J. Friedrich.

The counter-movement emphasized the comparison of dynamics of politics and political behaviour. The emphasis shifted towards interest groups and political movements. As a consequence of worldwide unrest and disobedience among the youth in the late 1960s new critical-dialectical and sometimes Marxist theories challenged the alleged conservatism of the behaviouralist mainstream which was blamed for only duplicating the alienated political world by its surveys. Political science discovered that the institutions were ill adapted but remained unchallenged by behaviouralists and functionalists. The scientific revolt started under the label of 'critique of parliamentarianism' and soon ended up in a dogmatic new political economy of revolution.

When the revolt petered out, neo-institutionalism and policy analysis became a minimal common denominator of leftists and mainstream scholars. The decline of communist regimes facilitated the change in theories and methods of comparative politics. New democracies were founded. In the era of the behavioural revolution nobody would have dared to talk about **constitutional engineering**. The breakdown of dictatorship in the 1970s and 1980s created the need to discuss old and new institutions. Even **rational choice institutionalism** was applied to the study of who took which option when creating a new constitutional order. Some former leftist scholars, such as Jon Elster, Claus Offe, or Adam Przeworski, developed an approach, dubbed as 'rational choice Marxism' which no longer accepted a 'telos of history' but worked out alternative options for the new elites in a post-communist world.

The breakdown of communism re-encouraged most distant systems designs. Transitions to democracy were compared in different areas and at different times. The theories of modernization and

transition to democracy were mostly modelled on developments in Southern Europe and South America in the 1970s. With the simultaneous transformations of both economic and political systems which had no precedent in recent history, old assumptions of modernization theories about the economic prerequisites of successful democratization were no longer applicable. New approaches were applied to the unique character of the peaceful revolutions in 1989, such as the testing of chaos theories from recent developments in biology and physics, although most of the applications remained metaphorical (Marks 1992).

Theories of various feasible roads to modernity in the tradition of Barrington Moore (1966) all of a sudden were outdated. On the other hand, typologies of transitions, such as 'liberalization', democratization, and 'consolidation', were prematurely generalized (see Chapter 5). They were difficult to find in many areas of the world and proved to be a generalization of those former dictatorships in Southern Europe which consolidated quickly because they were soon integrated in the European Union (O'Donnell and Schmitter 1986). They might apply only to the Western tier of states in East–Central Europe which recently became members in the EU. **Consolidology** as a subfield of **transitology** became a new branch of comparative politics. The normative equation—communism was a perversion of modernity, whereas post-communism is enlightened modernity—was quickly seen to be an untenable simplification. Soon comparativists discovered the 'defective democracies' which created another busy growth sector of comparativism (Merkel *et al.* 2003).

The acceptance of three worlds—the capitalist West, the communist world, and the Third World—until 1989 included the acceptance of a plurality of systems. After the breakdown of communism convergences are growing throughout the world (see the Introduction to this volume). The concept of a 'world society' emphasized by postmodern variations of systems theory seems to be more plausible than before 1989. When the biologist Maturana in the early 1980s developed the hypothesis that no country in the world was able to develop its communism fully because the world system was predominantly capitalist, this was taken as an abstract oddity of a non-social scientist. Nevertheless the hypothesis proved to be true. Oddly enough theories of post-modernity which emphasize plurality face an increasing streamlining of the world.

The consequences of this development for the methodology of comparative politics are not yet fully recognized. Political science mostly ignored the 'grand debates' on the level of macro-systems (see Chapter 24). Business as usual continued. Political science stuck to the middle level of mainly actor-oriented approaches. Recent revivals such as neo-institutionalism or rational choice had more impact on political science than the abstract peaks of a general theory in sociology. The status of institutionalism in comparative politics changed dramatically over the years. Institutionalism used to be an invective. At the turn of the century a new exaggeration was offered: 'we are all institutionalists now' (Pierson and Skocpol 2002: 706).

Rational choice approaches initially served as a counter-balance to the dominance of behavioural studies in the 1960s. It was easily combined with a multi-level analysis and with an enlightened neo-institutionalism which spread in the 1980s. It was linked with new attempts to reach the scientific level of neighbouring social sciences, such as economics: 'Rational choice institutionalism began as pure theft, lifting analytical tools from mathematics, operations research, and economics' (Shepsle 2006: 55). Rational choice approaches had the virtue of being applicable to any behaviour, from the most egoistic rationality to the most altruistic behaviour of saints. Against the assumptions of macro theories about autopoietic systems, the analysis of political actors remained meaningful. The strictly individualistic origin of the new approach was soon abandoned. Rational choice was applied to collective entities and even to whole states. The research programme of rational choice institutionalism conquered many departments in American universities, but never dominated in Europe. It was not unchallenged because of its abstractions, its simplifications, its analytical rigour, neglecting context. 'Context' was a new catchword of comparative studies which turned back to individual cases or to comparisons in a middle-range historical perspective.

KEY POINTS

☐ Theories, contents, and methods of comparative politics were influenced by political events. Especially after the Second World War there was a new interest in foreign institutions, groups, and movements.

☐ Modernization, decolonization, transitions to, and consolidation of, democracies influenced comparative politics and the practical application of its theories. Also the development after the Second World War of social welfare states had an impact on the move away from institutions towards policies and their impact on society.

Conclusion

The evolution of comparative politics was not a self-steering development, but one that proved to be deeply influenced by political events. The predicament of political science was that its capacity to forecast major events was limited. There was little anticipation of the student rebellion, the 'third-worldism', the technological and ecological revolutions, or the breakdown of communism. After 1945 the scope of American political science broadened to worldwide interests in area and systems studies.

The 'behavioural revolution' for a while seemed to develop into a kind of dominant paradigm—but only in the United States. The events after 1968 challenged the naïve trust in democratic institutions and an 'enlightened neo-institutionalism' had its revival. In combination with rational choice approaches, the two traditions merged in many ways. The crisis of policy-making under the impact of the oil crisis in 1973 strengthened the interest in transnational comparisons of public policies. The breakdown of communism renewed fields of comparisons which formerly had been treated under the auspices of modernization theories with a simplified analysis of dominant factors. Democratization and consolidation of the new democracies was one major interest. But soon the failure of consolidation ended in a new boom of studying defective democracy all over the world. If democracy was the final normative target of comparative studies, the scientific community had to face the fact that there are many defective democracies but nowhere a perfect democracy—not even in the world of consolidated states and representative governments in North America and Europe.

World trends

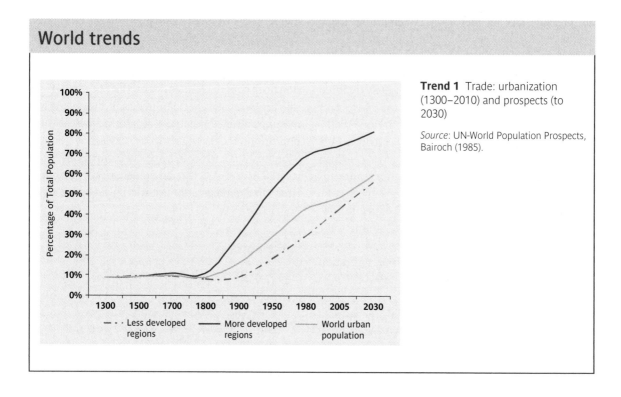

Trend 1 Trade: urbanization (1300–2010) and prospects (to 2030)

Source: UN-World Population Prospects, Bairoch (1985).

? Questions

1. Why can the evolution of comparative politics not be described as a sequence of paradigms?
2. What characterized comparative politics in pre-modern times? Who were the most important thinkers?
3. What characterizes comparative politics in modern times?
4. What was the contribution of the 'behavioural revolution' to the development of a scientific comparative political science?
5. Can experiments in comparative politics lead to a true scientific discipline?
6. Why are classifications and typologies important but problematic at the same time?
7. Why did comparative politics progressively shift its attention from polities to politics and policies?
8. Does politics determine policies or the other way round?
9. What is the influence of rational choice theory on comparative politics?
10. In what ways have political events influenced the evolution of comparative politics?

Further reading

For a more extensive treatment of the evolution of comparative politics see:

Almond, Gabriel A. (1997) *A Discipline Divided: Schools and Sects in Political Science* (Newbury Park, Calif.: Sage).

Apter, David E. (1996) 'Comparative Politics, Old and New', in Robert Goodin and Hans-Dieter Klingemann (eds.), *The New Handbook of Political Science* (Oxford: Oxford University Press), 372–97.

Blondel, Jean (1999) 'Then and Now: Comparative Politics', *Political Studies,* 47(1): 152–60.

Institutional theories

Chilcote, Ronald H. (1994) *Theories of Comparative Politics* (Boulder, Colo.: Westview, 2nd edn).

Daalder, Hans (1993) 'The Development of the Study of Comparative Politics', in Hans Keman (ed.), *Comparative Politics: New Directions in Theory and Method* (Amsterdam: VU University Press), 11–30.

——(ed.) (1997) *Comparative European Politics: The Story of a Profession* (London: Pinter).

Laitin, David, D. (2002) 'Comparative Politics: The State of the Subdiscipline', in Ira Katznelson and Helen V. Milner (eds.), *Political Science: The State of the Discipline* (Washington, DC: W. W. Norton and American Political Science Association), 630–59.

Munck, Gerardo, and Snyder, Richard (2007) *Passion, Craft and Method in Comparative Politics* (Baltimore, Md.: Johns Hopkins University Press).

Wiarda, Howard J. (ed.) (2002) *New Directions in Comparative Politics* (Boulder, Colo.: Westview Press, 3rd edn).

 Web links

www.politicalthought.com
Webpage called politicalthought.com. Particularly useful is the link to 'theorists'.

www.keele.ac.uk/depts/por/ptbase.htm
The Keele guide to political thought and ideology on the internet.

http://socialsciencedictionary.nelson.com/ssd/main.html
Online dictionary of the social sciences.

http://polsci.colorado.edu/RES/theory.html
Political theory resources, internet resources for political scientists (University of Colorado, Boulder).

www.political-theory.org/
Foundations of political theory (an organized section of the American Political Science Association).

Visit the Online Resource Centre that accompanies this book for more information:
www.oxfordtextbooks.co.uk/orc/caramani/

2 Approaches in comparative politics

B. Guy Peters

Chapter contents

Reader's guide

This chapter reviews the main theories, perspectives, and approaches in comparative politics. Theories and approaches are crucial in guiding research and the awareness of what specific perspectives imply is important to make sense of scientific results. The chapter discusses the five main approaches in comparative politics that evolved over time and still represent important contributions (the five 'I's): old and new institutional analysis, interests and actors' strategies to pursue them through political action, ideas (political cultures in particular, but also social capital), methodological individualism, and the influence of the international environment. The role of 'interactions' is also stressed. The chapter concludes by discussing the importance of looking at political processes as well as of defining what the 'dependent variables' are.

Introduction

The political world is extremely complex, involving a range of institutions, actors, and ideas that interact on a continuous basis to provide governance for society. The complexity of politics and government is compounded when we attempt to understand several different political systems, and to compare the ways in which these systems function. As comparative politics has moved beyond simple descriptions of individual countries or a few institutions, scholars have required substantial guidance to sort through the huge amount of evidence available, and to focus on the most relevant information. Thus, we need to develop alternative approaches to politics, and particularly to develop approaches that are useful across a range of political systems.

Political theories are the source of these approaches to comparison. At the broadest level, there is the difference between **positivist** and **constructivist** approaches to politics, and to social life more broadly (see Box 2.1). At less general levels a number of different theories enable the comparative political scientist to impose some analytic meanings on the political phenomena being observed, and to relate that evidence back to a more comprehensive understanding of politics. This chapter will first discuss some general questions about the use of theory in comparative political analysis, and then discuss a set of alternative approaches to politics. Each of the approaches discussed provides some important information about politics, but few if any are sufficient to capture the underlying complexity. The chapter, therefore, will also discuss the need to use multiple approaches and to assess the ways in which the approaches mentioned interact for more complex explanations.

KEY POINTS

❑ Given the high complexity of political systems and the wide range of variation between them across the world, it is important to develop approaches that are useful across them and not simply in single countries.

❑ Political theories are the main source of such approaches—the division between positivism and constructivism being the more general distinction.

Uses of theory in comparison

As is true for any other aspect of political science, theory is crucial for study of comparative politics. Although there is an important interaction between theory and empirical research in all areas of the discipline, that interaction is especially important in comparative politics. Although there is an increasing amount of statistical research in political science, a decreasing but still significant amount of case research, and a limited amount of experimental research, comparison remains in many ways the fundamental laboratory for political science.[1] Without the capacity to compare across political systems, it is almost impossible to understand the scientific importance of findings made in a single country (see Lee 2007), even one as large as the US.[2]

Without empirical political theory effective research might be impossible, or it certainly would be less interesting. Some questions that are almost purely empirical can and should be researched. It is interesting to know variations in the size of cabinets in European countries, for example, but if the scientific study of politics is to progress then research needs to be related to theory. The information on the size of cabinets can be related to the capacity of those cabinets to make decisions, for example, through understanding the number of 'veto players' in the system (Tsebelis 2002). Or the size of cabinets can be related to the capacity of social groups to achieve representation directly in the public sector.

Comparative political theory, therefore, is the source of questions and puzzles for researchers. For example, once we understand the concept of consociationalism, why is it that some societies have been able to implement this form of conflict resolution mechanism and others have not, even

BOX 2.1 Positivism and constructivism

Most of contemporary political science, and comparative politics, is founded on positivist assumptions. The most basic assumption of positivism is a fact value distinction, implying that there are real facts that are observable and verifiable in the same way by different individuals. Further, it is assumed that social phenomena can be studied in much the same way as phenomena in the natural sciences, through quantitative measurement, hypothesis testing, and theory formation. For example, the study of political attitudes across political cultures (beginning with work such as *The Civic Culture* (Almond and Verba 1963) and extending to contemporary work, has assumed that there are dimensions of individual political thought than can be measured and understood through surveys and rigorous statistical analysis.

Constructivism, on the other hand, does not assume such a wide gulf between facts and values, and considers facts to be socially embedded and socially *constructed* (see Finnemore and Sikkink 2001). Thus, the individual researcher cannot stand outside political phenomena as an objective observer but rather to some extent imposes his/her own social and cultural understandings on the observed phenomena. While most of the research undertaken from a positivist perspective assumes the individual is the source of social action (methodological individualism), constructivism asserts the importance of collective understandings and values, so that phenomena may not understood readily in the absence of that context. Rather than relying on variables to define the objects of research, constructive approaches focus more on dimensions such as scripts, or discourses, to promote understanding.

Each of these approaches to comparative politics can make major contributions to our understanding. The use of the variable-oriented research associated with positivism has added greatly to the comparative understanding of individual-level behaviour, as well as to understanding political parties and other mass-based organizations. On the other hand, much of the analysis of formal political institutions and processes of governing still relies on methods that, if not explicitly constructivist, do share many of the assumptions concerning collective understandings and the importance of ideas.

with relatively similar social divisions (see Lijphart 1996; Bogaards 2000)? Likewise, political systems that appear relatively similar along a number of dimensions may have very different experiences with maintaining effective coalition governments (Müller and Strøm 2000). Why? We have theories that help explain how cabinets are formed and why they persist but the anomalies and exceptions to these theories are crucial both for elaborating the models and enhancing our more general understanding of parliamentary democracies.

One of the crucial functions of theory in comparative politics is to link micro and macro behaviour. Much of contemporary political theory functions essentially at the micro-level, attempting to understand the logic of individual choice. The most obvious example is the rational choice paradigm that assumes utility maximization on the part of the individual, and uses that assumption about individuals to interpret and explain most political phenomena.[3] Likewise, cognitive approaches in political psychology are a central component of contemporary political science. In both cases, however, the individual behaviours are assumed to be channelled through institutions.

Further, there is some reciprocal influence as institutions shape the behaviour of individuals and individuals also shape institutions. For example, the institution of the presidency in the US is very different after the personal indiscretions of Bill Clinton, and will be different again after George W. Bush.

The link between the micro and the macro is crucial for comparative politics, given that one of our primary concerns is explaining the behaviour of political systems and institutions rather than individuals. Certainly variations in individual behaviour and the influence of cultural and social factors on that behaviour are important, but the logic of comparison is primarily having larger structures in play, and to think about how individuals interact within parliaments, parties, or bureaucracies. Indeed, one could argue that if a researcher went too far down the individualist route, then any comparison would become irrelevant, and all the researcher would care about would be the individual's behaviour. This problem is perhaps especially relevant for rational choice approaches that tend to posit relatively common motivations for individuals (but see Bates *et al.* 2002).

Theory is at once the best friend and the worst enemy of the comparative researcher. On the one hand, theory is necessary for interpretation of findings, as well as providing the puzzles and questions that motivate new research. Without having political theory research would simply be a collection of useful information and, although the descriptive information would be interesting, it would not advance the more analytic understanding of politics. Further, theory provides scholars with the puzzles and the questions that can be solved, or at least addressed, through comparative research. Theory predicts certain types of behaviour and if individuals or organizations do not behave in that manner we need to probe more deeply. We should never underestimate the role that simple empirical observation can play in setting puzzles, but theory is also a powerful source for ideas that add to the comparative storehouse of knowledge.

As important as theory is for interpreting findings and for structuring initial research questions, theory is also a set of blinders for the researcher. After we choose our theoretical approach and develop a research design based on that theoretical choice, most people find it all too easy to find support for that approach. This tendency to find support for a theory is not necessarily the result of dishonesty or poor scholarship. Rather, this tendency generally reflects a sincere commitment by the researcher to the approach, and the consequent inability to identify any disconfirming evidence, or even to look for it. Most research published in political science tends to find support for the theory or model being investigated, and although in many ways negative findings would be more useful, positive findings continue to be published more easily.[4]

Given the tendency to find support for theories, comparative research could be improved by greater use of triangulation.[5] That is, if we explore the same set of data with several alternative theories, or go into the field with alternative approaches in mind, we become more open to findings that do not confirm one or another of those approaches. Likewise, if we would collect several forms of data—substantiating the findings of quantitative research with those from case studies or other qualitative methods—then we could have a better idea whether the findings being presented were valid.[6] Doing this type of research can be expensive, involves a range of skills that many researchers may not possess, and may ultimately result in findings that are inconclusive and perhaps even confusing.

When we discuss theory for comparative politics, we have to differentiate between **grand theories** and more **middle-range theories**, or even analytical perspectives. At one stage of the development of comparative politics there was a great deal of emphasis on all-encompassing theories such as structural functionalism (Almond and Powell 1966) and systems theory (Easton 1965*b*; see Box 2.2). These theories became popular as comparative politics had to

---

BOX 2.2 Major approaches to comparative politics

Structural functionalism

The purpose of this approach was to identify the necessary activities (functions) of all political systems and then to compare the manner in which these functions were performed. As it was elaborated it had developmental assumptions about the manner in which governing could best be performed that were closely related to the Western, democratic model.

Systems theory

This approach considered the structures of the public sector as an open system that had extensive input (supports and demands) and output (policies) interaction with its environment.

Marxism

Class conflict is an interest-based explanation of differences among political systems. While offering some empirical predictions about those differences, Marxist analysis also posits a developmental pattern that would lead through revolution through a 'dictatorship of the proletariat'.

Corporatism

This approach stresses the central role of state and society interactions in governing, and especially the legitimate role of social interests in influencing policy. Even in societies such as Japan or the US that have not met the criteria of being corporate states, the identification of the criteria provides a means of understanding politics.

(continued)

BOX 2.2 (continued)

Institutionalism

Although there are several approaches to institutionalism, they all focus on the central role of structures in shaping politics and also in shaping individual behaviour. As well as formal institutional patterns, institutions may be defined in terms of their rules and their routines, and thus emphasize the normative structure of the institutions.

Governance

As an approach to comparative politics governance has some similarities to structural functional analysis. It argues that certain tasks must be performed in order to govern a society and then posits that these can be accomplished in a number of ways. In particular, scholars of governance are interested in the roles that social actors may play in the process of making and implementing decisions.

---

confront the newly independent countries in Africa and Asia, and find ways of including these countries in the same models as industrialized democracies. Those grand theories fulfilled their purpose of expanding the range of concerns geographically, as well as including less formal actors in the political process, but it soon became evident that by explaining everything they actually explained nothing. The functions of the political system and their internal dynamics discussed were so general that they could not produce meaningful predictions. Since that time there has been a tendency to rely more on mid-range theories and analysis, although the contemporary governance theories have some of the generality of functional theories.

Finally, as we engage in attempts to develop theory using multiple theoretical approaches, we need to be cognizant of their linkages with methodologies, and the possibilities for both qualitative and quantitative evidence. Comparative politics is both an area of inquiry and a particular method that emphasizes case selection as much as statistical controls to attempt to test its theories. Each of the approaches discussed below has been linked with particular ways of collecting data, and we must be careful about what evidence is used to support an approach, and what evidence is being excluded from the analysis.

KEY POINTS

❑ Theory is necessary to guide empirical research in comparative politics. It is also necessary to interpret the findings. It provides the puzzles and the questions that motivate new research.

❑ Without theory, comparative politics would be a mere collection of information. There would be no analytical perspective attempting to answering important questions. However, theories and approaches should never become blinders for the researcher. Ideally, we

should investigate the same question from different angles.

❑ An important distinction concerns grand theories and middle-range theories. With the behavioural revolution there was a great emphasis on all-encompassing theories. At present, there is a tendency to develop 'grounded theories' or middle-range theories that apply to more specific geographical, political, and historical contexts.

Alternative perspectives: the five 'I's

Institutions

The roots of comparative political analysis are in institutional analysis. Going back as far as Aristotle, scholars interested in understanding why governments

performed as they did, and seeking to improve that performance, concentrated on formal constitutional structures and the institutions created by those constitutions. Scholars documented in great detail differences in constitutions, laws, and formal structures of government, and assumed that, if those structures were understood, then the actual performance of governments could be predicted. Somewhat later scholars in political sociology also began to examine political parties as organizations, or institutions, and to understand them in those terms (Michels 1916).

With the behavioural revolution in political science, followed then by the increasing interest in rational choice models, the underlying paradigm in political science became more individualistic. The governing assumption, which is often referred to as *methodological individualism*, became that individual choices, rather than formal institutional constraints, produced observed differences in governments. It was difficult to avoid the obvious existence of institutions such as legislatures, but the rules of those organizations were less important, it was argued, than the nature of the individuals who inhabited them. Further it was argued that decisions emerging from institutions were to a great extent the product of the preferences of the members, and those preferences were exogenous to the institutions.

While many other areas of political science became almost totally absorbed by the concern with individual behaviour, comparative politics remained more true to its institutional roots. Even though some conceptualizations of behaviour within institutions was, and continues to be, shaped by individualistic assumptions, understanding structures is still crucial for comparative politics. With the return to greater concern with institutions in political science in general, the central role of institutions in comparative politics has at once been strengthened and made more analytical.

The 'new institutionalism' in political science (Peters 2000) now provides an alternative paradigm for comparative politics. In fact, contemporary institutional theory provides at least three alternative conceptions of institutions, all of which have relevance for comparative analysis. **Normative institutionalism**, associated with James March and Johan P. Olsen, conceptualizes institutions as providing sets of norms and rules that shape individual behaviour. **Rational choice institutionalism**, on the other hand, sees institutions more as aggregations of incentives and disincentives that influence individual choice. **Historical institutionalism** focuses on the role of ideas and the tendency of institutional choices to persist over long periods of time, even in

the face of their potential dysfunctionality. Each of these approaches to institutions provides a view of how individuals and structures interact in producing collective choices for the society.

Thus, merely saying that institutional analysis is crucial for comparative politics is insufficient. We need to specify exactly how institutions are conceptualized, and what sort of role they play in the analysis. At one level the concept of institutions appears rather formal, and not so different from some traditional thinking. That said, however, the contemporary work on those formal structures does examine their impact more empirically and conceptually than the more traditional work did. Also, the range of institutions covered has expanded to include elements such as electoral laws and their effects on party systems and the outcomes of elections (Taagapera and Shugart 1989).

Take, for example, studies of the difference between presidential and parliamentary institutions. This difference is perhaps as old as the formation of the first truly democratic political systems, but has taken on new life. First, the conceptualization of the terms has been strengthened for both parliamentary and presidential (Elgie 1999) systems, and the concept of divided government provides a general means of understanding of how executives and legislatures can interact in governing.[7] Further, scholars have become more interested in understanding the effects of the initial constitutional choice of presidential or parliamentary institutions. Some scholars (Linz 1990*a*; Colomer and Negretto 2005) have been concerned with the effects of presidential institutions on political stability, especially in less developed political systems. Others (Weaver and Rockman 1993*b*) have been concerned with the effects that presidential and parliamentary institutions may have on policy choices and public sector performance.

Although the distinction between presidential and parliamentary regimes is one of the most important institutional variables in comparative politics, other institutional variables are also useful for comparison, for example, the distinction between federal and unitary states (and among types of federalism, Schain and Menon 2006). Further, we can conceptualize the mechanisms by which social actors such as interest groups interact with the public sector in institutional terms (Peters 2000: ch. 5). The extensive literature on corporatism in its many manifestations has demonstrated the consequences of the way in which those interactions are structured. Likewise, the more recent literature on networks in governance also demonstrates structural interactions of public and private-sector actors (Sørenson and Torfing 2007).

The above discussion has concentrated on rather familiar institutional forms and their influence on government performance, but as already noted the development of institutional theory in political science has also brought greater attention to the centrality of institutions. Of the forms of institutional theory that have emerged in political science, historical institutionalism has had perhaps the greatest influence in comparative politics. The basic argument of historical institutionalism is that initial choices shape subsequent policies and institutional attributes of structures in the public sector (Steinmo *et al.* 1992). For example, the differences made in the initial choices about welfare state policies have persisted for decades and continue to resist change (Pierson 2001*b*). In addition to the fundamental observation about the persistence of programmes—usually referred to as path dependence—historical institutionalism has begun to develop theory about the political logic of that persistence (see Peters *et al.* 2005).

Institutional theory has been important for comparative politics and for political science more generally, but tends to be better at explaining persistence than explaining change. For some aspects of comparative politics we may be content with understanding static differences among systems, but dynamic elements are also important. As political systems change, perhaps especially democratizing and transitional regimes, political theory needs to provide the means of understanding this as well as predicting paths of change. While some efforts are being made to add more dynamic elements to institutional analysis, for example, the 'actor-centered institutionalism' of Fritz Scharpf (1997*c*), institutional explanations do remain somewhat constrained by the dominance of stability in the approach.

The above having been said, historical institutionalism can be related to important ideas about political change such as 'critical junctures' (Collier and Collier 1991; Cortell and Peterson 2000), and the need to understand significant punctuations in the equilibrium that characterizes most institutionalist perspectives on governing (see also Baumgartner and Jones 1993). In this approach change tends to be in the form of significant interruptions of the existing order, rather than through more incremental transformations. Much the same has been true of most models of transformation in democratization and transition, albeit with a strong concern about the consolidation of the transformations (Alexander 2002). This view contrasts with the familiar idea of incremental change that has tended to dominate much of the political science literature on public policy.

Interests

A second approach to explaining politics in comparative perspective is to consider the interests that actors are pursuing through political action. Some years ago Harold Lasswell (1936) argued that politics is about 'Who Gets What', and that central concern with the capacity of politics to distribute and redistribute benefits remains. Indeed, in political theory, the place of interest-based explanations has become more prominent, with the domination of rational choice explanations in much of the discipline (Lustick 1994; for a thorough critique see Green and Shapiro 1994). At its most basic, rational choice theory assumes that individuals are self-interested utility maximizers and engage in political action to receive benefits, usually material benefits, or to avoid costs (see Box 2.3). Thus, individual behaviour is assumed to be motivated by this self-interest and collective behaviour is the **aggregation of the individual behaviours**, through bargaining, formal institutions, or conflict.

Rational choice theory provides a set of strong assumptions about behaviour, but less deterministic uses of the general idea of interests can produce more useful comparative results. In particular, the ways in which interests in society are represented to the public sector and affect policy choices are crucial components of comparative analysis. The concept of corporatism was central to comparative analysis in the 1970s and 1980s (Schmitter 1974, 1989). The close linkage between social interests and the state that existed in many European and Latin American corporatist societies provided an important comparison for the pluralist systems of the Anglo-American countries. These differences produced a huge literature on the consequences of patterns of interest intermediation for policy choices and for political legitimacy.

BOX 2.3 Rational choice and comparative politics

Rational choice models have made significant contributions to the study of politics and government. By employing a set of simplifying assumptions, such as utility maximization and full information, rational choice models have enabled scholars to construct explanatory and predictive models with greater precision than would be possible without those assumptions. For example, if we assume that individuals act rationally to enhance their own self interest, then we can understand how they will act when they have the position of a 'veto player' in a political process (Tsebelis 2002). Likewise, if we assume voters engage in utility maximization then their choice of candidates becomes more predictable than in other models that depend more on a mixture of sociological and psychological factors, e.g. partisan identification.

By positing these common motivations for behaviour, however, rational choice adds less to comparative politics than to other parts of the discipline of political science. Comparative politics tends to be more concerned with differences among political systems and their members than with similarities. Comparative politics, as a method of inquiry (Lijphart 1971) rather than a subject matter, relies on selecting cases based on their characteristics and then determining the impact of a small number of differences on observed behaviours. If, however, everyone is behaving in the same way then important factors in comparative politics such as political culture, individual leadership, ideologies, and a host of others become irrelevant. Differences in institutions remain important, or perhaps even more important, in comparison because their structures can be analysed through veto points or through formal rules that create incentives and disincentives for behaviours.

The fundamental logic of corporatism was that many political systems legitimated the role of interest groups and provided those groups direct access to public decision-making. In particular labour and management were given the right to participate in making economic policy, but in return had to be reliable partners, with their membership living by the agreements, e.g. not striking. These institutionalized arrangements enabled many European and some Latin American countries to manage their economies with less conflict than was true for pluralist systems such as the United Kingdom.

The interest in corporatism in comparative politics also spawned a number of alternative means of conceptualizing both corporatism itself and the role of interests. For example, Stein Rokkan (1966) described the Scandinavian countries, and especially Norway, as being 'corporate pluralist', with the tightly defined participation of most corporatist arrangements being extended to involve a wide range of actors. Other scholars have discussed 'meso corporatism' and 'micro-corporatism', and have attempted to apply the concept of corporatism to countries where it is perhaps inappropriate (Siaroff 1999). In all its various guises corporatism provided a major thrust in comparative politics in the 1970s and 1980s.

The institutionalized pattern of linkage between social interests and the state implied in corporatism has been eroding and is being replaced by more loosely defined relationships such as networks (Torfing and Sørenson 2007; Klijn and Koopenjan 2005). The shift in thinking about interest intermediation to some degree reflects a real shift in these patterns, and also represents changes in academic theorizing. As the limits of the corporatist model became apparent, the concept of networks has had significant appeal to scholars. This idea is that surrounding almost all policy areas there is a constellation of groups and actors who seek to influence that policy, and who are increasingly connected formally to one another and to the relevant policy-making institution. The tendency of this approach has been to modify the self-interested assumption somewhat, in favour of a mixture of individual (group) and collective (network or society) interests.

Network theory has been developed with different levels of claims about the importance of the networks in contemporary governance. At one end, some scholars have argued that governments are no longer capable of effective governance and that self-organizing networks have become essential to providing this (Rhodes 1997; for a somewhat less extreme view see Kooiman 2003). For other scholars networks are in essence forms of interest involvement in governing, with formal institutions retaining the capacity to make effective decisions about governance. Further, the extent of democratic claims about networks varies among authors, with some arguing that these are fundamental extensions of democratic opportunities, and others concerned that their openness to membership is exaggerated and that networks may become simply another form of exclusion for the less well-organized elements in society.

Finally, we should note that, although there is a tendency to think of interests almost entirely in material terms, there are other important interests as well. Increasingly, individuals and social groups are defining their interests in terms of identity and ethnicity, and seek to have those interests accommodated within the political system along with their material demands.[8] This concern with the accommodation of socially defined interests can be seen, for example, in the literature on consociationalism (Lijphart 1968). Consociationalism is a mode of governing in which political elites representing different communities coalesce around the need to govern, even in the face of intense divisions across their communities. For example, this concept was devised originally to explain how religious groups in the Netherlands were able to coalesce and govern despite deep historical divisions.

Like corporatism, consociationalism has been extended to apply to a wide range of political systems, including Belgium, Canada, Malaysia, Colombia, Lebanon, and India. Likewise, it has been rejected as a solution for the problems of Northern Ireland and Iraq. The concept is interesting for comparative political analysis, but like corporatism may reflect only one variation of a more common issue. That is, almost all societies have some forms of internal cleavage (Posner 2004) and find different means of coping with those cleavages. In addition to strictly consociational solutions, social pacts (Higley and Burton 2002) have become another means of coping with difference and with the need to govern in the face of that difference.

Approaches to comparative politics built on the basis of interest tend to assume that those interests are a basis for conflict, and that institutions must be devised to manage that conflict. Politics is inherently conflictual, as different interests vie for a larger share of the resources available to government, but conflict can go only so far if the political system and the society are to remain viable. Thus, while interests may provide some of the driving force for change, institutions are required to focus that political energy in mechanisms for making and implementing policy.

Ideas

Although ideas are amorphous and seemingly not closely connected to the choices made by government, they are important and can have some independent effect on outcomes. That said, the mechanisms through which ideas exert that influence must be specified and their independent effect on choices must be identified. In particular, we need to understand the consequences of mass culture, political ideologies, and more specific ideas about policy. All of these versions of ideas are significant but each functions in different ways in the political process.

At the most general possible level, political culture exerts an influence on politics, but that influence is often extremely vague. Political culture can be the residual explanation in comparative politics—when everything else fails to explain the observed behaviours, then it must be political culture (Elkins and Simeon 1979). The real issue in comparative analysis, therefore, is to identify means of specifying those influences more directly and with greater accuracy. As comparative politics, along with political science in general, has moved away from behavioural explanations and more interpretative understandings of politics, there has been less analytic emphasis on understanding culture, so this important element of political analysis has been devalued.[9]

How, then, can we measure political culture and link this somewhat amorphous concept to other aspects of governing? The most common means of measuring the concept has been to use surveys, asking the mass public how they think about politics. For example, in a classic of political science research, *The Civic Culture* (Almond and Verba 1963) the public in five countries were asked a series of questions about their attitudes towards politics and particularly their attitudes about political participation. More recent examples of this approach to measurement include Ronald Inglehart's (1990, 1997) numerous studies using the World Values Survey, as well as studies that explore values existing in public and private organizations (Hofstede 2001).

Of course, before surveys for measuring political culture can be devised, scholars must have some

Table 2.1 Patterns of political culture

Grid	Group	
	High	*Low*
High	Fatalist	Hierarchical
Low	Egalitarian	Individualist

Source: Douglas 1968.

conceptual ideas about the dimensions that should be measured. Therefore, conceptual development must go along with, or precede, measurement. Lucien Pye (1968) provided one of the most interesting attempts at defining the dimensions of political culture, especially when viewed in comparative perspective. He discussed culture as the tension between opposite values such as **hierarchy and equality, liberty and coercion, loyalty and commitment**, and **trust and distrust**. Although these are expressed as dichotomies, political systems tend to have complex mixtures of these attributes that need to be understood to grasp how politics is interpreted within that society.

The anthropologist Mary Douglas (1968; see also Table 2.1) has provided another set of dimensions for understanding political culture that continues to be used (Hood 2000). She has discussed culture in terms of the concepts of **grid** and **group**, both of which describe the degree to which individuals are constrained by their society and its culture. Grid is analogous to the dimension of hierarchy in Pye's framework, while group reflects constraints derived from membership in social groups. As shown in Table 2.1, bringing together these two dimensions creates four cultural patterns that are argued to influence the performance of the public sector, and the lives of individuals. These patterns are perhaps somewhat vague, but they do provide means of approaching the complexities of political culture.

The trust and distrust dimension mentioned by Pye can be related to the explosion of the literature on social capital and the impact of trust on politics, a central concept in political culture. The concept of social capital was initially developed in sociology (Coleman 1973) but gained greater prominence with Robert Putnam's work on Italy and the United States

(Putnam 1993, 2000). This concept was measured through surveys as well as through less obtrusive measures. What is perhaps most significant in the social capital literature is that the cultural elements are linked directly with political behaviour, of both individuals and systems. Subsequent work in the social capital literature has emphasized the importance of different levels, and types, of trust on the performance of political systems.

As well as the very general ideas contained in political culture, political ideas also are important in the form of **ideologies**. In the twentieth century, politics in a number of countries was shaped by ideologies such as communism and fascism. Toward the end of the last century and into the current one an ideology of liberalism, or neo-liberalism, came to dominate economic policy in the industrialized democracies and was diffused through the less-developed systems by donor organizations such as the World Bank. Within the developing world, ideologies about development, such as Pancasila in Indonesia, reflect the important role of ideas in government, and a number of developing countries continue to use socialist ideologies to justify the strong position of the state in the economy.

Although ideologies have been important in comparative politics, there has been a continuing discussion of the decline, or end, of ideology as a force in political life. First, with the general acceptance of the mixed economy welfare state in most industrialized democracies the argument was that the debate over the role of the state in society was over (Bell 1965). More recently, after the collapse of the Soviet Union, a similar argument was made concerning the exhaustion of political ideas and the end of political conflicts based on ideas (Fukuyama 1992). This presumed end of the role of ideas, however, could be contrasted with the increased importance of some conservative ideologies and the increased significance of religion as a source of political conflicts.

A final way in which ideas influence outcomes in comparative politics is through specific policy ideas. For example, while at one time economic performance was considered, like the weather, largely uncontrollable, after the intellectual revolution in the 1930s governments had the tools to exercise that control (Hall 1989). Keynesian economic management was dominant for almost half a century, but then was supplanted by monetarism and to a lesser extent by ideas such as supply-side economics. Likewise, different versions of the welfare state, e.g. the Bismarckian model of continental Europe and the Beveridge model in the United Kingdom (see Esping-Andersen 1990), have been supported by a number of different ideas about the appropriate ways in which to provide social support. Many other policy areas have been guided by ideas that both justify and shape policy.

In summary, ideas do matter in politics, even though their effects may be subtle in a number of instances. This subtlety is especially evident for the impact of political culture, but tracing the impact of ideas is in general difficult. Even for policy ideas that appear closely related to the policy choices, it may be difficult to trace how the ideas are adopted and implemented (Braun and Busch 1999). Further, we need to think about policy learning (Sabatier and Jenkins-Smith 1993) and the social construction of agendas and political frames that can shape behaviour. Finally, for the purposes of comparative politics, we also need to consider why some political systems are more ideological than others, and how pragmatic and ideological styles may affect performance.

Individuals

I have already discussed the methodological individualism that has become central to theorizing in political science. Although I was arguing that an excessive concern with individual behaviour, especially when based on an assumption that individual motivations are largely similar, may make understanding differences among political systems taken as a whole more difficult, it is still impossible to discount

the importance of individuals when understanding how politics works, and how those regimes make decisions. The importance of political biography and political diaries as sources of understanding is but one of many indications of how important individual-level explanations can be in understanding governing.

Much of the individual level of explanation is rather naturally focused on political elites and their role in the political process. One of the more interesting, and perhaps most suspect, ways of understanding the behaviour of these political elites is through their personality. There have been a number of psychological studies, usually done from secondary sources, of major political figures (Freud and Bullitt 1967; Berman 2006). Most of these studies have focused on pathological elements of personality, and have tended to be less than flattering to the elites being considered. Less psychological studies of leaders, e.g. James David Barber's (1992; see also Simonton 1993) typology of presidential styles, have also helped to illuminate the role of individual leaders in the political process (see Table 2.2). Barber classifies political leaders in terms of their positive or negative orientations toward politics, and their levels of activity, and uses the emerging types to understand how these individuals have behaved in office.

A more sociological approach to political leaders has stressed the importance of background and recruitment, with the assumption that the social roots of leaders will explain their subsequent behaviour. Putnam (1976) remarked several decades ago that this hypothesis was plausible, but unproven, and that assessment remains largely true. Despite the absence of strong links between social background there is an

Table 2.2 Styles of political leaders

Orientation to politics	Activity	
	Active	*Passive*
Positive	Bill Clinton; Tony Blair	George H. W. Bush; Jim Callaghan
Negative	Richard Nixon; Margaret Thatcher	Calvin Coolidge; John Major

Source: Based on Barber (1992).

extensive body of research using this approach. The largest is the research on 'representative bureaucracy' and the question of whether public bureaucracies are characteristic of the societies they administer, and whether this makes any difference (Seldon 1997; Meier and Bohte 2001). While the representativeness of the bureaucracy is usually discussed at the higher, 'decision-making' levels, it may actually be more crucial lower down, where 'street level bureaucrats' meet citizens (Meyers and Vorsanger 2005). There is, however, some sense that the link between background and behaviour is strengthening, as programmes such as affirmative action emphasize the need for a more truly representative public service.

The ordinary citizen should not be left out of the consideration of the role of individuals in comparative politics. The citizen as voter, participant in interest groups, or merely as the consumer of political media plays a significant role in democratic politics, and perhaps less obviously in non-democratic systems. Therefore, we need to remain cognizant of the huge body of literature on voting behaviour across countries, and the insights about comparative political behaviour that have been gleaned from those studies. Further, the survey-based evidence on political culture already mentioned uses individual-level data to make some (tentative) statements about the system level.

In portions of political science that deal with the activities of government the role of the individual has become more apparent. Citizens are the consumers of public services, and the New Public Management has tended to place the individual citizens at the centre of public sector activity (see Chapter 8). This central role is true for the style of management that now is being pursued in the public sector. It is also true for a range of instruments that have been developed to involve the public in the programmes that serve them, and also for a range of instruments designed to hold public programmes accountable.

International environment

Much of the discussion of comparative politics is based on the analysis of individual countries, or components of countries. This approach remains valuable and important. That said, it is increasingly evident that those individual countries are functioning in a globalized environment and it is difficult if not impossible to understand any one system in isolation. To some extent the shifts in national patterns are mimetic, with one system copying patterns in another that appear effective and efficient (see Dimaggio and Powell 1991; see Chapter 24). In other cases the shifts may be coercive, as when the European Union has established political as well as economic criteria for membership.

The international influences on individual countries, although ubiquitous, are also variable across countries. Some, such as the US or Japan, have sufficient economic resources and lack direct attachments to strong supranational political organizations, and hence maintain much of their exceptionalism. The poorer countries of the developing world lack economic autonomy and their economic dependence may also produce some political dependence as well, so that their political systems may be influenced by other nations and by international organizations such as the World Bank and the United Nations.

The countries of the European Union represent a particularly interesting challenge for comparative politics. While most of these countries have long histories as independent states and have distinct political systems and political styles (see Peters 2006) their membership in the Union has tended to create substantial convergence and homogenization. The growing literature on Europeanization of the member states (Knill 2001; Schimmelfennig and Sedelmeier 2005; see also Chapter 23) has been attempting to understand these changing patterns of national politics in Europe and the increasingly common patterns of governance in the regimes. This is not to say that British parliamentary democracy and the presidentialism of Poland will merge entirely, but there is reciprocal influence and some difficulties in sorting out the sources of change.

The case of the European Union also points out the extent to which interactions among all levels of government are important for shaping behaviours in any one level. The concept of 'multi-level governance' has been very popular for analysing the policy-making of the European Union (Hooghe and Marks 2001; Bache and Flinders 2004). For individuals coming from federal regimes this characteristic of interaction might be considered a rather familiar feature of governing, and in many cases the sub-national governments have been the principal policy and political innovators. For many European countries,

COUNTRY PROFILE South Africa

Republic of South Africa

State formation

Dutch settlement at the Cape of Good Hope started with the foundation of a station by the Dutch East India Company in 1652. The region was seized by Great Britain in 1797 and annexed in 1805, but the Boers (of Dutch origin) resisted British rule throughout the 19th century. The second Anglo-Boer War ended in 1902, with Great Britain assuming sovereignty over the South African republics. In 1910, the Union of South Africa was created. From 1948 to 1990, the country was ruled under a regime of segregationist legislation (apartheid); the first multi-racial elections were held in 1994.
Constitution 1996, effective 1997 (but implemented in successive phases).

Form of government

Presidential socialist people's republic.
Head of state President elected by the National Assembly; term of 5 years (renewable once).
Head of government The President.
Cabinet Appointed by the President.
Administrative subdivisions 9 provinces.

Legal system

Based on Roman-Dutch law and English common law.

Legislature

Bicameral Parliament.
Lower house National Assembly: 400 seats; term of 5 years.
Upper house National Council of Provinces: 90 seats, 10 members elected by each of the nine provincial legislatures; term of 5 years.

Electoral system (lower house)

Proportional representation.
Formula Four seats for each percentage of the nation-wide vote; 200 members chosen from national party lists, the other 200 members chosen from regional party lists.
Constituencies 9 multi-member constituencies (4 to 43 seats).
Barrier clause None.
Suffrage Universal, 18 years.

Direct democracy

Three referenda have been held on the constitution and the reform process.

Party system Results of the 2004 legislative elections (National Assembly):

Electorate:	20,674,926	100.0%
Voters:	15,863,554	76.7%

Party	Valid votes	%	Seats
African National Congress (ANC)	10,880,915	69.7	279
Democratic Alliance (DA)	1,931,201	12.4	50
Inkatha Freedom Party (IFP)	1,088,664	7.0	28
United Democratic Movement (UDM)	355,717	2.3	9
Independent Democrats (ID)	269,765	1.7	7
New National Party (NNP)	257,824	1.7	7
African Christian Democratic Party (ACDP)	250,272	1.7	7
Freedom Front Plus (FF+)	139,465	0.9	4
United Christian Democratic Party (UCDP)	117,792	0.7	3
Pan Africanist Congress (PAC)	113,512	0.7	3
Minority Front (MF)	55,267	0.3	2
Azanian People's Organisation (AZAPO)	39,116	0.3	1
Others	113,161	0.7	0
Total	15,612,671	100.0	400

Notes: Category 'Others' includes parties with less than 1% nation-wide and no seats.
Source: Adam Karr's website.

however, multi-level governance is a more distinctive phenomenon that links both internationalization and the increasing political power of sub-national governments to the national political system.

The interaction among countries, and across levels of government, raises an analytic question for comparative analysis. When we observe a particular political pattern in a country, is that pattern a product of indigenous forces and national patterns, or is it a product of diffusion? The so-called 'Galton's problem' has been present for as long as there have been comparative studies, but its importance has increased as interactions have increased, and as the power of international organizations has increased (Seeliger 1996). Of course, we may never really be able to sort out all the various influences on any set of observed patterns in the public sector, despite the numerous answers that have been proposed to the problem (Braun and Gilardi 2006). Therefore, we can perhaps at best be cognizant of the existence of this problem and its potential impact on comparison.

While this copying among countries can be conceived as an analytic problem for social sciences, it is probably also a boon for governments and for citizens. If we conceptualize the international environment as a very large laboratory of innovations in both political action and policy, then learning from innovations in other settings becomes a valuable source for improving governing. A number of governments have attempted to institutionalize these practices through evidence-based policy-making.

Add a sixth 'I': interactions

To this point I have been dealing with five possible types of explanation independently of each other. That strategy is useful as a guide for research and for clarifying our thoughts about the issue in question, but it vastly understates the complexity of the real world of politics. In reality these five sources of explanation interact with one another, so that to understand the decisions made in the political process we need to have a broader and more comprehensive understanding. Given that much of contemporary political science is phrased in terms of testing specific hypotheses derived from specific theories, this search for complexity may not be welcomed by some

scholars, but it does reflect the reality of the political world.

Let me provide some examples. Institutions are a powerful source of explanations in comparative politics, and are generally our first choice for those explanations. Institutions, however, do not act—the individuals within them act, so we need to understand how institutions and individuals interact in making decisions. Some individuals who may be very successful in some political settings would not be so successful in others. Margaret Thatcher may have been a successful Prime Minister in the majoritarian British system, but her directive leadership style may have been totally unsuccessful in consensual Scandinavian countries, or even perhaps more consensual Westminster systems such as Canada. And these interactions can also be compared across time, with a bargainer such as Lyndon Johnson being likely to have been unsuccessful in the more partisan Congresses of the early twenty-first century.

Another example of interaction among possible explanations can occur between the international environment and institutions. Many of the states in Asia, and to a lesser extent Latin America, have adopted a 'developmental state' model to cope with their relatively weak position in the international market place and to use the power of the state for fundamental economic change (Evans 1995; Minns 2006). On the other hand, the more affluent states of Europe and North America have opted for a more liberal approach to economic growth, a model that better fits their position in the international political economy. For both countries their use of state power was to some extent influenced by the internationalization of markets, as well as of policy-making.

The literature on social movements provides a clear case for the interaction of multiple streams of explanation (see Chapter 16). On the one hand, social movements can be conceptualized as institutions, albeit ones with relatively low levels of institutionalization. These organizations can also be understood as reflecting an ideological basis, and as public manifestations of important ideas such as environmentalism and women's rights. Finally, some social movements also reflect underlying social and economic interests, although again in somewhat different ways than would conventional interest groups. Again, by using all these approaches to triangulate these organizations, the researcher can obtain a more complete understanding of the phenomenon.

The multiple streams of explanation and their interaction help to emphasize the point made at the outset of this chapter. The quality of research in comparative politics, and indeed in almost any area of the social sciences, can be enhanced by the use of multiple theories and multiple methodologies when examining the same 'dependent variable'. Any single analytical approach can provide a partial picture of the phenomenon in question, but only through a more extensive array of theory and evidence can researchers gain an accurate picture of the complex phenomena with which comparative politics is concerned. This research strategy is expensive, and may yield internally contradictory results, but it may be one means of coping with the underlying complexity.

KEY POINTS

❑ Comparative politics has institutional roots: more than other fields of political science it stresses the role of institutions in shaping and constraining the behaviour of individuals. The fundamental idea is that structures matter. It is however weak in explaining change.

❑ Rational choice analysis assumes that individuals are self-interested utility maximizers and engage in political action to receive benefits (and avoid costs). As an approach it is less relevant in comparative politics than in other fields.

❑ Although cultural explanations are often vague and 'residual', ideas matter and a great deal of research investigates the impact of specific cultural traits on political life (e.g. on democratic stability). Recent research stresses factors such as social capital and trust.

❑ As the last part of this volume stresses, single political systems are increasingly facing international influences—because of integration and globalization.

What more is needed?

The above discussion provides an idea of major approaches to comparative political analysis. These five broad approaches provide the means for an understanding for almost any political issues (whether within a single country or comparatively), yet they do not address the full range of political issues as well as they might. Indeed, there are at least two comparative questions that have not been explored as completely as they might have been. We can gain some information about these issues utilizing the five 'I's already advanced, but it would be useful to explore the two questions more fully.

Process

Perhaps the most glaring omission in comparative analysis is an understanding of the **political process**. If we look back over the five 'I's, much of their contribution to understanding is premised on rather static conceptions of politics and governing, and thus issues of process are often ignored. This emphasis on the more static elements of politics is unfortunate, given that politics and governing are inherently dynamic and it would be very useful to understand better how the underlying processes function. For example, while we know a great deal about legislatures as institutions, as well as about the individual behaviour of legislators, comparative politics has tended to abandon any concern about the legislative process.

Institutions provide perhaps the most useful avenue for approaching issues of process. If we adopt the common-sense idea about institutions, then each of the major formal institutions in the political system has a particular set of processes that can be more or less readily comparable across systems. Further, these various aspects of process may all come together and might constitute a policy process that, at a relatively high analytic level, has common features. Even if, however, we do have good understanding of the processes within each institution, we do not have as yet an adequate comparative understanding of the process taken more generally.

Outcomes

Having all these explanations for political behaviour, we should also attempt to specify what these explanations actually explain—what is the dependent variable for comparative politics? For behavioural approaches to politics the dependent variables will be individual-level behaviour, such as voting or decisions made by legislators. For institutionalist perspectives the dependent variable is the behaviour of individuals within institutions, with the behaviour shaped by either the values of the institutions or by the rule and incentives provided by those institutions.

Institutionalists tend to be more concerned about the impact of structures on the decisions taken by the public sector, while behavioural models are more likely to focus on the individual decision-maker and the attributes that might affect his or her choices.

As I have implied in several places above, one of the most important things that scholars need to understand in comparative politics is what governments actually do. If, as Harold Lasswell argued, politics is about 'who gets what', then public policy is the essence of political action and we need to focus more of our analytic efforts on policy. As Chapter 1 shows, this was indeed the case. However, policy outcomes are not just the product of politics and government action, but rather reflect the impact of economic and social conditions. Therefore, understanding comparative policy requires linking political decisions with numerous other social, economic, and cultural factors. Unfortunately, after having been a central feature of comparative politics for some time, comparative policy studies appear out of fashion. At one time there was a thriving interest in comparative policy studies (Heidenheimer *et al.* 1978; Castles 1998) but that interest has waned substantially. True, some of the same concerns appear as comparative political economy (Pontussen 1995), or perhaps as studies of the welfare state (Pierson and Myles 2001), but the more general concern with comparing policies and performance has disappeared in the contemporary literature in comparative politics.

If we look even more broadly at comparative politics, then the **ultimate dependent variable is**

governance, or the capacity of governments to provide direction to their societies. Governance involves *establishing goals for society, finding the means for reaching those goals, and then learning from the successes or failures of their decisions* (Pierre and Peters 2000). All of the other activities in the public sector can be put together within this general concept of governance. The very generality of the concept of governance poses some problems for comparison, as did the structural-functionalist and systems theories (Almond and Powell 1967) popular earlier in comparative politics. Still, by linking a range of governmental activities and demonstrating their cumulative effects, an interest in governance helps to counteract some attempts to overly compartmentalize comparative analysis. To some extent, it returns to examining whole systems and how the constituent parts fit together, rather than focusing on each individual institution or actor.

Governance comes as close to the grand functionalist theories of the 1960s and 1970s as almost anything else in recent attempts to develop comparative political analysis (see Box 2.2 above). Like those earlier approaches to comparative politics, governance is essentially functionalist, positing that there are certain crucial functions that any system of governance must perform, and then attempting to determine which actors are performing those tasks, regardless of the formal assignment of tasks by laws or constitutions. While some governance scholars have emphasized the role of social actors rather than formal actors in government in delivering governance, this must remain an empirical question that needs to be investigated rather than merely inferred from the theoretical presumptions of the author.

Governance also goes somewhat beyond the comparative study of public policy to examine not only the outputs of the system but its continuing capacity to adapt. One of the more important elements of the study of contemporary governance is the role of accountability and feedback, and the role of monitoring previous actions of the public sector. This emphasis is similar to the feedback loop in systems theory (see Figure I.1 in the Introduction to this volume), but does not have the explicit equilibrium assumptions of the earlier approach. Rather, governance models tend to assume some continuing development of policy capacity as well as institutional development to meet the developing needs.

KEY POINTS

❑ One of the weak points of comparative politics is its focus on static elements of the political system and a neglect of dynamic political processes. The field of comparative politics in which there is a greater attention to processes is that of comparative public policy analysis.

❑ The dependent variable in comparative politics varies according to approaches: but, perhaps, the ultimate dependent variable is 'governance', i.e. establishing the goals for society, finding the means to reach those goals, and then learning from the successes or failures of their decisions.

Conclusion

Understanding politics in a comparative perspective is far from easy, but having some form of theoretical or analytic guidance is crucial to that understanding. The discussion in this chapter has spent little time on grand theory but rather has focused on analytic perspectives that provide the researcher with a set of variables that can be used to approach comparative research questions. These five 'I's were phrased in rather ordinary language, but underneath each there is a strong theoretical core. For example, if we take the role of individuals in politics, we can draw from political psychology, elite theory, and role theory to explore the roles of individuals in politics.

Comparative politics should be at the centre of theory-building in political science, but that central position has to some extent been lost through the emphasis on individual-level behaviour. Further, the domination of American political scientists in the market place of ideas has tended to produce a somewhat unbalanced conception of the relevance of comparative research in contemporary political science. I would continue to argue that the world provides a natural laboratory for understanding political phenomena. We cannot, as experimenters, manipulate the elements in that environment but we can use the evidence available from natural experiments to test theory and to build theory.

?   Questions

1. What is the purpose of theory in comparative politics?
2. What is a functionalist theory?
3. What is meant by triangulation in social research?
4. What forms of institutional theory are used in comparative politics, and what contributions do they make?
5. Do institutions make a difference?
6. Both behavioural and rational choice approaches focus on the individual. Where do they differ?
7. Does political culture help to understand political behaviour in different countries?
8. Do people always act in self-interest in politics?
9. Will globalization make comparative politics obsolete?
10. Are the policy choices made by political systems a better way of understanding them than factors such as formal institutions or voting behaviour?

» Further reading

Basic discussions

Bates, R., Greif, A., Levi, M., Rosenthal, J.-L., and Weingast, B. (2002) *Analytic Narratives* (Princeton: Princeton University Press).

Geddes, B. (2002) *Paradigms and Sand Castles: Theory Building and Research Design in Comparative Politics* (Ann Arbor, Mich.: University of Michigan Press).

Peters, B. G. (1998) *Comparative Politics: Theory and Method* (Basingstoke: Palgrave).

Institutional theories

March, J. G., and Olsen, J. P. (1989) *Rediscovering Institutions* (New York: Free Press).

Steinmo, S., Thelen, K. A., and Longstreth, F. (1992) *Structuring Politics* (Cambridge: Cambridge University Press).

Interest-based theories

Sørenson, E., and Torfing, J. (2007) *Theories of Democratic Network Governance* (Basingstoke: Palgrave).

Tsebelis, G. (2002) *Veto Players* (Princeton: Princeton University Press).

Wiarda, H. (1997) *Corporatism: The Other Ism* (Armonk, NY: M. E. Sharpe)

The role of ideas

Hall, P. A. (1989) *The Political Power of Economic Ideas* (Princeton: Princeton University Press).

Putnam, R. D. (1993) *Making Democracy Work: Civic Traditions in Modern Italy* (Princeton: Princeton University Press).

Individual theories

Greenstein, F. I. (1987) *Personality and Politics* (Princeton: Princeton University Press).

The role of the international environment

Keohane, R. O., and Milner, H. (1997) *Internationalization and Domestic Politics* (Cambridge: Cambridge University Press).

Cowles, M. G., and Caporaso, J. A. (2002) *Europeanization and Domestic Change* (Ithaca, NY: Cornell University Press).

Governance

Pierre, J. (2003) *Debating Governance* (Oxford: Oxford University Press).

Web links

www.nd.edu/~apsacp
    Website of the Comparative Politics Section, American Political Science Association.

www.asu.edu/clas/polisci/cqrm
    Website of the Arizona State University Institute for Qualitative Methods.

www.rvc.cc.il.us/faclink/pruckman/pslinks
   Ultimate Political Science Links Page.

www.politicalresources.net
   Political Resources on the Net.

 Visit the Online Resource Centre that accompanies this book for more information:
www.oxfordtextbooks.co.uk/orc/caramani/

3 Comparative research methods

Hans Keman

Chapter contents

Reader's guide

In this chapter the 'art of comparing' is elaborated by means of a systematic treatment of how to relate a theoretically guided research question to a properly founded research answer. First, the role of variables in comparative research will be highlighted. Second, the specific meaning of 'cases' as well as their selection will be discussed in detail. These important steps in any type of comparative research are followed by explaining the 'core' of comparative method: the use of the different logics of comparative inquiry. Finally, some hazards and pitfalls common to the use of comparative methods will be highlighted and some possible solutions will be discussed.

Introduction

As the Introduction to this volume has stressed, comparative politics is characterized by both its substance and its method. The substance concerns the systematic study of phenomena that are representative for a political system (often countries, but not necessarily).[1] The method is the 'art' of comparing: what, when, and how to compare these systems or parts of systems. In this chapter the focus is on research methods as used in comparative politics: the concern is with the development of rules and the standards of how a comparative research design should be developed (Mair 1996: 310). Obviously the research design in comparative politics is a crucial step for developing theories, testing theories, and the verification of contesting or rival theories (Landman 2003: 4). Hence, as Peters emphasizes, '[t]he only thing that should be universal in studying comparative politics … is a conscious attention to explanation and research design' (Peters 1998: 26).

In short, theory and research design are closely interlinked in comparative politics. The crucial question therefore is: what is it that the student of comparative politics wishes to explain? In other terms: what is the *dependent variable* in the analysis? And what are the most likely 'causes' of the phenomenon under investigation? Which *independent variables* can account for the variation of the dependent variable across different political systems? The answer to this question rests heavily on the development of a 'proper' research design (RD). Comparative methods can therefore be considered as a 'bridge' between the research question (RQ) asked and the research answer (RA) proposed. This is what we label the 'triad' RQ → RA → RD.

Developing a research design in comparative politics is not an easy task and requires careful elaboration. First of all, the research design should enable the researcher to **answer the question** under examination. Second, the given answer(s) ought to **meet the 'standards' set in the social sciences:** are the results valid, reliable, and generalizable (King *et al.* 1994; Sartori 1994)? Third, are the research design and the methods used indeed **suitable for the research goals** set? In other words, has the 'art' of comparing contributed to finding an answer that is theoretically plausible and empirically correct (Landman 2003: 6–7)?

This chapter will elaborate these issues and attempt to guide the student in comparative politics towards linking research questions to research answers. A caveat is required though: a plurality of views exists on comparative research methods and there are many diverse views on the 'best' way to go. However, the same literature also shows that there is considerable agreement on what matters most as regard to applying comparative research methods in comparative politics. In this chapter I follow and elaborate these matters that are commonly viewed as being essential for doing research in comparative politics (see, for overviews, Dogan and Pelassy 1990; Mair 1996; Peters 1998; Landman 2003; Burnham *et al.* 2004; Pennings *et al.* 2006).

The chapter is organized as follows. In the next section the focus is on the role of variables in a research design representing theory: what is the role of and relationship between independent and dependent variables (X, and Y). Then, we turn to the 'carriers' of empirical information: **cases.** In addition to discussing what a case is in comparative

---

BOX 3.1 The triad RQ → RA → RD

Point of departure is that all research questions are theory guided (be it derived from existing theory, or challenging it, or attempting to develop a theory). The theoretical guidance is expressed in relating research questions (RQ) to research answers (RA) in the shape of logical relationships between a dependent variable (Y: what is to be explained) and the independent variables (X: the most likely causes, i.e. factors serving as an explanation). This 'bridge' between RQ and RA is the research

design (RD), taking into account the peculiarities of elements inherent to the RQ and RA. The comparative method is then a means to an end: to make choices as to which of the potentially vast mass of relevant empirical data (the evidence) and possible causes (the theory) are valid and reliable in arriving at a viable research answer. This implies that the triad is meant to design a relationship between cases and variables by means of the comparative method.

research, we will elaborate the process of case selection. This will be followed by discussing the different **logics of comparative inquiry,** that is, how to relate the empirical evidence to the research question asked and the research answers (originally) put forward. Subsequently, we will pay attention to a number of hazards that are related to some perennial problems in comparative research: conceptual 'travelling', equivalence, individual and ecological fallacies, as well as Galton's problem and over-determination. There are no easy answers to these problems, but knowing them may well mean avoiding them. In the final section I shall reflect on the advantages of using and applying comparative methods.

KEY POINTS

❑ The proper use and correct application of methods is essential in comparative politics.

❑ A correct application implies that the comparative method should meet the 'standards' set in the social sciences in terms of validity, reliability, and generalizability.

❑ The relationship between variables and cases in comparative research is crucial in order to reach empirically founded conclusions that further knowledge.

Linking theory to evidence

Comparative politics is considered by many as highly relevant for the development of theory in political science (see Chapter 2 above). Perhaps not all political scientists will fully agree with this statement, but most do. In particular, since the 1960s this point of view is widely acknowledged (see e.g. Almond 1996; Peters 1998; Burnham *et al.* 2004). This means that a research question (RQ) in comparative politics should always be either guided by theory or aiming at testing a theoretical argument. The comparative method is about observing and comparing carefully selected information (across space or time or both) on the basis of a causal relationship between a set of variables. The extent to which similarities and differences occur tells us about the plausibility of the theoretical relationships under review. One could say that the thrust of comparative methods is the application of quasi-experimental methods, where the researcher attempts to draw conclusions on the basis of some stimulus being absent or present (Burnham *et al.* 2004: 60–1).

In short, the comparative method allows us to test empirically hypothesized relationships among variables (Lijphart 1975: 159–60; Landman 2003: 10, even mentions prediction). In contrast to the methodology of the 'exact sciences', however, the conclusions are drawn from comparisons *not* experiments (this is why the comparative method is often labelled as 'quasi-experimental'). The real world of comparative politics is therefore the workplace for political scientists to examine how the complex world of politics

'turns' by demonstrating in a systematic and rigorous fashion **theoretical relationships among variables** (Pennings *et al.* 2006: ch. 1). Essential to applying comparative methods is therefore the awareness of what a theoretical relationship entails.

A theory in its simplest form is a meaningful relationship between two real-world phenomena: X, the independent variable, and Y, the dependent variable, where it is expected that change in one variable is related to change in the other. The conceptual and explanatory understanding of such a relationship is point of departure for conducting research by comparing empirical evidence across systems (see also Brady and Collier 2004: 309; Burnham *et al.* 2004: 57; Pennings *et al.* 2006: 34). In terms of the triad, the researcher first formulates a research question, such as: what factors contribute to the development of the welfare state?

This is the dependent variable, i.e. what the researcher seeks to explain. It is called dependent because we expect that its variation across systems is depending on one or more independent variables (some call a dependent variable the outcome).[2] As a tentative answer he/she comes up (often after extensive reading of literature on this topic) with a **hypothesis.** This tentative answer, or hypothesis, is a conjecture about the relationship between the dependent variable and the independent variable. This independent variable (or part of the research answer) is supposed to influence the outcome, i.e. the development of the welfare state. In a comparative research design (RD) the theoretical relationship is elaborated, preferably in causal terms, in order to account for the differences and similarities that occur in the 'real world' (see also Box 3.1).

Obviously, any type of 'X–Y' relationship in social science is a reduction from the complexities of the real world. This is deliberate. In comparative political science we develop hypotheses that account for explanations by isolating those factors that can account in a systematic way for the actual variation. This procedure not only allows for establishing by means of comparing evidence whether or not a relationship indeed exists, but also whether or not this relationship can be qualified as 'causal' or not (the relationship is then noted $X \rightarrow Y$).

Causality is a fraught concept in the social sciences and is in strict terms hard to come by. Yet, it is by now accepted that if the variation in the dependent variable (Y) is evidently and systematically related to the variation in (one of) the independent variable(s) (X) then we may assume causality—at least for the cases included in the analysis. This type of conclusion refers to the idea of 'internal validity' (see Box 3.2). Establishing causal relationships by means of comparative methods is considered as one of its major advantages. As I have already stated, comparative analysis is often labelled 'quasi-experimental', meaning that we can to a certain extent manipulate reality, enabling the researcher to conduct descriptive inference (King *et al.* 1994: 34 ff.). This implies that the empirically founded relationship between the

independent and dependent variable, based on a number of observations (i.e. the descriptive evidence) allows generalization over and beyond the cases under review. In these circumstances the researcher claims that his/her results are 'externally valid' (see Box 3.2). It is obvious that this 'leap' from the empirical evidence to a general, if not causal, explanation (the 'theory') is open to criticism and more often than not rival or contesting theories are developed to disprove or to enhance the theory.

Let us illustrate this with the debate on the research question 'does politics matter?' (For an overview of this debate see Castles 1998; Keman 2002*c*; as well as Chapter 22.) The origins of this debate go back to the 1970s. Researchers, working in the field of comparative political economy and public policy analysis, published their research on the emergence and cross-system variation of welfare states in industrialized democracies. The conclusion they shared was that the development and level of 'welfare statism' (commonly measured as public expenditures as a percentage of GDP) had less to do with 'politics' (e.g. the role and impact of parties, governments, ideologies) and more with the structural developments of the advanced capitalist countries (in fact all the member-states of the OECD).

What mattered most in explaining 'welfare statism' (the dependent variable Y; see Figure 3.1) were independent variables like the level of industrialization (the more industrialized a country, the higher the need for housing, health care, and

---

BOX 3.2 Internal and external validity in comparative methods

Internal validity refers to problems of specification of the research design (which variables are included in the model and which are omitted).

External validity is the question to what extent the results of the comparative research are also relevant for other cases that are not included in the research.

Both types of validity are equally important, but it should be noted that there is a trade-off (Pennings *et al.* 2006: 5–6). The more cases are included in the analysis that can be considered as representative, the more 'robust' the result will be (*external validity*). Conversely, however, the analysis of fewer cases may well be conducive to a more coherent conclusion for the set of cases that is included (*internal validity*).

The use of the term 'validity' in comparative politics is to some extent different from its usage in general social science methodology where it refers to measuring what we intend to measure. In comparative politics we mean to claim that the results are relevant for the cases under examination (Peters 1998: 48). Furthermore, the concepts of internal and external validity are of an *ideal-typical* nature: in a perfect world with complete information the standards of validity may well be met, but in practice this is hard to achieve. Yet, as Mayer (1989: 55) has rightly put forward, one should try to get as close as possible to these standards.

education); the rates of economic growth (the higher economic growth, the more fiscal room for welfare state spending); and the demographic composition of societies in terms of the proportion of younger and older people (Keman 2002*c*). This cluster of independent variables (represented as X_1 in Figure 3.1) was considered as the causal conditions explaining the variation in public policy formation for the development and level of welfare statism across OECD countries (e.g. Wilensky 1975). Political variables like party differences (e.g. left vs. right) and the relative strength of parties in government or the strength of trade unions (X_2 in Figure 3.1) were considered as only indirectly relevant (or merely coincidental) and neither necessary nor sufficient to explain the growth of a welfare state. In other words, the research conducted appeared to prove that 'politics did *not* matter' as an explanation for the development of the post-war welfare state.

A group of political science comparativists, however, were not convinced with the wider (generalizing) implications for political theory. A major objection concerned the finding that the *non*-political variables (X_1 in Figure 3.1) were insufficiently capable of explaining *why* the cross-system differences in the levels of spending on welfare statism differed, although in many instances the X_1 cluster of non-political variables was quite similar. Hence—in statistical terms—the explained variance (i.e. the proportion of non-political factors accounting for the differences in welfare statism, the outcome) was considered to be below par to allow for the conclusions. The descriptive inference was not homogeneous (i.e. the assumption that a given set of variables produces always the same outcome) in the opinion of these critics.

This criticism was supported by empirical observations of the levels of expenditures on welfare state related policy-making over time. It appeared that these levels tended to become more **divergent** whereas the explanatory variables (X_1) would predict otherwise: a **convergent** development would be expected to occur. Another criticism concerned the operationalization of the dependent variable. By examining the various policy components of 'welfare statism' (like expenditure on social security, education, and health care), it could be demonstrated that the **design** of the welfare state showed a large cross-system variation (see, for instance, Janoski and

Hicks 1994). In short: the dependent variable 'welfare statism' could not be systematically and causally linked to demographic factors, industrial growth, or economic development alone (the original explanation, or hypothesized relationship).

Summing up, the research answer given was neither convincing nor sufficiently explanatory. These criticisms based on the same type of empirical evidence have been conducive to the development of an alternative theory or 'rival' explanation as regards the development of the welfare state in the OECD world (see e.g. Schmidt 2002). This theory or research answer is depicted in Figure 3.1: in addition to the original explanation by means of non-political factors (X_1) another explanatory cluster of variables—representing politics (X_2)—was introduced into the equation.

The comparative analysis conducted demonstrated that political variables appeared to have a considerable (and statistical significant) impact as well (Swank 2002). Hence the 'new' research answer became: yes, it does matter! And this answer was found by means of a comparative research design based on a theory-informed research question and providing an alternative research answer. Note also that the research design not only concerns establishing the $X_2 \to Y$ relationship, proving that political variables played their role, but also controlling for the impact of 'politics' by including the original explanatory relationship $X_1 \to Y$. Hence, the comparative method was applied to test a theory *and* to develop it further.

In conclusion, no comparative research is useful without a theoretical argument underlying it, or without a methodologically adequate research

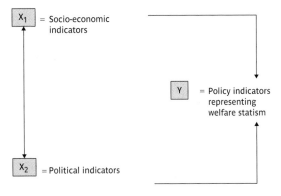

Fig. 3.1 Investigating 'does politics matter?'

Source: Adapted from Pennings *et al.* 2006: 34.

design to execute it. This shows the significance of comparative methods as well as the need to apply these carefully by rigorously and systematically considering the relation between research question and research answers in terms of causal relationships between dependent and independent variables $(X_n \rightarrow Y)$. The message conveyed here is that research in comparative politics requires a precise and detailed elaboration of a research design that connects research questions to research answers that are conducive to causal interpretation by means of descriptive inferences. In the next section I turn to a vital step in organizing a comparative research design: selecting the cases

suited for comparison that will direct the 'logic' of comparison.

KEY POINTS

❑ Theory comes before method and is shaped by the relationship between dependent (Y) and independent (X) variables.

❑ The research answers are (tentative) hypotheses that can be interpreted in causal terms by means of descriptive inference.

❑ The research design is meant to link systematically empirical evidence to theory by means of comparative methods.

Case selection

In the introductory section I referred to the terms 'quasi-experimental' and 'manipulation' in relation to developing and carrying out research in comparative politics. This points to a salient element of the 'art of comparison' (what, when, and how to compare). Recall that linking theory to evidence entails the purposeful reduction of real-world complexities so as to analyse the (logical) relationship between X and Y variables. Hence, the researchers must make decisions above **what** to compare, i.e. selecting the cases (the carriers of relevant information), and **how** this information can be adequately employed to reach conclusions as regards the research question and answer. The key to the development of a proper comparative research design is **which** cases can be useful for comparing and **how many** are to be selected. The answer to this question has led to many views and debates (see e.g. Przeworski 1987; Ragin 1987; Peters 1998; Brady and Collier 2004). The thrust of this debate focuses on an apparent trade-off between selecting many cases but few variables or few cases but many variables. This debate will not be repeated here, but I shall elaborate its practical implications for the concomitant logic of comparison. Below I shall first shed light on the meaning and features of what a 'case' is in comparative methods and how the selection of cases is made.

Cases

The term 'case' has a general meaning in social science methodology, but in comparative methods it

is used in a specific manner and is to some extent confusing (King *et al.* 1994: 116–17; Burnham *et al.* 2004: 146; Pennings *et al.* 2006: 34 ff.). In general, cases denote the units of observation at any given level of analysis (e.g. voters in a country: the country determines the level of analysis, whereas the voter is the unit of observation). In comparative methods we use this definition as well (see Box 3.3). The confusion stems from the distinction that is often made between research designs that are labelled 'comparable case strategy' (Lijphart 1975) or 'case study' (Peters 1998: 137).

In fact, here the researcher means the (comparative) study of 'systems' *within* which observations are made. For reasons of clarity, I propose to reserve the term 'case' in comparative methods for any type of **system** included in the analysis. In addition I refer to the **observations** as the values (or scores) of a variable under investigation. For example, if one analyses party behaviour in government then the system level or 'case' is that of governments and not countries. Conversely, if the welfare state is the focus of comparison, then this concerns the systems to be compared whereas the public expenditure on social security provisions is the empirical value for each system. In Box 3.3 the definition of a case is elaborated and illustrated by means of a data matrix (i.e. the organization of the empirical observations by case and by variable). It is important to be precise in this matter because the **number** of observations determines what type of (statistical) analysis is feasible given the available variation across the systems, or cases, under review (Pennings *et al.* 2006: 11)

In most literature on comparative methods the concern for the relationship between the cases selected and the variables employed to analyse the research question under review is considered as crucial in doing 'truly' comparative research. As stated above, this relationship is depicted as a choice between 'many cases, few variables' and 'few cases, many variables' (Przeworski and Teune 1970; Landman 2003). Yet, this choice is too simplistic and does not always concern a dichotomy. The first objection is that the type of data used (whether qualitative or quantitative) is not by definition conducive to a research design that is either a single case study based on qualitative data (by means of 'thick description') or one maximizing the number of cases and (thus) using quantitative data only (see also Brady and Collier 2004: 246–7). The second objection is that different types of data can be used within one research design regardless the number of cases. For example, the study of welfare states often combines qualitative elements with statistical data (e.g. van Kersbergen 1995), or take the study on 'social capital' by Putnam (1993) who deliberately combines survey data with historical analysis of the development of politics and society in Italy. Thirdly, it is often suggested that the choice for many cases and few variables would imply a Most Similar Systems Designs and, conversely, few cases and many variables would always imply a Most Different Systems Designs research design (I will discuss this distinction in more detail below). In summary, the

selection of cases and variables depends on a deliberate **choice** in relation to the research question and in consideration of the explanatory goals set (see also Fauré 1994; Ragin 2000).

Case selection

The first step in this process is case selection. Cases are the building blocks for the theoretical argument underlying the research design. Case selection and the number of cases included in the research design direct the type and format of comparison. This is illustrated in Figure 3.2.

Figure 3.2 shows that there are different possible research strategies depending on how many cases and how many variables are involved. **Intensive strategies** are those with many variables and few cases. **Extensive strategies** are those with few variables and many cases. In addition, the researcher should consider whether or not 'time' is a relevant factor to be taken into account (Bartolini 1993; Pennings *et al.* 2006: 40–1). This is often the case, in particular when change (or a process, development) is a crucial element of the research question. Finally, if the researcher aims at the use of statistical analysis, as many cases as feasible are required (King *et al.* 1994: 24; Burnham *et al.* 2004: 74).[3] In Figure 3.2 five options for choice are distinguished:

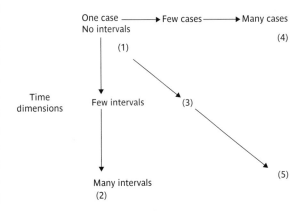

(1) Case study (at one time point);
(2) Time series (one case over time);
(3) Closed universe (relevant cases in relevant periods);
(4) Cross-section (all cases at one time point);
(5) Pooled analysis (maximizing cases across time and space).

Fig. 3.2 Types of research design

Source: Adapted from Pennings *et al.* (2006: 21).

The single case study

This cannot be considered as an explicit comparative research design. It may be part of a comparative research design, but standing alone it is at best implicitly comparative and its external validity is low or absent (see Peters 1998: 143–4; Landman 2003: 34–5). However it can be used for *post hoc* validation (to inspect whether or not the general results hold up in a more detailed analysis) or to study a **deviant** case (i.e. a case that appears to be an 'exception to the rule') and is also used as a **critical** case study (see e.g. Rueschemeyer *et al.* 1992). An advantage of a single case study can be that it allows for the inclusion of a larger variety of variables than is often feasible in a 'many cases' research design. Lijphart mentions the use of a single case study as a pilot for generating hypotheses, for instance, by means of a theory confirming or infirming analysis (Lijphart 1971: 691). This is called a **crucial** case study. Finally, single case studies often use information over time to generate comparable cases. This is similar to option 2 in Figure 3.2 (Hall 2006) where time is the defining category to develop comparable cases, that is, longitudinal analysis (or 'time series analysis').

Time series

Time series can be useful in two ways: one, to compare a specific configuration within one or a few systems in order to inspect not only change *per se*, but mainly to analyse which factors are (or become) relevant over time in terms of effect-producing capacities. An example is the analysis of Dutch corporatism for the period 1965–2000 (Woldendorp 2005). Another use is to replicate an earlier study by adding a time series to the existing one (King *et al.* 1994: 223).

Closed universe

The third option in Figure 3.2 concerns the 'few' cases and intervals comparison, taking into account change by defining periodical intervals based on external events (be it before or after a discrete event—like war or economic crisis—or comparing periods that are crucial for the development of political systems; Berg-Schlosser and de Meur 1996). A few(er) cases research design is developed as a 'focused comparison' that is derived from the research question under review (Lijphart 1975; Ragin 1991).

Cross-section

The fourth option in Figure 3.2 is frequently used: it concerns those cases that have more in common than they differ from each other, depending on the research question (Collier 1993). This means that the universe of discourse (i.e. the relevant cases in view of the theoretical relationship underlying the research design; Castles 1987) can be assumed to be constant, which would enhance the validity of the analytical results. For example, if the focus is the development and organization of party systems, then it follows that we only take into account representative democracies. This option is typically suited to so-called 'middle range' theorizing (Lane and Ersson 1994).

Pooled analysis

The final option is disputed among comparativists. On the one hand, the number of cases can be maximized by pooling cases across time and systems, but, on the other hand, there is the pitfall of the impact of time being assumed to be constant across all cases (or, at least, that change is consistent; Kittel 1999; Beck 2001). A possible fallacy is then the overdetermination of the results. This option is mainly used in sophisticated quantitative approaches and it requires skills in statistical methods at a more advanced level. Notwithstanding this caveat, this option can indeed help to increase the number of observations for the variables included in the research design (see e.g. Janoski and Hicks 1994).

All in all, the balance between the number of cases and variables in play is not as diverse as is often put forward. Rather, the message is that the range of choice is larger than is often thought (and practised): first, by combining the options available (options 3 and 5 are in fact combinations); second, by using the options in developing a research design sequential. For instance, following up a cross-sectional analysis (option 4) with a critical or a crucial case study as an in-depth elaboration of the broad comparative analysis (see e.g. Rueschemeyer *et al.* 1992). It should be noted, however, that the options for choice as depicted in Figure 3.2 are not completely free. For instance, if industrialization is seen as a **process**, it must be investigated **over time** in order to answer the research question whether or not this process results in the development towards welfare statism.

A good example of such a research design is Peter Flora's analysis of West European welfare states (Flora 1974). Various European societies were analysed from the time point that they slowly developed into more or less constitutional liberal democracies (1850–1970). In effect, in this research design the important point was not the actual number of cases or systems, but the information available for the whole period (i.e. option 2 in Figure 3.2). By comparing the rates of change with the rate of democratization it was possible to demonstrate when and under which conditions the welfare state developed. Another application can be found in Lane and Ersson (1997). They have employed a research design as depicted under options 4 and 3. Other examples could be highlighted and elaborated in terms of the options for choice as regards case selection as depicted in Figure 3.2 (see, for other examples, Landman 2003: part II; Pennings *et al.* 2006: ch. 2).

However, my main goal is to make clear that case selection is not only important for how many cases can or should be included in the analysis, but also that the choice is neither (completely) free nor unilaterally determined. First of all, the choice of cases depends on the theoretical relationship under review (X → Y) and, second, on what type of empirical data is available and required. The type of cases (systems) directs the type of variables and their level of measurement, resulting in a data collection suited for seeking the research answer to the question asked (see Box 3.3). Relating the cases and concomitant information (i.e. data) is the next step in performing comparative analysis. This stage of the research design concerns the assessment of the relationship between the evidence (data) collected across the selected cases for the independent and dependent variables in view of an explanation.

KEY POINTS

❑ In comparative research a case is the building block of research. It is important to keep in mind that the level of inquiry is related to the type of system under investigation. The variation across systems is empirically observed by means of indicators within and between systems.

❑ The balance between cases and variables is an important direction for organizing the case selection.

❑ Figure 3.2 shows the options for choice as regards case selection. The selection of cases depends on the research question and hypotheses that direct the research design. The choice of cases is finite and limits the (quasi-experimental) research design.

The logic of comparison and theory development

In comparative methods there are two basic research designs that employ a different type of logic: the Most Different Systems Design (MDSD) and the Most Similar Systems Design (MSSD). These designs relate directly to the type of cases under review and the selection of cases made by the researcher. Both approaches have been developed following John Stuart Mill's dictum: *maximise experimental variance—minimize error variance—control extraneous variance* (Peters 1998: 30).

Experimental variance

This points to the observed differences or changes in the dependent variable (Y) of the research question, which is supposed to be a function of the independent variable (X) included in the research design (as hypothesized by means of the research answer). Figure 3.1 above is an example of the basic structure of modelling the relationship between a research question and research answer. Recall that the question at stake was whether or not 'politics matters'. A crucial requirement for answering this question and attempting to settle this theoretical debate is that the dependent variable (Y = 'welfare statism') indeed varies across the cases and over time.

In addition, we must be sure that the variation in Y is sufficiently contrasting, otherwise we cannot tell whether or not the independent variables make a difference or not. If not, then the research design is flawed due to 'selection bias' on the dependent variable (Brady and Collier 2004). Obviously this would easily lead to 'error variance' since the researcher cannot tell whether the effect-producing variables (X) indeed account for the observed outcomes (in Y) or not. For example, if one analyses the research question of the retrenchment of the welfare state (Pierson 2001) and the research answer is that this is due to the introduction of the 'stabilization pact' by the EU, and only EU member-states (having agreed on the European Monetary Union) are selected as cases, then there is a real chance that the descriptive inference (establishing a X → Y relationship) cannot be tested sufficiently (King *et al.* 1994: 141; Landman 2003: 46).

Error variance

This is the occurrence of random effects of unmeasured variables that is almost impossible to avoid in the social sciences, given quasi-experimental designs that imply a reduction of 'real life' circumstances. Yet, it should be minimized as much as feasible (in statistical terms, the error term in the equation is constant or close to zero). One way to minimize, apart from a carefully executed case selection, is increasing the number of cases. However this is, in view of the research question under scrutiny, not always possible (e.g. there are no cases that fit selection criteria).

Extraneous variance

The final requirement in Mill's dictum is controlling for extraneous variance. If there is no control for other possible influences, the chances are high that the hypothetical relation X → Y is in part produced by another (unknown) cause. This is what we call a *spurious relationship* (a third variable affects the relationship under investigation: Pennings *et al.* 2006: 135). There is no foolproof remedy to prevent extraneous variance other than by having formulated a fully specified theory or by means of statistical significance tests and control variables (Figure 3.1 is to some extent a way to handle spuriousness: by controlling for social and economic factor = X^1, one could estimate the relative influence of politics X^2 in terms of a direct relationship; see also Peters 1998: 33–4). The best way to go in comparative politics, assuming that the case selection is properly organized in view of the theoretical relationship proposed, is to apply the principles of the Methods of Agreement and Difference. Using these methods we are in a position to draw causal conclusions by means of logically ordering the **differences** and **similarities** (i.e. variation across cases and/or time) between the

dependent and independent variables, based on the empirical evidence that has been collected.

Methods of Agreement and Difference

The logic of comparative inquiry is obviously linked to the issues of the type of variables developed (system level, within systems, or intra-system components) and the number of cases (many, few, one) selected for comparison. The level of inquiry indicates to what extent cases—countries, nations, years, or other units—are part of the universe of discourse (i.e. the number of cases). And, as we have already seen, case selection has implications for the differential use of the logics of comparison. In the literature on comparative method two logics are distinguished:

- [Indirect] Method of Difference
- [Indirect] Method of Agreement

These 'logics' refer to mode of descriptive inference to examine a theoretical relationship X → Y by means of comparing cases and the related information (data) as systematized in variables (see also Janoski and Hicks 1994; Ragin 2000; Pennings *et al.* 2006). The Methods of Difference and Agreement were developed by John Stuart Mill in his *A System of Logic* (1843). The basic idea is that comparing cases can be used to detect commonalities between cases and variables. The Method of Difference focuses in particular on the variation of certain features amongst others that do *not* differ (dramatically) across comparable cases. Hence, co-variation between the dependent and independent variables is considered crucial under the assumption of holding the context constant (the *ceteris paribus* clause: all other things are equal but for the hypothetical relationship). This is the Most Similar Systems Design (MSSD): locating variables that differ among similar systems, which account for observed political outcomes (the dependent variable).

Alternatively, the Method of Agreement consists of comparing cases (or systems) in order to detect those relationships between X → Y that are similar notwithstanding the differences on other features of the cases compared. Hence, all other things being different but for certain relationships that are considered to be causal (or effect-productive). This is the so-called Most Different Systems Design (MSDS). This distinction between 'most similar' and 'most different' is elaborated by Przeworski and Teune (1970) and is widely used in doing research in comparative politics.

The term 'indirect' methods points to more sophisticated versions of the original method. The **Indirect Method of Agreement** aims at eliminating those variables that all cases have in common, instead of focusing on an overall similarity *per se*. This elaboration is useful since it helps to avoid biased results by including more cases that are seemingly different (Janoski and Hicks 1994: 14). Alternatively the Indirect Method of Difference can be seen as an extension of the cases under review: some crucial variables are positive (sharing some values) and others are negative. This extension helps to refine the analytical results and is frequently used in quantitative research designs (see also the ideas on the so-called 'fuzzy-set logic' of comparison below).[4]

Both methods thus lead:

• either to MSSD → Method of Difference
• or to MSDS → Method of Agreement.

This 'logic of comparison' or, in our parlance, the relationship between research question and research design, runs in practice as follows: in a MSSD, where we assume that the cases have more circumstances in common (similar) than not, we interpret the research outcomes by concentrating on the **variation across the cases**, focusing explicitly on both the X and Y variables. Often this is called the 'cross-system variation' as the basis for explanation. A MDSD approach involves a comparison made on the basis of dissimilarity in as many respects as possible by concentrating on **commonalities across the cases**. The expectation is that this procedure is conducive to eliminate all other circumstances as possible explanations and one explanation emerges in which most, if not all agree. Skocpol and Somers (1980) have labelled this approach as the 'parallel demonstration of theory'.

In sum, the more circumstances the selected cases have in common, the more feasible it is to locate the variables that do differ and which can be considered as part of the explanation. Conversely, if dissimilarity in many respects is high across the cases, then these variables can be discounted as possible explanations, and there will be few (ideally only one) variables that

account for the comparative variation of the dependent variable (Pennings *et al.* 2006: 10). In Table 3.1 I summarize both logics of comparative inquiry and illustrate each logic and system design by means of an example based on published research.

In Table 3.1 both logics of comparison are presented in conjunction with respectively the MDSD and MSSD. The last two columns at the right-hand side concern the way conclusions are drawn by means of the 'method' and the descriptive inferences allowing for assessing the hypothetical relationship reflecting RQ → RA. The analysis of 'does politics matter' that was highlighted as an example was not only intended to settle a debate, but was originally developed as part of the study of the development of the welfare state. These studies focused mainly on the OECD area (Armingeon and Beyeler 2004; see also Chapter 22 below). These countries are considered to have more in common in terms of their features with respect to economy and politics than they are different. A major commonality is that they all share an identical political-economic system: democratic systems of representative government, on the one hand, characterized by a market economy, on the other hand. Over time, particularly after the Second World War, the welfare state emerged in these countries (Flora 1974; Esping-Andersen 1990; Castles 1998; as well as Chapter 21 below).

The research question under investigation concerned how to explain the **diversity** in welfare statism across these most similar countries. One of the hypothetical research answers concerned party differences (left versus right) especially as regards their presence or absence in government. Hence, the cases were selected in a MSSD format and the variables were constructed to measure the relative strength and ideological preferences of parties in government. The hypothesis under review became: the party differences between left and right will have an impact on and therefore affect the level and direction of welfare state related expenditures. By assuming that all other circumstances remained (more or less) the same or constant, the researchers were able to test this hypothesis by examining the **association** between party composition and degree and type of welfare statism. In short, the MSSD approach was used to apply the Method of Difference and by examining the co-variation between X and Y the conclusion was that the

Table 3.1 Features of the Most Similar and Most Different Systems Design

Type of design:	Case selection	Variables included	Logic of comparison	Descriptive inference
MSSD	Similar on features *not* part of X →Y relation: *ceteris paribus* clause	Dependent and independent variables: X and Y vary across the cases included	Method of Difference	X →Y relation shows co-variance (+ or −)
Example of research question: does politics matter?	Democracies that are members of the OECD assuming that these countries have more *in common* than differences.	Relative strength of left- and right-wing parties in government (X) influence level and growth of public expenditures on welfare (Y)	• Positive correlation between the left in government and level of welfare state expenditures. • Correlation tends to disappear over time: convergent development.	
MDSD	Dissimilar on many features *not* part of X →Y relation.	Dependent and independent variables: do *not* vary across the cases across the cases	Method of Agreement	X →Y relation remains constant.
Example of research question: do individual political rights promote stable democracy?	Members of the UN: selecting cases that are different in *most* features	Political rights of citizen exist (X_1) and are positively adhered to (X_2) promote stable democracy (Y)	• Political rights are effect-producing if they are positively adhered to. • If X_1 and X_2 co-vary, then democracy is enduring and undisturbed.	

Sources for examples: Schmidt (2002); Keman (2002*a, b*); Jagger and Gurr (1995).

'left in government' made a difference if compared cross-sectionally, but that this relationship weakened if inspected over time (see also Janoski and Hicks 1994; Schmidt 2002).

The other example in Table 3.1 concerns the research into the conditions of 'stable democracy' (Powell 1982; Lijphart 1994; Stepan and Skach 1994). The dependent variable used concerned a formal definition of democracy by Dahl (1971): polyarchy. This implied that all the cases included could (and did) vary to a large extent on other societal features: they were **dissimilar.** The hypothesis entertained was: the existence of and positive adherence to civil and political rights (freedom of speech, association, information, the right to vote and to public protest were not only laid down in law but also safeguarded in reality; Dahl 1971) would be conducive to establish democracy as 'the only game in town' and consequently be enduring and stable. This relationship between political rights and democratic performance was tested by means of a MDSD for as many different cases as feasible (in terms of available data)

using the Method of Agreement. This relationship was found to be indeed constant across most cases, notwithstanding many other features of the system being different (Keman 2002*a*).

In short, Table 3.1 demonstrates that, depending on the hypothetical relationship under review, the researcher must deliberate what cases and variables should be included in the comparative analysis if applying the Methods of Agreement or Difference. This will enable him of her to apply a logic of comparison in accordance with the information or data to **verify the hypothesis** by means of descriptive inference eliminating irrelevant and non-causal variables. This mode of comparative analysis is widely applied in comparative politics. Recently this logic has made important advances using Boolean algebra and fuzzy-set logic (Ragin 2000).

This type of analysis allows for the handling of many variables in combination with a relative high number of cases simultaneously (recall option 3 in Figure 3.2). Ragin claims that this type of research design (derived from the approach called **Qualitative**

BOX 3.4 Investigating economic performance using fuzzy-set comparison

Fuzzy-set analysis combined with ideal type analysis offers a new and innovative approach to examine qualitative and quantitative changes within cases, across cases, and over time (Kvist 1999). For example, Vis *et al.* (2007) employ this technique to gain meaningful and comparative information on economic performance (the dependent variable) by means of a conceptualization and operationalization of economic performance including economic growth (percentage of GDP per capita), total employment (percentage of the total population aged 15–64), and the level of gross public debt (percentage of GDP). Substantively, the argument is that the combination of these factors determines the level of economic performance. Different from other studies, it is argued that for a country to perform economically, it should excel on all three indicators.

A fuzzy-set ideal type analysis makes use of the 'corners' of the multi-dimensional property space. If there are 3 sets (growth, employment, and debt), the property space has 2^3 (= 8) *corners*, which are the ideal types (or models). The closer a case is to a corner, the larger the degree of membership to that model. An important feature of fuzzy-set theory is that the *membership* of the cases of the different sets can vary: anything

between full and no membership is possible. Whereas traditional quantitative variables are calibrated according to sample means or coefficients of variation, fuzzy-sets are calibrated in line with theoretical and substantive knowledge (Ragin 2000: 169).

The researcher establishes two qualitative *breakpoints*, 1 and 0, to determine when a case is, respectively, fully in or fully out of a set. An important question in fuzzy-set ideal type analysis is therefore how to operationalize these sets. In the study of the possible causes of economic performance continuous fuzzy-sets, meaning that all scores between 0 and 1 are possible, are used (see Ragin 2000: 158–60). Based on the three indicators selected and operationalized (growth, employment, public debt), the multi-dimensional property space consisting of eight ideal types (models) is determined.

Obviously, this method can be applied to both dependent and independent variables and can be considered as a means to enhance the validity and reliability of the data used as well as to be able to study more cases in a rigorous and systematic fashion. Hence, it can be considered as a potential solution of the trade-off between 'many versus few cases' and 'many versus few variables' (see also Pennings *et al.* 2006: 265–70).

Comparative Analysis; Ragin 1991; Kvist 1999) is a way to circumvent the apparent trade-off between the number of cases and variables: many cases/few variables versus few cases/many variables. The logic of comparison employed is based on Boolean logarithms by which qualitative and quantitative information is ordered in terms of **necessary and sufficient** conditions as regards the relationship under investigation. Additionally, this approach appears to be well suited to focus on intra-system variations (for example, on within-variation of 'whole' systems by means of multiple indicators). Instead of aiming at detecting one (at best) effect-producing circumstance (X) by means of a variable-oriented approach, the **homogeneity** of comparable cases directs the process of descriptive inference. This procedure and concomitant logic has been developed into what Ragin has labelled 'fuzzy-set logic' (see Box 3.4). According to

those who use this approach the advantage is that in comparative politics multiple causation is more likely to occur than mono-causal explanations. The fuzzy-set logic would be better equipped to deal with this and can therefore be considered as a promising development within the realm of comparative methods (Peters 1998: 173 ff.; Brady and Collier 2004: 133 ff.; Pennings *et al.* 2006: 137–41).

Concluding this section, it should be said that both logics of comparison (MSSD and MDSD) allow for drawing conclusions that help to develop or substantiate so-called middle-range theories (Chilcote 1994). Alternatively, the researcher may opt to adopt a case-based scenario by using Boolean analysis where several specific (intra-)*systemic* features are central to the argument made (e.g. electoral systems, party behaviour type of government, or policy variation within welfare states).

KEY POINTS

- ❑ Point of departure is a hypothesis concerning the relationship between two variables whose empirical validity we want to test through the use of real-world data.
- ❑ The Method of Agreement uses MDSD as its research design and to allow for descriptive inference in causal

terms. Conversely the Method of Difference derives its explanatory capacity from MSSD. The shared goal is to eliminate those variables that exemplify no systematic association between X and Y.

- ❑ An alternative logic of comparison has recently been developed: fuzzy-set logic.

Constraints and limitations of the comparative method

Although the comparative approach in political science is considered to be advantageous in linking theory to evidence and enhancing it as a scientific discipline, there are a number of constraints to the comparative method that limits its possibilities and impairs its usefulness to a certain extent. I have already mentioned a few of these and pointed to hazards and pitfalls.

A major concern is, for example, that we have too many theories that fit too few data. In other words, collecting **valid and reliable** data for the cases we have selected turns often out to be a daunting task. If this problem is insufficiently solved, it will undermine the quality and feasibility of the comparative method altogether. For instance,

we are confronted by the problem of **conceptual stretching and travelling** to develop valid and reliable data across all the cases we see fit for comparison (Sartori 1970, 1994). If this problem occurs (and it does) it may well affect the quality of the comparative analysis and thus the internal and external validity of the results. In conjunction with this hazard, it has been noted that reliability problems may arise as a result of *equivalents* that are used to widen the case selection. The problem is here to what extent a concept transformed into an empirical indicator has the same meaning across different settings or cultures (Van Deth 1998). Finally some caveats need to be taken into account when interpreting the comparative data available: (1) Galton's problem, (2) individual and ecological fallacies, and (3) over-determination (Przeworski 1987; Landman 2003: 40; Burnham *et al.* 2004).

These issues are all important for a proper use and solid application of the 'toolkit' of comparative methods. Yet, these limits and constraints should not be considered as insurmountable or invalidating the comparative approach within political science. On the contrary, one ought to **acknowledge** them and consider them as *caveats* to take into consideration whilst carrying out comparative research. Below I will elaborate these constraints and limitations of comparative methods.

Too many variables and too few cases

This is mainly a problem for a research design with few(er) cases (see Figure 3.2: options 1 and 3). Obviously one way to counter this problem is to enlarge the number of cases. However, this is often easier said than done. First of all, it depends on the research question and related answer whether or not this is feasible. Take for example Lijphart's study on consociational democracies (1977). Lijphart wished to enhance his original single case study (on the politics of accommodation in the Netherlands; Lijphart 1968) by replicating the explanatory mechanisms of that case to other cases (i.e. political systems) with similar societal features. Hence, by adding more cases he hoped to be able to enhance the external validity of his findings in the single case study.[5] In fact, on the basis of this comparative study, he developed his seminal *Democracies* (1984). However, this remedy is often not feasible and that is why comparativists have developed another way to solve the problem of too few cases: namely developing variables that can 'travel' across more cases.

Conceptual stretching

Conceptual stretching is the distortion occurring when a concept developed for one set of cases is extended to additional cases to which the features of the concept do not apply. Sartori (1970) illustrated this problem by means of the 'ladder of generality'. Enhancing a wider use of a theoretical concept by

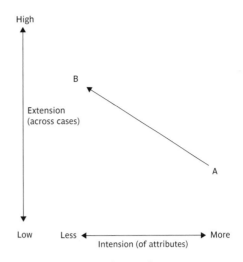

Fig. 3.3 Sartori's ladder of generality

Source: Pennings *et al.* (2006: 49).

extension (of its initial meaning, i.e. moving from A to B in Figure 3.3) involves a loss of intension (the observations reflect the original features of the concept, i.e. remaining close to B). Intension will obviously reduce the applicability of a concept in comparative research across more cases, but it enhances the internal validity of the cases compared. Extension will have the opposite effect, and the question is then whether or not the wider use (i.e. in a higher number of cases to be compared) impairs the claim for external validity of the analytical results. In Figure 3.3 the choice is visualized: the more the meaning of a concept moves due to the process of operationalization from position A to B, the less equivalent the information collected for each case may well be.

The choice to be made and the matter of dispute among comparativists is how broadly or extensively (i.e. from A to B) can we define and measure variables without a serious loss of meaning. There are different opinions on the degree of flexibility is allowed as regards to 'stretching' of concepts to make variables 'travel' across (more) cases. On the one hand, there is the constructivist *view* which tends to be critical of the possibility of comparing (and thus opt almost always for case studies). On the other hand, there is the **generalist** *view* claiming that in essence all empirical knowledge is based on 'methodological individualism' (see Chapter 2).

In a way, both positions are exaggerated in the sense that—following the metaphor of Sartori's 'ladder of generality'—for the 'generalists' A and

B are considered as almost interchangeable and for the 'constructivists' A and B are hardly ever the same. Sartori's idea is that there is a delicate balance between the two positions: **over**stretching is dangerous and not all concepts can travel all over the world and through all time (Sartori 1994). In other words there is no easy way out of this problem and the researcher has to make up his own mind. However, a few attempts have been made to develop methods to cope with the problem of overstretching and travelling.

Family resemblance

Some comparativists have suggested the method of categorizing by means of 'family resemblance' (Collier and Mahon 1993: 846–8). In its simplest fashion this method extends the initial concept by adding features which share some of the attributes of the original concept. How far this type of extension can go depends on how specific the research question is. For example, if we are investigating the behaviour of political parties and define these as actors that are vote-seeking (= A), office-seeking (= B), and policy-seeking (= C), then the concept of a party can be used in a wider sense, depending on the research question. Instead of requiring that all three characteristics are present *simultaneously*, we allow also the inclusion of parties as separate cases that have only two out of three in common. However, if we are examining all three dimensions of party behaviour simultaneously then we cannot stretch the concept.

Radial categories

The second option of going up the 'ladder of generality' is the use of **radial** categories. Here the underlying idea is that each step of extension, and thus including new comparable cases, is defined by a **hierarchy** of attributes belonging to the initial concept. In Figure 3.4 this is made visible by defining A as the essential attribute whereas B or C is considered as secondary. An example is the study of corporatism: the original concept and its meaning was quite specific, but gradually the operationalization widened to include more cases, but keeping the voluntary arrangement between employers' organizations and trade unions as an essential feature of the concept (Keman and Pennings 1995). All in all, Figure 3.4 demonstrates these two strategies for extension through which the

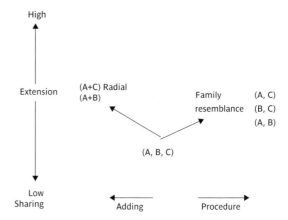

Fig. 3.4 Radial categorization and family resemblance

Source: Pennings *et al.* 2006: 50.

number of cases are to be increased. Family resemblance requires a degree of commonality and this produces three cases in comparison with one under the initial categorization, by sharing two out of the three defining features (AC, AB, BC). The radial method requires that the primary attribute (A) be always included. In Figure 3.4, this means two cases instead of the original one case (A + B and A + C).[6]

Equivalence

A related problem of transforming concepts into empirically based indicators concerns the question of whether or not the meaning of a concept stays constant across time and space. Landman (2003: 43–6) argues that this problem is less a matter of whether or not a concept is measured **identically** (which is a matter of reliability regarding the measurement across cases), but more to what extent it can be considered **equivalent**.

As with the issue of conceptual travelling, there are various views on accepting equivalence (assuming stability of the measured concept). The so-called **universalist** point of view departs from the idea that vital functions of a political system are fulfilled everywhere (Dogan and Pelassy 1990: 42). Conversely the **relativist** position is that the meaning of a concept is more often than not different across systems due to cultural and anthropological reasons. This difference of opinion appears difficult to reconcile. Again, there is no easy or straightforward solution. Several options are mentioned in the literature which suggest controlling for cultural differences (Van Deth

1998), raising the level of abstraction (Sartori's ladder of generality), or to limiting the case selection to those for which triangulation is feasible: comparing different types of indicators of the same concept (Peters 1998: 99–101). An example is to combine survey results on what the public in several countries think on the left versus right differences of their party system with the results of content analysis of party programmes (Keman 2007). Whatever solution is chosen, at the end of the day it is up to the researcher to decide whether or not the degree of equivalence is acceptable or not (Landman 2003: 46).

Interpreting results

Galton's problem, ecological and individual fallacies, and over-determination are all hazards that are related to the interpretation of the results of the comparative analysis.

Galton's problem

Galton's problem refers to the situation where the observed differences and similarities may well be caused by an often exogenous factor that is common to all the cases selected for comparison (see, for examples, Chapter 22), such as comparing fiscal policy-making across states in Europe after the introduction of the EMU requirements (Hix 2005), or the choice for a Westminster-style of parliamentary governance (Burnham *et al.* 2004: 74). Obviously, if diffusion is likely to be apparent, it will affect the process of causal inference because the explanation is corrupted by it (Lijphart 1975: 17).

Individual and ecological fallacies

These fallacies are likewise problematic *vis-à-vis* the causal interpretation of evidence. An ecological fallacy occurs when data measured on an aggregated level (e.g. at the state level) are used to make inferences about individual- or group-level behaviour. Conversely, individual fallacy is the result of interpreting data measured at the individual or group level as if they represent the 'whole' (e.g. using electoral surveys for party behaviour or even national

attitudes). This type of fallacy occurs regularly in comparative politics (Dalton 1996).

Over-determination and selection biases

Over-determination and selection biases are risks that emanate from case selection. In particular, when MSSD is used, the chances are high that the dependent variable is over-determined by another difference that is not actually catered for in the research design (Przeworski and Teune 1970: 34). Conversely, if the cases included in the analysis are quite homogeneous there is a chance of a selection bias which goes unnoticed. As King *et al.* (1994: 141–2) note, the worst-case scenario may occur if the similarities among the cases affect the degree of comparative variation of the independent and dependent variables.

To conclude this section, these constraints and limitations of the comparative method are serious and need continual attention. However, it would be wrong to conclude that—given the complexities discussed in this chapter—the comparative approach to politics is misdirected or inherently fallacious. If we accept the fact that most political science is comparative, even if not explicitly so (Mair 1996), then it is one of the **strengths** of the comparative method that both the advantages and disadvantages are widely acknowledged and debated.

KEY POINTS

❑ There are many hazards and pitfalls in comparative methods that ought to be taken into account to link theory and evidence in plausible fashion. Nevertheless the comparative method is a feasible and important approach for political science at large.

❑ Conceptual travelling is a sensitive instrument to widen the case selection as long as over-stretching is avoided. This could well be achieved by means of 'radial categories' or 'family resemblance'.

❑ Interpretation problems are due to biases like Galton's problem and over-determination, on the one hand, and to individual and ecological fallacies, on the other hand. Avoiding these problems as far as possible means reducing collateral damage of applying the comparative research.

Conclusion

Some time ago Gabriel Almond, a distinguished American comparativist, lamented the lack of progress in political science at large (Almond 1990). His main complaint concerned the lack of constructive collaboration among the practitioners. However, he made an exception as regards the field of comparative politics:

❝ Mainstream comparative studies, rather than being in a crisis, are richly and variedly productive.... In the four decades after World War II, the level of rigor has been significantly increased in quantitative, analytical, and historical-sociological work. (Almond 1990: 253) ❞

Not least the credit should go to those involved in the further development of the methodology of comparative politics. On the one hand, debates on difficult issues in the comparative method have been discussed for a long time now. On the other hand, new developments do take place and are widely welcomed. Rather than becoming involved in endless and bitter debates or forming competing 'schools', it seems that discussions are intended to make progress.

This chapter has attempted to demonstrate this. Throughout I have maintained that comparative politics is a (sub)discipline in political science where theory development is linked to empirical evidence by means of a rigorous application of the comparative method. Amongst other things this means that that the shared methodology is at the same time the means of communication between comparative political scientists.

Hence, developing a research design, formulating research question, and the pursuit of finding a valid research answer by means of a conscious selection of cases that can be made productive with the help of the logic of comparison, whilst being conscious of pitfalls and hazards, will enhance the progress of comparative politics. Therefore this chapter has approached the comparative method as the way to obtain as many of the advantages as possible, but has also acknowledged some common problems. Even if not all the problems—and they do exist—can be solved at this stage, I hold the view that the comparative method is the best way to go for political scientists.

? Questions

1. Why is the 'art of comparing' not only useful but also a necessary part of the toolkit of any political scientist? Give an example.

2. Can you explain why the comparative method is often called 'quasi-experimental' method? Can you give an example?

3. Try to elaborate whether or not the rules of internal or external validity are violated in the following statements:
   • Political parties and social movements are 'equivalents' and can be compared throughout the whole world.
   • The development of welfare states must always be researched cross-nationally and over time.
   • Party government in whatever political system is proper for analysing the process of government formation.

4. If you re-examine the debate on 'does politics matter' can you describe the research design used? And, are you able to develop a different one—in terms of variables and cases—to test the main issue of this debate alternatively?

5. There are different options as regards the type and number of cases needed to develop a research design. Can you think of a research question that would justify the choice of a single-case study where 'time' is not relevant and 'inter'-system references are unnecessary?

6. Can you think of examples that fit the proposed remedies to the problem of 'conceptual stretching' as visualized in Figure 3.4?

7. The distinction between 'many cases and few variables' and 'few cases and many variables' is frequently debated in comparative politics. List the pros and cons of the choice involved.

8. What is 'Galton's problem' and why is it a problem? Can you think of an example (e.g. by naming a process of diffusion across comparable systems)?

9. Describe the basic difference is between the Methods of Agreement and Difference? Give an example.

10. In the concluding section of this chapter it is stated that the comparative method is the 'best' way to go for a political scientist. Can you give reasons why this is indeed the case, or alternatively, can you argue that such a statement is too bold and does not fit 'all' political science?

» Further reading

General literature on methods in political science

Brady, H. D., and Collier, D. (2004) *Rethinking Social Enquiry: Diverse Tools, Shared Standards* (Lanham, Md.: Rowman & Littlefield). This edited volume discusses a wide variety of methodological concerns that are relevant for comparative methods. It is—in fact—a response to the quantitative oriented types of research methods in general and directed against the book by King, Keohane and Verba (see below).

Burnham, P., Gilland, K., Grant, W., and Layton-Henry, Z. (2004) *Research Methods in Politics* (Basingstoke: Palgrave Macmillan). This textbook discusses a variety of subjects within social science methods. There is one chapter on comparative methods, but other chapters are also useful.

King, G., Keohane, R. D., and Verba, S. (1994) *Designing Social Inquiry* (Princeton: Princeton University Press). This is a contemporary classic in social science methods and written by three political scientists. It is a basic introduction and uses much material taken from comparative politics.

Pennings, P., Keman, H., and Kleinnijenhuis, J. (2006) *Doing Research in Political Science: An Introduction to Comparative Methods and Statistics* (London: Sage, 2nd edn). This is a course book intended for students mainly at the MA and Ph.D. level. It is an introduction to the use of statistics in comparative research and contains a separate part where examples of published research are elaborated with numerous examples.

Specific literature on comparative methods

Dogan, M., and Pelassy, D. (1990) *How to Compare Nations: Strategies in Comparative Politics* (Chatham, NJ: Chatham House, 2nd edn). This useful introduction was originally published in the 1980s and takes the student to several of the problems mentioned in this chapter, making good use of existing research in comparative politics.

Peters, B. Guy (1998) *Comparative Politics. Theory and Methods* (Basingstoke: Macmillan). The goal of this book is to relate explicitly the various types of theories in political science to the comparative method. It offers a good overview of what types of research exist using comparative methods.

Landman, T. (2007) *Issues and Methods in Comparative Politics: An Introduction* (London: Routledge, 2nd edn). This introductory text starts form the basics of comparative research and its problems and then discusses various fields within comparative politics, focusing on different research designs by means of one, few, and many cases using many examples.

Lichbach, M., and Zuckermann, A. (eds.) (1997) *Comparative Politics: Rationality, Culture and Structure* (Cambridge: Cambridge University Press). A collection of essays that focuses on contemporary issues and debates regarding ontology, epistemology, and theory development in comparative politics. Interesting for students who wish to dig deeper into the theory–evidence linkage.

Mahoney, J., and Rueschemeyer, D. (eds.) (2003) *Comparative Historical Analysis in the Social Sciences* (Cambridge: Cambridge University Press). This reader contains many different views on developing qualitative types of comparative research with an emphasis on history and the use of case studies.

Ragin, C. (1987) *The Comparative Method* (Berkeley, Calif, University of California Press). The book centres on the alternative approach to using the comparative methods as discussed in this chapter (see also Box 3.4) and discusses the advantages of this approach in comparison with extant practices.

Ⓦ Web links

www.politicalresources.net
   Political Resources on the Net: provides links to a number of useful datasets for use in comparative politics.

www.parties-and-elections.de
   Parties and Elections in Europe.

http://freedomhouse.org
   Freedom House data on democratization.

http://phw.binghamton.edu/
   Political Handbook of the World: key information on national states regarding politics, economics, and demography.

www.cia.gov/redirects/factbookredirect.html
   CIA: The World Factbook is a regularly updated 'factbook' on most nation-states of the world.

www.ipw.unibe.ch/content/team/klaus_armingeon/comparative_political_data_sets/index_ger.html
   Two datasets on parties, party government, and political institutions as well as data on population, welfare policies, and trade unions; one set is on Western Europe, the other on Central and Eastern European countries; suitable for pooled time series analysis.

www.lisproject.org/publications/welfaredatat/welfareaccess.htm
   Comparative welfare states dataset, useful for comparing the performance of welfare state policies.

www.sp.uconn.edu/~scruggs/wp.htm
   This dataset is also on the welfare state but focuses on 'entitlements' of citizen in relation to welfare programmes.

www.sourceoecd.org
   OECD statistics on the economy, infrastructure, and social expenditures of most developed nation-states and Central and Eastern Europe.

http://epp.eurostat.cec.eu.int/
   Eurostat: aggregated statistical and individual level survey data on EU and member-states.

www.fsqa.com
   Concerns the website of Charles Ragin and gives access to the software to conduct Boolean analysis as used in Box 3.4.

 Visit the Online Resource Centre that accompanies this book for more information:
www.oxfordtextbooks.co.uk/orc/caramani/

SECTION 2

The historical context

4 The nation-state

Gianfranco Poggi

Chapter contents

Reader's guide

The most significant political units of the modern world are generally referred to as 'states' or 'nation-states'. It is within and between states that contemporary political business, in its various forms, is typically carried out. This chapter indicates to the reader where, when, why, and how this particular kind of political unit came into being and how it became dominant. It will thus provide conceptual and historical background knowledge useful for the reader's exploration of many other themes of the study of comparative politics. We suggest that this chapter is read in combination with Chapter 24 on 'Globalization and the nation-state' in which challenges to the dominance of this political unit coming from globalization processes are discussed.

Introduction

The comparative analysis of the arrangements under which political activity is carried out, and of its contents, refers chiefly to a multiplicity of interdependent but separate, to a greater or lesser extent autonomous, units—let us call them polities. Polities differ among themselves in numerous, relevant respects, and entertain with one another relations—friendly or antagonistic—which reflect those differences. These exist—and matter—against the background of considerable similarities. To point up the most significant of these, we might say that the polities making up the modern political environment, and whose internal and external activities give that environment its peculiar dynamics, all qualify for being called states.

The expression 'state' has been applied by scholars to polities which have existed in pre-modern contexts—say, to ancient Egypt, or to imperial China. This is of course a legitimate usage, but this chapter differs from it in assuming that 'state' is more appropriately used to designate the polities characteristic of what has been called the **modern political environment**. This came into being in Western Europe at the end of the Middle Ages, roughly between the thirteenth and the fifteenth century.

This chapter offers, in the first instance, a general, abstract, highly streamlined portrait of the state—a concept that sociologists inspired by Max Weber (whose work will be a prime source for much that follows) might call an ideal type. Such a concept may not fit closely some actual, historically given states, but points up some features which most of them share to a greater or lesser extent. Note also that our conceptual portrait of the state is bound to appear out of date on various counts, since a number of contemporary developments within the modern political environment have made less plausible some of the portrait's features, for instance the notion of state sovereignty (see Chapter 24).

I shall paint the conceptual portrait in two steps. First I consider the most fundamental aspects of the state, then amplify and qualify the portrait by adding other aspects, which generally have developed or become more visible over the last two or three centuries. After this, I shall address a different kind of question: assuming we now know what states *are like*, I will ask how they came into being and through what processes.

> **KEY POINTS**
>
> ❑ Most contemporary larger political units (or polities) share some aspects which justify calling them 'states'.
>
> ❑ To that extent, they all constitute present-day embodiments of a kind of polity which first developed in the modern West.
>
> ❑ On this account, a sustained scholarly engagement with 'comparative politics' should comprise a consideration both of the constitutive features of that kind of polity and of the major steps in its development.

A portrait of the state

Monopoly of legitimate violence

Let us begin with the more basic components of our conceptual portrait. States are in the first place polities where a single centre of rule has established its exclusive entitlement to control and employ the ultimate medium of political activity—organized violence—over a definite territory. Individuals and bodies operating within that territory may occasionally exercise violence, but if they do so without mandate or permission from the centre of rule, the latter considers that exercise illegitimate and seeks to suppress it. Typically, by mobilizing its own potential for violence, it overwhelms or threatens to overwhelm the potential wielded by those individuals or bodies, and compels them to 'cease and desist'. If it *cannot* do so, and if in the territory alternative seats of power can act with impunity on the assumption that it cannot, then you no longer have a state, but some other kind of polity.[1]

Territoriality

The territory itself is a most significant element in the state's conceptual portrait. To qualify as a state the polity must be able not only to 'police' a given portion of the earth by overwhelming any internal challenges that may arise to its own monopoly of legitimate violence. It must also claim that portion, against all comers, as exclusively its own, be able and disposed to protect and defend it, to patrol its boundaries, to confront and push back any encroachment by other states upon its territory's integrity and prevent any undue use of its resources. Needless to say, the ultimate medium of such activities is, again, organized violence.

On this account, the relation between state and territory is an intimate one. The territory is not simply a locale of the state's activities (violent or other), or its however cherished possession. Rather, it represents the physical aspect of the state's own identity, the very **ground** (this expression is itself a significant metaphor) of its existence and of its historical continuity. As an Italian jurist puts it, the state does not so much **have** a territory, rather it **is** a territory (Romano 1947: 56).

Sovereignty

It is with reference to its territory, furthermore, that the state establishes and practices its sovereignty—a somewhat mysterious and highly controversial attribute. Being sovereign signifies, for each state, that it recognizes no power superior to itself. It engages in political activity on nobody's mandate but its own, commits resources of its own, operates under its own steam, at its own risk. It is the sole judge of its own interests and bears the sole responsibility for pursuing those interests, beginning with the interest in its own security. Qua sovereign the state holds within the territory (and thus over the people residing in it) the ultimate authority, which another state can effectively challenge only (once more) by asserting the factual superiority of its own potential for violence. Sovereignty also means that each state accepts no interference from others in its own domestic affairs.

Plurality

It is thus a distinctive feature of the modern political environment that it consists in a plurality of territorially discrete, self-empowering, self-activating, self-securing states. Each of these presupposes the existence of all others, and each is in principle their equal, since it shares with them (and acknowledges in them) its own characteristics—sovereignty in particular. By the same token, since there does not exist over the states a higher layer of authority, a superior unit endowed with its own resources for violence, entitled to oversee and control the states, these necessarily tend to regard each other as potentially hostile, as constituting impending threats to their own security; and enter with one another into relations aimed in the first instance either to neutralize or to confront and defeat those threats.

Relation with the population

I should now make more explicit something I have so far barely hinted at. States exercise rule over people, issue commands to and expect obedience from people, pursue policies binding over people. But states, though they sometimes project themselves as self-standing, personified entities, are themselves **made of** people, operate exclusively within and through the activities of people—at bottom, indeed, of individuals. On this account the existence itself of states (as of other polities) involves a form of social inequality, a more or less stable and pronounced asymmetry between people exercising rule (a minority) and people subject to it (the great majority).

In the case of states, that asymmetry is to an extent bounded and justified by a hard-to-define sense in which the parties to it belong together, and jointly make up a collective entity. Together with the ruling minority, the ruled-over people constitute a **political community**. For this community the activities of rule, asymmetrical as they may be (and they are ultimately grounded in violence) constitute a medium for coming into being, for achieving and maintaining a shared identity, for pursuing putatively common interests. To this extent, as is the case for the territory, the relationship between the state and its population is not a purely factual one; the population is not perceived as a mere demographic entity but as a people (or, as we shall see, as a nation). As such it entertains a more significant, more intimate, one might say **constitutive**, relation with the state itself.

All this, of course, lends itself to much ideological mystification, for instance the notion that the people or the nation (see below) is the source and/or carrier of the state's very sovereignty. But Marx's aggressive debunking of the state itself as 'an illusory community' at some point ceases to be enlightening and may itself produce mystification; for how *illusory* can you call a commonality in the name of which feats of great magnitude and significance have been accomplished (for good or for evil) throughout modern history?

KEY POINTS

- ❑ Internally, states are characterized in the first place by a single centre of power that, however internally differentiated, reserves for itself the faculty of exercising or threatening legitimate violence.
- ❑ A state does not respond to any other power for the uses to which it puts the faculty of violence and other faculties.
- ❑ The state uses the faculty of violence in the first place to police and protect one portion of the earth which it considers its own territory. It claims exclusive jurisdiction over the population inhabiting that territory and at the same time considers itself the guardian of its interests.
- ❑ Externally, each state exists side by side with others, all endowed with the same characteristics, and treats them, according to its own judgement, as contenders, allies, or neutral parties.

A more expansive concept

A definition of the state appearing in Weber's *Economy and Society* provides both a retrospect on what I have said so far and a prospect on the points to be made in this section.

❝ The primary formal characteristics of the modern state are as follows: it possesses an administrative and legal order subject to change by legislation, to which the organised activities of the administrative staff, which are also controlled by regulations, are oriented. This system of order claims authority, not only over the members of the state, the citizens, most of whom have obtained membership by birth, but also to a very large extent over all action taking place in the area of its jurisdiction. It is thus a compulsory organisation with a territorial basis. Furthermore, today, the use of force is regarded as legitimate only so far as it is permitted by the state or prescribed by it. (Weber 1978: 56) ❞

This definition points us to a second level of conceptual discussion, where we consider some additional features of those states active in the nineteenth and twentieth century that were the main theme of the study of comparative politics during the latter century. Their practices of rule often displayed aspects not directly connected with the basic features already discussed, yet significant enough for our conceptual portrait of the state to take them into account—though of course individual states displayed them to a different extent and in different ways. This *diversity* is of course the main theme of the study of comparative politics.

The role of law

We may begin by noting that **law,** understood as a set of general, enforceable commands and prohibitions, has played a significant (though variable) role in the construction and management of states. In all societies, law so understood has chiefly performed two functions: first, to repress anti-social behaviour; second, to allocate between groups or individuals access to and disposition over material resources. In the West, however, law has been put to a further, third use in **establishing polities, deciding issues of policy, instituting public agencies and offices, activating and controlling their operations.**

These peculiar uses of law developed first in the Greek *polis*, then, more self-consciously and intensely, in the Roman Republic and Empire. Subsequently, European polities maintained a connection with the realm of law: rulers were expected to serve **justice,** observe it in their own conduct, and enforce it in adjudicating disputes and punishing crimes. But for a long time the commandments in question were seen to express the folkways and the moral values instilled by religion. Local judges themselves were said to **find** the law—sometimes with the assistance of popular juries—and were not meant to **make** it. Much less did the rulers do so. Instead, they mostly brought to bear the means of violence at their disposal and enforced the verdicts of judges and juries.

This arrangement, still observed in the early development of the state, subsequently changed. While continuing to declare themselves beholden to justice, rulers undertook to play a more active legal role. Increasingly assisted by officials trained in sophisticated, taught-and-learned law, they began to codify local, vernacular sets of customs and usages and to enforce them uniformly over the territory. Above all, they asserted themselves as the source of a new kind of law, **public** law. This regulated the relations on the one hand between the organs and offices of the state itself and on the other between the state and various categories of individuals and groups, generally asserting the supremacy of the former's interests over those of the latter.

There followed two developments that to an extent counter-balance one another. On the one hand, it was increasingly asserted that **all law was public** in so far only as it was produced by the state itself, through special organs and procedures. Law had become, so to speak, the exclusive speech of the state. On the other hand, **the state declared itself bound to its own laws.** The activities of its organs and the commands of state officials were seen as valid only if their content or, more often, the ways in which they were produced, conformed with some express legal principles, such as those contained in constitutions. Those responsible for deliberating state policy often framed their preferences by means of legal argument, referring to rights, rules, precedents. The implementation of policy was seen to involve largely the enforcement and implementation of laws.

On this account, particularly on the continent, academic credentials in law became the standard qualification for those aspiring to enter the state's administrative apparatus. In all these ways, though once more to an extent that varied in time and from region to region, the state—without ceasing to assert its own grounding in sheer might—became involved in producing and implementing (and, by the same token, complying with) arrangements expressed in legal instruments of diverse kinds: constitutions, statutes, decrees, judgments, ordinances, by-laws.

Centralized organization

These instruments, it will be noted, do not stand on the same plane, but make up a more-or-less explicit and binding hierarchy of legal sources. Typically, the constitution lies at the top, by-laws stand lower than statutes, and so on. This is so in three closely related senses:

1. Higher sources authorize and lay boundaries upon lower ones.

2. The products of lower ones can change without altering the content of higher ones, in so far as they articulate and specify it in different and thus variable ways.

3. The verified contrast between the content of a higher source and that of a lower one invalidates the lower one. Furthermore, this hierarchy may be matched by a more visible one. For instance, different judicial organs are empowered to issue judgments of different scope or gravity. Higher ones may review and nullify or revise the judgments of lower ones.

This hierarchical arrangement is intended to bring unity and coherence to a variety of legal instruments and related organs. But aspects of the state which have little to do with law reveal the same preoccupation with unity and coherence, and express it through hierarchy. For instance, the monopoly in the exercise of violence has a legal aspect (Weber speaks of 'legitimate force'). But much more significant are its organizational components, summarized in the contemporary expression **command, communication, and control,** without which that monopoly cannot be secured. Those components have sometimes a very loose relationship (if any) to legal constraints—witness the fact that 'command, communication, and control' are never as important as in warfare, a confrontation between the parties' capacity for exercising organized violence on whose outcome law has very little bearing.

More generally, the organizational blueprint of the state mostly reveals a managerial rather than a legal rationality. That is, it is chiefly intended to make the operations of all state agencies, numerous and diverse as they may be, as responsive as possible to the directives of the political centre, and to render them as far as possible uniform, prompt, predictable, and economical. Together, two rather different but equally common and persistent images of the state—respectively, the pyramid and the machine—convey, again, a preoccupation with unity and coherence which is reflected in its legal features but by no means only in these.

The distinction between state and society

The unity and coherence the state tries to achieve also has the effect of emphasizing its separateness with respect to the larger society.

The distinction between 'state' and '(civil) society', theorized by Hegel among others, is more or less expressly reflected in the constitution of several Western states. The state, in principle, is an ensemble of **institutional arrangements and practices** which on the one hand address all the political aspects of the management of a territorially bounded society, and on the other address only those aspects. So understood, the state represents and justifies itself as a realm of expressly political activities (legislation, jurisdiction, police, military action, public policy) complementary to a different realm—society—comprising diverse social activities which the state's organs do not expressly promote and control, for they are not considered political in nature.

Individuals undertake those activities in their private capacities, pursuing values and interests of their own, and in the process establish among themselves relations which are not the concern of public policy. At the centre of the realm of society stand two sets of concerns which for a long time the state saw very much as its own but subsequently, via lengthy and complex processes, released to that realm.

The state, religion, and the market

First, the state becomes increasingly secular. That is, it progressively dismisses any concern with the spiritual welfare of individuals, which previously it had fostered, mostly by privileging (and professing) one religion and associating itself with one church. (A critical reason for this development was the breakdown of the religious unity of the West caused by the Reformation.)

Second, the state progressively entrusts to the two central institutions of private law—property and contract—the legal discipline of the activities which relate to the production and distribution of wealth, and which increasingly take place via the market. Rule, religion, and the economy, thus differentiated, can each affirm its own autonomy and develop its rationality.

Not that these domains stand entirely on the same plane. One meaning of sovereignty is that the state's specific concern with external security and public order may override those of private individuals, especially in confronting emergencies. Furthermore, private activities are carried out within frameworks of public rules which the state is responsible for enacting and enforcing. But in principle those rules do not prejudge the outcome of the interactions taking place between individuals.

In the same way, it is the state's prerogative to fund its own activities by extracting resources from the economy. But typically the modern state is a 'taxation state'. That is: it extracts resources from the society's economic system chiefly by regularly levying moneys from stocks and flows of private wealth. Such levies have to be authorized by law and carried out by public officials. This renders them compatible with the security of private property and with the autonomous operations of the market. The name itself of another subsidiary form of extraction, the **public debt**, again suggests that compatibility: private individuals become creditors of the state and to that extent place a lien on public resources. Furthermore, the state plays an indispensable role in issuing and guaranteeing money, but is not supposed to allocate the wealth stored and vehicled by state-backed money.

With the progress of modernization, the differentiation between state and society is followed and deepened by further processes of differentiation, taking place within both realms. For instance, within the civil society there emerges a domain—science—which attends expressly and exclusively to the production and distribution of secular knowledge about nature, and as such operates autonomously with respect to the cognitive activities and concerns of theology or of other academic disciplines. Within the state itself, the so-called 'division of powers' between the legislature, the judiciary, and the executive constitutes the most express and self-conscious outcome of a process of differentiation. As a result the state, as we have already seen, increasingly presents itself as a complex ensemble of expressly differentiated and purposefully coordinated parts, each designed to perform as effectively as possible, on behalf of the whole, a specific task. The image of **the state as a machine**, and the growing significance of the vocabulary of **organization**, particularly convey this. The advance of differentiation produces its most visible effects in the context of the executive, with the development of bureaucratic systems of administration—a phenomenon to which I shall return (see also Chapter 8).

The public sphere

The visibility itself of these processes (often expressly theorized by jurists and other scholars) hides to an extent a further phenomenon—the formation of the 'public sphere' as a kind of hinge between state and society. As if to balance and complement the extent to which, as suggested above, the state monitors and assists the processes of the civil society, the subjects active in it acquire a capacity first to observe the activities of the state, then to communicate with one another about them, to criticize them, and finally to make significant inputs into them. This is only possible, at first, to a narrow minority within the population which possesses the leisure and the material and cultural resources necessary for taking part in these processes. But in the course of time that minority grows.

The public sphere comprises institutions such as the freedom of speech, of the press, of assembly, of association; rules that require some state organs to conduct their activities in public and thus to expose them to legitimate debate and criticism; above all, the institutions of 'representative' government.

Liberal and democratic arrangements for participation

Thanks to these institutions, the selection of the small minorities who directly and continuously operate some state organs comes to depend on registering and counting the preferences periodically expressed by much larger numbers of people making up the electorate. Again, at first only a narrow minority within the population can form and express such preferences, and even as, with the progress of liberalism, that minority grows, it remains long bounded by two qualifications: (1) material possessions (**census voting**) and (2) cultural attainments (**capacity voting**) (see also Chapter 5). We may characterize the progress of **democracy**, instead, as the progressive lowering and then elimination of those barriers. In the long run, the great majority of the adult population (for a long time, excluding women in many countries) acquires, through the suffrage, an equal (though minimal) capacity to express preferences and to make them affect the selection of political elites and, via these, the formation of public policy.

The new 'entrants into politics' are mobilized by expressly formed organizations—political parties—the competition between which determines directly who at a given time has the decisive say in legislative and executive organs, and indirectly the content of their activities. In other terms, the formation of public policy is made to depend on 'adversary politics'. This involves not only the periodic contest between parties for electoral support, but also the right of the party which has failed in a given contest to criticize the policies of the successful party, to propose alternative policies, and to seek success in the next contest.

The burden of conflict

Although we generally think of political participation chiefly as a **vertical** flow of influence from the society at large towards its political summit, we should never forget the etymological meaning of 'participation' itself: **taking sides**. This meaning points instead to a **horizontal** split, a division within the society itself. Put otherwise, through the public sphere the contrasts of opinion on political matters formed within the society map themselves onto the state, affecting particularly the operations of its legislative organs and of those charged with the initiation and implementation of policy. Such contrasts, though generally they do not express themselves through organized violence (given the state's monopoly of that) can be bitter and divisive, for expressly **political** alignments such as parties often derive their conflicting policy orientations from deep and long-standing **social** cleavages within the population where they compete with one another for support (see Chapter 13).

Such cleavages do not just represent different orientations of opinion concerning individual issues, but sometimes reflect serious cultural differences (say, between religious or between linguistic groups), tensions between a country's centre and its periphery, ethnic differences, or sharp class antagonisms. Such a situation is potentially threatening to sensitive political values, particularly when those cleavages do not cut across each other, but build on one another. Think of the Irish situation in the eighteenth century, when the native population often spoke a different language from the 'Anglo' upper stratum, practised a different religion, and was systematically excluded from positions having higher economic and social status.

In the modern political vocabulary, the significance of such a threat is particularly evident in negative expressions like 'sectionalism', 'factionalism', 'partisanship', or 'interest' and in the nearly obsessive contrasting emphasis on the necessity of protecting from such phenomena the state's 'unity', appealing instead to 'loyalty', 'discipline', and 'spirit of sacrifice'.

Citizenship and nation

In most modern states, this threat is countered by two different and to an extent complementary strategies: citizenship and the nation.

Citizenship

The first strategy consists in the institution of citizenship, which finds its primordial expression in the dictum **all citizens are equal before the law**. In fact, in its early formulations the principle did not refer to citizens; rather, it denied individuals of exalted status, without demoting them from that, some particular privileges they had long enjoyed, such as the exemption from certain forms of taxation and from the courts' jurisdiction, the right to be tried by their own peers or to be protected from certain kinds of punishment. But the principle came to signify the progressive inclusion of all individuals making up the people into a formally equal relationship to the state itself.

Individuals who found themselves placed under the same obligations and enjoyed the same entitlement *vis-à-vis* the state were made to feel more equal to one another. Furthermore their entitlements relating to the public sphere were put at the service of a new principle of equality, associated with the progress of democracy, and originally phrased as **one man, one vote**. Under this principle, as we have seen, broader and broader masses of individuals (again excluding women, for a long time) were able to enter the political process and make an input into the state's own activities via the electoral process and inter-party competition. Parties getting their support chiefly from economically disadvantaged strata promoted public policies—those we generally associate with the welfare state—that added to citizenship new entitlements toward the state. These to an extent reduced or compensated for inequalities generated among individuals by the workings of the market system and of the resultant class cleavages.

As a consequence, as one argument goes (but it is not an uncontested argument) those cleavages lost much of their power to threaten the state's unity. However, this happened by mobilizing class contrasts, by making the processes of creation and distribution of wealth an object of public contention and of policy, no longer shielded from the state by the separateness of the social realm.

Thus, in the first strategy the state acknowledges the significance of socio-economic cleavages and expressly works to reduce it by means of the growing structures of the welfare state. To this end it extracts from the economy greater and greater resources, and entrusts them to expressly created public organs, mandating them both to redistribute those resources and to assist the economy in producing further resources. The whole process is made possible by a historically unprecedented context, characterized by the capacity for sustained growth of industrial economies. Nonetheless, it presents problems of various kinds, at any rate from the standpoint of the elites which control those economies, although often those too benefit amply from the growing involvement of their state in economic affairs.

I have already mentioned one particular problem. The policies moderating the inequalities generated by the market by expanding the benefits of citizenship are activated by forces which, by denouncing those inequalities, often express and enhance the protest

BOX 4.1 Patterns of state formation

One can distinguish at least five paths in state formation:

1. Through *absolutist kingship* which obtained independent power through the build-up of armies and bureaucracies solely responsible to monarchs (e.g. France and Prussia).

2. Through *kingship facing judges and representative bodies* (and, within them, eventually political parties) which developed sufficient strength to become independent powers (e.g. England, Sweden).

3. State formation from below through *confederation or federation*, due to the maintenance of effective autonomy for the constituent 'states' and a general emphasis on the division of power within the centre through 'checks and balances' (e.g. Switzerland, US).

4. State formation through *conquest and/or unification* (e.g. Germany, Italy).

5. State formation through *independence* (e.g. Ireland, Norway, and cases of break-up of empires: Habsburg and Ottoman empires).

Source: Adapted from Daalder (1991: 14).

of the subaltern social strata, and thus threaten the unity of the state.

Nationhood

The second strategy addresses this problem directly, by seeking to generate in the whole society, across the classes, a shared sense of solidarity grounded on nationhood. To refer again to a concept introduced above, the political community typical of modern states is supposed to constitute a **nation**. Most of the polities with which this book deals define themselves as nation-states; the relations of states with one another make up international politics; the pursuit of the national interest by each state is supposed to be the key rationale for the varying content of those relations; finally, the largest international organization in the contemporary political environment is called the United **Nations**. Furthermore, nationalism is widely seen (for better or for worse) as a most significant determinant of political activity.

For all this, the concept of nation is notoriously hard to define. The etymology of the expression hints at a nation's origins in primordial phenomena, for it has the same root as 'nature' and *nasci*, Latin for 'to be born'. Most contemporary accounts of the concept, however, seem to agree that nations are **imagined and socially constructed** communities (Anderson 1983). That is: most nations have been brought into being by protracted, intense, diffuse communication processes, mostly activated by the state and carried out on its behalf, funded from the public purse, and carried out by modern intellectuals (historians, journalists, poets, musicians, teachers, political leaders). Their products are diffused by the compulsory public education system and vehicled by various symbolic practices (such as monuments, street names, public festivities, commemorations, and military parades). In so far as this operation is successful, it sustains in the members of the public a sense of trust, mutual belonging, and solidarity, a shared commitment to and pride in tradition.

As a result of those socialization processes, a people who generally had already lived for generations within the same framework of rule may come to share a value-laden, emotionally compelling image of its history and its destiny, a sense of its own uniqueness and superior value. It comes to perceive itself as a distinctively significant, binding, active, collective entity. It generally identifies closely with the territory of the state, which it considers its own cradle and its prime possession; or it aspires to make the territory on which it resides the seat of a new, self-standing state, intended to give political expression to its unity, to redeem its population from its painful and demeaning subjection to a state governed by foreign people.

The emphasis on nationhood counteracts the tendency of the public sphere to project into the political realm divisions arising from the diverse, often conflicting interests which motivate the activities of private individuals in the civil society. Such divisions tend to engender political loyalties which challenge the concern of rulers, once more, with unity and discipline. But the appeal to nationhood also has a more positive significance, which relates it to citizenship and the trend towards widening and enriching its significance.

Above, I have attributed that trend to the attempt by underprivileged social groups to reduce their disadvantage with respect to privileged ones. But a search for greater socio-economic equality can also impart more significance to nationhood itself. In the historical career of citizenship the rhetoric of 'one nation', in various formulations, has played at least as great a role as that of 'social justice'. In fact, the earliest modern, state-wide 'welfare' policies, those initiated by Bismarck in nineteenth-century Germany, were probably inspired more by the first concern than by the second. Even later, and in other countries, one may detect a connection between the burdens and sufferings the state's military ventures impose on a people, supposedly on behalf of the national interest, and the state's attempt to ease those burdens or compensate for those sufferings through welfare initiatives.

Civilianization

This awkward expression refers to a complex development which progressively affects political practice in established states. Although, I would argue, political power maintains its ultimate grounding in the exercise or the threat of organized violence, the latter ceases to manifest itself openly and harshly in everyday experience. Most of the people professionally involved in (so to speak) the business of politics no longer differ markedly (as they did in earlier stages of state development) in their attire, their posture, their speech, their demeanour, the ways they relate to one another and to other people, from individuals involved in other lines of business, be it commerce, management, or the liberal professions.

Most kinds of political and administrative activity are carried out in relatively peaceable and orderly sites (legislative bodies, courts, public agencies of various kinds), where people generally talk politely to one another, consult and refer to documents, argue about solutions to problems, negotiate arrangements, express reasons for their preferences, put forward proposals and suggestions. Even when superiors expressly give orders to their subordinates in the expectation of being obeyed, they refer at most in an implicit, covert manner to the sanctions which would follow from disobedience, and those sanctions rarely entail the exercise or the threat of violence. The highest and most general legal commands—say, statutes—are expressed in highly codified, sophisticated language. Lower level commands (say, a fine or an order to pay tax) are only valid and binding if they refer to higher level ones. And much of the activity

---

BOX 4.2 Wagner's law

Consider the following scattered indication of the validity of the so-called 'Wagner's Law', which states that government spending tends to rise faster than the growth of the national economy as a whole. In the UK government spending accounted for the percentages of GNP shown in the table.

Year	%
1890	8.9
1920	20.2
1938	30.0
1960	36.4
1970	43.0
1981	50.3
1983	53.5

Similarly, in the US the amount of government (federal, state, and local) spending as a proportion of the net national product almost tripled between 1926 and 1979. For all EECD countries over the period 1953–73 the average of the national product accounted for by government spending rose from 34 to 39 per cent.

Source: Poggi (1999: 109).

---

carried out by state agencies renders various kinds of services to individuals, assists their private pursuits, serves their needs, and is undertaken on their demand.

This does not mean that political activity has lost its sting, which (again and again) continues to consist in threatened or actual violence. The personnel routinely involved in that, however, are generally (not in times of war) a minority among the multitude of people carrying out the manifold political activity characteristic of a developed state.

Also, significantly, that minority operates within distinctive components of the state's political and administrative machinery. Generally, people serving in the police and in the armed forces are the only individuals authorized and expected to bear arms, to wear uniforms. They belong to bodies where the lines of authority are particularly clear, an imperious chain of command obtains, harsh sanctions may be promptly inflicted on those members who disobey or disregard orders. In this manner the threat or exercise of violence is entrusted to specialized personnel and separated—one might say segregated—from the normal practices of political authority, both materially (for instance, soldiers reside in specially designed buildings) and symbolically (see again the uniforms military people wear, with their markers of rank).

Punishment is no longer inflicted on miscreants in public places, in a particularly dramatic, cruel, visible manner. The most common among serious punishments—imprisonment—is mostly carried out in a routinized, silent, invisible manner, in separate buildings, often out of the public eye. And the decision to bring to bear the means of violence on criminals or on enemies belongs in principle to the **other** kind of political personnel, not themselves directly involved in practising violence—judges, members of representative bodies, top political officials.

Under this kind of 'civilianized' arrangement, incidentally, the state's capacity to unleash organized violence does not diminish, but if anything grows. For instance, a properly organized military unit, commanded by professional officers and fielding properly trained soldiers, equipped with the appropriate weaponry, can wield an amount of murderous firepower that in the past no traditional militia made up of volunteers and captained by local, non-professional leaders could muster. Paradoxically, this increase in the **potential** for violence may be accompanied by a decrease in the **actual** exercise of violence. As they go about the ordinary business of their lives, individuals may be spared the experience of fear by the very fact that the potential violence monopolized by the state becomes more, not less, fearsome.

The conceptual portrait recapped

The modern political environment is composed of a plurality of states which share some formal characteristics. Thanks to its monopoly of legitimate, organized violence, each state exercises sovereign power over a population which inhabits a precisely delimited territory, and constitutes a political community, often referred to as a nation. The interactions between states are normally peaceable, but since they are not overseen and regulated by a superior power capable of imposing sanctions, they ultimately depend on the might each state can bring to bear to oppose or overwhelm other states pursuing interests opposed to their own. Thus, those interactions are highly contingent and may periodically be adjusted by the threat or exercise of military action between the states involved.

Over the course of the last two or three centuries, many states have, to a greater or lesser degree, acquired additional traits. Their internal structure is generally designed and controlled by laws which each state produces and enforces, but which in turn regulate its own activities. These are very diverse, and are generally carried out by a number of organs and specialized agencies. They deal directly with a variable set of matters which the state considers of public significance, leaving instead to the initiative of individual subjects other matters making up the concerns of (civil) society.

Some state activities, however, including the making of laws and their enforcement, lay down frameworks for the pursuit by individuals of their own private concerns. Furthermore, the institutions of the public sphere may empower individuals to form and communicate opinions on state policies, and to organize themselves in parties which represent the diverse (and often contrasting) interests within the society, select the personnel of various state organs, and mandate their policies.

In the course of the last two centuries, most states have conferred on the individuals making up their populations a variable set of entitlements of citizenship, beginning with those relating to the public sphere, and comprising claims to various benefits and services provided by the state, but ultimately funded from the proceeds of the state's fiscal activities. The advance of citizenship has often entailed making a public issue of socio-economic differences between individuals, and committing state policy to their moderation. For this reason it has often been contested. One may consider the appeal to nationhood, and the state's positive efforts to 'push' that appeal, as a way of curbing the divisive effects of the contests over the reach and content of citizenship entitlements.

State development

All the conceptual features of the state presented above are the outcomes of numerous and complex historical events. These differed not just in their location in space and time, but in other respects: (1) the sequence in which those events occurred, (2) the degree to which their protagonists expressly sought to produce those outcomes, (3) the extent to which the features agreed or conflicted with one another. Such differences, in turn, affected the way in which the various features determined the patterns of political activity characteristic of each state, its relations to the civil society, its capacity to respond to new challenges.

Furthermore, as we have seen, all states-in-the-making operated in the presence of one another. Thus their mutual awareness led some states to imitate some aspects of others, or on the contrary to emphasize their differences from one another. This further complicated the historical processes. For instance, at a certain stage states previously unified by the successful efforts of royal dynasties sought to strengthen their unity by promoting in the populations over which they ruled a sense of nationhood. Later other states imitated such a nation-building project. Furthermore, populations which in spite of being ruled over by foreign powers had somehow acquired a sense of themselves as 'nations without states' sought, more or less successfully, to build states of their own. In other terms, in some cases state-building precedes nation-building, in other cases it is the opposite.

In dealing with these phenomena, the study of comparative politics necessarily tends to simplify them. It stresses, from time to time, either differences between relatively similar units or similarities between relatively different ones. It contrasts states built early, in late medieval or early modern Europe (for instance, England or France), with others built during a relatively late stage of modernization (for instance, in the second half of the nineteenth century, as in the case of Germany or Italy). It distinguishes states built upon successful conquest (for instance, England) from those owing their existence to the breakdown of larger polities (for instance, contemporary Serbia or Ukraine).

This section of the chapter simplifies the story of state formation and development by distinguishing three broad phases within it. This story, it must be remembered, unfolded first in Europe, then extended to polities built elsewhere by European powers (for instance, North America), and later encompassed other parts of world. However, the way in which it is narrated here reflects chiefly the European experience. Even in this context, let us say it once more, the succession of phases suggested below purposefully abstracts from a huge variety of events, incidents, episodes which a properly historical treatment would have to account for.

Consolidation of rule

We may label 'consolidation of rule' the first phase, which takes place, largely, between the twelfth and the seventeenth century. As it runs its course, with different timings in different countries, a decreasing number of political centres extend their control over a larger and larger portion of Europe. Each more or less expressly and successfully broadens the territorial reach of its own monopoly of legitimate violence and imposes it on other centres. The political map of the continent becomes simpler and simpler, for each centre now practices rule, in an increasingly uniform manner, over bigger territories. These, furthermore, tend to become geographically more continuous and historically more stable—unless, of course, they become themselves objects of further processes of consolidation.

Sometimes these are peaceful. For instance, the scions of two dynasties ruling over different parts of Europe marry, and the territorial holdings of one spouse become soldered with those of the other. Or a political centre temporarily hands over to another a part of its own territory as security for a loan, but then defaults and surrenders that security. But mostly consolidation is the more or less direct outcome of open conflicts between two centres over which one will control which territory. Such conflicts are mostly settled by war, which leads to conquest and forcible annexation of all or part of the loser's territory to the advantage of the winner. 'States make war', as someone memorably put it, 'and wars make states' (Tilly 1990: 42).

Thus, a decisive role in the consolidation of rule is played by military resources. But these in turn require the 'sinews of war', that is the financial capacity to muster those resources—troops, officers, *matériel*—and deploy them against opponents,

making them prevail in the clash of arms against the resources wielded by the enemy. Very often military innovation confers an advantage to armies and fleets that are larger, and can thus wage war over more than one front, and become internally differentiated into 'services' which can effectively perform distinct, complementary tasks in warfare. But such armies and fleets can be afforded only by rulers who marshal larger resources, and in turn this requires raising troops from larger populations, tapping the wealth produced by larger territories. This premium on size is a strong inducement to consolidation.

But one should not forget that the recourse to war, however frequent throughout European history, is by its very nature intermittent. When weapons are silent, however temporarily, resources of a different nature come into play. Often, political centres intent on consolidating rule do this in response to an appeal for peace which recurs most frequently in European history, often being voiced by religious leaders. Each centre argues (and seeks to prove) that by establishing its control over a larger territory it can put an end to rivalries between lesser powers which would otherwise occasion war. This does not always involve prevailing over those powers in battle. Diplomatic action, the game of alliances and coalitions, the ability to isolate opponents or to make them accept a degree of subordination, sometimes the recourse to arbitration by the empire or the papacy, also play a role.

Besides, military activity itself requires and produces rules of its own, the very core of an emerging

---

BOX 4.3 The bureaucratic state

Where the rule of law prevails, a bureaucratic organization is governed by the following principles:

1. Official business is conducted on a continuous basis.

2. There are rules in an administrative agency such that: (1) the duty of each official to do certain types of work is delimited in terms of impersonal criteria; (2) the official is given the authority necessary to carry out his/her assigned functions; (3) the means of compulsion at his/her disposal are strictly limited.

3. Official responsibilities and authority are part of a hierarchy.

4. Officials do not own the resources necessary for the performance of their functions but are accountable for their use. Official and private affairs are strictly separated.

5. Offices cannot be appropriated by their incumbents in the sense of private property that can be sold or inherited.

6. Official business is conducted on the basis of written documents.

Source: Bendix (1960: 418–19).

body of law seeking, more or less successfully, to regulate aspects of the relations between states. Another significant part of such law makes conflict over territory less likely by laying down clear principles for succession into vacant seats of power, which generally make the exclusive entitlement to rule depend on legitimate descent. Other developments contribute to the same effect, which we might call 'pacification'. In particular, thanks to remarkable advances in geography, in the measurement of terrain and in cartography, the physical reach of each centre of rule comes to be clearly delimited by geographical borders, in turn often determined by features of the terrain. It remains true, as Hobbes put it, that states adopt towards one another, even when they are not fighting, 'a posture of warre'. But they partitioned the continent of Europe, and later other continents, in a clear and potentially stable manner.[2]

Rationalization of rule

Historically, there is often an overlap between those I have called processes of consolidation, dominant in the first phase of state formation and development, and the distinctive processes of a second phase, which we might label the rationalization of rule. Consolidation, we have seen, produces larger, more visible, and stable containers of state power; rationalization bears chiefly on the ways in which such power is exercised. We can characterize such ways by distinguishing in turn three aspects of it: (1) centralization, (2) hierarchy, and (3) function. Let us take them in turn.

Centralization

In consolidating rule, and subsequently in exercising it, rulers had largely availed themselves of the cooperation of various subordinate but privileged power holders—chiefly, aristocratic dynasties, towns and other local or regional bodies, bishops and other ecclesiastical dignitaries. Often that cooperation was granted only after the subordinate powers had been forced to renounce some of their privileges—in particular, especially as concerns aristocrats, that of waging private wars.

All the same, cooperation generally had to be negotiated between the ruler and the privileged powers. These maintained a degree of autonomous control over various resources, and managed them in the first instance on their own behalf. They could be induced to do so on the ruler's behalf only on certain conditions, sanctioned by tradition or laid out in express agreements between themselves and the ruler. For instance, the cooperating lesser powers would extract economic resources from the population inhabiting the portions of the state's territory under their jurisdiction in order to convey them to the ruler. But they would do so only if they had given their consent to the purpose to which the ruler intended to commit those resources. They often kept a more or less large part of those resources for themselves, and controlled locally the ways in which the remainder of them were managed and expended in their respective part of the territory.

Obviously, such arrangements limit considerably the rulers' freedom of action, their ability to lay down policy for the state as a whole and have it promptly, reliably, and uniformly executed over the whole territory. They make the conduct of political and administrative business discontinuous and sometimes erratic, since who is charged with it at a given time—in particular, qua head of an aristocratic lineage—depends on the vagaries of hereditary succession. Thus, often those engaged in that business are individuals who have no particular inclination or capacity for it. Even the cooperation granted, as we have seen, by constituted, collective bodies (the so-called 'estates') tends to give priority to the particular interests of those bodies, and thus to preserve traditional arrangements, beginning with their autonomy. On this account it can be very difficult, for the ruler, to coordinate and render predictable the practices of a plurality of powers interposed between himself at the top and, at the bottom, a territory made larger by consolidation and its population.

To remedy this situation, rulers on the one hand progressively dispossess the existent individuals and bodies of their faculties and facilities of which they had traditionally availed themselves to perform political and administrative tasks.[3] On the other hand, they put in place alternative arrangements for performing both those tasks and those made necessary by new circumstances. Instead of relying on their former cooperators, they choose to avail themselves of **agents** and **agencies,** that is, individuals and bodies which the rulers themselves select, empower, mandate, activate, control, fund, discipline, and reward. In other terms, rulers build **bureaucracies.**

In principle, this process could greatly increase the hold upon social life at large of the political centre, enable the ruler to exercise power in an unbounded, arbitrary, despotic fashion, and expose all those subject to it to extreme insecurity. In fact, the previous cooperators who objected to the ruler's new arrangements often raised complaints to that effect, and sometimes rightly so. But more often their objections simply reflected their reluctance to give up some of their previous privileges. We would not characterize this phase as 'rationalization of rule' if its chief import had been solely to unbind rule.

It is an aspect of 'the European miracle' (the title of Jones 1981) that this phase of state-building has two apparently contrasting aspects. First, through the strategy we are discussing, rulers come to oversee, control, and to an extent manage, social life at large in a more and more intense, continuous, systematic, purposive, and pervasive manner. Second, to be legitimate, rule must appear to be oriented to interests widely recognized as general, and must be exercised in a more and more impersonal and formal manner. The notion of *raison d'état* conveys both aspects. It asserts that the might and security of the polity is a general and paramount interest, whose pursuit may occasionally override all others. But that interest is to be sought through self-conscious deliberation, grounded in an assiduous, careful, detached monitoring of circumstances.

In fact, the rationalization of rule itself is part of a broader process of rationalization of social existence at large. Each major sphere of society (beginning with the three already mentioned: politics, economy, religion) becomes the exclusive concern of a different institutional complex—a self-standing ensemble of arrangements, personnel, resources, principles, and patterns of activity. This differentiation allows (and perhaps demands) each concern to be pursued in such a way as to maximize a distinctive goal: respectively the might and security of the state, the profitability of economic operations, and the individual's prospects of spiritual salvation.

Hierarchy

In the political context, rationalization changes the basis of the routine exercise of power: the public understanding of its nature, its objective, its boundaries. As we have seen, that basis was traditionally constituted by the **rights and perquisites** of a number of privileged individuals and bodies (see Chapter 8). The new basis consists in the **duties and obligations** of individuals (we may label them 'bureaucrats' or 'officials') who have been appointed purposefully to established offices. Thus, the political and administrative activities of those individuals can be programmed from above by means of express commands. Those issuing such commands can reward those to whom they are issued if they comply with them, punish them if they do not. The commands themselves have two critical characteristics: (1) they tend to be general, that is they refer in abstract terms to a variety of concrete circumstances; and (2) their content can legitimately change, and thus respond to new circumstances (see also Box 4.3).

For this to happen, the new ensembles of individuals who carry out political and administrative activities—the bureaucratic units—must be hierarchically structured. At the bottom of the structure, even lowly office-holders are empowered to give orders (issue verdicts, collect taxes, conscript military recruits, deny or give permissions) to those lying below the structure itself. Those holders themselves, however, are supposed to do so in compliance with directives communicated to them by superiors. These monitor the activity of their direct subordinates, verify whether they conform with their directives, and if necessary override or correct their orders. And this arrangement can be replicated at various levels within the whole structure, which constitutes an ordered array where higher offices supervise, activate, and direct lower ones. In a related hierarchical arrangement, lower offices **inform** higher ones, make suggestions on how to deal with situations, and higher ones **make decisions** and transmit them downwards to lower ones for implementation.

As I have already indicated, law plays a significant role in structuring these arrangements for rule. First, law itself is a hierarchically structured set of authoritative commands, from those contained in a state's constitution at the top to the fine issued by traffic wardens at the bottom. Second, law can be taught and learned, and the knowledge of it (at its various levels) can determine, to a greater or lesser extent, the content of the agents' political and administrative operations.

This second aspect of the law points to a broader aspect of the rationalization of rule—the growing role of **knowledge** in the government and administration of the state. As rulers increasingly dispense with the cooperation of privileged individuals and bodies, the agents with which they replace them are largely chosen on account of what they know, or are presumed to know in so far as they have earned academic degrees and passed selective tests. Agents are expected to orient their practices of rule less and less to their own individual preferences or to local, particular tradition and lore, more and more to properly imparted and learned, systematic knowledge. Legal knowledge is the prototype of this, especially on the European continent, but it is increasingly complemented and supplemented by different kinds of knowledge—those relevant to, say, waging war, building roads and bridges, charting the country, collecting statistical data, keeping financial accounts, minting money, policing cities, safeguarding public health.

Function

Another principle structuring the centralized system of offices is **function**, that is, the system is internally differentiated so that its parts will deal optimally with a variety of tasks. To this end, the system parts must possess and put to use materially different resources; not only variously bodies of knowledge, acquired and brought to bear by appropriately trained and selected personnel, but artefacts as diverse as weapons at one end, printing machines at the other.

For all its diversity, the whole structure is activated and controlled, not only by knowledge, but by **money,** another public reality distinctly connected with rationality, chiefly acquired through **taxation**. The collaboration with rulers of traditional power-holders had usually engaged material and other resources which were part of their patrimony; thus, it was self-financed and unavoidably self-interested. Now, agencies operate by spending public funds allocated to them on the basis of express, periodic decisions (budgets) and are held accountable for the way those funds are spent. Office-holders are typically salaried, manage resources that do not belong to them but to their offices, and as they comply with their duties are not expected to seek personal gain, except in the form of career advancement.[4]

To the extent that it is rationalized, the exercise of rule becomes more compatible with the private individuals' pursuit of their interests. From the perspective of those individuals, rule, as exercised by

officials, appears more regular and predictable, and occasional deviations from rules can be redressed. Rulers are interested in increasing the resources available to the society as a whole, if only to draw upon them in funding their political and administrative activities. But to this effect they must at least recognize the requirements of the country's economic system, at best protect or indeed foster its productive dynamic, which rests chiefly on the market. To this end, as we have already seen, the extraction from the economy of private resources increasingly takes place chiefly by means of taxation.

The security of those resources and of their employment must be sustained by guaranteeing, through appropriate legislation and the machinery of law enforcement, the institutions of private property and contract. But other social interests and cultural concerns, too, not just economic ones, benefit from the limits rationalized rule sets on its own scope and from the arrangements it makes in order to become compatible with the autonomy of civil society.

The expansion of rule

In the third phase, states display a dynamic which we may label the 'expansion of rule'. For centuries, the activities of each state had been oriented to two main concerns:

1. On the international scene, it sought chiefly to secure itself from encroachments by other states on its territory and on its ability to define and pursue its own interests autonomously.

2. Within its territory, it was committed to maintaining public order and the effectiveness of its laws.

In the second half of the nineteenth and through the twentieth century, however, states brought their activities of rule to bear on an increasingly diverse range of social interests.

Essentially, the state no longer simply **ordains** through legislation the autonomous undertakings of individuals and groups or **sanctions** their private arrangements through its judicial system. Increasingly, it **intervenes** in private concerns by modifying those arrangements or by collecting greater resources and then redistributing them more to some parties than

COUNTRY PROFILE Germany

Federal Republic of Germany (*Bundesrepublik Deutschland*)

State formation

The German Empire was first unified in 1871. After the Second World War, Germany was divided into four zones of occupation administered by the UK, the US, the USSR, and France, respectively. The Federal Republic of Germany, which included the former UK, US, and French zones, was proclaimed in 1949. The former USSR zone became the German Democratic Republic and joined the Federal Republic in 1990.
Constitution Basic Law of 1949; became constitution of the united Germany in 1990 but is still referred to as the Basic Law.

Form of government

Federal republic.
Head of state President elected by a Federal Convention, including all members of the Federal Assembly and an equal number of delegates elected by the state parliaments; term of 5 years (renewable once).
Head of government Chancellor elected by an absolute majority of the Federal Assembly, term of 4 years.
Cabinet Federal Ministers appointed by the President on the recommendation of the Chancellor.
Administrative subdivisions 16 states (*Länder*).

Legal system

Civil law system; judicial review of legislative acts in the Federal Constitutional Court.

Legislature

Bicameral parliament.
Lower house Federal Assembly (*Bundestag*): 614 seats; term of 4 years.
Upper house Federal Council (*Bundesrat*): 69 members (each state government has three to six of the total 69 seats and must vote as a block).

Electoral system (lower house)

Mixed system of plurality vote and proportional representation.
Formula Hare/Niemeyer. The number of deputies elected in the individual constituencies is subtracted from the total of the seats to which their party is entitled. The remaining seats are allocated to the candidates on the party list, in the order enumerated. A party may have 'overhang mandates' when it wins more seats in the constituencies than it is entitled to according to the results of the proportional calculation.
Constituencies 299 single-member constituencies and 16 multi-member constituencies corresponding to the states.
Barrier clause 5 % unless at least 3 candidates of the party in question have been elected in single-member constituencies.
Suffrage Universal, 18 years.

Direct democracy

None.

Party system Results of the 2005 legislative elections (Federal Assembly):

Electorate	61,870,711	100.0%
Voters	48,044,134	77.7%

Party	Valid votes	%	Seats
Social Democratic Party	16,194,665	34.2	222
Christian Democratic Union	13,136,740	27.8	180
Free Democratic Party	4,648,144	9.8	61
Left Party	4,118,194	8.7	54
Greens	3,838,326	8.1	51
Christian Social Union	3,494,309	7.4	46
Others	1,857,610	3.9	0
Total	47,287,988	100.0	614

Note: In the federal institutions, the Christian Social Union (from the state of Bavaria) forms a joint faction with the Christian Democratic Union (present in all of the other states).
Source: Statistisches Bundesamt.

to others. Also, it seeks to **manage** social activities according to its own judgements and preferences, for it considers the outcome of those activities as a legitimate public concern, which should reflect a broader and higher interest (for example, the promotion of industrial development, of social equity, or of national solidarity).

The expansion of rule modifies deeply (and perhaps irreversibly) the relationship between state and society which characterized the previous phase. On this account, we can classify most of its explanations according to whether they locate the main source of the drive to expand in the state itself or in society.

The former accounts occur in various versions.

1. They may, first, impute to the state's administrative machinery an inherent tendency to grow, to avail itself of more resources, to take charge of more tasks, to address ever more, and more various, social interests, instead of leaving them to the market or to the automous pursuit of individuals and groups.

2. Or, second, they may see the main reason for state expansion in the dynamics of representative democracy and of adversary politics. Putting it simply, it pays for a party out of power to increase its support by promising, if voted into power, to devote more public resources to this or that new

state activity, and thus advancing the interests of social groups responding to its appeal. Typically, it is parties of the left which have successfully played this card, and have employed new forms of state activity and state expenditure in seeking to reduce the disadvantages inflicted on its supporters by market processes.

3. This interpretation fits closely with a third one, which imputes the expansion of the state chiefly to phenomena located in the society side of the state/society divide. Here, it is again underprivileged groups that stand to gain most by state expansion, and thus invoke it and favour it, through their suffrage or by other forms of mobilization.

4. But according to a rather different fourth interpretation, many aspects of state expansion support, rather than correct and counteract, the workings of the market economy, and are thus directly or indirectly in the interests primarily of firms and employers. For instance, the colonial ventures of some European states are imputed to the search by major economic forces for privileged access to the raw materials, the manpower, the market opportunities they saw in foreign lands, or to their seeking profit in supplying the state with military and naval hardware. Furthermore, for over a century now, many public resources have been committed to educational activities, which deliver to the labour market employees equipped with the diverse qualifications and skills the economy needs. In the second half of the twentieth century the state often underwrote, on behalf of firms and thus primarily of employers, the substantial research and developments costs necessary to sustain more advanced and profitable production processes.

More widely, this fourth interpretation attributes much state expansion to the fact that, left to itself, the market often does not generate enough demand for industrial products to sustain capital investment, does not ensure a reasonable level of employment and thus domestic demand for industrial products. From this perspective, the main beneficiaries of state expansion are, in the end, the more established and privileged social groups.

In fact the often evoked imagery of the state which expands by claiming as its own social tasks previously performed by autonomous social forces, and usurping them from society, is sometimes misleading.

BOX 4.4 Citizenship

❝ So far my aim has been to trace in outline the development of citizenship in England to the end of the nineteenth century. For this purpose I have divided citizenship into three elements, civil, political, and social. I have tried to show that civil rights came first, and were established in something like their modern form before the first Reform Act was passed in 1832. Political rights came next, and their extension was one of the main features of the nineteenth century, although the principle of universal political citizenship was not recognised until 1918. Social rights, on the other hand, sank to vanishing point in the eighteenth and early nineteenth century. Their revival began with the establishment of public elementary education, but it was not until the twentieth century that they attained to equal partnership with the other two elements of citizenship. (Marshall 1950: 27–8) ❞

Many of the activities carried out, well or otherwise, by the expanding state, respond to **novel** needs, potentialities, and opportunities generated by ongoing social developments—such as the demographic explosion, urbanization, increasing literacy, mass motorization, more mature industrialization, the increasing complexity of society itself. Already at the end of the nineteenth century, Durkheim had argued, in opposition to Spencer, that in the process of modernization the development of the private realm requires the development also of the public one.

Whatever the reasons for it, state expansion entails a growth in three interdependent aspects:

- The **fiscal take**, that is in the proportion of a country's yearly product extracted and managed by the state.

- The degree of **internal differentiation** of the organizational machinery of the state.

- The **total number of individuals** whom those units employ, and who possess increasingly varied qualifications and skills.

The two latter phenomena not only, as already suggested, displace the line between state and society. They also affect deeply the state itself, which comes to resemble an ever-growing, ill-coordinated ensemble of increasingly diverse units. The ordinary political processes—the articulation of collective interests via the parties and their periodic electoral competition, the determination of the executive by majorities, the formation of policies through the interplay between the executive and parliaments—can less and less effectively activate and steer an administrative machinery so vast, expensive, complex, and diverse.

Much in political decision-making and in the subsequent administrative activity responds to the interests of the units themselves, or those of the specific, often narrow, sections of society to which they correspond, rather than expressing a political project reflecting a comprehensive view of the society as a whole. Thus the administrative machinery becomes overloaded by multiple, ever-changing, conflicting demands. At the same time, some components of it are 'captured' by powerful and demanding social forces, and serve their needs rather than those of the public at large. All these phenomena make it more and more difficult for the political elites themselves to design and put into effect the policies for which the electorate has expressed a preference.

These phenomena manifest themselves in most contemporary states, but they do so to a different extent and in diverse ways. As the subsequent chapters show, one of the major tasks of the study of comparative politics is to establish empirically, and to account for, the variations present in the contemporary political environment, both in those manifestations and in the responses they find in the political authorities, the parties, the social movements.

BOX 4.5 Imagined communities

The nation is an 'imagined' political community:

- It is *imagined* because the members of even the smallest nation will never know most of their fellow-members, meet them, or even hear of them, yet in the minds of each lives the image of their communion.

- It is imagined as *limited* because even the largest of them, encompassing perhaps a billion human beings, has finite, if elastic boundaries, beyond which lie other nations.

- It is imagined as *sovereign* because the concept was born in an age in which Enlightenment and Revolution were destroying the legitimacy of the divinely-ordained hierarchical dynastic realm.

- It is imagined as a *community* because, regardless of the actual inequality and exploitation that may prevail in each, the nation is always conceived of as a deep, horizontal comradeship.

Source: Adapted from Anderson (1983: 6–7).

KEY POINTS

❑ One can distinguish, within the historical career of the modern state, three main phases, which different European states have followed in somewhat varying sequences.

❑ *Consolidation of rule*: within each larger part of the continent (beginning with its Western parts) one particular centre of rule asserted its own superiority over others, generally by defeating them in war, subjecting the respective lands to its control, and turning them into a unified territory.

❑ *Rationalization of rule*: each centre of rule increasingly relied on functionaries selected and empowered by itself, expressly qualified for their functions, and forming hierarchically structured units, their careers within which would depend on the reliability and effectiveness of their actions.

❑ *Expansion of rule*: states progressively took on broader sets of functions, both in order to confront social needs generated by ongoing processes of economic modernization, and to respond to requests for public regulation and intervention originating from various sectors of society. They added new specialized administrative units and funded their activities by increasing their 'fiscal take' from the economy.

Conclusion

One can safely assume that the vast majority of this book's readers live in a political environment which resembles more or less closely the portrait of 'the state' given in this chapter, and whose institutions and practices bear traces of the developments sketched in the last section. For this reason, those readers—whatever their feelings about their state, however they position themselves *vis-à-vis* the particular government which runs it—may take for granted its main features, including the fact that they are able, among other things, to study scientifically that state itself and to compare it with others. This chapter however, and others in this book, is intended to challenge the assumption that such matters can indeed be taken for granted.

The following statement by a notable German social theorist, Heinrich Popitz (1925–2002) entails such a challenge:

❝ The history of society shows only rare instances where the question, how can one lay boundaries around institutionalized violence?, has been confronted in a positive and viable manner. Essentially, this has happened only in the Greek polis, in the Roman republic and a few other city states, and in the history of the modern constitutional state. And the answers given to that question have been astonishingly similar: The principle of the supremacy of the law and of the equality of all before the law (the Greek named it 'isonomia'). The notion that the making of norms by the state encounters limitations (fundamental rights). Norms assigning different competences to various political organs (division of powers, federalism). Procedural norms (decisions by collective bodies, their public nature, appeals to and review by higher organs). Norms on the occupancy of offices (turn-taking, elections). Finally, norms concerning the public sphere (freedom of opinion, freedom of association and assembly). The similarity, or indeed the commonality among such answers suggests that there are systematic solutions of the problem, how to limit institutionalized power and violence, and that these solutions, although they presuppose certain premises if they are to hold, can to an extent hold across different contexts—as different, say, as city states and those ruling over extensive territories. (Popitz 1992: 65) ❞

Popitz's statement suggests some comments.

1. Although I have treated 'the state' as essentially a modern phenomenon (and its development as the chief political dimension of the broader phenomenon of modernization), some of its distinctive institutional arrangements had already manifested themselves in antiquity, as well as in the Middle Ages.

2. Both the earlier and the later (modern) arrangements appear at first as part of a distinctive Western story, for they originated in Europe and were subsequently transposed to parts of the rest of the world conquered and settled by European powers, especially in North America and Australia. (The US, however, was the first place where a peculiar arrangement, federalism, was more expressly and successfully experimented with and

served as a model for further experiments; see Chapter 11.) Since then, some such arrangements have become common to polities operating across the globe, although they differ in the manner in which they are interpreted and even more in the extent to which they are implemented.

3. The arrangements mentioned by Popitz, singly and together, succeed in an intrinsically difficult job—limiting, constraining, and 'taming' institutionalized political power.

This last point suggests a further consideration, left implicit in Popitz's statement. Such success cannot be taken for granted. It is a matter of degree, for it requires overcoming a built-in tendency of political power to grow upon itself, to escape limits and constraints, to 'go wild' as it were; and that tendency itself can appear in many circumstances and in many ways. In fact, some states which shared the characteristics mentioned in the first section of this chapter have not presented all those mentioned in the second section, which have appeared in later phases of political modernization and which (in the author's personal judgement) go a long way towards 'civilizing' the state itself.

For instance, the Tsarist empire refused to endorse many characteristic institutions of the constitutional, liberal, democratic states of Western Europe. Worse, even states which at a given point exhibited all those characteristics subsequently veered away from constitutionalism, liberalism, democracy, and underwent institutional changes generally associated with the notion of 'totalitarianism'—as happened in the twentieth century in Italy and Germany (see Chapter 6). And even some of the constitutive features of states listed in the first section, such as 'sovereignty', are currently put under stress by a number of developments, such as those associated with 'globalization' or with the formation of transnational polities (see Chapter 24).

Even apart from such dramatic developments, the liberal-democratic states themselves differ from one another in many relevant respects. For instance, some impart a centralized and some a federal structure to the relations between the state's political centre and its political periphery. States have differed (and differ) in the extent to which, in the course of time, they have broadened and enriched the entitlements of citizenship; or in the extent to which and the manner in which a given state seeks through its policies to support and plan the development of its national economy, as against leaving such development entirely to the workings of the market. The size of the so-called 'public sector' of the economy, and the way in which it has been managed, again have differed from state to state, as have their respective taxation policies.

These and other issues have often been fought over in significant, lasting confrontations between parties and between sectors of opinion; and the settlement they have attained has been more or less stable, has created affinities or contrasts between states. Besides being the themes of public life, those issues have long constituted the main topics of the scholarly study of politics, whether this study has focused on a particular state or on the diversity between states, on the range of possible and actual solutions. The latter, of course, is the main concern of this book as a whole.

World trends

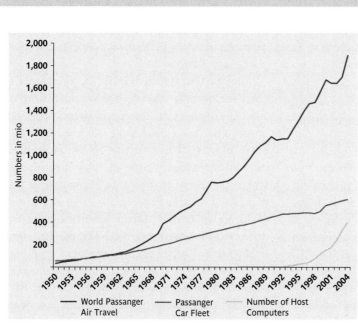

Trend 2 Communication and transportation (1950–2005)

Source: International Civil Aviation Organisation, American Automobile Manufactures Association, Ward's, Global Insight, Internet Systems Consortium.

―― World Passanger Air Travel   ―― Passanger Car Fleet   ------ Number of Host Computers

? Questions

1. What is meant by 'civilianization'?
2. How can one explain the fact that members of a state's population progressively acquired rights *vis-à-vis* the state?
3. What is civil society?
4. Do nations create states or vice versa?
5. What part did law play in the development of the modern state?
6. For what reasons did rulers come to rely on bodies of officials appointed and empowered by themselves?
7. What is meant by 'consolidation of rule'?
8. What is meant by 'sovereignty'?
9. What part did military force play in the making of European states?
10. How do states, typically, acquire the economic resources they use?

» Further reading

Elias, N. (2000) *The Civilizing Process: Sociogenetic and Psychogenetic Investigations* (Oxford: Blackwell Publishers; 1st edn 1938). The second, large volume of this most impressive work is dedicated to what it calls the 'sociogenesis of the state'.

Poggi, G. (1978) *The Development of the Modern State: A Sociological Introduction* (Stanford, Calif.: Stanford University Press, 1978). An accessible statement of its topic, ranging in its discussion from the Middle Ages to the contemporary era.

Tilly, C. (ed.) (1975) *The Formation of National States in Western Europe* (Princeton: Princeton University Press). A very influential collection of major contributions to its theme, including its military, fiscal, and economic aspects.

Weber, M. (1994) 'Politics as a Profession and Vocation' (1919), in *Weber: Political Writings,* ed. P. Lassman and R. Speirs (Cambridge: Cambridge University Press), 309–69. A compact but most illuminating and provocative discussion of the nature of politics and the modern state by one of the most significant modern social theorists.

 ## Web links

www.pipeline.com/~cwa/TYWHome.htm
Webpage of the Thirty Years' War which gave rise to the modern states after the Peace of Westphalia (1648).

http://userweb.port.ac.uk/~andressd/frlinks.htm
Webpage on the French Revolution.

www.arcaini.com/ITALY/ItalyHistory/ItalianUnification.htm
Webpage about the Italian unification, independence, and democratization.

http://americancivilwar.com/
Webpage about the American Civil War.

 Visit the Online Resource Centre that accompanies this book for more information:
www.oxfordtextbooks.co.uk/orc/caramani/

5 Democracies

Peter Mair

Chapter contents

Reader's guide

Since the fall of the Berlin Wall in 1989, scholars and institutional designers have become much more interested in understanding how democracies differ from one another. This chapter reviews the reasons for this new concern with comparing democracies, and also looks at the different definitions of democracy, paying particular attention to procedural definitions. Following a brief assessment of the different milestones that were reached on the path towards developing democracy, the chapter reviews the various attempts to model democracies as holistic systems and argues that most efforts in this direction are almost bound to be frustrated. The chapter concludes by looking at the notion of audience democracy as well as at the growing levels of popular dissatisfaction with democracy.

Introduction

Prior to the late 1970s the democracies of the world constituted a relatively small and homogeneous group of regimes. Figures published in a retrospective review by Freedom House[1] suggest that fewer than one in four of the world's polities were democratic in 1950, with most of these being in the West or having developed under the influence of Western models; three-quarters of the polities could therefore be defined as one or other of the then many varieties of non-democracy. Even as late as 1974, when Portugal launched the so-called third wave of democratization, just 27 per cent of the independent states in the world were democratic, including just 22 per cent of those states with populations greater than one million (Diamond 1999: 24).

For most of the early post-war decades, in short, more than 70 per cent of states could be counted in the non-democracy category, and it was the variation within this larger group that proved of greater interest to comparative political research (see Chapter 6). Hence, for example, the extended effort by Linz (1975) to specify the distinctions between authoritarian and totalitarian regimes, and Sartori's (1962: 148) earlier efforts to distinguish both of these regime types from a variety of alternatives that included tyranny, despotism, absolutism, dictatorship, coercion, and autocracy. In this period in particular, non-democracy was seen to take many forms, whereas democracy was simply democracy.

The particular variations embraced by the real existing democratic regimes of the earlier post-war years were mainly seen as relevant at the subsystem level. That is, the regime as a whole was often taken as read, and the differences which were analysed were those which operated across particular institutions within the polity (see also Chapter 1, as well as Keman 2002b).

To be sure, an ambitious and comprehensive country-by-country comparison of democratic development was organized by Dahl in the 1960s in his famous and still unrivalled *Political Oppositions* volume (Dahl 1966). But even here the burden of the analysis tended to focus on the subsystem level, in this case on the development of political parties, their support bases, and their patterns of competition both inside and outside parliament. Almond's (1956) classic categorization of democracies into Anglo-American, continental European, and what were later defined as 'working' multi-party systems (the Benelux, Switzerland, and Scandinavia), was also heavily influenced by an interpretation of the prevailing patterns of party competition, with the primary distinction in this case revolving around the question of whether the parties concerned represented closed and conflictual 'subcultures' or were more likely to engage in competition within shared electoral markets (see also Lijphart 1968b).

In other words, while particular institutions *within* democracies have always been compared and evaluated, little attention was paid to the comparison of models of democratic regimes *tout court*—at least beyond the many country-by-country configurative approaches that were then commonly found in the comparative politics literature (e.g. Beer and Ulam 1958; Finer 1970).

Today, however, there is an increasing concern to specify more clearly what is entailed by the notion of democracy as well as to compare different forms of democratic regime in terms of their policy performance, legitimacy, and stability. Within comparative politics, in other words, as well as in real-world discussions, variations *among* democracies are seen to have become much more important. What had been once a small and homogeneous group of regimes has now become large and heterogeneous. Hence, as we shall see below, the various attempts in the contemporary scholarly literature to establish new classifications and typologies of democracy.

KEY POINTS

❑ Having constituted fewer than one in four of world regimes in the 1950s and 1960s, democracies now count for almost three in four.

❑ What had been once a small and homogeneous group of democratic regimes has now become large and heterogeneous. Therefore, typologies and classifications are important in understanding how democracies function.

Comparing democracies

There are at least four important and related factors which have contributed to this new interest in comparing democracies.

The comparison of regimes

The first factor came from scholarship itself, with two important studies in the early 1980s by Powell (1982) and by Lijphart (1984) which sought to characterize and compare democratic regimes as a whole, joining measures of variation in cleavage patterns and party politics to those of institutional structures.

In Lijphart's case, this led him to elaborate the more all-embracing distinction between majoritarian and consensus models of democracy (see Table 5.1 and below), which was to prove a highly influential contribution to the literature on comparative democracy both in the first version from 1984, as well as in the revised and extended version that was published later (Lijphart 1999). This study also encouraged other scholars to think of democracies in more comprehensive terms, and to attempt to measure their survival and impact in terms of the entire complex of institutions that were involved.

The 'third wave' of democratization

The second major impetus came from the growing weight of the 'third wave' of democratization, and particularly from the explosion in transitions to

Table 5.1 Majoritarian and consensus models of democracy

Institutional feature	Majoritarian model	Consensus model
Executive	Concentration of executive power in single-party majority cabinets or minimum winning coalitions	Executive power-sharing in broad multi-party coalitions
Executive–Legislative relations	Executive dominates legislature	Balance of power in executive–legislative relations
Party system	Two-party system	Multi-party system
Electoral system	Majoritarian and disproportional electoral system	Proportional representation (PR)
Interest group system	Pluralist	Corporatist
Type of government	Unitary and centralized government	Federal and decentralized government
Legislature	Unicameralism	Strong and incongruent bicameralism
Constitution	Flexible and easily amended	Rigid and difficult to amend
Judicial review	Parliamentary sovereignty	Constitutional court
Central bank	Dependent on executive	Independent of executive

Note: In the updated and extended version of a typology originally introduced in 1984 with eight key features, Arend Lijphart (1999) identified ten features that distinguished between what he called the majoritarian (or Westminster) and consociational (or consensus) models of democracy.

democracy that occurred with, and in the immediate aftermath of, the fall of the Berlin Wall in 1989.

In a very influential study published soon after the fall of the wall, Samuel Huntington (1991) argued that democratization has historically developed in a series of bursts or 'waves', with a wave of democratization being defined as 'a group of transitions from democratic to nondemocratic regimes that occurs within a specified period of time and that significantly outnumbers transitions in the opposite direction' (Huntington 1991: 15). Much as a wave breaks on the beach, democratization has come in ebbs and flows, with the many transitions to democracy being followed by a smaller number of transitions back to non-democratic alternatives.

For Huntington, the first 'long' wave lasted from 1826 to 1926, and was then reversed in part by the rise of fascism and authoritarianism in the 1920s and 1930s; the second wave came after the Second World War and was reversed in the 1960s and 1970s; the third wave was initiated in Portugal in 1974 and reached explosive levels after 1989. Thus far, there have been no serious reversals (Huntington 1991; for a useful corrective on the actual counting of cases by Huntington, see Doorenspleet 2000). By the end of the century, therefore, the number of democracies had rapidly increased, and had come to constitute almost 75 per cent of the world's polities (Table 5.2).

Within this expanded universe, these democracies inevitably reflected an immense variety of institutional structures and forms.

With more cases, in other words, and with more fundamental variety, it became more important to classify democracies and to distinguish their variations. As Linz was to argue, some two decades after his earlier exploration of the differences between authoritarianism and totalitarianism, '[t]he fact that there is currently no alternative to democracy as a principle of legitimacy, and that so many countries have undergone a transition to democracy, compels us to look more closely at the variety of democracies and the ways they function' (Linz 1992: 182). By becoming 'the only game in town',[2] democracy developed into a new focus for inquiry precisely as the study of the alternatives to democracy faded from relevance.

One other side-effect of the explosion in the number of democracies around the world has been to wean research away from explanations of democratization. Prior to the 1980s, a large part of the literature on democracy was concerned with identifying the various structural factors that might help explain both transitions to democracy and the variation in the long-term stability of these regimes, with various authors emphasizing different combinations of economic, cultural, and social factors.[3] As the 'N' (the

Table 5.2 Democracies in the world

Year	Number of democracies*	Number of countries	Democracies as % of all countries
2005	123	192	64.1
2000	120	192	62.5
1995	117	191	61.3
1990	76	165	46.1
1974	39	142	27.5

* These are 'electoral democracies' as defined by Freedom House, a category that includes all of the polities they designate as 'free' and some of those designated as 'partly free'. The designation 'electoral democracy' is based exclusively on a judgement of the electoral process and ignores possible limits on civil liberties.

Source: Freedom House, *Democracy's Century* (LeDuc *et al.* 2002: 211).

number of cases) has grown, however, the interest, relevance, and sheer power of such explanations has tended to decline, and greater emphasis has been attributed to non-structural determinants such as actor strategies and preferences (e.g. Kitschelt 1992). Indeed, the major difference between the approaches to democratization that now prevail and those that were common through to the 1980s is that the conditions that favour democracy are now assumed to exist more or less everywhere, as a sort of default option, with the persistence of authoritarianism or the occasional reversion away from democracy now being the exceptions (see also Chapter 25).

Institutional engineering

The third major impetus was also related to the latter stages of the 'third wave', in that the sheer rapidity with which democracies became established after 1989, and the evident lack of democratic experience in many of the polities making this transition, led to a major resurgence in scholarly and practical interest in the question of 'institutional engineering' (Sartori 1994). In other words, in building democracies from scratch, it became an imperative for constitution-builders to gather advice about the likely implications of particular institutional choices, while the process also offered a new and unprecedented laboratory in which scholars could test theories concerning the causes and consequences of democratic design (e.g. Lijphart and Waisman 1996). The issue, in short, became one of evaluating the different models of democracy in terms of their effectiveness, stability, and legitimacy, and this clearly meant exploring them in the round, and assessing how one set of institutions might play off against another.

It was in this context, for example, that comparative political science witnessed the recrudescence of the debates between advocates of presidential and parliamentary models (e.g. Linz and Valenzuela 1994). In parliamentary systems, the executive is dependent on the confidence of the legislature, is usually a collective body, and is appointed or elected indirectly by the legislature. In a presidential system, by contrast, the executive usually enjoys a fixed term of office and cannot be dismissed in the ordinary course of events, is usually constituted by a single person, and is elected separately from the parliament by the direct (or, as in the US, somewhat indirect) vote of the citizenry.

The debates surrounding the merits of these alternative systems focused mainly on questions of representativeness (on which the parliamentary systems scored arguably higher) versus effectiveness and stability (on which presidential systems scored arguably higher), and were of crucial importance to many post-1989 constitutional engineers (Lijphart 1992; Sartori 1994).

Neo-institutionalism

The fourth impetus came again from developments within political science more generally, and was prompted in particular by the so-called new or neo-institutional turn in political analysis (March and Olson 1984; see also Chapter 2). Within comparative politics in particular, institutions had often tended to be seen as primarily dependent variables that could be explained by social, economic, or cultural factors. Democracy itself, most crucially, was believed to have its 'social requisites' (Lipset 1959). Within the emerging neo-institutional approach of the 1980s, by contrast, institutions came to be seen as independent variables which impacted directly upon outcomes and behaviour, almost regardless of the social and economic context. This, together with the new emphasis on the 'return to the state' in comparative politics (e.g. Almond 1988), led scholars to begin to inquire systematically into the effects of democracy rather than simply the sources of democracy, and to explore the way in which different forms of democracy exerted a differential impact on levels of economic growth, social stability, democratic satisfaction, and so on.

Following the institutional turn, in other words, democracy was no longer just democracy, but was a system rich in variation and potential capacities, and hence also something which, in its varied forms, could impact differently on performance, effectiveness, and legitimacy. This encouraged new modes of classifying democratic polities, and new ways of comparing the varied institutional architecture. By the late 1980s, it was the form and quality of democracy rather than its existence as such that were seen to matter (e.g. Diamond and Morlino 2005).

Defining democracy

By the end of the twentieth century the question of how some forms of democracy stacked up against others had begun to engage widespread attention among both scholars and policy-makers. This explosion of interest also led to a huge variety of suggestions about how to approach the comparison of democracies.[4]

As Collier and Levitsky (1997: 430–1) noted in a valuable early assessment of the emerging literature on the topic, the challenge of dealing with the sudden variety of post-authoritarian regimes provoked wide-ranging conceptual confusion, leading to a proliferation of alternative classifications and denominations, and an almost inevitable resort to the analysis of democracy 'with adjectives'. That is, democracy was no longer just democracy; now there was **electoral** democracy, **illiberal** democracy, **delegative** democracy, **deliberative** democracy, **reflective** democracy, and so on. But not only was there a large-scale variation in how democracy was beginning to be defined and qualified, there was also a great range of terms of reference through which such definitions were approached.

Procedural vs. substantive democracy

On the face of it, there are two distinct approaches to defining democracy. On the one hand, there are the many **procedural definitions** of democracy, which focus on how the regime is organized and the processes by which representation, accountability, and legitimacy are assured. On the other hand, there are the various **substantive definitions** of democracy, which deal also with the goals and effectiveness of the regime, and the extent to which the will of the people might be served in a more purposive sense.

Schumpeter, most famously, offered a strictly procedural definition of democracy: 'the democratic method is that institutional arrangement for arriving at political decisions in which individuals acquire the power to decide by means of a competitive struggle for the people's vote' (1947: 269). This has become one of the most widely used definitions of democracy, and Schumpeter went on to simplify it even further by stating that democracy entails 'free competition for a free vote' (1947: 271).

With substantive definitions, by contrast, particular goals are also envisaged, such that real democracy cannot be defined by process alone, but also entails efforts to promote equality, fairness, and inclusion. It was precisely this approach that Schumpeter sought to leave behind, in that he explicitly rejected an earlier and more normative eighteenth-century sense of democracy which viewed 'the democratic method [as] that institutional arrangement for arriving at political decisions which **realises the common good** by making the people itself decide issues through the election of individuals who are to assemble in order to carry out its will' (1947: 250; emphasis added).

Polyarchy

In practice, procedural definitions are usually preferred in comparisons of democratic regimes. Indeed, the employment of substantive definitions of democracy has become very rare in contemporary scholarly debates, despite Dahl's insistence that process and substance cannot really be separated: 'the democratic process is not only essential to one of the most important of all political goods—the right of people to govern themselves—but is itself a rich bundle of substantive goods' (Dahl 1989: 175).

It is perhaps for this reason that Dahl prefers not to refer to 'democracies' when addressing real-world cases, since that rich bundle of substantive goods is not always on offer, but instead to 'polyarchies' (Dahl 1971: 8), which he then goes on to define in primarily procedural terms. With Dahl, however, in contrast to Schumpeter, the procedural definition is maximalist rather than minimalist. That is, polyarchies are defined by more than simply an electoral process, but also by a more or less inclusive citizenship, and by the right of these citizens to oppose and vote out their governing officials. The definition of polyarchy goes beyond the free competition for the free vote to include the provision of complete rights of participation and contestation.

In his classic *Polyarchy* (1971: 3) Dahl specified eight institutional guarantees which were required in order that citizens (1) might formulate their preferences, (2) signify these preferences, and (3) have these preferences weighted equally in the conduct of government—the three elements that he deemed necessary if government is to be democratically responsive to its citizens. Later, in *Democracy and its Critics* (Dahl 1989: 221), he specified the seven institutions 'which must exist for a government to be classified as a polyarchy' and which included elected officials, free and fair elections, inclusive suffrage, the right to run for office, freedom of expression, alternative sources of information, and associational autonomy.

These conditions extend far beyond Schumpeter's earlier definition, even when that earlier definition is qualified by Schumpeter's own references to the need for free elections and institutional pluralism, and since then they have been expanded even further by other scholars. In an assessment of the developing democracies of Latin America, for example, O'Donnell (1996) has emphasized that the comparison of polyarchies also needs to take account of the degree of governmental accountability and the acceptance of the rule of law, suggesting an even weightier definition of democracy than that used by Dahl, or at least a more broad-ranging standard against which variations among real existing democracies might be analysed.[5] This is also the key element highlighted in an earlier and admirably clear definition proposed by Schmitter and Karl:

democracy is 'a regime or system of governance in which rulers are held accountable for their actions in the public domain by citizens acting indirectly through the competition and cooperation of their elected representatives' (1991: 76).

In the **thin** procedural version, then, mainly associated with Schumpeter, democracy is about elections and little more than elections;[6] in the **thick** procedural definition, mainly associated with Dahl, democracy (or polyarchy) also entails the provision of constitutional guarantees and controls on the exercise of executive power. This distinction also overlaps considerably with that sketched in Dahl's (1956) early contrast between **populistic democracy** (thin) and **Madisonian democracy** (thick), as well as that developed by Riker (1982) in his much-cited contrast between **populism** (thin) and **liberalism** (thick). In a more recent essay, Dahl (2000) also comes back to these versions when he distinguishes two 'dimensions of democracy'.

1. The first of these is characterized by an **enforceable set of rights and opportunities** on which citizens may choose to act if they wish, and which includes the rights of **association, belief, freedom of expression**, and so on: 'A country without these necessary rights and opportunities', notes Dahl (2000: 38), echoing his earlier arguments in *Polyarchy*, 'would as a consequence also lack the fundamental political institutions required for democracy'. This, then, is part of the 'thick' procedural version.

2. The second of Dahl's dimensions is where the 'thin' version comes in, and refers to **actual participation in political life**: 'The continuing existence of a democratic order would seem to require that citizens, or at least some of them, sometimes do actually participate in political life by exercising their rights and act on the opportunities guaranteed to them' (Dahl 2000: 38). However, to view democracy only in the light of this second dimension would be wrong, he adds, since the presence of fundamental rights and opportunities is also an intrinsic element of the definition.

In a similar vein, Mény and Surel (2002: 7–11) draw a distinction between **popular democracy** and **constitutional democracy** as two pillars which together determine the legitimacy and effectiveness of democratic regimes (see also Mair 2002: 81–4). The popular democracy pillar encompasses the role of the demos—the free association of citizens, the maintenance of free elections, the freedom of political expression and government 'by' the people. The constitutional pillar encompasses the institutional requirements of good government, such as the limits on executive autonomy, the guarantee of individual and collective rights, and the more generalized Madisonian system of checks and balances. This is government 'for' the people and for the public good and, following Mény and Surel, an ideal democracy needs to reflect an equilibrium between the two pillars.

Liberal and illiberal democracy

In one version or another, this distinction between what might be termed political participation and civil rights recurs throughout the debate on democracy. This is not the only reason to highlight it here, however. Rather, the distinction has now also become of immediate empirical importance in the comparison and evaluation of real-world democracies—particularly since the post-1989 explosion of 'third wave' transitions.

More specifically, among these newly emerging democracies, a new categorization has been suggested which distinguishes those democracies which conventionally foster both pillars, and which continue to be defined as liberal democracies or polyarchies; and those in which an acceptance of popular democracy and of government 'by' the people is combined with the persistence or even the re-introduction of restrictions and limits on individual freedoms and rights. These latter regimes have been defined as **electoral democracies** or **illiberal democracies**(see Diamond 1999; Zakaria 1997).

This new category of democracy, essentially unknown prior to the late 1980s, is characterized by the formal establishment of a democratic electoral process but with major shortcomings in terms of the provision of constitutional liberties and the establishment of any limits on the arbitrary exercise of executive power. For O'Donnell, for example, who underlines very clearly how this form of democracy differs from those established in the past, this new

> delegative democracy [is] more democratic, but less liberal than representative democracy...is strongly majoritarian...and consists in constituting, through clean elections, a majority that empowers someone to become, for a given number of years, the embodiment and interpreter of the high interests of the nation.... After the election, voters/delegators are expected to become a passive but cheering audience of what the president does. (O'Donnell 1994: 60)

Having studied the Latin American democracies in particular, he also adds that these new democracies 'exhibit a rather remarkable capacity for endurance' (p. 67).

Oversloot and Verheul (2006) identify a similar pattern in the Russian case, and also suspect it is becoming institutionalized. Here, democracy has become something which is managed by 'the party of power'—not an autonomous organization which has won power through elections as such, but rather a body constituted by 'the actual group whose members wield power in and through the executive branch of government, and which creates an "electoral branch" in order to hold on to power' (2006: 394; see also Cammack 1997). In other words, power flows from the executive downwards, rather than from the citizens upwards, unhindered by any serious constitutional curbs, and helped along by the lavish use of state resources.[7] For Zakaria, surveying the developing patterns of democracy in the world in the mid-1990s, 'illiberal democracy is a growth industry...And to date few illiberal democracies have matured into liberal democracies; if anything they are moving towards heightened illiberalism' (Zakaria 1997: 24).

With these real-world cases, we see not only a separation between the two pillars of democracy in theory, but also in practice. In other words, many new democracies are seen to have democratized only in terms of the elections, and to have neglected the building of corresponding constitutional guarantees and liberties. This is also seen to relate to the conditions of democracy and to the overall path of political development (see also Chapter 25).

Zakaria (1997) is very clear on this argument, suggesting that polities which establish constitutional liberties prior to full electoral enfranchisement are more likely to establish and maintain a stable liberal democratic order than those which open up the electoral process before—if at all—they seek to establish liberal constitutionalism: '[c]onstitutional liberalism has led to democracy, but democracy does not seem to bring constitutional liberalism', he argues (1997: 28; see also Chua 2003). In this reading, the path towards democratization taken by many of the Western European states—in which the civil or constitutional rights of contestation were established **prior** to the political rights of participation (Dahl 1971: 1–9, 33–47; see also below)—is seen as being much more benign than that in which the political rights of participation are established first.

In the event, however, as Møller (2007) clearly shows, the evidence of a growing divide between the liberal and illiberal worlds of democracy has ceased to be convincing, in that this specific and rather novel combination of electoral freedoms and constitutional restrictions is now beginning to prove thin on the ground. Møller's recent evidence, as well as that adduced by Diamond and Zakaria for the mid-1990s, is based on Freedom House data, in which detailed expert surveys of countries are used to score the different polities in terms of both political liberties and civil liberties.

In brief, the composite Freedom House scores in terms of both sets of freedoms range from 1 (completely free) to 7 (completely unfree), and these are then aggregated and averaged into an overall freedom score, in which Freedom House threshold for free polities (liberal democracies) is established at a score of 2.5 or lower (for example, the average of a score of 2 on the political liberties scale, indicating some minimal restrictions; and a score of 3 on the civil liberties scale, indicating more substantial restrictions but also something that is substantially removed from repression). Averages higher than this push the polity out of the 'free' category and into the category of 'partly free' or 'unfree'.

The West European democracies score 1 on both scales, and also average 1; North Korea scores 7 on both, and also averages 7.[8] The illiberal democracies were those in which acceptable levels of freedom on the political scale were combined with strong restrictions of freedom on the civil liberties scale, and it was this category which various observers believed to be increasing in frequency.

But while this category appeared common in the mid-1990s, it has now begun to fall back, with the proportion of electoral or illiberal democracies in relation to the total number of democracies dropping from over 27 per cent in 1998 to just 8 per cent in 2005. More specifically, if we take the most recent Freedom House data, and assume that a score of 1 or 2 on each of the two scales measures effective freedom, then some 41 per cent of the world's polities now score at the top of both scales at the same time; that is, they score at more or less the conventional liberal democratic and Western standard of democracy.

Moreover, no single polity scores 1 or 2 on the political rights scale, while also scoring 4 or more on the civil liberties scale. In other words, there is no single polity in 2005 that combines the provision of effective political rights with a substantial restriction in the provision of effective civil liberties. Indeed, there is only a handful of polities that score at the top of the range for political rights (1 or 2 on the Freedom House scale) while at the same time scoring worse (3 or more on the scale) in terms of civil liberties. It is this latter group which would form the basis for any illiberal democracy category, but even then, as can be seen from their common 2:3 scoring reported in Table 5.3, the levels of restrictions on civil liberties are not particularly pronounced. It is also worth noting that in only one polity, Burundi (3:5), is the political rights score at least two points better than the civil liberties score.[9]

In effect, therefore, this new category of democracy—combining free elections with limited constitutional freedoms—seems scarcely to exist any more. As in the long-standing Western democracies, the right to participate is increasingly found in combination with rights of association, free speech, and so on, and this appears to be true even when the rights of participation are established before those of the constitutional liberties. Conversely, when civil liberties are curtailed, as in contemporary Russia for example, political freedoms also tend to be restricted. It is only in Burundi that the two scores deviate in a manner that the illiberal democracy hypothesis might have suggested. Increasingly, therefore, as was the case prior to the 1990s, both dimensions of democracy are tending to coincide rather than to diverge, and to cumulate rather than to conflict. Democracies tend to be liberal and democratic, or not liberal and not democratic. Other combinations are simply infrequent (Møller 2007).

Table 5.3 'Illiberal' democracies in 2005

Country	Score on political rights	Score on civil liberties
El Salvador	2	3
India	2	3
Indonesia	2	3
Jamaica	2	3
Lesotho	2	3
Peru	2	3
Senegal	2	3

KEY POINTS

❑ Procedural definitions of democracy have become much more common than substantive definitions.

❑ The procedural definition of democracy advanced by Schumpeter specified very minimal electoral criteria, whereas the 'thicker' procedural definition of polyarchy advanced by Dahl identifies a long list of key conditions.

❑ Democracies have a popular participatory pillar and a liberal constitutional pillar.

❑ Since 1989, scholars and policy-makers have warned of the emergence of 'illiberal democracy', in which popular elections combine with limits on individual rights and freedoms.

❑ Recent evidence suggests that most democracies tend to be liberal and democratic, or not liberal and not democratic; the other combinations are relatively rare.

Developing democracy

According to Dahl (1966: xi), there have been three great milestones in the development of democracies: First, that of **incorporation,** when the mass of the citizenry was gradually admitted into political society; second, that of **representation,** when the right to organize parties was accepted; and third, that of **organized opposition,** when citizens won the right to appeal for votes against the government. Dahl was referring here primarily to the stages that were reached during Huntington's long first wave of democratization, in which these milestones were passed one by one, and often over an extended period of time. During the third wave transitions, by contrast, the milestones were reached more or less simultaneously.[10]

Incorporation

The first milestone was reached when citizens won the right to participate in governmental decisions by casting a vote, which implied a widening of political society and the opening up of the polity to the involvement of—eventually—all adult citizens. Among the older and more long-standing democracies, this milestone began to be passed in the mid-nineteenth century—France, Germany, and the Switzerland effectively introduced universal male suffrage for the first time in 1848, followed by the US in 1870, when former slaves were first enfranchised. By the end of the First World War, most of these political systems had accorded voting rights to their

---

BOX 5.1 The extension of voting rights

The right to vote was extented progressively until suffrage became universal. The percentage of males above voting age increased during the second half of the nineteenth century from around 3–5 to nearly 100 around the First World War (people who are imprisoned, some mentally ill people, and those supported by poor relief have been excluded from the right to vote for longer).

Beside gender and age the main restrictions to the right to vote were:

• *Census voting*: the right to vote was granted only to wealthy people (above a certain level of income or taxation, as well as property of real estate or land).

• *Capacity voting*: the right to vote was restricted to educated people (those with a given level of education, being able to read and write, as well as those who served in the army or were civil servants).

• *Race*: the non-white population was excluded from the right to vote, as for example in the US, in a number of Latin American countries and in South Africa until 1994 when the apartheid regime was abolished and the first multi-racial elections took place.

Sometimes, instead of restrictions in the right to vote, *plural voting systems* were used in which, based on wealth, different voters had the right to more or less votes. In Belgium between 1893 and 1918 voters had one, two, or three votes—depending on their wealth and profession (and whether or not they had a family). In Prussia between 1848 and 1870 there were three classes of taxation. Those who paid more taxes had also more votes. In the UK until 1950 university graduates had an additional vote in the so-called 'university constitutencies', a practice that is still maintained for Senate (upper house) elections in the Irish Republic. Plural voting systems run counter to the principle of 'one person, one vote'.

---

male citizens regardless of property or other status qualifications (see Box 5.1 and Table 5.4).

Female suffrage was slower to develop. The first countries to introduce universal female suffrage, and hence universal suffrage as such, were New Zealand in 1883, Australia in 1902, and Finland in 1907. A number of the other European democracies and the US followed in the wake of the First World War, often under pressure from militant women's suffrage organizations. Some were even later. The United Kingdom accorded women equal voting rights with men in 1928, France in 1945, Italy, after fascism and the Second World War in 1946, and Belgium in 1949. Switzerland accorded women equal voting rights in 1971, thus finally becoming a full-fledged democracy, but it was not until 1989 that one recalcitrant canton, under pressure from the Swiss federal government, adopted gender equality in voting also at local level. In most of these democracies, however, foreign residents are still denied voting rights, except at the local level. Suffrage is universal only among the national citizenry.

During the long first wave, in other words, democratization was signalled by the gradual abolition of the various restrictions to the right to vote—restrictions that had been defined by gender, status, capacity, and so on—such that the population

incorporated as full participants in the political society was substantially expanded. In the European democracies in particular, this was also the moment when the long-standing party systems became institutionalized or 'frozen', and when all the relevant actors were finally brought into the political arena (see Chapter 13). Among the democracies of the first and even the second waves, the only important subsequent change in voting rights came with the lowering of the age threshold, from 25 to 21 and eventually to 18 in most countries by the end of the 1970s. In the Austrian general election of 2007, in what is as yet a unique experiment for national-level elections, the age threshold was reduced to 16 years.

Representation

The second of Dahl's milestones was the right to be represented, that is, the right to organize parties and have these participate in parliament on equal terms with other parties. The organization of parties as such was never a very major obstacle, even in more restrictive polities, but their formal registration and recognition, and the ease with which they could participate in parliament, varied substantially from system to system. One useful if not wholly accurate indication of the passing of this milestone was the

Table 5.4 Voting rights

Country	Universal male suffrage first introduced	Universal female suffrage first introduced
Australia	1902	1902
Austria	1897	1919
Belgium	1894	1949
Canada	1918	1918
Denmark	1918	1918
Finland	1907	1907
France	1848	1945
Germany	1848	1919
Iceland	1916	1916
Ireland	1918	1923
Italy	1913	1946
Japan	1947	1947
Netherlands	1918	1922
New Zealand	1893	1893
Norway	1900	1915
Sweden	1911	1921
Switzerland	1848	1971
United Kingdom	1918	1928
United States	1870	1920

Source: Caramani (2000: 53); Therborn (1977); Inter-Parliamentary Union.

shift from the conventional majoritarian voting systems that characterized more exclusive regimes in the nineteenth century to more open and proportional voting formulae (PR).

As Rokkan (1970) and later Boix (1999) have argued, a large part of the impetus to adopt more proportional voting was because of the threat posed by the mobilization of new political parties to the dominance of the established alternatives. In other words, voting systems became more proportional as new opposition parties began to make significant inroads. Had the systems remained majoritarian, the new parties, often emerging with a strong base in the new and previously disenfranchised mass electorate, would possibly have enjoyed a massive advantage with respect to the more elite-based parties that were already in parliament.

It is therefore not surprising to see PR systems being adopted in many of the European countries at the same time as the franchise was universalized—1907 in Finland, 1918 in the Netherlands, 1919 in Germany (Table 5.5); the same logic later applied to the electoral system reforms that were introduced in South Africa in the lead-up to the abolition of apartheid. In a small number of countries, notably the United Kingdom, the United States, and Canada,

Table 5.5 The adoption of proportional voting formulae

Country	PR first introduced
Australia	1918/19*
Austria	1919
Belgium	1900
Canada	–
Denmark	1920
Finland	1907
France	1945
Germany	1919
Iceland	1959
Ireland	1922
Italy	1919
Japan	1947
Luxembourg	1919
Netherlands	1918
New Zealand	1993
Norway	1921
Sweden	1911
Switzerland	1919
United Kingdom	–
United States	–

* Alternative vote in single-member districts.
Source: Caramani (2000: 60); Mackie and Rose (1991).

one that affords the citizens the democratic means to 'throw the rascals out'.[11] In parliamentary systems, this milestone is reached when the executive becomes fully responsible to the legislature, and hence when it can be dismissed by a majority in parliament.

One rough indicator of when this milestone was first reached among the more long-standing democracies can be seen in the timing of the first acceptance of socialist or social democratic parties into government (Table 5.6). This has varied quite considerably

Table 5.6 Socialist parties enter cabinets

Country	First socialist party presence in cabinet
Australia	1904
Austria	1919
Belgium	1917
Canada	–
Denmark	1918
Finland	1926
France	1936
Germany	1919
Iceland	1947
Ireland	1948
Italy	1945
Japan	1993
Luxembourg	
Netherlands	1939
New Zealand	1935
Norway	1928
Sweden	1917
Switzerland	1943
United Kingdom	1924
United States	–

Source: Bartolini (2000: 360); various party websites.

the new parties were not seen as especially threatening, and the systems remained majoritarian and eventually also less fragmented.

Organized opposition

Dahl's third milestone was marked by the right of an organized opposition to appeal for votes against the government in elections and in parliament, a right which has been more crudely summarized as among the older democracies, especially beyond Europe, beginning in Australia in 1904 and coming finally in Japan in 1993. As yet, a party that might be defined as socialist or social democratic has failed to win executive office at the national level in either Canada or the US, while in most of the European polities access was achieved either in the inter-war years (Austria, Finland, France, Norway, the UK) or immediately following the Second World War (Iceland, Ireland, Italy). Given that these parties constituted the last major opposition to develop in most democracies prior to 1989, their acceptance

Table 5.7 Growing bipolarism among the long-standing European democracies

Bipolar Competition	1950s–1960s	1990s–2000s
Present	43.8 % ($n = 7$)	62.5 % ($n = 10$)
	Denmark	Austria
	France	Denmark
	Ireland	France
	Malta	Germany
	Norway	Ireland
	Sweden	Italy
	UK	Malta
		Norway
		Sweden
		UK
Absent	56.2 % ($n = 9$)	37.5 % ($n = 6$)
	Austria	Belgium
	Belgium	Finland
	Finland	Iceland
	Germany	Luxembourg
	Iceland	Netherlands
	Italy	Switzerland
	Luxembourg	
	Netherlands	
	Switzerland	

Note: Table entries refer to countries that have experienced bipolar competition for government at either some elections or all elections in the given period.

into executive office marked a crucial watershed in democratic development.

But although the right of opposition has by now been established in all liberal democracies, there remains significant variation in the everyday **capacity** of parliaments to effect full executive turnover. In particular, the fragmentation of the party system and the need for parliamentary majorities sometimes encourages a reliance on multi-party coalitions that cannot be displaced in their entirety. That is, given certain types of coalition, and given a multiplicity of parties, full-scale alternation becomes difficult, and hence only some of the rascals can be thrown out at any one time.

In two-party systems, by contrast, as well as in the various multi-party/bipolar systems that are characteristic of contemporary Italy and France, as well as of a number of the newer democracies, wholesale alternation in government is a normal expectation and a relatively frequent occurrence (Mair 2006b). In this case, opposition is clearly defined and effectively mobilized. It is also increasingly visible: as can be seen from Table 5.7 on p. 121, which reports the patterns that prevails among the long-standing European democracies, the traditional home of coalition government, bipolarism has become more common in recent decades. During the 1950s and 1960s, the majority of polities changed governments by means of shifting and overlapping centrist coalitions; during the 1990s, by contrast, almost two-thirds of these older polities had experienced at least some two-party or bipolar competition involving wholesale alternation in government. This has already been the prevailing pattern in

Table 5.8 Incumbency volatility in European democracies, 1950–2000

Countries	1950s	1960s	1970s	1980s	1990s
Austria	2.1	1.0	1.2	1.8	**6.6**
Belgium	3.1	**7.6**	3.1	2.8	6.8
Denmark	0.9	2.7	**7.8**	3.9	2.2
Finland	0.7	1.3	4.4	4.4	**4.7**
France	10.1	3.2	12.9	2.9	**13.4**
Germany	3.3	1.9	4.8	2.0	**5.0**
Iceland	2.8	1.3	8.1	**8.3**	5.0
Ireland	5.1	3.6	3.6	5.1	**5.8**
Italy	5.8	3.3	0.2	1.2	**15.0**
Luxembourg	**8.1**	7.2	4.1	5.5	2.1
Netherlands	2.3	3.0	3.2	3.2	**12.1**
Norway	1.3	1.9	**4.8**	4.7	2.3
Sweden	3.1	1.6	2.0	3.3	**6.6**
Switzerland	0.9	3.0	2.4	3.2	**4.7**
UK	1.7	5.0	**8.9**	0.8	5.7
Mean	3.4	3.2	4.8	3.5	6.5

Bold = peak.

Source: Author's calculations from Mackie and Rose (1991) and published election results.

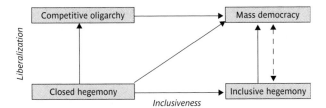

Fig. 5.1 Robert Dahl's typology of democratization processes (1971)

the older Commonwealth democracies—Australia, Canada, New Zealand—and it is rapidly becoming the norm in many of the newer democracies in southern and post-communist Europe.

Governing the European democracies is also increasingly a liability, at least as far as electoral support is concerned. Among the older European polities, for example, the net shift of votes from government to opposition—that is, the level of **incumbency volatility**—has doubled from little over 3 per cent in the 1950s and 1960s to 6.5 per cent in the 1990s (Table 5.8 on p. 122). These levels of electoral interchange across the government–opposition divide also reached a post-war peak in a majority of the individual polities during this period, with incumbency volatility recording a decade high in the 1990s in Austria, Finland, France, Germany, Ireland, Italy, the Netherlands, Sweden, and Switzerland. Putting it another way, some 60 per cent of the European polities recorded peak levels of incumbency volatility in the 1990s, as against just 20 per cent in the 1970s, and less than 10 per cent (just one case) in the other post-war decades. In this sense, we see Dahl's third major milestone beginning to loom larger in practice.

Paths of democratization

In a more schematic presentation, Dahl (1971: 6–9; 33–47) also charted the transformation of non-democratic regimes towards democracy along the two dimensions—that of **liberalization**, or public contestation (the right to be represented and to mobilise opposition), and that of **inclusiveness**, or participation and voting—to compare paths towards mass democracy. Non-democratic regimes (in most cases absolute monarchies) that liberalized without becoming more inclusive were classified by Dahl as *competitive oligarchies*. These included the parliamentary regimes with restricted suffrage in the UK and France prior to the First World War. Non-democratic regimes that became more inclusive without liberalizing were classified as *inclusive hegemonies*. These included the totalitarian

fascist and communist regimes in Nazi Germany and the Soviet bloc that regularly resorted to non-competitive mass electoral processes. The polities that became effectively democratic (the polyarchies) did so by *both* liberalizing *and* becoming more inclusive, whether simultaneously or in stages (Figure 5.1)

This is similar to the variation that was later highlighted by Zakaria (1997; see above) in his discussion of more recent paths towards democracy. For Zakaria, the most likely path towards liberal democracy was one in which *constitutionalism preceded participation*; when participation comes first, he argued, the process can become stalled, and may lead to the consolidation of illiberal democracy. Dahl had voiced similar concerns, warning of the risks that are involved 'when the suffrage is extended *before* the arts of competitive politics have been mastered and accepted as legitimate among the elites', adding that 'the liberalization of near-hegemonies will run a serious risk of failure because of the difficulty, under conditions of universal suffrage and mass politics, of working out a system of mutual security' (Dahl 1971: 38–9).

In a recent analysis of the development of party organizations in southern and eastern Europe, van Biezen (2003: 15–27) has returned to Dahl's initial distinction, contrasting the cases of Portugal and Spain, which moved from an authoritarian past and democratized on both dimensions at more or less the same time, and those of the Czech Republic and Hungary, which moved from a totalitarian but inclusive past (marked by the use of uncontested popular elections) and which then democratized on the dimension of public contestation. The latter is a seemingly risky scenario, and while the regimes in question and others in the similar post-communist circumstances have usually not failed, or fallen back from democracy, there is increasing concern about the quality of the democracies they maintain (Mungiu-Pippidi 2005). Moreover, they have also proved substantially less stable than Spain or Portugal in electoral and governmental terms (e.g. Gallagher *et al.* 2005: 298–303).

In other words, while Zakaria's concern about the rise of illiberal democracy may have come to nothing, it does appear that the character of the path towards democracy, and the particular sequencing of particular rights and freedoms may well have consequences for the stability and quality of the regimes concerned. The pace of democratization also marks a crucial distinction between the older and the newer democracies. Whereas the three milestones identified by Dahl were reached over a relatively extended period in the case of the older democracies (Tables 5.3, 5.4, 5.7 above), they were reached more or less simultaneously in the case of many of the newer democracies. That is, the right to vote, to be represented, and to organize opposition was won at one and the same time in many of the third wave polities, leaving little room for the party system and the institutional order more generally to settle.

> **KEY POINTS**
>
> ❑ The three great milestones on the path to developing democracy have been those of incorporation, representation, and opposition.
> ❑ The older and more established democracies reached these milestones one by one, and over a long period of time.
> ❑ The newer democracies have reached these milestones simultaneously.

Typologies of democracy

Majoritarian vs. consensus democracies

There have been only a handful of attempts by scholars to devise typologies of democracies as whole systems, and the most comprehensive of these has been the influential distinction between majoritarian and consensus democracies that was elaborated by Arend Lijphart in a series of key publications in the 1980s and 1990s (Lijphart 1984, 1999). This was in fact a development of an earlier approach that Lijphart had first developed in 1968 when he proposed a new typology of democratic systems as a corrective to the models then being developed by Gabriel Almond.

Almond's initial goal had been to build a classification of political systems throughout the world, including the many non-democracies, and within the democratic universe he had drawn a key distinction between what he called the Anglo-American democracies, on the one hand, and the continental European democracies, on the other. The former model was characterized by a secular, homogeneous political culture in which bargaining actors and associations were interdependent but autonomous, while the latter was characterized by a fragmented political culture with separate and non-overlapping political sub-cultures, in which independent actors came to politics not without bargainable differences but with 'conflicting and mutually exclusive designs for the political culture and the political system' (Almond 1956: 406). In the one case, the political system is likely to be centripetal, moderate, and stable; in the other, it is likely to be conflictual, polarized, and unstable.

Lijphart's (1968; 1977: 104–41) corrective to this basic model involved taking account of a second, cross-cutting, and quasi-institutional dimension, in which he distinguished two types of political elite behaviour, **coalescent** and **adversarial,** and through which he suggested that the choices and strategies pursued by political leaders could offset some of the problems posed by conflicts at the level of the political culture. In other words, divisions at the level of the society and culture could be tempered by certain types of political institutions and political behaviour.

Setting this new classification against that of Almond yielded a simple fourfold typology of democratic regimes, in which Lijphart's particular attention was devoted to what he deemed 'consociational democracies', that is, those systems in which coalescent elites sought to defuse the worst effects of social fragmentation and conflict.[12] Lijphart applied this model in particular to a number of the smaller European democracies that had been effectively passed over by Almond's typology—the so-called 'working' multi-party systems of Austria, Switzerland, the Netherlands, and Belgium—in which deep and potentially highly conflictual cleavages were controlled and accommodated by consensus-seeking political elites.

Table 5.9 Lijphart's 1968 typology of democracies

Elite behaviour	Structure of society	
	Homogeneous	*Plural*
Coalescent	Depoliticized democracy	Consociational democracy
Adversarial	Centripetal democracy	Centrifugal democracy

Source: Lijphart (1968*b*; 1977: 106).

Although much of Lijphart's later comparative work was devoted to developing and refining the theory of consociational democracy, the model remained necessarily tied to the original classification developed by Almond, and hence was seen as relevant only to those particular societies that were marked by so-called fragmented political cultures. Though highly insightful and very influential among constitutional engineers, it therefore enjoyed a relatively limited geographic application.

The new typology of democracies which Lijphart developed in the 1980s was more broad-ranging, and given that it was defined in almost exclusively political and institutional (rather than political cultural) terms, it also enjoyed almost limitless geographic application.[13] This was the distinction between majoritarian and consensus democracies, which was built on a broad-ranging and quite exhaustive set of political and institutional indicators (see Table 5.1 earlier on p. 110), particularly in the 1999 version when the interest group system and the degree of independence of the central bank were also added to the list of distinguishing criteria. In the original consociational model, by contrast, just four institutional characteristics were considered: proportionality, minority veto, segmental autonomy, and grand coalition.

The two approaches were closely related, however, and in work published in the late 1970s and early 1980s, Lijphart actually referred to the contrast as one between consociational and majoritarian models (Lijphart 2000: 228–30; Blondel 1988: 5–8). In brief, **majoritarian democracies** were regarded as those in which a winning party or coalition of parties could exercise virtually limitless power within a political system, in that executive authority was scarcely constrained. Among these democracies, in other words, there was a great difference between

winning and losing, and power was exclusive—the losers had no voice—rather than inclusive. In **consensus democracies**, by contrast, developing on the earlier notion of consociationalism, power was more likely to be shared rather than contested, minorities were formally included in decision-making processes, and executive power was limited by constitutional courts, powerful second chambers, and a decentralized system of territorial governance.

Lijphart developed his new framework by first identifying the various political and institutional features that could be associated with majoritarian democracy—and which were originally typified by the cases of the United Kingdom and New Zealand—and then by defining each of the features of consensus democracy as the opposite of that which prevailed in the majoritarian case. It was, to all intents and purposes, an inductive framework for the comparison of democracies, building out from two real-world cases and positing two extreme models at opposite ends of a notional continuum. Moreover, it represented one of the first serious attempts to construct a holistic model of democracy, taking into account not only the patterns of behaviour of the political elites, but also the institutional structures that defined the polity in which the elites operated and that constrained their behaviour.

It was also a problematic approach, however, and was not always internally consistent. The eight features associated with the majoritarian model in the 1984 version, and the ten adopted in 1999, fitted together very coherently in the particular political system from which they were inductively derived—the British system. Similarly, although with more careful adaptation, the eight (and then ten) features of consensus democracy also fitted together quite well at the opposite end of the spectrum—in the cases of Belgium and Switzerland. In between these two extremes, however, most other real-world systems reflected a sometimes confusing mix of both majoritarian and consensus features.

Lijphart tried to deal with this problem by separating what had been designed as a unidimensional model into two dimensions, which were also derived inductively (through factor analysis): a federal–unitary dimension, on which, for example, the US scored strongly on the consensus side, and an executive–parties dimension, on which the same US scored strongly on the majoritarian side. In other words, not all systems could be defined as consensus or majoritarian democracies: some were consensual and inclusive on both dimensions, and some were majoritarian and exclusive on both dimensions, but quite a number were mixed, being consensual on one and majoritarian on the other, while yet others were grouped in a poorly specified middle range.

What had begun as a comparison of distinct types or categories of democracies—majoritarian vs. consensus—therefore fell foul of a complex reality in which more-or-less values along each of a group of not necessarily congruent dimensions led to a host of equivocal cases. Indeed, typical of the problems involved in this approach is the treatment of party systems, which are included in the initial framework in terms of the familiar categoric distinction of two-party vs. multi-party, but which are then operationalized as the more-or-less 'effective number of parties' variable in a way that inevitably clouds the initial definitional clarity (Lijphart 1999: 62–9; see also the comments in Mair 2006a: 63–4).

Decentralist vs. centripetal democracies

Similar problems can be seen in Gerring et al.'s (2005) recent attempt to go beyond Lijphart and to develop an alternative whole-system categorization of democracies. This approach, which with Lijphart is one of the very few to attempt a holistic comparison of democracies, incorporates a more detailed range of institutional and political variables than does Lijphart, and proposes a categoric distinction between so-called 'decentralist' and 'centripetal' models of democracy. The **decentralist model** emphasizes several core features, including 'diffusion of power, broad political participation, and limits on governmental action'

(Gerring et al. 2005: 568). It is also marked by the fragmentation of both popular and political power: single-member districts and weak party cohesion are combined with Madisonian features such as a pronounced separation of powers and strong limits on executive authority. The **centripetal model**, by contrast, emphasizes the importance of inclusive but authoritative institutions, and builds strongly on the model of 'responsible party government' (Gerring et al. 2005: 569; Ranney 1962). It is marked by strong and unified government, along majoritarian lines, which combines with PR, centralized interest groups, and well-organized and strongly bounded political parties (Gerring et al. 2005: table 1).

Decentralized democracies are typified by the US case; centripetal democracies by the cases of Norway and Sweden, or by what Almond had formerly seen as the 'working multi-party systems' (see above). In fact, despite their different starting point, what Gerring and his colleagues offer here is almost the mirror image of the Lijphart distinction. That is, the categories of decentralized and centripetal fall almost squarely within the mixed categories created by Lijphart's crossing of the federal–unitary and executive–parties dimensions of his consensus and majoritarian models. What for Lijphart are mixed cases—combining federal (consensus) institutions with majoritarian cabinets, or unitary (majoritarian) institutions with consensus cabinets—are, for Gerring et al., the new models of decentralized and centripetal democracy respectively.

Inevitably, then, these alternative models also run into the same problems as those of Lijphart, although these prove more acute in the case of the centralist–centripetal distinction since more variables are involved (the authors list twenty-one possible features of each model) and since the models of democracy themselves are applied to more than 120 countries. Here too, but more evidently so, a relatively simple categoric distinction between models of democracy is diffused across a host of potentially incongruent institutional dimensions, with the result that we remain unsure whether any real-world examples of these types of democracy actually exist.

The problems of holistic models

The work of Gerring et al. and Lijphart is unusual in that in both cases an attempt is made to model democracies as whole systems. That said, these authors also tap into older and longer term concerns in comparative politics (Daalder 2002) in that they address the question of what makes for a 'better' democracy, a question that also links them to the more recent concerns with the quality of democracy (see above).

For Lijphart, for example, the key choice is between a majoritarian system that is responsive, accountable, and often efficient, but in which the representative channel may deny a voice to large proportions of the citizenry; and a consensus system which is inclusive and more representative, but that may prove less efficient in the longer term. Despite all the potential decision-making problems and veto points in Lijphart's consensus democracy, however, it remains for him a 'kinder, gentler' and hence more valued model of democracy (Lijphart 1999: 275–300). For Gerring *et al.*, it is the centripetal democracies that are superior: 'good governance arises from institutions that pull towards the center, offering incentives to participate and disincentives to defect' (Gerring *et al.* 2005: 580).

But this is by the way. What is more relevant to this present discussion is that both studies reach their conclusions having examined a large variety of institutional dimensions along which different individual polities could be placed, and it is here that the problems arise. For example, in neither approach is any single one of the various dimensions of comparison prioritized. Although Gerring *et al.* (2005: 571) refer to four dimensions in particular as being of 'primary interest' to their analysis—territorial sovereignty, legislative structure, the form of executive, and the electoral system—each of their twenty-one defining features weighs equally in their definition.

The same is true for the ten defining features specified by Lijphart (1999). And the principal difficulty in applying these models to the comparison of real-world democracies arises when these different dimensions prove incongruent, such as when a polity is majoritarian in terms of, say, its interest group system, but consensual in terms of its electoral system; or when, in the model proposed by Gerring *et al.*, a system is decentralized with respect to its legislative branch, but centripetal in terms of its use of referenda. Nor are these incongruities uncommon or exceptional. Gerring *et al.*'s misfits are Lijphart's ideal types, and vice versa.

But why should ostensibly coherent models of democracy prove so difficult to apply to real-world comparisons? Why should comparative politics face these problems when it seeks to model democracies *tout court*? After all, both sets of categories discussed above are strongly grounded in theory as well as in logic. Gerring *et al.* draw their models from reasoning associated with the founders of American democracy, for example, and from classic work in the history of political thought, while Lijphart infers his models from the standard-setting majoritarian system, as well as from his own exhaustive work on consociationalism.

In practice, however, and this is the most important conclusion to be drawn from this discussion, real-world democracies rarely prove as sharply bounded or as internally coherent as the various theoretically informed whole-system models might suggest. Indeed, there are few, if any, democracies which have been first constructed in the abstract in such a way that the different institutional elements knit together in forms that are both predictable and make sense. Even in the American case, as Dahl (2002: 66–7) emphasized, institutional design not only followed high-minded republican theories but was also strongly influenced the exigencies of day-to-day bargaining in the Convention. However persuasive the arguments of the *Federalist* in promoting the need for a separation of powers, for example, what proved decisive in the end was 'a group of baffled and confused men who finally settle on a solution more out of desperation than confidence [and who] had little understanding of how their solution would work out in practice' (Dahl 2002: 67; see also Rakove 1996).

Two centuries later, in the context of the extensive wave of post-communist constitution-making, and at a time when the institutional designers could call on a great deal more historical experience of democracy than was ever available to the Convention in Philadelphia, contingency also often proved decisive. As Grzymala-Busse (2006) has recently shown in the case of the oversight institutions that were established in the wake of the transition in East–Central Europe, for example, much of the real cross-national variation in what might have been theoretically expected to be a relatively uniform set of procedures came about as a result of the specifics of party competition as it developed in the different polities: 'Postcommunist political parties attempted both to build the state and to ensure their own survival', she concludes (2006: 297). And the result of this double-headed strategy was the collage or even mish-mash of different institutional arrangements that are now to be found among the post-communist polities.

Holistic models are also increasingly undermined by cross-national learning processes, and by the diffusion of particular institutional arrangements and solutions (Jahn 2006; see also Galton's problem in Chapters 22 and 23). As national borders become more porous, and as cross-national communication and lesson-drawing becomes more commonplace, this process of diffusion becomes all the more pronounced. Diffusion across neighbouring territories was one of the few structural factors highlighted by Doorenspleet (2005: 143–61), for example, in her comprehensive analysis of the factors that might explain the explosion of transitions to democracy in the early 1990s: 'States surrounded by democratic neighbors were generally more likely to make a transition to democracy states with nondemocratic neighbors' (2005: 168).

Diffusion also marks the cross-national learning processes that are increasingly noticeable among the long-standing democracies. One of the reasons why the Dutch held a referendum on the European constitution in 2005, the very first use of such a constitutional device in modern Dutch history, was because of Danish, French, and British examples; one of the reasons why the British government began to experiment with directly electing city mayors was because of the Canadian, US, and French examples; and one of the reasons why many polities have opted to free their central banks from direct political control is because of German and American examples.

Democracies, in short, are less and less likely to be closed or self-contained systems (as Chapter 24

shows), and in this sense they are also less and less likely to reflect totally consistent patterns when subject to comparative whole-system analysis. As Streeck and Thelen have argued:

> ❝[T]he institutional frameworks that exist in any particular society are never completely coherent. While some institutional arrangements may impose a dominant logic of action, these typically coexist with other arrangements, created at different points in time and under different historical circumstances, that embody conflicting and even contradictory logics. (2005: 19–20)❞

The problem in comparing democracies in this sense is not so much the problem of comparing apples and pears—something which can always be solved with the help of the ladder of abstraction (Sartori 1970 and Chapter 3); rather it is one of comparing apples which have become part pear with pears which have become part apple. The lack of progress made by comparative politics in developing whole-system models of democratic regimes therefore owes less to any intrinsic weaknesses in the discipline, and rather more to the increasing problems of complexity and exogeneity in the set of variables with which this sort of inquiry is concerned.[14]

KEY POINTS

❑ Developing typologies of democracy as whole systems has always proved very difficult.

❑ The most important attempt to develop a comprehensive typology is seen in Arend Lijphart's distinction between majoritarian and consensus democracy.

❑ The increasing transnational diffusion of institutions and ideas tends to make models of democracy less internally coherent and consistent.

Audience democracy?

Although democracy has now become the most common regime type across the world, there is a growing concern that its foundations are now less robust than before. One symptom of this emerging problem is the widespread evidence of citizen dissatisfaction with aspects of democracy (Table 5.10), as well as that of declining levels of participation and engagement.

These signs of citizen withdrawal from conventional political involvement are increasingly pervasive, and seem to stretch across many of the advanced industrial and post-industrial democracies as well as across many of the new democracies (e.g. Dalton 2004). Turnout at elections has fallen, particularly since the end of the 1980s; levels of party membership

Table 5.10 Satisfaction with democracy among democracies

Country (year of survey)	Score
Denmark (2001)	1.7
Netherlands (1998)	2.0
Australia (2004)	2.0
United States (2004)	2.0
Norway (2001)	2.1
Britain (1997)	2.1
Ireland (2002)	2.1
Canada (1997)	2.1
Switzerland (2003)	2.2
Sweden (2002)	2.2
Spain (2004)	2.2
Finland (2003)	2.3
New Zealand (2002)	2.3
Iceland (2003)	2.3
Belgium (2003)	2.3
Japan (1996)	2.4
France (2002)	2.5
Germany (2002)	2.5
Romania (1996)	2.5
Portugal (2002)	2.6
Hungary (2002)	2.6
Czech Republic (2002)	2.6
Lithuania (1997)	2.6
Israel (2003)	2.7
Poland (2001)	2.7
Slovenia (1996)	2.8
Mexico (2003)	2.9
South Korea (2004)	2.9
Brazil (2002)	2.9

Note: The countries are all those with scores of 1 or 2 on both the Political Rights and the Civil Liberties Freedom House scales in 2005, and for which CSES data on satisfaction with democracy are also available. The CSES scores for satisfaction with democracy are the mean values derived from responses to the survey question. 'On the whole, are you very satisfied, fairly satisfied, not very satisfied, or not at all satisfied with the way democracy works in [country]?'. The lower the score, the higher the satisfaction rating. For details and the data for the satisfaction levels, see CSES website.

have often sunk to record lows; and both the stability and strength of levels of partisan identity have become considerably weakened.[15] More generally, popular confidence in politics and politicians has dropped almost to the bottom of the scale, with a recent assessment of the data from across the EU showing that political parties are trusted less than any comparable social or political institution, including large companies, trade unions, the press, or the police (Dalton and Weldon 2005).

During the early post-war years, and probably through to at least the 1970s, conventional politics was seen to belong to the citizen, and was seen as something in which the citizen could, and often did, engage. By the beginning of the new century, on the other hand, conventional politics appears to have become part of an external world that people prefer to observe from the outside. There is a world of the parties, and a world of political leaders, that is increasingly separated from the world of the citizenry, and hence also one in which popular participation is becoming less relevant. As Bernard Manin (1997: 218–35) put it, what we now witness is the replacement of representative democracy or party democracy by audience democracy.

Although the democratic audience is occasionally taken with or moved by the spectacle that plays out before it, it is usually indifferent and passive. As Hibbing and Theiss-Morse put it in a discussion of the US case, '[a] vigorous democracy is the last thing people want, and forgetting entirely about politics is precisely what they do want' (2002: 232). It is this growing indifference to politics that has helped to encourage support for more 'non-majoritarian' decision-making, and for a greater role to be accorded to various non-partisan and non-political agencies—judges, regulatory bodies, central banks, international organizations, and the EU itself (Thatcher and Stone Sweet 2004). In other words, as citizens withdraw from politics, decision-making becomes more depoliticized.

At worst, the audience can be dissatisfied and somewhat angry, and it is this latter response which sometimes fuels the sort of populist anti-political protest that is now being experienced in many democracies, both old and new (Mény and Surel 2002;

Mudde 2004). In other words, largely because of growing citizen dissatisfaction, the functioning of democracy and the status of the political class itself have become issues of contention in political debates in many democratic polities, and have in turn encouraged more frequent institutional experiments with alternatives to representative democracy, including the use of referenda, citizens' juries, and other forms of participatory politics (Schmitter and Trechsel 2004).

In contemporary democracies, in other words, there is an increasing tendency to pass decisions back down to the citizens for their final approval, or to pass them up to non-political agencies and institutions, where they are subject to expert judgement and more technocratic evaluations. In neither of these circumstances is there much emphasis on the importance of conventional political mediation—elections, parties, or political competition more generally. This is therefore a challenge not only to Dahl's criteria for an effective polyarchy, and to his emphasis on the capacity to organize opposition, but also to Schumpeter's thinner definition of democracy. As citizens are offered more opportunities for direct participation, and as non-political agencies and 'guardian institutions' take on a more decisive role, it makes less sense to speak of power being acquired through a competitive struggle for the people's vote.

> **KEY POINTS**
>
> ❏ In recent years, audience democracy has tended to replace representative democracy and party democracy.
> ❏ Citizens have often withdrawn from political life and are now more likely to distrust their democratically chosen leaders.
> ❏ Decision-making procedures are now often depoliticized.

Conclusion

Since the fall of the Berlin Wall in 1989, and the explosion of transitions to democracy in the 1990s, scholars and policy-makers have become increasingly attentive to the differences among democratic systems. Treating democracy itself as the default option among political regimes, concern has shifted from focusing on the question of the quantity of democracy, in the sense of an older concern with explaining why some countries become democratic while others do not, to the question of the quality of democracy, which reflects a newer concern with explaining why some democracies seem 'better' than others.

At the same time, the capacity to compare democracies systematically has become undermined as democratic regimes themselves become subject to global and transnational influences, and as institutions are reformed or transplanted without much heed for coherence and consistency. What had been once a small and homogeneous group of democratic regimes has now become large and heterogeneous, and much less amenable to classification and modelling.

Democracies have also proved more troubled in recent years. Citizen disengagement from elections and other conventional modes of political participation, as well as the growing popular distrust and dissatisfaction with political leaderships, has tended to create a more passive, audience-oriented democracy. The electoral process, once seen as the defining feature of a democratic polity, has often become discredited and subject to challenge, with the result that decision-making rests increasingly in the hands of the judiciary and other non-majoritarian agencies. In an effort to encourage greater links to the citizenry, political leaders lay increasing emphasis on the use of referenda and primaries, diverting decision-making power away from the increasingly tarnished political parties which once epitomized democracy.

In these circumstances, the role of the constitutional pillar of democracy acquires a new resonance, while that of the popular pillar seems less and less relevant. Democracy, in other words, whether at the national or transnational level, now seems to be more about protecting people's rights, and less about ensuring that they still have a voice.

World trends

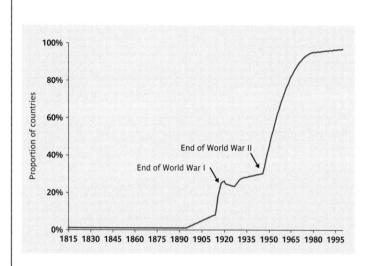

Trend 3 Democracy: proportion of countries with universal suffrage (1815–2000)

Notes: Universal suffrage includes both male and female adult population. Voting age varies over time and has been lowered progressively). Percentages are calculated on total number of countries. Number of countries are approximate for years in proximity to wars, major border changes (e.g., ex-Yugoslavia) and decolonisation processes. Universal suffrage disregards cases of unequal vote (i.e., *vote plural* in Belgium and *Dreiklassenwahlrecht* in Prussia).

? Questions

1. Why did authors increasingly feel that typologies of democracies are necessary?
2. When have the three 'waves' of democratization taken place, and where?
3. What do we mean by 'thin' and 'thick' definitions of democracy?
4. What do we mean by an electoral or illiberal democracy?.
5. What are the main milestones in the development of democracy?
6. What are the alternative 'paths' toward democratizations distinguished by Dahl?
7. What differentiates majoritarian from consensus democracies? Give real-world examples of both types.
8. What differentiates decentralised from centripetal democracies? Give real-world examples of both types.
9. Why is it difficult to compare democracies as whole systems?
10. Are representative democracies turning into audience democracies and, if so, why?

» Further reading

Definitions and typologies of democracies

Dahl, Robert A. (ed.) (1966) *Political Oppositions in Western Democracies* (New Haven, Conn.: Yale University Press).

—— (1971) *Polyarchy* (New Haven, Conn.: Yale University Press).

Lijphart, Arend (1977) *Democracy in Plural Societies* (New Haven, Conn.: Yale University Press).

—— (1984) *Democracies* (New Haven, Conn.: Yale University Press).

—— (1999) *Patterns of Democracy* (New Haven, Conn.: Yale University Press).

Mény, Yves, and Surel, Yves (eds.) (2002) *Democracies and the Populist Challenge* (Basingstoke: Palgrave).

Schumpeter, Joseph A. (1947) *Capitalism, Socialism, and Democracy* (New York: Harper & Brothers, 2nd edn).

Overviews of contemporary democracies

Keman, Hans (ed.) (2002) *Comparative Democratic Politics* (London: Sage).

LeDuc, Lawrence, Niemi, Richard G., and Norris, Pippa (eds.) (2002) *Comparing Democracies 2* (London: Sage).

Powell, G. Bingham (1982) *Contemporary Democracies* (Cambridge, Mass.: Harvard University Press).

Recent developments and topics

Diamond, Larry (1999) *Developing Democracy* (Baltimore, Md.: Johns Hopkins University Press).

—— and Morlino, Leonardo (eds.) (2005) *Assessing the Quality of Democracy* (Baltimore, Md.: Johns Hopkins University Press).

Huntington, Samuel P. (1991) *The Third Wave: Democratization in the Late Twentieth Century* (Norman, Okla.: University of Oklahama Press).

Manin, Bernard (1997) *The Principles of Representative Government* (Cambridge: Cambridge University Press).

Pharr, Susan, and Putnam, Robert (eds.) (2000) *Disaffected Democracies: What's Troubling the Trilateral Countries?* (Princeton: Princeton University Press).

Zakaria, Fareed (2003) *The Future of Freedom: Illiberal Democracy at Home and Abroad* (New York: Norton).

Web links

www.freedomhouse.org
   Website of Freedom House.

www.cia.gov/cia/publications/factbook/index.html
   Website managed by the CIA and detailing information about countries around the world.

www.electionworld.org/election/indexfrm.htm
   Website on elections and election outcomes.

www.psr.keele.ac.uk/election.htm
   Hugely comprehensive website detailing links and sources on elections and electoral systems.

www.idea.int
   Website of an intergovernmental organization promoting democracy around the world and an excellent source of data on voting and elections.

www.cses.org
   Website of the collaborative programme of research among election study teams from around the world.

www.ipu.org/english/home.htm
   The website of the Inter-Parliamentary Union.

www.constitution.org/cons/natlcons.htm
   Website giving details of constitutions around the world.

www.tol.cz
   Website offering coverage of events in the twenty-eight post-communist countries.

 Visit the Online Resource Centre that accompanies this book for more information:
www.oxfordtextbooks.co.uk/orc/caramani/

6 Authoritarian regimes

Paul Brooker

Chapter contents

Reader's guide

The concept of authoritarian regime is based on the residual notion throwing all the non-democratic political systems in together. However, the fact that they are *not* democracies means that these regimes share one other characteristic: they all use censorship and repression to maintain authority and to implement unpopular (or downright murderous) policies. Apart from this authoritarian characteristic they have little in common and, in fact, display a bewildering diversity, from monarchies to military regimes, from totalitarianism to semi-competitive elections, and from Cromwell to communist regimes. Furthermore, the concept of authoritarian regime covers a large slice of political history. The chapter begins with a historical introduction before looking at the key questions of who rules an authoritarian regime, why they rule, that is, their claim to legitimate authority, and how they rule, that is the mechanisms of control, the distinctive policies, and their ways of making policy. The conclusion discusses whether these regimes are becoming extinct or will come up with some evolutionary surprises.

Introduction

Until modern times states were normally ruled by authoritarian regimes and particularly by **monarchies**. These monarchical authoritarian regimes were based on an inherited and highly institutionalized form of personal rule that was restrained to varying degrees by traditional customs and institutions. However, the notion that rule over a state and its people could be inherited like private property—like a family business concern—would seem very primitive once democracy began to compete with the monarchies. They would increasingly be replaced by republics or converted into constitutional monarchies that reigned rather than ruled. But a different sort of authoritarian regime, namely **dictatorship by an organization or by its leader**, emerged at about the same time as democracy. Although these dictatorships would prove to be 'political dinosaurs' that are now facing extinction, they would collectively provide democracy with hard and sometimes bloody competition through much of the twentieth century.

The evolution of authoritarian regimes

Dictatorship by an organization or its leader first emerged in the form of the military personal dictatorship. The modern historical precursor was the rule of Oliver Cromwell (leader of the New Model Army) in seventeenth-century Britain but the more immediate and applicable prototype was the way in which General Napoleon Bonaparte became military dictator of France in the aftermath of the French Revolution. He not only seized power in 1799 through a military coup (see Box 6.1) but also used a plebiscite or referendum to legitimize this seizure of power—a stealing of democracy's clothes that would be typical of these new authoritarian regimes. Although he soon attempted to found a new hereditary monarchy under the title of Emperor of the French, Napoleon had actually pioneered a new type of personal rule: personal dictatorship by the leader of an organization.

BOX 6.1 Military seizures of power

Historical background

The seizure of power by a military organization or its leader is historically the oldest way of setting up a modern form of non-democratic regime. Napoleon's 1799 coup and the nineteenth-century seizures of power by the military or a military leader starkly revealed how the private ownership of public offices can occur in other ways than through ownership by a royal family—an organization or its leader can use force to take power from an old monarchy or a young democracy.

The seizure of power

This seizure of the country's public offices is carried out by means of an actual or threatened *coup d'etat*, which means literally a blow by/of the state but in practice an often bloodless attack by the military arm of the state against its own government.

Types of coup

- The *corporate coup*, which is carried out by the military as a corporate body and under the command of its most senior officers, such as the recent coup in Thailand;

- The *factional coup*, which is carried out by only a faction of the military and under the command of less senior and often only middle-ranking officers (and so is often described as a colonels' coup);

- The *counter coup*, which is launched against a *military* government by a disaffected or ambitious faction of officers.

Practical implications

Such distinctions are important practically as well as conceptually. For example, since most coups are factional and most factional coups fail, any government faced with a coup has no need to pack its bags unless and until it learns that this is *not* a factional coup but instead a corporate coup.

His nephew Louis Napoleon would pioneer another new type of personal dictatorship: the populist presidential monarchy (see below and Box 6.3; and Box: Misappropriation of power, in the Online Resource Centre). He was elected president of France in 1848 and three years later staged the classic example of an unconstitutional seizure of more power that is now generally described by its Latin American name: the *autogolpe* (self-coup). He followed his uncle's lead of presenting the country with a new constitution to be approved by plebiscite or referendum and during the short period that he retained the republican title of president (before copying his uncle and crowning himself emperor), he was a pioneering example of what is now termed the 'populist' form of presidential monarchy (McMillan 1991: 43–54). This quite rare type of personal dictatorship would also be found in Latin America and reached its peak nearly a century after Louis Napoleon with the self-coup of President Vargas of Brazil and his innovative period of populist presidential monarchy. But Latin America is better known as the region where military dictatorship became well-established during the nineteenth century, not only in the form of the personal military dictator but also as **rule by the military as an organization**—one of the two species of organizational dictatorship.

The other species did not appear until the twentieth century, with the evolution of **one-party rule** by a dictatorial political party claiming a permanent monopoly of power. In 1917 the Tsarist monarchy that ruled the huge Russian Empire was brought down by the military disasters and home-front privations of the First World War, opening the way for Lenin's Bolshevik party of revolutionary Marxists to seize power and establish one-party rule (see Box 6.2). Within a few years Lenin's renamed Communist Party ruled unopposed over a former Russian Empire that had been renamed the Union of Soviet Socialist Republics or simply 'Soviet Union'.

After Lenin's death in 1924, his party came to be dominated by General Secretary Stalin, the head of the party's administrative apparatus. Stalin would show that a communist party's leader could transform its organizational dictatorship into his personal rule despite the Leninist principle of collective leadership (by members of the party's elected executive committee and its political subcommittee, the Politburo). Collective leadership was replaced in practice by Stalin's personal rule as the acknowledged leader of party and regime. He also implemented the first Five Year Plan, which created a state-owned/planned economy in urban areas and a collectivized agriculture in the countryside. Although these political and

---

BOX 6.2 Revolutionary seizures of power

Comparison to the military coup

The revolutionary seizure of power by a political party is the civilian equivalent of the military coup. The party seizes the country's public offices by leading a successful revolution against what is usually a monarchical or military government. Although the revolution may be carried out by crowds of people taking to the streets in peaceful protests, most party-led revolutions have involved a military-style coup or civil war against the government.

The Russian Revolution: October 1917

The most famous case of a revolutionary coup is the Russian Revolution by the Bolshevik Party, later renamed the Communist Party. It used worker-militia Red Guards and some sympathetic military units to take control of the capital city and other major urban centres. The following civil war required the Communist Party to create and use

a large army to beat off the armies of their opponents and win control of the huge Russian countryside.

The Chinese Civil War: 1946–49

The most famous revolutionary civil war instead required a *rurally* based Chinese Communist Party to create and use large armies in 1946–9 to conquer the country's urban centres and establish a communist regime.

The Iranian Islamic Revolution: 1978–79

Perhaps the most 'incongruous' revolution was the relatively recent Islamic Revolution against Iran's monarchy. This revolution was not led by a political party but instead involved mosque-mobilized street demonstrations. It resulted in a regime dominated by Shiite Muslim clergy, most notably the personal rule of the Ayatollah Khomeini until his death a decade later.

economic developments are usually referred to as 'Stalinism', it is not surprising that they came to be seen as part of the model or template of a communist regime.

By the 1930s another threat to the democracies was coming from **fascism**. While communism had been able to expand into only Outer Mongolia, fascists had taken over the important democracies of Italy and Germany (see Box 6.5) and fascism seemed to have replaced communism as the political 'wave of the future' threatening democracy. On the other hand, the ideologically driven personal rule of Mussolini and Hitler would lead to their countries pursuing grandiose imperialist visions in the 1940s that were beyond their reach and eventually resulted in total military defeat.

The Second World War cost the lives of many millions of soldiers and innocent victims but the democracies and the Soviet Union were able to destroy the fascist challenge in a comprehensive and permanent fashion that would have taken much longer in peacetime, as was confirmed by the survival into the 1970s of Franco's quasi-fascist regime in Spain.

However, the Second World War also provided an opportunity for the spread of the communist model of dictatorship and the creation of a communist bloc of countries to compete with the dominant Western world. In Eastern Europe and the Balkans the opportunity arose from the 1944–45 destruction of Nazi Germany's rule by the Soviet Union's advancing armies and, in the Balkans, by local communist guerrilla forces. These newly liberated countries were taken over by the communists, using the disguise of electoral-coalition politics, and in most cases became 'satellite' states of the Soviet Union—formally independent countries with governments dependent upon and obedient to the Soviet Union. Similarly, in East Asia an opportunity for communist expansion arose from the destruction of the Japanese rule in the north of China and Korea by invading Soviet armies in the day, preceding Japan's August 1945 surrender. This led to the creation of the Soviet-sponsored communist state of North Korea and to a strengthening of the local communists in China that enabled them to win control of the whole country in the civil war of 1946–49. A quarter of the world's population was thereby brought under communist rule, which within a decade had clearly become the personal rule of Chairman Mao Zedong.

The post-war wave of communist expansion was largely brought to a halt with the onset of the Cold War between the new communist world and a Western world led by the US—which had become intent on containing the spread of communism. But its momentum was restored in the mid-1970s by the military victories in South Vietnam, Laos, and Cambodia, which were followed by the creation of several Marxist-Leninist regimes in parts of Africa and in Afghanistan. The communist Second World now politically and militarily rivalled the democratic and affluent First World and was much more powerful than the large Third World of politically non-aligned and economically developing countries.

The Third World, too, had produced a large number of authoritarian regimes since the Second World War, some of which had been quite innovative.[1] The dissolving of the British and French colonial empires created dozens of new states in the 1950s–60s that often became examples of the new 'African one-party state' dictatorship or of the old-fashioned military regime, which was finding a new niche for itself in Africa and Asia. In Latin America the military regime was a long-established form of government and began a new cycle of 'popularity' in the 1960s. By the mid-1970s in fact the Third World seemed virtually lost to democracy, as even in India the prime minister instituted a state of emergency that seemed to endanger the Third World's most important democracy. As this period also saw the beginning of the communist world's renewed expansion, it is only with hindsight that the origins of a global wave of democratization can be discerned in these years, the mid-1970s, when the authoritarian regime seemed to be not only numerically but also politically dominating the globe.

The global shift towards democracy in the final quarter of the twentieth century represented the most dramatic change in the political climate of the globe that has ever been recorded—and appeared to mean the extinction of the authoritarian regimes. The change began with the democratization of Portugal and post-Franco Spain in the mid-1970s and then swept through Latin America and Asia before returning to Europe in 1989 to democratize the communist regimes of Eastern Europe (Linz and Stepan 1996). Then in 1991 the democratizing process occurring in the Soviet Union led to this communist superpower peacefully disintegrating into its fifteen republics, which became independent and varyingly democratic countries (see Chapter 5 for the 'second' and 'third' waves of democratization). With the democratization of Africa in the first half of the 1990s, the global triumph of democracy seemed complete and the dictatorships seemed to be going the way of the dinosaurs, as Jowett had recently suggested in his theory of the 'Leninist extinction' (Jowett 1992: ch. 7). But if they were indeed becoming extinct, the dictatorships and the ruling monarchies could at least claim to have dominated the globe for nearly all of human history and to have appeared in an incredibly diverse range of species and subspecies.

KEY POINTS

❏ Pre-nineteenth-century states were normally authoritarian, usually monarchies.

❏ In the early nineteenth century there is the emergence of a new sort of authoritarian regime, namely dictatorship by (military) organization or its leader.

❏ Toward the mid-nineteenth century a new but rare type of personal dictatorship appears, namely populist **presidential monarchy** by an elected president who becomes dictatorial.

❏ In the first half of the twentieth century (with the decline of ruling monarchies) there is the emergence of dictatorship by a party or its leader, namely communist and fascist subtypes of one-party rule.

❏ In the third quarter of the twentieth century (after decolonization and the Cold War) there is the numerical preponderance of dictatorships as older varieties are joined by such new ones as the African one-party state.

❏ The final quarter of the twentieth century witnesses the triumph of democracy (and the 'mass extinction' of dictatorships?).

Who rules?

Personal rule

Personal rule is a particular form of authoritarian regime because its two main versions—the monarch and dictator—are so different in form and history. Not only had monarchies existed for thousands of years before the emergence of the personal dictatorships but also the hereditary and highly ceremonial nature of monarchical rule was quite different from the personal dictator's modern form of rule. The modern dictator was a professional soldier or politician who had come to power as the leader of a military or party organization or as an elected president. Nonetheless, there are interesting similarities between the monarch and the dictator, particularly the way their degree of personal rule varies from quite limited to absolutist. To use a well-known historical example, when King John's barons forced him to sign Magna Carta, they starkly revealed the difference between a feudal king and an oriental sultan.

Dictatorial monarchies

Monarchies are a good example of how institutions must be viewed in context in order to understand them. For while ruling monarchs and reigning monarchs are clothed in the same trappings of royalty, a **ruling monarch** exercises the same power as a personal dictator but a **reigning monarch** is a constitutional and largely ceremonial head of state. A ruling dictatorial monarchy seems even more primeval than a dictatorship and is restricted to a suitably specialized habitat. Apart from a few small kingdoms in such widely separated parts of the globe as Swaziland, Brunei, and Tonga, the ruling monarchies are concentrated in the Arab world and particularly the Gulf region, as in the case of the kingdom of Saudi Arabia, the United Arab Emirates, and the Sultanate of Oman. Furthermore, other Arab ruling monarchies, such as the Egyptian and Iraqi, managed to survive until the 1950s–60s and were usually ended by a military coup, not by democratization or a popular revolution like the 1978–79 Islamic Revolution in Iran (see Box 6.2) that overthrew the only Persian monarchy, the shah's rule over Iran.

The survival of so many Arab monarchies cannot be ascribed to the hold of timeless traditions, as most of these originated in the nineteenth or twentieth century and often as products of the British imperial rule over the region. The British established the Gulf emirates' monarchical rule in the nineteenth century through treaties that recognized some prominent families as royal and ruling families (Anderson 1991). After the First World War the British created the Hashemite monarchies of Jordan and Iraq 'from scratch' when carving out new states from the defeated Ottoman Empire—actually importing the Hashemite royal family from what is now the western region of Saudi Arabia. In contrast, the kingdom of Saudi Arabia was founded in 1932 as the culmination of decades of political and military endeavours by a great Arab tribal leader, Ibn Saud.

It is tempting to point to the Saudi and other Arab monarchies' oil wealth as an explanation for their survival. And indeed 'rentier state' theories argue that oil-rich authoritarian regimes survive by exploiting the 'rent' revenues from the oil industry. These revenues allow a regime to provide its subjects with substantial material benefits without the need for heavy taxation and therefore without the need for democratic representation: in other words, 'no representation without taxation'. But as Herb (1999) points out, oil wealth has proved neither a necessary nor sufficient condition for the survival of a ruling monarchy in the Middle East. For example, it has not been necessary for Jordan's monarchy and it was not sufficient for the shah of Iran.

Herb suggests that another explanation for the Arab ruling monarchies' survival is that often they are **dynastic monarchies**. They have very large royal families that have some collective choice in selecting able or reliable monarchs because they do not have to follow the rule of primogeniture (where the eldest son of the monarch automatically succeeds him) characteristic of Western monarchies. And the dynastic monarchies have ensured that any succession rivalries do not tear them apart and leave 'the family' vulnerable to outsiders, such as military officers, seeking to dispossess them of their power. An interesting structural feature of these dynastic monarchies is that the extensive royal families take key posts in the government and have members employed in the ministries and the military—in fact there is a 'profusion' of royals in the military (Herb 1999: 35). This gives the dynastic royal families the sort of extensive control over the state that is usually regarded as a characteristic of one-party rule or some forms of military rule.

Another interesting feature of some Arab monarchies is the emphasis on the subjects' right to present in person their grievances and requests to the monarch. It is a practice that has been trumpeted as 'desert democracy' (see Herb 1999: 41–2) but can hardly compensate for a lack of supposedly democratic parliamentary institutions like those found in the many dictatorships that have claimed an institutionally based democratic legitimacy. In contrast, the non-dynastic monarchies of Jordan and Morocco have not only established such institutions but also have allowed them more genuinely democratic elections than in dictatorships—and indeed have shared power with elected politicians. That both these successful monarchies lack oil but not political skill is another indication of the 'primacy of politics' in the survival of authoritarian regimes.

Monarchical dictators

Like a ruling monarch, a 'monarchical' dictator exercises some degree of personal rule and indeed is usually described as a personal or personalist dictator. Until the democratization of the 1970s–90s, a dictator was typically the leader of a military or party that had seized or misappropriated power (see Boxes 6.1, 6.2, and Box: Military juntas, in the Online Resource Centre). Instead of acting as the representative of the organization that carried or put him into power, this military or party leader had established a **personal** rather than organizational dictatorship. To use the language of 'new institutionalism', the personal dictator had loosened the principal–agent relationship between organization and leader to such a degree that he was actually able to 'shirk' his responsibilities to his organizational principal. Indeed he may have gone even further and reversed the relationship by converting the organization into merely an agent or instrument of his personal rule.

The reversal rather than only loosening of the principal–agent relationship is apparent in the two classic examples of absolutist personal rule by 'totalitarian' leader figures of the 1930s–40s: Hitler and Stalin.[2] Their nearest military equivalent was Generalissimo Franco's reversal of the principal–agent relationship with the army that he led to victory in the Spanish Civil War and then used as his key instrument of not totalitarian but certainly authoritarian personal rule.

However, the degree of personal rule exercised by monarchical dictators has varied just as much as it has among history's multitude of ruling monarchs. Some monarchical dictators have achieved an absolutist personal rule that is not institutionally constrained in any way, such as Hitler's rule over Germany or Mao's rule over China during the Cultural Revolution. At the other extreme there have been some merely personalist dictators, who could readily be removed or blocked by their organization or some other powerful institution in a modern version of King John and his rebellious barons.

A different sort of analogy with monarchy has been drawn by Linz's concept of **sultanism,** which has been applied to many personal dictators (Chehabi and Linz 1998). However, sultanism is concerned not with the degree of personal rule but with its methods and motivation—thus absolutist Hitler is never categorized as a sultanist dictator because he ruled a markedly ideological regime. The sultanist dictator's personal rule is not ideological or institutional and is based on intimidating and buying off key lieutenants or collaborators. The huge amount of financial corruption is a symptom of his **privatization of public power**, which often includes employing his family to wield power and reap the financial rewards of doing so. Such nepotism may well develop into hereditary succession to the position of dictator, as in the case of Haiti's 'Papa Doc' Duvalier being succeeded by his son, 'Baby Doc'. The standard type of sultanist dictatorship has historically been quite rare and found largely among the smaller states of Latin America, but the concept has been extended by Chehabi and Linz (1998) to a wider range of cases by viewing sultanism as a tendency that appears in different varieties of regime, to varying degrees, and in different stages of a personal dictator's career. In that sense it is quite similar to the institutionalist approach of viewing personal rule as a matter of degree that varies with the relationship between principal and agent.

Another analogy with monarchy is political science's long-established concept of **presidential monarchy**, sometimes described instead as a monarchical presidency (Brooker 2000: 147). The term 'presidential monarchy' was coined in the 1960s to describe the tendency of Third World personal dictators to institutionalize their personal rule in the post of president—the republican counterpart to the position of monarch. The personally dictatorial presidency had become prevalent in Africa and would soon become prominent in other parts of the Third World, with General Suharto in Indonesia, General Pinochet in Chile, and General Asad in Syria. It also appeared in the communist world, with Castro in Cuba, Kim Il Sung in North Korea, and Ceausescu in Romania becoming implicitly presidential monarchs 'for life' and even preparing the way for a family member to succeed to the presidential throne when they died or retired. A quite recent example of hereditary succession was Bashir Asad's inheriting the presidency of Syria from his father Hafiz Asad in 2000. The Kims in North Korea could be included as another relatively recent example except that Kim Jong-Il has taken over only his father's party and military positions and has left Kim Il-Sung as the country's 'Eternal President' (data on military can be found in comparative table 15 at the end of this volume).

However, the most important use of the concept of presidential monarchy is when it helps to define a historically unusual but increasingly important type of personal dictatorship: the **populist** form of presidential monarch. As the present global political environment favours democracy, the presidential monarchy is now most likely to come about through an elected president's personal misappropriation of power: the *autogolpe* or 'self-coup' (see Box: Misappropriation of power, in the Online Resource Centre). Unlike in cases of a military or party leader's personal dictatorship, the reversal of the principal–agent relationship involves the **electorate** as principal and the elected president as its agent. By reversing that relationship the president makes the electorate the instrument of his personal rule in the sense of providing him with a claim to democratic legitimacy, which he usually confirms by having himself re-elected through an undemocratic form of election (see below on non-competitive and semi-competitive elections). This is never an absolutist and is often a merely personalist dictatorship but it can be a quite durable form of personal rule, especially if it is backed up by a genuine popularity among the people. Such popularity may well be based upon populist or nationalist policies and propaganda, which are easier to maintain if the country is endowed with natural resources that are internationally in high demand.

COUNTRY PROFILE Chile

Republic of Chile (*República de Chile*)

State formation

Spanish conquerors arrived in the sixteenth century and founded the city of Santiago in 1541. Chile became part of the Spanish Viceroyalty of Peru. In 1810, when the Spanish throne had been toppled by Napoleon, a national junta was formed that proclaimed Chile an autonomous republic within the Spanish monarchy. Warfare continued until the royalists were defeated in 1817. Independence was formally proclaimed in 1818.
Constitution 1980, effective 1981; amended many times.

Form of government

Presidential republic.
Head of state Directly elected President; term of 4 years.
Head of government The President.
Cabinet Ministers appointed by the President.
Administrative subdivisions 13 regions.

Legal system

Derived from Spanish, French, and Austrian law; criminal justice system modelled on the US system.

Legislature

Bicameral National Congress (*Congreso Nacional*).
Lower house
Chamber of Deputies (*Cámara de Diputados*): 120 seats; term of 4 years.
Upper house
Senate (*Senado*): 38 seats; staggered elections (roughly one-half renewed every four years); term of 8 years.

Electoral system (lower house)

Closed party-list majority system.
Formula The majority party is entitled to the two seats of a constituency if it obtains more than two-thirds of the valid votes cast; otherwise the second seat goes to the second-placed party.
Constituencies 60 two-member constituencies.
Barrier clause Not applicable.
Suffrage Universal, 18 years; compulsory.

Direct democracy

Optional constitutional referendum can be called by the President if he/she has rejected a constitutional modification proposed by the Congress but the Congress insists on that modification.

Party system Results of the 2005 legislative elections (Chamber of Deputies):

Electorate	not available	100.0%
Voters	7,207,351	not available

Party		Valid votes	%	Seats
List A	Regionalist Action Party	26,698	0.4	1
	National Alliance of Independents	20,191	0.3	0
	Independents in List A	30,324	0.5	0
	Total List A ('Independent Regional Force')	**77,213**	**1.2**	**1**
List B	Christian Democratic Party	1,370,501	20.8	20
	Party for Democracy	1,017,956	15.4	21
	Socialist Party of Chile	663,561	10.1	15
	Radical Social Democratic Party	233,564	3.5	7
	Independents in List B	131,625	2.0	2
	Total List B ('Democratic Concertation')	**3,417,207**	**51.8**	**65**
List C	Communist Party of Chile	339,547	5.1	0
	Humanist Party	102,842	1.6	0
	Independents in List C	46,229	0.7	0
	Total List C ('Doing More Together')	**488,618**	**7.4**	**0**
List D	Independent Democratic Union	1,475,901	22.4	33
	National Renewal	932,422	14.1	19
	Independents in List D	148,063	2.2	2
	Total List D ('Alliance')	**2,556,386**	**38.7**	**54**
	Independents	62,387	0.9	0
Total		**6,601,811**	**100.0**	**120**

Source: Servicio Electoral.

The populist presidential monarchy has always been much more likely to emerge from democratization than from a consolidated or long-established democracy. Louis Napoleon was able to exploit the politically fluid aftermath of the democratizing 1848 revolution to have himself elected president and then stage an *autogolpe*. Similarly, the global spread of the populist presidential monarchy among democratizing states was a feature of the 1990s.

It is true that the Latin American tradition of *autogolpe* and populist presidential monarch was maintained in the 1990s by Fujimori in Peru and, his opponents might say, by Chávez in Venezuela. But populist presidential monarchy has been most common among the fifteen new states that were created by the disintegration of the Soviet Union.

Several of these countries seem to have evolved a new, more sophisticated version based upon a gradual or 'creeping' self-coup and a democratic disguise that uses seemingly competitive elections. By 2007 this sophisticated version was found in such places as Nazarbaev's Kazakhstan and, his opponents might say, Putin's Russia.

However, any version of populist presidential monarchy is inherently more vulnerable than a military or party leader's personal dictatorship, as was recently confirmed when President Akaev of Kyrgyzstan was overthrown by a popular uprising that was seeking real democracy. For a populist presidential monarch lacks the powerful organizational backing enjoyed by a leader of the military or of a strong political party.

BOX 6.3 The Latin American connection

Introduction

The Latin American contribution to the theory and practice of authoritarian rule includes more than just the concepts and examples of a 'junta' and an 'auto-golpe'. Two other contributions are (1) political scientists' concept of 'bureaucratic authoritarianism' (O'Donnell 1973) and (2) examples of populism's importance as ideology or regime.

Bureaucratic authoritarianism

Socio-economic characteristic

Bureaucratic authoritarianism occurs in societies with high levels of modernization, such as Argentina in the 1960s.

Economic explanation

The economy needs to shift to more intensive, 'deeper' industrialization. This in turn requires painful economic policies and a reduction in consumer demand.

Political implications

Consequently, there is a political need to end democracy and to control social sectors (e.g. labour) by excluding them from power, such as by encapsulating them in government-dependent interest groups.

Structural implications

It is a bureaucratic type of authoritarianism in which the key roles are played by military, civil-service and business-corporation bureaucrats, especially technocrats.

Populism as ideology or regime

Definition

Populism is usually associated with a democratic or dictatorial leader who favours and is favoured by 'the common people', who are also sometimes depicted by populism as the oppressed by the rich and powerful. Populism espouses a demagogic form of social equality that was associated with even the very first populist dictator, Louis Napoleon. His ideological supporters had 'egalitarian aspirations' that included a hatred of the rich, and Louis was depicted as 'the friend of the workers'—a supporter of their right to strike and unionize (McMillan 1991: 33, 142).

Latin American populism/Peronism and other variants

The Peronist populism of 1940s–50s Argentina was created by a husband-and-wife team of demagogic dictatorial rulers, Juan and Evita Peron. They favoured and were favoured by the labour unions and by the *descamisados* (shirtless) lower class. Although Peron was a military man, he was deposed by the Argentinean military in 1955. Similarly, ten years earlier the Brazilian military had deposed Vargas, the populist presidential monarch of Brazil, who had shown a paternalist concern for the poor and for labour unions. Nonetheless, the populist legacy has been very influential, though recent populists are less union-oriented and may espouse, like Chávez, a nationalism that views 'the oppressed people' as oppressed by the 'rich and powerful' US.

These organizations provide an element of political ballast that is even more evident in the case of the two types of organizational dictatorship: military rule and one-party rule. Often there is some overlap with cases of personal dictatorship by an organization's leader, because his personal rule has emerged *from* or *with* the rule of the military or party organization that he leads and may wholly overshadow the organization. But even these marginal cases are normally described in terms of the leader's organization—such as a 'military' or a 'fascist' regime—as well as in terms of the leader's personal rule. For any personal ruler retains some of the characteristics of his organization, particularly its form of rule or its ideological/policy orientation.

Military rule

Although the organizational dictatorship can be viewed as a single category, there are so many differences *within* as well as between the military and party versions of organizational dictatorship that they are better viewed as separate categories with their own types or subtypes. The **military dictatorship** is a very obvious case of rule by a 'distinctive' organization, which in this case has its own uniforms, barracks, career structure, and even legal system. In one sense it is surprising that there are not many more military dictatorships, considering Mao's famous aphorism that 'power grows out of the barrel of a gun' and the classic essay question: 'why doesn't the military rule every country?' There was a time in the 1970s when it appeared that the military was well on the way to ruling if not every country in the world at least every country in the Third World. For as Nordlinger (1977: 6) pointed out, during the previous thirty years the military had intervened in more than two-thirds of these countries and was exerting some form of rule over a third of them.

But the global wave of democratization that began in the mid-1970s seemed to put an end to military intervention in politics—the recent coup in Thailand appears a throwback to another age. Furthermore, military rule has always seemed to be a surprisingly weak and unstable form of regime, with an average lifespan of several *years* rather than decades (Nordlinger 1977: 139). Indeed militaries' tendency to lack either the intention or the determination to hold on to power is perhaps the most striking difference between the military and any political party that has established an organizational dictatorship.

Another illustration of the distinctiveness of the military as a ruling organization is that there are several different structural forms of military rule. As Finer (1976) pointed out, military rule has appeared in several different shapes and sizes, such as (1) the *open form* of military rule and (2) the *disguised forms* of military rule: (*a*) civilianized rule or (*b*) indirect rule through a civilian government.

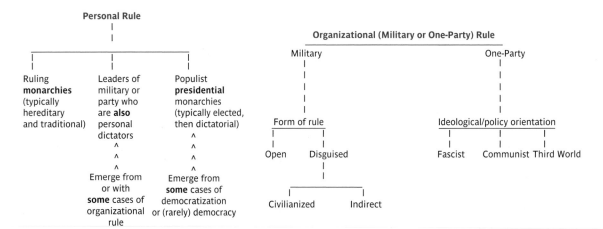

Fig. 6.1 Types of authoritarian regime

Open military rule

The military regime in Burma (Myanmar) is the most widely known and most durable contemporary example of the open-rule subspecies of military dictatorship. The Burmese military has continued to remain 'temporarily' in power for nearly twenty years, refusing to recognize the landslide victory that Suu Kyi's party won in the military-supervised 1990 elections. As in other examples of open rule by the military, its 1988 seizure of power resulted in military officers openly taking over the governing of the country. They established a junta that has acted as the country's *de facto* supreme government (see Box: Military juntas, in the Online Resource Centre) and they appointed themselves to key positions in the formal government, the Cabinet of Ministers. However, other examples of open military rule have *not* established juntas and have been content with military officers taking over the key positions in the government, such as president or prime minister. In these cases the military's senior commander may have ambitions to become a personal ruler and does not want to be constrained by a junta, which can become a highly institutionalized means of representing the military and its organizational dictatorship. On the other hand, establishing a junta is no guarantee of preventing some degree of personal rule, as the Chilean military discovered in the case of General Pinochet during his 1973–89 tenure as president of Chile.

Disguised military rule (civilianized or indirect rule)

The military's rule has been disguised either by civilianizing the regime or by ruling indirectly through behind-the-scenes influence over a civilian government.[3] The civilianization of a military dictatorship involves a very public and symbolic ending of such obvious features of military rule as the junta and the holding of the presidency or other government posts by military officers. However, the ending of the latter usually involves no more than the holder of the office retiring/resigning from the military rather than actually being replaced by a civilian.

Civilianization has usually taken the form of supposed democratization through semi-competitive elections to the legislature and/or presidency. But occasionally the civilianization has taken the form of a supposed shift from military rule to one-party rule, as occurred in Burma in the 1970s with the highly publicized shift to rule by the Burma Socialist Programme Party (BSPP). Thanks to the incompetence of the ex-officers who ran the BSPP, though, the military eventually ended up in the surreal situation of having to stage a coup against its own, civilianized regime. The coup of 1988 replaced this supposedly one-party rule with a caretaker military regime supposedly aimed at bringing about democratic elections and a return to the democracy the country had enjoyed in the 1950s. In reality the military probably thought the elections would be won by a renamed version of its BSPP and therefore would result in an era of indirect military rule.

The military's indirect rule disguises its dictatorship by controlling a civilian government from behind the scenes or, to continue with the metaphors, as a backseat driver or a puppet-master pulling the strings. As Finer pointed out, indirect rule can take the form of a continuous control of the government or, more commonly, of exerting control only intermittently and over a limited range of policies, such as military budgets and national-security policy (Finer 1976: 151–7). An important recent example was the Pakistani army's influence in the 1990s over its civilian government's policy towards the Taliban movement in Afghanistan.

One-party rule

The other type of organizational dictatorship, one-party rule, has not been as common as military rule but has produced more long-lasting dictatorships. After their seizure *or* misappropriation of power (see Box 6.2 and Box: Military Juntas, in the Online Resource Centre) dictatorial parties set up one of the various structural forms of one-party state, such as (1) the openly and literally *one*-party state in which all other parties are banned (in law or in practice) and (2) the disguised and effectively one-party state in which all other parties are (*a*) merely puppet parties or (*b*) prevented from competing properly against the official party (on single-party systems see Chapter 13). These differences between various structural forms of one-party state may seem similar to the differences between the open and disguised varieties of military dictatorship but the latter are forms of *rule* rather than simply forms of monopoly for a party that may or may *not* be ruling. For one-party states have been set up not only by dictatorial parties or their leaders but also by:

- Some military leaders who have become personal rulers, as in the case of General Hafiz Asad and the Syrian Baath party.
- Some military dictatorships, as in the case of the Burmese regime's BSPP civilianization described above.
- A few ruling monarchies, such as the shah of Iran's experiment with a one-party state a few years before he was overthrown by the Islamic Revolution.

Although the result in each case was the creation of a one-party state, the party was merely an instrument of what continued to be authoritarian rule by a military dictator, a military organization, or a hereditary monarch. It is true that a similar situation occurs when a ruling party leader becomes an absolutist dictator and converts his party into merely an instrument of his personal rule. But at least the personal dictatorship has emerged *from* or *with* rule by the party, and the dictator continues to display some of the characteristic features of his party—particularly, its ideological and/or policy orientation.

In that sense he also 'belongs to' the subtype of one-party rule that his party 'belongs to', as the three main sub-types are distinguished by their ideological/policy orientation. The fascist subtype has long been extinct, was very rare—Fascist Italy and Nazi Germany were the only examples—and involved very marginal cases in terms of being overshadowed by an absolutist personal ruler (see Box 6.5). The two other subtypes are the communist regimes and a virtually residual category that will be termed simply the 'Third World' sub-type.

Communist

The communist regime is historically the most important as well as most numerous sub-type. It produced one of the twentieth century's super-powers, the now defunct Soviet Union, and seems set to produce another super-power in the twenty-first century if China maintains its rate of economic progress—and its communist one-party rule. At their numerical peak in the 1980s there were nearly two dozen regimes that espoused the basic communist ideology of Marxism-Leninism (Holmes 1986: viii). But about a third of these regimes were actually military men's personal dictatorships and/or using Marxism-Leninism as only an ideological façade and symbolic claim to legitimacy. Even amongst the core examples of communist regime there were some marginal cases in terms of personal rule by the party leader overshadowing the communist party, such as with Castro in Cuba, Ceausescu in Romania, and Kim Il-Sung in North Korea. There were less than a dozen 'true' cases of communist organizational dictatorship and by 2000 only three still survived—China, Vietnam, and Laos.

Third World

This subtype is typified by the series of about a dozen 'African one-party states' that emerged from the decolonization of the British and French Empires in Africa in the 1950s–1960s. Each dictatorship's ruling party had won elections during the decolonization period and therefore had been the beneficiary of the colonial ruler's handover of power, soon misappropriating this power and establishing one-party rule. A form of 'elections' was retained and it was very much an exception when in 1965 President Nkrumah of Ghana could not be bothered going through the ritual of uncontested parliamentary elections and declared that all the Convention People's Party candidates should be considered duly elected.

However, African one-party states were soon either overthrown by military coups or converted into the presidential monarchy form of personal rule by their party leaders. The majority of these personal dictatorships survived for a generation before being removed by the wave of democratization that swept through Africa in the 1990s. Although it is true that the personal rule of President Mugabe of Zimbabwe has continued to survive, he came to power in the 1980s when Rhodesia/Zimbabwe was belatedly decolonized after decades of white-minority rule, and Mugabe had established a more sophisticated version of the traditional African one-party state.

There have also been some cases of Third World one-party rule outside Africa. Perhaps the best-known case is Baathist rule in Iraq, even though the Baathist one-party state was created by a military dictator and then became the basis for a civilian party administrator, Saddam Hussein, to make a Stalin-like bid for the succession and personal rule. In Latin America, several leftist or populist examples appeared at times after the Second World War, such as the Party of Institutionalized Revolution (PRI) in Mexico, the National Revolutionary Movement (MNR) in Bolivia, and the Sandinistas in Nicaragua. Not all succumbed to personal rule by their party leaders, and indeed during its 1940s–90s rule the Mexican PRI institutionalized a unique system of installing temporary presidential monarchs, with each president being allowed a degree of personal rule but only for a single six-year term of office.

KEY POINTS

❑ A ruling monarch is a royal dictator but a reigning monarch is a constitutional head of state.

❑ Dictatorship by an organization, such as the military or a party, is often transformed into personal rule by the organization's leader.

❑ Dictatorship can result from a military or revolutionary seizure of power or from a misappropriation of power by an elected party or individual.

Why do they rule?

Authoritarian regimes always claim that they exercise a **legitimate authority**. When they ask themselves the rhetorical question 'why do we rule?' they always have an answer ready, no matter how spurious or self-serving, that proclaims their right to rule and therefore the duty or moral obligation of the ruled to obey. From this perspective the ruled also can have no cause for complaint if their obedience is enforced by the regime's control mechanisms (see below on control).

Religious and ideological claims to legitimacy

Religion

The religious claims to legitimate authority have historically been the most common and are also the most interesting, if only in their intellectual ingenuity. Although religious claims to legitimacy became rare during the twentieth century, they had been associated with monarchies for more than a thousand years, as in the European monarchs' coronation anointing and their claims to rule by 'the grace of God' or 'the divine right of kings'.

The religious claim to legitimacy can still be seen in contemporary ruling monarchies, perhaps most obviously in the case of the Saudi monarchy's alliance with the Islamic Wahhabi movement (Anderson 1991). And religious claims to legitimacy re-emerged in a new guise with the 1978–79 revolution that overthrew the shah of Iran and established a self-proclaimed Islamic Republic (Brooker 1997: ch. 9). The new constitution included several religious elements, such as a Council of Guardians whose role has included (1) vetoing any of the elected parliament's proposed legislation that is not in accord with Islamic law and (2) vetting the Islamic qualifications of candidates for elected public office—a responsibility which the guardians have carried out in a conservative manner that has restricted the voters' choice of candidates. Another religious element in the new constitution was the novel and unique public office of supreme (religious) judge and leader of the revolution, which constitutionally outranked the elected president of the republic. It had been designed for the religious leader of the 1978–79 revolution, Ayatollah Khomeini, and is often described in the West as the post of spiritual leader. After Khomeini's death in 1989, the post and its spiritual responsibilities were transferred to another politically active member of the Shiite clergy in what appears to be another lifetime appointment.

Ideology

During the twentieth century, claims to legitimacy based on ideology virtually replaced claims based on religion. An ideology is similar to a religion in holding certain things to be sacred but is more concerned with 'this worldly' than 'other worldly' matters and with ideas, goals, and principles rather than rituals and symbols. Furthermore, an ideology usually lacks the social presence and influence of such long-established religions as Christianity or Islam, which also have a network of churches and mosques staffed by professional clergy who are expert in maintaining and propagating the religion. If an ideology is to be as effective as these religions in providing a basis for an authoritarian regime's legitimacy, the ideology will have to be given a similar social presence and influence by 'its' regime—through use of the mass media, the education system, and mass-mobilizing organizations, such as the regime's official party, youth movement, and labour unions.

The investment of time and energy may be quite acceptable to an ideologically driven authoritarian regime that already has a usable ideology and/or political party, as in the case of Hitler's personal dictatorship or the Burmese military dictatorship in its socialist adolescence. But an authoritarian regime that is not ideologically driven and lacks an ideology or party may well baulk at the costs of this investment—and of having ideological concerns influence its policy-making. It may well prefer instead to avoid ideological claims to legitimacy, as the post-1988 Burmese and many other military regimes have done. Another option is to invent a token ideology that provides a symbolic claim to legitimacy, as in the case of such sultanist dictators as the Haitian 'Papa Doc' Duvalier and his token 'black power' ideology of black consciousness and international black solidarity.

The ideological diversity of authoritarian regimes therefore includes not only the content of their ideologies but also the fact that many of these ideologies are not taken seriously and that many military regimes have never bothered with even a token ideology. Furthermore, when a claim to legitimate authority has been based on ideology, it may take one or more of three different forms. There have been ideological claims to legitimacy in:

- The personal sense of leaders claiming a prophetic legitimacy as ideologists.
- The organizational sense of parties or militaries claiming an ideological right to rule.
- The visionary or programmatic sense of a regime claiming that the goals and principles enshrined in its ideology give it a right to rule.[4]

Overlapping among the visionary, organizational, and personal forms of ideological claim to legitimacy has most commonly occurred when a communist personal dictator, such as Kim Jong Il of North Korea, has presented a prophetic new interpretation of communism's basic Marxism-Leninism—an ideology that provides both organizational and visionary forms of ideological legitimacy (see Box 6.4).

BOX 6.4 Communist ideological vision and Chinese economic practice

Communist ideology

The communist ideology has provided the most widely used **visionary** or programmatic form of legitimacy. It views rapid economic growth as an ideological, sacred goal because it will produce the material abundance required for the envisioned shift to a fully communist, classless society.

Stalin's influence

After Stalin's first Five Year Plan, the orthodox view of the transitional socialism stage leading to full communism was of a state-planned/owned economy with an emphasis on heavy industry and only a secondary role for light industry and agriculture.

The new pragmatism

In the 1980s the communist rulers of China produced a pragmatic reinterpretation of the communist economic approach. Their new economic doctrine, 'Socialism with Chinese Characteristics', argued that capitalist economic methods were a more effective way of attaining the rapid economic growth required in the socialist stage of

BOX 6.4 (continued)

progress towards full communism. There was a shift to an increasingly market economy with an increasing amount of private enterprise and private ownership (though land could only be leased). The economic emphasis shifted away from heavy industry and towards first agriculture and then increasingly the consumer and export sectors of the economy.

A long transition to full communism?

Any notion of a specifically 'Chinese way' was abandoned in 1987 with the new theory of a 'primary' stage of socialism. The main medium-term goal was to raise living standards and develop productive forces—through capitalist methods. But five years later the government predicted that China would remain in this primary, capitalist-like stage of socialism for a hundred years!

The communist ideology's organizational claim to legitimacy, Lenin's theory of the vanguard party, has been the basis of the most widely used ideological claim to legitimacy. After his 'vanguard party of the proletariat' (working class) had consolidated its revolutionary seizure of power, Lenin declared that it should lead the proletariat not only *to* revolution but also *after* a revolution. All the many communist regimes that arose during the twentieth century adopted his ideological justification of one-party rule as part of their commitment to Marxism-Leninism. Furthermore, several non-communist parties and regimes combined the Leninist doctrine of party leadership with *non*-Marxist socialist and/or nationalist doctrines, as in the case of the Baathist parties in Syria and Iraq.

In the 1960s a non-Leninist ideological justification for one-party rule appeared with the emergence of a cohort of African one-party states. There were various strands to their one-party ideology, such as an appeal to African traditions of consensual democracy and an attack on multi-party democracy's tendency to aggravate ethnic and tribal differences (Brooker 2000: 110). But the ideology's strong 'local appeal' also reduced its export potential to other parts of the Third World, and even within Africa it came to be overshadowed by Marxism-Leninism in the 1970s–80s.

There has been no equivalent of Leninism among the rare attempts to justify military rule ideologically. After the 1952 military coup against Egypt's ruling monarchy, Colonel Nasser claimed in somewhat Leninist fashion that the Egyptian military was acting as the temporary and transitional 'vanguard of the revolution'.[5] But Nasser's ideological justification of military rule was not espoused by other countries' coup-makers, except by the Nasser-emulating

Colonel Gadhafi when he overthrew Libya's ruling monarchy in 1969. An even less influential military equivalent of Leninism was the Indonesian military's 1960s–90s 'dual function' ideology that the army has a permanent political-social as well as military function. In general militaries have been wary of ideology and have preferred to express an 'ideological' commitment only to introducing or restoring democracy. Many non-military dictatorships, too, have presented 'democratic' claims to legitimacy in an implicit acknowledgement of that change in the world's political culture that first became evident as long ago as the American and French Revolutions—and whose influence can be seen in such seemingly unrelated areas as the ideological attractiveness of populism.

'Democratic' claims to legitimacy

Although many dictatorships have not claimed ideological legitimacy, since the time of Napoleon Bonaparte's plebiscites most of them have claimed a form of democratic legitimacy. Sometimes it has taken the ideological form of claiming to be a special or superior type of democracy, as in the communist regime's claims to be a 'proletarian democracy', the African one-party state's claim to be an 'African democracy', and the fascist regimes' claim to be an 'authoritative democracy' or a 'German democracy'. But always the claim to democratic legitimacy has additionally or alternatively taken an institutional form. There has been a claim **either to be employing democratic institutions,** such as an elected parliament or presidency, **or to be preparing the country for elections to democratic institutions** (having staged a coup to overthrow the country's undemocratic, corrupt or incompetent government). Even the fascist regimes retained revamped versions of their countries' parliaments, whether to rubberstamp legislation or just to provide a suitably significant audience for an important speech. And the many military dictatorships that have not employed democratic institutions have been quick to assure international and domestic audiences that military rule is only temporary and is preparing the way, such as by drafting a new constitution, for the successful (re)introduction of democracy.

Other dictatorships have introduced a new constitution or constitutional amendment in order to claim some legal legitimacy for their rule and their use of supposedly democratic institutions. In some cases there have even been constitutional provisions that legalize the official party's rule or monopoly, such as the recognition in the Soviet Union's 1936 and 1977 Constitutions of the leading role of the Communist Party. The other function of a new constitution or equivalent laws is to provide a claim to legal legitimacy for the dictatorship's state institutions and particularly its supposedly democratic institutions, such as an elected parliament or presidency.

But the dictatorship's claims that these parliamentary and presidential institutions in turn provide democratic legitimacy are undermined by a crucial 'detail': the elections for these public offices are not democratically competitive but only semi-competitive or even non-competitive. Although they have a modern democracy's universal suffrage, the right to vote is devalued by the refusal to allow competition for that vote—the 'people's choice' is merely a pretence at choice or simply no choice at all. Non-competitive elections, sometimes described as plebiscitary or one-candidate elections, give voters no choice between candidates or lists of candidates; the voters' only 'choice' is one of approving or rejecting the official candidate or (in the case of proportional representation elections) the official list of candidates. Some communist regimes have had a 'multi-party' official list drawn up by an electoral alliance or coalition composed of the regime's official party and one or more puppet parties. A few communist regimes and African one-party states have even allowed voters some 'choice' between official candidates, but of course any competition between them was a case of competing to be reliable supporters of the regime.

Semi-competitive elections are preferred by dictatorships seeking a 'serious', credible democratic disguise rather than resorting to non-competitive elections and somewhat defensive ideological claims to be a special or superior type of democracy. These elections involve some democratic competition between the official party and one or more other parties. Each party runs a separate and competing candidate or list of candidates. And the non-official parties have some autonomy, unlike the tightly controlled puppet parties seen in the 'multi-party' version of non-competitive elections. But the elections are only semi-competitive; the dictatorship ensures that its official party will win. The most blatantly unfair but effective method of ensuring that the official party wins elections is simply to rig the vote, while perhaps the most subtle but least reliable method is using the regime-controlled (through state ownership or other forms of control) media to provide a biased coverage of the elections and the country's 'democratic' politics.

In the 1990s a more sophisticated form of semi-competitive elections evolved in Kazakhstan and a few of the other new states created by the disintegration of the Soviet Union. It involves the use of two or more semi-official parties that compete against each other for parliamentary seats while remaining united in their support for the semi-competitively elected but 'above parties' populist presidential monarch. Any real opposition parties are dealt with by the usual methods of ensuring that non-official parties do not enjoy electoral success.

KEY POINTS

- ❏ Authoritarian regimes always claim they have a right to rule, have legitimate authority.
- ❏ Dictatorships always claim to be some form of democracy or to be preparing the way for democracy.
- ❏ Holding elections can be a sign of shrewd dictatorship rather than real democracy: it all depends on the type of elections.

How do they rule?

This section deals with the structure and processes of rule (control and policies) in totalitarian and authoritarian regimes.

Totalitarianism and authoritarianism

Totalitarianism

Totalitarianism is the most extreme way of dictatorship—and few authoritarian regimes have seriously attempted it. The term totalitarian was first popularized in the 1920s–30s, when Mussolini described the fascist state as totalitarian in the sense of 'everything in the State, nothing outside of the State, nothing against the State' (see Brooker 2000: 8). However, when the term was adopted by political scientists after the Second World War, they applied it not only to the now defunct fascist regimes but also to Stalin's communist regime in the Soviet Union. Occasionally, too, it would be applied to the new communist regimes that had emerged in China, North Korea, and Eastern Europe, though China's Chairman Mao had not yet implemented the 1958 Great Leap Forward and 1966 Cultural Revolution that would prove he was one of the most ideologically driven personal rulers.

The first generation of political science's theorists of totalitarianism, notably Arendt, Friedrich, and Brzezinski, emphasized that Hitler's and Stalin's regimes had created a very novel and ambitious type of dictatorship (Brooker 2000: ch. 1). For it sought to transform human nature through a 'totalitarian' organization of all aspects of life and through an official ideology that not only justified and guided this transformation of human nature but also provided a psychological means of carrying it out. The ideology's internal control of 'hearts and minds' would be assisted by external controls implemented by the regime's party and other organizations, especially the 'terror' inflicted by the secret police.

But the first-generation theorists did not emphasize the role of ideological indoctrination—through the mass media, education system, official party and various mass-mobilizing organizations—as much as might have been expected of theories that were highlighting the totalitarian regime's control of thought as well as action.[6] Perhaps their lack of emphasis on the regimes' ideological indoctrination was due to the fact that neither the theorists nor the regimes were part of the television era. Orwell's fictional *1984* vision of thought control through (two-way) 'telescreens' was science fiction and would not become even technologically feasible for decades. The totalitarian regimes in practice seemed to have relied more on social or organizational rather than technological means of indoctrination, and in fact it is the recent versions of democratically disguised dictatorship by populist presidential monarchs that have been most dependent on television for 'indoctrination'—using biased news programmes and other television items to sway voters in semi-competitive elections.

Instead of emphasizing totalitarian regimes' efforts at indoctrination, the theorists of totalitarianism tended to focus on the role of ideologically inspired leadership, such as the Hitler or Stalin leader figure who prophetically interprets and is driven by the ideology. But some first-generation and all second-generation theorists of totalitarianism had to reappraise the 'leader' factor and other aspects of the concept when the post-Stalin leadership in the Soviet Union not only eased repression and indoctrination but also criticized Stalin's personal rule or 'cult of personality'.

Authoritarianism

The difference between the totalitarian way of ruling and dictatorships' normal ways was highlighted by a sophisticated concept of authoritarianism developed by Linz more than forty years ago (Linz 1970). He described four defining elements or features of authoritarianism that delineated something much less controlling and less extreme than totalitarianism:

- The presence of some limited political pluralism.
- The absence of an ideology that is elaborate and/or used to guide the regime.
- The absence of intensive or extensive political mobilization.
- A predictably limited rather than arbitrary or discretionary leadership by a small group or an individual (though traditional monarchies were excluded from his concept of authoritarianism).

BOX 6.5 Fascist totalitarian leaders

Fascist Italy

Origins

In 1922 Mussolini led the militaristic counter-revolutionary Fascist party in a weak attempt at a coup, the March on Rome. The king of Italy was 'blackmailed' into appointing Mussolini as his constitutionally legitimate prime minister.

Consolidation

Mussolini took several years to convert what remained of Italy's democracy into a one-party state. He became a powerful head of government and a hierarchical party leader who was able to relegate his Fascist party to being the subordinate assistant of the new 'Fascist State'.

Personal rule

By the 1930s Mussolini was clearly the personal dictator as well as *Duce* (leader) of Italy. For example, his personal propaganda cult had become so prominent that *mussolinismo* seemed to overshadow Fascist ideology and such ideologically inspired innovations as the corporative state economic policy. But he never replaced the king as head of state, and was sacked by him in 1943 when the Allies invaded Italy and seemed certain to win the war.

Nazi Germany

Origins

The Nazi party came to power through a succession of **election** victories in the early 1930s when the country was suffering terribly from the social and economic effects of the Great Depression.

Consolidation

As the Nazis had become the largest party in parliament, the president appointed Hitler to the post of head of government in early 1933. Hitler took only several months to take over the parliament's legislative powers and legally enshrine a one-party state.

Personal rule

Hitler's regime became absolutist in 1934 under his new legal title of *Führer* (leader), which combined the powers and positions of head of state and government. This was accompanied by a personal oath of allegiance from all members of the military as well as from civil servants, police, and even the judiciary. Like Mussolini, he had the power to take his country into an ideologically driven war that would prove to be unwinnable and would bring an end to his regime.

These four features can be found in the great majority of dictatorships: from an African one-party state engaging in extensive political mobilization to a military regime whose junta is seeking to depoliticize a formerly democratic country. In fact Linz suggested that even totalitarian regimes might eventually develop into something that looked more like an authoritarian regime. He later coined the term 'post-totalitarian' to describe this development and to provide more differentiation *within* the very broadly applicable concept of authoritarianism (Linz and Stepan 1996).

Exercising control

Dictatorships have evolved some distinctive control mechanisms to ensure that, even if their claims to legitimacy are not effective, there *will* be obedience to their rule. These control mechanisms are the 'mailed fist within the velvet glove' of indoctrinating propaganda and supposedly democratic institutions. The control is exercised by monitoring and/or enforcing political loyalty and the obedient implementation of the regime's policies.

The most effective control mechanism is a competent political or secret police that uses various sanctions and methods of information-gathering to ensure obedience. Depending upon the regime and the circumstances, the sanctions range from execution or 'disappearance' to merely losing a job or career prospects, while the methods of information-gathering range from the use of torture to informers and electronic surveillance. Totalitarianism is more likely than authoritarianism to involve extreme sanctions and methods but any dictatorship may use extreme measures in a 'peak' period of repression (see Brooker 2000: 112–13). In these periods of extreme repression the political police may be so concerned with *potential* as well as *actual* disloyalty or disobedience that even loyal sectors of the population are 'terrorized' by the repression's scope and apparent arbitrariness.

The military has its own distinctive control mechanisms, notably the junta and the declaration of martial law. By bestowing policing and judicial powers upon the military, martial law creates a powerful mechanism for controlling the society at street and village level. In contrast, the military's junta (see Box: Military juntas, in the Online Resource Centre) acts as a control mechanism at the very highest level—the government of the country. The junta ensures obedience to military rule by counter-balancing the civilian influence upon and *within* the government, where often civilians hold a majority of the cabinet posts, particularly such technical posts as minister of finance or minister of health. A less common way of counter-balancing civilian influence has been to appoint military officers to important posts within the civil service and the regional administration of the country. The military may also use a political party as a means of extending control over state and society, but if a military's party is contributing to a civilianization strategy of democratically disguising military rule, it will be primarily concerned with mobilizing electoral support. Furthermore, often the military and its control mechanisms have been used to establish or strengthen a more personal military dictatorship, as in the case of General Pinochet in Chile or of Franco's use of Spain's military as an instrument of absolutist personal rule.

One-party rule's distinctive control mechanisms have been based on using a party rather than military to control state and society. Since Lenin's time the communist regimes have led the way in seeking strong and extensive party control. The party's Politburo is the equivalent of a junta and acts as the country's *de facto* government, with its decisions being passed on to the state's government, the council of ministers, for implementation.[7] The party also uses its extensive membership in the civil service and the military to ensure that its directives are carried out. Party members monitor policy implementation as well as political loyalty and in some cases party officials actually give 'guidance' to state officials—indeed regional and district party leaders have often been

the *de facto* governors of their areas. The communist party's leaders at all levels have appointment powers, which enables them to veto the appointment of politically unreliable personnel to state posts and also in practice allows them some patronage opportunities.

The Third World examples of one-party rule have seldom adopted the communist practice of strong and extensive party control. Not often has a party committee acted as a junta-like *de facto* government. And usually there has been less extensive party control, such as excluding the military from party membership, and/or a weaker party control that uses the party to monitor but not enforce political loyalty and policy implementation. The Baath parties in Syria and Iraq may appear to have been exceptions to this tendency but in the 1970s they, like several communist parties in other times and places, were converted into instruments of personal rule by their party leaders, respectively, military dictator Hafiz Asad and party boss Saddam Hussein.

Policies and policy-making

Policies

Most of the policies implemented by authoritarian regimes are similar to those of democracies. For example, it is unlikely that the design of a sewerage system or the procedures for ordering office stationery will be very different in a dictatorship than a democracy. It is true that authoritarian regimes in general have intervened in the economy and society more than have democracies, but it does not seem very valid or useful to suggest that therefore intervening in the economy or society is a typically 'authoritarian' rather than 'democratic' policy.

So the key question is whether authoritarian regimes have **distinctive** policies in the sense of social, economic, or foreign policies that one or more of these regimes have implemented but that democracies have avoided or never even considered. Many authoritarian regimes have not had any distinctive policies but at the other extreme there are several notorious one-off examples of distinctiveness: Nazi Germany's anti-Semitic genocide and racist 'living space' imperialism; the famine-producing callous collectivization of the peasantry in Stalin's Soviet

Union; the famine-producing Great Leap Forward in Mao's China; and the de-urbanization of Cambodian society by Pol Pot's communist regime. Aside from these extremes are groups of authoritarian regimes that have shared a distinctive policy.

The most well-known example is the Stalinist communist regimes' distinctive and shared *economic* policy approach, which produced the characteristically 'communist' economic structure: the centrally planned state-owned economy. Stalin's first Five Year Plan created a 'command' rather than market or mixed economy. It was a mixed economy only in the sense of combining a state-owned urban economy of industry and commerce with a state-controlled and collectivized agricultural economy composed of huge farms owned collectively by the peasants that worked them. However, the Stalinist economic structure was abandoned by China and Vietnam in the 1980s in favour of a market economy and some forms of privatization (see Box 6.4) and therefore is no longer characteristic of the few surviving communist regimes.

A well-known example of a distinctive social policy approach shared by some authoritarian regimes is their distinctive sexism. But the sexist approach of many Arab monarchies and the Iranian Islamic Republic is very different from the sexism of the two fascist regimes, which was linked to militarism and, in Nazi Germany, to racist eugenics. Perhaps the most useful conclusion to be drawn about authoritarian regimes' policies therefore is that in general they have been more diverse as well as more extreme and callous than the policies of democracies.

Policy-making

Authoritarian regimes' policy-making differs most from democracies' in not being influenced by the presence of democratic elections. The rulers of authoritarian regimes can afford to be more ideological or corrupt in their policy-making than can politicians whose careers depend upon success at the next elections. For example, if a personal dictator decides that he 'knows best' about economic policy, despite his lack of expertise or experience in this area of policy-making, he can instigate such a disastrous policy as Mao's Great Leap Forward without having to fear the consequences of policy failure.

Nonetheless, even the two classic cases of totalitarian personal rule differed dramatically in *style* and *scope* of policy-making. Stalin was a systematic workaholic who decided a huge range of policies down to the level of routine or even trivial decisions. In contrast, Hitler was a sloppy and lazy administrator who devolved most policy decisions to his trusted subordinates (acting as arbiter when they disagreed among themselves) and dominated policy-making only in the few areas that interested him or forced him to pay attention. But the policy-making style and scope of personal rulers usually lies somewhere between these two extremes. For example, during his thirty-year rule of Syria, President Hafiz Asad was a diligent administrator who took sole charge of national-security policy and internal-order policy but devolved most economic and administrative policy-making to his ministers and bureaucrats.

Differences in the style and scope of policy-making are less obvious among dictatorships that are *not* under personal rule. They tend to be governed by committee in a quite systematic fashion that is comparable to cabinet government in a democracy. In fact the shift to the non-personal, committee rule of 'collective leadership' in the Soviet Union and some other communist regimes in the 1960s–70s led some political scientists to apply models of bureaucratic politics or of 'institutional pluralism' to these regimes' policy-making (Hough 1977: ch. 2). If the party and state officials of state-owned/planned economies were engaging in a discreet form of sectional policy advocacy, it was likely to be even more prominent in dictatorships with mixed economies and their potential for discreet lobbying by an array of private-sector interests.[8] However, the presence of some form of collective leadership did not necessarily mean a resort to typically 'bureaucratic' incremental policy-making—sometimes there has been a surprising amount of radical change and policy experimentation. In particular, China's and Vietnam's economic liberalization in the 1980s saw the central authorities allowing or actually encouraging provincial and local administrators to experiment with innovative policies that, if successful, were used as a model for the whole country.

KEY POINTS

- ❏ Totalitarianism seeks total control, including control of thought, but is a historically rare way of dictatorship.
- ❏ Control mechanisms, such as the political or secret police, ensure obedience by monitoring/enforcing political loyalty and policy implementation.

- ❏ Authoritarian regimes are diverse in their policies and policy-making as well as their ideology and institutions.

Conclusion

The safest way to draw conclusions about authoritarian regimes is to present two differing perspectives: (1) the extinction interpretation and (2) the evolution scenario.

The **extinction interpretation** would concede that authoritarian regimes have shown a great ability to evolve new species and subspecies of dictatorship when the ruling monarchies seemed about to be replaced by democracy. But the extinction interpretation would depict these two centuries of diverse evolutionary responses as being doomed to failure. The authoritarian regimes are political dinosaurs in a world whose political climate is now clearly more advantageous to species of democracy. None of the new species or subspecies of dictatorship has been able to flourish for very long, and they all now seem headed towards extinction. Already the newest variation or subspecies, the more sophisticated versions of populist presidential monarchy, has begun to succumb to popular democratization (as in the Ukraine, Georgia, and Kyrgyzstan) aimed at ending or pre-empting such a regime. And the many cases of personal rule among the older, diehard authoritarian regimes will have problems with succession, as any personal rule that includes hereditary succession seems totally anomalous in the twenty-first century.

The **evolution scenario** adopts a very different historical perspective and different zoological comparisons from those used by the extinction scenario.

There is an obvious historical parallel between the catalysts of the contemporary US 'war on terrorism' and of the First World War—the 11 September 2001 attacks on the US and the assassination of Archduke Ferdinand in Sarajevo on 28 June 1914. The First World War was described by the US president of the time as a war that would make the world safe for democracy. But the Allies' victory was soon followed by an era in which authoritarian regimes actually strengthened their position, and their 'comeback' included the arrival of new types of authoritarian regime, the communist and fascist, that made the world much less safe for democracy.

If 9/11/2001 proves to be similar to 6/28/1914 in leading to a strengthening of the authoritarian regimes, this may take a comparable form to aspects of zoological evolutionary history. Not only have some primeval species, such as the crocodile and the cockroach, survived into the present century but even the dinosaurs avoided complete extinction by evolving into a very different family of species—the birds. They lack the fearsome appearance of a tyrannosaurus rex, and in fact have given us such attractive species as the wise old owl and the beautiful peacock. Similarly, the authoritarian regime may well survive and even flourish, not only because of the durability of its existing species and subspecies but also because the evolution of new species that are well adapted to survive in the new political climate.

World trends

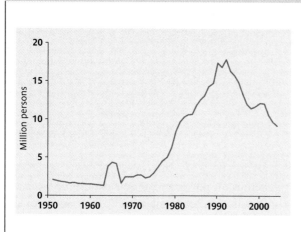

Trend 4 Conflicts: international refugees (1951–2004)

Source: United Nations High Commissioner for Refugees (UNCHR), World Watch.

Questions

1. Why have authoritarian regimes been more diverse and innovative than democracies?
2. Why did democracy take so long to win?
3. Can an authoritarian regime be popular—if so, how?
4. Why are there so many authoritarian regimes in the Middle East?
5. Was Saddam Hussein's dictatorship a case of sultanism, totalitarianism, or something else?
6. Why is the military more willing than a dictatorial political party to relinquish power?
7. How would a dictatorial politician set about misappropriating power?
8. Why is China still categorized as a communist state despite its apparently capitalist economy?
9. How would you know if your country's elections were only semi-competitive?
10. Why have authoritarian regimes been allocated only one chapter in this book?

» Further reading

Brooker, Paul (2000) *Non-Democratic Regimes: Theory, Government and Politics* (Basingstoke: Macmillan).

Chehabi, Houchang E., and Linz, Juan J. (eds.) (1998) *Sultanistic Regimes* (New York: Johns Hopkins University Press).

Herb, Michael (1999) *All in the Family: Absolutism, Revolution, and Democratic Prospects in the Middle Eastern Monarchies* (Albany, NY: State University of New York Press).

Holmes, Leslie (1986) *Politics in the Communist World* (Oxford: Oxford University Press).

Jackson, Robert H., and Rosberg, Carl G. (1982) *Personal Rule in Black Africa: Prince, Autocrat, Prophet, Tyrant* (Berkeley, Calif.: University of California Press).

Linz, Juan J. (2000) *Totalitarian and Authoritarian Regimes* (Boulder: Lynne Rienner).

Web links

www.freedomhouse.org
Website of Freedom House with assessments of global trends in democracy that also highlight cases of dictatorship.

www.amnesty.org
Website of the worldwide movement Amnesty International that campaigns for human rights and therefore also highlights cases of repression.

www.hrw.org
Website of Human Rights Watch that seeks to protect human rights around the world and therefore also highlights cases of repression.

www.wmd.org
Website of World Movement for Democracy that seeks to promote and advance democracy and therefore to help challenge dictatorships and democratize semi-authoritarian systems.

 Visit the Online Resource Centre that accompanies this book for more information:
www.oxfordtextbooks.co.uk/orc/caramani/

SECTION 3

Structures and institutions

7 Legislatures

Amie Kreppel

Chapter contents

Reader's guide

This chapter seeks to improve our understanding of the political roles and powers of legislatures. The first step is to define different types of legislatures on the basis of their primary functions and relationship with the executive branch. With these definitions as a foundation, the analysis then turns to examine the primary roles of legislatures within the political system as a whole, as well as several critical aspects of the internal organizational structures of legislatures. Finally, the relationship between the political power and influence of a legislature and the structure of the broader political and party system are discussed. Throughout the chapter the focus will be on legislatures within modern democratic political systems, although many of the central points apply to all legislatures regardless of context.

Introduction

The role of legislatures within the broader political environment in which they exist is far from universal or straightforward. Different scholars at different times have come to very different conclusions about the relative political power and legislative, or policy influence of legislatures. There are a number of reasons for this. General evaluations of the political power and influence of any type of institution will vary depending on particular cases are studied, the theoretical framework employed, the historical period under examination, and the precise definitions and understandings of 'power' and 'influence' invoked. All of these variables have played some part in the succession of very different understandings of legislatures and their role within the broader political environment.

In this chapter I examine the influence and importance of legislatures across a variety of different 'core' tasks including representing citizens and linking citizens and government, overseeing the executive, and, of course, policy-making. The importance of these tasks to the broader political system, and the variation between legislatures in their performance of them, make the understanding of legislatures a critical component of any attempt to understand politics more generally. In fact, legislatures exist in nearly every country on the planet, and have the potential to play an important political role even in non-democratic systems.[1]

> **KEY POINTS**
>
> ❑ Legislatures are present throughout the world and play a central role in almost all political systems.
> ❑ However, variations in their powers and structures are large.

What is a legislature?

The variety of terms such as 'assembly', 'congress', or 'parliament' that are often used interchangeably with the term 'legislature' increases the uncertainty about the roles and relative powers of legislatures. Clearly not all legislatures are the same or play the same role within their respective political systems. In fact, there are several distinctly different types of legislatures encompassing the full range of roles. Before we can begin to examine the types of legislatures it is necessary to concretely define not only what a legislature is, but also related words like assembly, parliament, and congress.

The problem that arises is that the exact meaning of these terms is not as clear as one might expect. For example, the definitions of assembly, legislature, parliament, and congress provided in dictionaries do not always clearly differentiate between these terms (see Box 7.1). All four are defined as 'a legislative body' or 'a body of persons having the power to legislate' making efforts to clearly distinguish between them difficult. And yet, most would agree that the terms are not interchangeable, and that there are different meanings implied by the use of one rather than the others.

> **BOX 7.1 Definitions**
>
> Assembly: A legislative body; specifically, the lower house of a legislature.
>
> Legislature: A body of persons having the power to legislate; specifically: an organized body having the authority to make laws for a political unit.
>
> Parliament: The supreme legislative body of a usually major political unit that is a continuing institution comprising a series of individual assemblages.
>
> Congress: The supreme legislative body of a nation and especially of a republic.
>
> *Source*: Merriam-Webster online (www.m-w.com).

Of these four terms 'assembly' is the most general. In fact, additional definitions of the word (uncapitalized) refer simply to the coming together of a group of people for some purpose, for example, a school assembly. It is only when we implicitly or explicitly add the qualifier 'political' or 'legislative' that we begin to think of assemblies in the same context as legislatures, parliaments, and congresses. By the same token, parliaments and congresses, generically, can be best understood as specific types of legislatures. This understanding of these four terms creates a hierarchy of institutions from the most general (an assembly) to the most specific (congresses and parliaments) which are understood as types of the mid-level category of 'legislatures' (see Figure: A hierarchy of institutions, in the Online Resource Centre).

Assembly

If we begin with the broadest definition of an assembly as 'a group of persons gathered together, usually for a particular purpose, whether religious, political, educational, or social', we can then designate legislatures as those assemblies for which the 'particular purpose' in question is political and at some level legislative in character (*The American Heritage Dictionary*, 4th edn). This understanding of legislatures is expansive enough to include a wide array of very different institutions, while still clearly distinguishing between legislatures and other types of assemblies organized for religious, educational, or social purposes.

However, precisely because of its inclusiveness, the term 'legislature' is too broad to help us distinguish between different types of legislative institutions. To accomplish this task we must move beyond dictionary definitions and concentrate on the structural characteristics of the political system in which the legislatures are located. Regardless of whether or not a political system can be categorized as democratic, **if there is a legislature in addition to an executive branch the relationship between the two will determine the core characteristics of the legislature.** The central determinative characteristic is the relative **level of interdependence** between the two branches.

Parliaments

In what are generally referred to as parliamentary systems the executive branch is selected from within, and by, the legislature. Furthermore, the executive branch or 'government' is formally responsible to the legislature throughout its tenure.[2] This means that it can at be removed from office any time should

a majority of the legislature oppose it, regardless of the electoral cycle. In turn, removal of the executive by the legislature may be accompanied by early elections in most systems. Because the executive branch is drawn from the legislative branch and there is a high degree of mutual dependence between them, these types of systems are known generically as fused-powers systems.

Legislatures in parliamentary systems are most commonly referred to as 'parliaments', regardless of their formal national title. This moniker reflects not only the type of system in which the legislature resides, but also its central task. The word parliament is derived from the French verb *parler*, to speak.[3] As we shall discover below, the name is well chosen as the institutional and political constraints on parliaments generally focus their activities on debate and discussion.

Congresses

In addition to the parliamentary type of legislature found in parliamentary systems, there is a different type of legislature, which are called 'congresses', within what are popularly referred to as presidential systems. Presidential systems are a type of separation-of-powers system (SoP). Although separation-of-powers systems are most often presidential in character (meaning that the executive consists of a single popularly elected president) this is not a requirement and non-presidential versions do exist (e.g. the European Union). In fact, all that is required is that the legislative and executive branches be selected independently and that neither has the ability to dissolve or remove the other from office (except in the case of incapacity or significant legal wrong-doing). The best-known separation-of-powers system is the US. The fact that the official name of the legislature of the US is 'the Congress' is neither an accident, nor a reason to avoid using the term congress to refer to a type of legislature more generally.

The word 'congress' is derived from the Latin *congressus*, 'a meeting or [hostile] encounter; to contend or engage' (Harper 2001). This is focused on the potentially conflict-ridden interactions between individuals. The use of congress to denote legislatures within separation-of-powers systems in general is justified by the policy-making focus of the primary activities they tend to pursue as well as the increased likelihood of a more conflictual relationship with the executive branch when compared to fused-power systems. Examples of both types of systems can be found in Table 7.1.

These more specific terms provide us with additional information, not only about the legislatures themselves, but also about the type of political system in which they exist (parliamentary/fused-powers systems or presidential/separation-of-powers systems).

Table 7.1 'Parliament' and 'Congress' type legislatures

Country	Lower Chamber	Legislature type	Regime
Argentina	Chamber of Deputies	Congress	SoP
Austria	Fedral Council	Parliament	Fused
Belarus	Chamber of Representatives		Non-democratic
Belgium	House of Representatives	Parliament	Fused
Bhutan	Tsgogdu		Non-democratic
Bolivia	Chamber of Deputies	Congress	SoP
Brazil	Chamber of Deputies	Congress	SoP
Canada	House of Commons	Parliament	Fused
Chad	National Assembly		Non-democratic
Chile	Chamber of Deputies	Congress	SoP
China	National People's Congress		Non-democratic
Colombia	Chamber of Representatives	Congress	SoP
Czech Republic	Chamber of Deputies	Parliament	Fused
Denmark	Folketing	Parliament	Fused
Egypt	People's Assembly		Non-democratic
Finland	Eduskunta	Parliament	Fused*
France	National Assembly	Parliament	Fused*
Germany	Federal Council	Parliament	Fused
Greece	Vouli	Parliament	Fused
Grenada	House of Representatives	Parliament	Fused
Guyana	National Assembly	Parliament	Fused*
India	Lok Sabha	Parliament	Fused

(continued)

Table 7.1 (*continued*)

Iran	Islamic Consultative Assembly		Non-democratic
Israel	Knesset	Parliament	Fused
Italy	Chamber of Deputies	Parliament	Fused
Japan	House of Representatives	Parliament	Fused
Korea, South	Kukhoe	Congress	SoP
Mexico	Chamber of Deputies	Congress	SoP
New Zealand	House of Representatives	Parliament	Fused
Pakistan	National Assembly	Parliament	Fused[a]
Peru	Congress	Congress	SoP
Poland	Sejm	Parliament	Fused*
Romania	Chamber of Deputies	Parliament	Fused*
Russia	State Duma	Parliament	Fused*
St Lucia	House of Assembly	Parliament	Fused
Singapore	Parliament		Non-democratic
Slovakia	National Council	Parliament	Fused
Spain	Congress of Deputies	Parliament	Fused
Switzerland	National Council	Congress	SoP[b]
Syria	People's Assembly		Non-democratic
Taiwan	Legislative Yuan	Congress	SoP
Tanzania	Bunge	Parliamentary	Fused
Turkey	Grand National Assembly	Parliamentary	Fused
United Kingdom	House of Commons	Parliament	Fused
United States	House of Representatives	Congress	SoP*
Venezuela	Chamber of Deputies	Congress	SoP

* These countries all have directly elected presidents. However, only France and Russia have semi-presidential systems. In Poland (especially before 1997 constitution) the president has a legislative role and at times has been quite politically active. In Guyana the president is the head of the electoral list that receives the most votes and, thus is directly elected, but not independently from the legislature.

[a] Although indirectly elected and historically primarily a figurehead, the current president of Pakistan, General Pervez Musharraf, wields significant political authority, dominating the legislative process.

[b] The executive in Switzerland is unique in that it is collegial (seven members) and indirectly elected by the legislature but it is not responsible to the legislature, nor can it dissolve the legislature. Thus, the two branches are independent.

Source: Kurian *et al.* (1998).

The role of legislatures

Legislatures serve a myriad of roles within a political system. Although the precise activities and roles they perform will vary significantly according to the broader political environment in which they exist, their activities can be loosely organized into three categories: (1) linkage and representation, (2) oversight and control, and (3) policy-making.

When fulfilling the first task legislatures serve as the 'agents' of the citizens they represent and are expected to act in their interests. In the second case legislatures become the 'principals' and are tasked with the monitoring and collective oversight of the executive branch (including the bureaucracy). Finally, when pursing the third type of activity legislatures engage in the act of legislating or policy-making. They may be either acting as agent, principal, or both when legislating, but the task is specifically focused on the policy process. What differentiates between legislatures is not which of these roles they play, but rather the degree to which their activities emphasize some roles over others.

In general an 'agent' is an actor who performs a set of activities and functions on behalf of someone else (the principal). The standard 'principal–agent problem' often studied in economics revolves around the fact that agents are likely to have both incentives and opportunities to shirk their duties and still receive the benefits associated with having done them. Thus, the principal has an incentive to devise some form of oversight to ensure that the agent is in fact performing their tasks in the manner expected.

In the political realm legislatures serve as both agents and principals in relation to the electorate and the executive branch respectively. And principals within the political system can have a variety of tools at their disposal to minimize the amount of agent shirking that actually occurs. Thus, the electorate (citizens) must act to control the legislature and the legislature must actively seek to control the executive branch.

Legislature as agent: linkage, representation, and legitimation

Linkage

Linking citizens to the government is one of the most fundamental tasks that legislatures perform within any political system. Even when the legislature is weak in terms of its other roles, it is almost always able to serve 'as an intermediary between the constituency and the central government' (Olson 1980: 135). In this context, legislatures act as a conduit of information allowing local-level demands to be heard by the central government and the policies and actions of the central government to be explained to citizens. The ability of legislatures to serve as **effective** tools of communication as well as the **relative importance** of this role varies.

The degree to which a legislature is able to serve as an effective means of communication between citizen and government depends critically on the level of regularized interaction between the members of the legislature and their constituencies, as well as the type and frequency of opportunities to convey information to the executive branch. In general, individual legislators will spend more time and be more actively engaged with their constituents when they are elected in single-member districts as opposed to multi-member districts (see Chapter 10). This is because they are the sole representative of the citizens in their constituency (the citizens within their district) at the national level.

Single-member districts also tend to be smaller geographically, and are frequently more homogeneous as a result. These characteristics make the representative's task easier as it reduces the diversity of interests that she must represent. If there is a high level of heterogeneity within a given district the likelihood that there will be conflicting preferences between groups increases, as does the probability that the legislator will be forced to support the preferences of one group of citizens over the others. Larger constituencies also reduce the ability of the legislator to form personal connections with the citizens, further reducing her ability to serve as an effective link between them and the central government.

The linkage role of the legislature will be more important in political systems in which citizens do not have the opportunity to communicate their preferences and satisfaction directly to the executive branch through the electoral process. Thus, in parliamentary systems (in which the executive branch is indirectly elected), as well as in most non-democratic regimes, the linkage function of the parliament type legislature is likely to be more important because it may be the only stable mechanism of communication between citizens and the central government.

Representation

In addition to providing a link between citizens and government, the individual members of a legislature are generally also expected to represent their constituents and work to protect their interests. In other words legislators are responsible for advocating for their constituents in their stead, ensuring that the opinions, perspectives, and values of citizens are present in the policy-making process (Pitkin 1967).

There are, however, different interpretations of the representative responsibility of legislators depending on whether they are understood to be **delegates** or **trustees**. In the former case members of legislatures are expected to act as mechanistic agents of their constituents, unquestioningly carrying messages and initiatives from them to the central government (with the goal of influencing policy outcomes in most cases). In contrast, if members of the legislature are viewed as trustees, the expectation is that they will serve as a more active interpreter of their constituents' interests and incorporate the needs of the country as a whole, as well as their own moral and intellectual,

judgement, when acting within the political, and especially policy, realm.

The large number of members within most legislatures (as compared to the executive branch) and the relatively small scale of their electoral districts make the effective representation of a variety of different minority communities possible. In contrast, smaller minority groups may have a more difficult time accessing or influencing the executive branch as a result of the latter's need to represent the broader interests of the country as a whole.[4]

Debating

This plural characteristic of legislatures not only increases their representative capacity, it also enables them to serve as public forums of debate, in which diverse opinions and opposing views can directly engage with one another, with the goal of influencing public opinion and policy outcomes. Legislatures within democratic political systems are likely to allow a broader spectrum of views to be expressed and debated openly (including those of the opposition) than most non-democratic systems. However, the debate function will be a more central and important activity in those legislatures with limited direct control over the policy-making process, which includes most non-democratic systems. This is because public debate within the legislature has the capacity to affect public opinion, thus providing legislators with an opportunity to potentially influence policy-making indirectly by increasing public awareness of critical issues.

In addition, by fostering debate and discussion legislatures can serve as important tools of compromise between opposing groups and interests within the society. As a result, the capacity of a legislature to effectively serve as a public forum of debate will be more important in heterogeneous societies in which there are significant policy-related conflicts between groups. Even when compromises are not achieved, the opportunity for minority or oppositional groups to openly and publicly express their views within the legislature may serve to limit conflict to the political realm, avoiding the much more detrimental effects of social unrest and instability.

Legitimation

Ultimately, the ability of a legislature to create links between citizens and government by providing adequate representation to critical groups and minority interests and fostering public debate will determine both its institutional legitimacy and its ability to provide legitimacy for the political system as a whole. The ability to mobilize public support for the government as a whole is an important aspect of a legislature's performance. In fact, even if legislatures 'are not independently active in the development of law, and even if they do not extensively supervise the executive branch, they can still help obtain the populace's support for the government and its policies' (Olson 1980: 13). This legitimizing function of legislatures is fundamentally a reflection of their linkage and representational activities, and depends critically on the successful achievement of these tasks (Mezey 1979).

Legislature as principal: control and oversight

Control

The ability of the governed to control the government is one of the foundational tenets of representative democracy. The primary tool used to achieve this goal is regularly scheduled free and fair elections. The type of executive oversight and control practised by the legislature is directly linked to the nature of the relationship between voters and the executive branch *and* between the legislature and the executive branch. The existence of an indirect mechanism of voter control over the executive branch in parliamentary systems in no way negates the democratic character of the system as a whole. It does, however, highlight the importance of the role of the legislature as a 'principal' overseeing the executive, in addition to its role as an agent and representative of citizens.

In effect, democratic political systems have two different 'principals' monitoring the executive branch, each of which has a different set of tasks. Voters directly or indirectly select the executive during elections. Between elections voters must monitor the actions of the executive to ensure that they have enough information to make future electoral decisions. However, in most cases citizens lack sufficient time, access, and information, as well as the technical skills needed, to effectively oversee the details of the daily political activity of the executive branch (including those agencies tasked with implementing policies within the executive branch). It is the task of the legislature to fill this lacuna.

Here, however, there is a greater degree of difference between presidential/separation-of-powers and parliamentary/fused-powers political systems.

1. The control and oversight functions of congress type legislatures in separation-of powers-systems tend to be more limited in scope than those in fused-powers systems, though they are still significant. The critical difference is the extent to which policy initiatives are a legitimate subject of control and oversight by the legislature. In separation-of-powers systems the policy agenda of the executive branch is not subject of legislative control or oversight. The executive cannot be removed from office because a majority in the legislature disapproves of its policy priorities. In fact, the legislature's ability to remove an executive from office in separation-of-powers systems is usually extremely limited, being restricted to cases of illegal activity and/or physical or mental incapacity. This type of formal **impeachment** of the executive (usually a president) is rare and usually a relatively complex legal process.

2. In contrast, parliament-type legislatures in fused-powers systems are explicitly tasked with policy-related control and oversight of the executive branch. Executives are responsible to the legislature for their policy agenda and may be removed from office if their policy goals are deemed unacceptable by a majority in the legislature. Removal of the executive in fused-powers systems is accomplished through a **motion of censure** or a **vote of no confidence**. This does not imply any legal wrong-doing. As a result, in most fused-powers systems the removal of the sitting executive by the legislature does not result in a crisis or systemic instability, although frequent recourse to censure of the executive can eventually lead to broader systemic problems.[5]

The significant difference between fused-powers and separation-of-powers systems in the policy-related control activities of legislatures is a function of the broader political system. More specifically, it is a result of the character of the legislative—executive relationship. In separation-of-powers systems voters select their legislature and executive independently from one another. In fused-powers systems voters cast votes only for the legislative branch. Selection of the executive occurs indirectly through the legislature. This difference is significant for the policy-related control functions of legislatures for two reasons.

First, the independent election of the executive and legislative branches makes it far more likely that there will be **substantial differences in their respective ideological or partisan identities**. For example, in the US the election of a president from one party and a congressional majority from the other is a relatively common occurrence (**divided government**). In fused-powers systems, however, it is impossible for the majority in the parliament and the executive branch to be from wholly distinct and opposing parties or coalitions. All governments in fused-powers systems *must* have the implicit or explicit support of a majority of the legislature to remain in office. The members of the executive branch (prime minister or equivalent and the cabinet ministers) are elected by, and generally from amongst, the members of the legislature. This process reduces the likelihood of policy-related conflict between the legislature and the executive branch.

The second reason for the difference in the control function of the legislature is tied to the requirements of the democratic process. Representative democracy requires that elected officials be responsible to those that elected them. In separation-of-powers systems voters elect the executive, and therefore only voters have the power to change or remove the executive. If a congress could remove a popularly elected president though a vote of censure or similar mechanism on the basis of policy disagreement it could easily undermine the democratic process as a whole. This threat does not exist in fused-powers systems since it is the parliament itself that elects the executive branch, and thus has the right to withdraw that support and select a new one.

Oversight

The absence of a strong policy legislative control function in separation-of-powers systems does not imply that the legislature has no role to play in policy oversight. In fact, legislatures in both separation-of-powers and fused-powers systems play a critical role in ensuring proper oversight of both the budgetary implications of policies and their timely and accurate implementation. Legislatures may be able to exercise these types of oversight and control functions in non-democratic systems, even if they are unable to effectively control the executive branch as a whole.

Legislative oversight of the executive branch is generally quite broad, entailing both the monitoring of executive agencies tasked with the implementation of policy decisions and regular engagement with the political executive to ensure it is meeting its commitments to the public and adequately addressing the various needs of the country. Although most legislatures engage in both types of oversight to some degree, in general the former task is of greater significance in separation-of-powers systems, while the latter takes precedence in fused-powers systems. The tools used to pursue these activities will vary between legislatures based on their resources and the characteristics of the broader political system (as discussed below), but there are some oversight mechanisms shared by most legislatures.

Question-time, special inquiries, hearings, and investigative committees are all frequently used by legislatures to gather information and, if necessary, hold various actors and agencies within the executive branch accountable for either a failure to act or inappropriate actions. On the whole legislatures have increased their executive oversight activities over time, largely in response to the growing complexity of government and the increased need to delegate many activities to other agencies.

1. **Question-time** is generally used in parliaments and provides a regularly scheduled opportunity for members of the legislature to present oral and written questions to members of the cabinet, including the prime minister or equivalent.

2. In contrast, **special inquiries and hearings** are organized on an *ad hoc* basis to investigate specific topics or issues that are considered important by some legislators and are present in both separation-of-powers and fused-powers systems.

3. **Investigative committees** are similar, but are more formalized; tend to address higher order issues and often have a longer duration. Like special inquiries and hearings, investigative committees exist in both fused and separation-of-powers systems.

4. In addition to all of these tools, legislatures may request or even require that the executive and/or its bureaucratic agencies provide it with **reports on specific issues** of concern, make presentations to the full legislature or relevant committees, or respond to specific inquiries in hearings.

Budget control

Legislatures may also engage in indirect oversight of executive policy initiatives through their control over the budgetary process.

The budgetary power of legislatures dates to the historical inception of legislative institutions. The earliest forms of legislatures were little more than groups of aristocratic lords called together by the king to approve new taxes and levies. Although monarchs had access to vast resources, they were often in need of additional funds to pay for the armies necessary to wage war and quell uprisings. In the Middle Ages these funds came largely from the taxes through the lords (see Chapter 4). Following the adoption of the Magna Charta in 1215 in England, the power of the monarchy to unilaterally levy taxes was curtailed somewhat through the creation of a committee consisting of twenty-five barons that could overrule the king. Its introduction created the norm of seeking approval for new taxes from among the lords of the time. This practice established the nearly ubiquitous norm of legislative control over the **power of the purse**. The result is that nearly all political systems require legislative approval of national budgets and tax policies.

Control and oversight of expenditure, even if limited by entitlements and other political artifices, is a powerful tool that can provide even the weakest of legislatures the opportunity to influence policy decisions.[6] There are few policy goals that can be achieved without some level of funding. As a result, the ability of the legislature to withhold or decrease funding for initiatives supported by the executive branch can become a useful bargaining tool. In fact, the need to obtain legislative approval for spending initiatives can even provide legislatures with the potential to influence decision-making in policy arenas traditionally reserved for the executive branch such as foreign and security policy.

In conjunction with executive control and bureaucratic oversight, the power of the purse provides legislatures with important opportunities to influence the policy process. However, in all of these activities legislatures are largely reactive and in many cases have only indirect policy influence. In many systems legislatures also have the ability to directly and even proactively participate in the policy-making process. To the extent that they are able to participate in the policy process in this manner, legisla*tures* become legisla*tors*.

Legislature as legislator: policy-making vs. policy-influencing

There are a number of ways that legislatures can be directly involved in the policy-making process ranging from simply giving opinions to making significant amendments and from initiating independent proposals to vetoing the proposals of the executive branch. Because of the central role of policy-making within the political process more generally, judgements about the comparative institutional power of legislatures are often based upon their relative ability to directly impact the policy process. As we have seen above, however, there are a broad variety of tasks regularly accomplished by legislatures, and in many cases legislating is not one of the most important (see Table: Legislative powers of legislatures, in the Online Resource Centre).

Consultation

The most basic, and generally least influential, type of legislative participation in the policy-making process is consultation. This power grants the legislature the authority to present an opinion about a specific legislative proposal, general plan of action, or broad policy programme. Consultation in no way guarantees that the executive branch will abide by the opinion of the legislature. Indeed, in some cases there is no guarantee that the opinion of the legislature is even taken into consideration. Despite this fact, the ability to present an opinion and to differentiate the views of the legislature from that of the executive can be important in many contexts. In particular, legislative opinions that are in conflict with the proposals put forward by the executive branch and are public in nature may serve as a tool of linkage and representation.

Delay

A common ability among even comparatively weak legislatures is the power to delay legislation.[7] This is a 'negative power' in that the legislature can only slow down the process, not provide positive input or substantive change directly. Despite this, the ability to delay passage of a proposal can be an effective bargaining tool when the executive branch prefers rapid action. Obviously the longer the allowable delay and/or the greater the urgency of the executive's proposal, the more powerful the potential bargaining position of the legislature will be.

Veto

In its most extreme incarnation the power of delay becomes the power of veto. Legislatures with veto power can definitively and unilaterally block policies from being adopted, regardless of the position of the executive branch. Like the power of delay, veto power is negative in character. As a result it will only be an effective bargaining tool for the legislature when the executive branch has a strong interest in changing the existing policy status quo. In fact, it should be noted that in cases when the legislature prefers (rapid) policy change the powers of delay and veto will be of little utility.

Amendment

The most important positive legislative tools are the power to amend and initiate proposals. The ability to substantively amend bills allows the legislature to actively change aspects of the executive branch's proposal to achieve an outcome more in line with the preferences of a majority of its members. The extent to which amendments are allowed, the ability of the executive to block or reverse amendments, and the existence of constraints on the subject of amendments will all influence how important the legislature's amendment capacity is. Frequent restrictions include limitations on the stage in the process at which amendments can be introduced (Spain), the number of amendments that can be introduced (Austria), or the ability of the legislature

to make changes that would incur additional costs (Israel).

Initiation

An independent power of initiative grants individuals or groups within the legislature the right to introduce their own policy proposals independent of the executive branch. In some legislatures all proposals must formally be initiated by the legislature (the US), while in others the legislature has no formal ability to independently initiate proposals (the European Union). Most political systems fall somewhere between these two extremes. Regardless of the formal power to adopt amendments or initiate proposals, the actual rate of legislative success in terms of the transformation of amendments or initiatives into law is likely to be the most accurate indicator of a legislature's ability to positively influence policy outcomes.

In most fused-powers systems independent member initiatives are rarely successfully adopted (or even fully discussed and debated). In Western European countries, for example, between 80 and 90 per cent of successful proposals are initiated by the executive branch. In some cases, such as Israel, private-member bills are estimated to account for less than 9 per cent of adopted proposals (Mahler 1998). In fact, the power to initiate a proposal is often of little use given the extraordinarily low rates of success. For example, in Belgium between 1971 and 1990 a total of 4,548 private-member bills were initiated, but just 7.3 per cent were ultimately adopted (Mattson 1995).

The centrality of the policy-making function of government has led to the development of a number of different attempts to categorize legislatures on the basis of their policy influence (see Table: Major classification of legislatures, in the Online Resource Centre). Thus, we can differentiate in a dichotomous way between **transformative legislatures** that have a high degree of direct policy-making influence and **arena type legislatures** that are more engaged in the linkage and oversight functions with little policy influence (Polsby 1975). Alternatively, legislatures can be understood in terms of their 'viscosity' or capacity to slow down and even block the executive in its attempts to make policy decisions (Blondel 1970).

KEY POINTS

- Legislatures engage in a wide variety of roles and tasks including providing a link between citizens and the central government, representing citizen interests, executive oversight, and participating in the policy-making process.
- While most legislatures in democratic systems perform all of these roles to some extent, the emphasis placed on the various roles and task will vary between legislatures.
- The very different character of the relationship between the executive branch and the legislature

in fused-powers and separation-of-powers systems influences which roles and tasks are emphasized by a legislature.

- There are a number of different tools that a legislature may employ within the policy-making process, including consultation, delay, veto, amendment, and initiation. While the powers of delay and veto are 'negative' in that they delay or block policies, amendment and initiation are 'positive' powers that create or alter the substance of a proposal.

The internal organizational structures of legislatures

Even legislatures that are formally granted considerable powers are likely to prove wholly ineffective if they do not also have an internal structure that allows for an effective division of labour, the development of specialized expertise, access to independent sources of information, and other basic organizational and operational resources. In most cases an analysis of the internal structures and resources of a legislature can provide a more accurate assessment of its general level of activity and influence than a similar review of just the formal powers granted to it in the constitution.

Number and type of chambers

One of the most obvious general structural variations that exist between legislatures is the number of chambers they have. In most cases legislatures have either one chamber (unicameral) or two (bicameral), although in a few rare cases legislatures have had more. Multi-chamber legislatures are generally created to insure adequate representation for different groups within the political system. The lower (and usually larger) chamber provides representation for the population as a whole, while the upper chamber represents specific socially or territorially defined groups. These can be the political subunits such as states (US), *Länder* (Germany), or cantons (Switzerland), or different groups of citizens such as aristocrats (UK) or ethnicities (South Africa under apartheid).[8] Unicameral legislatures are more likely to be found in unitary

political systems with comparatively homogeneous populations (such as Scandinavia).

More important than the actual number of legislative chambers is the relationship between them. In unicameral systems all of the powers of the legislative branch are contained within the single chamber. However, in bicameral systems these powers may be (1) *equally shared* (both chambers can exercise all legislative powers), (2) *equally divided* (each chamber has specific, but more or less equally important powers), or (3) *unequally distributed* (one chamber has significantly greater powers than the other). The first two cases are considered symmetric bicameral systems, while the latter are asymmetric bicameral systems. Table 7.2 provides some examples of bicameral systems.

Knowing how many chambers a legislature has and understanding the relationship between them (symmetric or asymmetric) is important because it can impact the broader policy-making process significantly. For example, if the chambers within a symmetric bicameral legislature have significantly different or opposing ideological majorities it may delay the legislative process since a proposal acceptable to the majority of both chambers must be developed, but it may also force increased political compromise and ensure a higher level of representation for minorities or territorial groups. Failure to reach a compromise, however, may block the policy process as a whole, or force the executive branch to attempt to govern without the legislature (through

Table 7.2 Representation and role/asymmetry of upper chambers

Country	Federal (Y/N)	Upper chamber	Size	Basis of representation	Mode of selection	Symmetric (Y/N)
Argentina	Y	Senate	72	Provincial	Directly elected	Y
Austria	Y	Bundesrat	64	Lander	Indirect election by provincial legislature by PR	N
Belarus	N	Council of the Republic	64	Regions	Indirectly elected 8 appointed by President	Y
Belgium	Y	Senate	71	Regions	Direct elections (40)—proportional and indirect selection (31)	N
Bolivia	N	Senate	27	Departments	Directly elected—top 2 parties (2/1) 3 seats per Admin. Dept.	Y
Brazil	Y	Senate	81	States	Directly elected—simple majority 3 seats per state	Y
Canada	Y	Senate	104	Regions	Appointed—by government	Y
Chile	N	Senate	47	Regions	Directly elected—majority (38) appointed (9)	Y
Colombia	N	Senate	102	National	Directly elected in a single national constituency—PR	Y
Czech Republic	N	Senate	81	National	Directly elected—simple majority 1/3 every 2 years	N
Egypt	N	Consultative Assembly	258	National	2/3 elected 1/3 appointed by President	N
France	N	Senate	321	Departments	Indirect election by electoral colleges in each Department	N
Germany	Y	Bundesrat	68	Lander	Indirectly selected by *Länder* governments	N
Grenada	N	Senate	13	National	Appointed—by governor general (on advice of prime minister)	N
India	Y	Rajya Sabha	245	States/ Territories	Indirectly elected (233) appointed by president (12)	N

(continued)

Table 7.2 (*continued*)

Country	Federal (Y/N)	Upper chamber	Size	Basis of representation	Mode of selection	Symmetric (Y/N)
Italy	N	Senate	315	Regions	Directly elected— PR and majority bonus within regions	Y
Japan	N	House of Councillors	252	National & Prefecture	Directly elected— nationally (100) and within prefectures (152)	N
Mexico	Y	Senate	128	States	Directly elected—modified majority (1 per state to 2nd party)	Y
Pakistan	Y	Senate	87	Provincial and Tribal Areas	Indirectly elected (4/province + 8/tribal areas + 3/Capital Territory)	N
Poland	N	Senate	100	Districts	Directly elected—simple majority 2 or 3 per district	N
Romania	N	Senate	143	National	Directly elected— two-ballots majority	Y
Russia	Y	Council of Federation	178	Federal Units	Indirectly selected (2/Republic, Oblast, Krais, Okrug and Federal City)	N
St Lucia	N	Senate	11	National	Appointed by Governor General PM selects 6 and opposition 3	N
Spain	N	Senate	257	Regional	Directly elected (208)—majority indirectly elected (49)	N
Switzerland	Y	Council of States	46	Cantons	Directly elected—simple majority	Y
United Kingdom	N	House of Lords	731	Class	Hereditary and by appointment	N
United States	Y	Senate	100	Federal Units	Directly elected—simple majority	Y

Both Taiwan and Venezuela have become unicameral legislatures since 1998. Data for Italian Senate updated to reflect 2005 electoral reforms. Data for Russian Federal Council updated to reflect post-2000 reforms instituted by President Putin. Data for UK House of Lords reflect most recent reforms. However, a vote in the House of Commons in March 2007 proposed that at least 80 per cent of the House of Lords be directly elected. This proposal was rejected by the House of Lords.

Source: Compiled by the author from Kurian *et al.* (1998). Updated from official national legislative websites.

decrees for example). In the worst-case scenario, such a blockage might even threaten the stability of the political system as a whole if necessary policies cannot be adopted.

Number, quality, and consistency of members

By their nature legislatures bring together a comparatively large number of people to enable them to engage in a broad variety of political activities. The legislature is usually the most numerous and most diverse of the primary branches of government. As a result, the tools and structures that it uses to organize itself are particularly critical and often quite informative in terms of assessing the effective roles of the legislature within the broader system.

Size

A few very basic descriptive statistics can reveal a good deal about the character and political role of a legislature. For example, the number of members relative to the size of the general population, the number of days per year the legislature is in session, the extent to which members are 'professional' legislators or maintain additional external employment, the rate of member turnover from one election to the next, and the general 'quality' of members can all provide information on the likely level of political influence that a legislature has within the political system and the policy-making process. The relationships between each of these characteristics and the general level of political influence and policy-making power of a legislature are outlined in Table: The impact of general characteristics on legislative influence, in the Online Resource Centre. Empirically, these variables have a high level of correlation with the general character and role of legislatures within their respective political systems.

The logic behind the relationships presented in the table is relatively straightforward in most cases. The relative size of the legislature is telling because of the inherent difficulty that large and diverse groups generally have in reaching coherent decisions. The more members a legislature has, the more time each decision is likely to require (as a result of the need to allocate individual speaking time for example). Additionally, more members are likely to lead to more complex mechanisms of internal organization and

more thinly spread institutional resources. Membership numbers must be interpreted in context, however, as very small countries will naturally tend to have much smaller legislatures while more populous countries will on average have larger legislatures (see Table: Major classification of legislatures, in the Online Resource Centre). Moreover, even numerically large legislatures can be quite powerful when their size is accommodated by presence of significant institutional resources and/or structures that facilitate decision-making.

Time

The amount of time that legislators actually spend attending to legislative tasks is also a useful indicator of the broader role of the legislature. At one extreme are legislatures which are formally or functionally 'in session' more or less year-round. On the other end of the spectrum are 'part-time' legislatures that meet for only a few days of the year and must accomplish all of their policy-making and oversight tasks during these limited periods (see Table 7.4). Clearly the greater the amount of time legislators have available to dedicate to their responsibilities, the more they will be able to accomplish, and the higher the probability that they will be able to exert significant political and policy influence.

The length of the annual session of a legislature is often directly tied to the type of members it attracts. Part-time legislatures that are in session for only short periods of the year not only provide the opportunity for their members to engage in other professional activities, they often make it a functional requirement. The average annual salary of a legislator is more likely to constitute a 'liveable' wage when the task performed constitutes a full-time job. Part-time legislatures more often than not provide only part-time wages, forcing members to maintain external professions. Of course there are also legislatures that are formally 'full-time' that nonetheless fail to provide members with salaries large enough to live on without recourse to additional external employment or personal wealth.[9]

The need for legislators to maintain additional external employment necessarily reduces the amount of time and effort they can dedicate to their legislative tasks. In some cases the role of the legislature may be so constrained that this does not represent a concern. In others, however, it will not only reduce

Table 7.3 Population and size of lower chamber in forty-five countries

Country	Lower chamber	Population	Size	Reps/citizens
Andorra	General Council of the Valleys	73,000	28	2,607
Argentina	Chamber of Deputies	34,673,000	257	134,914
Austria	National Council (Bundesrat)	8,023,000	183	43,842
Belarus	Chamber of Representatives	10,416,000	110	94,691
Belgium	House of Representatives	10,170,000	150	67,800
Bhutan	Tsgogdu	1,823,000	150	12,153
Bolivia	Chamber of Deputies	7,165,000	130	55,115
Brazil	Chamber of Deputies	162,661,000	513	317,078
Canada	House of Commons	28,821,000	301	95,751
Chad	National Assembly	6,977,000	125	55,816
Chile	Chamber of Deputies	14,333,000	120	119,442
China	National People's Congress	1,210,005,000	2978	406,315
Colombia	Chamber of Representatives	36,813,000	163	225,847
Czech Republic	Chamber of Deputies	10,321,000	200	51,605
Denmark	Folketing	5,250,000	179	29,330
Egypt	People's Assembly	63,575,000	454	140,033
Finland	Eduskunta	5,105,000	200	25,525
France	National Assembly	58,040,000	577	100,589
Germany	Federal Diet (Bundestag)	83,536,000	598	139,692
Greece	Vouli	10,539,000	300	35,130
Grenada	House of Representatives	95,000	15	6,333
Guyana	National Assembly	712,000	65	10,954
India	House of the People (Lok Sabha)	952,108,000	545	1,746,987
Iran	Islamic Consultative Assembly	66,094,000	270	244,793
Israel	Knesset	5,422,000	120	45,183
Italy	Chamber of Deputies	57,460,000	630	91,206
Japan	House of Representatives	125,450,000	500	250,900

(*continued*)

Table 7.3 (*continued*)

Korea, South	Kukhoe	45,482,000	299	152,114
Mexico	Chamber of Deputies	95,772,000	500	191,544
New Zealand	House of Representatives	3,548,000	120	29,567
Pakistan	National Assembly	129,276,000	217	595,742
Peru	Congress	24,523,000	120	204,358
Poland	Sejm	38,643,000	460	84,007
Romania	Chamber of Deputies	21,657,000	341	63,510
Russia	State Duma	148,178,000	450	329,284
St Lucia	House of Assembly	158,000	18	8,778
Singapore	Parliament	3,397,000	83	40,928
Slovakia	National Council	5,374,000	150	35,827
Spain	Congress of Deputies	39,181,000	350	111,946
Switzerland	National Council	7,207,000	200	36,035
Syria	People's Assembly	15,609,000	250	62,436
Taiwan	Legislative Yuan	21,466,000	164	130,890
Tanzania	Bunge	29,058,000	275	105,665
Turkey	Grand National Assembly	62,484,000	550	113,607
United Kingdom	House of Commons	58,490,000	659	88,756
United States	House of Representatives	301,102,000	435	6,921,188
Venezuela	Chamber of Deputies	21,983,000	203	108,291

Source: Kurian *et al.* (1998).

the effectiveness of legislators, it will also impact the type of individuals who desire and are able to join the legislature. This in turn impacts both the quality of members and the rate of membership turnover from one election to the next. When legislative wages are low it can serve to restrict membership to those with alternative sources of wealth, cause high-quality members to decide not to run for re-election, or even lead the most qualified individuals to simply never consider the legislature as a career option.

Committees

Almost without exception legislatures organize internally on the basis of committees. The variations that exist between these committees, however, can be enormous. Legislatures may have few or many committees and they may be created on an *ad hoc* basis or permanently established. In addition, there may be highly specialized subcommittees and/or temporary committees of inquiry created to address specific crises or questions. Committees can also vary in

Table 7.4 A comparison of annual session duration

Country	Lower chamber	Annual session(s)	Meeting days (sittings)
Argentina	Chamber of Deputies	Annual session from 1 March to 30 November	**
Austria	National Council (Bundesrat)	Annual session from mid-September to mid-July	**
Belarus	Chamber of Representatives	Variable	170 days
Belgium	House of Representatives	Annual session from 2nd Tuesday in October–20 July	Minimum of 40 days per session
Bhutan	Tsgogdu	Must meet at least once per year (May–June or October–November)	**
Bolivia	Chamber of Deputies	**	90 days (possible to extend to 120)
Brazil	Chamber of Deputies	2 sessions annually: 1 March–30 June and 1 August–5 December	**
Canada	House of Commons	***	**
Chad	National Assembly	2 sessions annually in April and October	90 days in session
Chile	Chamber of Deputies	1 annual session 21 May–18 September	**
China	National People's Congress	Once per year (usually in March)	14 days
Colombia	Chamber of Representatives	2 sessions annually: 20 July–16 December and 16 March–20 June	**
Denmark	Folketing	Annual session, October–October (no meetings in July, August, and September)	Approximately 100 plenary mtgs per year
Egypt	People's Assembly	2nd Thursday in November–30 June	**
Finland	Eduskunta	Spring and autumn sessions (recess December–January and summer)	**
France	National Assembly	Annual session, October–June	**
Greece	Vouli	Annual session from 1st Monday October (for not less than 5 months)	**
Grenada	House of Representatives	Must meet at least once every six months	**
Guyana	National Assembly	Officially in session every day except Saturday and Sunday	Meets on average two days per month

(continued)

Table 7.4 (*continued*)

India	House of the People (Lok Sabha)	3 sessions per year: February–May, July–August, November–December	**
Italy	Chamber of Deputies	Year-round (official vacations: 1 week for Easter, 2 weeks for Christmas, and August)	**
Japan	House of Representatives	Ordinary session January–May (extra ordinary sessions summer–autumn)	150 days/ordinary session (extraordinary ones vary)
Korea, South	Kukhoe	Regular session may not exceed 100 days (special session not to exceed 30)	Average of 45 days per year in plenary session
Mexico	Chamber of Deputies	2 sessions annually: 1 September–15 December and 15 March–30 April	**
New Zealand	House of Representatives	Session runs for full calendar year generally no sittings in January	**
Pakistan	National Assembly	2 annual sessions. Must not remain in recess for more than 120 days at a time	**
Poland	Sejm	Continuous, sittings determined by Presidium	26 sittings/year (1–4 days each) October 2001–October 2005
Romania	Chamber of Deputies	2 sessions annually: February–June and September–December	**
Russia	State Duma	2 sessions annually: mid-January–mid July and beg. October–end of December	Generally 2 days per week 3 weeks per month in session
Singapore	Parliament	No set calendar, 1 sitting/month 6 months maximum between sessions	**
Slovakia	National Council	2 annual sessions (spring and autumn)	**
Spain	Congress of Deputies	2 sessions annually: February–June and September–December	**
Switzerland	National Council	4 times per year (every 3 months) extraordinary sessions are allowed	3 weeks/ordinary session, 1 week/extraordinary session

(*continued*)

Table 7.4 *(continued)*

Syria	People's Assembly	3 sessions/year: October–December, mid-February–March, and mid-May–June	**
Taiwan	Legislative Yuan	2 sessions annually: February–May and September–December	2 sittings per week while in session
Tanzania	Bunge	Variable number of sessions lasting between 4 days and 2 weeks	25–30 days per year on average
Turkey	Grand National Assembly	Annual session: 1 October–30 September may recess for a max. of 3 months	meets Tuesday–Thursday in session
United Kingdom	House of Commons	Full year, adjourns for Christmas (3 weeks), Easter (1 week) and summer (10 weeks)	4–5 days per week while in session
Venezuela	Chamber of Deputies	Ordinary sessions: early March–early July and early October–late November	**

Source: Based on Kurian *et al.* (1998), updated from official national government and legislative websites.

terms of their role within the legislature. In some cases committees are responsible for reviewing and amending proposals before the full plenary discusses them, in others they are in charge of implementing the changes decided by the plenary.

As with legislatures themselves, committees may also have substantial or minimal resources at their disposal to support the achievement of their various tasks (see below). Each of these aspects of the committee system within a legislature can significantly impact the political and especially the policy influence of the legislature as a whole. These relationships are outlined in Table: The impact of committee characteristics on legislative influence, in the Online Resource Centre.

Permanency

One of the most important aspects of committees is their permanency. Committees that are created on an *ad hoc* basis not only tend to be less efficiently organized, but their members lack the opportunity to develop area-specific expertise or the contacts with external actors that facilitate independent and informed decision-making. Given the size of most legislatures committees often serve as the forum for the bulk of legislative activity, including the bargaining and coalition-building that must often be achieved between (or even within) political parties. The smaller size and less public nature of committees increase their utility as a forum for these types of activities. Frequent interactions between members, as well as the possible development of independent sources of information and expertise, further facilitate the legislative process. However, if the committees are not permanent they are unlikely to provide the necessary level of stability and structure required to reap these benefits.

Specialization

To make the most of their potential influence, ensure that the critical policy areas are covered, and that jurisdictional boundaries are as clear as possible, committees within influential legislatures also mirror the organization of the executive branch, with distinct committees for each cabinet portfolio. The association of specific committees with specific cabinet ministries can also serve to foster relationships between the members and staff of the legislature and the executive branch that may significantly improve inter-institutional cooperation.

Temporary committees

The potential for additional flexibility and specificity can be added through the incorporation of sub-committees and temporary investigative committees (sometimes referred to as committees of inquiry). These allow for still greater levels of specialization among members and permit the legislature to react to significant events or crises as necessary.

One of the surest indicators of the actual role of committees, and through them the legislative influence of the legislature as a whole, is the order in which proposals move between the full plenary and the committees. If legislation is fully vetted, including debate and even amendment, on the full floor *prior* to being sent to committee, committees are unlikely to play a substantial role in policy-making. Generally when this occurs the committee simply implements the decisions made in plenary and serves as an administrative and secretarial unit more than a policy-making one. Given the hurdles to fully engaging in a thorough analysis of policy proposals on the floor of the plenary, this process of vetting bills indicates a comparatively small policy role for the legislature as a whole as well. In contrast, when bills receive their first full analysis and amendment within the committees the likelihood is significantly higher that the legislature will have a more substantial influence on the final policy outcome. The policy review and revision process within committee offers the legislature an effective opportunity to influence outcomes that is unlikely to be available on the full floor.

Rules of procedure

The details of the internal organization and structure of a legislature, as well as the regulations that govern individual members and groups of members, are outlined within its Rules of Procedure (RoP). In most legislatures RoP are adopted internally and granted the status of legal regulation or statute, meaning that they serve as a kind of internal law applicable within the confines of the legislature. RoP can be an extremely useful source of information about the structure and character of the internal organization of a legislature, as well as the broader role of the legislature within the political system as a whole. Moreover, the RoP will reflect the internal balance of power within the legislature between the various political parties, as well as between individual members and the parties in general.

In principle, the RoP govern every aspect of legislative activity, from the opening of a legislative session and election of internal officers to the structure of the committee system, distribution of speaking time and the procedure for voting on legislation. In reality, there are almost always informal norms that regulate some activities, either instead of or in addition to the formal RoP. Despite the likely existence of some level of informal norms, the extent to which a legislature's RoP are well constructed, detailed, unambiguous, and comprehensive is a good indication of the breadth of legislative activity and the level of internal conflict.

Legislatures that are effectively engaged in the policy-making process must have an efficient internal structure capable of ensuring the timely review of proposals. An inefficient legislature is likely to find its opinions ignored and its influence diminished (Copeland and Patterson 1994). As a result, legislatures that have the capacity to impact policy will generally have mechanisms in place to limit debate on the floor, restrict amendments, and make use of the committee structure whenever possible. In contrast, legislatures that have little opportunity to impact policy outcomes directly will have rules that emphasize debate and discussion on the floor (the most public venue), making substantially less use of committees (if these exist) in the effort to sway public opinion and exercise indirect influence on policy decisions.

Similarly, legislatures are less likely to rely on informal norms as mechanisms of internal governance as the stakes of controlling the decision-making process *within* the legislature increase. Thus, when legislatures are more influential within the broader political system, there will be more competition between members to control that influence and as a result fewer aspects of internal organization will be allowed to remain unregulated or open to interpretation. As a result, the RoP in legislatures with effective legislative influence are generally significantly more detailed and comprehensive than those in less influential legislatures.

One final aspect of the legislature that can often be gleaned from an examination of the RoP is the relative roles of individual members versus political parties (as organized within parliamentary factions). The extent to which the RoP grant individuals the right to act independent of their party or parliamentary group provides significant insight into the relative partisan autonomy of the legislature as a whole. There are a broad variety of activities ranging from calling for a roll call vote, or raising a point of order, to offering an amendment from the floor that can theoretically be done by an individual member, some minimum number of members, or a specified subunit (such as a party group). Given the potential costs of high levels of individual action in terms of the overall efficiency of the legislature, some constraints on individual action may be imposed within legislatures even in the absence of external political party control.

Hierarchical structures and internal decision-making

Within every legislature there are a variety of internal positions of authority and power, even if the institution itself is relatively weak. At the level of the legislature as a whole there is generally a president, one or more vice-presidents, and in some cases questors or other secretarial/administrative positions. In addition, most legislatures will also have leadership positions within organized subunits, for example, chairs of committees, subcommittees, and/or specialized delegations and/or working groups.

The most fundamental difference between legislatures occurs between those that distribute internal positions of authority proportionally amongst all of the groups (usually political parties) represented, and those that use a 'winner-take-all' system, assigning positions only members of the majority (party or coalition). In the former case cooperation and compromise between government and opposition groups is facilitated by the requirements of working within an institution with clear power-sharing structures. In contrast, winner-take-all systems are more likely to foster a polarized environment that divides members based on their membership in the majority and resultant access to internal influence.

Majoritarian or winner-take-all systems discourage compromise. As a result, these types of legislatures will function well only when the majority in charge is reliable, either because of a high degree of party discipline or because of significant numerical superiority over the opposition. When parties are weak or undisciplined, and/or majorities are slim, individual member defections can lead to the defeat of majority proposals, and potentially to policy stagnation or legislative insignificance. On the other hand, when majorities are large and/or parties are disciplined, decision-making is likely to be more efficient and significant policy innovation easier to achieve. This **efficiency** will also make the most of the legislature's potential to impact the policy process.

In contrast, legislatures that distribute leadership positions among the parties and groups of both the majority and the opposition are more likely to witness frequent broad cross-party agreements and compromises and in some cases this may even be a requirement, given the proportional distribution of positions of power. This type of policy process is less likely to suffer significant negative consequences from individual member defections on particular issues or agreements because majorities will tend to be more centrally located by virtue of the need to build consensus. At the same time, however, this approach to policy-making is also likely to be more time-consuming and to lead to incremental policy reform based on compromise between opposing groups rather than sweeping ideologically informed policy innovations.

These are the two most extreme scenarios and there are, of course, a number of intermediate alternatives. For example, the majoritarian system is used to distribute internal positions of power in the US legislature; however, there is also a comparatively low level of party discipline. As a result, a number of different outcomes are possible depending on the size of the majority held by the largest party and the level of bi-partisan cooperation possible on a given issue. In general, however, legislatures that share internal positions of authority proportionally *tend* to be more consensual in character than those that use a winner-take-all system.

Institutional resources and distribution

Budget

The ability of a legislature to play an important independent role in the policy process or the broader political sphere will be deeply influenced by the type and extent of its resources. Many resources are tied to the level of funding at the disposal of a legislature. When legislatures set their own budgets (unsurprisingly) they are better funded than when this decision is left to the executive branch or some other external agency (Ranney 1981). There are some legislative resources that are not necessarily a direct function of institutional funding levels, such as popular support, institutional legitimacy, and member expertise, but even these are often improved indirectly by higher levels of institutional funding, which generally facilitates a more efficient and responsive legislature.

Space

At a very basic level the ability of legislatures to perform their tasks effectively is also impacted by the physical space they have at their disposal. The absence of sufficient space for meetings, offices, and other facilities such as libraries can have an extraordinary influence on the productivity of a legislature. If members must share office space they are unlikely to spend as much time within the legislature, insufficient meeting space may result in otherwise unnecessary delays in the policy process, and the absence of critical research facilities can significantly diminish the legislature's capacity for independent action. The type of space available to a legislature also transmits an important message to the general public about its importance relative to the other political institutions of the country. Obviously, however, even the most grandiose building is no guarantee of legislative power.[10]

Staff

The level of staff resources available to the legislature as a whole, as well as to individual members, is also indicative of the overall influence of the legislature. Staff can serve to facilitate the representative and linkage functions of individual members as well as increase the oversight and policy-making capacity of the legislature. The level of staffing needed by members will vary based on the size, type, and distance from the national capital of their electoral constituencies. Larger, more diverse districts are more complex and, as a result, more difficult to represent effectively. In proportional electoral systems (PR) with multi-member districts this concern is likely to be alleviated to some extent by the presence of a number of different representatives for each district. However, in single-member districts all linkage and representation functions have to be accomplished by a single legislator. In these cases especially, the extent to which a legislator can rely on staff support will have a significant impact on their ability to adequately perform these tasks.[11]

Suitable staff resources are also important for the legislature as a whole. As noted above, specialized staff within the committees can serve as independent sources of information for legislators, allowing them to maintain effective oversight of the executive branch and/or make informed decisions on policy proposals. In areas that are highly technical or detailed, such as the national budget, environmental protection, or welfare system reform, the availability of well trained staff is essential.[12] In addition, internal staffing resources can provide the technical support necessary to ensure that amendments and legislation initiated by members are well designed and comply with existing legal and administrative regulations. Without these resources an otherwise influential legislature is likely to waste its potential power, or worse, damage the system as whole through the promulgation of poorly constructed or contradictory laws.

KEY POINTS

❑ Understanding the internal organizational structures, membership, and resources of legislatures is a critical component of evaluating its overall influence and role within the broader political system.

❑ Most legislatures have one or two chambers. In the case of bicameral legislatures it is critical to understand both the representative function of each chamber and the relative distribution of power between them.

❑ The relative level of 'professionalization' of a legislature, including the amount of time it is in session each year, the character of its committees and other internal organizational structures, the type of members it attracts, and the resources they have at their disposal, is generally an accurate indication of its influence and power within the policy process and the broader political system.

Assessing a legislature's power

All legislatures, democratic or not, at least formally claim to fulfill the central representative/linkage, oversight, and legislative roles discussed above. Yet there are vast differences between legislatures in terms of the emphasis and centrality they ascribe to these various roles and, as a result, to the function they perform within the broader political system. There are legislatures for which the linkage and oversight functions are clearly pre-eminent (as in the UK, Greece, and Chile), while others place more emphasis on their legislative function (US, Italy, and the Netherlands). The next task is to understand the broader systemic characteristics that lead to these variations.

In spite of the great diversity and complexity of party systems, the underlying cause of the differences between legislatures is surprisingly simple, at least conceptually. Fundamentally, the extent to which a legislature is an active and effective participant in the legislative process versus assuming a more passive legislative role (focusing instead on oversight and linkage) is directly tied to the **degree of autonomy** it enjoys. More specifically, there are two aspects of a legislature's relative autonomy that are important:

- the independence of the institution as a whole;

- the independence of its members individually.

Institutional independence: executive–legislative relations

The level of institutional autonomy of a legislature is a function of its formal structural interaction with the executive branch. As seen above, fused-powers systems centralize legislative authority, while separation-of-powers systems tend towards decentralized legislative decision-making (see also Chapter 8).[13]

Fused-powers systems are structured hierarchically in so far as voters elect the members of the legislature and the members of the legislature, in turn, select the executive branch. In contrast, in separation-of-powers systems both the leader of the executive branch and the members of the legislature are elected by citizens (see Figure 7.1). The difference in the method of choosing the executive branch is of critical importance. The selection of the executive branch by, and from within, the legislature has significant implications for the latter's relative institutional autonomy within the broader political system. Perhaps counter-intuitively, the power to elect and dismiss the executive branch serves to *reduce* the independent policy influence of a legislature.

In a separation-of-powers system elections for the legislative and executive branches are not necessarily linked to each other in timing or, more importantly, outcome. This means there is no guarantee that the result will be a similar partisan distribution. In contrast, in a fused-powers system the election of the two branches are necessarily chronologically connected because following each legislative election the new legislature must select the executive branch. Furthermore, in a fused-powers system the need for the executive to be selected by and maintain the support of a majority within the legislature effectively requires a partisan link between the two branches. Even in systems with frequent minority governments, the implicit support (or lack of opposition) of a majority of the legislature is necessary to maintain the government in office.

In contrast, separation-of-powers systems structure the selection of the executive and legislative branches to be independent processes, even when they occur simultaneously. Citizens are given the opportunity to cast separate and distinct votes for each branch, despite the fact that these votes are often cast on a single ballot. By decoupling the two votes, separation-of-powers systems impose no restrictions on the partisan or ideological relationship between the two branches. As a result, any partisan distribution of majorities, from identical or contiguous to diametrically opposed, is possible. The absence of a partisan link between the executive and legislative branches, in combination with their structural independence, is essential in insuring that the legislature has the potential to play an active role in the policy-making process.

Fused power systems

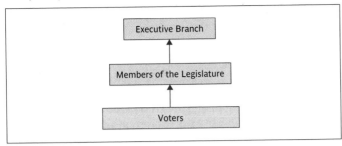

- Voters elect and may choose not to re-elect members of the legislature.
- Members of the legislature elect and may dismiss the executive branch through a vote of censure or no-confidence vote (restrictions may apply).
- The executive branch can dissolve the legislature (restrictions generally apply) and call for new elections. This results in dissolution of the executive branch as well)

Separation-of-power systems

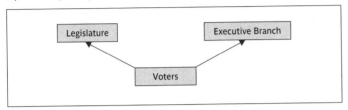

- Voters elect, and may choose not to re-elect, members of the legislature.
- Voters elect, and may choose not to re-elect, the executive branch (president)
- The executive *cannot* dissolve the legislature. The legislature can remove the executive *only* in case of legal wrongdoing.

Fig. 7.1 Powers systems

The impact of the interdependent relationship that exists between the executive and legislature in fused-powers systems is particularly important. The responsibility of the legislature for both installing and maintaining the executive branch severely constrains its ability to pursue independent legislative action. Majorities must remain comparatively stable in their support for the executive and by extension the executive's policy initiatives. In many (if not most) cases the defeat of an executive initiative of even moderate significance is considered a *de facto* vote of no-confidence with the potential to force the resignation of the government. The resulting instability, including the potential for new legislative elections, makes such actions risky for legislatures in fused-powers systems.

In contrast, separation-of-powers systems do not place any of these restrictions on the legislature. Because the executive branch is a wholly distinct institution unfettered by legislative control, there is no need for the legislature to maintain any form of support for it. The defeat of a policy proposal from the executive branch in the legislature, no matter how significant the policy, has no capacity to impact the tenure of the executive branch or the timing of legislative elections. The fixed term of office of both the legislative and the executive branches frees the legislature from the burden of maintaining the executive in office. At the same time it liberates both branches from any need for ideological affinity or policy consensus. The higher probability of partisan differences between the two branches in turn increases the likelihood that disagreements between them will occur and maintains the independence of the legislature even when their partisan identities are aligned.[14]

Member independence: the role of political parties

The ability of legislatures to take full advantage of the possibilities offered by a separation-of-powers system, as well as the degree to which those in fused-powers systems are able to make the most of their more limited legislative prospects, depends also on a less formal aspect of the political system. The character of the party system, and in particular the relative level of autonomy individual members of the legislature enjoy *vis-à-vis* their parties, can significantly affect the ability of the legislature as a whole to independently influence policy outcomes.

Unlike institutional independence, which is a function of the constitutionally defined structures of the

Table 7.5 Party and system characteristics related to member autonomy

Party characteristics	
Candidate selection	Centralized vs. decentralized selection by local units and/or activists, existence of leadership veto, self-nomination, etc.
Internal organization of political party	Hierarchical vs. decentralized party structures, role of legislative leadership in party structures (sharing of leaders)
Party system characteristics	
Electoral system	Party centred (i.e. party lists with or with out preference votes), candidate centred (usually single-member districts)
Sources of party and campaign funding	Existence of and rules regulating state financing, presence of fixed donor groups (labour), private resources, etc.

political system and the officially prescribed relationships between them, partisan autonomy depends on the characteristics of the party system. There are some particular elements of the party system that are especially important. These can be divided into two categories: (1) party specific characteristics and (2) systemic attributes of the party system. Examples of each type of variable are provided in Table 7.5. The underlying question addressed by each of these variables is fundamentally the same in all cases: to what extent is the political future and fortune of an individual member of the legislature controlled by his or her political party leadership outside of the legislature?

For most legislators there are two primary concerns or goals: (1) election/re-election and (2) the achievement of some set of policy outcomes (Fiorina 1996; Kreppel 2001). Both are intrinsically related to each other and central in determining legislator behaviour, regardless of the broader political system.[24] Secondary concerns often include the attainment of internal party or institutional positions of power such as a committee chairmanship or an internal party leadership role. Both the candidate selection mechanisms and the general internal organizational structure of political parties deeply impact the ability of individual members to achieve these goals if they lose the support of the leadership of their party.

Party organization

If re-election is important to legislators then their autonomy is reduced to the extent that the likelihood of their own re-election is controlled by the leaders of their party. Thus, if candidate selection (single-member districts) or the ordering of the party lists (multi-member districts) are controlled by the party elite, then those wishing to be re-elected must maintain the support of their party leaders (on electoral systems see Chapter 10). On the other hand, in parties that allow local party organizations and party activists to select candidates or in which the ordering of the party lists is either predetermined by set rules or determined by a broad spectrum of party members, individual legislators will enjoy a comparatively high level of independence from party leadership. In other words, the greater the party leadership's control over a member's re-election, the smaller the member's autonomy.

The impact of the centralization of a political party on member autonomy is less direct, perhaps, but equally important. At a very basic level, the more centralized a political party, the less room for independent decision-making by individual members. It is unlikely that an individual rank-and-file member will be able to influence the policy decisions of the party leadership in most cases. In decentralized parties there may be multiple centres of decision-making offering individual members both more opportunities to influence decisions and a broader array of party policy outcomes supported by some portion of the party leadership. Decentralized parties are also more likely to choose not to issue vote instructions, allowing members the independent vote in accordance with their personal preferences.

Another aspect is the relationship between organized party leadership within the legislature and the leadership structures that govern the 'electoral party' or the general party structure as a whole. Although ostensibly the party in the legislature is simply a subset of the larger electoral or popular party, in reality there are many cases in which the two-party organizations clash creating opportunities for individual members to act independently. It is not an uncommon phenomenon for the compromises required by the policy-making process within the legislature to cause alarm amongst party activists and leaders outside of the legislature. Parties that employ a single unified leadership structure within and outside of the legislature are less likely to face this type of intra-party strife, effectively decreasing opportunities for individual members to act independently.

Electoral laws

The impact of political parties is also mediated through aspects of the political system more generally. While the different scenarios discussed above can vary between political parties within a single political system, there are other elements that will generally affect all parties within a system (and thus all individual members of a legislature) in a similar manner. Two of the most important systemic variables are (1) the electoral system and (2) the rules regulating campaign funding.

Electoral systems influence member independence directly and profoundly by determining the nature of the voters' choices. In single-member districts voters are generally asked to select between individual candidates, while in PR systems the choice is usually between political parties. The latter method highlights the importance of parties and reinforces their primacy in mediating the citizen–government relationship. In contrast, in candidate-centred elections the political and personal attributes of the individual candidate are primary and in some cases may even overshadow the significance of party affiliation.

Thus, the relative autonomy of individual members of a legislature will increase as the electoral system offers opportunities for them to win re-election as a result of a high level of personal voter support, rather than simply a decision by party elite.

Elections that focus exclusively or even primarily on political parties significantly reduce the capacity of individual members to compete in the face of opposition or even indifference from their party's leadership. As important as electoral opportunity is, however, without access to sufficient financial resources no candidate will be competitive. As a result, it is also helpful to understand the rules and norms that regulate the electoral fundraising process.

The most important aspect regarding finance is the presence (or absence) of state funding and the rules that govern access to these funds (on party finances, see Chapter 12). Where state funding for electoral campaigns (and political parties more generally) is both the primary source of funds and easily accessible to new parties (or even independent candidates), the autonomy of individual members is likely to increase. Easily accessible state-financing for parties and campaigns increases the possibilities for new parties to form, and/or independent candidates to compete. As a result, the costs to members of leaving their party to run for election independently or to form a new party are reduced and political independence is increased. Even if members rarely choose to pursue either of these opportunities, the fact of that they exist is enough to diminish the capacity of the party to take action against members for failing to follow the party line.

Summing up, the combination of individual and institutional autonomy define the extent to which a legislature can effectively shape the policy process and help to determine legislative outcomes. These underlying relationships between the executive and the legislature and between the political parties and their members within the legislature create the broad structural constraints within which all of the other elements we have discussed operate. At one extreme are legislatures that are dominated by the executive branch (parliaments) with individual members largely controlled by their political parties. At the other extreme are legislatures that are formally independent from the executive branch (congresses) within political systems in which political parties are weak or decentralized and unable to effectively control the members of the legislature. These variables can be condensed into a simple 2 × 2 table such as Figure 7.2 overleaf.

	Centralized party system	Decentralized party system
Fused-powers system	**PARLIAMENT** UK Greece	**STRONG PARLIAMENT** Italy Poland
Separation-of-powers system	**WEAK CONGRESS** Colombia Argentina Bolivia South Korea	**CONGRESS** US

Fig. 7.2 Types of legislatures

KEY POINTS

❑ The institutional autonomy of the legislature (from the executive branch) and the individual autonomy of its members (from political parties) are the most fundamental variables affecting the policy influence of a legislature.

❑ Institutional autonomy is largely dependent on the formal political structures. In fused-powers systems in which the legislature selects the executive the two branches are mutually dependent and the institutional autonomy of the legislature is reduced. In separation-of-powers systems the legislature and the executive are both selected by the voters and the institutional autonomy of the legislature is increased.

❑ The autonomy of individual members of the legislature is a function of their dependence on political parties to achieve their electoral and policy goals. Individual members will have less autonomy in party-centred, PR electoral systems.

❑ Additional factors influencing the relative independence of individual members include the availability of state funding for electoral campaigns.

Conclusion

In the end, what difference does it make if a legislature is powerful or not? Why does it matter if the legislature has the capacity to independently affect policy outcomes? Is a strong legislature better or worse than a weaker one? Ultimately, there is no 'best' type of legislature, nor is there any reason that a more powerful legislature should be considered 'better' than one that is less influential. However, it is important to understand what type of legislature exists, particularly if there are concerns about key aspects of the political process, such as its 'representativeness', efficiency, or the quality of the policy outputs it produces.

The primary difference between the two general types of legislatures (parliamentary or congressional) and the variations of each presented in Table 7.1 is the relative importance of the core tasks performed by all legislatures—representation, linkage, oversight, and policy-making—in terms of the legislature's workload.

That said, the ability of the legislature to independently affect policy outcomes does have the potential to change the character of the political system as a whole by shifting the balance of power between the executive and legislative branches, and this carries with it potentially significant repercussions. For example, political systems with parliament-type legislatures that are focused primarily on their linkage and oversight functions will tend to have a more hierarchically structured policy-making process in which power is concentrated within the executive branch (and often within the political party hierarchy). This will tend to lead to more efficient decision-making because fewer actors are involved in the process. At the same time, however, the restricted level of access may result in the exclusion of key social groups from the policy-making process or may lead to large policy swings when a new government enters office.

In contrast, political systems that disperse power and facilitate the participation of a strong congressional-type legislature in the policy process are likely to be less efficient in terms of decision-making speed, but more inclusive. Because both the executive and the legislature participate in the legislative process, more coordination and compromise is likely to be necessary. This will certainly be the case when these institutions are controlled by different political parties (and/or when party control over individual members is weak). The result is likely to be a slower decision-making process with outcomes that represent broad compromises. Large policy swings are less likely and incremental change more common. Because of this, however, there is less likelihood that significant minority groups in society will be wholly excluded from the policy-making process or violently opposed to the resulting policy outcomes.

Thus, understanding the type of legislature that exists within a given political system, including both its formal relationship to the executive and less formal links to the political parties, can actually provide a good deal of information about the political system itself. Additional information about the legislature's internal organizational structures, the strength of its committee system, quality of its members, and access to resources will all provide significant additional clues about the type and relative policy influence of the institution as a whole.

? Questions

1. What is difference between an assembly, a legislature, a parliament, and a congress?
2. What are the core tasks of a legislature in a democratic society?
3. Why are legislatures generally better able to represent the interests of citizens than the executive branch?
4. What are separation-of-power systems and fused-power systems?
5. How are the oversight and control functions of legislatures different in fused powers and separation of powers systems?
6. What are the five possible tools that legislatures may have at their disposal to influence the policy-making process? Which are 'negative' and which are 'positive'?
7. What is the difference between a symmetric and asymmetric bicameral legislature? Why is it important?
8. Why is the structure and role of the committee system a good indicator of the policy-making influence of the legislature?
9. Why are political parties influential in determining the autonomy of a legislature?
10. What are the broader implications of having a strong legislature that is able to independently influence policy outcomes?

» Further reading

Döring, Herbert (ed.) (1995) *Parliaments and Majority Rule in Western Europe* (New York: Palgrave Macmillan).

Döring, Herbert, and Halleberg, Mark (eds.) (2004) *Patterns of Parliamentary Behaviour: Passage of Legislation Across Western Europe* (Aldershot: Ashgate).

Kurian, George Thomas, Longley, Lawrence D, and Melia, Thomas O. (1998) *World Encyclopedia of Parliaments and Legislatures* (Washington, DC: Congressional Quarterly).

Inter-Parliamentary Union (1986) *Parliaments of the World: A Comparative Reference Compendium* (Aldershot: Gower House, 2nd edn).

Loewenberg, Gerhard, and Patterson, Samuel (1979) *Comparing Legislatures* (Boston, Little Brown & Co.).

———— and Jewell, Malcolm (1985) *Handbook of Legislative Research* (Cambridge, Mass.: Harvard University Press).

Norton, Philip (1999) *Parliaments in Asia* (London: Routledge).

For a more extended bibliography see the works cited throughout this chapter. Students may also find useful material in journals such as the *American Political Science Review, British Journal of Political Science, Comparative Politics, Comparative Political Studies* and the specialized journals related to legislatures such as the *Journal of Legislative Studies,* and *Legislative Studies Quarterly.*

Web links

www.ipu.org/english/parlweb.htm
   The Inter-Parliamentary Union's websites of national parliaments.

www.electionworld.org/parliaments.htm
   Electionworld.org's Parliaments around the world website.

www.c-span.org
   C-span.org's clearinghouse of televised legislatures and legislature websites from around the world.

www.cqpress.com/product/Political-Handbook-of-the-World-2000.html
   Congressional Quarterly Press electronic version of the *Political Handbook of the World.*

 Visit the Online Resource Centre that accompanies this book for more information:
www.oxfordtextbooks.co.uk/orc/caramani/

8 Governments and bureaucracies

Wolfgang C. Müller

Chapter contents

Reader's guide

This chapter looks at decision-making modes of governments and their capacities to govern. Special attention is given to the relationship between the political and administrative parts of government. The chapter begins by addressing some definitional issues and distinguishing what constitutes government under different regime types. Next, the chapter presents different modes of government that reflect the internal balance of power: presidential, cabinet, prime ministerial, and ministerial government. The chapter discusses whether these models are appropriate for coalition governments. Then it addresses the autonomy of government, in particular from political parties and the permanent bureaucracy. Next, the chapter discusses the political capacity of governments, the relevance of unified vs. divided government, majority vs. minority government, and single-party vs. coalition government. Finally, the chapter highlights the bureaucratic capacities of government, addressing issues such as classic bureaucracy, the politicization of bureaucracies, and the New Public Management.

Introduction

The term 'government' has several meanings. In the broadest sense it refers to a hierarchical structure in any organized setting, including private clubs, business firms, and political institutions. Within politics a broad definition of government includes all public institutions that make or implement political decisions and that can be spread over several tiers, being called federal, state, and local government. That general understanding of government includes the executive, legislative, and judicial branches. Most common, however, is to refer to a country's **central political executive** as 'the government' and this will be this term's use in this chapter.[1]

The job of the government is to govern the country. Governing means ruling. It is not, as the term 'executive' might suggest, just implementing laws passed by the legislature. Rather, governing means the government having a strong imprint on the laws passed during its reign and more generally exercising overall control over a country and determining its direction. As we will see, governments are not always able to live up to very strong expectations about their ability to dominate political decision-making. Yet, even weak governments tend to be the political system's most important single political actor. This is a major reason why individuals and political parties mostly want to be in government. And because government is so important, positions in the central political executive tend to come with other goods that make them even more attractive: social prestige, decent income, public recognition, and privileged access to other powerful and/or famous people. The chance to govern the country and to enjoy these privileges is meant to motivate the best people to compete for government office. In democracies, such competition for government office ultimately is tied to elections. Either the government is directly elected or it is responsible to a parliament that results from general elections.

A few men and (increasingly also) women (see comparative table 10 at the end of this volume), distinguished and carefully selected as they may be, cannot run a country. Therefore, governments have bureaucracies to support them in their tasks of ruling and administrating the country. Thus, in functional terms, governing is not the exclusive task of the government. This has given rise to the notion of the **core executive**, which comprises 'all those organizations and procedures which coordinate central government policies, and act as the final arbiters of conflict between different parts of the government machine' (Rhodes 1995: 12). This implies that it is difficult to pin down the precise composition of the core executive. While the government in the narrow sense constitutes its centre, the core executive also comprises top civil servants, the key members of ministers' private cabinets, and a list of actors that varies over time and space. Realistically, the demarcation line between what constitutes the core and what belongs to the remaining parts of the executive also depends on the analyst's perspective and judgement. At the same time the core executive focus emphasizes coordination and negotiation rather than hierarchical relations among the units that constitute the core executive (Rhodes and Dunleavy 1995; Smith 1999).

> **KEY POINTS**
>
> ❑ The term 'government' has several meanings. Most common is to use it for the country's central political executive.
> ❑ Governing means ruling, exercising overall control over a country and determining the course it will take.

Types of government

Government and the separation of powers

Today's governments emerged through the piecemeal splitting-off of state functions from a traditionally undivided central government (mostly a monarch) (King 1975; Finer 1997). In order to limit the government's power, judicial functions were transferred to courts and legislative functions to parliaments. This process began in twelfth- and thirteenth-century England. It had many national variations and, in Europe, was not completed before the twentieth century. The constitutional doctrine of the separation of powers—as developed first and foremost by the political philosophers Locke, Montesquieu, and Madison—provides a normative justification for the separation of legislative, judicial, and executive institutions in order to guarantee liberty and justice (Vile 1967; see also Chapters 7 and 9).

In practice the state functions were never as neatly separated as envisaged by political philosophers. The executive has retained important legislative functions, in particular drafting legislation and issuing government decrees and ordinances (Carey and Shugart 1998). With the full democratization of polities and political parties establishing themselves as the main mechanism to structure elections and to coordinate incumbents, executives have gained almost a *de facto* monopoly in law-making in parliamentary systems. In presidential systems this is not true to the same extent, but executives also exercise large influence on legislation.

The normative foundations of democratic government rest on two premises: the government must be connected to the electoral process and work under constitutional constraints. Within these confines government can be organized in many ways. Three are quite common: **parliamentarism**, **presidentialism**, and **semi-presidentialism**. Another is connected with the successful Swiss model and deserves a mention: the **directorial** form cabinet government. Finally, government with a directly elected prime minister that may appear as 'natural' democratic improvement on parliamentarism has failed by all accounts in its only real-world test in Israel. Box 8.2 (p. 193) and Figure 8.1 (p. 194) show how these regime types can be distinguished.

As I have noted, in presidential systems the executives are not politically accountable to the legislature, but the legislatures do play a significant role in holding presidents accountable for judicial offences (see Box 8.1 below). Note, however, that often the decisions to investigate such offences and to proceeding with the impeachment of the president is primarily a political one.

BOX 8.1 Presidential impeachment rules in the US, Latin America, and Russia

US

Legitimate causes

Treason, bribery, or other high crimes and misdemeanors (Art. II).

Procedure

1. Any member of the House of Representatives can commence impeachment proceedings.

2. The House Committee on the Judiciary decides whether a floor vote will be held in the House of Representatives.

3. The House of Representatives then by majority vote decides whether the President should be impeached.

4. In the case of a positive vote the Senate can remove the President from office by two-thirds majority.

Argentina

Legitimate causes

Misconduct, crimes committed in the fulfilment of his duties and ordinary crimes (Art. 53).

Procedure

1. Only the House of Deputies has the power to impeach before the Senate the President (Art. 53).

2. The decision of House of Deputies requires a two-thirds majority (Art. 53).

3. The Senate can remove the President by majority vote and a quorum requirement of two-thirds of its members (Art. 59).

Brazil

Legitimate causes

Common offenses (Art. 86) and malversation during the performance of his functions. Crimes of malversation are those which attempt on the Federal Constitution (especially on the existence of the Union; the free exercise of the Legislative Power, the Judicial Power, the Public Prosecution and the constitutional Powers of the units of the Federation; the exercise of political, individual and social rights; the internal security of the country; probity in the administration; the budgetary law; compliance with the laws and with court decisions) (Art. 85).

(continued)

BOX 8.1 (continued)

Procedure

1. The Chamber of Deputies authorizes, by two-thirds of its members, legal proceedings to be initiated against the President (Art. 51).

2. The President can be submitted to trial before the Supreme Federal Court for common offenses or before the Federal Senate for crimes of malversation (Art. 86).

3. The President shall be suspended from its functions once the accusation or the complaint are received by the Federal Supreme Court or the Federal Senate, respectively (Art. 86).

4. If the trial has not been concluded after 180 days, the suspension of the President shall cease without prejudice to the normal progress of the proceeding (Art. 86).

Chile

Legitimate causes

Actions of his administration that may have gravely affected the honour and the security of the nation, or have openly violated the Constitution or the law (Art. 48).

Procedure

1. The accusation may be filed while the President is in office and within a period of six months following the expiration of his term. During the latter period he may not leave the country without the consent of the Chamber (Art. 48).

2. The majority of the Deputies in office decide whether the accusation brought against the President is or is not acceptable (Art. 48).

3. Two-thirds the Senators in office are required to declare the President guilty and hence remove him from office (Art. 49).

Mexico

Legitimate causes

Treason to the country and serious crimes of common order (Art. 108).

Procedure

1. The Chamber of Deputies conducts the proceeding and hears the accused (Art. 110).

2. The majority of the members present in session in the Chamber of Deputies proceeds with the accusation before the Chamber of Senators (Art. 110).

3. The Chamber of Senators hears the accused (Art. 110).

4. The Chamber of Senators, sitting as a court of judgement, applies the appropriate penalty by resolution of two-thirds of the members present in session (Art. 110).

Russia

Legitimate causes

High treason or some other grave crime.

Procedure

1. Confirmation of the crime in the President's actions by a ruling of the Supreme Court of the Russian Federation.

2. Confirmation of the procedure by the Constitutional Court of the Russian Federation.

3. Vote in the House of Representatives (*Duma*) on putting forward charges (at the initiative of at least one-third of the MPs with two-thirds of the total number of MPs).

4. Decision of the Federation Council on impeachment of the President (by the votes of two-thirds of the total number of MPs).

The government under different democratic regime types

What constitutes the government depends on the regime type. Presidentialism constitutionally provides for a one-person executive, but including his cabinet under the label of 'government' may be a useful working definition. Although the relations between the president and the cabinet are fundamentally different under fully fledged semi-presidentialism, both can be considered constituting the government. Yet, semi-presidential regimes offer a wide range of different working modes (Elgie 1999). Sometimes the president acts as the real head of government, relegating the prime minister to a mere assistant and occasionally scapegoat for things that do not go well, sometimes the holders of these two offices work together (or against each other) in complex power-sharing arrangements, and sometimes the president is hardly more than a powerful head of state, an authority in reserve to be mobilized only in crisis situations.

The archetypical case of semi-presidentialism, France, has seen the two former variants, while other countries, e.g. Austria, resemble the latter and combine a semi-presidential constitution with a parliamentary working of the system. Parliamentarism in many ways is a simple form of government: the cabinet is the government (Strøm *et al.* 2003). And although the mechanisms of creation and

---

BOX 8.2 Government creation and accountability under different regime types

Presidentialism

- Direct or quasi-direct popular election of the president for a fixed period.
- The head of state is identical with the head of government.
- President is not politically accountable to the legislature.
- Appointment of government members by the president (mostly with the consent of the legislature).

Parliamentarism

- The head of government (prime minister, chancellor, etc.) is different from the head of state (monarch or president).
- Most parliamentary systems allow for parliamentary dissolution by the head of state (typically on the prime minister's or government's proposal).
- Election of the prime minister by Parliament in some countries (e.g. Germany, Spain), appointment by the head of state (e.g. Italy, Ireland), or speaker of Parliament (Sweden) with subsequent vote of confidence in other countries, and appointment by the head of state without obligatory vote of confidence in another set of countries (e.g. UK, the Netherlands).
- The prime minister and the cabinet are politically accountable to the Parliament i.e. they can be removed from office by a vote of no-confidence at any time for no other reason that the Parliament no longer trusts the government. Some countries (Germany, Spain, Belgium, Hungary) require a *constructive* no-confidence vote, i.e. Parliament must replace the sitting government by an alternative government with the same vote.

Directorial government

- Currently, only Switzerland works with directorial government. The *Bundesrat* or *Conseil Fédéral* (Federal Council) consists of seven individuals who are elected individually by Parliament (the joint meeting of both chambers) for the entire term of Parliament.
- The federal president is head of government and head of state. This is inspired by US presidentialism, but the country's linguistic and religious diversity have required collegial government: the cabinet members rotate the presidency between them on an annual basis.
- The government is not politically accountable to Parliament.

Directly elected prime minister

- Only Israel practised this system from the elections 1996–2003 (with the decisions to introduce and abolish the system having been made in 1992 and 2001, respectively). Then the prime minister was popularly elected with absolute majority (in two rounds, if necessary) at the date of each parliamentary election and when the office of prime minister was vacant.
- The cabinet was nominated by the prime minister but required a parliamentary vote of confidence to get into office.
- The prime minister was politically accountable to Parliament. However, a successful vote of no-confidence also triggered the dissolution of Parliament and hence led to elections of both the prime minister and Parliament.

Semi-presidentialism

- The president is directly (or quasi-directly) elected.
- The president appoints the cabinet.
- The cabinet is politically accountable to Parliament.
- The president can dismiss the cabinet and/or dissolve Parliament.

accountability are fundamentally different, the cabinet also constitutes the government in systems with a directly elected prime minister (Israel) and in systems with directorial government (Switzerland).

Head of government's taking office rests on support of	Fixed term	
	Yes	No
Electorate	Presidential (US)	Parliamentary with directly elected PM (Israel)
		Semipresidentialism (F)
Parliament	Directorial government (Switzerland)	Parliamentary (UK)

Fig. 8.1 Regime types

Note: Only one example is included for each type.

KEY POINTS

❑ Today's governments constitute what remains of absolute monarchs, after splitting-off judicial and legislative functions.

❑ Notwithstanding the separation of powers doctrine, state functions are not fully separated. The government has retained important legislative powers, though differences exist between different regime types.

❑ Different regime types (or systems of government) also distinguish themselves by the definition of government. Constitutionally one-person executives and collective bodies can be distinguished. Some governments include the head of state while others have a separate one.

COUNTRY PROFILE Switzerland

Swiss Confederation (*Schweizerische Eidgenossenschaft/ Confédération Suisse/Confederazione Svizzera*)

State formation

The Swiss Confederation was founded as a defence alliance in 1291. Switzerland gained independence from the German Empire in 1499 and became a republic in 1848, turning from an alliance to a federal state.
Constitution 1999, effective 2000 (a revised version of the 1874 constitution).

Form of government

Federal parliamentary republic.
Head of state President and Vice President elected by the Federal Assembly from among the 7 members of the cabinet; term of 1 year (no consecutive terms).
Head of government The President.
Cabinet Federal Council (*Bundesrat/Conseil Fédéral/Consiglio Federale*) elected by the Federal Assembly from among its members; term of 4 years.
Administrative subdivisions 26 cantons including 6 half-cantons.

Legal system

Civil law system influenced by customary law; judicial review of legislative acts, except with respect to federal decrees of general obligatory character.

Legislature

Bicameral Federal Assembly (*Bundesversammlung/ Assemblee Fédérale/Assemblea Federale*).

Lower house National Council (*Nationalrat/Conseil National/Consiglio Nazionale*): 200 seats; term of 4 years.
Upper house Council of States (*Ständerat/Conseil des Etats/Consiglio degli Stati*): 46 seats (two representatives from each canton and one from each half canton); term of 4 years.

Electoral system (lower house)

Proportional representation, but single majority system for 5 single-member constituencies (two cantons, three half-cantons).
Formula Hagenbach-Bischoff method, with remaining seats being distributed according to the rule of highest average, in multi-member constituencies. Each elector can vote for a list as it stands or modify it by crossing out or repeating names appearing on it; he can moreover split his vote between different lists ('panachage') or select names from different lists in forming his own on a blank ballot paper.
Constituencies 26 multi- or single-member constituencies corresponding to the country's 20 cantons and 6 half-cantons.
Barrier clause None.
Suffrage Universal, 18 years.

Direct democracy

Mandatory referendum on constitution and international treaties, optional referendum on laws. Popular initiatives for the total or partial revision of the constitution. The 'general popular initiative' (introduced with a vote in 2003) allows 100,000 citizens to put not only constitutional changes, but also the implementation and modification of federal laws, on the political agenda.

(continued)

COUNTRY PROFILE Switzerland (*continued*)

Party system Results of the 2003 legislative elections (National Council):

Electorate:	4,779,733	100.0%
Voters:	2,161,921	45.2%

Party	Valid votes	%	Seats
Swiss People's Party	561,817	26.7	55
Social Democratic Party	490,388	23.3	52
Free Democratic Party	363,643	17.3	36
Christian Democrats	302,355	14.4	28
Green Party	160,209	7.6	13
Evangelical People's Party	47,839	2.3	3
Liberal Party	45,864	2.2	4
Federal Democratic Union	26,586	1.3	2
Swiss Democrats	19,263	0.9	1
Swiss Labour Party	18,930	0.9	2
Alternative List	12,523	0.6	1
Solidarities	10,563	0.5	1
Christian Social Party	7,358	0.4	1
League of Ticino	7,304	0.4	1
Others	27,416	1.3	0
Total	2,102,058	100.0	200

Notes: Category 'Others' includes parties with less than 1% nation-wide and no seats.
Source: Federal Assembly; Swiss Federal Statistical Office.

The internal working of government

The constitutional texts are typically silent about the internal working and decision-making of government. Although public lawyers may be able to fill such gaps by interpretation, in reality much is left to the political actors. Over time conventions may establish themselves. Conventions are normative rules that are generally respected although they are not backed up by law or other formally binding rules. Once conventions are ingrained, they may be as binding as formal rules provided by the constitution or ordinary laws. Yet constitutional conventions are binding only as long as the decision-makers respect them. Although breaking conventions typically is not cost-free for the breaker, respecting conventions cannot be forced upon them. Consequently, the more a mode of governing rests on formal rules, the more difficult it is to introduce change.

Political science has established a number of descriptive models of government. These models are partly derived from the constitutional order but try to highlight how the government actually works and arrives at decisions. The following models thus capture which actor or actors are typically able to leave their imprint on the outcome of the government decision-making process to a greater extent than other participants. They were developed with the background of the archetypal cases of presidential and parliamentary government—the US and UK—and subsequently applied to other cases. These are partly more complex and hence have given reason for conceptual refinement.

Presidential government

The principle of presidential government is to vest all executive power in a single, directly (or quasi directly) elected politician for a fixed term (i.e. the president is not political accountable to the legislature). As Article II of the US Constitution puts it: 'The executive Power shall be vested in a President of the United States of America.' Lijphart (1992) lists 'a one-person executive' among the defining principles of presidentialism. More realistically, the 'elected executive names and directs the composition of the government' (Shugart and Carey 1992: 19). Thus, within the executive domain, the president is sovereign. Different US presidents have developed their own styles. Some used their cabinet members mainly for executing their orders while others used them as advisers, but a collective decision-making system was never established (Warshaw 1996).

Cabinet government

While presidential government is the logical outflow of presidential system, cabinet government represents the traditional operating mode of parliamentary government as it emerged in Britain in the first half of the nineteenth century. Then the cabinet discussed and decided the important issues collectively. The prime minister was a chairman rather than a chief (Farrell 1971), a first among equals (*primus inter pares*). The background to that was the limited role of the state and the fact that the cabinet initially was the monarch's creation. A slim state kept the cabinet agenda manageable. The cabinet being the monarch's creation had three implications:

1. In many ways the monarch was his own 'prime minister', dealing with his ministers on an individual basis.

2. The ministers objected a strong prime minister undermining their direct link to the monarch.

3. So did parliament that was keen to avoid individual ministers' accountability being obscured by cabinet hierarchy (Mackintosh 1977: 56). Cabinet government continued to prevail when the

electoral reform gradually loosened the cabinet's tie with the monarch while strengthening that with the House of Commons (Macintosh 1977: 155–8, 257–343).

With the gradual increase of government tasks, however, more and more issues needed to be handled and decided. While their number clearly exceded what a cabinet could handle as a collective body, at the same time many issues became too technical to allow a meaningful discussion between non-specialists. This had two consequences. First, the proportion of government decisions going though cabinet declined. Second, many cabinet decisions became formal, only ratifying what was 'precooked' before the cabinet meeting within and between the ministries (Blondel and Müller-Rommel 1997, 1993). Thus **classical cabinet government** is a thing of the past. Yet this has not made the cabinet an empty vessel, making decisions only in name but not in substance. A number of authors have identified important issues that are still decided by the cabinet in substance and have stressed the role of the cabinet 'as court of appeal for *both* ministers radically out of sympathy with a general line, *and* for a premier confronted by a ministerial colleague who insists on ploughing her or his furrow' (Dunleavy and Rhodes 1990: 11). If a cabinet fulfills these functions, i.e. deliberates and decides important issues and also functions as court of appeal, then we can speak of **post-classical cabinet government**.

Prime ministerial government

Since the early 1960s, a transformation of the operating mode of British cabinets was noted. Richard Crossman, then a Labour MP with academic background, who himself served in the cabinet later on, coined the term prime ministerial government (Crossman 1963, 1972). In this model, collective deliberation and effective decision-making in and by the cabinet has been replaced by monocratic decision-making by the prime minister. Authors writing about other European states that experienced long stretches of single-party government, in particular Greece and Spain, have echoed the British diagnosis: cabinet government has given way to prime ministerial government.

But how can the prime minister play such a dominant role? Dunleavy and Rhodes have identified three different modes of prime ministerial government: (1) a generalized ability to decide policy *across all issue areas* in which the prime minister takes an interest; (2) by *deciding key issues* which subsequently determine most remaining areas of government policy; (3) by defining a *governing ethos*, 'atmosphere', or operating ideology which generates predictable and determinate solutions to most policy problems, and hence so constrains other ministers' freedom of manœuvre as to make them simple agents of the premier's will (Dunleavy and Rhodes 1990: 8).

Prime ministerial government suggests monocratic decision-making and hence resembles presidential government. Yet, the difference is that presidents have a constitutional right to do so while prime ministers need to go beyond their constitutional role. Also, presidents are unassailable, as their term is fixed, while prime ministers in principle can be forced out of office at any date. Such involuntary departure from office is not just a hypothetical possibility, as the most powerful British post-war prime minister, Margaret Thatcher, experienced in 1990, when she was ousted by her party.

Ministerial government

Finally, the transformation of cabinet government is seen to have occurred in the opposite direction. Rather than concentrating power in the prime minister, it has dispersed among the individual cabinet members. This is ministerial government or, in Andeweg's (1997) terminology, 'fragmented government'. As already noted, modern governments simply have to take too many decisions to bring the overwhelming majority to the attention of the cabinet. Decisions ending up in the cabinet typically are ratified only. Ministers are overworked and primarily concerned about getting their own act together. They are inclined to interfere in the business of other ministers only if the concerned decisions would produce negative fallout for their own department. Otherwise ministers refrain even from issuing their opinion, respecting a tacit rule of mutual non-intervention. This rule rests in the ministers' concern for their own department and career. As non-intervention is mutual, this rule helps them to get cabinet support for their own policies and it is the success or failure in directing their respective ministry that is crucial for the conduct of their careers. Recognizing this

development, Laver and Shepsle (1990, 1996) have made the strong assumption that ministers are 'policy dictators' within their own domain as the founding assumption for their theory of coalition formation.

Models of government and cabinet coalitions in parliamentary systems

Thus far party has been absent from the government modes presented here. Their implicit assumption is that no party line of division runs through government, though party-bonds may be important to overcoming other centrifugal forces (such as conflicting departmental interests). Indeed, cabinets consisting of more than a single party are unlikely to approach both full-blown prime ministerial and ministerial government.

To begin with, in the former the prime minister's dominance is partly due to his role as electoral leader and indeed victor when coming to office. The ministers' submission to the prime minster partly rests on his role as party asset that is not to be damaged by internal challenges. Coalition governments can come close to prime ministerial government when one party is dominant and the coalition builds on an electoral alliance that ties together the cabinet parties. Yet, in most cases the analogy to prime ministerial government in coalition governments is the establishment of an oligarchic leadership, consisting of the leaders of the coalition parties, with each party leader being on the one hand a 'prime minister' of his or her party team in government, and on the other hand deciding critical issues together with the other party leader(s). Note, however, that there are limits to collective leadership and 'sharing' the prime minister's powers. Party leaders cannot attend international summits—which are often the place where important decisions are made—in tandem. Nor can constitutional powers be formally shared. Thus, in the case of conflict, the prime minister can always invoke whatever powers the constitution has endowed the office.

Ministerial government in coalition regimes in strict terms would mean that 'the cabinet is not simply a *collection* of coalition partners, but instead it is a *distribution* of specific powers over policy formulation and implementation among those partners'

(Laver and Shepsle 1996: 282). In other words, each government party would implement its own policy in their departments and exercise no influence on the departments held by its partner or partners. This stark assumption underlies the coalition theory of Laver and Shepsle (1990, 1996; for a critique see Dunleavy and Bastow 2001) that predicts the formation of the government that allows each of the government parties full control over its most preferred policy dimension.

Coalition government works nowhere strictly according to the ministerial government model (see the contributions in Laver and Shepsle 1994). At least some policies get agreed between the parties—typically representing substantive compromises between the different party positions—before the coalition is set up. These deals are often fixed in coalition agreements. Moreover, coalition governance mechanisms such as coalition committees, watchdog junior ministers, and other scrutiny mechanisms are established to guarantee the deals are being observed by the coalition partners (Müller and Strøm 2000; Thies 2001; Timmermans 2003, 2006; Martin and Vanberg 2004; Strøm, Müller,

and Bergman 2007). Yet within these important confines even coalition governments can display a tendency to work according to the ministerial government mode.

Variability of government modes

Government modes are not fixed once and forever. The above discussion of the transformation of cabinet government into prime ministerial governent and/or ministerial government already suggests some long-term change. Yet government modes also vary according to political conditions and issues (Andeweg 1997). Thus single-party governments are more likely to become prime ministerial than coalition cabinets. One might be inclined to think that prime ministerial government requires suitable personalities, which need not always emerge. At the same time, each cabinet is likely to handle issues differently, depending on their relevance and potential of causing damage to the government. We therefore need to be precise whether a specific cabinet is classified by the most frequent decision mode or the decision mode that is applied to the most important issues.

KEY POINTS

❑ Constitutions are typically silent about the internal working and decision-making of government, leaving much to the political actors who adapt the government modes to changing circumstances.

❑ Presidential systems provide for presidential government (with its internal variations); parliamentary

systems offer a broader range of decision modes: cabinet government, prime ministerial government, and ministerial government.

❑ Coalition governments in parliamentary systems typically have developed more complex decision modes.

The autonomy of government

The previous section has looked at the government in isolation from its environment. When political parties were mentioned, the assumption was that there is no difference whatsoever between government members and their parties. Yet political parties are complex entities. They consist of (1) the mass organization (the 'party on the ground'), (2) the parliamentary party, and (3) the party team in government (both the latter are also referred to as 'party in public office'). None of the three must be united

internally nor fully agree with the other layers. To make it more complicated, there exists also the 'party in the electorate'. Although this layer lacks organization and therefore the quality of a political actor, it is a highly relevant reference point for politicians.

Again important differences can exist in the opinions held by party voters and one or more of the layers already mentioned (those of activists, MPs, and government members). Understanding governments thus requires exploring the autonomy they have from other actors or providers of essential re-sources without which they would not be able to govern. This section discusses political parties and, more briefly, the bureaucracy (which gets a more extended treatment in the following section). Parties are essential for getting a government into office and maintaining it there. And without the permanent bureaucracy the government could not govern.

Government autonomy: the party dimension

It is the electoral connection that makes government democratic and it is political parties which play a crucial role in structuring elections, even when the electoral system allows the choice of individual can-didates (Katz 1997). Modern democracies, therefore, have **party government** in a general sense. Yet, this understanding of party government can be contras-ted with a more specific one. According to Richard Rose (1976: 371):

> **❝** party government exists only in so far as the actions of office-holders are influenced by values and policies derived from the party. Where the life of party politics does not affect government policy, the accession of a new party to office is little more significant than the accession of a new monarch; the party reigns but does not rule. **❞**

What role parties have after the elections is subject to normative and empirical discussions. It is sufficient here to say that conflicting normative theories suggest both the full autonomy of elected officials from their party and, conversely, a strong role of the party in de-termining the course steered by the government. The former position can be associated with constitutional theory and liberal and conservative thinkers, the lat-ter one with much of constitutional practice and mostly socialist ideas (Birch 1967). The remainder of this section explores the issue empirically.

The key question is thus to what extent political parties can control the behaviour of their govern-ment teams. Three means of control are of particular importance (Rose 1976; Katz 1986; Müller 1994; Blondel and Cotta 2000).

Party programmes

Party control of the cabinet will be enhanced in situations where party programmes not only clearly state the intentions of the party, but also specify

appropriate means to the desired ends. In such cir-cumstances, ministers will have clear targets, whilst the party will have a yardstick for measurement of their performance.

Selection of cabinet members

Party control of the cabinet will be enhanced where cabinet ministers have internalized and act upon party values. The internalization of party values is hard to measure, but holding high party office is certainly a plausible indicator. Note that ministers who have good intentions of serving their party still need to be skilled executives in order to succeed.

Permanent control of the party over the cabinet

While the above conditions increase the likelihood of 'partyness of government' (Katz 1986), they do not guarantee the implementation of party policies. Parties therefore may want to exercise permanent control over their ministers. Naturally, the less the two above conditions are fulfilled—for instance, be-cause of the need to appoint technical experts rather than party leaders—and the more changed circum-stances (such as international crises und unexpected economic developments) have dated the party pro-grammes, the more important such control can be considered.

Empirical studies of party programmes and their relevance for government policy have a long tradi-tion, though most of them confine themselves to single countries and cabinets. In one of the few comparative and comprehensive studies, McDonald and Budge (2005) took a highly aggregated approach and compared party ambitions (programmes) in twenty-one countries with government ambitions (government declarations) and actual outputs in terms of budget priorities. In measuring party ambi-tion the methodology of the Comparative Manifesto Project (CMP) was employed: a frequency count of party statements in more than fifty coding categories (e.g. 'free enterprise', 'social services limitation', or 'regulate capitalism').

This study did not find relevant party impact on government in a short-term perspective. The inertia of public policy is simply too strong. In the words of McDonald and Budge (2005: 180): 'The reason is not that changes are not made but that they are slow, because of pre-existing budgets, contracts, commitments, and entitlements in the field of expenditures; time constraints, due process, legislative and social opposition, and administrative bottlenecks in the field of legislation.' Only when a party manages to hold on to government for a long time—McDonald and Budge list the New Deal Democrats in the US, the Thatcher–Major Conservatives in the UK, and the Scandinavian Social Democrats—will a party imprint on public policy be clearly visible.

Blondel, Cotta, and associates chose a less aggregated approach (Blondel and Cotta 1996, 2000). Conceptually, they considered both directions of influence: party on government and government on party. Three ideal types of party–government relations can be distinguished:

• Dominance—one of the two dominates the other.

• Autonomy—government and government parties coexist without exercising influencing on each other.

• Fusion—party and government become politically indistinguishable.

Empirically, this research was concerned with appointments (to the cabinet and the party executive), government patronage, and fifty policy decisions in a set of Western European countries. Unlike the CMP-based study, which extracted general policy concerns of parties from the manifestoes and the general direction of government policies from budget domains, this research was concerned with specific pledges and specific government policies. The aim was to establish to what extent government behaviour had a party origin and in what direction, if any, top-level recruitment takes place—from the party to the government (as the party government model suggests) or in the opposite direction.

Given the many methodological challenges and the small-N design, the Blondel and Cotta (1996, 2000) study has an exploratory character, indicating the potential value of some research directions for more comprehensive and methodologically refined attempts rather than providing final answers. Yet the study suggests that the ideal-typical picture of party government—with the party taking over government—needs correction. Specifically, after an initial period of **fusion** after a party entering government, new government appointments lead to increasing

autonomy of the two, though 'fast-track' appointments of government members to high party office suggest even a tendency towards **dependence** on the party. With regard to policy, the government is not just the technocratic executor of party policy. Rather, the government plays a significant role in shaping policies originating from the party and initiating its own ones. Patronage, it seems, is used to compensate the party for its desired policies that the government cannot deliver or does not want to deliver.

Presidentialization?

One recent attempt to capture the strengthening of the executive *vis-à-vis* political parties is the concept of presidentialization. Specifically, it means the strengthening of the chief executive. Although the term 'presidentialization' has been used earlier in studies of the British Prime Minister (Foley 1993, 2000; Pryce 1997) the most systematic comparative attempt has been made by Pogunke, Webb, and collaborators (Poguntke and Webb 2005). They associate presidentialization—in all regime types—with '(1) increasing leadership power resources and autonomy within the party and the political executive respectively, and (2) increasingly leadership-centred electoral processes' (Poguntke and Webb 2005: 5). In their analysis this process affects the internal working of the executive, the running of political parties, and the functioning of the electoral process.

Presidentialized government represents one ideal type of government. The 'partyfied' type of government occupies the opposite end of the continuum. The key question then is what is the role of individual leaders and of collective actors. Poguntke and Webb note that different regime types—parliamentarism, semi-presidentialism, and presidentialism—provide the actors with different power resources and hence constrain the place a specific government can take on the continuum. Thus, a parliamentary system under a strong prime minister can be more 'presidentialized' than a presidential system under a weak president, but never more so when the president is strong.

In their fourteen-countries empirical analyses Poguntke, Webb, and associates identify an almost uniform trend towards presidentialism. Specifically they recognize shifts in intra-executive power to the leader, increasing autonomy of the executive leader from the party, shifts of intra-party power to the leader, the leader's increasing autonomy from other party heavyweights, a growth of the leader's media coverage, increasing focus on the leader in electoral campaigns, and growing leader effects on voting behaviour. In combination these developments indeed suggest a major shift away from the 'partyfied' type of democracy.

Government autonomy: bureaucratic government?

The number of people who enter or leave government after elections (i.e. elected leaders and political appointees) differs from system to system. Yet in most systems their numbers are tiny compared to those of bureaucrats, even when lower rank civil servants are not considered. In many parliamentary systems hardly more than two dozen of posts changed hands when a wholesale government turnover occurred in the first post-war decades.

The idea of bureaucratic government (Rose 1969) rests on the assumption that such small a group cannot run the whole show and critically depends on the permanent bureaucracy. Bureaucrats can set the agenda of their political masters by identifying problems that need to be addressed; they can limit political choices by presenting a narrow set of alternatives and by undermining the viability of ideas that run counter to the department's common wisdom. Such ideas are labelled, for instance, as not workable, too expensive, having huge undesirable side effects, having already failed in earlier attempts, etc. The BBC comedy series *Yes, Minister*, originally broadcast in the 1980s, provides a masterful (though, of course, exaggerated) vision of bureaucratic government. More so than any other mode of government, bureaucratic government remains and need to remain invisible. Thus, politicians continue to dominate the public stage. They may even make consequential decisions (according to one of the above modes). Yet these decisions can be compared to choosing the flag to fly on a ship sailing on the ocean, while it is bureaucrats who determine its course. Moreover, most administrative decisions escape the politicians' attention altogether.

KEY POINTS

❑ Party government means that government actions are strongly influenced by the values and policies of the government party or parties.

❑ Political parties control their teams in government by the means of party programmes, the recruitment of party leaders into government office, and permanent oversight over and control of the government.

❑ Empirical studies mostly demonstrate that parties have only a limited impact on government. Initial fusion of party and government often gives room to government autonomy and occasionally party dependence on the government.

❑ Individual leaders tend to gain weight relative to the parties ('presidentialization').

The political capacity of government

Modern governments of rich nations can achieve much. They can maintain law and order, provide essential services to their citizens, strengthen the economy, and send men and women into orbit or explore outer space. Yet, whether governments can indeed do what is in the capacity of modern states depends largely on the political conditions that prevail during their reign. This section can discuss only a few selected topics. It leaves aside much of the often very consequential nitty-gritty details of institutional rules (see e.g. Weaver and Rockman 1993b; Strøm et al. 2003). Nor also it discuss systematically the reactions of citizens, interest groups, and the economy to government policy that at times have brought governments to their knees. It is sufficient here to refer to a few examples: the 2006 riots in the French banlieues (suburban housing complexes) which led the government to partly reverse its reform of the labour law; the mass strikes of the British trade unions that brought down the Heath government in 1974; and the less visible but much more common influence exercised by the investment decisions of firms in a globalized economy that have considerably constrained national governments' freedom of manœuvre.

Unified vs. divided government

The concepts of unified and divided government were invented in the US. Divided government means that the presidency is held by one party and at least one chamber of Congress is controlled by the other party; government is unified when all three are under the control of the same party (see also Chapter 7). The concepts of unified and divided government transfer easily to other presidential systems, although the multi-party nature of some of them requires some modification. Leaving aside non-partisan presidents, the (one-person) presidency by necessity must be under the control of one party and one party only. In contrast, no single party may control a majority in the legislature.

Yet a legislature passing a great number of detailed laws could make the president its mere servant. This could indeed be the case if no further provision were added to the definition of presidential government: some law-making authority of the president (Shugart and Carey 1992).

The US presidency represents the archetypal case of presidentialism. The formal law-making capacity of the president is a negative one: The president can veto any law passed by Congress. As long as no vote in both the House of Representatives and the Senate overrides the veto with two-thirds majority, the law is rejected and the status quo prevails. The US have seen divided government for most of the post-war period. Yet empirical studies suggest that this was not very consequential, as open battles between the Congress and the president resulting in vetos and occasional overrides have been very limited (Mayhew 1993; Binder 2003). While many studies of the US highlight the factors that prevent legislative immobilism, a comparative perspective can be particularly useful as it brings out many of the same factors more sharply and adds additional ones.

In Latin America the most powerful presidents enjoy a much richer set of legislative instruments than their US counterpart. Veto power can take the form of the line veto, enabling the president to veto specific clauses in legislation but accepting the rest,

and most presidents also enjoy decree power, the right of legislative initiative, and some procedural power in Congress (Mainwaring and Shugart 1997; Morgenstern and Nacif 2002). At the same time these systems are multi-party. Hence, the chances of a president to finding his party endowed with a legislative majority are often modest or non-existent. One influential study (Linz 1994) has seen here the main reason for the frequent breakdowns of democracy in Latin America. The institutional 'rigidity' of presidentialism—with fixed terms of both the president and the legislature—causes long periods of legislative gridlock followed by short periods of legislative overproduction. Both encourage frustrated political actors to resort to non-democratic means. Yet the specific assumptions about the behaviour of actors underlying Linz's theory have not withstood empirical scrutiny (Cheibub 2007). While it is true that democracy has had a rough life in Latin America, this is not just down to divided government. Presidents have found ways to cope with it, as Cox and Morgenstern (2002) demonstrate (see Table 8.1).

Depending on their own strength in terms of institutional empowerment and party support in the legislature, presidents employ four different stategies. I consider first the two extreme categories. The president uses unilateral powers if the legislature is hostile (**recalcitrant**). He uses presidential decrees to push forward his own policies (rather than making legislative proposals to the assembly) and vetoes laws passed by the legislature that run counter to his policy ambitions. In Cox and Morgenstern's typology this is the **imperial** president. This was the behavioural pattern of Chile's President Allende before General Pinochet's tragic military coup in 1973.

At the opposite end of the spectrum, if the president is sure that the assembly will follow his lead, he dictates his terms in the form of legislative initiative. Such a **dominant** president could be found in Mexico in the years of the Party of the Institutionalized Revolution (PRI) single-party dominance.

The two intermediate cases require the president to engage in give-and-take relations with the assembly. For the president this is more rewarding than unilateral action, as he does not need to push his powers to the very limits of constitutionality (or beyond) and because legislation is harder to overturn than presidential decrees. If the president meets a legislature that is **workable** he engages in legislative

Table 8.1 President–assembly relations under presidentialism

Presidential strategy	Assembly strategy			
	Reject	*Bargain*	*Demand payments*	*Acquiesce*
Undertake unilateral action	Imperial president, *recalcitrant assembly*			
Bargain		Coalitional president, *workable assembly*		
Pay-off			Nationally oriented president, *parochial assembly*	
Dictate				Dominant president, *subservient assembly*

Source: Cox and Morgenstern (2002: 455).

coalition-building. This requires policy deals (substantive compromises) and perhaps appointments from the coalitional parties to cabinet office. According to Cox and Morgenstern (2002), presidents in post-dictatorial Chile have followed that strategy.

Finally, if the president meets a legislature that largely consists of constituency-bound representatives who need to bring home immediate benefits for the purpose of their re-election, the president offers pork and large-scale patronage rather than policy concessions. Elected representatives then sell their policy-making powers for goods and services that they can allocate, in turn, in their districts to secure their re-election. Probably much of Brazil's recent history provides a good example of the relevance of a **parochial** strategy (Ames 2002).

As Cox and Morgenstern (2002) make clear, the same forces are at work in the US as in the two intermediary cases. Clearly, the office of the US president is not endowed with the institutional powers of imperial presidents in Latin America and elsewhere. But different presidents were in different situations

with respect to party support in Congress and other resources and chose their strategies accordingly. The record suggests that they were quite successful, although less so in more recent situations of divided government (Meyhew 1993; Binder 2003).

Attempts have been made to apply the concepts of unified and divided government to other regime types than presidentialism (Laver and Shepsle 1991; Elgie 2001). Accordingly, semi-presidential systems are treated in close analogy to presidential ones. The only difference is that the division line does not run between the executive and the legislature but between the legislature plus the cabinet on the one side and the president on the other. With regard to parliamentary systems, the authors identify minority governments as cases of 'divided government'. Here the division line runs between the cabinet (supported by a parliamentary minority) and the parliamentary majority. Without doubt these situations replicate some characteristics of divided government as it has emerged in presidential systems. Yet the very fact that the survival of government is not at stake in the latter while it it is in the two former make the analogy less than perfect and perhaps a case of 'conceptual stretching' (Sartori 1970; see also Chapter 3).

Majority vs. minority government

Governments that enjoy majority support—at least 50 per cent of the seats plus one—in parliament can not only survive in office but also enact their political programme. For a long time minority governments—governments comprising parties that collectively miss that mark—were considered an anomaly. They were considered as unwanted crisis symptoms, coming to power when no majority government could be formed. Such situations are also referred to as *immobiliste*, as they will be unable to produce political decisions (Laver and Schofield 1990: 72). Yet, as Strøm (1990) demonstated, minority governments are neither rare nor particularly unstable. This result is not driven by governments that have a *formal* minority status but can rely on a legislative (rather than government) majority coalition.

What is the rationale of minority governments? Laver and Schofield (1990: 77–81) suggest that minority governments occupying the ideological centre or, more technically, that hold the median legislator, are 'policy viable'. That means they can divide the opposition by policy proposals at the centre of the policy space. Although the left opposition will consider them too much to the right and the right opposition will find them too much to the left, these parties cannot joint forces to bring down the government and enact alternative policies.

Effective government by minority cabinets, of course, suggests that policy is the only or overwhelming motive that drives political parties. If office were dominant, parties of the extreme left and right would join forces to bring down any centrist minority government, as any new government would at least increase their chances for government office. In practice, most parties are indeed interested in government office in its own right (Müller and Strøm 1999). Yet, their behaviour is constrained by the anticipated reaction of their voters. The bringing down of a social democratic minority cabinet by parties further to the left in alliance with right-wing parties may not be well received by left voters, particularly when it results in a new government more to the right than the one replaced. Anticipated voter reactions also

matter in another sense: governing often results in electoral costs which some parties have good reasons to avoid (Strøm 1990). Indeed, as Narud and Valen (2007) show, there is a monotonic and strong trend for government parties to lose votes since the 1980s.

Table 8.2 provides a broad overview of the frequency of government types in democracies worldwide. The upper part of the table shows that minority situations—situations where no single party commands a parliamentary majority—are frequent, though more so in parliamentary than in presidential systems. The lower part suggests that about 45 per cent of these situations produce minority government in parliamentary systems and close to 78 per cent in presidential systems. Table 8.3 reports the majority status and government duration in a smaller set of countries in Western Europe, the heartland of parliamentary democracy. We see that minority cabinets account for about a third of the total. In their analysis of East Europen democracies—the ten new EU member-states and four Balkan countries—Druckman and Andrews (2007) report that 16 per cent (23 out of 76) had minority status (for the period from democratization until 2002). Yet, the more advanced East–Central European states that now belong to the European Union show about the same proportion of minority governments as their Western counterparts (see Table 8.4).

As Tables 8.3 and 8.4 reveal, overall majority cabinets enjoy a longer life than minority cabinets. Yet minority governments have a longer duration in some Western countries, particularly in those where they are a regular outcome of government formation. The figures also show that minority cabinets in most cases are clearly more than temporary solutions between two 'regular' majority governments.

As we have seen, minority government can be helped by their central location in the policy space. Institutional mechanisms such as presidential powers (already discussed in the context of divided government) can also increase their capacity. The French government is particularly lucky as the prime minister can draw on an arsenal of procedural rules that help the forcing through of government policy.

The strongest instrument is Article 49.3 of the constitution. It allows the government to turn any decision about legislation into a confidence issue, shifting the burden of proof to its opponents. Legislative proposals introduced under Article 49.3

Table 8.2 Coalitional status of governments under parliamentarism and presidentialism (1945–2002)

	Parliamentary regimes		Presidential regimes	
	N	%	N	%
Majority situations	215	43.2	121	55.5
Minority situations	283	56.8	97	44.5
Total	498	100.0	218	100.0
Government types in minority situations				
Majority coalitions	175	54.2	31	22.3
Single-party minority governments	83	25.7	49	47.6
Minority coalitions	65	20.1	31	30.1

Notes: The upper part of the table identifies government formation situations by counting the number of legislative seat distributions. Changes in the seat distribution are triggered by elections and splits and mergers of parties. The lower part records the government *type* that was formed in minority situations. Changes in the composition of government that did not affect its type—e.g. the switch from one majority coalition to another in a sitting parliament—are not registered. The number of government types exceeds that of minority situations because different government types were formed under the same seat distribution subsequently.

Source: Cheibub *et al.* (2004: 573–5).

are automatically adopted—without a vote on the proposal itself—as long as no no-confidence vote (requiring a majority of *all* MPs) unseats the government (Huber 1996). While this instrument is used frequently in France, most governments lack such strong instruments. In order to survive and get policies passed, minority cabinets therefore need to engage in negotiations with the oppositon. This limits their capacities, as is also reflected in government durations (Table 8.3). Overall, majority cabinets enjoy a longer life. In the aggregate they outlive minority cabinets by eight months. Yet, this is not true in every case.

Single-party vs. coalition government

Single-party governments have the distinctive advantage that no party line of division runs through the government. That implies that the government goals will be relatively uncontroversial internally. Any remaining differences are likely to be surpressed, given the common goal of survival in office.

Parties holding government office as result of their strong position—commanding a parliamentary majority or occupying a strategic position in the party system—are also likely to have strong leadership that can overcome internal difficulties. Hence, with everything else equal, governments consisting of a single party can be considered homogeneous. This implies that they can make decisions quickly, avoid foul compromises, and maintain a common front.

Coalition governments, in turn, need to satisfy at least some of the ambitions of each of the government parties. Even in the unlikely case of (almost) complete a priori agreement between the coalition partners about government goals, the fact remains that office-sharing means that the personal ambitions of some would-be ministers in the parties must be frustrated. This, in turn, may cause their only half-hearted support of the government (Sartori 1997). In most cases some of the party's policy ambitions will be compromised. This typically lengthens the internal decision-making process and often exposes internal divisons to the public, with the consequence

Table 8.3 Cabinet majority status and duration in Western Europe (1945–2007)

Country	Minority	Majority		Mean duration (in months)	
	N	*N*	%	*Minority*	*Majority*
Austria	1	23	95.8	18.2	31.6
Belgium	4	31	88.6	1.9	21.5
Denmark	29	4	12.1	23.0	26.5
Finland	17	31	75.6	6.7	20.1
France	7	21	75.0	14.5	23.0
Germany	3	25	89.3	0.8	27.8
Greece	2	11	91.7	21.7	23.8
Iceland	5	21	80.8	5.8	31.7
Ireland	11	12	52.2	28.5	36.8
Italy	24	28	54.9	9.2	15.2
Luxembourg	0	16	100.0		40.0
Netherlands	4	23	85.2	3.6	32.9
Norway	19	10	34.5	23.2	31.7
Portugal	5	10	76.9	29.2	20.3
Spain	8	2	22.2	35.5	41.6
Sweden	20	8	28.6	29.9	20.3
United Kingdom	3	19	95.0	27.1	35.0
Total	162	295	66.7	18.8	26.9

Note: Includes all cabinets that completed their term by 1 May 2007.
Source: Müller and Strøm (2000, updated).

of the government appearing divided and therefore weak. The alternative of one party quietly submitting would allocate the costs of coalition one-sidedly: that party would be considered to be selling out to its coalition partner by its activists and voters. These problems tend to remain modest in ideologically homogeneous coalitions but accelerate in heterogeneous ones. And they tend to be particularly tricky when they are fuelled not only by party policy ambition but also by office ambition. Whenever the most prestigious office—that of prime minister—is at stake *between* the coalition partners, coalitions tend to be seriously hampered by internal rivalry and conflict.

According to Table 8.2, in minority situations coalition governments are the dominant outcome in parliamentary regimes and still result in more than half such situations in presidential regimes. Tables 8.4 and 8.5 again detail the post-war record of East–Central and West European systems, respectively. We can distinguish countries with a

Table 8.4 Government duration in East–Central Europe (in months)

Country	Time	All governments	Single-party governments	Coalitions	Majority governments	Minority governments
Bulgaria	1991–1997	28	30	–	38	18
n (std. dev.)		4 (16)	3 (19)		2 (18)	2 (6)
Czech Republic	1993–2002	36	49	30	43	32
n (std. dev.)		3 (16)	1 (0)	2 (17)	1 (0)	2 (22)
Estonia	1992–2002	16	14	17	17	14
n (std. dev.)		8 (11)	2 (15)	6 (11)	5 (12)	3 (11)
Hungary	1990–2002	37	–	37	37	–
n (std. dev.)		4 (20)		4 (20)	4 (20)	
Latvia	1993–2002	11	–	11	12	10
n (std. dev.)		10 (8)		10 (8)	6 (10)	4 (6)
Lithuania	1993–2001	17	23	14	19	8
n (std. dev.)		6 (13)	2 (18)	4 (11)	5 (13)	1 (0)
Poland	1991–2003	16	17	16	19	11
n (std. dev.)		(8)	1 (0)	7 (9)	5 (8)	3 (6)
Romania	1992–2000	16	12	18	16	17
n (std. dev.)		6 (8)	2 (13)	4 (5)	3 (4)	3 (12)
Slovakia	1993–2002	20	8	22	761	9
n (std. dev.)		6 (22)	1 (0)	5 (24)	4 (25)	2 (1)
Slovenia	1993–2002	20	–	20	26	9
n (std. dev.)		6 (12)		6 (356)	4 (11)	2 (5)
Total	1990–2003	20	22	19	22	14
n (std. dev.)		61 (14)	12 (16)	48 (14)	39 (15)	22 (10)

Notes: Caretaker and governments in office at the time of the data collection are excluded. The Beron government in Bulgaria was non-partisan and supported by a minority of deputies. It is classified as minority government but not as coalition or single-party government.

Sources: Danzer (2007); Müller-Rommel *et al.* (2004).

uniform pattern of single-party governments from those that have experienced coalition governments only, and those with a mixed record.

Tables 8.4 and 8.5 again provide country means for government duration of both single-party and coalition cabinets. Leaving aside here the variation in the maximum length of parliamentary terms, the overall picture is remarkably balanced. In the aggregate, single-party governments do not last

significantly longer than coalition governments. Yet, this similarity should not prevent us from seing that very different forces are at work here. Coalition governments that do not reach the maximum possible duration mostly terminate over internal conflict and unbridgeable differences between the partners. In contrast, single-party governments tend to shorten their term because they feel strong and early elections are likely to return them to government (Strøm and

Table 8.5 Government form and cabinet duration (1945–2007)

	Single-party	Coalition		Mean duration (in months)		
	N	N	%	Single-party	Coalition	All
Austria	6	19	76.0	40.7	28.3	30.1
Belgium	5	30	85.7	10.2	20.8	19.2
Denmark	14	19	57.6	18.6	27.2	23.4
Finland	11	37	77.1	15.2	17.5	15.2
France	6	22	78.6	13.4	22.9	20.8
Germany	4	24	85.7	4.3	28.3	24.8
Greece	11	2	15.4	30.3	3.9	23.4
Iceland	4	22	84.6	4.3	30.8	26.6
Ireland	13	10	43.5	29.8	33.8	32.9
Italy	22	34	60.7	7.4	13.7	12.2
Luxembourg	0	16	100.0	–	40.0	40.0
Netherlands	0	28	100.0	–	27.8	27.8
Norway	19	10	34.5	27.5	22.7	26.0
Portugal	10	8	44.4	36.1	12.8	19.5
Spain	12	0	0.0	36.8	–	33.9
Sweden	20	8	28.6	28.5	24.2	27.4
United Kingdom	22	0	0.0	34.2	–	34.2
Total	179	289	61.8	24.9	24.0	

Note: Includes all cabinets that completed their term by 1 May 2007.
Source: Müller and Strøm (2000, updated).

Swindle 2002). In East–Central Europe the picture is remarkable similar, particularly given the lack of consolidation of both parties and party systems in most of the countries (Nikolenyi 2004).

KEY POINTS

☐ The political capacities of governments differ widely, depending on the government's support base in the political institutions and the society.

☐ In presidential regimes, 'unified government' suggests greater capacities. 'Divided governement' requires the president to use institutional prerogatives, bribe members of the legislature, or compromise with legislative parties.

☐ In parliamentary regimes normally single-party majority governments have the greatest political capacities.

Bureaucratic capacities

No government can achieve its goals, limited as they may be, without many helping hands. The modern state has developed the permanent bureaucracy as the prime instrument for that purpose (see Chapter 4). In order to fulfil the bureaucracy's mission, its members—the bureaucrats—need to be able and willing to do their job. In addition, the internal organization of tasks and processes can exercise a major influence on bureaucratic capacities.

Working from an idealization of the Prussian bureaucracy, Max Weber (1947) outlined the key characteristics of bureaucratic organization:

- *Personnel*: formal life-long employment of bureaucrats who receive a fixed salary and earn pension rights in return to their service and who are promoted largely on the basis of their seniority (the length of their service).

- *Organization*: specialization, training, functional division of labour, well-defined areas of jurisdiction, and a clear hierarchy among the bureaucrats.

- *Procedure*: impersonal application of general rules (mostly laws and government decrees); business is conducted on the basis of written documents, bureaucratic decisions are recorded, and the relevant documents carefully stored.

Each of these features has a specific function in making the bureaucratic organization an effective instrument. Weber indeed suggested that it is not only **effective** (i.e. getting things done) but, indeed, 'capable of attaining the highest degree of **efficiency**' (i.e. getting things done with a minimum of costs) (1947: 337). Life-long employment and career perspectives allow the administration to attract qualified staff and maintain it. Personnel stability, in turn, is one condition for a smooth working of the administrative machine that builds on division of labour and specialization. Well-trained bureaucrats who work on clearly defined issues and who are part and parcel of an unambiguous command chain are able to produce 'standardized' decisions. That means different bureaucrats when confronted with the same case would arrive at identical decisions derived from the general rules. Paying the bureaucrats a fixed salary and having strong rules of incompatibility aim at preventing personal interest intervening in their

decisions. Finally, the requirement that decisions get fully documented and hence can be checked at any time helps to keep bureaucrats on track.

A cornerstone of the bureaucratic system is **merit recruitment**. Accordingly, access to the administration is not restricted to particular segments of society; selection and promotion aim at appointing the best-qualified individuals. With regard to promotion, in the case of equal qualifications seniority is decisive. Although it is already covered in the above general characteristics of merit recruitment, it is worth pointing out that in such a system political affiliation and attitudes of job applicants and members of the bureaucracy do not play any role. Such considerations would not only be inappropriate but also unnecessary, as the bureaucracy is considered a neutral instrument. Within the confines of laws and regulations the merit bureaucrats serve every government loyally.

Problems of bureaucracy

To be sure, Max Weber's appraisal of bureaucracy rested on its comparison with pre-modern types of organization (including patrimonial systems, where offices were sold and, in turn, generated income for their holders). He was quick to add that real-life bureaucracies become inefficient when decisions need to take into consideration the individual characteristics of the cases to be decided. Indeed, the term 'bureaucracy', and even more so the adjective 'bureaucratic', in ordinary language implies excessive rules and complicated procedures, formalism, and rigidity in their application, hence delay and inefficiency in making decisions and consequently the waste of public money. It is true that each of the principles of bureaucratic organization can be overdone. The rule of law then degenerates to rigidity and inertia in procedures and over-regulation, specialization of bureaucrats leads to civil servants who perform acts without understanding their consequences, and personnel stability and arcane internal rules create a closed system out of touch with its environment. One possible consequence of the latter is groupthink. Groupthink means the unconscious minimizing of intra-organizational conflict in making decisions at the price of their quality, which can lead to disaster (Janis 1972; 't Hart 1990). A famous case of groupthink was the Kennedy administration's Bay of Pigs invasion and perhaps the same can be said about the more recent Iraq war planning of the Bush administration.

Theories of bureaucracy have been concerned with such phenomena but more often with less spectacular developments. Parkinson's Law is a famous formula for the creeping but consequential growth of the bureaucracy. Parkinson (1958) suggested that in a bureaucratic organization 'work expands to fill the time allotted'. Consequently, the development of bureaucratic organizations, such as the British Colonial Office, does not reflect its objective function. Indeed, that office increased its staff size considerably while the British Empire declined.

As we have seen, the principles of bureaucratic organization aim at separating the private interest of bureaucrats from the decisions they have to make. Yet to assume that human beings will ever be able and willing to separate completely their private preferences from their behaviour as officials would be naïve. Bureaucrats do have private interests and political preferences. They want to boost their income and prestige by climbing up the career ladder and will probably take account of their own political preferences when preparing or making decisions.

Let us consider first the growth of bureaucracy. Parkinson (1958) noted that officials want to 'multiply subordinates, not rivals'. The Public Choice School made the private interests of bureaucrats their starting point. Downs (1967) has provided us with a long shopping list of motivations and related behaviours of bureaucrats. Accordingly bureaucrats are interested in power, money income, prestige, convenience, and security, but they are also motivated by personal loyalties to their colleagues and institution, pride in proficient performance of work, desire to serve the public interest, and commitment to specific programs. This results in several types of bureaucrats—climbers, conservers, zealots, advocates, statesmen—with different motives and behaviours. Downs's over-complex taxonomy, however, has been less significant in terms of academic research and political fallout than the more parsimonious work of Niskanen (1971).

Niskanen built his theory on the simple assumption that bureaucrats have the goal of increasing their budgets. This is because most of the bureaucrats' personal incentives—salary, reputation, power, policy-making capacity—are positively related to the size of their organization's budget. The push of the bureaucrats is met by the pull from societal groups and their representatives who make increasing demands on government. Two reasons make it difficult to keep the growth of government at bay:

1. It is often hard or impossible to measure objectively the 'final outputs' of bureaucracies. With regard to many outputs it is hard to say when an optimal level is reached and to avoid overproduction. The super-powers' many-times overkill capacity built up during the cold war is a case in point.

2. Specific bureaucracies tend to be the only suppliers of particular (public) goods, e.g. defence or public health. This avoids wasteful duplication but also frees the bureaucracies from competitive pressure (which has negative effects on efficiency) and it deprives the politicians of alternative sources of information. All this contributes strongly to the growth of government.

Niskanen's theory is difficult to test. When confronted with empirical data, the evidence has been mixed. While some have found very little evidence conforming to the theory (Blais and Dion 1991), other studies remain sceptical about the power of bureaucrats to set the agenda in a way that results in ever-increasing budgets, but marshal impressive empirical evidence that production of services by private sector firms is considerably cheaper than that by bureaucrats (Mueller 2003: 371–80). In any case, with Niskanen serving on the Board of Economic Advisers under President Reagan and having inspired this president's thinking, his theory has been quite important for the recent efforts at rolling back the state.

I now turn to the effort bureaucrats bring to their job and to the question whether they diverge from the directions given by political officials. In recent years several studies have employed the principal–agent framework of micro-economics to address these issues (see also Chapters 7 and 9). Brehm and Gates (1997: 50) have nicely summarized the set of options bureaucratic agents have:

1. They may either work in the interest of their principal (no agency problem) or engage in leisure-shirking, dissent-shirking, or sabotage.

2. In the case of **leisure-shirking**, bureaucrats simply do not work as much as they are expected to do (and paid for). They may have a late start in the morning, enjoy an extended lunch break, and 'compensate' for this by leaving their office early, as a widespread stereotype of civil servants suggests (for an empirical example see Putnam 1993: 5).

3. **Dissent-shirking** means that bureaucrats do not do their best to implement the policies desired by their principals because they themselves have different preferences. This either means that the status quo is preserved or that the incumbent minister experiences an improvement from the status quo, but not enough to satisfy his or her ambitions.

4. While shirking leads to insufficient or no policies, **political sabotage** means the production of negative outputs. In this case, civil servants actively work against the interests of their principal.

Note, however, that it is not necessarily the fault of bureaucrats if politicians are not satisfied with their services. Simply, sometimes politicians demand more than a Weberian (neutral) bureaucrat can give: privilege the minister's constituency, help acquaintances of the minister obtain government permits to which they are not entitled, twist a public tender to benefit a sponsor of the minister's party, help mislead the opposition when preparing answers to parliamentary questions, and obstruct investigations of the Audit Court, parliamentary investigation committee, or the public prosecutor. There are indeed plenty of cases where members of government have suggested such behaviour to their civil servants. Of course, we know only those that eventually were exposed to the public, mostly ending with ministerial resignation. Yet it may be safe to assume that these cases constitute only the tip of the iceberg.

Politicians have responded in two ways to their uneasiness with the bureaucracy: (1) establishing spoils systems and (2) introducing New Public Management.

Spoils systems

In a spoils system the victorious party is free to appoint large layers of the administration after each election, with the jobs going to the party faithful.

Thereby the party rewards them for their work towards victory, either by providing their labour or making important financial contributions. An open spoils system was practised in the US in the nineteenth century, with President Andrew Jackson (1829–37) being crucial in its introduction. The claim was that the spoils system would be democratic in two ways:

1. It would allow the victor of the democratic contest to work with an administration that shares his political philosophy and hence would help him to live up to the promises made in the campaign.

2. It was radically democratic as it entrusted ordinary Americans rather than a closed elite of professional bureaucrats with the business of government.

In the second half of the nineteenth century the spoils system came under attack. Eventually, the Pendleton Civil Service Act (1883) established a merit system that was gradually introduced for the bulk of government positions. Only senior government jobs remained up for grabs for the victor. Yet, compared to most other systems, the US maintained a large degree of open politicization. Each change in the office of president is accompanied by the replacement of thousands of government employees by people more akin to the new incumbent and his party.

The major advantage of open spoils systems is that they provide the politicians with administrators who are committed to the government goals. Hence, if political faith would suffice to move mountains, the government would be enabled to achieve its goals. The disadvantage of bringing in cohorts of new people, often with little prior experience in public administration, is that the appointees do not know enough about their organization and its environment. Nor do they know each other, resulting in a 'government of strangers' (Heclo 1977). Moreover, political appointees often do not stay long enough to compensate for these disadvantages by learning 'on the job'.

While open spoils systems are rare, covert ones are more frequent. These are merit systems only in name, with the jobs in the civil service and more broadly in the public sector being allocated among party candidates. To provide just a few examples, such practices were widely applied in Austria, Belgium, and Italy for much of the post-war period, they have been reinvented in some of the post-communist systems, including Slovakia and Poland (O'Dwyer 2006: ch. 3), and they are endemic in Latin America and in the Third World in general. Party politicization affecting exclusively the top layers of the bureaucracy has been practised even more widely, e.g. in France, Germany, and Spain (Page and Wright 1999, 2007; Suleiman 2003).

Being formally merit systems means bureaucrats appointed as political trustees of a specific party stay on even when the government changes. The disadvantages are obvious: elected leaders have to work with bureaucrats who are not politically neutral but oppose the goals of the government and may indeed engage in dissent-shirking or political sabotage. Thus, while the problem of the bureaucrats' willingness can be resolved for those politicians who make the appointments, it may make things worse for their successors from different parties. One possible 'way out' for them is to strip the alien partisans of their most important functions, cut them off from politically critical communication—hence make them 'white elephants'—and hire another layer of partisans. The consequence will be an oversized bureaucracy for which the taxpayer will have to settle the bill.

New Public Management systems

New Public Management (NPM) systems represent a more fundamental challenge to the classic bureaucratic system than the undermining of merit recruitment. They aim at resolving the problems of both the bureaucrats' willingness and efficiency. Moreover, the proponents of NPM systems claim that establishing these systems can reverse the growth of the state.

NPM systems were first introduced in the US under the Reagan presidency in the 1980s. They were soon imported by the UK and New Zealand and later diffused throughout Western Europe. NPM builds on transferring methods from the market economy to the public sector.

Personnel

Top positions in the public sector are open to outside candidates who are hired on a fixed-term basis (rather than life-long employment). Consequently, salaries for public sector managers match those of the private sector and payment is tied to performance.

Organization

NPM methods aim at creating 'internal markets' in the public sector. This implies splitting large bureaucratic units into smaller ones and allowing for—indeed encouraging—competition between different public sector units (e.g. schools) and, where possible, between public and private sector units (e.g. agencies and firms). In other words, NPM aims at creating an environment that makes profit-seeking the survival strategy.

Procedure

According to NPM doctrine, it is no longer sufficient for a civil servant to observe administrative regulations in every detail, follow the specific instruction of his or her superiors, and not steal public money. Rather, accountability is based on the civil servant's performance in attaining the agency's goals. Thus public sector managers are expected to engage in managerialism and entrepreneurship (Suleimann 2003; Peters and Pierre 2001). Here at least two different approaches can be distinguished (Behn 2001). The 'let the managers manage' approach proceeds from assumption that previously the hands of public sector officials were tied by too dense regulations. It implicitly trusts civil servants 'to exercise their judgement intelligently, to employ their flexibility with prudence, and to be motivated primarily by the intrinsic rewards of public office'. This approach is largely based on *ex ante* controls, that is, on finding the right people to empower on these terms. In contrast, the 'make the managers manage' approach provides civil servants with 'specific, tightly written performance contracts that leave little room for trust' (Behn 2001: 30). Hence performance improvement is motivated by extrinsic rewards and the use of *ex-post* control mechanisms.

NPM schemes greatly enhance the potential for political control over the bureaucracy. Politicians (i.e. people whose positions are ultimately tied to the electoral process) control more financial and career incentives and can—by tying rewards to outcomes—more effectively align the preferences of civil servants with their own. Interestingly, the parliamentary accountability of ministers has not been enhanced in the sense of making them more directly responsible for the acts of their civil servants. Thus, one of the side effects of NPM schemes is the shoring up of politicians against scrutiny (Strøm *et al.* 2003). Critics of the NPM revolution focus on the deprofessionalization and politicization of the bureaucracy. As Suleiman (2003: 17–18) has put it: 'Political affiliation has once again become a determining criterion in appointments to top-level positions', with the tendency to view the bureaucracy 'as the instrument of the government *of the day* rather than of the government *of the state*'. Critics also suggest that the goal of the state organized along NPM lines 'is no longer to protect society from the market's demands but to protect the market from society's demands' (Daniel Cohen, quoted in Suleiman 2003: 16).

The quality of governance

Finally let us take a look at the performance of the bureaucracy. Table 8.6 reports the World Bank's government effectiveness index for selected countries and the earliest and the most recent years available. With regard to the developments outlined above, 1996 is a year when most Western administrations had been affected by some NPM reforms, while they already had a profound impact on the administrations of the pioneer countries—the US, UK, New Zealand. As noted earlier, the performance of bureaucracies is difficult to measure. Yet this index is the most ambitious attempt to do so to date. It draws on a wealth of cross-country data, mostly measures of perceptions the clients of government agencies and professional observers, such

as rating agencies. Governance is conceptualized as an overall measure of the quality of the public services and civil service, the degree of the civil service's independence from political pressure, the quality of policy formulation and implementation, and the credibility of the government's commitment to such policies. The data employed and the index construction is carefully documented in the paper cited at the bottom of Table 8.6 and a number of earlier papers that are available on the World Bank's webpage.

Table 8.6 shows that the quality of governance differs considerably between regions and countries (higher scores indicate better outcomes). Given that the more recent one includes more variables, not too much should be made out of small changes in the absolute values. What is more reliable is the relative placement of countries. Comparing the regions, we see that the Anglo-Saxon settler democracies and the countries of Western Europe can pride themselves on good governance, while the other established democracies (Israel, Japan, and India), the more recent democracies in Latin American and the Central and East Europen post-Soviet systems are clearly lagging behind. In Western Europe we observe a clear North–South decline of good governance. In Latin America the country with the longest democratic tradition, Chile, also provides the best governance. The positive thing about the post-Soviet states is that the quality of governance has improved considerably over the last decade.

KEY POINTS

❑ The government's capacities to implement is decisions critically depend on the ability and willingness of bureaucrats and the structures and processes of the public administration.

❑ Classic bureaucracy aims at making the civil service a neutral instrument. In practice, the including of individual political preferences by bureaucrats can lead to

agency loss; bureaucratic career concerns foster the growth of the state.

❑ The establishment of spoils systems and New Public Management methods can provide governments with greater grip on their bureaucrats. Yet both methods have their own problems.

Conclusion

Governments are key institutions in democratic states. Who occupies government normally determines the direction a country will take. This is

particularly true where cohesive political parties allow the fusion of executive and legislative power. This chapter has been concerned with three important

Table 8.6 Government effectiveness index (1996 and 2005)

	1996	2005
Non-European democracies		
Australia	2.00	1.88
Canada	2.03	1.92
India	−0.45	−0.11
Israel	1.49	0.95
Japan	1.33	1.16
New Zealand	2.46	1.90
Switzerland	2.53	2.03
United States	2.06	1.59
Western Europe		
Austria	1.99	1.60
Belgium	1.93	1.65
Denmark	2.09	2.12
Finland	2.04	2.07
France	1.94	1.46
Germany	2.01	1.51
Iceland	1.56	2.20
Ireland	1.70	1.63
Italy	0.93	0.60
Luxembourg	2.34	1.94
Netherlands	2.44	1.95
Norway	2.13	1.99
Portugal	1.03	1.03
Spain	1.70	1.40
Sweden	2.05	1.93
United Kingdom	2.33	1.70

(continued)

Table 8.6 (*continued*)

Post-Soviet systems		
Bulgaria	−0.64	0.23
Czech Republic	0.52	0.94
Estonia	0.53	1.03
Hungary	0.39	0.79
Latvia	−0.34	0.68
Lithuania	−0.16	0.85
Poland	0.50	0.58
Romania	−0.88	−0.03
Slovak Republic	0.17	0.95
Slovenia	0.52	0.99
Russia	−0.79	−0.45
Latin America		
Argentina	0.65	−0.27
Brazil	−0.25	−0.09
Chile	1.20	1.26
Mexico	−0.20	−0.01

Note: The World Bank's government effectiveness index includes measures of the quality of the public services and civil service, the degree of the civil service's independence from political pressure, the quality of policy formulation and implementation, and the credibility of the government's commitment to such policies. The mean of 213 countries is 0, and virtually all scores lie between −2.5 and 2.5. Higher scores indicate better outcomes.
Source: Kaufmann *et al.* (2006).

and interrelated questions: (1) how government decisions are made, (2) how autonomous governments are from the providers of key resources, and (3) what capacities governments have to rule the country.

Government decision-making depends on basic regime characteristics but within such confines can take different forms such as cabinet, prime ministerial, and ministerial government under parliamentarism. The modes of government change with functional requirements and according to the prevailing political conditions (e.g. single-party vs. coalition government).

Government autonomy *vis-à-vis* the parties that bring governments to office is controversial from a normative point of view. The party government model denies autonomy, while constitutional theory prescribes it. Empirically, government autonomy from parties has enormously increased. Part and parcel of that process is the tendency towards presidentialization, the vesting of more power in the chief executive.

Government capacities are high in situations of unified or majority single-party government and they are considerably constrained in situations of divided or minority government and when the government is a coalition. Institutional rules can partly compensate for the lack of party support. Governments depend critically on support from their bureaucracies. The classic model of a neutral bureaucracy, that serves any government equally well, has come under attack from two sides: one focuses on the self-interest of bureaucrats, and one denies the bureaucracy's neutrality or demands its 'democratization' so that politicians have an instrument in tune with their preferences.

? Questions

1. Which different meanings does the term 'government' carry?
2. What distinguishes prime ministerial government from cabinet government?
3. How can parties provide party government?
4. What distinguishes divided and unified government?
5. Why can minority governments survive?
6. What are the problems of coalition governance?
7. What are the problems of bureaucracy?
8. What are spoils systems and which forms do exist?
9. What distinguishes classic bureaucracy from New Public Management bureaucracy?
10. What is the presidentialization of politics?

» Further reading

Important texts on government not cited in this chapter:

Baylis, Thomas T. (1989) *Governing by Committee: Collegial Leadership in Advanced Societies* (Albany, NY: State University of New York Press).

Burch, Martin, and Holliday, Ian (1996) *The British Cabinet System* (London: Prentice-Hall/Harvester Wheatsheaf).

Edwards, George C., Kessel, J. H., and Rockman, Bert A. (eds.) (1993) *Researching the Presidency* (Pittsburgh: University of Pittsburgh Press).

Hayward, Jack, and Wright, Vincent (2002) *Governing from the Centre: Core Executive Coordination in France* (Oxford: Oxford University Press).

Hennessy, Peter (1986) *Cabinet* (Oxford: Blackwell).

Jones, G. W. (ed.) (1991) *West European Prime Ministers* (London: Cass).

Mackie, Thomas T., and Hogwood, Brian (eds.) (1985) *Unlocking the Cabinet: Cabinet Committees in Comparative Perspective* (London: Sage).

Peters, B. Guy, Rhodes, R. A. W., and Wright, Vincent (eds.) (2000) *Administering the Summit: Administration of the Core Executive in Developed Countries* (Houndmills: Macmillan).

Rose, Richard (2001) *The Prime Minister in a Shrinking World* (Cambridge: Polity).

—— and Suleiman, Ezra N. (eds.) (1980) *Presidents and Prime Ministers* (Washington, DC: American Enterprise Institute).

Weller, Patrick (1985) *First Among Equals: Prime Ministers in Westminster Systems* (Sydney: Allen & Unwin).

 Web links

www.psr.keele.ac.uk
   Richard Kimber's website on Political Science Resources (University of Keele).

www.gksoft.com/govt/en/parties.html
   Webpage of Government on the WWW devoted to political parties and party systems around the world. The main page includes additional information on heads of state, parliaments, executives, courts, and other institutions.

www.georgetown.edu/pdba
   Website of the Political Database of the Americas.

www.cia.gov/cia/publications/factbook
   Website of CIA's the World Factbook with information on institutions, social structures, economic data, and party systems for most countries of the world.

www.eiu.com
   Country Reports and Country Profiles published by the Economist Intelligence Unit are very useful for an overview and recent data.

 Visit the Online Resource Centre that accompanies this book for more information:
www.oxfordtextbooks.co.uk/orc/caramani/

9

Constitutions and judicial power

Alec Stone Sweet

Chapter contents

Reader's guide

This chapter compares the evolution of different national systems of constitutional justice since 1787. After introducing and defining key terms, it surveys different kinds of constitutions, rights, models of constitutional review, and the main precepts of 'the new constitutionalism'. The chapter then presents a simple theory of delegation and judicial power, focusing on why political elites would delegate power to constitutional judges, and how to measure the extent of power, or discretion, delegated. The evolution of constitutional forms is then presented comparatively. Beginning in the 1980s, the new constitutionalism took off, and today has no rival as a model of democratic state legitimacy. As constitutional rights and review have diffused around the world, so has the capacity of constitutional judges to control policy outcomes.

Introduction

This chapter provides an overview of the emergence, diffusion, and political impact of systems of constitutional justice. By system of constitutional justice, I mean the institutions and procedures, established by a constitution, for the judicial (third-party) protection of fundamental rights. In 1787, when the fully codified, written constitution was just emerging as a form, no such system existed anywhere in the world. At the dawn of the twenty-first century, one finds that virtually all new written constitutions include a charter of rights that is enforceable by a constitutional or supreme court, even against legislation. With very few exceptions, legislative sovereignty has formally disappeared. The new constitutionalism killed it, paradoxically perhaps, in the name of democracy.

Before we begin, some preliminary remarks on the comparative politics of our topic are in order. Until recently, comparative political scientists paid almost no attention to law, courts, and constitutions. The two major American journals in the field—*Comparative Politics* and *Comparative Political Studies* (both founded in 1968)—failed to publish a single article relating to courts or constitutions in their first twenty-five years of existence. In American political science, one finds a domain of inquiry devoted to 'judicial politics', but it is virtually a subfield of American politics. Outside the US, no equivalent field exists. Around the globe, academic discourse on law and courts is dominated by law professors. In this discourse, the fact that courts are political actors, and that they interact with other state institutions to make policy, is ignored or even actively resisted.

We can account for the indifference to 'things legal' by political scientists in several ways. As noted in Section 1 of this book, in the 1950s comparative politics began to turn away from approaches that Roy Macridis (1955) derided as 'formal-legal', in favour of research into how actors actually behaved or took decisions. Courts and constitutions are arguably the most 'formal' and 'legal', of state institutions. To take seriously what courts actually do—they produce a 'jurisprudence' or 'case law'—one has little choice but to immerse oneself in the formalism of legal reasoning and the rhetoric of justification. The neglect of judicial institutions may also be a consequence of the inherent difficulties of doing comparative research (language problems, for example), compounded by the professional-technical nature of legal discourse, and the sparseness or non-existence of native, politically relevant, scholarship.

All of this is to say that we have slight comparative understanding of judicial politics. There are, however, important indicators of change. Over the past twenty years, political scientists have gradually rediscovered law, courts, and constitutions, for various reasons. First, the new institutionalism—a broad interest in how rule systems and organizations structure political life—took hold across the social sciences (Hall and Taylor 1996; see also the Introduction to this volume, as well as Chapters 1 and 2). New institutionalists studied the state and so they could not help but encounter law and courts. Second, the concern for rules and organizations intersects with the emergence of rational choice and game theoretic approaches to politics, which emphasize how the 'rules of the game' shape the strategies of the actors playing the game and thus help to determine outcomes. When game theorists seek to explain how parts of political systems operate, it is almost always legal rules (constitutions, standing orders, electoral laws, and so on) that constitute the 'rules of the game'. Thus, many political scientists began to deal with law routinely, though they did not adopt traditional methods of legal scholarship.

Third, the salience to comparative politics of constitutions and rights exploded, especially after 1989. The huge wave of constitution-making in Central and Eastern Europe following the collapse of the Soviet Empire drew the attention of a field that had also become interested in democratization (see Chapters 5 and 25). New systems of constitutional justice began to emerge outside of North America and Europe, spurring interest even more. Law and courts have also become a significant component of international politics (Volcansek 1997), led by courts of the European Union (EU) and the World Trade Organization (WTO). Today, a growing field devoted to comparative judicial politics can be identified.

The chapter proceeds as follows. In the first section, I present basic concepts and define key terms. I then present a simple theory of judicial power, focusing on the potential for judges of the constitution to build and to exercise authority over all other state actors. I chart the diffusion of institutional forms associated with contemporary constitutionalism—the written constitution, the charter of rights, and constitutional (judicial) review—from 1787 to the present. Finally, I discuss some of the research findings of those who have studied the impact of rights adjudication on the greater political system.

Concepts and types

Definitions

There is no consensus on how to define concepts such as constitution, constitutionalism, and rights. My aim is to provide useful definitions of these and other terms to readers of this book (students of comparative politics), not to fix authoritative meanings. Students should note the discussion of alternative views and debate them; and they should remember that, in this field at least, virtually any attempt to carefully define concepts will be controversial.

Let us start with the word **constitution**. I prefer a broad, generic definition: a constitution is a body of meta-norms, those higher order legal rules and principles that specify how all other legal norms are to be produced, applied, enforced, and interpreted (Stone Sweet 2000: ch. 1). Meta-norms constitute political systems, as written constitutions do for the modern nation-state. In England (later the United Kingdom), whose constitution has evolved over centuries, meta-norms provide a simplified representation, or model, of how the political system has been institutionalized, and is expected to function.

In today's world, written constitutions are the ultimate, formal source of state authority: they establish governmental institutions (legislatures, executives, courts), and grant them the power to make, apply, enforce, and interpret laws. Constitutions tell us how lower order legal norms are to be made, especially statutes. They lay down legislative procedures; and they tell us how legislative authority is constituted (through elections, for example), and what the legislature can do (through enumerating powers). Constitutions also indicate how the various institutions are expected, if only ideally, to interact with one another (through separation of powers doctrines). New constitutions written over the last sixty years typically contain a catalogue of rights, which are, by definition, substantive constraints on government. These constitutions also establish an institutional means of protecting rights against governmental incursion, typically in the form of a supreme or constitutional court.

I use **constitutionalism** in two ways. First, the word refers to the commitment, on the part of any given political community, to accept the legitimacy of, and to be governed by, constitutional rules and principles. Constitutionalism is therefore a variable. The commitment to live under a constitution varies across countries. In any specific country, it can be strong or weak, and its character can change over time. Second, the word refers to those practices and understandings of government that are derivable from, or inhere in, any constitutional order. An American would focus on federalism and checks and balances between the branches of government, for example, while a Canadian would add an emphasis on the value of multi-culturalism.

It is worth noting other definitions. For the political scientist Carl Friedrich (1950: 25–8, 123), constitutionalism refers to 'limited government', situations wherein the constitution 'effectively restrains' those who control the coercive instruments of the state. Koen Lenaerts (1990: 205), a legal scholar and an EU judge, defines it as 'limited government operating under the rule of law'. Michel Rosenfeld (1994: 3), editor of the *International Journal of Constitutional Law*, notes that 'there appears to be no accepted definition of constitutionalism', and then states that 'modern constitutionalism requires imposing limits on the powers of government, adherence to the rule of law, and the protection of fundamental rights'. I will return to the 'limited government' formulation shortly, but for now it is enough to note that constitutions do not just limit state power, they constitute and enable it.

Others conceive of constitutionalism in wider terms (my second definition above), that is, as the whole of a community's practices and understandings about the nature of law, politics, citizenship, and the state. 'Constitutionalism is the set of beliefs associated with constitutional practice', Neil Walker (1996: 267) suggests; another constitutional theorist, Ulrich Preuß (1996: 11–13), defines it as 'the basic ideas, principles, and values of a polity [that] aspires to give its members a share in government'. In this view, constitutionalism encapsulates the fundamental notions of how, 'in our political system', 'we' organize the state (federal or unitary, republican or monarchical), constitute our government (separation of powers, checks and balances), provide for representation and participation (elections, referenda), protect minorities (rights and judicial review), promote equality (social welfare regimes), and so on. Here again, constitutionalism will vary. Institutional arrangements and public policies that are viewed as legitimate, and even required, in country X, for example, may be considered unacceptable in country Y.

Still others take an even broader cultural view,[1] conceiving it as an overarching ideology of politics, community, citizenship, and the state. In this tradition, constitutions are analysed in terms of their capacity to express the collective identity of the people—their values, aspirations, and idealized essence (Post 2000; Shaw 1999; Wolin 1989). A robust constitutionalism is a well-spring of legitimizing resources for the *demos*, the body politic, helping it to evolve as circumstances change. In contrast, a weak constitutionalism fails to represent collective identity, and fails to reconstruct the legitimacy of the state in times of crisis.

A typology of constitutional forms and the 'new constitutionalism'

Many notions of constitutionalism emphasize the good or proper functions that a constitution is supposed to perform: to limit government, to embody political ideals, to express collective identity. Where we see meta-norms, we observe a constitution.[2] Constitutionalism refers to the commitment of a polity to govern itself in conformity with the meta-norms, but this commitment may be absent in some places, at some times. A constitution can be 'bad' for democracy. Meta-norms could establish dictatorship and deny the people any say in their own governance; and a polity's 'constitutionalism' could help to legitimize authoritarianism. In world history, there are far more examples of constitutional regimes that have failed to sustain limited government and participatory democracy than there are examples of success.

Empirically, constitutions have differed a great deal, not least, in their capacity to constrain legislative power. Consider the following simple typology of constitutional models.

Type 1: the absolutist constitution

In this model, the authority to produce and change legal norms, including the constitution, is centralized and absolute. The controlling meta-norm is the fact that the rulers are 'above the law'. In such systems, the meta-norms reflect, rather than restrict, the absolute power of those who govern. The type 1 constitution typically rejects popular sovereignty, rights, and separation of powers. The archetype of the type 1 constitution in Europe is the French Charter of 1814, which other monarchies, especially in the Germanic regions, widely imitated (Dippel 2005: 162). In the twentieth century, many constitutions read as if they were full-scale constitutional democracies, when they in fact functioned as single-party or one-man dictatorships. Examples include the USSR and many Central European states under Communist Party control, and situations resulting after military coups in Asia, Africa, Central and South America. Although less prevalent in recent decades, there have been a few constitutions since 1980 that expressly enshrined one-person or one-party rule (Sri Lanka, Togo, Niger, among others).

Type 2: the legislative supremacy constitution

In this form, the constitution provides for (1) a stable set of governmental institutions and (2) elections to the legislature. Elections legitimize legislative authority, and legislative majorities legitimize statutory authority. Once adopted by the legislature, statutes are commands, until abrogated by subsequent legislative commands. The crucial meta-norm is the rule of legislative sovereignty, which has a number of important consequences. The first is that the constitution is not entrenched, that is, there are no special (non-legislative) procedures for revising it. Instead, the constitution can be changed through a majority vote of the parliament. In 1912, for example, the British House of Commons abolished the veto of the

House of Lords, removing the last important constraint on its own law-making powers. The second is that any act that conflicts with a statute is itself invalid. Judicial acts, too, are subject to this rule, so the judicial review of statutes is prohibited. The third is that there is no layer of substantive constraints—rights—in the constitution. Rights are, in effect, granted by parliament, in statutes. The British and New Zealand parliamentary systems, and the French Third (1875–1940) and Fourth Republics (1946–58), are almost pure examples of type 2 systems.

Type 3: the 'higher law' constitution

Type 2 and 3 constitutions share a common attribute: the constitution establishes (or recognizes the status of) state institutions and links these institutions to society, via elections. The type 3 form, however, adds substantive constraints on the exercise of public authority—in the form of constitutional rights—and establishes an independent, judicial means of enforcing rights, even against the legislature. Legislative sovereignty is expressly rejected. Type 3 constitutions are entrenched: they specify amendment procedures.

The type 1 constitution no longer exists as a viable model in the world today (Caenegem 1995), though constitutionalism may be non-existent in many authoritarian regimes. More controversially, one might argue that the type 2 constitution is all but extinct. One of the most remarkable developments in global politics over the past fifty years has been the consolidation of the type 3 constitution as a standard without rival. The point is not that all type 3 constitutions are the same; it is a fact that no two constitutions are exactly alike. What is important is the *broad global convergence around beliefs that only type 3 constitutions are considered to be 'good' constitutions*. This convergence has been called the **new constitutionalism** (Shapiro and Stone Sweet 1994).

The precepts of this new constitutionalism include the following:

• Institutions of the state are established by, and derive their authority exclusively from, a written constitution.

• This constitution assigns ultimate power to the people by way of elections or referenda.

• The use of public authority, including legislative authority, is lawful only in so far as it conforms with the constitutional law.

• The constitution provides for a catalogue of rights, and a system of constitutional justice to defend those rights.

• The constitution itself specifies how it may be revised.

Rights

Constitutions establish the procedures to be followed for producing various forms of law. These are procedural constraints: if the procedure is not followed, then the legal norm produced (statute, administrative determination, judicial decision) is not constitutionally valid. Rights are a different type of meta-norm, in that **they impose substantive constraints on the exercise of public authority**. When state officials make, interpret, and enforce law, they must respect rights, or their acts may be invalidated as law.

It is not enough to define rights simply as 'substantive constraints on law-making'. The nature of rights varies along a number of dimensions, two of which deserve special attention.

1. The first concerns the **hierarchical relationship** between a rights provision, on one hand, and the purposes for which public authority is exercised, on the other. A right might be conceived as more or less absolute: when an act of government violates the right, that act is unconstitutional. The right, being hierarchically superior, trumps any norm in conflict with it. Rights might also be conceived as relative values, to be balanced against other constitutional values, including state purposes. Because the constitution grants powers to state institutions to do certain things—to provide for the country's defence, roads and utilities, social security and welfare, for example—these purposes rise to constitutional status. In this conception, such purposes are not, *a priori*, hierarchically inferior to rights. Balancing is a basic technique that judges use to resolve tensions between a right and a state purpose, once judges have determined that a right is not absolute. The balancing judge weighs the cost of infringement of the right against the social benefits of the state action in

question, and then decides which value will prevail, in light of the facts of the case. When the state decides to build a new airport on existing farmland, for example, the property rights of the farmers whose land is to be expropriated may be outweighed by the 'public' or 'general' interest in the project.

2. The second dimension of variation concerns the **scope of the obligation** imposed on public authority by rights provisions. A right may impose a negative obligation: (1) the state may not infringe upon the right (an absolute version of rights), or (2) the state may not infringe upon the right more than is necessary to achieve a legitimate public purpose (a balancing version of rights). In some countries, rights provisions may impose a duty on the part of government, for example, to take measures to facilitate the enjoyment of a particular right. Or a right might entitle citizens to certain benefits—such as adequate health care, employment, and housing. One classic typology categorizes *rights as negative or positive*: the former constrains government not to do certain things; the latter encourages (or requires) government to act to accomplish certain goals. Older constitutions rarely contain positive rights; newer constitutions all do (see Chapter 4 for a description of the increasing numerous activities of states and bureaucracies over time).

Constitutional review

Once a polity decides to live under a type 3 constitution, the problem of how to guarantee the constitution's normative supremacy over other law arises. The type 3 constitution solves this problem by establishing a system of 'constitutional review': a 'judicialized' (third-party) mechanism for assessing the constitutional legality of all other legal norms.

Two modes of constitutional review are dominant in the world today.

1. The first is **judicial review**, the archetype of which is found in the US. American review is 'judicial' in that it is performed by the judiciary, in the course of resolving litigation.

2. The second mode has its origins in Austria and Germany: the powers of constitutional review are exercised by a special court—a **constitutional court**—while the ordinary (non-constitutional) courts are denied the authority to void legal norms, like statutes, when they conflict with the constitution.

BOX 9.1 The American vs. the European models of judicial review

American judicial review	European constitutional review
Constitutional judicial review authority is decentralized: all judges possess the power to void or refuse to apply a statute on the grounds that it violates the constitution law.	Constitutional review authority is centralized: only the constitutional court may annul a statute as unconstitutional. Judicial review of statute is prohibited.
The Supreme Court is a court of general jurisdiction: it is the highest court of appeal in the legal order, for all issues of law, not just constitutional issues.	The constitutional court's jurisdiction is restricted to resolving constitutional disputes. The ordinary courts handle civil suits and criminal matters.
Judicial review is defensible under prevailing separation of powers doctrines to the extent that it is 'case or controversy' review. Judges possess review authority because their legal duty is to resolve legal 'cases', some of which will have a constitutional dimension.	Review powers are defensible under separation of powers doctrines to the extent that it is not exercised by the judiciary, but by a specialized 'constitutional' organ, the constitutional court.
Judicial review is understood to be 'concrete', in that it is exercised pursuant to ordinary litigation. Abstract review decisions look suspiciously like 'advisory opinions', which are prohibited under American separation of powers.	Constitutional review is typically 'abstract': the review court does not resolve concrete cases between two litigating parties, but answers constitutional questions referred to it by judges or elected officials.

At this point, we confront radically different notions of separation of powers, which are constitutional conceptions of how the various state institutions, or branches of government, should function and interact with one another. Simplifying, in judicial review systems, the courts are understood to comprise a separate but co-equal branch of government, within a system of 'checks and balances'. The duty of American courts (their judicial function) is to resolve legal disputes: cases or controversies that arise under the laws of the US. The constitution is one of the laws. If litigants can plead the constitutional law before the courts, American judges will need to possess the power of judicial review in order to resolve the dispute, that is, in order to do their jobs. Such is the logic of *Marbury* v. *Madison* (1803), the Supreme Court decision that established constitutional review authority in the US.[3] The American model of judicial

review is also called the 'decentralized model', since review powers are held by all courts, not just the Supreme Court.

As we will soon see, giving review powers to all courts is not as popular as concentrating review authority in a specialized jurisdiction. Constitutional courts are favoured in countries where judicial review has traditionally been prohibited. Those who wrote new constitutions wished to enable rights protection while, at the same time, preserving legislative sovereignty as much as possible. In such polities (most of Europe and Latin America, for example), separation of powers doctrines take great pains to distinguish the **political function** (to legislate, to make law) from the **judicial function** (to resolve legal disputes according to legislation). The American checks and balances system appears to create a 'confusion of powers', since it permits the courts to participate in

Table 9.1 Regional distribution of models of constitutional review

Region	Constitutional judicial review (American model)	Constitutional court (European model)	Mixed[a]	Other[b]	None
Europe	5	31	3 (1)	1	2
Africa	12	29	1	6	3
Middle East	2	5	0	3	1
Asia and South East Asia	18	13	2	11	0
North America	2	0	0	0	0
Central America	3	3	3 (1)	0	0
South America	3	4	5 (3)	0	0
Caribbean	8	0	0	1	0
Total	53	85	14	22	6

[a] The number in parentheses refers to systems with European model constitutional courts, such as Portugal, but which also give review authority to ordinary judges. I have deferred to Dr Mavčič's classification, though I would normally count these states under the constitutional court column.
[b] Review mechanisms, often unique, that are unclassifiable.

Source: Data compiled by Dr Arne Mavčič, available on the web at www.concourts.net/, last updated in October 2005. French council-based systems were counted under the 'EM-CC' column, and Saudi Arabia, which is not included the Mavčič dataset, was counted under the 'None' column.

the work of the legislature. Because this system or review emerged in Europe and later spread globally, it is often called the 'European' or the 'centralized model'.

We can break down the centralized model of constitutional review into four constituent components.

1. Constitutional courts enjoy **exclusive and final constitutional jurisdiction**. Constitutional judges alone may invalidate a law or an act of public authority as unconstitutional, while the 'ordinary' courts (i.e. the judiciary, the non-constitutional courts) remain prohibited from doing so. In the US, review authority inheres in judicial power, and thus all judges possess it.

2. Constitutional courts **only settle constitutional disputes**. The US Supreme Court is a court of 'general jurisdiction'—it is the highest court of appeal for almost all disputes about rights in the American legal order. In contrast, constitutional courts do not preside over litigation, which remains the function of the ordinary judges. Instead, constitutional courts answer constitutional questions that are referred to them.

3. Constitutional courts are **formally detached from the judiciary and legislature** although they have links with these institutions. They occupy their own constitutional space, a space neither clearly judicial nor political in traditional separation of powers terms.

4. Some constitutional courts are empowered to **review legislation before it has been enforced**, that is, before it has actually affected any person negatively, as a means of eliminating unconstitutional legislation and practices before they can do harm. Thus, in the centralized model of review, the judges that staff the ordinary courts remain bound by the supremacy of statute, while constitutional judges are charged with preserving the supremacy of the constitution.

Modes of review: abstract and concrete

The American and the European models of review differ with respect to the pathways through which cases come to the judges. In the US, rights review is activated when a litigant pleads a right before a judge—any judge. In countries with constitutional courts, there are three main procedures that activate review, although not all constitutions establish all three procedures.

1. Abstract review is the pre-enforcement review of statutes. Some systems enable the statute to be reviewed before it enters into force (*a priori* review), others after promulgation but before application (*a posteriori* review). Abstract review is also called 'preventive review', since its purpose is to filter out unconstitutional laws before they can harm anyone. Abstract review is politically initiated. Typically, executives, parliamentary minorities, and regions or federated entities in federal states, possess the power to refer laws to the court.

2. Concrete review is initiated by the judiciary in the course of litigation in the courts. Ordinary judges activate review by sending a constitutional question—is a given law, legal rule, judicial decision, or administrative act constitutional?—to the constitutional court. The general rule is that a presiding judge will go to the constitutional court if two conditions are met: (1) that the constitutional question is material to litigation at bar (who wins or loses will depend on the answer to the question); and (2) there is reasonable doubt in the judge's mind about the constitutionality of the act or rule in question. Referrals suspend proceedings pending a review by the constitutional court. Once rendered, the constitutional court's judgment is sent back to the referring judge, who then decides the case on the basis of the ruling. In such systems, ordinary judges are not permitted to determine the constitutionality of statutes on their own. Instead, aided by private litigants, they help to detect unconstitutional laws and send them to the constitutional court for review.

3. The **constitutional complaint** brings individuals into the mix. Individuals or an ombudsman are authorized to appeal directly to the constitutional court when they believe that their rights have been violated, usually after judicial remedies have been exhausted.

Abstract review is 'abstract' because the review of legislation takes place in the absence of litigation, in American parlance, in the absence of a concrete 'case or controversy'. Concrete review is 'concrete' because the review of legislation, or other public act, constitutes a stage in ongoing litigation in the ordinary courts. In individual complaints, a private individual alleges the violation of a constitutional right by a public act or governmental official, and requests redress from the court for this violation. In American judicial review, all review is (at least formally) 'concrete', in that it is embedded in a concrete 'case'.

KEY POINTS

❑ A constitution is a body of legal norms—meta-norms—that governs the production and application of all other legal norms. Constitutionalism refers to a polity's commitment to abide by the constitution, and to the main principles found in any polity's constitution.

❑ A system of constitutional justice is a central component of the type 3 constitution and of the new constitutionalism. Such systems combine a written, entrenched constitutional text, rights, and a third-party mechanism—constitutional review—for the protection of rights.

❑ There are two main models of constitutional review today: the American model of judicial review, and the European model of review performed by a constitutional court. The models rest on different notions of separation of powers. American judicial review is expected to be fundamentally concrete, whereas European constitutional review is often abstract.

BOX 9.2 A normative debate: is rights review democratic?

Con	Pro
Rights review subverts majority rule, by allowing constitutional judges to substitute their policy choices for those of legislators.	Democracy does not simply mean the domination of the majority over everyone else. It also means basic standards of good governance which must include the protection of rights.
Rights provisions are vague and ill-defined. In a good democracy, elected officials will determine how rights should be protected in law.	It is precisely because rights provisions are not expressed as clear rules that we need judges to interpret them. Good constitutional rulings will lead legislators to care more about rights.
Judges can interpret rights in any way they wish, without being held democratically accountable for their decisions. We can expect an effective system of constitutional review to subvert, routinely, the will of the elected representatives of the people.	Rights are too important to be left to the protection of elected politicians. Judges are relatively more insulated from short-term political calculation, and are thus more likely to protect rights better than elected politicians.
The judicialization of politics through rights adjudication reduces the centrality of legislative debate, and therefore reduces the political responsibility of legislative majorities for their policy decisions. Such responsibility is basic to democratic legitimacy.	Judicialization means that legislatures govern, in dialogue with judges, in order to make rights protection effective. The legitimacy of the regime depends, in part, on how legislators and judges interact with one another to protect rights.

Delegation and judicial power

The power of constitutional judges is delegated power (Stone Sweet and Thatcher 2002): a written constitution expressly confers upon the judges review authority and indicates how it may be used. Why would political elites, those who draft a constitution and will live under it, choose to grant review authority to constitutional judges? Why should they choose to constrain themselves? This section discusses some of the consequences of this choice from the perspective of delegation theory, focusing on issues of agency and control. In doing so, it responds to a further question: to what extent can we expect political elites to remain 'in charge' of the evolution of the polity after delegating review powers?

The constitution as incomplete contract

People contract with each other in order to achieve benefits that they could not expect to realize on their own. Modern democratic constitutions can be conceived as contracts. They are typically negotiated by political elites—representatives of political parties—seeking to establish rules, procedures, and institutions that will enable them to govern under the cloak of political legitimacy, which reduces to constitutional legitimacy. In establishing a democracy, each contracting party knows that it will be competing with others for political power, through elections. Constitutional contracting also yields another crucial benefit: to constrain one's opponents when they are in power. The constitution thus produces two important common goods for the parties, in the form of a set of enabling institutions and a set of constraints.

Constitutional contracting, like all contracting, generates a demand for third-party dispute resolution and enforcement. Indeed, the social logic of contracts provides a logic of courts, more generally. Third-party enforcement of contracts is an institutional solution to a classic commitment problem (the prisoner's dilemma of game theory), which is one reason why we find it everywhere, at all times, in one form or another. The move to constitutional review is one way to deal with commitment problems associated with constitutional contracting. If the polity is federal, review will provide a means of resolving disputes between the federal government and the federated states, and among the federated states themselves. It is an old truism that federalism needs an umpire, which helps to explain why all federal constitutions provide for review. Contracting rights, too, heavily favours the delegation of review authority to a constitutional judge.

Take the following scenario, which is a simplified version of what in fact has occurred in many places since 1945. Once the contracting parties (political elites) decide to include a charter of rights in their constitution, not least to constrain their future opponents when the latter are in power, they face two tough problems. First, they disagree about the nature and content of rights, which threatens to paralyse the drafting process. The left-wing parties favour positive, social rights, and limits on the rights to property. The right-wing parties prefer to privilege negative rights, and do not want to restrict strong property rights. They compromise, drafting an extensive charter of rights that (1) lists most of the rights that each side wants, (2) implies that no right is absolute or more important than another, and (3) is vague about how any future conflict between two rights, or a right and a legitimate governmental purpose, will be resolved. Second, they have to decide how rights will be enforced. Delegating rights review authority to a constitutional court helps them deal with both problems. In agreeing to allow constitutional judges to decide how rights will be interpreted and enforced, they are able to move forward.

In this account, courts are (at least partly) an institutional response to the fact that most contracts are 'incomplete', and the new constitution, too, is an incomplete contract. Contracts can be said to be 'incomplete' to the extent that there exists meaningful uncertainty as to the precise nature of the commitments made (the rights and obligations of the parties under the contract), over time. Due to the impossibility of negotiating specific rules for all possible contingencies, and given that, as time passes, conditions will change and the interests of the parties to the agreement will evolve, all contracts are incomplete in some significant way.[4] Most agreements of any complexity are generated by what organizational economists call 'relational contracting'. The parties to an agreement seek to broadly 'frame' their relationship, by agreeing on a set of basic 'goals and objectives', fixing outer limits on acceptable behaviour, and establishing procedures for 'completing' the contract over time (Milgrom and Roberts 1992: 127–33).

Type 3 constitutions—complex instruments of governance designed to last indefinitely, if not forever—are paradigmatic examples of relational contracts. Much is left general, even ill-defined and vague, as in the case of rights. Generalities and vagueness may facilitate agreement at the bargaining stage. But vagueness, by definition, is legal uncertainty, which threatens to undermine the reason for contracting in the first place. The establishment of constitutional review is an institutional response to the problems of uncertainty and enforcement. Each party has an interest in seeing that the other parties obey their obligations, and that they will be punished for non-compliance. An important review function is to clarify the meaning of the constitution over time, and to adapt it to changing circumstances.

Principals, agents, trustees

Across the social sciences, as well as in the law and economics tradition, scholars use the 'principal–agent' framework to depict or model authority relations constituted by delegation (see, in particular, Chapter 7). The framework focuses on the relationship between those who delegate, who are called 'principals', and those to whom power is delegated, called 'agents'. For our purposes, let us assume that the principals are those who govern a political system, and that they will create institutions—agents—when they believe that doing so will help them govern more efficiently and effectively. Assume now that the political system is one of legislative sovereignty. The principals are therefore the legislators who produce the statutes that are meant to govern the polity. They decide, for good reasons, that it is too difficult to perform two governance functions at once, both making the laws, and enforcing and resolving disputes under the laws.[5] They therefore decide to delegate to agents—in this case, courts—to help them with the second set of governance functions.

Here is a stylized account of the ordinary courts as agents of the legislature in a system of parliamentary sovereignty, a type 2 constitutional system.

Judges are bound to enforce parliamentary statutes because they express the sovereign's will. The judge's principal is the parliament, and the norm the principal controls—the statute—constitutes the substantive terms of the judge's mandate to govern. The judge's formal governance function is to enforce the parliament's law. However, statutes can only be enforced—or 'applied' to resolve a legal dispute—once they have been interpreted; and, because statutory interpretation is a form of law-making, the law often comes to mean, in practice, what the courts have said they mean. Even where this is true, the principal still remains in charge. If the legislators notice that a judge has applied a statutory provision in a way that they did not intend and do not like, the law can be changed. Thus, so long as such agency 'errors' can be identified, they can be corrected. The principals may overturn judicial decisions by amending the statute to preclude the offending judicial interpretation. The decision rule governing the principal–agent relationship—a majority vote of the parliament—favours the principal's control. In type 2 systems, this rule is constitutionally frozen in place.

The traditional principal–agent framework loses much of its relevance when it comes to systems of constitutional justice. It is more appropriate to apply a model of 'constitutional trusteeship' to situations wherein the founders of new constitutions confer expansive, open-ended 'fiduciary' powers on a review court (Stone Sweet 2002). A trustee is a particular kind of agent, one that possesses the power to govern those who have delegated in the first place. Note that the ordinary courts do not govern the legislators, but are agents of the legislator's will. The constitutional court exercises fiduciary responsibilities with respect to the constitution. In most settings, they do so in the name of a fictitious entity: the sovereign people.

In systems of constitutional trusteeship, political elites—the political parties, the executive, members of parliament—are never principals in their relationship to constitutional judges. Depending upon the relevant decision rules in place, these officials may seek to overturn constitutional decisions or restrict the constitutional court's powers, but they can do so only by amending the constitution. But, as we have seen, the decision rules governing constitutional revision processes are typically more restrictive than those governing the revision of legislation; in many countries, amendment is a practical impossibility, especially when it comes to rights provisions.

Elected officials typically perform some of the functions usually associated with principals, as when they appoint members of the supreme or constitutional courts. Politicians can and do influence constitutional and supreme courts through appointments.[6] Nonetheless, by establishing (1) the normative superiority of the constitution, (2) a review organ, and (3) specific procedures for constitutional revision, they shifted the power to control constitutional development away from themselves, and to constitutional judges. In most situations, they are mere players within the rule structures provided by the constitution. They compete with each other in order to be in the position to govern and, once in power, they legislate—but under the control of the constitutional judge.

The zone of discretion

The points just made can be formalized in terms of a theoretical zone of discretion—the strategic environment—in which any court operates (see Stone Sweet 2002). This zone is determined by (1) the sum of powers delegated to the court and possessed by the court as a result of its own accreted rule-making minus (2) the sum of control instruments available for use by non-judicial authorities to shape (constrain) or annul (reverse) outcomes that emerge as the result of the court's performance of its delegated tasks. In situations of trusteeship, wherein the agent exercises fiduciary responsibilities, the zone of discretion is, by definition, unusually large. In some places and in some domains, the discretionary powers enjoyed by constitutional courts are close to unlimited.

We can compare the zone of discretion across courts and countries. The ordinary judge operating in a system of legislative sovereignty is an agent whose zone is relatively small compared to a trustee court of the constitution. The ordinary judge has delegated powers, to enable her to interpret and enforce statutes. But these powers must be understood in light of control instruments available to her principals—parliament—which reduce the agent's capacity to control outcomes considerably. Virtually all constitutional courts operate in larger zones of

discretion than our ordinary judge. The authority to review legislation, in general, is a vast power, but it varies in its particulars. In Europe, where the 'centralized' model of protecting rights reigns supreme, the widest zone of discretion will be found in a country where (1) the constitutional court has been delegated abstract and concrete review powers, as well as the authority to process individual complaints, and where (2) it is relatively difficult or impossible to amend rights provisions. This is the case of Germany and Spain. It is relatively easy for students of comparative constitutional politics, first, to read new constitutions, and then construct an account of a review court's zone of discretion, and to compare zones across countries.

Mapping a zone of discretion cannot tell us what constitutional courts will actually do with their powers. The best we can do is to predict that, given a steady case load, constitutional judges operating in a relatively large zone will come to exercise more influence over the evolution of the polity than those operating in relatively small zones. The prediction, of course, can be tested in comparative case studies. We should not expect our predictions to always be accurate, for the obvious reason that a zone of discretion does not take into account many factors that will be important in particular contexts. That said, research of this kind would be able to tell us a great deal about constitutional politics comparatively, such as why some systems are more effective than others. The last section of this chapter is devoted to the issue of effectiveness.

Other logics

To this point, the discussion in this section helps to explain why elites delegate to constitutional judges, but it presupposes that the elites want to establish constitutional democracy in the first place, and that they have decided that a mechanism of third-party rights protection is a good thing for them, in the future. Such an explanation does not work very well at helping us to understand why, in today's world, autocrats, dictators, and generals, too, write constitutions with rights and review, precisely because such rulers do not assume a peaceful, democratic competition for power with their opponents (see Ginsburg 2003). In general, courts can be useful to

BOX 9.3 The structural determinants of judicial power

The zone of discretion

The zone of discretion is a theoretical understanding of the strategic environment in which any court operates. The size of the zone is determined by (1) the sum of powers delegated to the court, and possessed by the court as a result of its past rulings, minus (2) the sum of control instruments available to overrule of otherwise constrain the court, by political elites who do not like the court's decisions, for example. The zone varies across countries, and it will vary across time in the same country, depending upon how the court interprets the constitution and its role in enforcing it.

France and Germany

The German Federal Constitutional Court enjoys one of the largest zones of discretion of any court. It possesses wide jurisdiction over all constitutional issues, defends both rights and federal arrangements, exercises abstract and concrete review, and receives constitutional complaints. In its case law, the court has made it clear that the German legislative authority must be exercised to enhance rights protection, wherever possible, given other constitutional values. Control instruments are extraordinarily weak. The German constitution does not allow an amendment to weaken rights provisions which, in practice, means that the court's decisions on rights are irreversible, except by the court itself. Because most important political issues make it to the court through one procedure or another, and since the court has adopted the posture of an aggressive defender of rights, German politics have become highly judicialized.

The French Constitutional Council exercises the abstract review of statutes adopted by parliament, prior to their entry into force. The council radically expanded its own zone of discretion in the 1970s, when it incorporated, against the founder's wishes, a charter of rights into the constitution. Compared with the German case, however, the council's zone is quite restricted. It does not handle referrals from the courts or individuals, thus reducing its capacity to control policy outcomes beyond legislative space. As important, the decision rules governing constitutional revision are more permissive than in the German situation: the constitution can be revised by a 3/5 vote of Assembly deputies and senators assembled in a special session. No important German decision on rights has, or can be, overruled, whereas two council decisions have been overruled in order: (1) to permit the right-wing majority to tighten immigration policy (amendment of 1993), and (2) to allow the left-wing majority to develop affirmative action policies for women

(amendment of 1999). The French Council reviews about one third of all laws adopted by parliament and has struck down at least one provision in half of all laws reviewed.

European countries with Kelsenian courts operate in large zones of discretion, given that (1) the courts possess broad powers to protect charters of rights, most of which are more extensive than the German, and (2) it is almost impossible to amend constitutional rights provisions.

The US and Canada

In the US and Canada, all courts may exercise the judicial review of statutes.

The US Federal Constitution provides for a short list of negative rights, although the Supreme Court has 'discovered' a longer list of unenumerated rights, such as privacy, thereby expanding its own zone of discretion. It is difficult to amend the US Constitution—readers should check out Article V! In practice, this means that the Court's case law on constitutional rights can only be changed if the Supreme Court changes its mind.

In 1982, Canada became fully independent from the United Kingdom, when it 'repatriated' its constitution and supplemented it with an extensive Charter of Rights and Freedoms. Repatriation radically expanded the judiciary's zone of discretion. The system of rights protection established by the Charter of Rights and Freedoms is an unusual one. The 'Notwithstanding Clause' of the charter permits the federal and provincial parliaments to 'override' a right, for a period of five years, renewable thereafter. Thus, there is no *de facto* judicial supremacy when it comes to rights, as there is in much of Europe and the United States. Canadian legislators can choose to violate a right, but their responsibility for doing so is complete. The Canadian Parliament has never chosen to do so, although some provincial legislatures have voted overrides.

Students should consider this question, to which there may not be a clear answer: is the zone of discretion of the US Supreme Court greater or smaller than that of the Canadian Supreme Court? On the one hand, the Canadian Constitution gives a privileged place for the Charter of Rights and Freedoms, which is a richer text than is the American Bill of Rights. On the other hand, a Canadian Supreme Court's ruling on rights can be more easily set aside, at least for five-year periods. But as this chapter emphasizes, the zone of discretion does not tell us what a court will actually do with its discretionary authority. Might a 'Notwithstanding Clause' encourage a court to be a more aggressive rights protector if it knows that it does not have the last word on a statute's constitutional legality?

those who run authoritarian states. Litigation, for example, may comprise a relatively cheap means of monitoring what is going on in the country, especially what the lower echelons of the bureaucracy are actually doing (Moustafa 2007: ch. 2). Courts may also help the ruler enforce new national policies in the face of regional resistance, thereby weakening

challenges to the ruler's power. But logics such as these do not apply to constitutional courts and rights review, which can directly challenge the ruler's power at its source. It is likely that rulers institute review for other reasons—to achieve a measure of international respectability, for example—never doubting their capacity to control the review courts.

KEY POINTS

- ❑ Constitutions are, among other things, incomplete, relational contracts. Delegating authority to constitutional judges is a means of dealing with various commitment problems, including interpretation and enforcement.
- ❑ Constitutional courts are a special kind of agent, called a trustee. A trustee court exercises fiduciary (caretaker) responsibilities over the constitution and is relatively insulated from the direct control of political elites.

- ❑ All courts operate in a strategic environment called a zone of discretion, which is determined by the authority given to the court minus the control instruments—in particular, the decision rules governing constitutional amendment—available for constraining the court. The bigger the zone, the less likely it is that political elites or the people will be able to reverse the court's rulings.

The evolution of constitutional review

In 1789, no system of constitutional justice existed anywhere on earth. After 1950, what I have called 'the new constitutionalism' emerged and then, in the 1990s, exploded into prominence. Between 1789 and 1950, the institutional materials that would solidify into the current 'models' of review were beginning to take shape, in the US, France, Austria–Germany, and in Scandinavia. I will briefly examine each of these cases in turn.

1789–1950

In America, the Federal Constitution of the US (1787) replaced the Articles of Confederation (1781), one of the first written constitutions of any modern nation-state. The new constitution established a Supreme Court and the judiciary as a separate branch of government, but the document neither contained a charter of rights nor expressly provided for the judicial review of statutes. The court's main purpose was to manage federalism, in particular, to secure national supremacy with regard to interstate commerce and finance. In 1791, the Bill of Rights was added to the text, as amendments, and constitutional review was added in 1803 through the Marbury decision.

Only in the 1880s did rights review begin to emerge. In its most important decisions during this period, the court defended the property rights of merchants and firms against state laws designed to regulate their commercial activities. During the First World War, the court began to deal with civil and political rights, but it did very little to protect them. In 1937, the court abandoned its opposition to market regulation of economic rights, after successive elections had cemented the power of New Deal Democrats, and in the face of President Roosevelt's threat to 'pack the Court' (Balkin 2005).

By the end of the Second World War, it would have been difficult to argue that constitutional experience in the US provided a respectable example of an effective 'system of constitutional justice', at least by today's standards. The constitution, after all, had formally sanctioned slavery. The Civil War led to slavery's abolition, and to the adoption of the 13th, 14th, and 15th Amendments (1865–70). Prior to 1950, the court made little of the 14th Amendment, which guarantees 'equal protection under the laws', for the purposes for which it was designed: to combat institutionalized racism and other forms of discrimination. Instead, the court, and therefore the constitution, was complicit in systematic rights abuses of the worst kind. In 1883, the court struck down as unconstitutional a Congressional statute banning discrimination against former slaves in hotels, the railroads, theatres, and so on; and in 1896, it bestowed constitutional legitimacy on the official apartheid that many Southern states had instituted after Reconstruction.[7] Apartheid would remain an important element of American constitutional law until well after the Second World War.

Although the American experience is increasingly irrelevant to global constitutionalism, it has had an impact. The US produced a model of judicial review that has been adopted by other polities. Further, the Supreme Court demonstrated to the world that constitutional review could survive and even prosper, not only through supervising federalism, but through protecting rights. In the 1950s, the court gradually moved to protect civil rights, especially freedom of speech and assembly, voting rights, 14th Amendment protections, and the rights of defendants in criminal cases. Indeed, by the end of the 1960s, the court had transformed itself into a formidable rights protector. This posture helped to create and sustain a rights-based, litigation-oriented politics in the US (Epp 1998), a politics that remains vibrant today. As important, Americans occupied post-Second World War Germany and Italy, and they insisted that these countries write constitutions that included a charter of rights and a review mechanism, thus helping to provoke the move to the 'new constitutionalism' in Europe.

In 1803, when *Marbury* v. *Madison* was rendered, the French were completing the destruction of independent judicial authority. That process began with the Great Revolution of 1789. In 1790, the legislature prohibited judicial review of legislation, and that statute remains in force today. By 1804, a new legal system had emerged. It was constructed on the principle—a corollary of legislative sovereignty—that courts must not participate in the law-making function. The judge was cast as a 'slave' of the legislature, more precisely, of the code system. The codes are statutes which, in their idealized form, purport to regulate society in a comprehensive way, not least, in order to reduce judicial discretion to nil. Through imitation, revolution, and war, the code system and the prohibition of judicial review spread across Europe during the nineteenth century (the British Isles and the Nordic region being the most important exceptions). Although the nineteenth century witnessed momentous regime change, a relatively stable constitutional orthodoxy nonetheless prevailed. In this orthodoxy, constitutions could be revised at the discretion of the law-maker; separation of powers doctrines subjugated judicial to legislative authority; and constraints on the law-maker's authority, such as rights, either did not exist or could not be enforced by courts.

BOX 9.4 Modes of constitutional review

The American model and judicial review

A legal 'case'—defined as a legal dispute brought to a court as litigation between two parties who have opposed interests—activates review, once one of the parties pleads the constitution, such as a right. Any court can, at the behest of either party, void a law as unconstitutional if that court determines that the statute violates the constitution.

The European model and abstract review

Abstract review is initiated when elected officials—typically the parliamentary opposition, the executive, or the government of a regional of federated state—refer a law for review after the law has been adopted by the legislature, but before it has been enforced. This mode of review is called 'abstract' because it proceeds in the absence of a concrete judicial case, since the law has yet to be applied. The review court compares the constitutional text and the statute, in the abstract, to determine if the latter conforms to the former. Abstract review is also called 'preventive review', since it allows the system to filter out unconstitutional laws before they can harm people.

The European model and concrete review

Concrete review is initiated when an ordinary judge, presiding over litigation in the courts, refers a constitutional question—for example, is law X, which is normally applicable to the dispute at bar, unconstitutional?—that the constitutional court must answer. The referring judge then resolves the dispute with reference to the constitutional court's ruling. This mode of review is called 'concrete' since it is related to a concrete case already under way in the ordinary courts. In comparison with American judicial review, however, concrete review still

(continued)

Curiously, the French Revolution did produce the first modern charter of rights. In 1789, the Constituent Assembly adopted the Declaration of the Rights of Man and of the Citizen before it completed its task of drafting the constitution of 1791. Since 1791, the French have lived under fifteen different written constitutions, but none provided for rights review, and none made the Declaration judicially enforceable. Constitutional review powers were periodically conferred on specialized state organs (never courts) in order to police the boundaries between executive and legislative authority, not to protect rights from legislative infringement. In the 1970s, the Constitutional Council incorporated the Declaration into the Constitution of the Fifth Republic (1959–present), against the express wishes of the founders (Stone 1990: chs. 3, 4).

The founders of the Fifth Republic established the Constitutional Council to help ensure the dominance of the executive (the government, named by the president) over the parliament (Chamber of Deputies and Senate) in legislative processes. Its role was transformed by two constitutional changes. First, as mentioned, the council incorporated a bill of rights into the constitution, where none previously existed, a process completed by 1979. The decision expanded the council's zone of discretion considerably. Second, in 1974 the power to refer statutes adopted by parliament before their entry into force was given to any sixty National Assembly deputies or sixty senators—that is, to opposition parties. The council exercises only politically initiated, pre-enforcement, abstract review of statutes. Once a statute has entered into force, it is no longer subject to constitutional review of any kind: legislative sovereignty thus remains formally intact.

The French experience is important for two main reasons. First, its code system and its conception of legislative sovereignty and separation of powers spread across Europe and would later take hold in Africa and Latin America, through the influence of French and Spanish colonialism. Second, like the Germans, the French experimented with models of non-judicial, politically activated, constitutional review in the form of specialized state organs. These experiments are cousins of the modern constitutional court, and a number of states use the 'constitutional council' model today.

In the area now comprised of Austria, Germany, and Switzerland, specialized state organs became a common feature of government in various federal polities during the nineteenth century. These bodies dealt primarily with jurisdictional disputes between state institutions, or among levels of government. The modern constitutional court is the invention of the Austrian legal theorist, Hans Kelsen, who developed the European model of constitutional review partly from these experiences. Kelsen drafted the constitution of the Austrian First Republic (1920–34), and he included a constitutional court among its most important state institutions. He was also a legal theorist whose writings and teachings turned out to be extraordinarily influential after the Second World War. As discussed below, the Kelsenian court, which is at the heart of the European model, is now the most popular institutional form of review in the world.

Some scholars speak of a Scandinavian model of review, and note that it is one of the world's oldest (Husa 2000). In Norway, the power of the judiciary to invalidate law as unconstitutional has been asserted since at least the 1860s, although the question of whether this power extended to judicial review of statutes was not definitively resolved until a Supreme Court decision of 1976 suggested that the answer was yes. Simplifying, the Danish Constitution of 1849 expressly provides for rights but not for review, and the Swedish Constitution (elements of which have been in place since 1809) provided for review but not for rights (until 1974). None of the courts in the region ever used review authority to any noticeable effect. Indeed, even today, these courts do almost no constitutional judicial review of any political consequence, and deference to the legislature is the rule (Husa 2000; Scheinin 2001).

The diffusion of higher law constitutionalism

During the inter-war period (roughly 1918–38), constitutional review was established in Czechoslovakia (1920), Liechtenstein (1925), Greece (1927), Spain (1931), and Ireland (1937); further, the German Supreme Court of the Weimar Republic also flirted with review (Stolleis 2003). Of these, only the Irish Supreme Court actually did much review, and only the Irish Court survived the Second World War. It is today one of the world's most effective review courts.

Review courts were established in Europe in successive waves of constitution-making, following the war, the end of fascism in Greece, Spain, and Portugal in the 1970s, and the fall of communism in Central and Eastern Europe after 1989. Apart from the Greek mixed system, every country adopted the Kelsenian constitutional court. The American model was rejected. Kelsenian courts were established in Austria (1945), Italy (1948), the Federal Republic of Germany (1949), France (1958), Portugal (1976), Spain (1978), Belgium (1985), and, after 1989, in the post-communist Czech Republic, Hungary, Poland, Romania, Russia, and other post-Soviet states, Slovakia, the Baltics, and in the states of the former Yugoslavia. The exception is Estonia, whose system mixes elements from the two models.

The American model is found in Africa, Asia, and the Caribbean, especially in those countries that had been colonized by Great Britain, or are part of the Commonwealth. In moving to rights and review, these systems, in effect, 'constitutionalize' the basic common law legal order. Judicial review is also found in countries that were under American occupation or influence after 1950, such as Japan and parts of Central and South America.

With decolonization, the number of states in the world expanded steadily throughout the 1950s and 1960s. Many of these new states were not very stable. Beginning in the 1970s, many post-colonial states in the developing world began to experiment with different constitutional forms. Written constitutions proliferated, most of which did not last, but they were almost always replaced with new written constitutions. By the 1990s, the basic formula of the new constitutionalism—(1) a written, entrenched constitution, (2) a charter of rights, and (3) a review mechanism to protect rights—had become standard, even in what most of us would consider non-democratic, authoritarian states.

Systems of constitutional justice in the twenty-first century

I will now survey the state of systems of constitutional justice worldwide.

1. The written constitution is the norm. There are 194 states in a recent data set compiled on constitutional forms,[8] 190 of which have written constitutions. Bhutan, Israel, New Zealand, and the United Kingdom do not have fully codified, entrenched constitutions. Israel nonetheless possesses a powerful Supreme Court that protects rights as part of the higher law (Gross 1998), and the Kingdom of Bhutan has drafted a constitution, which includes both rights and review (it awaits ratification). New Zealand (1990) and the UK (1998) adopted charters of rights in the form of statutes, but courts may not enforce these rights against the will of Parliament (Gardbaum 2001). Constitutions are currently suspended in four states: Thailand, Myanmar (Burma), Pakistan, and Somalia.

2. Out of the 194 states in the dataset 183 contain a charter of rights. Most constitutions written in the past three decades contain an extensive catalogue of rights that includes not only traditional civil and political rights, but positive or social rights. At present, few new constitutions omit rights. There have been 114 constitutions written since 1985 (not all of which have lasted), and we have reliable information on 106 of these. All 106 of these constitutions contain a catalogue of rights. It seems that the last constitution to leave rights out

was the racist 1983 South African constitution, hardly a model to emulate.

3. Of the 106 constitutions written since 1985 on which we can reliably report, all but five established constitutional review: those of North Korea, Vietnam, Saudi Arabia, Laos, and Iraq (in its 1990 constitution).

Table 9.1 presents data on the regional distribution of the various review mechanisms. The European model is clearly ascendant. Moreover, with few exceptions, the most powerful review courts in the world are Kelsenian courts. The spread of the European model has also meant the diffusion of abstract review. Mavčič (www.concourts.net) examined modes of review in 125 constitutions currently in force, and determined that 70 of them conferred abstract review authority on judges. Most of these also provide for individual, constitutional complaints. The American 'case or controversy' model is moribund, with little chance of being revived.

KEY POINTS

❏ Prior to 1950, there was little effective constitutional review outside of the United States, where it functioned more in favour of powerful economic interests and institutionalized racism than it did to protect minority rights.
❏ After 1950, the European model of review spreads from Austria and Germany throughout Europe and beyond.

❏ Today, nearly every country has a written constitution that provides for rights and rights review. The American model is found primarily in Commonwealth countries and in areas that have been under American influence. The European model, however, is far more popular.

Effectiveness

Many political scientists will not be interested in these developments if systems of constitutional justice do not influence broader political processes: the development of the constitution, the making of public policy, the competition among political elites. To the extent that constitutional review is effective, it will be central to these and other processes.

Constitutional review can be said to be effective to the extent that important constitutional disputes arising in the polity are brought to the review authority on a regular basis, that the judges who resolve these disputes give reasons for their rulings, and that those who are governed by the constitutional law accept that the court's rulings have some effect as precedents. Effectiveness varies across countries and across time in the same country.

Most review systems throughout world history have been relatively ineffective, even irrelevant. In weak systems, important political disputes may not be sent to constitutional judges for resolution, and decisions that constitutional judges do render may be ignored. Political actors may seek to settle their disputes by force, rather than through the courts, sometimes with fatal consequences for the constitutional regime. Put simply, elites may care much more about staying in power at any cost, or enriching themselves, or rewarding their friends and punishing their foes, or achieving ethnic dominance, than they care about building constitutional democracy. Constitutional regimes may also be overthrown by force. Since 1950, in Africa, Central and South America, and Asia, one finds over 100 examples. In some countries, the military *coup d'état* remains a constant threat. In the most recent decade (1997–2006), at least twenty-five coups were attempted in these areas, and at least fourteen were successful, including in Ecuador, Fiji, Guinée-Bissau, the Ivory Coast, Mauritania, Pakistan, Thailand, and Turkey. None of these proceeded with respect to constitutional principles. Nonetheless, despite the odds, some courts and constitutions have operated as constraints even on military dictatorship, as in Pinochet's Chile (Barros 2002).

Where constitutional review systems are relatively effective, constitutional judges manage the evolution of the polity through their decisions. There are several necessary conditions for the emergence of effective review systems; each is related to the court's 'zone of discretion'. First, constitutional judges must have a case load. If actors, private and public, conspire not to activate review, judges will accrete no influence over the polity. Second, once activated, judges must resolve these disputes and give defensible reasons in justification of their decisions. If they do, one output of constitutional adjudication will be the production of a constitutional case law, or jurisprudence, which is a record of how the judges have interpreted the constitution. Third, those who are governed by the constitutional law must accept that constitutional meaning is (at least partly) constructed through the judges' interpretation and rule-making, and use or refer to relevant case law in future disputes.

Why only some countries are able to fulfil these conditions is an important question that scholars have not been able to answer. The achievement of stable type 3 constitutionalism depends heavily on the same macro-political factors related to the achievement of stable democracy, and we know that democracy is difficult to create and sustain. Among other factors, the new constitutionalism rests on a polity's commitment to: elections; a competitive party system; protecting rights, including those of minorities; practices associated with the 'rule of law'; a system of advanced legal education. Each of these factors is also associated with other important socio-cultural phenomena, including attributes of political culture, which may be fragmented. Constitutional judges can contribute to the building of practices related to higher law constitutionalism, but there are limits to what they can do if they find themselves continuously in opposition to powerful elites, institutions, and cultural biases in the citizenry.

It is therefore unsurprising that one finds relatively effective review mechanisms in areas where one finds relatively stable democracy, which now includes the post-communist countries of Central Europe. Ranked in terms of effectiveness, I would place the systems of (1) Canada and the US in the Americas, (2) Germany, Ireland, and Spain in Western Europe, and (3) the Czech Republic, Hungary, Poland, and Slovenia in Central Europe at the top of the list. Outside these regions, there are probably only three courts that would make this list, those of India (Verma and Kumar 2003), Israel (Hirschl

2001), and South Africa (Klug 2000). The review courts of Colombia and Egypt (Moustafa 2007) are building effectiveness quite rapidly, despite operating in extremely difficult contexts.

The impact of constitutional review

There has been no systematic research or data collection on constitutions, rights, and rights protection, or on the politics of constitutional review. However, since 1990, scholars have produced a pile of single case studies, and a handful of small-N comparative treatments of these topics. I will not summarize all of this work here. Instead, I will focus on the impact of new review systems on politics in the two areas that have attracted the most attention.

Transitions to constitutional democracy

Since 1950, type 3 constitutions, rights, and review have been crucial to nearly all successful transitions from authoritarian regimes to constitutional democracy. Indeed, it appears that the more successful any transition has been, the more one is likely to find an effective constitutional or supreme court at the heart of it (Japan may be the most important exception). Review performs several functions that facilitate the transition to democracy. It provides a system of peaceful dispute resolution, under the constitution, for those who have contracted a new beginning, in light of illiberal or violent pasts. It provides a mechanism for purging the laws of authoritarian elements that have built up over many years, given that the new legislature may be overloaded with work. And a review court can provide a focal point for a new rhetoric of state legitimacy, one based on respect for rights and other values of the new constitution, and on the rejection of old rhetorics (fascism, one-party rule, legislative sovereignty, the cult of personality, and so on).

Today, constitutional democracy is defined in terms of the new constitutionalism, which assumes that constraining majority rule with rights and review is a good thing. Thus, it is hardly shocking that a new generation of scholars claim that constitutional courts have been—or simply are—more democratic than parliaments, and that they have cajoled or persuaded political elites to be more democratic than they would otherwise have been (e.g. Scheppele 2005). Moreover, many of today's newer and more successful review courts do not conceive of constitutionalism in restricted national terms, but in terms of an emerging 'global constitutionalism' with human rights at its core. The courts of Hungary, Poland, Slovenia, and South Africa do not hesitate to cite sources of law outside of their constitutions, including the decisions of other constitutional courts (Klug 2000).

The 'judicialization' of politics

A second important strain of research focuses on the impact of review on policy processes and outcomes. Most studies of judicialization proceed by conceptualizing constitutional review and rights adjudication as an extension of the policy process, and then observing and evaluating the impact of review on final outcomes and subsequent policy-making in the same area. The classic work is Martin Shapiro's *Law and Politics in the Supreme Court* (1964), but the basic approach has been applied to Europe (Shapiro and Stone 1994), and Latin America (Sieder, Schjolden, and Angell 2005), as well as many other specific countries.

Charles Epp (1998) has analysed the 'rights revolution' in four countries whose review systems would be classified under the American judicial review model. He shows that effective rights review does not just emerge spontaneously or naturally, but is the product of a constellation of structures and agency. Effective rights review depends on the building of a network of 'rights advocates' who are able to mobilize the resources necessary to litigate in the courts, often for causes that will benefit people who do not have such resources. The success of such litigation also rests on the shoulders of a critical mass of judges who are willing to embrace the roles of creative rights protector in the system. Epp argues that the rights revolution has gone furthest in the US and Canada, but his book also helps to explain development in India, and more recent changes in the UK and other Commonwealth countries. In every case he examines, the capacity of the judge to participate in policy processes, and often enough to control policy outcomes, has been enhanced.

It is easier to study the impact of rights review on legislative activity in centralized review systems than in decentralized systems, because constitutional judges and legislators interact with one another directly, through abstract review referrals and decisions. I have developed a theory of the constitutional judicialization of politics in Western Europe (Stone Sweet 2000), showing, among other things, that the impact of rights and the court on legislative activity will vary as a function of three factors: (1) the existence of abstract review, (2) the number of veto points in the policy process, and (3) the content of the court's case law. The more centralized the

---

BOX 9.5 The judicialization of politics through rights adjudication

The phrase 'judicialization of politics' refers to the process through which the influence of courts on legislative and administrative power develops, over time. In some places, in some sectors, policy is highly judicialized; in others, it may not be judicialized at all.

Rights review leads to the judicialization of legislative politics to the extent that (1) constitutional rights provisions have a legal status superior to statutes, (2) the review court receives important cases in which statutes are alleged to have violated rights, (3) the court sometimes annuls statutes on the basis of rights, and gives reasons for doing so. In judicialized settings, legislators worry about and debate the constitutionality of bills during the legislative process, and they will draft and amend their bills in order to insulate them from constitutional censure. In judicialized settings, constitutional courts routinely take decisions that serve both to construct the constitutional law and to amend legislation under review.

Some of the more controversial examples of highly judicialized politics around the world concern attempt to combat racial and gender discrimination, to liberalize and regulate abortion, and to criminalize 'hate speech', obscenity, and pornography.

In policy domains that are highly judicialized, courts and judicial process are part of the greater policy process. If political scientists do not pay close attention to courts, they will miss a big part of the action.

COUNTRY PROFILE Egypt

Arab Republic of Egypt (*Jumhuriyat Misr al-Arabiya*)

State formation

The modernization of Egypt started early in the 19th century after a brief invasion by Napoleon and a period of civil wars. An Ottoman viceroyalty since 1805, the country was informally controlled by Great Britain from 1882 and became a British protectorate in 1914. Following a revolution in 1919 and constant insurgency, Egypt was declared independent by Great Britain in 1922 but largely remained under British control until Colonel Gamal Abdul Nasser seized power in 1956, following a military *coup d'état* and the establishment of the Republic in 1953.
Constitution 1971, amended most recently in 2005 and 2007.

Form of government

Semi-presidential republic.
Head of state President, directly elected (since the 2005 reforms); term of 6 years (no term limit). Vice President appointed by the President.
Head of government Prime Minister; the leader of the majority party in Parliament, formally appointed by the President.
Cabinet Appointed by the President.
Administrative subdivisions 26 governorates.

Legal system

Based on European models, especially the French civil code, and Sharia law; familiy law corresponds with Islamic or Christian norms depending on the individual concerned.

Legislature

Bicameral Parliament.
Lower house People's Assembly (*Majilis Ash-Sha'ab*): 454 seats, half of which are reserved for farmers and workers; three-phase voting; term of 5 years if not dissolved earlier.
Upper house Advisory Council (*Majilis Ash-Shura*): 264 members (two-thirds directly elected, half of which must be farmers or workers; the remaining third appointed by the President); staggered elections (half of the elected members renewed every three years); term of 6 years.

Electoral system (lower house)

Mixed system of proportional representation and single candidate lists (since 2007 reforms).
Formula Since the 2007 reforms, 400 members are chosen by proportional representation while the remaining 44 are elected in local majority votes. (Prior to the reforms, 444 members were directly elected in 222 two-seat constituencies with one seat reserved for farmers and workers; the remaining 10 members were appointed by the President.)
Constituencies Both multi-member and 44 single-member constituencies since the 2007 reforms (222 two-member constituencies prior to the reforms).
Suffrage Universal and compulsory, 18 years.

Direct democracy

None.

Party system Results of the 2005 legislative elections (People's Assembly):

Electorate	31,253,417	100.0%
Voters	8,790,708	28.1%

Party	Valid votes	%	Seats
National Democratic Party (NDP)	n.a.	n.a.	320
Independents backed by the Muslim Brotherhood	n.a.	n.a.	88
New Wafd Party (NWP)	n.a.	n.a.	6
National Progressive Unionist Grouping (Tagammu)	n.a.	n.a.	2
Total 'National Front for Change'	n.a.	n.a.	96
Independents	n.a.	n.a.	26
Total	8,488,358	100.0	442

(The rows for Independents backed by the Muslim Brotherhood, New Wafd Party, National Progressive Unionist Grouping, and Total 'National Front for Change' are grouped under the label 'NFC'.)

Note: The candidates of the Muslim Brotherhood, which is illegal for its religious approach to politics, run as independents and made strong gains in the 2005 elections.
12 seats were vacant. Of nine members in all, four were directly elected and five others were appointed.
Source: IPU.

policy process—the greater the parliamentary majority, the more that majority is under the control of a unified executive, and the fewer veto points there are in legislative procedures—the more the opposition will go to the constitutional court to block important policy initiatives. Abstract review referrals are the most straightforward means of doing so. In many policy domains, legislative politics have become highly 'judicialized'. The web of constitutional constraints facing legislators has grown and become denser, as constitutional courts have processed a steady stream of cases, and built a policy-relevant jurisprudence. This orientation is also applicable to Central Europe (Sadurski 2005).

KEY POINTS

- Systems of constitutional review are effective in so far as constitutional judges are able to influence the development of the constitutional law and public policy through their interpretations of rights and other constitutional provisions. We do not find much effectiveness in countries that are not relatively stable democracies.

- In some places, including South Africa and Central and Eastern Europe, constitutional courts have been important to processes of democratization.
- In countries where review is highly effective, constitutional judges have become powerful policy-makers. Examples are mainly found in North America and Western Europe, although the courts of Colombia, Israel, and South Africa deserve mention.

Conclusion

Constitutional law is political law: it is the law that constitutes the state and governs acts of authority made in the name of the polity. Since the 1950s, the new constitutionalism—which combines (1) written, entrenched constitutions, (2) rights, and (3) constitutional review—has been consolidated as an unrivalled standard. Though we find provision for rights review virtually everywhere today, not all systems of constitutional justice are equally effective. Indeed, in many places they are irrelevant.

Where such systems are effective, constitutional judges govern. They do so through two linked processes. First, given a steady case load, they will adapt the constitution to changing circumstances, on an ongoing basis, through interpretation. Second, in applying their constitutional interpretations to resolve rights disputes, the judges will make policy, including legislative policy. The more effective any system of review is, the more judges will, inevitably, become powerful policy-makers. Both outcomes inhere in a simple legal fact, made real through effective review: the constitution is higher law and therefore binds the exercise of all public authority.

?   Questions

1. In what ways does a constitution constitute the state and the political system?
2. What are the main differences between a type 2 and a type 3 constitution?
3. What is 'the new constitutionalism' and what does it have to do with politics?
4. What is the difference between a court that is 'an agent of the legislature' and a court that is a 'trustee of the constitution'?
5. How does the American model of review differ from the European model?
6. Why is the zone of discretion, in part, determined by constitutional provisions that specify how the constitution is to be revised?
7. Do you think it is good for a country to have a big catalogue of rights and an effective system of review?

8. Would you rather live in a country whose politics are relatively more, or relatively less, constitutionally 'judicialized'?

9. Why do you think an authoritarian dictator might draft a constitution with rights and review?

10. Which are the most effective courts?

» **Further reading**

Recent comparative treatments of judicial politics and constitutional review

Epp, Charles (1998) *The Rights Revolution: Lawyers, Activists, and Supreme Courts in Comparative Perspective* (Chicago: University of Chicago Press).

Ginsburg, Tom (2003) *Judicial Review in New Democracies: Constitutional Courts in Asian Cases* (Cambridge: Cambridge University Press).

Hirschl, Ran (2004) *Towards Juristocracy: The Origins and Consequences of the New Constitutionalism* (Cambridge, Mass.: Harvard University Press).

Schwartz, Herman (2000) *The Struggle for Constitutional Justice in Post-Communist Europe* (Chicago: University of Chicago Press).

Sieder, Rachel, Schjolden, Line, and Angell, Alan (2005) *The Judicialization of Politics in Latin America* (New York: Palgrave Macmillan).

Stone Sweet, Alec (2000) *Governing with Judges: Constitutional Politics in Western Europe* (Oxford: Oxford University Press).

Tate, C. Neal, and Vallinder, T. (eds.) (1995) *The Global Expansion of Judicial Power* (New York: New York University Press).

See also the works cited throughout this chapter. *The International Journal of Constitutional Law* is the leading journal devoted to research on constitutional law and courts, though it only rarely publishes articles written by social scientists.

Ⓦ **Web links**

www.venice.coe.int/site/dynamics/N_court_links_ef.asp?L=E
 Hyperlinks to the constitutional and supreme courts of the world, maintained by the Venice Commission of the Council of Europe.

http://www2.lib.uchicago.edu/~llou/conlaw.html
 University of Chicago's 'Research Constitutional Law on the Internet'.

www.concourts.net
 Data, data analysis, and commentary on constitutional courts and review around the world.

www.jurist.law.pitt.edu/countries/
 University of Pittsburgh School of Law's website for 'legal news and research', country by country.

www.glin.gov/
 Global Legal Information Network, maintained by the US Library of Congress.

http://confinder.richmond.edu/
 'Constitution Finder', the University of Richmond.

www.findlaw.com/01topics/06constitutional/03forconst/index.html
 Find Law, constitutions.

 Visit the Online Resource Centre that accompanies this book for more information:
 www.oxfordtextbooks.co.uk/orc/caramani/

10 Elections and referendums

Michael Gallagher

Chapter contents

Reader's guide

This chapter covers the two main opportunities that people have to vote in most societies: elections and referendums. Elections are held to fill seats in parliaments or to choose a president, while at referendums citizens decide directly on some issue of policy. Elections are the cornerstone of representative democracy, in that the people elect others to make decisions. Referendums are sometimes perceived as the equivalent of 'direct democracy', but in practice they are deployed only as a kind of optional extra in systems of representative democracy, with hardly anyone suggesting that all decisions should be made by referendum. The chapter explores the variety of rules under which elections are held, and examines the consequences of this variation. It then looks at the use of the referendum and assesses its potential impact on a country's politics.

Introduction

We saw in Chapters 7 and 8 that parliaments and governments have the potential to be important actors. In this chapter we look at how governments and parliaments come into being in the first place. The process of election is an essential requirement of any political system that hopes to be regarded as possessing democratic credentials. Depending on the nature of the political system, parliament might then elect a government itself or, in a presidential system, the chief executive may be elected separately and have significant powers to appoint a government (see Chapter 8). Either way, the election is the main mechanism by which the people are able to express their views about how the country should be governed.

Not all elections are quite the same, though. Elections are governed by rules that determine, among other things, what kind of choices people can make when they turn out to vote and how those choices are converted into seats in parliament or the election of a president. Identical sets of voter preferences in two adjacent countries might have to be expressed differently if the electoral rules are different or, even if the ballot papers capture their preferences in the same way, the counting rules might deliver different results. Hence, it is important to understand what kind of rules are used and what consequences different rules have.

Governments and parliaments, produced by elections, make most of the political decisions facing a country, albeit within the constraints imposed by some of the other actors studied in this book, such as courts and interest groups (see Chapters 9 and 14 respectively). However, some decisions are taken not by these elected authorities but, rather, by the people themselves, in referendums on specific issues. Whereas the use of elections is universal among democracies, the use of referendums varies enormously. Many perfectly respectable democracies eschew the referendum; others use it only occasionally; some are quite regular users; and in one country, Switzerland, it is a central feature of the political system.

This variation is itself intriguing, as is the question of why some issues are put to referendums while others are not. The chapter examines the different kinds of referendum that are held or are provided for in countries' constitutions, and the kinds of issue that tend to be the subject of referendums. It looks at the reasons advanced for their use and at the concerns expressed by critics. There has been some dispute as to whether voters in referendums take much notice of the question supposedly at issue, and the chapter reviews the evidence before assessing the impact of referendums.

KEY POINTS

❏ Electoral laws and referendums are the two main opportunities that people have to vote.
❏ Elections are held to fill seats (representatives) in a parliament or some other institution.
❏ Referendums are votes on a specific issue to be approved or rejected.

Elections and electoral systems

Elections are a virtually universal feature of modern politics. Even regimes that cannot be considered democracies in any sense of the word, and that provide voters with little or no freedom of choice when they arrive at the polling station, have felt there might be some kind of legitimacy to be derived from holding elections.

In modern liberal democracies, elections are the central representative institution that forms a link between the people and their representatives. For the most part, ordinary people cannot participate directly in the process of making decisions on the great majority of issues, due to such obvious factors as size of population, policy complexity, and time constraints, among others. For the most part, the decisions that affect us all are taken by a tiny handful of individuals, such as members of parliament, government ministers, or presidents, sometimes known collectively as the 'political class'.

The reason why we (or, at any rate, most people most of the time) regard this state of affairs as legitimate rather than as an appalling usurpation of our rights is that the members of the political class are not simply imposed upon us but, rather, are elected by us to be our political representatives. Moreover, they face re-election and therefore can be voted out at the next election if they fail to satisfy us. This mechanism of achieving representation and accountability is central to the concept of modern democracy (see Chapter 5). A regime whose leaders are not elected and are not subject to the requirement of regular re-election cannot be considered democratic. Whether free and fair elections suffice to render a regime democratic is a matter of debate, but the absence of free and fair elections certainly renders it, by almost any definition, undemocratic.

By an electoral system I mean the set of rules that structure how votes are cast at elections and how these votes are then converted into the allocation of offices. I look first at electoral regulations (the rules governing the breadth of the franchise, ease of ballot access, and so on) and then specifically at electoral systems.

Electoral regulations

Among modern democracies, variations in the extent of the franchise are matters of detail rather than of principle (for an overview see Caramani 2000: 49–57). Generalizing somewhat, in the first half of the nineteenth century the male landed gentry constituted the bulk of the **electorate** (those who are entitled to vote), but from the middle of the century the franchise was gradually extended to the male section of the growing middle class. Around the turn of the century further advances meant that the male working class had the vote by the time of the First World War (1914). The struggle to secure the same rights for women took longer and, particularly in some mainly Catholic countries such as France and Italy, women did not get the vote on the same basis as men until after the Second World War (1945). The voting age was reduced steadily throughout the twentieth century, and in most countries these days stands at 18 (Caramani 2000: 56–7). Voting is generally voluntary, though in a few countries such as Australia and Belgium it is compulsory. Given that turnout in most countries is related to socio-economic status (SES), it has been argued that making voting compulsory would help eliminate the 'yawning SES voting gap' (Hill 2006) (see Box 10.1).

The ease of access to the ballot varies across countries and can be an important factor in determining whether new candidates or parties take the plunge and stand at an election. Most states impose some kind of requirement, such as a financial deposit, demonstrated support from a number of voters, or the endorsement of a recognized party. Generally speaking, the requirements are more demanding in candidate-oriented systems than in party-oriented ones (see Katz 1997: 255–61). High access requirements can be a significant deterrent for small parties or independent candidates; if not motivated simply by a desire to preserve the dominance of the established parties, they can be justified by the need to discourage a plethora of 'frivolous' candidates.

How much time may elapse between elections? Generally, the term of presidents is fixed while for parliaments constitutions specify a maximum period but not a minimum. The president of the US has a four-year term, while his or her French counterpart has five years (it was seven years prior to 2002). The term of some parliaments is fixed: for example, the parliaments of Norway, Sweden, and Switzerland have a four-year lifespan, while members of the US House of Representatives serve terms of only two years, which means in effect that they operate all the time in election campaign mode. Senators in the US, by contrast, have six years to savour the fruits of election. Most parliaments, though, do not have a fixed term; instead, the government (or prime minister, or in some cases the head of state) of the day has the power to dissolve parliament, and characteristically uses this power to call the election at the time most advantageous to itself. In many countries, once the parliament enters its last year of life (if it gets that far), election fever is in the air, and there is ceaseless speculation that a favourable opinion poll rating will induce the government to go to the country. The maximum time between elections is usually four years, though in a few (including Canada, France, Italy, and the United Kingdom) it is five years, while in Australia and New Zealand it is an exceptionally short three years.

BOX 10.1 Should voting be compulsory?

Arguments for compulsory voting	Arguments against compulsory voting
Our forebears struggled and died in order to win the right to vote, so people today have a duty to vote.	It is perfectly legitimate to take no interest in politics, or not to vote for whatever reason.
Politicians have a strong incentive to skew their policies towards those who will punish or reward them, depending on their record in office, and to neglect those who are unlikely to vote. When voting is optional, the better off are much more likely to vote than the poor, so policy outputs will favour the better off.	If everyone is compelled to vote, the votes of those who actually care about the outcome of an election are diluted by the votes of those with no interest in the outcome and who may be voting on a virtually random basis.
The role of money in politics is reduced since parties no longer need to motivate their supporters to turn out.	The onus should be on parties and candidates to persuade citizens that there is some reason why they should vote rather than being able to rely on the state to compel them to do so.
All citizens have a reason to inform themselves about the issues and about the performance of politicians, making for a better informed electorate.	Even those with no real interest in the election have to vote, so politicians have even more of an incentive than under optional voting to engage in attention-catching stunts to try to impress those who know nothing about the issues.
Compulsion is not a breach of principle: everyone has to pay taxes whether they want to or not, for example.	Freedom of choice implies the right not to turn out if you don't wish to, and this would be infringed by compelling people to turn out.

Electoral systems

The precise rules governing the conversion of votes into seats may seem a rather technical matter yet, as every writer on politics agrees, electoral systems matter. They can determine, or certainly have a major impact upon, whether a country has a two-party or a multi-party system; whether government is characteristically by one party or a coalition of parties; whether voters feel personally represented in a parliament by an MP willing to take up their case if they have a problem; whether women and minorities are heavily under-represented in parliament; and, perhaps, whether governments keep spending and taxes high or low.

This is not the place to supply a complete account of how all of the world's electoral systems work (see Farrell 2001; Gallagher and Mitchell 2005: appendix A; Reynolds *et al.* 2005). We can, though, sketch the main categories and the dimensions of variation, before moving on to examine the consequences of different configurations.

The main categories of electoral systems

There are many ways in which to categorize electoral systems, the most straightforward of which relates to the magnitude of the constituencies in which seats are allocated (a constituency is the geographic area into which the country is divided for electoral purposes). We may begin with the distinction between systems based on **multi-member constituencies**, in which the seats are shared among the parties in proportion to their vote shares, and those based on **single-member constituencies**, in which the strongest party in each constituency wins the seat. The former are often termed proportional representation (PR) systems, while the latter are termed majoritarian or non-PR systems.

Single-member plurality

The latter are simpler to explain and understand, which is why they were the earliest methods to be adopted. The simplest system of all is single-member plurality (SMP), also known sometimes as 'first-past-the-post' (FPTP). Here, voters simply make a mark, such as placing a cross, beside their choice of candidate, and the seat is then awarded to the candidate who receives most votes (i.e. a plurality). This is used in some of the world's largest democracies, such as India, the US, the UK and Canada; over 40 per cent of the world's population, and over 70 per cent of those in an established democracy, lives in a country employing this system (Reynolds *et al.* 2005: 30; Heath *et al.* 2005; Bowler *et al.* 2005*a*; Mitchell 2005; Massicotte 2005).

Alternative vote

Under the alternative vote (AV), which is used in Australia, voters are able to rank order the candidates, placing a '1' beside their first choice, '2' beside their second, and so on (Farrell and McAllister 2005). The counting process is a little more complicated. If one candidate's votes amount to a majority of all votes cast, that person is deemed elected. If not, then the lowest-placed candidate is eliminated from the count and his or her ballots are redistributed according to the second preference expressed on them. Supporters of this candidate are in effect asked 'given that your first choice lacked sufficient support to be elected, which candidate would you like to benefit from your vote instead?' The counting process continues, with successive eliminations of the bottom-placed candidate and transfers of their votes to the remaining candidates, until one candidate does have an overall majority of the votes. In consequence, AV is regarded as a majority system, given that the winner requires an absolute majority of the votes at the final stage, whereas under SMP a plurality suffices.

Two-round system

Another way of filling a single seat is by the two-round system (2RS): if no candidate wins a majority of votes in the first round, a second round takes place in which only certain candidates (perhaps the top two, or those who exceeded a certain percentage of the votes) are permitted to proceed to the second round, where whoever wins the most votes is the winner. This is employed to elect parliaments in over twenty countries, including France, Iran, and several former French colonies, and is widely used to elect presidents (Elgie 2005; Blais *et al.* 1997).

These three systems—SMP, AV, and 2RS—thus differ, yet in the context of the full range of electoral systems they have much more in common than differentiates them, as we shall see later, because they are all based on single-seat constituencies.

Proportional representation

PR systems vary a lot, but they have some things in common. PR is a principle, which can be achieved by any number of different methods, all of which have the aim, with some qualifications as we shall see, of awarding to each group of voters its 'fair share' of representation—or, putting it another way, of allocating to each party the same share of the seats as it won of the votes. The simplest way of achieving this would be to treat the whole country as one large constituency, as happens in Israel, the Netherlands, and Slovakia; then it is a straightforward matter to give, for example, 24 seats in a 150-member parliament to a party that receives 16 per cent of the votes (Rahat and Hazan 2005; Andeweg 2005). That guarantees a high level of proportionality, by which term we mean the closeness with which the distribution of seats in parliament reflects the distribution of votes. At the same time, it might leave voters feeling disengaged from the political system as they do not have a local MP. More commonly, then, the country is divided into a number of smaller constituencies, each returning on average perhaps five, ten, or twenty MPs. Now the seats are awarded proportionally within each constituency, but it cannot be guaranteed that the overall level of proportionality will be quite as high as when there is just one, national, constituency. Brazil, Finland, Indonesia, and Spain all exemplify this approach (Raunio 2005; Hopkin 2005).

A refinement of this is to retain sub-national constituencies but to keep some seats back in the light of the constituency allocations. Thus, if a party ends up somewhat under-represented overall, perhaps because it has just missed out on a seat in a number of constituencies, it can be awarded sufficient of the seats that were held back to ensure that it receives its due share overall. This is usually expressed in terms of 'tiers'; seats are awarded first in the lower tier, i.e. individual constituencies, and then the higher tier seats are allocated in such a way as to iron out the disproportionalities that the lower tier allocation produced. Using two tiers in this way ensures that proportionality can be as high as when the whole country is just one constituency, yet people still have constituency MPs who represent their own part of the country. Denmark and Sweden, among others, employ this two-tier approach (Elklit 2005).

There are different methods for awarding seats proportionally within each constituency, which are based on slightly different conceptions of what constitutes 'perfect proportionality' (Gallagher and Mitchell 2005: appendix A; see also Chapter 13). The two main groups of methods are known as 'highest averages' and 'largest remainders'.

Highest average

Highest average methods allocate seats sequentially by applying a series of divisors to a party's vote total. Each party's vote is divided by the first number in the series, and the first seat is awarded to the party with the highest average. That party's vote total is divided by the second divisor in the series, and the second seat is awarded to the party whose average is now largest. In general, the 'average' that each party presents at each stage equals its original number of votes divided by the nth number in the divisor series, where $(n-1)$ equals the number of seats it has so far been awarded.

The most widely used highest average method is that of D'Hondt, in which the series of divisors is 1, 2, 3, 4, 5, etc. The application of this method to a hypothetical set of votes is shown in Table 10.1.

The first seat goes to the largest party, the Socialists, and the second to the second largest party, that of the centre-right. For the third seat, the Socialists' 'average' of 17,000 is the largest, so they receive the third seat, with the Liberals taking the fourth. The centre-right party's average of 12,500 is now the highest unrewarded average, so that party is given the fifth seat, with the final two going to the Greens and the Socialists.

When some disproportionality is inevitable, as is nearly always the case, the D'Hondt method tends to favour larger parties; in this case the Socialists received 43 per cent of the seats with 34 per cent of the votes, for example. A highest averages method that is even-handed between larger and smaller parties is that of Sainte-Laguë, which employs the series 1, 3, 5, 7, 9, etc. Now the larger parties' averages are reduced more rapidly, and the prospects for smaller parties are improved. In the case above, the Socialists' third average is only 6,800 votes (34,000 divided by 5), so the Socialists do not receive a third seat until each party apart from the regionalist party has

---

Table 10.1 Allocation of seats by D'Hondt highest average method

	Votes won	Votes divided by first divisor (1)	Votes divided by second divisor (2)	Votes divided by third divisor (3)	Votes divided by fourth divisor (4)	Total seats
Socialist party	34,000	34,000(1)	17,000(3)	11,333(7)	8,500	3
Centre-right party	25,000	25,000(2)	12,500(5)	8,333		2
Liberal party	15,000	15,000(4)	7,500			1
Green party	12,000	12,000(6)	6,000			1
Radical right party	10,000	10,000				
Regionalist party	4,000	4,000				
Total	100,000					7

Source: Gallagher and Mitchell (2005: 586). The numbers in parentheses refer to the order in which the seats are allocated.

received one. The first two seats would be awarded as under D'Hondt, but then the Liberals would receive the third, the Greens the fourth, the Socialists the fifth, the radical right the sixth and the centre-right the seventh, so the distribution among the top five parties would be 2–2–1–1–1 rather than 3–2–1–1–1 as under D'Hondt. A variant employed in some countries is known as modified Sainte-Laguë: 1.4, 3, 5, 7, 9, etc. Compared with 'pure' Sainte-Laguë this makes it more difficult for smaller parties to win a first seat but is otherwise the same in its effects as the pure version.

Largest remainders

Largest remainders methods proceed by the calculation of a quota, after which each party is awarded a seat for each full quota it has and then the unallocated seats are given to the parties whose remainders, over and above their full quotas, are the largest. The best known version is based on the Hare, or 'natural', quota, which is the number of votes divided by the number of seats.

In the example in Table 10.2 the Socialist party has more than two full quotas, so it receives two seats and presents a remainder of 5,428 (its 'unused' votes). It turns out that four seats can be allocated

on the basis of full quotas, meaning that only three are unallocated; these three will go the three largest remainders. The Socialists' remainder is the fourth largest, so the party does not receive another seat. The method of largest remainders with the Hare quota (LR–Hare) is unbiased between larger and smaller parties, and usually gives the same results as the Sainte-Laguë method. Another largest remainders method (LR–Droop) is based on the Droop quota, calculated by dividing the number of votes by the number of seats plus one, so in this example 100,000 would be divided by 8 to give a Droop quota of 12,500. Here LR–Droop produces the same seat distribution as LR–Hare, though generally it favours larger parties over smaller ones.

The systems I have just described are known as list systems, because each party presents a list of candidates to the voters. While list systems are still the most common form of electoral system in the world (Reynolds *et al.* 2005: 30), in recent years a number of countries have adopted what are usually termed mixed systems (they are also known as mixed-member systems, the additional member system, and personalized PR). Here, characteristically, the voter casts two votes: one for a local constituency MP and one for a party list. A certain proportion of

Table 10.2 Allocation of seats by largest remainders method with Hare quota (LR–Hare)

	Votes won	Full Hare quotas	Votes accounted for by full Hare quotas	Remaining votes	Remainder rewarded?	Total seats
Socialist party	34,000	2	28,572	5,428	No	2
Centre-right party	25,000	1	14,286	10,714	Yes	2
Liberal party	15,000	1	14,286	714	No	1
Green party	12,000	0	0	12,000	Yes	1
Radical right party	10,000	0	0	10,000	Yes	1
Regionalist party	4,000	0	0	4,000	No	0
Total	100,000	4	57,144	42,856	3	17

Note: Votes: 100,000; seats: 7; Hare quota = 100,000/7 = 14,286
Source: Gallagher and Mitchell (2005: 587).

MPs are elected from local (usually single-member) constituencies and the rest from party lists; in Germany, the archetype of this category, the proportions are half and half, though in other countries the balance might tilt this way or that. The constituency seat is usually allocated under SMP rules.

The allocation of the list seats depends on whether the constituency part and the list part of the election are integrated or are separate (on mixed systems see Shugart and Wattenberg 2003). In the first case, the system is known as a **compensatory mixed system** (sometimes the word compensatory is replaced by corrective or linked, and the system may be known as mixed-member proportional, or MMP). The list seats are awarded in such a way as to rectify the under-representations and over-representations created in the constituencies, ensuring that a party's overall number of seats (not just its list seats) is proportional to its vote share. Typically, small parties fare badly in the single-member constituencies, winning hardly any seats, but are brought up to their 'fair share' overall by receiving the appropriate number of list seats, while the larger parties, which usually win more than their 'fair share' in the constituencies, are awarded few or none of the list seats because their constituency seats alone bring them up to or close to the total number to which they are entitled. Compensatory mixed systems can thus result in highly proportional outcomes. Germany, Albania, New Zealand, and Venezuela are examples of this system (Saalfeld 2005; Vowles 2005).

If the list part and the constituency part of the election are separate, though, we have a **parallel mixed system** (sometimes termed mixed-member majoritarian, or MMM). Now, the list seats are awarded to parties purely on the basis of their list votes, without taking any account of what happened in the constituencies. This benefits large parties, which retain the over-representation they typically achieve in the constituencies, and offers less comfort to smaller ones than a compensatory system would. Parallel mixed systems are more widely employed than compensatory ones, with Japan, Kazakhstan, Pakistan, and Russia among the users (Reed 2005; White 2005).

There is a third group of countries that cannot be fitted neatly into either category because, while there is some link between the list and constituency allocations, it is not as straightforward or as strong as in the compensatory systems: examples include Hungary, Italy from 1994 to 2001, and Mexico (Benoit 2005; D'Alimonte 2005).

While virtually all PR systems use party lists somewhere along the line, the **single transferable vote** (STV) in multi-member constituencies (PR-STV) dispenses with them. This takes the logic of the alternative vote and applies it to multi-member constituencies. That is, as under AV, voters are able to rank all (or as many as they wish) of the candidates in order of their choice and yet, as under a PR system, the results will reflect a high degree of correspondence between the votes cast for a party's candidates and its share of the seats. Any explanation of how the votes are counted under PR-STV tends to make the system sound more complicated than it actually is, and examining a specific example is the best way to understand the mechanics (examples are given in Gallagher and Mitchell 2005: 594–6; Sinnott 2005: 109–17). In brief, counting revolves around the Droop quota, defined earlier. Any candidate whose total of first preferences equals or exceeds this is deemed elected. Any 'surplus' votes an elected candidate has (that is, votes over and above the Droop quota and hence unnecessary for election) are transferred to other candidates, in accordance with the next preferences upon the ballot paper.

When a candidate's surplus votes are transferred, in practice the majority pass to other candidates of the same party, because most of those who cast their first preference for one candidate of their favoured party give their second preference to another candidate of the same party. If there are no surplus votes to distribute, the count proceeds by eliminating the lowest-placed candidate and transferring his or her votes in accordance with the next preference marked; again, typically, when one candidate of a party is eliminated from the count most of his or her votes pass on to another candidate of the same party because voters have voted along party lines. The process continues until all the seats are filled. The principle underlying this is that voters are able to specify, at each stage, which candidate they wish to benefit from their vote, in the event that their more preferred candidates turn out to be either so popular as not to require their vote or so unpopular as not to be able to benefit from it.

PR-STV differs from list systems not only in voters' power to rank but also in that it does not presuppose the existence of parties or their salience in voters' minds: voters may rank candidates on the basis of whatever factor is most important to them, which might be (and in parliamentary elections usually is) party affiliation but could also be views on a particular issue, perceived parliamentary or ministerial ability, gender, locality, and so on. Voters can thus convey a lot of information about their attitudes towards the candidates, rather than having, in effect, to say 'yes' to one and 'no' to the rest as under most systems. The 'discreet charm' of PR-STV lies in the paradoxical combination of its popularity among students of electoral systems (see below) yet its far from widespread use; only Ireland and Malta employ it to elect their national parliaments (Gallagher 2005).

Dimensions of variation

There are many different electoral systems, but they vary on a limited number of dimensions. Three are particularly important, The first is district magnitude, by which is meant the number of MPs elected from each constituency. A second is the degree of intra-party choice: the extent to which voters are able to decide which of their party's candidates take the seats that the party wins. A third concerns the difficulty of winning seats, expressed through the idea of thresholds.

District magnitude

District magnitude varies from one in countries that employ single-member constituencies up to the size of the parliament in those states in which the whole country is one large constituency. The higher the average district magnitude, the more proportional we can expect the election result to be. When there are more seats to share out it is easier to achieve a 'fair' distribution, whereas when there is only one seat the largest party in the constituency takes it and the other parties receive nothing. Moreover, in a ten-seat constituency, a party with only 5–10 per cent of the votes has a good chance of receiving a seat, whereas a party of this strength would not win a seat in any single-seat constituency if its support were spread evenly across the country. Proportionality will be expected to be higher when a country is based on two-seat constituencies (as is the case in Chile) than when it is based on single-seat constituencies; higher when based on three-seat constituencies than on two-seat constituencies; and so on. This means that there is no hard and fast dividing line between PR and non-PR systems. Conventional wisdom is that a high degree of proportionality will be hard to attain unless average district magnitude is at least five, though in practice systems based on two-seat, three-seat, or four-seat constituencies are usually regarded as variants of PR, with only the single-seat systems treated as non-PR.

Intra-party choice

Much of the discussion so far has been about how seats are shared among parties, but some voters may be at least as interested in which particular individuals fill those seats. How much intra-party choice among candidates is provided by the electoral system? Under all of the single-member constituency systems there is no intra-party choice for the simple reason that no party runs more than one candidate; if a voter likes a party but not its candidate, or likes a candidate but not her party, he simply has to grit his teeth and accept an unpalatable option.

Under PR systems, the degree of choice varies. Some list systems offer no intra-party choice; these are based on what are termed closed lists, where the party determines the order of its candidates' names on the list and the voters cannot overturn this. Under such a system, if a party wins, say, five seats in a constituency, those seats go to the first five names on its list, as decided by the party, whatever the voters think of those individuals. Closed lists are used in Israel, Portugal, and Spain, and in the overwhelming majority of countries that have mixed systems.

Other list systems, though, use preferential lists, in which the voters can indicate a preference for an individual candidate on their chosen party's list. In some cases the voters' preference votes determine which candidates win the seats; in others, it needs the preference votes of a certain number of voters to earn a candidate a seat ahead of someone whom the party placed higher on the list (Shugart 2005: 36–50). Belgium, Chile, and Poland are examples of countries where the voters have an effective voice in determining which of their party's candidates become MPs (De Winter 2005; Siavelis 2005). In most countries voters are confined to the list of their favoured party when indicating preference votes, but in Switzerland and Luxembourg the device known as *panachage* entitles them to award preferences for candidates on different party lists, and they are also able to 'cumulate' more than one preference on a particular candidate.

COUNTRY PROFILE Japan

Japan (*Nihon-koku/Nippon-koku*)

State formation

The foundation of Japan dates back to the Emperor Jimmu, 660 bc. After defeat in the Second World War, Japan adopted a democratic and pacifist constitution.
Constitution 1947, effective 1 January 1948; amended many times.

Form of government

Constitutional monarchy.
Head of state Emperor; the monarchy is hereditary.
Head of government Prime Minister, usually the leader of the majority party or coalition.
Cabinet Appointed by the Prime Minister.
Administrative subdivisions 47 prefectures.

Legal system

Modelled on European civil law system with some English and American ingredients; judicial review of legislative acts in the Supreme Court.

Legislature

Bicameral Parliament (*Diet* or *Kokkai*).
Lower house House of Representatives (*Shugi-in*): 480 seats; term of 4 years.

Upper house House of Councillors (Sangi-in): 242 seats; term of 6 years; staggered elections (one-half renewed every three years).

Electoral system (lower house)

Mixed system: 300 seats allocated by plurality, 180 seats allocated by proportional representation.
Formula D'Hondt method for the 180 seats allocated by propotional representation. Candidates may run in both the single-seat constituencies and the proportional represent-ation poll. However, the single-seat constituency must be located within their proportional representation block. Can-didates running in single-seat constituencies must obtain at least one-sixth of all valid votes to obtain a seat.
Constituencies 300 single-member constituencies (plurality vote) and 11 multi-member or 'block' constituencies (pro-portional representation vote).
Barrier clause None.
Suffrage Universal, 20 years.

Direct democracy

None.

Party system   Results of the 2005 legislative elections (House of Representatives):

Electorate:	103,067,966	100.0%
Voters:	69,532,186	67.5%

Party	Valid votes	%	Seats
Liberal Democratic Party	25,887,798	38.2	296
Democratic Party of Japan	21,036,425	31.0	113
Clean Government Party (Komei)	8,987,620	13.3	31
Japanese Communist Party	4,919,187	7.3	9
Social Democratic Party	3,719,522	5.5	7
New Party of Japan (Shinto Nippon)	1,643,506	2.4	1
People's New Party (Kokumin Shinto)	1,183,073	1.7	4
New Party Mother Earth (Shinto Daichi)	433,938	0.6	1
Others	–	–	18
Total	67,811,069	100.0	480

Notes: Category 'Others' includes parties with less than 1% nation-wide and no seats, and seats won in single-member plurality vote by independent candidates. Votes refer to PR vote, seats to total seats allocated in proportional representation and plurality vote.
Source: Inter-Parliamentary Union.

In PR-STV, the voters have complete freedom to award rank-ordered preferences for any candidate, not just within parties but also across party lines.

Thus, under closed list systems the key intra-party battle takes place at the candidate selection stages, since, in order to have a chance of election, aspiring MPs must ensure that the party gives them a high position on the list. Under preferential list systems and PR-STV, candidate selection is important but not all-important, because every party's candidates are competing with each other for support from the voters since they need to outpoll their running mates if they are to be elected.

Thresholds

Thresholds come into play when the electoral system does not aim to achieve a 'perfect' correspondence between vote shares and seat shares. Usually, electoral systems contain some inbuilt feature designed to prevent very small parties from winning seats; this can be justified on the ground that it is desirable to prevent undue fragmentation of parliamentary strength and to facilitate the formation of stable governments, though of course it can also be motivated simply by the larger parties' desire to discriminate against smaller ones.

A good example of a threshold is that employed in Slovakia, which as mentioned earlier has just one, national, constituency. This would make possible a very high degree of proportionality—except that the country also applies a 5 per cent threshold, meaning that no party that receives fewer votes than this wins any seats at all. At Slovakia's 2006 election, 12 per cent of voters cast a ballot for a party that did not reach the threshold, and so they were unrepresented in parliament. In Germany the threshold is a little more complicated: a party must win either 5 per cent of the list votes, or three constituency seats, to qualify for participation in the distribution of list seats. Thresholds in the range of 3–5 per cent are common; that of the Netherlands is unusually low (0.67 per cent) and Russia's, at 7 per cent, is unusually high. Thresholds tend to be applied at national level, but in some countries they exist at constituency level: in Belgium no party receives a seat in a constituency unless it has won 5 per cent of the votes there, while in Spain a constituency-level threshold of 3 per cent applies.

KEY POINTS

❑ The most basic distinction among electoral systems is between those based on single-member constituencies (non-PR systems) and those based on PR in multi-member constituencies.

❑ Single-member constituency systems all give an advantage to the strongest party in the constituency and leave supporters of other parties unrepresented.

❑ The main categories of PR systems are list systems, mixed systems, and the single transferable vote. PR systems can be made more proportional by using constituencies of larger district magnitude and by lowering or removing the threshold.

❑ PR systems vary in the degree of choice they give voters to express a choice among their party's candidates. Non-PR systems do not give voters any intra-party choice.

❑ Non-PR electoral systems are more likely to engender a two-party system, especially as regards the distribution of seats, while PR systems are more likely to lead to a multi-party system; though the shape of the party system depends on other factors as well, such as the nature of the politicized cleavages in society.

Referendums

Government today is representative government, meaning that the great majority of political decisions in all countries are taken by elected officials rather than directly by the people themselves. Nonetheless, some countries employ the device of the referendum, in which the people are able to vote on some issue.

We should be clear that this does not amount to 'direct democracy', a much-used but vague term. Rather, it is simply a question of whether a given country's system of basically representative government does or does not include provision for the referendum. The term 'direct democracy' has its roots in the idea that, under the institutions of representative government, the people's role in decision-making is only indirect, in that they elect representatives who then make the decisions. When the referendum is used, it seems that the people are making the decisions themselves. However, 'direct democracy' has many connotations, both positive and negative, and as a result many scholars tend to give the phrase a wide berth and confine themselves to a discussion of the referendum as an institution within the framework of representative democracy.

Types of referendum

In a referendum, as Butler and Ranney usefully define the term, 'a mass electorate votes on some public issue' (1994*a*: 1). We do not use the word for a vote on electing an individual to a position, such as president. The most useful typology designed to impose some order upon the potential chaos of a large number of referendums is that of Uleri (1996*a*; 2003: 85–109). This scheme identifies five important dimensions of referendums, none of them requiring a subjective judgement on the part of the observer.

The first three concern the question of whether a referendum should take place or not. First, the holding of a referendum might be according to prescribed rules or at the discretion of a political actor. Second, the referendum might be mandatory in the circumstances, or optional. Third, the referendum may take place at the request of a number of voters, or of a political institution.

A fourth dimension concerns the relationship between those calling the referendum and those whose proposal is being voted on. When the two are different, there is a distinction between referendums on proposals that have not yet come into force (these are termed **rejective** referendums), and referendums to change an existing state of affairs (**abrogative** or repealing referendums).

The fifth dimension is the significance of the referendum result, which may be binding or may be merely indicative of the public's views, with another actor such as parliament having the final say. This scheme can be represented as shown in Table 10.3.

We can illustrate this framework with some examples. *Ad hoc* referendums are those for which there is no fixed provision, such as the British vote in 1975 on whether to leave the European Community or any future vote on whether the country should join the eurozone. In contrast, the French and Dutch referendums of 2005 on the proposed EU constitution were procedural, in that they were conducted in accordance with pre-existing rules, and they were optional in that it was not legally or constitutionally necessary that a referendum be held. The referendums in Denmark and Ireland in 1972 on whether to join the European Community were procedural and mandatory, since both countries' constitutions specified the necessity for a referendum on an issue with such major implications for sovereignty.

Quite clearly, when all referendums are procedural and mandatory the institution of the referendum is relatively unpoliticized, in that no political actor has any say in whether the issue is decided by referendum or in some other way. In contrast, the use of *ad hoc* referendums, or even of optional procedural referendums, is open to partisan manipulation, for example by a government that decides to put an issue to a referendum in the hope of boosting its position or dividing the opposition. A well-known example is the French referendum in 1992 on whether to approve the Maastricht Treaty. Although parliament had the power to ratify the treaty, President Mitterrand put the issue to the people in the hope of exacerbating divisions among the right-wing opposition, but his tactic almost backfired disastrously as the people voted in favour by only a very narrow margin. The 2004 Taiwan referendum called by the president, Chen Shui-bian, to coincide with the presidential election, was also a politicized exercise; the opposition condemned the exercise and urged its supporters not to cast ballots (Hwang 2006: 117).

The distinctive feature of a people's initiative is clear: it enables a set number of voters to bring about a popular vote. The initiative is conspicuous by its rarity in the world's constitutions, though those few states that employ it do so on a large scale. Switzerland leads the way here, with most of its popular votes being initiated by voters; if a prescribed number (which varies from 50,000 to 100,000 depending on the nature of the proposal) signs a petition calling for a vote on amending the constitution or on

Table 10.3 Typology of referendums

Criterion	Value	Description
Promotion of referendum according to:	Prescribed rules	Procedural
	Discretion of some political actor	*Ad hoc*
Procedural referendum is:	Necessary to make or validate a decision	Mandatory
	Held at request of authorized actor	Optional
Popular vote is promoted by:	A number of voters	Initiative
	Other agent	Referendum
Promoter of vote and author of object to be voted on are:	The same actor	Decision-promoting (people called on to ratify)
	Different actors	Decision-controlling (people called on to veto)
Impact of referendum vote:	Must be accepted by relevant institution(s)	Binding
	Technically indicative as another actor has final say	Advisory

Source: Adapted from Uleri (1996a: 12; 2003: 107–8).

rejecting a bill recently passed by parliament, such a vote must take place.

Italy is the only other West European country to allow the initiative, and while the engaged citizenry brought about many popular votes in the 1980s and 1990s, the use of this weapon against the political class—for that was how many of these initiatives were perceived—has since declined. A number of post-communist countries have provision for the initiative in their constitutions, but the difficulty of mobilizing the population in most of these countries means that the initiative has not become significant. The initiative is also a prominent feature of state-level politics in parts of the US, especially the south-west. Since 1993 New Zealand has had provision for non-binding initiatives; in 1999 the people voted by more than four to one to reduce the size of parliament, but the advisory nature of the vote was emphasized when no such change was made.

The distinction between **decision-promoting** and **decision-controlling** referendums is an important

one. Provision for the former is rare; so-called 'plebiscitarian' referendums (see below), where an authoritarian leader makes a proposal and then calls a popular vote to endorse this, belong in this category. In Switzerland, the appropriate number of citizens may frame an amendment to the constitution (though not a proposed law) and secure a popular vote on the change. Decision-controlling referendums, where an actor opposed to some proposal may invoke the people as a potential veto player, are more common.

This distinction bears on the question of who gets to frame the precise question to be voted on, the 'agenda-setting' power that is important in many contexts. Those who frame the question can do so in such a way as to make retention of the status quo more likely, or less likely, depending on their preference. For example, in 1999 Australians voted on whether or not to retain the British monarch as their head of state. If republicans had been able to set the question, they would have offered the electorate a straight choice between the status quo and a republic, and opinion polls suggest that a majority of voters would have opted for change. But since the government, which preferred the status quo, had the power to set the question, it asked voters to choose between the status quo on the one hand and, on the other, a republic in which the president would be appointed by parliament. The latter option was opposed not only by monarchists but also by those republicans who felt strongly that the president should be directly elected by the people, leading to the defeat of the proposal and the retention of the monarchy.

Among decision-controlling referendums we may distinguish between abrogative referendums or initiatives (which aim to strike down an existing law or constitutional provision) and rejective ones (which aim to prevent some proposal from passing into law or the constitution). Switzerland has a widely used provision for the rejective initiative, under which, within ninety days of parliament's approval of a bill, 50,000 citizens may launch a challenge to it by calling a popular vote. Italy provides for the abrogative initiative, allowing citizens to call a vote on any existing law. In some other countries a minority of parliamentarians (as in Denmark or Spain) or a number of regional councils (as in Italy) may call a rejective referendum on certain proposals.

The existence of the decision-controlling referendum constitutes a potentially powerful check on government, which may have no option but to make concessions to its opponents in order to pre-empt the launching of a rejective referendum. The ease with which a political party in Switzerland can mobilize sufficient voters to launch a rejective initiative is one reason why Switzerland is governed by a more or less permanent grand coalition of the four major parties, to ensure that each party's concerns are addressed at an early stage of the policy-making process. The frequency of referendums thus diminishes the significance of elections; Swiss elections will not result in the ejection of a government, and even a large change in the relative strengths of the main parties will result only in the switching of a cabinet seat from one party to another.

One term that does not feature in most typologies these days is **plebiscite**, mainly because the word has taken on two completely different connotations. One is negative: for some people, it implies a referendum staged by an authoritarian regime with the aim of generating the appearance of popular support for a decision that in reality the people had no possibility of rejecting. Often, indeed, the vote is bound up with support for an individual as much as for the issue supposedly at stake. The referendums held in France by Napoleon and Louis Napoleon, or more recently in some post-communist countries such as Belarus and Turkmenistan on extending the rule of the incumbent president, would fit comfortably into this category. The 99.9 per cent vote recorded in favour of extending the late President Saparmurat Niyazov's term in Turkmenistan in a 1994 referendum is typical. The other connotation of 'plebiscite', derived from international law, is that it refers to a vote concerning a sovereignty issue such as independence, self-determination, or border definition (Deszõ 2001: 267).

The rationale of the referendum

Why use referendums? There are, of course, cases for and against, yet on the whole the evidence is strangely inconclusive and suggests that neither supporters or sceptics are on secure ground when they try to make a general case about referendums. We can categorize the arguments as related to **process** or to **outcome**. Process-related arguments suggest that, regardless of the decisions reached, the very fact that they have been reached through a referendum is important in itself, while outcome-related arguments suggest that the quality of decisions may be affected by the direct involvement of the voters (see Box 10.2). On the whole, supporters of referendums are more likely to invoke process-related arguments while opponents tend to emphasize the impact on outcomes.

Process-related arguments

The two main process arguments are, first, that certain policies can be fully legitimated only by their endorsement in a referendum and, second, that participation in a referendum is good in itself and also educates voters about issues.

The legitimation argument rests on the fact that, in modern states, people may have the opportunity to vote at regular intervals, but for the most part they are not expressing themselves directly on specific political issues. Rather, they are electing others to represent them in an office such as the presidency or governorship, or in an assembly such as a national parliament. Individual voters will take a number of factors into account when casting their ballot. Simply because a party includes a particular policy promise in its manifesto, we cannot conclude that anyone who votes for a candidate of this party necessarily wants to see that policy implemented. The policy may not have affected their vote at all, or they may have voted for the party despite rather than because of this particular policy.

This weakens the 'mandate' argument according to which the voters confer upon the winning party at an election a mandate to implement the policy platform on which it stood. In reality, given the number of different policies in each party's manifesto, not to mention the range of other factors (the appeal of the party leaders or of the local candidates, for example), what has been termed 'Ostrogorski's paradox' means that we cannot deduce people's policy preferences from the policy offerings of the parties they voted for (Setälä 1999: 14–16). Consequently, opponents of a policy might claim, when the government tries to implement it, that the government has no explicit mandate for it, or, conversely, a government that now regrets making the policy promise might claim, when resiling from it, that there is no evidence that the voters ever really expressed their support for it.

Hence, it is argued, we can only be sure that the people are in favour of a particular policy if they have actually endorsed it in a referendum. While no one except a referendum fanatic would suggest that this kind of validation process is needed for every piece of legislation or government decision, the argument has special force in the case of major choices facing a society: whether to join a transnational body such as the European Union (EU), whether to secede from an existing state and become independent, or whether to make a significant change to the political institutional regime or to the moral ethos of society.

For example, fourteen of the nineteen countries to join the EU between 1973 and 2004 held a referendum to decide whether to join, while Norway's people decided against joining in two referendums. The secessions of Norway from Sweden in 1905, Iceland from Denmark in 1944, East Timor from Indonesia in 1999, and Montenegro from Serbia in 2006 were all put to, and approved in, referendums.[1] The case for a referendum is even stronger if the proposal is one that did not feature prominently in the preceding election and that, if implemented, would be irreversible. In such cases a decision taken by political elites alone might not carry legitimacy or consent across society; many voters may simply feel that elites alone do not have the right to make such decisions on their behalf.

Enhancing the legitimacy of a major decision is one process argument in favour of the referendum, and the second is that the opportunity to vote in referendums increases political participation and is thus inherently a good thing. Given that it is commonplace to talk about widespread disengagement from the political process and about an attitude of cynicism towards the political class, the use of referendums might be able to reduce this feeling of alienation from the political process by involving people directly in decision-making. In addition, it is hoped, one result of empowering citizens to get involved in deciding an issue themselves will be that citizens educate and inform themselves about the subject, thus raising the level of political knowledge in society. Yet, it would be facile to imagine that unleashing a tranche of referendums on an indifferent populace will somehow create an engaged citizenry. Unless the issues at stake are important to electors, they are unlikely to make the effort to vote, perhaps feeling that their political representatives were elected precisely to decide such matters themselves.

Outcome-related arguments

Giving people more chances to take part in decision-making is cited as an argument in favour of referendums, as we have just seen, yet there is also a counter-argument. As Papadopoulos puts it, increasing the number of opportunities to participate also increases the opportunities for exclusion, and hence the use of referendums may lead to worse outcomes than purely representative democracy (quoted in Uleri 1996a: 17). Just as a committee that holds weekly meetings in the name of maximizing participation opportunities will end up being dominated by the handful of its members with nothing better to do with their time than attend every meeting, so an excessive provision of voting opportunities may in effect work against the interests of those who, for one reason or another, do not usually vote. If those of lower socio-economic status are the least likely to vote in referendums—as some data suggest, though the pattern is not universal (Qvortrup 2005: 31–5)—then the use of referendums, at least if it is excessively frequent, could work against the interests of the less well off.

Another outcome-related related argument against the referendum is the claim that, because the referendum is an inherently majoritarian device, it might result in infringement of the rights of minorities. Legislators, it is argued, are aware of the need for balance and for toleration even of groups whose behaviour they personally disapprove of. In contrast, the mass public, which bases its opinions on information fed to it by partisan sources or gleaned via the simplistic coverage of the tabloid press and their broadcasting equivalents, has no inhibitions about giving free rein to its prejudices in the privacy of the ballot box. As James Bryce summed up this line of thought, parliamentarians 'may be ignorant, but not so ignorant as the masses' (quoted in Gallagher 1996: 241).

However plausible this argument is in the abstract, empirical evidence does not support it. In order to evaluate it fully, we would require counterfactual evidence: that is, we would want to compare the policies actually made by legislatures with those that might have been made through referendums, and vice versa. While we cannot rerun history to see what would have happened under different decision-making rules, the frequency of state-level and local-level referendums and initiatives in the US allows us to come close to comparing the two. The evidence suggests that the key factor is not the mode of decision-making but the size of the unit making the decision: minority rights receive less protection in small local units than at state level (because the former are more likely to be homogeneous) regardless of whether the decision is made by referendum or by elected representatives, but there is no sign that referendums *per se* discriminate against minorities (Donovan and Bowler 1998: 264–70).

Moreover, there is often room for normative debate as to whether a particular decision amounts to unfair and discriminatory treatment of a minority or whether it is simply a perfectly legitimate choice by a majority of the voters. As defenders of the latter position are wont to say, majorities have rights too. Representative government is often criticized for being unduly responsive to pressure from well-organized and sometimes well-resourced minorities, who secure concessions at the expense of the public weal, and in principle referendums may help to counter this. Still, unbridled use of the referendum does have the potential to upset what may be a delicate balance within society, and consequently, in

most states employing it, there are devices to curb the danger of majoritarianism.

1. In most countries access to the referendum is highly restricted. Usually, it is the legislature that decides whether, and on what proposal(s), a vote is to take place, so it exercises an effective veto over the items that get onto the referendum agenda in the first place.

2. In countries that provide for the initiative, where a certain number of voters themselves can trigger a public vote without needing the consent of parliament, a judicial body such as a constitutional court is frequently accorded a veto role. The Italian constitutional court prevents around a third of referendum proposals being put to a vote, and constitutional courts are active in this area in a number of post-communist countries (Uleri 1996*b*: 107; Auer 2001: 351). In the US, too, courts play an important role, possessing the power (regularly used) to strike proposals from the ballot paper or, *post hoc*, to nullify the outcome of a vote on the basis that its implementation would be contrary to the state or federal constitution (Tolbert *et al.* 1998: 50–3; Magleby 1994: 235–6).

3. Some countries insist that a proposal achieve a 'super-majority' in order to be deemed to have been approved by the voters. This may require not only that a majority of voters support the measure but that turnout achieve a certain level (a figure of 50 per cent in Croatia, Czech Republic, Italy and Slovenia, for example). In federal countries, a 'double majority' is a common requirement: a proposal requires the support of a majority of voters and also a majority within at least half of the federal units (Australia, Switzerland).

There are two further outcome-related arguments levelled against the referendum. One is that it weakens representative institutions and might make 'joined-up government' more difficult, because a government's programme can be knocked off course by the public striking down one key aspect of it. This is more of a hypothetical concern than a real one, though, and in any case could apply only to countries that permit the voters to bring about a public vote without needing the approval of parliament.

The final criticism is that the referendum compels a stark choice between two conflicting alternatives and thus discourages the search for consensus. However, while such a criticism might be applicable to a referendum that sought to pre-empt negotiations, it does not amount to a case against referendums *per se*. Some issues, after all, do have to be resolved by a clear Yes–No decision, and a referendum is not inherently an unsatisfactory mechanism for making such a decision.

The outcome-related arguments, then, are largely critical of the referendum, but for the most part they are not convincing. The process-related arguments tend to be cited primarily by advocates of the referendum, but here too there is plenty of room for debate. The fact that it is impossible to point to clinching arguments on one side or the other helps to explain why there is such variation across the world in the use of the referendum, as we shall now see.

Empirical patterns

The use of referendums is widespread, albeit uneven. Legal and constitutional provision increased somewhat in the last three decades of the twentieth century (Scarrow 2003: 48) and there is evidence that the frequency of referendums is also increasing over time. LeDuc demonstrates a steady increase in the fifty-eight countries he covers from around 50 worldwide in the first two decades of the twentieth century to nearly 350 in the last two decades, partly as a result of an increase in the number of practising democracies (LeDuc 2003: 21). Even so, we should not exaggerate the use of referendums. Of the forty-four countries included in Table 10.4, nineteen have held two or fewer referendums since 1945. Switzerland is responsible for over half of the total number, and leaving it and its tiny neighbour Liechtenstein aside, the other countries have held on average only seven popular votes each over this period.

The variation in the frequency of referendums is striking. Some established democracies have held no national referendums at all (post-war Germany, India, Japan, the US) or very few (Netherlands, Spain, United Kingdom). In some others, such as Australia, Denmark, France, Ireland, and New Zealand the referendum has become established as a means by which

---

BOX 10.2 Referendums: arguments for and against

Arguments for the referendum	Arguments against the referendum
The referendum enhances democracy by enabling more people to become directly involved in decision-making.	Elected politicians have an expertise in policy-making that ordinary people do not, so taking decision-making out of the hands of political representatives is likely to lead to lower quality decisions.
Because of the way policies are bundled together at elections, only by a holding a referendum on an issue is it possible to get a clear verdict from the people on that issue.	In practice, many people decide how to vote in a referendum on the basis of extraneous factors, so we cannot draw inferences about policy preferences from voting behaviour in a referendum.
A decision made by the people directly has more legitimacy than one made by the political class alone, especially if the issue is a fundamental one for the future of society.	Referendums give insensitive or prejudiced majorities an opportunity to ride roughshod over minority rights.
The referendum process creates a more informed electorate as people are exposed to arguments on either side of the issue.	Those most likely to vote in a referendum are those who feel most strongly on an issue and the better off, so referendums work against the interests of moderates and the less well off.
All the evidence suggests that the referendum, sensibly used, can enhance representative democracy.	The use of referendums opens the door to the vision of a 'direct democracy' in which people cast votes on the 'issue of the day' without taking the trouble to inform themselves, thus trivializing the decision-making process.

Table 10.4 National referendums 1945–2006 in selected countries

Country	Number of referendums	Country	Number of referendums
Australia	26	Latvia	4
Austria	2	Liechtenstein	66
Argentina	1	Lithuania	18
Belgium	1	Luxembourg	1
Brazil	7	Malta	3
Canada	1	Mexico	11
Chile	2	Netherlands	1
Cyprus	2	New Zealand	28
Czech Republic	1	Norway	2
Demark	16	Poland	7
Estonia	4	Portugal	3
Finland	1	Russia	5
France	14	Slovakia	9
Germany	0	Slovenia	12
Greece	4	South Africa	0
Hungary	5	Spain	4
Iceland	0	Sweden	5
India	0	Switzerland	396
Ireland	28	Turkey	4
Israel	0	United Kingdom	1
Italy	63	United States	0
Japan	0	Uruguay	18
Total	776		

Notes: In cases of countries that have not been continuous democracies since 1945, the period covered is the time during which they were democracies. All figures refer to national-level referendums only.

Source: Site of the Research Centre on Direct Democracy (C2D) at University of Geneva (see web links at the end of the chapter).

the country reaches decisions on major questions. In others again a large and disparate range of issues, some major and some more or less trivial, have been put to a vote of the public; Switzerland and, to a lesser extent, Italy and Liechtenstein epitomize this pattern.

Explaining the variations is not easy. Worldwide, the largest countries make little use of the referendum, but within Europe large countries such as France and Italy are regular users. Some federal countries eschew the referendum, while others such as Australia and Switzerland embrace it. There are apparent cases of diffusion, or common roots, of patterns between neighbouring countries such as Switzerland and Liechtenstein, yet there is significant variation among the Scandinavian countries, which generally keep a close eye on each other's experiences.

The dramatic contrast between Switzerland and every other country represents a qualitative as well as a quantitative difference. Elsewhere, democracy is fundamentally representative in nature, and the referendum is a kind of 'optional extra' that modifies, to a greater or lesser degree, the way in which the political process functions. In Switzerland, in contrast, the referendum is woven deep into the fabric of democracy, and far from constituting an occasional 'shock to the system' it is an inherent part of that system.

Referendum subjects, outside Switzerland, do not usually cover the full range of political issues. In particular, conventional left–right issues such as the familiar tax-versus-spending trade-off do not habitually feature as items on referendum ballots. More characteristically, as I have already mentioned, referendum votes concern sovereignty-related questions such as independence, secession, or the pooling of sovereignty within the EU. The rationale is that these are non-partisan issues that transcend the day-to-day political warfare between parties and that the parties do not have the right to decide on the people's behalf.

The impact of referendums

In principle, referendums might make a significant difference to politics in a number of ways, most obviously to policy outcomes. The expectation is that in most cases it would be a conservative impact, in that the people are introduced to the decision-making process as an additional 'veto player'. A policy change agreed by the elite can potentially be prevented unless the people also approve it. Critics therefore warn of the danger of policy immobilism if the referendum is too readily available as a blocking mechanism to those opposed to change, asking whether any of the main advances of the past, such as extending the franchise to those with little property and to women, or the establishment of religious freedom, would have occurred had the eligible voters of the day been able to prevent it by a direct vote on the issue. Defenders argue that this is exaggerated, and that the endorsement of the voters is 'a powerful legitimiser of political decisions', depriving the outvoted minority of any sense that they have a valid grievance (Setälä 1999: 161). Major decisions involving sovereignty, or the allocation of values within a society, might not be regarded as fully legitimate by opponents if they are taken solely by the political class. Testing these propositions empirically—that policy innovation is slower in countries that employ the referendum, and that decisions made by a referendum enjoy greater legitimacy than those made by representative institutions alone—would of course be a challenge.

Where the initiative is available, the danger is of too much rather than too little policy innovation. Minorities might be able to get their superficially attractive but essentially populist schemes approved by a public that does not take the trouble to scrutinize them thoroughly or to ask how they will be funded, whereas elected parliamentarians would not be so gullible. This is a particular concern of elite theorists of democracy such as Giovanni Sartori, who refers to the 'cognitive incompetence' of most citizens, and of others who attribute great power to those who control the media and see referendums as merely 'devices for the political mobilization of opinion-fed masses by the elite' (Sartori 1987: 120; Hirst 1990: 33; Smith 1998). However, some of the arguments against allowing ordinary people to make decisions through referendums virtually amount to arguments against allowing people to vote at all. Moreover, the picture of voter incompetence can be disputed; even if voters do not possess comprehensive information about the case for and against the referendum issue, they may have acquired as much information as they actually need (Lupia and Johnston 2001). In addition, contrary to the claims that the media can exert power over easily led voters, overt attempts by the media to sway opinion may actually prove counter-productive (Aboura 2005).

Referendums could have a disastrous impact upon political parties which, in theory, might lose control of the political agenda, find themselves routinely racked by internal divisions over referendum issues, and, if in government, see their programme buffeted by random shocks from an unpredictable electorate. Yet, here too the dire outcomes that might occur in theory do not seem to happen in practice. In most countries, after all, there is no provision for the initiative, and so representative institutions such as parliament and government, which themselves are dominated by parties, can control access to the referendum. The evidence suggests that, far from being swept aside by referendums, parties can comfortably coexist with them and indeed often turn them to their advantage. Sometimes a referendum rescues a party from a damaging internal dispute, in that the responsibility for deciding the matter can be passed to the public at large. There is no sign that the frequent use of referendums weakens parties (Budge 2001), while parties, especially those with a distinct policy position, can expect to have some influence on the voting behaviour of their supporters (de Vreese 2006).

Finally, what about the impact of referendums on the quality of democracy? As I indicated earlier, it is possible to construct plausible arguments to the effect that the use of the referendum will greatly enhance, or greatly damage, the functioning of democracy. Yet the final verdict is that the quality of democracy seems to be little affected one way or the other by the incidence of referendums. The standard of democracy does not seem to differ so very much between Denmark (with 16 post-war referendums) and Finland (with 1), or between France (14) and Germany (0). It is difficult to find countries whose people feel their quality of democracy has been ruined by either the existence or the non-existence of referendums. Public attitudes, as far as we can tell, are broadly supportive (Dalton 2004: 182–4; Donovan and Karp 2006).

The referendum, then, is entirely compatible with the institutions of representative government. It is not an essential feature of a system of representative democracy but is, rather, an 'optional extra'. In the minds of some of its more fervent proponents and opponents, it might become the cornerstone of governance, transforming representative democracy into direct democracy, with citizens texting in their votes on the 'issue of the day'. This is not a realistic vision. Representative government has established itself across the developed world, and the evidence suggests that the referendum can play a significant role within it.

KEY POINTS

❏ Referendums take many forms, depending on whether or not the people themselves can initiate a popular vote, on whether parliament has discretion as to whether to decide a matter itself or put the issue to a referendum, and on whether the verdict of the people is binding or merely advisory.

❏ Supporters argue that referendums give the people the chance to make important decisions themselves and that being exposed to a referendum campaign increases people's information about the issue. Opponents maintain that referendums may discriminate against minorities and can result in incoherent policy choices.

❏ The frequency of referendums is rising over time, though they are still rare events in most countries.

❏ When people decide which way to vote in a referendum, their views on the issue at stake are usually the most important factor but they also take some account of cues from parties and politicians.

❏ Despite the fears of opponents and the hopes of proponents, there is little firm evidence to show that policy outcomes are affected greatly by the availability of referendums.

Conclusion

In this chapter we have looked at the two main voting opportunities in modern democracies: elections and referendums. Elections are central to any political system that claims to be democratic, while referendums, in contrast, are used extensively in some countries yet rarely or never in others.

Electoral regulations, the set of rules governing the holding of elections, tend to be quite similar among democracies, though there are some variations when it comes to the age at which one can vote or be a candidate, the ease of access to the ballot, and the term of office of elected representatives. The franchise was broadened steadily during the nineteenth and twentieth centuries, and the main debate now concerns not whether certain categories of citizens should be allowed to vote but, rather, whether people should be compelled to vote. Some argue that compulsory voting leads to more equitable policy outputs; others see it as an infringement of personal rights.

Electoral systems, the set of rules that structure how votes are cast at elections and how these votes are then converted into the allocation of offices, have the potential to play a significant role in influencing a country's political system. While there is a good deal of variation across countries, we have seen that electoral systems can be grouped into two main categories, PR and non-PR. Proportional representation systems provide a closer relationship between the distributions of votes and of seats, and are associated with multi-party systems; non-PR systems are more likely to produce single-party governments and something approaching a two-party system.

When we look at referendums we find a good deal of variation, not only in the frequency of use but in the kind of referendum. Some are initiated by the voters themselves, others by governments or parliaments. Some are held because the country's constitution declares that a referendum is necessary before a particular step can be taken; others are held at the whim of a government that hopes to derive some partisan advantage from the vote. Some are decisive, others merely advisory. While referendum issues can also cover a wide range, certain issues do seem to be regarded as especially suitable for popular votes: those concerning sovereignty, for example, or moral issues that cut across party lines.

The merits and demerits of referendums have been vigorously argued for many decades. One line of criticism casts doubt on voters' competence to reach a conclusion on the issues placed before them, suggesting that they are easily manipulated and tend to vote primarily on the basis of their attitude to the government of the day. The evidence does not support this, though undoubtedly voters' behaviour is affected by their evaluations of those arguing the case for and against the referendum issue. Referendums undoubtedly increase participation in the decision-making process, though proponents and opponents disagree as to whether this a good thing; for the former, it results in a more informed electorate, while for the latter it places decisions in the hands of those ill-equipped to make them. Proponents argue that a vote by the people legitimizes a decision in a way that a vote by parliament never could; opponents are concerned about the dangers of intolerant majorities trampling over the rights of minorities. The available evidence suggests that the hopes of proponents and the fears of opponents may both be exaggerated.

The two institutions are linked in that the significance of elections may be reduced when referendums are available to opponents of government measures. When there are no referendums, elections have greater potential to be a decisive arena, since they produce governments whose proposals cannot be blocked by a popular vote. In a country where major issues must be put to the people in a referendum, in contrast, elections settle less; the people retain veto power in certain areas regardless of the wishes of the government or parliament. If the opposition has the power to trigger a rejective referendum, the government has a strong incentive to make whatever concessions are necessary to prevent this from happening. Where there is provision for the initiative, the opposition has a further weapon to block the government, and the link between 'winning' an election and being able to impose one's policy preferences becomes even weaker.

? Questions

1. Should voting be made compulsory in modern democracies? What would be the main consequences of compulsory voting?
2. Do electoral systems shape party systems, or do party systems choose the electoral system that suits them?

3. What are the main consequences of electoral systems?

4. Taking any country as an example, what difference would we expect to see in its politics if it changed from a PR electoral system to a non-PR system, or vice versa?

5. Should the power of sufficient number of ordinary citizens to initiate public votes, which at present is confined to a few countries, be given to people in every country?

6. Are there certain subjects that are especially suitable, and certain subjects that are especially unsuitable, to be put to the people for decision by referendum?

7. Why is the referendum widely used in some democracies and rarely or never used in others?

8. How real is the danger that referendums will result in majorities infringing the rights of minorities?

9. Does the use of the referendum result in better policies than would be made without it?

10. Does the use of referendums threaten representative democracy, enhance it, or have little impact either way?

》 Further reading

Auer, Andreas, and Bützer, Michael (eds.) (2001) *Direct Democracy: The Eastern and Central European Experience* (Aldershot: Ashgate). Overview of the post-communist experience.

Bowler, Shaun, and Donovan, Todd (1998) *Demanding Choices: Opinion, Voting, and Direct Democracy* (Ann Arbor, Mich.: University of Michigan Press). Overview of the US experience.

Colomer, Josep (ed.) (2004) *Handbook of Electoral System Choice* (Basingstoke: Palgrave Macmillan). Comparative analysis of the origins of electoral systems.

Farrell, David M. (2001) *Electoral Systems: An Introduction* (Basingstoke: Palgrave).

Gallagher, Michael, and Mitchell, Paul (eds.) (2005) *The Politics of Electoral Systems* (Oxford: Oxford University Press).

—and Uleri, Pier Vincenzo (eds.) (1996) *The Referendum Experience in Europe* (Basingstoke: Macmillan).

LeDuc, Lawrence (2003) *The Politics of Direct Democracy: Referendums in Global Perspective* (Peterborough, Ont.: Broadview Press).

Lijphart, Arend (1994) *Electoral Systems and Party Systems: A Study of Twenty-Seven Democracies, 1945–1990* (Oxford: Oxford University Press).

Qvortrup, Matt (2005) *A Comparative Study of Referendums: Government by the People* (Manchester: Manchester University Press, 2nd edn).

Setälä, Maija (1999) *Referendums and Democratic Government: Normative Theory and the Analysis of Institutions* (Basingstoke: Macmillan).

Shugart, Matthew Soberg, and Wattenberg, Martin P. (eds.) (2003) *Mixed-Member Electoral Systems: The Best of Both Worlds?* (Oxford: Oxford University Press).

Web links

http://psephos.adam-carr.net/
   Adam Carr's site, based in Melbourne, describing itself as 'the largest, most comprehensive and most up-to-date archive of electoral information in the world, with election statistics from 175 countries'.

www.ipu.org
   Site of Inter-Parliamentary Union, with information on each member country's electoral system and electoral rules, plus links to national parliaments.

www.unc.edu/~asreynol/ballots.html
   Andrew Reynolds's site at University of North Carolina, with ballot papers from over 100 countries, showing the choices and constraints facing voters in different countries.

www.tcd.ie/Political_Science/Staff/Michael.Gallagher/ElSystems/index.php
Site with data on indices of disproportionality and party system fragmentation at elections in forty-two countries, plus information on electoral systems and downloadable files for calculation of indices.

http://c2d.unige.ch/
Site of the Research Centre on Direct Democracy (C2D) at University of Geneva, with data on past referendums worldwide and news about forthcoming ones.

www.iandrinstitute.org
Site of Initiative and Referendum Institute at the University of Southern California, Los Angeles: news and information about referendums (and research on them) across the US.

 Visit the Online Resource Centre that accompanies this book for more information:
www.oxfordtextbooks.co.uk/orc/caramani/

11 Federal and local government institutions

John Loughlin

Chapter contents

Reader's guide

The nation-state is the quintessentially modern form of political organization in which nations are meant to be co-terminous with states. The territorial organization of nation-states may be either federal or unitary, although each of these categories may be further categorized as being either more or less decentralized. Comparing territorial governance across states means constructing elaborate typologies. The welfare states of the post-war period represent the culmination of the nation-state-building process and tended to emphasize central control over sub-national levels of government. This, however, has been changing since the 1980s and sub-national authorities are today much less centrally regulated even if they still largely operate within the legal and constitutional structures of their national states. Nevertheless, the current period is characterized by a much greater complexity than was the case during the old welfare state period.

Introduction

Any analysis of contemporary territorial governance must begin with the territorial organization of the nation-state, which has been the quintessentially 'modern' form of political organization. But it is sometimes not realized that, from a longer term historical perspective, the nation-state is a relatively recent form of political organization. Most scholars date its appearance only to the time of the French Revolution (1789). But it consolidated its position throughout the nineteenth and twentieth centuries to become the dominant form up to the present. Previous to the nation-state, there existed other forms of territorial organization, such as the Holy Roman Empire, city-states such as Florence, Venice, and Genoa, city-leagues such as the Hanseatic League, and various types of ecclesiastical organization such as bishoprics and abbeys and, indeed, the papacy itself (Spruyt 1994).

The success of the nation-state may be gauged by a glance at the growth of the United Nations, essentially an organization of nation-states rather than of nations, contrary to its title, from its foundation until today. In 1945, when it was founded, it had 51 members. In 2006, there were 192 members. This growth has come about mainly because of the creation of new nation-states following decolonization after the Second World War, as well as the transition from communism in East and Central Europe after the collapse of the Soviet Empire after 1989. Even the failure of federations such as Czechoslovakia and Yugoslavia to remain together attest to the strength of the nation-state principle, since it was internal conflicts about this that led to their break-up.

Despite this success, the nation-state has not gone unchallenged and, indeed, in recent years there have been predictions of its demise (Ohmae 1995; Guéhenno 1995) because of pressures from above—globalization and (in Europe) the growth of the European Union (see Chapters 24 and 23 respectively)—and from below—the rise of regions and local authorities as political actors. Although the importance of these factors may have been exaggerated and it has been somewhat premature to write the obituary of the nation-state, there seems little doubt that the nation-state has changed significantly. Indeed, it is possible to speak of its 'transformation' in several important ways (Loughlin 2004*b*). If the nation-state has meant a certain form of territorial governance, then its transformation will have important consequences for the latter.

This chapter will explore the ways in which territorial governance has been understood and implemented within the nation-state model as well as how it may be affected by these transformations. It will end by discussing whether a new form of nation-state is emerging.

KEY POINTS

☐ The nation-state is the quintessentially modern form of political organization with distinctive features of territorial organization.
☐ Claims that is disappearing have been exaggerated.
☐ Nevertheless, it is true that, in recent years, the nation-state has been transformed in ways that affect territorial organization.

The modern nation-state and territorial governance

The modern nation-state

There were three distinctive 'moments' during the seventeenth and eighteenth centuries, each of which contributed something to the understanding of the modern state: its political organization, its relationship with civil society, and the forms of territorial governance linking state and society:

1. The English 'Glorious Revolution' of 1688 led to the installation of constitutional monarchy and the hegemony of the Westminster Parliament, followed by the Industrial Revolution which laid the basis of modern industrial capitalism and society.

2. In the American Revolution the thirteen British colonies in North America overthrew English rule

and established first a confederation and then the federation of the United States of America.

3. The third important historical moment was the French Revolution.

Each of these sets of events resulted in distinctive understandings of the state, political organization, and state–society relations. From the English constitutional and industrial revolutions emerged the United Kingdom of Great Britain and Ireland, built on a series of Acts of Union between England and the other three nations. This was a multi-national union state. The US became the first modern federal state. France produced the unitary state par excellence, characterized by 'unity and indivisibility' (Hayward 1983; Loughlin 2007b). Each of these state forms—union, federal, and unitary—would be imitated by almost all other modern nation-states. But it was the French state which developed the idea of the 'nation-state', from which modern nationalism arose and, in turn, affected both the British state form and modern federations. It is appropriate, then, to begin with France, even if it came chronologically last.

The French Revolution, beginning in 1789, was a vast, long-drawn-out series of events whose protagonists held several contradictory positions regarding the kind of state that should be adopted. Their ideological battles were fought against the background of a state which was already, in some respects, highly centralized. This was a result of the efforts of the French monarchy which, in previous centuries, and especially during the reign of Louis XIV, had sought to bring under control the nobles who dominated the provinces. The revolutionaries were divided into two main groups with radically differing positions with regard to the territorial organization of the new France: (1) the Jacobins, led by Robespierre, who wished to continue and complete the centralizing tendency of the monarchy; and (2) the Girondins, whose chief spokesman was Jacques Pierre Brissot, who wished to maintain some level of decentralization and diversity (Schmidt 1990; Ohnet 1996; Loughlin 2007b).

In the end, although each group was eliminated in turn by the Terror, including the Jacobins, who fell with the execution of Robespierre in 1794, it was the Jacobin conception that won the intellectual and political argument and gave rise to the celebrated description of France as the 'one and indivisible

Republic' (Hayward 1983). The Republic succumbed to the Napoleonic Empire, which, in turn, gave way to the restored monarchy, thus beginning a chain of regime changes in France which finally settled into the present-day Fifth Republic. But, whatever the regime, the basic ideas of 'unity and indivisibility' and the necessity of expressing this through a centralized state were retained. Furthermore, the Revolution and the Empire created the two basic institutions of the modern French state: (1) the *departments* set up at the Revolution as a way of abolishing the old system of provinces; and (2) the *prefectoral system* established by Napoleon as a way of exercising central control over these territorial entities. The old pre-revolutionary ecclesiastical parishes became the communes, which still, today, number around 36,000.

The French Revolution left another legacy to political thought and practice: nationalism, an ideology built on the assumption that nations ought to have states and states ought to be co-terminous with nations (Alter 1994; Guibernau 1996).

Unitary states and nationalism

Nationalism became a powerful movement throughout the nineteenth and twentieth centuries and was the driving force behind the unification of politically fragmented territories such as Germany and Italy, as well as the break-up of empires such as the Austro-Hungarian, Ottoman, British, and French. In the nineteenth century, the French model of the unitary state was a powerful example and influenced the territorial organization of many of these new states. In several countries, especially those of Catholic Europe, liberalism was associated with both nationalism and a strong centralized state capable of wresting control over education and social welfare from the church.

Some countries, such as the Netherlands, Spain, and Portugal, had already adopted the French model as a result of the Napoleonic conquests at the beginning of the nineteenth century. Greece adopted it when it achieved independence from the Ottoman Empire between 1821 and 1829. Despite, or rather because, of its highly fragmented character with thousands of islands, it has been strongly centralist ever since (Loughlin 2004a). Belgium broke away from the Netherlands in 1830 to become a monarchy but, despite the presence of a large Flemish-speaking population, opted for the model of a French unilingual and centralized state and Brussels became transformed by the end of the nineteenth century from a predominantly Flemish-speaking to a predominantly French-speaking city, situated entirely within Flanders.

The much diversified states of the Italian peninsula were unified between 1860 and 1870 in a movement known as the *Risorgimento*, under the leadership of the Piedmontese Camillo Cavour, who became the first prime minister of unified Italy. Although there were voices in favour of a decentralized federalist model, in the end, the new unified monarchy chose the French model precisely in order to overcome this diversity.

Germany, for its part, was no less fragmented than Italy but German nationalists were divided between those who followed Herder in defining nationhood in linguistic and cultural terms, and therefore wished to see a *Großdeutschland* (Greater Germany) and those liberals who were influenced by the French concept of civic nationalism, who were more in favour of a *Kleindeutschland* (Smaller Germany). The German-speaking lands, made up of many political entities from kingdoms to bishoprics, were also religiously divided between a Protestant north dominated by Prussia and a Catholic south dominated by Austria. This complexity led to ambiguities about what a German nation-state might look like and whether it should be federalist or unitary. The federalist tradition is probably the older one but, during the democratic Weimar Republic and the Nazi Third Reich, the model of the unitary nation-state was adopted, which, under the Nazis, evolved into a totalitarian state under the control of the Führer and the Nazi Party. This eventually led to the catastrophe of the Second World War.

Other states which opted for the French model were Albania, which became independent in 1912 (Bogdani and Loughlin 2007), Finland (1918), and many of the states of East and Central Europe (e.g. Moldova, Romania, and Bulgaria). Turkey, too, became, and remains, a French-style unitary state, with Ataturk's secularist state replacing the Ottoman Empire in 1921.

Federal states and nationalism

This does not mean that all modern nation-states adopted the unitary and indivisible French model. A minority chose the federal model. As noted above, already in the eighteenth century, the United States of America passed from being a confederation of colonies to a federal state. After their defeat in the Second World War, Germany and Austria reverted to their federal roots with the encouragement of the victorious allies, especially the US, for whom federalism was synonymous with democracy. Switzerland provides a much older model dating from the 'Old Confederacy', which existed between 1291 and 1523 and later confederal models, before it became, in 1848, the Helvetic Confederation, which, despite its name, is a federation rather than a confederation. The United Kingdom was neither a unitary state like France nor a federal state like the US but what is sometimes called a 'union' state, that is, a state which has been formed by a series of Acts of Union (Rokkan and Urwin 1982). Indeed, this was a common way of forming states through dynastic marriages or treaties before the arrival of the modern unitary state according to the French model. Examples are the Union between the duchy of Brittany and the French crown in pre-revolutionary France and the Austro-Hungarian Empire.

What is striking about all these cases of modern federations and union states, nevertheless, is that the nation-state model is retained with the 'national' dimension being represented at the federal or union level, where the representative assembly and government are responsible for those affairs which concern the nation as a whole—war, diplomacy, internal security, and national economic development—while the component entities of the state are responsible for those affairs dealt with most appropriately at that level—mainly education, health, social welfare, local government, etc. We shall examine below the different ways in which these functions are divided across levels of government. But the important point here is that, with regard to the unity of the nation, both unitary and federal states agree that this should not be compromised.

Not all unitary, federal, or union states have succeeded in maintaining this unity and there are numerous examples of failure or at least of incomplete unification. The 'first' United Kingdom of Great Britain and Ireland, which dated from the Act of Union between Great Britain and Ireland in 1801, gave way to the current United Kingdom of Great Britain and Northern Ireland with the partial independence of the southern part of Ireland in 1921. Several federations established by colonial powers after the Second World War also failed: the Malayan Union (1946–48); the Federation of Malaya (1948–63); the Federation of Rhodesia and Nyasaland (1953–63); the West Indies Federation (1958–62); the Mali Federation (1959–60); the Federal Republic of Cameroon (1961–72).

More recently, two former communist federations collapsed, one peacefully (Czechoslovakia); the other with great bloodshed (Yugoslavia). At least one of the principal reasons for the collapse of these federations, which aimed to unite a number of disparate states and nations, was their failure to construct an overarching and common **national** identity. Instead, the constituent units adopted individual nation-state-building projects, with some of the constituents, for example, the Czechs and the Serbs, dominating the federation, which led to a great deal of resentment among the others and undermined the unity of the whole. The Union of Soviet Socialist Republics (USSR) changed its federal structures (which, in any case existed largely on paper as it was a system under the strict control of the Communist Party of the Soviet Union) to form a looser Commonwealth of Independent States (CIS).

Belgium is an example of a unitary state which included two linguistic communities hostile to each other—the Dutch-speaking Flemish and the French-speaking Walloons—which in the 1980s became a highly decentralized federation in an attempt to hold the state together. It is unsure whether this attempt will succeed in the long run, mainly because the Flemish seem to have their own nation-building project, while the Walloons are divided and unsure of their political future.

Other unitary states have experienced difficulties because of internal nationalisms which challenge the legitimacy of the dominant nation-state, as is the case in Spain where there are powerful Catalan and Basque nationalist movements, and even in France there have been challenges from Breton and Corsican nationalist movements (Loughlin 1989). The lesson that may be drawn from the latter two cases is that even in countries with a strong unitary tradition, unification may still be incomplete. Spain, too, despite the Jacobin features of the Francoist state (at least with regard to the notions of unity and indivisibility of the Spanish nation) has been characterized as a multi-national society because of the continued resistance of Catalonia and the Basque Country to assimilation (Moreno 2001; Requejo 2005). On the other hand, the majority of nation-states, whether they be federal, unitary, or union, have succeeded in constructing a form of political organization in which the majority of the population do feel an attachment to the 'nation', however this is defined. This 'nation' is identifiable with a 'state', whether federal or unitary, with clearly differentiated borders and where the principal source of political legitimacy lies with the core central institutions.

> **KEY POINTS**
>
> ❑ The different kinds of modern state resulted from three distinctive historical 'moments' in the seventeenth and eighteenth centuries: the parliamentary and industrial revolutions in England (seventeenth century); the American Revolution in the United States (1776); and the French Revolution (1789).
>
> ❑ Each of these revolutions produced distinctive kinds of modern state: the union state in the United Kingdom; the federal state in the US; the 'one and indivisible' Jacobin state in France.
>
> ❑ The modern nation-state gave rise to the ideology and political movement of nationalism.
>
> ❑ In the nineteenth and twentieth centuries, nationalism has shaped the territorial organization of modern states—breaking up the older empires and uniting disparate territories into single states. Nationalism affected both federal and unitary states.

The welfare state

The establishment of welfare states, which began before the Second World War but which reached its peak in the post-war period, may be seen as the final stage of nation-state-building. In T. H. Marshall's formulation, welfare states added the final touch to national citizenship by adding *social rights* to the already existing *political rights* of representative democracy, and *civil rights* (Marshall 1950). There are various forms of welfare state (Esping-Anderson 1990; Castles 1993), but all have in common a number of basic features: the values of equality and equity for individuals, groups, and territories, and the duty of the state to intervene in the economy and society in order to achieve these values (see Chapter 21).

Territorial governance in welfare states

These developments had implications both for the organization of the central state and administration as well as for territorial governance (Loughlin 2004*b*). In order better to collect resources from the wealthier sections of society and stronger economic regions and to redistribute them to the weaker sections and to underdeveloped regions, the state found it necessary to centralize. The implication for territorial political organization was that central–local relations took on the form of a 'principal–agent' relationship: sub-national authorities, whether regions or local governments, increasingly became the 'agents' of their 'principal', the central state, in the delivery of these services. Furthermore, fiscal policy was controlled by the central government, thus decreasing local fiscal autonomy.

More specifically territorial policies, such as regional policy, were conceived mainly in 'national' terms, that is, in terms of how policies towards particular weaker regions might help the building up the overall national economy and society—the nation—rather than in terms specific to those regions themselves. During this period, the European Community was largely 'residual': it existed, but more in the background as a support for, and 'rescue' of, the nation-states which were rebuilding themselves after the war (Milward 2000). Other features of state organization and central–local relations during the heyday of the welfare state were territorial symmetry and standardization, and central regulation of sub-national authority activities to ensure that there would be no variation across the territory. The most extreme forms of this approach were in the unitary states of the Nordic countries and in the Napoleonic states of southern Europe. But these general trends could also be found in other states such as the Austrian and German federations and in the United Kingdom.

The crisis and reconfiguration of the welfare state (1970s–90s)

In the 1970s, the welfare state, and the old industrial capitalism which underlay it, went through a series of crises. The responses to these crises were increased economic globalization and financial deregulation, the shift from industrial capitalism to service industries (at least in the West), the arrival of neo-liberalism and New Public Management (NPM) as hegemonic policy paradigms, and the relaunch of the European Community in Western Europe (Jessop 2002; Loughlin 2004*b*; see also Chapter 8). These transformations had important consequences both for the conceptualization of the nature and functions of the state, and for territorial governance within the state. The state came to be seen less as a top-down, directive agency capable of bringing about the common good and realizing extensive welfare policy goals than as a stimulator from below of the forces of society and the economy that can achieve these themselves.

The shift from the old-style welfare state model to a more hybrid model to a new-style welfare state (since this has been changed but not abolished) entails significant shifts in territorial governance. These changes are summarized in Table 11.1.

Asymmetrical diversity vs. symmetrical uniformity

The old-style welfare state encouraged uniformity and standardization across the national territory in order to ensure there would be no deviation in the standards of services available to citizens of the nation. One of the most striking examples of this was in Sweden and the other Nordic states where, despite their huge geographical size, citizens in different parts of the territory benefited from similar standards of service. The same was true of the United Kingdom and, in some countries, such as Germany and Italy, there was a constitutional guarantee that this would be the case.

In Italy and Spain, there has been **political asymmetry** and diversity. Italy has its 'special' and 'ordinary' regions (this dates from the 1948 constitution). Spain, to some extent influenced by the Italian model, distinguished in its 1978 constitution between the

Table 11.1 Changes in territorial governance from the old-style to the new-style welfare state

The old-style welfare state	The new-style welfare state	Examples
Political, policy and functional centralization in the name of national unity	Political and functional decentralization	France, Spain, Italy, the NL, Sweden, the UK
Fiscal centralization	Fiscal decentralization but also some recentralization	Sweden, France
Administrative deconcentration rather than political decentralization	Political decentralization accompanied by administrative deconcentration	France, Spain, Belgium
Institutional and policy standardization: 'one size fits all'	'Customization', heterogeneity, and the right to experiment	Sweden, France, the UK
Territorial symmetry	Territorial asymmetry	Spain, Italy, the UK, Belgium
Hierarchical central–local relations	Non-hierarchical relations among regional and local governments	France, Sweden, the UK
Principal–agent relations between central and sub-national government	The 'choice' model	Sweden, the UK, France

'one and indivisible nation' of Spain, on the one hand, and the 'regions and nationalities on the other' (the nationalities being the Basque Country, Catalonia, and Galicia). The transition to the autonomic state distinguished between a fast track for the three nationalities (the Basque Country, Catalonia, and Galicia as well as Andalusia) who would achieve autonomous status early and a slow track for the rest (Aja 2004).

Political symmetry may coexist with **administrative asymmetry** as, for example, in the United Kingdom which had a highly centralized political system but an asymmetrical territorial administration, with the three territorial offices in Edinburgh, Cardiff, and Belfast which had distinctive relations with London. There is also a difference between political and administrative symmetry and asymmetry and **fiscal symmetry**/asymmetry. In the case of Spain, alongside the political asymmetry between the four special cases (Andalusia, Catalonia, the Basque Country, and Galicia) and the rest, there has been a fiscal asymmetry between the Basque Country and

Navarre and the rest of the country (including the three other special cases).

There is today a general tendency to increase asymmetrical diversity of all three kinds, although the combinations vary in different countries. Even the Scandinavian countries, previously marked by high levels of homogeneity, uniformity, and symmetry, despite the vast areas they cover (with the exception of Denmark), have been willing to accept some degree of diversity since the 1990s (Loughlin *et al.* 2005). The United Kingdom, a state with a high degree of administrative diversity, has also increased its political asymmetry by setting up devolved elected assemblies in Scotland, Wales, and Northern Ireland, and each new institution is quite different from the others. France changed its constitution in 2003 to define itself as a *République avec une organisation décentralisée* and also to incorporate the principles of subsidiarity and the right to experimentation by local authorities.

This is not to say that all these states are moving uniformly towards diversity! There are also contradictions and counter tendencies. In the Scandinavian countries, with their long-standing social democratic traditions, the commitment to provide uniform welfare services of a high level across the country remains very strong and there is an ongoing tussle between the social democrats (currently in opposition and who wish to maintain the older tradition) and the centre-right parties in power (most of whom seek greater diversity, although the Moderate Party leading the coalition is more 'Jacobin') as well as between the central authorities (in favour of uniformity) and the local authorities (in favour of diversity). In France, the central ministries have tried to recover some of their lost competences and there is still a strong *souverainiste* movement which is probably found in a minority of the political class but in a majority of the general population (Loughlin 2007). In Spain, the slow-track autonomous communities have sought to catch up with the fast trackers, who, in turn seek to maintain their distance, while the Madrid authorities seek uniformity and the autonomous communities stress diversity. The cases could be multiplied.

From the 'principal–agent' to the 'choice' model and the right to experiment

Central–local relations during the welfare state period were characterized by the 'principal–agent' model. This changed in the 1980s as central governments either reduced welfare services or even terminated some programmes of resource redistribution. In response to these challenges, many regional and local authorities made a virtue out of necessity and began to mobilize their resources and to form alliances with other local authorities both inside and outside their national states (Keating 1998*b*).

In Scandinavia, Sweden, followed by the other Nordic countries of Denmark, Norway, and Finland in that order, the central government launched the 'free commune' experiments, which aimed at reducing the regulatory burden of the central state on the activities of local authorities (Baldersheim and Ståhlberg 1994). The 'free communes' approach was an experiment which lasted from the mid-1980s until the early 1990s and allowed local authorities to adopt distinctive policies and even different kinds of

institutional organization in contrast to the previous highly rigid and standardized approach. Although the experiment officially ended in the 1990s, the principles underlying the experiment have become 'mainstreamed' and this has increased the diversity of the system in these countries. In Sweden, for example, there are two experimental regions in Skåne and Västra Gotaland which, although constitutionally on the same level, do have some distinctive characteristics not possessed by the 'ordinary' counties (Loughlin *et al.* 2005). In the UK, too, the devolution reforms initiated by the Blair government have included experiments in local authority organization including directly elected mayors and the abolition of the committee system, with the establishment of an executive separate from the assembly.

To some extent, these shifts have reflected the recognition that regional and local democracy are essential elements of democracy itself and that local autonomy implies some diversity and freedom from central government control (Council of Europe 1985). For the most part, however, the 'choice' model is also an expression of the neo-liberal approach which predominated in Western states during the 1980s and 1990s. Local autonomy, in application of the principle of subsidiarity, means deciding local policies at the appropriate level.

From a neo-liberal perspective, it also means adopting a competitive approach to local policy and politics. Without going as far as adopting the fiscal federalism of the US, where society functions quite differently from European countries, from the 1990s onwards, there has been a significant increase in competition among regional and local authorities, both within their own states, and with regional and local authorities more widely as they try to create the conditions necessary to attract inward investment. The acceptance of 'diversity' might also mean the acceptance of disparities in wealth and levels of socio-economic development at the territorial level in the same way that neo-liberalism accepts these at the level of individuals and social classes. As national governments have become less involved in developing explicit policies to reduce these disparities, the European Union has stepped in with its own structural action and cohesion policies. Even if these are conditional on matched funding from central governments, the latter are relieved of important

---

BOX 11.1 Subsidiarity

The term subsidiarity comes from Catholic social teaching and is based on the principle that decisions should be taken as close to the citizen as possible and should be taken by a higher level when the lower level is unable to perform a function or task.

It was first enunciated in an official document by Pius XI in his encyclical *Quadregismo Anno* (1931), which was a statement against the centralized states of the Fascist, Nazi, and Communist regimes of that period.

But the idea is older and may be found in the Tenth Amendment of the United States Constitution: 'The powers not delegated to the United States by the Constitution, nor prohibited by it to the States, are reserved for the States respectively, or to the people.'

It was also implicit in the 1985 European Charter of Local Self-Government of the Council Europe. Article 4, paragraph 3, states: 'This paragraph articulates the general principle that the exercise of public responsibilities should be decentralised.'

Its most famous contemporary formulation is in Article 9 of the Treaty on European Union (Maastricht, 1992):

The Community shall act within the limits of the powers conferred upon it by this Treaty and of the objectives assigned to it therein.

In areas which do not fall within its exclusive competence, the Community shall take action, in accordance with the principle of subsidiarity, only if and in so far as the objectives of the proposed action cannot be sufficiently achieved by the Member States and can therefore, by reason of the scale or effects of the proposed action, be better achieved by the Community.

Any action by the Community shall not go beyond what is necessary to achieve the objectives of this Treaty.

The Maastricht definition, however, has been interpreted to mean devolving functions back to national governments but not in its original meaning of devolving them from national to subnational levels of government.

---

functions which they had exercised during the heyday of the welfare state.

Changing patterns of fiscal relations

Local autonomy is viable only if it is accompanied by fiscal autonomy, that is, the right and capacity of local authorities to raise their own revenues or to have a degree of discretion over those fiscal resources they receive from central governments. There are two opposing arguments found in the academic literature with regard to the decentralization of control over local funding. The first was made in the 1950s in a situation of (national) welfare economics. It contends that 'only central governments could achieve local economic efficiency through policies of fiscal equalization and redistribution' (Caulfield 2000).

The counter-argument, known as fiscal federalism or fiscal decentralization, stresses that local fiscal autonomy is necessary as a way of increasing the accountability and responsiveness of sub-national governments. Fiscal federalism was the application of this notion to local authorities and was based on the idea that citizens could choose from among a variety of services offered by different local authorities by

simply moving residence from one authority to the other. This was meant to lead to the optimal allocation of resources in a market situation and to local authorities adapting services to local circumstances. It implied high levels of local political, policy, and fiscal autonomy and high levels of mobility among the citizenry. Of course, these conditions are more characteristic of the US than they are of most European countries. Nevertheless, there has been some attempt to apply principles of fiscal federalism within Europe (e.g. Switzerland).

These two approaches to fiscal policy reflect the above-mentioned difference between choice and agency models of local–central government relations. In the choice model, local authorities are seen as being best placed to make decisions that reflect the needs and preferences of their local communities. In the agency model, local authorities are seen first and foremost as agents carrying out policies on behalf of the principal, which is central government. Under the principal–agent model, local authorities had a low degree of discretion and the majority of grants received from central government were earmarked for specific purposes. But one of the underlying causes of the crisis of the welfare state model was, precisely, the 'fiscal crisis of the state', or the inability of the state itself to fund the ever-increasing demands of its own policy programmes (O'Connor 1973). Thus, among the first casualties of the crisis were the local authorities themselves. In the UK, under Mrs Thatcher's premiership, funding for local authorities was drastically reduced and one of their most important own resources, the business tax, was transferred to the national government.

More generally what has occurred in Europe is the application of a market-type approach, even if this is not full-blown fiscal federalism. The main expression of this has been the EU's single-market project, reinforced by the drive towards the creation of a common currency and the criteria of fiscal rectitude laid out in the Maastricht Treaty. These represent the arrival of a new financial orthodoxy which affects not just the countries of the Eurozone, but even those EU countries outside it, like Sweden and the UK, and even those outside the EU, such as Norway. National governments are held account-able (within the EU by the European Central Bank and, outside the EU, by organizations such as the International Monetary Fund) for the application of this new orthodoxy and, for this reason, have begun to regulate the activities of local authorities in areas such as borrowing and budgetary control. This leads to contradictory situations. While there has been greater political decentralization, there has also been increasing fiscal centralization. Furthermore, cent-ral governments have tended to offload burdensome tasks onto sub-national authorities without always providing the necessary financial and other resources to fulfil these tasks. This has been called the 'decent-ralization of penury', and often takes place under the guise of enhancing local democracy.

The situation is even more complex in that most countries today **combine** the 'agency' and 'choice' models, though most tend to emphasize one or the other as the dominant tendency (Caulfield 2000). This combination of models leads to a great deal of variety in the fiscal arrangements of European states but one overall trend has been an increase in grants from central governments and a decrease in 'own resources', such as local taxes and fees. This might suggest less local autonomy but it is also the case that central grants are becoming less earmarked and more general (Council of Europe 2000). This means that, despite losing some of their fiscal resources, local authorities may still retain a certain amount of fiscal autonomy if they have discretion over how the

grants are used. A good example is the Netherlands where about 80 per cent of local government funding comes in the form of central government grants but the majority of these are in the form of block grants. In the UK, by contrast, 75 per cent of funding comes from central government but there is a smaller per-centage that is discretionary. On the other hand, if a local authority raises its own resources but these may have to fund tasks decided by central government, then that local authority has less discretion.

From hierarchy to 'equality of levels'

A final trend to note in this survey of changes in territorial governance from the welfare state to a more pluralistic state model is the abandonment in a number of states of a hierarchical relationship among different levels of government. In Sweden, the counties and municipalities are on the same level and the two experimental regions do not have a hier-archical relationship with the municipalities found within them. In France, too, there is equality among the three sub-national levels of government: the re-gion, the department, and the municipality. This was a deliberate choice made when the regions were established, as the 'departmentalist' lobby in France feared that the regions might be in a superior position (as the departments had been over the communes). To avoid this, *all* hierarchy was abolished.

In the UK, there are no regions in England so the issue does not arise but it does in the case of Scotland and Wales. In these countries, the Scottish Parliament and National Assembly for Wales are responsible for local government funding and this gives them some leeway over their activities but, in theory anyway, they do not control them in a hierarchical manner. The relationship is managed rather through 'part-nership' arrangements—in Wales, the 'Partnership Council', and in Scotland there has been a growth of partnership working between the parliament and the local authorities. In the Netherlands, the provinces are relatively weak levels of government which do not dominate the municipalities (*gemeente*), while the latter have a kind of corporatist relationship with the central state. In other countries, such as Italy and Spain, the regions and autonomous communities are in a relationship of superiority over the provinces and municipalities but the general trend is towards non-hierarchical relations.

This can be explained by the increasing political and policy relevance of local authorities over the past number of years, as exemplified and promoted by the European Charter of Local Self-Government, which demands respect for local autonomy even by other levels of sub-national government such as regions. There has been a tendency in some cases, such as Flanders and Catalonia, for regions to adopt a kind of 'mini-Jacobinism', a regionalist centralism whereby they dominate and constrain lower levels of government. The European Charter deems such tendencies as unacceptable constraints on **local** autonomy. At the same time, this non-hierarchical model does make the division of powers among levels of government rather more complex as, given the complex nature of contemporary policy-making, many of these powers are shared. The French solution was to assign 'blocs' of competences to a particular sub-national authority, but this has not worked well in practice and has led to even greater confusion (Loughlin 2007).

Nevertheless, despite these difficulties, the development of 'non-hierarchical systems of governance', reflecting the wider shifts from 'principal–agent' to 'choice' models has meant that relations among levels of government now exist in new and varying configurations. This is both an opportunity and a danger for the sub-national entities as they are now more independent of each other and of the central state but also in competition with each other as they are largely responsible for their own economic, social, and political development, albeit usually in partnership with the central state. The opportunity is that they may become more developed; the danger is that they might fall behind. This calls for a new definition of the role of the state which still has the function of ensuring national unity and solidarity.

KEY POINTS

❑ The post-war welfare state was the final stage of the process of nation-state-building which began at the French Revolution.

❑ In both federal and unitary states, it implied a certain form of territorial organization, which emphasized centralization and central regulation of sub-national authorities.

❑ This has been termed the 'principal–agent' relationship whereby sub-national authorities were given responsibility for the delivery of social welfare services but highly regulated by the central state.

❑ This began to change in the 1980s with the arrival of neo-liberalism, leading to the freeing up to some extent of these central constraints and greater freedom for sub-national authorities.

❑ Territorial organization has been reconfigured with trends towards: asymmetry and diversity, greater choice, experimentation, greater local fiscal autonomy (albeit with some contradictory tendencies as well), less hierarchical relations among sub-national authorities.

Federal vs. unitary states

The classical distinction

Given these trends which have affected all states, the question arises as to whether the classical distinction between federal and unitary states is still useful. What are the differences between federal and unitary states?

It will be easier to begin with attempted definitions of what is a federal state. Kenneth Wheare, in a classic work on federalism, claimed that most of those who use the term 'have in mind an association of states, which has been formed for certain common purposes, but in which the member states retain a large measure of their original independence' (1963: 1). But, as the author points out, this definition may cover a wide variety of different types of associations of states, including entities such as the present-day United Nations but also previously existing political entities such as the German Empire or the Austro-Hungarian Empire which he denies were federations.

Wheare chooses the US as the prototype of a federation and judges other federations, such as the Australian, the Canadian, or the South African (as it existed before the transition to democracy) according to criteria derived from the US system. He argues that what distinguishes the US from other forms of political organization and what constitutes it as a federation is that '[t]he principle of

More unitary							More federal
Greece	Sweden Portugal	France Italy	UK	Spain		Austria Germany	Belgium
Ireland	Finland						Switzerland
Luxembourg	Denmark						US
	The Netherlands						
(Non-federal systems)			(Intermediate systems)			(Federal systems)	

Fig. 11.1 A spectrum of unitary and federal states

organization upon which [it] is based is that of the division of powers between distinct and co-ordinate governments' (ibid.: 2). What this means is that certain powers are exercised by the federal or 'general' government and other powers by the 'regional' governments of the constituent states. Each government is supreme in its own sphere. In this model of 'co-ordinate federalism' the powers of the federal government are circumscribed by the constitution and the remaining 'residuary' powers may be exercised by the regional governments. In theory, neither level of government may intervene in the sphere of the other. Both the general and the regional governments act directly on all the citizens depending on the issue and which level of government is responsible for this issue.

The use of the US as the template against which other political systems may be evaluated as federal or not has been challenged by more recent scholarship (Karmis and Norman 2005). First, as Hueglin argues, the US federalist tradition evolved out of an older confederal tradition so that there emerged two competing traditions of federalism (Hueglin 2003). Watts argues further that, although the US was the first modern federation and a reference point for subsequent federations, it is but one example of a wider phenomenon and needs itself to be placed in a comparative perspective (Watts 1996).

Watts accepts 'the basic notion [of federalism] of involving the combination of shared-rule for some purposes and regional self-rule for others within a single political system so that neither is subordinate to the other' but argues that '[t]here is no single pure model of federation that is applicable everywhere' (1996: 1). Besides the US model of 'co-ordinate' federalism, there is also the example of German 'co-operative' federalism. Furthermore, some scholars (Elazar 1991; Watts 1996) classify post-Franco Spain's 'Autonomic State' as a federation, although this would not be accepted by the

majority of Spanish scholars nor, indeed, is it recognized as such by the Spanish Constitution (Moreno 2001; Requejo 2005).

This is an important insight as it suggests that there may a spectrum ranging from complete unitary states, such as France or Portugal, to fully federal states, such as the US or Germany, with a range of options, for example, Spain, in between. A useful starting point to situating states on this spectrum is to employ the distinction, developed by King, between 'federalism' and 'federations' (King 1982; further developed by Burgess 1986 and Burgess and Gagnon 1993). 'Federalism' is a normative political ideology and movement which advocates the application of federalist principles in state organization. A 'federation' is a state which fully applies these principles, albeit in different forms, and leads to a variety of types of federation.

Federalism as a political movement may be found in unitary states such as France, Italy, or the United Kingdom which are not federations and where the dominant state ideology, as in France, may, in fact, be hostile to federalism (Loughlin 1986). On the other hand, even unitary states may have some 'federal characteristics' in their state organization. The examples which spring to mind are Spain after 1978 and the United Kingdom, especially following the devolution reforms of 1998. In Spain, there are strong federalist currents, for example, in the Spanish Socialist Party (PSOE), while in the UK there is less expression of federalist ideology but the configuration of the state following devolution has a 'quasi-federal' look.

Thus, our spectrum might have, at one end, the more completely unitary states such as Portugal, Ireland, and Greece, with France a little further on, and, at the other end, Belgium, the US, and Germany. Spain, Italy, and the UK would be placed somewhere in the middle (Figure 11.1). Of course, it is extremely difficult to find a method of measuring the degree of federation or not, just as it difficult to measure degrees of centralization and decentralization.

It is clear from this discussion that the simple division into unitary and federal states is inadequate to capture the complexities of modern state organization and that there is a variety of arrangements in between the two extremes. In order to capture this complexity, Watts adds the term 'federal political systems' to those of federalism and federation (Watts 1996). This new term describes a broad genus encompassing various kinds of non-unitary political systems, including federations. 'Federal political systems' differ from unitary systems in that there they have two or more levels of government 'which combine elements of **shared-rule** through common institutions and **regional self-rule** for the governments of the constituent units' (ibid.: 6–7). They include 'federations', 'quasi-federations', and 'confederations'.

The 'basic notion' of federalism—'the combination of shared-rule for some purposes and regional self-rule for others within a singe political system so that neither is subordinate to the other' (Watts 1996: 1–2)—has been applied in different ways to fit very different circumstances. This author provides a useful check-list of the dimensions along which there may be variation:

- The character and significance of the underlying economic and social diversities.

- The number of constituent units and the degree of symmetry or asymmetry in their size, resources, and constitutional status.

- The scope of the allocation of legislative, executive, and expenditure responsibilities.

- The allocation of taxing power and resources.

- The character of federal government institutions and the degree of regional input to federal policy-making.

- Procedures for resolving conflicts and facilitating collaboration between interdependent governments.

- And procedures for formal and informal adaptation and change.

The complexity of non-unitary states

Elazar lays out a list of 'federal-type' arrangements, which include constitutionally decentralized unions, federations, confederations, federacies, associated statehood, condominiums, leagues, and joint functional arrangements (Elazar 1995). Watts provides a useful explanation of these categories and a number of examples (Table 11.2).

Although some categorizations of particular states could be debated, this approach is useful since it highlights the complexity of contemporary territorial arrangements both within states and between them. Perhaps the greater conceptual danger, however, is that it interprets all political systems, whether unitary or federal, through the lens of federalism and may find 'federal arrangements' where they do not really exist. This is true especially of the categories 'unions' and 'constitutionally decentralized states' which are in fact unitary states with varying degrees of regionalization and decentralization (see Table 11.5).

Lijphart (1999: 189) has provided a more refined analysis of the degrees of centralization and decentralization in federal and unitary states as part of a wider analysis of democracy and government performance in thirty-six countries (Table 11.3). This illustrates that there is not a direct relationship between federalism/decentralization on the one hand, and 'unitariness'/centralization on the other, but that both federal and unitary states can be more or less centralized or decentralized. Lijphart's scheme also recognizes a difficult to categorize intermediate category which he calls 'semi-federal' (which is also 'semi-unitary'). Some of his allocations are questionable, for example, the placing of France, Italy, and the United Kingdom in the unitary/centralized box. But these may simply reflect the fact that the original research for this book was carried out in the 1980s and the table does not take into account recent developments such as the 'federal' constitutional reforms in Italy, the second phase of French decentralization culminating in the French constitution to describe France as a *République avec une organisation décentralisée*, or the 1998 devolution reforms in the UK.

Table 11.2 The variety of federal political systems

Type	Description	Examples
Unions	Polities compounded in such a way that the constituent units preserve their respective integrities primarily or exclusively through the common organs of the general government rather than through dual government structures.	New Zealand Lebanon Belgium (pre-1993)
Constitutionally decentralized Unions	Unitary in form in the sense that ultimate authority rests with the central government but incorporate constitutionally protected sub-national units of government which have functional autonomy.	China Italy Netherlands United Kingdom
Federations	Compound polities, combining strong constituent units and a strong general government, each possessing powers delegated to it by the people through a constitution, and each empowered to deal directly with the citizens in the exercise of its legislative, administrative and taxing powers, and each directly elected by the citizens.	Argentina Australia Austria Belgium (post-1993) Brazil Canada Germany Nigeria Switzerland United States
Confederations	Where pre-existing polities join together form a common government for certain limited purporse (foreign affairs, defence, or economic affairs), but the common government is dependent upon the constituent governments.	Commonwealth of Independent States (former USSR) Benelux (Belgium, the Netherlands, Luxembourg), European Union (but with some features of a federation) Switzerland (1291–1847) United States (1776–89)
Federacies	Political arrangements where a large unit is linked to a smaller unit or units, but the smaller unit retains considerble autonomy and has a minimum role in the government of the larger one, and where the relationship can be dissolved only by mutual agreement.	Azores (Portugal) Puerto Rico (US) Aaland Islands (Finland) Faroe Islands (Denmark) Isle of Man (UK)
Associated states	Similar to federacies, but can be dissolved by either of the units acting alone on prearranged terms.	Bhutan (India) Cook Islands (New Zealand) Liechtenstein (Switzerland) Marshall Islands (US) Monaco (France)
Condominiums	Political units which function under joint rule of two or more external states in such a way that the inhabitants have substantial internal self-rule.	Andorra between 1278 and 1993 (France and Spain)

(continued)

Table 11.2 (*continued*)

Type	Description	Examples
Leagues	Linkages of politically independent polities for specific purposes that function through a common secretariat rather than a government and from which members may unilaterally withdraw.	Arab League ASEAN Commonwealth of Nations NATO Nordic Council
Joint functional authorities	An agency established by two or more polities for joint implementation of a particular task or tasks.	International Atomic Energy Agency International Labour Organization
Hybrids	Political systems which combine characteristics of different kinds of political system.	Canada in 1867 South Africa after 1996 European Union after Maastricht

Source: Watts (1996: 8–13).

KEY POINTS

❑ There is a difference between federal and unitary states, based mainly on the constitutional division of labour between the national and sub-national levels of government.

❑ Both federal and unitary states must be further dis-aggregated into different kinds of federal and unitary state depending on their degrees of centralization and decentralization.

❑ There is an intermediate group of states which are neither federal nor unitary.

❑ There are different typologies available for organizing and classifying this complexity.

Trends towards regionalization and decentralization in unitary states

A general trend

As with federal states, unitary states exist along a spectrum between goes from highly decentralized to highly centralized and a range of possibilities in between (see Figure 11.1 above). It is necessary to make a number of conceptual clarifications before we can analyse more clearly where a particular state sits on this spectrum and also to evaluate specific sets of territorial reforms. First, it is necessary to distinguish between different kinds of region (Keating and Loughlin 1997). Second, we need to distinguish regionalism, regionalization, and decentralization (Loughlin 1996). Third, there are also different kinds of decentralization.

Political vs. administrative regions

The term **political regions** describes regional bodies with elected regional assemblies and governments responsible for budgetary and policy decisions (e.g. the French and Italian regions; the Spanish Autonomous Communities; the Polish regions; the Scottish Parliament and the Welsh and Northern Irish Assemblies) whereas **administrative regions** describes regions that perform certain tasks on behalf of the central state but which are not directly elected assemblies and governments. Examples of the latter include the French *établissements publics régionaux* before their upgrading to political regions in 1982; the English planning regions; Swedish regions (except for the two experimental regions of Skåne and Västra Götaland

Table 11.3 Degrees of federalism and decentralization in thirty-six democracies

Federal and decentralized [5.0]

Australia	Switzerland
Belgium (after 1993)	United States
Canada	
Germany	

Federal and centralized [4.0]

Venezuela

Austria [4.5]

India [4.5]

Semi-federal [3.0]

Israel	Papua New Guinea	
Netherlands	Spain	Belgium before 1993 [3.1]

Unitary and decentralized [2.0]

Denmark	Norway
Finland	Sweden
Japan	

Unitary and centralized [1.0]

Bahamas	Jamaica	France [1.2]
Barbados	Luxembourg	Italy [1.3]
Botswana	Malta	Trinidad [1.2]
Colombia	Mauritius	
Costa Rica	New Zealand	
Greece	Portugal	
Iceland	United Kingdom	
Ireland		

Note: The indexes of federalism are in square brackets with 5 being the most federal and 1 the least.
Source: Lijphart (1999: 189).

in Sweden, which do have directly elected governments) and Finnish regions; and the administrative regions in Ireland, Portugal, and Greece.

Regionalism

Regionalism is a political ideology and bottom-up political movement, which advocates greater control over the political, social, economic, and cultural affairs of the region by the inhabitants of the region or their representatives. Regionalism seeks to establish political regions. There may be links between regionalism and federalism but the difference is that traditional regionalism seeks political autonomy within the unitary state while federalism seeks the restructuring of the state itself.

COUNTRY PROFILE Nigeria

Federal Republic of Nigeria

State formation

Nigeria was run by the British Royal Niger Company until 1900, when it came under the rule of the British government. The country was formally united in 1914. Following the Second World War, successive constitutions legislated by the British government increased the autonomy of Nigeria. Independence was finally gained in 1960. From 1966, Nigeria was ruled by military regimes (except the Second Republic from 1979 to 1983); it returned to democracy in 1999. *Constitution* 1999; an amendment that would have allowed its president to serve more than two terms was blocked in 2006.

Form of government

Federal republic.
Head of state President, term of 4 years, renewable once.
Head of government The President.
Cabinet Federal Ministers appointed by the President.
Administrative subdivisions 36 states and 1 Federal Capital Territory.

Legal system

Based on English common law, Sharia law (in 12 northern states), and traditional law.

Legislature

Bicameral National Assembly.
Lower house House of Representatives: 360 seats; term of 4 years.
Upper house: Senate: 109 seats (the number of seats per state is determined by population); term of 4 years. Both chambers elected at the same time.

Electoral system (lower house)

Plurality.
Constituencies: 360 single-member constituencies.
Barrier clause Not applicable.
Suffrage Universal, 18 years. According to observers, elections fall short of international standards.

Direct democracy

None.

Party system Results of the 2003 legislative elections (House of Representatives):

Electorate	60,823,022	100.0%
Voters:	30,386,270	50.0%

Party	Valid votes	%	Seats
People's Democratic Party (PDP)	15,927,807	54.5	223
All Nigeria People's Party (ANPP)	8,021,531	27.4	96
Alliance for Democracy (AD)	2,711,972	9.3	34
United Nigeria People's Party (UNPP)	803,432	2.8	2
National Democratic Party (NDP)	561,161	1.9	1
All Progressives Grand Alliance (APGA)	397,147	1.4	2
People's Redemption Party (PRP)	222,938	0.8	1
Others	587,082	2.0	0
Total	29,233,070	100.0	359

Note: The results of the contested 2007 elections were not available at press time.
There was one vacant seat in 2003.
Source: African Elections Database.

Regionalization

Regionalization, on the other hand, is a top-down process in which central governments (or the European Union) develop a set of policies directed towards regions of various kinds (usually defined in administrative, statistical, or economic terms rather than cultural or historical). Regionalization may simply set up administrative regions without necessarily involving actors from the regions themselves. This kind of approach to regions was the usual one during the period of the welfare state examined in the first part of this chapter. In other words, regionalism and regionalization do not always coincide and can be in conflict with each other. Insensitive regionalization may provoke an outburst of regionalism as occurred in France from the 1960s onwards (Loughlin 1989). Furthermore, the increased emphasis on regions during the 1980s and 1990s in the EU and the growing popularity of the notion of 'multi-level governance' (Hooghe and Marks 2001) often masked the differences between the two processes, with the result that many regionalists were disappointed with the actual practice of EU regional policy which was much more a process of regionalization than one of regionalism. In recent years, there have been attempts both at the EU level and within member-states to ensure that both processes occur in harmony with each other. When this happens and regionalization and regionalism coincide, it usually results in the establishment of political regions.

Decentralization

The final term to be clarified is decentralization, which tends to be used rather loosely to cover a variety of phenomena. First, we may distinguish between **political** and **administrative** decentralization. Political decentralization means the transfer of decision-making powers from the central state to any of the sub-national levels of government. We need further to distinguish regionalism and regionalization, as defined above, from political decentralization. Although the establishment of political regions is always a form of political decentralization, the latter does not always mean setting up regions. Finally, political decentralization is not the same as administrative decentralization, or what is called in the Latin languages 'deconcentration' (as in the French *déconcentration*).

Deconcentration means the transfer of some administrative functions to sub-national levels of the administration. It can take place, however, without political decentralization, in the sense that it is the central organs of the administration which remain in control of policy-making and administrative behaviour. In France, *déconcentration* was used as a substitute for political decentralization at least until the 1982 decentralization reforms when there was an attempt to make it a tool of the latter (Loughlin 2007). With these conceptual clarifications in mind, we can now proceed to analyse the different territorial configurations of unitary states.

Occupying the 'meso'-level: the emergence of the region as a political 'actor'

The regional question is concerned with the 'meso'-level of territorial governance—that level that exists between the national and the local levels (Sharpe 1993b). In federal states, the component units of the federation are *ex officio* the 'meso' level and their position defines the nature of the federation. But in unitary states, the issue is less clear-cut. States have devised a wide variety of arrangements in the way in which they organize their 'meso' space. The larger unitary states, such as France, Italy, Spain, and the UK, have found it necessary to set up meso-level governments (regions in France and Italy; autonomous communities in Spain; a Parliament in Scotland and Assemblies in Wales and Northern Ireland, and possible future regions in England).

Italy adopted the regionalized model in its 1948 constitution, which distinguished between 'special' and 'ordinary' regions. The five 'special' regions were distinguished by their geographical/cultural features (the islands of Sicily and Sardinia) or simply by their linguistic/cultural specificity (Val d'Aosta; Friuli Venezia Giulia; and Trentino Alto Adige [South Tyrol]). These five regions began to function soon after the promulgation of the constitution. The remainder of Italy was divided into fifteen ordinary regions although they only began to operate in the 1970s.

When Spain made the transition to democracy with its 1978 constitution, it too distinguished between special regions, which the constitution described as 'nationalities' (these are the Basque Country, Catalonia, and Galicia—it does not call them 'nations', as it recognizes only Spain as the 'one and indivisible' nation—and also Andalusia) and the seventeen ordinary regions, which covered the rest of Spain. To some extent, the Spanish were influenced by the Italian example although the regional governments, known as autonomous communities, possess far greater powers than their Italian counterparts.

In France, what were in effect administrative regions, set up in the 1970s to promote economic development, were transformed by the 1982 decentralization reforms into fully fledged regional governments on a par with the departments and communes. They began to function as such after the first regional elections held in 1986 and have slowly emerged as an important level of French territorial governance (Loughlin and Mazey 1995). In Italy and Spain, the regional reforms were more a result of regionalism than simple regionalization, while in France they were initially more a form of regionalization, although, after 1982, there was an element of regionalism as well.

These processes occurred largely as a result of factors found within their respective states: in Italy and Spain, as responses to the excessive centralization of the Fascist and Francoist regimes respectively, and as part of a desire to accommodate the cultural and geographical diversity of each country; in France, as part of the Socialists' programme of modernizing the French state and also in line with their acknowledgement of some of the regionalists' demands (Loughlin 1989). The United Kingdom was the last of the large states in Western Europe to follow this trend when, after the election of Tony Blair at the head of a New Labour government in 1997, the devolution reforms were launched in 1998. Like the other large unitary states, there were internal factors behind these reforms, mainly the demand of the Scots for the 'return' of their parliament, but also as part of a perception that regions were necessary in the new Europe.

The acceleration of European integration from the mid-1980s did add a new element to these processes of strengthening regions, especially with the upgrading of EU Regional Policy in the form of the Structural and Cohesion Funds (Hooghe 1996). This led to a vast mobilization of regional and local authorities in the hope of obtaining some of this manna from heaven, but also to the placing of the 'Europe of the Regions' idea high on the agenda of both the EU and within member states. This strengthened the position of regions within the large unitary states who could argue that regionalism and regionalization were the appropriate forms of contemporary European governance. Some of the more extreme interpretations of these developments postulated that we are witnessing the disappearance of the nation-state. But when the result of this vast mobilization was little more than the setting up of the Committee of the Regions by the Maastricht Treaty, this notion faded away (Jeffery 1997).

The idea that regional government is an important element of the new model of European governance has also been influential both in the smaller unitary states of Western Europe as well as the new democracies of East and Central Europe. With regard to the former, and with the encouragement of the European Commission, it led to the setting up of administrative regions in Greece, Portugal, and Ireland in order to absorb the EU funds coming into these countries. In Denmark, Finland, and Sweden, it meant setting up both political and administrative regions, not so much to receive funds but in order that these regions might be stronger competitors in what was then perceived as the emerging 'Europe of competitive regions'. This trend has also been followed in the new democracies with Poland and Hungary also setting up regional levels of government.

Other former communist states such as Bulgaria, Romania, and Albania have programmes of decentralization aimed at strengthening local government but have hesitated about setting up elected regional governments. Among the reasons for this hesitation is the desire of national governments to retain control over the sub-national level but also the connivance of the European Commission which has quietly encouraged these governments to resist the setting up of political regions as it fears that this would endanger the effective and efficient administration of its funds. Table 11.4 illustrates the variety of situations with regard to regional government prior to enlargement. In order to assist comparison with federal states, these are also included in the table. The table shows what kind of region—political or administrative—exists in each state and how the regions relate to the central level.

Table 11.4 A typology of the pre-enlargement fifteen EU member states

Type of state	State	Political region[a]	Administrative/planning regions[b]	Right of regions to participate in national policy-making	Right of regions to conclude foreign treaties[c]	Political/legislative control over subregional authorities
Federal	Austria	Länder (10)		Yes	Yes (but limited)	Yes (not absolute)
	Belgium	Communities[d] (3)		Yes	Yes (but limited)	No
		Regions (3)		Yes	Yes (but limited)	Yes (not absolute)
	Germany	Länder (16)			Yes (but limited)	Yes (not absolute)
Regionalized unitary	Italy[e]	Regioni[f] (20)		Consultative	No	Yes
	France	Régions[g] (21)		Consultative	No	No
	Spain	Comunidades autonomas (17)		No	No	Yes
	United Kingdom[h]	Scottish Parliament	English standard regions	No with regard to English regions; through informal 'concordats'	No at present, but may evolve	Yes in Scotland and Northern Ireland
		Welsh National Assembly				No in Wales (so far)
		Northern Ireland Assembly				

(continued)

Table 11.4 (continued)

Decentralized unitary	Denmark	Faroe Islands	Groups of Amter	No	No	No
	Finland	Aaland Islands	Counties have a regional planning function	No	No (but has a seat in the Nordic Council)	Yes / No
	Netherlands	Rijnmond region[i]	Landsdelen	Consultative	No	No
	Sweden		Regional administrative bodies	No	No	No
Centralized unitary	Greece		Development regions (13)	No	No	No
	Ireland		Regional authorities (8)	No	No	No
	Luxembourg					
	Portugal	Island regions[j]	Potential planning regions	No	No	No

[a] This refers to regions and nations (as in Scotland, Wales, Catalonia, the Basque Country, and Galicia) with a directly elected assembly to which a regional executive is accountable.

[b] This refers to regions without a directly elected assembly, which exist primarily for administrative/planning purposes.

[c] There is a sharp distinction between the federal and non-federal states in this regard; however, the majority of non-federal states may engage in international activities with the approval of, and under the control of, the national governments.

[d] The Flemish linguistic community and the Flanders economic region have decided to form one body; the French-speaking community and the Walloon region remain separate.

[e] Italy is currently undergoing a process of political reform that involves the transformation of the old state into a new kind of state with some federal features. However, although the position of the regions will be strengthened, this will not be a federal state such as Germany or Belgium.

[f] In Italy there are seventeen 'ordinary' regions and five regions with a special statute because of their linguistic or geographical peculiarities: Sicily, Sardinia, Trentino-Alto Adige (South Tyrol, large German-speaking population), Val d'Aosta, and Friuli-Venezia Giulia.

[g] There are twenty-one regions on mainland France. However, to this one must add Corsica and the overseas departments and territories (the DOM and TOM). Since 1991 Corsica has a special statute and is officially a *collectivite territoriale* rather than a region. The TOM too have special statutes, and one of them, New Caledonia, was in May 1998 permitted to accede to independence within a period of twenty years.

[h] The United Kingdom was, until the referendums in Scotland and Wales in Sept. 1997, a highly centralized 'union' state. However, the positive outcome of the referendums meant there was a Scottish Parliament and a Welsh National Assembly by 1999. A referendum in 1998 on a Greater London Authority with an elected mayor was also successful, and this is seen as a precursor to possible regional assemblies in England. The successful outcome of the Northern Ireland peace process means there will be a Northern Ireland Assembly as well as other new institutions linking together the different nations and peoples of the islands.

[i] In 1991 it was decided to set up a new metropolitan region with an elected government in the Rotterdam area to replace the *Gemeente* of Rotterdam and the Province of South Holland. However, this was rejected by a referendum held in Rotterdam.

[j] Portugal, while making provision in its constitution for regionalization, has so far only granted autonomy to the island groups of the Azores and Madeira. The mainland remains highly centralized.

Source: Loughlin 2004.

KEY POINTS

❏ Unitary states, like federal states, vary according to their degree of regionalization and decentralization.

❏ It is useful to distinguish between regionalization (top–down approaches to regions by central states), regionalism (bottom-up political movements from the regions themselves), various kinds of decentralization (political, administrative, fiscal) as these describe different processes which may not also coincide.

❏ There are also different kinds of regions (political, administrative, economic, cultural) which do not always coincide with each other.

❏ In recent decades, there have been tendencies towards strengthening regionalism as well as political decentralization.

❏ The European Union has encouraged these tendencies, although its regional policies are more akin to regionalization than regionalism.

The local level

Local government and local autonomy

All states, with the exception of the Vatican, possess a level of local government but there is a great deal of variation in its position within the overall system of government. One important difference is between federal and unitary states. In federal states, as a general rule, local government does not have a direct relationship with the federal government but with the subfederal meso-government. In unitary states, there is usually a direct relationship between the central and local levels. However, in some cases (Italy, Belgium, Spain) the body occupying the 'meso' space—the region or the autonomous community—is the hierarchical superior of the local authorities. As remarked above, this has sometimes led, as in Catalonia and Flanders, to a kind of 'regional Jacobinism' or 'regionalist centralism', which may infringe local autonomy.

Political decentralization here means the strengthening of local government autonomy,.which is exercised both *vis-à-vis* the central state and *vis-à-vis* other sub-national entities such as regions or provinces. The Congress of Local and Regional Authorities of Europe (CLRAE), a body of the Strasbourg-based Council of Europe has been one of the main organizations encouraging greater political decentralization to the local level. The council has the tasks of promoting democracy and human rights and it has enriched the concept of democracy with the development of the notions of regional and local democracy. These are now seen as essential elements of democracy itself, which had hitherto been considered as primarily national democracy, that is, expressed in, and exercised through, national representative institutions. The main legal instrument in promoting local democracy is the European Charter of Local Self-Government (in French, La Charte Européenne de l'Autonomie locale) promulgated in 1985 and now signed and ratified by almost all of the current forty-six member-states. There is also a draft European Charter of Regional Autonomy but this has still not been accepted by all the member states of the council. Other bodies, in part inspired by the work of the congress, have also promoted regional and local democracy: the European Union's Committee of the Regions (CoR) has produced reports on the topic and the UN-Habitat Programme has drawn up a set of Guidelines of Effective Decentralization.

Comparing and typologizing local government

The trends outlined above simply deal with 'local governments' in general without specifying whether there are different kinds of local government. It is clear, however, that there is a wide variety of arrangements in different states and a range of ways of categorizing these arrangements.

In an influential comparative analysis of European local government, Page and Goldsmith (1987) use a combination of institutionalist and functionalist approaches. They first categorize the kinds of institutional relationships by distinguishing between 'political localism' characteristic of southern European countries and 'legal localism' found in northern European countries. They then explored the functional relationships within these two broad categories: the functions that central governments allocate to local governments; the degree of discretion (what we have called above 'autonomy') allowed local governments; and the access that local political actors have to the centre. In a system characterized by legal localism (the northern group), there is a high degree of administrative regulation from above (functions are determined by the centre); there is a high degree of discretion; and local political actors have limited access to the centre. Where there is political localism (the southern group), local governments have a general competence over local affairs, a low degree of discretion and local actors have easier access to the centre through informal relationships such as Italian clientelism or more formal arrangements such as the French *cumul des mandats* (Table 11.5).

The Page/Goldsmith typology, while useful in drawing attention to the different legal or political bases of local government in Europe, has been criticized for being too 'broad brush' to be capable of analysing with any degree of finesse the variety of situations (John 2001). John's analysis suggests that, while there are important differences between local governments in northern and southern Europe, the situation is more complex than this simple division would suggest.

There are important differences among countries in each group and even within a single country such as Germany. It may be that the Anglo-American group should be separated from the northern European group to form a group in its own right. Furthermore, the Scandinavian countries might also be distinguished from both Britain and Ireland on the one hand, and from Germany and the Netherlands on the other. Hesse and Sharpe (1991) try to capture this complexity by distinguishing three types of state:

- An Anglo group (UK, Ireland, North America).
- A Franco group (France, Italy, Spain, Belgium, Portugal, and, to some extent, Greece).
- A northern and middle European group (Scandinavian countries, the Netherlands, and Germany).

Similarly, Loughlin and Peters (1997) have used the concept of 'state tradition', drawing on the work of Dyson (1980), and postulating the existence of four state traditions: the Anglo-Saxon, the Germanic, the Napoleonic, and the Scandinavian. Each of these 'state traditions' conceives territorial organization in a distinctive manner based on a fundamental set of concepts related to the nature and functions of the state, its internal organization, and its relationship with civil society (Table 11.6).

Financial and fiscal trends

Fiscal local autonomy is the basis of political autonomy and it is important to examine recent trends in this regard (Loughlin and Martin 2003). First, there is an important distinction to be made between two principal sources of local revenue:

- 'Own resources' generated by local authorities themselves.
- 'Transfers' paid to sub-national governments by central government.

There is a variety of 'own resources' including local taxes (property, income, business, sales, consumption, environmental, property conveyance), fees, loans, and rent from property. 'Transfers' usually take the form of grants but some forms of shared taxation may also be transfers. The key issue in terms of local autonomy is the extent to which local authorities participate in the determination of such taxes and can influence both their base and rate. In the vast majority of cases, local authorities have little control over these. There are, though, regimes with relatively high levels of 'own' resources and low levels of transfers (e.g. Germany, Switzerland, the Nordic countries, and France) as well as others with low local resources and high degree of transfers (e.g. Austria, the Netherlands, and the UK).

Table 11.5 Functional allocation, discretion, and access in the local government systems of Western Europe

	Functions	Discretion	Access
North	High	High	Low
South	Low	Low	High

Source: John (2001).

Table 11.6 State traditions and their features

	Anglo-Saxon	Germanic	French	Scandinavian
Is there a legal basis for the state?	No	Yes	Yes	Yes
State–society relations	Pluralistic	Organicist	Antagonistic	Organicist
Form of political organization	Union state/limited federalist	Integral/organic federalist	Jacobin	Decentralized unitary
Basis of policy style	Incrementalist 'muddling through'	Legal corporatist	Legal technocratic	Consensual
Form of decentralization	State power (US); devolution/local government (UK)	Cooperative federalism	Regionalized unitary state	Strong local autonomy
Dominant approach to discipline of public administration	Political science/sociology	Public law	Public law	Public law (Sweden); organization theory (Norway)
Countries	UK; US; Canada (but not Quebec); Ireland	Germany; Austria; Netherlands; Spain (after 1978); Belgium (after 1988)	France; Italy: Spain (until 1978); Portugal; Quebec; Greece; Belgium (until 1988)	Sweden; Norway; Denmark

Source: Loughlin and Peters (1997).

Second, it is important to consider degrees of (1) political decentralization and (2) fiscal decentralization, since it is the combination of the two that determines the level of discretion that local authorities actually have over fundraising and expenditure. There are a number of countries in which there has been quite extensive political/administrative decentralization in the last ten to fifteen years, but this has not always been accompanied by fiscal decentralization.

Third, it is important to take account of the extent to which resources may be (1) 'earmarked' for specific purposes or (2) 'non-earmarked' or general. Both 'own resources' and 'transfers' may be ring-fenced. A key determinant of the level of local fiscal autonomy is therefore which tier of government determines the uses to which funding can be put. Thus, 'own resources' that are ring-fenced for specific purposes by a central government may allow less local control than transfers that are not ring-fenced.

Underlying these distinctions are the two contrasting models of centra–local relationships to which I have referred previously in this chapter: (1) a principal–agent model and (2) a 'choice' model (Caulfield 2000). The study by Loughlin and Martin (2003) suggests that there appears to be a general tendency towards the increasing use of 'transfers' and decreasing reliance on 'own resources'. Accompanying this trend, and apparently contradicting it, is a general move in favour of 'block' rather than 'ring-fenced grants'. The result has been that, in general terms, the level of local fiscal control has increased in recent years and the 'choice model' seems to have become more important, though most states continue to embody elements of the 'principal–agent' approach. The explanation of the apparent contradiction may be that the choice model is served by the element of fiscal control over transferred resources rather than by own resources. At the same time, from the point of view of strengthening local democracy, there are concerns about the decline in the level of 'own resources' and in most EU countries there have been attempts to keep down the overall level of local authority spending in order to meet the convergence criteria laid down in the Maastricht Treaty.

KEY POINTS

❑ There is a great variety of systems of local government which makes it difficult to classify.

❑ A classical way of typologizing local government in Europe is to distinguish between systems in northern Europe (legal localism) and southern Europe (political localism).

❑ This simple division needs to be complemented by more complex typologies which take into account the differences within the two broad categories: Anglo-Saxon, Germanic, French-Napoleonic, and Scandinavian systems.

❑ There are trends towards greater local fiscal autonomy but this has recently been somewhat tempered by the new fiscal orthodoxy which makes central governments responsible for their countries' fiscal rectitude (thus constraining local authorities).

Conclusion

Three points emerge from the above analysis:

1. The territorial dimension of governance is as important as ever and is growing in importance.

2. There are general trends which affect all political systems, whether unitary or federal and those in between.

3. These general trends are expressed in terms of the distinctive histories, political and administrative cultures, and traditions of the different states. In other words, there are patterns of convergence and divergence, thus making the territorial a highly complex phenomenon which is difficult to grasp and analyse empirically.

This is in line with the notion of the emergence of a new system of governance which does not abolish the traditional forms of governance of the classical nation-state, whether this is a federation or a unitary state, but does introduce alongside them new configurations and sets of relationships. This means that the rigid division between federal and unitary states is less relevant than in the past and that today we should think more of a spectrum with strong federal and unitary states at each end of the spectrum and, in between, a variety of types of state.

On a general level, the classical organization of the nation-state, which culminated in the welfare states of the *Trente Glorieuses* (1945–75), which implied a certain type of territorial organization, has been transformed from a hierarchical, symmetrical, and standardized model to one that is more non-hierarchical, asymmetrical, and diversified. This has led to the emergence of regions and local authorities as political actors in their own right and their position has been strengthened by the various decentralization and regionalization reforms that have taken place in all states since the 1980s. These processes and the new status of sub-national governments have, in turn, been strengthened by European bodies such as the EU and the Council of Europe as well as by the United Nations. These trends have important consequences for the nation-state itself and its forms of political representation, as well as its political and administrative organization. These political and institutional changes are also reflected in shifts in fiscal and financial relationships, where local authorities have greater discretion in the use of local finances but, at the same time, may be held more accountable by central governments and by the electorate for the use they make of these.

? Questions

1. How has the nation-state determined modern territorial organization?
2. Is the distinction between federal and unitary states still valid?
3. What are the different kinds of federal arrangements?
4. Is there an intermediate group of states that are neither federal nor unitary?
5. How has the post-war welfare state affected the territorial organization of nation-states?
6. What is the difference between regionalization and regionalism?
7. Does political decentralization lead to the establishment of political regions?
8. Are we seeing the emergence of a 'Europe of the Regions'?
9. How useful is the distinction between northern European 'legal localism' and southern European 'legal localism'?
10. Is there a contradiction between increased political decentralization and growing fiscal central control?

» Further reading

Starting point for discussion of federalism

Burgess, M. (2006) *Comparative Federalism: Theory and Practice* (London: Routledge).

Wheare, K. (1963) *Federal Government* (Oxford: Oxford University Press, 4th edn).

Useful contemporary analyses of federalism

Elazar, D. (1995) *Federalism: An Overview* (Pretoria: HSRC Publishers).

Karmis, D., and Norman, W. (eds.) (2005) *Theories of Federalism: A Reader* (Basingstoke and New York: Palgrave). This is a useful collection of publications ranging from the classical early texts to more contemporary theoretical debates.

Watts, R. (1996) *Comparing Federal Systems in the 1990s* (Kingston, Ont.: Institute of Intergovernmental Relations, Queen's University).

Regions and regionalism

Keating, M. (1998) *The New Regionalism in Western Europe: Territorial Restructuring and Political Change* (Cheltenham: Edward Elgar).

——(ed.) (2004) *Regions and Regionalism in Europe* (Cheltenham: Edward Elgar).

——and Loughlin, J. (eds.) (1997) *The Political Economy of Regionalism* (London: Routledge).

Swenden, W. (2006) *Federalism and Regionalism in Western Europe: A Comparative and Thematic Analysis* (Basingstoke: Palgrave). This is a useful reader.

For more literature on regionalism see Chapter 15.

Multi-level governance

Bache, Ian, and Flinders, Matthew (eds.) (2004) *Multi-Level Governance* (Oxford: Oxford University Press).

Hooghe, Liesbet, and Marks, Gary (2001) *Multi-Level Governance and European Integration* (Lanham, MD.: Rowman & Littlefield).

Overviews of local and regional government in the EU

Delcamp, A., and Loughlin, J. (eds.) (2003) *La Décentralisation dans les États de l'Union européenne* (Paris: La Documentation Française).

John, P. (1991) *Subnational Governance in Western Europe* (London: Sage).

Loughlin, J. *et al.* (2004) *Subnational Democracy in the European Union* (Oxford: Oxford University Press).

Page, E., and Goldsmith, M. (eds.) (1987) *Central and Local Government Relations: A Comparative Analysis of West European Unitary States* (London and Beverly Hills, Calif.: Sage).

 Web links

Federalism

www.indiana.edu/~speaweb/IPSA/article11.html
   International Political Science Association Comparative Federalism and Federation Research Committee.

Regionalism

www.essex.ac.uk/ecpr/standinggroups/regionalism/index.aspx
   European Consortium of Political Research Standing Group on Regionalism.

Local government

www.essex.ac.uk/ecpr/standinggroups/lgp/index.aspx
   Consortium of Political Research Standing Group on Local Government and Politics. This Standing Group has an electronic newsletter LOGOPOL which provides news of activities of the Group. To subscribe send a message to LOGOPOL-L@LISTS.UTWENTE.NL.

Organizations

www.coe.int/T/Congress/Default_en.asp
   Congress of Local and Regional Authorities of the Council of Europe.

www.cor.europa.eu/En/index.htm
   Committee of the Regions (of the European Union).

 Visit the Online Resource Centre that accompanies this book for more information:
www.oxfordtextbooks.co.uk/orc/caramani/

SECTION 4

Actors and processes

12 Political parties

Richard S. Katz

Chapter contents

Reader's guide

Political parties are among the central—some might even say the defining—institutions of modern democracy. But what is a political party? And what functions do parties perform that make them so central to democracy, and how are they organized to perform those functions? This chapter considers the definition, origins, and functions of parties. What role do parties play in the working of democracy? And what benefits do parties provide for those who organize them? The chapter then considers the ways in which parties are organized, regulated, and financed. Following this, the chapter discusses the relationships between parties and social cleavages, on the one hand, and political ideologies, on the other. It concludes with brief discussions of the role of parties in the stabilization of democracy in the late twentieth and early twenty-first centuries, and of challenges confronting parties in the new millennium.

Introduction

Throughout most of the twentieth century and into the twenty-first century, organizations that identified themselves as 'political parties' have been among the central actors in politics. Whether in power as the result of victory in regularly contested free and fair elections or as a result of *coups d'état* or revolutions, the governments of most countries effectively were in the hands of party leaders: Winston Churchill as leader of the British Conservative Party; Indira Gandhi as leader of the Indian National Congress; Adolf Hitler as the leader of the Nationalsozialistische Deutsche Arbeiterpartei (German Nazi Party); Mikhail Gorbachev as leader of the Communist Party of the Soviet Union; Ahmed Sékou Touré as leader of the Parti Démocratique de Guinée-Rassemblement Démocratique Africain.

When governments have not been in the hands of party leaders, most often because party government has been interrupted by a military takeover, the resulting juntas (see Chapter 6) have almost always immediately announced that their rule will be only temporary—until a regime of legitimate or honest or effective parties can be restored. And if, at the beginning of the twenty-first century, there is occasionally talk that the era of the political party is past, and that in a fundamental reconceptualization of democracy social movements and governance networks will supplant parties as the leading institutions channelling political participation and structuring government, experience to date offers little reason to suspect (or hope, depending on one's viewpoint) that this will happen any time soon.

> **KEY POINTS**
>
> ❏ Political parties are the central actors in democratic politics, as well as in many authoritarian and totalitarian regimes.
> ❏ It is unlikely that social movements or governance networks will replace the parties' many roles.

Definitions of party

Given their ubiquity, one might think that the definition of political party would be straightforward, but quite the reverse is true. Parties like the American Democrats, the Italian Fascists, or the Kenyan African National Union (KANU)—not to mention the myriad smaller parties like the Canadian Greens or the Polish Beer Lovers or the British Official Monster Raving Loony Party—are so different in motivation, organization, behaviour, and relevance as to raise the question of whether a single umbrella category can encompass them all. Indeed there are many scholars who would argue that some of the 'parties' cited above should not be included.

Taking Robert Huckshorn's (1984: 10) definition that 'a political party is an autonomous group of citizens having the purpose of making nominations and contesting elections in the hope of gaining control over governmental power through the capture of public offices and the organization of the government' as an example, one might legitimately ask whether the 'party' in a single-party state qualifies. While it may use the form of elections in an attempt to bolster its legitimacy, it does not contest elections precisely because it does not allow any other contestants. On the other side, only by assuming that they are delusional could one attribute the hope of gaining even a single office, let alone significant governmental power, to the myriad minor parties that appear on the ballots of many British, American, or Canadian constituencies.

The definition of party is significant both scientifically and normatively. **Scientifically**, a definition of party specifies the range of organizations or groups to which generalizations are expected to apply and from which data to test those generalizations should be drawn. **Normatively**, in the process of specifying what a party is, definitions of party often also specify what a party is expected to do (and hence can be criticized for not doing). This has been especially true of definitions that refer to parties in democratic systems, particularly when they define democracy in terms of inter-party competition; in these cases, democratic

BOX 12.1 Definitions of party

Bolingbroke (1841)	Parties, even before they degenerate into absolute factions, are still numbers of men associated together for certain purposes, and certain interests, which are not, or which are not allowed to be those of the community by others. A more private or personal interest comes but too soon . . . but such a party is then become a faction.
David Hume (1742)	Factions may be divided into personal and real; that is, into factions, founded on personal friendship or animosity among such as compose the contending parties, and into those founded on some real difference of sentiment or interest . . . though . . . parties are seldom found pure and unmixed, either of one kind or the other.
Edmund Burke (1770)	[A] party is a body of men united, for promoting by their joint endeavours the national interest, upon some particular principle in which they are all agreed.
Walter Bagehot (1889)	The moment, indeed, that we distinctly conceive that the House of Commons is mainly and above all things an elective assembly, we at once perceive that party is of its essence: there never was an election without a party.
Max Weber (1922)	'[P]arties' live in a house of 'power'. Their action is oriented toward the acquisition of social 'power,' that is to say toward influencing communal action no matter what its content may be.
Robert Michels (1911)	The modern party is a fighting organization in the political sense of the term, and must as such conform to the laws of tactics.
Joseph Schumpeter (1950)	A party is not . . . a group of men who intend to promote the public welfare 'upon some particular principle on which they are all agreed'. A party is a group whose members propose to act in concert in the competitive struggle for political power.
Anthony Downs (1957)	In the broadest sense, a political party is a coalition of men seeking to control the governing apparatus by legal means. By coalition, we mean a group of individuals who have certain ends in common and cooperate with each other to achieve them. By governing apparatus, we mean the physical, legal, and institutional equipment which the government uses to carry out its specialized role in the division of labor. By legal means, we mean either duly constituted or legitimate influence.
V. O. Key, Jr. (1964)	A political party, at least on the American scene, tends to be a 'group' of a peculiar sort. . . . Within the body of voters as a whole, groups are formed of persons who regard themselves as party members. . . . In another sense the term 'party' may refer to the group of more or less professional workers. . . . At times party denotes groups within the government. . . . Often it refers to an entity which rolls into one the party-in-the-electorate, the professional political group, the party-in-the-legislature, and the party-in-the-government. . . . In truth, this all-encompassing usage has its legitimate application, for all the types of groups called party interact more or less closely and at times may be as one. Yet both analytically and operationally the term 'party' most of the time must refer to several types of group; and it is useful to keep relatively clear the meaning in which the term is used.

(continued)

BOX 12.1 (continued)

Leon D. Epstein (1967)	Almost everything that is called a party in any Western democratic nation can be so regarded for the present purpose. This means any group, however loosely organized, seeking to elect governmental office-holders under a given label.
William Nisbet Chambers (1967)	[A] political party in the modern sense may be thought of as a relatively durable social formation which seeks offices or power in government, exhibits a structure or organization which links leaders at the centers of government to a significant popular following in the political arena and its local enclaves, and generates in-group perspectives or at least symbols of identification or loyalty.
Ronald Reagan (1984)	A political party isn't a fraternity. It isn't something like the old school tie you wear. You band together in a political party because of certain beliefs of what government should be. (Quoted in *Time Magazine*, 3 Sept.)
Joseph Schlesinger (1991)	A political party is a group organized to gain control of government in the name of the group by winning election to public office.
John Aldrich (1995)	Political parties can be seen as coalitions of elites to capture and use political office. [But] a political party is more than a coalition. A political party is an institutionalized coalition, one that has adopted rules, norms, and procedures.

values such as popular participation sometimes are incorporated into the definition of party in ways that imply particular organizational forms.

Although it is only one among an almost endless list of proposed definitions of party (see Box 12.1 for more examples), it is instructive to unpack Huckshorn's definition in order to highlight the issues involved in defining party. Huckshorn explicitly combines four elements, common to many definitions, and implicitly adds another.

The first explicit element concerns the **objective of parties**: 'gaining control over governmental power through the capture of public offices and the organization of the government'. There has been, however, considerable disagreement concerning the underlying motivation for this pursuit of power. For some (Lasswell 1960), the pursuit of power reflects psychopathology; others (Downs 1957; Schumpeter 1962; Schlesinger 1991) emphasize the pursuit of office essentially as an employment opportunity. From a more public regarding perspective, one finds Edmund Burke's (1770) classic definition of party as 'a body of men united, for promoting by their joint endeavours, the national interest, upon some particular principle in which they are all agreed'.

The second explicit element concerns the **methods** by which parties strive to achieve control of, or influence over, government: 'making nominations and contesting elections . . . and the organization of the government'. This points to two separable arenas in which parties operate, the electoral and the governmental, and as will be noted below, one significant question in the understanding of parties in general, and any single party in particular, is which came first.

The third explicit element of Huckshorn's definition is **competition**, expressed in the 'contesting' of elections and the 'hope [as opposed to the certainty] of gaining control'. But does the contesting of elections require free and fair competition among independent competitors or merely that the form of elections be observed? This is related to the fourth element, that the group of citizens be **autonomous**. At the extreme, these criteria appear to disqualify the parties of 'one-party' states, although on the other side these parties may claim to be facing real, if clandestine and illegal, opposition from 'counter-revolutionary forces'. Moreover, these parties' structures also may play a significant role in the organization and control of the government, more conventionally understood.

The implicit element of Huckshorn's definition is that the group of citizens has some level of coherence that allows them to coordinate their actions and to maintain an identity over time. While this does not require a formal organization, it certainly is facilitated by one, so that both some minimal level of organization and some minimal level of unity have become part of the definition of party.

The remaining question is whether 'party' should be regarded as a category, into which each specific instance either does or does not fit, or as an ideal type, to which each specific instance can more or less closely approximate. It is more common to take the first position, and to relegate the marginal cases like the American Prohibition Party or the Communist Party of the Soviet Union respectively either to a category of 'hard to classify but ultimately not very important parties' or to a separate category of 'non-democratic parties'. For some purposes, however, it is useful to recognize that all, or nearly all, of the elements of many definitions are matters of degree, and so to recognize variation in the level of 'partyness' even of organizations that clearly would be encompassed by a simple category of 'party'.

Thinking specifically about the meaning of party within the model of democratic party government, one can suggest a 'continuous concept of "partyness" of an organization or group, defined by three characteristics: (1) Exhibiting team-like behavior; (2) in attempting to win control over all political power; and (3) basing claims of legitimacy on electoral success' (Katz 1987: 8).

KEY POINTS

❑ Parties are ubiquitous in modern political systems.
❑ The definition of 'party' is contentious because it specifies which cases provide appropriate evidence for confirming or disconfirming empirical theories.
❑ Definitions centring on the objectives and methods of party, and emphasizing their role in political competition, reflect value-laden assumptions about the proper functioning of politics.

Origins of parties

Although there are references to groups that might today be recognized as parties in the histories of Athenian democracy, the Roman Republic and many of the city-states of medieval Italy—among other venues—the origins of modern parties lie first in the representative assemblies of the sixteenth–nineteenth centuries, and secondly in the efforts of those who were excluded from those assemblies to gain a voice in them. In both cases, parties arose in response to the fact that coordinated action is likely to be more effective than action taken by isolated individuals, even if they are in perfect agreement.

The earlier parties were **parties of intra-parliamentary origin,** evident for example in the British parliament in the seventeenth century—and even then the novelty was not the existence of factions but rather acceptance of the ideas that disagreement was not synonymous with disloyalty and that organization was not synonymous with conspiracy. Over time, these parties developed recognizable leadership cadres and became active in electoral campaigns. Their most significant contribution to the development of modern politics, as well as the greatest re-enforcement of their own strength, was to wrest control of the executive from the hands of the monarch and replace that control with responsibility to parliament, which ultimately meant that ministers would in fact be chosen by, and be responsible to, the parties (and especially their leaders) that controlled a majority of the parliamentary seats.

The rise of parliamentary government was far from equivalent to democratization, because well into the nineteenth, and generally into the twentieth, century, the right to participate in political life, including the right to vote, was highly restricted by a variety of economic, religious, and gender restrictions. The need to mobilize and organize large numbers of those excluded from legitimate participation to support leaders advocating for reforms—generally including the extension of political rights—gave rise to development of **parties of extra-parliamentary**

origin. The ultimate success of these parties in inducing the parties of the *régimes censitaires* to broaden the suffrage then was instrumental in converting the liberal regimes of the nineteenth century into the liberal democracies of the twenty-first century. Indeed, as Schattschneider (1942: 1) famously remarked, 'the political parties created democracy, and . . . modern democracy is unthinkable save in terms of the parties'.

The distinction between parties of intra- and extra-parliamentary origin (Duverger 1954) is not only a matter of timing, with parties of internal origin generally coming earlier—in the new democracies of East and Central Europe in the late twentieth century as well as in Western Europe and the Americas in the sixteenth to the early twentieth centuries. As will be discussed below, especially at their origins they often differ quite substantially in their organizations as well, and these 'genetic' differences tend to persist for many decades after parties of external origin win parliamentary representation, or parties of internal origin build membership organizations 'on the ground' (see Panebianco 1988).

Parties of internal and external origin have also tended to differ with respect to their social bases, with those originating in parliament representing the 'establishment' of upper and upper middle classes (or earlier, the nobility and gentry, and more recently, particularly in 'pacted' transitions to democracy in the former Soviet bloc, the clientele of the old regime), while those of external origin represent the middle, lower middle, and working classes, sometimes the adherents of dissenting religions, speakers of marginalized languages, the opponents of the old regime, etc.

In the late twentieth century, a new type of externally originating party has appeared in a number of countries—most notably and successfully in Italy. In these cases, a rich entrepreneur used his wealth and business empire in effect to create (or 'buy') a party in much the same way as he might create a chain of retail stores (Hopkin and Paolucci 1999). Although created outside of parliament, these parties tend to look more like older parties of internal origin, both in their balance of power between the central party organization (dominated by the entrepreneur through party officials who are in reality his employees) and ordinary members (if any), and in their conservative, or at least pro-business, policy profile. In particular, they are created to be 'cheerleaders' and supporters of an already established (albeit in the economy rather than in government) leader, who has little interest in or need for input of ideas or resources from below. Like the earlier parties of internal origin, and unlike most leader-centred parties of external origin, they depend on the material resources that the leader can mobilize, rather than on his or her personal charisma.

KEY POINTS

❑ Some parties originated within parliaments, while others originated outside of parliaments with the objective of getting in.

❑ The subsequent power relations of a party generally favours leaders whose positions in public office, or in an external party organization, are analogous to the positions of the leaders who originally built the party.

The functions of parties

Political parties perform a number of functions (see Box 12.2) that are central to the operation of modern states, and particularly of modern democracies. Indeed, as observed above, parties often are defined at least in part by the performance of these functions. At the same time, however, it should be recognized that these are not the only things that parties do (for example, parties may serve as social outlets for their members), nor do all parties effectively perform (or even attempt to perform) all of these functions—and that the fact that a function is

essential to the maintenance of a political regime does not mean it will be performed adequately; instead, its non-performance may be the reason for regime collapse.

Coordination

Historically the first function of political parties, and still one of the most important, is that of coordination, within government, within society, and between government and society at large.

BOX 12.2 Functions of Parties

Coordination	Maintaining discipline and communication within the parliamentary caucus.
	Coordinating action of the parliamentary caucus in support of, or opposition to, the cabinet.
	Organizing the political activity of like-minded citizens.
	Patterning linkage between representatives in public office and organized supporters among the citizenry.
Conducting electoral campaigns and structuring competition	Providing candidates, and linking individual candidates to recognizable symbols, histories, and expectations of team-like behaviour.
	Developing policy programmes.
	Recruiting and coordinating campaign workers.
Selection and recruitment of personnel	Selection of candidates for elections.
	Recruitment and/or selection of candidates for appointed office.
	Recruitment and socialization of political activists and potential office-holders.
	Integration of new citizens into the existing political system.
Representation	Speaking for their members and supporters within or in front of government agencies.
	Being the organizational embodiment in the political sphere of demographically or ideologically defined categories of citizens.

Coordination within government

Coordination within government (the 'party in public office') takes place in many venues. Most obviously, the coordination function is manifested in party caucuses (or groups, clubs, or *Fraktionen*) in parliaments, with their leaders, whips (party officials in charge of maintaining discipline and communication within the party's parliamentary membership, and 'newsletters' informing members of the expectations of their leaders), policy committees, etc. Parliamentary party groups also structure the selection of committee members and the organization of the parliamentary agenda. Whether in a system of formal separation of powers, like the US, or more pure parliamentary government, like New Zealand, parties provide the bridge between the legislative and executive branches. They also structure coordination between different levels (national, regional, etc.) of government. To the extent that parties perform this function comprehensively and effectively, it becomes reasonable to regard parties as organizations, rather than the individual politicians who hold office in their name, as central political actors.

Coordination within society

In addition to structuring coordination among like-minded public officials, political parties are one of the kinds of institutions (along with interest groups, NGOs, and the like) that organize and channel the political activity of citizens. Even in the absence of a formally organized 'party on the ground', party names and histories serve as points of reference and identification for citizens whose knowledge of and involvement in politics is often both sporadic and shallow. Where there are more formal organizations, these provide venues for political education, discussion, and the coordination of collective action.

Coordination between government and society

The third coordination problem addressed by political parties is the linking of the party on the ground as a group of active citizens supporting a particular political tendency (whether based on a coherent ideology, a common social grouping, a vague orientation, etc.) and the party in public office as a group of officials claiming to represent the same tendency. Within party organizations (see below), this function often is performed by a party central office. Whether this linkage takes, or is supposed to take, the form of control over the party in public office on behalf of the party on the ground, or direction of the party on the ground as an organization of supporters of the party in public office, varies among parties, as indeed does the effectiveness of the linkage whichever way it runs, as well as the level of coordination and discipline within either the party on the ground or the party in public office.

Contesting elections

A second major defining function of political parties is the conduct of electoral campaigns, and of political competition more generally. Parties provide most of the candidates in elections, and an even larger share of those with any real chance of being elected. In many political systems, parties are the formal contestants of elections—the ballot clearly identifies parties as the things among which the citizen is asked to choose—but even when the object of choice formally is individual candidates, the most relevant characteristic of those candidates usually is their political party affiliation. Ordinarily (the US, in which the organization and funding of campaigns is based primarily on individual candidates, being a notable exception), most of the funds required for a political campaign are raised and spent by parties, whether nationally or at the constituency level; campaign workers are recruited and directed by parties. The policy positions advocated in a campaign are generally those that were formulated and agreed to within parties. Between elections as well, parties generally act as the primary protagonists in political debates.

Recruitment

A third major function of parties is the recruitment and selection of personnel, with the balance between recruitment (finding someone willing to do the job) and selection (choosing among multiple aspirants) depending both on the party and the nature of the

position to be filled. The selection function is most significant with regard to candidacies for important offices, like the presidency, membership in the national parliament, or a regional governorship, and within parties whose candidates have a high probability of success. For minor offices (especially those that are unpaid), hopeless constituencies, or positions at the bottom of a party list of candidates, the primary function often is recruitment—avoiding the embarrassment of not being able to fill the position, or of filling it with someone who obviously is not up to the job (Sundberg 1987).

Taken together, these three functions of coordination (especially within the party in public office), conducting electoral campaigns (especially the formulation and presentation of policy programmes, platforms, or manifestoes), and recruitment of candidates for both elective and appointive office, to the extent that they are performed in a coordinated way (see the definition of party as an ideal type above), and to the extent that party elected officials effectively control the state, make the parties the effective governors, and give rise to the idea of 'democratic party government' (Rose 1974; Castles and Wildenmann 1986). Of course, not all democratic governments are democratic in this way. In the US, for example, the coherence of parties is much lower than in most other democracies, making individual politicians rather than their parties the real governors. In Switzerland, the referendum makes the citizens, and the variety of groups (including but by no means limited to parties) that can organize petitions demanding a referendum, the ultimate deciders of individual questions at the expense of party government.[1]

Parties have also been active in integrating new citizens into the political system. While this function was (and still is) particularly prominent in systems with rapidly expanding electorates, either because of suffrage expansion or significant immigration, the natural process of maturation means that there are always new citizens coming to political consciousness. Party youth movements often play a significant role in integrating the most politically interested and active members of each new generation into the existing party system. More generally, if frequently also (in the developed world) to a lesser degree than in the past, parties contribute to the connection of citizens to the established political order through the provision of services, ranging from ombudsman-like intervention with the bureaucracy to jobs and social services.

Representation

Finally, parties perform a variety of functions that may be classified as representation. First, parties speak and act for their supporters, in electoral campaigns, in the corridors of power, in the media and other public fora of discussion. Direct democracy being impossible in any but the smallest communities, parties serve as agents of the people, doing things that the people do not have the time, the training and ability, or the inclination to do for themselves. Parties also represent citizens in the sense of being the organizational embodiment in the political sphere of categories of citizens, as with a labour party, a Catholic party, the party of a language group or region, or even possibly a women's party.[2] Parties may, by analogy, represent the organizational embodiment of ideologies.

KEY POINTS

❑ Political parties play a central role in coordinating among public officials, among citizens with common political preferences, and between citizens and officials.

❑ Political parties are generally the central participants in elections, responsible for both the candidates and the issues among which voters will choose.

❑ Political parties are central participants in the recruitment of political personnel, both for the elective and appointive office.

❑ Political parties serve as representatives, both of social groupings and of ideological positions.

Models of party organization

Types of parties
Cadre or elite parties

The earliest 'modern' parties were the cadre (or elite or caucus) parties that developed in European parliaments. Because, particularly in an era of highly restricted suffrage, each of the MPs who made up these parties generally owed his election to the mobilization of his own, personal, clientele or the clientele of his own patron, there was little need for a party on the ground, and certainly not one organized beyond the boundaries of individual constituencies. Hence there was also no need for a party central office. Within parliament, however, the advantages of working in concert both to pursue policy objectives and to secure access to ministerial office led to the evolution of parliamentary party organizations, frequently cemented by the exchange of patronage (either personally for the MP or in the form of benefits for his personal supporters, patron, or constituency for which the MP could take credit to maintain his own local standing).

As electorates expanded, elite parties in some places developed more elaborate local organizations—most famously the 'Birmingham caucus' of Joseph Chamberlain—and some greater coordination (frequently taking the form of centrally prepared 'talking points' and centrally organized campaign tours by nationally known personalities) by a central office, but the heart of the organization remained, and to the extent that caucus parties continue to be significant remains, the individual MP and his or her personal campaign and support organization. At the level of the electorate, the concept of 'party membership' remained ill-defined. In the twenty-first century, parties that approximate the caucus format remain significant in the US and to a certain extent in Japan (the Liberal Democratic Party) and on the right in France.

Mass parties

The mass party developed from the second half of the nineteenth century (although some argue that the Jacobins of the French Revolution really were the first mass party, for example, Mavrogordatos 1996). In contrast to the intra-parliamentary origins of the caucus party, the 'genetic myth' of the mass party identifies it as a party of extra-parliamentary origin.[3] In the initial absence of either elected officials (a party in public office) or a network of local organizations

Table 12.1 Models of party

	Elite, caucus, or cadre party	Mass party	Catch-all party	Cartel party	Business firm party
Period of dominance	Rise of parliamentary government to mass suffrage.	Drive for mass suffrage to 1950s.	1950s to present.	1970s to present.	1990s to present.
Locus of origination	Parliamentary origin.	Extra-parliamentary origin.	Evolution of pre-existing parties.	Evolution of existing parties.	Extra-parliamentary initiative of political entrepreneurs.
Organizational structure	Minimal and local. Party central office subordinate to party in public office.	Members organized in local branches. Central office responsible to an elected party congress.	Members organized in branches, but marginalized in decision-making. Central office subordinate to party in public office.	Central office dominated by party in public office, and largely replaced by hired consultants. Decisions ratified by plebiscite of members and supporters.	Minimal formal organization, with hierarchical control by the autonomous entrepreneur and his/her employees.
Nature and role of membership	Elites are the only 'members'.	Large and homogeneous membership. Leadership formally accountable to members.	Heterogeneous membership organized primarily as cheerleaders for elites.	Distinction between member and supporter blurred. Members seen as individuals rather than as an organized body.	Membership minimal and irrelevant.
Primary resource base	Personal wealth and connections.	Fees from members and ancillary organizations.	Contributions from interest groups and individuals.	State subsidies.	Corporate resources.

Source: Adapted in part from Katz and Mair (1995) and Krouwel (2006).

(a party on the ground), the mass party begins with a core of leaders who organize a party central office with the aim of developing a party so as to be able to win elections and ultimately gain public office.

In contrast to the cadre party, which generally claimed to be speaking for the 'national interest' (although often based on a highly truncated view of who constituted 'the nation'), mass parties claimed to represent the interest only of a particular group (most often a social class),[4] and frequently built on the pre-existing organizations of that group (e.g. trade unions). Their primary political resource was numbers, with many small contributions of labour and money substituting for the few, but large, contributions available to elite parties. Both as a reflection of their subcultural roots and as a way of mobilizing their supporters, mass parties often pursued a strategy of 'encapsulation', providing a range of ancillary organizations (women's groups, after-work clubs, trade unions) and services (a party press, party-sponsored insurance schemes) that both helped isolate supporters from countervailing influences and made party support a part of the citizen's enduring personal identity rather than a choice to be made at each election.

Naturally, all of this required extensive organization. The archetypal mass party is organized on the ground in branches that, like other types of voluntary organizations of citizens, have a formally defined membership, made up of people who have applied for membership, been accepted (and potentially are liable to expulsion), and have certain obligations to the organization (most commonly including the payment of a subscription or fee) in exchange for which they acquire rights to participate in the organization's governance. In this regard, branches will elect their own officers, as well as delegates to higher levels of the party organization, including at the top the party's national congress (or convention or conference).

The national congress in principle is the highest decision-making body of a mass party, but as a practical matter can only meet for a few days every year (if that often), and therefore elects a party executive committee and/or chairman or president or secretary which is effectively at the top of the party hierarchy. The executive also manages the staff of the party central office. Again in principle, the representatives elected to public office under the party's banner are agents of the party, on the presumption that voters were choosing among parties and not individual candidates, and so are subject to the direction of the party congress and executive, which are also responsible for formulating the party's political programme or manifesto.

In reality, of course, things are often rather different with, as indicated by Michels' (1962) 'iron law of oligarchy', the very structures of internal party democracy leading to the domination of the party by its elite—a result that is less surprising when one remembers that the extra-parliamentary elite initially were the creators of the party. Moreover, in many parties that approximate the ideal type of the mass party, ancillary organizations as well as the parliamentary party and the central office staff are guaranteed representation in the national congress and/or the national executive, increasingly making the question of whether authority in the mass party flows from the bottom-up, or from the top-down, an open one.

Catch-all parties

The mass party originated primarily as the vehicle of those groups that were excluded from power under the *régimes censitaires*. It proved highly effective, however, first in securing broader rights of participation for its clientele groups and then in winning elections under conditions of broadly expanded suffrage, and in many cases this forced the cadre parties of the right to adapt or risk electoral annihilation.[5] Simply to become mass parties was not appealing, however. In general the social groups that they would represent were not large enough to be competitive on their own under mass suffrage and thus they had to be able to appeal across group boundaries. Moreover, the party in public office did not find the idea of ceding ultimate authority to a party congress and executive, even if in name only, attractive. The result was to create a new party model, with much of the form of the mass party (members, branches, congress, executive), but organized as the **supporters** of the party in public office rather than as its masters.

At the same time, many mass parties were forced to change, both by pressure from a party in public office anxious to free itself from the constraints of the mass party model and increasingly able to claim responsibilities and legitimacy based on a direct relationship with the electorate rather than one mediated by the external party organization, and by changes in society (e.g. breakdown of social divisions, spread of mass media) that made the strategy of encapsulation less effective and the resources provided by the parties' *classes gardées* less reliable and less adequate.

The result was (1) a reduction in the role of members relative to professionals, (2) a shedding of ideological baggage, (3) a loosening and ultimate abandonment of the interconnection of party and a privileged set of interest organizations (again, particularly unions), and (4) a strategy that reached across group boundaries for votes and resources. Particularly looking at these changes in mass parties of the left, Kirchheimer (1966) identified this new type as the 'catch-all party'. In fact, however, in both strategy and organization, Kirchheimer's catch-all party looks very much like that just described as the adaptation of the old cadre parties. As the catch-all party developed, it was accompanied by greater attention to the function of contesting elections, to the detriment of other party functions such as integrating or representing groups or opinions in politics or formulating and debating policy. It was also accompanied by increased reliance on political professionals—pollsters, media consultants, etc. (see Chapter 19)—leading to the idea of the electoral-professional party as an alternative to, or simply a variant of, the catch-all model (Panebianco 1988). Although most parties identified as being electoral-professional in fact have formal membership organizations, the emphasis has shifted so much toward the party in public office and the central office (or hired consultants who are not regular members of the party staff) that the membership is effectively superfluous, or maintained primarily for cosmetic reasons (i.e. the belief that having a membership organization will make the party look less elitist or oligarchic).

Cartel parties

By the last quarter of the twentieth century, even the catch-all model was under considerable pressure. Increasing public debts confronted ruling parties with a choice between dramatic increases in taxes and dramatic cuts in welfare spending. Globalization reduced the ability of governments to control their economies. Cognitive mobilization and the growth of interest groups, NGOs, etc., gave citizens both the abilities and opportunities to bring pressure to bear on the parties themselves, and on the state without requiring the intermediation of the parties. Party loyalties, and memberships, began obviously to erode. Shifts in campaign technology increased the cost of electoral competitiveness beyond the willingness of members and other private contributors to provide—at least without the appearance, and often the reality, of corruption that, when revealed, made parties even less popular.

These developments have inspired a number of adaptations and other initiatives. Katz and Mair (1995) have suggested that in many countries catch-all parties have been moving in the direction of what they call the 'cartel party'. This involves at least four major changes in the relationships among the parties, the citizenry, and the state, and between parties and their members.

1. The mainstream parties, that is, those that are in power, or are generally perceived to have a high probability of coming to power in the medium term, in effect form a **cartel to protect themselves both from electoral risks** (e.g. by erecting barriers to entry, by tacitly agreeing to keep divisive issues off the political agenda, by shifting responsibility away from politically accountable agencies so that they will not be held to account for them, by minimizing the difference in rewards to electoral winners and electoral losers) **and to supplement their decreasingly adequate resources with subventions from the state** (justified in terms of the parties' centrality to democratic government or of insulating parties from corrupt economic pressure).

2. The parties reduce the relevance of their role of bringing pressure to bear on the state on behalf of civil society (i.e. their role of representation), in favour of a part of their role as governors, defending policies of the state (including those made by bureaucrats, 'non-political' agencies like central banks, and even previous governments made up of other parties), in effect becoming **agencies of the state rather than of society**. This status tends to be particularly manifested in the proliferation of 'party laws' (see below) that regulate the internal practices of parties in ways that are more akin to state and quasi-state agencies than they are to private associations.

3. Cartel parties tend to increase the formal powers of party members, and indeed in some cases to allow increased participation by supporters who are not formal members. They do this, however,

not to increase the internal democracy of the parties, except perhaps in a plebiscitarian sense, but rather as a way of **preserving the form of internal democracy while disempowering party activists**—who are perceived to be more doctrinaire and policy-oriented, and hence less willing to accept the limitations implicit in a cartel. For example, leadership selection might be moved from the party congress, which allows a forum for internal opposition to be organized and expressed, to a direct mail ballot of the full membership.

4. In part simply extending the trends evident in the catch-all party, cartel parties also tend to replace the staff of the party central office with hired consultants, both **further privileging professional expertise over political experience and activism**, and **removing another possible source of challenge** to the leaders of the party in public office.

Anti-cartel parties

Although both Duverger (the principal elaborator of the idea of the mass party) and Kirchheimer (the elaborator of the idea of the catch-all party) presented their models as somehow representing an end-state of party development, each of the models has generated its own challenger. In the case of the cartel party, Katz and Mair (attributing the idea to Lars Bille), identify what they call the anti-party-system party as the cartel party's challenger. Parties of this type have also been identified as 'left-libertarian' or 'new right' parties, or as 'movement parties'. They tend to expect a much deeper commitment from their members than either catch-all or cartel parties, and in this way are similar to the mass party, but they are organized around an idea rather than a social grouping (although the idea may be differentially attractive/popular among different groups). Two of their primary appeals, however, are simply to a sense of frustration that substantive outcomes appear to change little, if at all, regardless of which of the mainstream parties wins an election, and to a sense that all of the mainstream parties are more interested in protecting their own privileges (for example, by voting themselves generous subventions) than in advancing the interests of ordinary citizens.

Particularly in their early days (before they faced the temptations of joining the cartel and enjoying public office), both Green Parties on the left and Scandinavian Progress Parties on the right exemplified anti-cartel parties.

Business-firm parties

An alternative form of challenger to established parties is represented by what Hopkin and Paolucci (1999) have called the 'business-firm party'. The prototypical example is Forza Italia, a 'party' created by Silvio Berlusconi—a businessman who became prime minister in Italy—essentially as a wholly owned subsidiary of his corporate empire, and staffed largely by its employees. While there may be an organization on the ground to mobilize supporters to cheer on the leader, it is only 'a lightweight organisation with the sole basic function of mobilising short-term support at election time' (1999: 315), and indeed in the case of Forza Italia the members of these organizations originally were not members of the party. Although Forza Italia developed from a previously existing firm, Hopkin and Paolucci argue that essentially the same model will typify 'purpose-built' parties in the future.

Parties in the US

Parties in the US present yet another model. From a European perspective, they appear to have much in common with the nineteenth-century cadre party, and Duverger famously identified them as a historical throwback or case of 'arrested development'. What they have in common with the cadre party is (1) a weak central organization, (2) a focus on individual candidates rather than enduring institutions, and (3) the absence of a formal membership organization. Where they differ profoundly, however, is in being extensively regulated by law, to the extent that Epstein (1986) reasonably could characterize them as 'public utilities', and in allowing the mass 'membership' (see below for an explanation of the quotation marks) to make the most important decision, that of candidate selection.

Reflecting the federal nature of the country, the basic unit of party organization is the state party. The national committees of the two parties, which control the national party central offices and elect the national chairmen, are made up of representatives of the state parties. The national conventions are not policymakers, even in form; they are called for the purpose of selecting—and effectively since the 1950s merely confirming the selection of—presidential candidates. Moreover, reflecting the separation of powers in the American constitution, both the parties have separate organizations in each House of the Congress, which not only serve as the equivalent of parliamentary party caucuses but also maintain their own, independent, fundraising, and campaign-mounting capacity, almost as if they were separate parties.

The three key features of the American legal system of party regulation are (1) the use of primary elections, (2) the vacuous definition of party membership, and (3) the candidate-centred nature of party regulation. In the decades around the turn of the twentieth century, reformers intent on breaking what they saw as the corrupt and excessive power of party bosses, 'democratized' the parties by putting power into the hands of ordinary party members (who they identified as party voters) through the use of primary elections. Today, each of the state parties is run (to the extent that they are run at all) by a party central committee, generally chosen in that party's primary election.

Virtually all of the party's candidates for public office, as well as the vast majority of delegates to its national nominating convention, are also chosen in primary elections, or in party caucuses which are essentially the same in terms of rights of participation. Unlike so-called primaries in other countries, these are public elections, run by the state and structured by public law rather than party rules. The second element of these reforms was to deny the parties the right to define or control their own memberships. Rather than having formal members (who make an application to join, pay a membership fee, and in theory could be rejected or expelled), American parties only have 'registrants', that is voters who have chosen to affiliate with one of the parties in the process of registering to vote—if, indeed, there is even that much of a formal attachment between 'members' and party, given that not all states have partisan registration of voters.

American law generally treats registrants as if they were members in a more substantive sense, but the party has no control over who registers as a 'member', and the member takes on no obligation by enrolling. Moreover, some states do not have partisan registration, and even in some states that do have partisan registration any voter can claim the right to participate in a party's primary elections (open primary)

without even the pretence of prior registration in it. Generally, the choice between open and closed (only party registrants may participate) primaries is determined by state law, although the parties have won (in court) the right for each party to determine for itself whether to allow voters who are not registered as 'members' of any party to participate in its own primary. Finally, even when ostensibly dealing with parties, American legal regulations focus on candidates as individuals. The overwhelming majority of the money spent in American campaigns is controlled by the candidates' own committees, and in general the parties are regarded merely as a privileged class of 'contributor'.

Even though eligibility for the public support given to finance presidential campaigns is based on the vote shares of their parties' candidates in the previous election, the money itself is given to the campaign committees of the candidates, not to the party organizations. The right to call oneself the candidate of a party is won in its primary election, with the party organization unable to bar any qualified voter who presents the requisite number of petition signatures and/or fee from competing and often is barred even from expressing a preference among the primary candidates (although party 'clubs', which are formal membership organizations but are not formally part of the party, may do so).

The result of all of this is to make it unclear whether the United States should be described as having a two party (Democrats and Republicans), six party (Presidential Democrats, House Democrats, Senate Democrats, and the same for the Republicans), or hundred party (Democrats and Republicans in each state) system—or alternatively whether it might not to some extent be appropriate to characterize the United States as having no political parties at all.

Membership

Although the original parties of intra-parliamentary origin had no members other than the MPs who aligned themselves with a party caucus, virtually all modern parties claim to have a membership organization. The modes of acquiring membership, the role played by members both in rhetoric and in practice, the size of the membership organization (and indeed the degree to which it is an organization at all), however, vary widely among parties.

BOX 12.3 Types of American primaries

Closed primary	Only those who have registered in advance as 'members' of the party may participate.
Modified primary	Those who have registered as 'members' of the party, and—at the party's discretion—those who are registered as 'Independent' or 'non-affiliated' voters may participate.
Open primary	All registered voters may participate in the primary election of the one party of their choice.
Blanket primary	All registered voters may participate, choosing if they wish among the candidates of a different party for each office. The candidates of each party with the most votes become the nominees.
Louisiana 'primary'	All registered voters may participate, choosing among all of the candidates for each office. If a candidate receives an absolute majority of the votes, that person is elected, and the 'primary' in effect becomes the election for that office. Otherwise, the two candidates with the most votes, regardless of party, become the candidates for the (run-off) general election.

As suggested above, the prototypical membership-based party is the mass party. In its simplest form, the members of a mass party are individuals who have applied and been accepted as members of local branches or sections (based either on local government boundaries or electoral districts—which generally are the same except in cases where an obsession with population equality forces subdivision boundaries to be crossed in the construction of constituencies). In some parties, this form of direct individual membership is or was supplemented by indirect membership acquired as part of membership in an affiliated organization. Most commonly these were trade unions affiliated with social democratic parties, such as the British Labour Party.

Affiliated membership might come automatically and inescapably as part of union (or other group) membership, or it might require an explicit choice by the potential member either to acquire party membership ('contracting in') or to decline party membership ('contracting out'); membership rights such as voting for members of the party executive might be exercised by the individual, or indirectly through representatives of the affiliated organization. With the development of the catch-all party model and the weakening of social class as the basis of party politics, affiliated memberships have been dropped by some parties, for example the Swedish Social Democrats, leaving only individual membership.

As elite parties transformed into, or were replaced by, membership-based parties of the centre and right, they too adopted the local branch model, although the relationship of the branches to the party itself might differ. For example, the National Union of Conservative and Unionist Associations in the UK remained organizationally separate from (although housed in the same building as) the Conservative Party *per se*. Similarly, the 'clubs' of Forza Italia are distinct from the party itself, as are the Democratic and Republican clubs found in the United States. In each case, the membership organization may more properly be described as an organization of party supporters than as the base of the party itself.

Particularly in the first half of the twentieth century, Communist and Fascist parties developed their own forms of membership organization. For the Communists, the dominant form was the cell, based on the workplace rather than on residence; for the Fascists, it was the militia.

Membership remains important to the self-understanding of many parties, and the idea that party leaders should be responsible to a membership organization has been widely embraced as a necessary element of democratic governance, although there are prominent dissenters from this view (e.g. Sartori 1965). Traditionally, membership has been measured in three ways.

COUNTRY PROFILE United States

United States of America

State formation

American colonies were founded by Spanish, French, and English settlers since the 16th century. The US was founded by 13 colonies declaring their independence from Great Britain in 1776. It expanded to the western coast of the continent and has since been receiving more immigrants than the rest of the world combined.
Constitution: 1787, effective 1789; amended 27 times.

Form of government

Federal republic.
Head of state President and Vice President elected on the same ticket by a college of representatives who are elected directly from each state; term of 4 years (renewable once).
Head of government The President.
Cabinet Appointed by the President with approval of the Senate.
Administrative subdivisions 50 states and 1 district.

Legal system

Based on English common law; each state has its own legal system; judicial review of legislative acts.

Legislature

Bicameral Congress.
Lower house House of Representatives: 435 seats; term of 2 years.
Upper house Senate: 100 seats (2 members from each state); staggered elections (one-third renewed every two years); term of 6 years.

Electoral system (lower house)

Simple majority vote in one round (absolute majority in the states of Georgia and Louisiana).
Constituencies 435 single-member constituencies. Each representative represents roughly the same number of citizens, provided that each state has at least one representative.
Barrier clause Not applicable.
Suffrage Universal, 18 years.

Direct democracy

Referendums at state level.

Party system Results of the 2004 legislative elections (*House of Representatives*):

Electorate:	221,285,099	100.0%
Voters:	123,535,883	55.8%

Party	Valid votes	%	Seats
Republican Party	55,713,412	49.2	232
Democratic Party	52,745,121	46.6	202
Independent	674,202	0.6	1
Others	4,059,551	3.6	0
Total	113,192,286	100.0	435

Notes: Category 'Others' includes parties with less than 1% nation-wide and no seats.
Sources: US House of Representatives; US Elections Project, George Mason University (for electorate and turnout).

1. The most obvious is simply a raw **count of members**. This is useful for organizational purposes: is membership growing or shrinking? How much income should be expected from membership fees? Are representative institutions necessary, or can all members attend a party congress and speak for themselves?

2. In comparative terms, however, this measure suffers from its dependence on the scale of the system.

If every citizen of Luxembourg were a party member, the absolute number of members would still be less than 25 per cent of German party membership, which represents less than 3 per cent of the German electorate. More generally comparable across space and time is the **ratio of party membership to the size of the electorate**.

3. Finally, comparisons between parties may be based on their **organizational density** (the ratio of

members to voters), the problem here being that an increase in this ratio can be the result either of an increase in membership (an indicator of party strength) or of a decline in vote (an indicator of party weakness).

Regardless of how membership is measured, however, and despite its perceived importance, party membership has generally been declining, often in absolute terms but almost always in relative terms (for examples, see Table 12.2). Although some scholars (e.g. Katz 1990) argue that members may cost a party more than they are worth—and that the value to a citizen of being a party member may also exceed its cost—this has commonly been regarded as a problem, for which however no real solution has yet been found.

Regulation

Whether or not they reflect the merging of parties with the state, an increasing number of countries have enacted special 'party laws', either supplementing or replacing legal regimes that treated parties as simply one more category of private association. In some cases, these party laws are embedded in the national constitution, while in others they are ordinary statutes or bodies of regulations.

A number of specific justifications have been offered in favour of special party laws. These can, however, generally be categorized into three groups. The first is the **centrality of parties to democracy**. In several cases (Germany, France, Spain, Portugal, Greece, Italy), this is specifically acknowledged in the national constitution, while in others it has been acknowledged either in the law or in the parliamentary debates when the law was enacted. In general, the importance of parties to democracy has been a justification for giving the parties special rights, protections, or privileges beyond those that would normally be granted to an 'ordinary' private association.

The second, albeit closely related, justification is the **power of parties**. Because of their central position in democratic government, a party that is anti-democratic or corrupt may pose a particularly serious threat to democracy. Hence if their importance justifies special privileges, the dangers they pose justify special oversight and restrictions.

Third, a party law may be justified as a matter of administrative convenience or necessity. Most commonly, this justification has revolved around the twin problems of ballot access (the right to place candidates on the ballot) and control over the party's name or symbols (particularly on the ballot), although the related question of the right to form a parliamentary group may also be involved. (Alternatively, this may be regulated by the parliament's own Rules of Procedure—see Chapter 7.)

Where there is a party law, one of the first issues to be dealt with is the definition of party—to determine whether a group is entitled to the privileges and subject to the regulations of the law. Unlike the definitions discussed above, legal definitions generally are procedural and organizational, and may indeed distinguish between parties in general and parties that are entitled to special treatment. For example, while the Canada Elections Act defines a party simply as 'an organization one of whose fundamental purposes is to participate in public affairs by endorsing one or more of its members as candidates and supporting their election', the 'real' definition is that of a 'registered party'. To be a registered party, an organization must file an application declaring that it meets the definition of party just quoted, but also declaring its full name, a short-form name or abbreviation (that will appear on the ballot), its logo (if any), plus the names, addresses, and signed consent of the party's leader, officers, auditor, chief agent, and 250 electors. Finally, it must endorse at least one candidate.[6] In other countries, official recognition may require that the party 'offer sufficient guarantee of the sincerity of their aims' (German Law on Political Parties of 1967, § 2(1)), and/or adhere to prescribed norms of internal democracy.

Continuing with the Canadian example, once a party is registered it acquires a number of privileges, including: (1) contributions to the party become eligible for tax credits; (2) the party's name appears on the ballot (but only if the nomination is confirmed by the party leader, giving the central party organization control over the use of its name); (3) if it has received at least 2 per cent of the valid votes nationally or 5 per cent of the valid votes in the districts in which it had candidates, half of its election expenses can be reimbursed by the federal treasury and the party can receive a quarterly subvention based on its vote at the previous election. The requirements for ballot access in Canada are the same for party and non-party candidates (except that a candidate

Table 12.2 Party membership

Country	Membership/electorate %			
	Time 1	%	*Time 2*	%
Austria	1980	28.48	1999	17.66
Belgium	1980	8.97	1999	6.55
Czech Republic	1993	7.04	1999	3.94
Denmark	1980	7.30	1998	5.14
Finland	1980	15.74	1998	9.65
France	1978	5.05	1999	1.57
Germany	1980 (West only)	4.52	1999 (whole)	2.93
Greece	1980	3.19	1998	6.77
Hungary	1990	2.11	1999	2.15
Ireland	1980	5.00	1998	3.14
Italy	1980	9.66	1998	4.05
Netherlands	1980	4.29	2000	2.51
Norway	1980	15.35	1997	7.31
Portugal	1980	4.28	2000	3.99
Slovakia	1994	3.29	2000	4.11
Spain	1980	1.20	2000	3.42
Switzerland	1977	10.66	1997	6.38
United Kingdom	1980	4.12	1998	1.92

Source: Mair and van Biezen (2001).

wishing to have a party designation on the ballot must submit a letter of endorsement from the party leader in addition to the required signatures and deposit), but in some countries the candidates of a registered party, or a party that already has some level of representation in parliament, may be given a place on the ballot without having to satisfy the requirements imposed on non-party or new-party or very-minor-party candidates.

On the other hand, acquiring official status often also subjects a party to a number of obligations. Canadian registered parties, for example, are required to submit frequent, and audited, financial reports. German law requires membership participation in the selection of party leaders and that candidates be selected by secret ballot, requirements that are not imposed in equivalent detail on other private associations.

Finance

As is implicit in the preceding section, one field in which state involvement in the affairs of parties has been particularly prominent is that of finance. Traditionally, this has taken the form of regulation, and most specifically of prohibitions—against taking money from certain sources, or using it for certain purposes. Although they were directed at candidates rather than parties *per se* (which the law did not explicitly recognize), the British Corrupt Practice Prevention Act of 1854 and the Corrupt and Illegal Practices Prevention Act of 1883 were early examples. Often these were supplemented by requirements of public disclosure of sources of income, objects of expenditure, or both. In recent decades, these regulatory regimes have in many countries been supplemented by programmes of state support for parties. Some of these take the form of 'tax expenditures' (by making contributions to parties eligible for tax deductions or credit, some of the cost of those contributions is effectively transferred to the state in the form of revenue that is foregone), while in other cases parties receive either partial reimbursement of expenses or subventions directly from the state, frequently accompanied by even more invasive regulations justified as monitoring the use of public money.

Regulation of spending

Regulation of party spending has been more-or-less synonymous with regulation of **campaign** spending—although, of course, parties spend money on many things that are at best indirectly related to campaigns (for example, social events that help cement member commitment but have no overt connection to a campaign). These regulations take three general forms: bans on particular forms of spending; limitations on total spending; required disclosure of spending.

Aside from bans on such obviously corrupt practices as vote buying or bribery, the most significant prohibition of a specific form of expenditure (more recently in some countries, this has been a limitation rather than a total ban) concerns the buying of advertising time on the broadcast media. Limitations on total spending generally are based on the size of the electorate and the type of office involved. Expenditure reports are frequently required, and provide some element of transparency, but differ widely among countries with regard to the categories of expenditure that are reported, the degree of detail (e.g. specific recipients or only category totals), the frequency and currency of reports, and the degree

to which reports are audited or otherwise subject to independent verification.

Beyond these questions of reporting, all forms of regulation of party spending confront a number of inter-related problems concerning exactly whose spending is to be controlled. Is it parties as organizations, or candidates as individuals, or everyone, including those without formal ties to either candidates or party organizations? To exclude parties (or to include national party organizations but not their local affiliates) is likely to make regulation nugatory, but to include them requires a level of official recognition that until recently was rare in countries with single-member district electoral systems. To include everyone may be seen as an unacceptable limitation on the political speech rights of citizens, but to include only formal party organizations and their candidates risks the explosion of spending by organizations (such as the American 527s in the 2004 presidential election)[7] that are simply the party in another, but now un- or less regulated guise.

Once party and campaign spending are equated, a further problem becomes the definition of the campaign. This involves two questions. First, when does the campaign begin? If the regulated campaign period is too short, its regulation may be of little consequence. Japan, for example, has a very short formal campaign period during which virtually everything is prohibited, but it is preceded by a real campaign subject to very little regulation. Second, what activity is campaign activity? As with the question of regulating non-party spending, an excessively broad definition of campaigning may subject all political speech to burdensome regulation, but an excessively narrow definition, such as the American 'magic words' doctrine (only messages containing words or phrases like 'vote for', 'elect', 'Smith for Congress', 'vote against', 'defeat', and referring to a specific candidate, count as campaigning) may defeat the purpose of the regulations.

Regulation of fundraising

Contribution limits are designed to prevent wealthy individuals or groups from exercising undue influence over parties (although, of course, the meaning of 'undue' often is in the eye of the beholder). In various places, foreigners, corporations (sometimes only public corporations or only firms in heavily regulated industries; in other cases all businesses), or trade unions are barred from making, and parties from accepting, political contributions. Anonymous contributions also are generally barred, perhaps from fear that the anonymity will be in name only.

Regardless of who is allowed to make contributions, there may also be limits on the size of contributions from an individual donor, either to an individual recipient, in aggregate, or both. Both kinds of limits are, however, relatively easy to evade: rather than making a corporate contribution, a corporation can 'bundle' (collect centrally and then deliver together) what appear to be individual donations from its officers or employees; an individual can give many times the individual legal limit by 'arranging' to have donations made in the name of his or her spouse, children, and other close relatives. Moreover, the definition of 'contribution' itself is problematic. Money is obvious, but should in-kind contributions be included (and how should they be valued)? What about the donation of services? And perhaps most vexing of all, if a person or group independently advocates the election of a party or candidate (what in the United States are called 'independent expenditures'), does that count as a contribution subject to limitation, or free speech that must be protected? Finally, whether or not contributions are restricted, their subversive (of democracy) effect may be limited by requirements of public disclosure.

Public subventions

A growing number of countries provide support for parties, through their tax systems, through the direct provision of goods and services, or through direct financial subventions. In some cases, these supports are specifically tied to election campaigns (or alternatively limited to non-campaign related research institutes) while in others they are unrestricted grants for general party activities (see Chapter 7).

The earliest and most common public subventions are the provision of staff to parliamentary parties or their members, ostensibly to support their official functions but often convertible to more general political purposes. Particularly in countries in

which broadcasting was a public monopoly, parties generally are given an allocation of free air time; other examples of free provision of services include the mailing of candidates' election addresses (e.g. UK), free space for billboards (e.g. Spain, Israel, and Germany), free use of halls in public buildings for rallies (e.g. UK, Spain, Japan), and reduced rates for office space (e.g. Italy). Although these raise some problems, the more contentious question was the direct provision of money, which is nonetheless becoming nearly universal.

Public support for parties raises two questions (beyond the somewhat specious question of whether people should be compelled through their taxes to subsidize causes with which they do not agree). First, is the primary effect of state subventions to allow parties better to perform their functions of policy formulation, public education, and linkage between society and the government? Or is it to further the separation between parties and those they are supposed to represent by making the parties less dependent on voluntary support? Second, do systems of public support (in which the levels of support are almost always tied to electoral support at the previous election),[8] as well as rules limiting individual contributions, further fairness and equality, or do they unfairly privilege those parties that already are dominant ('to those that have, more shall be given')?

KEY POINTS

- Party organizational types have evolved over time as suffrage was expanded and societies changed.
- Rather than reaching an end-point, organizations continue to evolve, and new types continue to develop.
- Party membership, and involvement of citizens in party politics more generally, appears to be declining virtually throughout the democratic world.
- Parties are increasingly the subject of legal regulation, which while justified in the name of fairness may also contribute to the entrenchment of the parties that currently are strong.

Parties and the stabilization of democracy

Parties were central to the transition from traditional monarchy to electoral democracy in the first wave of democratization (primarily in the late nineteenth and early twentieth centuries), but they have also been central actors in the third wave (see Chapter 5). In the older democracies, where the liberal rights of contestation were established before suffrage was expanded to the majority of citizens, parties helped to integrate newly enfranchised citizens into the established patterns of competition. While enfranchisement generally led to the rapid growth of parties (most often socialist) appealing specifically to the new voters, even what are now identified as 'bourgeois parties' found it in their interest to appeal to the new voters—for example as citizens, or Christians, or members of a peripheral culture rather than as workers.

In immigrant societies such as the US, Canada, Australia, or in South America, the parties also contributed to the integration of arrivals into their new country. The degree to which parties (and other institutions) could perform this function successfully was strongly influenced by the magnitude of the load placed upon them by the rapidity of suffrage expansion. Where the franchise was broadened in several steps spaced over decades, as in the United Kingdom, the existing parties generally were able to adapt, with the result that would-be demagogues or revolutionaries found a very limited market. When franchise expansion was more abrupt, as in France in 1848 or Italy in 1913, the twin dangers that masses of new voters would be mobilized by radicals and that this possibility would be perceived by others to be a threat requiring drastic measures often led to the collapse of democracy.

This function of integration and stabilization is also potentially important in the new democracies of the late twentieth century. Particularly in the formerly communist bloc (but not only there), the process of democratization has differed from that in the earlier waves in that political mobilization of the citizenry preceded the development of public contestation (Enyedi 2006: 228). Moreover, the levels of literacy, general education, access to mass media, and international involvement far exceed those of earlier waves. Coupled with this has been a deep distrust of the whole idea of political parties, rooted in the unhappy experience of the communist party state. Among the results have been extremely low rates of party membership (giving rise to the idea of a 'couch party'—one whose membership is so small that they could all sit on a single couch) and quite high electoral volatility.

Not only has the attachment of voters to particular parties been problematic, so too has the attachment of elected politicians, with parliamentary party groups (tellingly usually identified in Eastern and Central Europe as 'clubs') showing such low levels of stability that in some cases parliamentary rules have been changed specifically to discourage party splits or defections. Whether integration into the system of European Union party groups will bring some stability to this situation, and whether this weakness and fluidity of party systems will be detrimental to the performance or continuity of democracy in the region, remain to be seen.

A second major area in which the role of parties in stabilizing democracy is in doubt is the Islamic world, where the question is whether the electoral success of Islamist parties helps to integrate their followers into democratic politics, or alternatively threatens to undermine democracy altogether (Tepe 2006). The underlying conflict of values—the will of God as articulated by clerics versus the will of the people as articulated at the ballot box—is hardly unique to the Islamic world (and indeed was important throughout the nineteenth century in Europe), but now appears particularly pressing there.

One of the features of the late twentieth century has been the proliferation of international, national, and non-governmental democracy assistance agencies (e.g. the UN Electoral Assistance Division; the Center for Democracy and Governance of the USAID; the International Institute for Democracy and Electoral Assistance; see Chapter 25). Given the recognized centrality of parties to the stabilization of democratic regimes, not to mention the tendency simply to identify democracy with inter-party electoral competition, these agencies have seen the promotion and support of parties as part of their mandate.

While these agencies unsurprisingly only want to support 'democratic' parties, beyond an obvious distaste for parties that show disdain for civil liberties or threaten to suppress/oppress their opponents, there is some uncertainty regarding what a 'democratic' party is. Most particularly, however, this disagreement focuses on the question of internal party democracy: whether it is important that the party's members somehow elect the party's leaders and decide on, or at least ratify, its policy positions. Ironically, many of these agencies appear wedded to the mass party model of organization and democracy, even though they recognize that the social conditions that gave rise to that model in Europe are not found in the emerging democracies (and those same agencies would oppose those conditions if they were) and even though the standard of internal democracy they would like to apply in emerging democracies was not satisfied by many of the parties of the now-established democracies at the time that their democracies were emerging.

KEY POINTS

- ❑ Parties have played, and continue to play, a vital role in stabilizing democracy by integrating new citizens (whether new because they have come of age, immigrated, or benefited from expansion of the rights of citizenship) into the existing political system.
- ❑ Whether the electoral success of anti-democratic parties helps to moderate them and to integrate their followers into democracy, or instead serves to undermine democracy, is an unresolved but pressing issue.
- ❑ Whether a party can be internally oligarchic and yet also be an asset for system-level democracy remains a contentious issue, particularly for democracy-promoting agencies deciding which groups merit their support.

Conclusion

Political parties remain central to democratic government in the twenty-first century. It is still parties that contest elections and identify most of the candidates. It is still parties that structure the coalitions required to enact legislation and support governments. Nonetheless, parties face a number of potentially serious challenges.

As already suggested, party membership is declining almost everywhere (Mair and van Biezen 2001). One result has been to force parties to become more dependent on financial contributions and other forms of support (e.g. the 'loan' of labour or 'independent' campaign advertising) from corporations and organizations of special interests, and more recently to 'feed at the public trough' through direct public subventions. This decline in party involvement has not been limited to formal members, however, but is also reflected in declining party identification, and perhaps most significantly in the growth of hostility not just to the particular parties that happen to exist in a given country at a given time, but to the whole idea of parties and of partisanship. One manifestation of this is the growth of anti-party-system parties; another is the number of new parties that eschew the use of that word in their names and even of existing parties that try to 'rebrand' themselves without the party denomination (e.g. 'New Labour' instead of 'Labour Party').

The growing popularity of such ideas as 'consensus democracy' (Lijphart 1999) and 'deliberative democracy' (e.g. Guttmann and Thompson 2004; Budge 2000), like the complaint of former President Carter that the 2004 US presidential election campaign was 'too partisan', are reflective of a desire for amicable agreement that denies the existence of real conflicts of interest and opinion. But if one accepts Finer's (1970: 8) definition of politics as what happens when 'a given set of persons . . . require a *common* policy; and . . . its members advocate, for this common status, policies that are *mutually exclusive*', this is in effect to want to take the politics out of democracy.

Although rarely put overtly in these terms, the alternative to contentious and partisan politics is generally some form of government by experts or technocrats. Often these 'reforms' have been advocated and enacted by the parties themselves as a way of avoiding responsibility for unpopular but unavoidable decisions or for outcomes that are beyond their control. Even when the parties remain centrally involved in policy, increasingly their role (and the basis upon which they compete) is defined in terms of management rather than direction. By reducing the policy stakes of elections, however, the parties have also decreased the incentives for citizens to become active in the parties (Katz 2003) and given ammunition to those who ask why the state should provide subsidies and other special privileges (Mair 1995).

The role of parties as representatives of the people, or as links between the people and the state, has been challenged as well by the increasing range of interest organizations that compete with them as 'articulators of interest'. Rather than being forced to choose among a limited number of packages of policy stances across a range of issues—some of which may be of little interest, and others of which he or she may actually oppose—the modern citizen can mix-and-match among any number of groups, each of which will reflect his or her preferences more accurately on a single issue than any party could hope to do. With improved communications skills, and especially with the rise of the internet, citizens may feel less need for intermediaries at all; they can communicate directly with those in power themselves.

Many parties have themselves tried to adapt to more sophisticated electorates and to new technologies, giving rise to the possibility of 'cyber parties' (Margetts 2006; see also Chapter 19). In its initial stages, this may be little more than the use of mass e-mailings to 'members' (now of mailing lists rather than of real organizations) and the use of the mechanisms of e-commerce to facilitate fundraising from individuals. In a more developed form, it is likely to include chat-rooms and discussion list-servers. In theory, the technology might allow what would amount to a party meeting that is always in session. To date, however, there has been more evidence of people at the grass roots using the internet to send messages to those in positions of authority than there has been evidence of those in authority actually listening. And as with the party congresses of the last century, even if the internet (or simply the regular mail) is used to allow party members or supporters to make decisions, real power will continue to rest with those who frame the questions. It remains unlikely that the internet will somehow lead to the repeal of the Iron Law of Oligarchy.

Overall, then, there are two challenges facing parties at the beginning of the twenty-first century. One is the increasing complexity of problems, the increasing speed of social and economic developments, increasing globalization—all making the problems facing parties as governors less tractable. The other is the increasing political capacity of citizens (cognitive mobilization) running into the ineluctable limitations of individual influence in societies of the size of modern states—expectations of effective individual involvement, even if restricted to the minority who are politically interested, often are unrealistic. Both challenge widely held views of how democratic party government should work. How parties adapt to these changing circumstances, whether by redefining their roles or by altering public expectations, will shape the future of democracy.

? Questions

1. Is a group that nominates candidates in order to put pressure on other parties, but not with a real hope of winning an election itself, properly called a political party?

2. Is 'political party' better understood as a category, into which each case either does or does not fit, or as an ideal type, which each case can more or less closely approximate?

3. Is democracy conceivable without political parties?

4. What is the 'iron law of oligarchy'?

5. How do cartel parties differ from catch-all parties?

6. Does the United States have 'real' political parties?

7. Is the regulation of political parties' finance compatible with political freedom?

8. What is the meaning of 'left' in political terms?

9. Do political parties play the same role in new democracies as in the established democracies?

10. Must a democratic political party be internally democratic?

Further reading

Katz, Richard S., and Crotty, William (eds.) (2006) *Handbook of Party Politics* (London: Sage). Extensive discussions of many of the topics raised.

——and Mair, Peter (1992) *Party Organizations: A Data Handbook on Party Organizations in Western Democracies, 1960–90* (London: Sage). Extensive, but somewhat dated, data concerning party organizations.

Classics on political parties

Duverger, Maurice (1954) *Political Parties* (New York: John Wiley).

Hershey, Majorie R. (2006) *Party Politics in America* (New York: Longman, 12th edn).

LaPalombara, Joseph, and Weiner, Myron (eds.) (1966) *Political Parties and Political Development* (Princeton: Princeton University Press).

Panebianco, Angelo (1988) *Political Parties: Organization and Power* (Cambridge: Cambridge University Press).

Sartori, Giovanni (1976) *Parties and Party Systems: A Framework for Analysis* (Cambridge: Cambridge University Press).

Annual reports (from 1991) on party politics in most established democracies are available in the *Political Data Yearbook*, published as the last issue each year of the *European Journal of Political Research*. In addition, the *European Journal of Political Research, West European Politics,* and *Party Politics* focus heavily on issues concerning political parties.

Ⓦ Web links

www.electionresources.org
  Manuel Álvarez-Rivera's Election Resources in the Internet.

www.psr.keele.ac.uk
  Richard Kimber's website on Political Science Resources (University of Keele).

www.parties-and-elections.de
  Database of Parties and Elections about parliamentary elections, parties, and political leaders in Europe.

www.electionworld.org
  Website includes information on political parties around the world with up-to-date election results and other information on the party system and the main institutions.

www.gksoft.com/govt/en/parties.html
  Webpage of Government on the WWW devoted to political parties and party systems around the world. The main page includes additional information on heads of state, parliaments, executives, courts, and other institutions.

www.epicproject.org
  Website of the EPIC Project on election process information collection which includes also information on parties and party systems.

www.georgetown.edu/pdba
  Website of the Political Database of the Americas including information on parties and party systems.

http://dodgson.ucsd.edu/lij
  Website of the Lijphart Election Archive with information on party systems, electoral systems, and recent election results around the world.

www.cia.gov/cia/publications/factbook
  Website of CIA's the World Factbook with information on institutions, social structures, economic data, and party systems for most countries of the world.

www.idea.int
   Website of the International Institute for Democracy and Electoral Assistance (IDEA).

www2.essex.ac.uk/elect/database/aboutProject.asp
   Website of the project on Political Transformation and the Electoral Process in Post-Communist Europe
   (University of Essex).

www.eiu.com
   Country Reports and Country Profiles published by the Economist Intelligence Unit are very useful for an
   overview and recent data.

 Visit the Online Resource Centre that accompanies this book for more information:
www.oxfordtextbooks.co.uk/orc/caramani/

13 Party systems

Daniele Caramani

Chapter contents

Reader's guide

This chapter looks at the interactions between parties and how party competition leads to different types of party systems. First, the chapter looks at the *origins* of party systems. Historical cleavages between left and right, the liberal state and religious values or ethno-regional identities, agrarian and industrial sectors of the economy, led to socialist, liberal, religious, regionalist, and other party families. Why are these old party families still the main actors in our time? Second, the chapter looks at the *format* of party systems, some of which include two large parties (two-party systems) while others are more fragmented (multi-party systems). What is the influence of the electoral system, and what are the consequences for governmental stability? Third, the chapter analyses the *dynamics* of party systems. To maximize votes parties tailor their programmes to voters' preferences and converge towards the centre of the left–right axis. Is this why parties propose increasingly similar policies and programmes?

Introduction

This chapter views parties in their connections and relationships within a system. As in planet systems the focus is not on single planets but on the constellations they form: their number, the balance of size between them, and the distance that separates them. Parties can be ideologically near or distant, there are systems with many small parties or few large ones or even—to pursue the analogy further—one large party with 'satellites' (as in some authoritarian systems). Over time some systems change while others remain stable. The variety of party 'constellations' is thus very large.

Whereas the dynamic principle of planets is gravity, the motor of political interactions is competition for power. In liberal democracies this competition is based on popular votes. The shape and dynamics of party systems are determined by the electoral game in which parties are the main actors. A party system is therefore first and foremost the result of **competitive interactions** between parties. As in all games there is a goal: the maximization of votes to control government. In this sense, party systems are much more dynamic (changeable) than star systems. The set of interactions between parties, however, is not exclusively composed of competition, but also of **cooperation**. Parties, for example, cooperate when they build a coalition to support a government.

Three main elements of party systems are important:

1. **Which parties exist?** Why do some parties exist in all party systems (e.g. socialists) whereas others only in some (e.g. regionalists, agrarians, or confessional parties)? This relates to the origin, or genealogy, of party systems.

2. **How many parties exist and how big are they?** Why are some systems composed of two large parties and others of many small ones? This relates to the format, or morphology, of party systems.

3. **How do parties behave?** Why in some systems do parties converge towards the centre whereas in others they diverge to the extremes of the ideological 'space'? This relates to the dynamics of party system.

An obvious but important point is that party systems must be composed of several parties. There is no 'system' with one unit only. The competitive interaction between parties requires pluralism. If the goal is to get the most votes, there must be free elections, some degree of enfranchisement, and pluralism without which competition cannot exist. This chapter therefore focuses on democratic systems and excludes totalitarian or authoritarian regimes with single parties (such as China or Syria).

KEY POINTS

❑ Party systems are sets of parties that compete and cooperate with the aim of increasing their power in controlling government.

❑ What determines interactions is (1) which parties exist, (2) how many parties compose a system and how large they are, and (3) the way in which they maximize votes.

❑ It is appropriate to speak of a party system only in democratic contexts in which several parties compete for votes in open and plural elections.

The genealogy of party systems

The 'national' and 'industrial' revolutions

Most contemporary parties and party families originated from the radical socio-economic and political changes between the mid-nineteenth century and the first two decades of the twentieth. Lipset and Rokkan (1967) distinguish two aspects of this transformation: (1) the **Industrial Revolution** refers to changes produced by industrialization (a radical change of the economy) and urbanization (cities and new family structures); (2) the **National Revolution** refers to the formation of nation-states (culturally homogeneous and centralized political units), and liberal democracy (parliamentarism, individual civil and voting rights, equality, and secular institutions). These two sets of transformations caused unprecedented levels of social and political mobilization.

The Industrial and National Revolutions created socio-economic and cultural divisions opposing different social groups, elites, sets of values, and interests. Lipset and Rokkan name these conflicts cleavages (see Box: What is a cleavage?, in the Online Resource Centre). With the birth of modern parliaments and free elections, and with the progressive extension of franchise, political parties developed and reflected the socio-economic and cultural divisions created by the two 'revolutions'. Modern party families appeared as the 'political translation' of social divisions in systems in which conflict is increasingly settled through vote. Cleavages in modern states can be classified according to two dimensions:

- **territorial:** at one end are territorialized conflicts that oppose peripheral regions to the centre of the state (its elites and bureaucracy); at the opposite end are non-territorial conflicts between groups within the very centre of the state;
- **functional:** at one end are conflicts about resources and their (re)distribution between social groups (e.g. economic interests); at the opposite end are conflicts on moral principles (e.g. religious values).

Cleavages and their political translation

Lipset and Rokkan distinguish four main cleavages created by the two 'revolutions' (see Table 13.1). These revolutions have each produced two main cleavages. Subsequent transformations have produced additional cleavages, namely the 'International Revolution' triggered by the Soviet Revolution of 1917, and the 'Post-Industrial Revolution' in the 1960s–1970s, which led to a value cleavage between generations and globalization since the late 1990s.

In the transformation of the nineteenth century socio-economic and cultural conflicts emerged simultaneously with democratic reforms: the creation of modern parliaments, free competitive elections, and the extension of civil and political rights. Conflicts

of that time were expressed in organizations that were typical of this new regime. Political parties are the product of the parliamentary and electoral game, and party systems reflect the social oppositions that characterize society when parties first appear. The fundamental features of today's party systems were set during the early phases of mobilization of, at first, restricted electorates (only very few people had the right to vote when liberals and conservative dominated in the nineteenth century) and, later, of 'massifying' electorates when socialist parties mobilized the vast working class that emerged from the Industrial Revolution.

The National Revolution produced two cleavages.

Centre–periphery cleavage

This conflict emerged when nation-states formed and integrated in the nineteenth century, and political power, administrative structures, and taxation systems were centralized. It also brought about—sometimes artificially—national languages and the adoption of a national religion. Italy in 1860–70, Germany in 1870, Switzerland in 1848 unified as nation-states. Others formed through independence (Ireland in 1922 from the United Kingdom, Norway in 1906 from Sweden, Finland in 1907/17 from the Russian Empire). The new national territories were heterogeneous with different ethnicities and languages, and administration was fragmented. Nationalist and liberal elites carried out state formation and nation-building, facing resistance from subject populations in peripheral territories in two aspects.

1. **Administrative:** peripheries were increasingly incorporated in the bureaucratic and fiscal system of the new state (for example, with the creation of provinces or departments through which the central state controlled the territory of and extracted taxes), implying a loss of autonomy for regions.

2. **Cultural:** religious, ethnic, and linguistic identities in peripheral regions were replaced by the allegiance to the new nation-state fostered through compulsory schooling, military conscription, and other means of national socialization. As the first Italian prime minister said in 1870 after Italy unified, 'we have made Italy, let us make Italians'. Nation-building took place also in old established states. In France in 1863, according to official

Table 13.1 Stein Rokkan's cleavages and their partisan expression

Revolution	Timing	Cleavage	Divisive issue(s)	Party families	Examples
National	Early 19th century (restricted electorates)	Centre–periphery	Liberals and conservatives face resistance to state/administrative centralization and cultural standardization (language/religion).	Regionalists, ethnic parties, linguistic parties, minorities.	Scottish National Party, Bloc Québéquois, Partido Nacionalista Vasco.
		State–church	Conflict between liberal and secularized state against clerical and aristocratic privilege, and over religious education, influence of church in politics, democratic institutions.	Conservative and religious parties (Catholic mainly), Christian democracy.	Austrian People's Party, Christian-Democratic Union, Swiss Catholic Party, Partido Popular.
Industrial	Late 19th century (suffrage extension)	Rural–urban	Conflict between industrial and agricultural sectors of the economy on trade policies: agrarian protectionism vs. industrial liberalism (free trade vs. tariffs).	Agrarian and peasant parties.	Finnish Centre Party, Australian Country Party, Polish Peasant People's Party.
		Workers–employers	Employers vs. the rising working class on job security, pensions, social protection, degree of state intervention in economy.	Workers' parties, socialists and social democrats, labour parties.	British Labour Party, Argentinian Socialist Party, Swedish Social-Democratic Workers' Party, Spanish PSOE.

(continued)

Table 13.1 (*continued*)

Revolution	Timing	Cleavage	Divisive issue(s)	Party familes	Examples
International	Early 20th century (mass electorates)	Communists–socialists	Division within the 'left' (workers' movement) over centrality of the Soviet Union Communist Party and its international leadership, and over reformism vs. revolution.	Communists.	Partito Comunista Italiano, Izquierda Unida, Parti Communiste Français, Japan's Communist Party.
Post-industrial	Late 20th century (demobilized electorates)	Materialist–post-materialist values	Generational cleavage over policy priorities: new values of civic rights, pacifism, feminism, environment.	Green and ecologist parties.	Die Grünen, Austrian Grünen/Grüne Alternative, Democrats '66, Women's Party.
		Open–closed societies	Globalization of the economy, opening up of labour markets, competition from cheap Asian labour, fiscal and monetary integration in Europe, and anti-Americanization of culture.	Protest parties, nationalist parties, extreme right-wing parties, neo-populist parties.	FPÖ, Front National, Danish Progress Party, Fifth Republic Movement (Hugo Chávez), Movement for Socialism (Evo Morales).

figures, only 22 per cent of the communes spoke French, all located around the Paris region (Weber 1976: 67).

Resistance to administrative centralization and cultural standardization was expressed in regionalist parties such as the Scottish National Party, the Swedish Party in Finland, the various Basque and Catalan parties in Spain, the parties of the German- and French-speaking minorities in Italy, the Bloc Québéquois in Canada, and so on, opposing nationalist/liberal parties.

State–church cleavage

Nation-states in the nineteenth century were not only centralized and homogeneous, but also based on the liberal ideology promoting secular institutions (no church influence), individualism, and democracy (sometimes republicanism). Liberal reforms and the abolition of estates (clergy, aristocracy, bourgeoisie, peasantry) of pre-modern parliaments, as well as individual vote and free elections, put an end to clerical and aristocratic privilege. Liberals were opposed by conservatives who refused democracy and defended the monarchy. To a large extent, this was a conflict between the rising industrial bourgeoisie and the corporate privilege of clergy and aristocracy.

The new liberal secular state fought against the long-established role of the church in education. Compulsory education by the state was used to 'forge' **citizens** with new (non-religious) values. Especially in Catholic countries this led to strong conflicts, whereas in Protestant countries—where churches belong to the state—the cleavage focused on moral principles. The church was also expropriated of land and buildings and, in Italy, it lost its temporal power and state (about a fourth of the Italian peninsula) when Italy unified from the previous state mosaic in 1860–70.

The conflict characterized the opposition to liberals against the conservatives, who believed in a return to the old pre-democratic regime. In some countries, Catholics took the place of conservatives, as in Belgium, Switzerland, Germany. In other countries, Catholics were banned through papal decree from participating in the political life of the liberal nation-state (by being candidates, voting, or creating a party). For this reason Catholic parties did not appear in Italy and France until the early 1920s. In fact,

it was not until after the breakdown of democracy and the inter-war fascist period that the Catholic Church fully accepted democracy. 'Christian democracy'—in Italy, France, Germany, Austria—is the family that appears from this evolution after the Second World War.

An interesting case is that of countries with mixed religious structures. In the Netherlands there was one unified Catholic party and a number of Reformed and Calvinist parties reflecting the fragmentation of Protestantism. Religious parties merged in 1972 into the Christian Democratic Appeal. In Germany, too, an inter-confessional party developed (the Christian Democratic Union). In Switzerland a major Catholic party emerged from the opposition to the Protestant Radicals/Liberals.

The Industrial Revolution produced two additional cleavages.

Rural–urban cleavage

The first was the contrast between landed rural interests (agriculture) and the rising class of industrial and trading entrepreneurs. This cleavage focused on trade policies, with agrarians favouring trade barriers for the protection of agricultural products (protectionism) and industrialists favouring free market and trade liberalization with low tariffs (liberalism). This cleavage was reinforced by cultural differences between countryside and urban centres where industries concentrated. Cultural openness/closure added to the division between primary and secondary sections of the economy.

As a general rule, weak sectors of the economy tend to be protectionist because of the threat of imports, whereas strong sectors favour the opening up of economic borders which favour exports (Rogowski 1989). Agriculture was threatened by technological progress and acceleration of productivity. The defence of agrarian interests—when peasant populations received the right to vote—was expressed from the end of the nineteenth century through agrarian parties (also called peasants' or farmers' parties). Large or small agrarian parties existed everywhere in Europe but were particularly strong in Eastern Europe and in Scandinavia. They were also common in Latin America.

The period after the Second World War witnessed both the decline and transformation of these parties. On the one hand, in most countries peasants' parties disappeared. On the other, the large agrarian parties of the north and east abandoned the agrarian platform and changed into centre parties. The recent reawakening of this cleavage is most notable in Latin America where opposition to multi-national companies, defence of raw materials and resources, and the threat of globalization has led to protectionist policies (e.g. gas and oil nationalization in Bolivia and Venezuela). In the 1990s a number of upheavals of peasants took place in the Chapas region in Mexico. This cleavage is also present in the European Union where farmers' pressure groups lobby for protectionist trade agreements and for state subsidies.

Workers–employers cleavage

This is the cleavage between the industrial entrepreneurial bourgeoisie who started the Industrial Revolution and the working class that resulted from it. It is the opposition between 'capital' and 'labour' which, up to the present, characterizes the left–right alignment. In so far as this split is present in all countries, it is the most important one. Left–right is the most common ideological dimension along which parties are placed (even in the US where a socialist party never developed: see Box 13.1).

Industrialization had a very deep impact on Western societies. It radically changed the production mode, it caused unprecedented levels of geographical mobility through urbanization (the dislocation of people from countryside to urban industrial centres), it transformed family structures from extended to nuclear. Workers moved to new industrial centres where living conditions were extremely poor. They were therefore easy to mobilize through trade unions, with socialism providing a unifying ideology. With the extension of voting rights social democratic and labour parties gained parliamentary representation.

Socialist parties campaigned for labour protection against the capitalist economy. They promoted *social rights* and *welfare state* provisions on top of civil and political rights, and a substantial equalization of living conditions besides formal legal equality (Marshall 1950; Kitschelt 1994). These claims concerned under-age and female labour, wages, working hours, contract security, protection in the workplace and during periods of unemployment or illness, progressive taxation, abolition of heritage, accident insurance, pension schemes. Socialists favoured economic policies with a strong intervention of the state in steering the economy and public investments (later Keynesianism) against the liberal free-market ideology. They looked for state ownership of infrastructure (railways, energy), industries, and sometimes financial institutions.

Many socialist and labour parties originate from previously existing trade unions, the main organizations of the working class before universal suffrage. With restricted franchise most workers did not have the right to vote. The state was therefore controlled for most of the nineteenth century by liberals and conservatives who were able to impose their policies. Unions responded to a number of needs of the working class, increased solidarity and cooperation within it, and provided a wide range of 'services'. With enfranchisement, workers' parties developed as an 'electoral branch' of trade unions.

The Soviet Revolution of 1917 produced a cleavage within the workers' movement.

Communism–socialism cleavage

In the aftermath of the First World War and the Russian Revolution that led to the Soviet Union and the single-party regime controlled by the Communist Party, in all countries communist parties formed as splinters from the socialists. The main issue was the acceptance of the lead of the Soviet Communist Party in the international revolutionary movement and also ideological differences, namely whether a revolution would be necessary to take the proletariat to power, or if this goal would be achieved through electoral means.

As a reaction against the radicalization of the working class and its powerful action through a new type of mass party organization, fascist parties emerged in a number of European countries and, more or less directly, dominated government during the 1930s. These parties favoured the nation over class and 'internationalism', and private property against communism. Fascist parties were the product of the radicalization of the industrial upper bourgeoisie threatened by socialist policies, and of the aristocracy threatened by the redistribution of land and agrarian reforms.

BOX 13.1 Why is there no socialism in the US?

A number of classical studies have addressed this question. The main factors explaining the absence of a socialist ideology and workers' party in the the most advanced capitalist country are:

- *Open frontier*: geographical and social mobility gave American workers the possibility to move on in search of better conditions.

- *Party machines*: dominance of Democrats and Republicans in the nineteenth century made the rise of third parties difficult.

- *The free gift of the vote*: working-class white men all had the right to vote, were integrated in the political system, and had a say in government's actions.

- *Roast beef and apple pie*: the American working class was more affluent than the European and all socialist utopias come to grief with a satisfied working class.

- *No feudalism*: the absence of aristocracy in America made the working class very similar to the European bourgeoisie.

Read:

Lipset, S. M. (1977) 'Why No Socialism in the United States?', in S. Bialer and S. Sluzar (eds.), *Sources of Contemporary Radicalism* (Boulder, Colo.: Westview Press), 131–49.
—— and Marks, G. (2000) *It Didn't Happen Here: Why Socialism Failed in the United States* (New York: Norton).
Sombart, W. (1976) *Why is there No Socialism in the United States?* (London: Macmillan), translated from the German 1906 text.

Finally, the 'Post-Industrial Revolution' (Bell 1973) created two more recent cleavages.

Materialism–post-materialism cleavage

A cleavage between generations over sets of socio-political values emerged in the 1960s and 1970s as a consequence of the protracted period of international peace, economic wealth, and domestic security since the end of the Second World War (Inglehart 1977). The younger cohort developed 'post-materialist values' focused on tolerance, equality, participation, freedom of expression, respect for the environment, fair international trade, peace, Third World aid, as opposed to the 'materialist' values of the war generation centred around themes of national security, law and order, full employment, protection of private property, tradition, and authority (within the family and the state).

These new values were primarily expressed in a number of new social movements (see Chapter 16): the civil rights movement in the US in the 1950s, pacifism from the Vietnam War in the 1960s, feminism in the 1970s claiming equality in the labour market and family, environmentalism in the 1980s. In the 1990s, new anti-globalization movements developed against the globalization of the economy and the Americanization of culture (Della Porta *et al.* 1999). From a party politics perspective, however, there are only a few examples of a significant impact of these 'new left' movements, the main being green parties (Müller-Rommel and Poguntke 2002). A more pervasive impact of the Post-Industrial Revolution is on the 'new right'.

The globalization cleavage

Economic globalization has created a further post-industrial cleavage between sectors of the economy that profit from the blurring of economic boundaries, and sectors that are negatively affected by the competition from new markets and cheap labour from the East and Asia. 'Losers' in globalization and—in the European Union—integration (Betz 1994) have reinforced support for neo-populist protest parties who favour trade barriers to protect local manufacture and 'locals-first' policies in the labour market. These groups are the small and medium enterprises, unskilled workers, craftsmen, and agricultural producers.

The economic defensive attitude of these groups is reinforced by cultural, anti-immigration, and xenophobic prejudice stressing religious and national values against multi-ethnic society and cosmopolitanism. Many of these parties rely upon an extreme right-wing heritage, such as the Austrian Liberal Party, the French and Belgian National Fronts, the Italian National Alliance (Kitschelt 1995). Others are more sporadic parties, such as the One-Nation Party in Australia. In Latin America neo-populist tendencies have a left-wing 'Bolivarian' character as the movements led by Morales in Paraguay and Chavez in Venezuela (Burgess and Levitsky 2003). Neo-populism is also a reaction to changing security conditions which—since the terrorist attacks in the early 2000s—have created a resurgence of materialist values, the need for internal police and external control.

Variations in cleavage constellations

Cleavage constellations change through space (from country to country) and over time.

Space

Not all cleavages exist in all countries. There is a variety of constellations, and thus of party systems. Why do some cleavages exist in specific countries while not in others? It is difficult to summarize the explicative part of the Lipset–Rokkan's model here. Whereas the left–right cleavage exists everywhere and is a source of similarity, the state–church cleavage developed especially in Catholic countries in Europe and Latin America. The rural–urban cleavage was strong in regions with small farming and independent units, where farmers were not under the control of landlords. The centre–periphery cleavage appears where there are ethno-linguistic minorities.

Country-specific cleavage constellations are therefore determined by:

- differences in objective factors such as diverse social structures: multiple ethnicities or religious groups, structure of the peasantry, class relations;
- the extent to which socio-economic and cultural divisions have been politicized by parties, that is, by the action of elites (Rose 1974; Lijphart 1968*b*);
- the relationship between cleavages: their existence and strength can prevent the development of new ones (agrarian claims have been incorporated by Catholic parties or by conservative parties where, like in England, agriculture had been commercialized early).

Generally, two types of constellations are distinguished: (1) **homogeneous constellations** where there is one predominant cleavage, namely the left–right cleavage on the distribution of resources between classes (for example, Britain), and

(2) **heterogeneous constellations** in which various cleavages—economic, ethno-linguistic, religious, territorial—overlap or cut across one other in plural democracies such as Belgium, Canada, India, the Netherlands, Switzerland (Lijphart 1984).

Time

Lipset and Rokkan do not take into account developments that took place after the 1920s as, over time, cleavage constellations and party systems have remained extraordinarily stable. Up to the present even party labels have not changed (liberal, socialist, conservative), as a sort of political *imprint* that crystallized. Lipset and Rokkan have formulated the so-called freezing hypothesis:

> [T]he party systems of the 1960s reflect, with few but significant exceptions, the cleavage structures of the 1920s ... [T]he party alternatives, and in remarkably many cases, the party organizations, are older than the majorities of the national electorates. (1967: 50; italics omitted)

Today's party systems reflect the original conflicts from which they emerged (see Box: Party families, in the Online Resource Centre) in spite of a decline in cleavage politics with the blurring of social divisions (Franklin 1992). In the 1920s the full mobilization of the electoral market through universal suffrage and PR caused its saturation. With the extension of suffrage citizens were incorporated in the political system. Voters acquired strong political identities through partisan identification and socialization processes that proved stable over time. As in all markets, in the electoral market too there are entry barriers. Little room was left for new parties. Existing parties were thus able to maintain their control over electorates through the generations.

Empirical research has confirmed the basic stability of electoral patterns over time, rejecting the thesis of increasing *dealignment and realignment* of Western electorates (Dalton *et al.* 1985). Rose and Urwin (1970) and, in a long-term perspective, Bartolini and Mair (1990) have analysed trends of electoral volatility (the change of votes from one election to the next) from 1885 to 1985. First, they found that general levels of volatility are stable supporting the freezing hypothesis. Second, they found that volatility between left and right declines, confirming the stabilizing of ideological identities. Third, however, they found that volatility within the left and within the right increases which means that, whereas left and right identities persist, the identification with a specific party declines (see also Kriesi 1998). Therefore, in spite of secularization and post-industrial economies—and in spite of some degree

of change within Western electorates—a dramatic realignment along new cleavages does not seem to have taken place, maintaining the validity of the freezing hypothesis.

KEY POINTS

- Modern party families originate from socio-economic and cultural cleavages created by industrialization, urbanization, and the formation of centralized liberal states.
- The centralized and democratic liberal state creates conflicts with the church and with peripheral regions, leading to religious and regionalist parties. Industrialization opposes liberal economic interests to the rural world as well as to the working class, leading to agrarian and labour parties. Parties of the working class divide in the 1920s into communist and social democratic parties.

- The introduction of universal suffrage and PR after the First World War 'freezes' the party constellations that remain stable until the present. After the Second World War the end of the state–church conflict leads to the emergence of Christian democracy.
- The most significant examples of realignment in recent time are the generational cleavage over (post-)materialist values and the economic changes triggered by globalization that led to new party families: the greens and the neo-populist parties.

The morphology of party systems

An important element of the competitive interaction between parties is the shape of party systems (sometimes called format). The two main elements of the morphology of party systems are: (1) the *number* of competing units, that is, parties, and (2) the *size* of these units. How many are the players and how strong are they? The number and strength of actors can be observed at two levels: the **votes** parties get in elections and the **seats** in parliament. A 'variable' that must be considered is therefore the electoral system through which votes are translated into parliamentary seats.

It is important to distinguish *types* of party systems. Two types of party systems are not considered in this section because they do not fulfil the democratic conditions that allow competition:

1. Single-party systems in which one party only is legal: these are the totalitarian and authoritarian experiences of the Communist Party in the Soviet Union, the Nationalist-Socialist Party in Germany in the 1930s, or the Baathist Party in Iraq until 1993 and in Syria.
2. Hegemonic-party systems in which other parties are legal but are 'satellites', under the strict control

of the hegemonic party with whom they cannot compete to control government: these are also totalitarian or authoritarian systems existing in Egypt or Algeria today, and in many former communist regimes before 1989 in Central and Eastern Europe.

The other four types are: (1) dominant-party system, (2) two-party system, (3) multi-party system, and (4) bipolar system.

Dominant-party systems

Dominant-party systems are characterized by one very large party that dominates all others with a *large majority* (well above the absolute majority of 50 per cent of parliamentary seats) over *protracted periods of time* (several decades). In these systems all parties are legal and allowed to compete in free elections with universal suffrage to challenge the dominant party. However, no other party receives enough votes to come close to 50 per cent. Electors vote massively for the dominant party. There is therefore no alternation in power and the dominant party does not need to build coalitions to form a government. In dominant-party systems it is in fact irrelevant how many other parties exist.

An example of a dominant-party system is India between 1947 and 1975. After Independence and the end of colonial rule the Congress Party received electoral support above 50 per cent and was able to rule unchallenged until 1975–77 when the 'state of emergency' was declared. Over the long period of uncontested rule forms of patronage developed and in 1977 the Congress Party was eventually defeated. A more recent example of a dominant-party system is South Africa since the end of apartheid in the early 1990s. The African National Congress, initially led by Nelson Mandela, has been able to secure the absolute majority of the votes because of the role it had in enfranchising the black population. In Europe a case of a dominant-party system is Sweden. The Social Democratic Workers' Party formed almost all governments from 1945 until 1998, with around 45 per cent of the votes on average. Only in a few cases did it have to form a minority government or rely on small coalition partners such as the formerly communist Left Party. In Mexico, the Institutional Revolutionary Party was in power from the revolution of 1917 until the 2000 election when it was defeated for the first time.

Between 1946 and 1994 the Italian Christian Democracy was uninterrupted in power. However, only until 1953 did this party receive an absolute majority of the seats and was able to form a single-party government. After 1953 it relied on small coalition partners. A similar case is the Liberal Democratic Party in Japan between 1953 and 1993. Factions developed within both parties and, because of the lack of alternation, they became less responsive to the demands from the electorate with forms of patronage (Shiratori 2004: 105).

Two-party systems

A two-party system is one in which two fairly equally balanced large parties dominate the party system and alternate in power. The two parties have comparable sizes and equal chances of winning elections. Even a small amount of votes changing from one party to the other (electoral swing) can cause a change of majority. Alternation in power is therefore frequent. These are very competitive systems. Because both parties are large, the winning party is likely to receive

the absolute majority of seats and form single-party governments without the need for partners.

The features of two-party systems are those listed in Table 13.2. The two large parties have similar sizes around 35–45 per cent of the votes each, that plurality electoral systems transform in absolute majorities of seats for the largest party. This does not mean that these are the only parties. A number of other smaller parties compete in the elections. However, they are marginal as they are not necessary to form a government. In the United Kingdom, the Liberal Democratic Party, Scottish National Party and Plaid Cymru (the Welsh national party), and various parties in Ulster compete but do not have a strong impact on the party system.

In two-party systems single-party governments tend to alternate from one legislature to the next. This is, to a large extent, an effect of plurality electoral systems. Because the threshold in first-past-the-post (FPTP) systems is very high, the two main parties have a majoritarian vocation. Parties propose policies and programmes that are acceptable to a large part of society. Plurality leads to ideological moderation and similarity of programmes. In turn, this similarity makes it easier for voters to switch from one party to the other and creates alternation.

There are not many cases of two-party systems. These systems are typical of the Anglo-Saxon world where—unlike continental Europe where around the First World War all countries changed from majoritarian to PR electoral systems—plurality in single-member districts has been maintained. In addition, the trend seems to be declining. Only the US provides today a 'perfect' example of a two-party system where Republicans and Democrats have dominated since 1860.[1] Australia maintains a strong two-party system with the Australian Labour Party and the Liberals. In Great Britain the Conservatives and the Labour Party have been increasingly challenged by 'third' parties like the Liberal Democratic Party. Other examples include Costa Rica (National Liberation Party and Citizens' Action Party) and Malta (where the Labour Party and the Nationalist Party receive together close to 100 per cent of the votes). In Canada Conservatives and Liberals dominated until 1993 (with a strong New Democratic Party), since when the Bloc Québéquois and the Reform Party have been increasing their support.

Table 13.2 Types of party systems in democracies

Type of party system	Features	Cases
Dominant-party	One large party with more than absolute majority of votes and seats. No other party approaching 50%. No alternation. One-party government.	India until 1975, Japan between 1955 and 1993, Mexico until 2000, South Africa since 1994.
Two-party	Two large parties sharing together around 80% of votes and seats. Balanced (35–45% each) with one of the two reaching 50% of seats. Alternation between parties. One-party government.	Austria, Britain, Costa Rica, Malta, New Zealand until 1998, Spain, South Africa until 1989, US.
Multi-party	Several or many parties, no one approaching 50% of votes and seats. Parties of different sizes. Parties run for elections individually and form coalitions after elections. Alternation through coalition changes. Coalition government.	Belgium, Canada, Colombia, Czech Republic, Denmark, Finland, Germany until 1989, Hungary, Italy before 1994, Netherlands, Poland, Russia, Switzerland, Turkey.
Bipolar	Two large coalitions composed of several parties sharing together around 80% of votes and seats. Coalitions are balanced (40–50% each). Coalitions are stable over time and run elections as electoral alliances. Alternation between coalitions. Coalition government.	France in the Fifth Republic, Germany since 1990, Italy since 1994, Portugal.

Two-party systems can be found also in countries with PR electoral systems. Austria since the Second World War has been dominated by two parties—the Austrian People's Party and Austrian Socialist Party—receiving around 40 per cent of the votes and seats each, and able to form single-party governments in many legislatures. In addition, alternation has taken place frequently. After the transition from Franco's regime to democracy in 1977, the party system of Spain moved towards a two-party system. In spite of many (but small) regionalist parties, the party system in Spain presents two large parties

of a similar size: the Spanish Socialist Workers' Party and the People's Party.

For years Germany came close to a two-party system and was named a 'two-and-a-half party system' with two large parties collecting together more than 80 per cent of the votes (the Christian-Democratic Union and the Social Democratic Party) and a smaller Liberal Party party (around 5 per cent) with a pivotal position and able to decide—through alliance—which of the larger parties would be in charge of government. With the rise of the Greens the system turned towards a bipolar system. Israel has used a

PR electoral system since the creation of the state in 1948. Yet until the end of the 1990s the system was structured around two main parties: the Likud and the Labour Party.

Multi-party systems

Multi-party systems are the most frequent type of party system. In the majority of countries multi-party systems exist. This is also the most complex type of party system. In a multi-party system the number of parties ranges from three to double-digit figures. Three to five parties exist in Canada, Ireland, Japan, and Norway. Party systems in which the number of parties approaches ten (or even more) are Belgium, the Netherlands, and Switzerland. None of the parties in a multi-party system is majoritarian (with 50 per cent of the votes or seats). Furthermore, the parties that compose a multi-party system are of different sizes: some are large (say, 30 per cent of the votes) some small (less than 5 per cent).

Because in multi-party systems no single party has an overall majority the result is that parties must form coalitions in order to support a government. In parliamentary systems (see Chapters 5 and 7) the vote of confidence requires a 50 per cent majority of seats. Parties run individually in elections (contrary to bipolar systems) and governmental coalitions are negotiated after the results are in.

Unlike plurality in single-member constituencies, PR does not hinder small parties from addressing small segments of the electorate, sometimes through extreme ideologies and programmes. PR therefore does not lead to ideological moderation which, in turn, makes it more difficult for voters to switch from one party to the other and cause a government change. In addition, PR does not provide the 'amplification' effect of electoral swings as does plurality. As a consequence, government change rarely takes place through electoral change but rather by swaps of coalition partners.

While multi-party systems are considered to represent better socio-political pluralism in countries with religious, regional, and ethno-linguistic cleavages, their negative aspects have been at the forefront since the Second World War. Multi-party systems were held responsible for instability, frequent coalition 'crises', and poor responsiveness, with no single party clearly accountable. Classical political scientists such as Finer (1932), Hermens (1941), Duverger (1954), and Almond (1956) blamed PR and multi-party systems for the lack of ideological moderation in the 1920s and 1930s which eventually led to the breakdown of democracy in most continental European countries.

Positive aspects of PR and multi-party systems have been stressed since analysis in the 1960s and 1970s including small countries such as Belgium, the Netherlands, Switzerland, and the Scandinavian countries. Studies on 'consensus democracies' showed that multi-party systems are stable, functioning, and peaceful. In plural societies PR and multi-party systems are the only viable ways to involve minorities in decision-making processes and reach consensus.[2] As Chapter 5 shows, consociational or consensus democracies represent a different model of democracy from the majoritarian or 'Westminster' model. Both have advantages and disadvantages (see Box 13.2).

The way in which multi-party systems function largely depends on the degree to which parties are ideologically polarized. Sartori (1976) has distinguished two main types of multi-party systems.

Moderate multi-party systems

The logic is similar to that of two-party systems. First, the number of parties is limited (below five) and, second, the direction of the competition is centripetal, that is, the main parties tend to converge toward the centre of the left–right scale to attract the support of the moderate electorate. At the centre are one or more small parties with whom the two big ones on either side may form a coalition. The role of these small parties is 'pivotal' in that they can decide whether the coalition is going to be centre-left or centre-right. The ideological distance between parties is limited so that all coalitions are possible. This type of party system is named 'moderate' because of the absence of extreme parties.[3]

BOX 13.2 A normative debate: advantages and disadvantages of party systems

Two-party systems	Multi-party systems
Historically positive connotation Two-party systems are the main cases that resisted the breakdown of democracy between First and Second World Wars: Britain and US.	*Historically negative connotation* After the First World War in Italy, Weimar Germany, Spanish Second Republic, and in the French Fourth Republic (1946–56) instability led to crisis of democracy.
Effective Produces governments immediately after elections. Governments are stable because they are formed by a single party.	*Ineffective* Governments take long to form after elections because of negotiations between parties. Coalitions lead to unstable governments.
Accountable Because there is only one party in government responsibility is clearly identifiable by the electorate.	*Non-accountable* Because governments are formed by many parties responsibility is obfuscated.
Alternation Two main parties alternate in power. Voters influence directly the formation of goverment: a small shift can cause government change.	*No alternation* Coalition negotiations are out of the reach of voters' influence and shift of votes are not necessarily followed by changes of government.
Non-representative FPTP under-represents minorities and over-represents large mainstream parties of left–right.	*Representative* PR fairly represents minorities in societies with ethno-linguistic and religious minorities.
Moderate politics All main parties have a chance to govern and thus avoid extreme claims. Need to gather votes from large moderate segments of the electorate.	*Extreme politics* Multi-party systems allow representation of extreme (anti-system) parties. Some do not have any government prospect and do not hesitate to radicalize their claims.
Discontinuity Decisions are made by majority with a clear strategy but there can be discontinuity between subsequent goverments. Legislation is often reversed.	*Continuity* Decisions are made by consensus through consultation. More difficult to find a clear strategy but more continuity in legislation.

Polarized multi-party systems

There are three main features in polarized systems.

1. **Polarization.** There is a large ideological distance between parties with a strong dose of dogmatic radicalism. Extreme *anti-system parties* aim not only to change government but also the *system of* government (the regime). These parties do not share the principles of the political system and aim to change its institutions (Capoccia 2002). Given the ideological distance between parties not all coalitions are viable. Some parties are continuously excluded. Such parties know they are in constant opposition, become irresponsible, and radicalize their discourse with promises they cannot maintain (and know that they will never be called to put into practice).

2. **An occupied centre.** There is one main party placed at the centre of the left–right axis which represents the 'system' against which extreme anti-system parties are opposed. The centre party is always in power and becomes also irresponsible and unaccountable. This party is not punished electorally because of the absence of viable alternatives.

3. **Centrifugal competition.** The occupation of the centre discourages a centripetal move on the part of other parties because, ideologically, the centre is already occupied. As a consequence, there is divergence. The competition is centrifugal and accentuated by a bilateral opposition on both sides of the centre.

Examples of polarized multi-party systems are the Weimar Republic in Germany, from 1919 until 1933, and Italy between 1946 and 1992. Italy in particular has often been taken as an ideal type. A strong centre party, Christian Democracy, was opposed on both sides by unreformed anti-system parties: the Italian Communist Party and Italian Social Movement (a post-fascist party). Coalitions between Christian Democracy and either anti-system parties were not viable and Christian Democracy ruled uninterrupted until 1992, although the Communists had a large share of votes (35 per cent).

Bipolar systems

Bipolar party systems combine elements of both multi- and two-party systems. As in multi-party systems there are many parties, none of which has a majority. And, again, coalition governments are the rule. However, coalitions—rather than single parties—are the important players. These form before elections and run as electoral alliances. They remain stable over time. There are usually two large ones of evenly balanced size alternating in power. Competition therefore resembles that of two-party systems.

In France left and right have alternated in power since 1958.[4] The left includes Socialists, Radicals, Communists, and Greens, whereas the right includes Gaullists and Liberals (they merged in 2003 as the Union for a Popular Movement). In Italy since 1994

the centre-left coalition is composed of Social Democrats, Communists, Greens, and Catholics, whereas the centre-right coalition is of Silvio Berlusconi's Forza Italia, the Northern League, a Catholic and the post-fascist party. The coalitions have alternated in power in 1996, 2001, and 2006. In Germany, finally, two coalitions oppose each other: Social Democrats and Greens on the one hand, Christian-Democratic Union, Christian-Social Union, and Liberals on the other.

The number of parties

So the number of parties is important, but how, exactly, should parties be *counted*? If all parties that run in an election are counted (or even only those that get some votes) their number would be extremely large and useless in building a typology. In every election there are dozens of parties and candidates that do not get any votes or very few. It is therefore necessary to have reasonable rules to decide whether a party is 'relevant' or not, and counted or not. There are two ways to count parties: (1) *numerical* with indices based on the *size* of parties; (2) *qualitative* with rules based on the *role* of parties in the system.

Numerical rules

These rules represent quantitative attempts to classify party systems on the basis of the number and size of parties that compose them. Various indices have been devised to summarize this basic information: are there many small parties (a *fragmented* party system) or few large parties (a *concentrated* party system)?

The most straightforward way of counting is obviously done by deciding to include all parties above a given threshold (say, 1 per cent). This method, however, has many problems, namely parties with 2 and 49 per cent are counted one-to-one. Similar methods include Rokkan's method (1968) to classify party systems through an index based on the distance of the largest party from the 50 per cent absolute majority, the distance of the second party from the first, and so on. Lijphart (1968b) devised an index based on the sum of parties' percentages in decreasing order until 50 per cent is reached: the larger the number of parties needed to reach the absolute majority, the more fragmented the party system.

COUNTRY PROFILE Italy

Italian Republic (*Repubblica Italiana*)

State formation

The Kingdom of Italy was proclaimed in 1861; Italy was finally unified in 1870. The monarchy was abolished by a popular referendum in 1946.
Constitution 1947, effective 1 January 1948; amended many times.

Form of government

Parliamentary republic.
Head of state President elected by an electoral college consisting of both houses of Parliament and 58 regional representatives, term of 7 years (no term limit).
Head of government President of the Council of Ministers, appointed by the President and confirmed by Parliament.
Cabinet Council of Ministers, nominated by the Prime Minister and approved by the President.
Administrative subdivisions 15 regions and 5 autonomous regions.

Legal system

Civil law system; judicial review under certain conditions in Constitutional Court.

Legislature

Bicameral Parliament.
Lower house Chamber of Deputies (*Camera dei Deputati*): 630 seats, the winning national coalition receiving 54 per cent of them; term of 5 years.

Upper house Senate (*Senato*): 315 seats, the winning coalition in each region receiving 55 per cent of that region's seats.

Electoral system (lower house)

Proportional representation.
Formula If the political coalition or party with the highest number of votes fails to win 340 seats, it is given 'bonus' seats to meet the 340-seat requirement. The 277 remaining seats are distributed among the other coalitions or lists using the whole number quotient and highest remainders method.
Constituencies 26 multi-member constituencies for 617 seats, 1 single-member constituency and 1 multi-member constituency for Italians abroad.
Barrier clause 10 per cent nation-wide for a coalition, 2 per cent for a party within a coalition, 4 per cent for an independent party; for language minority lists, 20 per cent of the votes cast in their constituency. A list obtaining the highest number of votes among all lists and which fails to win 2 per cent of the votes cast is also entitled to a seat.
Suffrage Universal, 18 years (25 in senatorial elections).

Direct democracy

A consultative referendum can be called by Parliament, and an abrogative referendum (with a quorum of participation of 50 per cent) can be called by 500,000 citizens or 5 Regional Councils. An optional constitutional referendum has never been practised.

Party system Results of the 2006 legislative elections (Chamber of Deputies):

Electorate:	47, 160, 264	100.0%
Voters:	39, 425, 981	83.6%

Party		Valid votes	%	Seats
The Union	Olive Tree	11, 928, 362	31.2	220
	Communist Refoundation	2, 229, 604	5.8	41
	Rose in the Feast	991, 049	2.6	18
	Italy of Values	877, 159	2.3	16
	Party of Italian Communists	884, 912	2.3	16
	Federation of the Greens	783, 944	2.1	15
	Populars (UDEUR)	534, 553	1.4	10
	South Tyrolean People's Party	182, 703	0.5	4
	Autonomy (Vallée d'Aoste)	34, 167	0.1	1
	Others	590, 533	1.5	0
	Total 'The Union'	19, 036, 986	49.8	348

(continued)

COUNTRY PROFILE Italy (*continued*)

Party		Valid votes	%	Seats
House of Freedom	Go Italy	9,045,384	23.7	137
	National Alliance	4,706,654	12.3	71
	Union of Christian and Centre Democrats	2,582,233	6.8	39
	Northern League	1,749,632	4.6	26
	Christian Democracy-New Socialists	285,744	0.7	4
	Others	626,050	1.6	0
	Total 'House of Freedom'	18,995,697	49.7	281
Others		197,381	0.5	1
Total		38,230,064	100.0	630

Source: Ministry of Interior.

The most used indices are Rae's **fractionalization index** (Rae 1971) and the **effective number of parties** (Laakso and Taagepera 1979). The fractionalization index (F) varies from 0 (full concentration of seats or votes in one party) to 1 (total fragmentation with each seat or vote going to a different party). The effective number of parties (E) indicates the number of parties in a system and does not have an upper limit.

The two formulas are the following:

$$F = 1 - \Sigma p_i^2 \qquad E = 1/\Sigma p_i^2$$

where p is the percentage of votes or seats for party i and Σ represents the sum for all parties. The percentages for all parties are squared to weight parties through their size. If there are two parties A and B, receiving each 50 per cent of the seats, one calculates first the square for party A (.50 × .50 = .25) and for party B (.50 × .50 = .25) and then adds them together (.25 + .25 = .50). Thus:

$$F = 1 - .50 = .50 \qquad E = 1/.50 = 2$$

In this example, F is exactly between 0 and 1 (.50) and E counts perfectly that there are two parties only. In the real world, the distribution of power among parties is obviously more complex.

Table 13.3 lists the effective number of parties (based on seat distributions) in a number of countries for recent elections.[5] As one can see there is a great variation between countries. The less fragmented countries are those using plurality/majoritarian or

transferable vote systems in single-member districts (Australia, France, Great Britain, Hungary, Malta, the US), whereas the most fragmented countries are those with PR and many religious and ethno-linguistic parties (such as Belgium, Finland, the Netherlands, New Zealand, Norway, Switzerland).

Table 13.3 Rae's parliamentary fractionalization index (F), effective number of parliamentary parties (E), and Gallagher's index of disproportionality (LSq)

Country	Election	F	E	LSq
Australia	2004	.60	2.4	8.7
Austria	2002	.65	2.9	1.6
Argentina	2005	.81	5.3	13.5
Belgium	2003	.86	7.0	5.9
Brazil	2002	.88	8.5	3.7
Canada	2006	.69	3.2	8.7
Chile	2005	.82	5.6	6.8
Czech Republic	2006	.68	3.1	6.3
Finland	2003	.80	4.9	3.5
France	2002	.55	2.2	22.2

(*continued*)

Table 13.3 (*continued*)

Country	Election	F	E	LSq
Germany	2005	.75	4.1	3.3
Greece	2004	.54	2.2	7.4
Hungary	2006	.58	2.4	4.4
India	2004	.86	7.1	3.9
Ireland	2002	.70	3.3	6.6
Israel	2006	.87	7.8	3.2
Italy	2006	.81	5.1	3.5
Japan	2005	.56	2.3	19.0
Malta	2003	.50	2.0	1.8
Mexico	2006	.67	3.0	6.4
Netherlands	2003	.79	4.8	1.4
New Zealand	2005	.66	3.0	1.4
Norway	2005	.78	4.6	2.9
Poland	2005	.77	4.3	9.8
Portugal	2005	.61	2.6	5.9
Russia	2003	.70	3.4	10.7
Spain	2004	.58	2.4	7.3
Sweden	2002	.76	4.2	2.5
Switzerland	2003	.80	5.0	2.4
Turkey	2002	.46	1.9	27.4
United Kingdom	2005	.59	2.5	16.8
United States	2004	.50	2.0	3.9
Mean		.69	3.9	7.3

Notes: For calculations parties rather than alliances have been considered (France, Chile, Italy). Seat figures always based on final allocation. For mixed electoral systems, PR votes have been taken (Japan, Mexico, Hungary). For Germany *Zweitstimmen* have been used and in France first-ballot figures for votes. As a general rule for including parties in the calculation, all parties polling at least 1%, or securing at least one seat, have been taken into account.
Source: Author's calculations based on results in 'Country Profiles' (see also the Online Resource Centre).

Qualitative rules

In many cases it is not appropriate to consider numerical criteria only to decide whether or not a party is relevant. Often small parties—that quantitative rules would not count—have far-reaching consequences for coalitions, influencing important decisions, mobilizing people in demonstrations, and so on. In many cases, small parties are much more important than their sheer size would suggest. Sartori (1976) has developed two criteria—or rules—to decide which parties really 'count' and should be 'counted':

1. **Coalition potential:** a small party is irrelevant if over a period of time it is not necessary for any type of governmental coalition. On the contrary, a party must be counted if, disregarding its size, it is pivotal and determines whether or not a coalition is going to exist and which.

2. **Blackmail potential:** a small party must be considered relevant when it is able to exercise pressure on governmental decisions through threats or veto power and by doing so alter the direction of competition.

The influence of electoral laws on the format of party systems

Given the impact of party system fragmentation on government stability, accountability, and responsiveness, as well as on the type of consensus vs. majoritarian decision-making, a large amount of comparative politics has been concerned with establishing the causes for varying numbers of parties and their size. Two sets of causes have been identified: (1) the electoral system and (2) the number of cleavages in the society.

Electoral systems

Electoral systems are mechanisms for the translation of votes into parliamentary seats. Chapter 10 shows that there are two main 'families' of electoral systems: (1) majoritarian systems in single-member constituencies; (2) PR systems in multi-member constituencies. The first and best-known formulation of the causal relationship between electoral and party systems is Duverger's Laws from his classic book *Les Partis Politiques* (1951, translated in 1954). As can

---

BOX 13.3 The influence of electoral systems on party systems

Duverger's 'laws' (1954)

First Law

'The majority [plurality] single-ballot system tends to party dualism'.

Second Law

'The second ballot [majority] system or proportional representation tend to multipartyism'.

Mechanical effects

Electoral systems with high thresholds of representation (first-past-the-post) exclude small parties from parliament whereas PR allows small parties to win seats.

Psychological effects

Under plurality systems voters vote strategically avoiding small parties; parties have an incentive to merge to pass high thresholds of representation; under PR voters vote sincerely for small parties which are not penalized and have no incentive to merge.

Rae/Riker's 'proposition' (1971, 1982)

'Plurality formulae are always associated with two-party competition exept where strong local minority parties exist'.

Sartori's 'tendency laws' (1986)

Law 1

'Given systemic structuring and cross-constituency dispersion (as joint necessary conditions), plurality systems cause (are a sufficient condition of) a two-party format'.

Law 2

'PR formulas facilitate multipartyism and are, conversely, hardly conducive to two-partyism'.

Cox's 'coordination argument' (1997)

'Why . . . would the same two parties necessarily compete in all districts [cross-constituency dispersion or national-ization]?' Local candidates link together because of the need to coordinate in order to compete more effectively for (1) seats to implement policies, (2) support presidential candidates, (3) elect the prime minister, (4) obtain more upper-tier seats, and (5) obtain more campaign finances.

'If a system (1) elects legislators by plurality rule in single-member districts; (2) elects its chief executive by something like nationwide plurality rule; and (3) hold executive and legislative elections concurrently, then it will tend to . . . have a national two-party or one-party-dominant system'.

---

be seen in Box 13.3, the two laws are simple: plurality or majoritarian electoral systems favour two-party systems whereas PR leads to multi-party systems. This causal relationship between electoral and party systems is due to both mechanical and psychological effects.

Mechanical effects refer to the formula used to translate votes into seats. In single-member constituencies to win the one seat is difficult. One party with the most votes gets the single seat. The second, third, fourth, and so on, do not get any seat (first-past-the-post). If in a constituency Party A receives 29.4 per cent of votes, Party B 29.3 per cent, and all other parties even less, only Party A is represented (winner-takes-all). This means that the threshold is high and all parties but the first one are eliminated. With PR, on the contrary, in each multi-member constituency many seats are allocated in proportion to the votes. If Party A receives 32.4 per cent of votes, it has a right—more or less—to a third of the seats allocated in that constituency. Small parties are not

excluded (a party with 5 per cent of votes gets roughly 5 per cent of seats) and the overall number of parties that end up in parliament is much higher than under single-member plurality systems.

Psychological effects refer to the awareness of voters and parties of mechanical effects:

1. On the **demand** side (voters), in electoral systems in which only large parties have a chance to win seats, voters tend to vote **strategically** (not necessarily their first party preference) to avoid wasting votes on small parties with no chance of getting seats. Converging votes on large parties reduces their overall number. On the contrary, with PR in which small parties can win seats, voters vote **sincerely** (their first preference) because their vote is not wasted. This increases the vote for small parties and thus their overall number.

2. On the **supply** side (parties), with plurality small parties have an incentive to merge with others to increase their chances to pass the threshold,

reducing the number of parties. On the contrary, with PR parties have no incentive to merge: they can survive on their own and small splinter parties are not penalized. This increases the overall number of parties.

Rae (1971), Riker (1982), and Sartori (1986) have questioned these laws by asking whether the reductive effect of majoritarian electoral systems works at *the constituency level or at the national level*. At the constituency level the high threshold reduces the number of parties. But does this always translate into a reduction at the national level?

Suppose a parliament has 100 seats from 100 single-member constituencies. If in each constituency a different party wins the seat, we would end up with a fragmented parliament. The question thus is: under which conditions does the reductive effect of FPTP at the constituency level, also reduce the number of parties at the national level? The answer is: majoritarian systems produce two-party systems at the national level only if parties are 'nationalized', i.e. receive homogeneous support in all constituencies (see Cox in Box 13.3). If there are parties with territorially concentrated support, this leads to fragmentation in the national party system. Under plurality, a nationally small party can be strong in specific regions and thus win seats and create fragmentation in the national parliament. If many parties are territorially concentrated the national fragmentation is larger.

An example is Italy. In 1994 a new, mostly plurality, electoral law in single-member districts was introduced with the aim of reducing party-system fragmentation. Yet this did not happen. Many of the parties have regional strongholds such as the Northern League in the north, the Catholics in the north-east, the Left Democrats in the centre, and the post-fascist party National Alliance in the south. In addition, many small parties base their support on local clienteles.

In most countries party systems nationalized with the beginning of competitive elections in the mid-nineteenth century, so the support parties receive is increasingly homogeneous across regions and territorialized support has declined. This can be observed in Europe, North America, but also in India and Latin America (Caramani 2004; Chhibber and Kollman 2004; Jones and Mainwaring 2003) due to the development of national party organizations and increasing candidate coordination (Cox 1997). Where plurality systems exist, therefore, the reduction of the number of parties did take place. Plurality systems *distort* party votes when they translate them into seats:

- they *over*-represent large parties (the share of seats for big parties is larger than their share of votes);
- they *under*-represent small parties.

How can we measure the empirical level of (dis)proportionality between votes and seats? Various indices have been devised: the most used one is the Least Square index of disproportionality or LSq (Gallagher 1991; Gallagher and Mitchell 2005: appendix B):

$$\text{LSq} = \sqrt{1/2 \Sigma (v_i - s_i)^2}$$

where v is the percentage of votes for party i, s is the percentage of seats for party I, and Σ represents the sum for all parties. This index varies between 0 (full proportionality) and 100 (total disproportionality). Take, as an example, the results of the 2005 New Zealand election in Table 13.4. If the total of the squared differences is halved ($3.9/2 = 1.9$) and then the square root is taken, the result is 1.4, that is, an almost perfect proportionality between votes and seats.

In the last column of Table 13.3 values of the LSq index are given. In countries with plurality systems (Canada, Great Britain, India) there is a stronger distortion of the popular vote. The same applies for other systems based on single-member constituencies such as France with a two-ballot majoritarian system. On the contrary, disproportionality is lower for countries with PR systems.

The number of parties in parliament is always smaller than the number of parties that run for elections. All electoral systems—also PR systems—have a reductive effect on the number of parties. Differences among PR systems are large. Spain's system is more disproportional than others. This is because in Spain the **magnitude of constituencies** is small. The magnitude refers to the number

Table 13.4 Results of the 2005 New Zealand election and Gallagher's LSq index of disproportionality

Party	Votes (%)	Seats (N)	Seats (%)	Difference (% seats– % votes)	Squared
Labour Party	41.1	50	41.3	0.2	0.0
National Party	39.1	48	39.7	0.6	0.3
New Zealand First	5.7	7	5.8	0.1	0.0
Green Party	5.3	6	5.0	−0.3	0.1
Māori Party	2.1	4	3.3	1.2	1.4
United Future	2.7	3	2.5	−0.2	0.1
ACT New Zealand	1.5	2	1.7	0.2	0.0
J A's Progressive	1.2	1	0.8	−0.4	0.1
Others	1.3	0	0.0	−1.3	1.7
Total	100.0	121	100.0		3.9

Note: Votes refer to party lists votes whereas seats include both party list seats and electorate seats.

of seats allocated in a given constituency. The larger the magnitude, the higher the proportionality between votes and seats. If the magnitude is small, the few seats go to few parties and are harder for small parties to win. Some PR systems artificially increase the number of seats (those using the Droop quota or the Imperiali quota) in order to make it easier for small parties to get represented. In these systems the correspondence between votes and seats is greater.[6]

Cleavages

Large numbers of parties are also the result of social and cultural pluralism. The presence of numerous cleavages leads to more parties than in culturally homogeneous countries. PR electoral systems were introduced in plural societies to incorporate minorities in the representation circuit and in decision-making processes. Plurality systems would have excluded large segments of the society which then—dangerously—may have looked for other (non-institutional) channels of action. As a recent article by Colomer (2005) argues, PR electoral systems are the result of an already existing political fragmentation, and not the other way round.

Finally, radical changes in the morphology of party systems due to new electoral systems are rare. Examples are the change from majoritarian to proportional as in New Zealand in 1998 (leading to an increase in the number of parties), or the other way round in France with the 1958 new constitution (leading to a bipolar structure). When in 1986 PR was reintroduced for one election only, small parties such as the National Front received many more seats than under the majoritarian system and thus caused a greater party fragmentation.

KEY POINTS

❑ The morphology of party systems is important for understanding the competitive interactions between parties: it concerns the number of players and their size. The main types are dominant-party, two-party, multi-party, and bipolar systems.

❑ In two-party systems, moderate multi-party systems, and bipolar systems competition is centripetal and alternation between parties or coalitions takes place. In dominant-party systems and polarized multi-party systems there is no alternation and competition is centrifugal.

❑ Measures of fragmentation are based on the number and size of parties. However, small parties, too, can be important if they have coalition or blackmail potential.

❑ The format of party systems is influenced by electoral systems. Through mechanical and psychological effects plurality tends towards two-party systems (large parties are over-represented) and PR to multi-party systems (which are less disproportional).

The dynamics of party systems

In the wake of Joseph Schumpeter's (1943) definition of democracy—a set or rules for selecting political leaders and making decisions by means of competition for votes—authors have developed analogies between **electoral competition** and **market competition**. In the electoral market, parties and candidates compete for 'shares' of the electorate as happens in the economic world where firms compete for shares of the market. Parties are organizations whose main motive is the *maximization of votes*, and the exchange between represented and representatives is similar to that between demand and supply in the economy (see Table 13.5).

The market analogy

Anthony Downs's *An Economic Theory of Democracy* (1957) is a pioneering book in which the basic elements of these models were spelled out for the first time. It is one of the most influential works in the comparative party systems literature (see Further reading). In this model, actors (parties and voters) are **rational.** Parties calculate their strategies by formulating platforms with the goal of maximizing votes and being elected or re-elected, disregarding policy priorities. Parties are coalitions of individuals seeking to control institutions rather than the implementation of programmes. Parties act self-interestedly to gain office. Like firms in the economic market, they are indifferent to the 'product' they offer but interested in making profit (monetary in the economic

market and votes in the electoral one). To maximize votes parties offer programmes that appeal to a large part of the electorate.

Voters, like consumers, face alternatives which they order from most to least preferred and choose the alternative that ranks highest. Voters make a rational choice by voting for parties whose programmes are closest to their policy preferences, because they are close to their interests or to their values and moral orientations. Voters vote on the basis of the *proximity* between parties' positions and their preferences

Table 13.5 The analogy between economic and electoral competition

Dimensions	Economy	Elections
Market	Economic	Electoral
Actors {	Firms	Parties
	Consumers	Voters
Profit	Money	Votes
Supply	Goods, services	Programmes, policies
Demand	Product preferences	Policy preferences
Communication	Advertising	Campaigns

and so they know what the alternative proposals by different parties are, that is, they are *informed* about their possible choices.

Rational citizens vote on the basis of a self-interested calculation, like consumers who calculate the benefit between 'packages'. On the other hand, parties are like businesses competing for customers. They establish what people 'like' so they can sell more. Following a logic of *supply and demand,* parties offer policies that voters can either choose to 'buy' or not. Once elected, parties seek re-election through policies appealing to large segments of the electorate. The parties' goal is to make a 'profit' in terms of votes; the voters' goal is to maximize *utility* by buying a product that increases their satisfaction. As in economic theory, the search for individual advantages produces *common goods*, namely responsiveness and accountability.

Rational choice competition models were first devised for two-party systems—mainly the US. However, vote-maximizing strategies have been observed in multi-party systems, too. To maximize votes is the main motive also in systems in which governments are coalitions. The more votes, the better the chances to enter a coalition, control governmental institutions, and place individuals in key official positions.

The spatial analogy

The idea of proximity/distance between individual preferences and parties' policies indicates that players move in a space of competition. The second element that Downs 'imported' from economic models of competition is their spatial representation. In particular, Downs adapted models of the dynamics of competition between firms, that is, where firms locate premises according to the physical distribution of the population.

Let us take the simple case of a village in which there is only one street (the example is from Hotteling 1929). On each side of the street there are evenly spaced houses (the square dots in Figure 13.1). What are the dynamics between two competitors, say two bakeries A and B? Assuming that both bakers offer

the same quality of bread for the same price and that consumers will rationally try to reduce their 'costs' by buying bread in the nearest shop (proximity), if A and B are located as they are in the figure, B will have a larger share of the market. The share of B's market goes from the right-side end of the street to the M-point which is the middle between the locations of A and B. Residents on the right of the M-point will buy bread in bakery B and residents on the left of the M-point will buy bread in bakery A. The dynamic element in this model consists of A's move to increase its share of the market. By relocating the bakery in AA, the baker is able to gain the share of the market indicated by the dashed area. Obviously, B too can move toward the centre (BB) and win back part of the lost share of the market. Both bakers seek to *optimize their location.*

An additional element introduced by Smithies (1941) concerns the elasticity of the demand. The further away from the grocery, the higher the 'costs' for buyers. To what extent is a relocation towards the centre tolerated by residents of the extremes? Incentives for a new bakery at the edges of the village increase as people feel that AA and BB are too distant. The risk of strategies of relocations toward the centre is that a new bakery C appears taking away part of B's share of the market (the dark shaded area). In these models there are therefore two dynamic elements: (1) the movement caused by the search for the optimal location and (2) the appearance of new competitors in spaces left uncovered. Equilibrium is reached when no competitor has an interest in changing its position along the axis.

Downs's model

Through the spatial analogy between physical and ideological space, Downs imports these analyses into electoral studies. Most elements are maintained: (1) the one-dimensionality of the space, (2) the principle according to which costs are reduced by choosing the nearest option (proximity), (3) competitors' search for the optimal location through a convergence toward the centre.

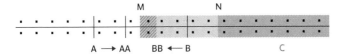

Fig. 13.1 Hotteling's model (1929)

Downs represented the ideological space through a 0 to 100 scale ranging from left to right. As will be seen, one-dimensionality is maintained, even if it is not always a realistic assumption, because it summarizes other dimensions and is the most important one (in terms of size of parties that define themselves according to this dimension), and because it is present in all party systems (thus allowing comparisons).

Both Hotteling and Smithies had previously applied spatial models to politics through analogies with the ideological space and were able to predict that parties tend to converge towards one another in the effort to win the middle-of-the-road voters, and to present increasingly similar programmes and policies. Downs adds one crucial element to the models: the **variable distribution of voters** along the left–right continuum. Voters are not distributed regularly along the scale but concentrate in particular ideological positions, namely around the centre. For Downs this is the crucial explanatory and predictive element of

party systems' dynamics: 'if we know something about the distribution of voters' preferences, we can make specific predictions about how ideologies change in content as parties maneuver to gain power' (1957: 114). If one assumes a normal (or 'bell-shaped') distribution of the electorate with many voters at the centre of the scale and fewer at the extremes (see type A in Figure 13.2), the prediction of the model is again that parties will converge toward the centre.[7]

The first dynamic element of these models is that they predict the convergence toward the centre and the increasing similarity of platforms and policy actions. This centripetal competition (Sartori 1976) is determined by the parties' aim to win the *median voter* (see Box 13.4). Examples are the progressive convergence of previously radical left-wing workers' parties toward the centre to attract moderate voters (the German Social Democrats in 1959, the French Socialists in the 1970s, the New Labour Party under Tony Blair, or the US Democrats under Bill Clinton).

Type A: Downs's basic model (1957): the bell-shape (or normal) distribution of the electorate: centripetal competition

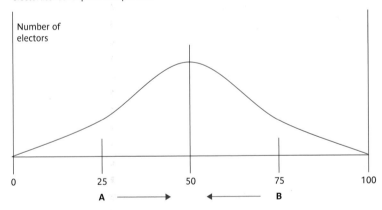

Type B: A two-modal distribution of electors: centrifugal competition

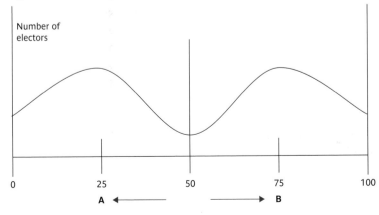

Fig. 13.2 Types of voter distributions (*continued*)

Type C: A skewed distribution of electors: enfranchisement in the nineteenth century and new parties

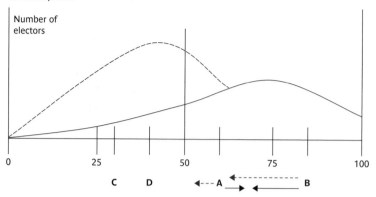

Type D: Polymodal distribution in multi-party systems

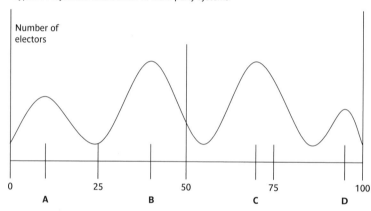

Fig. 13.2 *(continued)*

The second dynamic element consists of centripetal competition arising not only because of the proximity principle, but also because there are more voters in the centre. Parties' strategy does not only depend on the logic of the model (the assumption of proximity voting) but also on the **empirical distribution of the electorate**. The potential loss of voters at the extremes does not deter parties from converging because there are few voters at the extremes. This is not the case if the distribution of the electorate is different, a two-model distribution as depicted in type B. This is a case of ideological polarization within a political system (for example, the Weimar Republic and Italy during the 'first republic'). The distribution of the electorate therefore determines the *direction* of competition (centrifugal or centripetal).

The third element of the dynamics of party systems is that in the middle of the left–right axis voters are more *flexible* than at the extremes where they are firmly encapsulated in strict ideologies and/or party organizations. 'Available' voters (Bartolini and Mair 1990), located in the middle, are less ideologized

---

BOX 13.4 The median voter

The median voter is the voter who divides a distribution of voters placed on a left–right scale into two equal halves. In a distribution from 0 to 100 in which for each point there is a voter (including position 0), the median voter is on position 50 (with 50 voters on each side). Suppose, however, that there are 50 voters on position 100, and the remaining voters distribute regularly between positions 49 and 99 (one voter on each position). In this case the median voter is on position 99.

and have weak party identifications. These voters are ready to change their minds and, therefore, are very appealing to parties seeking to 'seduce' them.

The wider application of rational choice models

What are the links of these models with other aspects of parties and party systems? Four are particularly important as they show the range of their potential application.

Party organization

Rational choice models help to interpret the transformation of parties from mass parties to 'catch-all parties' (see Chapter 12). This transformation can be seen as the organizational and ideological adaptation to competition.

Dealignment

These models also help to interpret patterns of dealignment, that is, the loosening of the relationship between parties and specific segments of the society (workers for social democrats, peasants for agrarians, middle classes for conservatives and liberals). Centripetal competition and the maximization of votes lead parties to make their programmes and ideologies more vague to attract support from other groups. This blurs the connection between groups and parties and causes a higher propensity to change vote from one election to the next.

Enfranchisement and democratization

In both types A and B the distributions are symmetrical. In type C, on the contrary, we have a **skewed distribution**. The solid curve represents an electorate that is skewed toward the right of the axis. Here the median voter is around position 65 rather than 50, and parties A and B would accordingly converge toward this point. This is a situation typical of restricted electorates in the nineteenth century when lower classes were excluded from the franchise. A and B would therefore be the typical parties of the periods of restricted electorates, namely Liberals and Conservatives as the parties of 'internal origin' (Duverger 1954) of the bourgeoisie and aristocracy. Enfranchisement and democratization processes in the second half of the nineteenth century and first

two decades of the twentieth radically changed the shape of the distribution of electors as represented by the dashed curve, making it more similar to a normal curve. This new distribution explains the emergence of new parties C and/or D of 'external origin' (such as social democrats and agrarians).[8]

The dream of reformists (as against revolutionary socialists) was that socialism and the proletariat could come to power through votes ('paper stones') and the extension of the franchise rather than through revolution (real stones!). For analytical Marxists the development of the industrial society would naturally lead workers to power through sheer numbers. Since, however, numbers of industrial workers did not grow—in fact, they declined—socialist parties faced a dilemma between moving toward the centre to maximize their appeal to the middle classes—thus relaxing their programme—and giving up their ideology and losing voters from workers (Przeworski and Sprague 1986).

PR and multi-party systems

Under FPTP convergence is likely because the threat of other parties appearing at the extremes is low, given the high threshold required to win a seat. Rather than new parties, under these systems, the model predicts *high abstention levels* as is the case in the US. Is it different in PR electoral systems?

First, multi-party systems occur when PR electoral systems allow a lower threshold of representation. Second, multi-party systems develop when the distribution of the electorate is polymodal, with more than one or two peaks (type D). With electors' distributions of this type the dynamics of the competition is not centripetal. PR is no hindrance to new parties. Existing parties have no incentive to converge toward the centre since they would lose part of their support to 'neighbouring' parties and because the position they would be moving to is already busy. It is therefore less likely than in two-party systems that parties will look like each other ideologically.

Downs assumed that the ideological space was fixed and not elastic, that is, ranged from 0 to 100. Observing multi-party systems, Sartori (1976) was on the contrary able to establish that **ideological spaces are elastic,** that is, they can stretch, with extremes becoming more extreme and an increasing ideological distance between parties. Parties may adopt the strategy of becoming more extreme to distinguish themselves from moderate parties. This leads to the radicalization of parties wishing to maintain a distinctive character.

In Italy between 1989 and 1992 the two main 'anti-system parties' underwent processes of ideological deradicalization, with the Italian Communist Party dropping the communist ideology and label, and transforming into a modern social democratic party (as the German SPD did in 1959 at the famous Bad Godesberg congress), and the Italian Social Movement abandoning its former neo-fascist ideology. For both parties the centripetal move led to splinter parties which maintained radical ideologies (the Party of Communist Refoundation and the fascist Tricolor Flame). Both are small but PR did not prevent them from existing and stretching the ideological space.

In conclusion, the crucial determinant is the distribution of the electorate. If we know the shape of the curve we can predict the behaviour of parties. However, to know what the voters' distribution looks like is a matter of **empirical investigation**—not of deductive models—namely through surveys asking respondents to place themselves on a left–right scale (Budge and Farlie 1977; Laver 2001).

In spite of critiques (see Box 13.5) these models remain useful. In all electorates a number of less ideological voters are ready to change their vote. This is an available electorate around which competition turns and on which these models focus. This electorate

---

BOX 13.5 Critiques to rational choice models

Assumption	Critique
Rationality	The relationship between parties and voters is determined by a number of 'non-rational' or 'irrational' factors: socio-economic conditions, party identification, political socialization, influence of the media. Empirical research shows that most voters vote according to these factors rather than rational ones (Budge *et al.* 1976).
Full information	Voters are not fully informed about the proposal parties present in their platforms and programmes, and are unable to evaluate the extent to which they correspond to their own preferences. Also, do voters know what their preferences are? With technical issues this often proves unlikely.
Vote maximization	Parties are not vote maximizers: • Parties as office seekers do not require to maximise votes but to get just enough. There is the need to win but the magnitude of the victory is not important. Parties 'seek to maximize only up to the point of subjective certainty of winning' (Riker 1962: 33). • Parties may just seek to influence public policy rather than aim for office. As de Swann notes, '[c]onsiderations of policy are foremost in the minds of the actors . . . [T]he parliamentary game is, in fact, about the determination of major government policy' (1973: 88). • Vote maximization faces resistances within parties to keep a less 'cynical' attitude and a more coherent ideology. The influence of militants, activists, and 'rank and files' should not be underestimated. Müller and Strøm (1999) find that only half of the parties they examine follow a strategy of vote maximization.
One-dimensionality	It is not realistic that all parties compete along the left–right dimension. This may be true in two-party systems in which the electoral system reduces the variety of parties. In multi-party systems, however, the number of dimensions is larger. Several empirical analyses show that the space of competition is in most cases pluri-dimensional, as genetic models show.

is composed of **opinion voters** or 'pocket-book voting', that is, based on private interests, values, and opinions, rather than **identity voters** or 'socio-tropic voting' based on socio-economic and identification factors. The models described in this section apply less to segments that are encapsulated in strong identifications. For this reason these models apply to the left–right dimension along which voters are available rather than other dimensions (ethnic, linguistic, religious) along which identities are stronger and voters less available (Sartori 1976). Even if these models apply to parts of the electorate only, they are crucial as they determine the direction of competition.[9]

A more fundamental question, however, is how to interpret the convergence of parties and the increasing similarity of their programmes. From a methodological point of view it is difficult to separate the impact of competition from other factors such as (1) the development of a large and homogeneous middle class and the disappearance of other classes, namely the working class; (2) the reduction of social inequalities and the secularization of society with the disappearance of religious conflicts; (3) the integration of societies and the disappearance of ethnic and linguistic particularities through nationalization and globalization. In this respect the elasticity of the space is central. The space of competition seems to have become smaller with extremes falling away. Is the convergence of parties a result of this evolution rather than a product of competition?

KEY POINTS

❑ In the electoral market parties (the supply side) present programmes and platforms to appeal to a large number of voters whose vote is determined by the proximity of their preferences (the demand side) with the parties' offer. Voters are assumed to be rational, that is, informed about alternative party proposals and able to chose the alternative closest to their top preferences.

❑ The dynamics of party systems is determined by parties' search for the optimal location on the left–right axis. Depending on the distribution of the electorate along the scale, parties move to a position where the support in votes is largest.

❑ The prediction of competition models is that parties converge toward the centre of the left–right axis as the optimal location, as the point where most votes concentrate, and as the point where voters are less rigidly ideologized.

Conclusion

Understanding party systems requires the combination of the various perspectives presented in this chapter.

1. The **macro-sociological** approach must be combined with **institutional** and **actor-oriented** models. They complement each other and are not mutually exclusive. We cannot understand party systems without reference to the social cleavages from which parties have emerged. However, we must also take into account parties' capacity to act independently from social conditions—in fact, to shape them—through ideology and policy. The motivations of parties are not entirely determined by their origins. Parties' strategies, in turn, must take into account the rules of the game—electoral laws being the most important ones—influencing the number and size of players.

2. Both **descriptive** and **explanatory research** are needed. The ultimate goal of research is to account for the shape and dynamic of party systems. However, before searching for causes, party systems should be described carefully. As seen with counting parties, this is often more complicated than appears at first sight.

3. Finally, we cannot understand party systems in isolation. We need **comparison** to assess whether or not they are fragmented or unstable, as well as a **long-term** perspective rather than a myopic focus on just the most recent elections. This is the only way of assessing how exceptional a given party system or a given change really is.

? Questions

1. What are the National and the Industrial Revolutions?
2. What are Stein Rokkan's four main social cleavages and which party families emerged from them?
3. How should the number of parties in a system be counted?
4. What are the characteristic features of a two-party system?
5. What does 'effective number of parties' mean?
6. What is the effect of electoral systems on the shape of party systems?
7. What does it mean that parties are 'vote-maximizers'?
8. Describe centripetal and centrifugal party competition in Downs's model.
9. Are voters really rational?
10. Can the space of competition be reduced to one left–right dimension?

» Further reading

Classical texts on party systems

Downs, Anthony (1957) *An Economic Theory of Democracy* (New York: Harper Collins).

Duverger, Maurice (1954) *Political Parties* (New York: Wiley).

Lipset, Seymour M., and Rokkan, Stein (1967) 'Cleavage Structures, Party Systems, and Voter Alignments: An Introduction', in Lipset and Rokkan (eds.), *Party Systems and Voter Alignments* (New York: Free Press), 1–64.

Sartori, Giovanni (1976) *Parties and Party Systems: A Framework for Analysis* (Cambridge: Cambridge University Press).

For a more extended bibliography see the works cited throughout in this chapter.

In addition, up-to-date reports on party systems can be found in journals. Detailed country-by-country developments from 1991 onwards are reported in the *Political Data Yearbook*, an annual supplement of the *European Journal of Political Research*. Students may also find useful material in journals such as the *American Political Science Review, British Journal of Political Science, Comparative Politics, Comparative Political Studies Electoral Studies, Party Politics*, and *West European Politics*.

Web links

www.electionresources.org
Manuel Álvarez-Rivera's Election Resources in the Internet.

www.psr.keele.ac.uk
Richard Kimber's website on Political Science Resources (University of Keele).

www.parties-and-elections.de
Database of Parties and Elections about parliamentary elections, parties, and political leaders in Europe.

www.electionworld.org
Website includes information on political parties around the world with up-to-date election results and other information on the party system and the main institutions.

www.gksoft.com/govt/en/parties.html
> Webpage of Government on the WWW devoted to political parties and party systems around the world. The main page includes additional information on heads of state, parliaments, executives, courts, and other institutions.

www.epicproject.org
> Website of the EPIC Project on election process information collection which includes also information on parties and party systems.

www.georgetown.edu/pdba
> Website of the Political Database of the Americas including information on parties and party systems.

http://dodgson.ucsd.edu/lij
> Website of the Lijphart Election Archive with information on party systems, electoral systems, and recent election results around the world.

www.cia.gov/cia/publications/factbook
> Website of CIA's the World Factbook with information on institutions, social structures, economic data, and party systems for most countries of the world.

www.idea.int
> Website of the International Institute for Democracy and Electoral Assistance (IDEA).

www2.essex.ac.uk/elect/database/aboutProject.asp
> Website of the project on Political Transformation and the Electoral Process in Post-Communist Europe (University of Essex).

www.eiu.com
> Country Reports and Country Profiles published by the Economist Intelligence Unit are very useful for an overview and recent data.

 Visit the Online Resource Centre that accompanies this book for more information:
www.oxfordtextbooks.co.uk/orc/caramani/

14 Interest groups

Timothy Werner and Graham K. Wilson

Chapter contents

Reader's guide

The study of interest groups spans many subfields in political science and is often accused of being overly amorphous. Placing this body of work in a comparative context only further increases this ambiguity. This chapter begins by reviewing just what constitutes an interest group and briefly surveys how this definition differs in the cross-national context. The chapter proceeds by detailing the role of interest groups in various political settings, including mass participation and elections, institutions and lobbying, and state–society relations. Touched on throughout the chapter and emphasized in its last section are the normative implications of the interest group system. Important questions to ponder when thinking about the role of interest groups in politics include: how is power distributed, is any one political player privileged over others, and what are the positive benefits that accrue to individuals and societies through interest group membership?

Introduction

The glory and the challenge of the study of interest groups is that it lies at the intersection of many different fields of political science. Political science often associates interest group studies with the study of political participation, linking to the study of electoral politics, campaigns, and elections (Rosenstone and Hansen 1993; Goldstein 1999). On the other hand, interest group studies linked to Europe or countries such as Japan become almost a form of political economy, exploring linkages between state and society (Johnson 1982; Samuels 1987; Pempel 1998). Particularly in the US where interest group activity is often assumed to be focused on Congress, interest group studies can be seen as adjacent to legislative studies (Wright 1996).

The cost of this diversity is ambiguity in terms, ambiguity even about what the term 'interest group' means and whether it is preferable or inferior to alternatives such as 'pressure group', 'organized interests', or 'state and society'. Box 14.1 traces the historical development of the term interest group, and Table 14.1 provides some sense of the composition of the interest group community in the US. Given all of this diversity, one may wonder if there are any subjects political scientists examine that do not fall under this rubric.

The benefit of this diversity is the existence of a large number of impressive studies that contribute much to our understanding of politics and government. In addition to the numerous and varied empirical studies of interest groups, their study has inspired large bodies of literature in formal theory, especially on collective action, and in normative political theory, including most famously pluralism,

the belief that power is and ought to be widely dispersed among numerous groups all with a capacity to influence public policy (Polsby 1960; Dahl 1956, 1961). We shall proceed by examining in turn interest groups as a form of political participation, interest groups in association with individual political institutions (such as Congress), and interest groups as an expression of state–society relations.

Table 14.1 Classification of interest groups in the US (%)

Citizen sector	23.9
Profit sector	37.8
Nonprofit sector	32.5
Mixed sector	5.8
Total	100.0

Source: Walker (1991: 59).

KEY POINTS

- ❑ Interest groups are membership organization and advocacy groups that make policy-related appeals to the government.
- ❑ The study of interest groups is at the intersection of many fields of study—such as political parties, electoral politics and public policies—as well as different theoretical approaches—such as collective action, normative theories and pluralism.

BOX 14.1 What is an interest group?

The definition of an interest group has been in flux since the early twentieth century. Bentley's (1908) definition of a group consisted of little more than a collection of individuals. Truman (1951) defined an interest group as any group that, on the basis shared attitudes, makes certain claims upon other groups in the society based on its shared attitudes. Both of these definitions are flawed in that they do not distinguish political parties

from interest groups. Walker (1991), attempting to more clearly delineate parties and interest groups, defined an interest group as a functioning association that is open to membership and concerned with public policy at the national level. Baumgartner and Leech (1998) have further refined Walker's definition, defining interest groups as membership organizations and advocacy groups that make policy-related appeals to the government.

Interest groups and political participation

For many students of politics, the phrase 'interest group' still conjures up an image of an organization composed of individual citizens focused on a particular interest or area of politics. Common Cause, Friends of the Earth, or the Campaign for Nuclear Disarmament are exemplars of this approach to interest groups. The classic questions for this concept of interest group study are the reasons why people join interest groups and the consequences of these reasons for the political system.

Interest group formation and maintenance

The reasons why people do or not join interest groups have been the object of investigation for nearly two hundred years. Tocqueville (1835) famously argued that Americans were unusually likely to join voluntary associations. In recent years, Putnam (1995, 2000) worried that Americans were losing this characteristic and that in consequence social capital was declining. Neither Tocqueville nor Putnam focused on interest groups as such; yet, undoubtedly, these studies do include interest groups among the ranks of their subjects.

Skocpol (2003) in contrast argued that voluntary organizations were related to developments in the nature of the American state rather than a natural enthusiasm of Americans to join. Curtis *et al.* (1992) also found the high levels of participation in civic life in America to be linked not to a unique culture but to religiosity—in a fifteen-country study, they found Americans' level of participation to be roughly equal to (or less than) those of citizens in other advanced industrial nations when religious memberships were removed. In short, there have been continuing discussions of whether or not the propensity of citizens to join voluntary organizations has changed over time and of whether or not Americans join such organizations at higher rates than others.

Most discussion of interest groups and political participation focuses on why some people join interest groups and others do not. We should note at the outset that, although to many the term conjures up images of mass membership organizations that citizens join voluntarily, many if not most of the organizations that function as interest groups are not of this type. As Salisbury (1984) noted, institutions dominate interest group activity. Most lobbyists in Washington, DC, work for business corporations, not mass membership organizations. This dominance of institutions is even greater if we add to their number lobbyists who represent organizations such as universities. Finally, there are difficult, transitional cases such as labour unions or professional organizations such as medical societies in which membership is required as a condition of employment. Thus much interest group activity is conducted by institutions in which membership, if not participation, is not a voluntary activity.

Olson's *The Logic of Collective Action* and responses to it

Much of the work on interest groups has been focused, however, precisely on understanding voluntary participation in interest groups. One of the most stable findings in social science has been the positive relationship between political participation and socio-economic status. In what became a very familiar saying, E. E. Schattschneider (1960) commented that in the pluralist heaven the choir sang with an upper class accent. An even more familiar problem formulated by Mancur Olson (1965) is that joining an interest group is an irrational act.

BOX 14.2 Alexis de Tocqueville on groups in America

Americans of all ages, all stations of life, and all types of disposition are forever forming associations. There are not only commercial and industrial associations in which all take part, but others of a thousand different types—religious, moral, serious, futile, very general and very limited, immensely large, and very minute...In democratic countries knowledge of how to combine is the mother of all other forms of knowledge; on its progress depends that of all the others.

Olson argued that interest groups are formed and maintained in response to 'selective incentives' or by-products that benefit the individual member. It is not rational for someone to join an interest group in pursuit of a collective good because he or she will have no reason believe that the costs the individual incurs will result in offsetting gains in performance by the group. The likelihood that, for example, the 99,999th person to join an interest group will make much difference to its power by joining is negligible. However, that person will still incur the costs of membership.

Olson's book emphasized the importance of this problem for economic groups. Farmers' organizations needed to attract members by offering benefits to individual members such as use of a grain elevator, because individuals did not have a plausible reason to join to promote public policy goals such as higher farm subsidies, even if they were to be the material beneficiaries of them. After all, they would receive the subsidies whether or not they joined the interest group that campaigned for them. However, the most important application of Olson's theory seemed to be to the difficulty of forming interest groups that pursued widely dispersed, non-excludable benefits such as clean air or water, generally termed 'public goods'. The collective action problem seemed to preclude interest group activity in pursuit of public interests. In consequence, pluralism seemed to be unlikely to provide for the common good and instead to favour more concentrated, narrower interests that had a better chance of overcoming collective action problems (see Chapter 18).

The Owl of Minerva seems to fly disconcertingly often in political science. No sooner was Olson's book published than public interest groups flourished, first in the US, then elsewhere. One of the favourite statistics about political participation in the UK is that the environmental group, the Royal Society for the Protection of Birds (RSPB), has more members than all the political parties combined. Did the growth of public interest groups invalidate Olson's arguments? A body of work by Jack Walker and his students (1983, 1991) suggested not. Public interest groups evaded the collective action problem through the support of sponsors or patrons, possibly rich individuals but more often foundations, and not through like-minded citizens spontaneously banding together.

Nonetheless, the continued strength of public interest groups suggests either that although they may rely on a patron for mobilization, they maintain themselves either though the adept supply of individualized benefits (such as attractive calendars as a reward for membership) or, more probably, a willingness on their members' part to incur the costs of membership, perhaps as an expression of their beliefs and values (Nownes and Cigler 1995). James Q. Wilson (1974) provided a valuable advance on Olson by setting out the variety of motives that can underpin the decision to join interest groups:

- **instrumental reasons** in order to obtain the benefits that Olson emphasized;
- **purposive reasons** in pursuit of the goals of the organization;
- **expressive reasons**, seeing in their membership subscriptions a means of making a statement in support of their beliefs or, more often, against policies or values they dislike.

For many interest groups today, membership amounts to nothing more than going online or responding to a phone call and paying a subscription (Skocpol 2003). Those who do so frequently have no intention of going to meetings or being active in the organization. Anger is a great motivator; groups solicit memberships by emphasizing the danger posed by familiar 'hate figures' such as Hillary Clinton for American conservatives and George W. Bush for liberals. American environmental groups experienced a surge in membership in the early 1980s as the anti-environmental policies of the Reagan administration unfolded; joining an environmental group was a convenient way of sending a message that such policies were unacceptable.

Groups and elections

The success of public interest groups in an era in which political parties in Western democracies have struggled to attract and retain members has drawn attention to the importance of groups as a means of political participation. Interest groups have long been active in political campaigns. The Committee on Political Education (COPE) of the union federation, the AFL-CIO, has provided equipment and workers to support candidates (nearly always

Democrats) in campaigns. Individual unions—the United Auto Workers (UAW) and more recently teachers unions such as the National Education Association and its state affiliates—have been equally important. In more recent years, the role of interest groups in providing financial contributions has been more controversial.

A huge amount of effort has been expended by political scientists in trying to show that campaign contributions made by the political action committees (PACs) that are the legally required subsidiaries of these groups change or do not change votes by members of Congress. The ideological predispositions of incumbents and the interests of their constituents are competing explanations for how legislators vote and are difficult or impossible to isolate from the impact of campaign contributions. In consequence, the almost innumerable studies of the impact of PACs have failed to demonstrate a clear impact (Ansolabehere *et al.* 2003; Wright 1985, 1996).

There have been periods in which PAC contributions were not the predominant means by which groups contribute to campaigns. At times campaign finance law in the US has allowed interest groups to make larger contributions. For a time, interest groups were able to make 'soft money' contributions from their general treasuries to political parties which could then funnel the money to specific candidates. These payments dwarfed the small amounts PACs could contribute and were prohibited by the McCain-Feingold Act of 2002 (Franz 2005), but much like PAC donations, soft money contributions do not appear to have provided firms with tangible benefits (Ansolabehere *et al.* 2004) and some executives felt that soft money donations were more a result of a political 'shakedown' by the parties than a strategic move on their own part (Sitkoff 2003). Despite its reform impulse and ban on soft money, McCain-Feingold increased 'hard money' donation limits, allowing individuals and PACs to contribute more to individual candidates than previously. Further, lobbyists—especially business lobbyists—frequently and increasingly 'bundle' large number of contributions from executives together to provide a coordinated donation far larger than a PAC can make. As Table 14.2 shows, business interests dominate both in terms of the number of PACs and the total value of campaign contributions in the US.

Table 14.2 Distribution of PACs and PAC giving by organizational type (%)

Organization type	PACs	PAC giving
Publicly held corporations	40.8	36.3
Labor unions	7.9	21.8
Trade associations	17.7	28.6
Cooperatives	1.3	1.5
Private corporations	3.2	2.1
Nonconnected organizations	29.1	9.7
Total	100.0	100.0

Source: Wright (1996: 124).

Currently, organizations that might be considered interest groups, the '527s' (see Chapter 12), are able to solicit and spend money without significant controls so long as they operate separately from but in effect in support of (or in opposition to) candidates. Perhaps the most important restriction is that their advertisements cannot explicitly call for the election or defeat of a named person within sixty days of an election. In practice it is easy to design campaign advertisements that evade this control, and this restriction was weakened by the Supreme Court decision in *Federal Election Commission v. Wisconsin Right to Life, Inc.* in June 2007. In consequence, it is more effective for very rich individuals to give large amounts of money to interest groups such as MoveOn.org than to give to parties or candidates the organization supports. Groups such as MoveOn.org have been important factors in the 'air wars'—television campaign commercials—of presidential and congressional campaigns.

There are of course analogies to this in other countries. Unions have long been the primary source of finance for the British Labour Party and businesses in certain industries (for example, brewing) were the traditional source of money for the Conservative Party. However, the limited scope for paid television commercials and availability of free television time to the parties have precluded interest groups from playing as important a role in financing elections as in the US. Whether this will remain the case as other campaign costs—opinion polling, focus groups, etc.—continue to rise remains to be seen. The spread of 'capital intensive' campaigning

based on focus groups, opinion polls, and cleverly designed party-political broadcasts certainly creates a universal need among politicians for more money.

KEY POINTS

- ❏ The formation of interest groups depends upon institutional and cultural factors (e.g. religiosity). From an individual perspective, joining an interest group is irrational and occurs only if accompanied by selective incentives.
- ❏ There are several kinds of reasons for joining interest groups, the most important being instrumental (to obtain benefits), purposive (belief in the goals of the

group), and expressive (manifesting values through membership of the group).
- ❏ Depending on the national regulations about party finances and campaigns (most notably, television commercials), interest groups are closely involved in the electoral process through donations to political parties.

Interest groups and institutions

Interest groups, as Olson noted, often exist for reasons other than to influence public policy. The American Automobile Association in the US or Automobile Association in the UK attract members primarily through offering assistance in breakdowns, insurance discounts, and trip planning, not by lobbying for better roads. Political scientists, however, are attracted to the study of interest groups primarily because of their potential impact on political institutions and public policy.

Whom to lobby?

Interest groups are by and large purposive organizations that focus their energies in ways and places that maximize their chances of success. The qualification 'by and large' is necessary because a significant number of interest groups must act in ways that impress members and increase the likelihood that they will renew subscriptions—to use James Q. Wilson's terminology, these are 'expressive' organizations. The old Campaign for Nuclear Disarmament in the UK was never likely for this reason to move off the streets and into discreet discussions with the Ministry of Defence and Foreign Office.

It has been argued similarly that the intensely competitive world of US interest groups can prompt groups to engage in high-profile activity that impresses the membership and provides the resources necessary to ensure group autonomy and survival, rather than to maximize the chances for policy impact

(Berry 1977). For example, the constructive engagement between the US Chamber of Commerce and the Clinton administration on health insurance came to an end when the Chamber decided its moderation was losing it members to the National Federation of Independent Business (Skocpol 1996).

However, it is safe to argue that, when interest groups try to influence public policy, they intend to succeed. It follows, therefore, that interest groups will focus their efforts on those institutions that have the most power and on which they can exert influence. Interest groups may therefore decide not to focus their efforts on an institution either because that it is relatively unimportant in public policy-making or because they doubt their capacity to have much impact on it. Traditionally, therefore, interest groups have paid less attention to Parliament in the UK (though there has been some increase in recent decades) because of its limited role in formulating the details of most public policy and to the presidency in the US because they doubt the capacity of these institutions to have much impact. When institutions gain power, they nearly always attract greater attention from interest groups so long as the groups have a plausible for strategy for exerting influence. Thus the considerable increase in the importance of decisions made in Brussels by the European Union over the domestic policies of member-states has lead to dramatic growth in the amount of lobbying undertaken there by interest groups (Coen 2007).

COUNTRY PROFILE Argentina

Argentine Republic (*República Argentina*)

State formation

Argentina was first explored by Europeans in 1516, became a Spanish colony in 1580 and part of the Viceroyalty of the Rio de la Plata in 1776. After two unsuccessful invasions by the British Empire in 1806 and 1807, the First Government Junta was established in Buenos Aires when King Ferdinand VII had been overthrown by Napoleon in 1810 (May Revolution). Formal independence was gained on 9 July 1816. *Constitution* 1853; amended many times.

Form of government

Presidential republic.
Head of state President and Vice President elected on the same ticket; term of 4 years (renewable once).
Head of government The President.
Cabinet Ministers appointed by the President.
Administrative subdivisions 23 provinces and 1 autonomous city.

Legal system

Mixture of US and West European legal systems.

Legislature

Bicameral National Congress (*Congreso Nacional*).
Lower house Chamber of Deputies (*Cámara de Diputados*): 257 seats; staggered elections (129 or 127 renewed every two years); term of 4 years.
Upper house Senate: 72 seats; staggered elections (one-third of the members elected every two years); term of 6 years.

Electoral system (lower house)

Proportional representation.
Formula D'Hondt. A third of the candidates of each party must be women.
Constituencies 24 multi-member constituencies corresponding to the provinces.
Barrier clause None.
Suffrage Universal and compulsory, 18 years.

Direct democracy

Optional but binding legislative referendum can be called by Parliament. Other non-binding referenda can be called by the President or the Congress. A non-binding legislative popular initiative is possible.

Party system Results of the 2005 legislative elections (Chamber of Deputies):

Electorate	26,098,546	100.0%
Voters:	18,513,717	70.9%

Party	Valid votes	%	Seats
Front for Victory	5,071,094	29.9	50
Radical Civic Union	1,514,653	8.9	10
Alternative for a Republic of Equals	1,227,726	7.2	8
Justicialist Party	1,142,522	6.7	9
Republican Initiative Alliance	1,046,020	6.2	9
Justicialist Front	670,309	3.9	7
Progressive, Civic and Social Front	625,335	3.7	5
Alliance Union of Cordoba	530,115	3.1	4
Federalist Unity	372,843	2.2	2
Alliance New Front	347,412	2.0	3
Front of Everyone	316,294	1.9	6
Civic Front for Santiago	185,733	1.1	3
Front for the Renewal of Concordia	189,327	1.1	2
Popular Movement of Neuquen	85,700	0.5	2
Others	3,647,997	21.5	7
Total	16,973,080	100.0	127

Source: Adam Carr's website.

The dominance of the 'executive' part of government in parliamentary systems—the permanent bureaucracy plus the elected politicians (ministers)—at the top of government departments has made them almost universally the primary focus of interest groups in those countries. It is now half a century since pioneering political scientists such as S. E. Finer (1958) and Samuel Beer (1965) drew attention to the importance of interest groups in policy-making in Britain through their close and recurring contacts with government departments.

The importance of interest groups in policy-making in the UK has fluctuated over time in both the 'micro' level of individual policies and the 'macro' level of styles of governance. The National Farmers' Union (NFU) was an integral part of agricultural policy-making, almost indistinguishable from the Ministry for Agriculture, Fisheries and Food (MAFF) during the period of food shortages during and for some time after the Second World War. From the 1960s onwards, as plentiful food supplies were taken for granted, its influence slipped. Both the Conservative Heath government (1970–74) and the Labour governments of 1964–70 and 1974–79 attempted to establish extremely close relationships with interest groups representing employers and workers.

The Thatcher government in contrast explicitly committed itself to decreasing the role of interest groups in policy-making, reducing the frequency and closeness of contacts with both the Trade Union Congress (TUC) and the employers' organization, the Confederation of British Industry (CBI). The Labour government led by Tony Blair (1997–2007) took care not to reverse this change (Grant 2000). Similarly in Japan, the relationship between the Ministry of International Trade and Industry (MITI) and both the general employers organization, the Keidanren and trade associations representing specific industries, was extremely close during the period of state-led economic growth (1950s to *c*.1990) (Johnson 1982). Thereafter, as this model of economic development seemed to falter, the relationship became less close and MITI was reorganized (Pempel 1998).

Yet a reduction in the power of interest groups is not the same as them becoming totally insignificant. Ironically, it was during the Thatcher years that British political scientists began to adopt a network model of governance, describing policy-making as the result of interactions between mutually dependent governmental and non-governmental actors, including interest groups (Rhodes and Marsh 1992).

How do we make sense of these trends in interest group politics on the one hand and the popularity of network perspectives in political science on the other? Perhaps the end of conspicuous monopolies on influence (such as that of the NFU with the MAFF in the UK) and the demise of even more conspicuous attempts at neo-corporatist policy-making at the level of the national economy obscure the continuing importance of networks that include interest groups in more prosaic policy areas. However, networks encompass many more actors than interest groups, including local governments, experts, and specialist journalists. It might be possible, therefore, to argue that the growth in the importance of networks that include interest groups is compatible with an argument that the influence of interest groups now has to be shared with influence for other non-governmental actors.

In the US, the focus of interest groups on Congress is so well known that some are still surprised that interest groups seek to influence other institutions as well. Congress plays a much more important role in policy-making than other legislatures (see Chapter 7). The relatively strong focus of its members on their own constituencies makes them attentive to the views of interest groups important within them. The role of interest groups in providing campaign finance or in participating directly in elections has increased yet further their prominence in congressional life. Although congressional committees have lost some of their autonomy and power as party leaders have become more important in recent years, they remain the locus of congressional policy-making on most issues most of the time, particularly in the House of Representatives.

Congressional committees are generally constituted of legislators whose constituencies are most affected by the policies and who are therefore most receptive to interest groups who represent them (Grier and Munger 1993). The combination of the power of congressional committees over agencies' budgets and legislative requests and the influence of interests affected by the agencies over legislators was often said to create 'sub-governments' or 'iron triangles', three-sided relationships between legislators, agencies, and interest groups that led to public policy being directed towards satisfying the interest group, not the public interest (McConnell 1966). For example, the Bureau of Land Management which controls federal land in the West of the US was said to follow policies of low rents and high grazing densities that satisfied the National Cattlemen's Association and western legislators on House and Senate Interior committees that oversaw the agency. Yet these high-density grazing and low-rent policies were probably bad for the environment and the taxpayer.

In recent decades, the iron triangle approach has fallen out of favour. Divisions on Congressional committees have become more frequent, often along party lines and the emergence of public interest groups has ended the monopoly once enjoyed by 'producer' groups (Berry 1999). To return to the example of ranching, the Interior Committees now include liberal environmentalists as well as conservative supporters of ranchers; the Cattlemen's Association must now deal with the criticisms of environmental groups. More amorphous policy networks have replaced homogeneous subgovernments (Heclo 1978).

Empirical studies of lobbying

The empirical study of lobbying has lagged behind that of other forms of political activity, probably because of its somewhat veiled character. A large-scale case study of trade politics was conducted by Bauer *et al.* (1963) in the 1950s and early 1960s; more comprehensive studies were undertaken by Heinz *et al.* (1993), Schlozman and Tierney (1986), and Walker (1991) in the 1970s and 1980s. These datasets are still being used with good effect today. Questions that have been explored include the degree to which lobbyists focus on mobilizing friends rather than persuading the undecided or legislators who are hostile and the formation of coalitions by interest groups (see e.g. Austen-Smith and Wright 1994, 1996; Baumgartner and Leech 1996a, b) and, as Table 14.3 demonstrates, how the definition of the lobbying community can vary widely based upon the policy domain.

Walker's work and its extension posthumously particularly by Baumgartner and his co-authors (e.g. Baumgartner and Leech 1998, 2001) has yielded a much richer understanding not only of interest groups but of policy change more generally. Baumgartner and Jones (1993) in particular have shown how policy change is dependent on changes in the understanding and definition of a policy with the effect of shifting the locus of decision-making to a less favourable environment to that which used to benefit the dominant interest. Pesticides and nuclear power, for example, were both redefined in ways that shifted the understanding of these issues from

Table 14.3 Organizational activity across four policy domains (%)

Organization type	Agriculture	Energy	Health	Labour
Business	20	54	15	8
Citizen	14	11	7	4
State/local government	3	5	6	1
Labor union	5	1	3	34
Minority group	3	0	14	11
Nonprofit	1	4	21	7
Professional	1	3	17	4
Trade association	51	22	16	26
Other	2	0	1	6
Total	100	100	100	100

Source: Heinz *et al.* (1993: 63).

being almost miraculous benefits of science to be-ing imminent dangers from which the public needed protection. This change in turn resulted in changes in the location of decision-making, the actors involved, and, finally, in policy outcomes. Bosso (1987) has documented such a pattern in pesticide regulatory policy.

Approaches to lobbying other institutions

Comparative political scientists have not ignored the relationships between interest groups and other in-stitutions but have in general paid less attention to them. It is, for example, scarcely novel to point to the role of interest groups in judicial politics (see Chapter 9). Interest groups have been highly visible actors in some of the tumultuous confirmation fights over nominations to the Supreme Court (and less conspicuously to lower courts, especially the Appeal Courts). The rejection of the nomination of Robert Bork in 1987 and the bruising but successful fight to place Clarence Thomas on the court in 1991 wit-nessed large-scale mobilization of the public as well as intensive lobbying by interest groups both in favour of and against the nominations (Silverstein 1994; Caldeira and Wright 1998).

It is also well known that interest groups are heavily involved in litigation either in bringing cases them-selves, funding and organizing the filing of cases by suitable individuals, or by filing *amicus curiae* briefs in support or opposition to claims filed by others. Caldeira and Wright (1988) have shown that the fil-ing of a large number of *amicus curiae* briefs makes it more likely that the Supreme Court will hear the case. Interest group involvement in filing or organizing the filing of cases has been associated with high-profile decisions such as the NAACP's successful pursuit of an end to legally based segregation through the courts, culminating in *Brown* v. *Board of Education of Topeka*.

Less well known but of great importance is the activity of interest groups in contesting regulations is-sued by agencies such as the Occupational Safety and Health Administration (OSHA) or Environmental Protection Agency (EPA). Under the Administrative Procedures Act or the legislation creating the indi-vidual regulatory agency, those affected by a new regulation (often interest groups and businesses) can

challenge it in the courts, either on the basis that there were procedural failings in its adoption or that the agency lacked adequate evidence on which to base the regulation. Both the actual challenges to regulations and the threat of such challenges can have a substan-tial impact on the behaviour of regulatory agencies (Wilson 1985). These challenges are important not only in their impact on a specific regulation but in influencing the capacity of the agencies to regu-late; agencies tied up in court defending proposed regulations are less able to develop additional ones.

Do interest groups make significant use of the courts in other countries? The courts in the US have a degree of power in policy-making unmatched in any other democracy. However, there has been a clear trend towards an increased role for the judiciary in policy-making in many democracies, including those such as Canada and the UK long regarded as minim-izing its power. Both countries have taken important steps towards instantiating basic rights and freedoms as a higher form of law. Presumably this will provide a means by which interest groups can bring or support challenges to ordinary legislation. The judicial arm of the EU, the European Court of Justice, has tre-mendous opportunities to exert influence on a wide range of issues such as environmental and industrial policies, as it decides whether member-states have complied with EU regulations (directives) or with the fundamental treaties creating the EU.

Relations between interest groups and executive agencies in general remain poorly explored. Students of the American bureaucracy, notably Aberbach and Rockman (2000), have noted the frequency of interactions between interest groups and executive officials. Journalists have drawn attention to the highly privileged position that business groups have enjoyed under the administration of George W. Bush. Not only have these business groups been given privileged access in drafting policies, but they have also been able to have their officials appointed to key positions within the agencies themselves. The trucking (lorry) industry has had several of its officials appointed to key positions in the agencies that set safety policies for the industry (such as maximum driving hours for truck/lorry drivers) and these appointees in turn have followed policies that serve the economic interests of the industry, arguably at the cost of increased risk to the public (*New York Times,* 3 December 2006). And in May 2007, the chief lawyer of the National Association of Manufacturers was appointed to run the Consumer Products Safety Commission (*New York Times,* 17 May 2007).

Comparative politics has generally shied away form purely partisan explanations for the power of interest groups in the executive branch (Peterson 1992). We have already encountered one perspective on interest groups and the executive branch, namely the iron triangle or subgovernment formulation. Largely concentrated on agencies that are rarely in the mind of the president, that is, outside the core executive of the OMB, NSC, State Department, etc., the iron triangle subgovernment perspective suggested that interest groups and their congressional allies, not the White House, would shape how agencies behaved. We discussed above the view that the iron triangle/subgovernment perspective described the past, not present, of interest group politics. However, in spite of its initial appeal, the network perspective that displaced it also has troubles describing the relationship between interest groups and the executive branch today.

The initial appeal of network perspectives derives from its emphasis on shared values and frequent contacts. As Aberbach *et al.* (1981) demonstrated, the American senior civil service is very different from the British, Japanese, or French. Rather than consisting (as in those examples) of people traditionally drawn from the most prestigious universities, with an education aimed at producing generalists, the American higher civil service consists of specialists with technical educations drawn from a wide variety of universities. They have more in common with people with similar backgrounds in industries or interest groups with whom they deal than with each other. Moreover, the well-known 'revolving door' of Washington politics takes people who have had successful careers in government and places them in higher paid jobs in the private sector, often working for interest groups or businesses dealing with the agency for which they worked.

What, then, of the limitations of a network perspective? Its problems derive from ignoring ideology, partisanship, and their impact on executive branch politics. A vast number of subjects are understood very differently by people depending on their ideology and partisanship. Two very different policy areas, climate change and education, illustrate the point. In the US conservative Republicans deny that climate change is occurring, or, if it is, that the behaviour of Americans plays any significant role in causing it; liberal Democrats believe the opposite. Conservative Republicans believe that public schools should be replaced by private schools and parents be given vouchers to use pay for tuition; liberal Democrats believe that children should attend public schools.

In this highly ideological and partisan atmosphere, the idea of a civil service providing 'neutral competence' is hard to sustain (see Chapter 8). Instead, more and more political appointments are made to government agencies with the intent of either subjugating the civil servants within them or of providing a potential for policy-making that is independent of them. This 'thickening' of government (to use Light's 1995 term), removes the permanent civil service from the making of key decisions and facilitates (as in the decisions on going to war with Iraq) the demand that any information or advice supplied be fitted to the preconceptions of the political appointees. In turn, the political appointees limit access to those interest groups that their party favours and insist that the interest groups employ lobbyists who are supporters of their party. In short, whereas network approaches postulate the linkages of civil servants and interest groups on the basis of education and shared expertise, Washington in recent times has seen numerous examples of policy areas characterized by competing liberal/Democratic and conservative/Republican networks. At least in the case of the conservative/Republican network, power has been used to exclude the alternative network from influencing key debates and decisions; it remains to be seen what would happen were the Democrats to control the White House and Congress simultaneously in this new environment.

Determinants of interest group strategies

Most of the writing on interest groups and political institutions has been descriptive rather than theoretical and uninterested in comparisons between countries. Perhaps the closest most studies of interest groups come to theorizing about their relationship with political institutions is to approach the question of what determines interest group strategies.

Wyn Grant (2000) asked a crucial question about British politics: why do some interest groups in the UK cultivate an **insider** strategy and others an **outsider** approach? Interest groups that follow an insider approach attempt to establish a close, confidential relationship with a government department and eschew militant tactics or large-scale demonstrations. Those using an outside strategy do the opposite. Ken Goldstein (1999) asked a similar question in the US: why do some interest groups in the make large-scale campaign contributions whereas others focus on the 'grass roots'? Goldstein finds that, in many ways, mass outside participation is just as choreographed as insider strategies, but that an outside strategy is more explicitly premised on stressing the electoral connection than traditional lobbying. Grant and Goldstein remain exceptions, however, leaving scholars to debate as to whether the 'network' perspective is a form of theorizing or merely sophisticated description.

A question that is surprisingly rarely asked by comparative political scientists is what effect political institutions have in shaping interest groups or interest group systems. At the most obvious level, interest groups in many countries have been sponsored and promoted by government (Nownes 1995; Browne 1998). At moments in their history, groups as diverse as the American Farm Bureau Federation (AFBF), American Medical Association (AMA), and National Rifle Association (NRA) all received support from government institutions. An obvious topic for more theoretical consideration could be the conditions under which government institutions actively promoted the development of interest groups.

At a deeper level, an argument can be made that interest group structures are to an important degree shaped by the character of the political institutions they confront. Thus the overlapping, fragmented political institutions of the US facilitate the existence of an interest group system that is also highly fragmented (Wilson 1990). There are usually several organizations competing for the title of being the authentic representative of sectors of society such as farming or business. In contrast, countries that have political institutions which centralize power to a greater degree also have more unified interest groups; there is clearly a single dominant group representing sectors in the UK such as agriculture and business. How far this correlation between the character of interest group systems and the political institutions on which they operate is due to strategic calculation by the groups ('We better unite to have an impact') and how far it is due to choices by governments ('We don't want to be bothered dealing with numerous competing groups') could be an interesting question to explore further.

> **KEY POINTS**
>
> ❑ Interest groups lobby the institutions that have the most power and the institutions on which they can exert most influence. These may be either or both legislatures or executives. Interest groups lobby also other institutions, namely judicial ones or bureaucracies.
>
> ❑ The interaction between interest groups and state institutions can be described in different perspectives: iron triangle, subgovernment, network. Interest group strategies can be either insider strategies or outsider strategies.
>
> ❑ Institutions have a strong effect in shaping interest group configurations. In many cases, interest groups have been sponsored and promoted by government. More generally, institutional frameworks shape interest group structures: fragmented institutions lead to fragmented interest group systems; political institutions that centralize power lead to more unified interest groups.

Interest groups and state–society relations

The early great studies of interest groups such as V. O. Key (1942) and David Truman (1951) paid considerable attention to the relationships between capital, agriculture, labour, and government. In part this was a reflection of the realities of interest group politics at the time; the public interest groups that so often spring to mind in the US when interest groups are mentioned did not then exist in significant form. In part, however, this reflected the traditional concern of political sociology with these relationships.

The central role of business

Capital and, to a lesser extent, farmers and unions are key players in the interest group politics of all democracies. The vast majority of lobbyists work for business organizations or individual companies (Berry 1997). Business is by far the largest player in campaign finance through its PACs and whatever other means for making contributions happen to be available at the time. The collective institutions representing business in the US—the competing peak associations such as the National Association of Manufacturers (NAM), Chamber of Commerce, and Business Roundtable—are less powerful *vis-à-vis* member companies than their counterparts in, for example, continental Europe. Much the same is true of American trade associations, with a few exceptions such as the American Chemistry Council. However, American businesses, their trade associations, and umbrella groups are very active practitioners of standard interest group politics—lobbying, mobilizing public support, making campaign contributions.

In contrast, business organizations in most other democracies play a less overt role in politics. This is not to say, of course, that business is not important politically. The long dominant Liberal Democratic Party in Japan and the Conservative Party in the UK both used to receive large-scale financial support from business. Business contributions to the Conservative Party always tended to come from a limited number of businesses and in recent decades this support has declined too. However, in most democracies business has tried to avoid overt political involvement in order to cultivate an image of non-partisan expertise. The goal has been to present a picture of business as an indispensable partner, not merely an interest group (on party finance see Chapter 12).

This image of business as a 'social partner', not a mere interest group, has often, indeed usually, characterized the strategy of the CBI in the UK (Grant 2000). It is even more the case in those countries characterized as having coordinated market economies (CMEs) by Hall and Soskice (2001*b*). CMEs are those in which the allocation of resources including investment capital is made not only or even primarily through market mechanisms but through the integrated, coordinated activities of firms, banks, and governments. Much of the growth of Japanese business was funded at low cost by the savings of citizens lodged in the Post Office bank. Investment decisions on Volkswagen are made by the bank associated with the firm that is in turn an offshoot of the *Land* (state) in which the firm is primarily located.

In turn, the firm will accept a degree of responsibility for the long-term nurturing of the region in which it is based that US companies would find strange. On a day-to-day basis, large-scale enterprises in countries such as Japan and Germany are indeed not merely interest groups but participants in the governance of their locales.

The idea that some interest groups, especially business and unions, are not merely interest groups but are social partners is much more widely accepted in the CMEs than in what Hall and Soskice term the liberal market economies such as the US and UK. Business organizations and large firms are not merely interest groups outside the state exerting pressure on it; they are partners in governance that participate in providing essential services and solving problems. The most visible expression of this idea has been in the neo-corporatist countries, as described by Schmitter (1985, 2000). An essential point to grasp is that neo-corporatism is not only a forum in which key policy is formulated by government in partnership with business but is a societal system in which businesses, business organizations, and unions take responsibility for addressing societal problems. In the Covenant system in the Netherlands, for example, businesses and their organizations commit to solving problems in formal agreements with government. Covenants provided one way in which the Netherlands could try to meet its commitments under the Kyoto Treaty. Large-scale users of energy around Rotterdam, for example, agreed to become either the best in the world or equal to the best in the world within five years in terms of reducing greenhouse gases. In Germany, trade associations have long accepted responsibility for regulating their members' performance in health and safety or the protection of the environment. Their role in environmental protection has been codified in the Eco Management and Auditing System (EMAS) authorized by the EU.

The argument that business is not merely an interest group is also made in liberal market economies but in a different form. In these countries the concern is that, as Lindblom (1977) argued some thirty years ago, business has a 'privileged position' in part because it can switch investment to different locations in response to how it is treated. States or countries that treat business less favourably will receive less investment or experience capital flight and, in consequence, will suffer a decline in their standard of living. Politicians, regardless of ideology, eager for re-election will ward off this catastrophe by giving business what it wants and will do so, Lindblom stressed, without being pressured, bribed, or pushed by interest group activity. In a sense, therefore, business did not even need to undertake conventional interest group activity.

Lindblom was probably focused on the opportunities that American federalism provided for businesses to exert leverage by moving or even just threatening to move away from high tax or strict regulatory environments. The advent of globalization gave his arguments more general applicability. Cheap and easy communications such as email, the safe and easy transport of products in containerized shipping, and rapid, low-cost movements of capital facilitated both by modern technology and the removal of government controls made it easier than ever before for businesses to move around the globe. There was much fear that, in consequence, there would be a 'race to the bottom' as government reduced taxes and weakened regulations in order to attract or retain investment (Greider 1997). The degree to which these fears have been well founded remains to be seen (Kahler and Lake 2003). Many countries have reduced taxation on businesses and highly paid people (usually business executives). It is possible that governments have been deterred from adding to what businesses like to call 'the regulatory burden'. There is, however, no evidence that there has been any significant move to roll back regulations on safety and health or the environment; indeed, Vogel (1995) argues that globalization has tended to raise, not lower standards overall. The 'privileged position of business' argument has additional weaknesses, however.

1. It ignores major differences between industries in the ease with which they can move around (Chapman and Walker 1991). It is relatively easy to shift garment manufacturing (shirts, jeans, etc.) around the world. It is much less easy to move an industry dependent on extracting rare resources (e.g. diamonds) or on scarce skills (e.g. computer development).

2. Business's needs or wishes are often more complicated than lower taxes or weaker regulations. In general, it has been lower skill industries such as textile manufacturing that have moved readily, whereas high value added, high skill industries

have not. Perhaps because effective government services such as education are important to them, high tech industries have flourished and remained in higher tax, stricter regulation states such as California rather than moving to lower tax, weaker regulation states such as Mississippi.

3. As briefly mentioned above, ease of movement for business between states and countries is not something that just happens but is the result of deliberately adopted policies (Vogel 2006). Globalization was only to a limited extent the unplanned product of technological change; it was more the consequence of agreements between governments to more or less abolish tariffs on manufactured goods and controls on capital movements.

Nonetheless, the 'privileged position' argument does make a compelling case for seeing business as not just another interest group.

The changing and weakening role of labour

Labour unions also have had a somewhat special character as interest groups. At different times and in different places, unions have defined their role as mere bargaining agents for higher wages, as organizations for the promotion of the working class both through wage bargaining and through lobbying for legislation that would benefit it, and finally as agents of social transformation towards a better society. In consequence, their political role has also varied tremendously (Wilson 1979; Asher 2001).

In the American craft union tradition of Gompers and the American Federation of Labor (AFL), the only (though often considerable) political task for unions was to secure a legal environment that allowed them to exert power in collective bargaining. Similar concerns prompted British unions to create the Labour Representation Committee prior to the First World War to promote the selection and election of pro-union members of parliament (MPs) within the Liberal Party. The Congress of Industrial Organizations (CIO) tradition in the US gave unions a wider role as champions of policies benefiting the less affluent, including policies such as Medicare as well as collective bargaining. Unions have also supported and sustained the creation of parties such as the Labour Party in the UK, nominally dedicated to social transformation. Finally, and most obviously (but not exclusively), in the neo-corporatist countries, unions have wanted to be recognized as a social partner on a par with business, involved in tripartite discussions on major policy issues and accepting responsibility for administering services such as health insurance or apprenticeship training.

Unions have often had some trouble in deciding which of these roles they wish to adopt. While British unions have wanted to preserve a sense that the Labour Party which they sustain through their financial contributions should be controlled by them, they have also wanted to function as an expert lobby commanding attention from both Conservative and Labour governments. One Secretary General of the TUC boasted that he had taken unions out of Trafalgar Square (the traditional rallying point for demonstrations) and into Whitehall (the location of top-level government offices). In the neo-corporatist countries, the unions have often traded off wage increases in tripartite discussions with government and business for government promises to expand the welfare state. And as the size of the traditional working class (never, as Przeworski [1985] argued, a majority of the population) has declined, the political costs to labour or social democratic parties of being perceived to be controlled by unions has increased.

Unions have lost strength around the world (for data see Chapter 18). This is in part due to the decline of employment in traditionally unionized industries such as coal mining. The decline of unions also demonstrates, however, the importance of government policies on interest groups in contrast to the impact of interest groups on government policies. Some of the decline in the power of unions is attributed to the risks of outsourcing or shifting production overseas that are an aspect of globalization. In some countries such the UK and US, the power of unions has been reduced consciously by legislation that erodes their power in collective bargaining by, for example, changing the law to limit strikes and picketing. One reason why British unions accepted a diminution of their unpopular power in the Labour Party was their desperation to see an end to Conservative governments that had done so much to reduce their industrial power through numerous statutory changes in the rights of unions. A similar dynamic captured the relationship between

American unions and the Democratic Party from the 1950s onward (Davis 1986).

Interest groups and normative theory

The political economy perspective on interest groups therefore directs our attention away from their narrower, more strictly defined political roles and towards their broader position in the economy and society. It links their status and power not only to their ability to lobby, raise money for candidates or parties, and mobilize members to vote 'the right way' but to social responsibilities and the variety (form) of capitalism that exists.

There has been a tendency in the US and, to a certain degree in the UK, to see interest groups, particularly interest groups such as businesses or unions, as inevitably deleterious to economic success. Interest groups create policies that interfere with market efficiencies by providing them with 'rents', that is, unwarrantable incomes (Godwin and Sheldon 1998). Mancur Olson (1982) argued that the accrual of benefits by interest groups at the expense of economic efficiency over time would ultimately cause the decline of nations. As we have seen, such perspectives are misleadingly simple. The roles as well as powers of business groups and unions are deeply embedded in the varying forms of capitalism that exist. At least at some times and in some places (such as the neo-corporatist countries), extensive power for these interest groups can be associated with them playing an important, constructive role in governance (see Chapter 20).

An important stimulus to the study of interest group politics is the clear relevance of its subject matter to normative political theory. Interest group scholars ask how much power minorities hold and what differentiates the minorities that are and those that are not represented by interest groups. As we have seen in passing, empirical studies of interest groups have often been related to these normative concerns.

Most American writing on interest groups has been explicitly or implicitly related to the debate about whether the American polity is one in which power is widely dispersed among competing interests that encompass more or less all of American society or not. Many studies have tried to show that, in spite of the variety and number of interest groups in the US, pluralism is not an accurate description of the polity (Mills 1956; Bachrach and Baratz 1962; Lowi 1969; Lukes 1974). Others have tried to show the opposite (Truman 1951; Latham 1952; Dahl 1956, 1961). Much of the focus has been on the degree to which there are important interests that are not represented in the interest group system or, in contrast, that there are interests—usually business—that enjoy privileged status or power in the interest group system, power that is hard to reconcile with democratic values (Schlozman 1984; Schlozman and Tierney 1986).

The rich pluralist tradition is not limited to the impact of interest groups on policy, however, but has also focused on the impact of groups on their own members. Tocqueville famously argued that groups could be training grounds for citizens, providing experience at a direct, more limited level, of practices vital to democracy. Groups have been credited with the capacity to counteract the anomie of mass society. The development of groups providing a 'civil society' that stands between the individual citizen and the state has been seen as a key part of a transition from totalitarian or authoritarian dictatorships to a truly democratic society. This aspect of theorizing about transitions draws in part on the Tocquevillian view of interest groups as training grounds for democracy and partly on the belief that involvement in groups promotes social capital, the willingness of citizens to work with and trust each other (see e.g. Putnam 1993 or Encarnación 2001). As we noted above, there has been much discussion of whether or not the associational life of Western democracies has been declining as citizens watch more television and engage less with each other (Putnam 1995; see also Chapter 17).

Debates about declining social capital have focused largely on questions such as whether or not citizens are indeed less involved in *any* groups or whether they are merely involving themselves with *different*

groups. Perhaps soccer clubs have displaced bowling clubs. There has been less attention paid to the characteristics of groups themselves and therefore their capacity to provide the benefits that social theorists have hoped they would. Most interest groups in the US today are far from the participatory organizations Tocqueville and others have celebrated (Skocpol 2003). The sole act linking many members to many groups is writing a cheque or giving a credit card number online or over the phone in order to express anger with a hate figure that the group promises to campaign against. There is not much such groups do to decrease anomie or foster social capital.

Nonetheless, the debates in normative theory continue to provide a welcome stimulus to interest group studies. In consequence, interest group scholars should have little difficulty in answering the 'so what?' question about their work.

KEY POINTS

❑ Interest groups play an important role in linking state and society. They are much more than pressure groups. Rather they have roles as 'social partners' in governance that participate in providing services and solving political problems.

❑ The role of trade unions as social partners has declined over time. Their role as social partner remains important in neo-corporatist countries in which unions are recognized on a par with business and the state.

❑ The role of interest groups as social partners and their influence in decision-making processes is democratically important as it represents a form of pluralism and of diffusion of power outside the state. Interest groups also have an important function as training grounds for citizens, providing direct experiences of social participation and democratic practice.

Conclusion

This chapter has suggested that the glory and the problem of interest groups as a field of comparative politics is that it is a meeting ground for scholars motivated by contrasting interests. As the numerous cross-references with other chapters in

this volume show, these include the study of political participation, political institutions, political parties, elections, policy-making, and that of political economy. No doubt other contributions to interest group studies could be identified. It is obviously tempting to give the field greater coherence by dropping one or more of these interests and saying that the study of interests groups is or ought to be properly limited to merely one. However, those more concerned with understanding interest groups than with comparative politics as a discipline should resist such arguments. Every one of these contributes something to understanding interest group politics and the ideal study of both specific interest groups and interest group systems should take them all into account.

World trends

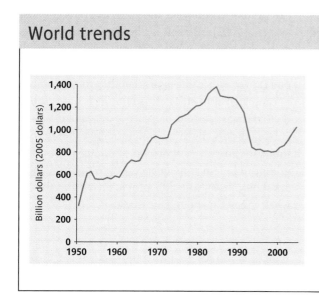

Trend 5 Trade: world military expenditures (1950–2004)

Source: Bulletin of Peace Proposals, Worldwatch, Bonn International Center for Conversion, Stockholm International Peace Research Institute.

? Questions

1. How has the nature of group membership changed since the time that Alexis de Tocqueville wrote *Democracy in America*? What are the consequences of these changes?
2. How does the collective action problem apply to interest groups? What are the principle means that interest groups have for overcoming the collective action problem?
3. Who are the targets of interest groups' lobbying efforts in the Europe and US? What factors determine who interest groups lobby in these different settings?
4. What are iron triangles and issue networks? Does either term describe the interactions between interests and the government in the US or Europe?
5. How do the differing natures of various national bureaucracies (e.g. in the US, the UK, France, and Japan) affect the ways in which interest groups approach lobbying the government?
6. How do interest group systems vary with different countries' economic systems?
7. What are the principal objections to the notion the business holds a privileged position in the political system? Does the evidence presented in the tables for this chapter support or refute these claims?
8. How has globalization affected the 'privileged position of business'?
9. How do interest groups contribute to the fostering of social capital and a civil society?
10. How accurate a depiction of the American interest group system and American society does pluralism provide?

» Further reading

Baumgartner, Frank R., and Leech, Beth L. (1998) *Basic Interests: The Importance of Groups in Politics and in Political Science* (Princeton: Princeton University Press). The most recent, comprehensive review survey of the study of interest groups in American political science.

Berry, Jeffery M., and Wilcox, Clyde (2006) *The Interest Group Society* (New York: Longman, 4th edn). A textbook-like treatment of the place and power of interest groups in American politics.

Coen, David (2007) *Lobbying the European Union: Institutions, Actors and Policy* (Oxford: Oxford University Press). A new study that focuses on the increasing presence and importance of lobbying in Brussels.

Dahl, Robert A. (1961) *Who Governs?* (New Haven, Conn.: Yale University Press). The classic articulation of the pluralist argument.

Heinz, John P., Laumann, Edward O., Nelson, Robert L., and Salisbury, Robert H. (1993) *The Hollow Core: Private Interests in National Policy Making* (Cambridge, Mass.: Harvard University Press). An empirical re-examination of the Washington, DC, lobbying community that challenged many accepted arguments about lobbying in the US.

Lindblom, Charles E. (1977) *Politics and Markets: The World's Political–Economic Systems* (New York: Basic Books). The seminal work on the political power of business within global society.

Olson, Mancur (1965) *The Logic of Collective Action* (Cambridge, Mass.: Harvard University Press). The major challenge to the pluralist tradition; most work on the formation and maintenance of interest groups begins by addressing Olson's argument.

Putnam, Robert D. (2000) *Bowling Alone: The Collapse and Revival of American Community* (New York: Simon & Schuster). A recent work lamenting the decline of social capital amongst the American public, primarily due to its increasing focus on activities, such as watching television, that do not involve the broader community.

Walker, Jack L., Jr. (1991) *Mobilizing Interest Groups in America* (Ann Arbor, Mich.: University of Michigan Press). A major empirical study of all aspects of the political behaviour of interest groups, based upon surveys of groups throughout the 1980s.

Wilson, Graham K. (1990) *Interest Groups* (Cambridge, Mass.: Blackwell). A comparative empirical study of interest groups.

Ⓦ Web links

http://herrnson.cqpress.com/IGs.htm
    CQ Press is a leading political science publisher in the US; this website provides hyperlinks to the websites of many major American political interest groups, including the AFL-CIO, the Chamber of Commerce, the League of Conservation Voters, and the National Rifle Association.

http://ec.europa.eu/civil_society/index_en.htm
    The European Commission is the executive arm of the European Union. In 2006, the Commission began the European Transparency Initiative, which focused on reforming lobbying activities, amongst other political and policy activities.

www.fec.gov
    The Federal Election Commission is responsible for the enforcement of campaign finance law at the federal level in the US. They also collect and distribute data free of charge to the public.

http://lobby.la.psu.edu
The Collaborative Research Project on Lobbying and Policy Advocacy is led by Frank R. Baumgartner. The project examines and provides information on the policy issues on which federal lobbyists in the US were active in the late 1990s and early 2000s.

 Visit the Online Resource Centre that accompanies this book for more information:
www.oxfordtextbooks.co.uk/orc/caramani/

15 Regions

James Bickerton and Alain-G. Gagnon

Chapter contents

Reader's guide

This chapter examines the concept of region and starts by reviewing the main theories and approaches that are used to understand the political role and importance of regions. It then discusses the various dimensions and aspects of regions and regionalism. Regionalism from below concerns the political mobilization of regional identities, whether by movements or political parties. Looking at regional institutions involves an examination of how regions have been recognized, accommodated, and sometimes created by states through a process of regionalization 'from above', undertaken by central governments with administrative and governance purposes in mind. Finally, the chapter focuses on the political economy of regions, tracing the changing economic role and place of regions within the national and global economy. Of particular note is the emergence of a new regionalism tied to the economic, technological, and political changes associated with increasing integration and globalization.

Introduction

What is a region? It is a geographical space. But beyond that there are many meanings attached to it, and many approaches used to understand it. It has been called 'a multiple abstraction, and a slippery idea for those who use it as a conceptual tool' (Rasporich 1997: 322). According to Keating, it may relate to an identity; it often has a cultural element; it may sustain a distinct society and a range of social institutions. It can be an economic unit or a unit of government and administration. And all these meanings may coincide, to a greater or lesser degree (Keating 2004: xi).

The idea of region is both simple and highly ambiguous. We are reminded that:

> **❝** in most states, the region is a contested area, both territorially and functionally. Spatially, it exists between the national and the local and is the scene of intervention by actors from all levels, national, local, regional and now supranational. Functionally, it is a space in which different types of agency interact and, since it is often weakly institutionalized itself, a terrain of competition among them. (Keating 1997: 17) **❞**

Sometimes used when referring to intermediate levels of political representation or governance (provinces, states, *Lander*, counties, supra-urban areas), region also has been employed to refer to a spatial area within a state encompassing more than one political unit (New England), or a supra-national area stretching across state boundaries (for example, the Great Lakes or Cascadia regions of North America). It may not be demarcated by political boundaries at all but by particular cultural or economic characteristics (such as the Acadian region in Canada or Silicon Valley in California). The latter use of the term denotes 'a territorial entity having some natural and organic unity or community of interest that is independent of political and administrative boundaries' (Stevenson 1980: 17).

Not surprisingly, then, geographers, economists, sociologists, and political scientists all define region using different criteria, leading Simeon to argue that 'regions are simply containers . . . and how we draw the boundaries around them depends entirely on what our purposes are: it is an *a priori* question, determined by theoretical needs or political purposes' (1977: 293). With such a malleable nature, 'political entrepreneurs themselves seek to shape the definition of region to reflect their values and interests' (Keating 1997: 17). So, while the concept of region must always be associated with territorial space (as it traditionally has been), it also must be understood as a social, economic, and political construction; that is, the historical work of human actors and actions. Regions and regionalism are not static, unchanging, and geographically determined; they are the continuous creation of human history, the product of complex interactions between the region's external environment (economic, political, institutional) and its internal life. This makes the task of delineating regions—their number, shape, and character, and the identities associated with them—dependent upon a host of factors.

That regions and regionalism exist politically is an irrefutable fact of political life, in most if not all states. Therefore their study is an important part of the collective effort to understand politics in all its complexity at the local, national, and supra-national levels. In Europe, North America, and other areas of the world, regions have influenced the composition and practices of political party systems, set political agendas, shaped constitutions, legislatures, and administrative structures, contested national identities, and been the cause or stimulus for a wide range of public policies and governance mechanisms. Its impact on both government structures and political processes has been significant. Yet its multiple and overlapping meanings, its pervasive character, and its often elusive and intangible quality—both as a concept and a political phenomenon—make its study a challenging and often imprecise exercise. Nonetheless, the various manifestations of region, and the complicated dynamics of regionalism, have never been as important an aspect of European and global politics as they are today.

KEY POINTS

❑ Region is a concept with multiple meanings, though always referring to a territorial space. Its exact meaning is determined by the theoretical needs or political purposes for which it is being used.

❑ Regions exist as political, economic, cultural, and administrative units. Regionalism, which is the political mobilization of individuals based on their common attachment to, identification with, and interest in the region, can manifest itself in one or all of these dimensions simultaneously.

❑ Regions and regionalism can have an effect on and interact with all the various structures and processes that define the political system.

Theories and approaches

The modernization paradigm

Until the 1960s, the study of regions in social science was dominated by the modernization paradigm and development theory. Industrialization, bureaucratization, and the emergence of the nation-state had generated a scholarly focus on functionalism and national integration as the hallmarks of modern societies. These concepts were theorized and applied by a long line of social scientists, including Weber (1968), Smelser (1966), Deutsch (1966), Shils (1975), and many others. Regions and regionalism were seen as remnants of pre-industrial, pre-modern societies, fated to be eclipsed by the inexorable march of progress in the form of the homogeneous, functionally organized, nationally integrated nation-state (Caramani 2004). This fit well with the predictions of neo-classical economists who held that the establishment and maintenance of free markets would lead eventually to the even spatial diffusion of investment and employment, creating a situation of equilibrium where levels of economic growth and development would differ little from region to region.

For modernization theorists such as Shils, cultural homogenization is a key process in the inevitable decline of regionalism and territorially based conflict. Regional peripheries are seen as isolated, distant from the centre, and oppressively traditional in their cultural values. The challenge for elites is to diffuse their 'modern' values to the peripheries, thereby securing adherence to a central value system. Ruling in this model consists of the universalization within society of the values and the rules inherent in the ordering of modern societies. As noted by Tarrow, this approach provides the elites at the centre who seek to control, regulate, and reform regional peripheries with an ideology that turns their domination over these regions into legitimized hegemony (1977: 20; for data on national communication networks see Comparative table 1 at the end of this volume).

In conjunction with the functionalist approach of sociologists like Shils, a behaviouralist regional science emerged that increasingly emptied region of its historical and social content, substituting an abstract notion of space defined by one or more criteria, such as population density or income, as the delineators of region. This allowed economists to apply micro-economic models to these spatial units unfettered by concerns such as regional history, culture, or social conflict. As purely economic development units, regions could be subjected to technocratic forms of planning. Out of this grew such notions as 'stepping down' the economic dynamism of the core to peripheral regions, first elaborated by Perroux (1950) and Myrdal (1957), leading to the spread of growth centre strategies as the international leitmotiv of regional planning in the 1960s and 1970s. Despite its immodest attempts at scientific precision and its shunning of the insights of other disciplines, regional science was an important innovator in the realm of the spatial dimension, particularly 'the insight that the proximity or remoteness of economic agents to each other . . . is a central feature of regional life' (Markusen 1987: 253–5).

If the pervasive influence of the modernization paradigm led to the neglect of regions in social science, or their reduction to mere spatial units emptied of history and social content, interest in regions and regionalism was reinvigorated from the 1960s with the critique of this perspective. Stein Rokkan and others began to challenge the notion that territorial cleavages were of declining significance and relevance by demonstrating the persistence of earlier territorial cleavages into modern times. In the 1970s and 1980s, these cleavages spawned peripheral protest movements and concentrations of territorial-cultural opposition to ruling elites. Seeking more autonomy, self-determination, and special recognition, these movements were sometimes successful in stimulating **federalizing** strategies of accommodation in response (Rokkan 1980).

Culturalism and minority nationalism

One way scholars have understood the persistence of regionalism, contrary to the expectations of the modernization paradigm, is to view it from a cultural perspective. Distinct regional cultures can sustain a sense of regional community and provide the basis for values and policy preferences that differ from other regions or the larger national community. This cultural approach has long informed the historical treatment of regions and the phenomenon of regionalism. In the US, Frederick Jackson Turner's provocative essay, 'The Significance of the Frontier in American History', provided an explanation for regional dissent in the American West that emphasized the unique conditions and experience of the frontier. This encouraged distinctive cultural values such as self-reliance, ingenuity, and participatory democracy that in turn fed a sense of political alienation towards what was perceived to be an old-world, corrupt, and domineering East (1894). In more recent times, similar arguments have been deployed to help to explain the persistence of western regionalism in Canada (Gibbins and Berdahl 2003).

Almond and Verba (1963), Hartz (1955, 1964), Lipset (1990), and others have used a culturalist approach to explain cross-national variations in political life based on differences in national values (see Chapter 17). Widely shared identities and values are thought to structure a society's political behaviour. This general approach has also been used to explain regionalism within countries, whether through reference to different regional political cultures or the cultural effects of different initial settlement patterns (in Hartzian terms, 'founding fragments'). This is argued to have produced spatially distinct value

systems capable of supporting different regional outlooks and policy preferences (for Canada, see McRae 1964; Elkins and Simeon 1974; Wiseman 1981).

Regions as cultural spaces, however, cannot be definitively located or pinned down to a single spatial context. Regional sensibilities, outlooks, or identities can exist within a number of different spatial contexts simultaneously. The core elements of such multilayered identities are nested in such factors as physical geography, economy, institutions, and social characteristics such as class, religion, language, ethnicity, and community heritage (Soja 1989). To the extent that regional identities exist, however, they are available to be mobilized politically, given the right conditions and the availability of means and resources for giving voice to a particular regional identity and the interests and concerns linked to it. In this way a region's history, mythologies, and cultural symbols become a discursive and ideological resource for political actors.

In North America, Europe, and elsewhere, the role of culture in shaping the distinctiveness if not the singularity of the regional experience is magnified by the presence of ethnic minorities with claims to historic nation status. In such circumstances, the myth of the nation-state has been countered by the assertion of the existence of plural identities within state boundaries, contradicting assumptions and expectations about the assimilation of minorities within majority identities. Certainly, minority nationalism tends to be more freighted with emotion and provides individuals with a political and cultural identity that differs from that associated with being a resident of a region. Accordingly, the claims of regions tend to be more modest than those of minority nations, both for individuals and towards state authorities.

Not surprisingly, regions that are home to minority nations—such as Québecois, Scots, or Catalans—are where the most persistent and politically potent forms of regionalism can be found (Gagnon and Tully 2001). Moreover, that cultural differences *per se* may be diminishing over time does not seem to herald any similar decline in the salience of regional or national identities. In Canada, Québecois, Western Canadian, and Aboriginal identities became more politicized precisely at a time when inter-regional and inter-group cultural differences were much less significant than they had been historically (Gibbins 1980; Cairns 2004). The same could be said about the recent upwelling of various regionalisms and minority nationalisms in Europe. This suggests that cultural distinctiveness and political identity formation are separate phenomena, and need not operate in tandem. Identities are not single or exclusive, but multiple and complex, in both individuals and communities. The human capacity to sustain and compartmentalize multiple identities is a highly developed skill of contemporary citizens. Indeed, with appropriate institutional arrangements, cultural convergence and the increasing commonality of values can expand the basis for people with distinct identities to share institutions; can increase their potential for living together and living apart at the same time.

Elsewhere in the world, Indonesia provides an example of a country with a fragmented geography and an ethnically diverse polity that has been confronted by autonomy-seeking movements in various far-flung regions, including Aceh, East Timor, Sumatra, and Sulawesi. The latter, in turn, have encountered strong central government resistance, if not outright assertion of Javanese dominance (Bertrand 2004: 35).

Marxism and uneven economic development

Marxism has provided yet another theoretical jumping off point for the study of regions, one critical of both the modernization paradigm and cultural approaches. A variety of class and dependency theorists share in common the premise that the unfettered market does not operate in a spatially impartial way, and that political power has been a key factor in structuring unequal relations in the market place. Certainly the market into which regional industries and workers have had to insert themselves has always been a political creation, the parameters and rules of which have been shaped and reshaped through the exercise of political power. Initially developed to explain continuing conditions of underdevelopment in the Third World, Marxist-inspired regional theories also have been applied to explain the situation of less-developed regions within industrialized countries. Generally, Marxists have argued that regions cannot be studied in isolation from their larger national and world settings, and in particular the dynamics inherent within capitalist development and global capitalism.

There are contending approaches to regions within Marxism. What might be termed the 'logic of accumulation' approach sees regional underdevelopment as structural, just one of several forms of uneven development under capitalism, and a necessary condition of accelerated **capital accumulation**. In other words, development and underdevelopment are two sides of the same coin, and just as capitalism produces a global system of metropolitan domination and periphery subordination that victimizes Third World countries because of their dependent position within an international division of labour, so too does it produce regional disparities and inequalities within the developed countries (Carney 1980; Clark 1980).

Other scholars have contested this mechanistic approach and instead advocate historical and detailed case studies looking at the set of forces shaping the development of each specific region. A foremost early example is Vilar's monumental study of Catalonia (1977). Another group argues that areas of the world with older, slower developing modes of production become victims of imperialist exploitation by advanced capitalist countries (Wallerstein 1979). Yet another stresses the existence of prior modes of production as barriers to regional development under capitalism (Brenner 1977). Hechter's study of the Celtic fringe in Britain applies some of these concepts, including notions of unequal exchange between the metropolitan centre and peripheral regions, to describe how military, political, and economic coercion, as well as cultural and ideological symbols, are used to create, enforce, and legitimate cases of internal colonialism (Hechter 1975).

This disagreement over regions and regionalism to some extent reflects Marxism's theoretical difficulties with the concepts of nation and nationalism. The Hobsbawm–Nairn debate over the meaning of emergent neo-nationalist movements is instructive here. Hobsbawm links such movements to the gradual disintegration of national economies within global capitalism, a process which has created a situation of greater vulnerability and exploitability for the small and economically dependent states that are the probable outcome of territorial movements pursuing separatist agendas (Hobsbawm 1977). Nairn agrees that the socio-political fragmentation set into motion by minority nationalist movements is a response to the highly uneven development of capitalism in the modern era which stimulates peoples to respond to their own particular grievances. He argued that in the case of Britain this would lead eventually to the country's break-up, a prospect which (unlike Hobsbawm) he viewed as both positive and inevitable (Nairn 1977).

Certainly, the Marxist debates over how to understand regionalist and ethno-territorial nationalist movements illustrate the benefits of historical specificity for students of regionalism, as well as how a theory of the economy can inform the study of territorial movements (Markusen 1987).

Despite prognostications of imminent political fragmentation emanating from a number of sources, Urwin has shown the limited success of political mobilization of ethno-national minority groups within Western liberal democratic states. There are instances where greater regional autonomy has been won, such as Belgium, Spain, and the United Kingdom; and Quebec's impact clearly has altered the Canadian political agenda and federalism practices. Yet no Western liberal democratic state has come to an end, and over time some ethno-nationalist movements actually have become less dynamic and threatening to these states (Urwin 1998). They have successfully contained regionalist and minority nationalist sentiment, their resilience borne of institutional inertia and a willingness to bend if necessary, 'prepared to accommodate either symbolically or in limited ways the demands of minorities, though not necessarily admitting the need for institutional change or territorial adjustment' (Urwin 1998: 226). What Urwin claims this experience shows is that the interplay of state, territory, and ethno-national identity is constrained by some basic facts: 'powerful and influential structures and institutions; broad and positive acceptance of pluralism and difference; tolerance as an integral element of democratic practice; and the ability of many people to live reasonably comfortably with dual identities' (1998: 240).

Institutionalism

The societal focus of various cultural and economic approaches to the study of regions has been subjected to a useful corrective in the form of institutional approaches, in particular neo-institutional and new institutional theorists who argue that political analysis is best conducted through a focus on institutions. In terms of the study of regions, institutionalists proclaim the central importance of a range of institutions—constitutions, bureaucratic and governance structures, courts, party and electoral systems—not only for providing the basic framework for regions, but for explaining the extent and form of regionalism in a society. In short, institutional design can entrench and strengthen territorial politics and regional identities in a society, or undermine and weaken this base of identity.

Take for example the US and Canada. Both are geographically and demographically diverse federations on the North American continent. Canada, however, is a country in which regionalism is strong and pervasive, whereas its existence in American politics is muted at best. This can be explained in part by differences in the two countries' constitutional frameworks and party systems. The American Constitution fragments its broad geographic regions into a multitude of states, and aside from the Civil War, 'no constitutional or institutional attempt has been made to put the potential regional Humpty Dumpties back together again' (Gibbins 2004b: 40). Regional communities such as the South, Midwest, Southwest, East Coast, Sunbelt, or Rustbelt exist conceptually but have little or no institutional structure. In Canada, the federal division of the country has been into fewer and larger provinces and territories, with significantly more powers than their American counterparts. Indeed, the large provinces of Ontario, Quebec, and British Columbia virtually constitute their own regions, a fact recognized by legislative revisions to Canada's constitutional amendment formula (Gibbins 2004a).

More important than this, however, is that 'the Canadian constitutional order **inadvertently** encourages regionalism through the impairment of territorial representation, whereas the opposite is true for the United States' (Gibbins 2004b: 42). This is because in the US intra-state federalism—the representation of territorial interests within national parliamentary institutions by national politicians—is strong, while in Canada this function is sacrificed for responsible government that comes with cabinet solidarity, tight party discipline, and *de facto* unicameralism (since the regionally constituted Canadian Senate is an empty shell in terms of power and effectiveness). As a result, Canadian federalism is of the *inter-state* variety, where regional conflict is externalized to the realm of intergovernmental relations, with provinces assuming the role of defenders of the regional interest. This is reinforced by a party system that has become increasingly regionalized and twisted out of shape by Canada's single-member, simple plurality electoral system, which punishes smaller parties with diffuse national support, while rewarding parties with regionally concentrated support (Cairns 1968; Gibbins 2005).

In the 1990s, an institutionalist perspective on regional economic development was developed, centring on the experience of prosperous regions and recognizing the collective and social foundations of economic behaviour. Building on the insights of endogenous growth theory and institutional economics, and sensitive to local path dependencies, this perspective uncovers the key role within regions of local networks of association and stresses the importance to the success of regions in the current global economy of 'intermediate forms of governance to build up broad-based, local "institutional thickness" that might include political institutions and social citizenship' (Amin 1999: 313).

The institutionalist approach is now used to explain human action, behaviour, and outcomes within a wide range of political and economic contexts, and can be found in three distinct varieties: *historical institutionalism* (located within the political science tradition) emerged in reaction to behaviouralism and can be associated with the idea of path dependency, 'which is the idea that once institutions are formed, they take on a life of their own and drive political processes' (Lecours 2005: 9); *rational choice institutionalism* (from rational choice theory), which emphasizes the importance of institutions—seen as rules governing the political game—in the strategic calculations of actors; and *sociological institutionalism* (linked to organization theory), which defines institutions in terms of norms, values, culture, and ideas, and sees institutions as shaping the perceptions of actors, leading to behaviour that reinforces and reproduces those very same institutions (Lecours 2005: 16–17).

KEY POINTS

- ❏ The modernization paradigm defined regions as spatial units to be integrated and absorbed into the mainstream, but regions have resisted homogenizing and centralizing pressures.
- ❏ Regions also can be understood as cultural spaces, with distinct value systems and multilayered regional identities. Cultural convergence has not led to the decline of regional political identities.
- ❏ Regions have been shaped and reshaped by the dynamics of capitalist development and global capitalism. Attention to the historical specificity of regions

and a theory of the economy can inform the study of regionalism.
- ❏ Western liberal democratic states have proven highly resilient in the face of autonomist and secessionist movements.
- ❏ Institutions, once established, exercise an independent bias or effect on political processes and behaviour. Institutional design can strengthen or weaken territorial politics and regional identities.

Regionalism from below: identities and parties

Regional identities and political parties constitute the main focus of this section. First we discuss the notion of regional political cultures and examine a variety of examples drawn from different national contexts and political systems. While feeling some attachment to a particular place or territory is a nearly universal phenomenon, this takes different forms and is embedded in different social, cultural, and historical experiences worldwide. We next study the political mobilization

of these identities through movements and political parties, and examine how and why these identities become politicized.

Cultures and identities

Studies pertaining to regional political cultures have received much coverage in Canada (Elkins and Simeon 1980). Researchers have been interested in describing those cultures and explaining how they emerged and evolved through time. Naturally, those studies have been produced at a given moment and tend to reflect dominant interpretative biases in the literature at that time. As a result, such accounts are not culturally neutral though they constitute an important contribution to our understanding of political realities.

Regional political cultures have been studied in terms of their differential intensity with respect to political behaviour as it pertains to trust, efficacy, and modes of political participation, as Gabriel Almond and Sidney Verba formulated it in their classic study (Almond and Verba 1963). However, Almond and Verba neglected to study the link between the dyad 'trust and efficacy' and types and intensity of political participation, a weakness in some political culture studies that others, such as William Gamson (1968: 48), have identified. More recently, scholars have started to pay attention in their study of political cultures to differentiation of various kinds of cultural difference. Bannerji probably best depicts this emerging trend when arguing that some cultural differences not only 'distinguish' but 'encode' and

are 'structured through power relations' (Bannerji 2000: 131–3).

The situation experienced by members of minority nations is highly relevant here as political attitudes and beliefs can be solicited from at least two sources: the majority and minority nations. Political leaders, social actors, and institutions are all involved in the processes of socialization, cultural differentiation, and political education. It is difficult to gauge how receptive citizens are to these invitations to mobilize. What is easier to measure is the extent to which citizens can acquire dual or even multiple identities. Dual identities are frequent in the context of multinational states such as Canada, the United Kingdom, and Spain. In these cases we see some overlap between sub-national (ethno-territorial) and state (national) identities. At times, it is the state identity that prevails, at other times the ethno-territorial. Failing to maintain a balance between these two allegiances is an important variable in determining the stability or precariousness of a state. Table 15.1 suggests the tensions that exist between ethno-territorial and state identities in the regions of Quebec, Catalonia, and Scotland.

Table 15.1 Dual identity in Catalonia, Scotland, and Québec (1997–2005)

	Catalonia 1998	Catalonia 2005	Québec 1998	Québec 2005	Scotland 1997	Scotland 2005
Only*	11.5	14.5	12.0	19.0	23.0	32.0
More* than**	23.4	23.4	31.0	32.0	38.0	32.0
As* as**	43.1	44.8	32.0	35.0	27.0	22.0
More** than*	7.6	8.2	17.0	7.0	4.0	4.0
Only**	13.0	7.7	5.0	6.0	4.0	5.0
Do not know or refuse to answer	1.4	1.6	3.0	2.0	4.0	5.0

* = Catalan, Québécois, Scots   ** = Spanish, Canadian, British

Source: Luis Moreno, Ana Arriba, and Araceli Serrano, *Multiple Identities in Decentralized Spain: The Case of Catalonia*, Madrid, Instituto de Estudios Sociales Avanzados (CSIC), Working Paper 97–06; Spanish Center for Sociological Research (CSI Studies nos. 1523, 2286 et 2455); Paul Wells, 'Quebecers? Canadians? We're Proud to be Both', *The Gazette* (4 Apr. 1998). Data came from a poll conducted by CROP on behalf of *The Gazette* between 27 Mar. and 1 Apr. 1998; Sondage Léger Marketing, *The Globe and Mail*, *Le Devoir*, *Sondage Québécois*, press release available at: http://legermarketing.com/documents/spclm/050427fr.pdf; Scottish Social Attitudes Surveys (National Centre for Social Research: www.natcen.ac.uk/natcen/pages/or_socialattitudes.htm#ssa.

Explaining the rise of regional parties

There is a general trend all over Europe that can be identified concerning regionalist parties. They have been gaining prominence due to three processes: (1) the democratization of state structures and political practices; (2) the resurgent articulation of local and regional interests in the wake of the retrenchment of the welfare state and the turn to neo-liberalism; and (3) the politicization of minority nations (nations without states).

Democratization

Let us first look at the process of democratization as an explanatory variable. In the case of Spain, the emergence of regionalist parties is the result of the claims for autonomy that were witnessed at the beginning of the 1980s (Gunther *et al.* 1986). This is especially so within the historic nations of Catalonia, Galicia, and the Basque Country where demands for autonomy have been more forceful and fed by a strong sentiment of shared identity and culture. It should be stressed, as pointed out by Lancaster and Lewis-Beck, that 'regional parties should not be equated with extremist, violent, or anti-sentiment. Nor should regional parties always be viewed from the dominant centrist perspective, as an impediment to national integration' (1989: 31, 33). In the Canadian case, it is worth noting that, although the Bloc Québécois has as its principal goal the secession of Quebec from Canada, other federal parties have not contested the legitimacy of their elected representatives within the House of Commons. This political stance has worked well since 1993 as Bloc Québécois members have illustrated that it is possible for a regionalist party to promote an **independentist** stance within the political institutions of the state while making a valuable contribution to the overall performance of the federation in its day-to-day work (Gagnon and Hérivault 2007).

Neo-liberalism

Second, parties of national integration have been challenged by regional forces with renewed vigour since the early 1980s (Smith 1985: 1–68; Wilson 1983; Bickerton 2007: 412). During the heyday of the welfare state, stretching from 1945 to 1975, political parties pursuing national objectives tended to be more successful with voters (see Chapter 11). With globalization and implementation of a neo-liberal agenda, regionalist political parties have gained in popularity in several countries that were already fragmented along ethnic, religious, cultural, or economic lines. A case in point is the Lega nord that advocates the establishment of an autonomous region, known as Padania, in Northern Italy (Brouillaud 2005: 119–46).

Scots, who generally were very critical of Westminster's neo-conservative policies during the Thatcher years, began to consider the idea of secession as a means to establish a more progressive regime. The same argument served Quebec independentists well during the 1995 referendum on Quebec secession (Gagnon and Lachapelle 1996). The strength of the country can be measured by the central state's capacity to cast political debates at a different level through the implementation of public policies that have repercussions across the land (environment, energy, health and welfare, constitution, charter of rights, and the like). In that sense one wonders how best to describe the situation in Belgium where there are no longer any national parties in Brussels, leaving the national parliament entirely occupied by regionalist political parties (Peeters 2007: 38).

Minority nations

Third, during the last three decades, we have witnessed a strong politicization of minority nations which have accessed various democratic means to advance their cause. Electoral campaigns and referenda have been two key tools used by nationalist leaders to give added legitimacy to their claims. Implementation of autonomous communities throughout Spain has led to the development of nationalist parties at the regional level. For example, Convergencia i Unió has held power in Catalonia, under Jordi Pujol's leadership, for most of the last twenty-five years. Similarly, the Basque National Party has done particularly well during the same period. Catalonia with Esquerra Republicana and Convergencia i Unió and the Basque Country with Partido Nacionalista Vasco, Euzkadiko, and until 2002 (when its right to run candidates was denied) Herri Batasuna, have generated the largest number of regional parties in Spain. Other autonomous regions, with the notable exception of Galicia, have generally adhered to the national party system (see Table 15.2).

Table 15.2 Spanish general elections

	1977	1979	1982	1986	1989	1993	1996	2000	2004
National parties									
Alianca Popular/Coalicion Democratica Partido Popular	8.2 % (16)	6.0 % (9)	26.5 % (107)	26.2 % (105)	25.1 % (101)	34.6 % (138)	38.8 % (156)	44.5 % (183)	38.3 % (148)
Union de Centro Democratico (UCD)	34.5 % (166)	35.0 % (168)	6.5 % (11)	—	—	—	—	—	—
Centro Democratico y Social (CDS)	—	—	2.8 % (2)	9.3 % (19)	7.9 % (14)	—	—	—	—
Partido Socialista Obrero, Partido Socialista de Catalunya (PSOE/PSC)	29.4 % (118)	30.5 % (121)	48.4 % (202)	44.1 % (184)	5.5 % (20)	33.6 %* (141)	37.6 % (141)	34.1 % (125)	43.3 % (164)
Partido Communista/Izquierda Unida (PCE/IU)	9.4 % (19)	10.8 % (23)	4.0 % (4)	4.5 % (7)	8.0 % (14)	8.1 % (15)	10.5 % (21)	5.5 % (8)	5.3 % (2)

(continued)

Table 15.2 (continued)

	1977	1979	1982	1986	1989	1993	1996	2000	2004
Regional parties									
Convergencia i Unió (CiV)	2.8 % (11)	2.7 % (8)	3.7 % (12)	4.7 % (18)	5.0 % (18)	5.0 % (17)	4.6 % (16)	4.2 % (15)	3.3 % (10)
Partido Nationalista Vasco (PNV)	1.6 % (8)	1.5 % (7)	1.9 % (8)	1.5 % (6)	1.2 % (4)	1.3 % (5)	1.3 % (5)	1.5 % (7)	1.6 % (7)**
Basque Left (HB, EE, EA)	0.3 % (1)	1.4 % (4)	1.4 % (3)	1.6 % (7)	2.3 % (8)	1.4 % (3)	1.2 % (3)	0.4 % (1)	0.3 % (1)
Partido Socialista de Catalunya (PSC)						5.5 % (18)			
Bloque Nacional Popular Gallego/Coalicion Gallega/Bloque Nacionista Gallego	0.12 %	—	—	0.4 % (1)	—	—	0.9 % (2)	1.3 % (3)	0.8 % (2)

* The Partido Socialista Catalunya is listed independently as a regional party in the 1993 general elections.

** Herri Batasuna was not allowed to run candidates in the general elections of 2004.

Source: Lancaster and Lewis-Beck 1989; www.congreso.es/elecciones/.

The role of regionalist parties in national party systems

Beyond the minority nationalism that so marks politics in Quebec, Scotland, and Catalonia, regionalism more generally has played a key role as a maker of political identity in Canada, the United Kingdom, and Spain. Canada has long experienced distinct regional patterns of voting behaviour as illustrated by support obtained in federal elections by the Western-based Progressives, Social Credit, and CCF parties from the 1920s to the 1950s, the Reform Party in the 1990s, and the Bloc Québécois during the last fifteen years (Bickerton *et al.* 1999). The classic works of Lipset (1968) and Macpherson (1953) on the emergence of regional parties in the Canadian West during the first half of the twentieth century were influential in accounting for the sources and impact of regionalism on Canadian politics. Their conclusions were that class structure and economic conditions were central to the emergence and persistence of right-wing and left-wing agrarian parties in Alberta and Saskatchewan respectively. These initial studies have since been joined by many others (Simeon 1977; Forbes 1979; Brym 1986; Bickerton 1990; Young and Archer 2002), all of whom highlight the continuing importance of regionalism in Canadian politics.

Political parties are known to exercise a variety of functions, including aggregation of interests, elaboration and dissemination of political ideas, electoral campaigning, and ultimately assuming power (see Chapter 12). In federal or federalizing countries such as Belgium, Canada, Spain, and the United Kingdom, political parties are involved at multiple levels of governance, and electoral success at one level is not necessarily replicated at the other level; indeed, parties may compete exclusively at one level or the other.

The structuring of political parties at the country-level often takes decades, as their leaders attempt to build coalitions of voters across linguistic groups, classes, religions, and regions to secure their election. In Canada, there has long been some push and pull between two major trends. One trend suggests that political leadership on major issues most properly belongs with federal politicians operating within the central state, and that member states of the federation should accept a subordinate role. A counter-trend is that regional politicians know

best the needs and interests of their regions and communities, and therefore are best positioned to protect and promote these interests on a broad range of issues.

This tension between centralist parties and regionalist parties has too often been neglected by students of party politics. Recently, there has been some added interest, perhaps due to a desire by nation-states to play a stronger role in the globalizing world. Pierre Trudeau, Canada's Liberal prime minister for virtually the whole period from 1968 to 1984, was fond of saying that Canada was more than the sum of its parts. This stance contributed to intense political clashes with Quebec-centred parties, whether federal parties such as Ralliement Créditistes and the Bloc Québécois, or provincial parties such as the Union Nationale, Parti Liberal, or Parti Québécois (Bickerton *et al.* 1999: 164–92). During the last two decades, the Bloc Québécois and the Reform/Canadian Alliance Party are two regionalist parties that have been quite successful bringing forward regional issues and interests within the federal parliament, whereas the previous period had been largely dominated by party representation with an almost exclusively national focus (Bickerton 2007: 412).

Similar behaviour has been witnessed in Spain where both the Partido Socialista Obrero de España (PSOE) and the Partido Popular (PP) have taken a centralist stand, alienating as a result large segments of voters in the Basque Country, Galicia, or Catalonia after Franco's death, at the beginning of the democratization process. Concomitant with this democratization process, we find the emergence of numerous regionally based political parties. Most studies of political parties in Spain have explored the 'national' party system *per se* rather than investigating regional parties or regional political behaviour. As a result, we tend to ignore issues at the regional level, although 'regional parties are part of the Spanish party system and yet are also distinct, competitively pitting themselves against the national parties' (Lancaster and Lewis-Beck 1989: 29–43).

In the cases of Canada and Spain, we see that regionalist parties have played a key role in the political stability of the political system. For example, over the past several years in Canada, during Liberal and Conservative minority governments, the Bloc Québécois has sided several times with the governing party in order to avoid triggering an election. In

Spain, Convergencia i Unió (CiU) was doing the same, while negotiating more accommodating measures from Madrid. Regional parties such as these have done extremely well—in the case of the Bloc Québécois outperforming since 1993 all other federal parties in the province of Quebec. In the case of Spain, with the return of democracy, regional parties have bested the Partido Popular in Catalonia, and have done better than the Spanish Communist Party in national elections.

Regional parties have demonstrated their relevance and usefulness in different ways over the years. They have addressed issues of representation in the case of fragmented societies. They have influenced the policy process, making governing parties accountable to a larger population by forcing them to address issues of redistribution in Canada, social security in Belgium, political rights in the Basque Country, and environmentalism in most countries.

Pascal Delwitt, in a thorough account of regional parties within eight European countries, found that in the thirty-two regional parties that have obtained at least 4 per cent of the vote at a national election, twenty-two have assumed responsibilities within the executive branch of government, either at the regional or the national level. Three of those parties (Volksunie, Front Démocratique, Rassemblement Wallon, Lega Nord) have assumed political leadership at both the regional and the national levels. Three others have been part of the executive only at the national level, namely Democratic Union of Hungary, Swedish National Party, and Rassemblement Wallon. The remaining sixteen have been involved at the executive level within the regions (Delwitt 2005: 51–84; see also Table 15.3).

The emergence and strengthening of regional parties can be connected with the mobilization of ethnic and nationalist movements or else it is due to the sense of alienation within regional electorates in countries that are as varied as Belgium, Canada, the United Kingdom, Finland, Italy, and Spain, and where voters have perceived themselves to be poorly represented by traditional political elites in national parties. In short, the prevalence and role of regional parties constitutes an important phenomenon that requires our attention. No longer can we reduce the study of party politics to the major/minor dichotomy or to national party systems *per se*; there is an urgent need for a more sophisticated analysis of party dynamics to account for the emergence and continuing salience of this regionalist trend.

KEY POINTS

❑ 'Regionalism from below' has its roots in distinctive cultures and identities, which can be described in terms of differences in terms of values, beliefs, attitudes, orientations, and patterns of participation. Members of minority nations often have dual identities which coexist in varying states of accommodation and tension.

❑ The rise of regionalist parties can be explained in terms of three general factors or trends: the democratization of societies, the crisis of the welfare state and the turn toward neo-liberalism, and the political mobilization of minority nations.

❑ Regional parties in multi-national countries like Canada and Spain tend to be integral parts of their respective national party systems, as often constituting an element of stability as disruption.

Regionalization from above: institutions

To the variety of regionalisms that exist correspond different modes of regional government and governance, with the institutionalization of regions varying widely from country to country. The relations between regional and central institutions within any given political system (unitary, federalizing, or federal) can be seen as a complex interplay of centrifugal and centripetal pressures. Particular governmental and societal arrangements can be understood as different strategies of territorial management, with various ways and means being identified to represent and respond to regional communities.

Table 15.3 European regional parties within national and regional executives

	National government	Regional government		National government	Regional government
Swedish Popular Party, Finland	Yes	–	Canary Islands Coalition, Spain	No	Yes
Volksunie, Belgium	Yes	Yes	Union Valenciana, Spain	No	Yes
New Flemish Alliance, Belgium	No	Yes	Bloque Nacional de Valencia, Spain	No	Yes
Vlaams Belang, Belgium	No	No	Social Democratic Labour Party, UK	No	Yes
Rassemblement Wallon, Belgium	Yes	–	Sinn Fein, UK	No	Yes
Front Démocratique des Francophones, Belgium	Yes	Yes	Welsh Party, UK	No	No
Convergencia i Unió, Spain	No	Yes	Scottish Nationalist Party, UK	No	Yes
Esquerra Republicana de Catalunya, Spain	No	Yes	South Tyrolian People's Party, Italy	No	Yes
Partido Nacionalista Vasco, Spain	No	Yes	Sardinian Action Party, Italy	No	Yes
Herri Batasuna, Spain	No	No	Valdotanian Union, Italy	No	Yes
Euzkal Alkartasuna, Spain	No	Yes	Lega Nord, Italy	Yes	Yes
Partido Regionalista de Cantabria, Spain	No	Yes	Bavarian Party, Germany	No	No
Partido Aragonese, Spain	No	Yes	Electoral Committee of Schelswig, Germany	No	No
Chunta Aragonista, Spain	No	No	Democratic Union of Hungarians in Romania, Hungary	Yes	–
Partido Andalusian, Spain	No	Yes	Alsace d'Abord, France	No	No
Bloque Nacionalista Gallego, Spain	No	No	Ligue de Savoie, France	No	No

Source: Delwitt (2005).

Regionalism and federalism

Regional government, meaning autonomous institutions elected by universal suffrage, is most advanced in federal countries like Canada, the US, Germany, Austria, Belgium, Switzerland, and increasingly Spain. In federal countries regions are constituted as autonomous political entities with constitutionally protected powers and the right to participate in national politics through a second legislative chamber at the national level, or through mechanisms of institutionalized cooperation between governments. In unitary systems, regional administrative institutions are simply decentralized arms of the state. In France and Italy, there are regions with limited powers and without great autonomy, created through processes of *deconcentration* and existing alongside more traditional administrative units (large cities, departments, communes, provinces). However, some of these regions (Sicily, Sardinia, Valle d'Aosta, Trentino-Alto Adige, Friuli-Venezia-Giulia, Corsica) have been granted a special status and forms of asymmetric regionalization in response to their specific territorial demands (see Chapter 11).

Canada stands out as an interesting case due to its combination of federalism and parliamentarism. As in Belgium and Spain, Canada has used its system of intergovernmental relations to strike deals pertaining to national issues through a variety of mechanisms including constitutional conferences, regular meetings of federal-provincial committees, joint initiatives and accords (the 1999 social union framework, and the like), and more recently a revamping of fiscal relations between the central state and the provinces to address a perceived imbalance. Belgium and Canada are considered today to have decentralized federations with a strong capacity on the part of the member states to raise revenues to cover their expenditures (Watts 1999: 119). The regions in Belgium are surely the ones that can exert more powers among federal countries, as illustrated by the fact they are allowed to make representations on behalf of their respective community within international fora. However, when compared to the US, it becomes clear that Canadian provinces can exercise an extensive array of powers that American states are prevented from assuming within their federation.

Clearly, regions take on a multiplicity of forms in different historical contexts. Quebec has seen its frontiers evolve over the centuries, as have other historic regions such as the Basque Country or Catalonia. Nor is there universal agreement on the meaning and status of these ethno-territorial regions. For instance, Quebec has been portrayed by some as an autonomous political entity best understood as a region state, if not nation-state in waiting, while it is represented by others as the *foyer* of the French-Canadian culture in Canada. The same pattern of contestation applies to Catalonia. In some cases what matters are the political institutions through which a political community can organize and assert itself; in other cases it is a region's cultural role and influence that most matters.

With regional differences such an essential characteristic of Canada, regionalist movements in Atlantic Canada and the West have consistently pursued the goal of increasing their capacity to exercise influence over the central government, and their perceived failure to do so has incited claims of unfair treatment and regional alienation. Quebecers, who couch their demands in terms of national affirmation, for the most part have pursued an alternate course of demanding increased autonomy and freedom from the centre. These differences in regionalist objectives and agitation are ultimately linked to differences in fundamental values, visions, and identities. The vision that tends to dominate among the majority of English-speaking Canadians, particularly since the adoption of the Canadian Charter of Rights and Freedoms in 1982, is that Canada is comprised of a single national political community or *demos*. This national vision creates ongoing tensions in Quebec since it tends to undermine the notion of dualism, considered by francophone Quebecers to be a founding pillar (if not sacred covenant) of the Canadian federation.

Due to its federal and multi-national make-up, several authors are of the view that Canada is a country constituted by several *demoi* (Gagnon and Iacovino 2007). Quebecers and Aboriginals have a high degree of national self-consciousness and make self-governance claims based on their status as nations within a multi-national federation, whereas other Canadians tend to view themselves as members of an encompassing political community within which all are considered to be on the same footing. It follows from this that everyone ought to be considered as a resident of a single, large country and be treated identically as the citizens of a single *demos*. In 2006, the election of a Conservative government under Prime Minister Stephen Harper led to the formal granting of 'nation' status to the Québécois, contributing to the easing of tensions between Quebec and Ottawa. With this initiative the Conservatives symbolically broke with a long-standing practice for federal governments in Canada in the field of territorial management by diverting from the one-nation policy and opening the door to greater federal **asymmetry.**

Federalizing processes in unitary states

In the United Kingdom, formally still a unitary system, a process of devolution has been under way for more than a decade and has begun to show results (Loughlin 2007). Such developments have made it more difficult to clearly distinguish the patterns of territorial management and power-sharing arrangements that exist within some unitary states versus federal systems. Spain is probably the best example of this, considering that it remains a unitary system that has acquired many of the features of a multi-national federation (Moreno 2001).

In Britain, where Scottish, English, and Welsh identities coexist, each acknowledges the presence and legitimacy of the others as distinct nations. Political interactions in this case take place within the constitutional and political context of a state union (Forsyth 1981). Over the years tensions have appeared at different historical junctures, based on the political attitudes of Westminster towards regional claims emanating from the periphery. The work of Colley (1992), Hechter (1975), and Nairn (1977) here is particularly revealing. With the purpose of attenuating these tensions, the Labour government of Tony Blair launched in 1997 a major devolution project with a view responding to different needs by providing varying forms of power within Britain to different representative assemblies. On 13 September 1997, two days after the Scottish Referendum on Devolution, Blair declared: 'This is a good day for Scotland, and a good day for Britain and the United Kingdom . . . the era of big centralised government is over!' (Leeke *et al.* 2003: 18).

It is worth underlining that, until the late 1990s,

> 66 the United Kingdom was alone among the larger European Union states in lacking elected regional governments. . . . The development here is highly asymmetrical: inevitably so, given the very different histories of the four countries of the Union. . . . Seen in comparative perspective, this is a weak form of devolution, yet it is also transformational in view of the limited prior development of a distinctive Welsh polity. (Rawlings 2001: 481) 99

In the Spanish case, a unitary state that underwent several transformations after its transition to democracy in the late 1970s, a variety of federalizing measures have been implemented (Moreno 2001). In the process, the central state has recognized the existence within Spain of four historic nations (Catalonia, Galicia, Basque Country, and recently Andalusia). The main objective pursued by Madrid has been to try to provide each autonomous community with identical powers (an idea that is best conveyed by the expression *café para todos*) so as to avoid granting even more distinct status to the historical nations. This has led to major conflicts between central and regional authorities over the years and has encouraged historic nations to ask for an asymmetrical devolution of powers to their respective regions, or more simply a demand for greater autonomy (Guibernau 2006).

Varying self-definitions stimulate regions to make distinct political claims. Catalonia, the Basque Country, and Galicia make regional claims as historic nations and on this basis call for the further devolution of powers from the central government in Madrid, prompting other regional communities to seek similar status. Amongst these, only Andalusia has been successful so far in obtaining national status from the central government. Madrid's decision to grant Andalusia nation status can be explained in part by its desire to entice other political communities to make similar claims, thereby reducing the extent of asymmetry and therefore the political significance of granting national status to a region. Central government attempts to water down the implications of such recognition is an example of the territorial management strategies employed by central authorities, which not surprisingly has produced some backlash from Spain's three historic nations.

COUNTRY PROFILE Australia

Commonwealth of Australia

State formation

James Cook took possession of eastern Australia in the name of Great Britain in 1770. Beginning in 1788, six colonies were successively established that federated and became the Commonwealth of Australia in 1901.
Constitution 1900, effective 1901.

Form of government

Federal state.
Head of state English monarch, represented by a Governor General. The monarchy is hereditary.
Head of government Prime Minister appointed by Parliament.
Cabinet Ministers appointed by the Prime Minister, responsible to Parliament.
Administrative subdivisions 6 states and 2 territories.

Legal system

English common law with a High Court (the chief justice and six other justices are appointed by the Governor General).

Legislature

Bicameral Parliament.

Lower house House of Representatives: 150 members; term of 3 years.
Upper house Senate: 76 members (12 from each of the 6 states and 2 from each of the 2 territories); staggered elections (one-half of state members are elected every 3 years by popular vote; territory members are elected every 3 years); term of 6 years.

Electoral system (lower house)

Instant-run-off voting (referred to as 'preferential vote' in Australia).
Formula Single non-transferable vote.
Constituencies 148 single-member constituencies plus 2 territories.
Barrier clause None.
Suffrage Universal and compulsory, 18 years.

Direct democracy

Constitutional referendum must be initiated through parliamentary bill. Requirement of double majority of states/territories and voters. In addition, non-binding 'plebiscites' are held on non-constitutional matters.

Party system Results of the 2004 legislative elections (House of Representatives):

Electorate	13,064,678	100.0%
Voters	12,354,983	94.6%

Party	Valid votes	%	Seats
Liberal Party of Australia	4,741,458	40.5	74
Australian Labor Party	4,409,117	37.6	60
Australian Greens	841,734	7.2	0
National Party of Australia	690,275	5.9	12
Independents	288,206	2.4	3
Family First Party	235,315	2.0	0
Australian Democrats	144,832	1.2	0
One Nation Party	139,956	1.2	0
Country Liberal Party–The Territory Party	39,855	0.3	1
Others	184,384	1.7	0
Total	11,715,132	100.0	150

Notes: Category 'Others' includes parties with less than 1 % of the votes nation-wide and no seats.
Source: IFES Election Guide; Australian Election Commission.

This brief survey suggests a competition for ascendancy between two approaches to defining the political community. On the one side, there are those who believe in a single *demos*, despite the presence of minority communities (Canada and Spain). These majority populations cling to political arrangements based on territorial and symmetrical federalism. In contrast, supporters of multiple national communities or *demoi* (generally members of the minority communities) wish to install or move toward different arrangements based on a multi-national and asymmetrical model of federalism (Kymlicka 1998).

Naturally, these competing visions have led to conflict and tensions in countries such as federal Canada, Belgium, and Switzerland, as well as in federalizing Spain and in the United Kingdom (Moreno 2001). Federalism here is a key component to take into account. As we are reminded by Richard Simeon, '[f]ederalism is not only a **response** to regionalism, but also ensures that it will continue. . . . it provides an institutional focus for loyalty and identity' (1975: 508). As a result, economic, social, and political interests can be mobilized behind a given set of institutions, challenging from time to time the stability of a political regime, especially when sought-after recognition for national communities is being denied.

It is worthwhile referring to the Belgian case here as it has undergone no less than five major constitutional reforms since 1970 that transformed radically the country from a unitary to a (con)federal state in which linguistic matters are generally managed at the community level, and economic matters at the regional level. Now, as Article 1 of the Constitution stipulates: 'Belgium is a federal state, composed of communities and regions'. Those reforms were instrumental in allowing, through constitutional means, each layer of the Belgian state apparatus (central, regional, community) a legitimate role, within their own spheres of jurisdictions at the international level (Paquin 2003: 625–6).

The role of federalism should not be neglected in accounting for the international activities of regions, as is suggested by Simeon's take on the issue. But what matters most, we believe, is 'the importance of nationalism in explaining the breadth, scope and intensity of a region's international activity in the former [multinational states] and its absence, or lesser prominence, in the latter [nation-states]' (Lecours and Moreno 2003: 268). This understanding goes a long way towards explaining the increasing presence of regions such as Bavaria, Catalonia, Flanders, and Quebec in various international fora.

KEY POINTS

❑ In general, regions have attained the greatest degree of autonomy where there are constitutionally protected federal institutions.

❑ Asymmetric regionalization has occurred in some unitary states, and an institutional 'blending' is under way that blurs the difference between multi-national

unitary states and federal systems, in terms of the power-sharing arrangements instituted for regions.

❑ Regional autonomy and asymmetry in the national treatment of regions has proceeded furthest where minority nations are present, whether or not the country in question is formally a federal state.

Political economy of regions

A central theme in the study of the political economy of regions is the degree to which regional inequality and dependence have been internally determined—related to some indigenous characteristic of the region or its people—or alternatively ordained by structures and conditions that have been externally imposed on those regions that are less economically advantaged. This section will introduce the reader

to the history of this topic and survey the range of research and opinion to which it has given rise.

Regional differentiation: causes and consequences

From the mid-nineteenth to the mid-twentieth centuries, the industrializing states of the Western world were transformed by processes of political, social, and economic integration associated with the consolidation of nation-states, bureaucratic modernization, and capitalist development focused for the most part on protected national economies (with or without attached colonial empires). Diverse regions at uneven levels of development were incorporated into these emergent national political economies, though not on equal terms. Location, initial resource endowments, transportation links, population base, and previous rounds of investment in productive capacity, and various forms of infrastructure were all relevant factors in determining the advantages or disadvantages accruing to regions in subsequent phases of growth and development. The migration of labour to growing urban and industrial centres, and the stimulus this gave to new rounds of investment, produced agglomeration effects that reinforced the initial advantages of some regions, while draining capital and human resources from others, leading to their further differentiation (Massey 1998).

The role that politics and state policy played in all this was not negligible. It was national politicians who initiated, planned, and supervised the incorporation of lands and peoples into consolidated nation-states; it was through politics that the policy frameworks that supported and directed national development were created, installed, and maintained. These multi-generational state and nation-building projects were sustained and legitimized with nationalist visions, symbols, and rhetoric, and the political promise of security and economic prosperity. Regionalist resistance was sometimes violent and dramatic (as with the nineteenth-century wars of unification in Europe, the American Civil and Indian Wars, the Métis-led rebellions in Canada, or the Spanish Civil War), but more often was limited to periodic episodes of political contestation through social movements or regional political parties (see the discussion of regional movements and parties above).

In the post-war era of economic expansion and relatively full employment (1945–75), regional concerns about inequality and fair representation tended to be subsumed if not completely submerged under the class politics and social policy agenda associated with the construction of national welfare states. The problem of regional inequalities was dealt with primarily, if at all, as a residual matter for state

managers focused on the 'main game' of full employment and price stability, which they pursued in good Keynesian fashion through the manipulation of the fiscal levers of centralized taxation and spending. The residents of less developed regions benefited, like other citizens, from the redistribution of income enabled by progressive tax systems and the public provision of basic health and social services. Economic growth and social spending did alleviate poverty, while equalization schemes in most federal states (based on intergovernmental transfers) contributed to the standardization of public services across regions. But neither of these mechanisms succeeded in eliminating regional disparities in economic growth, per capita income, and unemployment rates.

The rise and decline of regional development policy

In the 1950s and 1960s, regional planning, described by Friedmann as 'the process of formulating and clarifying social objectives in the ordering of activities in supra-urban space—that is, in any area larger than a single city' (Wannop 1997: 154), became common in most Western industrialized countries. Initiated as part of post-war reconstruction and often focused on the development of satellite communities to relieve urban congestion, in the 1960s priorities shifted towards the development of growth centres in peripheral regions. These initiatives, supported by emerging economic theories such as variants of Perroux's strategy of 'growth poles', were meant to foster industrial growth to address regional disparities. Such decentralization was made palatable by the growing diseconomies of metropolitan locations for industry, and the benefits of diverting some of the growth from the often overheated economies of economic and industrial core areas. Throughout Europe—in France, Italy, Germany, the UK—regions were viewed primarily as units for spatial planning, to be managed by central states (Keating 2004: xii). In the US, sub-state regional councils became eligible for federal planning and economic development funds, as well as other conditional grants. By 1980, almost the entire US was covered by regional planning organizations, though only weakly empowered and with no popular base (Wannop 1997). In Canada, a spate of development agencies and programmes were consolidated in 1969 in a new Department of Regional Economic Expansion, focused initially on reducing economic disparities between the Atlantic region (inclusive of eastern Quebec) and the rest of Canada (Savoie 1986).

The economic logic of regional development policies was to make regions self-sustaining, whereupon active regional policy would no longer be necessary and regions could positively contribute to national economic growth. In the meantime, the costs of congestion and stress in booming areas could be relieved. But there also were separate political and social logics at work in the creation of these policies. The political weight of poorer regions was used to counter their economic weakness, and their demands to bring work to the workers rather than vice versa could not be easily ignored, especially when their political importance to national governing coalitions was significant or they harboured the potential for disruption or separatism. As well, in advanced industrial countries citizenship was increasingly undergoing a 'thickening' process, with the state assuming responsibility for the social integration of all its citizens by equalizing opportunities and living standards, thereby preventing or reversing the marginalization of groups or places (Keating 1997: 18–20).

In its early phases this form of **regional policy** being pursued by central states was largely depoliticized and technocratic, left in the hands of bureaucrats. However, it soon became more interventionist, with more sophisticated policies covering larger areas. Planning frameworks became more elaborate and growth centres within regions were chosen based on their growth potential rather than their lagging economic performance. Local political and economic elites were drawn into the process, and regional planning, policy, and funding issues increasingly became subject to political contestation. 'Once local and regional interests were brought formally into the process of policy making and implementation, it became apparent that regional preferences and priorities were not always consistent with those of central governments' (Keating 1997: 22–3).

Regional policy went into decline with the widespread onset of stagflation (low growth, simultaneously rising unemployment, and inflation) and growing international competitive pressures from the mid-1970s onward. This first disrupted then gradually brought to an end the national systems of mass production and welfarist politics of the post-war era. As the governments of Western industrialized countries began to shift their attention and concern to shoring up their national competitiveness, which was dependent upon the economic health and vitality of their core industrial areas and sectors, the post-war model of territorial management broke down. Reducing regional disparities suddenly became much less of a priority.

As Keating has noted, into this growing policy and political vacuum three types of regionalist politics

Table 15.4 Old and new regionalism

Old regionalism	New regionalism
Formed in a bipolar context	Taking place in a multipolar world
'From above' process or top-down	'From below' process or bottom-up
Inward oriented and protectionist	Open and compatible with an interdependent world economy
Specific with regards to its objectives	More comprehensive and multi-dimensional societal process
Concerned with relations between group of neighbouring nation-states	Takes place in a context of globalization, in which a variety of non-state actors are operating at all levels of the global system

Source: Hettne (2003).

emerged: first, a *defensive regionalism* committed to resisting change, that was tied to traditional economic sectors and the threatened communities that depended on them; second, an *integrating or modernizing regionalism* aimed at adapting to change and reinserting the region into the national economy; third, an *autonomist regionalism*, particularly in regions with historic claims to nation status, seeking a distinctive path to modernization by combining autonomy, cultural promotion, and economic modernization (1997: 24). From the 1970s to the 1990s, these modes of regionalism coexisted within many countries, often disharmoniously due to the basic contradictions between them at the level of policy.

Globalization and the new regionalism

There is now a new international context for regions, creating for them opportunities but also dangers, and providing the conditions for the incubation of a new regionalism. A number of interrelated changes have contributed to this altered context: falling international trade barriers, the adoption of a neo-liberal policy framework with its agenda of deregulation and free markets, the creation of free trade and economic union agreements (e.g. the North American Free Trade Agreement [NAFTA] and the EU), and in general the sweeping economic, technological, political, and cultural changes associated with globalization. In many ways these changes have undermined or threatened to destroy the traditional employment base of peripheral regions, as well as the established programme supports for these regions.

The Janus-faced nature of globalization for regions, however, is that it has opened up new possibilities and potentials that practically speaking were not previously available. This has occurred because of the changing character of international economic competition, itself a function of changes in technology, production methods, corporate organization, and the removal of restrictions on international trade and investment. This has made accessible to regions, in a manner never before possible in human history, global markets that absorb an increasingly diverse range of products and services. As a result, the determinants of regional competitiveness in the contemporary global economy have shifted. Traditional factors of comparative advantage, such as economies

of scale, plentiful supplies of labour, access to cheap raw materials, and proximity to markets, may still matter, but these are now joined and often superseded by the entrepreneurial, technological, social, and cultural strengths of a region (Piore and Sabel 1984; Porter 1990).

In response to these changes, regional policies in many jurisdictions have been revamped. To be more specific, governments have recognized that changes in the nature of production, in technology, and in patterns of trade have altered the basis of regional development, such that the competitive imperative is now not only greater and more immediate for all economies (because of their greater exposure to international economic forces and markets), but also different in terms of the structure of constraints and opportunities which it presents for regions, as well as the factors and resources that are directly relevant to long-term regional competitiveness. This means that governments have found it necessary to adapt to the new context by supporting new forms of regionalization of policy-making and implementation, involving partnerships between various levels of government (supra-national, national, provincial/regional, local), as well as the private sector and key actors in civil society, in order to create collaborative regional policy frameworks.

The phenomenon of devolved governance and regionalization is one that varies greatly in practice. Certainly, the EU has been very active in this area, insisting on the creation of regional partnerships in the management of EU funds made available for regional development purposes. As a result, regionalization has become a controversial issue in many EU states, especially in the accession countries recently admitted to the Union (Trigilia 1991; Sharpe 1993*a*; Keating 1998*a*; Brusis 2002).

This trend to regionalization has been accompanied by a reprioritization of the key factors in regional development, with much greater significance now being accorded to so-called **endogenous** factors based on the character and quality of a region's human, social, and cultural capital, what some have called a **socially embedded growth model** (Amin 1999). This revalues the development significance of high-quality health and education services, cultural amenities, entrepreneurial and managerial training, information and innovation networks, as well as supports for marketing, technology transfer, and business start-ups.

Table 15.5 Exogenous and endogenous development models

Characteristics	Exogenous model	Endogenous model
Source of development impetus	External to the region, large corporations sourcing finance, technology, and expertise globally	Internal to the region, locally owned firms or activities drawing on local resources and expertise
Spatial focus	Regional metropoles, major urban centres	Community-based: cities, towns, rural areas, neighbourhoods
Sector focus	Large unit production, branch plants, capital intensive	Small and medium-sized enterprises (SMEs); manufacturing, personal and business services, owner-operated small unit production
Agents of development	National or foreign corporate capital, multinational firms	Local/regional entrepreneurs (both capitalist and social); worker/producer cooperatives
Programme instruments	Grants, large loans, tax concessions, payroll rebates, infrastructure	Social infrastructure, education and training, small loans, mechanisms for region and community-based networking, planning, financing, marketing and technology transfer
Site and mode of governance	National or international; central government bureaucrats; top-down, externally imposed decisions	Local or regional: region and community based development agencies; collaborative partnering arrangements between government, private sector and civil society actors

Selective financial and industrial incentives and physical infrastructure are still an important part of the regional development 'toolbox' that governments use, but both the dynamics of regional development and the policy focus of governments is changing. In general terms, this seems to be the consensus reached by many regional development researchers in Europe and elsewhere (Stohr 1990; Putnam 1993; Storper 1995; Amin 1999; Florida 2003).

In summary, the contemporary understanding of regional development has four aspects: economic development, social integration and redistribution, cultural development and identity, and environmental considerations (Keating 1997: 31). The new approach is to involve a broader range of actors and policies than previously, and to create more region-specific strategies tailored to local needs, circumstances, and potentials. This in turn requires a high degree of decentralization and regionalization of governance, involving extensive cooperation at the regional/local level between various levels of government, as well as private sector and civil society actors. Creating this new institutional and fiscal nexus for regional development requires all levels of government to acknowledge that the policies and decisions most likely to nurture sustainable regions will emerge from a strong network of regional actors (public and private) brought together on the basis of a shared territorial and cultural identity and a direct interest in the economic fate of the community and its residents. If regions can cohere socially and culturally, and if they are actively supported by government, they will be more capable of adapting to and taking advantage of the new economic challenges and opportunities.

KEY POINTS

- ❑ The differentiation of regions within nation-states occurred over an extended period of time. Ongoing state and nation-building projects were met by regional resistance in the form of military conflict, minority nationalism, territorial movements, and party-based politics.
- ❑ The construction of welfare states in the post-war era included a regional dimension. At first largely submerged by class-based and redistributive politics, persistent regional economic disparities led to the introduction of regional development policies as a complement to national social programmes. Changes in the international political economy in the 1970s

led to the decline of regional development policy, giving rise to defensive, modernizing, and autonomist modes of regionalism.

- ❑ A new regionalism emerged in the 1990s in the context of globalization. The traditional determinants of regional economic competitiveness based on comparative advantage is now supplemented by an endogenous, 'socially-embedded' growth model that requires regionalized governance in order to nurture collaborative regional policy frameworks. This adds social, cultural, and environmental dimensions to the traditional economic aspects of regional development.

Conclusion

Region as a concept for political scientists can be malleable and abstract, as well as mundane. Its pliability and amorphous character is due to its multiple potential meanings. Political actors will define it to reflect their values and their particular interests and needs. In this sense, though region may be tied to geographic space, it is very much a product of human construction.

There are a number of different theories and approaches that have been used to describe and inquire into the meaning of regions as economic, social, cultural, and last but not least, political phenomena. Mainstream modernization and development theory ascribed diminishing significance to regions, since the differences they represented were inevitably fated to fade as the integration processes linked to modernity and capitalism proceeded apace. Other approaches and perspectives remained sceptical of this outcome. Culturalists described the persistence of spatially distinct value systems that continued to define regions as cultural spaces, a persistence that was especially notable for regions populated by minority nations. In these cases, individuals frequently espouse multiple political identities, which continue to be available to political elites for mobilization purposes, despite a trend over time toward cultural convergence. Marxists are less sanguine than

modernization theorists about the convergence of regions undergoing development within a global capitalist system, though there remains disagreement on this point. What is shared within this approach is certainty about the necessity to understand the past, present, and future of regions within the broader national and international context, particularly as this pertains to the economic forces acting on and within regions. Institutional theorists of various persuasions bring to the study of regions their insights into the independent shaping effect on regions and regionalism exerted by the design and workings of political and social institutions.

'Regionalism from below' refers to the societal forces that have given cultural and identity content to regions and regionalism. Whether these are located within regional political cultures or the multiple identities nurtured within individuals who are members of minority nations, they can help to explain the rise and role of regionalist parties in Western liberal democratic states, especially those that feature ethno-territorial minorities or regions with claims to historic nation status, such as Spain, Canada, Belgium, and the United Kingdom.

The degree of institutionalization of regions, and the extent of their autonomy from central governments, is directly related to two factors:

- Whether the country in question is a federal state with a constitutionally protected division of powers between central and regional governments and autonomous, democratically elected representative assemblies.

- Whether the state in question is a multi-national one, in the sense of having one or more clearly defined ethno-territorial minorities with claims to historic nation status.

Either or both of these conditions within liberal democratic states virtually ensures over time the progressive development of power-sharing arrangements between central and regional authorities, as democratic elites seek to accommodate regionalist sentiment. In those states with minority nationalist movements or parties, the tendency will be for this accommodation to take the form or evolve in the direction of asymmetrical power-sharing arrangements, as illustrated in the cases of Catalonia, Scotland, and Quebec.

Finally, the economic differentiation of space conjointly produced by the processes of capitalist development and the state policies put in place to provide the framework for this development can be seen to have had a determinant effect not only on the formation of regions, but on the timing and forms of regionalism which subsequently emerged. The rise, decline, and transformation of regional development policy, despite national variations, can be related to changes in the macro-political economy of states, most recently the economic, political, cultural, and technological changes associated with globalization. As the determinants of regional economic success have come to rely more on the social, cultural, and technological strengths of regions existing and competing in a global market place, a more complex understanding of regional development has taken shape, initiating movement towards more devolved or regionalized forms of governance.

? Questions

1. Why is the concept of region so difficult to define?
2. What are some of the different theoretical approaches that can be used to understand the meaning and significance of regions?
3. What is the relationship between regional political identities and distinct regional cultures?
4. Can it be argued that the nation-state is becoming a thing of the past?
5. How are changes brought about by national minorities affecting the prospects for democracy in the Western world and beyond?
6. Do strong regions produce federalism, or does federalism produce strong regions?
7. Unitary and federal states have more in common than it seems at first glance. What accounts for this?
8. What are the contributions of minority nations in Canada, the United Kingdom, and Spain to the development of federal practices in their respective contexts?
9. How has the process of capitalist development affected the formation and uneven development of regions?
10. What is the 'new regionalism' and how does it reflect the changing role of regions, and the economic challenges they face?

» Further reading

Brodie, J. (1990) *The Political Economy of Canadian Regionalism* (Toronto: Harcourt Brace Jovanovitch).

Gagnon, A.-G., and Tully, J. (eds.) (2001) *Multinational Democracies* (Cambridge: Cambridge University Press).

Gibbins, R. (1982) *Regionalism: Territorial Politics in Canada and the United States* (Toronto: Butterworths).

Keating, M. (2001) *Plurinational Democracy: Stateless Nations in a Post-Sovereignty Era* (Oxford: Oxford University Press).

——(ed.) (2004) *Regions and Regionalism in Europe* (Cheltenham: Edward Elgar).

——and Loughlin, J. (eds.) (1997) *The Political Economy of Regionalism* (London: Frank Cass).

——and McGarry, J. (eds.) (2001) *Minority Nationalism in the Changing State Order* (Oxford: Oxford University Press).

Markusen, A. (1987) *Regions: The Economics and Politics of Territory* (Totowa, NJ: Rowman & Littlefield).

Young, L., and Archer, K. (eds.) (2002) *Regionalism and Party Politics in Canada* (Don Mills, Ont. Oxford University Press).

 Web links

www.essex.ac.uk/ecpr/standinggroups/regionalism/index.aspx
The website of the Standing Group on Regionalism, which organizes conferences, seminars, and workshops on various aspects of regionalism. The group's publishing outlets are the journal *Regional and Federal Studies* and the Frank Cass book series on regionalism.

www.sagepub.com/journalsProdDesc.nav?prodId=Journal200838
The website of the journal *European Urban and Regional Studies*. The journal's mandate is to provide a means of dialogue between different European traditions of intellectual inquiry on urban and regional development issues, highlighting the connections between theoretical analysis and policy development.

www.curs.bham.ac.uk
The website of the Centre for Urban and Regional Studies (CURS), at the University of Birmingham, an international centre for research and teaching in regional and local economic development, urban policy, and regional and urban regeneration.

www.umoncton.ca/icrpap/index_icrdr.html
The Canadian Institute for Research on Regional Development promotes informed public debate and disseminates objective analyses and information on regional development in Canada. The Institute encourages a multidisciplinary approach, including economics, economic geography, political science, public policy, and sociology.

 Visit the Online Resource Centre that accompanies this book for more information:
www.oxfordtextbooks.co.uk/orc/caramani/

16 Social movements

Hanspeter Kriesi

Chapter contents

Reader's guide

This chapter looks at a phenomenon that is usually not part of the core business of comparative political scientists, but which deserves to be taken seriously in a world that is increasingly shaped by non-state actors, such as social movements. The chapter begins with a discussion of what we mean when we speak of social movements and a conceptualization of key terms. It then moves on with the presentation of three theoretical approaches which have successively shaped the debates of the specialists: the classical model, the resource mobilization model, and the political process model. It pays particular attention to the political process approach that is most promising from the comparativist's point of view. This approach is elaborated in the third section. The final section presents some results about the emergence, the level of mobilization, and the success of social movements.

Introduction

Starting on 17 September 1991, right-wing thugs violently attacked hostels of asylum seekers in Hoyerswerda, in Northern Saxony, and initiated a wave of right-wing violence against asylum seekers and other ethnic minority groups across Germany, in which several dozen immigrants were killed. These events, in turn, provoked one of the largest mass movements in German history, involving millions of citizens in rallies, nightly candle-lit marches, and vigils in front of asylum seekers' hostels to protect them against attacks. On 8 November 1992, more than 300,000 people gathered in Berlin to demonstrate against extreme right violence (Koopmans 2001).

On 15 February 2003, two and a half million Italians marched past the Coliseum in Rome in protest at the impending war in Iraq. On the same day in Paris, 250,000 people protested against the war, and half a million people walked past the Brandenburg gate in Berlin. In Madrid, there were a million marchers, in Barcelona 1.3 million; in London, 1.7 million people—the largest demonstration in the city's history. Even in New York, more than 500,000 people assembled on the east side of Manhattan. 'On that day in February, starting from New Zealand and Australia and following the sun around the world, an estimated 16 million people marched, demonstrated, sang songs of peace, and occasionally—despite the strenuous efforts of organizers—clashed with police' (Tarrow 2005: 15).

On 6 October 2006, red was the colour of the day in Berlin, where workers at the Bosch-Siemens household machine factory demonstrated for their jobs. Of the workforce of 1,050, 570 were about to lose their jobs. The demonstration was only the beginning of a 'solidarity march' to the Bosch-Siemens head office in Munich, where the protest activities ended with a large gathering of Siemens workers in front of the corporation's head office.

These are examples of protest events organized by social movements of various stripes—movements of the extreme right and anti-racist movements in the first example, the transnational peace movement in the second, and the German labour movement in the third. Traditionally, social movements have not been considered part of comparative politics. The study of social movements has been the preserve of sociologists dealing with collective behaviour such as panics, crazes, fads, or crowds. As we shall see, social movements are specific forms of collective behaviour. They have action repertoires of their own distinguishing them from established political actors. But they cannot be reduced to their particular action repertoires. To the extent that political scientists paid attention to movements at all, they considered them as public interest groups, i.e. as interest groups defending the collective interests of the general public, and proceeded to analyse them as if they were nothing more than interest groups.

Social movements have organizations which often closely resemble interest groups or, for that matter, political parties. But they cannot be reduced to their organizational component. Comparativists have for too long disregarded social movements. As pointed out in Chapter 24, the current master process of globalization, among other things, widens the resources available to non-state actors, including social movement organizations. Local, regional, national, and transnational social movements have become regular participants in the political process at all levels of polities.

Our society has become, according to some (Meyer and Tarrow 1998b), a 'social movement society': social protest has become a perpetual element of modern life, protest behaviour is employed with greater frequency, by more diverse constituencies, and is used to represent a wider range of claims than ever before, and professionalization and institutionalization may transform the social movement into an instrument within the realm of 'conventional' politics. Even if somewhat exaggerated, this idea reflects well the current tendencies in the political process of democratic polities.

KEY POINTS

❑ Social movements constitute an integral part of the contemporary political process in democratic polities.

❑ Social movements are not simply another type of interest group.

❑ Social movements have action repertoires of their own that distinguish them from established political actors.

Social movement as regular participants in political processes

Defining social movements

Although everybody seems to have a fairly good idea of what a social movement is, the concept is not easy to define. By a social movement, we often mean a group of people involved in a conflict with clearly identified opponents, sharing a common identity, a unifying belief or a common programme, and acting collectively. In other words, the concept of social movement includes at least three component elements: (1) a group of people with a conflictual orientation towards an opponent, (2) a collective identity, and a set of common beliefs and goals, and (3) a repertoire of collective actions.

The various definitions of social movements (Box: What is a social movement?, in the Online Resource Centre, provides three examples) all emphasize that **movements are engaged in conflicts with some opponents**, but scholars are not of one mind when it comes to specifying the character of the conflicts involved. Some leave the question open-ended; others narrow the range of opponents primarily to those within the political arena, as reflected in the recent conceptualization of movements as a variant of 'contentious politics' (McAdam *et al.* 2001; Tilly and Tarrow 2007). This narrower view excludes movements within established institutions, such as religious movements within established churches that attempt to reform the church or to block such reforms (e.g. Tarrow 1988), or challengers of cultural authorities. Snow *et al.* (2004) propose a more inclusive, yet not entirely open-ended definition by considering as social movements challengers or defenders of 'existing institutional authority—whether it is located in the political, corporate, religious, or educational realm—or patterns of cultural authority, such as systems of beliefs or practices reflective of those beliefs' (Snow *et al.* 2004: 9).

Since most conflicts involve some aspect of politics, however, the narrower view may not be so narrow after all. The women's movement, for example, challenges cultural authorities—patriarchal values and beliefs—but it also mobilizes women as women 'to demand equal rights from Fiji to Finland ... to confront authoritarian rule (e.g. Mothers of

the Disappeared in Argentina and El Salvador), to demand peace (e.g., Women in Black in Bosnia and Israel), to call for handgun control (e.g., the Million Moms March in the US), and to address a variety of social problems across their communities' (Ferree and McClurg Mueller 2004: 578). In comparative politics, in any case, we are primarily interested in movements which in one way or another target the political process.

Movements vs. organizations

As to the group of people constituting the social movement, the question of how to define its boundaries proves to be particularly difficult (see also Chapter 18). The boundaries of social movements are inherently disputed, unstable, and ultimately dependent on mutual recognition by the members of the group involved. The people participating in a movement must somehow be connected to one another and they must share a common goal. Diani and Bison (2004) propose that we speak of a social movement only in cases of conflictual collective action which is based on dense informal interorganizational networks. No single actor can claim to represent a movement as a whole. Instead, a social movement is constituted by a network of multiple individual and organized actors who, while keeping their autonomy and independence, engage in a sustained, coordinated effort to achieve collective goals.

This distinguishes social movements from organizations such as political parties or interest groups, who are more formally constituted. Parties and interest groups may be part of the network that constitutes a social movement, but movements may not be reduced to them. In addition, for a social movement to exist, Diani and Bison require that all participants in the dense, informal network share a strong common identity. Collective identities take shape on the basis of the informal networks and, in turn, reinforce them. Organizational and individual actors with a common identity no longer merely pursue specific goals, but come to regard themselves as elements of much larger and encompassing processes of change—or resistance to change.

This element distinguishes social movements from coalitions, which are formed for specific campaigns and do not have the sustained character of social movements. We do not speak of social movements in the case of 'episodic' events of protest or single campaigns that do not have a certain duration in time. Social movements involve a protracted series of protest events produced by more or less stable networks of organizational actors. Clearly, there is a considerable variability in their careers and trajectories, as some movements do indeed last for a comparatively short time only, as with most neighbourhood NIMBY oppositions ('Not In My Back-Yard'), while others endure for decades, as with the labour movement or the women's movement. However, the kind of changes movements pursue, whatever their degree or level, typically require some measure of sustained, organized activity.

The most distinctive of the three defining elements of the social movement is probably the collective action component. At its most elementary level, collective action consists of any goal-directed activity engaged in jointly by two or more individuals. It entails the pursuit of a common objective through joint action. The common objective may be of an economic (as in a firm), religious (as in a church or a sect), cultural (as in an opera orchestra or a rock-band), or political nature (as in a party or an interest group). To identify the specificity of social movements, it is useful to distinguish those collective actions that are institutionalized from those that are not and that fall outside institutional channels (Snow *et al.* 2004: 6). In pursuing their collective political objectives, social movements typically engage in *non-institutionalized* collective action, because they do not have regular access to the decision-making arenas in parliament and in the state administration. Social movements are forced to draw attention to their cause by mobilizing in the public sphere and addressing themselves to the general public.

Social movements and media

Very generally, the public sphere can be defined as the arena where the political communication between the decision-makers and the citizens takes place (Neidhardt 1994). Although no decisions are taken in the public sphere, the public debate is part and parcel of the political process. The political contest in the public sphere focuses on the attention of the public to specific political issues, on its support for specific political actors, and their issue-specific positions (public opinion).

As Schattschneider argued a long time ago, the 'expansion of conflict' beyond those immediately concerned plays a crucial role in democratic polities. Conflicts are 'frequently won or lost by the success that the contestants have in getting the audience involved in the fight or in excluding it, as the case may be' (1988: 4). The agenda-setting approach has adopted and developed this basic idea. It considers the struggle for the attention of the public as the central element of democratic representation and attention shifts as key mechanisms for the development of (political) conflicts. Under contemporary conditions, where the media play a key role in politics, the struggle for public attention involves all political actors. However, those who do not have regular access to the decision-making arenas—such as social movements—are particularly dependent on it.

In general, social movements have two types of strategies to draw attention to their cause (Keck and Sikkink 1998*b*: 226–30):

- **Protest politics**: mobilizing for protest events in the public sphere.
- **Information politics**: collecting credible information and deploying it strategically at carefully selected sites.

Protest events sometimes directly challenge the movement's opponent, such as in a strike. More often, however, they address the public more generally. The publicity created by protest events pursues two objectives (Gamson *et al.* 1992: 383): it is intended to create a public debate and to increase the 'standing' and the 'legitimacy' of the social movement in the conflict in question. To be able to have some impact on the political process or on any other decision-makers, social movements must draw the attention and support of the public, i.e. they need to become visible in the media and their ideas have to obtain resonance and legitimacy in the citizen public. The challengers need to gain 'standing', i.e. a voice in the media, and they need to do the right 'framing', i.e. develop central organizing ideas (frames) that some part of the citizen public understands and supports (Ferree *et al.* 2002: 86, 105). Public debate is not the ultimate goal, however. In the final analysis, the social movement seeks, via public support, to have an impact on the decision-makers in the conflict in question. Creating controversy is a way of increasing opportunity by opening media access to movement spokespersons and allies (Gamson and Meyer 1996: 288).

While non-institutionalized 'protest politics' constitute the distinctive characteristic of social movements, they do not only engage in these forms of collective action. They typically combine **protest politics** with **information politics** and the two elements tend to support each other. On the one hand, protest provides the opportunity for 'information politics': only when a movement has obtained a certain public visibility can it successfully employ an 'information strategy'. As Meyer and Tarrow (1998*a*: 18) point out, today, the organizational and technical requirements for the 'information strategy' are less restrictive than they have been in the past, which means that resource-poor organizations can pursue efficient information strategies.

Given the media's fascination with controversy and conflict, providing controversial information about a given issue—in addition to protest politics—often constitutes a promising strategy for social movements. Efficient protests, in turn, often presuppose a credible information policy. Greenpeace—an organization of the environmental movement—for example, before mobilizing does its own research, acquires the necessary expertise, and searches for alternative solutions. In the course of the subsequent campaign, this background information is offered to the public and decision-makers. The action repertoire of social movements is, however, typically skewed in the direction of non-institutional lines of action.

As Charles Tilly (1978: 10) has pointed out, a central problem for students of social movements is that the three constitutive components of a social movement do not always change together. What happens when the same group of people continues to pursue its original goals, but increasingly abandons protest politics, because it has acquired more resources and is able to obtain institutionalized

access to the decision-making arenas and increasingly uses 'insider' strategies such as lobbying, participation in elections, and lawsuits? Do we still speak of a social movement? The labour movement is a case in point. It has created very powerful organizations—labour unions, social democratic and communist parties, who have become key actors in the decision-making arenas. The opposite development is also possible: an established actor who loses political power may have recourse to non-institutionalized forms of action in an attempt to gain more weight in the decision-making arenas. This happened in Germany in the early 2000s, when the oppositional Christian-Democrats (CDU-CSU) launched a petition campaign to stop the coalition government of the Social-Democrats and the Greens from adopting a new naturalization code. In the audience democracy (see Chapter 5), this is likely to happen more frequently, which means that the line between established political actors and social movements is becoming increasingly blurred.

KEY POINTS

- ❑ The concept of the social movement includes three constitutive components: (1) a group of people with a conflictual orientation towards an opponent, (2) a collective identity, and a set of common beliefs and goals, and (3) a repertoire of collective actions.
- ❑ The conflicts may be of a cultural or a political nature. We are focusing here on movements who target the political process.
- ❑ The group of people constituting a social movement are connected by a dense, informal inter-organizational network and share a strong common identity.
- ❑ They engage in a sustained series of non-institutionalized collective action, since they do not have regular access to the decision-making arenas in parliament and in the state administration.
- ❑ To be able to have some impact on the political process, social movements have to draw the attention and support of the public. They do so by a combination of protest politics and information politics.

Theoretical approaches

The theoretical approaches to social movements have been conveniently divided into three models (McAdam 1982)—the classical model, the resource mobilization model, and the political process model.

Classical model

The classical model, in fact, refers to a *set of theories* with a common denominator: they all start from the notions of 'structural strain' or 'breakdown'. These notions imply a social order whose normal condition is one of integration. If the social order remains sufficiently integrated, strain and breakdown may be avoided and collective behaviour—the classical model speaks of collective behaviour rather than collective action—may not take place. In this logic, as observed by Buechler (2004: 48), 'all roads lead to Durkheim's overriding concern with social integration and the problematic consequences of insufficient integration in modern societies' (Durkheim 1964). Durkheim's analysis of anomie and egoism identified breaches in the social order that could lead to chronic strains or acute breakdown.

Anomie is Durkheim's name for the gap between the emergent division of labour (social differentiation) and the extent of regulation of social relations (social integration). While Durkheim said little about collective action, his analysis provided a major foundation for subsequent theories of strain and breakdown as explanations for such behaviour. Such theories all presume that structural strain and breakdown of standard routines of everyday life have a disruptive psychological effect on individuals, which triggers some form of collective behaviour (Figure 16.1). The motivation for movement participation is held to be based not so much on the desire to attain political goals as on the need to manage the psychological tensions of a stressful social situation.

The most general of all the classical models is the theory of collective behaviour, which is associated with authors such as Smelser (1962), and Turner and Killian (1987). Other variants include the theory of mass society (Kornhauser 1959) or theories of relative deprivation (Gurr 1970). All variants have in common that collective behaviour is sharply set off from conventional behaviour, with elements of contagion, excitability, spontaneity, and emotionality as prevalent. In some versions of the theory, collective behaviour is seen as irrational, disruptive, dangerous, and excessive.

McAdam (1982: 11–19) summarized the critique to these models. First of all, they leap from invidious social conditions to discontent and from discontent to revolt. At best, as McAdam points out, social strain is a necessary, but insufficient cause of social movements. These models are too deterministic and leave no room for political actors and they do not take into account the larger political context. To say that social movements presuppose discontent is true, but trivial: you need discontent to feed any political challenge, it is a necessary condition. To say that discontent causes social movements, however, is plainly false: discontent is nowhere near a sufficient condition (Aya 1990: 32).

Second, the atomistic focus of this model on the individual is problematic on a number of counts. Perhaps the most glaring is the assimilation of movement participants to deviant or marginal persons who are characterized by their social isolation. Social movements are viewed as emergent collections of discontented individuals. But this is to ignore that they are collective phenomena. It is not isolated individuals who become movement participants, but social movements develop within established interaction networks. Third, the critique stresses that movement participants are not primarily motivated by psychological rewards, but that they are engaged in political action.

Resource mobilization model

In sharp contrast to the classical model, the resource mobilization theory views social movements

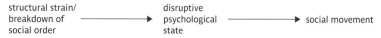

Fig. 16.1 Classical model (McAdam 1982: 7)

as normal, rational, political challenges by aggrieved groups. The predecessors of this approach are John Stuart Mill and the utilitarians, Weber and Marx rather than Durkheim.

The new approach implies a shift from a deterministic to an agency-oriented paradigm. Attention turns from the social forces and conditions that produce movements to the question of how movements mobilize and produce their success. Students of social movements are no longer preoccupied by the question of social order, but adopt the point of view of those engaged in purposeful efforts at social change. This theory claims that discontent is more or less constant over time and thus inadequate as a full explanation of social movements. The proponents of this approach assume that there is always enough discontent in any society to supply the grass-roots support for a movement if the movement is effectively organized and has at its disposal the power and resources of some established elite group.

The entrepreneurial-organizational variant of this approach even allows for the possibility that grievances and discontent may be defined, created, and manipulated by political entrepreneurs and organizations. At the most fundamental level, social movements develop not from an aggregate rise in discontent but from a significant increase in the level of resources available to support collective protest activities. Solidarity and organization as well as external support are treated as key resource for social movements and receive central places in the theory; the more organization, the better the prospects for mobilization and success.

Tilly's explanation focuses on **group solidarity** as the key factor accounting for collective action (Tilly *et al.* 1975). He seeks to undermine any sharp distinction between routine political struggle and violence by arguing that the same political dynamics and solidarity processes underlie both. Oberschall (1973), Gamson (1975), and McCarthy and Zald (1977) all stress the fundamental importance of organization, or, more generally, of mobilization structures for the transformation of grievances into successful collective action. In insisting on the importance of organizations, proponents of the resource mobilization model reject the classical theorists' exclusive focus on the movement's mass base in favour of an analysis of the crucial role played by segments of the elite in the generation of the challenge.

Tilly (1978: 62–4) casts the organizational preconditions for the mobilization of social movements in a neat formula based on Harrison White's concept of a 'catnet'—a set of individuals comprising **both a category** (such as 'women' or 'blacks') **and a network**: the more extensive the 'groupness' of the category, i.e. the greater the group's inclusiveness and the more pronounced its common identity, and the denser its internal network, the more organized it is:

CATNESS x NETNESS = ORGANIZATION

Note that this formula does not only include formal organizations, but also the range of everyday life social locations that are not aimed primarily at movement mobilization, where micro-mobilization may take place: friendship networks, voluntary associations, family and work units, and elements of the state structure itself. It is not a particular form of organization that is emphasized by resource mobilization theory, but the overall structure of the discontented group (Figure 16.2).

In addition to organization, the resource mobilization perspective also puts the emphasis on the tactical and standardized action repertoires of social movements. Protest politics can take different forms, but the repertoire at a given moment in a given context proves to be highly standardized. In past centuries, challengers of authorities typically engaged in short-term, local, and highly variable forms of contention. Tilly (1995) has described how these modular

Fig. 16.2 Resource mobilization model (adapted from Tilly *et al.* 1975; Tilly 1978)

action forms first shifted towards a new repertoire of long-term, national, and generally applicable forms in Great Britain during the late eighteenth and early nineteenth century. Thus, demonstrations, assemblies, and strikes became modular forms of collective action as British politics increasingly nationalized during the period in question.

Today, the capacity to create protest events of a certain news value constitutes the key resource of a social movement actor. There are three main factors which contribute to the news value of a protest event: the originality of an event (its surprise effect), the number of participants, and their radicalism (Rochon 1990: 108; Koopmans 1995: 149-52). These three factors correspond to the three main forms in the action repertoire of contemporary social movements: (1) **confrontational types of action** (new or illegal types of protest, not characterized by violence, but provoking surprise, and generating tensions or feelings of defiance among the authorities or the public, e.g. occupation of public buildings, street blockades); (2) **demonstrative types of action** (e.g. demonstrations, marches, meetings); (3) **violent types of action** (involving material or human damage, e.g. sacking stores or killing public officials).

McAdam's (1982) critique of the resource mobilization approach points to the failure of its proponents to adequately differentiate organized change efforts by excluded groups from those of established interest groups. By emphasizing the similarities between conventional action and protest politics, the resource mobilization perspective normalized protest too much. While this was a salutary corrective against the tendency to assimilate protest and deviant behaviour, the distinction between **conventional** and **unconventional** forms of protest was seriously blurred and the role of **organizations** in protest was exaggerated.

In a similar vein, Piven and Cloward (1977) do not quarrel with the assumption of the resource mobilization approach that social movement actors are rational political actors, but, defending Rosa Luxemburg's position on the role of organizations in bringing about revolutionary change in the great Marxist debate between her and Lenin, they maintain that protest is not created by organizers and leaders, but wells up spontaneously in response to momentous changes in the institutional order. Their point is that efforts to build organizations are not only futile

but that 'by endeavouring to do what they cannot do, organizers fail to do what they can do' (1977: 36–7).

McAdam also criticizes the 'consistent failure by many of its proponents of resource mobilization to acknowledge the political capabilities of the movement's mass base' (1982: 29). In particular, resource mobilization theorists fail to acknowledge the power inherent in the disruptive tactics of the truly powerless. They tend to overlook the crucial importance of the indigenous resources of the aggrieved population and to put the emphasis on external resources of allies and other external supporters. Next, McAdam criticizes the approach for its failure to distinguish between objective social conditions from their subjective perception: the link between objective conditions and action is seldom straightforward, the meaning people attach to their objective situation is crucial for their mobilization. Finally, the approach has to some extent failed in its own terms, because it has tended to neglect the role of leadership in social movements. In particular, it has failed to analyse the influence of leadership on the strategy of social movements (Ganz 2000).

Political process model

Based on his critique of the resource mobilization model, McAdam (1982) formulates a third perspective on social movements—the political process model. This model shares the basic assumptions of the resource mobilization approach and it also considers the level of organization within the aggrieved population as a crucial element for its mobilization. Therefore, it is often treated as just another variant of the resource mobilization approach. However, it adds two elements to the previous model.

1. First, the political process model puts the group into its **political context** and focuses on the **political opportunities and constraints** structuring the way it interacts with its adversaries. The political process model is based on the idea that the social processes of the classical model do not directly promote the mobilization of social movements, but do so only indirectly through a restructuring of existing power relations. Proponents of the model see the timing and fate of movements as largely dependent upon the opportunities afforded the challengers by shifting the institutional structures

and ideological dispositions of those in power. The concept of political opportunity emphasizes resources external to the group that can be taken advantage of even by weak or disorganized challengers. Social movements form, according to this perspective, when organized citizens respond to changes in opportunities that lower the costs of collective action or increase its likely benefits.

2. The second element added by the political process models refers to the **subjective meaning** people attribute to their situation. The emergence of a social movement implies a transformation of consciousness within a significant segment of the aggrieved population. Before collective action becomes possible, people must collectively define their situations as unjust and subject to change through collective action. McAdam (1982: 51) refers to this condition as a **cognitive liberation**, which is facilitated by expanding political opportunities, by the internal solidarity and organization of the aggrieved group, and by strategic attempts by political entrepreneurs. The last facilitating condition has been elaborated by the 'cultural turn' in social movement research, which has focused on the analysis of framing processes—the social construction of grievances and discontent by social movement actors (Snow *et al.* 1986; Snow and Benford 1988). Figure 16.3 presents the schematic outline of the political process model as proposed by McAdam (1982: 51). This model has subsequently been elaborated into a more encompassing 'social movement paradigm' which attempts to integrate the various models, but tends to neglect the elements of the

classical models. Political opportunities, mobilizing structures, cultural framings and repertoires of contention became integral parts of this more encompassing perspective—the 'social movement paradigm' (McAdam *et al.* 1996).

The political process model and its successor have also met with criticism.

1. The concept of 'political opportunity structure' has been criticized for its all-inclusive character. It tends to become a sponge that soaks up virtually every aspect of the social movement environment—political institutions and culture, crises of various sorts, political alliances, policy shifts. Used to explain so much, it may ultimately explain nothing (Gamson and Meyer 1996).

2. Critics have pointed out (Goodwin and Jasper 1999: 34) that not all social movements are equally focused on the political process and, therefore, dependent to the same degree on political opportunities for their mobilization and success. Thus, movements challenging cultural authorities will have a greater degree of autonomy from the political context and thus be less adequately explained by the present approach. The women's movement, or at least part of it, is an obvious and important example, and it is probably no coincidence that this movement has received less attention from the political process approach than it deserves, although this situation is changing (e.g. Banaszak 1996).

3. It has been pointed out that the concept of opportunity often serves as a substitute for breakdown (Buechler 2004: 61). Opportunities emerge when the established order becomes vulnerable to the

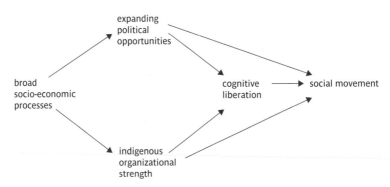

Fig. 16.3 The political process model of movement emergence (McAdam 1982: 51)

actions of social movements and when their costs of acting are reduced. What constitute opportunities from the perspective of the movement actors represents a **breakdown of social control mechanisms** from the point of view of the established authorities and the defenders of the status quo.

What actually happened with social movement theory is a re-evaluation of collective action: it has come to be increasingly painted in a positive light. This shift:

> ❝followed larger disciplinary trends as approaches stressing values, integration and consensus gave way to those emphasizing conflict, domination, and resistance. And these larger trends were themselves linked to social changes and political challenges beginning with the civil rights movement and expanding into the myriad social movements and legitimation challenges of the 1960s. (Buechler 2004: 51) ❞

While an earlier generation of social scientists had been traumatized by the rise of fascism and the mobilization of various right-wing groups, the successes of the civil rights movement, anti-war movement, the women's movement, and the environmental movement attracted a new generation of social scientists who supported the aspirations of participants.

Several authors sympathetic to the general framework of the political process approach have criticized the 'structural bias' and the determinism involved in much of the recent work in this area (e.g. Goodwin and Jasper 1999; McAdam *et al.* 2001). Such critics wish to put more emphasis on the processual elements. They insist on the particularities of the movement-specific contexts, on the dynamics of the interaction between the actors in one and the same context, and on the subjective interpretations of the actors involved.

Finally, two additional defects were identified with the political process model and its successor—the social movement paradigm (McAdam *et al.* 2001; Tilly and Tarrow 2007):

- Their single-minded focus on **single-actor movements** and their indifference to the broader field of contentious politics (which includes phenomena such as ethnic conflicts, nationalist episodes, and revolutions, too).

- The overwhelming tendency of their practitioners to study movements at the **national level.**

McAdam *et al.* (2001) tried to address these last defects by a deliberately dynamic approach to contentious politics all over the world. They sought to deduce key processes and mechanisms that constitute contentious politics (see Box 16.1).

BOX 16.1 Contentious politics

Contention, collective action, and politics overlap in contentious politics (p. 23):

> ❝interactive, collective making of claims that bear on other people's interests and involve governments as claimants, objects of claims, or third parties. Social movements qualify as a form of contentious politics, but so do revolutions, civil wars, and a wide variety of other struggles. In all these forms of contention, distinctive claim-making performances and repertoires vary from setting to setting and regime to regime. Some of those performances are modular; as with street demonstration, they transfer easily from setting to setting and regime to regime. They build on social bases belonging to the setting or regime. ❞

Some generalizations about contentious politics (pp. 196–7):

- Although it generally occurs in different sorts of regimes, revolutions, civil wars, lethal ethnic conflicts, social movements, and other forms, contentious politics results from similar causes in different combinations, sequences, and initial conditions.

- We can usefully break those causes into recurrent mechanisms and processes. Explaining contention means identifying the mechanisms and processes that lie behind it.

- In all sorts of regimes, from low capacity to high capacity and from undemocratic to democratic, routine interactions between governments and political actors produce political opportunity structures that greatly limit what forms of contention different potential makers of claims can actually initiate.

(continued)

KEY POINTS

- There are three basic theoretical approaches to social movements: (1) the classical model, (2) the resource mobilization model, and (3) the political process model.
- Classical theories presume that structural strain and breakdown of standard routines of everyday life cause discontent among the individual members of the group to trigger collective behaviour.
- According to the resource mobilization theory, social movements develop not from an aggregate rise in discontent but from a significant increase in the level of resources available to support collective protest activities of the aggrieved group. Solidarity, organization,

and external support are key resources for social movements.
- The political process model builds on the resource mobilization approach, but with two additional elements. First, it puts the aggrieved group into its political context and focuses on the political opportunities and constraints structuring the way it interacts with its adversaries. Second, it recognizes that the emergence of a social movement implies a transformation of consciousness within the aggrieved population.
- Although the political process model has, like the other two models, met with serious criticism, it holds out the greatest promise for comparative politics.

The comparative analysis of social movements

For comparative politics, the political process model holds considerable promise. By putting social movements into their political context, it brings the study of social movements into the mainstream of political science. This section discusses the specific ways of how social movements are determined by and interact with their political context. Figure 16.4 provides a framework for the comparative political analysis of social movements. This framework distinguishes between three sets of variables—political opportunity structures, configurations of power, and interaction contexts. Let us look at the different elements of each set.

Political opportunity structure

The political opportunity structure constitutes what we could call the hard core of the political process framework. The basic idea of the framework is

that 'political opportunity structures influence the choice of protest strategies and the impact of social movements on their environment' (Kitschelt 1986: 58). Since Eisinger (1973) first introduced the notion of political opportunity structures, students of social movements have distinguished between 'open' and 'closed' structures, that is, structures which allow for easy access to the political system or which make access more difficult. Kitschelt (1986) introduced the additional distinction between **input** and **output** structures, that is, structures referring specifically either to the openness of the political system in the input phase of the policy cycle or to its capacity to impose itself in the output phase. In practice, it proved to be difficult to separate these two types of structures clearly from one another. Open systems at the same time tend to have only a limited capacity to act, whereas closed systems tend to lack such a capacity.

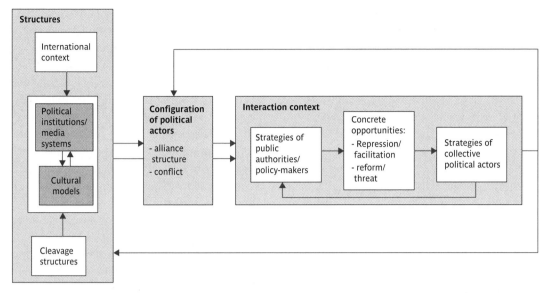

Fig. 16.4 A framework for the study of the impact of the political context (adapted from Kriesi 2004: 70)

The core of the structures, in turn, is made up of formal political institutions. The degree of openness of the political system is a function of its (territorial) centralization and the degree of its (functional) separation of power. The greater the degree of decentralization, the wider the formal access and the smaller the capacity of any one part of the system to act. Decentralization implies a multiplication of state actors and, therefore, of points of access and decision-making. In federal states, such as those of Germany, Switzerland, or the US, there are multiple entry points at the national, regional, and local level. In centralized states, such as those of France, the Netherlands, the UK, or Sweden, regional and local entry points are rather insignificant. In addition, the system's openness is closely related to the (functional) separation of power. The greater the separation of power between the legislature (parliamentary arena), the executive (government and public administration), and the judiciary, and the greater the division of power within each one of these branches of government (e.g. between partners in the governing coalition as a result of the electoral system), the greater the degree of formal access for movement actors and the more limited the capacity of the state to act. The overall accessibility of the political institutions can be summarized by the usual models in comparative politics (see Section 3 of this volume).

Given the key importance of the media, the political process approach has paid surprisingly little attention to the structure of the media system in a given country. Hallin and Mancini (2004) provide a comparative framework for the study of the impact of media systems on the political process. They propose four dimensions along which media systems can be compared (see also Chapter 19):

- The development of **media markets** with particular emphasis on the strong or weak development of a mass circulation press.

- **Political parallelism**, i.e. the degree and nature of the links between the media and political parties or, more broadly, the extent to which the media system reflects the major political divisions in society.

- The development of **journalistic professionalism**.

- The degree and nature of **state intervention** in the media system.

Based on these criteria, they distinguish between three models of media systems:

- The Mediterranean or Polarized Pluralist Model.
- The North/Central European or Democratic Corporatist Model.
- The North Atlantic or Liberal Model.

In the past, the European media systems had been closer to the world of politics than the North Atlantic systems but, under the impact of secularization and commercialization, they are shifting away from it and towards the world of commerce. Commercial media create powerful new techniques of representation and audience creation, which not only established political actors, but also social movement actors must adopt in order to prevail in the new communication environment. Two of the most important of these techniques are **personalization** and the tendency to privilege the point of view of the 'ordinary citizen'. The implications for social movements are certainly ambivalent. The highly problematic impact of the media's 'star system'—its tendency to personalize politics—on social movements has, in particular, been shown by Gitlin (1980). He showed that the New Left in the US lost its ability to certify and control its own leaders, as they became celebrities who used their newly won fame as a personal resource. Greenpeace, by contrast, demonstrates how a social movement organization can use the media's commercial interests to its own advantage.

The extent to which social movement actors obtain access to the decision-making arenas not only depends on the formal institutional structure, but also on more informal preconditions, which I propose to call **cultural models**.

A first example of such cultural models refers to the prevailing strategies of the authorities with regard to social movements, i.e. to the procedures typically employed by members of the political system when they are dealing with challengers. We may distinguish between **exclusive** (repressive, confrontational, polarizing) and **integrative** (facilitative, cooperative, assimilative) strategies. These prevailing strategies have a long tradition in a given country and they are related to its institutional structure. Thus political authorities in consensus democracies are rather more likely to rely on integrative strategies than their colleagues in majoritarian democracies (for the distinction between these two types of democracy, see Chapter 5).

In consensus democracies, the tendency to rely on integrative strategies is the result of a collective learning experience that reaches back to the resolution of the religious conflicts which have torn these countries apart for centuries. The resolution of these conflicts provided the models for dealing with political challenges for centuries to come. Similarly, the tendency to rely on repressive strategies is a result of historical experiences, as is argued by Gallie (1983), who traces the repressive reactions of the French ruling elites to

the challenge by labour movement protest after the First World War back to the earlier experience of repressing the Parisian Commune in 1870.

A second major category of cultural models concerns the political-cultural or symbolic opportunities that determine what kind of ideas become visible for the public, resonate with public opinion, and are held to be 'legitimate' by the audience. Koopmans and Statham (1999: 228) proposed the term **discursive opportunity structure** to denote this second type of cultural models. They apply the concept to the mobilization by the extreme right—a social movement that uses an ethnic-cultural model of citizenship and national identity to mobilize against immigration in Western Europe. Ethnic-cultural models of national identity assert that people belong to a nation because of their ethnic or cultural (e.g. linguistic or religious) origin. This kind of model contrasts with civic-political models of citizenship, which conceive of the nation as a political community of equal citizens to which everybody who has been born into the community in question belongs. Comparing the differential success of the extreme right in post-war Italy and Germany, Koopmans and Statham test and confirm the hypothesis that the resonance of the extreme-right frame, and consequently its chances of mobilization and success in a given country, depends on the dominant model of national identity and citizenship. Its mobilization and success turn out to be greater (1) the more the dominant discourse on national identity and citizenship corresponds to and legitimates the ethnic-cultural ideal type of national identity, and (2) the less the dominant conception of the nation is grounded in and legitimized by civic-political elements (1999: 229).

The cultural models can be combined with the political institutional structures in order to arrive at more complex and more focused opportunity sets. Table 16.1 provides an example of a typology of context conditions based on institutional structures and prevailing strategies.

Both institutional structures and cultural models are influenced by even more fundamental structures, which we should include in our conceptualization of the structural political context in the broader sense of the term. Thus, political institutions and cultural models are influenced by the country-specific political cleavage structures and by the country's international context. As discussed in Chapter 13,

Table 16.1 The general settings for the mobilization of social movements

Dominant strategy	Formal institutional structure	
	Weak state	*Strong state*
Exclusive	*Formalistic inclusion:*	*Full exclusion:*
	formal, but no informal, facilitation of access; strong repression;	neither formal nor informal facilitation of access; strong repression;
	possibility of veto, but no substantive concessions	possibility of neither veto nor substantive concessions
	(Germany, Brazil, US)	(France, Japan, Argentina)
Inclusive	*Full procedural integration:*	*Informal cooptation:*
	formal and informal facilitation of access; weak repression;	no formal, but informal, facilitation of access; weak repression;
	possibility of veto, but no substantive concessions	no possibility of veto, but substantive concessions
	(Switzerland, Canada)	(Netherlands, Sweden)

Source: Kriesi (1995: 177).

the specific political cleavage structure of a country, in turn, is rooted in the history of social and cultural conflicts. Traditional social and cultural cleavages constitute the basis of the political cleavage structure even today. To the extent that traditional conflicts are still salient and segment the population into mutually exclusive adversarial groups, there is little manœuvring space for new types of challengers who attempt to articulate a new kind of social or cultural conflict. Comparing the mobilization of new social movements (see Box 16.2) in four Western European countries in the 1970s and 1980s, there is evidence for the existence of such a 'zero-sum' relationship between traditional and new political cleavages (Kriesi *et al.* 1995).

BOX 16.2 New social movements

The so-called 'new social movements' have been responsible for the bulk of the mobilization that has taken place in Western Europe from the 1970s up to the 1990s. Most authors would probably agree that this family of movements includes the **ecology movement** (with its anti-nuclear energy branch), the **peace movement**, the **solidarity movement** (solidarity with developing countries), the **women's movement**, the **human rights movement**, the **anti-racist movement**, the **squatters' movement**, as well as various other movements mobilizing for the rights of discriminated-against minorities (such as the gay movement).

These movements were called 'new' at the time in order to distinguish them from the 'old' labour movement, which had dominated the mobilization for collective action in Western Europe up to the 1960s.

On the one hand, these movements go back to the new left, the new generation of radicals who were the protagonists of the anti-authoritarian revolt of the late 1960s. On the other hand, they are an offspring of the citizens' action committees that had started to articulate more specific grievances of local or regional populations in the early 1970s. These citizens' action committees were much more pragmatic and at the same time much broader in scope than the new left proper. Thanks to their dual political roots, the new social movements have managed to achieve what the new left has never been able to do on its owh—namely, the political mobilization of masses of citizens on behalf of their emancipatory goals.

Source: Kriesi *et al.* (1995).

Moreover, even if today the national political context is still the most significant one for the mobilization of social movements, it is important that we do not lose sight of sub-national as well as international contexts. On the one hand, nation-states are subdivided in regional and local levels of governance. The variance of the opportunity structure between regions or member-states is of great importance above all in federal states, but the significance of the variations in local contexts for the mobilization of social movement is highly relevant everywhere. On the other hand, nation-states are increasingly inserted into supra- or international systems of governance that impose constraints and open opportunities for social movement actors. Thus, Tarrow (2005) argues that rapid electronic communication, cheaper international travel, diffusion of the English language, the spread of the 'script' of modernity, and 'internationalism' facilitate transnational activism. Internationalism 'both makes the threats of globalization more visible and offers resources, opportunities, and alternative targets for transnational activists and their allies to make claims against other domestic and external actors' (pp. 8–9). In other words, internationalism offers a wide range of venues for conflict.

According to Tarrow, the unusual character of the contemporary period is not that it has detached individuals from their societies or created transnational citizens but that it has created what he calls 'rooted cosmopolitans' and 'transnational activists'. This is a stratum of people who are able to combine the resources and opportunities of their own societies into transnational networks, leading to an 'activism beyond borders' (p. 43). Transnational activism and transnational movement organizations are, as he shows, a growing phenomenon even if, as I would add, the bulk of social movement campaigns still take place in a national context and address domestic targets. Examples of transnational movements include the resistance to the war in Iraq which was mentioned at the outset of this chapter, and the global justice movement which mobilizes against the World Trade Organization (WTO), the World Economic Forum (WEF), or the G8 meetings and organizes its own yearly Social Forums (originally in Porto Alegre, Brazil, more recently in different locations across the world).

Configuration of power

The next set of variables refers to the configurations of actors. From the point of view of a mobilizing social movement, this configuration has three major components:

- **Protagonists:** the configuration of allies (policy-makers, public authorities, political parties, interest groups, the media, and related movements).
- **Antagonists:** the configuration of adversaries (public authorities, repressive agents, counter-movements).
- **Bystanders:** the not directly involved, but nevertheless attentive audience.

Actor configurations represent what we know of the set of actors at a given point in time—their capabilities, perceptions, and evaluations of the outcomes obtainable (their 'pay-offs' in terms of game theory), and the degree to which their interests are compatible or incompatible with each other. The configuration describes the level of potential conflict, the 'logic of the situation' at that point in time, but it does not specify how the situation is going to evolve, nor does it say how it has been created.

The configuration of political actors at any given point in time is partly determined by the **structures of the political context**. Thus the new social movements in Western Europe faced a very different alliance structure depending on the configuration of the left, their natural ally (the new social movements essentially were 'movements of the left', see Box 16.2), which was, in turn, decisively shaped by the **heritage of the prevailing strategies** to deal with challengers in a given country (Kriesi *et al.* 1995).

The heritage of exclusive strategies in a country like France caused the radicalization and eventual split of the labour movement into a moderate, social-democratic left and a radical communist left. This split in the labour movement, in turn, contributed to the continued salience of the class conflict, which, at the time of the emergence of the French new social movements in the latter part of the 1970s, limited the availability of the left for the mobilization of the new social movements. In the French situation, where the left was dominated by the Communist Party up to the late 1970s, the Socialists could not become unconditional allies of the new social movements. They had to continue to appeal to the working class in traditional class terms to ward off Communist competition, and both the Socialists and the Communists tended to instrumentalize the new social movements—especially the peace movement and the solidarity movement—for their own electoral purposes.

However, the configuration of political actors is less stable than the structural component of the political context. The alliance structure of a given movement may, for example, change decisively at any election, depending on whether the political party which constitutes a natural ally for the social movement in question is elected into power or loses its government position. Thus, the social democrats tended to support the Western European new social movements when they were in opposition, but were much less reliable allies when in government. Moreover, it is also much easier for social movements to modify the configuration of political actors than to modify the structural context.

While authors who analyse the mobilization of social movements in a comparative (cross-national, cross-regional, or cross-local) perspective rely heavily on explanations involving structural elements, authors who do case studies within national contexts tend to put the accent more on configurations of political actors. Most importantly, they tend to adopt a longitudinal perspective involving comparisons across time and important shifts in the configurations of political actors. In their view, it is the shifts in the configurations of political actors—the instability of political alignments—which create the opportunity for successful mobilization (Tarrow 1994: 87–8). Such instability may relate to the changing electoral fortunes of major parties.

The civil rights movement in the US provides a well-known example for the leverage created by electoral realignments: both the decline of their Southern white vote and the movement of African-American voters to the Northern cities increased the incentive for the Democrats to seek black support. With its 'razor-thin electoral margin, the Kennedy administration was forced to move from cautious foot-dragging to seizing the initiative for civil rights, a strategy that was extended by the Johnson administration to the landmark Voting Rights Act of 1965' (Tarrow 1994: 87).

The instability of political alignments may also refer to a policy-specific situation. In other words, shifting opportunities for mobilization and success may be policy-domain specific. Some exogenous shock, such as changes in socio-economic conditions, natural catastrophes, system-wide governing coalitions, or policy outputs from other subsystems may destabilize the domain-specific equilibrium. Social and cultural shifts and unpredictable catastrophic events may cause policy failures in the domain in question, system-wide power shifts may cause corresponding domain-specific shifts, and policy outputs of other subsystems may cause disarray in the traditional problem-solving routines in the domain in question.

Following the model of Baumgartner and Jones (1993), the policy process in a given policy-domain can be conceptualized as a 'punctuated equilibrium': long periods of stability and incremental policy-making under the auspices of a dominant coalition are interrupted by shorter intervals of major policy change. As the policy monopoly of the dominant coalition destabilizes, established policy paradigms weaken their hold on the policy-makers' minds and controversy is introduced. This provides a 'window of opportunity' (Kingdon 1984: 173–204) for policy change in general and for the intervention of social movement actors in particular.

American nuclear power is an example of the construction and collapse of a policy monopoly. Baumgartner and Jones (1993: 70) maintain that the opponents of nuclear energy in the US won primarily by getting their vision of the issue accepted and by altering the nature of the decision-making process, by expanding the range of participants involved. When the venue had been expanded by opponents to include licensing, oversight, and rate making, the industry lost control of the issue and the future was determined. Whatever the ultimate reason for the breakdown of the nuclear power coalition in the US (see below), the case of US nuclear power illustrates the opportunities that open up for social movements as the hold of dominant coalitions over a policy domain loosens up.

Interaction contexts

The third level of analysis concerns the interaction context. This is the level of the mechanisms linking structures and configurations to agency and action, and it is at this level that the **strategies of the social movements and their opponents** come into view. 'Strategy' is the conceptual link actors make between the places, the times, and the ways they mobilize and deploy their resources and the goals they hope to achieve. Strategy is a way of 'framing' specific choices about targeting, timing, and tactics. Movement actors will make their strategic choices on the basis of their appreciation of the specific chances of reform and threat, and the specific risks of repression and facilitation they face. Box 16.3 defines these mechanisms and describes how they are expected to operate with regard to the level of mobilization.

A striking illustration of how repression operates and how social movements may use its anticipated effects in their own strategic choices is provided again by the civil rights movement. This movement deliberately chose a strategy of demonstrating in cities in the South of the US, where an unmistakably repressive reaction to peaceful demonstrations could be expected. The violent clashes that followed brought the movement more media attention than it would otherwise have received, and conveyed the movement's message in a most powerful way, which consequently led to increased external support. Although, at least in democratic regimes, repression may not reduce the level of movement mobilization, it can be expected to have a considerable effect on the action repertoire. It will reduce the amount of radical mobilization.

As Gamson and Meyer argue, the definition of opportunity, that is, the appreciation of the concrete situation, is typically highly contentious within a social movement and they suggest that 'we focus on the process of defining opportunity and how it works' (1996: 283). The debates within movements typically turn around questions of 'relative opportunity' for different courses of action. Opportunity may shift in favour of some specific part of the movement, the radicals for example, and may result in a radicalization of the movement as a whole. According to

---

BOX 16.3 Four mechanisms linking the context structure to the mobilization of social movements

Four mechanisms involved in linking the general structural setting to the mobilization of social movements:

- **facilitation**: any action by other actors that lowers the costs of mobilization;
- **repression**: any external action that increases such costs;
- **chances of success**: the likelihood that collective action will contribute to the realization of a movement's goals;
- **threat/reform**: a situation where collective benefits are expected even if no collective action is undertaken/where collective 'bads' are expected if the movement does not act.

Impact on the volume of mobilization:

Facilitation:

This will generally lead to an incrase in the level of mobilization.

Repression:

Extremely high levels of repression will make collective action unattractive for the large majority of potential activists.

At lower levels, increased repression may not be able to reduce the amount of mobilization; in the literature several examples of movements can be found that were actually stimulated by repression.

Chances of success:

The level of mobilization is likely to increase with the chances of success; there are two types of success:

> **proactive success**: implies the introduction of new advantages; it is diffcult to achieve under any kind of circumstances;

> **reactive success**: implies the avoidance of new disadvantages; may be more easily achieved, which is why defensive mobilization is more likely to occur than proactive mobilization.

Threat/reform:

The level of mobilization is likely to increase with the intensity of threat; the level of mobilization is likely to decrease with the chances of reform; threat contributes to the likelihood of 'defensive' mobilization.

Source: Adapted from Tilly (1978); Koopmans (1992).

the political process approach, however, the 'relative opportunities' are to a large extent determined by the configuration of actors and the structural context. In other words, the outcome of the internal debates of the movements is constrained by the larger political context, which the strategically oriented movement actors will not fail to take into account in their deliberations.

Ganz (2000) adds the important notion of **strategic capacity**, i.e. the movement's capability of developing effective strategy. He distinguishes between three key influences on strategic choices: salient knowledge, heuristic processes, and motivation. First, **salient knowledge** is the precondition that actors deal effectively with the problems they face. Second, **heuristic processes** permit them to use this knowledge imaginatively. Third, **motivation** is critical because of its effect on the actors' ability to concentrate their effort for extended periods of time.

These three elements, in turn, are a function of **leadership** and **organization.** Ganz (2000: 1015–16) argues (1) that leaders who are personally committed to the cause because of their own biographical experience are likely to be particularly motivated; (2) that leadership teams who combine 'strong' ties to their own constituency with 'weak' ties to a variety of people are more likely to combine personal commitment and local knowledge with innovative ideas; and (3) that leaders with knowledge of a diversity of salient collective action repertoires are more likely to develop effective strategy than those without such knowledge.

With respect to organizational structures, he suggests that structures that 'afford leaders venues for regular, open, and authoritative deliberation; draw resources from a diversity of salient constituencies; and hold leaders accountable to those constituencies—and to each other—are more likely to generate effective strategy than those that do not' (Ganz 2000: 1016). Moreover, he stresses that it is not sufficient simply to describe the strategy, it is important to study it in context: since strategy unfolds as a process, it is important to pay attention to the mechanisms that generate it. Box 16.4 provides excerpts from a famous speech by Martin Luther King Jr., which may serve as an illustration of the strategic capacity of this great leader of the American civil rights movement.

Differences in strategic capacity may explain why some new organizations fail while others survive,

---

BOX 16.4 Excerpts from the speech delivered by Martin Luther King Jr. on the steps at the Lincoln Memorial in Washington, DC on 28 August 1963

Five score years ago, a great American [Abraham Lincoln], in whose symbolic shadow we stand signed the Emancipation Proclamation. This momentous decree came as a great beacon light of hope to millions of Negro slaves who had been seared in the flames of withering injustice. It came as a joyous daybreak to end the long night of captivity.

But one hundred years later, we must face the tragic fact that the Negro is still not free. One hundred years later, the life of the Negro is still sadly crippled by the manacles of segregation and the chains of discrimination. One hundred years later, the Negro lives on a lonely island of poverty in the midst of a vast ocean of material prosperity. One hundred years later, the Negro is still languishing in the corners of American society and finds himself an exile in his own land. So we have come here today to dramatize an appalling condition.

. . .

I am not unmindful that some of you have come here out of great trials and tribulations. Some of you have come fresh from narrow cells. Some of you have come from areas where your quest for freedom left you battered by the storms of persecution and staggered by the winds of police brutality. You have been the veterans of creative suffering. Continue to work with the faith that unearned suffering is redemptive.

Go back to Mississippi, go back to Alabama, go back to Georgia, go back to Louisiana, go back to the slums and ghettos of our northern cities, knowing that somehow this situation can and will be changed. Let us not wallow in the valley of despair.

I say to you today, my friends, that in spite of the difficulties and frustrations of the moment, I still have a dream. It is a dream deeply rooted in the American dream. I have a dream that one day this nation will rise up and live out the true meaning of its creed:

(continued)

BOX 16.4 (continued)

'We hold these truths to be self-evident: that all men are created equal'.

I have a dream that one day on the red hills of Georgia the sons of former slaves and the sons of former slave-owners will be able to sit down together at a table of brotherhood. I have a dream that one day even the state of Mississippi, a desert state, sweltering with the heat of injustice and oppression, will be transformed into an oasis of freedom and justice. I have a dream that my four children will one day live in a nation where they will not be judged by the color of their skin but by the content of their character.

I have a dream today. I have a dream that one day the state of Alabama, whose governor's lips are presently dripping with the words of interposition and nullification, will be transformed into a situation where little black boys and black girls will be able to join hands with little white boys and white girls and walk together as sisters and brothers. I have a dream today.

---

and they may at the same time account for less adaptive behaviour among older organizations. Ganz uses the example of the unionization of Californian farm workers (1959–66) to show the importance of strategic capacity for the movement's success. Explanations relying on changing political opportunity structures or resources, or references to Cesar Chávez's charismatic leadership cannot account for the United Farm Workers' (UFW) success, while more resourceful organizations had failed. The UFW's strategy turned out to be more effective than that of its rivals because of the way in which it was developed. It adapted familiar repertoires to new uses. It drew on elements of an ethnic labour association (reminiscent of earlier organizing attempts by farm workers of colour), a union, and community organizing drives in a new synthesis that went far beyond its individual components. It developed a 'dual strategy' based on the mobilization of farm workers (the discontented group) and of urban supporters (external allies who brought in material and political resources). By reaching beyond the fields to the cities, the UFW exposed what growers considered to be a legitimate exercise of their authority as illegitimate in the public domain.

An array of specific mechanisms links the general structural setting to the mobilization of social movements. They constitute what we could call 'concrete opportunities'. Tilly (1978) introduced the pair of mechanisms 'facilitation and repression', Koopmans (1992) added 'success chances and reform/threat'. McAdam *et al.* (2001) pursued this line of reasoning further and introduced several additional mechanisms, which allowed linking the structural context to the concrete episodes of mobilization (see Box 16.3).

KEY POINTS

❑ The political context for the mobilization of social movements can be broken down into political opportunity structures, configuration of actors, and interaction contexts.

❑ The formal institutional political structures and the cultural models such as prevailing strategies combine to define the overall structural context.

❑ The configuration of power refers to the shifting configurations of allies, adversaries, and bystanders who exist at the level of authorities and policy-makers in the policy-specific context or in the polity at large and who constitute the alliance and conflict structures facing the movement.

❑ The overall context is linked by specific mechanisms to the strategic choices made by the social movements in the interaction context: facilitation vs. repression, and success chances vs. reform/threat are examples of such mechanisms.

COUNTRY PROFILE Brazil

Federative Republic of Brazil (*República Federativa do Brasil*)

State formation

Independence from Portugal was gained in 1822. In 1889 the Republic was established. An authoritarian regime prevailed from 1930 to 1945. After the Second World War, democratization took place, but in 1964 the military overthrew the President and Brazil was ruled by a succession of military governments that suspended constitutional guarantees. Civilian government was restored in 1985.
Constitution 1988; amended many times.

Form of government

Presidential, federal republic.
Head of state President and Vice President elected on same ticket with two-ballot system (run-off between the two candidates with most votes in first ballot); term of 4 years.
Head of government The President.
Cabinet Appointed by the President.
Administrative subdivisions 26 states and 1 federal district.

Legal system

Civil law based on Roman and Germanic traditions.

Legislature

Bicameral parliament: National Congress (*Congresso Nacional*).
Lower house Chamber of Deputies (*Câmara dos Deputados*): 513 members; term of 4 years.
Upper house Federal Senate (*Senado Federal*): 81 members (3 members from each constituency, majority vote); staggered elections (one-third elected after a four years, two-thirds elected after the next four years); term of 8 years.

Electoral system (lower house)

Proportional representation.
Formula D'Hondt (highest average) and open list (preferential voting).
Constituencies 27 (the states and federal district).
Barrier clause 5% nation-wide (since 2006).
Suffrage Universal and compulsory, 18 years; voluntary between 16 and 18 years and over 70; military conscripts do not vote.

Direct democracy

The National Congress can call non-binding referenda and plebiscites. Legislative popular initiative is not binding either.

Party system Results of the 2006 legislative elections (Chamber of Deputies):

Electorate:	125,827,119	100.0%
Voters:	104,778,751	83.3%

Party	Valid votes	%	Seats
Partido do Movimento Democrático Brasileiro (PMDB)	13,580,517	14.6	89
Partido dos Trabalhadores (PT)	13,989,859	15.0	83
Partido da Social Democracia Brasileira (PSDB)	12,691,043	13.6	65
Partido da Frente Liberal (PFL)	10,182,308	10.9	65
Partido Progressista (PP)	6,662,309	7.1	42
Partido Socialista Brasileiro (PSB)	5,732,464	6.2	27
Partido Democrático Trabalhista (PDT)	4,854,017	5.2	24
Partido Liberal (PL)	4,074,618	4.4	23
Partido Trabalhista Brasileiro (PTB)	4,397,743	4.7	22
Partido Popular Socialista (PPS)	3,630,462	3.9	21
Partido Verde (PV)	3,368,561	3.6	13
Partido Comunista do Brasil (PC do B)	1,982,323	2.1	13
Partido Social Cristão (PSC)	1,747,863	1.9	9
Partido Trabalhista Cristão (PTC)	806,662	0.9	4
Partido Socialismo e Liberdade (PSOL)	1,149,619	1.2	3

(*continued*)

COUNTRY PROFILE Brazil (*continued*)

Party	Valid votes	%	Seats
Partido da Mobilização Nacional (PMN)	875, 686	0.9	3
Partido de Reedificação da Ordem Nacional (PRONA)	907, 494	1.0	2
Partido Humanista da Solidariedade (PHS)	435, 328	0.5	2
Partido Trabalhista do Brasil (PT do B)	311, 833	0.3	1
Partido dos Aposentados da Nação (PAN)	264, 682	0.3	1
Others	1, 295, 380	1.5	0
Total	88, 290, 718	100.0	513

Notes: Category 'Others' includes parties with less than 1% nation-wide and no seats.
Source: electionresources.org

Emergence, mobilization, and success of social movements

Social movement studies intend to explain three aspects of social movements—their emergence, mobilization, and eventual success.

Emergence

The political context has above all been used to account for the emergence of social movements. A famous example of the kind of reasoning involved is Skocpol's book, *States and Social Revolutions* (1979). At the origin of the three social revolutions she studied—the French, Russian, and Chinese Revolutions—Skocpol finds a conjunction of two key factors: (1) a political crisis and (2) agrarian socio-political structures (i.e. a given form of national cleavage structures) that gave rise to widespread peasant discontent and facilitated insurrections against landlords. The political crisis is brought about by the intensification of international pressure (shifts in the geopolitical context structure) that leads to a military and fiscal crisis of the state (institutional strain and even breakdown), which in turn gives rise to profound divisions in the ruling elites over how to respond to the state's declining effectiveness and fiscal problems (realignments in the configuration of actors). The peasant revolts become uncontrollable at the moment when regime defections become widespread and when the elite loses its cohesion and is no longer capable of exercising its social control (by repressive measures).

Skocpol (1979: 154) claims to have identified the sufficient causes of social revolutionary situations. However, the various elements of the political context define only a set of necessary conditions for the emergence of contention—its 'opportunity set'. The transformation of a potentially explosive situation into the unfolding of events within the interaction context is historically contingent, and, therefore, quite unpredictable. Precipitating factors, exogenous shocks, contingent or catalysing events, and suddenly imposed grievances play a crucial role in such a transformation. In addition to the 'opportunity set', the unfolding of events crucially depends on the choices made by actors on the basis of their preferences.

Thus the events leading up to the French Revolution were set in motion by the king's move to invite the population to submit its grievances to the authorities (*cahiers de doléances*)—a 'window of opportunity' with quite unanticipated consequences. The death of Franco set off the transition to democracy in Spain—a somewhat more predictable outcome. The incident with Rosa Parks launched the Montgomery Bus Boycott, which marked the beginning of the civil rights movement. The declaration of the state of emergency in Kenya in 1952 resulted in the arrest of nationalist leader Jomo Kenyatta and 145 other Kenyan political figures, which unleashed the Mau Mau revolt. The assassination of opposition leader Benigno Aquino was the origin of the Philippines Yellow Revolution. The accidents at Three Mile Island and Chernobyl were crucial for the mobilization of the anti-nuclear movement.

The contingency of the precipitating event may vary from one occasion to another. As McAdam *et al.* (2001: 147) observe, the catalytic event is often neither accidental, nor the primordial starting point of the episode, but the culmination of a long-standing conflict. To the extent that the build-up of a political conflict systematically increases the opportunity for mobilization, we are more likely to be able to account for the unfolding of subsequent contentious episodes.

Mobilization

The political opportunity structures are ideally suited to the explanation of the volume and form of a movement's mobilization. In a cross-national study of four Western European countries, we have shown that the level and form of collective action vary quite closely as a function of the openness of the political system of the respective countries (Kriesi *et al.* 1995). We found that the openness of the Swiss system facilitates the mobilization for collective action. The existence of direct democracy institutions in particular invites citizens to mobilize collectively. At the same time, the openness of the system and the availability of conventional channels of protest, such as the direct-democratic channels, have a strong moderating effect on the strategic choices of the Swiss movement actors. They have learned to use the available direct democracy instruments, and they continue to use them even if they are not very successful in doing so. By contrast, the relative closure of the French system provides little facilitation for the mobilization by collective actors, which not only dampens the level of mobilization, but also contributes to the radicalization of the movement's action repertoires. Table 16.2 presents these results.

Another example illustrates the importance of the media for the level of mobilization of social movements today. Holmes Cooper (2002) compares three different campaigns by the German peace movement: the very effective mobilizing campaign against cruise missiles in the early 1980s, the less impressive campaign against the first Gulf War, and the weak

Table 16.2 Action repertory of social movements per country (% of total number of protest events)

Action form	Switzerland	Netherlands	Germany	France
Direct democracy	8.1	–	–	–
Petitions	8.1	2.8	2.7	1.2
Festivals	5.5	1.4	2.2	1.4
Demonstrations	52.5	49.7	60.6	41.7
Confrontations	13.4	35.0	19.3	24.5
Light violence	7.7	5.1	6.2	5.8
Heavy violence	4.7	6.0	9.0	25.4
All	100.0	100.0	100.0	100.0
N	1,322	1,319	2,343	2,132

Source: Kriesi *et al.* (1995: 50).

campaign against German intervention in Bosnia in 1995. She focuses on the **congruence between frames used in media reporting and the social movement's own frames**: congruence between the two types of frames, she argues, increases the mobilizing capacity of the movement, while lack of congruence imposes restrictions on this capacity. The underlying mechanism accounting for this relationship is provided by the presumed impact of media reporting on individual patterns of perception and on debates in the social networks—the 'micro-mobilization contexts', where individual mobilization processes in fact take place. A high congruence between media reporting and the framing by the movement reinforces the empirical credibility and the resonance of the movement frames.

Holmes Cooper largely confirms her hypothesis: there is, indeed, a close relationship between the congruence of media frames and framing by the peace movement, on the one hand, and the level of mobilization in the three campaigns by that movement, on the other. But this does not establish a causal connection between the two. It could be that the degree of mobilization by the movement itself has had a decisive influence on media reporting. Holmes Cooper attempts to exclude this possibility by showing that media reporting had already adopted certain frames before the mobilization for the respective campaigns by the movement.

There is, however, yet another possible explanation of her result: quite generally, the issue-specific debates in the media are part and parcel of the more encompassing political conflict about the control of the corresponding issue (Wolfsfeld 1997). Thus, media reporting of the three foreign-policy controversies which gave rise to the respective campaigns by the German peace movement reflected the corresponding conflicts which existed within and between the established political actors.

Given that the left has always been a key ally of the peace movement, the left's issue-specific positions are likely to have had a decisive influence on the level of mobilization achieved by the movement. It is, therefore, important to note that the left was unified in its opposition to the stationing of cruise missiles, and still relatively unified during the brief period of the Gulf War (even if it was characterized by deep divisions after the end of the war). By contrast, the left was deeply divided with respect to German participation in international interventions in Bosnia in June and December 1995. After the impact of the massacre in Srebrenica, prominent figures such as Joschka Fischer pronounced themselves in favour of German intervention.

It is, of course, true that potential participants in campaigns organized by the peace movement do not simply accept the positions and interpretations adopted by the leading speakers of the left, about which they learn in the media. But the left's degree of unity or division with regard to the issue taken up by the peace movement is likely to play a key role (Kriesi *et al.* 1995: 73 ff.). It is also true that media reporting does not simply reflect the degree of unity or division of the left. But in the press most often read by potential movement participants, the issue-specific situation on the left has a high news value and receives much attention. In my view, we can barely distinguish between media-frames and the framing used by established political actors (on the left and on the right) in issue-specific political debates.

Success

Social movements do not only intend to successfully mobilize. Ultimately, they want to have an impact on political decision-making or on society at large. In comparative politics, where we primarily deal with instrumental movements that seek to influence politics, their impact on policy decisions is of key importance. Outcomes are still less often studied than the emergence and mobilization of social movements. The field is not as empty, however, as many observers have claimed (Giugni 1998).

There is one movement in particular whose success has been the object of several studies with a comparative political process perspective—the anti-nuclear movement. It provides an excellent illustration of how the different aspects of the political context have been used to explain a movement's outcomes. Kitschelt's (1986) influential analysis put the accent on the structural element and compared the movement's impact in four countries with quite distinct political opportunity structures: Germany, France, Sweden, and the US. He made the general point that there is **no one-to-one correspondence between** the level of mobilization and the success of social movements: strong mobilization does not necessarily lead to profound impacts if the political opportunity structures are not conducive to change. Conversely, weak mobilization may have a disproportionate impact owing to properties of the political opportunity structure.

More specifically, Kitschelt argued that in Germany, Sweden, and the US, where political opportunity structures were conducive to popular participation, greater responsiveness to the anti-nuclear opposition invariably led to extremely tight and often changing safety regulations. Once formulated, these new safety standards allowed opponents to intervene and insist that they be complied with. Construction delays were the result, especially in the US and Germany—the two countries with fragmented implementation structures. Much shorter delays were typical in France and Sweden, where tight implementation procedures offered few opportunities for outside intervention in the construction process. In Sweden, nuclear policy was ultimately changed, too, not by disrupting the policy implementation process, but by the shifting electoral fortunes of major parties and changes in government. In the open Swedish system, the anti-nuclear movement finally prevailed, because it was largely supported by the institutional structure, the prevailing cultural models, and the configuration of power in the Swedish system.

KEY POINTS

❑ The emergence of a social movement or radical transformations such as revolutions can be explained by the combination of structural preconditions and contingent events (precipitating factors, suddenly imposed grievances, exogenous shocks).

❑ The volume and form of social movement mobilization is heavily conditioned by the relative openness of the political context and by the congruence between media frames and movement frames, which in turn is conditioned by the political context in which it is embedded.

❑ There is no one-to-one correspondence between the level of mobilization and the success of social movements. Strong mobilization does not necessarily lead to profound impact if the political opportunity structures are not conducive to change. Conversely, weak mobilization may have a disproportionate impact owing to properties of the political opportunity structure.

Conclusion

There are very good reasons not to treat social movements as a distinct set of phenomena to be dealt with by a specific subfield of social sciences. It is fruitful to include them in the comparative analysis of the political process, since they have become regular participants in policy-making in democratic societies.

Among the specialists of social movements, there is currently a tendency to enlarge the perspective beyond social movements to **contentious politics** (or protest politics, as I have called it here) and to focus less on social movements as such and more on the mechanisms and processes through which contentious politics operates (McAdam *et al.* 2001; Tilly and Tarrow 2007; see Box 16.1). In this perspective, social movements are only one version of contentious politics, which ranges from small-scale protest events to large-scale revolutions. This is a promising perspective as long as we do not lose sight of the fact that social movements constitute distinctive social processes in their own right.

The political process approach is of particular interest for the integration of these distinctive processes into the mainstream of comparative politics. A number of mechanisms contribute to integrate contemporary social movements into the political process of liberal democracies, i.e. to institutionalize them (Meyer and Tarrow 1998*a*: 23–4): social movement activists have learned to employ conventional and unconventional collective actions; police practices increasingly encourage the routinization of contention; the tactics used by movement organizations and those used by more institutionalized groups increasingly overlap.

Such mechanisms at the same time contribute to the increasing integration of social movement actors into the policy-making process and to the adoption of social movement strategies by routine participants in policy-making. Moreover, the attention social movement scholars increasingly pay to the outcomes produced by popular claims-making and contention (Giugni 1998; Giugni *et al.* 1999) also brings them closer to the analysis of public policy-making, which in turn, enhances the usefulness of the political process approach.

? Questions

1. What is a social movement? What is its relation to interest groups, political parties, and the media?
2. What is the difference between a movement challenging political authorities and a movement challenging cultural authorities? Discuss this question on the basis of the feminist movement.
3. Describe the three major models for the analysis of social movements and discuss the weaknesses of each.
4. What are political opportunity structures and cultural models?
5. What are configurations of power and how do they change?
6. In which countries does the peace movement face favourable context conditions, and in which countries are these context conditions rather unfavourable?
7. Describe some aspects of the interaction context.
8. Under which conditions do movements emerge?
9. What kind of conditions favour the mobilization capacity of social movements and under what kind of conditions do they radicalize?
10. When do social movements have success, i.e. under what conditions are they able to reach their goals?

» Further reading

Classical texts on social movements

Gamson, William A. (1975) *The Strategy of Social Protest* (Homewood, Ill. Dorsey).

McAdam, Doug (1982) *Political Process and the Development of Black Insurgency, 1930–1970* (Chicago: University of Chicago Press).

Tarrow, Sidney (1994) *Power in Movement. Social Movements, Collective Action and Politics* (Cambridge: Cambridge University Press).

Tilly, Charles (1978) *From Mobilization to Revolution* (Reading, Mass.: Addison-Wesley).

Turner, Ralph A., and Killian, Lewis (1987) *Collective Behavior* (Englewood-Cliffs, NJ: Prentice-Hall, 3rd edn.).

Useful collections of articles

McAdam, Doug, McCarthy, John D. and Zald, Mayer N. (eds.) (1996) *Comparative Perspectives on Social Movements: Political Opportunities, Mobilizing Structures, and Cultural Framings* (Cambridge: Cambridge University Press).

Snow, David A., Soule, Sarah A., and Kriesi, Hanspeter (eds.) (2004) *The Blackwell Companion to Social Movements* (Oxford: Blackwell).

For a more extended bibliography see the works cited throughout this chapter.

In addition, up-to-date reports on social movements can be found in specialized journals such as *Mobilization* (published in the US), *Social Movement Studies* (published in the UK), and *Forschungsjournal Neue Soziale Bewegungen* (published in Germany). Students may also find useful material in the major journals in American sociology: *American Sociological Review, American Journal of Sociology, Social Forces,* and *Social Problems.*

Web links

www2.bc.edu/~gamson/Homepage(Frames).html
   Website of the Boston College Media Research and Action Project (directed by William Gamson).

www.amnesty.org
   Website of Amnesty International, a worldwide campaigning movement that works to promote all the human rights enshrined in the Universal Declaration of Human Rights and other international standards.

www.wz-berlin.de/zkd/zcm/default.en.htm
   Website of the research group on Civil Society, Citizenship, and Political Mobilization in Europe (in German).

www.greenpeace.org/international/
   Website of Greenpeace International.

www.edgehill.ac.uk/Research
   Website of the Social Movement Group.

www.globalfundforwomen.org
   Website of the Global Fund for Women. Makes grants to seed, support, and strengthen women's rights groups around the world, envisioning a just and democratic world where women and men can participate equally in all aspects of social, political, and economic life.

www.earth22.com
   Website of Building a Better World by independent activists with links to Progressive Urgent Actions, most of which can be done by email.

www.webactivemagazine.co.uk
   Website of WebActive, a weekly publication designed to offer progressive activists an up-to-date resource on the web to find other organizations and individuals with similar values and interests.

www.alexanderstreet6.com/wasm
   Website of Women and Social Movements in the United States, 1600 to 2000, from Alexander Street Press and the Center for the Historical Study of Women and Gender at SUNY Binghamton.

www.wcml.org.uk
   Website of the Working Class Movement Library.

www.wsu.edu/socmov
   A site for the study of progressive social movements, particularly the cultural dimensions of social change.

www.euromovements.info
   Website of the European Social Forum and Surroundings.

http://montgomery.troy.edu/rosaparks/museum
   Website of Rosa Parks Library and Museum.

http://depts.washington.edu/civilr/index.htm
   Website of Seattle Civil Rights and Labor History Project.

www.usm.edu/crdp
   Website of the Civil Rights Documentation Project.

www.wsu.edu/~amerstu/smc/smcframe.html
   Website of Social Movements and Culture—A Resource Website.

www.globaljusticemovement.org
   Website of the Global Justice Movement.

www.psr.keele.ac.uk/parties.htm
   Political parties, interest groups, and other social movements. Contains many links to parties and social movements.

www.nathannewman.org/EDIN/

Economic Democracy Information Network. Contains links to social movements, sorted by issue area.

www.vcn.bc.ca/citizens-handbook

The Citizen's Handbook: 'As far as we know, this is the best quick guide to community organizing on the web' (quoted from website).

www.mobilization.sdsu.edu/index.html

The Mobilization Homepage: '*Mobilization* is an international journal of research and theory specializing in social movements, protests and collective behavior. *Mobilization* was created to fill the void that there was no scholarly journal of research and theory with an interdisciplinary and international scope that dealt exclusively with social movements, protest and collective action.'

www.igc.org/index.html

Institute for Global Communications. Network of several social movements.

 Visit the Online Resource Centre that accompanies this book for more information:
www.oxfordtextbooks.co.uk/orc/caramani/

17

Political culture

Svante Ersson and Jan-Erik Lane

Chapter contents

Reader's guide

This chapter looks at the role of political culture in political life. First it surveys different fields within political science studying political culture. Next the issue of defining political culture is addressed. Each country has its political culture, i.e. a set of unique beliefs and values concerning the political regime of the country and its politics. To unpack this notion of politics as attitudes, the study of political culture includes ethnicity, religion, historical legacies, and secular values. Recently, the debate on political culture has dealt with social capital, or the role of free associations in a democracy, and the divisive nature of gender politics and homosexuality. The chapter concludes with a discussion about how political outcomes are related to the basic items of culture.

Introduction

To study culture and politics examines diversity in values among different communities and theorizes its political consequences. It includes ethnicity and religion, but also 'new politics', for example, environmentalism and feminism. Theorizing culture and politics is a timely preoccupation given the coming of a multicultural society with its politics of recognition. The concept of political culture is a key tool in the analysis of how communities engage in politics. The employment of large-scale survey research permits the discovery of value orientations and change among citizens.

A number of cultural theories about politics predict political consequences from cultural phenomena, to be discussed here with the support of new empirical data, following our general approach of unpacking the culture concept into values, ethnicity, and religion. The occurrence of **political effects of culture** is here substantiated in a novel way on the basis of new empirical information from various levels

of aggregation (macro, meso, and micro), showing both cross-country cultural differences and within-country differences in nations with strong social cleavages. It is the mass belief and value orientations that matter for politics and democracy, like party choice, democratic viability, and political stability, for example. The ultimate values of citizens show up in their secular policy stances concerning participation, lifestyles, and gender (see Comparative table 10 at the end of this volume for data on gender).

> **KEY POINTS**
>
> ❑ In increasingly multicultural societies, the concept of political culture acquires new scope and relevance.
> ❑ The main dimensions of political cultures are value orientations, religion, and ethnicity.

The field of political culture

Theorizing culture and politics goes back to classical political theory. Montesquieu speculated in *Persian Letters* (1721) about the role culture played in political life. A century later Tocqueville in *Democracy in America* (1835) claimed that the workings of American democracy were partly due to the 'habits of the heart' of American citizens, i.e. their propensity to form free associations. Durkheim identified 'collective consciousnesses' as the common core for members of a society (in *The Division of Labour in Society,* 1893). In *Community and Society* (1887), Tönnies spelled out how communities and associations were the basic social systems in any society. In the post-modern world both communities and associations count, but it is the ethnic and religious communities that are on the rise in political saliency. Max Weber in his monumental *Economy and Society* underlined the social consequences of religion but played down those of ethnicity (Weber 1978: 385–98).

Studies of national characters were conducted during the Second World War, reviewed by Margaret

Mead (1951). The first systematic study of political culture is Almond and Verba's *The Civic Culture* (1963), followed by Pye and Verba (1965). In their influential book, Almond and Verba suggested that countries inherit different political legacies that shape attitudes towards government and participation in public affairs, permeating the political institutions. They argued that democracies were nourished by a political culture of bargaining and civic activism, called civic culture. According to Almond and Verba, various combinations of three attitudes form a few basic types of political cultures: (1) **parochial attitudes** (deferent and alienated towards the political system); (2) **subject attitudes** (passive relation to the political system); (3) **participant attitudes** (active and allegiant citizens).

The value orientations characteristic of the civic culture include 'a set of political orientations that are balanced' and harbour norms of trust and tolerance. *The Civic Culture,* however, met with criticism, partly confronted in *The Civic Culture Revisited* (1980), as scholars from the Third World could not accept that ordinary people in their countries were characterized by deference and alienation. Political cultures can be identified for a country as a whole (national political cultures) or for a region in a country (regional political traditions). The civic culture is the set of attitudes and beliefs that support the democratic regime.

Making Democracy Work (1993) by Putnam poured new wine into the theme of a civic culture, linking it with the study of trust and the existence of a civil society. There is also a bridge between the studies of civic culture from the 1960s and the studies of social capital in the 1990s. Social capital is looked upon as a synonym to civic culture, but social capital may in addition be tapped by attitudes towards trust as well as the presence of social networks (Jackman and Miller 1998, 2004). Thus, one type of political culture discussed early in the political science literature was the civic culture, which is now connected with the study of trust, linked to the Coleman concept of social capital (Coleman 1990). Yet, the concept of political culture is today more encompassing than the free associations of civil society, covering also the politics of all kinds of communities, ethnic, religious, and sex-based ones.

Social capital theory, with its hypotheses about trust, has attracted major interest. Putnam's research in *Making Democracy Work* (1993) on Italy and *Bowling Alone* (2000) on the US deals with the variation of social capital across regions or provinces (space) as well as over time. For Italy his major finding was that 'the performance of a regional government is somehow very closely related to the civic character of social and political life within the region' (Putnam 1993: 99). Similar research on the American states has suggested that there is 'strong evidence that social capital influences governmental performance' (Knack 2002: 782).

The study of political culture includes also the analysis of ethnicity and religion, which both have long constituted core fields of study with high relevance in political science. The identity of ethnic and religious communities is of utmost importance for their political mobilization, resulting in ethnic and religious cleavages with major political repercussions such as sectarian tension. Today cultural analysis in politics now proceeds along two lines. On the one hand, there is massive **micro** research using surveys into values, i.e. value orientations, as with *Culture Shift in Advanced Industrial Society* (1990) by Inglehart. On the other hand, there is the **macro** study of entire cultures, such as with Huntington's *The Clash of Civilizations* (1996).

Douglas and Wildavsky attempted with **new cultural theory** a general synthesis of traditional and new approaches to political culture (Thompson *et al.* 1990), arguing that social groups have a basic tendency to maintain their ways of life. The combination of both micro (citizen attitudes) and macro (country studies) inquiries into political cultures adds greatly to the dynamism in this field of political science (Van Deth and Scarbrough 1995).

Political culture also includes gender and homosexuality, in so far as these are culturally embedded and politically important. Political culture was much stimulated by the emergence of **new politics** in advanced countries, where substantial groups of people looked to express values beyond the traditional left–right scale (see Chapter 16). To capture these new value orientations, such as environmentalism, the search for quality of life, and the emergence of feminism, scholars resorted to the massive employment of survey research. Moreover, Huntington's idea of a clash between civilizations in the twenty-first century stimulated a worldwide debate about religion and its social and political consequences. Did he issue a warning, a more or less probable prediction or an ominous direction to follow in action by the US, like the invasion of Iraq?

Finally, political culture is today highly popular in the discipline, with several alternative theoretical frameworks to choose from, which responds well to the emergence of a multi-cultural society (Kymlicka 1996), involving huge migration from developing countries to the advanced ones.

As the concept of political culture has to be **unpacked**, we suggest that it be decomposed into the central elements of culture, as studied in sociology and anthropology, namely **ethnicity, religion, and value orientations**. Research into political culture presents a few challenges that are both conceptual and methodological. They will be pinned down here in relation to the most discussed theories in a rapidly swelling literature.

The cultural approach to politics may be contrasted with the rational choice approach, which looks upon human behaviour as utility maximization. The new cultural frameworks deal with questions concerning the search for the meaning of life as well as for social and personal identity in ever more rational social systems. The cultural approach complements rational choice, as it goes beyond action as self-centred rational strategy to inquire into how communities shape individuals and how shared meanings and symbols arise. It deals with social construction, interpretations, and imagined identities as well as the symbols and myths of communities (see Chapter 4). Culture does not take preferences as given, like rational choice, but focuses precisely upon how groups form the basic allegiances of people. Political cultural theory theorizes the basic political commitments, beliefs, and norms of people acting in various social systems, having philosophical roots in communitarianism, postmodernism, and in the civil society framework (Etzioni 1990).

KEY POINTS

❑ Political culture stands for the basic attitudes of people towards politics, policy, and the polity. One political culture—the civic culture—has been much researched in democracy theory and has stimulated recent theories of social capital and trust.

❑ The diversity of political cultures stems from ethnicity, religion, and value orientation. Ethnicities, nations, and race have been of core interest to political science.

Religion shows in the interest in civilizations, their conflicts, and modes of cooperation. Value orientations have been researched, looking for the sources of new cleavages such as gender and environmentalism ('new politics').

❑ Theories of culture have two major sources: one in civil society theory (value orientations) and another in communitarianism (ethnicity, religion, tradition).

Definitions of political culture

A variety of elements

Political culture analysis investigates the implications of ethnicity, religion, and value orientations for government, the polity, and governance. Political culture is part of the more general phenomenon of culture, for which there are several definitions in the social sciences, focusing upon different phenomena: mind, behaviour, or artefacts. For sociologists and anthropologists, culture embraces all that constitutes 'ways of life'. Political scientists tend to focus more upon culture as attitudes or belief systems. An inclusive conception of culture as ways of life tends to be too broad, as it is difficult to say that certain social phenomena do not constitute a way of life. What counts is the variety of cultural phenomena and their **political consequences**.

Political culture should be unpacked into the key elements of culture. The variety of political culture appears in ethnicity, religion and value orientation. Ethnicity is for instance a major source of electoral support for regionalist political parties. Ethnicity also harbours nationalism and racism, which both were powerful political forces in the twentieth century. The political consequences of religion enter the sociology of religion, as conceptualized by Weber (1920, 1963), and are at the core of the analysis of the civilizations of the world. The relevance of religion for politics is today linked with the rise of fundamentalisms—especially in Islam but also in Hinduism and Protestantism. Finally, the immense employment of survey research in the social sciences has opened up a whole new field: the study of attitudes or value orientations. To understand politics in the post-modern society, it is necessary to survey the secular values or value orientations that people bring to politics, such as post-materialism, egalitarianism, and gender attitudes.

The immense global migration after the Second World War has made ethnic minorities much more relevant politically, as they organize as modern **diasporas**, claiming rights in their new country while retaining an image of their homeland (Sheffer 2003). This is the theme of multiculturalism. Kymlicka (1996) insists upon the new social carpet of politics in advanced Western societies. One cannot, as Barry (2000) does, deny that historical minorities, immigrant groups, and religious diasporas have become much more politically vocal. It is an open question whether their demands can be met within the precepts of liberalism or whether these cultural claims require a new 'politics of recognition' (Parekh 2000).

There are several definitions of **culture** focusing upon thought, law, customs, architecture, values, or achievements (see Box 17.1). They target:

- either **customs** in general (Thompson *et al.* 1990: 1) and **ways of life**, i.e. culture as referring to the whole way of life of a people, their interpersonal relations as well as their attitudes, their social behaviour;

- or they focus upon **attitudes:** culture as composed of values, beliefs, norms, rationalizations, symbols, ideologies, i.e. so-called mental products.

Political culture too is defined in various ways. One definition reads: 'The political culture of a society consists of the system of empirical beliefs, expressive symbols, and values which defines the situation in which political action takes place' (Verba 1969: 513).

Methodological issues

A basic problem in cultural research is that of finding tenable evidence for the existence of cultural items.

Thus, research into political culture presents certain challenges that are of a methodological nature. To talk about culture and its impact upon politics and society, one needs evidence or data about cultural phenomena. When political culture is defined as **ways of life**, then data may be taken from behavioural evidence of almost any kind, as in the theory of basic attitudes to risk in society (food, medicine, pollution) as determined by culture (Wildavsky 1997) or different kinds of American presidents expressing various types of culture (Ellis and Wildavsky 1987).

The comparative analysis of culture and its implications for politics need not be restricted within a cross-sectional approach. An analytical framework for cultural analysis with an emphasis upon politics may be based upon a longitudinal approach to culture, as with the idea of specific historical legacies. A historical tradition would be a cultural force that acts through time, shaping the politics of a country, such as colonialism or the family system. One can distinguish between different colonial experiences as well as their time duration. Similarly, a variety of culturally embedded family systems may be identified around the world, as in Todd's analysis of the basic components of the family (Todd 1983).

BOX 17.1 Definitions of 'culture'

Malinowski (1931: 621)

This social heritage is the key concept of cultural anthropology...It is usually called culture.... Culture comprises inherited artifacts, goods, technical processes, ideas, habits and values.

Kroeber and Kluckhohn (1963: 357)

Culture consists of patterns, explicit and implicit, of and for behavior acquired and transmitted by symbols, constituting the distinctive achievement of human groups, including their embodiments in artifacts; the essential core of culture consists of traditional (i.e., historically derived and selected) ideas and especially their attached values; culture systems may, on the one hand, be considered as products of action, on the other as conditioning elements of further action.

Geertz (1973: 89)

[Culture] denotes an historically transmitted pattern of meanings embodied in symbols, a system of inherited conceptions expressed in symbolic forms by means

of which men communicate, perpetuate, and develop their knowledge about and attitudes towards life.

Almond and Verba (1965: 13)

Here we can only stress that we employ the concept of culture in only one of its many meanings: that of *psychological orientation toward social objects*.

Huntington (2000: xv)

Hence we define culture in purely subjective terms as the values, attachments, beliefs, orientations, and underlying assumptions prevalent among people in a society.

Gerring and Barresi (2003: 209)

[Culture] is any phenomenon that is social, ideational or symbolic, patterned and shared by the members of a social group.

Here, the purpose is to tie some key problems in the research into value orientations by means of large-scale surveys. The methodological problem of finding adequate evidence recurs in research upon value orientations. Macro indices are all constructed on the basis of micro response items from surveys to individual persons. The best research theory from the point of view of empirical evidence is post-materialism, but it is difficult to reconcile with the evidence about rising ethnic and especially religious communitarianism. Post-materialist theory really does not have a theoretical core of key propositions about attitudes, from which many interesting implications can be generated.

For most of the value orientations discussed in political culture, there is both a distinct cross-national variation and a stable pattern of variation over time. Due to the large samples employed in the World Values Surveys (WVS) one can safely say that data are reliable. At the same time we must also be aware of that within each country studied there is a variation. All in all, the **variation within the countries is often larger than the variation between the countries**. The political cultures of nation-states are not homogeneous, coherent, or compact, although it is less heterogeneous in terms of attending religious services than is the case for interpersonal trust. The founders of the study of political culture also acknowledged this. Verba noted: 'The degree to which basic political attitudes are shared within a political system thus becomes a crucial but open question' (Verba 1969: 526).

Cultural analysis includes both the **micro analysis of peoples' attitudes** and the **macro analysis of country differences**. Inglehart employs the immense WVS to uncover the value orientations of individuals in some eighty countries around the globe. Using this micro information, he moves on to construct two indices—rationality/secularization vs. post-materialism/self expression—that allow him to rank all these countries in a two-dimensional macro cultural space. The broad claim in this research is that a post-materialist culture matters for economic, political, and social development. Inglehart's position in 1997 was that a 'given society's culture plays an important role in economic growth' (Inglehart 1997: 235), and in 2005 Inglehart and Welzel conclude that their 'findings strongly support a cultural explanation of democracy' (Inglehart and Welzel 2005: 209), explaining for example gender empowerment and

democratic development (see Comparative table 8 at the end of this volume).

Thus, there are a number of highly relevant hypotheses about political values that are worth examining with survey data, such as for instance: post-materialism, trust or social capital, and egalitarianism/individualism or the fatalism/achievement orientation. Yet, any research into value orientations must respect the following methodological principles for attitudinal research using mass data (e.g. the Eurobarometers or the WVS):

- **Converse's principle**: value orientations are the product of correlations among response items;
- **Robinson's principle**: macro values may deviate from micro values.

Converse realized that to find an evidential base strong enough for testing hypotheses about attitudes and the existence of values, one needs a battery of questions that tap a dimension among all the response items. Moreover, the value orientation is nothing less or more than the coherence in the reliance upon numerous response items. Thus, attitudinal research is in need of quantitative techniques in order to test key hypotheses about the existence of values with human beings. The necessary data would have to be generated through surveys, which opens up the possibility of large-scale empirical research in culture, using micro-level data.

Yet, comparative cultural analysis has always had a great interest in macro-level considerations. Thus, macro cultures could be aggregated up from micro-level data, as when countries are compared in terms of the number of the adherents of post-materialist values. But macro cultures could also be identified, using macro-level information only, such as the variety of colonial experiences or the degree of gender empowerment, as measured by gender favourable legislation, etc. It is here that Robinson's principle becomes relevant, warning against any automatic conclusion about the micro level from the macro level. The possibility of a so-called **ecological fallacy** is constantly present in cultural research that can only be countered by the employment of survey-generated data.

The next section presents in a comprehensive way the key aspects of political culture, as they have been uncovered in cultural research, employing recently available data. We have selected a set of highly relevant themes in the literature that bring out the political impact of cultural phenomena. The selection of themes is ours, but it follows closely the debate among scholars engaging in cultural research. We substantiate these cultural effects with new data.

KEY POINTS

❑ Two kinds of data are employed in political culture: interpretation of behaviour and survey research into people's attitudes.

❑ Culture as ethnicity or religion often employs historical information, whereas culture as value orientation uses the survey with many response items in order to tap and verify the existence of key values (Converse's principle).

❑ Political culture can deal with macro or micro values. Make sure you understand this distinction and the

danger in confusing the micro (individual level) and the macro (society level) in cultural analysis (Robinson's principle).

❑ The employment of survey data to uncover value orientations raises questions about what 'value orientations' really stand for but also how values at an individual (micro) level may be related to aggregate values at the national (macro) level.

Dimensions of political culture

To understand politics it is not enough to analyse the institutions of a country or the preferences of political elites chasing political power. Cultural theories argue that the attitudes and beliefs of ordinary citizens play a fundamental role in shaping political outcomes. These basic commitments relate to the support for the state and cover value orientations that shape the policy-making process, defining the saliency of issues. What, then, is the political culture of a democratic regime and country?

Value orientations

During recent decades, a new type of cultural research has been conducted, namely the analysis of value orientations, based upon survey research into the attitudes of citizens. In the post-modern society, people act on the basis of values that cannot be accounted for by traditional political culture, such as ethnicity, religion, or political ideology (left–right). To understand the values that people bring to 'new politics', only surveys of peoples' attitudes can provide the necessary information about how different values such as individualism, nationalism, egalitarianism, and gender equality are supported in various groups (Kaase and Newton 1995; Van Deth and Scarbrough 1995; Borre and Scarbrough 1995; Klingemann and Fuchs 1995).

Theories of value orientations differ considerably in analytical depth and empirical foundation. The best-researched theory from the point of view of empirical evidence is **post-materialism**. Post-materialist theory has been generalized to account for other attitudes besides environmentalism, personal autonomy, and quality of life. Let us look at the cross-national variation of some central value orientations discussed in the literature, relying upon data from the four waves (from around 1980, 1990, 1995, and 2000) of the WVS (data on environment can also be found in Comparative table 9 at the end of this volume).

Support for political institutions

Attitudes towards the political system are central in political culture. These may range from support for leading political actors to general support for the political system itself. A key question is which mass attitudes result in political satisfaction with government. Measuring (1) satisfaction with government and (2) satisfaction with democracy, the survey data from WVS, presented in Figure 17.1, suggests that the country variation in terms of support for political institutions is strongly linked with the satisfaction with democracy. If democracy works well, there is political satisfaction, and vice versa. Russia and Ukraine come out low on both dimensions. Vietnam is an outlier with high scores on both dimensions, which

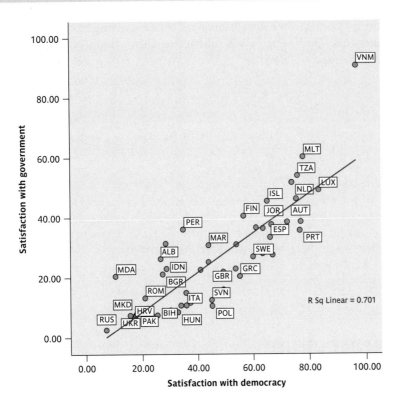

Fig. 17.1 Satisfaction with democracy and government

Source: Inglehart *et al*. (2004). Variables employed are: e110 (satisfaction with democracy) and e111 (satisfaction with political system).

indicates that survey data must be interpreted with caution. Yet, it is true that macro measures on satisfaction with government as well as with democracy go together when other surveys like national election studies are compared with the WVS data.

Satisfaction with government changes over time, even within stable democracies. Citizens in Europe are, according to the Eurobarometers, slightly more satisfied with the way democracy works in their own country in 2005 than was the case in 1995. Similar data for Latin America based on the Latinobarometro displays a slight downward trend and data for African countries also display a downward trend when figures for 2005 are compared with figures for 2000. For most countries in the post-industrial world, trust in government has been going down. Yet the pattern is not uniform. In the US, trust for government, according to the American National Election Studies, went steadily down from the early 1960s to reach the lowest scores in 1980 and 1994, but then recovered; in 2004 some 45 per cent said that they trusted the government in Washington just about always or most of the time. In the UK, the trust in government as measured by the British Social Attitudes has been decreasing steadily over the last twenty years.

Trust in government should be separated from general trust in social relationships—so-called interpersonal trust or social capital.

Interpersonal trust

Researching the cultural sources of democracy, scholars have attempted to uncover the mass beliefs that are conducive to a democratic culture in the social interactions among anonymous individuals. Thus, horizontal relations within a society may be described through the presence of interpersonal trust. Interpersonal trust is measured with a response item where the respondent agrees either that most people can be trusted or that 'you can't be too careful'. The percentage of a sample saying that most people can be trusted is expressing the national score on generalized interpersonal trust. This item, entered into *The Civic Culture* study, has been used in all four waves of the WVS. Figure 17.2 shows that there is a firm cross-national variation between countries with respect to the distribution of interpersonal trust. Countries scoring high on trust in 1981, like the Scandinavian countries, do so also in year 2000, whereas countries like Mexico, Argentina, and South Africa score low on both dimensions.

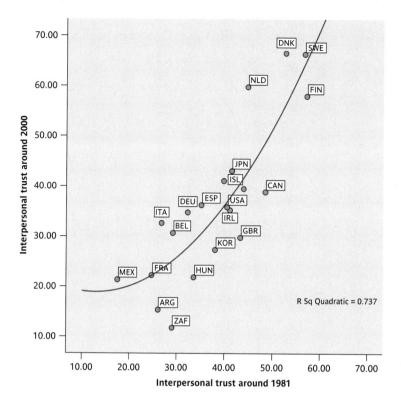

Fig. 17.2 Interpersonal trust, 1981 and 2000

Source: Inglehart *et al*. (2000, 2004). Variables employed are: v27 (trust 1981) and a165 (trust 2000).

Is trust declining in our societies? Scholars have attempted to measure the health of the democratic regime by inquiring into the dynamics of interpersonal trust. Looking at the change in the level of interpersonal trust over time, it is possible to go back to the late 1950s for the five countries included in *The Civic Culture* study. In both the US and United Kingdom, the downward trend is clear, going from levels around 50 per cent in 1959 to around 30–5 per cent in 2000. Germany and Italy show the opposite trend, going from lower values (less than 20 per cent) to higher values (more than 30 per cent). In Mexico the score for 1995 was higher than for 1960, whereas the lowest scores stem from 1980 and 2000. For eleven countries reporting this item in the four WVS waves the mean score was 38 per cent in 1981 and it slightly decreased to 35 per cent in 2000, but among them six had higher scores in 2000 than in 1980. Therefore, one should be careful when talking of a general decline of social trust.

Post-materialism

Perhaps the most discussed value orientation is post-materialism, because it is very relevant to policy-making changes (Box 17.2). If mass attitudes towards environmental and economic-policy issues change

in a major way, then the political parties have to integrate this in their electoral campaigns. Inglehart introduced the concept of post-materialism in the early 1970s. Post-materialist orientations were to begin with measured with four attitudinal items, where the respondent was asked to prioritize two of the items (see Box 17.2). Later on, a twelve-item battery was employed. Those who were classified as post-materialists preferred giving people more to say and protecting freedom of speech over maintaining order in the nation and fighting rising prices, whereas those with the opposite preference order were classified as materialists, and the other combinations were labelled as mixed orientations. With the advent of a post-industrial society, post-materialist orientations were expected to increase over time, but economic crises with increasing unemployment could dampen the increase.

Survey data from the WVS presented in Figure 17.3 suggest a cross-national variation with respect to level of post-materialist orientations in different countries. Italy had a rather high proportion of post-materialists in 2000, but that proportion was much lower in 1981. Finland had a high level in 1981 but a much lower one in 2000. It is only in countries like Hungary, Korea, and South Africa that the level of post-materialism

BOX 17.2 Post-materialism

Post-materialism is a concept developed in relation to new politics. It is based on survey data summarizing the attitudes of citizens towards a number of phenomena. The following four response items have been used as one indicator of this value orientation.

First choice. 'If you had to choose, which one of the things on this card would you say is most important?'

1. Maintaining order in the nation

2. Giving people more say in important government decisions

3. Fighting rising prices

4. Protecting freedom of speech

Second choice. 'And which would be the next most important?'

The index is constructed from these response items in the following way: Those choosing maintaining order (1st choice) and fighting prices (2nd choice) are classified as **materialists**; those choosing giving people more say (1st choice) and protecting freedom (2nd choice) are classified as **post-materialists**; those making other choices are classified as belonging to a **mixed group**.

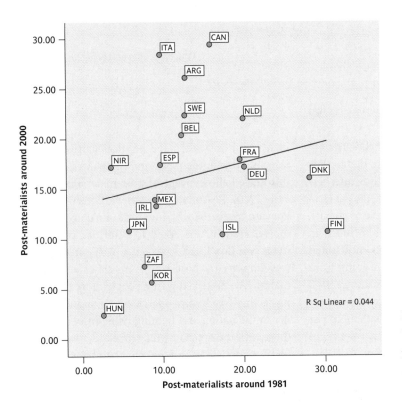

Fig. 17.3 Post-materialist orientations around 1981 and 2000

Source: Inglehart *et al*. (2000, 2004). Variables employed are: v1000mpm (post-materialism 1981) and y002 (post-materialism 2000).

remains low at both periods of time. The expectation in post-materialist theory of a steady increase in the number of citizens holding post-materialist orientations has not been fulfilled. From 1981 to 1995, the post-materialist proportion increased from 13 to 20 per cent among the nine countries represented in the four waves, only to go down to 14 per cent in 2000. Thus, post-materialism displays no stable direction of change over time, looking back over the last two to three decades.

Secularization

Decisive for the stability of the democratic regime is the support for a secular conception of politics, where the legitimacy of the regime is based upon a legal-rational view of the state. Scholars have tried to tap how strongly secular values are entrenched in mass attitudes. As societies are modernizing, one would expect that the role of religion would diminish, in the form of secularization. This was actually one basic tenet in modernization theory. To trace secularization one may inquire into developments within religious behaviour and attitudes. A low rate of attendance at religious services is often used as a crude indicator for the presence of secular orientations in society. Survey data from WVS indicate that there is a distinct cross-national variation between countries, and that this variation is quite stable over time. Poland and Ireland report high rates of attendance both in 1990 and in 2000, but the highest rates come from Nigeria. More countries report lower rates, like Iceland, Finland, Sweden, Russia, Latvia, and Japan.

A question on attending religious services was also part of *The Civic Culture* five-nation study. Comparing 1960 with 2000, it is obvious that in four of the five countries the rates of attendance have decreased—the US deviate from this pattern with an attendance rate around 45 per cent in both 1960 and 2000. The drop in attendance is more pronounced in Germany and Italy than is the case for United Kingdom (from a low rate) and Mexico (from a high rate). WVS data also indicate a slight decline in attendance rates over time, but the mean value only changes from 17 to 16 per cent over a twenty-year period for the nine countries reporting at all four waves. Other evidence shows a similar direction. Over the last two or three decades there has only been a slow decline in religious attendance, as the sharp decline actually occurred in the 1960s and the 1970s in the post-industrial countries. An increase may be found in a Third World country like Nigeria where religious fundamentalism counts. Typical of religion today is both increased secularization and stronger fundamentalism.

Ethnicity

Culture as ethnicity harbours such classical fields of political science as nationalism and racism. The study of the political implications of ethnicity covers the activities of the many **ethnies** (ethnic minorities) around the world. The field of ethnicity was much stimulated by theories of the nation for a long time, racism mainly in the past, and multi-culturalism today. Today global migration makes ethnic politics highly salient in advanced societies, but ethnic mobilization is also to be found in the Third World, such as with tribes and historical minorities. As ethnic communities are mobilizing around the world, seeking political recognition for their special identity and

destiny, the growing saliency of ethnies has stimulated a new debate about the meaning of citizenship (Van Gunsteren 1998) as well as on the concept of a nation in a multicultural society (Miller 1997; data on language can be found in Comparative table 3 at the end of this volume).

Understanding ethnicity poses a major challenge for the conceptualization of the nation. The long debate about the basic characteristics of nations—natural, imagined, biological, mythical, ancient, modern, popular, elitist—is far from resolved (Smith 1998, 2004; Anderson 2006). Penetrating into the depths of ethnies and nations may require hermeneutical methods of social research, interpreting the meaning of myths, signs, and logos. On the other hand, race has been completely discarded, but racism is an important theme in for instance the theory of legal practice in the US (Bell 2004).

Ethnicity, especially language, has implications for party choice and the development of party systems. Lijphart showed that in the 1970s language was a strong determinant of party choice in 'divided countries' (1979*a*: 453; see also Chapter 13). As Horowitz underlined: 'Whether ethnic parties emerge—and when—how many of them, their relative strength, and their interactions all have much to do with group division and cohesion. And the contours of the party system in an ethnically divided society have a profound effect on the ethnic outcomes of party politics' (1985: 293). The field of ethnic studies has always included the nation and nationalism as a core concern.

The two dimensions employed in the following example refer to **national pride** and **identity with the nation**. Survey data in Figure 17.4 suggest a distinct cross-national variation, as it is also obvious that to a certain extent national identification goes together with national pride. Pakistan and Germany are examples of two contrasting cases, Pakistan scoring high on both dimensions whereas Germany scores low. Most countries score higher on national pride than on national identity and this fact indicates that there are competing identifications in many countries.

Questions about national orientations have been asked in all four waves of the WVS. Among the countries participating in the four waves national pride is higher in 2000 (mean of 54 per cent saying they are very proud) than in 1981 (46 per cent). National identity is basically similar over time, with 33 per cent

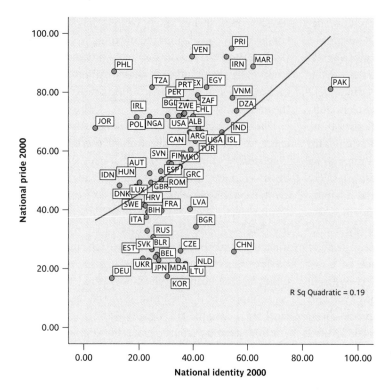

Fig. 17.4 National identity and national pride (1999 and 2002)

Source: Inglehart *et al.* (2004). Variables employed are: g001 (national identity) and g006 (national pride).

claiming that they identify with the national level in 1981 and 30 per cent in 2000. How politically sensitive the question of national identification tends to be appears well from Huntington's recent book (2005) on the United States, where he issues a warning against divided loyalties among the quickly expanding group of *Latinos*. However, coherent national identities or compact nations are a thing of the past, as multiculturalism and globalization in combination propel an irresistible migration wave.

Ethnic minorities often turn an ethnic cleavage in a country into a manifest vehicle for political mobilization, as has happened with strong political consequences in Belgium and Canada (see Chapter 15). Another well-known case is the Basque region of Spain, where ethnic mobilization has had not only constitutional consequences but also considerable political violence. Here the link between culture and politics has two elements: first, there is a consistent pattern of voting in the various Basque districts, with support for the Basque radical nationalist parties, Herri Batasuna (HB), Euskal Herritarrok (EH), and, since 2005, the Basque Communists (PCTV-EHAK); second, there is a connection between the support for the radical Basque parties and the size of the Basque-speaking population in a region.

At the first election to the Basque Parliament in 1980 HB received about 14 per cent of the vote and its highest support was recorded in 1990 with 18 per cent. At the 1998 and 2001 elections HB was part of the EH-coalition, and after the party was declared illegal in 2003 its supporters aligned to the Basque Communists in the 2005 election, when they received roughly 12 per cent. There is no doubt that the radical Basque nationalist votes go to this party using shifting party labels (Elections in Euskadi 2006).

It is also true that Basque language is associated with Basque nationalism. The number of Basque-speaking population has increased over time, according to the Basque censuses from 21 per cent in 1981 to 39 per cent in 2001 and the higher the proportion of Basque-speaking population in a municipality, the higher is the support for Basque radical nationalists (EUSTAT 2006).

Ethnicity is not only captured through language. Also historical legacy and an orientation towards ethnic or national entity are used as ethnic markers. Race may also be entered as a dimension of ethnicity, at least when ethnies are conceptualized as imagined communities. The debate about the scientific status of the concept of race has not decreased in intensity despite the forceful rejection of all forms of racism. For the social sciences, race remains a relevant category in so far as it is culturally embedded and surfaces in the distribution of power, privilege, and resources. Interestingly, a few countries, including the US and several countries in Latin America, employ race as official designators of groups of people, although modern biology denies any major, genetically derived, differences between such groups, since the between-group variation is smaller than the within-group variation (Cavalli-Sforza 2001).

Let us examine the example of South Africa, where ethnicity and race figure prominently even after the abandonment of the apartheid system. Table 17.1 sets out the connection between party support and language group. Although the dominant party, African National Congress (ANC), receives votes from all language groups, there is a clear ethnic pattern in party support in 2000. The table shows that the ANC mobilizes the black vote, being successful in splitting the Zulu vote between itself and the Inkatha Freedom Party (IFP). Table 17.2 has the vote distribution by race, according to standard classifications in official South African statistics.

It is stunning how strong race is expressed in the support for the political parties. Only non-whites vote in a balanced manner for almost all parties. Interestingly, the Indian minority leans less towards the ANC than one may have expected, given the long common struggle against racial discrimination based upon white hegemony. Political stability in the new South Africa rests upon a constitutional democracy, with strong mechanisms guaranteeing the rule of law plus so-called consociational devices meaning power-sharing among different ethnies.

What about ethnic politics in the US, which employs an official race classification of the population? Table 17.3 has the information about voting in the presidential election in 2004. Here we only focus on electors voting for the two major candidates George W. Bush (Republican) and John Kerry (Democrat). In the US case, race is expressed more clearly in the presidential vote than is the case for religion. As we know from the 2004 election, this does not mean that religion or religious issues are unimportant, but rather that ethnicity as race was an important factor to consider when accounting for the 2004 presidential election outcome.

Table 17.1 Languages and party support in South Africa in 2000 (%)

Party	Languages					
	Afrikaans	*English*	*Xhosa*	*Zulu*	*African other*	*Total*
ANC	19.1	16.1	86.3	65.9	85.9	64.9
IFP	1.1	0	0	22.4	0	5.8
African-minor	8.1	12.6	12.1	6.7	8.5	9.0
DP + DA	34.2	46.0	1.6	2.3	3.6	11.2
NNP	23.9	23.0	0	2.5	1.8	6.8
White-minor	13.6	2.3	0	0.2	0.2	2.3
Total	100.0	100.0	100.0	100.0	100.0	100.0
N	272	174	313	478	658	1895

ANC = African National Congress, IFP = Inkatha Freedom Party, DP = Democratic Party, DA = Democratic Alliance, NNP = New National Party; among minor African parties we count: African Christian Democratic Party, Pan Africanist Congress, United Democratic Movement; as minor White parties we count: Freedom Front, Afrikaner Unity Movement.

Source: Based on data from Afrobarometer, round 1, 2000.

Table 17.2 Race and party support in South Africa in 2000 (%)

Party	Race				Total
	Black/African	White/European	Coloured	Indian	
ANC	79.3	2.0	46.2	15.7	64.9
IFP	7.4	1.2	0	0	5.8
African-minor	8.7	7.2	9.7	23.5	9.0
DP + DA	2.8	58.6	10.3	23.5	11.2
NNP	1.7	15.3	33.8	33.3	6.8
White-minor	0.2	15.7	0	3.9	2.3
Total	100.0	100.0	100.0	100.0	100.0
N	1,450	249	145	51	1,895

Source: Based on data from Afrobarometer, round 1, 2000.

Table 17.3 Race and vote at the US 2004 presidential election (%)

Candidate	Race				Total
	Black	Asian	Hispanic	White	
John Kerry	90.1	37.5	67.4	41.5	49.9
George W. Bush	9.9	62.5	32.6	58.5	50.1
Total	100.0	100.0	100.0	100.0	100.0
N	111	24	46	595	778

Source: ANES (American National Election Study) 2004.

Religion

The relevance of religion for politics has increased dramatically in recent years with the emergence of fundamentalism. It has implications for global governance and the possibilities of cooperation among the civilizations of the world. On a day-to-day basis, religion impacts upon politics in two different ways. On the one hand, **religious cleavages** exist in many societies, as religious fragmentation in a society or country may follow divisions between the major world religions, such as Christianity versus Islam in Nigeria and Lebanon, Buddhism against Hinduism in Sri Lanka, Islam versus Hinduism in India, Malaysia, and Indonesia and secular communism against Buddhism in Tibet and China. Religious heterogeneity also involves strong political tensions between creeds or sects within the major world religions, such as Orthodoxy against Catholicism in Ukraine, the Sunni versus the Shi'a in the Muslim world, the Hindus versus the Sikhs in India, and Protestantism against Catholicism in the US and Brazil.

On the other hand, even when there is religious homogeneity, religion impacts strongly upon society and politics through its influence upon the 'mind' of a country. Culture conceived as **civilization** forms the broadest field of inquiry, which tends to link up with the analysis of the major world religions and their social consequences. In attempts to classify the world into a parsimonious set of civilizations (Lane and Ersson 2005), the world religions, measured in terms of numbers of believers, are employed. Thus, Judaism frames the politics of Israel, Islam the politics of the Arab civilization, whereas Confucianism as well as Shintoism matters for the political style in China and Japan (see Comparative table 2 at the end of this volume).

Today the political focus concerning religion is directed towards the rise of religious fundamentalism and its political implications, within Islam (Muslim Brotherhood), Protestantism (the US, Brazil), and Hinduism (*Hindutva*). It is a major challenge to the social sciences to explain the new religious communitarianism, as the great sociologists of the twentieth century all predicted a seminal decline of political salience for religion, as for instance in modernization theory focusing upon the impact of secularization. The most debated form of fundamentalism is the twentieth-century movement called Muslim Brotherhood, originating in Egypt (*al-Banna* 1928) and Pakistan (*Mawdudi*). It has its own ideology, covering most aspects of private life including Islamic finance, as well as public action. Political parties adhering to the Muslim Brotherhood, albeit with very different forms of radicalism, have participated in elections in several countries and sometimes scored victory (in Palestine Hamas and in Turkey the Justice and Development Party). These parties, though, are not allowed to operate in all Muslim countries, which has caused political violence, for instance in Algeria (the Islamic Salvation Front) and Egypt as well as Syria.

A case for the growing relevance of religion is made by Norris and Inglehart (2004), although Protestantism or Calvinism has not been able to maintain its support in Western Europe. Secularization has been on the rise during the twentieth century, but this is mainly a phenomenon of the industrial and post-industrial world. They conclude that 'there is no evidence of a worldwide decline of religiosity or the role of religion in politics' (2004: 212), since also in industrial and post-industrial society one can note that religion continues to influence the electoral behaviour of British as well as US citizens.

Ethnicity and religion are in most instances easy to distinguish, but there are some countries where they are almost indistinguishable. These are cases of 'mutually reinforcing cleavages'. Let us first look at the modern state of Israel. In the Online Resource Centre, the Table: Ethnicity and party support in Israel in 2003, indicates that various social groups vote differently, including the sizeable Arab minority citizens within Israel, but there one also finds a split between the European Jews (Ashkenazi) and the Sephardic Jews (Mizrahim). The Ashkenazi Jews vote relatively more left than right. The support for the centre right (Likud) is stronger among the Sephardic Jews. The recent immigration of Russian Jews into Israel has also strengthened the centre right. Israel is an example where religious belonging is another word for ethnicity, as for example those adhering to other religions are chiefly Arabs (and Muslims), supporting the far left parties, which also are the Arab parties. A second example is the Ulster conflict, which ranks high among examples of political tension in deeply divided societies. One easily associates it with the examples of Lebanon, Sri Lanka, and Kashmir. In the Online Resource Centre, the Table: Religious orientation and party support in Northern Ireland in 2004, indicates a clear match between religious affiliation (Protestant–Catholic) and party allegiance in election results for the Ulster province.

Now, the political effects of religion are today ambiguous, with the themes of secularization and of the rise of religious fundamentalism. In the Ulster conflict, besides religion, there is a pure political value orientation, namely tradition (see next section). In fact, it is two political traditions or conceptions of the nation that clash, namely nationalism with the groups who adhere to the idea of a united Ireland against unionism with the groups who wish Ulster to remain within the United Kingdom. Which weighs the most in the Ulster conflict, religion or nationalism? It is the ethnic cleavage: unionism versus nationalism that outweighs religion as a determinant of party choice.

Tradition

The study of political culture emphasizes the present, searching for how ways of life or beliefs and attitudes impact upon political participation and the political system. But it also probes into how the past impacts

COUNTRY PROFILE China

People's Republic of China (*Zhōnghuá Rénmín Gònghéguó*)

State formation

The first unification under the Qin Dynasty dates back to the year 221 BC. A Republic of China was established in 1912 after the unsuccessful Qing Dynasty had been overthrown, but no political stability was achieved. From 1927 to 1950 the Kuomindang (or Nationalist Party) opposed the Chinese Communist Party in a civil war. The People's Republic was established under the leader of the latter, Mao Zedong, in 1949.

Constitution 1982; amended several times.

Form of government

Communist state. The Communist Party and its internal institutions are generally superior to the state institutions that are described here.

Head of state President and Vice President elected by the National People's Congress; term of 5 years (renewable once).

Head of government Prime Minister, nominated by the president and confirmed by the National People's Congress.

Cabinet State Council appointed by the National People's Congress.

Administrative subdivisions 23 provinces, 5 autonomous regions, and 4 municipalities. Hong Kong and Macau have the status of Special Administrative Regions.

Legal system

Derived from Soviet and continental European civil code.

Legislature

Unicameral National People's Congress (*Quánguó Rénmín Dàibiao Dàhuì*): about 3,000 members elected by municipal, regional, and provincial people's congresses; term of 5 years. There is also a Chinese People's Political Consultative Conference which is not anchored in the constitution but in some sense fulfils the functions of an advisory upper house.

Electoral system

A half-year-long series of layered indirect elections is conducted, beginning from local popularly elected people's congresses up to the National People's Congress. In practice the selection of members for the higher people's congresses is controlled by the Communist Party. Approximately one-third of the seats of the National People's Congress are informally reserved for non-party members such as technical experts and members of the smaller allied parties.

Constituencies The delegates from each of the 34 administrative subdivisions form a delegation.

Suffrage Universal, 18 years.

Direct democracy

None.

Party system　Results of the 2002–2003 elections:

Electorate	not available	100.0%
Voters	not available	not available

Party	Valid votes	%	Seats
Communist Party of China	n.a.	n.a.	n.a.
Revolutionary Committee of the Kuomintang	n.a.	n.a.	n.a.
China Democratic League	n.a.	n.a.	n.a.
China Democratic National Construction Association	n.a.	n.a.	n.a.
China Association for Promoting Democracy	n.a.	n.a.	n.a.
Chinese Peasants' and Workers' Democratic Party	n.a.	n.a.	n.a.
China Zhi Gong Party	n.a.	n.a.	n.a.
September 3 Society	n.a.	n.a.	n.a.
Taiwan Democratic Self-Government League	n.a.	n.a.	n.a.
China Democracy Party (banned)	0	0	0
China Green Party (seeking to become a political party)	0	0	0
Total	n.a.	100.0	about 3,000

(Rows from Revolutionary Committee of the Kuomintang to Taiwan Democratic Self-Government League are marked as *Registered allied parties*.)

Note: Besides the dominant Communist Party of China, eight registered minor parties exist which however do not form any political opposition.

Source: Wikipedia.

upon the present in the form of lingering political traditions. Cultures inherited from the past may have a great relevance for the present, if they form part of the present collective consciousness.

An exercise in constructing holistic political cultures building on historical traditions is Elazar's typology (1966) of different political cultures in the US. Elazar's types—**moralistic, individualistic,** and **traditionalist** cultures—refer to some of the analytical aspects of culture discussed above, such as for instance religion (moralistic culture with Protestant sects) and historical legacy (traditionalist culture in the Deep South). According to new cultural theory value orientations tend to exhibit one of four kinds of logic: (1) fatalism, (2) hierarchy, (3) individualism, and (4) egalitarianism (Thompson *et al.* 1990).

Elazar's typology is strongly linked with religion as well as the historical path of immigration into the American continent. The moralist culture would be the Puritan or Lutheran North, the traditionalist culture is the Deep South with its members from the Anglican Church, and the individualist culture is composed of the remaining parts of the US including New York and Pennsylvania (with the Quakers for instance). Elazar's typology, when used in empirical research, employs the Sharkansky scale, running from '1' for the moralist culture to '9' for the traditionalist culture with '5' for the individualist culture.

If hierarchy is the basis, then traditionalist cultures should come close to '9', but if communitarian values count as the denominator, then individualist cultures should come as '1' and moralist cultures as '9'. To speak with Wildavsky, the South would be hierarchy, the North egalitarian, and the West individualist—we need a more complex typology than simply a dichotomy. Fatalism is hardly to be encountered in the US, except perhaps for the 'Uncle Tom attitudes' during and after the period of slavery.

Let us now combine the hypothesis of three major American political cultures from Elazar with the trust theme of Putnam. When social capital is measured by means of the existence of a civil society—free associations of all kinds, and the presence of social trust (Putnam 2000: 291)—then one finds a strong variation from the Dakotas to Georgia and Mississippi. Interestingly, this variation seems to follow the Sharkansky scale, based upon Elazar's typology: *moralism* (strong civil society), *individualism* (medium civil society), and *traditionalism* (weak civil society). It is an open question what lies beneath the Sharkansky scale: is it religion, immigration meaning ethnicity, or Wildavsky's value orientations? Does Elazar's political culture have any political implications?

Figure 17.5 presents one example of a political effect, namely how the political culture identified by Elazar is related to women's representation in the

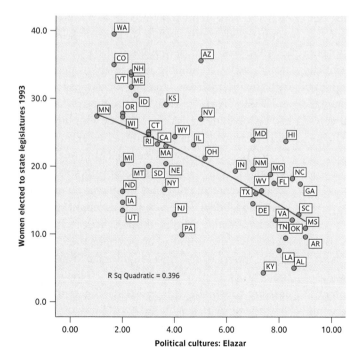

Fig. 17.5 American political culture and women's representation in US state legislatures (1993)

Source: Political culture scores come from Sharkansky (1969) and Koven and Mausolff (2002); women's representation come from Center for American Women and Politics (2006).

state legislatures. It appears that there was a correspondence between the political culture score and women's representation in 1993. States with more of a traditionalistic culture have less women represented in the state legislatures, while states with a moralist culture have higher representation. Since these political cultures are expressions of historical legacies, one would expect weaker connections over time. And comparing the political culture with women's representation in 2005 there is a much weaker relation.

Besides mass attitudes or ways of life, political legacies may be identified as harboured in country-specific institutions or models of governance such as the Westminster legacy and consensus (see Chapter 5). A field yet to be explored in detail is the analysis of the social consequences of colonialism. Although there are some challenging hypotheses here (Fanon 1966; Said 1978), the variety of outcomes of different colonial experiences has not been researched in depth.

> **KEY POINTS**
>
> ❑ The political implications of ethnicity, propelled by the relevance of multi-culturalism for present-day societies, appear neatly in the political support for ethno-political parties or social movements.
> ❑ Religion has micro implications both for how citizens orientate themselves in politics and macro consequences with respect to how civilizations may be able to coexist or tend to clash.
> ❑ Political cultures may emerge from peculiar traditions, which have implications for political outcomes and policy-making.
> ❑ Political traditions may be found that play a role for both policy-making and electoral behaviour, e.g. in the US and Northern Ireland. In the Third World, various colonial legacies make up important political traditions for today's politics.

Current issues in political culture theory

The analysis of political culture is a dynamic field of study with new hypotheses and findings regularly emerging. Since the early 2000s, attention has chiefly focused upon three topics causing much debate among social scientists. First, the notion of **social capital** has stimulated scholars to try to pin down what it really stands for. Second, there is much talk about the **clash of civilizations**. Third, the **politics of sex** is no longer on the fringe of politics, but it is a central concern for policy-making and law, following the recognition that gender and homosexuality may be culturally embedded. In this final section, we shall briefly debate these three themes.

Social capital

Trust theory aims at explaining performance outcomes—political and economic ones. The expectation is that a political culture with a strong dose of social trust is conducive to democratic stability. Deliberations on this theme end up in models at an aggregate national level where higher levels of social capital (interpersonal trust) are associated with

higher levels of democracy (Newton 1997, 2004; Paxton 2002). Data displayed in Figure 17.6, however, only partly support this expectation. It is true that high levels of democracy are to be found among countries where the level of social trust is high (the Scandinavian countries). But it is also true that there are countries combining high levels of democracy with low or medium levels of social trust (Austria and Chile) as well as that other countries combine low or medium levels of democracy with high levels of social trust (China and Iran are two examples).

Social capital theory has emerged from one form of cultural analysis, namely the enquiry into trust, where the occurrence of trust may be measured either by institutional data or survey analysis of attitudes. Institutional data indicating the presence of social trust argues that the more free associations there are, the higher interpersonal trust would tend to be. When trust theory employs survey data, then the respondents are presented with questions concerning how they interact with neighbours, as well as whether they have confidence in other persons (the **explanans**). Institutional performance of regional government

Our chapter has illustrated that scholars have amassed a great deal of knowledge about political participation over the past half century. If we had to bet on avenues of research where scholars can make the most advance in throwing light on the mechanisms and dynamics of political participation we would nominate three subjects.

1. We need to understand better the interaction between the capacities and motivations of individuals to engage in political participation and the socio-economic, institutional, and political-strategic context in which such actors are embedded. As the example of education and voter turnout in different electoral systems and under conditions of differential socio-economic inequality in the last section illustrates, political behaviour cannot be explained merely in terms of individual-level traits or macro-level conditions and rules, but has to understand the contingent interaction between micro and macro level.

2. We need to understand more clearly why everyday political actors and political entrepreneurs who produce selective incentives for others to participate in politics opt for different modes of political participation in different circumstances and in light of different demands. Sure, there are grey zones between social movements, interest groups, and political parties that make it hard to discern distinctive modes of political participation. Nevertheless, it is a fascinating and by and large under-studied question why political actors sometimes invest in trajectories of political involvement that crystallize more around volatile social movements, or durable interest groups, or programmatically complex parties.

3. The differentiation between modes of political action appears to grow in post-industrial democratic polities. Consider the contrast to labour movements in the early twentieth century. The same actors who were activists in socialist parties also tended to lead labour unions—regardless of whether these were the 'transmission belt' of parties or whether parties were the electoral mouthpieces of labour unions. Furthermore, these core cadres also organized disruptive extra-institutional street politics that sustained labour mobilization as a social movement. By the late twentieth century, however, socialist parties and unions rarely ever engage in protest events. And even the relationship between labour mobilization as a functional interest group and as an electoral undertaking has become an arm's length affair where all sides struggle to preserve their mutual autonomy.

Not only the causes, but also the consequences of increasing differentiation between modes of political action deserve more attention. What takes place is a 'decentring' of democratic politics across diverse sites and modes of action, a pluralization of political democracy and political involvement. Why is there so much and such diverse political activism? This is a real and unresolved puzzle when thinking about political participation. Perhaps the best answer we can give is: because they don't want to see Hamlet without the Prince.

? Questions

1. Why do people participate in politics?
2. What are the three principal sites of participation and what are the three principal modes of participation?
3. What is the 'paradox of collective action'?
4. What are the solutions to the paradox of collective action?
5. Why is union membership higher in Ghent systems?
6. Which factors are known to increase levels of turnout?
7. Do you think that low turnout rates are a threat to democracy?
8. Why do political entrepreneurs sometimes initiate social movements, sometimes build interest organizations, and sometimes found parties?

9. What are the three different types of micro-level factors for participation? Give examples for each.

10. Should theories of collective action start from the premise that participation is a 'cost' or should theories reverse the premise and treat participation as a 'benefit'?

» Further reading

As classics on political participation that especially emphasize the cross-national variance in patterns of political involvement, consult Barnes and Kaase (1979) and Verba *et al.* (1978). Formal theories of collective action can be traced from Olson (1965) via Hardin (1982) to Lichbach (1995), followed by further refinements over the past ten years. On turnout in cross-national perspective, see the classics by Powell (1986) and Jackman (1987) and the most recent comprehensive analysis by Franklin (2004). As a survey of political participation in electoral politics and beyond within advanced industrial democracies, see also Dalton (2002), a textbook regularly updated through new editions.

Barnes, Samuel H., and Kaase, Max (1979) *Political Action: Mass Participation in Five Western Democracies* (Newbury Park, Calif.: Sage Publications).

Dalton, Russell J. (2002) *Citizen Politics: Public Opinion and Political Parties in Advanced Industrial Democracies* (Chatham, NJ: Chatham House Publishers/Seven Bridges Press, 3rd edn.).

Franklin, Mark N. (2004) *Voter Turnout and the Dynamics of Electoral Competition in Established Democracies since 1945* (Cambridge: Cambridge University Press).

Hardin, Russell (1982) *Collective Action* (Baltimore, Md.: Johns Hopkins University Press).

Jackman, Robert W. (1987) 'Political Institutions and Voter Turnout in the Industrial Democracies', *American Political Science Review*, 81(2): 405–24.

Lichbach, Mark Irving (1995) *The Rebel's Dilemma: Economics, Cognition, and Society* (Ann Arbor, Mich.: University of Michigan Press).

Olson, Mancur (1965) *The Logic of Collective Action: Public Goods and the Theory of Groups* (Cambridge, Mass.: Harvard University Press).

Powell, G. Bingham, Jr. (1986) 'American Voter Turnout in Comparative Perspective', *American Political Science Review*, 80(1): 17–43.

Verba, Sidney, Nie, Norman H., and Kim, Jae-on (1978) *Participation and Political Equality: A Seven-Nation Comparison* (Cambridge, Mass.: Cambridge University Press).

Web links

Parties

http://psephos.adam-carr.net
   Carr's election archive. Contains electoral information from 175 countries.

http://dodgson.ucsd.edu/lij
   Lijphart Elections Archive. Contains information about electoral systems, election results, and the like.

www.electionresources.org/
   Election Resources on the Internet. Collection of links to websites around the world which provide complete and detailed national and local election statistics.

www.duke.edu/~mms16/DistrictLeveldatasources.htm
   District Level Electoral Data on the Internet (by Matthew M. Singer). Contains links to online sources of complete electoral results at the constituency levels.

www.janda.org/ICPP/index.htm
   International Comparative Political Parties Project. Impressive data collection on parties around the world.

Unions

www.ilr.cornell.edu/library/research/subjectGuides/laborUnions.html
   Labor Unions and the Internet. Commented link collection maintained by the Catherwood Library (Cornell University). While this link collection focuses on the US, there are some very useful links to international sites as well.

http://eurofound.europa.eu/eiro/
   European Industrial Relations Observatory. Offers news and analysis on European industrial relations.

www.dol.gov/ILAB/media/reports/flt/main.htm
   Foreign Labor Trends (ILAB). Website maintained by the US Department of Labor Bureau of International Labor Affairs, with information from about twenty countries around the world.

www.cf.ac.uk/socsi/union
   Cyber Picket Line. Comprehensive collection of links to union-related matters, including links to (some) unions around the world (World Trade Union Directory).

www.unionstats.com
   The Union Membership and Coverage Database. Data resource for the US, providing private and public sector labour union membership, coverage, and density estimates.

www.ilo.org
   The International Labour Organization. A UN specialized agency which seeks the promotion of social justice and internationally recognized human and labour rights. Contains a wealth of data on union-related matters; see especially www.ilo.org/public/english/bureau/stat/portal/index.htm.

http://eurofound.europa.eu/emcc/
   Collective Bargaining Europe. 'The ''Collective Bargaining Europe'' website from the European Trade Union Institute aims to ensure the supply of information on current bargaining developments related to the coordination of collective bargaining, especially at the European level. The site contains country reports on bargaining developments in the previous year from all EU countries and some of the candidate countries. These country reports are then summarized in the annual report *Collective Bargaining in Europe*. Various articles on the economic background of collective agreements, as well as good practice examples, are available under the heading 'Special Features' (quoted from website).

www.etui-rehs.org/
   European Trade Union Institute. Their mission is 'to become the single best and most respected European knowledge and competence centre in relation to the world of labour' (from their site). Many links, reports, data, and the like on labour-related matters.

Social movements

www.psr.keele.ac.uk/parties.htm
   Political parties, interest groups, and other social movements. Contains many links to parties and social movements.

www.nathannewman.org/EDIN/
   Economic Democracy Information Network. Contains links to social movements, sorted by issue area.

www.euromovements.info/english/index.htm
   Guide for Social Transformation in Europe: European Social Forum and Surroundings. Example of how social movements try to coordinate on the web.

www.vcn.bc.ca/citizens-handbook
   The Citizen's Handbook. 'As far as we know, this is the best quick guide to community organizing on the web' (quoted from website).

www.mobilization.sdsu.edu/index.html
   The Mobilization Homepage: '*Mobilization* is an international journal of research and theory specializing in social movements, protests and collective behaviour. *Mobilization* was created to fill the void that there was no scholarly journal of research and theory with an interdisciplinary and international scope that dealt exclusively with social movements, protest and collective action.'

www.igc.org/index.html

Institute for Global Communications. Network of several social movements.

Data

www.idea.int/vt/survey/voter_turnout_pop2-2.cfm

Website of International IDEA. Comprehensive set of data on turnout.

www.cses.org

Website of the Comparative Study of Electoral Systems.

www.worldvaluessurvey.org

Website of the World Value Survey.

www.lisproject.org/publications/welfaredata/welfareaccess.htm

Comparative Welfare States Data Set assembled by Evelyne Huber, Charles Ragin, and John D. Stephens and updated by David Brady, Jason Beckfield, and John Stephens.

http://stats.oecd.org/wbos/Default.aspx

OECD Statistics. Contains, besides many other data, information on union membership.

 Visit the Online Resource Centre that accompanies this book for more information:
www.oxfordtextbooks.co.uk/orc/caramani/

19

Political communication

Rachel K. Gibson and Andrea Römmele

Chapter contents

Reader's guide

Political communication is a new and exciting area of research that is located at the crossroads of the study of communication, political parties, and electoral behaviour. This chapter reviews these different subdisciplines, drawing out their relevance in shaping this emergent field, with an emphasis particularly on their comparative perspectives. Starting with the broad question of what purpose communication serves in modern democracies, we profile and seek to synthesize the various answers that have been voiced by scholars from across the discipline. Arguing that campaign communication constitutes a particularly rich 'springboard' for discussion of the evolution of political communication research, we track the historical development of this area of study as well as the practices and behaviours it has sought to document. As well as profiling the changing nature of the media system, this approach leads us to the 'new political communication'—that is based around the new information and communication technologies (ICTs). We examine the work that has been done on the uses of the new media by parties and politicians across a range of democratic contexts and offer some insights into the strong challenges they introduce for the established manufacturers of political communication.

Introduction

The characterization of modern societies as 'information societies' has become commonplace; in general, all societies are constituted by communication, as all social processes are performed by exchanging information. But more than ever before, the control of information and communication has become a central determinant of political power and social structure (Bell 1973; Salvaggio, 1989). Success and failure of individual and collective actors alike depend increasingly on their ability to communicate properly. One of the most detailed definitions of what political communication actually is comes from Franklin: 'The field of political communication studies the interactions between media and political systems, locally, nationally, and internationally' (1995: 255). Franklin argues that political communication focuses on the analysis of: (1) the political content of the media; (2) the actors and agencies involved in the production of content; (3) the effect; (4) the impact of the political system on the media system; and (5) the impact of the media system on the political system.

From the view of comparative politics, the focus of political communication is on the connection between politicians, voters, and the media. It is the connection and interdependency between politics, media, and society that will structure this chapter. We will first talk about the role of communication in democracies. Why do politicians and voters need to communicate at all? Why is communication a necessary pre-condition for representative democracy to function? In a second step, we will show what different disciplines come together in the field of political communication, putting an emphasis on communication

effects. We will then present a newly developing field within political communication: campaign communication. In this part of the chapter, we present different phases of campaign communication and discuss the Americanization and modernization hypothesis. In addition, we also offer an overview of media system development, a feature which is developed further when we turn to the impact of the new information and communication technologies (ICTs) for political communication.

We argue here that the new media technologies are leading to the emergence of a new form of political communication, one that is more citizen-driven but not necessarily 'mass-based', as it might be traditionally thought of. Whether this bodes well or ill for the quality of political communication as a whole is something of a 'wait and see' scenario. Throughout the chapter we strive to refer to sources that allow us to take a comparative approach to the subject of political communication. Such an approach is crucial for promoting a wider critical perspective on politics as a whole, enhancing and enriching one's analytical focus and the validity of one's conclusions.

KEY POINTS

❑ The control of information and communication is a central determinant of political power and social structure.
❑ New media technologies are leading to the emergence of a new form of political communication, one that is a more citizen-driven but not necessarily mass-based.

Communication and democratic politics

In representative democracies communication between leaders and citizens is a necessary condition for the political system to work. Voters need to be informed about the political programmes, policy issues, and political alternatives presented by the candidates and/or political parties (opinion formation); on the other hand, political representatives need to know the wishes and demands of those

whom they are supposed to govern (interest mediation).

In modern mass democracies it is political parties that connect government and the governed with one another: 'Citizens in modern democracies are represented through and by parties' (Sartori 1976: 24), which means that communication occurs through political parties and comes from them. Sarcinelli

(1998: 277) ascribes a 'communicative hinge function' to parties in the democratic process; they perform a middle-man service in the communication between state agencies and citizens, in both the process of opinion formation and interest mediation. 'Parties can best be conceived as a means of communication' (Sartori, 1976: 29). Although parties have been, and still are, the main actors in the political communication process, candidates are now playing an increasingly important role. This is due to a range of factors, principal among which are arguably technological developments and the rise of television as a visual medium. The personalization of political messages offers voters an 'information shortcut' in deciphering and making sense of complex policy issues (Popkin 1991).

Although parties are the key organizations linking citizens to government they are by no means the only organizations that engage in political communication. The communicative behaviour of non-governmental organizations (NGOs) and protest movements has also attracted scholarly attention, especially with the rise of new ICTs. A number of studies have indicated that the most likely beneficiaries of the new media are loosely organized *ad hoc* protest groups (Bonchek 1995; Bimber 1998). In part, this is because of the relative low cost of the net and the lack of editorial control, which means that fringe campaigns have greater opportunities to voice their concerns and get the message across than they do via the traditional media. Moreover, e-mail and hypertext links make it easier than before to mobilize protest quickly and link together previously unconnected individuals, even breaking down traditional barriers of time and space (see Chapter 18). We return in greater depth to the role played by new ICTs in the last part of this chapter.

When one studies political communication, three actors appear to occupy the centre stage: the media, political elites, and voters. All of these are dependent

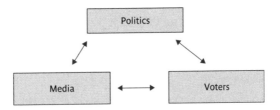

Fig. 19.1 Political communication and its main actors

upon and influence one another. Changes and developments occurring to one actor naturally then have an influence on the other actors.

In this chapter we concentrate primarily on the roles of two of those actors—the media and political elites. This does not mean that we regard the voters as playing an unimportant role; throughout the chapter we mention how changes at the mass level, and particularly the decline of party identification, have affected the way in which political actors communicate. In addition, in the last part of the chapter we consider how the new ICTs are changing the ways in which citizens and politics (can) communicate, both in terms of the mode and also the message. However, these changes to the citizen body are documented more explicitly elsewhere in this volume and are not explored systematically here.

KEY POINTS

❏ In representative democracies communication between leaders and led is a necessary condition for the political system to work. Political parties are the key actors in performing this function.

❏ However, new actors such as NGOs and social movements are increasingly important in linking citizens to government, and are the biggest beneficiaries of ICTs.

Approaches to political communication

Communication research

Communication research is a very broad research field linking many other subdisciplines, such as psychology, literature, business administration, and political science. From the perspective of political communication, a heavy interest obviously lies in the effect communication has on citizens (and potential voters). Although there is common ground that the mass media are a powerful instrument of influencing

COUNTRY PROFILE Mexico

United Mexican States (*Estados Unidos Mexicanos*)

State formation

Spain ocuppied what is now known as Mexico in 1519 and conquered the Aztec capital in 1521. Mexican independence was declared in 1810, when Spain was occupied by Napoleon's army, but only recognized after a long war in 1821. The first republic was established in 1824. *Constitution* 1917.

Form of government

Federal presidential republic.
Head of state President, elected by popular vote; term of 6 years (not renewable).
Head of government The President.
Cabinet Appointed by the President; the appointment of the Attorney General requires approval of the Senate.
Administrative subdivisions 31 states.

Legal system

Mixture of civil law system and US constitutional theory; judicial review of legislative acts.

Legislature

Bicameral National Congress (*Congreso de la Unión*).

Lower house Chamber of Deputies (*Cámara de Diputados*): 500 seats; term of 3 years.
Upper house Senate (*Cámara de Senadores*): 128 seats; 96 members are elected by popular vote and 32 seats are allocated on the basis of each party's popular vote; term of 6 years.

Electoral system (lower house)

Mixed system: 300 seats allocated by plurality, 200 seats allocated by PR.
Formula Simple quotient plus greatest remainder for the 200 seats allocated by PR. However the majority party will not obtain more than 300 seats (or 315 with more than 60% of popular vote).
Constituencies 300 single-member constituencies (plurality vote) and 5 multi-member or 'block' constituencies (PR vote).
Barrier clause None.
Suffrage Universal and compulsory (but not enforced), 20 years.

Direct democracy

Referendums on constitutional matters, administrative reforms, and political issues.

Party system Results of the 2006 legislative elections (Chamber of Deputies):

Electorate:	71,351,123	100.0%
Voters:	41,531,750	58.2%

Party	Valid votes	%	Seats
National Action Party (PAN)	13,876,499	34.3	206
Party of the Democratic Revolution (PRD) in alliance with the Labour Party and Convergence (Alliance for the Good of All)	12,040,698	29.7	159
Institutional Revolutionary Party (PRI) in alliance with the Green Party (Alliance for Mexico)	11,704,639	28.9	122
New Alliance Party	1,887,667	4.7	9
Social Democratic and Peasant Alternative Party	852,849	2.1	4
Others	129,209	0.3	0
Total	40,491,561	100.0	500

Notes: Category 'Others' includes parties with less than 1% nation-wide and no seats, and seats won in single-member plurality vote by independent candidates. Votes refer to PR vote, seats to total seats allocated in proportional representation and plurality vote.
Source: Instituto Federal Electoral.

opinion and effects on behaviour, there is great difficulty in predicting effects, or in proving that they have happened, after an event.

The development of thinking about media effects may be said to have a 'natural history', in the sense of it being strongly shaped by the circumstances of time and place. It has also been influenced by several environmental factors, including the interests of governments and law-makers, changing technology, and historical events. McQuail (2005) distinguishes four phases of media effecting history, starting from the phase of regarding media as a very powerful tool for influencing public opinion.

In the first phase, ranging from the turn of the nineteenth/twentieth century until the 1930s, the media were credited with considerable power to shape opinion and belief, to change habits of life, and to mould behaviour more or less according to the will of their controllers (Bauer and Bauer 1960). In Europe, the use of media by First World War propagandists, by dictatorial states in the inter-war years, and by the new revolutionary regime in Russia, all appeared to confirm that the media could be immensely powerful. 'Within the life of the generation now in control of affairs, persuasion has become a self-conscious art and a regular organ of government' (Lipmann 1922). In the 1930s the Payne Fund Studies in the US looked at the impact of movies on delinquency, aggression, and prejudice, while early experimental studies by Hovland *et al.* (1949, 1953) examined the impact of the media for planned persuasion. Popular accounts in the inter-war years reinforced the notion that the mass media could have a direct and decisive impact upon shaping public opinion, and ultimately voting choices.

In the second phase, roughly to be located from the 1930s to the 1960s, we find a shift to sophisticated empirical studies (Blumer 1933; Blumer and Hauser 1933). Many different studies were carried out investigating effects of different types of content and media. The findings suggested a much more modest role for media in causing any planned or unintended effects. The still influential and useful summary of early research by Joseph Klapper appeared to set the seal on this research phase. It summarized that 'mass communication does not ordinarily serve as a necessary or sufficent cause of audience effects, but rather functions through a nexus of mediating factors' (1960: 8).

Hardly had the 'minimal effects' conclusion been written into communication textbooks when it was being challenged. The third phase of media effects can be titled (leaning on an article by Elisabeth Noelle-Neumann 1973): 'Return to the Concept of Powerful Media'. Those with political or commercial motives for using or controlling the media did not feel they could risk accepting the message of relative media impotence which research had produced. In relation to public opinion effects, Lang and Lang argue that the 'minimal effect' conclusion is only one particular interpretation which has gained undue currency: 'The evidence available by the end of the 1950s, even when balanced against some of the negative findings, gives no justification for an overall verdit of "media impotence"' (1981: 659).

One obvious reason for the reluctance to accept a 'minimal effect' conclusion was the arrival of television in the 1950s and 1960s as a new medium with even more power of attraction than its predecessors and with seemingly major implications for social life. However, systematic survey analysis emphasized that the overall impact of mediated communiations was essentially one of reinforcement not change (Trenaman and McQuail 1961; Blumler and McQuail 1968; Matterson and McClure 1976).

The new attempt to study media effects, the fourth phase, was marked by a shift of attention towards long-term change, towards *cognitions rather than attitude*, and towards collective phenomena such as climates of opinion, structures of belief, definitions of social reality, and ideologies (in more detail see McQuail 2005: 460).

> In essence, this involves a view of media as having their most significant effects by constructing meanings. These constructs are then offered in a systematic way to audiences, where they are incorporated (or not), on the basis of some form of negotiation, into personal meaning structures, often shaped by prior colletive identifications. Meanings (thus effects) are constructed by receivers themselves. This mediating process often involves strong influence from the immediate social context of the receiver. The break with 'all powerful' media is also marked by a methodological shift, especially away from quantitative survey methods. (McQuail 2005: 461)

One approach playing a dominant role in this phase is agenda setting. Theories of agenda setting suggest that the news drives the public's issue priorities, thereby not telling people 'what to think' but 'what to think about' (McCombs and Shaw 1972). The theory implies that stories which get most attention in the news become the problems which the public regards as most important. The theory focuses only on the amount of coverage, not its tone or content.

There are, of course, many other ways of systematically looking at media effects from the perspective of political communication. We have chosen the historical perspective. Perse (2001) strongly critizises this approach since it does not recognize the differences between various research areas. Instead of the historical approach she proposes to deal with key differences in terms of alternative models of effect. The four models she names are: (1) *direct effects*; (2) *conditional effects* (varying according to social and psychological factors); (3) *cumulative effects* (gradual and long-term); and (4) *cognitive-transactional effects* (with particular reference to schemata and framing). As McQuail rightly points out though, these models correspond quite closely to the four phases described

above. Table 19.1 summarizes the main features of these models.

Research on political parties and communication

Political communication is also a focus taken up from a party research perspective. The question here is, by and large, how political parties are adapting to the changes and demands the media system and media society is making. The focus of much of the discussion is on the demise of the mass party and its replacement by new models of organization, showing a shift in focus of the parties away from inward concerns with party members and acitivists towards more outward concerns with voters.

The expanding role of political consultants, computer databases, telephone opinion polling, and the media—the process of professionalization—is seen as reducing the role of parties as mobilizers and conduits for popular participation and opinon. Drawing

Table 19.1 Four models of media effects

Types of effects	Nature of effects	Media-content variables	Audience variables
Direct	Immediate, uniform; short term; emphasis on change.	Salience.	Not relevant.
Conditional	Individualized; reinforcement as well as change; long or short term.	Not relevant.	Social categories; social relationships; Individual differences.
Cumulative	Based on cumulative exposure; cognitive or affect; enduring effects.	Consonant across channels; repetition.	Not relevant
Cognitive-transactional	Immediate and short term; Based on one-shot exposure; cognitive and affective, behavioural effects possible.	Salience of visual cues.	Sheama make-up; mood; goals.

Source: Perse (2001: 51).

on the example of the American parties, where this type of campaigning is regarded as having reached its zenith, observers warn of the dangers to party relevance and vitality that professionalization represents. Indeed, one commentator wrote that parties have witnessed nothing less than a 'destruction of their status' in recent years (Johnson-Cartee and Copeland 1997: 12). Not all accounts are so doom-laden, with some authors preferring to talk less normatively about party change rather than party decline as a result of professionalization. The principal approach is to explore the role of parties in the new campaign process, as well as the way the new campaign process affects the parties (Farrell 2006: 123).

The picture of party decline and/or party passivity is problematic on a number of fronts. Most obviously, it is clear that parties at some stage must be consciously involved in the uptake of the new ways of political communication. It is a process that involves extensive senior-level decision-making, organizational reform, and financial muscle—consultants have to be hired, polls and focus groups commissioned, and media training undertaken. Such a change could not simply be foisted on parties, but would require consent. This consent would inevitably be influenced by organizational outlook and capability.

Beyond these logical objections, however, if systemic factors were solely responsible for professionalization then we would expect all parties to be at a similar stage in their use of the techniques. The empirical evidence suggests, however, that there is considerable variance within party systems over the timing and pace of professionalized political communication in general and professionalized campaigning in particular. In the US, for example, the Republicans were credited with professionalizing their campaign operation at least a decade before the Democrats. Similarly, the Conservatives in Britian were considered the first exponents of the new campaigning style in the late 1970s, whereas Labour actively resisted them. Finally, in Germany, although the 1998 campaign by the Social Democratic Party (SPD) under the leadership of Gerhard Schröder seemed to mark the new era of professionalized campaigning in Germany, stirrings were detected in the Christian Democratic Union as early as 1972.

Given these objectives, we have argued elsewhere that parties' role in the process of professionalizing political communication may be more active than has hitherto been recognized (Gibson and Römmele 2001). Relating political communication to the party goals literature, we argued that:

> ❝ it is evident that parties with vote maximization as their primary goal would be most likely to adopt the new techniques. Major changes to electoral strategy are undertaken to shore up and increase a party's vote share. Thus, it is the large catch-all type of parties that we would expect to most readily embrace professional campaigning. (Gibson and Römmele 2001: 36) ❞

There is a young body of literature dealing with these issues (Farrell 2006; Gibson and Römmele 2001; Panebianco 1986) showing that parties expand and equip themselves organizationally. Party research has shown that due to the growing relevance of 'staying on message', of organizing the permanent campaign, the party headquarters become more and more important. Due to the growing relevance of television the candidate gains more importance. The fact that new campaign styles have required political parties to adapt their organizational dynamics as well as their communication strategies does not of itself imply that the parties are somehow weaker as a consequence, but what certainly cannot be disputed is that they have been forced to adapt. Standing still was never an option (Farrell 2006: 131).

KEY POINTS

❏ Research on communication effects distinguishes four phases. In the first phase scholars see the media as having a direct and decisive impact on citizens' beliefs and orientations. The second phase regards the media as having only minimal effects, interpersonal communication is considered of more impact. The third phase of media effects returns us to the concept of a powerful media, and is based strongly around the perceived influence of television. The fourth phase of media effects is marked by a shift in scholarly attention towards changing cognitions rather than attitudes (i.e. agenda setting and priming).

❏ Research on political parties has shown that parties quite openly adapt to the changing demands of the media and society; parties have strengthened their party headquarters to be able to cope with the new demands.

Electoral campaigns

The research on political campaigns is a rather young research field. It brings together research on political parties, electoral research, and communication research. Scholars focus on campaigns as the prototype situation of political communication. Political actors do not behave and communicate differently in campaign periods compared with non-campaign periods. However, during a campaign, one can see communication patterns, strategy, and effects much more clearly.

The pioneer study in the area of campaign communication no doubt is the work conducted by Paul Lazarsfeld and his colleagues in *The People's Choice* (1944). This study focuses on the formation, change, and development of public opinion in a presidential election, more precisely: what impact do campaigns have on voters' decisions. The overall message from the Lazarsfeld study was that theories of propaganda had largely exaggerated the effect of political communications on the mass public.

❝ In summary, then, the people who did most of the reading and listening not only read and heard most of their own partisan propaganda but were also most resistant to conversion because of strong predispositions. And the people most open to conversion ... read and listened least .... The real doubters—the open-minded voters who make a sincere attempt to weigh the issues and the candidates dispassionately for the good of the country as a whole—exist mainly in deferential campaign propaganda, in textbooks on civics, in the movies, and in the minds of some political idealists. In real life, they are few indeed. (Lazarsfeld *et al.* 1944: 95–100) ❞

If we think about the different phases of media effects discussed earlier in this chapter, the Lazarsfeld findings clearly are an example of the second phase.

It was a pioneering study, combining in a very convincing way electoral research and communication research. The effect of campaigns on voters' decisions has since then been of limited interest, most likely because of the difficulty of relating campaign and media effects to individual (voting) behaviour. 'The study on election campaigns, as opposed to elections, is a major gap in the literature' (Harrop and Miller 1987: 240). This quite correctly describes the situation for campaign research in the late 1980s.

Although practitioners of course always state that campaigns are important and make a big difference, this view was and is not shared within the academic community. For a long time, political scientists did not give political campaigns much importance. Since voters had a strong party identification and other predispositions, campaigns had little effect, despite of course getting out the votes. It was taken up again in the edited volume by Farrell and Schmitt-Beck with the eloquent title *Do Campaigns Matter?* (2002).

As the authors rightly point out, since the seminal work of Lazarsfeld *et al.*, there had been little analysis of how voting behaviour is influenced by the communication activities of political parties and other political actors. 'Whether campaigns matter is certainly an under-researched question' (2002: 16). Together with their contributors, the editors come to the conclusion that campaigns may not be of such predominant importance as is assumed by the political actors (whose outlook is glued to the superficial back and forth of day-to-day political debate), but they do count for something in the political process. They are one factor among many others that are important for how and what people decide. While it would be a clear exaggeration to state that campaigns are of prime importance in determining the election result, it seems pretty incontrovertible that campaigns do, indeed, matter for the behaviour of citizens at elections and referenda.

The major gap in the literature which was pointed out earlier has been filled by a number of outstanding and highly recognized studies. Edited volumes (Bowler and Farrell 1992; Swanson and Mancini 1996), articles in mainstream academic journals (*Electoral Studies, Party Politics, Press/Politics, European Journal of Political Marketing*) as well as monographs (Norris 2000; Römmele 2005; Plasser 2002) have taken up the subject of campaign research from a comparative perspective. The general notion in these scholarly works is the change that can be observed in a historical as well as an international perspective. How can this change be described and empirically measured and what implications does it have? According to most academic observers, there have been two broad phases in political campaigning that have preceded the current one.

1. In the first or 'pre-modern era' (Norris 2000), political communication was based on the strength of the **local party organization and face-to-face contact.**

2. The second wave of campaigning, in contrast, saw a **shift from communication via the party organization to mass media communication between parties and voters.** Citizens do not receive their information directly from party meetings or rallies, but through the mass media. With the mass media, parties can communicate their message to a broader audience. Because party identification and party attachment have declined, parties not only have to mobilize their electorate, they also have to convince the undecided voters of their party programme.

Since the early 1990s, parties are seen as facing new challenges. With the rising number of swing voters and weakening party identification, the processes of individualization and modernization are increasingly pushing political campaigns into the limelight. Such trends are clearly reflected in the voting and communications research literature, which have become increasingly intertwined. This new era of uncertainty is marked by increasing efforts by the parties to reach individual voters via the internet, direct mail, and telemarketing. Extensive use is made of survey research, focus groups, and public relations experts to better package the parties' message.

While initially this new campaign era was referred to in generic terms as an Americanized style of campaigning (Negrine and Papathanassopoulos 1996), recently it has had more historical or developmental labels applied to it, such as post-modern (Norris 2000), phase 3 (Farrell and Webb 2000), post-Fordism (Denver and Hands 2000), or professionalized campaigning (Gibson and Römmele 2001). Despite these differences in nomenclature, there is considerable agreement between these authors as to the central features of this new era in party campaigning.

Whereas the above-mentioned scholars describe and measure the change from campaigning from a historical perspective, others discuss a potential convergence of campaigning to the US campaign model; is there an **Americanization** to be observed? Authors putting forward this thesis argue that 'campaigning in democracies around the world is becoming more and more Americanized as candidates, political parties, and news media take cues from their counterparts in the US' (Swanson and Mancini 1996: 4). Scammell suggests that Americanization is 'useful as a shorthand description of global trends ... the US is a leading exporter and role model of campaigning' (1997: 4).

The **modernization** perspective takes a broader view. All established democracies are facing a decrease in party identification (although to a different degree), a rise in late deciders in election campaigns, etc. Hence methods of professionalized campaigning are taken up. Plasser (2000) distinguishes between a *shopping model* and an *adoption model*. The most widespread model of adopting selected innovations and techniques of US election campaigns might be the shopping model, whereby certain techniques and organizational routines of professional campaigning practice are imported from the United States and are modified and implemented taking the national content of political competition into account. The shopping model primarily focuses on down-to-earth techniques that can easily be implemented in the national context while maintaining country- and culture-specific campaign styles and philosophies (Plasser 2000: 35).

No one would seriously question US campaign practices having an impact on campaign activities of parties and candidates in other countries. During US presidential elections party employees and campaign consultants from other countries head to the US to closely monitor 'cutting-edge electioneering' (Blumler *et al.* 1995: 59). However, whether US campaign features can and are transported one-to-one to other countries is a question of comparative campaign communication (see, for more detail, Farrell 2006: 124–5). Comparative work is in its infancy in that field, but a few studies have already proven that structural filters (electoral laws, party systems, media system, governmental make-up) as well as cultural restraints limit the Americanization trends (Römmele 2005). Due to different electoral systems a campaign can follow a completely different logic (Zittel and Gschwend 2007).

Especially differences in the media system and media logic bring about different styles of political communication. In their very thorough and rich comparative analysis on the comparison of media systems Hallin and Mancini (2004) distinguish three

Table 19.2 Political campaigning in historical perspective

	Pre-modern: mid-19th century to 1950s	Modern: early 1960s–late 1980s	Professionalized: after 1990s
Campaign organization	Local and decentralized party volunteers	Nationally coordinated with greater professionalization	Nationally coordinated but decentralized operations
Preparations	Short-term, *ad hoc*	Long campaign	Permanent campaign
Central coordination	Party leaders	Central party headquarters, more specialist advisers	Special party campaign units and more professional consultants
Feedback	Local canvassing and party meetings	Occasional opinion polls	Regular opinion polls plus focus groups and interactive websites
Media	Partisan press, local posters and pamphlets, radio broadcasts	Television broadcasts through main evening news	Television narrow casting, targeted direct mail, targeted ads
Campaign events	Local public meetings, whistle-stop leadership tours	News management, daily press conferences, controlled photo-ops	Extension of news management to routine politics and government
Costs	Low budget	Moderate	Higher costs for professional consultants
Electorate	Stable social and partisan alignments	Social and partisan dealignment	Social and partisan dealignment

Source: Adapted from Norris (2000: 138); Römmele (2005); Gibson and Römmele (2001).

types of media systems and link the way politics is communicated to the origin of these systems. In the **Mediterranean or pluralist model**, predominant in Southern Europe, the media system, due to its historical development, is closely tied to the world of politics. Once democracy was consolidated in those countries a high degree of political parallelism prevailed, with the media serving to represent a wide range of political forces that contended for influence. Newspaper circulation in these countries remains relatively low and electronic media correspondingly high. In the **democratic corporatist model** (including Scandinavia, the Low Countries, Germany, Austria, and Switzerland) we see strong mass circulation of commercial media and of media tied to political and civil groups; the coexistence of political parallelism and journalistic professionalism, and the coexistence of liberal traditions of press freedom and a tradition of strong state intervention in the media, which are seen as a social institution and not as purely private enterprises.

The third model put forward by Hallin and Mancini is the **North Atlantic or liberal model**, with the US being the prime example. There we observe a strong development of a commercial press and its dominance over other forms of press organization, as well as early development of commercial broadcasting and relatively strong professionalization of journalism. The media have been institutionally separate from political parties and other social groups and state intervention has been limited by comparison with the other two models.

KEY POINTS

❑ The new field of campaign communication distinguishes three historical phases: the pre-modern campaign, the modern campaign, and the professionalized campaign. The latter phase is characterized by a high degree of personalization, targeted information, and a more business-like approach to communication with the electorate.

❑ Scholars have also used the terms Americanization and modernization of political campaigning to describe this third phase of communication. The focus

in these accounts is largely upon the external and contextual dynamics that are driving the processes of change, rather than comparing the internal changes taking place within the actors (parties, candidates) themselves.

❑ Hallin and Mancini (2004) distinguish three key models of media system: the Mediterranean or pluralist model, the democratic or corporatist model, and the North Atlantic or liberal model.

Table 19.3 Structural filters and the potential for diffusion of US campaign techniques in Western Europe

Country	Governmental structure	Party system	Electoral system	Private TV spots	Access to state campaign finance	Internet access (more than 40% are online)	Campaign limits
Austria	Parliamentary	Multi-party	PR	Allowed	Yes	No	No
Belgium	Parliamentary	Multi-party	PR	Not allowed	No	No	Yes
Denmark	Parliamentary	Multi-party	PR	Not allowed	No	Yes	No
Finland	Semi-pres.	Multi-party	PR	Not allowed	No	Yes	No
France	Semi-pres.	Two-party	Two ballot	Not allowed	Yes	No	Yes
Germany	Parliamentary	Multi-party	PR	Allowed	Yes	No	No
Ireland	Parliamentary	Multi-party	STV	Not allowed	Yes	No	Yes
Italy	Parliamentary	Multi-party	Mixed	Allowed	Yes	No	Yes
Netherlands	Parliamentary	Multi-party	PR	Allowed	No	Yes	No
Norway	Parliamentary	Multi-party	PR	Not allowed	Yes	Yes	No
Sweden	Parliamentary	Multi-party	PR	Allowed	No	Yes	No
Switzerland	Parliamentary	Multi-party	PR	Not allowed	No	No	No
UK	Parliamentary	Two-party	Plurality	Not allowed	No	No	Yes

The new political communication

In this section we look at the developments taking place in political communication as a result of the rise of the new media, focusing particularly on the changing context of election campaign communication and efforts by parties and candidates to reach voters through new **internet-related technologies**.

While such appeals seem relatively commonplace in the first decade of the new millennium, it is striking to think that barely ten years ago parties and politicians using the new media were considered to be a highly avant-garde if rather eccentric minority. Now having a website is a staple component of any attempt at voter outreach, and campaigners are under increasing pressure to find new and innovative ways to present themselves and their policies online.

The effectiveness of these efforts in mobilizing support is not entirely clear, but the implications of such developments for the traditional 'one to many' understanding of political communication, as we reveal below, are profound. In the remainder of the chapter we discuss these changes by documenting the evolution of online political communication from its early experimental days in the mid-1990s through to its second phase, or what is increasingly termed Web 2.0.

Essentially our argument is that we are now seeing a new era in 'digital communication' in which political institutions and organizations are facing an increasingly difficult task in disseminating their message across a range of new media fora and platforms. The ability of the traditional players to control the flow and dosage of political information circulating to the masses is being eroded as more independent news sources emerge to rival the mainstream media outlets. The rise of social networking tools such as blogs, wikis, and shared personal profiles on **Myspace, YouTube,** and **Bebo** herald a radical new form of distributed and decentralized mass communication that challenges traditional modes of dissemination. Gaining a foothold in this new labyrinthine media environment could yet prove a crucial step for conventional political forces in their quest to re-engage a growing number of apathetic and disengaged citizens.

The early days: Web 1.0 communication

At the start of the web revolution, which we can date essentially from 1993 and the release of the graphical browser Mosaic by the National Center for Supercomputing Applications,[1] most attempts at online political communication consisted of a basic homepage and a few e-mail contacts. Parties and candidates were among some of the first political actors to establish a presence in cyberspace with the earliest reports of launches of websites emerging in 1994 around the US Congressional mid-term elections (Foot and Schneider 2006; Bimber and Davis 2003; Howard 2006). National party organizations in other democracies appear to have begun their colonization of the web by a roughly similar time point, from mid to late 1994 onward (Gibson 2004; Gibson *et al.* 2003).

Beyond the parties, grass-roots-inspired and issue-based campaigns also started to take notice of the power of the new medium to mobilize support. Pre-web internet-related technologies such as Usenet[2] had already been utilized by the US computing community to protest against a range of commercial and governmental software and encryption initiatives that were perceived as infringements of so-called 'cyber-rights and liberties' (Akdeniz 2000; Chadwick 2006: 116). Their use and effectiveness expanded dramatically in the post-web era, however, from more localized efforts to stop the overlay of a new telephone area code in Los Angeles (Lin and Dutton 2003) to more globalized forms of protest against the failure of world leaders to address problems of the world's poorest nations (Capling and Nossal 2001; Meikle 2002; Pickerill 2003; Surman and Reilly 2003).

At the executive level, governments proved rather slower in adapting to the new media environment. The US government's pioneering **Firstgov** portal site went live only in 2000, offering little more than a basic menu of links to other departments and services and a search facility. While services have progressed significantly since then, in the US and numerous other countries, towards a more seamless user interface (West 2005, 2006), in general, e-government initiatives (as they have become known) have been seen as promoted by a more managerial and 'consumerist' agenda, rather than the opportunities it presents for fostering two-way or multi-way dialogue between and with citizens (Chadwick and May 2003; Musso *et al.* 2000; Needham 2003; Stanley and Weare 2004). In addition, as recent reports from the United Nations (UN) have highlighted, the potentially harmful effects of e-government expansion in widening the technological divide between rich and poor countries is a matter of increasing concern.[3]

Academic analyses: production and content

As these developments have taken place academic study has attempted to keep pace, with some of the earliest studies in online political communication emerging in the mid to late 1990s in the campaigns and elections sphere.

Robert Klotz (1997) produced a study of candidate web pages produced for the 1996 Senate race in *PS*, the news magazine of the American political science professional body. His findings pointed to a surprisingly high level of activity in regard to website establishment, with over 80 per cent of major party candidates offering some type of home page, although this dipped markedly for minor party and independent candidates. In addition, the generally positive stance taken towards opponents was noted, breaking with the growth of negative advertising used in other media (Chang *et al.* 1998; Merrit 1984; Sabato 1981). In general, however, the contents appeared to vary little, with most sites offering a *mélange* of candidate photos, biographies, issue profiles, and contacts. More adventurous sites featured press releases and calendars.

Studies of electioneering online spread rapidly across a variety of contexts from Western to Eastern Europe, Asia, and Oceania (Gibson and Ward 1998; Roper 1999; Voerman 1999; Newell 2001; Semetko and Krasnoboka 2003). These analyses essentially confirmed and expanded Klotz's initial findings, particularly with regard to the **increasing uniformity of web page contents**. National differences notwithstanding, an informal template for online electioneering appears to have taken hold, with most sites comprising a short party history or candidate biography, some key policy statements and

documents to download (e.g. manifesto), as well as a special media/newsroom section for press release distribution.

On the interactive front, most campaigners played it safe, offering e-mail contacts, search facilities, and channels for supporters to pledge their support and/or make a donation. Chat-rooms and opportunities for genuine interactivity were generally thin on the ground, the opportunities for abuse and negative headlines proving too great a risk for most of those interested in winning voter support, particularly among the mainstream players.

Within this largely static picture of message construction and dissemination, however, some signs of awareness of the more dynamic and personalized communication facilities offered by the new medium were emerging. Sign-up e-mail news bulletins started to appear more widely post-2000, allowing parties and candidates to target their message, particularly to the faithful, and create a continuous and updated flow of information. For the more technologically ambitious, opportunities provided by wireless news feeds via Personal Digital Assistants (PDA) and/or RSS (Really Simple Syndication) have proved a logical next step.

Viral marketing methods also started to be exploited, whereby the peer-to-peer networks that have grown up online are set in motion via offering users the opportunity to 'forward on' campaign advertisements as well as requests for assistance (Painter and Wardle 2001). More aggressive attempts by groups to market themselves using blanket e-mailing techniques or 'spamming', however, are quite rare, with most campaigners fearing the backlash from disgruntled voters whose inboxes are already bulging under an increasing amount of unsolicited impersonal e-mail messages seeking their custom or support (Fallows 2003).

Net effects?

As the above review makes clear, much of the academic study of the new political communication has focused on content (particularly of websites) and the development of new analytical tools and methodologies to study it (Gibson and Ward 2000; Foot and Schneider 2004).

More limited attention has been devoted to the effects of new media, particularly in terms of user or audience effects. Initial studies focused instead on elites, looking at the structural and reforming consequences for political institutions and organizations. Taking their cue from the early visionary theorizing that preceded the web era, when writers entertained utopian vistas of the internet bringing about a return to the days of direct democracy (Dyson 1998; Negroponte 1995; Rheingold 1995), scholars put forward a range of revolutionary and reformist scenarios for the state and its various branches. Egalitarian possibilities for a rebalancing of the communication system were set out whereby smaller, more marginal, players gained a greater voice (Gibson and Ward 1998; Bimber 1998; Grossman 1995). Alternatively, more dystopian perspectives on the dangers of new ICTs for enhancing elite power and fears of reducing democracy to a gameshow were also outlined by concerned observers (Lipow and Seyd 1995).

The empirical findings that rolled in thereafter, however, proved to be somewhat more prosaic in nature. The so-called 'normalization' thesis emerged as an explicit counterweight to ideas of any equalization, calling attention to the increasing dominance of mainstream parties, news organizations, and commercial internet service providers (ISPs) in the online environment (Margolis and Resnick 2000). Content-wise, the major players were found to offer the most sophisticated and up-to-date sites, particularly during election periods. Also presence-wise, the bigger parties (in the UK and US at least) were found to enjoy far more links into their sites than the average minor party (Gibson *et al.* 2003; Margolis *et al.* 1999). Findings from more sophisticated web link analysis tools gave further support to the structure of dominance in identifying what was termed as WWW 'power law', whereby a very small number of sites within a given policy domain received a disproportionately high number of inbound links (Hindman *et al.* 2003).

Much to the disappointment of the e-democracy proponents, the findings of 'no change' were then replicated across the wider effects spectrum once the audience research started to filter through. Survey data of online users' habits and attitudes proliferated and indicated for the most part that it was generally the more engaged people who were using the internet to promote their views (Bimber 2001; Davis 2005, 1999; Norris 2003). Subsequent studies have emerged that question blanket acceptance of this

'reinforcement' paradigm, pointing to the growing prominence of internet skills and familiarity as resources in and of themselves that promote increased participation (Krueger 2000).

Young people in particular, it was noted, could be mobilized through the increasing opportunities for participation online (Owen 2006; Gibson *et al.* 2005). Survey data gathered by the Pew Center in the US revealed that, while young people (18 to 29 years old) had lower levels of consumption of network and local television news and daily papers, they were the most frequent consumers of internet news (Pew Report 2003). In the UK a joint BBC/MORI poll for the 2005 general election revealed that those in the youngest age bracket (18 to 34 years) were the most likely to seek out election news on the internet (Schifferes 2006). In addition, younger voters in the UK showed signs of being more inclined to vote or contact their elected representatives in the online environment (Hansard Society 2002).

On the specific question of whether or not voters were influenced by what they viewed online, the picture becomes murkier, however. Pew Center data on this question has certainly shown a growing appetite for online political information among US voters. Starting in 1996 they revealed that a mere 4 per cent of the overall population paid attention to election news online. By 2004 this had risen to 29 per cent (Rainie *et al.* 2005). In general voters do confess to being influenced by what they see online, with four out of ten US internet users saying the internet gave them important information to decide their vote and one in five reporting that it actually made a difference to their vote decision (Rainie *et al.* 2005: 10). A more systematic analysis of this question was undertaken by Farnsworth and Owen (2004) who concluded online news consumption had a significant effect on voter decisions in the 2000 US presidential election. Adopting a 'uses and gratifications' perspective, the authors found that those voters who actively looked for information online were more likely to perceive their decision-making as being influenced by what they saw.

In other countries a growth in those paying attention to online political news and information has similarly been reported, albeit not to the high levels witnessed in the US. In the Australian 2004 federal election 12 per cent of the public claimed to have paid some attention to the internet as a news source, this rising to 18 per cent among internet users (Gibson and McAllister 2006). In the UK in 2005, the figure was slightly higher at 15 per cent (28 per cent of internet users) (Ward and Lusoli 2005). In other European countries, such as Germany, the rates of interest among internet users at least are somewhat higher. According to figures from the federal election of 2005, 36 per cent of internet users sought political information online.[4]

In terms of the communicative value of candidate and partisan websites specifically as tools for voter recruitment, the evidence so far does suggest some influence can be detected. An early analysis by D'Alessio (1997) of the 1996 House and Senate races reported that candidates with websites enjoyed a significantly higher level of support than those without. Subsequent in-depth survey research by Bimber and Davis (2003) of voters who viewed particular candidate sites in the US during 2000, however, largely negated this conclusion, arguing that most people were not affected by what they viewed online, particularly in terms of being mobilized to vote. More recent analysis by Gibson and McAllister (2006) of the 2004 Australian federal election, using a more fully specified model of campaign preparedness than D'Alessio, reinforced his more positive conclusion that web presence did matter—in this context by as much as two percentage points. Given the relatively small audience for the sites, however, the authors concluded that the effects were likely to be indirect, and perhaps that websites themselves were capturing some more intangible quality of professionalized campaigning among candidates, not measured by other variables.

Political communication 2.0?

The story of online political communication up until the middle of the first decade of the new millennium is largely one of limited innovation among elites and minimal, albeit growing, relevance for citizens. For the most part, political actors, great and small, have been content to set out their virtual stalls to attract voters, with occasional forays into 'viral' techniques to help to push their message to a wider audience of less interested voters. Reliance on this fixed 'point to mass' model of dissemination, however, has come under increasing strain with the rise

of next generation web tools to arrive in the hands of users.

The emergence of Web 2.0

The term 'Web 2.0', although decried by purists in the industry as a vacuous buzzword, has become synonymous with the significant shift in web design and use.[5] It was coined at a commercial conference on web development in the US in October 2004 which was held to demonstrate that the internet was alive and kicking despite the dot.com crash. The organizers of the conference sought to bring together some of the major survivor companies on the basis that they shared a common approach and philosophy about how the web could be used. In essence, therefore, the term does not refer to a particular type of technology or infrastructure but to a developmental moment in internet history, and a point of paradigm shift in the functionality of the web.

From a technical standpoint, the key shift is that the web itself has now become the platform for accessing tools and services, replacing the desktop personal computer. Through the browser it becomes possible to select the software and data needed to manage and automate online activities including maintaining a home page, uploading and circulating photographs, as well as ensuring one receives the latest news and entertainment sources direct to the personal computer. A secondary and associated practical development is that these applications are all increasingly able to 'talk' to one another behind the scenes through advances in new inter-operability software (primarily AJAX), creating a more seamless interface and enhanced user experience.

From a human or societal perspective, the consequences are possibly even more profound, involving a significant increase in the level of autonomy and control that individuals bring to their media use and consumption. Through what is increasingly now described as 'social software', everyday users can create, distribute, and value-add to online media content. In practical terms this means widespread use of new applications such as 'blogging', 'tagging', and 'wikis', all of which are seen to embody the spirit of Web 2.0.[6] A hallmark of these applications is the devolution of creative and classificatory power to 'ordinary' users in developing online tools and resources. This shift has led to the Web 2.0 being alternatively known as the 'participatory' web.

From political communication 1.0 to 2.0?

The key question for this chapter in relation to the Web 2.0 era is what it means for political communication. There are four key developments in the nature of political communication that the rise of Web 2.0 technologies herald.

1. The move **from a 'one to many' to a 'many to many'** mode of message distribution. Those seeking to influence popular debate and attitudes will need to find ways of gaining entry into the social networks growing up around the new collective spaces that users, and particularly younger users, congregate and inhabit (e.g. Myspace or Bebo). This could entail parties, social movements such as MoveOn.org in the US, or governments even becoming more neutral hosts for such citizen network formation, rather than guiding and directing those activities.

2. A rising role for **aggregator or information 'broker' services.** With the growing volume of information available online, people increasingly need trusted search tools and aggregator services to help them locate, sort, and collate the information that they need. Conversely, then, while the number of news sources may be proliferating, individuals' need for authoritative and credible material may replicate or even drive a further concentration of information providers. Political communicators, therefore, will need either to invest in developing their reputation as sifters and sorters of relevant information (a possibility for established government bodies), or at least ensure that they are linked to major news feed services such as Feedster.

3. A focus on the production of dynamic political content that can be **distributed via different media and across different platforms and an erosion of any offline/online division** in developing communication strategy. The convergence of internet technologies with previous media is already taking place through innovations such as web television, interactive cable, and net-connected mobile phones. While it is not quite a return to the medium being the message, considerations of distribution and dissemination will loom large in content design and campaign tactics. The manufacturers of political messages will need to adopt a more integrated or 'whole of media' approach that ensures their widespread and rapid delivery.

4. An increase in **channels for bottom-up communication to policy-makers** and enhanced scrutiny of elites. The harnessing of new ICTs to social network formation, the rise of citizen journalism, and populist encyclopedias such as Wikipedia, places an upward pressure on the agents of representation to look at ways of enhancing their transparency and accessibility. One example of such developments is the incorporation of a searchable website within the US Federal Funding Transparency and Accountability Act which will allow the public to trace how their federal taxes are spent. In Estonia, the 'Today I Decide' website allows anybody to send in their ideas for policy to the government.

Of course the provision of such tools does not mean that the input will directly or even indirectly inform policy development. Indeed a proliferation of such mechanisms without any procedures for following up on concerns raised could misfire, with democratic hopes being raised and then swiftly dropped. However, the opportunities now offered by the technology for feeding *vox populi* into the political process and letting the 'wisdom of crowds' speak are undeniably growing. And with reports that Wikipedia was proved almost as accurate as *Encylopaedia Britannica* in *Nature* during 2005, along with the robustness of open source software, the argument against using the technology for more direct democracy appears to be waning.

In short, it appears that the dominant thrust of this second phase in new political communication is to place ordinary citizens increasingly in the driver's seat. The role of parties, government departments, politicians, and candidates becomes one of assisting voters and supporters in their quest for information, social interaction, and self-expression. As a corollary, while content is not unimportant, its crown is slipping. The audience for the new political communication is big and growing. It is not however, a mass audience in the sense of a bulk of people consuming a fixed and predetermined diet of information. Nor is it even an audience, given the growth of user-generated content. Recent Pew Center figures report that almost one in ten of the online audience (7 per cent) have created their own web-based journal or log (now commonly referred to as 'blogs').[7] Getting a message, any message, across to these busy individuals constitutes the major challenge for communicators working in the Web 2.0 era. The counter-trend, however, as noted above is that this rising 'noise' level means that citizens increasingly need moderating and legitimating bodies. The emergence of 'A-list' bloggers for instance indicates a new concentration of power and influence with an information technology elite.

These changes may take decades to be fully realized and will not see the wholesale displacement of traditional political communication approaches. Already, however, we can discern some movement toward their realization. From beginnings in the form of subscription-based e-newsletters, parties and candidates have graduated on to more continuous and direct communication through RSS news feeds from their site, allowing users to feed through updates direct to their desktop or into their own web pages. Blogs are being embraced by the political class, albeit with varying degrees of authenticity, as a key means of content distribution. While many leading politicians now run a blog, few occupy the A-list. More typical, and seemingly more effective, is the Howard Dean approach of securing favourable mentions on the most prominent few: a process which

entails some sustained and careful coordination of net-savvy supporters who blanket the net with positive statements of support. The social networking sites appear to remain largely a politics-free zone, which may say something about the outlook and average age of those using these spaces.

KEY POINTS

- ❑ The 'early days' of political communication online (i.e. middle of the 1990s) saw a rapid embracing by political actors of the internet and particularly the World Wide Web (WWW). Most efforts, however, reproduced the logic of previous models of media communication with a single point (web page) being used to disseminate out to the mass audience.
- ❑ From the middle of the following decade this model of 'point-to-mass' communication is increasingly challenged and we are seeing a new era in 'digital communication'.
- ❑ Political institutions and organizations are facing an increasingly difficult task in disseminating their message across a range of new media fora and platforms.
- ❑ The successful candidates and parties will be those that can find and authentically reach out to voters in the new social spaces that have blossomed in the Web 2.0 era.

Conclusion

Thus far the actual impact of Web 2.0 on political communication remains to be seen. There are, as we note, some conflicting trends at work, with a proliferation and fragmentation of the public space, countered by persistent trends among users to seek out established voices. Overall, it does seem that the technology at the heart of the new political communication allows the smaller parties and advocacy groups to attract more notice and be heard. Judging by the minor parties' own expressed views, they do

not count themselves as 'losers' in the online communication stakes. While it certainly appears to be true that the 'old faces' are better connected and have a higher level of visibility, the internet gives smaller groups a far cheaper means to reach a possible global audience. Just being out there and on the radar is a 'win' for them. In the 'old' media, this type of unedited, always on, direct, and two-way communication channel to supporters just did not exist.

?   Questions

1. Which disciplines and subfield issues have played a key role in defining political communication?
2. What have been the contributions of these various perspectives to shaping our understanding of political communication?
3. Who are the central actors in political communication?
4. What different phases of media effects has political communication identified?
5. What do we mean when we talk about the Americanization or modernization of political campaigning?
6. How would you describe the shopping model? And the adoption model?
7. What is personal communication? What is mediated communication?
8. What are some of the key traits of the new political communication?
9. How far are new ICTs truly changing the nature of political communication?
10. Which types of political actor are most likely to benefit from using the new media to communicate with the public?

»   Further reading

Bimber, B. (2004) *Information and American Democracy: Technology in the Evolution of Political Power* (Cambridge: Cambridge University Press).

Chadwick, A. (2006) *Internet Politics: States Citizens, and New Communication Technologies* (Oxford: Oxford University Press).

Esser, Frank (ed.) (2004) *Comparing Political Communication* (Cambridge: Cambridge University Press).

Farrell, David, and Schmitt-Beck, Rüdiger (eds.) (2002) *Do Campaigns Matter?* (London: Routledge).

Hallin, Daniel C., and Mancini, Paolo (2004) *Comparing Media Systems* (Cambridge: Cambridge University Press).

Lazarsfeld, P., Berelson B., and Gaudet, H. (1944) *The People's Choice: How the Voter Makes up his Mind in a Presidential Campaign* (New York: Columbia University Press).

McQuail, Denis (2005) *Mass Communication Theory* (London: Sage, 5th edn).

Norris, P. (2000) *A Virtuous Circle: Political Communications in Postindustrial Societies* (Cambridge: Cambridge University Press).

Swanson, David, and Mancini, Paolo (eds.) (1996) *Politics, Media and Modern Democracy. An International Study of Innovations in Electoral Campaigning and their Consequence*s (Westport, Conn.: Praeger).

In addition, students can refer to the following specialized journals: *Harvard International Journal on Press/Politics, European Journal on Communication, Journal of Political Marketing, Journal of Communication, Political Communication,* among others.

Web links

www.wpfc.org
   World Press Freedom Council.
www.indexonline.org
   Index on Censorship.
www.ifj.org
   International Federation of Journalists.

www.freemedia.at
  International Press Institute.

www.pewinternet.org/index.asp
  Pew Internet and American Life Project.

www.governmentontheweb.org
  Government on the Web Project.

www.protest-cultures.uni-siegen.de/engl/index.html
  Changing Protest and Media Cultures.

www.hansardsociety.org.uk/eDemocracy.htm
  UK Hansard Society's E-Democracy Programme.

 Visit the Online Resource Centre that accompanies this book for more information:
www.oxfordtextbooks.co.uk/orc/caramani/

SECTION 5

Public policies

20 Policy-making

Christoph Knill and Jale Tosun

Chapter contents

Reader's guide

The process related to public policy-making touches the core function of democratic politics, namely the elaboration and discussion of solutions to societal problems. This chapter provides an overview of the different stages of policy-making. In doing so, we seek to offer a theoretical entrée to the analysis of policy-making as well as to highlight the determinants of 'real' policy choices. To this end, we combine the illustration of the policy cycle framework with an analysis of some country-specific factors. Further, we discuss the effects of international factors on the design of domestic policies and present empirical findings for the relative importance of both national and international factors.

Introduction

Public policies follow a particular purpose: they are designed to achieve defined goals and present solutions to societal problems. More precisely, policies are government statements of what it intends to do or not to do, including law, regulation, ruling, decision, or order (Birkland 2001: 132). Public policy, on the other hand, is a more specific term, which refers to a long series of actions carried out to solve societal problems (Newton and van Deth 2005: 263). Hence, (public) policies can be conceived of as the main output of political systems (see Figure I.1 in the Introduction to this volume). But how are these policies actually made? Does policy-making differ across policy fields or countries?

The classic policy analysis literature approaches these questions by using policy typologies as 'analytical shortcuts' for the underlying processes. The most influential approach to this has been the typology developed by Lowi (1964), who distinguishes between (1) **distributive policies** (measures concerning the distribution of new resources), (2) **redistributive policies** (measures that modify the distribution of existing resources), and (3) **regulatory policies** (measures that specify conditions and constraints for individual or collective behaviour, for instance, standards for car exhaust emissions or requirements applicants have to fulfil to obtain an authorization to trade goods or offer specific services on the national or international market).

Another widely used concept is James Q. Wilson's (1973, 1989, 1995) typology in which costs and benefits related to a policy are either widely distributed or narrowly concentrated. Each of the four possible combinations yields different implications for policy-making. When both costs and benefits of a certain policy are widely distributed, a government may encounter no or only minor opposition, indicating majoritarian politics as the likely outcome. When both costs and benefits of a certain policy are concentrated, a government may be confronted with opposition of rival interest groups, which signals interest-group politics (i.e. political processes are dominated by the lobbying activities and strategic interaction of the involved interest groups). If costs are concentrated and benefits diffused, a government may encounter opposition from dominant interest groups. In this case, entrepreneurial politics are the probable outcome. This implies that policy change requires the presence of political entrepreneurs who are willing to develop and put through political proposals despite strong societal resistance. When costs are diffuse and benefits concentrated, a government is likely to face a relevant interest group favourable to its endeavour, which makes clientelistic politics the likely outcome.

There exist, in fact, many other ways of classifying public policies, which also make implicit assumptions about the corresponding policy-making process (Anderson 2003: 5–13). Another related concept is the analysis of **policy instruments**, which links instrument choice—i.e. the selection among voluntary, compulsory, or mixed instruments—to the likelihood of resistance to a particular policy (Howlett and Ramesh 2003: 195).

Opposition or consent to policy by the addressees of the same policy is of course an essential question of general interest. Nonetheless, there is more analytical leverage to the analysis of public policies by focusing more explicitly on the political processes, since this perspective enables us to gain a fuller understanding of their causes and consequences. This politics perspective involves scrutinizing the roles of the executive and legislative branches of government, whose relationship is at the heart of policy-making. But it also implies theories of decision-making and the exploration of public policy structures for understanding how social and economic interests also shape the content of policies. Thus, studying policy-making in terms of comparative politics can enhance our scientific understanding, as it gives us powerful tools for scrutinizing both the determinants and impacts of policy decisions (see Chapter 22). It grants us the possibility of analysing the effects of new developments, such as globalization or 'internationalization', on policy arrangements. Further, this theoretical approach to policy-making may be used for solving real-world policy problems, and hence improving the overall quality of public policies.

BOX 20.1 Types of policies

Lowi's typology (1964)

Type of policy	Definition	Examples
Regulatory policies	Policies specifying conditions and constraints for individual or collective behaviour	Environmental protection; migration policy; consumer protection
Distributive policies	Policies distributing new resources	Agriculture; social issues; public works; subsidies; taxes
Redistributive policies	Policies modifying the distribution of existing resources	Land reform; progressive taxation; welfare policy in more general terms

Wilson's typology (1973, 1989, 1995)

Costs	Benefits	
	Concentrated	Diffuse
Concentrated	Interest group politics ('zero sum game')	Entrepreneurial politics
Diffuse	Client politics ('iron triangles')	Majoritarian politics

KEY POINTS

❑ Public policies are the outputs of the political system; they come along in different forms, including laws, regulations, or rules.

❑ The policy analysis literature relies on policy typologies and distinction between policy instruments as 'analytical shortcuts' for the underlying policy-making process.

❑ By studying the policy-making process from a comparative politics perspective, we gain a fuller understanding of the causes and consequences of policy decisions.

Conceptual models of policy-making

What would an ideal policy look like? What is the best policy design that can be achieved? Both questions are crucial to policy-making. The first one refers to the functionality of a policy to be made, i.e. which design a particular policy should have in order to meet an *ex ante* defined goal. The second one touches upon the constraints that appear when policies are actually made, which are principally given by politics, i.e. the process by which the actors involved make decisions. Therefore, it is essential for our purpose to examine how politics shapes public policies.

There are a number of conceptual models that help to clarify our understanding of the relationship between politics and public policies. The major models that can be found in the literature are (1) the institutional model, (2) the rational model, (3) the incremental model, (4) the group model, (5) the elite model, and (6) the process model. These models are not competitive but rather complementary as they focus on different aspects of political life, and hence help us to understand separate characteristics of public policies (Dye 2005: 12).

The main implication of these models is that they make different assumptions about the importance of the actors involved—institutions, politicians, bureaucrats, interest groups, and the public—and their rationality. If we conceive of policy-makers as entirely rational actors that search for maximizing solutions to policy problems, our analytical focus would rather be on the quality of available information, decision procedures, etc. If we, however, model policy-makers as imperfectly rational actors, the research interest should rather shift to the role of other aspects, such as mechanisms of finding compromises. We now shortly explain these models—except the process model, which we address in the next section—to provide an initial theoretical access to policy-making.

Institutional model

For a long time, the central interest of political science was on how institutional arrangements influence the content of public policies. The institutional model conceives of policies as institutional outputs. The focus of analysis is primarily on the balance between executives and legislatives, which show notable variation across political systems. In this context, the United Kingdom is generally perceived to have a dominant executive, whereas Denmark and Switzerland are generally regarded as balanced systems (Newton and van Deth 2005: 106). From the institutional perspective, public policies are formulated and implemented exclusively by these institutions. Hence, policy-making should be a smooth and largely technical process, which merely involves executives and legislatives. All the intra-institutional processes, however, remain a 'black box'.

Rational model

First developed in the field of economic analysis, the rational model of decision-making formulates guidance on how to secure 'optimal' policy decisions, which means that a decision is rational if no other alternative is better, according to the decision-makers'

preferences (Shepsle and Bonchek 1997: 25). To select a rational policy, a policy-maker should:

- Define a set of societal problems that are independent from other problems.
- Formulate goals that guide the decision-makers.
- Examine all feasible alternatives.
- Investigate all alternatives in terms of their outcomes, and the costs and benefits.
- Compare all alternatives with the other alternatives.
- Make the best choice among the alternatives so that optimal outcome can be achieved (Anderson 2003: 121).

The rational model is also associated with a particular mode of learning, namely Bayesian learning. According to this perspective, governments update their beliefs on the consequences of policies with all available information about policy outcomes in the past and elsewhere and choose the policy that is expected to yield the best results (Meseguer Yebra 2003, 2006: 39). Rational policy-making involves a number of demanding assumptions, for example, policy-makers are expected to have perfect information, which has provoked strong criticism (Simon 1955). Nonetheless it remains important for analytical purposes as it helps to contrast ideal policy decisions with actual ones.

By assuming that all political actors behave rationally, i.e. reduce costs and maximize benefits, the rational model also provides the starting point for public choice approaches to policy-making. Public choice theory examines the logic and foundation of actions of individuals and groups that are involved in the policy-making process. In this regard, the main objects of analysis are voting behaviour and party competition, coalition and government formation, the involvement of interest groups and bureaucracy in policy-making (e.g. Buchanan and Tullock 1962; Dunleavy 1991; Laver and Hunt 1992; Müller 2003).

Moreover, game theory, which is also related to the rational model, serves to analyse decisions in situations in which two or more rational players interact, and where the outcome depends on the choices made by each (Munck 2001). The most widely used games for analysing strategic situations are the 'prisoner's dilemma' and the 'chicken game'. In both games, the mutual solution is unstable since both players individually tend to stray from it (Axelrod 1984; Rapoport and Chammah 1966).

Incremental model

Incrementalism emerged as a response to the rational model. Rather than an ideal, it purports to be a realistic description of how policy-makers arrive at their decisions (Lindblom 1959, 1977; Wildavsky 1964). This is related to its foundation on 'bounded rationality', i.e. an alternative concept to rational choice that takes into account the limitations of both knowledge and cognitive capacity of decision-makers. Incremental decisions involve limited changes to existing policies (Anderson 2003: 123).

Similar to rational learning, there is also a concept of bounded learning. In that case, governments likewise engage in information-gathering activity but do not scan all available experience and instead use analytical shortcuts and cognitive heuristics to process the information (Meseguer Yebra 2003, 2006; Weyland 2004). An example of such heuristics is the adoption of policies from countries that are considered to be particularly successful or the emulation of policies that have already been adopted by a large number of other states.

The Achilles heel of the incremental model is that it does not explain how decision-makers arrive at these incremental adjustments. In response to this central shortcoming, Jones and Baumgartner (2005) propose a model of choice that combines incrementalism and punctuated equilibrium theory, which states that political processes are generally characterized by stability and incrementalism, but occasionally produce large-scale departures from the past. In fact, this explanatory model performs well for explaining the development of the US budget.

Group model

Group theory hypothesizes that policies are the result of an equilibrium reached in group struggle, which is determined by the relative strength of each interest group (Truman 1951; Latham 1965). Groups can be distinguished concerning several aspects, such as income, membership size, membership density and recruitment, organizational aspects, whether they are united, e.g. by 'umbrella institutions', divided, whether they use sanctioning mechanisms, and aspects of leadership (Newton and van Deth 2005: 170). Accordingly, changes in the relative strength of the single interest groups involved may trigger policy changes. Group theory presupposes that policy-makers are constantly responding to group pressures, which motivates politicians to form majority coalitions for which they have the competence to define what groups are to be included (Dye 2005: 21).

More importantly, the potential effect of groups for policy-making depends on particular structures. Generally, in (neo-)corporatist systems, for instance, economic interests are strongly integrated in policy-making (Schmitter and Lehmbruch 1979). The pluralist model regards politics as a market place with more or less perfect competition, where individuals, political parties, and interest groups compete for influence over policy domains. It assumes equal access to the policy-making arena, fragmentation of the market place, a competitive process for determining policies, and the neutrality of government (Thomas 1993).

Elite model

Related to group theory is the view that policy-making is determined by the preferences of governing elites (Mills 1956). The elite model is narrower in a sense as it claims that the electorate is generally poorly informed about public policies and that the elites shape the public opinion on policy questions. It mainly highlights the potential source of bias in policy-making in terms of the adoption of policy alternatives that rather correspond to the preferences of the elite than of the general public. This view, however, contradicts the popular median voter theorem, which conveys that—under the condition that simple majority rule is used—opinion held by the median voter will become the policy decision (Black 1948; Downs 1957).

KEY POINTS

❑ The literature of political science offers a number of conceptual models of policy-making, which enhance our understanding of policies and politics.

❑ The models can be separated in terms of their model of policy-makers as either fully or partially rational actors.

❑ Further, the models differ concerning their focus on the relevance of political institutions and societal groups.

Analysing policy-making as a process: the policy cycle

What are the main characteristics of policy-making? Basically, three features can be identified. First, policy-making occurs in presence of **multiple constraints**, e.g. shortage of time and resources, public opinion, and of course the constitution. Secondly, policy-making involves the existence of **various policy processes**. Governments are not unitary actors but consist of different departments that overlap and compete with each other. Thirdly, these policy processes form an **infinite cycle of decisions and policies**. Current policy decisions are not independent of decisions taken before, and policies under discussion today may have 'knock-on effects' leading to further policies tomorrow (Newton and van Deth 2005: 265–6).

Given this nature of policy-making, it is convenient to conceive of policy-making as a process model, which is also often labelled **policy cycle**. It models the policy process as a series of political activities, consisting of (1) agenda setting, (2) policy formulation, (3) policy adoption, (4) implementation, and (5) evaluation. Each policy cycle begins with the identification of a societal problem and its placement on the policy agenda. Subsequently, policy proposals are formulated, from which one will be adopted. In the next stage, the adopted policy is taken to action. Finally, the impacts of the policy are evaluated. This last stage leads straight back to the first, indicating that the policy cycle is continuous and unending. This sequential model of the policy cycle represents a simplification. In the real world different political actors and institutions may be involved in different processes at the same time. Yet the policy cycle provides a useful heuristic for breaking policy-making into different units to illustrate how policies are actually made.

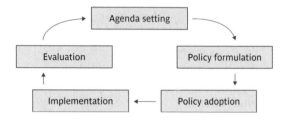

Fig. 20.1 The policy cycle

Agenda setting

The first stage in policy-making refers to the identification of a public problem, which requires the state to intervene. In fact, there are many problems, but only a small number will be given official attention by legislators and executives. Those public problems that are chosen by the decision-makers constitute the policy agenda. In this context, Cobb and Elder (1972: 85–6) distinguish between the systemic agenda and the institutional agenda. The systemic agenda refers to all societal problems that demand public attention, hence forming the 'discussion agenda'. The institutional agenda, by contrast, contains a set of problems that are up for the serious consideration of decision-makers. Thus, the institutional agenda is the 'action agenda', which is more specific and concrete than the systemic agenda. Setting the agenda is an important source of power as it is policy consequential, i.e. legislative institutions grant an advantage to the first movers as compared to the second movers (Shepsle and Weingast 1987).

The factors determining whether an issue reaches the agenda may be cultural, political, social, economic, or ideological. In this respect, Schattschneider (1960) argued that disadvantaged groups need to expand the 'scope of conflict' if they want to gain access to the agenda. A notable advance was contributed by Bachrach and Baratz (1962), who studied decision-making with particular emphasis on what was excluded from the agenda, i.e. 'non-decisions'.

However, none of these **univariate** models generated testable hypotheses, which triggered the development of multivariate **models** (Howlett and Ramesh 2003: 131). These approaches include, for instance, the **funnel of causality model** (King 1973), which integrates several variables into a unified framework. A major theoretical achievement is based on the three policy initiation models formulated by Cobb *et al.* (1976):

1. The **outside-initiative model** refers to a situation where citizen groups gain broad public support and get an issue onto the formal agenda.

2. The **mobilization model** describes a situation in which initiatives of government need to be placed on the public agenda for successful implementation.

3. In the **inside-initiation model**, influential groups with access to decision-makers present policy proposals, which are broadly supported by particular interest groups but only marginally by the public.

According to Kingdon (1995: 19), agenda setting can be regarded as 'three process streams flowing through the system—streams of problems, policies, and politics. They are largely independent of one another, and each develops according to its own dynamics and rules. But at some critical junctures the three streams are joined, and the greatest policy changes grow out of that coupling of problems, policies, and solutions.'

The result of the convergence of the three streams is the opening of a 'policy window', which allows advocates of a certain issue to put it on the policy agenda. Similar to the **garbage can model** (Cohen *et al.* 1972), Kingdon's conception of agenda setting emphasizes the relevance of chance, and therefore qualifies the notion about the rationality of agenda setting.

Baumgartner and Jones (1991, 1993, 1994) modified Kingdon's model by extending it to the notion of 'policy monopolies', in which particular subsystems control the interpretation of a problem. These subsystems comprise both governmental and societal actors. The members of specific subsystems seek to change policy images in order to weaken the stability of existing policy arrangements. In doing so, the subsystem members can either publicize a problem and encourage the public to demand its resolution by government ('Downsian strategy'), or they can modify the institutional arrangements within which the subsystem operates ('Schattschneider strategy') (Howlett and Ramesh 2003: 139).

In most cases, the policy agenda is set by four types of **actors**: (1) public officials, (2) the bureaucracy, (3) the mass media, and (4) the interest groups (Gerston 2004: 52). Elected public officials, e.g. the president, the parliament, the ministries and courts, are the most obvious agenda builders since their position enables them not only to make policies, but also to place certain issues on the agenda. However, actual agenda setting is related to the larger political game in terms of power and the intensity of ideological conflict both within and between the (coalition) government and parliament. In this context, it must be highlighted that there is a high degree of variation of rules and practices of agenda building in Western European parliaments (Döring 1995: 224; 2001).

In the literature there is a virtual consensus that bureaucracies have an impact on policy-making at both the planning and implementation stage (Hammond 1986). However, recent studies have shown that bureaucrats also have the ability to affect the organization of the political agenda. In this context, Schnapp (2000) demonstrates that bureaucracies can stand in as effective agenda setters under clearly identified circumstances, i.e. if no political actors put forward a proposal on a certain problem, and therefore chances exist for the bureaucracy to increase its utility by advancing a policy proposal, and if the minister is willing to sponsor the bureaucratic proposal into the political process of decision-making.

Agenda setting is also frequently associated with the role of mass media (McCombs and Shaw 1972; McCombs 2004). However, not all media topics are placed on the policy agenda, which highlights that a public discussion of a more or less relevant societal problem must not necessarily become a political problem.

This leads us to the fourth source of agenda-setting power: the interest groups. Agenda-setting theory generally requires advocates to expand interest in a particular issue or policy (Cobb and Elder 1983: 105–8). That interest groups place issues on the public agenda seems to be indisputable, yet the question emerges whether and to what extent their interests are compatible with public needs. Most importantly, the success of various interest groups depends on those in positions of power.

Over the years, research on agenda setting has become increasingly sophisticated. More recent works cover a wide range of new research questions. Various scholars ask how representation affects agenda setting (Jones and Baumgartner 2004; Penner *et al.* 2006). Another aspect is about the role of political parties for agenda setting (John 2006; Walgrave *et al.* 2006; Green-Pedersen 2007). A further fashionable perspective on agenda setting scrutinizes the effects of experts and the scientific community (Pralle 2006; Timmermans and Scholten 2006).

Policy formulation

The second stage in the policy cycle—policy formulation—involves the definition, discussion, acceptance, or rejection of feasible courses of action for coping with policy problems. Generally, policy formulation is strongly related to policy adoption—the subsequent stage here—and in fact a clear-cut distinction between them is often impossible. However, we decided to present them separately since they do refer to different stages. Policy formulation deals with the **elaboration of alternatives of action**, whereas policy adoption refers to the formal adoption to take on a policy.

Hence, policy formulation implies the definition of policy objectives and the selection of the most appropriate policy instruments, as well as their settings (Hall 1993). It takes place within the broader context of technical and political constraints of state action. The political constraints can be either substantive or procedural. Substantive constraints refer to the nature of the problem, while procedural constraints are about procedures involved in adopting a policy. These procedural constraints are related to as both institutional and tactical constraints (Howlett and Ramesh 2003: 147–8).

Policy formulation generally involves a number of actors. But basically policy formulation brings the relationship between executives and legislatures to the forefront. There are in fact good reasons to believe that there is a dominance of executives over legislatures and parties. Executives can rely on more

---

> **BOX 20.2** Formulating policy
>
> **Thomas R. Dye (2005: 42)**
>
> Policy formulation occurs in government bureaucracies; interest group offices; legislative committee rooms, meetings of special commissions; and policy-planning organizations otherwise known as 'think tanks'. The details of policy proposals are usually formulated by staff members rather than their bosses, but staffs are guided by what they know their leaders want.

---

resources than parties and their representatives in the legislature. Especially with regard to deepening European integration, it is expected that the weight of executives in relation to parliaments will increase (cf. Fabbrini and Donà 2003). Conversely, the dominance of the executive in national political systems paved the way for the success of European integration.

With their comparative analysis of legislative activity in Belgium, France, Germany, and the United Kingdom between 1986 and 2003, Bräuninger and Debus (2007) show that the legislature is also still highly involved in policy formulation. These findings suggest that the influence of the opposition and of parliaments in particular is at least not as insignificant as is often argued.

Earlier studies (Dogan 1975) emphasized the role of ministerial bureaucracy and top civil servants in policy formulation. However, policy formulation can rather be conceived as a more or less informal process of negotiation between ministerial departments and interest groups (Jann and Wegrich 2006). Interest groups play a major role in policy formulation as they often work with executive and legislative officials to develop a policy draft. Interest groups may play a big part in formulating legislation about complex and technical issues, and when government institutions lack time and staff to cope with such matters (Anderson 2003: 105–7). This is, for instance, the case with the European Commission, which has developed sets of informal and formal rules that emphasize the key role that consultation with interest groups plays in European policy-making (Mazey and Richardson 2001). This illustrates the relevance of bargaining among different actors for policy formulation.

Table 20.1 Legislative bills by initiator and country

Country	Government	Government parties	Opposition parties	Government and opposition parties	Total
Belgium	1,010	1,700	2,089	297	5,096
	(19.8%)	(33.4%)	(41.0%)	(5.8%)	(100%)
	[90.9%]	[8.7%]	[4.2%]	[36.7%]	
France	1,444	1,867	2,421	14	5,746
	(25.1%)	(32.5%)	(42.1%)	(0.2%)	(100%)
	[67.9%]	[5.7%]	[0.9%]	[7.1%]	
Germany	1,573	426	658	110	2,767
	(56.9%)	(15.4%)	(23.8%)	(4.0%)	(100%)
	[90.2%]	[79.6%]	[2.0%]	[84.6%]	
UK	519	705	785	16	2,025
	(25.6%)	(34.8%)	(38.8%)	(0.8%)	(100%)
	[95.0%]	[12.6%]	[4.2%]	[93.8%]	

Notes: $N = 15,634$. Figures are numbers of bills introduced by government or (groups of) MPs of lower chamber of parliament. Share of bills by initiator in parentheses; share of successful bills in brackets.
Source: Bräuninger and Debus (2007).

Another aspect of policy formulation refers to the impact of policy advice and scientific knowledge (Martin and Richards 1995). In this regard, it is an interesting research question how this division of tasks between policy-makers and advisory organs affects policy outcomes, which might be modelled in game theoretical terms. In this context, the role of 'think-tanks' also started to attract considerable attention. Their functioning is related to ideas about policy networks, epistemic communities, and policy learning (Marin and Mayntz 1991; Haas 1992; Meseguer Yebra 2003, 2006). To influence policies, think-tanks can only rely on the generation of ideas about policy problems. Thus, in contrast to interest groups that also offer resources, think-tanks operate by using communication (Stone 2005).

Policy adoption

In contrast to preliminary stages of decision-making, the final adoption of a particular policy alternative is determined by government institutions. The adoption of a policy option is determined by a number of factors. Of these, two sets of factors are of major relevance. First of all, the set of feasible policies can be reduced by the necessity to build majorities for the approval of a policy option, which implies considerations about values, party affiliation, constituency interests, public opinion, deference, and decision rules (Anderson 2003: 126).

Party loyalty is an important decision-making criterion for most members of parliament (Bowler *et al.* 1999; Benedetto and Hix 2007 for qualifications). Therefore, party affiliation is an important indicator for the likelihood of a member of parliament to approve a policy draft. Nevertheless, we must keep in mind that commonly there is a considerable variation in the cohesion of parties within national parliaments (e.g. Janda 1980). According to a comparative study by Bräuninger and Debus (2007), a small but significant share of law proposals are initiated by bipartisan or even opposition parties and adopted by a parliamentary majority (Table 20.1). This finding somewhat contradicts the branch of research that argues that the government is the sole and decisive actor in policy-making (see e.g. Döring 1995, 2001; Döring and Hallerberg 2004).

Another important decision criterion is given by the expected costs and benefits of a policy proposal for the constituency. In this context, Weingast *et al.* (1981) show in the case of distributive politics, a strong reliance on a re-election constituency may imply larger projects and programmes than are economically efficient. Generally, a member of parliament is expected to adopt a policy option, if the benefits for the constituency prevail. Further, considerations about the public opinion also affect policy choices as well as decision rules, values, and perception of deference. Generally, however, policy adoption should be dominated by bargaining and compromise, and, therefore, the most plausible decision-making theory appears to be incrementalism rather than rational models (Hayes 2001).

The second set of factors refers to the allocation of competencies between the actors involved in policy-making. Cross-national research concludes that the type of state organization, whether federal or unitary, affects the success, speed, and nature of governmental policy-making.

In analysing this aspect of the policy-making process, Tsebelis's (1995, 2000, 2002) concept of 'veto players' is particularly useful. In presidential systems, 'divided government' can impede decision-making as there are generally insufficient incentives for political parties to cooperate and build policy-making coalitions (see also Chapter 8). But other states are also prone to this kind of constraint. Germany's bicameral legislature limits governmental policy-making to the consent of a set of veto players (Tsebelis and Money 1997). In this context, Bräuninger and König (1999) show that German governmental potential for policy change is determined by the formal rules of bicameralism as well as domain-specific distribution of legislators' party-orientated policy positions.

Implementation

Implementation represents the conversion of new laws and programmes into practice. Without proper implementation, policy has neither substance nor significance. Thus, policy success depends on how well bureaucratic structures implement government decisions. At the first glance, implementation appears

as an automatic continuation of the policy-making process. Nevertheless, there often exists a substantial gap between the passage of new legislation and its application, which reveals that the relationship between decision-making and implementation is tenuous at best (Pressman and Wildavsky 1973; Hill and Hupe 2005).

Consequently, it is the explicit objective of implementation research to open the 'black box' between policy formation and policy outcomes. To this end, various theoretical approaches were elaborated to the study of implementation, which Pülzl and Treib (2006) divide into three categories (also Hill and Hupe 2005: 41–84):

- Top-down models (Pressman and Wildavsky 1973; Bardach 1977; Mazmanian and Sabatier 1983) primarily emphasize the ability of policy-makers to produce unequivocal policy objectives and control the implementation process.

- Bottom-up models (Lipsky 1971, 1980) regard local bureaucrats as the central actors in policy delivery and view implementation as negotiation processes within networks.

- Hybrid models (Mayntz 1977; Windhoff-Héritier 1980) integrate elements of both previously mentioned models and other theoretical models.

For successful implementation, there must be an entity with sufficient resources, which is able to translate the policy objectives into an operational framework and that is accountable for its actions (Gerston 2004: 98). Often bureaucracies emerge as principal actors during implementation. In his study of the US bureaucracy, Meier (2000) finds implementation depends on the policy type, i.e. whether it is regulatory, distributive, or redistributive in nature (Lowi 1972). Hence, when implementing regulatory policies, most agencies are responsive to the communities over which they preside, while distributive policies are implemented with some bureaucratic discretion, with congressional subcommittees and organized interest groups exercising continuous oversight. In the area of redistributive policy, however, little discretion is left to bureaucracy since Congress puts in a lot of effort when designing these policies. In conclusion, the very design of a policy seems to be of relevance for implementation success.

Related to the policy types is the choice of policy instruments used in legislation. According to Mayntz (1979) different policy instruments are vulnerable to specific kinds of implementation problems. This finding stimulated a notable body of literature on the effects of policy instruments for reducing the 'implementation deficit' of European Union policies (Knill 2006).

But it is not only the policy design and the instrument choice that determines the likelihood of proper implementation. In federal systems, for instance, implementation efforts may move between the levels of government as well as within levels of government (Gerston 2004: 103). If implementation is a matter of horizontal implementation, in which a national legal act must be applied solely by an agency in the executive branch, the number of actors remains low and implementation can be attained smoothly. But if vertical implementation is concerned, implying that various segments of the national government must interact with different levels at the sub-national level, the undertaking may become challenging.

The relevance of bureaucracy during the implementation phase reveals a contradictory picture of great interest. On the one hand, bureaucracies are essential for making policies work. On the other hand, senior bureaucrats are often more experienced and better trained than their political masters (Newton and van Deth 2005: 118), which paves the way for 'bureaucratic drift'. This term describes the phenomenon that policy will drift towards the liking of bureaucracy and away from what was originally intended by legislation. The threat of a bureaucratic drift is mainly found in cases of coalition government where the drift might be to the ideal position of one of the coalition partners without this being suspected (Hammond and Knott 1996). Sometimes, this discrepancy between intended and actual results is also referred to as 'agency problems', originating from the principal–agent theory (Grossman and Hart 1983).

In this context, Schnapp (2001) reveals that bureaucratic drift is likely in countries with coalition governments that have a high number of coalition parties, namely Finland, Switzerland, Belgium, and Japan. By contrast, it seems unlikely in Spain, Canada, New Zealand, Greece, and the United Kingdom since their governments are composed of one party only. A number of instruments were introduced to control bureaucrats: politicians can appoint their own political advisers; bureaucrats are trained in a public service ethos; scrutiny and auditing schemes were introduced as well as 'open government' and ombudsmen (Newton and van Deth 2005: 130).

Evaluation

After a policy is passed by the legislature and implemented by the bureaucracy, it becomes a subject of evaluation. The main question at this stage is whether the output of the decision-making process—a given public policy—has attained the intended goals. Evaluation is often a formal component of policy-making and is generally carried out by experts who have some knowledge about the processes and objectives pertaining to the issue undergoing review (Gerston 2004: 124).

Evaluation can be carried out in different ways. In this context, Munger (2000: 20) differentiates between (1) purely **formal** evaluations (monitoring routine tasks), (2) **client satisfaction** evaluation (performance of primary functions), (3) **outcome** evaluation (satisfaction of a list of measurable intended outcomes), (4) **cost–benefit** evaluation (comparison of costs and impacts of a policy), and (5) evaluation of **long-term consequences** (impact on the core societal problem, rather than symptoms alone). In more general terms, policies should be evaluated for their efficiency (using the least resources to the maximum effect) and effectiveness (achievement of the intended goals).

Policy evaluation provides a feedback loop, which enables decision-makers to draw lessons from each particular policy in operation. This feedback loop identifies new problems and sets in motion the policy-making process once again, creating an endless policy cycle. This turns policy evaluation into a powerful tool of the policy-making process: it possesses the potential to reframe an issue once thought to be resolved by policy-makers, but as we will see it can also lead to the termination of public policies. In this respect, policy evaluations can pave the way for policy learning and evidence-based policy-making (Sanderson 2002).

The systematic evaluation of a policy—or more specifically of a programme—comprises five areas, namely (1) the need for a particular programme, (2) the programme's design, (3) its implementation, (4) its impact or outcomes, and (5) its efficiency

(Rossi *et al.* 2004: 18). These domains are mainly dealt with in scientific evaluation. Administrative evaluations are conducted or initiated by the public administration and political evaluation is carried out by diverse actors in the political arena, including the public and the media (Howlett and Ramesh 2003: 210–16). Most government agencies make some effort to evaluate their own policies and programmes. The most common type of evaluation is based on hearings and reports. Another common approach is given by the analysis of citizens' complaints. Occasionally teams of high-ranking administrators or consultants visit sites and collect impressionistic data about how policies are carried out, or government agencies themselves gather data on policy output measures. And in some policy fields, governmental entities evaluate the performance of certain policies by comparing them with professional standards. However, most policy evaluations are unsystematic and do not satisfy minimal requirements formulated by scientific evaluation research, before and after comparisons (Dye 2005: 335–39). The need for systematic policy evaluation is expected to grow since contemporary concern over the allocation of scarce recourses makes it essential to evaluate the effectiveness of policy interventions.

In practice, policy evaluation presents numerous challenges to the evaluators. Citizens and governments alike tend to interpret the actual effects of a policy so as to serve their own intentions. Often governments avoid the precise definition of policy objectives because otherwise politicians would risk taking the blame for obvious failure (Jann and Wegrich 2006). Further, public policy decisions cannot be limited to intended effects only. In fact, they are often characterized by a number of unintended effects (Newton and van Deth 2005: 272–3). However, evaluators can be confronted with more general problems: 'Program circumstances and activities may change during the course of an evaluation, an appropriate balance must be found between scientific and pragmatic considerations in the evaluation design, and the wide diversity of perspectives and approaches in the evaluation field provide little firm guidance about how best to proceed with an evaluation' (Rossi *et al.* 2004: 29).

The results of the evaluation procedure can also lead to the termination of a certain policy. In theoretical terms, policy termination should be likely when a policy problem has been solved, or if evaluation studies reveal the dysfunctionality of a policy. Nonetheless, the empirical findings show that, once a policy is institutionalized within a government, it is hard to terminate it (Bardach 1976; Jann and Wegrich 2006). This immortality of public policies stems from various sources. The most rampant view—which is analogous to Wilson's (1973, 1980) policy typology—is that inefficient programmes continue because their benefits are concentrated in a small, well-organized constituency, while their greater costs are dispersed over a large, unorganized group. Moreover, legislative and bureaucratic interests may impede termination. This is also related to the concept of incrementalism, which implies that attention to proposed changes focuses on parts of existing policies and not on their entirety (Dye 2005: 344–45). Further reasons are cognitive aversion, institutional longevity, dynamic conservatism, anti-termination coalitions, legal obstacles, and high costs of initiation (Biller 1976; deLeon 1978). Thus, termination should become more likely if a government experiences some kind of shock, justifying drastic measures, such as economic crises (Geva-May 2004).

Studies of policy termination are therefore frequently concerned with the question why policies and programmes continue to exist (Jann and Wegrich 2006). The systematic explanation for the persistence of policies in light of their obvious inefficiency is a further challenge and could substantially complement the revised policy termination approach—in particular by means of systematically integrating non-termination phenomena in the face of the suboptimal provision of services (Bauer 2006). Overall, the analysis of policy termination needs further theoretical and empirical substantiation.

KEY POINTS

- In analytical terms, it is helpful to view policy-making as a series of political activities encompassing agenda setting, policy formulation, policy adoption, implementation, and evaluation.
- The number of actors involved decreases when we move from agenda setting to implementation.
- Evaluation is a rather formal component of policy-making and often carried out by experts.
- The concept of policy termination yields some interesting implications; however, this aspect is both theoretically and empirically still underdeveloped.

COUNTRY PROFILE Russia

Russian Federation (*Rossiyskaya Federatsiya*)

State formation

Independence 24 August 1991 (from Soviet Union). *Constitution* 1993.

Form of government

Federation.
Head of state President; term of 4 years (renewable once). There is no vice president; the Prime Minister serves as acting president until a new presidential election is held.
Head of government Prime Minister appointed by the President with the approval of the Duma.
Cabinet Appointed by the President.
Administrative subdivisions 48 oblasts, 21 republics, 7 autonomous okrugs, 7 krays, 2 federal cities, and 1 autonomous oblast.

Legal system

Based on civil law system; judicial review of legislative acts.

Legislature

Bicameral Federal Assembly (*Federalnoye Sobraniye*).

Lower house State Duma (*Gosudarstvennaya Duma*): 450 seats; term of 4 years.
Upper house Federation Council (*Soviet Federatsii*): 178 seats (members appointed by the top officials in each of the 88 federal administrative units); term of 4 years.

Electoral system (lower house)

Mixed system of plurality vote and PR (until December 2007 elections).
Formula 225 seats allocated by plurality in single-member constituencies, 225 seats allocated by PR. From 2007, all seats are to be elected by PR.
Constituencies 225 single-member constituencies and 1 multi-member constituency; from 2007, one multi-member constituency.
Barrier clause 5% nation-wide; from 2007, 7%. A 25% voter turnout is required to validate the poll.
Suffrage Universal, 18 years.

Direct democracy

The constitution provides the possibility for the President to call an extraordinary referendum under procedures established by federal constitutional law.

Party system Results of the 2003 legislative elections (State Duma):

Electorate:	108,404,870	100.0%
Voters:	59,297,970	54.7%

Party	Valid votes	%	Seats
United Russia	22,529,459	38.0	221
Communist Party	7,622,568	12.9	51
Liberal Democratic Party	6,923,444	11.7	37
Homeland Union	5,443,053	9.2	37
Russian Democratic Party (Yabloko)	2,601,549	4.4	4
Union of Right Forces	2,390,868	4.0	3
Agrarian Party of Russia	2,201,806	3.7	3
Russian Pensioners' Party	1,869,729	3.2	1
Rebirth of Russia	1,137,193	1.9	3
People's Party of the Russian Federation	707,434	1.2	16
Others	5,870,867	9.9	74
Total	59,297,970	100.0	450

Notes: Category 'Others' includes parties with less than 1% nation-wide and no seats. Seat figures include both 225 district seats (including 74 that were won by non-partisan candidates) and the 225 list seats.
Source: Russian Election Commission.

The importance of institutions, framing, and policy styles

While we scrutinized rather generally the different stages of policy-making in the first section, we now refine our analytical focus and examine how certain structures in different countries can impact policy decisions. This perspective adopts a comparative perspective on the analysis of the policy-making process. We concentrate on institutions, cognitive and normative determinants, and national policy styles (Jamison and Baark 1999).

The role of institutions

In a broader sense, we can interpret policy-making as a strategy for resolving societal problems by using institutions. At the same time, however, it is also a process for modifying those same institutions in order to meet these goals. Generally, policy institutions serve to reduce complexities inherent to the policy-making process (Simon 1957; March and Olsen 1984; Luhmann 1985). They shape the behaviour of actors and the use of policy instruments (Weaver and Rockman 1993b). From a rationalist perspective, institutions can structure the interaction and avoid the suboptimal solutions they are given by the prisoner's dilemma. From a sociological point of view, institutions can support cooperation through the provision of moral or cognitive templates (Hall and Taylor 1996).

Hence, the relationship between public policy and institutions is a close one, since policy does not become a public policy until it is adopted, implemented, and enforced by government institutions. Institutions lend legitimacy, universality, and coercion to policies (Dye 2005: 12). The core institutions in democracies and semi-democracies—elections, executives, and legislatures—are important for framing the entire policy-making apparatus. 'These core institutions provide the method by which rulers and those being ruled accept some understood rules of the game and then seek to employ these rules to make policy' (Considine 2005: 105).

As policy interventions in democratic systems originate in electoral systems, it is the most essential formal institution when scrutinizing policy-making. Electoral competition is largely party competition, which turns political parties into important actors (see Chapter 13). One of their main functions is to structure and articulate public opinion. Most frequently, political parties are described by a left–right dichotomy, implying that they have diametrically opposed policy preferences. In fact various studies—based on expert judgements as well as content analysis of party manifestoes—found a level of consistency with this dichotomy (Laver and Hunt 1992; Budge and Klingemann 2001; Laver *et al.* 2003; Debus 2007).

Strongly related to this is the relevance of the voting systems, of which we can distinguish between three main types:

- **Plurality-majority systems**, in which the elected candidates get more votes than any other (e.g. United Kingdom).
- **Proportional representation**, in which seats are allocates according to a formula that seeks to ensure proportionality (e.g. Germany).
- **Mixed systems** that combine plurality-majority with proportional representation aspects (e.g. Japan).

Each system has strengths and weaknesses (see Chapters 5, 10, and 13 for further discussions of these models). While the proportional system ensures the representation of all societal groups, including small parties, plurality-majority systems are usually associated with stable and effective governments. These aspects have strong repercussions on the quality of policy-making.

The relationship between legislative and executive is also of crucial importance for policy-making. In parliamentary models, the executive is a group of ministers elected from the very parliament, while in pure presidential systems, the two branches of government are separate. In this context, Lijphart (1999) claims that, despite strong variations among countries, democratic systems tend to fall into two categories: majoritarian and consensus democracies. The majoritarian system—which is generally associated with the United Kingdom, and hence is also known as the 'Westminster model'—concentrates power and fuses executive and legislative powers in the classic parliamentary manner (e.g. Colombia, Costa Rica, France, Greece, New Zealand (before 1996)). By contrast, the consensus model focuses on sharing power by separating and balancing executive and legislative power (e.g. Austria, Germany, India, Japan, the Netherlands, and Switzerland). Consensus democracies score higher in terms of democratic quality as well as the state's generosity in social welfare, environmental policy, criminal justice, and foreign aid (Lijphart 1999: ch. 16).

Role of cognitive and normative frames

The concepts on normative and cognitive frames are crucial for explaining how actors understand and interpret policy-making situations. Cognitive frames refer to the schemes through which actors view and interpret the world (Campbell 1998: 382). Normative frames are about values and attitudes that shape the actors' view of the world (Fischer 2003). Both cognitive and normative frames can enable but also constrain policy action.

Thus, to gain a more comprehensive understanding of policy adoption, we need to supplement our analytical framework—which is mostly the rational choice model—by the consideration of normative and cognitive determinants. Although rational motivation may explain the adoption of new policies, cognitive and normative factors may be essential for understanding better the decision-making at each stage of the policy-making process (Miller and Banaszak-Holl 2005: 214). The characteristics of cognitive and normative frames can be linked to sociological institutionalism, in which legitimacy-seeking actors are confronted with institutional pressures to conform to a set of cultural rules, norms, and expectations (Miller and Banaszak-Holl 2005: 195).

In this context, Surel (2000) discusses three concepts, i.e. those on **policy paradigms** (Hall 1993), **advocacy coalitions** (Sabatier and Jenkins-Smith 1993; Sabatier 1998), and **référentiel** (Jobert and Muller 1987). According to Hall (1993), there are certain policy paradigms present in the real world that imply distinct policy goals. These goals—that are intertwined with the paradigm—then define the choice and specification of instruments. The advocacy coalition framework, by contrast, assumes a similar construct to affect the entire society, which is the 'deep core'. Subordinated to it is the 'policy core', which refers to the belief systems within a subsystem of public policy. From this perspective, 'secondary aspects' are the instrumental decisions that are necessary to implement the policy core. The *référentiel* equals a paradigm as it comprises values and norms.

Cognitive and normative frames produce a sense of specific identity. However, certain actors have a privileged role in public policy-making as they generate and diffuse cognitive frames. Since elites and other privileged actors frame policy ideas to convince each other as well as the public, they are important for the adoption of policies (Campbell 1998: 380). This category of actors is labelled 'mediators' (Jobert and Muller 1987) or 'policy-brokers' (Sabatier 1998). Further, cognitive and normative frames help to reduce tension and conflict by marking out 'the terrain for social exchanges and disagreements, rather than simply supporting an unlikely consensus' (Surel 2000: 502). Dobbin (1994), for instance, shows that the differences in how decision-makers promoted railway development in the late nineteenth century can be explained by variations in cognitive frameworks. An instructive approach is presented by Campbell (1998), who models the role of ideas for policy-making against the background of cognitive and normative framing. In this way, he shows that ideas can both enable and constrain policy-making. At the cognitive level, ideas can either help policy-makers to define a clear course of action, or they can impede policy-making if they are used as cognitive constraints. As concerns the role of ideas at the normative level, they possess the ability to legitimize policy solutions to the public, but simultaneously ideas can potentially constrain the normative range of legitimate solutions.

National policy styles

The concept of policy styles—or also regulatory styles—refers to the routines and choices of actors involved in policy-making and implementation (Richardson 1982: 12). To a certain extent, this concept takes up the discussion about institutional characteristics (Lijphart 1999) as well as Dyson's (1980) elaboration on 'strong' and 'weak' states.[1]

Further, it is related to the ideas of 'policy communities' and 'administrative culture' (Hill 2005: 69; van Thiel 2006: 118). Thus, it is the main idea of this section to elucidate that, for the analysis of policy-making, nations matter (Feick and Jann 1988).

Richardson (1982) distinguishes policy styles along two dimensions. The first dimension is about how policy-makers respond to the issues on the policy agenda. Do decision-makers anticipate societal problems (technocratic approach), or do they merely react to them (diplomatic approach)? The first notion presupposes that the government is perfectly informed and able to foresee and forestall policy problems before they become critical. By contrast, the second notion about the government's approach is built around the concept of imperfect information and hence seems to be more realistic. The second dimension is about the relative autonomy of the state *vis-à-vis* other actors involved in policy-making and implementation. Here, the question is whether decision-makers seek to ensure consensus among the parties involved, or whether they simply impose their decisions on the executing actors (Richardson 1982: 12–13).

These core elements of their analytical framework can also be found in other conceptualizations. Van Waarden's (1995) typology of regulatory styles, for instance, comprises six sub-dimensions that refer to the 'what', 'how', and 'who' questions of policy-making:

1. Liberal-pluralist versus étatist versus corporatist style: the first style prefers 'market' solutions to policy problems, while étatism implies a preference for 'state solutions'. Corporatism, by contrast, favours 'associational' solutions to policy problems.

2. Active versus reactive styles: active styles are higher in their degree of intensity, radicalism, and innovation as compared to reactive ones.

3. Comprehensive versus fragmented or incremental styles: comprehensive policies are integrated into larger plans, while the latter are not.

4. Adversarial versus consensual paternalistic styles: the first type strongly relies on coercion and imposition, while the latter is based on consultation.

5. Legalistic versus pragmatic styles: legalistic styles are characterized by formalism, detailed regulation, and rigid rule application. The pragmatic style, on the other hand, is informal and flexible in both policy formulation and implementation.

6. Formal versus informal network relations between state agencies and organizations of state agencies.

In comparison, the typology proposed by Knill (1998) is more parsimonious. National regulatory styles are basically defined by the mode of state intervention and administrative interest intermediation. With respect to state intervention, he further distinguishes between (1) hierarchical versus self-regulation, (2) substantive versus procedural regulation, as well as (3) uniform and detailed requirements versus open regulation allowing for administrative flexibility and discretion. In a similar way, he subdivides administrative interest intermediation into (1) formal versus informal, legalistic versus pragmatic, and (2) open versus closed relationships between administrative and societal actors.

Policy styles provide an analytically useful concept for determining the design of policies, for example, the choice of instruments (Howlett 1991; Arentsen 2003) as well as the mode of implementation (Freeman 1985). Yet, assessing the extent of impact of national policy styles augers for systematic comparative analysis (Freeman 1985). Different policy styles can exist within countries, at different government levels as well as in different policy fields (Richardson 1982; Howlett and Ramesh 2003).

Richardson's (1982) volume itself, however, could not deliver empirical evidence for existence of national policy styles. In fact, the single case studies showed remarkable degrees of intra-national variations in policy styles. Conversely, when evaluating the success and failure of four policy areas (steel, health care, finance, HIV and the blood supply) in six European countries, namely France, Germany, the Netherlands, the UK, Spain, and Sweden, Bovens *et al.* (2001) found some evidence that different national policy styles affect how policies are formulated. Most importantly, policy styles in some countries tend to be more stable and clearly defined than are those of others, even though very much also seems to depend on the policy sector.[2]

The concepts of national policy styles are linked to legal, political, and administrative institutions and cultures. Given this strong rootedness, national

	Anticipatory	Reactive
Consensus-seeking	Netherlands, Spain	Germany, Sweden
Imposing	United Kingdom	France*

Fig. 20.2 Richardson's (1982) typology of policy styles

*Concerning financial regulations, the French style is anticipatory.
Source: Based on Bovens *et al.* (2001: 645–7).

regulatory styles are generally expected to be resistant to change, even with increasing economic and political internationalization (van Waarden 1995). These persistent differences in national regulatory styles can have important effects, especially with respect to European integration. This aspect explains why the study of national regulatory styles has been expanded to the study of Europeanization research (see e.g. Mazey and Richardson 1996; Knill 2001; Jordan and Liefferink 2004).

In sum, we can conclude that the notion of national policy styles is not unproblematic. Similarly to the concept of policy cycles, we should rather refer to it as a heuristic tool for identifying common policy-making patterns, but not as explanatory factors.

KEY POINTS

❑ Policy-making can be thought of as a strategy for resolving societal problems by using institutions; simultaneously policy-making is also a process for modifying those same institutions for attaining these goals.

❑ Cognitive and normative framing fulfils important functions during the policy-making process.

❑ Similar to the policy cycle, the concept of policy styles also serves as a useful heuristic tool for identifying common policy-making patterns among countries; nonetheless, it must also be regarded as another 'analytical shortcut'.

The role of international factors for domestic policy-making

In this section, we dismiss the assumption that policy-making is merely influenced by domestic factors and concentrate on the impact of international factors on domestic policy-making. The notion that countries do not constitute independent observations has been known for a long time in comparative politics, and became discussed as 'Galton's problem' (Naroll 1961; Braun and Gilardi 2006; Jahn 2006; Caramani 2008 for an overview).

In consequence, scholars are increasingly paying attention to how actors, institutions, and economic forces that extend beyond state borders can shape domestic politics and hence public policies (Bernstein and Cashore 2000: 67). This recognition has led researchers to scrutinize more carefully the link between domestic policy processes and the international arena (Risse-Kappen 1995). Such scholarship is, however, still at an early stage and the challenge before political scientists is to develop theoretical conceptions of how internationalization affects domestic public policies and policy-making (Howlett and Ramesh 2003: 55).

Despite these limitations in terms of theoretical literature, we can approach the policy effects of internationalization 'through the back door' by turning to the concepts of policy diffusion and policy transfer, and to the analysis of cross-national policy convergence as related concept (see also Chapter 22 on these concepts).

Theories of policy diffusion, policy transfer, and cross-national policy convergence

Diffusion is generally defined as the socially mediated spread of policies across and within political systems, including communication and influence processes which operate both on and within populations of adopters (Rogers 1995: 13). Diffusion studies typically start out from the description of adoption patterns for certain policy innovations over time. In a subsequent step, they analyse the factors that account for the empirically observed spreading process.

According to this context of diffusion, no distinction of different forms of 'spread mediation' is made.

In terms of the domestic policy-making process, diffusion mainly affects the stages of agenda setting, and to a lesser degree policy formulation. However, the mere placing of these issues on the policy agenda does not imply that they will be adopted. Therefore, some authors emphasized that the likelihood of policy adoption increases if the policy proposal originates from a country that is culturally similar to the receiving country (Strang and Meyer 1993; Strang and Soule 1998). Other scholars stress the relevance of administrative traditions and capacities (Kern *et al.* 2000). Lenschow *et al.* (2005) argue that the extent to which a policy innovation is accommodated by a given country can be explained by three aspects: institutional, cultural, and socio-economic. In their analytical framework, institutional factors—defined as organizational structures, formal and informal rules, and policy-making procedures—are expected to facilitate or constrain policies (Thelen and Steinmo 1992). Culture is included for understanding how policy discourses are developed, interpreted, and eventually integrated into the domestic policy-making context, whereas socio-economic structure and development points to the general capacity of state for policy actions.

However, we have to keep in mind that once a diffusing policy idea—either with or without modifications—has been placed on the agenda or became a policy proposal, its further development is then mainly influenced by domestic politics. Hence, domestic factors, such as considerations about values, party affiliation, constituency interests, public opinion, and decision rules come into play again.

Policy transfer can best be described as 'processes by which knowledge about policies, administrative arrangements, institutions and ideas in one political system (past or present) is used in the development of policies, administrative arrangements, institutions and ideas in another political system' (Dolowitz and Marsh 2000: 5; see also Rose 1991; Dolowitz and Marsh 1996; Radaelli 2000). Policy transfer is not restricted to merely imitating policies of other countries, but can include profound changes in the content of the exchanged policies (Rose 1991; Kern *et al.* 2000). In fact, there are basically four degrees of transfer (Rose 1993; Dolowitz and Marsh 1996: 351; 2000: 13):

- Copying (direct and complete transfer).
- Emulation (transfer of the ideas behind the programme).
- Combinations (mixture of different policies).
- Inspiration (final policy does not draw upon the original).

The focus of transfer studies is on the analysis of the specific processes and factors that influence the way and degree to which one country learns from other countries with regard to policy-making in a certain area. Here again domestic factors come into play. In terms of decision-making it is important which actors engage in policy transfer, which negotiation power they possess, and therefore whether they can build a supportive coalition for adopting a policy developed elsewhere. Another crucial aspect for the success of a policy import might be its regulatory legitimacy (Majone 1996: ch. 13). It is indeed reasonable to hypothesize that some countries have more problems in regarding external policy proposals as legitimate than others.

Policy diffusion and policy transfer share a number of assumptions, for example, that governments do not learn about policy practices randomly, but rather through common affiliations, negotiations, and institutional membership (Simmons and Elkins 2004). Both transfer and diffusion processes hence require that actors are informed about the policy choices of others (Strang and Meyer 1993: 488). Given these conceptual overlaps, diffusion is often equated with policy transfer (Kern 2000; Tews 2002).

Notwithstanding these conceptual overlaps, however, analytical differences between diffusion and transfer should not be overlooked. Diffusion studies typically start out from a rather general perspective. While analyses of policy transfer investigate the underlying causes and contents of singular processes of bilateral policy exchange, the dependent variable in diffusion research refers to general patterns characterizing the spread of innovations within or across political systems. The diffusion literature focuses more on the spatial, structural, and socio-economic reasons for particular adoption patterns rather than on the reasons for individual adoptions as such (Bennett 1991: 221; Jordana and Levi-Faur 2005). Diffusion studies often reveal a rather robust adoption pattern, with the cumulative adoption of a policy innovation over time following an S-shaped curve (Gray 1973; Berry and Berry 1990).

Both transfer and diffusion represent processes that might result in policy convergence, which can be defined as 'any increase in the similarity between one or more characteristics of a certain policy (e.g. policy objectives, policy instruments, policy settings) across a given set of political jurisdictions (supranational institutions, states, regions, local authorities) over a given period of time' (Knill 2005: 768). It has close proximity to the concept of isomorphism which has been developed in organization sociology and is defined as a process of homogenization that 'forces one unit in a population to resemble other units that face the same set of environmental conditions' (DiMaggio and Powell 1991: 66). The central question underlying studies on isomorphism refers to the mechanisms through which organizations become more similar over time. There is thus a broad overlap between studies on policy convergence and isomorphism, with the major difference between the two concepts being on their empirical focus. The literature on isomorphism concentrates on increasing similarity of organizational and institutional structures and cultures. Studies on policy convergence, transfer, or diffusion, by contrast, focus on changes in national policy characteristics.

But transfer and diffusion do not necessarily lead to converging policy outputs. This would imply that policy ideas were equally transposed into domestic policy proposals, and subsequently adopted through the same or similar political processes. Admittedly, this is an unrealistic scenario. Van Waarden (1995: 334), for instance, points out that policy diffusion does not automatically lead to convergence as foreign models usually need to be modified to correspond to national institutional structures and regulatory styles. How can we explain similar policies across different countries otherwise? Apparently, there are different sources of international influence with a varying degree of constraints on domestic policy-making and public policies.

International sources that affect domestic policy-making

Internationalization (Hirst and Thompson 1996) does not only affect policy sectors that are generally associated with externalities, such as environmental policy, but also policy fields with no immediate international connection, such as social policy. Yet, internationalization is a highly complex phenomenon with varying effects on different policy sectors and states. To disentangle the mechanisms behind internationalization, we rely on the concepts introduced by Holzinger and Knill (2005), who distinguish between (1) imposition, (2) international harmonization, (3) regulatory competition, and (4) transnational communication.

Imposition—sometimes also labelled 'coercive isomorphism' (DiMaggio and Powell 1991), or 'penetration' (Bennett 1991)—occurs whenever an external political actor forces a government to adopt a certain policy. This presupposes asymmetry of power, and often policy adoption is accompanied by an exchange of economic resources. Policies can either be unilaterally imposed on a country by another, or imposition can occur as a condition of being part of an international institution (Dolowitz and Marsh 2000: 9). Unilateral imposition happens rarely and only in extreme situations, such as wars. Conditionality, on the other hand, can be observed more frequently, as where applicant countries for membership in the European Union have to adopt the entire *acquis communautaire*, i.e. the total body of European law accumulated thus far. Imposition implies that the country forced to adopt a certain model has not much choice in modifying the policy. As a consequence, imposition can generally be expected to lead to complete similarity of the policies of the submitting country and the policies of the imposing country or institution. In such cases, domestic politics are mainly bypassed.

International harmonization refers to a situation in which member states voluntarily engage in international cooperation, and hence corresponds to 'negotiated transfer' (Dolowitz and Marsh 2000: 15). This mechanism implies that countries comply with uniform legal obligations defined in international or supranational law. International harmonization presupposes the existence of interdependencies or externalities which push governments to resolve common problems through cooperation within international institutions, thus sacrificing some independence for the good of the community (Drezner 2001: 60; Hoberg 2001: 127). Once established, institutional arrangements will constrain and shape the

---

BOX 20.3 International harmonization and domestic politics

Bernstein and Cashore (2000: 79–80)

The importance of domestic politics is largely limited along this path to the stage of rule creation/ratification and to the decision of whether to comply or not in specific circumstances. In the two-level game of international negotiations, governments balance, and sometimes play off, the interests of their negotiating partners and domestic constituencies. Domestic policy-making structures are also important when states require domestic ratification of international agreements or implementing legislation.

However, once rules are in place, assuming states view them as legitimate, they create a 'pull toward compliance' regardless of domestic political factors.

Contravening the rule could result in costly disputes in international adjudication bodies or domestic courts or sanctions of various sorts. It could also erode the legitimacy of other related rules that a state may want others to obey or, in utilitarian terms, erode general reciprocity that creates a broad incentive to obey international rules in the long run. The rule also becomes a resource on which transnational and/or coalitions of domestic actors can draw when governments do not comply. For example, they can publicize non-compliance, pressure governments to live up to their commitments or press governments to launch disputes against other countries which do not fulfil their obligations.

---

domestic policy choices, even as they are constantly challenged and reformed by their member-states. As a result, international institutions are not only the object of state choice, but are consequential for subsequent governmental activities (Martin and Simmons 1998: 743).

The mechanism of regulatory competition is closely related to the notion of internationalization as economic globalization. Regulatory competition is expected to homogenize the policy outputs of countries when these are mutually faced with competitive pressures. Thus, this mechanism presupposes economic integration among countries. The competitive pressure arises from (potential) threats of economic actors to shift their activities elsewhere, inducing governments to lower their regulatory standards. In this way, regulatory competition among governments may lead to a race to the bottom in policies (Drezner 2001: 57-9; Hoberg 2001: 127; Simmons and Elkins 2004).

Theoretical work, however, suggests that there are a number of conditions that may drive policy in both directions (Vogel 1995; Scharpf 1997*d*; Kern *et al.* 2000; Holzinger 2002, 2003), including, for example, the type of policy concerned (e.g. product or process standards), or the presence of other interests than business in national politics.

Often a distinction is made between product and production process standards (Scharpf 1997*d*; Holzinger 2003; Murphy 2006). In the case of production standards, we find a widely shared expectation

that states will gravitate towards the policies of the most *laissez-faire* country (Drezner 2001). If the regulation of production processes implies an increase in the costs of production, potentially endangering the international competitiveness of an industry, regulatory competition will generally exert downward pressures on economic regulations (Scharpf 1997*d*: 524). It is assumed that governments are ready to lower environmental standards in the face of lobbying and exit threats exerted by the respective industry (Hahn 1990).

Expectations are yet less homogeneous for product standards. While industries in both low-regulating and high-regulating countries have a common interest in harmonization of product standards to avoid market segmentation, the level of harmonization can hardly be predicted without the examination of additional factors. Most important in this context is the extent to which high-regulating countries are able to factually enforce stricter standards. If it is possible to erect exceptional trade barriers, as for example for health or environmental reasons under EU and WTO rules, stricter policies can be expected (Vogel 1995; Scharpf 1997*d*). Otherwise competitive pressure may induce governments to lower their standards (Holzinger 2003: 196).

So far, most empirical findings for different policy sectors, such as environmental and social policy, do not support the race to the bottom scenario but rather give hints for the occurrence of a race to the top, i.e. upward ratcheting of regulatory standards (see

Chapter 21 on the welfare state and Chapter 22 on the impact of public policies). International economic factors alone yet do not determine the direction of policy responses. Various domestic factors, such as the nature of policy-making institutions, mediate internationalization (Bernstein and Cashore 2000: 73). In this respect, Risse-Kappen (1995) stressed the mediating function of domestic policy networks.

Transnational communication consists of a number of mechanisms, which are purely based on communication among countries, namely lesson-drawing, transnational problem-solving, emulation, and the transnational promotion of policy models. Lesson-drawing refers to constellations of policy transfer in which governments rationally utilize available experience elsewhere in order to solve domestic problems (Rose 1991). This concept is closely related to rational decision-making and Bayesian learning (Meseguer Yebra 2003, 2006).

Transnational problem-solving is also based on rational learning. It is driven by the joint development of common problem perceptions and solutions to similar domestic problems as well as their subsequent adoption at the domestic level. In doing so, transnational elite networks or epistemic communities, international institutions, and common educational and normative backgrounds play an important role in forging and promulgating transnational problem-solving (DiMaggio and Powell 1991; Haas 1992; Elkins and Simmons 2004).

Emulation, on the other hand, is motivated by the desire for conformity with other countries rather than the search for effective solutions to given problems. States might sometimes copy the policies of other states simply to legitimate conclusions already reached (DiMaggio and Powell 1991; Bennett 1991). Finally, policy adoption can be driven by the active role of international institutions, for example, the EU, the OECD, or the World Bank, that are promoting the spread of distinctive policy approaches they consider particularly promising (Keck and Sikkink 1998). The adoption of internationally promoted policy models can be a tool for policy-makers to reduce uncertainty by simply doing what other governments have done (Tews et al. 2003: 594).

Similar to all the other mechanisms, the effects of transnational communication strongly depend on mediation by domestic politics (Radaelli 2005). Thus, as concerns the national effect of these mechanisms

of internationalization, we must conclude that the political context matters (Steinmo et al. 1992). As already argued for policy diffusion, it can be expected that if the cultural, institutional, or socio-economic similarity between communicating countries and international institutions is high, the adoption of the corresponding policy proposals should become more likely. Another strategy for enhancing the likelihood of policy adoption is given by the infiltration of the domestic policy-making process, for example by penetrating domestic policy networks (Bernstein and Cashore 2000: 83). However, general statements are hardly possible.

Empirical illustration

In this final section we seek to show that internationalization and its related mechanisms actually occur in the real world. There is a considerable body of empirical literature, which we cannot discuss in full (but see Heichel et al. 2005 for a systematic overview). Instead, we limit ourselves to some selected empirical examples illustrating the analytical concepts already presented.

Policy diffusion

Guler et al. (2002) show that the adoption of ISO 9000 quality certifications can be explained by diffusion theory and isomorphism. Their results support their hypothesis that states as well as foreign multinationals are involved in coercive isomorphism. Additionally, there is also evidence for the importance of mimetic isomorphism, which leads to policy imitation.

The diffusion of regulatory agencies has also attracted notable attention. Gilardi et al. (2006) examine the diffusion of economic and social regulatory agencies across Europe and Latin America. An interesting implication of their research is that the main explanatory factor depends on the type of regulatory agency. As concerns the spread of economic agencies, the theory of regulatory competition fits well. By contrast, the diffusion pattern of agencies operating in the field of social policy can best be explained by the essential role of transnational networks of professionals. Thus, transnational communication appears as the central causal mechanism in the latter case.

Oberthür and Tänzler (2002) concentrate on the role of international institutions in processes of diffusion by examining their effects on the spread of three climate policy instruments, namely climate protection plans and strategies, emissions trading schemes, and carbon dioxide energy taxes. International institutions generate pressure and provide incentives for the adoption of policy innovations. Hence policy promotion at the international stage does matter. This finding is substantiated by Tews *et al.* (2003), who analyse the diffusion of eco-labels, energy or carbon taxes, national environmental policy plans or strategies for sustainable development, and free access to information. Moreover, the authors present empirical support for the upward-driving effects of regulatory competition for product standards.

As concerns the diffusion of pension privatization, Brooks (2005) suggests that policy decisions in states are strongly interdependent on policy actions undertaken by peer nations, that is, countries that are structurally comparable and that participate in the same economic and political organizations. This finding can be interpreted in two ways. First, since peer nations usually trade extensively, this result can point to the relevance of competitiveness considerations for policy adoption. Thus, her results would show the relevance of the regulatory competition. Or, secondly, adoption can also be triggered by cultural similarity. These findings match with the outcomes of a study by Simmons and Elkins (2004) on the spread of models of foreign economic policy-making. The authors show that economic competition, as well as the policies of a country's socio-cultural peers, determines the adoption of liberal economic models.

Policy transfer

Dolowitz (1997) uses the policy transfer framework for explaining the main changes in the British employment policy during the 1980s, which culminated in the enactment of the Social Security Act in 1989. The government's motivations for policy transfer were (1) growing public concern over high level of unemployment, hence problem pressure, (2) electoral uncertainty, related to the threat of electoral defeat, (3) competition pressure, and (4) perceived dysfunctionality of the existing system. In response to these challenges, the British government transferred core elements of the American and Swedish welfare-to-work systems.

Jones and Newburn (2002) clarify the impact of the United States on recent developments of British crime control policy. To this end, they conduct document analysis and find evidence that in this case policy transfer actually took place. Also dealing with the United Kingdom, Pierson (2003) scrutinizes the policy transfer between the British and the Australian Labour Party in terms of welfare-to-work systems and student funding during the 1990s. His review of empirical evidence reveals that the main driving force behind policy transfer was the desire to solve policy problems, and hence the main mechanism turned out to be learning. The relevance of policy-oriented learning is also emphasized by Hulme (2005), who clarifies the use of the policy transfer approach for the analysis of social policy.

Lavenex (2002) shows how Central and Eastern European candidate countries have transferred refugee policy from the European Union, despite practical difficulties in their implementation and important differences with regard to past and present experiences with refugees. While domestic factors explain variation with regard to the timing of the countries' implementation of asylum laws and the general asylum practice, the mainly triggering factors for this reform can be conditionality.

Policy convergence

Holzinger *et al.* (2008) analyse the development of forty environmental measures across twenty-four countries between 1970 and 2000, by concentrating on international economic and institutional interlinkages between nation-states. Whereas economic interlinkages are associated with regulatory competition, institutional interlinkages refer to both international harmonization and transnational communication within institutions, which stimulates learning processes among member countries. Their results show that in general similarity grows considerably from 1970 to 2000. These developments can be explained in particular by the effects of international harmonization and transnational communication.

International harmonization contributes most to the explanation of convergence. In this context, the explanatory power of the EU variables is much less pronounced than accession to international institutions, which is a rather surprising result. The effects of transnational communication on environmental policy convergence are of almost the same size as those of international harmonization. Communicative interaction within international organizations obviously has very strong effects on the convergence of environmental policies. Hence compared to the institutional variables, there is little support for effects of regulatory competition on cross-national policy convergence. The explanatory power of the other variables controlled for in the analysis is limited. In fact, only income and cultural similarity seem to matter, but their effect strongly depends on the model specification.

KEY POINTS

❑ As internationalization is a complex phenomenon, it is useful to approach its underlying mechanism via the concepts of policy diffusion, policy transfer, and cross-national policy convergence.

❑ There are four main mechanisms: imposition, harmonization, regulatory competition, and transnational communication.

❑ There is considerable empirical evidence that internationalization affects domestic policy-making, especially the effect of international harmonization and transnational communication.

❑ For candidate countries for EU membership, conditionality is an essential driving force for adopting external policies.

Conclusion

Policy-making is extremely complex. Therefore, the analysis of policy-making usually focuses on single stages of the complete policy-making process. But this simplification is not a genuine cure. In fact, policy processes in the single stages remain complex. Problem definition and agenda setting ensure important strategic advantages, turning this stage into a highly competitive one. Many actors—formal and informal ones—participate in the selection of suitable items from an undefined universe of societal problems. Power fragmentation also affects policy formulation and adoption, which are characterized by negotiation and the search for compromise. If the political system is a rather cooperative one, decision-making in the political process remains unchallenging. Otherwise, there can be harmful delays in decision making. The number of actors involved decreases at the implementation stage. However, legislators always feel discomfort with regard to the dominating role of bureaucracy at this stage. In the subsequent evaluation stage, the floor is opened to experts and their appraisal of whether a policy performs well or poorly.

We must also keep in mind that there are structures present in the political sphere that help to reduce the complexity of policy-making. Political institutions, for instance, fulfil such a function. In a similar manner, framing mechanisms, such as cognitive or normative schemes, serve to structure politics. Finally, the development of routines and particular styles of making public policies helps to establish a stable negotiation framework and hence ensures the continuity of policy-making.

However, policy-making cannot be conceived in domestic terms only. It is not exclusively a response to policy problems or the outcome of domestic bargaining processes. As we discussed, policy-making is also affected by internationalization, implying a variety of stimuli and corresponding reaction patterns. In more general terms, internationalization can either enable or constrain policy-making. How these effects are translated into policy outcomes, however, mainly depends on domestic policy-making processes. In light of the analytical challenges outlined in this chapter, research on policy-making will remain stimulating for scholars of comparative politics.

? Questions

1. How can we think of policy-making in terms of theory?

2. In which ways are policy typologies related to the policy-making process?

3. What are the main stages of the policy cycle, and how does this concept enhance our understanding of policy-making?

4. Which actors—societal and political ones—participate, or even dominate, in the single stages?

5. What is the role of political institutions in policy-making?

6. How can we define normative and cognitive frames?

7. What are national policy styles, and how do they better the policy output?

8. Which theoretical concepts cope with the effects of internationalization on domestic policy-making?

9. What are the mechanisms behind these concepts? And how do they interact with domestic policy-making?

10. Does internationalization matter empirically?

» Further reading

Arce, Moisés (2005) *Market Reform in Society: Post-Crisis Politics and Economic Change in Authoritarian Peru* (University Park, Pa.: Pennsylvania State Press). This is an excellently written in-depth analysis of neo-liberal policy reform in Peru, which combines theory and process tracing in a remarkable way. It is really worth reading—and not only for those interested in Peruvian politics.

Baumgartner, Frank R., and Jones, Bryan D. (1993) *Agendas and Instability in American Politics* (Chicago: University of Chicago Press). This is an important book that provides several new ways of looking at politics and policy-making.

Bryce, Herrington J. (2005) *Players in the Public Policy Process: Nonprofits as Social Capital Agents* (Basingstoke: Palgrave Macmillan). This book develops a convincing framework for scrutinizing the increasing role of non-profits in governance.

Compston, Hugh (ed.) (2004) *Handbook of Public Policy in Europe: Britain, France and Germany* (Basingstoke: Palgrave Macmillan). Gives a comprehensive overview on the content of public policy in Britain, France, and Germany across a wide range of policy fields.

Fischer, Frank, Miller, Gerald J., and Sidney, Mara S. (eds.) (2006) *Handbook of Public Policy Analysis: Theory, Politics, and Methods* (Boca Raton, Fla.: CRC Press). A valuable volume that successfully explores methodologically the policy-making process under theoretical considerations.

Gilmour, Robert S., and Halley, Alexis A. (eds.) (1994) *Who Makes Public Policy: The Struggle for Control between Congress and the Executive?* (Chatham, NJ: Chatham House). Consists of a number of case studies on a variety of policy issues, providing insightful illustrations of policy-making in the United States.

Lijphart, Arend (1999) *Patterns of Democracy: Government Forms and Performance in Thirty-Six Countries* (New Haven, Conn.: Yale University Press). This is simply a 'must read' book.

Munger, Michael C. (2000) *Analyzing Policy: Choices, Conflicts, and Practices* (New York and London: W. W. Norton). This is an accessible and comprehensive introduction to the principles of public-policy analysis from an economics perspective.

Sabatier, Paul A. (ed.) (2001) *Theories of the Policy Process* (Boulder, Colo.: Westview Press). A remarkable anthology that gives a great overview of theoretical approaches to the study of policy-making.

Weiner, David, and Vining, Aidan R. (2004) *Policy Analysis: Concepts and Practice* (Upper Saddle River, NJ: Prentice-Hall). A superb textbook with a very instructive section on 'doing' policy analysis.

Web links

www.policyagendas.org
   The Policy Agendas Project.
http://webhost.ua.ac.be/m2p/
   Media, Movements and Politics research group.
www.uni-konstanz.de/FuF/Verwiss/knill/projekte/envipolcon/project-homepage.php
   Environmental Policy Convergence in Europe.
www.defendingscience.org/
   Project on Scientific Knowledge and Public Policy.
www.policyhub.gov.uk/
   British Government Social Research Unit.
http://ec.europa.eu/yourvoice/index_en.htm
   'Your Voice in Europe'.

 Visit the Online Resource Centre that accompanies this book for more information:
www.oxfordtextbooks.co.uk/orc/caramani/

21 The welfare state

Kees van Kersbergen and Philip Manow

Chapter contents

Reader's guide

The welfare state is important for our comprehension of democratic politics in modern societies, just as knowing about modern politics is crucial for understanding the causes, sources of variation, and consequences of the state's social interventions into markets and families. The chapter focuses on the key issues of the emergence, expansion, variation, and transformation of the welfare state. It explains that studying the welfare state necessarily means engaging in debates about some of the most fundamental and enduring questions of comparative political science and political economy.

Introduction

Why is the welfare state interesting for comparative political science? Because it represents the single most important transformation of advanced capitalist democracies in the period after the Second World War. Understanding the welfare state is key for understanding modern politics, just as an understanding of modern politics is key if we want to understand the causes of welfare state formation and growth, as well as the various social and economic effects that social interventions into the market and family display. What is more, the study of the welfare state confronts us with some of the most fundamental and enduring questions of political science and political economy.

From different normative perspectives, classical political economy (John Stuart Mill as well as Karl Marx) was convinced that capitalism and democracy were incompatible. But the mature welfare states of the West prove that capitalism and democracy indeed can go together—even with beneficial consequences for both. High social spending does not need to have detrimental effects on economic competitiveness, as the combination of a generous welfare state and a competitive market economy in a country like Sweden demonstrates. The 'democratic class struggle' (a term originally coined by Anderson and Davidson [1943], then adopted by Lipset [1960: 220], and taken to the realm of welfare state studies by Walter Korpi [1983]) obviously allows for a beneficial class-compromise, and the welfare state seems to be its most prominent embodiment.

Comparative politics has studied the origins, growth, and crises of the welfare state, testing various theories of political mobilization and development. What and who were pivotal in this process: social classes, the workers' movement, historical legacies of state structures, wars, economic development, demographic pressures, employers' interests? Are the various forms of political structures, actors, and struggles responsible for differences in size, type, and quality between welfare states? Comparative political scientists (especially political economists) have also looked at the impact of the welfare state (its performance) in an endeavour to grasp to what extent politics matters for social and economic output and outcomes. Does politics (e.g. the strength of political movements and parties or the composition of a government) matter for the type of social and economic policies (output) carried out in a country? And do these policies influence social and economic variables (outcome) such as economic growth, unemployment, inequality, and poverty (see next chapter)?

There is finally also a straightforward substantial and practical interest in the study of the welfare state. Many people care whether they live in a society in which the ratio between the highest and the lowest income decile is around 5.7 (US) or around 2.5 (Germany) (Smeeding and Gottschalk 1999). Also, many people care whether they live in a society in which taxation and welfare state transfers reduce poverty by 13 (US) or by 82 per cent (Sweden, see Iversen 2006; see also Comparative tables 5 and 6 at the end of this volume). The study of the welfare state addresses fundamental questions of social fairness, basic notions of a good society and of non-tolerable degrees of inequality and social exclusion. This discussion has of course also its technical side: assumed we agree on certain political aims (like a reduction of the unemployment rate below the 5 per cent level), we would like to know how to best achieve this goal. Thorough comparative studies of the working of social protection programmes promise to provide us with this kind of practical 'how to' knowledge.

KEY POINTS

❑ The welfare state is the product of the interplay between political equality (democracy) and economic inequality (capitalism).

❑ The welfare state represents a fundamental transformation of advanced capitalist democracies in the post-1945 period.

❑ Comparative politics tries to explain the emergence, growth, and consequences of welfare states, but also addresses fundamental issues of social justice and the good society.

What is the welfare state?

What do we mean when we talk about the welfare state? Let us start with the classic definition by Harold L. Wilensky, who described 'the essence of the welfare state' as 'government-protected minimum standards of income, nutrition, health, housing and education, assured to every citizen as a political right, not charity' (Wilensky 1975: 1). Here the welfare state is first and foremost a democratic state that—in addition to civil and political rights (see Marshall 1950 and Box 21.1)—guarantees social protection as a right attached to citizenship. Most political scientists tend to think along the state-centric lines that Wilensky advocated and agree that social policy must be seen as 'lines of state action to reduce income insecurity and to provide minimum standards of income and services and thus to reduce inequalities' (Amenta 2003: 92). Moreover, nation-states that 'devoted most of their fiscal and bureaucratic efforts in these directions were and are considered to be "welfare states"' (Amenta 2003: 92).

Such a definition and approach are typical for political science analyses of the welfare state. The advantage of state-centred definitions was that they were clear-cut, while operationalizations for empirical research were relatively straightforward, too. No surprise that in the literature the predominant way of operationalizing the welfare state, its growth and expansion, was in terms of public social spending, expressed as a proportion of total state spending or of the Gross Domestic Product (GDP). There were many drawbacks of this approach, however. An exclusive focus on social policy tends to overlook

the fact that, although the state plays an important role in providing welfare, it is certainly not the only institution doing so. Moreover, it is not easy to draw a clear line between social policies and other types of policies promoting welfare. Finally, not all social policies actually promote welfare, even though their intention may be to do so (Hill 2006: ch. 1).

Esping-Andersen (1990) has criticized the political science literature for its exclusive focus on the state and social spending, arguing that the welfare state 'cannot be understood just in terms of the rights it grants' and the amount of money it spends. It is hardly conceivable that 'anybody fought for spending per se'. What we need to know instead is for which purpose the money is used. Moreover, we have to avoid studying welfare state activity in isolation, because 'we must also take into account how state activities are interlocked with the market's and the family's role in social provision' (Esping-Andersen 1990: 21). It is the specific institutional mixture of market, state, and family that characterizes how a nation provides work and welfare to its citizens, and various nations do this in very different ways. The question how much a state spends (welfare effort) is much less relevant than the questions (1) **on what** it spends its public resources, (2) **how it influences the distribution of resources and life chances** in other ways than through spending (e.g. via tax expenditures; through the 'hidden welfare' state—Howard 1993; Hacker 2002), and (3) **what other social institutions** play a role in social provision.

BOX 21.1 Marshall's three elements of citizenship

'I propose to divide citizenship into three parts. I shall call these three parts, or elements, civil, political and social.

The civil element is composed of the rights necessary for individual freedom—liberty of the person, freedom of speech, thought and faith, the right to own property and to conclude valid contracts, and the right to justice. . . .

By the political element I mean the right to participate in the exercise of political power, as a member of a body invested with political authority or as an elector of the members of such a body. . . .

By the social element I mean the whole range from the right to a modicum of economic welfare and security to the right to share to the full in the social heritage and to live the life of a civilized being according to the standards prevailing in a society. . . .

It is possible, without doing too much violence to historical accuracy, to assign the formative period in the life of each to a different century—civil rights to the eighteenth, political to the nineteenth and social to the twentieth.'

(Marshall (1965: 78 and 81))

All welfare states, Scharpf and Schmidt (2000: 7) have argued:

> provide free primary and secondary education, and all provide social assistance to avoid extreme poverty. Beyond that, the 'golden age' models differ fundamentally from one another along two dimensions: the extent to which welfare goals are pursued through the regulation of labour markets and employment relations or through the 'formal welfare state' of publicly financed transfers and services, and the extent to which 'caring' services are expected to be provided informally in the family or through professional services.

We agree with Esping-Andersen (1990, 1999, 2002) that in order to understand social policy and the welfare state it is crucial to appreciate that the market, the state, and the family can all be the main welfare providers. It is the specific interaction between these institutions in the provision of work and welfare that we define as a welfare regime. It is a **complex system of managing social risks**, where each institution represents a radically different principle of doing this: 'Within the family, the dominant method of allocation is, presumably, one of reciprocity ... Markets are governed by distribution via the cash-nexus, and the dominant principle of allocation in the state takes the form of authoritative redistribution' (Esping-Andersen 1999: 35–6). What one institution does, affects what the others can, will, or must do. Esping-Andersen gives a succinct example:

> a traditional male bread-winners family will have less demand for private or public social services than a two-career household. But when families service themselves, the market is directly affected because there will be less labour supply and fewer service outlets [for data on labour markets see Comparative table 13 at the end of this volume].

In turn, if the state provides cheap daycare, both families and the market will change: there will be fewer housewives, more labour force participation, and a new demand multiplier caused by double-earner households' greater propensity to purchase services. (1999: 36)

Certain risks of life potentially become **social** risks and subject to political struggles, (1) because they are shared by many people and therefore affect the welfare of society as a whole (say loss of income because of disability and/or old age), (2) because they are interpreted as a threat to certain strata of society (say poverty that causes protest and uprisings against the ruling elite), and (3) because the risks are beyond the control of any individual (say mass unemployment in a market society). These are specific conditions for risks to become social risks. Why and how this happens, however, has been the topic of several decades of empirical research that has generated fascinating debates in comparative politics on theory, methods, and data to which we now turn.

KEY POINTS

- Welfare states provide citizens with free education and protect them against extreme poverty. Beyond this minimum social protection welfare states differ with respect to the generosity and the scope of social protection against the risks of sickness, invalidity, unemployment, and old age.
- The state is not the only institution providing welfare.
- Market, state, and family influence each other in how much of the task of providing work and welfare they assume. They form a welfare regime, which is a complex system of managing social risks.

The emergence of the welfare state

What drives the emergence and development of the welfare state? Three theoretical perspectives can be identified, (1) a functionalist approach, (2) a class mobilization explanation, and (3) a literature emphasizing the impact of state institutions and the relative autonomy of bureaucratic elites.

Functionalist approach

'The welfare state is an answer to problems created by capitalist industrialization': functionalist theories understand the emergence and expansion of the welfare state in developed nations as an answer of the state to the growing needs of its citizens. These needs emerge with the vanishing of traditional means of subsistence and of traditional bonds of mutual assistance (in families, through guilds, or charities) and the expansion of the risks of modern, industrial society: industrial accidents, cyclical unemployment, the inability to gain one's own living due to sickness or old age.

In a rapidly modernizing society, demands for social and economic equality become pressing. In

---

BOX 21.2 The emergence of the welfare state

The modern welfare state is a European invention—in the same way as the nation state, mass democracy, and industrial capitalism. It was born as an answer to problems created by capitalist industrialization; it was driven by the democratic class struggle; and it followed in the footsteps of the nation state.

(Flora (1986: xii))

---

catering to such demands, the scope of state intervention was increased tremendously and the nature of the state was transformed. As Flora and Heidenheimer (1981: 23) argued:

  With the structural transformation of the state, the basis of its legitimacy and its functions also change. The objectives of external strength or security, internal economic freedom, and equality before the law are increasingly replaced by a new raison d'être: the provision of secure social services and transfer payments in a standard and routinized way that is not restricted to emergency assistance. (Flora and Heidenheimer 1981: 23)

The increased demand for socio-economic security came from a system of industrial capitalism that dislodged masses of people and made them dependent on the whims of the labour market, thus destroying forms of social protection that had existed traditionally. Modernization involved rapidly changing working conditions, the emergence of the free labour contract, and the loss of income security. Welfare state development was related to the problem of social disorder and disintegration that was created by the increasing structural-functional differentiation of modern societies. Such differentiation 'involves a loosening of ascriptive bonds and a growing mobility of men, goods, and ideas. It leads to the development of extensive networks of exchange and greater disposable resources. As differentiation advances and breaks down traditional forms of social organization, it changes and exacerbates the problem of integration' (Flora and Alber 1981: 38). Modernization was seen as causing social disintegration. The welfare state steps in to solve problems of social integration.

The major assumption of the functionalist literature was that different nations will adopt similar social and economic policies once they reach comparable levels of social and economic development.

In other words, functionalist theories expected policy **convergence** among the developed nations. If welfare states differed with respect to the coverage they provided and the benefits they granted, the causes of variation were assumed to be 'chronological', namely explained by the **different timing of industrialization and modernization** in the various countries. These differences would disappear in the long run.

Class mobilization

'Welfare state growth was driven by the democratic class struggle': class mobilization and interest group theories rather emphasized that collective political actors, such as labour movements, special interest groups, and political parties, demand and fight for social policies in the interest of their clientele. In this perspective the welfare state is seen as the outcome of political struggles between social classes and their political organizations, each with their own power base.

In a market economy, in which income stems from selling one's labour power in the labour market, anything which hinders labour from being 'marketable' turns into an existential threat for the worker: unemployment, sickness, invalidity due to accidents or old age, etc. The market could neither cope with this new type of social risks directly (e.g. through private insurance) nor provide the collective goods needed to solve these problems. If many of the new risks therefore stemmed from treating **labour as a commodity,** the main task of the welfare state seemed to lie in **decommodifying labour,** that is, in granting labour temporal relief from the pressure to sell itself on the labour market. Such a decommodifying effect of welfare state intervention lay in the interest of workers, so it seems straightforward to identify the labour movement as the main political driving force behind welfare state formation and growth.

Not convergence, but rather **variation** among welfare states was emphasized by these approaches, a variation which is mainly explained with power differentials, with cross-country difference in the strength of key political actors. The causes for variation are 'synchronic', i.e. they are expected to persist in the longer run—or at least as long the power differentials themselves persist.

State institutions and bureaucracy

'The welfare state followed in the footsteps of the nation state': institutionalist theories, finally, point to those rules and regulations of (democratic) policy-making and state structures that operate relatively autonomously from social and political pressures as the main determinants of the emergence and growth of the welfare state.

Scholars belonging to this school of thought have emphasized the 'state building' aspect in welfare states (Skocpol 1985, 1992; Skocpol and Orloff 1986). When countries for the first time were confronted with the social problems generated by modern industrial society it mattered whether their bureaucratic elite was relatively autonomous, like in Japan (Garon 1987) or Sweden (Heclo 1975), or whether the lack of bureaucratic autonomy led to a 'politicization' of early welfare state formation and to welfare clientelism. The harsh critique that the US progressive movement voiced against political clientelism in US veteran pensions for long delegitimized and delayed state social protection in the US (Skocpol 1992). Early welfare state building therefore exemplifies the importance of historical sequencing. What came first: the formation of a Weberian bureaucracy or mass democracy (Kamens 1986)? From an institutionalist perspective, which looked at how the state took over social responsibility for its citizens, it also proved easier to acknowledge that early welfare state programmes were not always exclusively targeted at workers, but often at other social categories whose risks did not coincide with class—like soldiers or mothers (Skocpol 1992). Especially those studies which showed that early welfare programmes often focused on mothers and families (Pedersen 1990, 1993) inspired a wave of contributions to the comparative welfare state literature in which gender gained much more prominence than it had played before.

The literature took the previous contributions to task for largely ignoring the fact that, in order to get decommodified, you have to be commodified first (Pedersen 1990; Lewis 1992; Orloff 1993; Sainsbury 1994, 1996; O'Connor *et al.* 1999; Morgan 2002, 2003, 2006). Decommodification as an analytical concept ignored the fact that many women remained excluded from the labour market in the first place. Despite the claim that welfare production has to be analysed within the context of the triad of state, market, and family (Esping-Andersen 1990), the family actually played only a minor role in mainstream welfare state analysis. Only after the challenge to the welfare state literature posed by the feminist critique did concepts like 'de-familialization' gain wider attention, concepts which discussed how and to what extent state provision of welfare may substitute those social services traditionally provided in the family (Esping-Andersen 1999).

The insights of the institutionalist school nicely squared with earlier observations in the modernization literature, namely that often it was the **least** democratic countries where suffrage was *not* yet extended which had actually pioneered in building the modern welfare state. Also, it was not always the most economically advanced countries which took the lead in the introduction of state social protection programmes. It is rather the early pre-emptive strategy of state elites who anticipate workers' unrest that explains much of the pioneering role of not yet fully democratic and economically less advanced nations like Germany and Austria around the last two decades of the nineteenth century. In these states social rights were not granted because of the extended political-participatory rights of workers, but as a kind of **compensation** for the lack of such participatory rights (Flora and Alber 1981; Alber 1982).

The power resources approach and the institutionalist literature reacted to the fact that the causal link between industrialization (or modernization more generally) and welfare state development was not always elaborated well theoretically and not often confirmed empirically (see Wilensky and Lebeaux 1965; Kerr *et al.* 1973; Cutright 1965; Pryor 1968; Rimlinger 1971; Jackman 1975; Wilensky, 1975). In order to demonstrate the great variety among western welfare states Figure 21.1 locates countries in two dimensions: first, according to the **chronological** point in time at which they have introduced the first major social insurance programme and, secondly, according to the **economic** point in time, i.e. according to the level of economic development and prosperity, at which they introduced such a programme.

As Figure 21.1 shows, it is impossible to detect any clear relationship between the level of modernity, industrialization, or prosperity (here measured as GDP per capita) and the relative 'earliness' or 'lateness' of

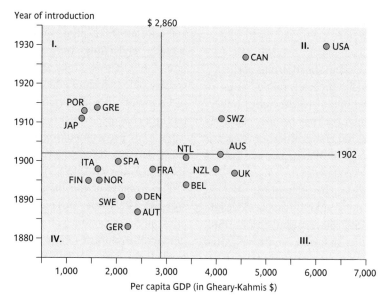

Fig. 21.1 Level of economic development at the time of introduction of the first major social protection programme

Sources: Schmidt (1998: 180) and Maddison (1995: 194–201), cf. Wagschal (2000: 49).

welfare state formation. The Anglo-Saxon countries (UK, US, Canada) appear as countries that introduced social protection programmes relatively late and at a relatively high level of economic development. They are joined by Protestant–liberal countries like the Netherlands or Switzerland which qualify as welfare latecomers as well (Manow 2004). Countries like Germany or Austria were welfare pioneers in a chronological sense, but a couple of countries introduced first social insurance programmes at even lower levels of economic development than those two countries (e.g. Japan, Portugal, Finland, Italy). But how do the political and social forces which can be held responsible for early or late welfare state building also explain the different paths of further welfare state development? It is to this question that we would like to turn in the following section.

> **KEY POINTS**
>
> ❑ The welfare state has been understood as the (functional) response to the social problems generated by modernization, as the result of the political conflicts between capital and labour in modern capitalist societies, and as a central element in modern nation-state building.
>
> ❑ There is no obvious connection between the level of economic well-being or democratization of a society and the development of its welfare state.
>
> ❑ Different approaches have different explanatory goals or problems: the functionalist approach tries to explain the convergence of modern welfare states; the power resources and institutionalist approaches attempt to account for the enduring variation among welfare states.

The expansion of the welfare state

The impact of social democracy

In the 1980s and 1990s a new generation of research primarily took issue with the logic of industrialism thesis, but increasingly also with the median voter-view that democratic politics as such can explain the expansion of the welfare state (Jackman 1975, 1986). The theoretical goal was to demonstrate how politics mattered for the different welfare state paths that countries had followed in the post-war period, focusing particularly on the question whether differences in party-political government composition can explain differences in welfare state expansion. Hewitt (1977), for instance, demonstrated that the mere presence of democratic structures could not sufficiently explain the growth of social expenditures and gains in equality, but that *social democratic rule was a necessary condition of expansion and egalitarian outcomes*. The explanatory importance of party politics was also underlined by the predictive failure of economic models based on the median-voter theorem. In one of the classical economic contributions to the literature, Meltzer and Richard (1981) put forward a model that predicted that welfare state redistribution should increase with increases in income inequality. With the typical right-skewed income distribution, the income of the median voter is below the average income, so she should develop an interest in redistribution—an interest that should become stronger with increasing income inequality. However, it is not the highly unequal societies which redistribute the most. On the contrary, countries like Sweden or Norway have both an already highly compressed wage and income structure *and* a generous welfare state, and countries like the US combine an unequal income distribution with a rather residual welfare state.

A large number of studies corroborated the causal effect of social democratic power on welfare state performance and discovered the conditions under which these movements were actually capable of refracting the working of the market through social protection programmes. Decommodification was found to be strongest if the *left was strong* (Stephens 1979) and the *right was divided* (Castles 1978). Moreover, social democratic attempts to expand the welfare state were seen to be particularly effective if the party was supported by a strong and coherent union movement (Stephens 1979; Higgins and Apple 1981).

Cross-national quantitative studies extensively tested the thesis that it was primarily politically organized labour (social democracy) which was responsible for the social transformation of capitalism. In most cases, the political parties were identified as the chief causal agents (Hewitt 1977; Korpi 1983, 1989; Stephens 1979; Hicks and Swank 1984; Esping-Andersen 1985; Alvarez *et al.* 1991; Griffin *et al.* 1989; Hicks 1999; for an encompassing study see Huber and Stephens 2001). The more the mass of the population is organized as wage-earners within the social democratic movement, the higher the quality (universalism, solidarity, redistribution) of the welfare arrangements tended to be and, as a result, the higher the extent of equality. A developed welfare state, therefore, was interpreted as evidence for a decisive

shift in the balance of power in favour of the working class and social democracy.

Many of these studies assumed the social democratic welfare state to be a leap in the direction of socialism or, indeed, an early image of the future 'good society' (Shalev 1983). Since the early study by Hewitt (1977), there was considerable evidence in favour of a social democratic effect on income distribution (Björn 1979; Stephens 1979; Hicks and Swank 1984; Swank and Hicks 1985; Muller 1989; Hage *et al.* 1989). Still, income distribution was for several reasons a problematic variable. On technical grounds, aggregate data available until the arrival of the Luxembourg Income Study (Smeeding *et al.* 1990; Mitchell 1990) were not truly comparable. On theoretical grounds, income distribution was problematic to the extent that the kinds of universalistic and generous welfare programmes associated with successful social democratic politics tended to lose their redistributive effect because they increasingly favoured the middle classes (LeGrand 1982; Goodin and LeGrand 1987; Esping-Andersen 1990; Korpi and Palme 1998).

There was some evidence to suggest that the social democratic effect was more evident when measured against institutional characteristics of welfare states. This is the case in Myles's (1989) study of pension systems, Korpi's (1989) and Kangas's (1991) studies of sickness insurance, Palme's (1990) study of pension rights, and Esping-Andersen's (1990) study of welfare state attributes such as universalism, the public–private mix, the importance of means-tested social benefits, and active labour market policies. Yet as research moved in the direction of studying the institutional properties of welfare states, it also moved away from the kind of linear 'more or less' or 'the bigger, the better' social democratization conception that dominated the literature in the 1980s. Thus Kangas's (1991: 52) study of social expenditure and social rights concludes that 'the biggest are not necessarily the best, but the best are rarely the smallest'.

Neo-corporatism and the international economy

Others argued that the political efficacy of left parties to decommodify labour and to promote welfare state expansion depended not only on the extent to which they counted on strong trade unionism, but also more structurally, on the development of centralized, neo-corporatist industrial relations systems (Cameron 1978, 1984; Schmidt 1983; Scharpf 1984, 1987; Hicks *et al.* 1989).

Cameron (1978, 1984) suggested that the association between strong social democracy and welfare states was linked to a country's position in the international economy. Specifically, he has argued that the vulnerability that small, open economies faced favoured the expansion of the public economy so as to reduce uncertainty via social guarantees, full employment, and more active government management of the economy. As elaborated more fully in the work of Katzenstein (1985), the real causal chain appeared to be that **small open nations developed democratic corporatist structures as a way to enhance domestic consensus, facilitate economic adjustments, and maintain international competitiveness.** While democratic corporatism was promoted by the presence of strong social democratic labour movements, Katzenstein pointed to Switzerland and the Netherlands to suggest that they did not constitute a necessary condition. At this point it became increasingly difficult to separate the neo-corporatist argument from the social democratic thesis (Keman 1990; Garrett 1998).

Cameron's argument has often been mistakenly interpreted as an outright rejection of the social democratic thesis: the explanatory power attached to 'openness' seemed to suggest that the effect of social democracy was spurious. However, the gist of his thesis (Cameron 1984) was more deeply historical, suggesting that the openness of an economy favoured the concentration of industry, which in turn enhanced the power of labour since workers were easier to mobilize and organize in an economy with a few large and concentrated employers instead of many small and fragmented ones.

The importance of neo-corporatist arrangements for social democratic success has been stressed in the studies by Schmidt (1983), Keman (1988), and Hicks *et al.* (1989). They have suggested that social democracy was most likely to promote the expansion of the welfare state if its parliamentary power was matched by **strong consensus-building mechanisms** in both the polity and economy. These studies also suggested that neo-corporatist intermediation came to play an especially important role in maintaining welfare policies during economic crisis periods: the distributive battles that erupt when growth declines were better managed with 'all-encompassing' interest organizations.

Studying income distribution, Hicks and Swank (1984) and Muller (1989) suggested that the strength of left parties (and economic openness) influenced income distribution directly, while trade unionization and centralization of wage bargaining had decisive indirect effects by providing the electoral basis for social democracy. By the end of the 1980s a consensus had grown that parties or unions alone had little effect and that successful social democratization required a configuration of strong left parties in government supported by an encompassing and centralized trade union movement (Alvarez *et al.* 1991; Garrett 1998). Only in the 'coherently' liberal political economies, in which a weak labour movement met with a political dominance of conservative parties, or in the coherently social democratic political economies, where a strong labour movement went hand in hand with left governments, were macro-economic policies, wage bargaining, and welfare expenditures expected to function well because complementing each other. 'Incoherent political economies', on the other hand, were expected to perform much less well, when right governments that pursued neo-liberal economic policies met with strong union resistance, causing industrial strife, or when the attempt at macro-economic management of left governments was counteracted by fragmented and particularistic unions that proved unable to engage in concerted wage restraint. Today's debate about the impact of globalization on the sustainability of generous welfare state programmes in many respects reflects this earlier corporatist debate about economic vulnerabilities in open economies and the concomitant need for welfare compensation (see below and Chapter 24).

Risk redistribution

In one of the more fundamental challenges to the literature Baldwin (1990) rejected the causal link between social democracy and solidaristic social policies altogether. Baldwin showed that, while growing equality may have been a characteristic feature of modern welfare states, it has not been its goal. The welfare state was more about reapportioning risks than about the redistribution of wealth. Equality referred to risk redistribution. The theory of risk and distribution allowed for a rejection of what Baldwin called the labourist (i.e. class mobilization) account for its narrow focus on the working class as the only risk category. The critical insight was that class may, but rarely does, coincide with a risk category. The labourist view mistakenly assumed that welfare policies were explained in terms of a victory of the working class over the bourgeoisie.

Baldwin's crucial claim was that what historically had determined the solidarity of social policy was not working-class strength, but, on the contrary, the fact that 'otherwise privileged groups discovered that they shared a common interest in reallocating risk with the disadvantaged' (Baldwin 1990: 292). Similarly, Heclo and Madsen (1986) and Therborn (1989) argued that the principles of solidarity and equality that characterize Swedish Social Democracy had less to do with socialism than with the Swedish historical tradition. Thus, it may very well have been Swedish history, and not social democracy, that constituted the root cause of reform. The implication was that the Swedish model was inapplicable elsewhere (Milner 1989).

Christian democracy and Catholic social doctrine

One of the major problems of the social democratic model was that several countries (e.g. the Netherlands or France) pursued equality and had a big welfare state without the advocacy of a strong social democratic labour movement (Castles 1978, 1985; Stephens 1979; Wilensky 1981; Skocpol and Amenta 1986). Both the incapacity to explain early reforms of capitalism by liberal and conservative state elites and the fact that other political parties also behaved as pro-welfare actors made clear that the political process of welfare state construction and expansion needed to be reconsidered. One answer came from those who showed that Christian democracy (or political Catholicism) constituted a functional equivalent or alternative to social democracy for expanding the welfare state (Wilensky 1981; Schmidt 1982). This point was raised early on by Stephens (1979: 100), who argued that 'it seemed possible that anti-capitalist aspects of catholic ideology—such as notions of fair wage or prohibitions of usury—as well as the generally positive attitude of the catholic church towards welfare for the poor might encourage government welfare spending'. As a result, one of the basic assumptions of the social democratic model, namely that the power of labour equals the power of social democracy, had to be relaxed. Christian democratic parties operating in the centre enjoyed considerable working-class support and were commonly backed by powerful Catholic unions (see van Kersbergen 1995). This political constellation was highly favourable to welfare state development.

Secular trends

Emphasizing political agency against the functionalist approaches has of course the danger of falling into the other extreme of neglecting how much the growth of the welfare state is influenced by secular processes beyond the control of single political actors. Some of them include:

1. Demographic ageing: longer life expectancy and lower birth rates lead to demographic ageing and increase the demand for social spending on health, pensions, and care. Medical progress is costly and puts an increasing strain on health care spending.

2. Baumol's disease: productivity increases slower in services than in manufacturing, which means that the (social) services will gain in relative economic performance. At the same time, economies with a larger service sector will grow at a slower pace (Pierson 2001).

3. De-industrialization: with job losses in agriculture and industry, the secular process of de-industrialization increases the demand for welfare state compensation (job protection, re-training; active labour market policies) (Iversen and Cusack 2000).

4. Wagner's law, named after the German economist Adolph Wagner (1835–1917), predicts an ever-increasing share of public expenditures in developed industrial economies, causing a secular trend towards higher public spending in all developed economies.

5. 'Politics for profit' (see e.g. Buchanan 1977): public choice approaches maintain that politicians aim at expanding public spending to maximize their 'political income' and to increase their re-election prospects.

6. Programme maturity, 'positive feedback', and ratchet effects—each welfare programme breeds its own supporters, so once introduced, it is almost impossible to abandon it later (Pierson 1994, 1998; Huber and Stephens 2001).

While all advanced welfare states have to cope with these secular challenges, their vulnerabilities and opportunities in coping with them vary according to their institutional set-up. It is to this that we turn next.

KEY POINTS

- ❑ Social democratic rule was a necessary condition of expansion and egalitarian outcomes.
- ❑ The political impact of left parties on the welfare state depended on the development of centralized, neo-corporatist industrial relations system that helped to enhance domestic consensus, facilitate economic adjustments, and maintain international competitiveness.
- ❑ Important criticisms of the social democratic or labourist model: (1) the welfare state is about

reapportioning social risks and the working class is only one risk category; (2) there are countries that pursued equality and a developed welfare state, but did not have a strong social democratic labour movement.

- ❑ There are other pro-welfare state actors (e.g. Christian democracy) and important non-political processes (e.g. demographic ageing) that promote expansion and development.

Variations among developed welfare states

Each welfare state is a 'unique' combination of regulations and institutions. However, in comparative politics we are not interested in uniqueness, but in comparability and systematic variation. In order to compare welfare states, some simple dimensions of variation can be distinguished. They comprise at least the following: (1) Is the welfare state tax-financed or contribution-financed? (2) Is it that every citizen is protected or is it rather that every worker (and his or her dependants) is insured? (3) Are benefits a right, gained either through previous contributions to social insurance programmes or attached to the status of citizenship, or do benefits depend on proven need, i.e. are they granted conditional on means testing? (4) Are benefits uniform (flat rate) or do they reflect prior income, in other words, are pension or unemployment payments temporary substitutes for wages or do they aim at securing some 'minimum' or 'decent' standard of living?

That welfare states come in a limited variety can be partly explained by the fact that choosing a particular institutional solution in one dimension simultaneously narrows the choice set in others. The advanced welfare states represent packages or bundles of institutional and regulatory answers to the social problems of modern society. There are only so many

possible options to protect against certain social risks like unemployment, sickness, inability to work due to old age or invalidity, and the various protective measures cannot be combined freely.

Take for example welfare state financing: if the welfare state is tax-financed, eligibility should be linked to the citizen status (with or without means testing), but not to the employment relation. But this would also mean that benefits are unlikely to reflect prior income but rather a social notion of a socially fair and accepted (minimum) standard of living. In a contribution-financed welfare state, in contrast, proportional deductions from the payroll justify differentiated benefits that reflect the length of the previous contribution period and the level of the contributions paid. If social protection is primarily linked to the employment relation, it seems to be a 'natural' solution to insure those who are not in dependent employment (e.g. spouse, children) via the family member who is dependently employed.

Since welfare states represent bundles or packages of institutional or regulatory solutions to social problems, scholars have proposed to distinguish specific welfare state **models or regimes**. One of the earliest proposals was that of Richard M. Titmuss (1958),

COUNTRY PROFILE India

Republic of India (*Bhārat Gaṇarājya*)

State formation

From the 16th century, Indian colonies were established by several European countries. By 1856, most of the country was under the control of the British East India Company. It became a colony of the British Empire after a failed insurrection in 1857. In the 20th century, the Indian National Congress and other political organizations engaged in a non-violent struggle for independence, which was finally won in 1947. However, India lost the territories that became independent Pakistan and, later, Bangladesh; over 7 million Indian Muslims moved to these countries after the partition, another 7 million Hindus and Sikhs moving the other way. *Constitution* 1949, effective 1950; amended many times.

Form of government

Federal republic.
Head of state President elected by an electoral college (elected members of both houses of Parliament and the legislatures of the states); term of 5 years (no term limits).
Head of government Prime Minister, chosen by the members of Parliament of the majority party.
Cabinet Appointed by the President on the recommendation of the Prime Minister.

Administrative subdivisions 28 States and 7 Union Territories.

Legal system

Based on English common law; judicial review of legislative acts.

Legislature

Bicameral parliament (*Sansad*).
Lower house People's Assembly (*Lok Sabha*): 545 seats (543 elected by popular vote, 2 appointed by the president); term of 5 years.
Upper house Council of States (*Rajya Sabha*): 250 members (up to 12 appointed by the president, the remainder chosen by the elected members of the state and territorial assemblies); term of 6 years.

Electoral system (lower house)

Plurality
Constituencies 543 single-member constituencies.
Barrier clause Not applicable.
Suffrage Universal, 18 years.

Direct democracy

None.

Party system   Results of the 2004 legislative elections (People's Assembly):

Electorate	671,487,930	65.4%
Voters	389,948,330	38.0%

Party	Valid votes	%	Seats
Total 'National Democratic Alliance'	140,524,231	36.1	186
Total 'United Progressive Alliance'	139,194,294	35.7	221
Total 'Left Front'	30,609,574	7.9	59
Others and independents (with seats)	66,954,259	17.2	77
Others (less than 1% nation-wide and no seats)	12,497,426	3.2	0
Total	389,779,784	100.0	543

Note: Each of the alliances consists of a leading party (the *Baharatiya Janata Party*, the *Indian National Congress*, and the *Communist Party of India (Marxist)*, respectively) and a number of smaller parties which cannot be listed in the textbook for reasons of space.
Source: Election Commission of India.

who already in the late 1950s suggested distinguishing the following:

- The **residual welfare model**, in which social protection 'comes into play only after the breakdown of the private market and the family as the "natural" channels for the fulfilment of social needs' (Flora 1986: xxi).

- The **industrial-achievement-performance model**, in which welfare rights and benefits are linked to the employment relation and reflect 'merit, work performance and productivity' (ibid.).

- An **institutional redistributive model**, in which social welfare institutions are an integral part of society, providing 'universalist services outside the market on the principle of need' (ibid.).

There is obviously considerable overlap between the Titmuss's welfare state typology and the one proposed by Gøsta Esping-Andersen in his seminal *Three Worlds of Welfare Capitalism* (1990). In this book, Esping-Andersen distinguished three regimes.

Anglo-Saxon liberal regime

In a liberal or residual welfare state regime, benefits tend to be low and flat rate. They are means-tested or targeted at clearly delineated groups in society. The welfare state is predominantly tax-financed. More encompassing protection against the vagaries of life has to be purchased individually on the market (e.g. life insurance or private pension plans), as the welfare state only protects the small group of the most destitute and needy. Overall public spending on social protection is comparatively low. This welfare regime is to be found where conservative parties are often in government, in the US and the UK and to some extent also in Australia and New Zealand (see below).

Scandinavian social democratic regime

The social democratic welfare state regime is predominantly tax-financed as well, but in contrast to the residual-liberal model, benefits are granted without means testing. They are a citizen's right and benefit levels tend to be much more generous: it is 'a welfare state that would promote an equality of the highest standards' (Esping-Andersen 1990: 28). Subsequently, overall levels of public spending tend to be much higher, too. Besides relatively generous funding, social democratic regimes provide a lot of welfare services in care, health, and education, the welfare state itself becomes a major employer, and it creates in particular much female employment (Huber and Stephens 2000). This kind of welfare state regime is found mainly in Scandinavian countries in which social democratic parties are strong, often in government, levels of unionization high, and the political right divided.

Continental conservative regime

The conservative continental regime, finally, comes close to Titmuss's 'performance achievement' model.

BOX 21.3 Esping-Andersen's three welfare state regimes

'[In the liberal welfare state,] means tested assistance, modest universalist transfers, or modest social insurance plans predominate. Benefits cater mainly to a clientele of low-income, usually working-class, state dependents. ... In turn, the state encourages the market, either passively—by guaranteeing only a minimum—or actively—by subsidizing private welfare schemes ... In ... conservative and strongly 'corporatist' welfare states, the liberal obsession with market efficiency and commodification was never pre-eminent and, as such, the granting of social rights was hardly ever a contested issue. What predominated was the preservation of status differentials; rights, therefore, were attached to class and status. This corporatism was subsumed under a state edifice perfectly ready to displace the market as a provider of welfare; hence, private insurance and occupational fringe benefits play a truly marginal role. ... The third ... regime-cluster is composed of those countries in which the principles of universalism and decommodification of social rights were extended also to the new middle classes. We may call it the 'social democratic' regime-type since, in these nations, social democracy was clearly the dominant force behind social reform. ... the social democrats pursued a welfare state that would promote an equality of the highest standards. ... This model crowds out the market, and consequently constructs an essentially universal solidarity in favour of the welfare state. All benefit, all are dependent; and all will presumably feel obliged to pay.'

(Esping-Andersen (1990: 26–28))

Here, social rights are not based on citizen status, but on the employment relation. The welfare state is contribution-financed rather than tax-financed. Those not dependently employed are covered via their employed spouse or relatives. Welfare benefits are differentiated according to income and record of contributions to the social insurance fund. The conservative welfare state is transfer heavy and service lean. Being based on occupational principles, conservative welfare states display a high degree of programme fragmentation. The major occupational groups (white collar- and blue collar-workers, civil servants, free professions, self-employed, etc.) all have their own social insurance schemes (see Table 21.1).

Esping-Andersen's welfare state typology has become extremely influential in the comparative welfare state research literature and it is successfully orienting research to the present day. Whether studies analysed patterns of employment growth in the service economy (Scharpf 1997*b*), or different political picks between full employment, balanced budgets, and income equality (Iversen and Wren 1996), or patterns of income inequality among the OECD countries (Korpi and Palme 1998), in all of these and many other studies the 'three world' heuristic was time and again confirmed.

The voluminous literature about Esping-Andersen's welfare state typology (see for a summary Arts and Gelissen 2002) has therefore mainly discussed whether additional regime types should be added to it rather than putting Esping-Andersen's typology itself into question. It has been convincingly argued that we should add a distinct **southern European welfare regime** (Italy, Spain, Portugal, Greece) and that we should treat the two antipode welfare states, the welfare states of **Australia and New Zealand**, as special cases, too (Castles 1989; Castles and Mitchell 1992; Ferrera 1996, 1997).

Southern Europe

The southern-European welfare regime distinguishes itself from the rest of continental-conservative welfare states by:

- The long-time absence of a nation-wide, uniform social assistance scheme.
- The dominance of pension spending among total social spending.
- Highly segmented labour market with the highest protection standards for the 'happy few' in the state sector and in state enterprises, combined with large segments of low protection in the private sector, plus unregulated employment in the large shadow economy.
- Finally, by national health systems which are rather untypical for the conservative welfare regimes on Europe's continent.

Australia and New Zealand

Castles has argued that the welfare states of New Zealand and Australia represent a type ('radical') of their

---

Table 21.1 Esping-Andersen's Three Worlds of Welfare Capitalism

Esping-Andersen's welfare regimes (Titmus' welfare models)	'Liberal' (residual model)	'Conservative' (achievement-performance model)	'Social Democratic' (institutional redistributive model)
Prime example	US, UK	Germany	Sweden
Decommodification	Low	Medium	High
Social rights	Need based	Employment related	Universal
Welfare provision	Mixed services	Transfer payments	Public services
Benefits	Flat benefits	Contribution-related	Redistributive

Source: Ebbinghaus and Manow (2001: 9).

Table 21.2 Decommodification scores in the Three Worlds of Welfare Capitalism

	UE	Sick	Pension	Total Decom		UE	Sick	Pension	Total Decom
					Benefit generosity index results				
Australia	4.0	4.0	5.0	13.0	United States	7.4	0	11.3	18.7
United States[a]	7.2	0	7.0	13.8	Japan	4.5	6.2	9.4	20.0
New Zealand	4	4.0	9.1	17.1	Australia	5.0	5.0	10.1	20.1
Canada	8	6.3	7.7	22.0	Italy	3.2	7.3	10.0	20.5
Ireland	8.3	8.3	6.7	23.3	Ireland	6.9	6.2	8.3	21.4
United Kingdom	7.2	7.7	8.5	23.4	United Kingdom	7.2	7.2	8.5	22.9
Italy	5.1	9.4	9.6	24.1	New Zealand	5.0	5.0	13.3	23.3
Japan[a]	5.0	6.8	10.5	27.3	Canada	7.2	6.4	11.4	25.0
France	6.3	9.2	12.0	27.5	Austria	6.9	9.7	11.2	27.8
Germany	7.9	11.3	8.5	27.7	France	6.3	9.5	12.0	27.8
Finland	5.2	10.0	14.0	29.2	Finland	4.9	10.0	13.0	27.9
Switzerland	8.8	12.0	9.0	29.8	Germany	7.5	12.6	8.7	28.8
Austria	6.7	12.5	11.9	31.1	Netherlands	10.6	9.7	11.5	31.8
Belgium	8.6	8.8	15.0	32.4	Switzerland	9.2	11.0	12.0	32.2
Netherlands	11.1	10.5	10.8	32.4	Belgium	10.2	8.6	14.0	32.9
Denmark	8.1	15.0	15.0	38.1	Denmark	8.6	12.6	11.8	32.9
Norway	9.4	14.0	14.9	38.3	Norway	8.5	13.0	11.9	33.4
Sweden	7.1	15.0	17.0	39.1	Sweden	9.4	14.0	15.0	38.4
Mean	7.1	9.2	10.7	27.2		7.1	8.6	11.3	27.0
Standard Deviation	1.9	4.0	3.4	7.7		2.1	3.5	1.9	5.8
Coefficient of variation	0.27	0.44	0.32	0.28		0.29	0.41	0.17	0.21
					Correlation with original scores	0.87	0.95	0.70	0.87

Correlation between programmes	Correlation between programmes
UE-Sick r = 0.44	UK-Sick r = 0.45
UE-Pension r = 0.23	UE-Pension r = 0.36
Sick-Pension r = 0.72	Sick-Pension r = 0.30
Cronbach's α = 0.72	Cronbach's α = 0.59

Note[a] 'Total Decom' score is amount in table 2.2 of Esping-Andersen (1990), not sum of programme scores.

Source: Adapted from Scruggs and Allan (2006a: 68).

own as well (Castles 1989, 1996; Castles and Mitchell 1992). While targeting does play a prominent role in them, which led Esping-Andersen to classify them as liberal welfare regimes, eligibility rules are not particularly restrictive. Moreover, state social protection in both countries often works 'through the market', especially via state arbitration of industrial conflicts, securing high employment protection and compressed wages, which makes post-hoc welfare intervention and redistribution often unnecessary.

Esping-Andersen's typology was based on his **index of decommodification** and used 1980 data. Recently, Scruggs and Allan (2006*a*) have reopened the discussion about the regime classification by replicating Esping-Andersen's original study with new data and gathering data for the 1990s (see web links below and Table 21.2). They find that several countries seem to have been misplaced and that the coherence within the clusters of countries is less strong than Esping-Andersen assumed. However, they overemphasize their results somewhat when they conclude that there is limited empirical support for the regime classification. This is because in many instances their replication does confirm the original analysis and because—as they readily admit—they have so far not included stratification, i.e. the other important dimension on which the regime typology was based. Still, theirs is a very welcome critical contribution that will improve the quality of the debate tremendously.

KEY POINTS

❑ The advanced welfare states represent packages or bundles of institutional and regulatory answers to the social problems and risks of modern society, such as unemployment, sickness, inability to work due to old age or invalidity.

❑ Five welfare regimes are distinguished: (1) an Anglo-Saxon liberal regime; (2) a social democratic regime found in Scandinavia; (3) a conservative model that is typical for continental Europe; (4) a Southern European regime; and (5) a 'radical' type found in Australia and New Zealand.

The effects of the welfare state

Where (political) economists have primarily been interested in how the state (the public sector in general) has influenced economic behaviour (economic growth, labour market participation, investments, etc.), comparative political science research has focused on welfare and has tended to take a broader approach when studying the effects of social policies. Theoretically, they have been inspired by T. H. Marshall (1950; see Box 21.1). His concept of social citizenship not only stresses social *rights*, but also how the granting of such rights structures and restructures **stratification** and **status** relations in society. The main questions were whether the welfare state (1) modifies social inequality; (2) alleviates poverty; (3) reduces social risks; and (4) whether different welfare states have varying consequences for social stratification.

(In)equality and redistribution

When we talk about inequality and poverty, we talk about the social divisions and stratification that cause a differential distribution of social risks. The relevant social stratification in our societies concerns status or occupational groups, social classes, gender, ethnicity. Social policies, their design and content, are likely to be affected by the prevailing differentiation in society and may or may not influence social stratification and inequality. Research in the field of comparative social policy analysis and the welfare state deals with the question whether social policies structure, cause, reproduce, reinforce, or moderate social inequality.

Class, gender, and ethnicity as concepts are supposed to capture systematically how society is structured in such a way that certain groups of people are clearly privileged or disadvantaged in terms of their occupational position, income, wealth, status, skills, education, and above all power. These structural characteristics are expected to determine to a large extent the life chances of the individuals within these groups and they are affiliated (or thought to be affiliated) with many other things, including health, happiness, death rates, lifestyle, culture, political preference, etc.

With respect to class, the debate is whether and to what extent it is possible to 'escape' one's own class.

The use of the concept for analytical purposes only makes sense if there is a certain level of class closure, i.e. if mobility, both within a generation and between generations, is rare. To assume that the welfare state can have an effect on social stratification is to assume that social policies are capable of pulling down barriers to mobility and of decreasing closure. Similar considerations hold for other structural social divisions. Are people locked in a social position and are the privileges or disadvantages of such positions passed on from generation to generation? Do welfare state interventions support social mobility and break up closure? Or if such interventions do not have much effect, is there perhaps an impact on the life chances associated with class, gender, or ethnic position? Do social policies reduce social inequalities or do they, in fact, reproduce differences or even reinforce them? Do the different welfare regimes (re)structure social divisions differently?

Universalism vs. targeting

Many people naturally associate social policies and the welfare state with redistribution and equality. However, it is important to realize that redistribution does not always imply more equality. For instance, saving money during periods of relative prosperity (e.g. when in a job) for periods of need (e.g. when old and retired) is a form of redistribution, but does not lead to more equality. Redistribution is not necessarily from the rich to the poor. With respect to equality, the intellectual debate has revolved around the issue whether social policies **targeted at specific groups** (e.g. the working class, women, migrants) have the effect of reducing inequalities or whether **universalism** in social policy, that is to say 'the provision of a single, relatively uniform service or benefit for all citizens regardless of income or class' (Hill 2006: 192), actually does a better job.

The question is not trivial, because the different welfare regimes vary precisely in this respect, with the **social democratic model being a universal system and the liberal regimes the most strongly targeting.** Moreover, in all regimes, but especially in the conservative regime, social inequalities and status differentials are intentionally reproduced in the welfare system, through occupational and earnings-related social insurance schemes. Inequalities are reproduced also in the universalist schemes, because

the better-off and highly educated people with higher skills and competences are much better capable of taking advantage of universal services (health care, education) than poorer and less educated people.

At face value, it seems that targeting is ultimately better for the poor or the less well-off, primarily because social policies are designed exclusively for those who need it most. Redistribution via targeting, moreover, is fair and efficient because it does not waste resources by transferring money to people who do not need aid. However, targeting is a kind of **Robin Hood strategy** ('stealing' from the rich, giving to the poor) that antagonizes the rich and provokes them to defect the system. As Korpi and Palme (1998: 672) explain: 'By discriminating in favour of the poor, the targeted model creates a zero-sum conflict of interests between the poor and the better-off workers and the middle classes who must pay for the benefits of the poor without receiving any benefits'.

An alternative is a **simple egalitarian system** with flat-rate benefits for all, giving relatively more to the poor than to the better-off. However, also this system (known as the Beveridge system), has incentives for the middle classes to opt out and look for private insurance. Finally, there is the evangelical **Matthew strategy** ('For unto every one that hath shall be given, and he shall have abundance: but from him that hath not shall be taken away even that which he hath') of earnings-related provision that give relatively more to the rich than to the poor. The Matthew effect is most pronounced in services, for instance in (higher) education of which the rich profit much more than the poor, not only because they get the service, but also because education greatly advances earnings capacity.

When empirically comparing welfare state regimes, we find the **paradox of distribution**: 'The more we target benefits at the poor only and the more concerned we are with creating equality via equal public transfers to all, the less likely we are to reduce poverty and equality' (Korpi and Palme 1998: 681–2). Encompassing models that combine a simple egalitarian system with the Matthew strategy are the most redistributive systems that also have a high level of political support and legitimacy. How is this possible?

❝ By giving basic security to everybody and by offering clearly earnings-related benefits to all economically active individuals, … the encompassing model brings low-income groups and the better-off citizens into the same institutional structures. Because of its earnings-related benefits, it is likely to reduce the demand for private insurance. Thus the encompassing model can be expected to have the most favourable outcomes in terms of the formation of cross-class coalitions that include manual workers as well as the middle classes. By providing sufficiently high benefits for high-income groups so as not to push them to exit, in encompassing institutions the voice of the better-off citizens helps not only themselves but low-income income groups as well. (Korpi and Palme 1998: 672) **"**

Similarly, Smeeding (2005) in a recent paper shows that the targeting welfare state regimes, especially the US, have the highest levels of poverty and inequality and that this is a **political** effect. Speaking about the US, Smeeding (2005: 980) says: 'if one decides to make poverty or inequality an active policy goal, one can make a difference. We have more inequality and poverty than other nations because we choose to have more.' Smeeding, too, argues that when the distance between the rich and the less well-off becomes too great, as happens in a targeted system, the rich opt out and cater for themselves: they get private insurance, get the best health care and make sure their children get the best education available. This reproduces and even reinforces social divisions. As Smeeding puts it (2005: 980): 'higher income inequality produces lower levels of those publicly shared goods that foster greater equality of opportunity and greater upward mobility: income insurance, equal educational opportunity, and more equal access to high-quality healthcare'.

Recent empirical research (e.g. Kenworthy 1999; Korpi and Palme 2003; Brady 2005; Scruggs and Allen 2006*a*) underscores the differential impact of various welfare state regimes on equality and poverty. Although some (e.g. Brady 2005: 1354) find that the welfare state, regardless of the period or the type one studies, strongly reduces poverty, there seems to be a consensus that **univeralism in particular produces the most pronounced effects.** The mechanisms behind this are manifold (see Hill 2006: 192–4). For instance, good benefits and services (especially education and health care) that tailor to the standards of the better off rather than to the poor are good for the poor and increase social mobility. Also, fragmented, targeted, or particularist systems (i.e. separate systems for separate groups) actually **reinforce** inequality and may imply that the state or politics is

associated with the promotion of inequality, causing severe problems of legitimacy. In addition, universal provision of services protects both the poor and the better off from sudden attacks on their budgets (e.g. health care), so that the poor get the service they otherwise would be forced to give up, while the income of the better off is protected so they do not become poor. Finally, some universal transfers, such as child benefits or family allowances, serve society at large, even for those people who have no children, because other people's children will contribute to their pension.

This explains why an earlier generation of comparative (quantitative) studies failed to find a linear relationship between welfare state and post-tax and post-transfer income equality, but when we account for the different types of welfare states and understand the paradox of redistribution, this finding is no surprise. However, we note that the issue of inequality is predominantly phrased in terms of income and market position and in this sense can be said to address especially the class issue in social divisions and stratification.

Feminist critiques pointed to the more general weakness of class analysis, namely that class theory had great difficulty in dealing with the class position of women, particularly housewives not active on the labour market. The feminist critique of Esping-Andersen's *Three Worlds* has made clear that, if one really wants to understand the working of the regimes in terms of market, state *and* family, one also needs to develop theoretical tools that can make sense of the gender dimension of social stratification and how social policies presuppose and affect the relations between men and women (see Bussemaker and van Kersbergen 1994).

Social policies assumed the distribution of labour between men and women and tended to reinforce these. For the position of women it is crucial whether they are entitled to benefits as individuals or whether rights are tied to families in which men are often the sole income earner. Also, women have different types of risks and needs (e.g. think of single parenthood). As a result, the outcomes of welfare state interventions in terms of equality and poverty and in terms of labour market behaviour are markedly different for men and women. Just to give a few examples, in the European Union (except in Finland and Sweden), although the welfare state reduces the risk of poverty everywhere, the poverty risk for women is considerably larger than for men (European Commission 2004: 188). Only in the social democratic welfare regime does the rate of employment of women approach the male rate. Everywhere women earn less than men.

In the golden age of the welfare state (1960s and 1970s), the income security and redistribution that the welfare state offered was considered to be not simply a matter of social justice, but also of macro-economic efficiency. Welfare state expenditures could be viewed as part of the Keynesian demand management logic that helped maximize economic performance, particularly economic growth and the prevention of unemployment. Moreover, many of the welfare state's programmes contribute to the supply of labour. It is no exaggeration to say that the welfare state's jobs and programmes (such as child care, parental leave, sickness benefits) have played a crucial role in increasing the supply of female labour. Or, to put it differently, the welfare state has helped women to enter the labour market at a scale that without it would have been impossible. The welfare state also facilitated economic reconstruction and adaptation by offering 'easy' exit routes for redundant workers in non-competitive industries via disability schemes and early retirement.

> **KEY POINTS**
>
> ❑ The welfare state is itself a system of social stratification: it can counter, reproduce, or reinforce social (class, gender, ethnic) inequalities.
> ❑ The impact of social policies on poverty and inequality varies enormously per regime, with the universalist social democratic regime the most and the liberal targeting regime the least redistributive.
> ❑ Paradoxically, the more benefits are targeted exclusively at the poor and the more public policies are devised to create equality via equal transfers to all, the less likely it is that poverty and equality are reduced.
> ❑ Men profit more than women from welfare state interventions to reduce equality and poverty and to improve chances in the labour market.

The challenges and dynamics of contemporary welfare states

Today, the welfare state seems to be under pressure from many sides: population ageing, sluggish economic growth, mass unemployment, changing family structures, the transformation of life cycle patterns, post-industrial labour markets, the erosion of systems of interest intermediation and collective bargaining, the rise of new risks and needs, and international pressures (globalization) (see for a particularly enlightening overview Schwartz 2001). Especially the globalization literature started from the assumption that an increasingly internationalized market would force the generous welfare states of the Western world into a common downward movement (see Chapter 24).

Globalization: efficiency vs. compensation

However, it seems that the advanced OECD-economies have maintained their ability to 'tax and spend' to a surprising degree. What is most remarkable from the viewpoint of the early pessimistic predictions is that the welfare state basically survived (Kuhnle 2000) rather than proved to have outlived itself. This has led to an as-yet unresolved debate between, on the one hand, those researchers who think that globalization is indeed a major challenge that potentially is damaging the economic foundations of social policies, at the very least prohibiting the efficiency–equality solution still possible in the Keynesian era, and, on the other hand, those scholars who argue that the challenges and threats for the welfare state such as ageing are essentially endogenous and have little to do with globalization.

Today's debate about the impact of globalization in many respects reflects the earlier corporatist debate: while one side of this debate holds that the internationalized market and the intensified economic competition it triggers has rendered high levels of welfare spending unsustainable (the **efficiency hypothesis**), others argue that welfare state compensation of those who (fear to) lose from economic openness has historically been a social and political precondition for the liberal post-war trade regime (the **compensation hypothesis**) (Rodrik 1996; Rieger and Leibfried 1998, 2001; Glatzer and Rueschemeyer 2005).

The small states' experience of economic vulnerability in an internationalized market is today shared by all. Adherents of the compensation hypothesis argue that economic openness and a liberal trade regime rested on the domestic political promise to compensate the losers of economic integration via the welfare state. In this perspective the threat that the internationalized economy poses for generous redistributive regimes is that it risks undermining the social and political legitimacy of economic openness itself. With downward pressures on the advanced welfare states, economic openness is endangering the very social and political preconditions on which it rests. As of yet we lack clear empirical evidence for 'race to the bottom' effects commonly attributed to globalization. Also, the causal link between economic openness and domestic social protection has not yet been convincingly established (Iversen and Cusack 2000). For instance, it remains far from clear whether international economic integration comes with increased domestic risks and economic volatility, which then would call for compensation by the domestic welfare state, as the compensation hypothesis claims.

Moreover, it seems still possible to implement social and economic policies that redistribute wealth and risk in such a manner that the potential victims of the global market are protected. Such policies can be beneficial to economic growth, because they yield collective goods that the market cannot produce. These especially concern investments in human capital and the infrastructure. It was especially the 'varieties of capitalism' literature which highlighted this important contribution of the welfare state to skill-intensive production regimes (Hall and Soskice 2001a; Iversen and Soskice 2001). Workers invest in those special skills on which skill-intensive production regimes in coordinated market economies depend only when they have a guarantee that their investments will pay off in the long run. Generous unemployment payments that take into account the previous wage level and that can be drawn for relatively long periods of time, as well as generous early retirement rules, make sure that investments into special skills will

not be lost even in the case of unemployment. At the same time, comprehensive (corporatist) labour market institutions seem to be crucial to prevent employees exploiting the policy of social protection and investment by driving up wage claims. It also turns out that a nation's economic, political, and social stability is increasingly important for investment decisions, particularly for those investors who are forced to take their decisions under conditions of uncertainty and high risk (Garrett 1998: 130). Certainty and predictability are highly valued in an increasingly uncertain and volatile global economy. This view, however, is contested by other prominent welfare state researchers (Huber and Stephens 2001; Stephens 2005: 63).

The 'efficiency versus compensation' debate has not been settled. But after more than ten years of debate on the effects of globalization on the generous welfare states of the West at least the competing hypotheses are now more clearly distinguished (Glatzer and Rueschemeyer 2005):

1. The **compensation hypothesis** holds that markets tend to disrupt traditional forms of social security and create a need for new compensatory policies that (democratic) governments may supply. Moreover, social policies can also be productive assets as they foster a better educated, trained, and healthier workforce and contribute to the development of a more equal and less conflictuous society.

2. The **efficiency hypothesis** says that globalization hampers social policy. International competition forces national governments to reduce costs by scaling down taxes and social policies. Because what matters is the share of wage costs per unit of production, competition in the world market requires a permanent improvement of productivity. Of more consequence for social policy is that globalization increases the power of capital over labour and national government because of the credible threat of investment strike by exit.

Garrett and Nickerson (2005) test these hypotheses in a quantitative comparative analysis of the relationships between government spending, international market integration, and democratization in middle-income countries. The findings are that also in these countries there is a positive relationship between exposure to the world market and 'big' government, but that early and quick removal of capital controls inhibits the expansion of the public economy. The most important finding from a political science perspective, however, is that in this process politics matters enormously, as it was only in the countries that democratized that public spending grew. Hence, the 'consequence of democratization and globalization, the two sweeping changes in middle-income countries since 1980s, has been to accelerate, rather than retard, public spending growth in these countries' (Garrett and Nickerson 2005: 48).

A similar 'politics matters' conclusion is reached by Huber and Stephens (2001) and Stephens (2005) in a study on the welfare state in north-western Europe. Trade openness leads to the expansion of the welfare state only under social democratic or Christian democratic leadership. If the secular right is in power, it does not happen. The social democratic and Christian democratic welfare states were not only compatible with competition on the world market, but 'to the extent that they enabled wage restraint and provided collective goods valued by employers, such as labor training, the generous social policies actually contributed to competitiveness' (Stephens 2005: 70). It is soaring unemployment and budget deficits that cause public spending cuts. Welfare state retrenchment is caused by globalization only to the extent that rising unemployment is an effect of globalization. But these effects are mediated by politics, for instance because policy mistakes played a crucial role in the crisis of the most developed welfare states of Scandinavia in the early 1990s, just as better policies have contributed to their more recent turnaround. In so far as the internationalized economy undermines generous welfare states, it is in the process of undermining its own social and political legitimacy.

Most recent studies indicate that domestic politics and institutions are of great consequence for how the pressures of globalization make themselves felt in social policy and the welfare state. It does not seem to be the case that globalization *always* undermines the welfare state. Under favourable political conditions, increasing openness can imply welfare state development, but if such conditions are absent, the compensation hypothesis fails to convince too. This makes social policy outcomes more dependent on raw political struggles. According to Glatzer

and Rueschemeyer, welfare state outcomes are predominantly the result of the complex *interplay* of international economic forces and domestic politics and institutions.

> The actual trajectories of social policy development will rely primarily on conditions within countries. Welfare states are in the first instance shaped by the wealth of nations, by state–society and state–economy relations, and by power relations within countries. If these factors are fundamentally changed by international openness of the economy, we should expect fundamental changes in social welfare policy. (Glatzer and Rueschemeyer 2005: 215)

Even in the light of international pressures, domestic institutions and politics remain the key for understanding social policy development.

Welfare defence: the politics of retrenchment

This is precisely the target at which those who are critical of the globalization argument direct their critical arrows. Since the early 1990s, comparative political scientists have documented empirically that welfare states have been remarkably resistant to change, notwithstanding the mounting challenges they face. They readily admit that the challenges are formidable and that retrenchment and reform are real and important, but they also point to the fact that we simply have not observed the radical overhaul or the breakdown of the welfare state that some of the more speculative globalization theories were expecting. So an interesting new puzzle was formulated: how is it possible that the major institutions of the welfare state persist in the light of all the pressure for change?

As Green-Pedersen and Haverland (2002) rightly stress, the debate on retrenchment and austerity, particularly since the publication of Paul Pierson's (1994) instant classic on the topic, has been almost entirely a political science affair. Paul Pierson (1996: 178), who analyses retrenchment policies at the level of single programmes, has argued that 'frontal assaults on the welfare state carry tremendous electoral risks' and that retrenchment should not be misunderstood as the mirror image of the growth of the welfare state. Welfare expansion usually generated a popular politics of credit claiming for extending social rights and raising benefits to an increasing number of citizens, while austerity policies affront voters and networks of organized interests. In other words, welfare state reform tends to induce **political backlash** and this has been taken to explain the striking inertia of social programmes.

The post-1945 welfare state has also produced an entirely novel **institutional context**. Once welfare programmes, like social housing and health care, were solidly established, they created their own programme-specific constituencies of clients and professional interests. As a consequence, 'the emergence of powerful groups surrounding social programs may make the welfare state less dependent on the political parties, social movements, and labour organizations that expanded social programs in the first place' (Pierson 1996: 147). They potentially become veto-players in the game of retrenchment. Specialized social programmes in the policy areas of social housing, health care, education, public assistance, social security, and labour market management have indeed developed into institutionally separated and functionally differentiated policy domains. Therefore, a general weakening of social democratic and Christian democratic parties and the trade union movement—the main political supporters of welfare state expansion—need not translate into a commensurate weakening of social policy. The old politics of the welfare state has been replaced by a new politics of welfare state defence. The programme-specific constituencies of clients and professional interests have developed into powerful defenders of the status quo welfare state and the main sources of political controversies over reform.

Supported by strong popular attachments to specific policies, professional policy networks are able to muster substantial veto powers against reform efforts. Moreover, given the political salience and popularity of social policy, it is not easy to turn a political preference of 'dismantling the welfare state' into an electorally attractive proposition. Shifting the goals from expansion to retrenchment imposes 'tangible losses on concentrated groups of voters in return for diffuse and uncertain gains' (Pierson 1996: 145). On average, 'retrenchment advocates thus confront a clash between their policy preferences and their electoral ambitions' (Pierson 1996: 146). In his later work, Pierson (2001: 428) stresses that different welfare regimes constitute different settings for the 'new politics' of welfare state reform,

and recognizes that as a result of this he may have underestimated the continuing political salience for welfare state politics of organized labour in some regimes.

The former 'politics matters' researchers as well as those who adhered to the 'power resources approach' (see Huber and Stephens 2001) empirically corroborate Pierson's thesis and conclude that for austerity and retrenchment (public employment in Scandinavia is the exception) traditional class and politics matter less and less, because an institutional rather than a political logic governs the adaptation of welfare states. If this is the case, then it makes sense to turn again to the first, 'pre-political' generation of research as a source of inspiration for understanding current developments in welfare state restructuring. The 'logic of industrialism' approach, for instance, would suggest that population ageing, one of the correlates of industrialization, has clearly been a major factor governing recent welfare state retrenchment and restructuring. In this sense, old theory is still relevant. However, current change is as much economic and social as it is demographic, if only because of the existing massive institutional commitments to pensions (Myles and Quadagno 2002: 51). Post-industrial development, too, has a whole set of new 'correlates', of which the increasing labour market participation of women, changing family structures, and declining fertility rates are the most important ones.

There is another way in which we can learn from the 'logic of industrialism' approach, which stressed that rapid economic growth created not only the **need** for welfare state intervention, but also the **resources** to do so. Scarbrough (2000) has stressed that trends associated with industrial development (urbanization, individualization, changes in family structures, increasing reliance on wage labour) are still paramount and hence permanently reinforce needs or generate new demands. At the same time, affluence, continued (although slower) economic growth, and the still considerable administrative capacity of the state all provide the resources and means for the welfare state.

Scarbrough also points to the continued relevance of those theories that see the welfare state as an aspect of modernization and development, especially nation-building. In her analysis, welfare states are still appropriate elite strategies of social and political incorporation and developments such as internationalization reinforce the threat of social exclusion. Her conclusion is that there are 'good grounds for the presumption that state intervention to ensure some degree of security and equity among its citizens remains central to societal cohesion and political order' (Scarbrough 2000: 240). The central role the welfare state plays in social integration and nation-building is underscored in several recent studies (e.g. Ferrera 2005; McEwen and Moreno 2005).

In Esping-Andersen's (1999) analyses, postindustrialism leads to serious trade-offs, particularly between protecting labour market insiders and creating opportunities for outsiders and, more generally, between employment and equality. Iversen and Wren (1998) even identify a post-industrial *tri*lemma between (1) budgetary restraint, (2) wage equality, and (3) employment growth, where only two of these three policy goals can be successfully pursued simultaneously:

  ❝ Because budgetary restraint precludes any rapid expansion of public sector employment, governments wedded to such discipline must either accept low earnings equality in order to spur growth in private service employment or face low growth in overall employment. Alternatively, governments may pursue earnings equality and high employment, but they can do so only at the expense of budgetary restraint. (Iversen and Wren 1998: 513) ❞

The changing welfare state

In the retrenchment and welfare state reform literature there has been an important debate on how to best conceptualize and operationalize welfare state change, reform, and retrenchment. The problem is known as the 'dependent variable problem' (see Green-Pedersen 2004; Kühner 2007). This is an important issue and needs to be clarified to answer the question how much welfare states have actually changed since the Golden Age of growth, that is to say, roughly since the 1980s. Some (e.g. Pierson 1996), on the basis of aggregate expenditure data, particularly transfer payments, concluded that there has been no radical dismantling of welfare state arrangements. But looking at the organization of the public sector, particularly the delivery of social services and the development of public employment, Clayton and Pontusson (1998) observed that current reforms (retrenchment) tended to have an anti-service bias

which was not picked up when studying transfer payments.

Pierson (2001) has done a lot to clarify the 'dependent variable problem'. Very helpful is his insight that welfare state change cannot be measured along a single scale. This would reduce the problem of welfare state retrenchment and reform to a dichotomy of 'less' versus 'more' and 'intact' versus 'dismantled', which is an unwarranted theoretical simplification. Pierson proposed to look at three dimensions of welfare state change:

• Recommodification: the attempt 'to restrict the alternatives to participation in the labour market, either by tightening eligibility or cutting benefits' (Pierson 2001: 422), that is to say strengthening the whip of the labour market.

• Cost containment: the attempt to keep balanced budgets through austerity policies, including deficit reduction and tax moderation.

• Recalibration: 'reforms which seek to make contemporary welfare states more consistent with contemporary goals and demands for social provision' (Pierson 2001: 425).

Of course, it is very difficult to distinguish between the various dimensions in practice, but a number of hypotheses that relate these dimensions to the welfare state regimes have been helpful in guiding empirical research in the first decade of the new millennium. Pierson (2001) argued that each regime (social democratic, liberal, or conservative) is characterized by its own specific 'new politics' of welfare state reform. In the liberal regime voters are less likely to be attached to the welfare state than in the conservative or social democratic models. Recommodification is here the pivotal feature of welfare state reform. In the social democratic welfare regime, voters are highly attached to, and dependent on, the welfare state. Recommodification is not so much on the political agenda of reform, but—if only because of the sheer size of the public sector—cost containment is. The conservative regime is probably the most ill-adapted model of the three worlds of welfare capitalism, as a result of which recalibration and cost containment are the two dimensions of reform that dominate. Here the issues are how to stimulate job growth in the underdeveloped service sector and how to contain the exploding costs of pensions, disability, and health.

Conclusion

Most recently, researchers have focused on newly emerged problems. Institutional and electoral analyses have come a long way in explaining why—in spite of the challenges and pressures—welfare states have been capable of resisting (radical) change or reform. However, there are many empirical examples of substantial changes that seem momentous in the light of mainstream institutional theory. So the question is how this happens or, in other words, how and under what conditions it is possible to override the mechanisms of sclerosis and resilience. Some have offered answers by describing specific institutional mechanisms or political conditions under which substantial reform is possible (e.g. Kitschelt *et al.* 1999; Levy 1999; Ross 2000; Bonoli 2000, 2001; Green-Pedersen 2001; Kitschelt 2001; Swank 2001; Vis and van Kersbergen 2007), others suggest that ideational factors, discourse (e.g. framing), and policy learning can prevail over electoral and institutional resistance against major policy reform (Cox 2001; Schmidt 2002; see Green-Pedersen and Haverland 2002; van Kersbergen 2002; Starke 2006). In the next decade or so, researchers will document empirically how welfare states change in various dimensions, what their causes are, and what effects or consequences follow from such changes.

The welfare state will remain interesting for comparative political science, because in the next decades we will witness another important transformation that will decide about the quality of life of citizens in advanced capitalist democracies. Welfare state reform is a political process in which power struggles are crucial, not only for understanding why and how reform occurs, but also for grasping what politics is all about: who gets what, when, how. In this sense, the study of the welfare state will continue to offer us essential and never-ending questions of comparative political science and political economy.

? Questions

1. Why is the welfare state an important topic for comparative political science?

2. Why is an exclusive focus on the welfare state misleading if one tries to understand how a nation provides work and welfare?

3. What makes a risk a social risk?

4. Are left parties that promoted the expansion of the welfare state also the main defenders of the welfare state?

5. What non-political processes have stimulated the growth of the welfare state?

6. Why is it that the more we target benefits at the poor only and the more concerned we are with creating equality via equal public transfers to all, the less likely we are to reduce poverty and equality?

7. Does the welfare state reduce poverty and inequality?

8.   Why does globalization not necessarily lead to the downsizing of the welfare state?

9.   Why are welfare states so resilient?

10. Which are the three worlds of welfare capitalism?

》 Further reading

Baldwin, P. (1990) *The Politics of Social Solidarity: Class Bases of the European Welfare State 1875–1975* (Cambridge: Cambridge University Press). A beautifully written historical analysis of how solidarity was produced 'through the backdoor' and the major challenger of the social democratic model of welfare state development.

Esping-Andersn, G. (1990) *The Three Worlds of Welfare Capitalism* (Oxford: Polity Press). The classic work that introduced the welfare regime typology and a central work of reference.

Flora, P., and Heidenheimer, A. J. (eds.) (1981) *The Development of Welfare States in Europe and America* (New Brunswick, NJ and London: Transaction Books). An early, but still highly relevant work in the tradition of modernization theory that is very rich in historical data.

Hacker, J. S. (2002) *The Divided Welfare State: The Battle over Public and Private Social Benefits in the United States* (New York: Cambridge University Press). A highly informative analysis of US social policy.

Huber, E., and Stephens, J. D. (2001) *Development and Crisis of the Welfare State: Parties and Politics in Global Markets* (Chicago and London: University of Chicago Press). An encompassing book that combines quantitative comparisons and detailed case analyses and gives the best overview of welfare state development currently available.

Korpi, W. (1983) *The Democratic Class Struggle* (London: Routledge & Kegan Paul). The study that firmly founded the social democratic/power resources approach to welfare state development.

O'Connor, J., Orloff, A., and Shaver, S. (1999) *States, Markets, and Families: Gender, Liberalism and Social Policy in Australia, Canada, Great Britain and the United States* (New York: Cambridge University Press). An analysis of the liberal regime from a gender perspective.

Pierson, P. (1994) *Dismantling the Welfare State? Reagan, Thatcher, and the Politics of Retrenchment* (Cambridge: Cambridge University Press). Why was it impossible, even for those who really tried, to dismantle the welfare state? The classic statement on the new politics of the welfare state.

Rimlinger, G. V. (1971) *Welfare Policy and Industrialization in Europe, America and Russia* (New York: Wiley). A still relevant historical study of how industrialization is linked to the emergence of the welfare state.

Scharpf, F. W., and Schmidt, V. A. (eds.) (2000) *Welfare and Work in the Open Economy*, i. *From Vulnerability to Competitiveness*, ii. *Diverse Responses to Common Challenges* (Oxford: Oxford University Press). An impressive book that collects theoretically sophisticated essays and valuable country studies of how welfare states adjust to their changing economic and social environment.

Ⓦ Web links

www.sp.uconn.edu/~scruggs/wp.htm
Scruggs welfare state entitlement data set.

www.lisproject.org/
Luxembourg Income Study.

www.ssa.gov/international/links.html
Social Security in Other Countries, social security online.

www.ilo.org/
International Labour Organization.

www.oecd.org
  OECD webpage.

www.bertelsmann-stiftung.de
  Bertelsmannstiftung on social policy reform.

 Visit the Online Resource Centre that accompanies this book for more information:
www.oxfordtextbooks.co.uk/orc/caramani/

22 The impact of public policies

Jørgen Goul Andersen

Chapter contents

Reader's guide

This chapter takes public policies as the independent variable and looks at their effects. It analyses different policies of regulation of the economy and the welfare system, and their impact on economic performance and social equality. The chapter discusses not only the impact of concrete policies, but also the impact of broader patterns and principles of policies. First, the chapter describes the overriding historical change in approaches to the economy, from Keynesian ideas of macro-economic steering, towards more market-oriented economic perspectives. Second, the chapter presents the main typologies of welfare regimes, varieties of capitalism, and flexicurity. Thirdly, the chapter addresses some of the empirical analyses of the effects of welfare policies and the tension between welfare and economic efficiency. Finally, the chapter discusses the feedback mechanisms from policy effects to new demands for policy change.

Introduction

Whereas political decisions (also called policy or output) were traditionally taken as the final result of the political process, comparative political science has increasingly turned attention towards 'outcomes' or the impact of policies (see Chapter 1). This change in focus has entailed a great interest in the implementation of political decisions, on the one hand, and in the relationship between politics and the economy—the economic and social effects of public policies—on the other. In this chapter I deal with the latter question (on implementation see Chapter 20).

Many of these issues are on the borderline between politics and economics. The so-called 'new political economy' approach seeks to combine insights from both disciplines. To some extent, this holds also for comparative **welfare state** research (see previous chapter). Substantial parts of what follows are drawn from these approaches. In addition, I shall discuss the political impact of public policies, that is, the political feedback effects of policies, which is a field of increasing concern in political science.

Many of these discussions revolve around the theme of reconciliation between welfare and economic efficiency in the broadest sense. In the 'golden age' of the welfare state from the 1950s to the 1970s, governments in the rich industrial countries applied Keynesian macro-economic steering to secure economic growth, full employment, and social welfare (Zürn and Leibfried 2005; see Chapter 21). After the unsuccessful attempts to combat unemployment by traditional Keynesian measures in the 1970s, however, economists began searching for alternative diagnoses and solutions. In the fields of welfare, labour market, and tax policies, economists became increasingly concerned with the impact on economic incentives. The 1980s saw a revival of neo-classical thinking, with focus on distortions of the smooth functioning of the market and the corresponding loss of economic efficiency. When Ronald Reagan was elected president of the US, and Margaret Thatcher became prime minister of

the UK, this sort of criticism of the welfare state moved from the margins to the mainstream of politics.

This turn in policies set the stage for many subsequent debates about the impact of **public policy**. What is the **impact of various public policies**? How should it be measured? Are equality and efficiency compatible, or is there a trade-off? Some researchers have claimed that globalization aggravates such negative economic side effects and enforce a harmonization towards more market conformity. Some have even questioned whether welfare policies have the intended welfare effects for those in need.

Addressing such questions, researchers have built various conceptualizations of clusters of policies that tend to go together because they are mutually connected. Such configurations of policies that are complementary may also be labelled **regimes**. In one branch of research, scholars have formulated conceptions of **welfare regimes**, emphasizing (re)distribution and taking their point of departure in a 'politics against markets' way of thinking. Others have focused on the positive interplay between the state and different types of market economies, arguing that there are different types of state regulations (or absence thereof) that work equally well—but differently. Still others have discussed various conceptualizations of **flexicurity** in labour market policies, that is, combinations of economic flexibility and social security.

Policies also impact on politics, and on future policies. In the last section, we discuss such feedback effects on interest constellations and power relations, and on the paths of public policy development. Besides this, we briefly discuss policy transfer and policy diffusion from one national context (or one policy field) to another, and finally, we return to the issue of convergence between public policies amid common exogenous pressures such as ageing, Europeanization, and globalization.

Economic paradigms and approaches to welfare

The aftermath of the Second World War witnessed a steady long-term expansion of the public sector, absolutely and relatively, in particular social expenditure (whereas traditional expenditures for the 'nightwatch state' went down, relatively). This took place in a climate of rapid economic growth. After the protectionist policies during the crisis of the 1930s which dramatically lowered international trade and economic growth, the Western capitalist countries had in 1944 decided for the so-called Bretton Woods system which linked the American dollar to gold at a fixed price, and other currencies to the dollar at (in principle) fixed exchange rates.

This system, alongside a gradual lowering of tariffs, contributed to long-term uninterrupted economic growth, almost full employment, and relatively stable prices. For twelve European countries where statistics are available for the entire period, average annual growth in GDP 1950–73 was 4.6 per cent, as compared to 1.6 per cent in 1890–1913 and 1.4 per cent in 1913–50. From 1973–92 growth rates slowed down—but only to 2.0 per cent (Table 22.1).

Until the 1970s, the growth in public sector and social expenditure (see Table 22.2) was largely regarded as a 'natural' concomitant of industrialization, economic growth, and modernization in general, including ageing of the population (Wilensky 1975: 47). Political scientists, usually taking a somewhat more conflictual and less functionalist view, also emphasized the political mobilization of the lower social

Table 22.1 Economic growth in Europe, 1890–1992

Periods	Average annual growth in real GDP		
	total	*per capita*	*per person-hour*
1890–1913	1.6	1.7	1.6
1913–1950	1.4	1.0	1.9
1950–1973	4.6	3.8	4.7
1973–1992	2.0	1.7	2.7[a]
1890–1992	2.5	1.9	2.6[a]

Notes: Countries: Germany, France, Italy, Austria, Belgium, Netherlands, Switzerland, UK, Sweden, Finland, Denmark, and Norway. For 1992–2005, real annual growth rate for EU-15 was 2.1% (as against 3.2% in the US); per capita in EU-15 was 1.7% (as against 2.1% in the US) (OECD 2007: tables A3 and A.9). It is mainly low growth in Germany, Italy, and France that accounts for the lower per capita growth rate in EU-15.
[a]Last year for the calculation of GDP per person-hour is 1987.
Source: Maddison (1991) quoted in Crafts and Toniolo 1996; Crafts and Toniolo (1996: 2).

Table 22.2 Social expenditure as % of GDP

Countries	Historical calculations[a]		OECD old series[a]			OECD social expenditure database (2007)			
	1900	*1930*	*1960*	*1970*	*1980*	*1980*	*1990*	*1998*	*2003*
Germany	0.6	4.8	18.1	19.5	25.7	20.3	20.3	27.3	27.3
Austria	0.0	1.2	15.9	18.9	23.3	23.3	25.0	26.8	26.1
France	0.6	1.1	13.4	16.7	22.6	21.1	26.5	28.8	28.7
Belgium	0.3	0.6	13.1	19.3	30.4	24.2	24.6	24.5	26.5
Netherlands	0.4	1.0	11.7	22.5	28.3	27.3	27.9	23.9	20.7
Sweden	0.9	2.6	10.8	16.8	25.9	29.0	31.0	31.0	31.3
Finland	0.8	3.0	8.8	13.6	19.2	18.5	24.8	26.5	22.5
Denmark	1.4	3.1	12.3	19.1	27.5	29.1	29.3	29.8	27.6
Norway	1.2	2.4	7.9	16.1	21.0	18.5	26.0	27.0	25.1
Italy	0.0	0.1	13.1	16.9	21.2	18.4	23–9	25.2	24.2
Greece	0.0	0.1	10.4	9.0	11.1	11.5	21.6	22.7	21.3
Spain	0.0	0.1	—	—	—	15.8	19.3	19.7	20.3
Portugal	0.0	0.0	—	—	—	11.6	13.8	18.2	23.5
Czech Rep.	—	—	—	—	—	—	16.8	19.4	21.1
Poland	—	—	—	—	—	—	16.2	22.8	22.9
Switzerland	—	1.2	4.9	8.5	14.3	15.2	19.8	28.3	20.5
UK	1.0	2.2	10.2	13.2	16.4	18.2	21.6	24.7	20.1
Ireland	—	3.7	8.7	11.9	19.2	16.9	19.0	15.8	15.9
Australia	0.0	2.1	7.4	7.4	12.8	11.3	14.4	17.8	17.9
NZ	1.1	2.4	10.4	9.2	15.2	19.1	22.5	21.0	18.0
Canada	0.0	0.3	9.1	11.8	15.0	13.3	18.2	18.0	17.3
US	0.6	0.6	7.3	10.4	15.0	13.1	13.4	14.6	16.2
Japan	0.2	0.2	4.1	5.7	11.9	10.1	10.8	14.7	17.7
Turkey	—	—	—	—	—	4.3	6.4	11.6	13.2

[a] Quoted from Lindert (2004a: 12–13).

classes and the strength of socialist parties (Korpi 1983)—the so-called 'power resources explanation'. Cameron (1978) described this as a sufficient but not necessary condition; economic openness and corporatist coordination was more important (see also Katzenstein 1985).[1] But there was a strong optimism about politics prevailing over markets (Ringen 2006). Apart from some scholars complaining about insufficient redistribution (LeGrand 1982; Goodin and LeGrand 1987), few questioned the impacts on equality, welfare, and employment, and few were concerned about possible negative side effects.

This changed after the breakdown of the Bretton Woods system in 1971 when the US had to suspend the convertibility of dollars to gold (which eventually made currencies free-floating), and after the first oil crisis in 1973–74 which released mass unemployment in most countries, often for the first time in a generation. In the first place, the largely unsuccessful attempts to combat unemployment by traditional Keynesian policies (such as stimulation of aggregate demand) and the anomaly of stagflation (stagnation combined with inflation)[2] paved the way for theories of rational expectations (Lucas 1972, 1973). These theories implied that economic actors would anticipate the inflationary effects of fiscal and monetary policies and adjust their behaviour accordingly. Thereby, the negative effects of stimulating demand would, so to speak, come before the positive ones.

Further, more and more economists began questioning the assumption of economic neutrality of redistribution (Sandmo 1991). Previously, economic redistribution via taxes and cash transfers to households had been described in textbooks as a matter of transferring a bucket of water from one person to another. This was challenged by Okun (1975) who argued that the 'bucket is leaking', i.e. there was an inevitable loss in economic efficiency entailed to this redistribution as it distorted the market mechanisms.

This was the beginning of a paradigmatic change in economic theory, away from a focus on macroeconomic steering, towards a more 'neo-classical' focus on the micro level and the supply side. The interpretation of unemployment is a case in point. Previously, it was seen as the responsibility of governments to ensure full employment. Unemployment was an effect of insufficient demand for labour power, because of too low levels of consumption or investments (to be solved, for example, by

stimulating effective demand), or because of insufficient competitiveness (to be solved primarily by wage moderation). But the legacy of policy failures constituted a kind of 'learning process' that could pave the way for new ideas.

From now on, economists and governments increasingly focused on the supply side of the economy, not least on the economic incentives that could stimulate labour supply and growth. Unemployment in Europe came largely to be seen as 'structural' or 'natural' unemployment, i.e. as an employment that would *not* disappear even if domestic demand or export-induced demand for labour power increased. Only structural changes towards more market conformity in social policies, tax policies, labour market regulation, and wage formation could help.

The impressive work *The OECD Jobs Study* (OECD 1994) summarized the new approaches and underlined the constraints of globalization which would make it more and more difficult for governments to avoid the necessary labour market reforms. This was disputed, however. Rather than seeing this policy change as an instance of social learning, Korpi (2002) maintained that this was much more a matter of political choice. In his view, the shift should be interpreted mainly in terms of changing power balances between capital and labour.

At any rate, the policy impacts of the welfare state came to a large extent to be seen as adverse: unintentionally, social protection aggravated the very problems which it was supposed to solve. Due to the phenomenon called 'hysteresis' (Blanchard and Summers 1986)—loss of skills during long-term unemployment—persistent unemployment would furthermore tend to generate large-scale **unemployability** which, in turn, might lead to the development of an underclass characterized by a dependency culture (Murray 1984). Even researchers who had previously evaluated the welfare state positively began speculating whether the price of equality would in fact be less wealth *plus* less equality if some groups were chronically marginalized from the labour market (Esping-Andersen 1996; Esping-Andersen *et al.* 2002).

This diagnosis could furthermore be convincingly illustrated by the different employment/unemployment records of the EU and the US. In the 1960s and 1970s, the US seemed to suffer from a 'structural' unemployment problem which

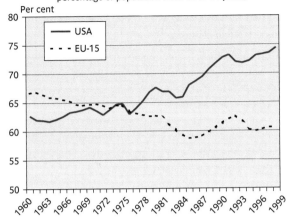

(a) Employment rates (total employment as a percentage of population from 15 to 64 years)

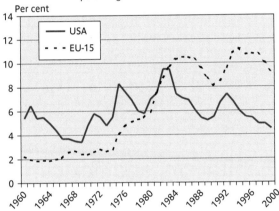

(b) Unemployment rates (unemployment as a percentage of total labour force)

Fig. 22.1 Employment rates and unemployment rates: EU-15 and USA (1960–1999)

Source: OECD (Historical Statistics, 1999 CD-Rom) and OECD (2000) Economic Outlook.

Europeans used to explain by the poverty caused by the underdeveloped welfare state in the US (see Figure 22.1). From the 1980s, however, it was the other way around: unemployment in Europe was chronically higher than in the US, approaching twice the American level. Looking at employment, the situation seemed even worse. Employment rates in the US were steadily increasing whereas the European figures were constantly declining. Europe had tried to solve its unemployment problems by early retirement and other arrangements to reduce the active labour force, but (in accordance with the new economic theories) the long-term dynamic effect seemed to be fewer jobs rather than lower unemployment. Declining employment rates only aggravated the future ageing crisis—which for purely demographic reasons (not to mention pension systems) was also much more threatening in Europe than in the US, due to lower fertility and immigration rates (see Comparative tables 4 and 14 at the end of this volume).

In short, during the 1980s and 1990s it was more and more often argued that the US had the most efficient welfare system: they had the market. Europe, on the other hand, was hit by stagnation or at best faced a trade-off between equality and employment. Apparently, the European welfare states were less sustainable in a globalized economy (OECD 1994; Nickell 1997; Jackman 1998). They had their successes in the 1950s and 1960s, but now they were sometimes described as 'virtual "time bombs" waiting to explode' (Ljungkvist and Sargent 1998: 546). European countries could choose to prioritize equality and security, but only at the price of persisting unemployment and long-term unsustainability of the welfare state. The welfare state and compressed wage structures with high minimum wages may have been beneficial in the 1960s and 1970s, it could be argued, but under intensified global competition after 1980, the effects were adverse. Similar arguments about loss of efficiency have repeatedly been put forward regarding the effects of taxation, not least in a context of global competition.

However, even though wage differentials typically increased (Förster and d'Ercole 2005), and incentives were strengthened, most European countries were not willing to lower minimum wages or give up substantial elements of social protection. As can be seen from Table 22.2, social expenditure has stopped growing as a proportion of GDP, but there are few instances of decline in proportions and virtually no examples of genuine cuts in aggregated budgets (see also Pierson 1994). In the Luxembourg Employment Strategy 1997, and at the Lisbon summit in 2000, the European Union (EU) confirmed its devotion to pursuing a somewhat different path in its employment strategy with more emphasis on education and training, (state-supported) innovation, and social cohesion.

The question of reconciliation between regulation, welfare, and equality on the one hand, and employment or economic growth on the other has been a core theme of discussion in comparative research on the impact of public policies. Theoretical arguments are clear, but modern economics has often been accused of putting too much emphasis on theoretical arguments and on model-based calculations. As argued by Lindert against the key findings of much neo-classical economics:

> such findings ... are not really findings. Contrary to the words offered ... none of these authors actually 'found' or 'showed' their results. Rather, *they chose to imagine* the results' as they are based on 'a theoretical model laden with assumptions. It is educated, intelligent, plausible fiction—but fiction nonetheless ... We need empirical tests that can choose among competing views on the basis of factual evidence. (Lindert 2004*b*: 82)

KEY POINTS

❑ The failure of Keynesian policies to combat unemployment after 1973 paved the way for new economic perspectives focusing on the negative economic side effects of welfare/tax policies.

❑ European governments have been reluctant to reduce social expenditures; at best, they have managed to reduce the growth in expenditures to the growth in GDP.

Welfare regimes, varieties of capitalism, and flexicurity

One of the differences between analyses of the impact of public policy from an economic and from a political science perspective is that the latter more often addresses the effects of institutions from a 'regime' perspective. That is, they often take their point of departure in ideal types of welfare states or political economies that build on a combination of variables that are seen as interdependent or complementary. The two most well-known are the concepts of **welfare regimes** (Esping-Andersen 1990, 1999) and varieties of capitalism (Hall and Soskice 2001*b*). In addition, there is a variety of concepts at a somewhat lower level of abstraction, among which the notion of **flexicurity** has been much debated. These approaches bear many similarities, but they differ in their ideas about causes, classifications, and impacts of policies. As far as causes are concerned, welfare regime theory puts the main emphasis on politics (interest conflicts) whereas varieties of capitalism theory are more 'functionalist' (with emphasis on what is beneficial for the economy). Theories of flexicurity are vague on causes but add the possibility that causes may be rather accidental. However, it is the questions about classifications and in particular about impact that are our concern here.

The concept of welfare regimes

The concept of welfare regimes builds on the observations (1) that welfare state characteristics tend to cluster, and (2) that there is a strong relationship between **labour markets, the family, and the welfare state**.[3] 'Welfare regimes' refers to the interaction, or the unison between these three elements (Esping-Andersen 1999: 4). What differs between welfare states is not just the level of expenditure (Table 22.2) but even more the division of tasks and the ways entitlements and expenditures are structured. I shall focus here on the social and economic impact of these welfare regimes.

Inspired by the classical works of Titmuss (1974), Gøsta Esping-Andersen distinguished between three ideal types of welfare regimes in his seminal book on

The Three Worlds of Welfare Capitalism (1990; see also Chapter 21).

Conservative welfare regimes (mainly found in continental Europe)

In the **conservative** model ('invented' by the German chancellor Otto von Bismarck in the 1880s), benefits are normally financed by mandatory social contributions, usually on a 50–50 basis, by employers and workers, paid to social insurance funds (often jointly controlled by the unions, employers, and the state, sometimes slightly state-subsidized). Eligibility depends on contributions, and entitlements depend on contribution record. Duration of unemployment benefits, for instance, is often related to employment record, and the level of pensions is more or less proportionally (actuarially) related to contributions. The main aim is to secure income replacement, that is, the conservative model is aimed at security rather than equality. As pointed out by Iversen (2005), however, insurance almost inevitably has some redistribution as a side effect.

The conservative model was designed to support—and maintain—a male breadwinner family structure with a marked family responsibility and gender division of labour. Male breadwinners should be able to support their family even in a situation of temporary or permanent loss of income (unemployment, disability, etc.). Women should be responsible for family care. Thus, the conservative model for long managed to maintain low labour force participation rates among married women, and as care was seen mainly as a family duty, this welfare regime tends to have an underdeveloped public service sector. Even when there is a collective responsibility for financing, the work is often delivered by families, e.g. in old-age care (Theobald 2007).

As to labour market regulation, this model logically corresponds with uninterrupted careers and strong employment protection of core workers (Esping-Andersen 1999: 18). Like several other aspects of this model, employment protection is often claimed to come under pressure. This holds also for financing via social contributions which is often considered less 'employment-friendly' due to the high 'social wage' in terms of social contributions that are levied on top of the actual wage (Scharpf 2000: 79–91). Also the male breadwinner assumption has definitely come under pressure, and the same holds for the low provision of social services, not least what can also be termed low 'social investments' in childcare. Many scholars agree that the conservative model is in profound crisis (Esping-Andersen *et al.* 2002).

Liberal welfare regimes (mainly found in Anglo-Saxon countries)

The liberal model is based on selective support for those who cannot provide for themselves. Benefits are usually tax-financed and, even though benefits are targeted, coverage is in principle universal for all citizens, men and women alike. By its very residual nature, this model is aimed only at alleviating poverty, not at large-scale redistribution, let alone decommodification. But it does involve a higher degree of de-familialization and a lower degree of gender segregation than the conservative model.

When it comes to labour market regulation, the liberal model is intrinsically linked to weak unionization and weak wage coordination. The labour market is to a large extent allowed to function as a market with a minimum of public regulation.

A transitional stage between the liberal and the social democratic welfare model (described below) is the Beveridgean social liberal model (named after Lord Beveridge who in 1942 issued a report about the future of social security in the UK). The core element is **basic security**—a system of universal but rather low flat-rate benefits which prevents poverty but encourages people to make additional arrangements for themselves, for instance private supplementary insurance.

Social democratic welfare regimes (mainly found in Scandinavia)

This model went one step further, either with very high basic security levels (as in Denmark) or—more typically—by adding an earnings-related tier on top of the basic security protection (as in the other Nordic countries), all based on citizenship and financed through general taxes. The ideal is an encompassing model covering the entire population, enabling everybody to maintain a high standard of living regardless of employment record (decommodification), and enabling even the middle classes to gain adequate protection by common public arrangements in order to avoid 'crowding in' of privately financed welfare. High social protection for all individuals regardless of employment record by itself implies de-familialization, but this is taken much further by the actions of the state to expand the public care sector in response to—and with the deliberate aim of facilitating—women's labour force participation. In a social democratic welfare regime, dual earner models based on two life-long full-time (or almost full-time) salaries is the standard.

As to labour market regulation, this model goes together with relatively centralized—or at least strongly coordinated—wage bargaining. Because of the dual earner model, and the comprehensive coverage by the welfare state, however, the need for employment protection is lower. In actual practice, social democratic welfare states differ on the latter point. Unemployment protection is uniformly high, but employment protection legislation is unusually liberal in Denmark, whereas Norway, Sweden, and Finland have moved towards rather strong employment protection. Danish trade unions were heading in the same direction—supported also by EU regulations—but eventually decided for what came to be labelled 'flexicurity'—a combination of low ('flexible') employment protection, generous social protection for those unemployed, and active labour market policies to bring people back to employment (see below).

The realization of these aims depends, it has often been claimed, first and foremost, on the political mobilization of the working class and its ability to forge alliances with the middle classes (Korpi 1983; Esping-Andersen 1990). Welfare states express 'politics against markets' (Esping-Andersen 1985). Some scholars (e.g. Baldwin 1990) have objected to this 'power resources model', claiming that universalism was rather the effect of a dialectic between working class representatives instinctively wanting to target benefits to the working class, and bourgeois parties who wanted to grant access to these social rights for the middle classes as well—given that these social rights were already there and had to be paid for anyway.

Varieties of capitalism

Whereas neo-classical economics regards large welfare states as economically inefficient and welfare regime theory emphasizes 'politics against markets', varieties of capitalism theory claims that large welfare states, apart from being redistributive, could also have highly beneficial economic impacts. According to the varieties of capitalism theory, highly regulated economies with large welfare states develop competitive advantages of their own which can make for equal or even superior economic performance. The attraction of this approach is, first and foremost, that it provides explicit theoretical arguments for this claim which seems more in accordance with real-world observations than, for example, neo-classical economics.

Rather than decommodification, the point of departure for varieties of capitalism theory is companies' interests in using the market as the main instance of coordination, *vis-à-vis* using other forms of coordination (Hall and Soskice 2001*b*). These mechanisms tend to be self-reinforcing and create a permanent divide, the authors contend, between liberal market economies (LME) and coordinated market economies (CME). The propensity of institutional traits to **cluster** or reinforce each other because they work together well (like in the case with welfare regimes) is called **institutional complementarities**.

The key variable, according to this theory, is the nature of skills needed in production. Where companies demand specialized skills that are not transferable between branches and perhaps not even between companies, they are highly dependent on workers' willingness to invest in these skills. The willingness among workers to invest in specific skills, in turn, depends on some kind of insurance against the risk of losing jobs. Therefore employers are at least as dependent on such protection as workers—in particular unemployment protection for those who become unemployed, but also employment protection against the risk of unemployment. Where companies demand general skills, by contrast, they are not interested in such protection, but prefer simple market regulation. Even workers do not have a sufficiently strong interest in social protection in this instance.

Accordingly, theorists in this tradition have criticized power resources theories of welfare regimes for their notion of 'politics against markets'. Social protection, according to Iversen (2005: 8), 'can improve the operation of markets as well as undermine them'. Some researchers claim that historically, employers have been at least as supportive of social protection as workers (Baldwin 1990; Swenson 2002).

Explicitly trying to bridge between varieties of capitalism and welfare regime theory, Iversen (2005) underlines the common insurance interests of workers and employers in different types of economies. When wage earners have invested in specialized qualifications specific to a particular company, employers and employees have joint interests in insurance—otherwise both workers and employers would be reluctant to invest in such skills. In short, Iversen argues that the level and composition of human capital is the core determinant of welfare state characteristics (Iversen 2005: 13; see also Estevez-Abe *et al.* 2001). However, insurance and redistribution are impossible to separate. Redistribution entails insurance, and conversely, insurance inevitably involves redistribution.

Needless to say, protagonists of the power resources theory are critical of this theory. Korpi (2006) claims that historical accounts are flawed and points out that, even if the theory of qualifications is accepted, it has a much more narrow range than the entire welfare state, let alone the entire system of political regulation. Besides, the allegation that power resources theory builds on a zero-sum concept of interests is simply wrong, according to Korpi.

Even though most of these arguments are quite convincing, they concern only the question of causes which is of secondary interest here. Korpi is far less critical of the arguments about **impact,** and here the varieties of capitalism theory has quite a lot to add. Thus, the institutional differences constitute **comparative institutional advantages** (Hall and Soskice 2001*a*: 36–44). LMEs, where skills tend to be general, develop competitive advantages in 'radical innovation'. CMEs, by contrast, with their strong emphasis on co-specific skills—including, not least, a strong emphasis on skilled work (like the German *Facharbeitertradition*), find themselves being particularly competitive in specialized quality production—in what the Volkswagen car company has sometimes marketized as *Bessermachen*.

This also explains why LMEs and CMEs have reacted very differently to globalization—in fact, over the last forty to fifty years, key indicators such as the proportion of GDP spent on government outlays do not reveal any convergence except for countries that are catching up (Table 22.3); in particular, there has been an increasing **difference** between the US and Europe since the 1960s. Apparently, LMEs have found one way of adapting to globalization, CMEs another (Swank 2002).

Welfare regime theory would have similar arguments, but is slightly less elaborated at this point. However, the variaties of capitalism theory is silent on the question of the relationship between family structure, the state, and the labour market. The varieties of capitalism approach also differs from the welfare regime approach by operating with only two worlds of capitalism. The Nordic welfare states, in this perspective, are at least as much CMEs as the continental European countries, in spite of their universal welfare arrangements which tend to produce somewhat less poverty and more equality.

Flexicurity

The concept of flexicurity simply refers to the combination of flexibility and security (Bredgaard *et al.* 2005). It was developed as political discourse after the 1995 Dutch labour market reform, as a kind of *post hoc* rationalization of what had been decided. In academic theory, it was introduced by Wilthagen (1998) and carried on, for example, by Auer (2000) and Madsen (2002).

Theories of flexicurity are narrower in scope and less theoretically ambitious than the theories above. In particular, they contain no grand theory of the origin of various arrangements—but they add the observation that welfare and labour market institutions are not always deliberately constructed. For example, until the concept of flexicurity was invented, few experts in Denmark had noticed that the country had a particular combination of policies/institutions which could constitute a comparative advantage. Rather, the country was typically considered a 'laggard' in the development from 'numerical' to 'functional' flexibility (Piore and Sabel 1984; Porter 1990). At any rate, the development of the Danish flexicurity model was not intentional from the outset. Theories of flexicurity are strong about 'politics for markets' but implicitly criticize the varieties of capitalism approach by introducing new divisions among the CMEs. The theories have been formulated, however, in both a narrow and a much broader version. The broader version is more compatible with the varieties of capitalism approach than the former as it identifies varieties of flexicurity as well (e.g. numerical vs. functional).

The narrow concept of flexicurity refers to a specific combination of (1) liberal employment protection legislation (flexibility), (2) generous

Table 22.3 Total outlays as % of GDP

Countries	OECD Old Series[a]				OECD Economic Outlook[b]			
	1960	*1968*	*1980*	*1990*	*1990*	*1995*	*2000*	*2005*
Germany	32.4	39.1	48.8	45.8	44.5	48.3	45.1	46.8
Austria	35.7	40.6	48.9	49.3	51.5	56.0	51.4	49.6
France	34.6	40.3	47.0	49.9	49.3	54.4	51.6	54.4
Belgium	34.5	41.7	50.7	53.2	52.2	51.9	49.1	50.1
Netherlands	33.7	43.9	56.9	57.5	53.1	49.7	43.7	45.7
Sweden	31.0	42.8	61.9	60.8	61.3	67.1	56.8	56.4
Finland	26.6	32.8	36.4	46.8	48.3	59.0	48.8	50.8
Denmark	24.8	36.3	56.9	58.6	55.9	59.5	53.9	53.0
Norway	29.9	37.9	50.7	51.3	54.0	51.5	42.7	42.9
Italy	30.1	34.7	42.0	53.9	53.5	52.5	46.1	48.2
Greece	17.4	23.5	30.5	49.6	50.2	51.0	52.2	46.7
Spain	13.7	21.3	33.1	43.0	42.6	44.2	39.0	38.2
Portugal	17.0	20.9	39.5	40.6	40.0	42.8	43.1	47.8
Czech Rep.	—	—	—	—	—	53.9	42.0	43.9
Poland	—	—	—	—	—	47.7	41.0	42.8
Switzerland	17.2	20.7	—	28.8	30.0	34.5	33.9	36.4
UK	32.2	39.3	45.2	42.3	42.2	45.0	37.5	45.1
Ireland	28.0	35.2	—	40.9	43.1	41.4	31.6	34.6
Australia	21.2	24.1	—	37.5	35.2	38.2	34.8	34.9
NZ	—	—	—	—	49.6	43.5	40.4	40.6
Canada	28.6	34.2	—	49.3	48.8	48.5	41.1	39.3
USA	26.8	30.3	34.1	36.2	37.1	37.0	34.2	36.6
Japan	17.5	19.2	33.0	31.9	31.8	36.5	39.2	36.9

[a] OECD Historical Statistics (1999); Andersen and Christensen (1991).
[b] OECD Economic Outlook 79 (June 2006).

employment protection, high compensation levels, long duration (security), and (3) active labour market policies aimed at solving matching problems between supply and demand of qualifications. This is sometimes described as a 'golden triangle'. Key countries are Denmark and to some extent the Netherlands (Auer 2000; Madsen 2002).

Like newer economic approaches, the narrow notion of flexicurity acknowledges the need for flexibility. When employers are free to fire, they are less reluctant to hire. And when workers can rely on solid protection, they are more inclined to change jobs. Besides, they do not lose much protection in terms of seniority as they can easily be fired anyway.

However, there is also another, much broader conception of flexicurity. Wilthagen *et al.* (2003) distinguish between four types of flexibility:

- External numerical flexibility (as above).
- Internal numerical flexibility (working time, overtime, etc.).
- Functional flexibility (workers move between tasks in the organization).
- Wage flexibility (wage dispersion according to productivity).

They also add different aspects of security:

- Job security (as above).
- Employment security.
- Income security (as above).
- Combination security (combination of work, family, etc.).

According to this conception, there is a 4 × 4 matrix of various flexicurity arrangements, and those countries which appear 'inflexible' on some combinations may be flexible on others. Whereas Denmark and to a lesser extent the Netherlands tend to substitute job security with employment security and income security, other labour market regimes maintain job security but seek to enhance functional flexibility and/or internal numerical flexibility. As it recognizes the existence of some kind of flexicurity in most European countries and makes no *a priori* assumptions that any model is superior, Wilthagen's conception of flexicurity is largely in accordance with varieties of capitalism theory.

Small state theory

The compatibility with varieties of capitalism theory also applies to the small state theory launched by Katzenstein (1985). Basically, it is argued that small states are open economies which are vulnerable to international competition and therefore in extra need of coordination. Such states tend to develop consensual corporatist structures which serve to stabilize these economies and to enhance competitiveness. The argument resembles those of varieties of capitalism, only it spells out why some countries are particularly inclined to develop those kinds of structures.

> **KEY POINTS**
>
> ❑ Welfare regimes refer to particular combinations of the welfare state, the family, and the labour market.
> ❑ Varieties of capitalism refers to different methods of coordination in the economy: via the market, or via negotiations and regulation. A key variable is the types of skills (general vs. specific) and, accordingly, the need for protection in order to secure willingness to invest in those skills.
> ❑ Welfare regime theory emphasizes conflict whereas varieties of capitalism is more functionalist and emphasizes common interests between employers and workers and beneficial impacts on the economy.
> ❑ Flexicurity in the narrow sense refers to a particular hybrid between liberal and coordinated market economies.

Tensions between welfare and economic efficiency

As mentioned, a substantial part of the research about the impact of policy—including the theories referred to in the preceding section—is concerned with what can in broad terms be described as the tension between equality and welfare on the one hand and economic growth and employment on the other. What is the impact of public welfare policies (taxation, cash benefit systems, and public services) and labour market policies/institutions on various aspects of economic performance? Below, I survey a few main issues and findings. I first describe a few findings from the literature that compares welfare regimes or varieties of capitalism. Next, I address the issues of welfare/tax expenditure, equality, and economic growth. Finally, I discuss the impact of labour market policies.

Comparing social and economic impact of regimes

One line of research is preoccupied with comparing the social and economic impact of regimes—welfare regimes, varieties of capitalism, etc. In an often quoted study, Goodin *et al.* (1999) compared the social and economic accomplishments of three welfare states (US, Germany, and the Netherlands), representing three welfare regimes (liberal, conservative, and social democratic, respectively). As far as equality and reduction of poverty is concerned, the authors find significant differences, confirming the predicted rank order, with the social democratic regime being the most redistributive and the liberal regime being the least. Moreover, the American welfare state, in spite of being targeted to the poor, turns out to be extremely inefficient in redistributing income and alleviating poverty (Goodin *et al.* 1999: 152 – 86; see also Korpi and Palme 1998; Kenworthy 2004: 102 – 5; and Box: The distributional impact of welfare regimes, in the Online Resource Centre). This corresponds with OECD studies showing an almost linear association between non-health social spending (towards working age population) and poverty rate in percentages (Förster and d'Ercole 2005: 29).

Goodin *et al.* (1999) also demonstrate that the social democratic regime has the highest score on social integration, stability in life, and on securing autonomy in life, whereas the liberal model fails in most of these respects as well. More recent studies show a decline in social capital (indicated by social trust) in nearly all liberal welfare regimes—and almost nowhere else (Larsen 2006).

The economic performance of the liberal model is better. In particular, it performs well in terms of labour market integration (see also below). But contrary to predictions by economic theory, Goodin *et al.* (1999) find little difference in terms of economic growth and prosperity, confirming the classical statement that 'incentives are not behaviours' (Marmor *et al.* 1990: 219).

In their book about European unemployment regimes, Gallie and Paugam (2000*a*) examine the impact of different welfare policies on the social conditions of those unemployed. They build on roughly the same regime clustering, but they single out the 'sub-protective' southern European welfare states from the 'ordinary' conservative ('employment-centred') model in continental Europe (Gallie and Paugam 2000*b*: 17). Almost regardless of indicator: poverty, financial hardship, life satisfaction, etc., they find the best conditions for the unemployed in social democratic regimes, followed by the conservative regimes. In several respects, however, the long-term unemployed are worse off in the 'sub-protective' regimes than in the liberal ones.

Whereas the findings regarding the social impact of welfare regimes are extremely robust, the conclusions regarding the impact on economic performance are sensitive to the delineation of time periods, data sources, and to methods. This is even more significant when we come to the distinction between LMEs and social market economies (SMEs) in the varieties of capitalism literature (Hall and Soskice 2001*b*). This theory claims that SMEs have competitive advantages of their own which can make for equal or even superior economic performance.

The prediction that SMEs are not economically inferior is largely confirmed in empirical analyses, for example, in Pontusson's study of 'Social Europe' vs. 'Liberal America'. Comparing averages, Pontusson finds that GDP growth rates have been roughly similar in the 1980s and 1990s; during the 1960s and 1970s, there were even superior growth rates in the SMEs (Pontusson 2005: 5–9). On average, the two regime types also perform equally well as far as unemployment rates are concerned. However, at least in the 1990s, LMEs have been the most successful when it comes to employment rates and decline in unemployment (Pontusson 2005: 71, 81–2). Again, however, these figures are averages. Some SMEs—notably the Nordic countries and the Netherlands—have managed very well also in this respect. At the same time we may note that, in accordance with small state theory (Katzenstein 1985), economic performance and in particular employment performance has generally been quite good in small states with open economies, that is, large export and import rates.

Whether or not this is a temporary phenomenon remains to be seen, but Pontusson contends that one has to take the balance of payments into account. In the 1990s most SMEs had surpluses on their balance of payments which means that they were underspending; most of the LMEs, on the other hand, were overspending and had deficits (Pontusson 2005: 95). This has even continued after 2000 where the Nordic SMEs have caught up on employment.

Tax/welfare system, equality, and economic efficiency

To what extent do taxes and transfers harm economic efficiency, as claimed by Okun (1975) and by innumerable theoretical contributions since then? Theoretically, there are several arguments that welfare spending would also have beneficial effects on economic performance. Possible positive mechanisms are several. Everybody seems to agree that welfare expenditure has positive effects up to a certain limit, and that some welfare expenditure, for instance in childcare, not to mention education, should be seen as an important investment in human capital or social capital. Social security may help in avoiding child poverty and the transmission of poverty from one generation to the next. Unemployment insurance may boost 'good jobs' and make workers more willing to take risks. Thus, Korpi (1985) has protested against Okun's metaphor of a leaking bucket and stated that it should rather be seen as an irrigation system. At any rate, effects must be assessed empirically. Below, I address a small sample of empirical studies.

Among the most thorough studies is Peter Lindert's two-volume book *Growing Public* (2004) that treats the economic impact of welfare state growth over more than a century and the technically more simple book of Pontusson (2005) referred to above. An earlier overview of findings and arguments is provided in Atkinson's (1999) *The Economic Consequences of Rolling back the Welfare State*. In his book on *Egalitarian Capitalism*, Kenworthy (2004) has addressed the issue of compatibility of equality and indices of economic efficiency.

As it emerges from the overview in Table 22.2, there is a large variation in social expenditure between countries. However, there are many pitfalls in such statistics, as some countries pay most benefits as taxable incomes whereas others usually pay net benefits. However, when these differences are corrected (OECD 2007; see also Adema 2000; Adema and Ladaique 2005) the ranking looks somewhat different (see Table 22.4). Further, if we include private welfare expenditure, the order changes almost completely. In particular, the US moves from the low-spending countries to the high-spending countries. The difference is that welfare in the European welfare states is mainly publicly financed, by taxes that are strongly dependent on income. In private insurance, people pay the same amount per head. Taxes, by contrast, are much higher on high incomes than on low incomes. This holds not only for proportional or progressive income taxes, but even for the most regressive ones, such as taxes on consumption.

By avoiding high taxes and economic disincentives, countries with high private welfare expenditures instead of public expenditures should theoretically be more efficient. However, no significant correlations are found between social expenditures on the one hand and level or growth of GDP on the other (see Table 22.5). Summarizing empirical tests, Atkinson (1999: 32–3) and Lindert (2004b: 86–8) demonstrate that most studies have found no significant associations. In his own more sophisticated test, including only genuinely **social** expenditures, Lindert (2004b: 172–93) found no significant associations either.

Lindert's analysis only covers the period until 2000, and one may ask whether his findings are not contradicted by more recent evidence indicating that, not least after 2000, the American economy has been performing much better that the European ones. From 1992 to 2005, growth rates in the US moved significantly ahead of Europe (3.2 per cent as compared to 2.1 per cent). However, when population growth is discounted, the difference in per capita growth is much smaller: 2.1 per cent as compared to 1.7 per cent (Table 22.1). Moreover, as pointed out by Pontusson (2005), the US has generally been over-consuming in this period. Further, Pontusson (2005) adds that high productivity increases in the US, relative to Europe, should be discounted by the long working hours in the US; by contrast,

Table 22.4 Net social expenditure as % of GDP (2003)

Countries	Public expenditure	Total publicly mandated expenditure (net)	Net social expenditure including private expenditure on welfare
Germany	27.3	29.5	30.8
Austria	26.1	23.9	25.0
France	28.7	29.8	32.2
Belgium	26.5	26.0	29.5
Netherlands	20.7	20.6	26.0
Sweden	31.3	29.2	30.9
Finland	22.5	22.7	23.6
Denmark	27.6	23.8	25.2
Norway	25.1	23.8	24.4
Iceland	18.7	23.2	23.2
Italy	24.2	25.3	25.6
Greece	21.3	—	—
Spain	20.3	19.6	19.7
Portugal	23.5	23.2	24.3
Czech Rep.	21.1	21.5	21.6
Poland	22.9	—	—
Switzerland	20.5	—	—
UK	20.1	22.8	28.2
Ireland	15.9	15.6	16.0
Australia	17.9	20.6	23.4
NZ	18.0	17.2	17.7
Canada	17.3	19.5	24.0
USA	16.2	18.9	27.0
Japan	17.7	19.7	22.2
Turkey	13.2	—	—

Source: OECD social expenditure database 2007.

Table 22.5 Correlations between social expenditure as proportion of GDP and economic performance

Periods	Correlation between social expenditure and . . .	
	Growth of GDP per capita	Level of GDP per capita
1880s	0.10	−0.18
1890s	0.34	−0.05
1900s	−0.23	0.09
1910s	0.12	0.31
1920s	−0.24	0.49
1960s	−0.17	−0.07
1970s	0.14	0.00
1980s	−0.07	0.12
1990s	0.01	0.12
Simple average	0.00	0.09

Social expenditure (1880–1930: welfare, employment, pensions, health, and housing subsidies) as % of GDP, initial year in decade.

Source: Lindert (2004a: 17).

Europeans have enjoyed a significant shortening of weekly hours as well as longer holidays. As can be seen from Table 22.1 above, measuring GDP per working hour also gives a more optimistic picture of economic growth after 1973 more generally. In short, there are few signs in these data that emerging new pressures like globalization force welfare states to adjust.

Why is the bumblebee flying? In line with these findings, Kenworthy (2004) demonstrates that there is no obvious tension between equality and economic performance. Adjusting for catch-up effects, Kenworthy actually finds the highest growth rate 1980–2000 in countries with low inequality. The same association is found in comparisons between American states (2004: 56).

As to the association between equality and employment, findings are more ambiguous. Many studies indicate a negative association between equality and private sector service job growth, sometimes also between the difference between pre- and post-tax income and total job growth (Kenworthy 2004: 90). Indeed, one of the major concerns in a period of globalization and deindustrialization is the potential surplus of unskilled labour (Esping-Andersen *et al.* 2002). However, surprisingly few studies consider the possibility that the number of unskilled workers may be reduced even faster than the number of jobs. In Denmark, about 20 per cent of all unskilled jobs disappeared from the early 1990s to the early 2000s. But the number of unskilled workers, due to generational replacement of lower educated generations by higher educated ones, dropped at an even faster speed (Andersen 2006).

Impact of labour market policies and institutions

This brings us to the impact of labour market policies. As mentioned, the reinterpretation of unemployment has been one of the core issues of the paradigmatic change in policies from Keynesian demand-side policies to what has been called supply-side economics. It should be added, though, that many economists underline that their interest in disincentives and distortions does not necessarily imply that Keynesian insights are scrapped. It can be an add-on policy rather than a replacement (Nickell *et al.* 2004).

In many countries, in accordance with *The OECD Jobs Study* (1994), focus in economic policies and employment policies was shifted to the issue of structural unemployment. In economic terms, structural unemployment is defined as the non-accelerating inflation (or wage) rate of unemployment, that is, the lowest level of unemployment compatible with stable price or wage increases (Elmeskov and Mac-Farland 1993). The level of structural unemployment will always be well above zero due to so-called 'frictional unemployment', that is, the fact that people switch between jobs. Workers are involuntarily dismissed and cannot always find a new job immediately. Indeed, in a flexible labour market the absolute minimum level of structural unemployment is bound to be slightly higher than in an inflexible labour market due to a larger job exchange.

However, in most countries, structural unemployment is assumed to be far above that minimum level. In the mid-1990s it was typically estimated that structural unemployment was close to the actual level of unemployment in most countries (OECD 1997), indicating that only structural reforms could bring about any significant improvement (see Table: Calculated structural unemployment in 1996 and subsequent development of unemployment (1996–2002), in the Online Resource Centre).

Theoretically, there may be several causes of structural unemployment:

- High minimum wages, which mean that low-productive labourers will not be hired.
- Insufficient incentives: too generous levels, and too long duration of unemployment benefits, social assistance, etc.
- Employment protection legislation preventing employers from hiring when they cannot fire, and enabling the core labour force to demand high wage increases without meeting competition from those unemployed who would be willing to work for less (the so-called 'insider-outsider' problem, see Lindbeck and Snower 1988).
- Insufficient mobility between geographical areas, or across trade borders, creating coexistence of unemployment and demand for labour power.

The recommendations in the 1990s from the OECD and others generally focused on more flexibility: more wage flexibility, more flexible employment protection legislation (i.e. less protection), more mobility across geographical regions, trades, and occupations, and stronger work incentives and/or sanctions to make workers more flexible. Empirical research in the determinants of employment and unemployment has come up with somewhat more nuanced answers, however.

In the first place, it could be questioned whether the estimations of structural unemployment tend to be misleading. As can be seen from Table: Calculated structural unemployment in 1996 and subsequent development of unemployment (1996–2002), in the Online Resource Centre, some countries have experienced significant and rapid decline in unemployment levels. Of course, this could be attributed to structural reforms. But it also seems that the estimations that are in fact extrapolating from historical associations between unemployment and wage increases

may exaggerate the risks of inflation and thus the level of structural unemployment.

Next, systematic studies of the impact of labour market and social policies give somewhat mixed results. As far as policy impact on unemployment is concerned, studies have focused on the following effects, among others (Nickell and Layard 1999; Nickell *et al.* 2004; OECD 2006).

Unemployment protection

There is consensus from most comparative studies that duration of unemployment benefits tends to have adverse effects; in particular, it tends to increase duration of unemployment spells and the proportion of long-term unemployed (OECD 2006: 61). As regards the effects of replacement rates, evidence is more mixed but overwhelmingly confirms the conventional wisdom (Nickell 1997; Blanchard and Katz 1996; Holmlund 1998; Nickell and Layard 1999; Nickell *et al.* 2004; OECD 2006: 61). However, it is also underlined in the OECD (2006: 190–1) that some countries have achieved low unemployment in spite of generous benefits, in particular if they are combined with a strict work test. Lindert (2004*b*: 119) adds that high replacement rates may harm employment, but tend to boost productivity, so that economic growth impact is small.

Minimum wages

This was a main concern in *The OECD Jobs Study* (1994). However, no studies indicate that high minimum wages are associated with higher unemployment rates (Holmlund 1998; Galbraith *et al.* 1999), and more recently, the OECD (2006: 88) has de-emphasized this factor. Besides, there is increasing awareness of dangers of entrapment in low-paid work (OECD 2006: 174–9).

Employment protection

In actual practice, employment protection does not, on average, seem to have any impact on the **level** of unemployment (OECD 2006: 95–6), but it has a strong impact on the **structure** of unemployment. Long-term unemployment is most widespread in countries with strict employment protection (Bertola *et al.* 1999; Nickell and Layard 1999; Esping-Andersen 2000). This does not falsify theories of flexicurity, but it does mean that these systems should be analysed in relation to specific national contexts.

Taxation

There is some evidence that, in particular, targeted reductions in taxes may have effects on unemployment—and perhaps even more on employment; but this remains a contested issue (Jackman *et al.* 1996; Blanchard and Katz 1996: 67; Disney 2000; Davieri and Tabellini 2000). The OECD (2006: 95) was reluctant to give any strong advice on this issue, including the balance between social contributions and income taxes. However, it is underlined that negative effects of taxes may depend on corporatism and a feeling of responsibility among union leaders.

Activation

Activation was pointed out by the OECD (1994) as a good second-best solution. However, both micro- and macro-level evaluations of the impact of activation have been rather disappointing (Martin 2000; OECD 2006: 68). It is far from being a panacea as was believed in the mid-1990s. In particular, effects often seem small in relation to costs. However, some activation measures work in some contexts, and countries that put emphasis on activation generally do tend to perform better, even if micro-level measures fail to document significant effects.

Corporatism

Probably the most robust finding in the literature is that corporatism and wage coordination have beneficial impacts on employment. The OECD (1994) used to be sceptical about corporatism because it tended to lead to 'compressed wage structures' with high minimum wages. But facing quite unambiguous empirical evidence, the OECD (2006: 82) has modified its view. Some studies indicate that **unionization** as such has a negative impact on employment (OECD 2006). But it is the **coverage and centralization** of bargaining that count, probably because they inflict a sense of responsibility for the economy on union leaders. This leads to wage moderation, in particular in periods with a high demand for labour power. It is also important to underline that unionization is not straightforwardly related to collective bargaining coverage. In most continental European countries, collective bargaining results among the minority of organized workers are extended to most of the labour market by so-called *erga omnes* arrangements. Often collective bargaining coverage is more than 80 per cent, even if unionization is only 30, 20, or even 10 per cent.

It is a quite stable finding that the relationship is U-shaped or 'hump-shaped' (OECD 2006: 84–5; Calmfors and Driffill 1988; Scarpetta 1996; Elmeskov *et al.* 1998; see also Hemerijck and Schludi 2000; Nickell and Layard 1999; Scharpf 2000). Both completely unorganized (market-determined) and centralized bargaining have beneficial impact, whereas bargaining at the company or sectoral level is detrimental. The ability of trade unions to moderate wage demands even has a positive effect on the level of structural unemployment. This is basically in accordance with the varieties of capitalism predictions.

The preferred type of analysis in this type of research is analyses of aggregate data on country variations, time series—and, increasingly, on both. But one can also choose a very different point of departure in micro-level survey-based studies. This is what we find in search theory which examines the impact of various types of incentives (possibly including non-economic incentives) on job search and transition to job. As such studies are most often conducted within individual countries, it may be impossible to find any direct policy variations, at least in cross-section studies. However, even if the unemployment benefit system has to be treated as a constant, there may still be individual variations in compensation rates. Such studies serve to bring out some of the micro-level mechanisms that mediate macro-level associations, and they also present an additional way of testing hypotheses (Clement and Andersen 2007). Furthermore, there are examples of cross-national studies that may bring out the effects of macro-level policy variations.

Policy feedback and path dependence

Until now, we have only looked at policy feedback on welfare or on economic measures. However, policies also have impacts on future politics and policy. This is also labelled policy feedback (Pierson 1994: 39–50; and see Figure I.1 in the Introduction). During the last couple of decades, there has been an immense increase in political science interest in comparative studies of the dynamic impact of policy and policy change. This section elucidates how policy change affects politics, how policy learning takes place, and how feedback mechanisms may often mean that policy changes follow a particular course determined by pre-existing policy programmes. This is what has become known as path dependence. Finally, policies are **diffused** and **transferred** from one country to another, or from one policy field to another.

Policy feedback on politics

The most obvious feedback effect of policies is the impact on the constellation of interests in society and thereby on future inputs to the political process. This may happen in several ways:

• Policies generate 'vested interests' in maintaining particular programmes.

• Policies create entirely new interest groups (see Chapter 14).

• Policies change distribution of power resources between interest groups.

• Policies create divisions of interests as well as unity of interests.

• Policies open or close access opportunities to influence future policies and shape actors' perceptions of interests.

These effects may be intentional or unintentional. All welfare programmes generate interest groups, many of which become organized. Perhaps the best example of unintentional generation of vested interests is found in early retirement policies in Europe in the 1980s. At that time, it became a popular strategy to combat unemployment, in particular youth unemployment, by means of various programmes giving older workers an incentive to retire before pension age. Very soon, however, most such arrangements came to be seen as vested interests, so that it could involve substantial political costs to change them. This is one of the main reasons why policy change is often nearly irreversible (Pierson 1994).

Sometimes policy change involves the creation of entirely new interests which may contribute to new dynamics. A case in point is outsourcing of public services to private providers. Almost instantly, such policies create a new interest group of private service providers which will lobby for further increase in outsourcing. If these service providers manage to capture a substantial proportion of the market, there may also be a division in interest between privately and publicly employed service workers in such services.

Power distribution between interest groups is also strongly related to policy. For instance, trade unions have remained extremely strong in countries with voluntary state-subsidized unemployment insurance organized by trade unions (the so-called Ghent system; see Chapter 18 and Figure 18.1). Another key example is universal vs. targeted welfare arrangements. Most likely, targeting would not in the short run leave those who are most in need worse off than before. It could even be legitimized by the intention to improve conditions for those 'really' in need. But in the long run, those 'really in need' often find themselves worse off. In the first place, if welfare arrangements are universal, their numerical basis of support is broader. Further, they may enjoy larger legitimacy as more people find it easy to identify with those receiving benefits when this group includes people like themselves. But perhaps most importantly, as noticed by Titmuss (1974), if the middle classes are enrolled in a programme, they will not only make larger demands but also have more resources to have such demands heard.

Policy learning, social learning

Another important instance of policy feedback is 'policy learning' or 'social learning'. The notion of learning is based on Hugh Heclo's classical remark that '[g]overnments not only "power" . . . they also puzzle' (1974: 305). They try to find out how policies work and which policies can produce the intended effects. Sometimes the terms 'policy learning' and 'social learning' are used interchangeably, as describing 'the process by which civil servants, policy experts, and elected officials evaluate the performance of previously enacted policies' (Béland 2006: 361).

The broad definition includes learning that is relatively 'detached and technocratic in nature' (idem) and is aimed at more narrow adjustments of policies after evaluation of their impact. However, comparative research has been more concerned with broader changes in ideas and perceptions of entire policy networks (Sabatier 1988), with change of the basic ideas and paradigms that define problems and possible solutions (Hall 1993), or with development of 'epistemic communities' of people sharing the same general framework of ideas (Haas 1992). Bennett and Howlett (1992) distinguished between 'government learning', 'lesson drawing', and 'social learning' on the basis of a classification of who learns what. They reserve the label 'social learning' for paradigm shift in an entire policy community.

At any rate, paradigm shift is particularly interesting from a comparative politics perspective. The concept of policy paradigm, which is borrowed from Kuhn's (1962) famous work on *The Structure of Scientific Revolutions,* includes several aspects. A paradigm is an all-inclusive interpretation of the world which includes not only goals but also:

- problem definitions;
- interpretation of causal mechanisms;
- possible solutions;
- a framework for interpretation of evidence;
- exclusion of alternative worldviews.

A shift in paradigm may have several sources. Generalizing from the Reagan/Thatcher experience, Pierson (1994: 49) suggests that learning is less important in this instance. Still, a standard source is some sort of crisis for the old paradigm which includes its particular set of problem definitions and possible solutions, i.e. policy instruments. When these instruments successively fail, the old paradigm comes into crisis. For instance, in Denmark, any thinkable Keynesian policy instrument was adopted between 1975 and 1986 to combat unemployment (Andersen 2002). When all these instruments had failed, this paved the way for a paradigm change which redefined unemployment not as a matter of insufficient demand for labour power or excessive supply, but as a matter of 'structural' problems such as too high minimum wages in relation to qualifications, too low mobility, too weak incentives to work, and so on.

This interpretation gave meaning to unexpected phenomena such as wage inflation beginning at a high level of unemployment. The new paradigm explained this as evidence that the 'structural' level of unemployment had been reached. Curiously, this paradigm shift was accepted by all major political actors in a very short time, partly because it included a variety of policy options, some of which were highly acceptable also to social democrats, not least 'active' labour market policy with its emphasis on enhancing qualifications and facilitating mobility for those unemployed.

It is important to underline that such policy learning is not always rational. As pointed out by Weyland (2005) and Béland (2006), the search for alternative paradigms is often steered by a 'logic of availability' where political actors make cognitive shortcuts because they **need** new ideas that can give meaning to anomalies, 'reduce uncertainty [and] propose a particular solution to a moment of crisis' (Blyth 2002: 11).

Once accepted, the new policy paradigm also installs its own standards of evaluating policy impact. This is by no means just an 'objective' assessment. The crucial premises are seldom questioned. If the expected results appear, nobody asks whether they may have been caused by other factors. And even if a certain policy *does not* work, this rarely leads to a questioning of the underlying causal assumptions, but rather towards focus on implementation problems, of problems of giving the medicine in sufficient doses, etc. In short, a paradigm carries its own learning and mislearning from observed policy impacts (Larsen 2002).

Path dependence

Policy learning in relation to paradigm shift is one among several mechanisms that tend to make policies path dependent. Path dependence in the broadest sense means that policies at one point of time tend to impact on, or indeed determine, policies at a later point of time because of high switching costs. This also implies that initial policy choices are often very crucial as they determine or at least constrain later policy choices (Powell 1991: 192–3). Thus, it is no accident that current variations in European welfare systems to a large extent reflect initial differences in choices that were made more than 100 years ago.

The theory of path dependence is borrowed from institutional economics where it was developed with the aim of explaining, for example, why inferior technologies survived in the competition with superior ones. For instance, if a certain technology, say, a particular software steering system, obtains a dominant position in the market, compatibility with this software by itself becomes a survival criterion for other products, and this in turn becomes an argument for adhering to this software. Or take the instance of a computer keyboard where the position of letters is determined by their previous position on the typewriter. Allegedly, the position of the letters on the typewriter was not designed with the aim of enabling typists to type as quickly as possible; on the contrary, it was deliberately developed with the aim of slowing down the speed of typing because

a mechanical typewriter cannot function beyond a certain speed: the types will simply jam (Pierson 1994: 43). Thus, it would seem rational to change the position of letters on the computer keyboard as this could increase the speed of typing. But once everybody has learned this system, the switching costs are too high.

In politics too, there are switching costs. Quite a few of these costs may be mainly practical/administrative, but the most important switching costs are of course political ones: switching policies usually involves losses and gains. For instance, incumbent governments will almost certainly be punished by those voters who suffer significant losses whereas they are far less likely to be rewarded by those who experience gains.

There are four main lines of interpretations of path dependence in comparative social research.

1. The first one emphasizes 'lock in' effects and the 'stickiness' of policies—not least welfare policies—analogous with the example of the keyboard: policies rarely change, except in extraordinary situations where external pressures and/or political conjunctures enable path-breaking reforms. In particular, vested interests tend to block major reforms.

2. Decisions at one point of time tends to impact strongly on decisions at a later point of time. This is why comparative policy analysis should be extremely sensitive to history. However, this notion of path dependence has been criticized for being too indiscriminate and too vague; certainly, it does not run any risk of falsification.

3. More in line with economic institutionalism, Pierson (2000) has attempted to develop path dependence into a theory. Here the concept refers to a model of 'positive feedback' which is basically analogous to the example of competing technologies. What we should do is to look systematically for those **mechanisms** which produce path dependence, that is, positive feedback where each new policy step reinforces the current path.

4. Still others acknowledge the importance of identifying mechanisms but adhere more to the notion of path dependence as a **perspective** which draws attention to such mechanisms whereby previous policies determine later policy choices. Probably this is the most realistic approach.

To take a classic example, universal flat-rate pensions have one great disadvantage, namely that they do not cover the pension needs of the new middle classes sufficiently. As a consequence, a pension system of purely flat-rate pensions tends to 'crowd in' private pension arrangements if it is not supplemented by some kind of earnings-related scheme (Esping-Andersen 1990; Myles and Pierson 2001). The predictable consequence is that those countries which seek to maintain universal flat-rate state pensions will eventually find themselves ending up with a 'multi-pillar' pensions system with a large private component. By the same token, however, those countries who introduce a supplement will find themselves under pressures towards switching to a purely contribution-defined system. In short, due to mechanisms of path dependence, universal tax-financed flat-rate pensions as we knew them, with or without earnings-related supplements, tend to eliminate themselves. Even though some of the intervening variables do not completely match these expectations, this is basically what has happened to the universal tax-financed pensions in Scandinavia (Larsen and Andersen 2007).

However, this example is rather difficult to generalize beyond the field of pensions; other mechanisms of path dependence are found in other fields, and it seems unlikely that more broad-ranging theories can be developed to account for this. Often path dependence is more about changing interest constellations and power resources. Furthermore, some instances of path dependence really do match the very static view which has been widespread in welfare state research, resembling more a negative feedback model than a positive one.

Alongside differences in interest constellations and differences in exposure to exogenous or societal pressures, not least economic pressures, path dependence is the main explanation of continuing cross-national differences in policies, in particular welfare policies. However, there may also be instances of policy feedback that lead to convergence.

Policy transfer and policy diffusion

Policy transfer and policy diffusion are examples of such policy feedback mechanisms that may lead to convergence between policies in different countries. Often the two concepts are used interchangeably (see Chapter 20).

We should reserve **policy transfer** for the use of knowledge about policies and their impact in one system (or in one policy field) to deliberately change policies in another country (or in another policy field). Thus, policy transfer is about processes which do not always involve imitation or emulation but may indeed occasionally involve substantial change while implanting policies from one institutional and cultural context to another (Knill 2005). It is a matter of deliberate cross-national or cross-sectoral policy learning.

Policy diffusion is a broader concept that refers to all conceivable channels of influence between countries (or between policy fields). Major emphasis is on studying various mechanisms of diffusion, from imposition to voluntary adoption of policy models that are communicated across borders or across policy fields in one way or another (Knill 2005; Rogers 1995).

The interest in diffusion of policies has increased, not least with the intensification of European integration. What is most interesting here from a policy feedback perspective is not so much the imposition of common rules by joint decision-making or by the Court of the European Communities, but perhaps even more the open method of coordination (OMC) which is an instance of so-called 'soft law' regulation based on recommendations rather than sanctioned rules. Studies of the impact of OECD have been conducted from such perspectives (Armingeon and Beyeler 2004). The OMC which was given this label in the EU summit in Lisbon, 2000, is a deliberate attempt to encourage policy transfer by bringing actors together to formulate common goals on the basis of recognition of institutional differences. OMC builds on policy learning and policy transfer (de la Porte *et al.* 2001).

Policy convergence

Policy diffusion constitutes a sort of disturbance in some cross-national research aiming to explain policy as an effect of structural, institutional, or political forces (Knill 2005). For instance, country variations in policy are often interpreted as an effect of either variations in economic pressures, variations in institutions, or variations in strength of political parties. But in addition to these determinants comes the problem that countries may simply have learned from each other. In purely quantitative analyses, this constitutes a serious 'disturbance' that is almost impossible to control.

However, there are some important problems relating to the issue of policy convergence by itself. In the first place, should convergence be measured by policy or institutions on the one hand, or by the *impact* of policies—policy outcomes—on the other? Secondly, four different patterns are conceivable (Kautto and Kvist 2002):

- **Convergence:** policies or policy outcomes become more and more similar.

- **Divergence:** policies or policy outcomes become more and more different.

- **Persistent difference:** policies or policy outcomes remain as they are.

- **Parallel trends, persistent differences:** policies or policy outcomes change in the same direction, but differences are maintained.

The last mentioned pattern is often conflated with convergence. For instance, Gilbert (2002: 138) notes a common trend towards more targeting (means-testing) of social benefits in nearly all welfare states. However, if we are to trust his indicators, this common trend is combined with persistent or even increasing difference between those (mainly Anglo-Saxon) countries that target mostly, and those countries (in particular Scandinavian ones) that only resort to targeting in rather exceptional instances.

At a meta-level, there may more easily be convergence. Welfare states have developed very differently, but if we add the private and public net expenditures, we find striking similarities across countries. Also if we look at the profile of the entire pensions system, it is obvious that, in nearly all countries, some kind of earnings-related system has developed, either within the state arrangements, or as a private proliferation of the welfare state. One could say that such highly different policies may nevertheless be **functionally equivalent** in the sense that they tend to produce relatively speaking similar outcomes.

KEY POINTS

- ❏ Policies shape politics and shape future policies.
- ❏ Policies affect power resources and generate vested interests, or even new interest groups.
- ❏ Policies are path dependent, at least in the broad sense that past decisions structure and constrain new ones, often also in the more narrow sense that precise mechanisms can be identified.
- ❏ Policy learning often takes place within a paradigm, but even paradigm shifts may be ascribed to learning.
- ❏ Policy convergence may derive not only from 'functional necessity', but also from policy transfer.

Conclusion

The study of the impact of policy is a relatively novel branch of comparative politics. It is also one of the most difficult because it is often very complicated to disentangle effects of policies from all sorts of other effects. Furthermore, it is difficult in the sense that it often involves cross-disciplinary insights in both politics and economics. Nonetheless, it is also a very important field of research. To determine what are the outcomes of different types of policies and how policies should be designed to obtain desired outcomes is one of the most challenging fields of research in political science. Furthermore, it is a field where economists increasingly begin to learn from comparative politics, not least from the insights in complementarity between policies or institutions that are mutually interconnected.

When it comes to the political impact of policies, this is also a rapidly expanding field of research that helps understand policy change in general, and not least policy change across nations. It helps to illuminate why countries exposed to the same external pressures often pursue quite different roads, as the theory of path dependence teaches us. It helps to understand some of the **political** forces behind policy convergence across programmes or across nations. And it helps to understand the **dynamics** of policy change.

? Questions

1. What does institutional complementarity mean?
2. What is the difference between welfare regimes and the regimes of varieties of capitalism theory?
3. What is understood by flexicurity?
4. How does corporatism impact on unemployment, and why?
5. How do different welfare models impact on equality, and why?
6. What is structural unemployment?
7. What generated a paradigm shift in the interpretation of unemployment?
8. How may policy changes affect the mobilization of interests?
9. What does path dependence mean, and are policies always path dependent?
10. What contributes to policy transfer between countries, and between policy fields?

» Further reading

Classical texts on policy regimes

Esping-Andersen, Gøsta (1990) *The Three Worlds of Welfare Capitalism* (Cambridge: Polity Press).

Hall, Peter A., and Soskice, David (eds.) (2001) *Varieties of Capitalism: The Institutional Foundations of Comparative Advantage* (Oxford: Oxford University Press).

Titmuss, Richard (1974) *Social Policy: An Introduction,* ed. Brian Abel-Smith and Kay Titmuss (New York: Pantheon Books).

Useful guides to impact of policies

Iversen, Torben (2005) *Capitalism, Democracy, and Welfare* (Cambridge: Cambridge University Press).

Lindert, Peter A. (2004) *Growing Public: Social Spending and Growth since the Eighteenth Century* (Cambridge: Cambridge University Press).

OECD (1994) *The OECD Jobs Study* (Paris: OECD).

——(2006) *Employment Outlook 2006: Boosting Jobs and Incomes* (Paris: OECD).

Classical texts on policy feedback

Heclo, Hugh (1974) *Modern Social Politics in Britain and Sweden: From Relief to Income Maintenance* (New Haven, Conn.: Yale University Press).

Pierson, Paul (1993) 'When Effect Becomes Cause: ''Policy Feedback'' and Political Change', *World Politics*, 45(3): 595–628.

Ⓦ Web links

www.lisproject.org/publications/welfaredata/welfareaccess.htm
   Luxemburg Income Study (LIS) Comparative Welfare States Data Set.

www.oecd.org/document/2/
   OECD Social Expenditure Database.

www.sp.uconn.edu/~scruggs/wp.htm
   Comparative Welfare Entitlements Dataset (Lyle Scruggs).

http://naticent02.uuhost.uk.uu.net/archive/index.htm
   European Social Survey (ESS): free downloadable data from 2002, 2004, 2006 and following years.

www.scp.nl/users/stoop/ess_events/links_contextual_data2003.htm
   Overview of websites with free information on European countries (links).

www.issp.org/
   International Social Survey Programme (ISSP).

www.worldvaluessurvey.org/
   World Values Survey (WVS).

 Visit the Online Resource Centre that accompanies this book for more information:
www.oxfordtextbooks.co.uk/orc/caramani/

SECTION 6

Beyond the nation-state

23 The EU as a new political system

Simon Hix

Chapter contents

Reader's guide

This chapter analyses the development and operation of the European Union (EU) as a political system. I start by looking at the evolution of the EU and how the process of European integration has traditionally been understood. The chapter then discusses what it means to think of the EU as a political system from the point of view of comparative politics. As in other multi-level polities, there are two basic dimensions of the EU system: (1) the vertical dimension—the allocation of policy-making power between the EU and the member-states; and (2) the horizontal dimension—the design and operation of EU decision-making. These two dimensions are considered separately before we turn to the 'missing link' in the EU system: the lack of genuine 'democratic politics'.

Introduction

In the early twentieth century, Europe suffered the two most destructive wars in human history, as the pinnacle of centuries of bitter political and economic rivalries between the states of Europe. At the beginning of the twenty-first century, in contrast, the states of Eastern and Western Europe are united in a continental-scale political system, where certain executive, legislative, and judicial powers are collectively pooled at the European level, and national governments' choices are heavily constrained by the rules and decisions of the EU. There are certainly problems with the EU. In particular, decision-making amongst twenty-seven states is difficult, and the democratic foundations of the EU remain weak. However, the EU is one of the most remarkable political achievements of modern times. The EU single market guarantees the economic prosperity of almost half a billion people, and most EU citizens take for granted the investment, consumption, educational, travel, and lifestyle opportunities that exist because of the EU. Above all, for the first time in human history, a war between the major states of Europe is almost unimaginable.

How did this happen? When six European states decided in the early 1950s to place their coal and steel industries under collective supra-national control, few would have expected that this would have led within fifty years to a new continental-scale political system. Box 23.1 lists the key stages in the development of European integration. A few stages are worth highlighting. In the 1960s, Western Europe became the first region in the world to establish a customs union, with an internal free trade area and a common external tariff. Added to this 'common market' was the first genuinely supranational public expenditure programme: the Common Agricultural Policy (CAP). European integration then took a major step forward in the 1980s. The first, and so far only, continental-scale 'single market' was created by the early 1990s, with the removal of internal barriers to the cross-border flow of goods, services, capital, and labour, a single European competition policy, and a single European currency (the euro). In parallel to, and partly as a consequence of, the single market, in the 1990s the EU developed common social and environmental policies, common policies on the movement of persons between the EU states and across the EU's external borders, and began to coordinate national macro-economic, justice and policing, and foreign and security policies.

As the first genuinely supra-national political system, many aspects of the EU are unique. On the other hand, from the point of view of comparative politics, there are many things the EU shares with other multi-level polities. For example, the division of powers between the lower (national) and higher (European) levels of government determines how policy-making works and the room for manœuvre of the two levels of government. Moreover, at the European level, the design of agenda setting and veto powers in the decision-making process determines which actors are most likely to secure the policies they most prefer and how easy or difficult it is to change existing policies. The field of comparative politics has developed analytical tools to understand these and other aspects of multi-level political systems which are increasingly applicable to the EU.

KEY POINTS

❏ In half a century the EU has evolved from an organization governing coal and steel production and a common market to a continental-scale political system, with extensive executive, legislative, and judicial powers.

❏ The process of European integration began with six member states, the EU now has twenty-seven members and may enlarge to thirty or even thirty-five in the next decade or so.

❏ The EU shares many characteristics of other multi-level political systems, which enables the tools of comparative politics to be applied to the EU.

BOX 23.1 Key dates in the development of the European Union

18 February 1951	Belgium, France, Germany, Italy, Luxembourg, and the Netherlands sign Treaty of Paris, launching the European Coal and Steel Community (ECSC).
23 July 1952	Treaty of Paris enters into force.
1 January 1958	Treaties of Rome enter into force, establishing the EEC and Euratom.
30 July 1962	Common Agricultural Policy starts.
5 February 1963	Van Gend en Loos ruling of the ECJ, establishes the 'direct effect' of EEC law.
15 July 1964	*Costa* v. *ENEL* ruling of the ECJ, establishes the 'supremacy' of EEC law.
29 January 1966	Luxembourg compromise, which effectively means Council must decide unanimously.
1 July 1967	Merger Treaty, establishing a single set of institutions for the three communities.
1–2 December 1969	Hague Summit, governments agree to push for further economic and political integration.
1 January 1973	Denmark, Ireland, and the United Kingdom join.
27 October 1970	Governments start foreign policy cooperation (European Political Cooperation).
10 February 1979	Cassis de Dijon ruling of the ECJ, establishes 'mutual recognition' in the provision of goods and services in the common market.
13 March 1979	European Monetary System begins.
7–10 June 1979	First 'direct' elections of the European Parliament.
1 January 1981	Greece joins.
26 June 1984	Margaret Thatcher negotiates the 'British rebate' from the annual budget.
1 January 1985	First 'European Communities' passports are issued.
1 January 1986	Portugal and Spain join.
19 May 1986	European flag used for the first time.
1 July 1987	Single European Act enters into force, launching the single market programme.
13 February 1988	First multi-annual framework for the EC budget agreed.
9 November 1989	Berlin Wall falls.
1 January 1993	Single European Market starts.
1 November 1993	Maastricht Treaty enters into force, launching the EU and the plan for EMU.
21 July 1994	European Parliament rejects a piece of EU legislation for the first time.
1 January 1995	Austria, Finland, and Sweden join.
1 January 1999	EMU starts.
15 March 1999	Santer Commission resigns before a censure vote is held in the European Parliament.
1 May 1999	Amsterdam Treaty enters into force, starting the 'area of freedom, security and justice'.
24 March 2000	European Council agrees the 'Lisbon strategy' to promote growth and productivity.

(continued)

BOX 23.1 (continued)

1 January 2002	Euro notes and coins replace national notes and coins for ten member-states.
1 February 2003	Nice Treaty enters into force, launching defence cooperation and reforming the institutions in preparation for enlargement.
1 May 2004	Cyprus, Czech Republic, Estonia, Hungary, Latvia, Lithuania, Malta, Poland, Slovakia, and Slovenia join.
26 October 2004	European Parliament blocks the election of a new Commission.
29 October 2004	Treaty establishing a Constitution for Europe signed.
29 May/1 June 2005	'No' votes in referenda in France and the Netherlands on the Constitutional Treaty.
1 January 2007	Bulgaria and Romania join.

Explanations of European integration

In the early period of the EU's development, social scientists attempted to explain the process of economic and political integration in Europe. Several scholars expected in the 1950s and 1960s that 'regional integration' would happen in many parts of the world, as relations between states changed dramatically in the aftermath of the Second World War and with the onset of the cold war. However, by the mid-1960s, the extent of institution-building and the intensity of political and economic cooperation were far greater in Western Europe than in any other region. As a result, an explanatory framework developed for the sole purpose of understanding the EU, rather than for the purpose of explaining a general social or political phenomenon. Broadly speaking, and grossly simplifying a diverse set of research and scholarship, explanations of European integration fall into two main camps: (1) **intergovernmental approaches**, which see the preferences and decisions of the national governments as primary; and (2) **supra-national approaches**, which see supra-national political, social, and economic forces beyond the control of the national governments as primary.

Intergovernmental approaches

The basic assumption of these approaches is that main actors in the EU are the governments of the member-states (e.g. Hoffmann 1966, 1982; Taylor 1982; Moravcsik 1991). National governments have a clear set of preferences about what policies they would like to see allocated to the European level, and what the content of the policies should be. For example, British governments have traditionally preferred economic integration to political integration, while German governments have wanted both. Moreover, British governments have wanted the EU to adopt a free-market approach to economic integration, while German governments have looked for the EU to adopt a 'social market' approach, with harmonized social and labour market regulations.

Another assumption of the intergovernmental approaches is that governments 'bargain hard' with each other on the basis of these preferences, and only agree to outcomes at the European level if these outcomes promote their preferences. This assumption is usually matched to a corollary assumption, that governments possess enormous political and informational resources (for example, they have large public administrations), and so have a good understanding of the likely consequences of their actions. For example, governments understood that establishing a single market and economic and monetary union would inevitable create constraints on a range of important domestic economic and social policies.

At face value, one might assume that, if governments are self-interested, have varying preferences, and are determined not to lose any ground when bargaining at the European level, nothing will ever be done in the EU. Indeed, this was one of the conclusions of some of the early intergovernmental theorists, who assumed that European integration could not progress beyond a very minimal level (e.g. Hoffmann 1966). Nevertheless, more recent intergovernmental approaches argue that there are good collective reasons for member-state governments to hand over significant powers to the EU institutions, well beyond the expectations of the early theorists (Moravcsik 1993, 1998; Pollack 1997). For example, it is often in all the governments' interests to have a common policy for the single market (such as a common standard for car emissions), yet agreement cannot be reached as each government has their own particular policy preference which they are reluctant to give up. This 'coordination problem' can be resolved by delegating agenda-setting power to the European Commission, where the Commission works out which is the best policy option for the EU as a whole, which all the governments then agree to support. This helps explain why delegating agenda-setting power to the Commission in the creation of the single market was both in the self-interest of the EU governments and crucial for the process of European integration.

The intergovernmental approaches explain well why the process of integration stalled in the 1970s, as governments preferred national to European solutions to the economic problems in that period. These approaches also explain how a convergence of governments' preferences in favour of a continental-scale market, and the careful design of a set of new decision-making rules, enabled European integration to be relaunched in the 1980s and 1990s.

Nevertheless, there are several aspects of European integration that these approaches have not been able to explain so well. They cannot explain the increase in the powers of the European Parliament (EP) in the treaty reforms since the mid-1980s. In addition, if the governments are in control of the process of European integration, and there are no long-term consequences beyond the collective intentions of the governments, it is hard to explain why there is declining support for European integration. Indeed, from an intergovernmental perspective, since the governments run the EU, and the governments are elected by the citizens, then there is no 'democratic deficit' in the EU (Moravcsik 2002). Finally, although

intergovernmental approaches may be very useful for understanding the 'grand bargains' in the process of European integration, such as the Single European Act or the Maastricht Treaty, they seem less useful for understanding day-to-day decision-making, where there are multiple actors and interests and a more complex set of preferences and decision-making rules.

To understand how the EU works on a day-to-day basis, it is more useful to think of the EU as a political system, and apply tools and approaches from the study of comparative politics along the lines of national systems on which comparative politics has traditionally focused.

Supra-national approaches

The basic assumption of these approaches is that the process of European integration is a deterministic process driven by underlying political, economic, and social forces. In the early period of European integration, Ernst Haas proposed what he called a 'neo-functionalist' theory of economic and political integration (Haas 1958, 1961; cf. Lindberg 1963). At the heart of this theory was the concept of 'spillover', whereby 'a given action, related to a specific goal, creates a situation in which the original goal can be assured only by taking further actions, which in turn create a further condition and a need for more, and so forth' (Lindberg 1963: 9). For example, a common market in coal and steel would work much more efficiently if there was a common market in other goods and services used in the production and distribution of coal and steel. Similarly, once the free movement of labour is established as part of the single market, with the effective abolition of controls on the movement of people once they are inside the EU, there was pressure on the member-state governments to agree common justice and home affairs policies.

One variant of this approach was Bela Belassa's (1961) theory of economic integration. Belassa argued that, once a customs union had been established, the potential economies of scale from such a union could not be met unless all barriers to the free movement of goods and services had been removed (in other words in a single market). Then, once a single market had been established, the market would function more effectively if a single currency could be established, which would allow for greater price transparency and reduced transaction costs of doing business across borders. Then, if a single currency were established, economic shocks to the currency union could no longer be addressed through monetary policies, so there would need to be fiscal transfers from high growth regions to low growth regions. These fiscal transfers would need to be legitimized somehow, which would require the establishment of genuine political union, with democratic elections for the central institutions. In other words, Belassa predicted a logical teleological development from a customs union to a political union.

Most scholars within the supra-nationalist approach were not as economically determinist as Belassa, in that they assumed that integration would not proceed without the input of actors or groups of actors. In other words, economic forces are insufficient on their own to force states to take major integrationist steps. However, in contrast to the intergovernmental view, which emphasizes the supremacy of states and governmental actors, most scholars within the supra-national framework emphasize the role of 'non-state' actors, such as economic and social interest groups and the supra-national institutions of the EU themselves (e.g. Marks *et al.* 1996; Pierson 1996; Sandholtz and Stone Sweet 1997; Pollack 2003). For example, transnational businesses in the early 1980s put pressure on the governments to support the creation of a genuine single market in Europe (e.g. Sandholtz and Zysman 1989).

Meanwhile, the Commission, led by President Jacques Delors, played an important role in shaping the single market programme, the reform of the EU budget in the late 1980s, the plan for economic and monetary union (e.g. Pollack 2003). Similarly,

by establishing the doctrines of the 'direct effect' and 'supremacy' of EC law in the early 1960s, the European Court of Justice (ECJ) has fashioned a quasi-federal legal framework for the EU, beyond the intentions of the signatories of the early treaties (e.g. Weiler 1991). And the EP has interpreted the decision-making rules of the EU in a way that has maximized its influence under the various legislative procedures (e.g. Hix 2002).

Supra-national approaches explain very well the evolution from the coal and steel community to the customs union. They also explain the development from the single market to economic and monetary union, and how a market on a continental scale has spillover effects on governments' taxing, spending, immigration, and policing policies. Overall, supra-nationalism does well to capture the remarkable, and perhaps teleological, evolution of the EU from a customs union in the 1960s to a full-blown political system by the end of the twentieth century. Nevertheless, the inherent determinism of the supra-nationalist approaches means that they are less able to explain why the process of European integration slowed between the late 1960s and the mid-1980s, or why some member-states decided to join the EU at different times or indeed remain largely outside the process of European integration (such as Norway and Switzerland). These approaches are also less able to explain why the EU is more able to adopt common policies in some areas, such as environmental policy, than in other areas, such as social policy.

Again, thinking of the EU as a political system helps us to understand its internal workings in detail, which in turn has implications for understanding the general process of European integration.

KEY POINTS

❑ For most of its history, the EEC/EU has been mainly understood by social scientists as a unique case of political and economic 'integration' between sovereign nation-states.

❑ Intergovernmentalism focuses on how the policy preferences and actions of the European governments, and particular the three most powerful governments

(Germany, France, and Britain), shape the design of the EU at the various stages of integration.

❑ Supra-nationalism focuses on how the underlying economic, political, and social factors and the behaviour of interest groups and the EU institutions constrain the choices of governments and so further economic and political integration.

COUNTRY PROFILE Israel

State of Israel (*Medinat Yisra'el*)

State formation

In the late 19th century, the Austro-Hungarian Jew Theodor Herzl founded the Zionist movement that strived for the establishment of a national Jewish state. By the end of the Second World War, some 500,000 Jews immigrated to Palestine, mostly from Russia and Europe following pogroms and outbreaks of anti-semitism. Palestine became a League of Nations mandate administered by Britain in 1920. Independence was gained in 1948.
Constitution No formal constitution. A parliamentary committee has been working on a draft constitution since 2003.

Form of government

Parliamentary democracy.
Head of state President elected by Parliament, term of 7 years (no term limits).
Head of government Prime Minister assigned by the President; traditionally the leader of the party that holds most of the seats in parliament.

Cabinet Ministers selected by the Prime Minister and approved by Parliament.
Administrative subdivisions 6 districts.

Legal system

Mixture of English common law, British Mandate regulations, and Jewish, Christian, and Muslim legal systems.

Legislature

Unicameral parliament (*Knesset*): 120 seats, term of 4 years.

Electoral system

Proportional representation.
Formula D'Hondt.
Constituencies 1 multi-member constituency for 120 seats.
Barrier clause 2% nation-wide.
Suffrage Universal, 18 years.

Direct democracy

None.

Party system Results of the 2006 legislative elections:

Electorate:	5,014,622	100.0%
Voters:	3,186,739	63.5%

Party	Valid votes	%	Seats
Kadima (Forward)	690,901	22.0	29
Labour	472,366	15.1	19
Shas (Sephardi)	299,054	9.5	12
Likud	281,996	9.0	12
Our Home Israel	281,880	9.0	11
National Union-National Religious Party	224,083	7.1	9
Age-Pensioners of Israel to the Knesset	185,759	5.9	7
United Torah Judaism	147,091	4.7	6
Vigor-Together	118,302	3.8	5
United Arab Lists-Arab Renewal Movement	94,786	3.0	4
Hadash (United Front for Peace and Equality)	86,092	2.7	3
Balad (National Democratic Assembly)	72,066	2.3	3
The Greens	47,595	1.5	0
Green Leaf	40,353	1.3	0
Others	94,740	3.0	0
Total	3,137,064	100.0	120

Note: Category 'Others' includes parties with less than 1% nation-wide and no seats.
Source: Knesset.

Understanding the EU as a political system

A political system but not a state

A key insight of modern social science, as it began to emerge as a discipline at the start of the twentieth century, was that democratic and effective government can only work within a state: which Max Weber and others understood as a hierarchical organization, where power is concentrated at the centre, and where the central authorities can use the 'forces of violence' (the police and the army) to enforce the law and maintain political stability (see Chapter 4). However, this ideal type of political organization only really existed in a relatively small number of countries (such as France, Britain, and Sweden) and in a rather short period of human history (from the seventeeth to the mid-twentieth centuries). For many societies in Europe and throughout the world, and for most of human history, power and authority has been split between multiple different actors and levels of government. And with the widespread decentralization of authority to local and regional governments and non-state organizations, and with the delegation of authority to supra-national bodies such as the EU and the World Trade Organization (WTO), political power is now dispersed or 'shared' in multiple settings (see Chapter 24). This does not mean that the 'state' as traditionally understood does not exist. However, it does mean that politics, government, and policy-making now exist in many contexts either outside or beyond the classic Weberian state (Badie and Birnbaum 1983).

This is precisely the situation with Europe, where the gradual process of economic and political integration has produced a complex allocation of executive, legislative, and judicial policy-making powers at multiple levels of government, including the European level. For sure, the EU is the first genuine 'supra-national polity' to exist in human history, and as such is certainly unique. However, all political systems are to some extent unique. The US has a unique model of the separation of executive and legislative power, France has a unique semi-presidential model of government, Germany has a unique model of interlocking federalism, and so on (see Chapter 11 on the diverse forms of territorial organization). What is more important from the point of view of comparative political analysis is that all political systems face a common set of issues, such as what powers are allocated to the central institutions relative to the lower institutions, and how decision-making should work in the central institutions.

This was one of the insights of comparative political scientists in the 1950s, who tried to develop a common framework for defining and analysing the complex array of political systems that existed throughout the world (e.g. Almond 1956; Easton 1957; see also the Introduction to this volume). There are four essential characteristics of all democratic political systems:

1. There is a clearly defined set of institutions for collective decision-making and set of rules governing relations between and within these institutions.

2. Citizens seek to achieve their political desires through the political system, either directly or through intermediary organizations like interest groups and political parties.

3. Collective decisions in the political system have an impact on the distribution of economic resources and the allocation of social and political values across the whole system.

4. There is a continuous interaction between these political outputs, new demands on the system, new decisions, and so on.

The EU possesses all these characteristics. First, the level of institutional development and complexity in the EU is far greater than in any other international or regional integration organization. One might even say that the EU possesses the most formalized and complex set of decision-making rules of any political system in the world. Second, a large number of public and private groups, from multi-national corporations and global environmental groups to individual citizens, are involved on a daily basis in trying to influence the EU policy process. Third, EU policy outcomes are highly significant and are felt throughout the EU. The direct redistributive capacity of the EU is indeed small, since the EU budget is only about 1 per cent of the total GDP of the EU. However, the single market, European social and environmental regulations, the single currency, justice and interior affairs policies, and the myriad of other policy outputs of the EU system have an enormous indirect impact on the allocation of resources and social relationships in European society. Fourth, the EU political system is a permanent feature of political life in Europe. The quarterly meetings of the heads of government of the member states in the European Council may be the only feature that many citizens and media outlets notice. Nevertheless, EU politics is a continuous process, within and between the EU institutions in Brussels, between national governments and Brussels, within national public administrations, between private interests and governmental officials in Brussels and at the national level, and between private groups involved in EU affairs at the national and European levels.

Conceptualizing the EU as a political system rather than a unique example of regional integration enabled social scientists in the late 1980s and early 1990s to start to apply tools and methods from the comparative study of political systems to the EU (e.g. Scharpf 1988; Streeck and Schmitter 1991; Sbragia 1992; Tsebelis 1994; van der Eijk and Franklin 1996; Majone 1996; McKay 1996). These tools helped provide answers to a new set of generalizable questions, such as which actors are most influential in the EU legislative process, how independent from political control is the ECJ, why do some citizens support the EU while others oppose it, why does the EU produce some policy outcomes but not others? As a result, conceptualizing the EU as a political system enabled social scientists to answer new questions, discover new facts, draw new analytical inferences, and bring together scholarship on the EU with the general field of comparative politics (Hix 2005).

The constitutional architecture of the EU

The Treaty establishing a Constitution for Europe, which was signed by the member states in October 2004 and renegotiated in June 2007, was an effort to simplify and codify the existing rules governing the allocation of competences between the EU and the member-states and the operation of the EU institutions. Even before this treaty, however, the EU already had a basic 'constitutional architecture'

because there is an established division of policy competences and institutional powers which results from the existing treaties and how these treaties have been interpreted over the years. Indeed, one of the remarkable things about the new treaty is how little of the established policy and institutional architecture of the EU it would in fact change if it entered into force.

Box 23.2 describes the basic policy architecture of the EU. This 'catalogue of competences' is not set out in any one article of the existing treaties, but is a widely accepted interpretation by legal and political scientists of the design of the basic policy framework in the EU. The EU level has exclusive responsibility for the creation and regulation of the single market, and for managing the competition and external customs and trade policies that are inherently derived from this task. The EU level is also responsible for the monetary policies of the member-states whose currency is the euro, for the common agricultural policy, and the common fisheries policy. In these areas, the EU governments no longer have any power to make policy at the national level.

A wide array of policy competences are 'shared' between the EU and the member-states. In these areas, policies are made at both the national and European levels and the European-level policies usually aim to supplement existing or ongoing policies at the national level. This is the case, for example, in the areas of labour market regulation, regional spending, and immigration and asylum. The third area of policies can be described as 'coordinated competences', in that these are policies where action remains primarily at the member-state level, but the governments have accepted that they need to coordinate their domestic policies collectively at the European level because there are inevitable effects on each other from keeping these policies at the national level. For example, for the states with a single currency there is a need to coordinate their macro-economic policies, and with the freedom of movement of persons inside the EU there is a need to coordinate some policing and criminal justice policies. Finally, all the major areas of taxation and public spending, such as education, health care, transport, housing, welfare provision, and pensions, remain the exclusive preserve of the member-states, with very little EU interference in how these policies are managed.

BOX 23.2 The basic policy architecture of the EU

Exclusive EU competences

Regulation of the single market, including removing barriers and competition policy.

Customs union and external trade policies.

Monetary policy for the member states whose currency is the euro.

Price setting and subsidy of production under the Common Agricultural Policy.

Common fisheries policy.

Shared competences (where action is taken at both the national and European levels)

Social regulation, such as health and safety at work, gender equality, and non-discrimination.

Environmental regulation.

Consumer protection and common public health concerns, such as food safety.

Economic, social and territorial cohesion.

Free movement of persons, including policies towards third-country nationals.

Transport.

Energy.

Coordinated competences (where national actions are coordinated at the EU level)

Macro-economic policies.

Foreign and defence policies.

Policing and criminal justice policies.

Health, cultural, education, tourism, youth, sport, and vocational training policies.

Exclusive member state competences

All other policies, for example, most areas of taxation and public spending.

Turning to the institutions, put simply, executive powers at the European level are shared between the Council and the Commission (see Box: The basic institutional architecture of the EU, in the Online Resource Centre). Whereas the Council sets the medium-term and long-term policy agenda (particularly via the heads of state and government in the European Council), the Commission has a formal monopoly on legislative initiative. The Commission and the member states are also jointly responsible for the implementation of EU policies. Legislative power is also shared between two institutions: the

legislative meetings of the Council and the EP. The EP has equal power with the Council under the main legislative procedure, the so-called co-decision procedure. However, some highly sensitive areas of policy, such as tax harmonization, are passed under the **consultation procedure**, under which the Council is only required to consult the EP before passing legislation. Finally, judicial power in the EU is shared between the ECJ and national courts, which are primarily responsible for enforcing EU law (as part of domestic law) and refer cases to the ECJ if a domestic case raises a significant point of EU law.

KEY POINTS

☐ The EU is not a state, in the traditional meaning of this word, in that powers are shared between the EU and the member-states, the EU is based on voluntary cooperation between the member-states, there is no direct EU taxation, the EU budget is small relative to its GDP, and the EU relies on the forces of coercion of its member-states to enforce its decisions (there is no 'Euro FBI' or 'Euro army').

☐ The EU can be understood, nevertheless, as a political system, in that it possesses a basic constitutional

architecture which determines the balance of powers between the EU and the member-states and between the institutions at the European level, and the policies of the EU have significant direct and indirect implications on the economy and society in Europe.

☐ Conceptualizing the EU as political system allows tools and methods from the comparative study of political systems to be applied to the EU.

Vertical dimension: the EU as a 'regulatory state'

The dominant policy goal of the EU is the creation and regulation of a market on a continental scale. EU environmental and social policies, the single currency, budgetary policies, and even justice and internal affairs policies are in many respects 'flanking' policies of this dominant policy goal. These policies make Europe's continental-scale market work more effectively (the single currency), or correct potential market-failures (environmental and social policies), or compensate potential losers from market integration (budgetary policies), or address potential social and security externalities from market integration (justice and interior policies). Given the primacy of the single market and the centrality of EU market regulation policies, the EU is often described as a 'regulatory state' (Majone 1996). This conception nicely captures the contrast between the EU and the 'welfare states' at the national level in Europe, where the main policy instruments of government are taxation and public spending rather than market regulation. Whereas a welfare state deliberately aims to redistribute resources from one group of citizens in society to another, the aim of a regulatory state is to benefit all citizens more or less equally.

Creation and regulation of the single market

The single market notionally started on 1 January 1993, after the passage of almost 300 pieces of legislation to enable the basic elements of the single market to be established. However, in practice the single market is an ongoing project, as major areas of the economy (such as the provision of services and the professions) still operate in separate national markets rather than in a single European-wide market.

The creation of the single market has both deregulatory and reregulatory elements. On the **deregulatory** side, creating the single market involves the removal of barriers to the free movement of goods, services, capital, and labour between the EU member states. Three types of barriers had to be removed to enable this free movement to take place.

1. The single market required the removal of certain **fiscal barriers**, such as the harmonization of value added tax and excise duties (on goods like alcohol and tobacco).

2. The single market required the removal of **physical barriers** on the movement of goods and persons, such as the abolition of customs formalities, paperwork, and inspections at borders between the member-states. Removing border controls on the movement of persons was also an original aim of the single market programme, however several member-states (including Britain, Ireland, and Denmark) refused to accept that it was necessary to remove border controls in order for the free movement of persons to function effectively—all that was needed, they contended, was the right to move, reside, and work anywhere in the EU. In response, the other member-states agreed to remove their border controls as part of the Schengen Accord, which was initially outside the formal framework of the EU but was brought into the EU framework by the Maastricht and Amsterdam treaties.

3. The single market required the removal of **technical barriers** to the free movement of goods and services, such as separate national product standards that could be used as 'non-tariff barriers'. The EU had tried to establish common standards via harmonized rules throughout the EU. However, in the landmark *Cassis de Dijon* judgment in 1979, the ECJ established the principle of 'mutual recognition', whereby any product meeting the standards of one member-state can be legally sold in all other member-states. This principle became the basis of a 'new approach' to the creation of the single market, whereby harmonization was limited to minimum technical and health and safety standards. Another key area of removal of technical barriers was in public procurement, where rules were established which prevent governments from favouring home companies in public contracts. A host of directives have also been passed to liberalize air, water, and road transport, and to open up national energy, telecoms, and television markets. Regarding the movement of capital, controls on the free flow of capital between the member states were abolished, and the European

Company Statute was adopted in 2001, which enables multi-national companies to be registered as a single European-wide entity.

On the **reregulatory** side, as part of the single market programme, the EU replaced existing national regulations with new European-wide regulations. The three clearest examples of this are EU competition policies, environmental policies, and social policies. On competition policies, the EU has anti-trust regulations (which outlaw a variety of agreements between companies that would restrict competition, such as price-fixing or predatory pricing), prohibits government subsidies to industry that threaten competition and trade between the member states, and the Commission is required to review and vet mergers between companies with a combined worldwide and EU-wide turnover of a certain size. On environmental policy, common EU regulations cover, among other things, air and noise pollution, waste disposal, water pollution, chemicals, biodiversity, environmental impact assessments, eco-labelling and eco-audits, and natural and technological hazards. Also, the European Environment Agency was set up in 1994 in Copenhagen to collect environmental data and develop environmental forecasts. On social policy, EU legislation covers rights of workers to free movement, health and safety at work, working conditions, worker consultation, equality between men and women, general provisions of anti-discrimination (which cover race, ethnic origin, religion, disability, age, and sexual orientation), and labour markets (such as rights of part-time and temporary workers).

The single market more or less benefits all EU citizens. The deregulatory side of the 'project' enables the economy to function more efficiently, which benefits businesses and consumers, creates jobs, and produces higher growth rates. Some uncompetitive firms are put out of business by the new competitive rigours of the single market. However, these losses are far outweighed by the new firms, new opportunities, and new jobs that are created by the world's largest market.

The EU's reregulatory policies are also usually regarded as aimed to benefit all EU citizens rather than any particular group of citizens. EU regulatory policies do this by correcting certain 'market failures' that might arise in a continental-scale market. For example, harmonized consumer protection standards enable consumers to gain information about the quality of products that would otherwise not be publicly available. Health and safety standards and environmental standards reduce the adverse effects ('negative externalities') of market transactions on individuals not participating in the transactions. Competition policies prevent monopolistic markets from emerging, market distortions, and anti-competitive practices. And industry regulators, through such instruments as price controls, ensure that 'natural monopolies' operate according to market practices. Put this way, EU 'social regulations' are very different to national 'social policies', in that while the latter are usually geared towards providing benefits to particular social groups, the former aim to allow the labour market to function more efficiently (Majone 1993).

Nevertheless, there are significant indirect redistributive consequences of a market on a continental scale and the growing network of European-level social policies (Leibfried and Pierson 1995; Streeck 1996; Scharpf 1997a; Kleinman 2002). The EU does not have the direct redistributive capacity of national welfare states (see Chapter 21), but the emerging EU regulatory regime reflects a particular 'welfare compromise' at the European level that constrains existing welfare compromises and choices at the domestic level. For example, the single market places downward pressure on states with higher labour market standards (such as Germany and Scandinavia), and upward pressure on states with lower labour market standards (such as Britain and southern Europe). In addition, the redistributive capacities of the national welfare states are further constrained by the restrictions on national fiscal policies as a result of economic and monetary union.

Economic and Monetary Union and the European Central Bank

The Maastricht Treaty established in 1993 a three-point plan for Economic and Monetary Union (EMU):

1. This plan involved a timetable, with the launch of EMU on 1 January 1999 and the introduction of euro notes and coins on 1 January 2002.

2. It established four 'convergence criteria', which member-states have to meet to be able to join the single currency: (1) a stable currency, (2) a convergent economic cycle with the EU average cycle, (3) an annual government deficit of less than 3 per cent of GDP, and (4) a gross public debt of less than 60 per cent of GDP.

3. The plan established an institutional design of EMU.

In this design, the European Central Bank (ECB) has the sole responsibility of defining and implementing monetary policy (including setting interest rates) for the member-states whose currency is the euro, with the sole aim of maintaining price stability. The ECB comprises a six-member Executive Board, appointed by the European Council, and a Governing Council, of the Executive Board members and the governors of the national central banks of the EMU member-states. Meanwhile, the governments, meeting in the Council of Economic and Finance Ministers, have the final say over interventions in foreign exchange markets, adopt common economic policy guidelines for the EU as a whole, and monitor the national economic policies of the EU member-states.

Not all EU member-states are members of EMU. Eleven states launched EMU in 1999—Austria, Belgium, Finland, France, Germany, Ireland, Italy, Luxembourg, Netherlands, Portugal, Spain. Greece became the twelfth EMU member in 2001. Of the 'old fifteen' states, the United Kingdom, Denmark, and Sweden chose to stay outside EMU, and none of the 'new ten' were allowed to join EMU when they became members of the EU in 2004, although several of the new member states pegged their currencies to the euro.

A key element of the EMU framework, which was added after the Maastricht Treaty, is the Stability and Growth Pact (SGP). The German government, in particular, was concerned that once states had met the initial convergence criteria and entered EMU they might then be tempted to run large public deficits, which would undermine the stability of the euro, and so negatively affect the more fiscally responsible states. The SGP was hence agreed in 1997 as a way to limit this problem, by requiring that member states must maintain an annual budget deficit of less than 3 per cent of GDP, or otherwise face a fine (established

as a percentage of national GDP). However, one problem with the pact was that a fine could only be imposed by collective agreements amongst the governments. When France and Germany, the two largest economies in EMU, were the first major breakers of the SGP rules, no fine was imposed, which brought its credibility into question.

The main theoretical framework for understanding economic and monetary integration both generally and in the specific context of the EU is the 'optimal currency area' (OCA) theory, developed by Robert Mundell (1961). According to this theory, independent states will form a monetary union if the benefits of joining exceed the costs. The main cost of a monetary union is the loss of an independent exchange rate. With a 'one-size-fits-all' monetary policy, differential economic cycles between states have to be tackled by other policies, such as labour mobility (from states in recession to states growing more quickly), wage flexibility (where workers in the state where there is low demand reduce their wages), or fiscal transfers (from high growth to low growth states). If labour mobility is low, if there is limited wage flexibility, and if fiscal transfers are small, then a group of states do not form an OCA. Put this way, the EU is clearly not an OCA!

However, for some states, the economic benefits of EMU might outweigh some of these potential costs. A single currency lowers transactions costs in the economy (by removing the need to change money), produces a more efficient market, leads to greater economic certainty, and in general creates lower interest rates and higher growth rates. When deciding whether to join EMU a state will weigh the extent of these benefits against the probability that it will find itself in a recession while the other EMU states are booming, and so will be forced either to lower wages or suffer the consequences of low labour mobility and small fiscal transfers. The convergence criteria can consequently be seen as an attempt to create a degree of economic convergence, which would limit the need for wage flexibility, labour mobility, or fiscal transfers. In general, for states with high levels of trade integration with the Eurozone, the benefits of joining EMU outweigh the costs, since higher trade integration means higher economic convergence and greater transaction costs benefits of a single currency (e.g. Krugman 1990). In contrast, for states with lower trade integration and less convergent

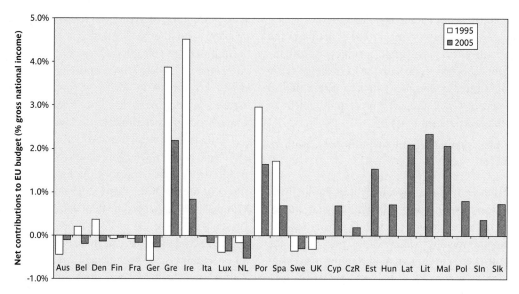

Fig. 23.1 Net contributions to the EU budget, 1995 and 2005

Source: Calculated from data in European Commission (2006).

economic cycles, the costs of joining EMU are likely to outweigh the benefits—which is broadly speaking the situation of the United Kingdom, although this might change.

EU expenditure policies

In contrast to the powerful direct and indirect effects of the single market and EMU on EU citizens' lives, and in contrast to the huge public spending programmes of the national governments, the direct spending power of the EU is small, since the EU budget represents only about 1 per cent of the total GDP of the EU member-states. Spread across all EU citizens, the costs of the EU budget are absolutely tiny. However, for those who receive money out of the EU budget—namely poorer states, farmers, backward economic regions, and research scientists—the sums can be staggeringly huge.

The EU adopts multi-annual budgets: see the Table: Size and main expenditure categories of the EU budget, 2007–13, in the Online Resource Centre, for the plan for 2007–13. The budget categories are a little misleading. The main EU spending policy is the CAP, which is a system of price support for a wide range of agricultural products and other subsidies to farmers. The CAP consumes more than 30 per cent of total EU spending. The second main area of EU

spending is on regional policy, covered under the heading 'economic and social cohesion'. Spending in this area is targeted in economically backward regions, regions with high levels of unemployment, and regions undergoing major industrial restructuring. EU regional funds are mainly spent on infrastructure projects in these regions, such as building roads, schools, airports, and telecommunications systems, and together consume about the same proportion of the EU budget as the CAP. The third main area of EU spending is on scientific research. Most of the EU's research and development funds are distributed to networks of researchers working on some of the leading areas in the natural sciences, such as biotechnology and telecommunications.

Figure 23.1 shows 'who got what' under the EU budget in 1995 and 2005 as a proportion of each member-state's gross national income. In general, there are six main net contributor states: Austria, Germany, Luxembourg, the Netherlands, Sweden, and the United Kingdom. Prior to the 2004 enlargement there were four main net beneficiary states: Greece, Ireland, Portugal, and Spain. These states were the main recipients of EU regional funds, and for Greece and Ireland in particular the proportion of their national income received from the EU budget is large: about 4 per cent of total gross national income for these two states. Nevertheless, after the

2004 enlargement, the benefits to Greece, Ireland, Portugal, and Spain fell considerably, as the regional funds began to be targeted towards the poorer regions in many of the new member-states. Also, after enlargement, the Netherlands replaced Germany as the largest net contributor to the EU budget as a percentage of its GNI and as a percentage of the Dutch population, which played a significant role in the anti-Europe campaign in the 2005 referendum in the Netherlands on the EU Constitution.

In general, the best way to understand EU spending policies is to see them as a combination of 'solidarity' and 'side payments'. On the **solidarity** side, transfers through the EU budget have generally passed from the richer states to the poorer states, on the grounds that the EU is more than simply an economic union, and so there should be some mechanism for redistributing wealth from the richer parts of Europe to the poorer parts. On the **side-payments** side, however, most EU spending policies are the result of specific intergovernmental bargains, where member states who expect to lose (or who do not expect to win as much as other states) from major policy changes in the EU demand some compensation out of the EU budget. For example, in the Treaty of Rome negotiations, France proposed the CAP, as a subsidy regime mainly for French farmers, because the common market was expected to benefit Germany's manufacturing-based economy more than France. Similarly, in return for agreeing to the single market programme, which was expected to benefit the main exporting economies of central and northern Europe, Spain, Italy, Portugal, Ireland, and Greece requested a doubling of EU spending under the regional funds, to enable them to compete on a level playing field.

In addition, once spending policies have been set up they are very difficult to change, even if the original policy aims are no longer justified. This is because any change to the EU budget requires unanimous agreement amongst the governments. The clearest example of this is the CAP, which encourages overproduction and overintensive land-use, benefits larger farmers more than smaller farmers, creates numerous trade disputes with the EU's partners, and depresses world agricultural prices by subsidizing the export of EU agricultural products, and so devastates large parts of the developing world. As long as unanimity is maintained for budgetary agreements, the French government will not agree to any changes to the CAP unless it receives something else in return.

Interior policies and external relations

Finally, there are two main areas of EU policy-making that are not strictly related to the EU's main economic policies:

- The array of justice and interior affairs policies, which includes immigration, asylum and other policies on the free movement of persons, as well as police and judicial cooperation.
- The EU's external relations policies, which include trade policies, development and humanitarian aid, the Common Foreign and Security Policy (CFSP), and European Security and Defence Cooperation (ESDP).

While in economic terms the EU is more a 'regulatory state' than a 'welfare state', where the EU's interior and external relations policies are concerned, the EU is developing some elements of a 'security state', in that these policies influence how the EU member-states manage the **internal and external** political rights, responsibilities, and security of their citizens.

Internal side

On the internal side, the Maastricht Treaty established the Justice and Home Affairs pillar of the EU, which brought into the legal framework of the EU a number of existing intergovernmental cooperation arrangements between the interior ministries of the EU member-states. These provisions covered the removal of border controls between the member-states, immigration and asylum policies and common policies towards 'third-country nationals', and police and judicial cooperation to combat drug-trafficking, terrorist activities, cross-border crime, and illegal immigration. Initially EU policies in these areas were made by 'intergovernmental' decision-making procedures: the governments in the Council had to agree unanimously, the Commission shared the right of legislative initiative with the member-states, the EP had very little influence, and there was almost no judicial review by the ECJ.

This model was then reformed in the Amsterdam Treaty, which separated the policies covering the movement of persons (immigration, asylum, internal and external borders, etc.) from the police and judicial cooperation policies. The free-movement policies were set up in the main body of the EU treaty in the framework of a new 'area of freedom, security and justice', where the Commission now had a monopoly on legislative initiative, some policies were adopted in the Council by qualified majority voting, the EP had some legislative power, and the ECJ exercised judicial review. Since the Amsterdam Treaty, the EU has adopted a large number of legislative acts in this area covering, among other things, common rules for non-EU nationals working in the EU, the right of third-country nationals to family reunification, an EU long-term residence status for third-country nationals who have resided in a member state for five years, and the admission of third-country nationals as students, vocational trainees, or volunteers.

External side

On the external side, since the establishment of a common market, the EU has had a single external trade policy, where the Commission represents the EU in the World Trade Organization (WTO) and in bilateral and multilateral trade negotiations. The EU has also developed an array of external economic policy instruments that it uses to project 'soft power' on the world stage (see Chapter 25). These include direct humanitarian and economic assistance as well as various preferential-trade agreements, such as the European Economic Area (EEA), association agreements, free trade agreements, partnership agreements (for example, with the EU member-states' former colonies in Africa, the Caribbean, and the Pacific), inter-regional association agreements with other regional trade blocs, and mutual recognition agreements (mainly with the US).

External security and defence policies developed more slowly. Defence cooperation was mainly managed through NATO rather than the EU. However, foreign policy cooperation between the EC member states began in the 1970s, and the Maastricht Treaty formally established the CFSP pillar of the EU, to which the Nice Treaty added the ESDP—as the 'European pillar' of the NATO transatlantic defence alliance. Under CFSP, the EU member-states adopt 'common strategies' and 'common positions' by unanimity, which set out the EU's position on a key foreign policy issue. Then, the EU member-states only require a qualified majority vote to adopt a 'joint action' implementing a common position. This combination has allowed the EU to act in a wide variety of areas. For example, the EU adopted a common strategy towards Russia in 1999 and the Mediterranean in 2000, the EU took an active collective role in the conflict in the former Yugoslavia, and in 2003 the EU adopted a common European Security Strategy, which sets out how and why EU security policies differ from the US administration's 'pre-emptive strike' doctrine. Nevertheless, a genuinely 'common' EU foreign policy is inevitably hampered by the conflicting security and foreign policy preferences of the key EU member-states, as was so clearly demonstrated in the internal rift in the EU over whether to support the US in the second Iraq war.

KEY POINTS

❑ Regulation of the free movement of goods, services, capital, and labour is the main policy instrument, as part of the creation and organization of the single market.

❑ Economic and monetary union is a complement to the single market, in that a single market functions more effectively with a single currency, and a single currency govern by an interdependent central bank ensures economic stability.

❑ EU expenditure policies, in contrast, are a secondary policy instrument of the EU, and have mainly been used to enable major steps in the process of economic integration by consensus.

❑ The EU has begun to expand beyond economic policies, into justice and interior affairs policies and foreign and security policies, but policy-making in these areas has developed much more slowly.

❑ The basic policy architecture of the EU, where a continental-scale market is created and regulated at the European level while spending and security policies remain largely at the national level, means that the EU is more a 'regulatory state' than a welfare state or security state.

Horizontal dimension: a hyper-consensus system of government

The main determinant of how policies are made by the central institutions in a political system is how far the power to set the agenda and the power to veto decisions from being taken are centralized in a single actor or dispersed between multiple actors. At one extreme, a political system can have a single 'agenda-setter' and 'veto-player', for example where there is single-party government and executive dominance of the legislature. At the other extreme, multiple actors could potentially veto any change to existing policies, for example where there is coalition government between several political parties or where there is a separation of powers between the executive (the president) and the legislature (Tsebelis 2002). In the EU, agenda-setting powers are split between two institutions and multiple actors have the ability to block policy changes in the EU's legislative process. As a result, the EU has an extremely consensual model of government.

Executive politics: competing agenda setters

First of all, agenda-setting power—in terms of who sets the overall policy agenda of the EU—is split between the heads of government in the European Council and the Commission. The heads of government, meeting in the European Council, decide on treaty reforms, which determine the allocation of powers between the EU institutions, and set the medium-term policy agenda, by inviting the Commission to initiate legislation in a particular policy area. The European Commission, meanwhile, has a formal monopoly on the initiative of most EU legislation.

In the European Council, political leadership, in the form of the presidency of the Council, rotates every six months between the member-states (Hayes-Renshaw and Wallace 2006; Tallberg 2006). Some member-states are clearly better at running the presidency of the Council than others. For example, larger member-states generally have larger administrative capacity to manage the business of the EU. However, the largest member-states tend also to try to place their domestic political issues on the EU agenda, and are less concerned about coordinating the overall policy agenda with the Commission and the other member-states. Furthermore, the powers of the Council presidency are actually quite limited. This is because the presidency cannot initiate legislation, and must deal with legislation that has already been initiated by the Commission and may already have been through several stages of negotiations. Nevertheless, every member-state tries to make progress on several key policy issues during its period in the presidency, and so tries to coordinate its policy ideas with the Commission well before taking over the leadership reins in the Council.

The Commission, on the other hand, has traditionally been regarded as being politically and institutionally committed to the process of European integration, and so is often assumed to have policy preferences that are more 'integrationist' than most member-states. For example, in the process of creating the single market, the Commission generally wanted legislation that promoted further market integration or a high level of EU-wide regulation. Nevertheless, this view of the Commission as an 'integrationist preference outlier' may be unfounded. The commissioners are appointed by national governments and most commissioners have strong ties to the political parties who chose them and seek to return to domestic politics after their careers in the Commission. Hence, commissioners are unlikely to be very much more pro-integrationist than the governments that appoint them. Also, below the level of the commissioners, research has shown that the senior officials in the Commission bureaucracy have policy preferences that are typical of politicians from the member-states from which they come and from the national political parties they support (Hooghe 2001).

In addition, since the college of commissioners formally decides by a majority vote, the Commission generally initiates policies that are close to the policy preferences of the median member of the Commission (Crombez 1997; Hug 2003). Nevertheless, whereas the average member of the Commission is probably not a policy outlier on the question of the speed and extent of European integration, the left–right policy location of the Commission has changed dramatically in recent years. The Table: Make-up of the Prodi and Barroso Commissions, in the Online Resource Centre, shows that whereas the Prodi Commission was relatively evenly balanced between left and right, a clear majority of the members of the Barroso Commission were on the centre-right. This change is partly explained by the shifting make-up of the governments (who appoint the commissioners): from a centre-left majority in the late 1990s to a centre-right majority in the early 2000s. However, the shift is also explained by a change introduced by the Nice Treaty, whereby the larger member-states no longer have two commissioners each. It was common practice for the larger member-states to appoint one commissioner from each side of the political divide, which inevitably led to a balanced Commission. Now that each member state has only one commissioner, the make-up of the Commission mirrors the political make-up of the Council at the time that the commissioners are appointed.

Bicameral legislative politics: rising power of the European Parliament

The most significant change over the last twenty years in the way the EU institutions work has been the steady increase in the powers of the EP. Originally, the governments in the Council dominated the legislative process, and the EP had a limited right to be consulted. However, with the programme to establish the single market, which required the adoption of over 300 pieces of legislation, the EP was granted two readings of most major pieces of legislation and, as a result, was able to have a significant impact on how the single market was designed (Tsebelis 1994). The Maastricht Treaty then established the co-decision procedure, which was extended and reformed by the Amsterdam Treaty. As a result, today the EP and the Council have equal power in the adoption of most pieces of EU legislation.

Figure 23.2 describes the main stages in the co-decision procedure. The Commission is responsible for proposing legislation to the Parliament and Council. The Parliament then adopts an 'opinion' on the legislation, in the form of a series of amendments. These amendments are prepared in one of the Parliament's committees, where one of the members of the EP (the 'rapporteur'), is responsible for writing the Parliament's report on the bill and shepherding the legislation through the committee and the full plenary. Once the plenary of the Parliament has adopted the report the Council then takes a 'common position' on the bill. If the texts adopted by the Council and Parliament are identical after the first readings, the legislation is adopted and becomes law. If the texts are not identical, the legislation passes back to the Parliament for a second reading and back to the Council for a second reading. If the two institutions still cannot agree a Conciliation Committee is convened, which is composed of twenty-seven members of the EP (MEPs) and one representative from each of the twenty-seven EU governments. If the Conciliation Committee reaches an agreement on a 'joint text', this is then put to the Parliament and the Council for a final, third, reading. This may sound complicated. However, the procedure is remarkably efficient, in that the EU adopts approximately 100 pieces of legislation a year, about fifty of which pass through the co-decision procedure. Also, about half of the bills through the co-decision procedure are adopted after just the first reading. Furthermore, because the majority in the EP is independent from both the Commission and the Council, the EP is an extremely powerful legislative actor under the co-decision procedure.

When voting on legislation the Council usually acts by a system of weighted voting known as qualified-majority voting (QMV). Unanimous voting is kept for some highly sensitive policy issues, such as tax harmonization. (Table: Qualified-majority voting in the Council, in the Online Resource Centre, shows how the QMV system works.) In general, larger states have more votes than smaller states, which translates into a greater chance of being on the winning side in a vote—as represented by the 'power' column. The system was reformed by the Nice Treaty, where the larger member-states gave up one of their two commissioners in return for more influence under QMV in the Council. The decision-making threshold was also raised slightly, making it more difficult. Voting rarely takes place in the Council, as there are strong incentives for the governments to decide by 'consensus' (Hayes-Renshaw and Wallace 2006). However, when votes

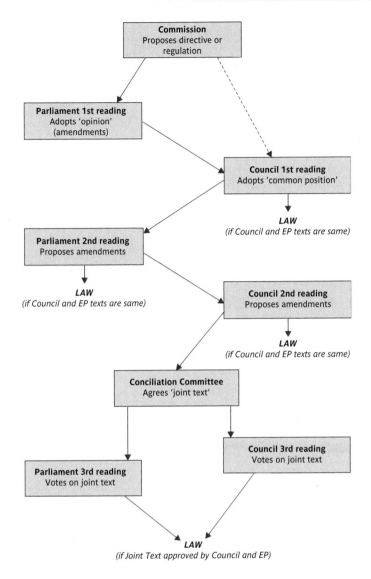

Fig. 23.2 The co-decision procedure

do take place, divisions in the Council split the governments along geo-political, economic, as well as ideological lines: for example, north vs. south, east vs. west, net contributors vs. net beneficiaries, and left governments vs. right governments (e.g. Mattila 2004).

Table 23.1 shows the number of seats per member-state in the EP. The size of the Parliament has increased tenfold since it was first established in the early 1950s, and has almost doubled in size since it was first elected in June 1979. The number of seats per member-state has also been changed with successive enlargements.

However, these numbers are misleading, in that the MEPs do not sit or vote along national lines.

Ever since the first session of the Parliament in September 1952, the MEPs have formed transnational political groups, and sat in the Parliament along left–right lines. As Figure 23.3 shows, the European People's Party-European Democrats (EPP, which brings together all the main Christian Democratic and conservative parties) was the largest group in the 1999–2004 and 2004–09 Parliaments, with the Party of European Socialists (PES, which brings together all the socialist, social democratic, and labour parties) the second largest. Between these two groups is a coalition of centrist and liberal parties: the Alliance of Liberals and Democrats for Europe. There are two smaller parties who sit to the left of the PES: a coalition of green and left-regionalist parties (the

Table 23.1 Member-states' seats in the European Parliament

	Sept. 1952	Mar. 1957	Jan. 1973	June 1979	Jan. 1981	Jan. 1986	June 1994	Jan. 1995	May 2004	June 2004	Jan. 2007	June 2009
Germany	18	36	36	81	81	81	99	99	99	99	99	99
France	18	36	36	81	81	81	87	87	87	78	78	72
Italy	18	36	36	81	81	81	87	87	87	78	78	72
Belgium	10	14	14	24	24	24	25	25	25	24	24	22
Netherlands	10	14	14	25	25	25	31	31	31	27	27	25
Luxembourg	4	6	6	6	6	6	6	6	6	6	6	6
United Kingdom			36	81	81	81	87	87	87	78	78	72
Denmark			10	16	16	16	16	16	16	14	14	13
Ireland			10	15	15	15	15	15	15	13	13	12
Greece					24	24	25	25	25	24	24	22
Spain						60	64	64	64	54	54	50
Portugal						24	25	25	25	24	24	22
Sweden								22	22	19	19	18
Austria								21	21	18	18	17
Finland							16	16	16	14	14	13

(continued)

Table 23.1 (*continued*)

	Sept. 1952	Mar. 1957	Jan. 1973	June 1979	Jan. 1981	Jan. 1986	June 1994	Jan. 1995	May 2004	June 2004	Jan. 2007	June 2009
Poland									54	54	54	50
Czech Republic									24	24	24	20
Hungary									24	24	24	20
Slovakia									14	14	14	13
Lithuania									13	13	13	12
Latvia									9	9	9	8
Slovenia									7	7	7	7
Cyprus									6	6	6	6
Estonia									6	6	6	6
Malta									5	5	5	5
Romania											35	33
Bulgaria											18	17
Total	78	142	198	410	434	518	567	626	788	732	786	732

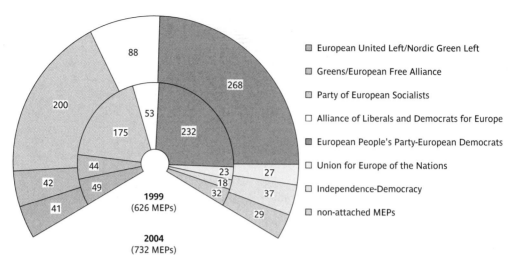

Fig. 23.3 Party make-up of the European Parliament, 1999 and 2004

Greens/European Free Alliance), and a group of left-socialist and ex-communist parties (the European United Left/Nordic Green Left). A coalition of national-conservative parties (the Union for a Europe of the Nations) sits just to the right of the EPP, and a group of anti-European parties (Independence-Democracy) sits even further to the right. Finally, almost thirty 'non-attached' MEPs sit on the furthest right, since most of these members come from extreme right parties.

Judicial politics: a powerful and independent court

The ECJ, together with national courts, provides a powerful check on the EU's executive and legislative institutions. The ECJ played a significant role in the development of the legal basis of the EU political system, in particular by developing **the doctrines of the direct-effect and supremacy of EU law.** The ECJ

is independent from the governments in the Council, and national courts often support the ECJ against their own governments. For example, on several occasions the ECJ has struck down legislation adopted by the Council and Parliament on the grounds that the treaties did not give the EU the right to adopt legislation in a particular area. Nevertheless, like all supreme courts, the ECJ is not completely isolated from external pressures, since it knows that if it strays too far from the meaning of the treaties, the governments can act collectively to rein in its powers. The ECJ is also aware that national courts, particularly the German Constitutional Court, are protective of their right to interpret whether EU law is in breach of fundamental human rights as set out in national constitutions (see Chapter 9). The EU's Charter of Fundamental Rights is an attempt to provide a set of basic rights for the ECJ to apply, although until the EU Constitution is implemented the Charter is not binding.

KEY POINTS

- With multiple actors and checks and balances, the EU has a hyper-consensus system of government.
- On the positive side, the checks and balances mean that legislation cannot be adopted without overwhelming support in the Commission, amongst the governments in the Council, the parties in the EP, and with the approval of the ECJ.

- On the negative side, the checks and balances mean that the EU is prone to 'gridlock' and lowest-common-denominator policy outcomes, and these problems are likely to increase with the enlargement of the EU from fifteen to twenty-seven or more states.

Democratic politics: the missing link?

Procedurally, the EU is 'democratic', in that the governments in the Council and the MEPs are elected by EU citizens, the EU's decision-making procedures are fair and transparent, and the checks and balances in the EU system ensure that policy outcomes from the EU are inevitably close to some notional EU-wide median voter (Moravcsik 2002). In a substantive sense, however, the EU does not have real 'democratic politics', meaning that there is competition between political elites for political office and in the policy process, there are identifiable winners and losers of this competition, and there is participation and identification of the public with one side or another in the political process (Føllesdal and Hix 2006).

Low public support for the EU

One of the key problems facing the EU is the relatively low and declining support for the project. Since the early 1970s, Eurobarometer polls of public attitudes towards the EU have been conducted every six months in every member-state. Figure 23.4 shows the percentage of respondents who said that they felt that their country's membership of the EU is a 'good thing'. Public support for the EU rose in the late 1980s with the widespread enthusiasm for the single market project, but then declined rapidly until the mid-1990s, and has remained at a relatively low level ever since. These days, only about one in two EU citizens think that their country's membership of the EU is a good thing. There is a widespread belief that the EU is an elitist project and European citizens no longer trust their political leaders to 'go off to Brussels' and negotiate on their behalf, as was starkly shown in the French and Dutch referendum rejections of the EU Constitution.

Part of the pattern in support for the EU can be explained by economics: the EU is popular when the European economy is booming and is blamed when the economy is performing badly. However, as the dotted line in Figure 23.4 shows, public support for the EU and the annual growth rate of the EU economy have followed different trends since the late 1980s. Clearly the economy does not tell the whole story. At an individual level, research has shown that those with higher incomes and higher levels of education (who benefit most from the single market) are more

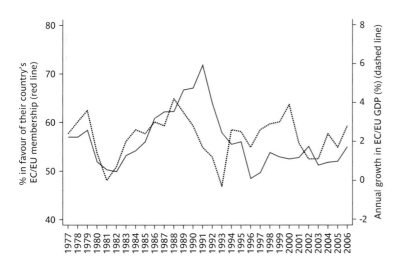

Fig. 23.4 Public support for the EU and EU GDP growth

Source: Calculated from Eurobarometer surveys and Eurostat data.

likely to support the EU than those on lower in-comes and with lower levels of education (Gabel 1998). Also, political extremists tend to be more anti-EU than political centrists. However, political parties and domestic institutions can influence which people like the EU. For example, the political party a person supports, and the position that party takes towards the EU, has a strong influence on whether that person is 'pro' or 'anti' EU (Anderson 1998). Concerns about a 'democratic deficit' in the EU also have a significant impact on attitudes towards the EU in countries that have strong domestic democratic institutions (Rohr-schneider 2002). Nevertheless, public support for the EU has declined in all EU member-states and across all groups in society since its peak in the early 1990s.

A competitive party system in the European Parliament

Democratic politics has begun to emerge inside the EU institutions. As discussed, the policy direction of the Commission is influenced by whether it is domin-ated by left-wing or right-wing politics. Also, votes in the Council split along ideological as well as national-interest lines. However, it is in the EP that a genuine 'party system' has emerged. As discussed above, the MEPs have always sat in transnational political, rather national, groups. Over the last twenty years, these groups have gradually become more powerful and more competitive. For example, votes in the Parlia-ment increasingly split along left–right lines, and the two largest groups now vote against each other as often as they vote together, which places the Liberals in the centre of the Parliament in a powerful posi-tions, since they determine whether a centre-left or a centre-right majority wins in a particular vote (e.g. Hix *et al.* 2007).

The party groups in the Parliament have also be-come highly 'cohesive'. The Figure: Voting cohesion of the main political groups in the European Par-liament, in the Online Resource Centre, shows how cohesive the main political groups were in recorded ('roll-call') votes in the first five directly elected EPs, where a score of 1 means that all the MEPs in a par-ticular group voted the same way in every single vote in a parliament and a score of 0 means that the MEPs in a particular group were split down the middle in every vote in a parliament. Voting along party lines

was already relatively high in the first directly elected Parliament, but rose dramatically between the third and fifth Parliaments. As a comparison, the main political groups in the EP are now more cohesive in votes than the Democrats and Republicans in the US Congress, and are almost as cohesive as party factions in national parliaments in Europe.

The 'failure' of European Parliament elections

Despite the growing levels of party competition and cohesion in the EP, elections do not provide a very effective link between the citizens and the behaviour of the MEPs and the transnational political parties. This is because EP elections are less important than national parliamentary elections and so are gener-ally regarded by political parties, the media, and the voters as 'second-order' contests (esp. van der Eijk and Franklin 1996). Because they are second-order national contests, like regional or local elections, EP elections are fought by national parties and on the performance of national party leaders and national governments, rather than by European parties and on the performance of the European Commission or the political groups in the EP.

This has two significant implications:

1. Turnout in EP elections is approximately 20 per cent lower than in national parliament elections, and turnout in EP elections has fallen steadily, to about 45 per cent of EU citizens in the June 2004 elections.

2. Voters use EP elections to express their views on national rather than European political issues, and so vote to punish unpopular governments or vote to express their views on particular issues, and so vote for smaller single-issue parties.

As a result, throughout the EU, governing parties tend to lose votes in EP elections, while opposi-tion parties tend to gain votes (see Table: Governing party performance in European Parliament elections, 1979–2004, in the Online Resource Centre). For example, in the 2004 elections, the British Labour government received 19 per cent fewer votes in the EP elections in that year than it received in the 2001 British general election. Moreover, despite the dra-matic increase in the powers of the EP over the past twenty years, the evidence suggests that EP elections have become increasingly rather than decreasingly second-order (in terms of the proportion of votes lost by governing parties across the EU in each set of European elections).

Interest groups in Brussels: an EU civil society

One aspect of democratic politics which is highly developed in the EU is interest group organization and mobilization. In terms of the number of interest groups trying to influence government and policy-making, Brussels is more like Washington, DC, than any national capital in Europe (see Chapter 14). This is partly because many groups in society have stakes in how the single market is regulated, and so have an incentive to try to shape EU legislation in their pre-ferred direction. It is also because there are multiple points of access in EU decision-making for interest groups, whereas at the national level in Europe, policy-making tends to be dominated by governmental and party-political elites, with only limited access for particular interest groups.

Table 23.2 shows the type and number of interest groups registered in Brussels. Together these groups employ over 10,000 people. In other words, there are as many people on the outside in Brussels trying to influence the EU institutions as there are on the inside involved in drafting and negotiating EU policies. These numbers might suggest that business interests dominate Brussels. However, this is misleading, as many groups representing 'public interests', such as the environmental lobby, the consumer lobby, and the trade unions, are part-funded directly from the EU budget and also have direct access to many governments and the party groups in the EP. As a result, the EU has a very vibrant civil society, with more or less equal access for every major group in society.

Table 23.2 Type and number of interest groups in Brussels, *c.* 2001

Type	N
Formal European level interest groups addressed to the EU, representing:	
business	950
public interests (e.g. NGOs)	285
professions	158
trade unions	43
public sector	14
Individual companies in Brussels (with public affairs offices geared towards the EU)	250
Offices of member states' regions in Brussels	171
National interest groups in Brussels	170
Commercial public affairs consultancies in Brussels	143
EU law firms in Brussels	125
Total	2,309

Source: Calculated from data in Greenwood (2003).

KEY POINTS

- There are growing concerns about a 'democratic deficit' in the EU, in that many citizens feel that they have little influence over the direction of EU policies.
- Public support for the EU has declined since widespread enthusiasm for the single market programme in the late 1980s, and the EU is widely perceived as an elitist project which benefits highly educated and highly skilled citizens.

- Although EP elections do not provide an effect link between EU citizens and EU policy-making, there is growing political contestation inside the EU institutions, particularly in the EP, where the political groups compete and coalesce along left–right lines.
- There is a vibrant and representative civil society in Brussels, in terms of the number and extent of interest groups involved in the EU policy process.

Conclusion

The EU was established by sovereign nation-states primarily to create and govern a Europe-wide market and to tackle the policy questions that arise at both the European and national levels from the free movement of goods, services, capital, and persons on a continental scale. As such, the EU is a remarkable and unique achievement: the only genuinely supranational polity that is the result of voluntary choices of citizens and democratic governments. However, the EU possesses many of the features and processes of other democratic political systems. As in other multi-level polities, policy powers are divided between the European and national levels. Also, how policies are made by the EU institutions is similar to other political systems that have a separation of powers between the executive and the legislature and where large coalitions are required for legislation to pass. Multiple checks and balances guarantee broad consensus, but also make it difficult for policies to be changed. Nonetheless, in comparison to other democratic political systems, the connection between citizens' policy preferences and policy outcomes from the EU is extremely indirect. Citizens elect national governments and the EP, but in no sense do citizens have a choice about who governs them at the European level and the direction of the EU policy agenda.

? Questions

1. Is the EU a political system?
2. Why is regulation the main policy instrument of the EU?
3. Who are the winners and losers from the EU budget, and why?
4. Who is the main agenda-setter in the EU: the Council or the Commission?
5. How powerful is the European Parliament?
6. Is the European Court of Justice beyond political influence?
7. Why has public support for the EU declined since the early 1990s?
8. Why do European parties vote cohesively in the European Parliament?
9. Why are European elections 'second-order national elections'?
10. Which interest groups are most influential in the EU, and why?

》   **Further reading**

Classics in European integration and EU politics

Haas, Ernst B. (1958) *The Uniting of Europe: Political, Social, and Economic Forces, 1950–1957* (South Bend, Ind.: University of Notre Dame Press, 2004 edn).

Majone, Giandomenico (1996) *Regulating Europe* (London: Routledge).

Milward, Alan S. (2000) *European Rescue of the Nation-State* (London: Routledge, 2nd edn).

Moravcsik, Andrew (1998) *The Choice for Europe: Social Purpose and State Power from Messina to Maastricht* (Ithaca, NY: Cornell University Press).

Pollack, Mark A. (2003) *The Engines of European Integration: Delegation, Agency, and Agenda Setting in the EU* (Oxford: Oxford University Press).

Weiler, Joseph H. H. (1999) *The Constitution of Europe: 'Do the New Clothes have an Emperor?' and Other Essays on European Integration* (Cambridge: Cambridge University Press).

General reference books

De Grauwe, Paul (2005), *Economics of Monetary Union* (Oxford: Oxford University Press, 6th edn).

Corbett, Richard, Jacobs, Francis, and Shackleton, Michael (2005) *The European Parliament* (London: John Harper Publishing, 6th edn).

Dinan, Desmond (2004) *Europe Recast: A History of European Union* (Basingstoke: Palgrave).

Hix, Simon (2005) *The Political System of the European Union* (Basingstoke: Palgrave, 2nd edn).

Rosamond, Ben (2000) *Theories of European Integration* (Basingstoke: Palgrave).

Wallace, Helen, Wallace, William, and Pollack, Mark A. (eds.) (2005) *Policy-Making in the European Union* (Oxford: Oxford University Press, 5th edn).

Books on specific aspects of the EU system

Alter, Karen J. (2001) *Establishing the Supremacy of EU Law: Making of an International Rule of Law in Europe* (Oxford: Oxford University Press).

Eijk, Cees van der, and Franklin, Mark (eds.) (1996) *Choosing Europe? The European Electorate and National Politics in the Face of Union* (Ann Arbor, Mich.: University of Michigan Press).

Franchino, Fabio (2007) *The Powers of the Union: Delegation in the EU* (Cambridge: Cambridge University Press).

Gabel, Mathew J. (1998) *Interests and Integration: Market Liberalization, Public Opinion, and European Union* (Ann Arbor, Mich.: University of Michigan Press).

Greenwood, Justin (2003) *Interest Representation in the European Union* (Basingstoke: Palgrave).

Hayes-Renshaw, Fiona, and Wallace, Helen (2006) *The Council of Ministers* (Basingstoke: Palgrave, 2nd edn).

Hix, Simon, Noury, Abdul, and Roland, Gérard (2007) *Democratic Politics in the European Parliament* (Cambridge: Cambridge University Press).

Hooghe, Liesbet (2001) *The European Commission and the Integration of Europe* (Cambridge: Cambridge University Press).

Hug, Simon (2002) *Voices of Europe: Citizens, Referendums, and European Integration* (Atlanta, Ga.: Rowman & Littlefield).

Thomson, Robert, Stockman, Frans N., Achen, Christopher H., and König, Thomas (eds.) (2006) *The European Union Decides* (Cambridge: Cambridge University Press).

(W)   **Web links**

EU institutions

http://europa.eu
   Web portal of the European Union.

http://ec.europa.eu
   European Commission.

www.consilium.europa.eu
   Council of the European Union.

www.europarl.europa.eu
   European Parliament.

www.curia.europa.eu
   European Court of Justice.

www.ecb.eu
   European Central Bank.

EU data, legislative tracking, and documents

http://epp.eurostat.ec.europa.eu
   Statistical office of the EU (Eurostat).

http://ec.europa.eu/public_opinion/index_en.htm
   Eurobarometer opinion polls.

http://eur-lex.europa.eu
   Portal to EU law and the Official Journal of the EU (Eur-lex).

http://ec.europa.eu/prelex
   Commission's legislative tracking website (Prelex).

www.europarl.europa.eu/oeil
   EP's legislative observatory (Oeil).

EU news

http://euobserver.com
   EU observer.

www.euractiv.com
   EurAktiv.

www.europeanvoice.com
   European Voice: a weekly newspaper on the EU.

Research groups and datasets

www.eu-newgov.org
   New modes of governance project (NewGov).

http://dosei.dhv-speyer.de
   Domestic Structures and European Integration project (DOSEI).

www.lse.ac.uk/collections/EPRG
   European Parliament Research Group (EPRG).

http://personal.lse.ac.uk/hix/HixNouryRolandEPdata.htm
   Hix–Noury–Roland dataset of roll-call votes in the European Parliament.

Academic journals

www.uni-konstanz.de/eup
  European Union Politics.

www.uaces.org/JCMS.htm
  Journal of Common Market Studies.

www.tandf.co.uk/journals/routledge/13501763.html
  Journal of European Public Policy.

 Visit the Online Resource Centre that accompanies this book for more information:
www.oxfordtextbooks.co.uk/orc/caramani/

24 Globalization and the nation-state

Georg Sørensen

Chapter contents

Reader's guide

Processes of globalization and other forces significantly increase connections and exchanges between nation-states at all levels: social, economic, political, and cultural. As a result, states become much more dependent on their surroundings. The old distinction between a First, a Second, and a Third World is being replaced by a new typology of states: the *advanced capitalist state* is today post-modern rather than modern, and a group of *weak post-colonial states* in the South are increasingly marginalized, fragile, and unable to stand on their own feet. Between these two groups are a number of *modernizing states* in Asia, Eastern Europe, Latin America, and elsewhere. These changes are critical for the study of comparative politics. First, the state units that comparativists compare have changed significantly. Second, 'international' and 'domestic' politics are now intimately related. This calls for an approach which emphasizes both; so the disciplines of comparative politics and international relations need to work much closer together, maybe even merge.

Introduction

The standard image of the sovereign nation-state is that of an entity within well-defined territorial borders: a national polity, a national economy, and a national community of citizens. The focus of **comparative politics** is on politics *within* countries; the focus of **international relations** is on politics *across* countries. Each discipline has developed a specific set of approaches and theories (see the Introduction to this volume). Many of these approaches and theories rest on the premise 'other things being equal' (Riggs 1994: 1); that is to say, comparative politics researchers can safely ignore what takes place outside of the borders of the countries they are studying and international relations researchers can equally ignore what takes place inside countries. This in turn is predicated on the idea that domestic politics and international politics are two qualitatively different things; the former takes place in an environment where there is an ultimate locus of final authority (see Chapter 4), the latter takes place in an environment where there is no such authority: 'anarchy' is the label of international relations scholars for that situation.

This division of labour has certainly yielded many good results in terms of insights about domestic and international affairs. But it was always clear that the distinction between 'inside' and 'outside' was made for analytical convenience. 'Other things' are *not* equal; what takes place inside countries is comprehensively important for international relations; and what takes place in the international realm is often decisive for the destiny of single countries. A number of questions related to comparative politics can possibly be studied without considering the international context (and vice versa for international relations), also in the future. But many of the most interesting research questions, including the core issue of the fate of the state itself, can only be studied if the relationship between 'domestic' and 'international' is taken into serious consideration. That is because the standard image of a sovereign nation-state does not apply anymore: the national polity, the national economy, and the national community are no longer neatly separated from the outside in

the way that the traditional approaches and theories would have us believe. Even sovereignty is changing in ways that indicate the decreasing significance of borders.

The focus in this chapter is on globalization and the changes in sovereign statehood that it has helped bring about. The next section briefly introduces the debate that is taking place about the consequence for states of globalization; in that connection we must look closer at the core concepts for analysis—globalization and the sovereign state. Then, the following three sections trace the modalities of statehood as they have developed over the last several decades.

First, the **advanced capitalist states** are transforming from modern into post-modern states. That involves changes at the levels of economics, politics, and nationhood (i.e. the transformation of community). It also involves changes in the institution of sovereignty; a new 'sovereignty game' is in the making.

Second, the **weak post-colonial states** were created out of special circumstances: the globalization of the institution of sovereignty in the context of decolonization. The core features of weak statehood will be identified below. Weak states also play a special sovereignty game which reflects their fragility; they remain highly dependent on the international community.

Third, the **modernizing states,** such as China, India, Russia, and Brazil, amalgamate features of modern, post-modern, and weak post-colonial statehood in different combinations. In economic terms, the international context is increasingly important for them, but in broader political terms their relationship to international society is more unstable.

Finally, against the background of this new typology of states, the last section speculates about the pursuit of comparative politics in a new setting. The conclusion argues that purely 'domestic' or purely 'international' analysis should be avoided; that calls for changes in the discipline of comparative politics.

KEY POINTS

- ❑ Globalization has considerably contributed to the change in sovereign statehood.
- ❑ The fate of the state can only be assessed if the relationship between 'domestic' and 'international' is taken into consideration.

- ❑ As a result of state transformation due to globalization, a new typology of states is proposed: (1) post-modern, (2) weak post-colonial, and (3) modernizing states.

COUNTRY PROFILE Saudi Arabia

Kingdom of Saudi Arabia (*Al-Mamlaka al-Arabiyya as-Saūdiyya*)

State formation

The Kingdom of Saudi Arabia is characterized by a strong alliance of secular and clerical structures that was initiated in 1744 by Muhammad bin Saud. During the first decades of the 20th century, Abdul Aziz bin Saud was able to settle some regional rivalries by the successive conquest of important parts of the Arabic peninsular. He became the first King of Nejd and Hejaz, recognized by the United Kingdom in 1927. The Kingdom of Saudi Arabia was founded in 1932 when the regions of Al-Hasa and Qatif joined the realm.
Constitution Formally the Qur'an; a Basic Law of Government, promulgated in 1992, articulates the government's rights and responsibilities.

Form of government

Monarchy.
Head of state The King, chosen by the royal family from among its members and approved by the clergy (*ulema*).
Head of government The King is also the Prime Minister.
Cabinet Council of Ministers, appointed by the monarch every four years; includes many members of the royal family.

Administrative subdivisions 13 provinces.

Legal system

Sharia law; several civil and commercial codes exist.

Legislature

Council of Ministers (*Majlis as-Shura*): 150 members and a chairman, appointed by the monarch; term of 4 years. However, the Council of Ministers is not an actual legislature, for its resolutions have to be ratified by royal decree. Its main function is to advise the King.

Electoral system

To date, no national elections have been held. Municipal elections were held for the first time in 2005.
Suffrage Males; 21 years.

Direct democracy

None.

Party system

No political parties exist except the clandestine Green Party; political opposition is generally prevented.

The debate about globalization and states

There are three major positions in the debate about globalization and states. First, there are scholars who think that states are losing power and influence as a result of globalization. There is a **retreat of the state** in the sense that 'the domain of state authority in society and economy is shrinking . . . [W]hat were once domains of authority exclusive to state authority are now being shared with other loci of sources of authority' (Strange 1996: 82), because 'globalization erodes the power of states' (Julius 1997: 454).

Second, there are **state-centric** scholars who believe that states remain in charge of globalization and have even managed to expand their capacities for regulation and control (Hirst and Thompson 2000; Weiss 1998). At the same time, very few 'retreat' scholars would claim that the state is 'losing' out to the extent that states are withering away or becoming entirely powerless. And very few 'state-centric' scholars would maintain that states are always 'winning' and are all-powerful.

BOX 24.1 'Retreat' vs. 'state-centric' scholars

Three 'retreat' scholars	Three 'state-centric' scholars
Kenichi Ohmae	*Linda Weiss*
The nation-state has become an unnatural, even dysfunctional unit for organzing human activity and managing economic endeavour in a borderless world. It represents no genuine, shared community of economic interest. It defines no meaningful flows of economic activity. (1993: 78)	There are now sufficient grounds to suggest that globalization tendencies have been exaggerated, and that we need to employ the language of internationalization to understand better the changes taking place in the world economy. In this kind of economy, the nation-state retains its importance as a political and economic actor. (1998: 212)
John Naisbitt	*Robert Gilpin*
The nation-state is dead. Not because states were subsumed by super-states, but because they are breaking up into smaller, more efficient parts—just like big companies . . . We are moving toward a world of 1,000 countries because many people of the new tribalism want self-rule and every day they see others getting self-rule, or moving toward it. (1994: 43)	[M]ost of the social, economic, and other problems ascribed to globalization are actually due to technological and other developments that have little or nothing to do with globalization. Even though its role may have diminished somewhat, the nation-state remains prominent in both domestic and international economic affairs. To borrow a phrase from the American humorist Mark Twain, I would like to report that the rumors of the death of the state 'have been greatly exaggerated'. (2002: 350)
Susan Strange	*Ethan Kapstein*
[T]he domain of state authority in society and economy is shrinking . . . what were once domains of authority exclusive to state authority are now being shared with other loci of sources of authority. (1996: 82)	Economic actors look to states in order to gain market access and to level the playing field of international competition. (1994: 6) [S]tates continue to adapt to ongoing changes in the world economy . . . and firms continue to value their national identity . . . (1993: 503)

Therefore, most scholars support some version of a third pragmatist middle position; instead of a zero-sum view of either 'winning' or 'losing', it is accepted that both can take place at the same time. As a result of globalization states are becoming stronger in some respects and weaker in others. There is a process **of state transformation** taking place and it plays out differently in different states (Held and McGrew 2002; Jessop 2002; Brenner *et al.* 2003). This idea makes it possible to study the changes which states undergo, both in their internal make-up and in the relations with other actors, without making the false assumption that it is a game of only 'winning' or 'losing'. It is a game of change, of transformation, which is almost always more complex. The 'transformationalist' position is more open than the 'retreat' and the

'state-centric' views; but it is not very precise. If states are indeed changing, what exactly is going on and what are the larger implications? That is the central question in what follows.[1]

There is an extreme diversity of views on globalization. Some see it primarily as an ideology (sometimes called globalism) designed to promote neo-liberal measures of deregulation and open economies (e.g. Herman 1999). Others put it in context of a larger process of capitalist development and expansion where globalization is the most recent phase (e.g. Hoogvelt 2001). But these are merely two examples from debates related to the economic aspects of globalization. Sociologists, anthropologists, geographers, political scientists, students of law, historians, and others all have debates on globalization which link

BOX 24.2 Definitions of globalization

Globalization refers to all those processes by which the peoples of the world are incorporated into a single world society, global society.   (Albrow 1996)

The world is becoming a global shopping mall in which ideas and products are available everywhere at the same time.   (Kanter 1995)

Globalization can be defined as the intensification of worldwide social relations which link distant localities in such a way that local happenings are shaped by event occurring many miles away and vice versa.   (Giddens 1990)

---

up with each other. They have surely provided fresh insights compared with other, more compartmentalized, research undertakings (Scholte 2005 has a good overview of the vast literature); they have also led to strong critiques of research undertakings based on a concept that is not very precise (e.g. Rosenberg 2005).

To be sure, globalization is a contested concept; it has been described as a 'polyvalent, promiscuous, controversial word that often obscures more than it reveals' (Jessop 2002: 113; Sørensen 2004: 23–6). There is general agreement about what it means in the broadest sense, namely the expansion and intensification of all kinds of social relations across borders: economic, political, cultural, and so on (Holm and Sørensen 1995: 1). Globalization is uneven in terms of cross-national intensity, geographical scope, and national and local depth. It is driven by various forces, including governments, corporations, popular groups, and many others; they help shape what globalization is and what it does. In other words, globalization is both a cause and a consequence. It is no anonymous entity that has all of a sudden taken control of peoples and states. At the same time, globalization increasingly shapes the context for inter-state relations as well as for the everyday lives of ordinary citizens.

Here I want to concentrate on the consequences of globalization for salient aspects of sovereign statehood. What is a state? It is a *sovereign, territorial entity with a population and a government*. For present purposes, it is relevant to focus on four aspects of statehood.

1. All states have **political-administrative** (including military) **institutions of government,** but there are huge differences between them in terms of efficiency, capacity, and legitimacy. It cannot be taken for granted, for example, that all states enjoy a monopoly on the legitimate use of force.

2. The **economic basis of the state** comprises the ability to design, construct, produce, finance, and distribute economic goods. Some states have well-defined national economies, others do not. Weak states are highly dependent on the world market and have extremely heterogeneous economies.

3. The definition of **nationhood and identity** must be examined. Nationhood means that people within a territory make up a community. The community is based on nationality or 'sentiment' (meaning a common language and a common cultural and historical identity) as well as on citizenship (including political, social, and economic rights and obligations).

4. **Sovereignty** is an institution which defines the rules that, in turn, define the locus of political authority and set the context for relations between states. We must trace the major changes in sovereignty related to processes of globalization.

KEY POINTS

❑ Globalization is a contested concept. In the broadest sense, it means the expansion and intensification of all kinds of social relations across borders.

❑ As a result of globalization, a process of state transformation is taking place. States are becoming stronger in some respects and weaker in others.

❑ Four aspects of statehood are in focus when discussing the transformation of the state: (1) the political-administrative institutions of government; (2) the economic basis of the state; (3) nationhood and identity; and (4) the institution of sovereignty.

Advanced capitalist states

From modern to post-modern

Since the debate about globalization and state transformation has primarily concerned the advanced capitalist states it is appropriate to begin with them. In order to be precise about how these states have been transformed, it is necessary to have an idea about how they looked in the past. This of course opens another source of controversy, because our picture of the state in the past must be constructed and the construction we come up with is crucial for estimating the transformations that are taking place in the present (Cameron and Palan 2004). Some 're-treat' scholars tend to overestimate the power and influence of the state in the past because it serves to re-emphasize what they see as the current predicament of the state. 'State-centric' scholars, by contrast, underline that states were never all-powerful (e.g. Krasner 1999) and that reduces the contrast between states today and states in the past.

But even if it is controversial, some notion of what advanced capitalist states looked like by the mid-twentieth century is necessary in order to appreciate the changes in the wake of globalization (see also Chapter 4). It is common to focus on the Peace of Westphalia at the end of the Thirty Years' War in 1648 as the birthplace of the modern sovereign state. That peace accord undermined the power of the church and strengthened secular power. The power and authority of kings was further strengthened in a context of fierce competition and violent conflict with rivals. The build-up of state power changed the relationship between the state and the people. A large group of individuals within a defined territory, subject to one supreme authority, became 'the people'. They are subjects and citizens of a particular state; at the same time they have a shared idea of themselves as a cultural and historical entity; they are an 'imagined community' (Anderson 1991), or a nation. A modern state is a nation-state in the sense that the population shares the characteristics of *citizenship and nationhood*. A nation-state is not necessarily based on a homogeneous ethno-national group of people. Very few modern states are nation-states in this more narrow sense.

The modern state is based on a national economy. The state rulers helped create a national space for economic development by removing local barriers to exchange and supporting both industry and infrastructure. The modern national economy is characterized by the combined presence within its territory of the major economic sectors, that is, means of production and distribution as well as means of consumption. What particularly defines a national economy is the fact that the most important inter- and intra-sectoral links are domestic. There is

---

BOX 24.3 The birth of the 'Westphalian state'

The Thirty Years War (1618–48)

Starting initially in Bohemia as an uprising of the Protestant aristocracy against Spanish authority, the war escalated rapidly, eventually incorporating all sorts of issues.... Questions of religious toleration were at the root of the conflict.... But by the 1630s, the war involved a jumble of conflicting stakes, with all sorts of cross-cutting dynastic, religious, and state interests involved.... Europe was fighting its first continental war.

Quoted from Holsti (1991: 26–8)

The Peace of Westphalia (1648)

The Westphalian settlement legitimized a commonwealth of sovereign states. It marked the triumph of the *stato* [the state], in control of its internal affairs and independent externally. This was the aspiration of princes [rulers] in general—and especially of the German princes, both Protestant and Catholic, in relation to the [Holy Roman or Habsburg] empire. The Westphalian treaties stated many of the rules and political principles of the new society of states.... The settlements was held to provide a fundamental and comprehensive charter of all Europe.

Quoted from Watson (1992: 186)

Table 24.1 Four types of state

State dimensions	Modern state	Post-modern state	Weak post-colonial state	Modernizing state
Government	A centralized system of democratic rule, based on a set of administrative, policing, and military organizations, sanctioned by a legal order, claiming a monopoly of the legitimate use of force, all within a defined territory.	Multi-level governance in several interlocked arenas overlapping each other. Governance in context of supra-national, international, transgovernmental, and transnational relations.	Inefficient and corrupt administrative and institutional structures. Rule based on coercion rather than the rule of law. Monopoly on the legitimate use of violence not established.	The modernizing states combine features of the modern, the post-modern, and the weak, post-colonial state.
Nationhood	A people within a territory making up a community of citizens (with political, social, and economic rights) and a community of sentiment based on cultural and historical bonds. Nationhood involves a high level of cohesion, binding nation and state together.	Identities less exclusively national. Collective identities 'above' and 'below' the nation reinforced. Transformation of citizenship. Less coherent 'community of citizens'.	Predominance of local/ethnic community. Weak bonds of loyalty to state and low level of state legitimacy. Local community more important than national community.	Brazil, China, India, and Russia are major examples of modernizing states.
Economy	A segregated national economy, self-sustained in the sense that it comprises the main sectors needed for its reproduction. The major part of economic activity takes place at home.	National economies much less self-sustained than earlier because of 'deep integration'. Major part of economic activity embedded in cross-border networks.	Heterogeneous combination of traditional agriculture, an informal petty urban sector, and some fragments of modern industry. Strong dependence on the global economy.	Additional examples include Argentina, Mexico, and Venezuela in Latin America, as well as Indonesia, Malaysia, and Thailand in Asia.
Sovereignty	National authority in the form of constitutional independence. The state has supreme political authority within the territory. Non-intervention: right to decide without outside interference.	From non-intervention towards mutual intervention. Regulation by supranational authority increasingly important.	Constitutional independence combined with 'negotiated intervention' (donor control of aid, supervision by international society). 'Non-reciprocity' (special treatment of weak states because they cannot reciprocate).	Each of these countries contain a unique mixture of different types of statehood.

external trade, of course, but the economic structure is introvert rather than extrovert (for data on trade see Comparative table 16 at the end of this volume).

The political-administrative institutions of government were considerably strengthened in the course of major wars, in particular the world wars of the twentieth century. State intervention in the economy was pushed by a need to mitigate social tensions via redistribution and to procure the necessary means for the war effort. That had to be combined with great increases in the level of taxation (Zürn 1998; Porter 1994).

The core characteristics of the modern, Westphalian state as it had developed mainly in Western Europe and North America around 1950 are summarized in Table 24.1. This ideal type provides an image of the previous shape of the state against which later changes can be assessed.

How do these characteristics transform in the context of globalization? Let us begin with the economy. No one denies that the national economies of the advanced capitalist countries are more interconnected than ever before (for statistical evidence, see Dicken 1998 and Maddison 2001). The question is sooner

about the larger significance of these developments. 'State-centric' scholars will maintain that this is not new: these economies were already densely interconnected at the eve of the First World War (Hirst and Thompson 2000). 'Retreat' scholars will argue that a qualitative shift is taking place: a truly global economy is in the making.

Technological changes in transport, communication, and production, together with a more liberalized world economy, means that 'shallow integration' manifested in arm's length trade between independent firms is being replaced by 'deep integration' where production chains (i.e. the various stages in the production of goods and services, from procurement of inputs to sales and service) are globally organized within the framework of a single, transnational corporation (UNCTAD 1993: 113). As a result, trade increasingly takes place within the context of the same company or network of companies. Such intra-firm trade now accounts for roughly one-third of world trade.

The real world is probably a mixture of old and new in the terms described here, uneven across countries and economic sectors. On the one hand, a unified,

Table 24.2 Selected top 100 transnational companies (TNCs), 1995

Corporation	Economy	Industry	Transnationality index
Nestlé SA	Switzerland	Food	94.0
Electrolux AB	Sweden	Electronics	88.3
Shell, Royal Dutch	UK/Netherlands	Oil, gas, coal	73.0
Bayer AG	Germany	Chemicals	69.3
Sony Corporation	Japan	Electronics	59.1
IBM	US	Computers	54.9
Honda Motor Co.	Japan	Automotive	52.6
Top 100 TNCs in the world			*51.0*
Daewoo Corp.	Korea	Diversified	47.7
GTE Corp.	US	Telecommunication	14.9

Notes: TNCs are ranked by transnationality index. The transnationality index is calculated from the average ratios of foreign assets to total assets, foreign sales to total sales, and foreign employment to total employment.

Source: Based on United Nations (1997).

BOX 24.4 Economic globalization as a mixture of old and new

Most observers will agree with the summation by Bob Jessop (2002: 115–16), indicating that economic globalization takes place in the following ways:

- Internationalization of national economic spaces through growing penetration (inward flows) and extraversion (outward flows).

- Formation of regional economic blocs embracing several national economies—notably the formation of various formally organized blocs in the triadic regions of North America, Europe, and East Asia—and the development of formal links between these blocs—notably through the Asia-Pacific Economic Cooperation forum, the New Transatlantic Agenda, and the Asia–Europe meetings.

- Growth of more 'local internationalization' or 'virtual regions' through the development of economic ties between contiguous or non-contiguous local and regional authorities in different national economies—

ties that often bypass the level of the national state but may also be sponsored by the latter.

- Extension and deepening of multi-nationalization as multinational companies, transnational banks, and international producer services firms move from limited economic activities abroad to more comprehensive and worldwide strategies, sometimes extending to 'global localization' whereby firms pursue a global strategy based on exploiting and/or adjusting to local differences.

- Widening and deepening of international regimes covering economic and economically relevant issues.

- Emergence of globalization proper through the introduction and acceptance of global norms and standards, the adoption of global benchmarking, the development of globally integrated markets together with globally oriented strategies, and 'deracinated' firms with no evident national operational base.

homogeneous and fully integrated global economy has not emerged. On the other hand, 'national' economies are less self-sustained than they used to be because of the processes of 'deep integration' which have been combined with more intense integration in other economic sectors, not least the financial sector.

We turn to the political level. What has happened to national government? There is an interplay between economic and political developments: economic globalization tends to increase the demand for political cooperation across borders because states are increasingly dependent on activities outside their territory. More cooperation is a way of gaining influence outside of the state's jurisdiction (Zürn 1998). At the same time, political initiatives, such as creation of the single market in the European Union (EU), or liberalizations in context of the World Trade Organization (WTO), also significantly push economic globalization.

Several observers point to the combined growth of transnational, transgovernmental, international, and supra-national relations. Transnational relations are cross-border relations between individuals, groups, and organizations from civil society. Transgovernmental relations are relations between governments

at different levels. External relations are no longer the prerogative of foreign ministries and heads of state. Sector ministries, regulatory agencies, officials responsible for corporate supervision, and so on are connected with their counterparts in other countries (Slaughter 1997). The growth of conventional inter-state relations is evidenced in the growth of International Governmental Organizations (IGOs) from 123 in 1951 to 260 by the mid-1990s (Table 24.3). The most far-reaching form

Table 24.3 Number of international governmental (IGO) and international non-governmental organizations (INGO)

Year	IGOs	INGOs
1909	37	176
1951	123	832
1996	260	5,472

Source: Zacher (1992: 65); Held *et al.* (1999: 53).

of political cooperation across borders is supra-national governance. Governance—in contrast to government—refers to activities everywhere (local, national, regional, global) involving regulation and control. Supra-national refers to the fact that some institutions—such as for example the EU—have the powers to write the rules for member-states in some areas. Rulings by the European Court of Justice, for example, take priority over rulings by national courts.

The EU, then, is the clearest example of what could be called multi-level governance (see Chapter 23), that is, a situation where political power is diffused and decentralized. Instead of a purely national political regulation, a complex network of supra-national, national, and sub-national regulation has developed. The EU is in a class of itself in terms of the intensity and extensity of regional cooperation among member-states. Other regional initiatives are primarily based on conventional forms of inter-state cooperation. At the global level, supranational elements can be found in some places, for example, the dispute settlement system in the WTO or in the International Criminal Court (jurisdiction over persons for the most serious crimes of international concern), but the bulk of global governance continues to be of a more conventional kind.

In any case, there appears to be a general trend away from national government within a defined territory towards multi-level governance in several interlocked arenas overlapping each other. Some of that governance reflects a more intense conventional cooperation between independent states. Some of it reflects a more profound transformation towards supra-national governance in a context of highly interconnected societies.

BOX 24.5 Settlement system of the WTO

By reinforcing the rule of law, the dispute settlement system makes the trading system more secure and predictable. Where non-compliance with a WTO agreement has been alleged by a WTO member, the dispute settlement system provides for a relatively rapid resolution of the matter through an independent ruling that must be implemented promptly, or the non-implementing member will face trade sanctions.

Source: WTO Website

BOX 24.6 The International Criminal Court

The International Criminal Court (ICC) is an independent, permanent court that tries persons accused of the most serious crimes of international concern, namely genocide, crimes against humanity and war crimes. The ICC is based on a treaty, joined by 100 countries.

The ICC is a court of last resort. It will not act if a case is investigated or prosecuted by a national judicial system unless the national proceedings are not genuine, for example if formal proceedings were undertaken solely to shield a person from criminal responsibility. In addition, the ICC only tries those accused of the gravest crimes.

Source: ICC Website

National identity

As regards nationhood and identity, the modern state is based on two kinds of community: (1) a **community of citizenship** concerning the relations between citizens and the state, including political, social, and economic rights and obligations; (2) a **community of sentiment**, based on a common language and a common cultural and historical identity.

What happens to these two types of communities in context of globalization? The community of citizens transforms in the sense that civil and other rights are no longer being granted solely by the sovereign state. At the global level, a set of universal human rights has been defined. In some regional contexts, common rights for citizens of different countries have emerged. The EU has established a common citizenship which grants of number of rights to EU citizens in all member-states (Soysal 1994: 148). The process is not confined to Europe. According to one scholar the increasing adherence to universal human rights mean that national citizenship is in the process of being replaced by 'postnational membership' based on these universal rights. This indicates a transformation of citizenship 'from a more particularistic one based on nationhood to a more universalistic one based on personhood' (Soysal 1994: 137). It goes together with a much increased forging of transnational links among people that practise 'citizenship without moorings' (Rosenau 1993: 282) in order to address issues of common concern (e.g. environment, equality, or security problems). In sum, there

It is indicated in this analysis that the emergence of a Western civic identity is concentrated among the elite groups of Western societies because they are the ones who have engaged in circulation and educational exchange. Possibly the creation of self-identities analysed by Giddens, taking place in sophisticated processes of reflexive endeavour, is also primarily an elite phenomenon. If so, what happens with collective identities among those for whom economic globalization is more of a threat than an opportunity? According to Manuel Castells, such groups frequently develop a 'resistance identity' (Castells 1998: 60). They might be nationalistic groups turning against immigration and seeking to emphasize a narrow understanding of national identity, such as the Front National in France or the Alleanza Nazionale in Italy. They might also be regional community organizations, religious, or ethnic movements (see also Chapter 13 on neo-populist parties).

In sum, globalization would appear to reinforce collective identities both 'above' and 'below' the nation. Identities are less exclusively national and the emergence of a Western civic identity is an indicator of that. But more defensive 'resistance identities' are also gaining importance, among them nationalistic and local identities.

Sovereignty

Finally there is the issue of sovereignty. The juridical core of sovereignty is constitutional independence. The sovereign state stands apart from all other sovereign entities. There is no final political authority outside or above the state (James 1999: 461). Even in the face of globalization, the international system continues to be organized in this manner: it consists of sovereign states that have final political authority within their territory.

But this does not mean that the institution of sovereignty has remained completely unchanged (Sørensen 2001). Sovereignty can be seen as a special kind of game played by states who have it. Constitutional independence defines what the game is all about (i.e. political authority and its appropriate distribution among the players). The rules regulating the game stipulate how the players should behave towards each other in various situations. There are many such rules (Jackson 1990: 35), the most important one being **non-intervention**, that is, the right for states to choose

is no breakdown of national citizenship, but there are different forces at work to transform the coherent community of citizens as it existed in context of the modern state.

What about the community of sentiment, the cultural and emotional attachment to the nation? According to Anthony Giddens, the creation of identity is increasingly becoming an individual project. Religious and other beliefs, for example, are not simply taken over from previous generations. Rather, they are reflected upon, evaluated, and then actively accepted or rejected. When identity is something that has to be actively created and sustained by individuals, the result may be less commitment to the national community of sentiment. At the same time, new collective identities 'above' the nation could be in the process of emerging. One analysis speaks of a 'Western civic identity' that is an 'essential component of the Western political order'; at its core is a 'consensus around a set of norms and principles, most importantly political democracy, constitutional government, individual rights, private property-based economic systems, and toleration of diversity' (Deudney and Ikenberry 1999: 193).

their own path and to conduct their affairs without outside interference. The rule of non-intervention has been changed or at least strongly modified because of the more intense political cooperation across borders that globalization has stimulated.

The EU is a good example in this respect. Instead of non-intervention, the EU member-states undertake comprehensive intervention in each other's affairs. During the past decade, institutions at the European level have gained considerable influence over areas that were traditionally thought to be prerogatives of national politics: currency, social policies, border controls, law and order. A key player in this development is the European Court of Justice which has helped push supra-national governance by establishing the supremacy of European law in several important areas (Caldeira *et al.* 1995).

This does not mean that we approach the 'twilight of sovereignty' (Wriston 1992) as some 'retreat' scholars have implied. States do consent to comply with supra-national regulation, but they do it in their own best interest because, as a group, states are themselves the sources of that regulation, and seen from the single state, the new set-up allows for increased influence over fellow states. Supra-national regulation gives the single state new possibilities for controlling events outside its territorial jurisdiction. The price is that outsiders get to influence the regulation of affairs at home. States can withdraw from this kind of cooperation if they want to—they do retain constitutional independence. But because of the demand for more cooperation spurred by globalization, it is unlikely that they would wish to do so.

Having gone through changes in salient aspects of changes in sovereign statehood among the advanced capitalist states, we can summarize the result and compare them to the characteristic features of modern statehood as they were presented above. The modern state was first and foremost a national entity, with national government, national community, national economy, and national sovereignty. The emerging entity is less 'national' on all counts. At the same time, it is not certain where the processes of change will eventually lead. Together with several others, I prefer to speak of 'post-modern' states (Holm and Sørensen 1995: 187) in order to indicate these processes of transformation. The 'post-' terminology indicates that the traditional picture of the modern state needs revision, but we remain unsure about what exactly is taking its place.

Some state-centric scholars will argue that the image of the post-modern state is merely applicable to the members of the EU. It is a regional phenomenon not very relevant for larger advanced states outside Europe, such as the US and Japan (Waltz 1999). The counterargument is that these latter states are deeply involved in economic and other processes of globalization (Foreign Policy/Kearney 2006) and that even super-powers cannot 'go it alone' (Nye 2002) in an increasingly integrated world. These views reflect the ongoing debate about globalization and state transformation.

KEY POINTS

❑ In order to be precise about how the advanced, capitalist states have been transformed, it is necessary to have an idea about how they looked in the past. By the mid-twentieth century these states were *modern*.

❑ Modern states are based on: (1) a national economy, the major part of economic activity takes place at home; (2) a national government, a centralized system of democratic rule within a defined territory; (3) a nation, a people within a territory making up a community of sentiment and a community of citizens. Modern states are sovereign and emphasize non-intervention, that is, the right to decide without outside interference.

❑ Modern states are transforming into *post-modern* states. That transformation is pushed by a variety of economic, political, and other forces.

❑ Post-modern states are less 'national' on all counts: (1) a major part of economic activity is embedded in cross-border networks; (2) national government is being replaced by multi-level governance in several interlocked arenas; (3) identities are less exclusively national. Post-modern states emphasize mutual intervention instead of non-intervention.

Weak post-colonial states

The lack of 'stateness'

The debate between 'state-centric' and 'retreat' scholars about consequences of globalization for sovereign states is focused on the advanced states in Western Europe, North America, and Japan. As discussed in the previous section, that debate concentrates on the extent to which there has been a transformation away from the traditional modern state towards a type of state that is less 'national' in basic respects. This is not a relevant debate for weak post-colonial states in the Third World. They were never 'modern states' in the first place and they are not on the way to becoming 'post-modern'. The weak states display a different trajectory of state formation. Since most of these states are in Sub-Saharan Africa, I shall focus on that region. But the ideal type of the weak state defined below is relevant for other areas as well.

Before colonization, these areas were not states with distinct territories. They were tribal and other communities with no clearly defined jurisdictions. So borders were created from the outside and the surprisingly straight lines on the map were drawn by the colonizers. The colonial powers took no particular interest in the political and economic development of the areas they took into possession. They were more interested in maximizing profits, so the focus was on the extraction and export of natural resources, combined with an effort to curtail the cost of controlling the colonies. In some places, colonial rule involved building some infrastructure, together with some political as well as social and economic institutions; in the worst cases, such as for example the Belgian King Leopold's rule in Congo, the colonizers left nothing in terms of development.

After the Second World War, the prevailing view on colonies changed dramatically. Before the war, colonial rule was considered legitimate and even necessary, given the backward condition of the colonized areas. After the war, colonialism came to be considered fundamentally wrong, even 'a crime' (UN General Assembly Resolution 3103, quoted from Jackson 1990: 107). That normative change led to decolonization, which in turn meant the globalization of the institution of sovereignty. For the first time, sovereign statehood became the only form of political authority worldwide.

Several factors help explain the replacement of colonialism with the right of colonies to self-determination.

1. The old colonial powers had been reduced to second rank in the international system. The new leading powers in the system—the US and the Soviet Union—generally supported the promotion of independence for the colonies.

2. Some colonial areas had supported the Allied war effort. That strengthened ideas about equality and independence.

3. An ideology of nationalism gained strength in elite circles and the young United Nations (UN) provided a new forum where the aspirations for independence could be expressed and find support.

The modern states introduced in the previous section were, in a manner of speaking, **created from the inside**. The struggle between various state-seeking groups ended with victory for one group or coalition of groups that went on to achieve—in Max Weber's expression—a monopoly of the legitimate use of force within a defined territory. At the same time, states were constantly at each other's throats. War between states was an important aspect of state-building, as emphasized in Charles Tilly's well-known phrase: 'states made war and war made states' (Tilly 1990: 20–8; see also Chapter 4). An important ingredient in war was the conquest of enemy territory: the stronger swallowed the weaker.

Fundamentally, this kind of competition was a basic driving force in European state-making and development. The preparation for war forced power-holders into a series of compromises with their subject populations which constrained their power and paved the way for rights of citizenship. Citizenship in turn meant material benefits for the population. Combined with the creation of domestic order and the promotion of capital accumulation, these processes furthered the building of bonds of loyalty and legitimacy between kings and people.

In the case of weak states in the Third World, by contrast, decolonization gave independence (i.e. recognition as a sovereign state) to entities which had very little in terms of substantial statehood (Jackson 1990). In that sense these states were **created from the outside** when the international society rejected colonialism. Power-holders in weak states faced no serious external threat. Both states and regimes were protected from outside threat by the strong international norms, created in context of decolonization and strengthened during the cold war. Recolonization, annexation, or any other format of strong states in the North taking over weak states in the South is not on the agenda. For most post-colonial leaders, the situation at independence was one of no severe external threats against the state and the regime, combined with few domestic institutional constraints. It was under those circumstances that a large number of leaders chose the path that led to the formation of weak states. Why?

After the successful anti-colonial struggle, there was little left to create unity. It was a huge task to bring together diverse ethnic groups with different languages and traditions. The state elites quickly gave up trying. At the same time, institutional structures were generally weak, lacking capacity, competence, and resources. In this context, a system of 'personal rule' emerged (Jackson and Rosberg 1982) where key positions in the state apparatus are manned by loyal followers of the leader. State elites do not primarily seek to provide public or collective goods. The state apparatus is sooner source of income for those clever enough to control it. The spoils of office are shared by a group of followers making up a network of patron–client relationships.

Lack of 'nationness'

Ethnic identities connected to tribal, religious, and similar characteristics continue to dominate over the national identity in weak states. Because the state does not deliver on political, social, and legal rights, it creates no bonds of loyalty leading to state legitimacy. When the ethnic community becomes the primary focus for the satisfaction of people's needs, loyalties are projected in that direction, and ethnic identities are reinforced; the national 'community of citizens' fails to develop. Similarly, the national 'community of sentiment' is in trouble because local

(ethnic, tribal, religious) communities are primary. They provide sources of identification via rituals and myths. Patron–client relationships serve to reinforce ethnic loyalties: 'An example is traditional oaths, which affirm identity and obligation within the ethnic community but which often have a purpose in the state arena, such as securing electoral victory or political succession. These oaths are recurrent motifs in national politics in Kenya' (Ndegwa 1997: 602).

The weakness of the economy

The economy in weak, post-colonial states is a heterogeneous amalgamation of traditional agriculture, an informal petty urban sector, and some elements of modern industry, frequently controlled by external interests. In both urban and rural areas large parts of the population are outside of the formal sectors, living in localized subsistence economies. Exports consist of few primary products and the economies are highly dependent on imports of manufactured and technology-intensive products. In Sub-Saharan Africa, for example, primary products accounted for 92 per cent of total export production in both 1970 and 1991.

Weak states are not attractive sites for foreign investment. There is no dynamic domestic market, no adequate supply of skilled or semi-skilled labour, no developed physical infrastructure, and they do not offer stable, market-friendly conditions of operation. A little more than 2 per cent of total Foreign Direct Investment (FDI) goes to Sub-Saharan Africa (World Bank 2006). In other words, the circuits of global capital—often thought to be the spearheads of globalization—do not include the weak states in any major way. In that sense, they are marginalized bystanders in the process of economic globalization. At the same time, they remain deeply dependent on the global economy. On the one hand, export earnings from primary products are of great importance for the economies. On the other hand, economic aid makes up an increasing share of the means they have at their disposal. Official Development Assistance (ODA) increased from 12 per cent of GDP to 18.6 per cent of GDP in Sub-Saharan Africa between 1990 and 2003 (UNDP 2005). In some countries, more than half of the state budget is financed by ODA.

The weakness of sovereignty

Weak states have formal sovereignty, understood as constitutional independence granted in the context of decolonization. Formal sovereignty is of great importance for weak states, because sovereignty offers access to international institutions, including the UN system where states are legally equal (e.g. every country has one vote in the General Assembly). It also provides access to economic, military, and other forms of aid. In formal terms, sovereignty leaves supreme legitimate power in domestic affairs to the government. Therefore, rulers of weak states seek to emphasize and confirm the principles and rules of sovereignty (Ayoob 1995: 3). This emphasis amounts to a demand to be treated as **equals** in the international society of states, to have their sovereignty respected and count on par with every other country in the international system, irrespective of the fact that these states are terribly weak and able to do very little on their own.

But rulers of weak states also seek to be considered **unequal** as they are at the losing end of the international system. To compensate for that situation, weak states demand special treatment in terms of economic aid, market access, compensation for natural resources and colonialism, and so on. That is, weak states want to be allowed to receive extra resources from the developed world. The demand is that economic aid, for example, should be a clear international obligation for the developed countries and not something that the weak states have to respectfully apply for.

So even if weak states have sovereignty in the form of constitutional independence, they cannot play the classical game of sovereignty based on non-intervention. Aid flows mean that donors will want to make sure that the resources they provide are used according to plan. That creates a pressure in the direction of 'negotiated intervention' for that kind of supervision to take place. Weak states can say no, of course, but that might cut them off from significant funding. The most obvious cases of external intervention are the so-called 'humanitarian interventions' in 'failed states' such as Somalia, Liberia, Rwanda, or Sierra Leone. International society steps in primarily for humanitarian reasons when domestic conflict has got out of hand.

There is another respect in which the fragility of weak states influences their sovereignty game. The classical sovereignty game is based on reciprocity: states are equals and deal with each other on an equal, *quid pro quo* basis. Weak states cannot do that because they are not in a position to reciprocate. They want something (for example, economic aid) but are unable to give anything in return. Sovereignty is built on the assumption that states who have it **can basically take care of themselves**. Weak states fail to meet that requirement; they cannot play a game of self-help. They play a different game of 'non-reciprocity' and 'negotiated intervention' and that is a source of tension in the international society of states.

It is the combined presence of the elements summarized in Table 24.1 above that amount to a 'lack of stateness'. Even if the ideal type is inspired mainly by the weak states in Sub-Saharan Africa, lack of stateness is a problem elsewhere also, for example, in such countries as Afghanistan, Colombia, Burma, Bangladesh, Haiti, Nepal, Kyrgyzstan, Uzbekistan, and Yemen.

The concept of 'weak post-colonial state' is more precise than the general concepts of 'Third World' countries or 'developing' countries, or even 'the South', because it singles out states with particular problems in three areas:

1. There is a **security gap** in the sense of inability and/or unwillingness to maintain basic order (protection of the citizens) within the state's territory.

2. There is a **capacity gap** in the sense of inability and/or unwillingness to provide other basic social values, such as welfare, liberty, and the rule of law.

3. There is a **legitimacy gap** in that the state offers little or nothing in terms of services, and thus gets no support in return.

The larger question is whether weak states are also developing countries, that is, are they really on the road to development? The idea that every country can get development is an ideology created in context of decolonization. We only have to go back to the 1930s to find an entirely different ideology, dominating especially in the colonial motherlands. On that view, only some, maybe even rather few, colonies would ever be able to stand on their own feet and thus achieve development. Most peoples in the colonies were seen to require 'an indefinite period of European tutelage' and some were likely to 'remain wards of the states-system for centuries, if not forever' (Jackson 1990: 73). That outlook was sustained by a Western belief in its own superiority which was rejected with decolonization. But the adoption of a new outlook does not alter the empirical conditions for development which continue to be highly wanting in the weakest states. Those conditions are behind the processes of state breakdown or the emergence of 'failed states', a notion indicating the breakdown of states in various ways (Gros 1996).

KEY POINTS

❑ Decolonization gave independence (i.e. recognition as a sovereign state) to entities which had very little in terms of substantial, empirical statehood.

❑ Weak post-colonial states are plagued by political institutions that are inefficient and corrupt, and by weak bonds of loyalty to the state and a low level of state legitimacy.

❑ The economic basis is fragile and dependent on links to the outside.

❑ Weak states play a special sovereignty game focused on 'negotiated intervention' and 'non-reciprocity'.

❑ It is an open question whether the weak states are on the road towards development or to further breakdown and 'state failure'.

Modernizing states

Between post-colonialism and post-modernism

The sections above argue that in the current international system there are two, radically different modalities of sovereign statehood. On the one hand, the advanced capitalist states are transforming from modern to post-modern. On the other hand, the weak post-colonial states display a particular set of features that amount to a lack of 'stateness'. Between these ends of the spectrum is a large group of states that will be called 'modernizing' states. They combine features of the three ideal types of state presented so far: the modern, the post-modern, and the weak, post-colonial state. The term 'modernizing' is meant to indicate that such states are in a general process of transition. It is not meant to indicate that they will surely discard every aspect of weak statehood, and graduate to modern and then to post-modern. No such teleology is implied as transitions can move in different directions and change may not mean change for the better.

Brazil, China, India, and Russia are major examples of modernizing states; additional examples include Argentina, Mexico, and Venezuela in Latin America, as well as Indonesia, Malaysia, and Thailand in Asia.

Each of them contains a unique mixture of different types of statehood. Many parts of India, for example, display the economic characteristics of weak statehood (i.e. a heterogeneous combination of traditional agriculture, an informal petty urban sector, and some fragments of modern industry), but the country also has larger elements of a modern industrial structure. It even has advanced economic sectors that are now seeking active integration in cross-border networks via direct investment and much more involvement in economic globalization. A similar mixture can be found in China, but this country is already a highly active participant in economic globalization. Russia may have modernized even more, but its relationship to the global economy remains more like that of a member of the Organization of Petroleum Exporting Countries (OPEC), in that it exports energy and raw materials and imports more sophisticated products.

The mixture of state types also applies to the political level. Massive corruption and weak state structures remain a serious problem in all four states, but in other areas there is a higher degree of effective national government. The countries are all seeking closer integration into the global economy and also to some extent into the international organizations and networks of multi-level governance. The question then is what the consequences will be of this economic and political globalization for their trajectories of development.

New global competitors: India and China

Compared to the weak states discussed in the previous section, modernizing states are better positioned to benefit from economic globalization. International firms today are looking for a range of facilities when they invest, including

> ❝ an adequate supply of cost-effective semi-skilled or skilled labour, a good physical infrastructure, government policies which are market-friendly, and minimal distance related transaction costs.... In the 1990s FDI is determined less by the country-specific costs of factor endowments or size of local markets, and more by those variables which facilitate firm and/or plan economies of scale and scope; and the effective exploitation of regional and/or global markets. (Dunning 2000: 29) ❞

Many modernizing states are able to offer that package. At the same time, they possess companies of their own that are able to participate in strategic alliances and economic networks and that increases their prospects for gaining from economic globalization in terms of technology transfers, market access, product upgrading, and competence development. The host states possess sufficient regulatory capacity for establishing the necessary frameworks concerning relations to foreign operators.

The liberalizing measures that have widely opened the doors to comprehensive participation in economic globalization have surely boosted economic growth in both India and China. India began liberalization in 1991. According to two well-known observers, India's opening up to globalization represents a crucial breakthrough for India's development (Singh and Srinivasan 2003). Yet serious problems remain. There have not been significantly positive effects on employment because the traditional sectors are being squeezed while the modern sector provides only a limited increase in the workforce. With 35 per cent of the population on less than $1 a day (and as much as 80 per cent on less than $2 a day; UNDP 2005), poverty continues to be widespread.

Table 24.4 Economic growth in India and China

Indicators	China	India
GNP per capita 1989, dollars	330	340
Real GDP per capita 2005 (PPP$)[a]	5,530	3,100
Annual growth rate, GDP per capita (%)		
1965–80	6.9	3.6
1980–90	10.2	5.8
1990–2003	8.5	4.0

[a] PPPs are Purchasing Power Parities, an attempt to measure real GDP in terms of domestic purchasing powers of currencies, thereby avoiding the distortions of official exchange rates.

Source: UNDP (1996; 2005).

China began liberalizing much earlier and has been able to attract a much higher level of foreign investment. Economic growth has averaged more than 9 per cent annually over the last twenty-five years, an unparalleled achievement; and the number of extreme poor (less than $1 a day) has dropped to 16 per cent of the population (UNDP 2005). But even in China, economic globalization is a mixed blessing. Inequality has risen sharply: 'by 2005, the top 10 percent earned 45 percent of the income, while the bottom 10 percent earned only 1.4 percent' (Wen 2005: 2). The Gini ratio rose from 0.20 in 1980 to 0.45 in 2005 (see Comparative tables 5 and 6 at the end of this volume).

Another aspect of globalization in both China and India are sweatshop factories with poor working conditions, low job security, low wages, and long hours of work. In the Pearl River and Yangtze River delta regions in China, for example, 'migrant workers routinely work 12 hours a day, 7 days a week; during the busy season, a 13- to 15-hour day is not uncommon' (Wen 2005: 3). In other words, even in relatively successful modernizing states, a significant part of their participation in economic globalization has nothing to do with upgrading and sophisticated production. It might sooner be called 'downgrading', with deteriorating conditions for labour. Some will argue that there is improvement in the sense that previously unproductive work in stagnant and inefficient public enterprises is being replaced by more productive work in a competitive world market, but from the point of view of the labour force it is hardly a great leap forward.

Economic globalization in China has led to serious environmental problems because rapid economic growth takes place with little or no attention to the environment. Some 60 per cent of China's major rivers are classified as being 'unsuitable for human contact'. China's deputy minister of the environment recently stated that 'cities are growing, but desert areas are expanding at the same time; habitable and usable land has been halved over the past 50 years' (Wen 2005: 10). Seven of the ten most polluted cities in the world are in China. More than one-third of industrial wastewater enters waterways without any treatment.

The economic changes in China have pushed some political change. For example, private entrepreneurs, that is, 'capitalists', have been allowed to become members of the Communist Party since 2002. There is less direct party control of people's daily lives. But still, independent trade unions are not permitted and freedom of assembly and association is highly restricted. The judiciary is not independent; it is controlled by the party. Human rights abuse remains widespread (Freedom House 2006). This might help explain why a strong increase in social unrest is combined with a new popularity of Maoism, especially in the poorest sections of society. According to one sceptical report, '27 years of reform has not only significantly liquidated the natural and human resources of China, it has also liquidated the political capital of the Party and the state. The legitimacy of the government is being challenged' (Wen 2005: 42).

So economic liberalization has not produced a large amount of political liberalization. The question is how this divergence between economic freedom and political control will develop in the future. China's participation in economic and political globalization will be one important element in that equation. The Chinese president, Jiang Zemin, declared in 2000 that participation in economic globalization was 'an objective requirement' for economic development (quoted from Garrett 2001: 409). There is also a tension in China's approach to international order. On the one hand, China has increasingly adopted a more liberal view, according to which continued participation in economic globalization and further integration into the institutions of international society is the appropriate course for the country. On the other hand, a strict realist view, according to which international politics is essentially a struggle for power and relative advantage, continues to dominate among Chinese decision-makers. They continue to 'view the world as essentially conflict-prone, interstate relations as zero-sum power struggles, [and] violence is by no means a less common solution' (Deng 1998: 316).

The international community, meanwhile, demands in principle that China should pay more respect to civil and political rights in order to become a fully legitimate member of international society. But because of China's economic importance, such demands are formulated in a low voice and not backed by strong political or economic pressure. In sum, even if modernizing states are able to benefit from globalization, the process of participating in it is no panacea. It does not open a smooth course to economic and political change. Involvement in globalization increases several tensions in the process of development that present new challenges both to the modernizing states and to the international community.

KEY POINTS

❑ Modernizing states combine features of the three ideal types of state: the modern, the post-modern, and the weak post-colonial state.

❑ The term 'modernizing' is meant to indicate that such states are in a general process of transition; transitions can move in different directions; change may not mean change for the better.

❑ Brazil, China, India, and Russia are examples of modernizing states.

❑ Modernizing states are in a better position than are weak states to benefit from participation in globalization. But such participation is no cure-all; it can also increase tensions in their process of development.

Comparative politics in a new setting

Methodological implications

The discipline of comparative politics is built on the idea that 'comparison is the methodological core of the scientific study of politics' (Almond *et al.* 2004: 31). Political systems exist within the framework of sovereign states; for this reason comparison is understood to be comparison between countries (i.e. sovereign states). The principle that comparative politics compares countries is so entrenched that major introductions to the discipline (e.g. Almond *et al.* 2004; Landman 2003) do not find it necessary to explain why that is the case: it is considered self-evident. Similarly, a dominant view in the discipline of international relations is that the international system is a system of sovereign states: they are the basic components of the international system (e.g. Waltz 1979).

Both disciplines have a point. As Chapter 4 shows, almost every individual on earth is the citizen or subject of a state. Whether or not people are provided with basic social values—security, wealth, welfare, freedom, order, justice—strongly depends on the ability of the state to ensure them. Furthermore, states have not withered away because of globalization and other forces. They continue to be overwhelmingly important for the lives of people. It is not attractive to live in a very weak or 'failed' state; it can even be mortally dangerous. So states continue to be utterly significant for any kind of political or social analysis.

At the same time, states are constantly in a process of change. Therefore, it is always relevant to ask questions about the current major modalities of statehood, not least because such modalities help explain how and why states are able or unable to provide basic social values. During the cold war, the prevalent distinction was between the advanced capitalist states in the First World, the communist states in the Second World, and the remaining states in the Third World. With the collapse of most communist states, some use a distinction between the rich countries of the North and the poor countries of the South. That is not a very precise categorization. This chapter has suggested a different one: (1) the advanced capitalist states are in a process of transition from modern to post-modern statehood; (2) the weak post-colonial

states display a serious lack of 'stateness'—and they are by no means on a secure path to the development of more substance; (3) the modernizing states are different combinations of these three ideal types. Of course, even this categorization can be further refined.

The typology suggested here is not meant to replace any other possible distinction. It will remain relevant—depending on the research question—to differentiate between big and small states, nation-states and non-nation states, old and new states, states from various regions and sub-regions, and so on. But the modalities put forward here help explain how sovereign states have transformed in the context of globalization. It has also been emphasized that 'globalization' is itself a complex entity that must be explained; it is not an anonymous force that throws states around at will. To the extent that 'globalization' applies pressures on single states, that pressure often originates in actions undertaken by other states, as demonstrated by several examples above.

So the first recommendation to comparativists is to be aware of the larger context in which political, economic, and other processes play out. This is not a very dramatic proposition as awareness of context is nothing new to comparative politics. The add-on here is merely the suggestion of a different distinction between types of state. The second recommendation is to accept that 'international' and 'domestic' are intimately connected and this requires that both elements are taken into the analysis of the development and change of sovereign statehood. The proposition can be translated into two practical guidelines for future study:

1. Proceed on the assumption that the core values pursued by states, that is, security, wealth, welfare, freedom, order, justice, each contain 'domestic' as well as 'international' aspects. None of these values can be reduced to a purely 'domestic' or a purely 'international' issue.

2. Therefore, avoid purely 'systemic' or purely 'domestic' analysis. Put the international–domestic interplay at the centre of inquiry and ask questions about 'outside–in' and 'inside–out' relationships.

Analytical implications

Let us finally look at one of the core aspects of statehood, that is, democracy. Democratic rule has always developed within the context of independent states. The emergence of multi-level governance raises the question whether and how that new context can be democratic. According to one view, 'the only forum within which genuine democracy occurs is within national boundaries' (Kymlicka 1999: 124). The reasoning is that outside of that context there is no obvious *demos*, no well-defined political or moral community. An opposing view argues that such community can be created, just as it had to be created within national boundaries in the early phases of sovereign statehood (Habermas 1999). In any case, the emergence of multi-level governance means that the previously well-defined national context for democracy is being replaced by a new context that integrates 'domestic' and 'international' elements in a different kind of polity.

Some optimist liberal scholars argue that democratic problems in that new setting can be relatively easily confronted by designing international institutions in such a way as to 'preserve as much space as possible for domestic political processes to operate' (Nye 2001: 3). For those who more strongly emphasize the changes invoked by globalization, however, a whole new structure of cosmopolitan democracy must be created, based on an ensemble of organizations at different levels, bound by a common framework of cosmopolitan democratic law with a charter of rights and obligations (Held 1995).

In weak states institutions at the national level are fragile and ineffective. They are controlled by state elites who do not primarily seek to provide public or collective goods. At the global level, international institutions and stronger states increasingly attempt to constrain, influence, and direct policy measures in weak states. Their ticket to influence is the high level of external dependence, economically and otherwise, of weak states. Again, political developments including attempts at democratization are decided in an interplay between 'domestic' and 'international' elements.

The economic basis of sovereign statehood has also been transformed. In the modern state, there was a segregated national economy, self-sustained in the sense that it comprises the main sectors needed for its reproduction. The major part of economic activity took place at home. In the post-modern state, national economies are much less self-sustained than previously because of 'deep integration' and major parts of economic activity are embedded in cross-border networks. In other words, the economic basis of the post-modern state contains a 'domestic' as well as an 'international' component. That creates a new setting for the provision of wealth and welfare—a key feature of mass democracy (see Chapter 21). Economic globalization underscores the tension between vulnerability and efficiency which is at the core of all areas of economic security (Buzan 1991: 237). When 'national' economies are integrated to an extent where opting out of the world market is no longer a viable option, there must be substantially higher vulnerability. Such vulnerability has permanently been a characteristic of weak post-colonial states, because they were always highly dependent on the global economy.

The changes discussed here are reflected in the transformation of the institution of sovereignty. In context of the modern state, sovereignty is closely connected with the 'golden rule' of non-intervention (Jackson 1990). But multi-level governance is quite the opposite of non-intervention; it is systematic **intervention** in national affairs by supra-national and international institutions. It means something else to be sovereign under conditions of multi-level governance than it did under traditional conditions of national government. In weak states, sovereignty has changed as well. Traditionally, sovereignty means international legal equality: equal rights and duties of member-states in the international system. But weak states are highly **unequal** so they need help from the developed world. A number of weak states are unable to take care of themselves, but sovereignty—which they have—assumes that they can. They possess sovereignty without being able to meet its requirements. That is behind new practices of 'humanitarian intervention' and trusteeship. In short, the institution of sovereignty changes to make room for a situation where 'domestic' and 'international' affairs can no longer easily be separated.

In conclusion, the sovereign state is alive and doing well. By no means has it been obliterated by forces of globalization. But it has been transformed in ways which closely connect 'domestic' and 'international'. That insight must be taken on board when conducting comparative analysis of political systems.

KEY POINTS

❑ States continue to be utterly significant for any kind of political or social analysis. But states are constantly in a process of change. It is necessary to ask questions about the current modalities of statehood, not least because such modalities help explain how and why states are able or unable to provide basic social values.

❑ Changes in statehood places the discipline of comparative politics in a new setting. In particular, it is

necessary to accept that 'international' and 'domestic' are intimately connected.

❑ The core values pursued by states, that is, security, wealth, welfare, freedom, democracy, order, and justice each contain 'domestic' as well as 'international' aspects. That insight must be taken on board when conducting comparative analysis of political systems.

World trends

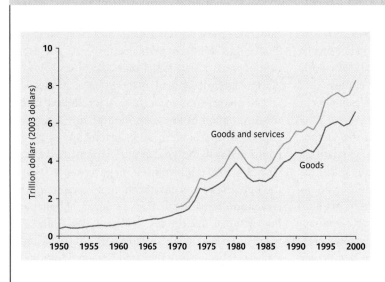

Trend 7 Trade: world export of goods and services (1950–2003)

Source: International Monetary Fund.

?   Questions

1.   Set out the standard image of the modern state. Does that image apply to your own country?

2.   What is globalization? Why is there such an intense debate about globalization and its consequences?

3.   What are the major aspects of statehood that are relevant in a debate about globalization and states?

4.   Describe the changes involved in the transformation from modern to post-modern statehood. Identify three states that you would consider post-modern.

5.   Are identities changing so that we are increasingly becoming citizens of the world rather than nationals belonging to our countries?

6.   Identify the characteristics of weak post-colonial statehood. Where can we find such states?

7.   Are weak post-colonial states on the road to development or are they on the road to further breakdown and 'state failure'? Discuss examples.

8.   Will modernizing states gain from participating in economic globalization or will it further aggravate their problems? Discuss the case of China.

9. Can multi-level governance be democratic? Why or why not?

10. Will the process of state transformation lead to a more peaceful and prosperous world?

» Further reading

Dicken, Peter (1998) *Global Shift: Transforming the World Economy* (London: Paul Chapman, 3rd edn). Provides a detailed introduction to all major aspects of economic globalization.

Held, David, and Anthony, McGrew (2002) *Globalization/Anti-Globalization* (Cambridge: Polity). Presents the pro- and anti-views in the debate on globalization and state transformation.

Jackson, Robert (1990) *Quasi-States: Sovereignty, International Relations and the Third World* (Cambridge: Cambridge University Press). Explains the emergence of weak states in the context of decolonization.

Scholte, Jan Aart (2005) *Globalization: A Critical Introduction* (Basingstoke: Palgrave Macmillan, 2nd edn). Presents a sociological overview of all major dimensions of globalization.

Sørensen, Georg (2001) *Changes in Statehood: The Transformation of International Relations* (Basingstoke: Palgrave Macmillan). Explains the dynamics of state transformation and the emergence of post-modern and weak post-colonial states.

Weiss, Linda (1998) *The Myth of the Powerless State* (Ithaca, NY: Cornell University Press). Argues that states remain strong and able to regulate the development of economic globalization.

Recent papers available online

http://carlisle-www.army.mil Martin van Creveld discusses 'The Fate of the State'. The paper is provided by the US Army War College.

www.theglobalsite.ac.uk/press/107colas.pdf Another paper concerning the future of statehood, written by Alejandro Colás, is provided by the Global Site. The paper is entitled 'The Promises of International Civil Society: Global Governance, Cosmopolitan Democracy and the End of Sovereignty?'

www.vuw.ac.nz/atp/articles/Luke_9608.html A paper, written by Timothy W. Luke, entitled 'Nationality and Sovereignty in the New World Order'. The paper is provided by the Department of Politics at Victoria University of Wellington.

http://sacred-sovereign.uchicago.edu/jbe-sovereignty.html A thorough discussion of the nature of 'Sovereignty at the Century's End' and an excerpt from J. B. Elshtain's *New Wine and Old Bottles: International Politics and Ethical Discourse*. The paper is provided by University of Chicago Divinity School.

www.mtholyoke.edu/acad/intrel/walglob.htm To find out more about Kenneth Waltz's view on the future role of the state, read his paper 'Globalization and Governance'. The site is maintained by Mount Holyoke College.

www.mtholyoke.edu/acad/intrel/drucker.htm A paper written by Peter F. Drucker entitled 'The Global Economy and the Nation State' and provided by Mount Holyoke College.

www.ippu.purdue.edu/ A paper written by Michael Nicholson on 'Globalization, Weak States and Failed States'. The paper is provided by Purdue University.

Web links

www.globalpolicy.org/nations/
A comprehensive collection of links on sovereignty, provided by Global Policy Forum.

http://europa.eu.int/
The official website of the European Union.

http://plato.stanford.edu/entries/nationalism/
Here one can find a thorough introduction to nationalism. The site is maintained by Stanford University.

www.gapresearch.org/
Globalization and Poverty (GAP) Research is a UK government funded project.

Websites with data on globalization

www.worldbank.org/data
Extensive website of World Bank 'Data and Statistics' including World Development Indicators. The 'Data by Country' and 'Data by Topic' pages also have good links to other sources of data. See also the 'World Ban Group Inequality Around the World' data page, and the 'Research Datasets'.

www.developmentgateway.org/node/244175/
Development Gateway. Extensive set of links, possibly all one could ever want.

www.wto.org/
World Trade Organization 'Trade Statistics'.

www.undp.org/poverty/
UNDP's 'World Income Inequality'.

http://utip.gov.utexas.edu/
University of Texas Inequality Project (UTIP) with Galbraith's datasets on inequality based on industrial pay rates.

www.childinfo.org/index2.htm
Website of UNICEF Progress for Children. Includes child survival and health, water and sanitation, education, and maternal health.

www.unctad.org/Templates/Page.asp?intItemID=1584&lang=1
UNCTAD 'Statistics Overview' with price, trade, and trade barrier data available through their statistical databases.

www.fao.org/waicent/portal/statistics_en.asp
Food and Agriculture Organization (FAO) 'Statistics' with data on agriculture, fisheries, and nutrition.

http://papers.nber.org/papersbyprog/ITI_archive.html
National Bureau of Economic Research ('International Trade and Investment Archive').

www.gtap.agecon.purdue.edu/default.asp
Global Trade Analysis Project Purdue. The GTAP produces a publicly available and regularly updated dataset and CGE model tailored for the analysis of trade policy changes.

www.cid.harvard.edu/cidtrade/index.html
Global Trade Negotiations Homepage at the Center for International Development: Harvard University.

www.princeton.edu/~deaton/
Angus Deaton's homepage on 'Poverty in the World and in India'.

www.iie.com/research/globalization.htm
The 'Globalization Page' of the Institution for International Economics.

 Visit the Online Resource Centre that accompanies this book for more information:
www.oxfordtextbooks.co.uk/orc/caramani/

25 Promoting democracy

Peter Burnell

Chapter contents

Reader's guide

Of all the big issues in comparative and international politics few are more topical, controversial, and important than those surrounding the international promotion of democracy. The subject lies at the juncture between the study of politics on the one side and the twin worlds of public policy and those people whose profession is to promote democracy on the other. This chapter explains what 'promoting democracy' means and why it has become so prominent. Different rationales and policy drivers are compared, as are the principal institutions and actors and various methods or approaches. The record of promoting democracy is assessed in the light of the methodological difficulties that make rigorous evaluation problematical. There are major questions concerning the kind of democracy that is being promoted. How can the activity be justified? Do the Europeans offer a distinctive approach that compares favourably with American endeavours? And does democracy promotion work? Finally, in a world of increasing globalization should ideas and approaches to democracy promotion be recast if they are to be relevant and effective in the future?

Introduction: comparing definitions

The increasing number of democracies in the world (described in Chapter 5) is a distinctive feature of the contemporary era and a major component of the political dimension of globalization understood in its broadest sense. These developments have not come about purely by chance. From the late 1980s onwards democracy has been promoted to a degree and in ways that have no precedent in history. Emblematic is the formation of the Community of Democracies, which began as a global gathering of 106 governments in Warsaw in 2000.

Basic vocabulary

Because the basic vocabulary of democracy promotion is rather recent and confused, some key terms must be clarified before I proceed.

The idea of promoting democracy has an active and a passive sense, corresponding to the distinction between the promotion of democracy and democracy being promoted. The **active** sense comprises deliberate actions undertaken with a view to achieving a democratic purpose. There is intentionality. This frames questions about which actors in the international democracy promotion 'industry' are doing what, and how, as well as to what effect. The **passive** sense orients us more towards how far democratic

---

> **BOX 25.1 Democracy and democracy promotion in the twenty-first century**
>
> The idea of democracy as a universal commitment is quite new, and it is quintessentially a product of the twentieth century...While democracy is not yet universally practiced, nor indeed uniformly accepted, in the general climate of world opinion, democratic governance has now achieved the status of being taken to be generally right. (Sen 1999: 5)
>
> Democracy promotion as a foreign policy goal has become increasingly acceptable throughout most of the international community...an international norm embraced by other states (than the US), transnational organisations, and international networks...in the community of democratic states the normative burden has shifted to those not interested in advocating democracy promotion. (McFaul 2004: 148, 158)

> **BOX 25.2 Community of democracies**
>
> The Community of Democracies is a grouping of over 100 states from diverse regions, cultures, and religions, 'dedicated to a core set of democratic principles and to support cooperation among democracies worldwide'. It claims to work to extend democracy's realm, develop democratic processes in its members, and strengthen fledgling democracies. Collaboration at the United Nations in the form of a UN democracy caucus is a central element. The initial gathering in Warsaw (2000) was followed by further meetings in Seoul (2002) and Santiago (2005). A non-governmental Council for a Community of Democracies, based in Washington, DC, has been formed to support this global movement. A Nongovernmental Coalition for the Community of Democracies engages a wide variety of NGOs in lending support and encouragement to the Community of Democracies.

---

trends are occurring in prospective, emerging, and new democracies, the kind of democracy that is emerging (for instance, is it a high-quality democracy?), and whether the trends are being influenced by such external forces as outside actors and international events.

Intentionality is central to the active sense of promoting democracy. In the passive sense, however, democratic impulses could come about in a country as the accidental by-product of its international and transnational dealings. For example, political developments taking place inside other countries might have 'spillover' effects, as reflected in terms such as demonstration effect, democratization by emulation, and (somewhat perversely given that democracy has such positive normative connotations), 'contagion'. All these are part of the international dimensions of democratization. They are not insignificant.

The intentional promotion of democracy employs a wide range of methods or approaches. An initial distinction is between direct and indirect promotion. The **direct approach** targets some defining political characteristics of democracy, whether political values, norms, and principles or more concrete organizational forms. The **indirect approach** seeks to work on the conditions for democratization, for example, the socio-economic requisites or prerequisites. Direct approaches must embody some idea about what democracy means and its institutional manifestations. Indirect approaches demand an understanding of what makes democracy possible and how it comes about—a theory of democratization. There, the discourse is characterized by competing accounts. The precise relevance of social-economic conditions for instance is the subject of much argument. A further complication is disagreement over the importance of phenomena like civic culture that seem very significant for democracy and democratization but may be considered either as part of the definition or as a 'cause', or even as a consequence.

This chapter concentrates on political strategies for promoting democracy, while recognizing that one possible approach, and a plausible account of how democratization comes to be promoted, is through forms of international development cooperation that further the economic, social, and human development of countries receiving foreign aid.

Democracy promotion

The instruments, methods, or approaches that are employed in promoting democracy directly can be placed along a continuum running from soft power to hard power (Nye 2005). However, if power is defined in narrowly coercive terms, then the full continuum spans assistance, persuasion, influence, and incentives on the one side. On the other side it includes: pressure ('diplomatic pressure' for instance); political conditionalities, especially negative conditionalities that embody threats in the event of non-compliance (not the positive conditionalities that stress incentives or inducements); sanctions, either threatened or actual; and covert and overt military intervention. One approach to simplifying such diversity is to allocate the approaches to either *linkage* or *leverage* (Levitsky and Way 2005). In practice different methods or approaches are often employed simultaneously by the same democracy promotion actor or by different actors. Alternatively they may be employed in sequence depending on the political circumstances and political trajectory of the countries on the receiving end. Thus assistance may be offered in the form of democracy-building projects after external pressure on the government has made it receptive to these kinds of initiative.

Given that the democracy promoters themselves comprise different kinds of organization—governmental, intergovernmental, semi-autonomous, and non-governmental—they vary greatly in their mandates and their access to different instruments for promoting democracy. United Nations (UN) initiatives can employ a form of international legitimacy that other actors lack, but in contrast to the private political foundations who are likely to specialize in providing democracy assistance the US government can, and often does, operate a more 'muscular' approach.

Democracy assistance

Democracy assistance is usually consensual: it belongs to the 'linkage' category. It comprises grant-aided support that can take the form of technical, material, and financial assistance to pro-democracy initiatives. Assistance includes what Carothers (2004) calls 'institutional modelling': attempts to transfer blueprints of democratic practice, procedure, and organizations that resemble working models already familiar in the established democracies. For Carothers assistance should also extend to giving encouragement and support to pro-democracy activists in their efforts to challenge authoritarian and semi-authoritarian rulers. This comes very close to direct involvement in domestic political struggles. When combined with the application of external pressure on the rulers to open up political space for reformers, it moves in the direction of harder forms of power.

Democracy assistance is a sizeable international industry. It is impossible to know exactly how big it is in financial terms, because figures have not been collected on a comprehensive and systematic basis, using precise and standardized definitions. For example, the US Agency for International Development (USAID), which is one of the most assiduous, provides consolidated data for 'democracy and governance assistance'; and the figure of $1.4 billion provided by the United Nations Development Programme (UNDP) is for programmes the UNDP calls 'democratic governance'.

There is also the question of whether human rights and related programmes should be included in the figure or not. The total volume of European Community support for democracy, human rights, judicial reform, governance, and civil society during 2000–04 is around $4.5 billion. EU states individually

Table 25.1 Total USAID general (non-democracy) and democracy and governance assistance (DG) by region, 1990–2004 (in millions of 1995 dollars)

Region/number of countries receiving DG assistance	DG assistance	Other assistance	DG as % of Total
Africa/39	1,089	9,790	10.0
Asia/16	579	7,039	7.6
Eurasia/12	995	6,631	13.0
Europe/16	998	5,732	14.8
Latin America and Caribbean/22	1,313	8,019	14.1
Middle East and Mediterranean/14	606	29,999	2.0
Oceania (Pacific Islands)/1	0.06	164	0

Source: Finkel *et al.* (2006: 31).

add a further total of around twice that amount. All in all the grand total of all providers' democracy assistance very loosely defined could be as much as $10 billion annually. However, the cost of promoting democracy directly by all possible means, which includes diplomatic interventions and the like, although impossible to gauge is bound to be even higher. Yet even that expenditure is small relative to total official development assistance, which was around $106 billion inclusive of debt relief in 2005.

Political conditionality

The European Union has been a major exponent of political conditionality as a distinctive approach to promoting democracy. The EU's Copenhagen criteria (1993) lay down conditions referring to 'stability of institutions guaranteeing democracy, the rule of law, human rights and respect for the protection of minorities' for eligibility to join the EU. While close observers differ on the details, most acknowledge that as a structure of incentives to undertake democratic reform this conditionality has been very effective in pushing the democratization of post-communist countries in Central and Eastern Europe (Pridham 2005; Vachudova 2005). The EU 'speaks softly and carries a big carrot' is one way of describing this approach.

However, while conditionality can be deployed on its own, in the EU's case some analysts also attach considerable weight to what has been called 'normative power Europe' (Manners 2002). This refers to the effects of socialization or social learning, which change attitudes and beliefs or behaviour, if necessary through manipulating the cost-benefit calculations that target governments make about their international reputation. The result may lead newly adopted democratic practices to become deeply embedded even after the prize of positive conditionality such as EU membership has been won and its incentive power has obsolesced. By comparison Vachudova (2005) gives more emphasis to how 'active leverage' by the EU empowered pro-reform actors in the prospective accession countries.

The United States and the European Union

Notwithstanding the EU's successes in Central and Eastern Europe, it is the US government and its instruments that have the larger profile in promoting democracy around the world. It is the one superpower with the capacity and political will to deploy the full range of methods or approaches, including the harder forms of power, where the US has a comparative advantage. From the time of President

Reagan's interest in promoting democracy as a way of combating Soviet influence around the world, to President G. W. Bush making freedom and democracy the centrepiece of his foreign policy rhetoric after 9/11, the US has tended to set agendas in democracy promotion. The prominence of the US in this is reflected in what Melia (2006) calls the US 'democracy bureaucracy', which has developed a proliferation of institutional actors or 'moving parts', especially during the Bush years. Box 25.3 below gives some leading examples.

The Europeans have found themselves struggling to know how best to respond to the US role in democracy promotion outside of the candidate countries for EU membership. Multilateral cooperation offers certain advantages but the deployment of a distinctive approach that renounces the use of force and offers one or more uniquely European variants on liberal democracy also seem attractive. In 2006 there were moves in the European Parliament to establish a European Foundation for Democracy through Partnership. The aim would be to provide an EU counterpart to the National Endowment for Democracy (NED), which is a leading US institution, although perhaps with less emphasis on providing grants. Key European actors seemed divided over the idea, in particular the European Council's interest in tying such a foundation to Europe's main security and other strategic concerns. That would replicate what some critics believe is a major weakness in contemporary US policy towards democracy promotion.

KEY POINTS

❏ Promoting democracy abroad has developed over the last twenty years, not just in respect of many post-communist countries but in other parts of the developing world too.

❏ The active promotion of democracy is intentional and deliberate although not necessarily successful; in addition democratic trends may be positively (or negatively) influenced by a wide range of other international factors, in short, passive democracy promotion.

❏ Active democracy promotion employs a variety of methods that span a continuum from soft power to hard power. Direct approaches address political objects; indirect approaches address the economic and cultural conditions for democracy.

❏ The US and Europe have different reputations in respect of democracy promotion. The EU prides itself on political dialogue and working in partnership, although its greatest successes have involved the use of political conditionality. In contrast, the US is sometimes described as pursuing a more 'muscular' approach.

Explanations of democracy promotion

A strong sense of the value of democracy and a desire to see it spread far and wide have never been absent from the Western world during the period since 1945. Even before then, the dismantling of European empires in Africa and Asia saw attempts to implant formal democratic structures of government. But it was the end of the cold war that signalled a quantitative shift in willingness to adopt democracy promotion as a foreign policy goal. The erosion of Soviet influence followed by the collapse of the Soviet Union made it safer for Western governments to demand human rights, democracy, and good governance in countries that previously had been valued primarily as Western allies. Former client states of the USSR too became more vulnerable to Western political interference. These international developments were enabling factors.

More important, sizeable mobilizations of support for political change began to take place inside many societies in the Third World and the former Second World. Often this was spurred as much by growing social and economic discontent as by grievances over political oppression and human rights abuse. International promotion of democracy gained legitimacy from this **pull-factor**, that is to say the call for political reform by people living in societies with non-democratic regimes, even if certain **push-factors** or determinants in the countries promoting democracy have supplied the main policy drivers.

Idealism

Idealism offers one possible reason for promoting democracy. The intrinsic value of freedom and democracy may be considered so great that societies which already enjoy these properties feel obliged to help other societies share them too. It is a disinterested act, even when not tinged with missionary zeal. Historians see a close association of the US and democratic idealism dating to the presidency of Woodrow Wilson (1913–21). One view is that the US is 'born to lead'; that promoting freedom and democracy is the US's 'manifest destiny'. Sceptics draw a distinction between the rhetoric and the reality.

Democracy promotion and US imperialism

A more critical view sees the US defining its aims in such a way as to pursue global hegemony. When backed by all the resources available to the US, the promotion of democracy abroad serves the purpose of US imperialism. Other countries then follow. It is true that in the 1980s efforts in support of democratization were part of a strategy to confront Soviet power and influence. However, that situation no longer exists. And it is not obvious why the many countries that now officially support international democracy promotion would do so if the main goal is US domination. Undoubtedly governments shape their foreign policies in accord with their view of the national interest, but it is also worth mentioning that many ordinary people support efforts to promote democracy too. Thus a sample survey of respondents carried out in the US and in nine European Union countries and Turkey found support for 'soft power' approaches reached 74 per cent (The German Marshall Fund of the US 2005).

Developmental arguments

Paradigms depicting the relationship between development in the developing world and democracy or democratization underwent a double shift from the 1980s. Prior to then, the dominant economistic reasoning maintained that developing countries must address their economic needs before they could expect to sustain democracy. By trying to democratize prematurely they would jeopardize their prospects of development. What made this 'cruel choice' seem inevitable was the belief that economics determines politics. In so far as some particular kind of political rule is most favourable to development, then authoritarian regimes have the edge. The economic 'miracle' of East Asia's 'dragons' appeared to be illustrative.

However, this chain of reasoning has since come to be questioned, on two grounds. Many African countries were simply not developing. Just as important was the rise of the intellectual proposition that politics can make a difference. This was connected with a more general movement in the social sciences to recognize that institutions and human agency do matter; not everything is determined by structural 'causes'. Furthermore, development was increasingly defined not just as economic growth but in terms of improved social conditions and human development (for data on education and literacy see Comparative table 7 at the end of this volume). Attention turned to the ways in which democracy, human rights, and good governance might benefit such development. The debate about these complex issues has not yet been conclusively resolved.

Nevertheless something of a double paradigm shift did take place: away from a belief in the economic merits of authoritarian rule within an 'economics first' approach to development, towards a belief that democratic reform can be helpful. Indeed, in many cases democratization could even be essential to unlocking the developmental potential, in North Korea for instance. Ultimately that would enable these countries to graduate from international aid of all kinds. That is a stated objective of the aid donors.

However, some major international development agencies like the World Bank continue to stress most of all the importance of better governance, not democracy. This builds on arguments that the rule of law and secure property rights are more important for development than are other civil liberties or extensive political rights. Lipset's (1959) enduring thesis that stable democracy is more difficult to maintain in the absence of social modernization and economic development continues to command widespread support, which means that a considerable raft of social and economic as well as political changes must ultimately go hand in hand.

Democracy promotion and international capitalism

Just as the developmental case for promoting democracy has fluctuated in accordance with changes in thinking about development, so the same is true of the policy drivers that are framed in more expressly political terms. Marxist and neo-Marxist perspectives explain democracy promotion as an instrument of global capitalism. And it is true that the kind of democracy that figures most pervasively in democracy promotion resembles what Marxists criticize as bourgeois democracy, lacking the more rigorously egalitarian and popular participatory content of radical models of democracy that embrace a strong commitment to absolute socio-economic equality and 'people power'.

So democracy promotion has been portrayed as a handmaiden of capital, international capital and transnational capital in particular (Robinson 1996). It is likened to a Trojan horse for economic liberalization. It brings down regimes that had socialist pretensions and puts in their place governments that look more likely to render account to private economic interests. Political liberalization, democratization, and economic marketization have indeed moved forward in parallel in many parts of the world. Market economics certainly do not dictate market politics, but Western-style democracies do seem to respect and require the economic freedoms that are associated with capitalism. Even so, there are other and possibly more compelling answers to questions seeking an explanation of democracy promotion.

Democratization, international peace, and national security

The democratic peace thesis was strongly endorsed in President Clinton's support of democratization and has regularly featured in the policy rationales of most official actors. The thesis maintains that democracies do not go to war with one another (Russett 1993). Thus everyone gains as more states become democratic.

The thesis has generated an enormous literature, some of it highly critical. Critics dispute its validity or contest its applicability to democratization in the twenty-first century. One objection is that the thesis holds only under certain limiting conditions, for example on a restrictive definition of war, or during the cold war era, or when most democracies were wealthy industrial societies. There is no consensus on the principal reasons why democracies rarely go to war with democracies. No one denies that democracies have initiated wars against non-democracies. Democratization can increase the likelihood of internal turmoil, which in turn might impact adversely on external relations. The bloody transformation of former Yugoslavia after the end of communism is an example.

Nevertheless, views resembling the democratic peace thesis continue to play a part in the justifications advanced for promoting democracy. Furthermore, after the terrorist events of 9/11 and the policy of the US government to embrace freedom and democracy as major objectives in the Middle East and elsewhere, democratization—and hence democracy promotion—have come to be presented as antidotes to international terrorism. President Bush has harnessed the promotion of democracy to national security objectives in a very particular way. The Advance Democracy Act (2005) proposed to strengthen the State Department's commitment to democracy promotion for this very purpose. The government's national intelligence strategy was reformulated in ways that now enumerate bolstering the growth of democracy and sustaining the peaceful development of democratic states as strategic mission objectives of the Office of the Director of National Intelligence (Central Intelligence Agency). As with the democratic peace thesis more broadly, the anti-terrorism case for promoting democracy soon came to be echoed in the public policy pronouncements of governments elsewhere in the West.

However, once again, the theory fails to convince everyone. Although in some places illiberal or oppressive rule might share responsibility for the emergence of political extremism in society and a willingness to pursue political ends by violent means, these may not be the only or even the primary 'causal' influences. They are probably most potent when linked to other enabling conditions, stimuli, or catalysts. For instance other theories draw attention to the radicalizing effects of poverty and resentment at global social injustice, or to the militant tendencies of extremist religious and nationalist views. In the Middle East a satisfactory resolution to the conflict between Israel and the Palestinians could be a necessary condition before the perceived threat to the West from Islamic terrorism starts to recede. European leaders are more willing to make these connections than the US government, and are less inclined to portray democracy promotion in the region as the main solution.

What is more, the possibility that largely free and fair elections might bring about an elected government that itself appears to sponsor terrorism or, at the very least pursues policies that seems to be threatening in some other way, cannot be discounted. The victory of Hamas in the first Palestinian parliamentary election in January 2006 is an example of the first. The popularity of President Hugo Chávez in Venezuela might be considered an example of the second, given his constant criticism of the US role in regional and world affairs. The result is that some Western governments appear to be inconsistent in their support for the democratic process, depending on the electoral outcomes.

KEY POINTS

❑ No single theory appears to capture well all the actors or cover the entire period since the late 1980s, not least because the actors disagree among themselves on exactly what they are trying to achieve and why.

❑ After 9/11, the contribution of democratization to securing peace within and between nations has gained prominence in the context of a global war on terror, especially in the rhetoric of politicians.

❑ Commentators question the sincerity of the political rhetoric. Analysts question the social scientific reasoning upon which various theories claim to be based.

Actors on the supply side

On the supply side, the international 'democracy industrial complex' has grown considerably over the last twenty years or so to include some very different kinds of organization, governmental, intergovernmental, autonomous but largely publicly funded, and genuinely non-governmental actors who are either not-for-profit or commercially motivated.

One way of distinguishing between the actors is in terms of those for whom democracy support is one of many activities, the UNDP for instance, and those for whom it is their sole rationale, like Britain's Westminster Foundation for Democracy (WFD). Another is to distinguish between the kinds of activities they engage in. For example, even within just the realm of democracy assistance, several organizations mainly give grants, some offer technical support, and some are operational. Different again is the intergovernmental International Institute for Democracy and Electoral Assistance (IDEA), based in Sweden, which works at the interface between analysing democratic trends and disseminating advice; it is not operational and does not award grants.

Intergovernmental actors

The UN is the one truly multilateral organization of great note that is prominent in international democracy promotion. The UN's contribution ranges from broad statements of support for democratic values by the Office of the Secretary-General through to a considerable practical experience in helping stage, monitor, and observe elections, especially in new states (see Newman and Rich 2004). Within the UN family the UNDP has grown to possibly the largest provider of democratic governance assistance in the world, and is involved in over 130 countries. In 2005 Secretary-General Kofi Annan announced the creation of a separate UN Democracy Fund. Initial pledges received from twenty-six countries totalled $41 million.

Regional-level organizations that express a strong commitment to support democracy in the member-states include the Organization of American States (OAS) and the African Union, through its New Partnership for Africa's Development (NEPAD) and African Peer Review Mechanism. The Commonwealth offers some practical assistance to its members by way of exchanging experiences in matters like parliamentary training and legislative oversight of the executive. The Organization for Security and Co-operation in Europe (OSCE) has been centrally involved in elections observation in southern-east and eastern Europe.

COUNTRY PROFILE Turkey

Republic of Turkey (*Türkiye Cumhuriyeti*)

State formation

After defeat in the First World War, the constitutional Republic of Turkey succeeded to the 600-year-old Ottoman Empire under the leadership of its founder and first president Mustafa Kemal (honorifically rebaptized Atatürk, Father of the Turks, in 1934). Since the establishment of a multi-party system in 1945, the country has suffered several military *coup détats*; the current constitution was ratified by popular referendum during a military junta that lasted until 1983. *Constitution* 1982, amended many times.

Form of government

Republican parliamentary democracy.
Head of state President, elected by the National Assembly; term of 7 years.
Head of government Prime Minister appointed by the President from among the members of parliament.
Cabinet Council of Ministers appointed by the President on the nomination of the Prime Minister.

Administrative subdivisions 81 provinces.

Legal system

Civil law system derived from various European continental legal systems.

Legislature

Unicameral Grand National Assembly of Turkey (*Türkiye Büyük Millet Meclisı*): 550 seats; term of 5 years.

Electoral system

Proportional representation.
Formula D'Hondt.
Constituencies 79 multi-member constituencies.
Barrier clause 10% nation-wide.
Suffrage Universal, 18 years.

Direct democracy

Since the 1982 constitutional referendum, two more referenda have been held, most recently in 1988.

Party system Results of the 2002 legislative elections (Grand National Assembly):

Electorate:	41,452,823	100.0%
Voters:	32,733,410	79.0%

Party	Valid votes	%	Seats
Justice and Development Party (AKP)	10,779,489	34.3	363
Republican People's Party (CHP)	6,099,083	19.4	178
True Path Party (DYP)	3,004,842	9.5	0
Nationalist Movement Party (MHP)	2,622,545	8.3	0
Youth Party (GP)	2,277,651	7.2	0
Democratic People's Party (DHP)	1,953,627	6.2	0
Motherland Party (ANAP)	1,610,708	5.1	0
Democratic Left Party (DSP)	385,950	1.2	0
Others	2,714,533	8.6	9
Total	31,448,428	100.0	550

Source: Adam Carr's Website.

Governmental actors

The governments of established liberal democracies try to promote democracy through a number of institutional channels, including their foreign affairs ministries and development aid agencies, and by funding private, autonomous, or quasi non-governmental organizations that have been set up to promote democracy. The governments include those of the US, Britain, the Netherlands, Germany, Canada, Denmark, and the Nordic countries.

The US government has easily the highest profile. The executive commitment has grown under successive presidents, from Ronald Reagan onwards, to become a flagship of President George W. Bush's second term. Of all government departments, USAID is the one that enjoys the most prominent reputation for work in the democracy and governance area. USAID receives overall foreign policy guidance from the Secretary of State. USAID counts democracy, conflict prevention, and humanitarian assistance as one of three main ways in which it advances US foreign policy objectives. But under 10 per cent of all USAID aid spending, which is less than 1 per cent of the entire federal government budget, goes on democracy and governance.

Stiftungen and foundations

Germany's *Stiftungen* and democracy foundations in such countries as the US, the Netherlands, and Britain share with one another some combination of formal autonomy, private or quasi-governmental status, with extensive reliance on central government funding. The relationship between what they do and government policy may not be wholly transparent, but their collected experience in offering practical support to democratic development is considerable.

In Germany, after being funded in the federal Parliament for two consecutive elections, a political party is entitled to receive government funding for civic education work at home and certain international activities. Each one of the *Stiftungen* is then close to one of the main parties. Together they have long experience in developing contacts abroad at the non-governmental level. For example, the Friedrich Ebert *Stiftung* was founded in 1925. The foundations work with actors in civil society and other groups including parties. They are unusual in that they establish permanent field offices in countries abroad. They have a reputation for developing partisan links with ideologically like-minded parties, which is difficult to achieve in some countries in Africa for instance, where the parties may have ethnic or regional identities but no clear or distinctive programmatic commitment.

Germany's foundations accounted for over three-quarters of the combined annual overall budget spent

---

BOX 25.3 The US democracy bureaucracy

US government actors inherited by the Bush administration

US Agency for International Development (USAID)

State Department, includes: Bureau for Democracy, Human Rights and Labor Affairs; Special Coordinator for Assistance to Europe and Eurasia; Bureau of Educational and Cultural Affairs

Voice of America and other broadcasting arms

Programmes managed by the Department of Justice and Dept. of Labor

Defense Department functions, e.g. International Military Education and Training

US Intelligence Community

Additions during the Bush presidency include

Millennium Challenge Corporation

Middle East Partnership Initiative

Broader Middle East and North Africa Initiative

New Midddle East broadcasting programmes

Coordinator for Reconstruction and Stabilization

Deputy National Security Advisor for global democracy promotion

US Congress

Works with counterpart legislatures

Nongovernmental organizations funded by government grant

National Endowment for Democracy (NED): NED affiliates such as the National Democratic Institute; International Republican Institute. Also houses the International Forum for Democratic Studies; *Journal of Democracy*

Freedom House

Carter Center (founded by President Jimmy Carter)

Non-profit and for-profit enterprises operating mainly as government contractors

For example Management Systems International; Chemonics.

Private organizations

Open Society Institute: 31 country specific foundations financed by American philanthropist George Soros.

Source: Adapted from Melia (2006).

governance in the Pacific region, with Indonesia being a major partner.

Friedrich Ebert *Stiftung*	Social Democratic Party
Konrad Adenauer *Stiftung*	Christian Democratic Union
Heinrich Böll *Stiftung*	Green Party (Bundnis 90/Grüne)
Friedrich Naumann *Stiftung*	Free Democratic Party
Hans Seidel *Stiftung*	Christian Social Union
Rosa Luxemburg *Stiftung*	Party of Democratic Socialism

BOX 25.4 The *Stiftungen* are close to Germany's political parties

by Europe's political foundations on democracy-related work in 2004 (van Wersch and de Zeeuw 2005). The Olof Palme Foundation, linked to Sweden's Social Democratic Party, is somewhat similar. In addition, political parties in many established Western democracies contribute to democracy-building more directly through transnational co-operation with parties in new and emerging democracies, even if they do not have special foundations.

In the US, the NED was established as a non-profit organization with public funding voted annually by Congress in 1983. As well as making its own grants, it works closely with four core institutes, two of which, the National Democratic Institute for International Affairs (NDI) and International Republican Institute (IRI), are especially prominent in the world of democracy assistance.

Other European countries that have dedicated democracy foundations funded by government include Britain. The WFD, founded 1992 is active mainly in post-communist Europe and anglophone Africa. In the Netherlands the Institute for Multiparty Democracy (NIMD), founded in 2000 following Dutch party involvement in South Africa's transition from apartheid, specializes in strengthening party politics in around fifteen countries. A Centre for Democratic Institutions (CDI) established by the Australian government in 1998 is based at the Australian National University. It too emphasizes support for party development and parliamentary

The European Union as distinctive hybrid

As Chapter 23 above makes clear, the EU is not a state. And until quite recently foreign policy analysts were not all convinced that the lens of foreign policy could be used to illuminate the EU's external behaviour. However, the EU is becoming more than just one more intergovernmental actor. It has moved towards the adoption of a common foreign and security policy; and is now one of the world's largest foreign aid donors. Its formal commitment to promoting democracy has grown apace. One of the most visible institutional expressions is the European Initiative for Democracy and Human Rights (EIDHR), which dates from 1994 and disburses grants totalling approximately 120 million euros annually to around thirty-two countries. Although EIDHR monies can be disbursed to non-governmental organizations in countries without seeking their government's consent, this happens very rarely. The institution has focused mainly on human rights support.

The EU's role in promoting democratic political reform in Central and Eastern European countries in the 1990s, and extended most recently to the Balkans, has already been noted. This was no disinterested act. Just as many people in the transition and post-communist societies saw democratization as an aid to recovering national independence—freedom both from authoritarian rule and from political domination by the Soviet Union (subsequently Russia)—so Western Europeans saw democratic reform in the 'near abroad' as a plus for their own security. Both economic and political transformations are considered essential for countries to be considered eligible for membership of the EU. And EU expansion appealed to many existing members, although not all for the same reasons. The EU has also had a strong dynamic of its own, with increase in membership potentially helping the institution to become a more powerful actor in world affairs in its own right. Democracy promotion in nearby states has served this objective. In fact promoting democracy anywhere can be seen both as a symbol and tool of powerful actor status in world affairs.

Aside from Central–East Europe, democratic progress in other regions including but not only what since the 2004 enlargement is called the 'European neighbourhood', remains a desideratum, even in countries that will never be considered for EU membership. Just like EU enlargement, the European Neighbourhood Policy (ENP) can be interpreted as a domain-expanding policy, by the European Commission specifically (Kelley 2006). Other rationales include democracy's claimed ability to secure domestic political stability and predisposition towards peaceful external relations. This remains an important challenge in the Balkans. Then there is the belief that democracies are less likely to export political asylum seekers and terrorists to countries in the EU. This is relevant to North Africa especially. The ENP offers governments to the east and on the southern and eastern shores of the Mediterranean and Caucasus a 'privileged relationship' in return for political as well as economic reform.

Finally in Europe there is some political commitment to present democracy as a core European value. This centres on the conviction that Europe offers a model of political harmony both within and among states that is highly relevant to some other parts of the world, not least the zones of conflict, because it shows how to rise above centuries of interstate violence—Europe having been at the heart of two 'world wars' and one 'cold war' in the twentieth century alone. The political values on which this stability in Europe has been constructed are for Europe to demonstrate and to share, not by exporting democracy aggressively but by engaging in processes defined by 'partnership' and ideological suasion. In so far as this strategy achieves results, the international standing of the EU can be reckoned to benefit accordingly.

Democracy promotion by new democracies

If the EU is distinctive if still less prominent than the US, then some of the newer democracies that have joined the cause of international democracy promotion warrant individual mention too. Collectively they provide the main membership of the Community of Democracies and several regional bodies already mentioned. South Africa and Poland are examples of new liberal democracies that have been active in trying to influence politics in nearby states, although South Africa's inability to persuade Zimbabwe's President Mugabe to relax his oppressive rule or leave office has occasioned much disappointment in the West.

Poland's politicians and civic groups have been active in countries to the East. Ukraine is one such country, and it illustrates the considerable assortment of foreign and international actors that may be at work over time, acting separately and together. Poland's President Krasniewski played a leading role in resolving the political crisis in the Ukrainian capital, Kiev, in late 2004, when hundreds of thousands of Ukrainian protesters crammed the central thoroughfare. They were demonstrating peacefully against the fraudulent electoral victory claimed by Viktor Yanukovitch, the Russian-backed candidate hand-picked by outgoing president Leonid Kuchma, against his rival, Viktor Yushchenko, who was preferred by the West. A rerun of the November election took place in late December, which Yushchenko won easily.

The 'orange revolution' is often cited as a triumph for international democracy promotion and an inspiration to other countries. But the Ukrainian case illustrates the difficulty of assigning responsibility to any single external actor or initiative in such a complex and dynamic situation. Moreover close observers like Åslund and McFaul (2006) and Youngs (2006) question how much support the outside actors really have given. They agree that it was domestic Ukrainian actors and events who were and are the primary influence on political developments, including in the period leading up to and during the 'orange revolution'.

What is more, political in-fighting among the political elite since 2004 has dispelled some of the euphoria. Continued opposition by the EU to the government's policy of applying for EU membership means that one potentially very strong incentive for it to push democratic change further forward is absent. Since 2004 much international attention has moved to other regions, principally the Middle East. The continuing political uncertainties in Ukraine after 2004 serve to underline the point that we need to consider very carefully the choice of census date when seeking to pass judgement on the success or failure of international intervention.

KEY POINTS

❑ Many different kinds of organizations are involved in promoting democracy. Development agencies stress 'democratic governance'; democracy foundations focus on democracy and may value it for its own sake.

❑ The EU's distinctive contribution to democratization in Central and Eastern Europe has reflected national

interests and an EU motivation. We cannot be sure the European Neighbourhood Policy will be anything like as effective.

❑ The US has the highest profile worldwide, and it is not obvious that the EU has been more effective in promoting democracy, outside the European arena.

The market for democracy promotion

The market for democracy promotion is more difficult to describe. The term 'demand side' offers a neat counterpart to 'supply side'. But even in semi-authoritarian regimes, let alone the more autocratic examples, the people in power are often not keen on foreign offers of support for democratization. And it is worth considering whether the voices and driving forces that determine most the size and shape of democracy promotion come from the promoters and providers as they go about pursuing their own and their country's political, bureaucratic, and other interests. The charge that it is the providers who shape the market and strongly influence the demand or the way the demand is expressed, as well as their response to the demand, has long been levelled in the case of international development cooperation for instance.

People who live under oppressive rule find it difficult to openly make demands for international help. Nevertheless democracy promoters tend to assume there is popular hunger for more freedom and democracy in such countries and moreover that international endeavours to help them gain these ends is desired. However that demand may not coincide exactly with what the democracy promoters mean by democracy or the kind of democratization they are keen to support. An illustration is the unresolved debate about the status of Islamic perspectives on democracy, which insist it is the will of God and not the people who must be sovereign and in addition contest the idea of equal rights for women. A grievance that is often given voice by putative beneficiaries of democracy assistance projects and their representatives is that decisions on project design and the like are determined on the supply side. Indeed, they say they structure their 'demand' to coincide with

what they believe will resonate most strongly with the providers rather than in accord with their own understanding of what is wanted or what is best.

In principle, establishing which countries are not democracies or where people have fewest freedoms should not be difficult. Here, the academic literature on democratization and organizations involved in promoting democracy both make considerable reference to the country data that Freedom House publishes each year. However, it would be unrealistic to expect to find a perfect fit between such data and the actual patterns of allocation in democracy promotion and assistance, for reasons to do with the policy drivers that lie behind democracy support.

Over time, however, there have been major changes in the market for democracy promotion that have followed the political trends inside countries. Thus whereas in the first half of the 1990s countries in the former Second World were heavily targeted, many of the European examples have now 'graduated', while some others, like the Central Asian Republics, appear to have become less accessible. Several states in the Balkans became candidates for democracy support as they emerged from the violent break-up of Yugoslavia and began to look like possible candidates for EU membership.

Elsewhere in the world a few African countries have moved beyond the need for concentrated democracy support, South Africa for instance. Some continue to be the focus of modest attention, such as Zambia, and others like Zimbabwe and Sudan seem impossible to reach. Most Latin American and Caribbean countries already qualify as democracies and, while receiving international assistance in particular sectors such as judicial reform, they are not the most prominent candidates. While the OAS is a positive force for democratic consolidation within the region, at the present time Cuba and Haiti appear to be beyond external influence. Recent efforts by the US have focused on oil-rich Venezuela, where the populist leadership of President Hugo Chávez and his condemnations of US imperialism are seen as a threat to democracy and to US interests. Meanwhile China, which by virtue of its demographic weight makes the largest single contribution to lack of freedom and democracy, is largely off limits to democracy promotion, although some outside actors try to improve China's adherence to human rights.

The region that in the twenty-first century has come to the fore in the thinking of democracy promotion's supporters is the Middle East. This is both because liberal democracy has made least progress there and because political reform in countries like Egypt, Syria, and Iran is now seen to be vital to Western security interests. And although its strategy

for promoting democracy there has not succeeded and has drawn strong criticism (Diamond 2005) the US continues to pour resources into Iraq. Countries around the southern shore of the Mediterranean are a focus for EU thinking, while Turkey's accession to the EU can be viewed as important to securing that country's democratic consolidation. The Middle East and Afghanistan present today's frontier for international promotion of democracy but no one is very confident that they know how to this. In the past there has been some political liberalization in countries like Jordan and Egypt that was not sustained. There is considerable debate over whether external democracy interventions pushed by the West could turn out to be more of a hindrance than a help, given the past history of troubled relationships, the cultural differences, and all the suspicions and misunderstandings fuelled by the invasion of Iraq, the US's support for Israel, the growth of radical Islam, and the 'war on terror'.

KEY POINTS

❑ The true demand for democracy promotion is hard to fathom even if people in the established liberal democracies believe their choice of political system is a universal value.

❑ Democracy promotion efforts have never corresponded very closely to patterns of greatest democratic deficit. Reasons grounded in *realpolitik* are partly responsible. In many countries the challenge of promoting democracy promotion looks very difficult.

❑ The allocation of democracy promotion and assistance efforts has changed over time. This is partly an opportunistic response to political developments like the collapse of the Soviet Union followed later by the democratic graduation of many former communist countries, and partly a function of new thinking such as about the main threats to national, regional, and international security.

Democracy promotion strategies

The variety of available methods or approaches to democracy promotion that range from democracy assistance, soft power, and linkage, all the way to attempts to impose democracy by force, suggest that governmental and intergovernmental democracy promoters in particular face major questions of strategy. That means questions about what to do, where, and more especially how to go about it (Burnell 2005). The major donors are still grappling with these issues and none claim to have found all the answers, even as events around them continue to move on and the challenges become increasingly complex.

Constraints on intervention

Democracy promotion is not licence to do anything in the name of advancing the cause. There are, at least in principle, constraints in international law. Not even the UN is legally entitled to try to impose democracy by force. The limited circumstances whereby the UN Security Council may authorize military intervention in the internal affairs of a country against the will of its government were narrowly defined at a time when the idea of state sovereignty was paramount. In the first instance they require that the country be regarded as a threat to others, such as exporting instability to the surrounding region. The post-cold war world has seen increasing discussion among legal scholars and theorists of international politics of the rights that peoples have to democratic government. That the UN might have a responsibility to protect and enforce those rights is one possible corollary. However it is contentious. The grounds for physical intervention by the UN or another intergovernmental actor like the North Atlantic Treaty Organisation (NATO) have tended to be stretched most in situations where there has been massive abuse of human rights, the Balkans for example. But there has been no consistency of intervention, as the failure to prevent the Rwandan genocide in 1994 demonstrates. In the space of around four months up to one million Rwandans were massacred in inter-tribal warfare. The major Western powers looked on; the UN seemed powerless to intervene.

Moreover the UN does not have the military capability to spread democracy at gunpoint, even if that was a feasible strategy. And the evidence suggests that such an approach is more likely to fail than succeed. Of sixteen US military interventions abroad since 1898 in only four cases was democracy sustained ten years after the departure of US forces (Pei and Kasper 2003). Events resembling a slide to civil war in Iraq post-Saddam do not bode any better. Furthermore the occupation of Iraq and all its costs mean that even the US military is overstretched. Securing Afghanistan's very fragile new democracy against a resurgent Taliban is sorely taxing NATO.

Of course military intervention to end internal war can contribute to peace-building and thereby offer a service to democracy-building. For example British military deployment in Sierra Leone from 1999 was critical to ending the civil war that had broken out there and restoring elected civil rule. But most military adventures abroad initially have little to do with wanting to export democracy, even if they end up furthering the conditions in which democracy-building can be advanced and allow that to be used retrospectively as the rationale.

Types of democracy assistance

If governmental and intergovernmental actors and the US government especially have a comparative advantage in using the widest possible range of approaches to promoting democracy, then democracy assistance is the one method that is available to the greatest number and variety of actors, the foundations included. Assistance also tends to be much more visible than say diplomatic pressure, or 'diplomatic dialogue' even, which often take place behind closed doors and are difficult to measure.

Carothers (2004) offers a useful categorization of democracy assistance in the shape of a 'democracy template'. This distinguishes three sectors: electoral process, state institutions, and civil society. For each sector there are sector goals, and typical forms of democracy aid that relate to them. Boxes 25.5 and 25.6 present concrete examples of how UNDP and USAID respectively classify their activities. The area of civil–military relations have by and large been relatively neglected by democracy assistance. Although quite critical to the democratic prospect in some countries like Pakistan, the subject appears to have been viewed more as matter for international security cooperation.

Broadly speaking, democracy assistance has evolved along a path from electoral support through an emphasis on civil society to an increased willingness in some circles to regard support for party strengthening as essential to democracy-building. This evolution reflects progress in our understanding of democratization—what it is and what makes it happen or, more specifically, what is needed if a democratic opening is to be sustained. A lesson grasped fairly early on was that elections do not make a democracy. There are many cases where the election result is largely predetermined by illiberal and anti-democratic manœuvres by the government long before ballot day, irrespective of whether the actual proceedings meet the international benchmarks for good practice. Zimbabwe is an example.

Although democratic consolidation is a concept that has no precisely agreed meaning, it involves change along behavioural and attitudinal as well as institutional dimensions that go well outside—while helping to underpin—a free and fair electoral process. So the contribution made by international election observation, and the more interventionist practice of election monitoring, should be kept in perspective. Nevertheless they are significant in the overall conspectus of democracy assistance, and many organizations take part.

BOX 25.5 United Nations Development Programme democratic governance

Main services: responding to the requests and needs of developing countries, UNDP offers services in the following:

- parliamentary development;
- electoral systems and processes;
- justice and human rights;
- e-governance and access to information;
- decentralization, local governance, and urban/rural development;
- public administration and anti-corruption.

UNDP supports transitions through:

- providing policy advice and technical support, such as on the cost of elections and party organization;
- capacity development of institutions and people, such as training parliamentarians;
- advocacy, communications, and public information campaigns;
- promoting dialogue among conflicting groups;
- knowledge networking to share good practices.

Source: UNDP, Fast Facts: Democratic Governance (2006).

BOX 25.6 USAID's democracy promotion toolbox: illustrative and concrete examples of how USAID says it supports democratization

Promoting justice and human rights through the rule of law

Improve laws, institutions, and the judiciary as checks on the executive.

Support due process, non-discrimination, and representation of all segments of society.

Strengthening the institutions of democratic and accountable governance

Encourage effective, transparent provision of goods and services; avenues for participation and oversight; separation of powers with checks and balances.

Support anti-corruption in all institutions and sectors.

Strengthen effective oversight and democratic functioning of authorities responsible for security.

Expanding political freedom and competition

Promote free, fair, transparent multi-party elections.
Promote representative, accountable political parties.

Engaging society through the voice, advocacy, and participation of citizens

Promote effective private voluntary associations and a strong civil society.
Promote vigorous independent media.

Source: USAID, *At Freedom's Frontiers: A Democracy and Governance Strategic Framework* (December 2005).

Partly because the electoralist fallacy came to be so widely recognised, civil society support became a major area of democracy assistance throughout the 1990s. The attraction for democracy promoters was that it seemed to avoid direct interference in a country's internal politics. However the more resources were put into trying to create and strengthen institutional capacity in civil societies, the greater was the realization of the dangers involved in pursuing this goal. Much evidence of donor dependency came to light: civic groups unlikely to be sustained after foreign support ceased. In many cases such groups tended to comprise elites who were neither representative of their society nor committed to developing wide and deep roots in society: external orientation was their rational response to the donor incentive structure.

Finally, the notion that support to civil society is a politically safe way to promote democracy has come to be discredited on two counts. First, civic actors can be very political and may well have to deal with politically powerful people, perhaps provoking intense hostility in the process. There are countries like Zimbabwe where overt support for any actors who oppose the government increases the chances that those actors will face increased repression. Secondly, authoritarian rulers have other stratagems for co-opting, limiting, or simply ignoring, if not actually repressing, civil society actors. They may be able to maintain the appearance of political liberalization without conceding meaningful democratization. Egypt is often cited as an example. In societies that lack well organized political parties for channelling

Table 25.2 Total USAID democracy assistance by subsector, 1990–2003 (in millions of 1995 dollars)

Civil society	2,438
Governance	1,458
Rule of law	1,219
Elections	687

Source: Finkel *et al.* (2006: 34).

Table 25.3 Political party assistance by thirty-two European political foundations, by type, 2004 (%)

Strengthen party organization	33
Strengthen party capacity for electoral campaigning	15
Promote women's participation	12
Training of party poll-watchers or election staff	8
Strengthen parliamentary role of parties	11
Strengthen overall party system	9
Other	12

Source: Van Wersch and de Zeeuw (2005: 16).

political mobilization in a manner compatible with orderly democratic rule, authoritarian breakdown may not proceed smoothly to the installation of democracy. Instead, there is turmoil, creating opportunities for illiberal groups ('uncivil society') to take charge, as happened in Iraq.

For all these reasons there is more talk now than formerly of the imperative to strengthen political parties. Parties must provide the political leadership if good governance is to be possible; and opposition parties must have the capability to hold government to account. Thus more democracy promoters are thinking about the parties dimension, although the majority of efforts to date have not systematically aimed at connecting support to parties individually with the development of an effective and competitive party system appropriate to the society in question (Burnell 2006*b*). Rather than work with the parties directly it may be more effective to seek to improve

their institutional and regulatory environment. For instance in many countries, especially in Africa, support for legislative strengthening may be a prerequisite to a more truly competitive party system. The funding regime, both the public funding of parties and controls on political expenditures, is another crucially important area for advice.

Democracy promotion and state-building

Democracy promotion faces enormous challenges in societies coming out of violent conflict and especially those where the state is fragile or still not very effective, that is, failing or, even worse, close to collapse. An increasing number of such cases from Afghanistan to the Democratic Republic of Congo have come to attention in the unstable politics of the post-cold war world; the cases examined in detail by de Zeeuw and Kumar (2006) include Sierra Leone, Uganda, Ethiopia, Mozambique, Guatemala, Cambodia, Rwanda, and El Salvador as well.

Sub-state violence or at minimum very weak governance have been placed under the spotlight that previously focused on threats of large-scale inter-state war and East–West conflict in particular. Where multiple weaknesses exist, the solutions tend to be interconnected, even though they are often not well understood. They may include not just state-building (or re-building) but also nation-building, economic reconstruction and development, the resolution of humanitarian crises, in addition to installing democracy, good governance, and human rights. The correct order of priorities, the trade-offs, and sequencing issues between these processes pose big and complex theoretical and practical questions for the societies themselves and for international actors who wish to render help. The issues lie at the interstices of several literatures, including those on humanitarian intervention, conflict, and peace-making, democratization and democracy promotion, and development, which means that no single discipline, school of thought, or body of advisers can pretend to have all the answers.

Democratization vs. state-building

One of the larger theoretical questions is whether state-building should take precedence in situations where public order is weak, especially if the political instability endangers neighbouring countries too. Insisting on moving rapidly towards a participatory and competitive political system could risk mobilizing uncivil elements into the political process. Populist leaders may take advantage and align party political cleavages with the ethnic, racial, religious, or sectarian divisions that have brought about violent conflict in the past. Some of the hallmarks of stateness, monopoly of the means of violence for instance, might be difficult to achieve at the same time as rival politicians resort to the arbitrary use of force. External encouragement to adopt some form of political decentralization may end up handing power to regional warlords or local despots who do not share democratic values.

However, the alternative of pursuing a 'state first' approach that concentrates on strengthening the powers of central government and seeks to establish the rule of law ahead of building democracy, is not without risks either. It can create an accumulation of vested interests in power concentration; the force of path dependence then takes over and makes it more difficult to democratize and disperse power later, once public order has been secured. While more inclusive participation in the political process can help the cause of nation-building, political leaders may use the democratic process in ways that actually promote inter-communal conflict, for instance by appealing to their own ethnic group and portraying other groups in very negative terms. By comparison, a less representative and more authoritarian form of government would be able to suppress the potential for conflict. President Milošević's promotion of Serb nationalism which contributed to the disintegration of the formerly stable communist state of Yugoslavia shows that democratization can harbour dangers.

International actors should be sensitive to these dilemmas. At the very least when advising the institutional architecture for building democracy after conflict or in the presence of centrifugal tendencies, they should take account of the way different electoral systems, regulations governing the formation of political parties, and the behaviour of the media can all influence whether the new political order turns out to be inclusive and harmonious or divisive and exclusionary. Reynolds (2002) surveys the different approaches; Bastian and Luckham (2003) show how difficult it can be to alight on the right solution even in countries that once looked like stable democracies, Sri Lanka for instance. International actors are usually reluctant to make sufficient resources available to address the issues, especially where the country is of no great strategic importance. Also, international assistance of all sorts should be aware that the capacity of broken-backed states and lawless societies to put support to good use is bound to be limited. The chances are that material aid will be misused and may fuel corruption, while the external political interference takes way a meaningful sense of political self-determination. International involvement in Bosnia-Herzegovina since the Dayton Peace Accords (1995) brought peace to the area has been widely portrayed in this way, notwithstanding all the good intentions.

So, where violent internal conflict has existed, possibly because serious political discrimination, oppression, and human rights abuse have been rife, the moral that democracy and peace should go together looks obvious. After all, democracy is a way of managing conflict peacefully. However, getting to the point where peace and democracy are both firmly established is the major problem. Conflict-resolution, peace-building, and democratization can require some hard choices to be made, especially when calculated from the different perspectives of the short, medium, and longer terms. Tactics and strategy for solving one set of problems can be at odds with what is required to address other equally important sets of issues. Political deals that accommodate bullies may be essential to seal peace but can come back to haunt democratization later. If 'war criminals' from the past are pursued zealously in the interests of showing a newfound commitment to justice, human rights, and the rule of law, then a new democracy may risk alienating the supporters of those people and may delay the onset of stable communal relations, on which stable democracy must ultimately rest. Thus democracy promoters should proceed with care and be prepared to envisage that every case will be different.

KEY POINTS

❑ External imposition is not generally considered to be an effective way of promoting sustainable democracy.

❑ Civil society has been a privileged recipient of democracy assistance, because it seemed to offer opportunities for foreign involvement without offending the sensitivities of governments. However, experience has shown that non-democratic regimes are increasingly wary of foreign involvement with civic actors in their country.

❑ Democracy projects and programmes have changed from focus on elections and institutions of government, through civil society, to increasing attention to the need to strengthen political parties, key players in building stable democracy.

❑ Promoting democracy in fragile states and post-conflict societies is especially problematical. International actors must reflect carefully on how the various requirements of peace-making, peace-building, democratization, and development may not all harmonize.

The record of promoting democracy

Promoting democracy has lasted long enough for it to be reasonable to ask 'does it work?' However, although the short answer is that its performance has probably been very modest, the question is actually far too simple, for the following reasons.

What should be evaluated?

In addressing questions about what should be evaluated the distinction between an **active** and **passive** sense of democracy promotion is highly relevant. The first involves intentionality, where performance can be assessed against the objectives of the democracy promoters, assuming they are coherent and well defined. The second sense refers to where democracy is affected by many different kinds of external influence, for example, the encouragement that might come from residing in a 'good neighbourhood'. Here the evaluator first has to determine the yardsticks for measuring democracy's trajectory

and set the benchmarks against which to measure progress.

Another important distinction that is relevant especially but not only to active democracy promotion is between the consequences for democracy on the one hand and the contribution those democratic consequences make to realizing the further objectives that democratization is supposed to serve: economic development, international peace, enhanced security, and so on. There is no guarantee that effective support to democratization will procure these other ends. The continuity of a regime other than Western style liberal democracy might serve these other ends better, as it has done in Singapore, one of the world's most affluent, stable, and technologically advanced countries.

How to evaluate?

Evaluating democracy assistance has been found to be fraught with methodological difficulties. But these look relatively trivial when compared with the challenge of assessing democracy promotion *tout court*. The different methods of promoting democracy are so diverse as to defy easy comparison, whether in terms of the kinds of resources they employ which encompass money, technical know-how, and 'political capital', or the approaches they use which range from quiet diplomacy to armed might.

Compared to international development cooperation the art of evaluating democracy assistance (and even more so the evaluation of democracy promotion) are still in their infancy, although not for want of trying (Green and Kohl 2007). The inability to attribute causality with any great certainty is a big conundrum in assessing impact, which should include any unintended and negative effects, and in evaluating the effectiveness of assistance. By comparison identifying the outputs of a project or programme and constructing some observable measure of the immediate effects, or outcomes, look straightforward. For instance the number of election observers who have been 'trained' or the number of new civic associations that have been launched can be counted easily. But the contribution these make to democratization is extremely difficult to assess. Many influences will have a bearing on that. And assigning attribution to a specific instance of democracy assistance or promotion while discounting all the others is exceptionally tricky in situations where several democracy promoters or assistance initiatives have been in play. Naturally the counterfactual—what would have been the outcome in the absence of a democracy intervention—cannot be known.

Moreover a sensitive comparison of interventions should take account of differences in the degree of difficulty, resistance, or obstacles encountered along the way. The analysis might have to refer to the kind of legitimacy and amount of support that even a non-democratic regime may enjoy among its own people. These properties can suggest useful guidance to choices of democracy promotion strategy (Burnell 2006*a*). For instance an autocracy founded on religious beliefs may be impervious to any attempts at democracy promotion. Eroding the power of an authoritarian regime, encouraging a process of political liberalization, supporting democratic transition, aiding democratic consolidation, helping secure a fragile democracy against subversion, and combating headlong democratic reversal are all very different

endeavours. Yet examples of each one can be found in the history of democracy promotion. What might be considered a very marginal achievement in one country could be a major turning point in the political evolution of another.

Why evaluate?

Evaluation is always done for some purpose. The reasons can differ significantly from one context to another: they usually shape the exercise, the assessment design, conduct, and what happens to the results. Accountancy style audits of expenditure are the least ambitious. But invariably where public money has been spent the demands for political accountability go further and look for evidence of achievement. Democracy assistance practitioners in the foundations are just as likely to value the process of evaluation as a learning tool. That is to say, evaluation is an opportunity to find out what did and did not work well, in order to do better next time. In some organizations evaluation may also serve as a defence mechanism against unhelpful political interference that would divert the organization from adopting a strictly professional approach.

Finally there is a view that evaluations of democracy assistance must themselves be democratic. They should be occasions to demonstrate and share fundamental democratic values. That usually means a participatory approach, which involves the 'stakeholders' in the country that is supposed to benefit. How extensive should that participation be: designing and implementing the questionnaires, analysing the findings, writing the conclusions, and formulating the recommendations that evaluations lead to and which should determine the shape of new programmes? Few democracy promotion organizations are ready to go to these lengths.

The evaluation findings to date

The single largest **quantitative** study of the effectiveness of democracy assistance has concentrated on the democracy and governance (DG) assistance programmes of USAID, covering 195 countries during 1990–2003 (Finkel *et al.* 2006). The report claimed to find consistent and clear positive impacts, with both lagged and cumulative effects. However, the overall effect was very small because only limited resources have been put into DG: the average eligible country during the period received only $2.07 million per year, rising to half as much again in 2003. Notwithstanding Finkel *et al.*'s endorsement of the proposition that increased DG aid would be justified, the record revealed by the evaluation accords closely with the view Carothers (2004) draws from doing **qualitative** assessments over many years. Carothers's view is that internal factors generally outweigh external factors. He believes the potential for democracy assistance to make a difference should not be exaggerated.

The democracy assistance foundations also commission their own evaluations, although the results are not always released into the public domain. The *Stiftungen* for instance tend to be rather shy of publicity. Two European exceptions in 2005 were the NIMD and WFD. A comparison is revealing. The WFD attracted a critical report from an independent consultancy commissioned by the Foreign and Commonwealth Office (FCO), the main source of the WFD's income. The FCO's response was to confirm that WFD should remain in existence. This was because of the organization's value in enabling democracy interventions in countries at arm's length from the British government. Yet the report also indicated there have been occasions when the FCO has been called on by a foreign government to account for the WFD's conduct in lending support to political opponents.

The NIMD in contrast received very favourable comment in an independent evaluation, which praised its pioneering approach. And whereas WFD has been under pressure from the FCO to adopt a more 'strategic' approach to selecting countries, partners, programmes, and projects, the NIMD was encouraged to reconfirm its principled commitment to a more demand-led, locally driven approach. Such an approach fits the NIMD's core philosophy of giving priority to 'partnership' and local ownership, something that also resembles how the UNDP claims to go about doing democracy assistance. That said, the report advised NIMD to reflect more on how to strengthen programme implementation and incorporate the lessons from experience.

The future may see increasing attention paid to issues of evaluation, even if on present evidence there are considerable weaknesses in the policy chain between the *ex post* assessment of democracy assistance and the *ex ante* appraisal of policies and strategies for promoting democracy more generally, the goal of promoting democracy included (see Burnell 2007).

KEY POINTS

❑ Credible evaluation methodologies for democracy assistance are under construction but still beg the larger challenge of how to do sound comparative assessment of the different approaches to promoting democracy, that is, comprehensive strategic analysis.

❑ Different rationales for evaluating democracy support can lead to different consequences.

❑ Most analysts tend to be sceptical about claiming great credit for democracy assistance in promoting democracy especially in comparison to domestic influences, and they emphasize more the interactions between the external and internal influences. Ukraine's celebrated 'orange revolution' is an example.

Future of democracy promotion

Democracy promotion has worked best where the conditions were favourable and the tide was already running or about to run in a pro-democracy direction anyway: in short, where it was least needed. The most challenging cases remain. There are many of them. To illustrate, Freedom House in its annual surveys reckons the number of states still 'not free' remains on average around fifty, and they include the most populous of all, China. Another fifty or so states are classified as only 'partly free'. The Middle East and Africa contain the majority of examples.

Backlash against democracy promotion?

There is enormous scope for democracy to make more progress around the world, but suspicions abound that democracy promotion might already have had its day. This would be consistent with the view that democracy promoters are no longer well received in many places, contrary to the situation in the first half of the 1990s when post-communist Europe in particular was very welcoming (Carothers 2006). What explains this?

The military invasion of Afghanistan and Iraq and the resulting confusion of ideas between democracy promotion and 'regime change' have been held responsible for arming authoritarian rulers with a rallying cry against foreign interference. These rulers can now portray democracy promotion as an assault on sovereignty and statehood. They can mobilize nationalist sentiments in the cause of opposing democratic reform. The governments of China and Russia are seen to be leading the way in this democracy promotion backlash. By inference the ebbing of the tide for democratization may not be too far behind. Civil society activists find themselves particularly vulnerable (Gershman and Allen 2006). A further cause for confusion in Arab eyes was added by Israel's military aggression against Lebanon in 2006. Although strongly supported by the US administration as a drive for freedom in the Middle East, this adventure threatened to destabilize the elected civilian government and the very state of Lebanon, which only recently had gained freedom from Syria's heavy-handed domination.

We should not confuse attitudes towards democracy assistance, which is offered by a wide range of actors with different interests, with what is widely speculated to be a growth in anti-American sentiment around the world following the Bush administration's unilateral approach to foreign policy and hard power interventions overseas. Nevertheless, there are other reasons for saying democracy promotion's future may compare unfavourably with its past.

Negative international influences

One reason is that a preoccupation with the active sense of promoting democracy and an interest in democracy promotion organizations mobilizes bias against giving due weight to all the features of the international system that are pushing the other way. The negative incentives, countervailing forces, and subversive factors that work against democratization and undermine democracy promotion should not be neglected. At the lowest level there is non-assistance: the non-democracies that are neglected, Myanmar for instance.

There are also perverse examples of assistance and promotion where, despite good intentions, the efforts prove counter-productive, perhaps through poor judgement, bad strategy, or flawed implementation. And there are examples of concrete financial, economic, technical, or political support being extended to political institutions or practices that are known to be adverse to democracy but are prized for serving other goals. As an illustration of anti-assistance or counter-promotion, the 'war against terror' has led the West to support Pakistan's ruler General Musharraf as a key strategic ally, although Pakistan is not a liberal democracy. International support for efforts to combat coca growing in Colombia boost the military in that country, where the security forces have been widely accused of infringing human rights.

Also, there are of course authoritarian rulers and illiberal regimes that lend practical and political support to like-minded governments in other countries, in a sort of transnational network of dictators. The relationship of China to North Korea and Myanmar is illustrative. China's great economic success advertises the benefits of its political model, making it look attractive to countries where liberal democracy could threaten instability, undermine governmental effectiveness, and retard development, Uganda for instance. Despite Sen's (1999) claim that democracy is a universal value and is not ethnocentric, promoting democracy is certainly not 'the only game in town' (see also Chapters 5 and 6).

A further major reason why democracy promotion or its direct promotion specifically could come to be discredited is the way the structure of the global political economy subjects many countries to forces and events way beyond their control. Although economists do not all agree on the merits and limitations of global capitalism, there is little doubt that the effects of the market can make large numbers of people poor. They are certainly increasing both the international and domestic inequalities between rich and poor; and inequalities in turn may be responsible for disempowering the most vulnerable people. The kind of democracy that is being spread by the promotion of democracy may be no match for the way these larger economic and social trends are creating and recreating relations of political inequality, contributing to powerlessness at the national and sub-national levels. At minimum the quality of democracy suffers; at worst its very survival is put at risk. The problem here is globalization.

The problem of globalization

The meaning of globalization and its consequences are much debated (Baylis and Smith 2005; see Chapter 24 above). For some globalization is reducible to global economic integration powered by the triumph of neo-liberal economics and the increasing domination of all manner of social relations by market forces. This could have profoundly anti-democratic consequences, in so far as the disequalizing economic and social effects translate into substantial inequalities of political influence and power. Political self-determination may be made more difficult for whole societies and individual groups of people.

The cultural side of globalization might be no less pernicious. There is for instance the spread of individual consumerism which displaces the civic engagement and public service ethos on which the strength and depth of liberal democracies so heavily depend. 'Negative social learning' from the more unattractive and dysfunctional features of established Western democracies may be considered under this heading. High levels of distrust in and cynicism towards politicians is a worrying example.

An even more expansive notion of globalization says that in the current era power is being redistributed away from national states to institutions of multi-level and polycentric governance. While not accountable to ordinary people these institutions are taking decisions that have significant consequences for the lives of people almost everywhere. Put differently, a growing appreciation that pressing regional and global problems can be addressed only through regional or global solutions means that responses confined to the national level look increasingly inadequate. Of course, globalization is not happening at the same pace everywhere, and so the haemorrhaging of power is affecting some states more than others. For the more powerful states, that have most control over the intergovernmental, transgovernmental, and even many of the extra-governmental institutions, the state is not so much being weakened as being transformed. But for many smaller, weaker, and especially the heavily indebted and aid-dependent

countries, their ability to exercise meaningful choices between different ways of addressing their problems is heavily constrained. In this context, replacing a non-elected ruler by a liberal democratic government might not make a great deal of difference to the majority of people's lives or convince them that they can now take control of their own destiny.

Democracy promotion's response to globalization?

The implications for democracy promotion could be enormous. On the one side, there is the possible inference that the most effective way to promote democracy is by rethinking our theories and polices towards international development cooperation. This suggests a dramatic improvement in efforts to end world poverty is what is needed. On the other side, more attention needs to be given to promoting democracy beyond the national state. In some countries that would mean trying to correct the 'democratic deficit' of the European Union. For many more countries it means exploring ways of democratizing major institutions of global governance like the World Trade Organization, World Bank, and International Monetary Fund. The UN is another arena ripe for democratization, given the disproportionate power that is held by the permanent members of the Security Council who are few in number and not very representative of humankind.

The scope for creative thinking about how to combine the values, principles, and practices of democracy with the political dynamics of a globalizing world is then enormous. If promoting democracy within prospective, new, and emerging democracies has been found to be a great challenge, then promoting democracy at levels beyond the nation-state is probably immeasurably more difficult. Maintaining society's appetite for democratic engagement in the longer established democracies like Britain, and educating democracy promoters in the West to think more imaginatively about how to realize democratic visions in an increasingly globalized world, could be good places to start.

Conclusion

Following the end of the Cold War and collapse of Soviet power, the international promotion of democracy has become a significant feature of international politics. The US and European actors are easily the most prominent contributors. However many countries, including some of the newer democracies and a range of regional and intergovernmental organizations including the UN, are also taking part. The different institutions have their own distinct characteristics. The working relationships between government or other official departments and notionally autonomous or private foundations funded by government are not wholly transparent. This reflects the confusion of purpose behind democracy promotion.

A large market for democracy promotion still exists in the sense that many countries and a very large number of people do not live in liberal democracies. The presumption that the majority of these societies would welcome greater freedom and the opportunity to freely elect their governments may be correct. However that does not necessarily mean they endorse Western style liberal democracy or agree with all the methods of democracy promotion.

Although commentators offer different explanations for the increase in democracy promotion, none put it down to principled idealism alone. They link it to agendas of national interest of the democracy-promoting countries, defined in various ways. These range from economic considerations to a reduced exposure to state-led aggression and other threats to security, such as international terrorism.

Democracy is being actively promoted by a variety of approaches or methods, some more coercive than others. However, there is a widely held view that strategic analysis and direction have been weak. While the 'soft option' of democracy assistance projects and programmes has probably received the most attention in the literature, its actual contribution to democratization should not be exaggerated. There is still much to learn about its impact and effectiveness. The challenge of how to compare the effectiveness of endeavours that have different objectives, such as changing attitudes, changing behaviour, and transplanting formal organizational structures, is daunting in itself.

Moreover, democracy promotion could become even more challenging in the future. The most receptive countries have now become democracies, particularly the states that have joined the European Union. Strong opposition from the ruling elites and unfavourable socio-economic conditions characterize many of the world's remaining non-democracies. Too little attention has been given to the collateral damage to democracy and democratization that increasing globalization is likely to bring. Structural forces in the global political economy impact adversely on political entitlements, and movements towards regional and global governance are making democratic self-determination increasingly difficult to achieve at the level of the national state. If it is to offer an adequate response, thinking and practice about international democracy promotion needs to move to a new plane.

World trends

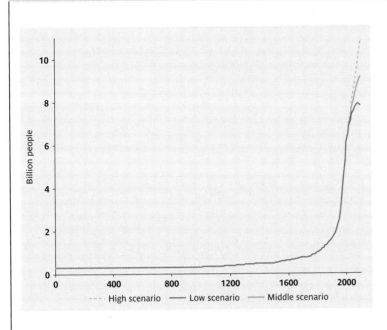

Trend 8 Demography: world population (1–2000) and prospects (to 2050)

Note: Population estimates are based on different assumptions about future fertility rates.
Source: United Nations World Population Prospects, US Bureau of Census.

? Questions

1. What different ways of promoting democracy are there and how significant are the differences?

2. How persuasive are the principal explanations of why democracy promotion has become so prominent over the period since 1989?

3. Do the Europeans have a different approach to promoting democracy to the Americans, and have they been more successful?

4. How can strategies for promoting democracy take account of the fact that the world's non-democracies differ greatly among themselves?

5. What makes democracy promotion in fragile states and post-conflict societies especially problematical?

6. What difficulties impede a rigorous assessment of the impact and effectiveness of democracy assistance?

7. Does the phenomenon of globalization have specific implications for the idea and practice of promoting democracy?

8. Why are some countries witnessing a backlash against democracy assistance and what lessons do you draw for the future of international democracy promotion?

9. Should primary responsibility for promoting democracy in non-democracies rest with the UN?

10. Could international democracy promotion advance democratic models different to those based on Western liberal democracies?

》 **Further reading**

Burnell, Peter (ed.) (2000) *Democracy Assistance: International Co-operation for Democratization* (London: Frank Cass). Wide-ranging survey of ideas, institutions, and cases.

Carothers, Thomas (2004) *Critical Mission: Essays on Democracy Promotion* (Washington, DC: Carnegie Endowment for International Peace). Critical reflections on US democracy promotion 1994–2003 by the acknowledged leading authority.

Cox, Michael, Ikenberry, John, and Inoguchi, Takashi (eds.) (2000) *American Democracy Promotion: Impulses, Strategies and Impact* (Oxford: Oxford University Press). A major collection of diverse interpretations predating 9/11.

de Zeeuw, Jeroen, and Kumar, Krishna (eds.) (2006) *Promoting Democracy in Post-Conflict Societies* (Boulder, Colo.: Lynne Rienner).

Newman, Edward, and Rich, Roland (eds.) (2004) *The UN Role in Promoting Democracy: Between Ideals and Reality* (Tokyo and New York: United Nations University Press). A substantial critical assessment of the UN's role and performance.

Ottaway, Marina, and Carothers, Thomas (eds.) (2000) *Funding Virtue: Civil Society Aid and Democracy Promotion* (Washington, DC: Carnegie Endowment for International Peace). Lessons of experience from several countries in a major sector for democracy assistance.

Pridham, Geoffrey (2005) *Designing Democracy: EU Enlargement and Regime Change in Post-Communist Europe* (Basingstoke: Palgrave). A systematic in depth account of EU democratic conditionality.

Schraeder, Peter (ed.) (2002) *Exporting Democracy: Rhetoric vs. Reality* (Boulder, Colo.: Lynne Rienner). Comparison of democracy promotion by several European countries, US, and Japan.

Vachudova, Milada (2005) *Europe Undivided: Democracy, Leverage and Integration after Communism* (Oxford: Oxford University Press). Detailed comparison of EU approaches to influencing politics in pre-accession states.

Youngs, Richard (2006) *Survey of European Democracy Promotion Policies 2000–2006* (Madrid: Fundación para las Relaciones Internacionales y el Diálogo Exterior). Revealing comparison of the policies of seven European countries and the main EU institutions.

 Web links

www.ned.org
  The National Endowment for Democracy is the US's leading private non-profit organization for promoting democracy. The website gives access to Democracy Newsletter, World Movement for Democracy, and much more.

www.idea.int.se
  The International Institute for Democracy and Electoral Assistance provides a bridge between democracy research and strengthening new democracies and democratization.

www.usaid.gov
  Contains the 2006 report for USAID by S. Finkel, A. Pérez-Liñán, and A. Seligson, with D. Azpuru, *Effects of US Foreign Assistance on Democracy Building: Results of a Cross-National Quantitative Study. Final Report*.

www.ccd21.org
  Council for a Community of Democracies, a leading advocate of the World Community of Democracies movement.

www.ndi.org
  National Democratic Institute, a prominent affiliate of the National Endowment for Democracy, supporting democratic initiatives around the world.

www.nimd.org

    Netherlands Institute for Multiparty Democracy, which pursues a distinctive remit to bring political parties together, especially in divided societies.

www.wfd.org

    Westminster Foundation for Democracy, an independent public body for promoting democracy, funded by the British government.

www.undp.org/governance

    United Nations Development Programme democratic governance programme.

www.oas.org

    Organization of American States account of 'key issues' such as strengthening democratic commitment, protecting human rights, building democratic institutions, elections observation, and civil society participation.

 Visit the Online Resource Centre that accompanies this book for more information:
www.oxfordtextbooks.co.uk/orc/caramani/

Comparative tables

Comparative table 1 Communication

Country	Telephone lines (per 1,000 people)	Internet users (per 1,000 people)	Roadways (km)	Railroads (km)	Airports
Albania	71	21	18,000	447	11
Algeria	77	58	108,302	3,973	142
Argentina	218	248	229,144	31,902	1,381
Australia	561	718	810,641	47,738	455
Austria	452	567	133,718	6,011	55
Belgium	462	491	150,567	3,521	43
Brazil	223	136	1,751,868	29,252	4,276
Canada	547	656	1,042,300	48,467	1,337
Chile	211	411	79,605	6,585	363
China	265	93	1,870,661	74,408	486
Colombia	173	107	112,988	3,304	984
Costa Rica	336	242	35,330	278	157
Cyprus	533	378	14,496	n.a.	16
Czech Republic	315	499	127,747	9,572	121
Denmark	613	688	72,257	2,673	92
Egypt	129	62	92,370	5,063	88
Estonia	336	524	56,856	958	24
Finland	405	627	78,189	5,741	148
France	603	470	956,303	29,085	477
Germany	668	614	231,581	47,201	554

(continued)

Comparative table 1 (*continued*)

Country	Telephone lines (per 1,000 people)	Internet users (per 1,000 people)	Roadways (km)	Railroads (km)	Airports
Greece	589	355	114,931	2,571	82
Hungary	337	306	159,568	7,937	46
Iceland	642	854	13,028	n.a.	98
India	44	53	3,383,344	63,230	341
Indonesia	54	68	368,360	6,458	662
Iran	290	115	179,388	7,256	321
Ireland	495	501	96,602	3,312	36
Israel	457	576	17,446	853	53
Italy	431	496	484,688	19,459	133
Japan	461	677	1,183,000	23,556	175
Korea (South)	484	691	100,279	3,472	107
Latvia	323	456	69,532	2,303	46
Lebanon	252	178	7,300	401	7
Lithuania	224	342	79,497	1,771	91
Luxembourg	509	656	5,227	274	2
Malta	503	317	2,227	n.a.	1
Mexico	180	171	235,670	17,562	1,839
Netherlands	459	652	134,000	2,808	27
New Zealand	437	777	92,931	4,128	118
Nigeria	9	37	194,394	3,505	69
Norway	460	678	92,513	4,077	99
Peru	78	160	78,829	3,462	268
Philippines	38	86	200,037	897	256
Poland	306	275	423,997	23,072	122
Portugal	398	731	78,470	2,850	66

Comparative table 1 (*continued*)

Country	Telephone lines (per 1,000 people)	Internet users (per 1,000 people)	Roadways (km)	Railroads (km)	Airports
Romania	197	222	198,817	11,385	61
Russia	284	168	871,000	87,157	1,623
Senegal	21	43	13,576	906	20
Slovakia	220	459	42,993	3,662	36
Slovenia	406	542	38,451	1,229	14
South Africa	107	116	362,099	20,872	731
Spain	453	475	666,292	14,873	157
Sweden	714	753	424,947	11,481	255
Switzerland	678	675	71,297	4,583	65
Syria	150	57	94,890	2,711	92
Turkey	267	225	426,906	8,697	117
Ukraine	262	114	169,477	22,473	499
United Kingdom	542	619	388,008	17,156	471
United States	890	682	6,430,366	226,605	14,858
Uruguay	289	196	77,732	2,073	64
Venezuela	139	117	96,155	682	375
Vietnam	186	154	222,179	2,600	32

Note: Data refer to 2006.

Source: International Telecommunication Union; World Bank; United Nations Education, Scientific and Cultural Organization.

Comparative table 2 Religion

Country	Majority religion (% of total)		Second religion (% of total)		Third religion (% of total)		Other religions (% of total)	
Albania	Muslim	70.0	Orthodox	20.0	Roman Catholic	10.0		
Algeria	Muslim	99.0	Christian	0.5	Jewish	0.5		
Argentina	Roman Catholic	92.0	Protestant	2.0	Jewish	2.0	Other/None	4.0
Australia	Roman Catholic	26.4	Anglican	20.5	Other Christian	20.5	Other/None	32.6
Austria	Roman Catholic	73.6	Protestant	4.7	Muslim	4.2	Other/None	17.5
Belgium	Roman Catholic	95.0					Other/None	5.0
Brazil	Roman Catholic	73.6	Protestant	15.4	Spiritualist	1.3	Other/None	9.7
Canada	Roman Catholic	42.6	Protestant	23.3	Other Christian	4.4	Other/None	29.7
Chile	Roman Catholic	70.0	Evangelical	15.1	Jehovah	1.1	Other/None	13.9
China	Buddhist	43.0	Daoist	20.0			Other/None	37.0
Colombia	Roman Catholic	90.0					Other/None	10.0
Costa Rica	Roman Catholic	76.3	Evangelical	13.7	Jehovah	1.3	Other/None	8.7
Cyprus	Orthodox	78.0	Muslim	18.0			Other/None	4.0
Czech Republic	Roman Catholic	26.8	Protestant	2.1	Other	12.1	Unaffiliated	59.0
Denmark	Evangelical	95.0	Other Christian	3.0	Muslim	2.0		
Egypt	Muslim	90.0	Coptic	9.0	Other Christian	1.0		

Comparative table 2 (*continued*)

Estonia	Evangelical	13.6	Orthodox	12.8	Other Christian	1.4	Other/None	72.2
Finland	Lutheran	84.2	Orthodox	1.1	Other Christian	1.1	Other/None	13.6
France	Roman Catholic	85.0	Muslim	7.5	Protestant	2.0	Other/None	5.5
Germany	Protestant	34.0	Roman Catholic	34.0	Muslim	3.7	Other/None	28.3
Greece	Orthodox	98.0	Muslim	1.3			Other/None	0.7
Hungary	Roman Catholic	51.9	Calvinist	15.9	Lutheran	3.0	Other/None	29.2
Iceland	Lutheran	87.6	Roman Catholic	2.0	Other Christian	2.7	Other/None	7.7
India	Hindu	80.5	Muslim	13.4	Christian	2.3	Other/None	3.8
Indonesia	Muslim	86.1	Protestant	5.7	Roman Catholic	3.0	Other/None	5.2
Iran	Muslim	98.0					Other/None	2.0
Ireland	Roman Catholic	88.4	Other Christian	4.6			Other/None	7.0
Israel	Jewish	76.4	Muslim	16.0	Other Christian	2.1	Other/None	5.5
Italy	Roman Catholic	90.0					Other/None	10.0
Japan	Buddhist	84.0					Other/None	16.0
Korea (South)	Christian	26.3	Buddhist	23.2			Other/None	50.6
Latvia	Lutheran	55.0	Roman Catholic	24.0	Russian Orthodox	9.0	Other/None	
Lebanon	Muslim	59.7	Christian	39.0			Other/None	1.3
Lithuania	Roman Catholic	79.0	Russian Orthodox	4.1	Protestant	1.9	Other/None	15.0

(*continued*)

Comparative table 2 (*continued*)

Country	Majority religion (% of total)		Second religion (% of total)		Third religion (% of total)		Other religions (% of total)	
Luxembourg	Roman Catholic	87.0					Other/None	13.0
Malta	Roman Catholic	98.0					Other/None	2.0
Mexico	Roman Catholic	76.5	Protestant	6.3			Other/None	17.2
Netherlands	Roman Catholic	31.0	Reformed	13.0	Calvinist	7.0	Other/None	49.0
New Zealand	Anglican	14.9	Roman Catholic	12.4	Presbyterian	10.9	Other/None	61.8
Nigeria	Muslim	50.0	Christian	40.0	Indigenous	10.0		
Norway	Church of Norway	85.7	Pentecostal	1.0	Roman Catholic	1.0	Other/None	12.3
Peru	Roman Catholic	81.0	7th Day Adventist	1.4	Other Christian	0.7	Other/None	16.9
Philippines	Roman Catholic	80.9	Muslim	5.0	Evangelical	2.8	Other/None	11.3
Poland	Roman Catholic	89.8	Orthodox	1.3	Protestant	0.3	Other/None	8.6
Portugal	Roman Catholic	84.5	Other Christian	2.2			Other/None	13.2
Romania	Orthodox	86.8	Protestant	7.5	Roman Catholic	4.7	Other/None	1.0
Russia	Russian Orthodox	17.5	Muslim	12.5	Other Christian	2.0	Other/None	68.0
Senegal	Muslim	94.0	Christian	5.0	Indigenous	1.0		
Slovakia	Roman Catholic	68.9	Protestant	10.8	Greek Catholic	4.1	Other/None	16.2
Slovenia	Roman Catholic	57.8	Muslim	2.4	Orthodox	2.3	Other/None	37.5

Comparative table 2 (*continued*)

Country	Religion	%	Religion	%	Religion	%	Religion	%
South Africa	Zion Christian	11.1	Pentecostal	8.2	Roman Catholic	7.1	Other/None	73.6
Spain	Roman Catholic	94.0					Other/None	6.0
Sweden	Lutheran	87.0					Other/None	13.0
Switzerland	Roman Catholic	41.8	Protestant	35.3	Muslim	4.3	Other/None	18.6
Syria	Muslim	90.0	Christian	10.0				
Turkey	Muslim	99.8					Other/None	0.2
Ukraine	Orthodox	45.7	Greek Catholic	6.0			Other/None	48.3
United Kingdom	Christian	71.6	Muslim	2.7	Hindu	1.0	Other/None	24.7
United States	Protestant	52.0	Roman Catholic	24.0	Mormon	2.0	Other/None	22.0
Uruguay	Roman Catholic	66.0	Protestant	2.0	Jewish	1.0	Other/None	31.0
Venezuela	Roman Catholic	96.0	Protestant	2.0	None	2.0		
Vietnam	Buddhist	9.3	Roman Catholic	6.7	Hoa Hao	1.5	Other/None	82.5

Sources: CIA World Factbook.

Comparative table 3 Language

Country	Majority language (% of total)		Second language (% of total)		Third language (% of total)		Other languages (% of total)	
Albania	Albanian	94.4	Romani	4.5	Mazedonien	1.1		
Algeria	Arabic	86.8	Kabylish	6.7	Tamazight	3.3	Other	3.2
Argentina	Spanish	62.3	Aimará	9.7	Quechua	2.5	Other	25.5
Australia	English	96.5	Italian	2.7	Chinese	0.5	Other	0.3
Austria	German	98.0	Turkish	1.0	Croatian	0.6	Other	0.4
Belgium	Dutch	52.7	French	39.2	Italian	4.9	Other	3.2
Brazil	Portuguese	96.7					Other	3.3
Canada	English	59.3	French	23.2			Other	17.5
Chile	Spanish	92.0	Indian	7.2			Other	0.8
China	Mandarin	87.6	Zhuang	1.1	Tibetish	0.4	Other	11.9
Colombia	Spanish	87.5	Indian	12.5				
Costa Rica	Spanish	85.7	English	2.9			Other	11.4
Cyprus	Greek	80.0	Turkish	19.8			Other	0.2
Czech Republic	Czech	94.3	Slovak	4.9	German	0.5	Other	0.3
Denmark	Danish	96.9					Other	3.1
Egypt	Arabic	89.8					Other	1.1

Comparative table 3 (*continued*)

Estonia	Estonian	67.3	Russian	29.7		Other	2.3
Finland	Finnish	90.0	Swedish	9.6		Other	0.4
France	French	94.6				Other	5.4
Germany	German	93.6	Turkish	3.0		Other	3.4
Greece	Greek	96.1	Albanian	1.9		Other	2.0
Hungary	Hungarian	92.7	Romani	5.0	German	2.0	Other	0.7
Iceland	Icelandic	99.0				Other	1.0
India	Hindi	35.8	Marathi	7.2	Bengali	6.1	Other	50.9
Indonesia	Indonesian	83.7				Other	16.3
Iran	Farsi	52.0	Aserbaid-shanian	30.1	Kurdish	11.5	Other	6.4
Ireland	English	70.3	Irish	29.7			
Israel	Hebrew	65.4	Arabic	25.0	Russian	8.3	Other	1.3
Italy	Italian	97.2	German	0.9	Slovene	0.2	Other	1.7
Japan	Japanese	99.1	Korean	0.8	Chinese	0.1	
Korea (South)	Korean	100.0					
Latvia	Latvian	61.0	Russian	38.8		Other	0.2

(*continued*)

Comparative table 3 (*continued*)

Country	Majority language (% of total)		Second language (% of total)		Third language (% of total)		Other languages (% of total)
Lebanon	Arabic	92.9	Armenian	5.7	Kurdish	1.4	
Lithuania	Lithuanian	82.4	Russian	14.8	Belorussian	2.7	Other 0.1
Luxembourg	Luxembourgish	69.1	German	23.8	French	7.1	
Malta	Maltese	95.5	English	4.5			
Mexico	Spanish	90.7	Indian/Maya	7.1			Other 1.2
Netherlands	Dutch	92.3	Frisian	6.4			Other 1.3
New Zealand	English	95.0	Maori	2.6			Other 2.4
Nigeria	Hausa	16.7	Igbo	15.0	Fulfulde	6.7	Other 61.6
Norway	Norwegian	98.5	Saamish	1.1			Other 0.4
Peru	Spanish	87.5	Quechua	12.1			Other 0.4
Philippines	Cebuano	21.3	Tagalog	20.0	Hiligaynon	10.7	Other 48.0
Poland	Polish	95.3	German	2.6	Ukrainian	1.3	Other 0.8
Portugal	Portuguese	99.9					Other 0.1
Romania	Romanian	91.0	Hungarian	6.7	Romani	1.1	Other 1.2
Russia	Russian	94.4	Tatarian	3.4	Ukrainian	1.4	Other 0.8
Senegal	Wolof	44.4	Serere-Sine	22.2	Fulacunda	11.1	Other 22.3

Comparative table 3 (*continued*)

Slovakia	Slovak	83.9	Hungarian	10.5	Romani	1.8	Other	1.2
Slovenia	Slovenian	92.6	Serbo-Croatian	4.5	German	2.5	Other	0.4
South Africa	Zulu	23.8	Xhosa	17.6	Afrikaans	13.3	Other	45.3
Spain	Spanish	73.1	Catalan	17.0	Galician	7.0	Other	2.9
Sweden	Swedish	98.4	Finnish	0.7			Other	0.9
Switzerland	German	63.7	French	20.4	Italian	6.5	Other	9.4
Syria	Arabic	66.7	Kurdish	6.7	Armenian	3.3	Other	23.3
Turkey	Turkish	80.0	Kurdish	15.0	Arab	2.0	Other	3.0
Ukraine	Ukrainian	70.5	Russian	27.5			Other	2.0
United Kingdom	English	97.0	Hindi	1.7			Other	1.3
United States	English	88.1	Spanish	10.7			Other	1.2
Uruguay	Spanish	99.2	Portuguese	0.8				
Venezuela	Spanish	94.7	Indian	5.3				
Vietnam	Vietnamese	93.2	Khmer	1.3	Mandarin	0.7	Other	4.8

Note: Percentages indicate first languages disregarding whether or not people also speak other languages.

Source: Haarmann (2002).

Comparative table 4 Demography

Country	Population (million)	Population (million) 2015 (projection)	Aged 65 or above (%)	Fertility rate	Life expectancy at birth	Infant mortality (per 1,000 births)
Albania	3.6	3.3	4.9	2.3	73.7	18
Algeria	33.3	38.1	5.3	2.5	71.0	35
Argentina	40.3	42.7	10.1	2.4	74.3	17
Australia	20.4	22.2	12.6	1.7	80.2	6
Austria	8.2	8.3	16.4	1.4	78.9	4
Belgium	10.4	10.5	17.5	1.7	78.8	4
Brazil	190.0	209.4	n.a.	2.3	70.3	33
Canada	33.4	35.1	13.0	1.5	79.9	5
Chile	16.3	17.9	7.9	2.0	77.9	8
China	1,321.9	1,393.0	11.9	1.7	71.5	30
Colombia	44.4	52.1	6.0	2.6	72.2	18
Costa Rica	4.1	5.0	5.7	2.3	78.1	8
Cyprus	0.8	0.9	11.9	1.6	78.5	4
Czech Republic	10.2	10.1	14.1	1.2	75.5	4
Denmark	5.5	5.6	14.9	1.8	77.1	3
Egypt	80.3	88.2	6.1	3.3	69.6	33
Estonia	1.3	1.3	16.3	1.4	71.2	8
Finland	5.2	5.4	15.7	1.7	78.4	4
France	63.7	62.3	16.6	1.9	79.4	4
Germany	82.4	82.5	18.3	1.3	78.7	4
Greece	10.7	11.2	18.0	1.3	78.2	4
Hungary	10.0	9.8	15.1	1.3	72.6	7
Iceland	0.3	0.3	11.7	2.0	80.6	3
India	1,129.9	1,260.4	3.4	3.1	63.1	63
Indonesia	234.7	246.8	3.1	2.4	66.5	31

Comparative table 4 (*continued*)

Country	Population (million)	Population (million) 2015 (projection)	Aged 65 or above (%)	Fertility rate	Life expectancy at birth	Infant mortality (per 1,000 births)
Iran	65.4	79.9	4.3	2.1	70.2	33
Ireland	4.1	4.7	10.9	1.9	77.7	6
Israel	6.4	7.8	10.1	2.9	79.7	5
Italy	58.1	57.8	19.7	1.3	80.0	4
Japan	127.4	128.0	19.2	1.3	81.9	3
Korea (South)	49.0	49.1	9.0	1.2	76.9	5
Latvia	2.3	2.2	16.6	1.3	71.4	10
Lebanon	3.9	4.0	15.8	2.3	71.9	27
Lithuania	3.6	3.3	15.2	1.3	72.2	8
Luxembourg	0.5	0.5	13.8	1.7	78.4	5
Malta	0.4	0.4	13.3	1.5	78.3	5
Mexico	108.7	119.1	5.2	2.4	74.9	23
Netherlands	16.6	16.8	14.0	1.7	78.3	5
New Zealand	4.1	4.3	12.2	2.0	79.0	5
Nigeria	135.0	160.9	2.3	5.8	43.3	98
Norway	4.6	4.8	15.0	1.8	79.3	3
Peru	28.7	32.2	7.5	2.9	69.8	26
Philippines	91.1	96.8	5.7	3.2	70.2	27
Poland	38.5	38.1	12.8	1.3	74.3	6
Portugal	10.6	10.8	16.9	1.5	77.2	4
Romania	22.3	20.9	14.6	1.3	71.3	18
Russia	141.4	136.7	4.0	1.3	65.4	16
Senegal	12.5	14.5	4.0	5.0	55.6	78
Slovakia	5.4	5.4	11.7	1.2	74.0	7

(*continued*)

Comparative table 4 (*continued*)

Country	Population (million)	Population (million) 2015 (projection)	Aged 65 or above (%)	Fertility rate	Life expectancy at birth	Infant mortality (per 1,000 births)
Slovenia	2.0	1.9	15.4	1.2	76.3	4
South Africa	44.0	47.9	3.9	2.8	49.0	53
Spain	40.4	44.4	16.5	1.3	79.5	4
Sweden	9.0	9.3	17.1	1.6	80.1	3
Switzerland	7.6	7.3	15.7	1.4	80.5	4
Syria	19.3	23.8	4.3	3.5	73.2	16
Turkey	71.2	82.6	3.7	2.5	68.6	33
Ukraine	46.3	41.8	2.9	1.1	66.1	15
United Kingdom	60.8	61.4	15.9	1.7	78.3	5
United States	301.1	325.7	12.3	2.0	77.3	7
Uruguay	3.5	3.7	13.2	2.3	75.3	12
Venezuela	26.0	31.3	7.2	2.7	72.8	18
Vietnam	85.3	95.0	5.4	2.3	70.4	19

Note: Data refer to 2006.

Sources: United Nations; World Bank; United Nations Conference on Trade and Development; International Monetary Fund.

Comparative table 5 Development

Country	Human Development Index (HDI)	Public debt as % of GDP (2006)	Share of income or consumption (%)		Inequality measures (richest 20% to poorest 20%)
			Poorest 10%	Richest 10%	
Albania	0.78	n.a.	3.8	22.4	4.1
Algeria	0.72	18.6	2.8	26.8	6.1
Argentina	0.86	61.0	1.1	39.6	17.6
Australia	0.96	14.1	2.0	25.4	7.0
Austria	0.94	63.0	3.3	23.0	4.4
Belgium	0.95	90.3	3.4	28.1	4.9
Brazil	0.79	50.0	0.8	45.8	23.7
Canada	0.95	65.4	2.6	24.8	5.5
Chile	0.85	3.9	1.2	47.0	18.7
China	0.76	22.1	1.8	33.1	10.7
Colombia	0.79	45.3	0.7	46.9	25.3
Costa Rica	0.84	53.4	1.3	38.4	14.2
Cyprus	0.89	64.8	n.a.	n.a.	n.a.
Czech Republic	0.87	29.1	4.3	22.4	3.5
Denmark	0.94	28.1	2.6	21.3	4.3
Egypt	0.66	102.9	3.7	29.5	5.1
Estonia	0.85	3.6	2.5	27.6	6.4
Finland	0.94	37.7	4.0	22.6	3.8
France	0.94	64.7	2.8	25.1	5.6
Germany	0.93	66.8	3.2	22.1	4.3
Greece	0.91	104.6	2.5	26.0	6.2
Hungary	0.86	68.6	4.0	22.2	3.8
Iceland	0.96	23.5	n.a.	n.a.	n.a.
India	0.60	52.8	3.9	28.5	4.9

(*continued*)

Comparative table 5 (*continued*)

Country	Human Development Index (HDI)	Public debt as % of GDP (2006)	Share of income or consumption (%)		Inequality measures (richest 20% to poorest 20%)
			Poorest 10%	Richest 10%	
Indonesia	0.70	43.8	3.6	28.5	5.2
Iran	0.74	25.3	2.0	33.7	9.7
Ireland	0.95	22.8	2.9	27.2	5.6
Israel	0.92	89.0	2.1	28.8	7.9
Italy	0.93	107.8	2.3	26.8	6.5
Japan	0.94	176.2	4.8	21.7	3.4
Korea (South)	0.90	31.9	2.9	22.5	4.7
Latvia	0.84	11.0	2.5	29.1	6.8
Lebanon	0.76	209.0	n.a.	n.a.	n.a.
Lithuania	0.85	18.0	2.7	27.7	6.3
Luxembourg	0.95	n.a.	n.a.	n.a.	n.a.
Malta	0.87	n.a.	n.a.	n.a.	n.a.
Mexico	0.81	20.7	1.6	39.4	12.8
Netherlands	0.94	50.8	2.5	22.9	5.1
New Zealand	0.93	19.9	2.2	27.8	6.8
Nigeria	0.45	10.4	1.9	33.2	9.7
Norway	0.96	44.8	3.9	23.4	3.9
Peru	0.76	33.8	1.1	43.2	18.6
Philippines	0.76	61.6	2.2	36.3	9.7
Poland	0.86	49.0	3.1	27.0	5.6
Portugal	0.90	67.4	2.0	29.8	8.0
Romania	0.79	21.4	3.3	24.4	4.9
Russia	0.80	8.0	2.4	30.6	7.6
Senegal	0.46	17.8	2.6	33.5	7.5
Slovakia	0.85	36.1	3.1	20.9	4.0

Comparative table 5 (*continued*)

Country	Human Development Index (HDI)	Public debt as % of GDP (2006)	Share of income or consumption (%)		Inequality measures (richest 20% to poorest 20%)
			Poorest 10%	Richest 10%	
Slovenia	0.90	29.0	3.6	21.4	3.9
South Africa	0.66	32.9	1.4	44.7	17.9
Spain	0.93	39.9	2.6	26.6	6.0
Sweden	0.95	46.4	3.6	22.2	4.0
Switzerland	0.95	51.0	2.9	25.9	5.5
Syria	0.72	37.9	n.a.	n.a.	n.a.
Turkey	0.75	64.7	2.0	34.1	9.3
Ukraine	0.77	12.7	3.9	23.0	4.1
United Kingdom	0.94	42.2	2.1	28.5	7.2
United States	0.94	64.7	1.9	29.9	8.4
Uruguay	0.84	70.6	1.9	34.0	10.2
Venezuela	0.77	28.4	1.6	32.8	10.6
Vietnam	0.70	47.5	3.2	29.9	6.0

Note: HDI is a measure of general well-being devised by the United Nation Development Programme (UNDP). It provides a composite measure of three dimensions of human development measure through various indicators: (1) living a long and healthy life, (2) being educated, and (3) having a decent standard of living. It does not include dimensions of rights and democracy.

Sources: United Nations Development Programme; World Bank.

Comparative table 6 Economy

Country	GDP per capita (US$)	GDP growth (% change) 1990–2004	GDP per capita (PPP, US$)	Inequality (Gini index)
Albania	2,439	4.8	5,700	28.2
Algeria	2,616	0.9	7,600	35.3
Argentina	3,988	1.3	15,200	52.8
Australia	31,690	2.5	33,300	35.2
Austria	35,766	2.0	34,600	29.1
Belgium	33,807	1.7	33,000	33.0
Brazil	3,284	1.2	8,800	58.0
Canada	30,586	2.1	35,600	32.6
Chile	5,836	3.7	12,700	57.1
China	1,490	8.9	7,700	44.7
Colombia	2,176	0.5	8,600	58.6
Costa Rica	4,349	2.5	12,500	49.9
Cyprus	18,668	3.0	23,000	n.a.
Czech Republic	10,475	2.7	21,900	25.4
Denmark	44,673	1.7	37,000	24.7
Egypt	1,085	2.5	4,200	34.4
Estonia	8,331	4.3	20,300	35.8
Finland	35,562	2.2	33,700	26.9
France	33,896	1.7	31,100	32.7
Germany	33,212	1.5	31,900	28.3
Greece	18,560	2.6	24,000	34.3
Hungary	9,962	3.1	17,600	26.9
Iceland	41,893	2.0	38,000	n.a.
India	640	4.0	3,800	32.5
Indonesia	1,184	1.8	3,900	34.3
Iran	2,439	2.3	8,700	43.0

Comparative table 6 (*continued*)

Country	GDP per capita (US$)	GDP growth (% change) 1990–2004	GDP per capita (PPP, US$)	Inequality (Gini index)
Ireland	44,644	7.3	44,500	34.3
Israel	17,194	1.6	26,800	39.2
Italy	29,143	1.3	30,200	36.0
Japan	36,182	0.8	33,100	24.9
Korea (South)	14,136	4.5	24,500	31.6
Latvia	5,868	2.8	16,000	37.7
Lebanon	6,149	3.7	5,700	n.a.
Lithuania	6,480	1.4	15,300	36.0
Luxembourg	70,295	5.4	71,400	n.a.
Malta	13,256	3.6	21,000	n.a.
Mexico	6,518	1.3	10,700	49.5
Netherlands	35,560	2.1	32,100	30.9
New Zealand	24,364	2.1	26,200	36.2
Nigeria	560	0.8	1,500	43.7
Norway	54,465	2.5	46,300	25.8
Peru	2,490	2.1	6,600	54.6
Philippines	1,036	0.9	5,000	46.1
Poland	6,346	4.0	14,300	34.5
Portugal	15,970	2.1	19,800	38.5
Romania	3,374	1.4	9,100	31.0
Russia	4,042	−0.6	12,200	39.9
Senegal	683	0.9	1,800	41.3
Slovakia	7,635	2.7	18,200	25.8
Slovenia	16,115	3.6	23,400	28.4
South Africa	4,675	0.6	13,300	57.8

(*continued*)

Comparative table 6 (*continued*)

Country	GDP per capita (US$)	GDP growth (% change) 1990–2004	GDP per capita (PPP, US$)	Inequality (Gini index)
Spain	24,360	2.3	27,400	34.7
Sweden	38,525	1.8	32,200	25.0
Switzerland	48,385	0.2	34,000	33.7
Syria	1,293	1.5	4,100	n.a.
Turkey	4,221	1.6	9,000	43.6
Ukraine	1,366	−3.2	7,800	28.1
United Kingdom	35,485	2.2	31,800	36.0
United States	39,883	1.9	44,000	40.8
Uruguay	3,842	0.8	10,900	44.9
Venezuela	4,214	−1.2	7,200	44.1
Vietnam	550	5.5	3,100	37.0

Note: Data refer to 2006 unless otherwise indicated.

Source: World Bank.

Comparative table 7 Environment

Country	Carbon dioxide emissions	
	per capita (metric tons)	share of world total (%)
Albania	1.0	0.1
Algeria	5.1	0.7
Argentina	3.4	0.5
Australia	18.0	1.4
Austria	8.6	0.3
Belgium	8.3	0.3
Brazil	1.6	1.2
Canada	17.9	2.3
Chile	3.7	0.2
China	3.2	16.5
Colombia	1.3	0.2
Costa Rica	1.5	0.1
Cyprus	8.9	0.1
Czech Republic	11.4	0.5
Denmark	10.1	0.2
Egypt	2.0	0.6
Estonia	13.6	0.1
Finland	13.0	0.3
France	6.2	1.5
Germany	9.8	3.2
Greece	8.7	0.4
Hungary	5.7	0.2
Iceland	7.6	0.1
India	1.2	5.1

(*continued*)

Comparative table 7 (*continued*)

Country	Carbon dioxide emissions	
	per capita (metric tons)	share of world total (%)
Indonesia	1.4	1.2
Iran	5.6	1.5
Ireland	10.3	0.2
Israel	10.6	0.3
Italy	7.7	1.8
Japan	9.7	4.9
Korea (South)	9.6	1.8
Latvia	2.9	0.1
Lebanon	5.4	0.1
Lithuania	3.7	0.1
Luxembourg	22.0	0.1
Malta	6.2	0.1
Mexico	4.0	1.7
Netherlands	8.7	0.6
New Zealand	8.8	0.1
Nigeria	0.4	0.2
Norway	9.9	0.2
Peru	1.0	0.1
Philippines	1.0	0.3
Poland	7.9	1.2
Portugal	5.6	0.2
Romania	4.2	0.4
Russia	10.3	5.9
Senegal	0.4	0.1
Slovakia	7.0	0.1
Slovenia	7.8	0.1

Comparative table 7 (*continued*)

Country	Carbon dioxide emissions	
	per capita (metric tons)	share of world total (%)
South Africa	7.8	1.4
Spain	7.3	1.2
Sweden	5.9	0.2
Switzerland	5.6	0.2
Syria	2.7	0.2
Turkey	3.1	0.9
Ukraine	6.6	1.3
United Kingdom	9.4	2.2
United States	19.8	23.0
Uruguay	1.3	0.1
Venezuela	5.6	0.6
Vietnam	0.9	0.3

Notes: Information as of 15 Apr. 2005. The Cartagena Protocol on Biosafety was signed in Cartagena in 2000, the United Nations Framework Convention on Climate Change in New York in 1992, the Kyoto Protocol to the United Nations Framework Convention on Climate Change in Kyoto in 1997, and the Convention on Biological Diversity in Rio de Janeiro in 1992.

Sources: United Nations; Carbon Dioxide Information Analysis Center.

Comparative table 8 Gender

Country	Female economic activity rate (aged 15 and above) 2004	Ratio female/male income 2006	Seats held by women (%) 2006
Albania	49.4	0.54	7.1
Algeria	34.8	0.33	6.2
Argentina	52.2	0.53	35.0
Australia	56.1	0.70	24.7
Austria	49.3	0.44	33.9
Belgium	43.4	0.63	34.7
Brazil	56.3	0.57	8.6
Canada	60.2	0.63	20.8
Chile	36.4	0.39	15.0
China	69.2	0.64	20.3
Colombia	60.5	0.58	12.0
Costa Rica	43.7	0.46	38.6
Cyprus	53.0	0.59	14.3
Czech Republic	51.7	0.51	17.0
Denmark	59.4	0.73	36.9
Egypt	20.1	0.23	2.0
Estonia	52.2	0.62	18.8
Finland	56.9	0.71	37.5
France	48.2	0.64	12.2
Germany	50.4	0.58	31.8
Greece	42.7	0.55	13.0
Hungary	42.1	0.64	10.4
Iceland	70.9	0.71	33.3
India	34.0	0.31	8.3
Indonesia	50.7	0.45	11.3

Comparative table 8 (*continued*)

Country	Female economic activity rate (aged 15 and above) 2004	Ratio female/male income 2006	Seats held by women (%) 2006
Iran	37.2	0.38	4.1
Ireland	51.9	0.51	13.3
Israel	49.7	0.64	14.2
Italy	37.0	0.46	17.3
Japan	48.5	0.44	9.0
Korea (South)	50.1	0.46	13.4
Latvia	49.1	0.67	21.0
Lebanon	31.7	0.31	4.7
Lithuania	51.8	0.69	22.0
Luxembourg	44.1	0.49	23.3
Malta	32.5	0.48	9.2
Mexico	39.9	0.39	25.8
Netherlands	55.8	0.63	36.7
New Zealand	59.8	0.70	32.2
Nigeria	45.6	0.41	6.4
Norway	63.1	0.75	37.9
Peru	58.2	0.41	29.0
Philippines	53.8	0.60	15.7
Poland	47.9	0.59	20.4
Portugal	55.2	0.59	21.3
Romania	50.7	0.65	11.2
Russia	54.3	0.62	9.8
Senegal	56.5	0.53	19.2
Slovakia	51.9	0.58	16.7

(*continued*)

Comparative table 8 (*continued*)

Country	Female economic activity rate (aged 15 and above) 2004	Ratio female/male income 2006	Seats held by women (%) 2006
Slovenia	53.4	0.61	12.2
South Africa	46.4	0.45	32.8
Spain	44.2	0.50	36.0
Sweden	58.8	0.81	45.3
Switzerland	60.1	0.61	25.0
Syria	38.0	0.33	12.0
Turkey	27.8	0.35	4.4
Ukraine	49.9	0.53	7.1
United Kingdom	55.0	0.65	19.7
United States	59.6	0.62	15.2
Uruguay	55.7	0.55	11.1
Venezuela	55.9	0.51	18.0
Vietnam	72.4	0.71	27.3

Sources: World Bank; International Labour Organization.

Comparative table 9 Labour

Country	Unemployment (% rate)	Labour force sectors (%)		
		Agriculture	Industry	Services
Albania	13.8	58.0	15.0	27.0
Algeria	15.7	0.0	13.4	72.6
Argentina	8.7	n.a.	n.a.	n.a.
Australia	4.9	3.6	21.2	75.2
Austria	4.9	3.0	27.0	70.0
Belgium	8.1	1.3	24.5	74.2
Brazil	9.6	20.0	14.0	66.0
Canada	6.4	2.0	22.0	76.0
Chile	7.8	13.6	23.4	63.0
China	4.2	45.0	24.0	31.0
Colombia	11.1	22.7	18.7	58.5
Costa Rica	6.6	20.0	22.0	58.0
Cyprus	5.5	7.4	38.2	54.4
Czech Republic	8.4	4.1	37.6	58.3
Denmark	3.8	3.0	21.0	76.0
Egypt	10.3	32.0	17.0	51.0
Estonia	4.5	11.0	20.0	69.0
Finland	7.0	4.4	17.5	78.1
France	8.7	4.1	24.4	71.5
Germany	7.1	2.8	33.4	63.8
Greece	9.2	12.0	20.0	68.0
Hungary	7.4	5.5	33.3	61.2
Iceland	1.3	5.1	23.5	71.4
India	7.8	60.0	12.0	28.0
Indonesia	12.5	43.3	18.0	38.7

(continued)

Comparative table 9 (*continued*)

Country	Unemployment (% rate)	Labour force sectors (%)		
		Agriculture	Industry	Services
Iran	15.0	30.0	25.0	45.0
Ireland	4.3	8.0	29.0	64.0
Israel	8.3	1.8	21.0	77.1
Italy	7.0	5.0	32.0	63.0
Japan	4.1	4.6	27.8	67.7
Korea (South)	3.3	6.4	26.4	67.2
Latvia	6.5	13.0	19.0	68.0
Lebanon	20.0	n.a.	n.a.	n.a.
Lithuania	3.7	15.8	28.2	56.0
Luxembourg	4.1	1.0	13.0	86.0
Malta	6.8	3.0	22.0	75.0
Mexico	3.2	18.0	24.0	58.0
Netherlands	5.5	2.0	19.0	79.0
New Zealand	3.8	10.0	25.0	65.0
Nigeria	5.8	70.0	10.0	20.0
Norway	3.5	4.0	22.0	74.0
Peru	7.2	9.0	18.0	73.0
Philippines	7.9	36.0	15.0	49.0
Poland	14.9	16.1	29.0	54.9
Portugal	7.6	10.0	30.0	60.0
Romania	6.1	31.6	30.7	37.7
Russia	6.6	10.8	29.1	60.1
Senegal	48	77.0	n.a.	n.a.
Slovakia	10.2	14.8	29.3	55.9
Slovenia	9.6	4.8	39.1	56.1
South Africa	25.5	30.0	25.0	45.0

Comparative table 9 (*continued*)

Country	Unemployment (% rate)	Labour force sectors (%)		
		Agriculture	Industry	Services
Spain	8.1	5.3	30.1	64.6
Sweden	5.6	2.0	24.0	74.0
Switzerland	3.3	4.6	26.3	69.1
Syria	12.5	26.0	14.0	60.0
Turkey	10.2	35.9	22.8	41.2
Ukraine	2.7	25.0	20.0	55.0
United Kingdom	2.9	1.4	18.2	80.4
United States	4.8	16.5	22.9	60.6
Uruguay	10.8	14.0	16.0	70.0
Venezuela	8.9	13.0	23.0	64.0
Vietnam	2.0	56.8	37.0	6.2

Note: Data refer to 2006.

Sources: World Bank; United Nations Conference on Trade and Development; International Monetary Fund.

Comparative table 10 Migration

Country	Net migration rate (migrants per 1,000 population)
Albania	−4.54
Algeria	−0.33
Argentina	0.40
Australia	3.78
Austria	1.91
Belgium	1.22
Brazil	−0.03
Canada	5.79
Chile	0.00
China	−0.39
Colombia	−0.29
Costa Rica	0.48
Cyprus	0.42
Czech Republic	0.97
Denmark	2.50
Egypt	−0.21
Estonia	−3.22
Finland	0.78
France	1.52
Germany	2.18
Greece	2.34
Hungary	0.86
Iceland	1.43
India	−0.05
Indonesia	−1.27

Comparative table 10 (*continued*)

Country	Net migration rate (migrants per 1,000 population)
Iran	−4.29
Ireland	4.82
Israel	0.00
Italy	2.06
Japan	0.00
Korea (South)	0.00
Latvia	−2.27
Lebanon	0.00
Lithuania	−0.72
Luxembourg	8.64
Malta	2.04
Mexico	−4.08
Netherlands	2.63
New Zealand	3.43
Nigeria	0.26
Norway	1.72
Peru	−0.99
Philippines	−1.48
Poland	−0.46
Portugal	3.31
Romania	−0.13
Russia	0.28
Senegal	0.00
Slovakia	0.30
Slovenia	0.76

(*continued*)

Comparative table 10 (*continued*)

Country	Net migration rate (migrants per 1,000 population)
South Africa	−0.08
Spain	0.99
Sweden	1.66
Switzerland	2.66
Syria	0.00
Turkey	0.00
Ukraine	−0.13
United Kingdom	2.17
United States	3.05
Uruguay	−0.21
Venezuela	−1.28
Vietnam	−0.40

Note: Includes the figure for the difference between the number of persons entering and leaving a country during 2006 per 1,000 persons (based on mid-year population).

Source: United Nations.

Comparative table 11 Military

Country	Military expenditure (% of GDP)		Conventional arms transfers 1990 prices	
	1990	2005	Imports (US$ million) in 2004	Exports (US$ million) in 2004
Albania	5.9	1.5	31	n.a.
Algeria	1.5	3.3	149	n.a.
Argentina	1.2	1.3	67	0
Australia	2.1	2.4	396	50
Austria	1.0	0.9	21	3
Belgium	2.4	1.3	0	173
Brazil	2.5	2.6	142	62
Canada	2.0	1.1	112	365
Chile	4.3	2.7	456	0
China	2.7	3.8	2,697	129
Colombia	2.2	3.4	11	n.a.
Costa Rica	0.0	0.4	0	n.a.
Cyprus	5.0	3.8	0	0
Czech Republic	n.a.	1.8	630	10
Denmark	2.0	1.5	78	2
Egypt	3.9	3.4	596	0
Estonia	n.a.	2.0	10	0
Finland	1.6	2.0	77	22
France	3.5	2.6	3	2,399
Germany	2.8	1.5	216	1,855
Greece	4.7	4.3	1,114	0
Hungary	2.8	1.8	12	70
Iceland	0.0	0.0	n.a.	0

(continued)

Comparative table 11 (*continued*)

Country	Military expenditure (% of GDP)		Conventional arms transfers 1990 prices	
	1990	2005	Imports (US$ million) in 2004	Exports (US$ million) in 2004
India	2.7	2.5	1,471	0
Indonesia	1.8	3.0	19	8
Iran	2.9	2.5	403	0
Ireland	1.2	0.9	4	n.a.
Israel	12.4	7.3	1,422	160
Italy	2.1	1.8	224	827
Japan	9.0	0.8	250	0
Korea (South)	3.7	2.7	544	38
Latvia	n.a.	1.2	7	0
Lebanon	7.6	3.1	1	0
Lithuania	n.a.	1.9	9	0
Luxembourg	0.9	0.9	0	n.a.
Malta	0.9	0.7	18	0
Mexico	0.5	0.5	35	n.a.
Netherlands	2.5	1.6	129	840
New Zealand	1.9	1.0	8	0
Nigeria	9.0	1.5	0	0
Norway	2.9	1.9	9	13
Peru	1.0	1.5	368	0
Philippines	1.4	0.9	38	n.a.
Poland	2.7	1.7	96	124
Portugal	2.7	2.3	406	0
Romania	4.6	2.5	579	17
Russia	12.3	4.3	0	5,771

Comparative table 11 (*continued*)

Country	Military expenditure (% of GDP)		Conventional arms transfers 1990 prices	
	1990	2005	Imports (US$ million) in 2004	Exports (US$ million) in 2004
Senegal	2.0	1.4	0	n.a.
Slovakia	n.a.	1.9	0	0
Slovenia	n.a.	1.7	2	n.a.
South Africa	3.8	1.7	606	39
Spain	1.8	1.2	281	113
Sweden	2.6	1.5	104	592
Switzerland	1.8	1.0	144	74
Syria	6.9	5.9	0	0
Turkey	3.5	5.3	746	28
Ukraine	n.a.	1.4	n.a.	188
United Kingdom	4.0	2.4	94	791
United States	5.3	4.1	387	7,101
Uruguay	2.5	1.6	18	0
Venezuela	n.a.	1.2	7	0
Vietnam	7.9	2.5	291	n.a.

Source: Stockholm International Peace Research Institute.

Comparative table 12 Trade

Country	Imports of goods and services (% (% of GDP)	Exports of goods and services (% of GDP)	Manufactured exports (% of exports)	High-technology exports (% of exports)
Albania	43.0	21.0	82.0	1.0
Algeria	26.0	40.0	2.0	1.0
Argentina	18.0	25.0	29.0	8.0
Australia	21.0	18.0	25.0	14.0
Austria	46.0	51.0	84.0	12.0
Belgium	81.0	84.0	81.0	8.0
Brazil	13.0	18.0	54.0	12.0
Canada	34.0	38.0	60.0	14.0
Chile	30.0	36.0	13.0	5.0
China	31.0	34.0	91.0	30.0
Colombia	22.0	21.0	38.0	6.0
Costa Rica	49.0	46.0	63.0	37.0
Czech Republic	72.0	72.0	90.0	13.0
Denmark	38.0	43.0	66.0	20.0
Egypt	29.0	29.0	31.0	1.0
Estonia	86.0	78.0	77.0	14.0
Finland	32.0	37.0	83.0	21.0
France	26.0	26.0	83.0	19.0
Germany	33.0	38.0	84.0	17.0
Greece	29.0	21.0	59.0	11.0
Hungary	68.0	64.0	88.0	29.0
Iceland	43.0	37.0	17.0	6.0
India	23.0	19.0	73.0	5.0
Indonesia	27.0	31.0	56.0	16.0
Iran	30.0	32.0	9.0	2.0

Comparative table 12 (*continued*)

Country	Imports of goods and services (% (% of GDP)	Exports of goods and services (% of GDP)	Manufactured exports (% of exports)	High-technology exports (% of exports)
Ireland	65.0	80.0	86.0	34.0
Israel	49.0	44.0	94.0	19.0
Italy	26.0	27.0	88.0	8.0
Japan	10.0	12.0	93.0	24.0
Korea (South)	40.0	44.0	92.0	33.0
Latvia	60.0	44.0	61.0	5.0
Lebanon	41.0	21.0	68.0	2.0
Lithuania	61.0	54.0	58.0	5.0
Luxembourg	125.0	146.0	86.0	10.0
Malta	83.0	76.0	90.0	58.0
Mexico	32.0	30.0	80.0	21.0
Netherlands	60.0	65.0	70.0	29.0
New Zealand	29.0	29.0	31.0	14.0
Nigeria	37.0	55.0	2.0	2.0
Norway	30.0	44.0	19.0	18.0
Peru	18.0	21.0	20.0	2.0
Philippines	51.0	52.0	55.0	64.0
Poland	41.0	39.0	81.0	3.0
Portugal	38.0	31.0	85.0	9.0
Romania	46.0	37.0	82.0	3.0
Russia	22.0	35.0	21.0	9.0
Senegal	40.0	28.0	39.0	6.0
Slovakia	79.0	77.0	86.0	5.0
Slovenia	61.0	60.0	90.0	6.0

(*continued*)

Comparative table 12 (*continued*)

Country	Imports of goods and services (% (% of GDP)	Exports of goods and services (% of GDP)	Manufactured exports (% of exports)	High-technology exports (% of exports)
South Africa	27.0	27.0	58.0	6.0
Spain	29.0	26.0	77.0	7.0
Sweden	38.0	46.0	81.0	17.0
Switzerland	37.0	44.0	93.0	22.0
Syria	34.0	35.0	11.0	1.0
Turkey	35.0	29.0	85.0	2.0
Ukraine	54.0	61.0	67.0	5.0
United Kingdom	28.0	25.0	76.0	24.0
United States	14.0	10.0	82.0	32.0
Uruguay	28.0	30.0	32.0	2.0
Venezuela	20.0	36.0	12.0	3.0
Vietnam	74.0	66.0	53.0	6.0

Note: Data refer to 2006.

Sources: World Bank; United Nations Conference on Trade and Development; International Monetary Fund.

Glossary

Abstract review Refers to a procedure of constitutional review in the absence of a concrete judicial case and before the law has been enforced. Also called 'preventive review', since it allows the system to filter out unconstitutional laws before they can harm people.

Active democracy promotion Promotion action resting on intentionality.

Advanced capitalist democracies Political and economic systems that combine a highly developed (industrial/post-industrial) economy with a democratic political system.

Agenda setting Processes through which attention is directed towards a particular public problem.

Agents In the context of political science, institutions or persons to whom power is delegated. Trustees are a particular kind of agent possessing the power to govern those who have delegated in the first place.

American judicial review A model of judicial constitutional review carried out by all types of courts (decentralized) expected to be fundamentally concrete.

Americanization (of communication) The political, economic, social, and cultural influence of the US political communication techniques on other countries.

Ancillary organization An organization such as a trade union or women's club that is formally affiliated with a political party through such mechanisms as overlapping memberships or formal representation on governing boards.

Assembly Any group or gathering of people drawn together for a common purpose or reason. Assemblies can be of numerous types including religious, educational, social, or political, based on the character of their objectives and the subject of their activities.

Asymmetric chambers A bicameral system in which the two legislative chambers are not equal in power. In most cases in the modern era the lower chamber (representing the people as a whole) is the more powerful chamber.

Asymmetric regionalism The uneven or imbalanced distribution of powers, responsibilities and/or revenues between regional governments within that state. This often occurs in states with politicized ethno-territorial minorities or minority nations that consistently demand a range of powers and responsibilities that differs from those exercised by other regional governments populated by members of the ethno-linguistic majority.

Audience democracy Term coined by Bernard Manin (1997) to indicate a contemporary form of democracy in which citizens are not actively engaged in the process but view their political leaders as if they were performing on a distant stage.

Ballot access The requirements (such as support of electors as expressed through signatures, or a financial deposit) that must be met before a party or candidate is allowed to stand for election.

Behavioural revolution Important turn in the 1940s–50s when empirical political theories replaced normative theories, data were collected through means of surveys and analysed by statistical and computerized instruments. Linked to the structural-functional paradigm, with broad concepts applicable to a large number of diverse cases.

Bicameral legislature A legislature that consists of two chambers, with a lower chamber that represents the people as a whole and an upper house that represents either the sub-units (in a federal system), the regions within a country, or even a particular class or group in society.

Bipolar party systems A party system in which two large and equally balanced stable coalitions of parties run for elections and alternate in government.

Cabinet government Collective and collegial government, with all important decisions to be made by the full cabinet and the prime minister acting as first among equals.

Cadre (elite) party A form of party with little formal organization, that is primarily an alliance of politicians and their patrons (or clients) to coordinate activities within government.

Capital accumulation Dynamic process that underlies economic growth and the transformation of the production process within a capitalist economy. This occurs because the competitive business units within capitalism must 'accumulate' in order to survive, forcing them to reinvest a portion of the economic surplus produced by their workers to keep up with the new efficiencies and technological breakthroughs being made by other firms in the national and global economy.

Catch-all party A form of party characterized by appeals, both for votes and for material support, that cross cleavage lines and by a shedding of the 'ideological baggage' associated with the mass party model.

Centralization The policy undertaken by a political entity in order to restrict and eliminate the extent to which other, peripheral, regional entities seek to preserve their traditional entitlements, and thus limit its own initiative and its own disposition over political practices and resources.

Central–local relations The way in which relations between central and local governments are organized. These differ in different types of state (federal/unitary) and in different state traditions (Anglo-Saxon, French, Scandinavian). Today, local authorities are less constrained by central governments (the 'principal–agent' model) and are given greater freedom over policy choices and forms of organization (the 'choice' model).

Centrifugal and centripetal competition Alternative dynamics of competition with parties either distancing themselves from the centre of the left–right axis towards the extremes or converging toward the centre and increasingly resembling each other.

Christian democracy Political movement that is inspired by the Christian faith and has as its main goal the provision of order in society by promoting a harmonious relationship between all classes and layers of society.

Citizenship Historically variable set of rights and obligations which, in the course of modernization, individuals come to possess *vis-à-vis* the state.

Civic culture Type of political culture that emphasizes social activism, participation in networks of free associations, democracy, and a vibrant civil society.

Clash of civilizations Theory stating that the cultural, ethnic, and religious differences replace the ideological division of the cold war as the primary source of international conflict.

Classification Process and result of grouping cases by minimizing differences within each class and maximizing differences between classes, according to a dimension or property. Classes are mutually exclusive and jointly exhaustive.

Cleavage A division of interest and values within a polity opposing groups structurally, culturally, and organizationally.

Co-decision procedure The main legislative procedure of the EU under which the Commission makes legislative proposals and legislation must be passed by a majority of MEPs and a qualified-majority vote in the Council. The European Parliament and the EU Council have two readings of legislation and if they still disagree a conciliation committee is convened to try to reach a compromise.

Collective action Type of action in which more than one individual is required to contribute to an effort in order to pursue a goal or achieve an outcome.

Collective action paradox Mancur Olson's argument that, under certain conditions it is not rational for individuals to join interest groups, as they can enjoy the benefits that stem from the group's existence without having to pay the cost to create or maintain the organization (i.e. they can free ride). The ultimate consequence is that, unless a group provides an additional incentive for members to join, no one will join the group, meaning that no one will receive the collective benefit in the end, as the group will not exist to advocate for it.

Comparative method Method for testing against empirical evidence alternative hypotheses (and thereby either corroborate or reject them) about necessary and sufficient conditions for events to occur based on the association between configurations of values of different independent variables across cases, and the values of the dependent variable.

Comparison The inquiry of similarities and differences. It is a tool for building empirically falsifiable explanatory theories. In the course of scientific development, systematic and inductive comparison has replaced anecdotal and deductive approaches.

Conceptual stretching Distortion occurring when a concept developed for one set of cases is extended to additional cases to which the features of the concept do not apply.

Concrete review When an ordinary judge refers, within a specific litigation, to a constitutional question.

Congress General term for a legislative assembly within a separation of powers political system. Congresses can consist of one chamber or two, if bicameral they may be symmetrical or asymmetrical.

Consensus democracy Form of democracy in which the emphasis is placed on the inclusion of minorities at all stages in the decision-making process and in which the most widespread possible agreement is sought for public policies and programmes.

Consociationalism Different societies find different means of coping with their respective internal cleavages. Consociationalism is a mode of governing in which political elites representing different communities coalesce around the need to govern, even in the face of intense divisions across their communities.

Constituency The unit, usually defined territorially, into which the country is divided for electoral purposes and from which MPs are returned. Single-member constituencies return just one MP, whereas multi-member constituencies return several MPs.

Constitution Statute in which the fundamental political institutions, procedures, and principles of a state are established and in which the basic rights are guaranteed.

Constitutionalism Refers on one hand to the commitment of a political community to accept the legitimacy of constitutional rules and principles and, on the other hand, to an understanding of government that is derivable from a specific constitutional order. Typical examples are federalism and checks and balances.

Constructivism Basic assumption that social realities are not primordially given but constructed in the course of history.

Control Process through which the influence of some variables on the relationship between operational (independent and dependent) variables is reduced or entirely eliminated (*coeteris paribus* clause).

Conventional and unconventional participation Political participation describes activities that have the intent or effect of influencing government action. Conventional participation is expressed within accepted institutional channels (e.g. voting); unconventional participation takes place through activities that range from public events (demonstrations, sit-ins) to direct physical attacks on property or people.

Corporatism Institutionalized patterns of linkage between social interests and the state, focusing especially on the legitimate role of social interests in influencing policy. A common denominator of the many definitions is the close coordination in law-making and wage formation between the state and interest organizations which are granted a privileged and more or less monopoly status as representatives. Trade unions and employers' associations are usually the key players at the nation level.

Coup A *coup d'état* is literally a blow by/of the state but is typically an attack by the military arm of the state against its own government and aimed at seizing power, whether as a 'corporate' coup by the military as a united, corporate body or as a 'factional' coup by part of the military.

Decentralization A process whereby power is transferred from the central level of government and/or administration to other levels. Political decentralization means the transfer of political decision-making powers and functions to lower levels of government, while administrative decentralization means the transfer of administrative tasks without political decentralization.

Democracy assistance Concessionary and largely consensual provision of support for democracy and democratization from a state or international organization by way of projects and programmes.

Democracy promotion Attempts to influence democratization by a variety of methods and approaches that can include linkage and leverage and various measures of soft and hard power.

Democracy promotion backlash Growing opposition to external democracy assistance and promotion in the twenty-first century, evident in several countries including China and Russia.

Democratic deficit The notion that the EU institutions are not as democratically accountable as national institutions. Common allegations associated with the democratic deficit are that the European Commission is appointed rather than elected, that Council decision-making is not as transparent as it could be, that national parliaments cannot control their governments when they do business in Brussels, and that citizens are not as well connected to the European Parliament as they are to their national parliaments.

Democratic disguise The disguise that an authoritarian regime uses to hide the fact that it is a non-democratic regime—a disguise that now typically involves the use of semi-competitive multi-party elections.

Democratic peace thesis Statement that democracies tend not to go to war with one another.

Democratization The process by which non-democratic institutions or polities become democratic.

Descriptive analysis Type of analysis aimed at establishing empirical patterns: the degree to which phenomena occur, variations between cases, and change over time.

Devolution Process by which political, administrative, and/or judicial powers are transferred from central state authorities to regional authorities. Whereas decentralization or deconcentration results in no diminution of central state authority, but merely alters the spatial context within which such authority is effectively exercised, devolution does involve a reduction of power and authority for the centre and more political autonomy for the region.

Digital communication The transmission of digital data through independent new sources that rival mainstream media channels.

Direct promotion of democracy Action employing political methods and engaging with political institutions.

Disguised military rule The military's rule can be disguised either by civilianizing the regime (such as by ending the junta and having officers in government retire/resign from the military) or by ruling indirectly through behind-the-scenes influence upon a puppet civilian government.

District magnitude The number of MPs returned per constituency.

Divided government Configuration of power in which at least one of the chambers of the legislature is controlled by a party that does not hold the presidency.

Electoral market Hypothetical space where political parties present programmes and policies (offer) and voters choose on the basis of their preferences (demand), with the former aiming at maximizing votes and the latter aiming at maximizing utility deriving from specific policies.

Electoral system The set of rules that structure how votes are cast at elections and how these votes are then converted into the allocation of offices/seats.

Empirical research Type of research based on evidence from the real world and disjoined from any type of moral, normative, or value judgement.

Equivalence Feature of concepts and properties whose connotation is similar for all the cases compared.

European model of constitutional review A model of judicial constitutional review carried out by constitutional courts (centralized 'Kelsenian' courts) allowed to be abstract.

Evaluation (of policy) Procedure asking whether the output of a given public policy has attained the intended goals.

Explanatory analysis Type of analysis that relates two or more variables (phenomena) with the aim of formulating general causal statements about their relationship. Also referred to as multi-variate analysis.

Extension (or denotation) Set (or class) of cases to which a concept refers.

External (extra-parliamentary) origin (of parties) Parties of external origin were founded outside government in order to contest elections and thereby first make demands on government and ultimately to elect officials from among their own ranks.

Federal state State where sovereignty is shared across several levels of government and in which one level may not intervene in defined areas of competence of the other. There are different kinds of federal states (e.g. dual federalism in the US and cooperative federalism in Germany).

Federalization Process that leads toward the transformation of a unitary state into a federal state. This generally involves constitutional as well as political and administrative changes that enhance the autonomously exercised powers and responsibilities of one or more regions within the state.

Flexicurity Combination of flexibility and social protection. In a narrow version, this refers to the combination of liberal employment protection, generous social protection, and active labour-market policies. In a broader version, it refers to a multitude of combinations between different modes of flexibility and security.

Fractionalization Degree of fragmentation in a party system. The higher the number of parties, the higher fragmentation in a party system.

Free-rider problem A problem faced when public, non-excludable goods are provided. Free-riders are individuals who consume a good, but let others pay for its production.

Freezing hypothesis Consolidation of party alternatives and electoral alignments from the 1920s until the 1970s due to the saturation of the electoral market caused by full franchise and PR electoral systems.

Functionalism The functionalist approach aimed to identify the necessary activities (functions) of all political systems and then to compare the manner in which these functions were performed. This theoretical paradigm, coupled with structuralism and systems theory, aimed at bridging diverse empirical contexts but it was built on assumptions that turned out to be closely related to the Western, democratic model.

Fused-powers system Regime in which the executive is selected by the legislature, usually from those within the legislature, and is dependent upon the 'confidence' of the legislature to remain in power. In many cases the executive may also dissolve the legislature by calling for new elections.

Generalizations Law-like statements about relationships between social and political phenomena independent from the specific spatial or temporal context.

Ghent system A system of voluntary unemployment insurance which is administered by trade unions. The name of the system comes from the Belgian town Ghent, where it was first introduced.

Global economy, globalization Terms that refer to the increasing interdependencies between national economies that challenge existing domestic social policy arrangements.

Good governance A commonly used term in the development discourse that, at its most expansive meaning, it embraces inclusive and participatory democracy and at minimum is used to denote freedom from corruption.

Governance Approach in comparative politics that argues that certain tasks must be performed in order to govern a society and then posits that these can be accomplished in a number of ways. In particular, scholars of governance are interested in the roles that social actors may play in the process of making and implementing decisions.

Hard power A country's military and economic might.

Human development index The UNDP's human development index is a summary measure comprising life expectancy, adult literacy rate, and a decent standard of living measured in income per capita terms: it falls short of the definition provided.

Implementation The conversion of new laws and programmes into practice.

Incomplete contract Contract allowing for uncertainty as to the precise nature of commitments (e.g. the rights and obligations of the parties under the contract).

Indirect promotion of democracy Action focusing on conditions or pre-conditions for democratization that may be described as non-political, for example, economic variables.

Information and Communication Technologies (ICTs) The study, design, development, implementation, support, or management of computer-based data systems, particularly software applications and computer hardware.

Initiative (popular) Referendum held at the behest of a prescribed number of ordinary citizens.

Inside lobbying Refers to the traditional tactics employed by interest groups to influence governmental policy-making through institutional channels, including lobbying the executive and bureaucracy, meeting with members of the legislature and their staffs, and filing court briefs.

Institutional competitiveness The fact that different regimes develop different comparative advantages. There is not one single road to competitiveness (or to employment), but different strategies that fit into different institutional contexts.

Institutional complementarity Clusters or configurations of (policy) institutions that are mutually supportive (for instance, combinations of various welfare arrangements, or combinations of regulation of the economy). The fact that institutions tend to cluster—and to have a combined impact beyond simple addition (interaction)—is embodied in the notion of 'regime'.

Institutionalism Set of approaches focussing on the central role of structures in shaping politics and individual behaviour. As well as formal institutional patterns, institutions may be defined in terms of their rules and their routines, and thus emphasize the normative structure of the institutions.

Institutions Formal rules of political decision-making and less formal standard operating procedures. These serve to reduce complexities inherent in the policy-making process, shaping the behaviour of actors and the use of policy instruments. In the policy literature 'institutions' also refers to policies, or to the 'programmatic structure' of policies (for instance, contributory vs. tax-financed welfare arrangements, pension systems, etc.).

Intention (or connotation) Set of properties shared by cases to which a concept applies.

Intergovernmentalism One of the two main modes of EU decision-making. Key features of intergovernmentalism are that decisions are reached by unanimous agreement between the EU governments, the European Parliament plays a consultative rather than a legislative role, and the European Court of Justice does not have full judicial review power.

Internal (inter-parliamentary) origin (of parties) Parties of internal origin were originally organized within parliament to coordinate the activities of their members (MPs) in pursuing legislative goals and supporting or opposing cabinets.

International leverage Authoritarian governments' vulnerability to external democratizing pressure. Three important determinants are: the state's raw size and military and economic strength; the existence of competing issues on Western foreign policy agendas; access to support from an alternative regional power.

International linkage Concept composed of five dimensions: economic; geopolitical; social; communication; and transnational civil society. Linkage raises the cost of authoritarianism by (1) heightening the salience in the West of authoritarian rule; (2) increasing the probability of an international response; (3) creating domestic constituencies with a stake in adhering to democratic norms; (4) strengthening democratic forces in relation to their opponents.

Internationalization (of policies) Describes the processes of policy diffusion, policy transfer, and cross-national policy convergence.

Iron law of oligarchy 'Who says organization, says oligarchy.' The fact of organization leads all parties, including those that proclaim themselves to be democratic, to be dominated by their leaders.

Iron triangle Depiction of the role of interest groups in policy-making. Within a given issue area, a sub-system consisting of a key bureaucrat, a key legislator, and a key interest group would form and set the contours of governmental policy, allowing for little input from outside this group of three.

Judicialization of politics Process through which the influence of courts on legislative and administrative power develops over time.

Junta Spanish term for a council or committee and is used by political scientists to describe the political committee of military leaders that is formed during a coup to represent the military in its new role as a ruling organization.

Labour movement Social movement that began during the industrial revolution, fighting for better working conditions and higher living standards for industrial workers. For this purpose, it was organized in labour and trade unions.

Ladder of generality Representation of the relation between intension and extension obeying a law of inverse variation. The larger the extension (and the smaller the intension), the higher the level of abstraction of a concept.

Legislature A kind of assembly in which individuals and/or groups are gathered together for explicitly political purposes. At least one of the political goals of a legislature will entail policy-making or legislating.

Legitimate violence In principle, violence operates on a factual basis, wherever a given subject finds itself unable to resist and override the force brought to bear upon it by another subject. The exercise of violence may be facilitated and regularized by the extent to which those exercising it can plausibly claim that its exercise is authorized by some generally recognized value or principle, which renders it legitimate, and resistance to it illegitimate.

Liberalism A complex of political values and principles which, through varied constitutional arrangements, seeks to lay relatively narrow boundaries on the activities of the state, committing them first and foremost to respecting and fostering the autonomy of private individuals in their capacity as economic actors.

List systems The most common method of implementing the principle of proportional representation; voters choose between lists of candidates presented by different parties.

Majoritarian democracy Form of democracy in which the emphasis is placed on one side winning an outright (if also temporary) victory over the other, and in which success at the polls offers political control over all the key institutions.

Majority government The parties represented in government hold at least 50 per cent of the seats plus one in parliament.

Mass party (of integration) A party form characterized by the formal dominance of the extra-governmental membership organization, and a strategy of mobilization and encapsulation aimed at a well-defined social constituency (the *classe gardée*).

Media system The social and technological systems through which information is created, gathered, processed, and disseminated.

Merit system Access to the administration is not restricted to particular segments of society; selection and promotion aim at appointing the best-qualified individuals.

Method of agreement Logic of comparison of cases with similar values on as many variables as possible in order to account for the variation in the dependent variable through the association with independent variables that also vary.

Method of difference Logic of comparison with cases with different values on as many variables as possible in order to account for the invariance in the dependent variable through the association with invariant independent variables.

Ministerial government Type of government in which decision-making power is dispersed among the individual cabinet members ('fragmented government').

Minority government Type of government in which the parties represented in government hold less than 50 per cent of the seats plus one.

Minority nations Cultural minority groups deprived of their own state (or stateless nations) within a country in which another group is majoritarian and with whom they share the state institutions.

Misappropriation of power (by a party) Usurpation arising when (1) a democratic election victory gives a party access to the key public offices and then (2) the party misappropriates its newly acquired public offices by misusing public powers to ensure that it cannot be defeated in any future elections.

Mixed systems Electoral systems in which some MPs are returned by plurality from local (usually single-member) constituencies and others by PR from national or regional lists (usually multi-member).

Mobilization Attempts by political entrepreneurs (in parties, interest groups, and social movements) to encourage political participation of others.

Most Different Systems Design Research design in which the cases selected are characterized by different values on a large number of independent variables.

Most Similar Systems Design Research design in which the cases selected are characterized by similar values on a large number of independent variables.

Multi-national state Type of country comprised of a populace that has two or more ethnically differentiated, culturally distinct, and territorially concentrated political communities that have historic claims to nationhood.

Multi-party systems A party system in which many parties exist, with at most only one party approaching the absolute majority of seats, and therefore need to form coalitions to support a government that are negotiated after the elections.

Nation A political community may be considered a nation when it is unified not only by the shared subjection to a system of rule but also by a complex and historically variable set of social and cultural bonds of diverse nature (commonalities of ethnic origins, of language, of religion, of customs, of historical experience, of political values) which generate among individuals a significant feeling of affinity and distinctiveness.

National and industrial 'revolutions' Concepts indicating broad political changes in the nineteenth century in politics (formation of nation-states and the democratization and secularization of political systems) and in economy (industrialization and urbanization, and the emergence of a working class).

Nationalism An ideology and political movement based on the nation-state principle in which those who consider themselves to be members of a nation seek to obtain an independent state. A distinction may be made between 'majoritarian nationalism', which refers to established nation-states such as France or Germany, and 'minority nationalism' which refers to stateless nations such as Scotland or Catalonia.

Nation-building Sometimes conflated with state-building, refers to attempts to bring a common sense of national belonging and solidarity to plural communities who reside in the same state.

Nation-state A form of political organization, first advocated during the French Revolution, which links together 'state' and 'nation', whereby each nation should have a single state and each state should correspond with a nation.

Neo-institutionalism Theory that puts forward the role of institutions and norms. Institutions are sets of rules and structures that shape individual behaviour. Other types of institutionalism stress the incentives that institutions set for individual behaviour. In a historical perspective, institutions persist over time and determine future choices (path dependence).

Networks Corporatist patterns of linkage between social interests and the state are being replaced by more loosely defined relationships such as networks. Different claims about this have been developed (self-organizing networks instead of state-led government, networks as a form of interest involvement in governing, networks as a form of inclusion or exclusion from democratic participation).

New constitutionalism New model of democratic state legitimacy, based on the following three elements: (1) a written constitution, (2) a charter of rights, and (3) a judicial review mechanism.

New political communication The changes in political communication induced by the emergence of new media based on information and communication technologies.

New Public Management The application of market mechanisms in the public sector: fixed-term contracts, 'internal markets' and competition, encouragement of managerialism and entrepreneurship, and performance-related contracts.

New social movements Social movements since the mid-1960s which departed from the 'old' labour movement. These movements include the ecology, peace, solidarity, women's, human rights, and squatters' movements, as well as various other movements mobilizing for the rights of discriminated minorities (such as the gay movement).

One-party rule This arises when a political party rules dictatorially as some form of open or disguised one-party state and operates a (1) communist, (2) fascist, or (3) Third World type of one-party rule.

Open military rule The open form of military rule occurs when the military seizure of power leads to military officers openly taking over the governing of the country, such as by establishing a junta or appointing themselves president or prime minister.

Outside lobbying Refers to more recent techniques, such as grass-roots campaigns, in which elites attempt to use mass memberships or the public more broadly to influence key political players.

Over- and under-representation Distortion between the proportion of votes parties receive and the proportion of seats they are allocated, caused by different types of electoral systems. Through over-representation large parties receive a share of seats that is larger than their share of votes, and through under-representation small parties receive a share of seats that is smaller than their share of votes.

Over-determination Insufficient number of cases to test for all potentially relevant independent variables (low degree of freedom).

Paradigm Dominant mainstream approach including a set of assumptions and possible research questions. Of the evolutionary stages of comparative politics, only the dominance of the 'behavioural revolution' came close to Kuhn's idea of a paradigm change.

Parliament A legislative assembly within a fused-powers system. Parliaments can consist of one chamber or two, if bicameral they may be symmetrical or asymmetrical.

Parliamentary systems Regimes in which the executive is not directly elected by the citizens, but is placed in office and held accountable through parliament, which is directly elected.

Party government Regime in which the actions of office-holders are determined by values and policies derived from their party.

Party system Set of political parties within a democratic system competing with each other for the largest share of the electoral vote, with the aim of winning elections and controlling government.

Passive democracy promotion Type of democratization influenced by external and international forces that do not have democratic outcomes as their aim.

Path dependence Concept originally developed in institutional economics, referring to the large political, as well as practical, costs of changing policy. In addition to this strict notion of path dependence as a theory, with emphasis on mechanisms, one also finds 'softer' versions that apply path dependence as a perspective.

Personal dictatorship The leader of a military or party that has seized or misappropriated power but instead of acting as its representative has established a personal dictatorship.

Pluralism A school of thought that argues that groups within society form to influence government through a process of competition. Across issues and times different groups are allied differently, and thus no one group is believed to dominate the government's decisions. Individuals themselves are believed to belong to multiple and competing groups, thus further ensuring the stability of the system.

Policy feedback Concept covering feedback effects from output and outcomes of policies to new input to policies. It includes path dependence, policy learning, policy diffusion, and changing power relations between political actors.

Policy formulation The definition, discussion, acceptance, or rejection of feasible courses of action for coping with policy problems.

Policy learning A 'change in thinking' about a specific policy issue.

Policy paradigms Overall worldview underlying policies. The notion of paradigm is borrowed from the study of revolutions in the worldview of natural sciences (e.g. from a geo-centric to a heliocentric paradigm). Policy paradigms provide particular problem definitions, and to a large extent solutions.

Political action committees PACs are vehicles formed by entities such as corporations and unions that bundle contributions from their employees or members and then distribute them to politicians running for office in the US. PACs are necessary because corporations and unions are not allowed legally to contribute directly to candidates.

Political communication The study of the interactions between media and political systems, locally, nationally, and internationally.

Political communication 2.0 The changes in political communication induced by the emergence of internet-related technologies.

Political conditionality Attachment of democracy, human rights, and governance conditions to offers of assistance to development. Certain political conditions may also be applied to membership entitlement to intergovernmental organizations like the European Union and Organization of American States.

Political culture The orientation of the citizens of a nation towards politics, and their perceptions of political legitimacy and the traditions of political practice. Set of values, attitudes, and beliefs related to state authority and the political system.

Political entrepreneurs Individuals who instigate collective action without receiving selective benefits, but often induce others with such benefits to participate in the mobilization.

Political opportunity structures The degree to which social movements have access to the political system.

Political process approach Approach that interprets social movements as a form of mass politics. The chances of the movement achieving success are discussed in terms of the 'opportunities' that are available.

Politics, policy, polity Politics is the struggle for power within a system of rules, institutions, and norms (polity) to be exercised (policies) in order to achieve given outcomes.

Polyarchy Term developed primarily by Robert Dahl (1971) to indicate a system of government that is the closest that real existing polities come to democracy. Polyarchies offer inclusive participatory rights to citizens and also guarantee full and fair competition between alternative groups and leaders.

Population An ensemble of human individuals which reproduces itself biologically and which normally occupies, over several generations, the same territory.

Post-materialism Value orientation that emphasizes quality of life, social equality, protection of the environment, participation in social and political life and that is expressed in a number of new social movements such as pacifism and feminism.

Post-modernism Stage of modernity which implements the basic principles of modernity (e.g. the constructivist approach) in a radicalized way. It is characterized by a set of theoretical assumptions rather than a clearly discernible new structure of society.

Prediction Scientific statements about the relationship between social and political phenomena should include elements of prediction, i.e. statements about outcomes if certain conditions are fulfilled.

Preferential voting Opportunity, under some list systems, for voters to cast a preference vote for an individual candidate on a list rather than just for the list as a whole.

Presidential systems Systems in which the chief executive, usually an individual political leader, is directly elected by the citizens and enjoys a fixed term of office.

Presidentialization of politics Strengthening of the chief executive in his or her party and executive functions and increasingly leadership-centred electoral processes.

Prime ministerial government Monocratic decision-making by the prime minister, by taking up issues at will or by deciding key issues with subsequent implications on government policy or by defining a governing ethos which generates solutions to most policy problems.

Privileged position of business Argument that business has more political influence than any other interest group due to its ability to have a much greater effect on the economy and thus the re-election hopes of incumbents. There is an ongoing debate as to whether globalization has enhanced business' power or not.

Procedural democracy Form of democracy in which the definition emphasizes the process by which political leaders are elected and held accountable rather than the political or ideological goals that are set by the regime.

Professionalization The social process by which the communication occupation transforms itself into a true profession and by which the qualified are demarcated from unqualified amateurs.

Proportional representation The principle that the distribution of seats among parties brought about by an election should closely correspond to the distribution of votes among those parties. This principle can be effected by a wide range of different specific methods.

Proportionality Degree of correspondence between parties' vote shares and their shares of seats.

Protest events Means for social movements to draw attention to their cause. Ranging from petitions, festivals, demonstrations to violent confrontations.

Public interest groups Groups that seeks to achieve a non-self-interested collective goal (e.g. clean air) that will benefit society at large and not just the members of the interest group.

Public policies A long series of actions carried out to solve societal problems. They are the main output of political systems.

Public sphere A public sphere exists when a large number of autonomous individuals find themselves enabled by the resources they possess, activated by their interests, and authorized by the existing constitutional arrangements (especially the freedoms of speech, of assembly, of organization, of the press) to communicate to one another their opinions on political issues and policies, to articulate both their disagreements and their agreements, and to align themselves accordingly.

Qualified-majority voting System of weighted-voting in the EU Council, where each member state government has a number of votes in proportion to its population. Votes are cast en bloc. Under the QMV rules of the Nice Treaty, decisions require a 'triple majority': of 258 votes out of the total of 345 votes of the 27 member states, 50 per cent of the member states, and 62 per cent of the EU population. QMV is used for most social and economic legislation.

Quasi-experimental research design The comparative method is called 'quasi-experimental' because conclusions are inferred from empirically informed comparisons and not from experiments.

Rational choice A set of (more or less formal) deductive models based on assumptions of rationality: ordering of preferences, maximization of utility, and full information.

Rationalization The tendency to engage in action, individual or collective, in a deliberate manner, so as to optimize its bearing on one's interests and preferences. In the case of political and administrative activity, the attempt to optimize the relationship between costs and benefits of public activity by rendering that activity as far as possible uniform, predictable, and economical.

Redistribution Reallocation both of social risks and of material resources, either from one social group to another or over the life-course.

Referendum Vote held not to elect a parliament but to decide on some specific issue.

Regional autonomy The location of state powers and responsibilities with authorities and institutions at the regional level. The extent of regional autonomy varies from state to state and constitutes a key element of power-sharing arrangements in both federal and non-federal countries.

Regional policy Range of policies, programmes, and fiscal arrangements the objective of which is to reduce economic and social disparities between regions within a nation-state, a sub-national state, or an affiliated group of nation-states.

Regionalism The social, cultural, economic, and political expression of a spatially distinct pattern of values, attitudes, orientations, opinions, behaviours, preferences, interests, and/or actions that reflect the sense of belonging or attachment to, and the personal and community interests that are vested in a particular territorial space. Also an ideology and political movement whereby regional populations or key groups within them demand greater autonomy over the affairs of their region, usually by the establishment of elected regional governments.

Regionalization Process of organizing along regional lines or at the regional level, the political and administrative structures of the state, and/or other policy, decision-making, and representational mechanisms within state and society. It is usually carried out as a top-down initiative.

Registration requirements Obligations in order to receive the right to vote. They increase the cost of voting. The low turnout in the US is partly explainable by time-consuming registration requirements compared to other rich democracies.

Rejective referendum Type of referendum in which the people vote on a proposal that some measure of government or parliament should be rejected.

Repertories of contention The means groups choose to protest. Include demonstrations, general strike actions, or civil disobedience.

Research design Basic organization of a research programme which formulates hypotheses concerning the relationship between variables, identifies the relevant indicators, selects cases and data, discusses measurement and comparability problems, and identifies the suitable techniques for data analysis.

Resource mobilization The amount of people, money, and media coverage that a particular social movement can mobilize.

Riskiness of participation Attribute to classify political participation by the sanctions political authorities might impose on it, from monetary fines and minor harassments to incarceration and death.

Ruling monarchy A ruling monarch exercises the same sort of power as a personal dictator and, unlike a reigning monarch, is not a constitutional and largely ceremonial head of state.

Secularization The decline of religious values as well as the institutional separation of state and church. Hence the historical tendency of modern states to disregard, in planning and justifying their activities, those criteria and rules relating to mundane matters and public concerns, which ecclesiastical authorities traditionally claimed to derive from their privileged knowledge of divine truths.

Selection bias (1) Distortion affecting the inference from sample to population arising from the non-random inclusion in the analysis of a number of cases chosen from a larger pool that are not representative of the population (external validity); (2) over-representation of cases at one end or the other of the distribution of the dependent variable (internal validity).

Selective incentives 'Private' benefits political entrepreneurs can direct to those who help to overcome the free-rider problem in the production of a collective good. These incentives can be material (e.g. a gift), expressive (e.g. a sense that one is doing the right thing), or solidary (e.g. the comfort that comes from being part of the group).

Semi-competitive elections Low level of democratic competition between the official party and one or more other parties but the dictatorship ensures by various subtle or not so subtle means that its official party will win the elections.

Separation-of-powers system Regime in which the legislative and executive branches are selected independently from one another and neither can dismiss the other (with certain rare exceptions for criminal activity or incapacitation). Both branches are generally elected by citizens through distinct votes.

Single market A single market to replace the separate markets of the member-states is the main aim and achievement of the EU. The creation of the single market involved the removal of technical, physical, and fiscal barriers to the free movement of goods, services, capital, and labour in Europe.

Social capital Positive outcomes generated by the networks that bind a community together. The more of these and the stronger these connections are, the greater the social and political benefits they generate and hence civil society and quality of life have a higher potential to flourish. Social capital is a key component for building and maintaining democracy.

Social democracy Political movement that has as its main goal the material and immaterial improvement of the position of workers and employees in capitalist society by stressing equality.

Social movement Streams of public collective unconventional participation that target demands at policy-makers primarily through community, street, and media events, often involving a disruption of regular social life, e.g. through blockades and sit-ins.

Social movement organization (SMO) Conscious, collective, organized groups that attempt to bring about, or resist, large-scale change in the social order by non-institutionalized means.

Social networks Connection of several individuals, tied by one or more types of relation, such as values, partisanship, or friendship. Social networks are thought of as enabling political participation in various ways (mobilization, group pressure, monitoring).

Social risks Risks that are shared by many people and affect the welfare of society as a whole are interpreted as a threat to certain strata of society, and are beyond the control of any individual.

Socially embedded growth model Various institutional and political-economy theories about the new regionalism. The emphasis within this model is on the internal or endogenous social and economic factors responsible for regional economic success, such as the character and quality of a region's human, social, and cultural capital.

Soft power Strategy based on attraction and persuasion rather than coercion. It arises from the attractiveness of a country's culture, political ideals, policies, and practices, both domestic and as displayed in how it conducts external relations.

Sovereignty A principle originally articulated by rulers involved in early state-making who (1) claimed that within their territories their political faculties and prerogatives overrode all those claimed by lesser powers; (2) acknowledged no centre of rule operating outside those territories as having political faculties and prerogatives superior to their own.

Spoils system System through which the victorious party appoints large layers of the administration after each election, with the jobs going to party trustees.

       Originally a subfield of legal studies, it was among the precursors of modern political science. However, its affirmative, somewhat metaphysical, focus on the state was soon left behind.

State A polity which claims in law (and is able to assert in fact) that within a given portion of the earth its properly constituted organs are exclusively entitled to practise legitimate violence in the pursuit of political interests, beginning with the maintenance of public order and defence of the territory from foreign encroachments.

State-building Activities intended to create the essential conditions for, and the substance of, a state, defined in terms of a monopoly of the means of violence and an ability to procure certain basic functions like security throughout the territory.

State subvention State subventions are subsidies from the public treasury to support the activities of political parties.

Supra-nationalism One of the two main modes of EU decision-making involving a monopoly on legislative initiative by the European Commission, co-equal power in the adoption of legislation by the governments (in the Council) and the European Parliament (under the co-decision procedure), and judicial review of EU legislation by the European Court of Justice.

Symmetric chambers Bicameral legislatures in which both chambers have exactly the same powers, both in terms of investiture/censure of the government and as regards the policy-making process.

Systemic functionalism Theoretical paradigm based on the functions of structures within a social or political system.

Systems theory General empirical theory replacing the narrow concept of state and its institutions with the broader concept of the political system as a set of structures (institutions and agencies) whose decision-making function is to reach the collective and authoritative allocation of values (*output*, i.e. public policies) receiving support as well as demands (*inputs*) from the domestic as well as the international *environment* which it shapes through outputs in the *feedback loop*.

Territoriality Each states rules over a clearly bounded portion of the earth (and the adjoining waters), and its commands and other practices of rule apply in principle to all individuals operating, at a given time, over that territory.

Third wave Term coined by Samuel Huntington (1991) to distinguish the wave of democratic transitions that took place between 1974 and 1990 from earlier waves of democratic transitions that took place between 1828 and 1926 and between 1942 and 1962.

Threshold Level of support (usually expressed as a percentage of the total vote) that a party must reach in order to achieve representation.

Traditions Cultural elements inherited from the past and maintained through recurrent rituals.

Transnational social movements Deal with issues that exceed the local and national level and that are trans-boundary or 'global' in their character. Typical examples are ecology or human rights movements.

Triangulation Research strategies aiming at exploring the same set of data with several alternative theories or to go into the field with alternative approaches in mind in order to become more open to unexpected findings.

Trust Type of social relationship based on reliance. The relationship can be horizontal (trust in fellow citizens) as well as vertical (trust in political, cultural, social, and economic elites and authorities).

Turnout The ratio between voters and electorate. The electorate can be defined in different ways: all residents in a polity, all citizens, and all citizens who are also registered to vote.

Two-party system A party system with two equally balanced parties that receive almost all votes and alternate in power, forming single-party governments.

Unicameral legislature A legislature that consists of only one chamber. Unicameral legislatures are never found in federal political systems and are often associated with smaller, more homogeneous societies.

Unified government All three branches of presidential government—the presidency and both houses of the legislature—are under the control of the same party.

Union state A pre-modern form of state organization constructed through 'acts of union' between political entities.

Unitary state State in which sovereignty is concentrated at the level of a single central government. Unitary states may be centralized, decentralized, or regionalized.

Variables A property or attribute that has been made measurable.

Varieties of capitalism Different methods of coordination between economic actors. The concept is parallel to the welfare regime concept, but the cornerstone is completely different: it is the interest of firms in using the market vs. negotiations and public regulation as the main instance of coordination. This underlies a dichotomization into LMEs and CMEs.

Web 2.0 Synonymous with the significant shift in web design and use.

Welfare regime Specific configuration of state, market, and family that nations adopt in their pursuit of work and welfare and the management of social risks. Three or more such clusters are usually identified: conservative, liberal, social democratic.

Welfare state Type of democratic state, influenced by Keynesianism, that offers (some) protection to its citizens against the hardships of the (labour) market (e.g. unemployment) and life (e.g. sickness).

Welfare state reform Generic term to refer to the political interventions that are meant to adjust existing welfare arrangements to changing social (e.g. ageing) and economic (e.g. globalization) conditions, ranging from the incremental fine-tuning and correction of policy instruments to radical measures such as the abolishment of old and the introduction of new social programmes.

Endnotes

Introduction

1 Not all authors would agree with such a division of disciplines, stressing that fields like public administration, policy analysis, political behaviour, as well as political economy are not part of comparative politics (see e.g. the titles of the volumes in the Oxford Handbooks of Political Science listed in the 'Further reading' section to this Introduction). More importantly, perhaps, this division in three main disciplines disregards methodology as a separate field. However, opinions diverge as to whether or not methods should be considered within the field of political science—as they largely overlap with methods in other sciences, such as economics, sociology, social psychology, and so forth.

2 These are the years in which the first studies on political culture were published (see, as an example, Banfield 1958), followed by others stressing the differences in political cultures other than the Anglo-Saxon culture—namely based on clientelism and patronage. For a recent example of cultural analysis see Putnam (1993).

3 Numbers are a universal language and thus, from a comparative point of view, the least problematic level of measurement of phenomena in diverse contexts.

4 Within the new-institutionalist theory different positions have emerged and have been summarized by Hall and Taylor (1996). (1) **Historical new-institutionalism** devotes more attention to the time dimension and the constraints set by past developments (path dependence) with a strong impact on public policy analysis. (2) **Sociological new-institutionalism** stresses how institutions model politics, influence preferences by narrowing expectations and orientations. Institutions thus influence individual and collective strategies. (3) **Rational choice new-institutionalism** focuses on how institutions result from the aggregation of individual preferences and on institutions' contribution to solving collective action problems.

5 These cycles correspond to what Ch. 1 names pre-modern, modern, and post-modern comparative politics or what Chilcote (1994) calls traditional, behavioural, and post-behavioural comparative politics.

6 This is also the period in the 1950s and 1960s when modern political science started developing in Europe on the US model. New departments, new chairs of comparative politics, and new degree programmes were created. This contributed both to the widening and expansion of cases and fields, and to the fragmentation and specialization of the discipline.

7 Charles Tilly's critique of Stein Rokkan's model points precisely to Rokkan's failure in genuinely analysing the *interactions* between countries (Tilly 1984a: 129).

Chapter 2

1 This classification of research types comes from Arend Lijphart's seminal (1971) article.

2 A great deal of political science theory has been developed in reference to the US, given the size and importance of the political science profession. A good deal of that theory, however, does not appear relevant beyond the boundaries of the US (in some cases not within those boundaries either).

3 This is something of an oversimplification of the assumptions of rational choice approaches, but the central point here is not the subtlety of some approaches but rather the reliance on individual-level explanations. For a more extensive critique of the assumptions see Box 13.5 in this volume.

4 That is, if we could reject more theories and models then we could focus on the more useful ones. As it is, we are overstocked with positive findings and theories that have credible support.

5 The classic example of a study that uses triangulation explicitly is Allison (1971). This book, however, uses multiple theories but it does not verify the results through multiple research methods.

6 See e.g. Adcock and Collier (2001) who stress the need for common standards of validity for all varieties of measurement, as well as the interaction of those forms of measurement.

7 Lijphart (1999) has provided a slightly different conceptualization by distinguishing between majoritarian and consensual political systems (see Ch. 4 on Democracies). Some parliamentary systems such as the Westminster system are majoritarian, designed to produce strong majority governments that alternate in office. Others, such as in the Scandinavian countries, may have alternation in office but the need to create coalitions and an underlying consensus on many policy issues produces less alternation in policy.

8 These shifts are to some extent a function of changes in political culture, especially the movement towards 'post-industrial politics' (Ingelhart 1990).

9 This is more true for American political science than for European political science. Discourse theory and the use of rhetorical forms of analysis have been of much greater relevance in Europe than they have in North America, and qualitative methodologies remain more at the centre of European political analysis.

10 One exception to this rather broad generalization is that different legislative processes create different numbers of veto points, with bicameral legislatures e.g. having many more barriers to legislating than unicameral (Tsebelis and Money 1997).

11 This is true if one adopts the familiar 'stages' model (Hill and Hupe 2005), or more analytic conceptions of stages (Dunn 1994).

12 The interest in these phenomena has to some extent come back in through the back door, with the high level of interest in performance studies in comparative public administration.

Chapter 3

1 In the comparative politics literature the term 'cross-national research' is often used to depict the units of observation or cases used in the comparative analysis (e.g.

Dogan and Pelassy 1990; Landman 2003). In this chapter we shall however deliberately use 'cross-*system* analysis', for—as Lijphart (1975: 166) pointed out—this term avoids the idea that 'nations' are the only units of observation to be used in a comparative politics research design.

[2] There are many names in use for independent variables: exogenous, effect-producing, antecedent variables, etc. They all have in common that a change in X affects Y. In this chapter we will use the term dependent (Y) and independent (X) variables.

[3] This is the distinction that is made between *variable-oriented and case-oriented designs* (Przeworski and Teune 1970: 130; see also Keman 1993a; Ragin 2000).

[4] In the literature on comparative methods it is often suggested that MSSD is best suited for comparing many cases using quantitative variables and, alternatively, MDSD can be applied to a few(er) cases comparison which would make use of qualitative information (e.g. Landman 2003: 29). Yet the logic of comparison is not directive in this sense nor is it a necessary requirement. It has more to do with the debate on the advantages and disadvantages of the qualitative and the quantitative approach (see Brady and Collier 2004; Ragin 2000).

[5] It should be noted that the research design including only consociational democracies appears to suffer from a selection bias on the dependent variable (see Brady and Collier 2004: 79–81): only those political systems were included that were characterized by features that define consociationalism. Lijphart's defence is that it concerned an **explorative** analysis. In his later work on types of democracies (e.g. *Patterns of Democracy*, 1999) this selection bias was not present any more.

[6] In fact this method of increasing the number of cases is close to, and by and large similar to, developing conceptual classifications for comparative use. A **classification** (often also called typology or taxonomy) is constructed by using two rules: (1) the species identified (e.g. types of democracy) are mutually exclusive, and (2) the species observed are jointly exhaustive. The main difference with family resemblance and radial categorization is that a classification is derived from 'real' cases, whereas the other method argues on the basis of operational definitions. This gives more leverage for enhancing the number of cases and is considered as equally valid. See also Pennings *et al.* (2006: 148–50); Peters (1998: 93–97).

Chapter 4

[1] One often speaks, today, of 'failed' states (see Ch. 25).

[2] The same rules of delimitation apply to the sea.

[3] They mostly do that, however, without depriving those individuals and bodies of their private resources and of their status advantages.

[4] Since not only more significant faculties and responsibilities correspond to higher offices but also greater material and status rewards, the hierarchical structure we have talked about also constitutes a career system. It is a ladder which by climbing up office-holders can satisfy their legitimate ambitions.

Chapter 5

In preparing this chapter I have benefited from many useful discussions with Alex Trechsel and Jørgen Møller. The usual disclaimer applies.

[1] See the Freedom House report *Democracy's Century: A Survey of Global Political Change in the 20th Century*, published on 7 Dec. 1999. See also Box 5.1.

[2] This famous observation is also from Linz, and seems to have first been used in a 1990 essay (Linz 1990: 158).

[3] For a valuable review of how this literature developed, as well as an empirical assessment of how the weight of these different factors has changed over time, see Doorenspleet (2005). On 'transitology' and 'consolidology' see also Ch. 1.

[4] The explosion was also reflected in the successful launch of two new journals devoted to the comparison of democracies and democratisation: the *Journal of Democracy*, founded in 1990, and *Democratization*, founded in 1993.

[5] The combination of Dahl and O'Donnell's criteria also comes close to the lengthy list of political and civil liberties used by Freedom House in its contemporary ratings of polities across the world. See also Coppedge and Reinicke (1990).

[6] Although even Schumpeter accepted the need for elections in democracy to be free and fair, and also accepted that this required at least some degree of institutional pluralism (1947: 292–93).

[7] In a recent assessment, Perry Anderson (2007: 10) cites the Russian observer Dmitry Furman who defines the contemporary regime in Russia as 'managed democracy'—a system in which 'elections are held, but the results are known in advance; courts hear cases, but give decisions that coincide with the interests of the authorities; the press is plural, yet with few exceptions dependent on the government'. See also Ekiert *et al.* (2007).

[8] See www.freedomhouse.org/uploads/ Chart83File137.pdf (11 Jan. 2007) for the 2006 data.

[9] For recent evaluations of the different measures used to classify democracies, see Munck and Verkuilen (2002) and Bogaards (2008); for a review of the advantages and disadvantages of dichotomizing the distinctions between democracies and non-democracies, see Collier and Adcock (1999). For a more broad-ranging evaluation of recent approaches see Berg-Schlosser (2004).

[10] In a similar approach to Dahl, but also one that is more narrowly specified, Lipset and Rokkan (1967: 26 ff.) have traced the relationship between the sequencing of democratic developments in the different polities of Western Europe and the character of the party system that subsequently developed in these polities (see also Ch. 13).

[11] Note also Przeworski's (1991: 10) widely cited definition of democracy as 'a system in which parties lose elections'. Dahl's milestones can also help make sense of the European Union as a quasi-democratic polity: one that affords the rights of participation and representation but that limits the scope for organized opposition *within* the institutions (see Mair 2007).

[12] Lijphart developed the term 'consociationalism' from the work of the late Reformation philosopher Johannes Althusius who had argued in the early 17th century for a form of

federalism in which distinct communities within a single polity could work together by retaining a large degree of autonomy. See Hueglin (1979).

13 In the 1984 version of his new framework, Lijphart included a reference to the number of dimensions of party competition, and, by extension, the cleavage structure, as one of the eight relevant characteristics of the two models of democracy. All other features were strictly political and/or institutional. This feature is not included in the more extended version of the models in 1999, however, even though it is used to help explain variation in party numbers, which remains one of the relevant characteristics. By 1999, in other words, social factors are no longer seen to play a direct role in distinguishing between the two forms of democracy.

14 This is also sometimes true even when comparing a more limited range of institutions, as the confusion over the classification of presidential, semi-presidential, and parliamentary systems testifies. See e.g. Elgie (1998).

15 For a recent review and discussion of the European evidence, see Mair (2006c), from which some of the following paragraphs are drawn.

Chapter 6

1 Innovative ideologies or structures had already appeared in Turkey and Mexico in the 1930s, with visionary military dictators seeking to Westernize the former and to civilianize the latter's military-dominated politics into democratically disguised one-party rule.

2 Reversing the principal–agent relationship is not sufficient, though, to produce absolutist personal rule if the dictator's party or military is a relatively weak institution; e.g. Mussolini's fascist party was too weak to control or counterbalance Italy's military and reigning monarch.

3 Civilianization and indirect rule have also been favourite strategies of military **personal** rulers in, respectively, the Middle East and Latin America.

4 The visionary ideological claims to legitimacy have been diverse and have included: the communists' vision of a world of classless, affluent, and internationalist societies; the Baathist vision of a united and socialist Arab nation; Ataturk's vision of a westernized and democratic Turkey; Mussolini's vision of a new Roman Empire for Italy; and Hitler's vision of a German-led Aryan master-race ruling the world.

5 The military's temporary vanguard role was converted into a civilianized presidential monarchy for Nasser, who was succeeded by his deputy, ex-Colonel Sadat, who was in turn succeeded by his own deputy, ex-General Mubarak, who continues to rule Egypt in a unique example of third-generation civilianized presidential monarchy.

6 Historical research would later show that, in fact, Hitler's and Stalin's regimes failed to achieve even a total control of actions, let alone thought, and were in this sense less totalitarian than a few of the more recent communist regimes, such as Pol Pot's Cambodia and Kim's North Korea.

7 The Politburo is usually similar in size to a large junta but may have a standing committee, as in China, that is about the size of a small junta and does the week-to-week decision-making.

8 However, some mixed-economy regimes are almost as state-dominated in their policy making as a Stalinist communist economy. For example, the Asad Baathist regime's state-dominated economic policy making has been described as 'bureaucratic politics' because this 'virtual presidential monarchy' had devolved most economic policy-making to state and party officials who also seem to have been wholly autonomous from the weak private-sector economy (Hinnebusch 1994: 105, 98).

Chapter 7

1 Currently Saudi Arabia and Myanmar (Burma) are the only two internationally recognized countries that do not have some form of legislature.

2 Throughout this chapter the word 'Government' (capitalized) refers to the actual occupants of the executive branch (such as the prime minister and her cabinet), while use of the same word uncapitalized refers to the generic structures of the political system as a whole that constitute the governmental structures of the country.

3 The term is also related to the Anglo-Latin 'parliamentum', although the French '*parlement*' predates this construction (Harper 2001).

4 This is especially true in presidential systems and those parliamentary systems in which a single party wins an absolute majority of seats in the parliament. In contrast, coalition governments that include parties representing a variety of minority interests can serve to increase the representative function of the executive branch as a whole.

5 There are a number of institutional structures that can increase or decrease the ease with which a legislature can successfully adopt a motion of no-confidence, such as the requirement for all such motions to also include a simultaneously adopted motion for the investiture of a new executive (the German **constructive vote of no confidence**). In some parliamentary systems use of censure votes is very rare (Germany, the UK) in others is occurs more regularly (France) while in still others use of the mechanism is so common as to cause concern for the system as a whole (Italy).

6 Entitlements, as opposed to discretionary funds, are pre-existing financial commitments that cannot be withdrawn or decreased. Programmes such as Social Security that guarantee citizens financial support at a specified level in the future are entitlements. These types of commitments can account for a significant portion of the overall budget of a political system.

7 The power of delay is particularly common in upper chambers. In these cases the legislative power of delay is as likely to be used against the lower chamber as it is to be used against the executive branch.

8 For example, under the previous apartheid regime South Africa had a tripartite legislature with each chamber's membership drawn from a distinct racial group.

9 The British House of Lords is a well-known example.

10 The British House of Parliament is a striking architectural achievement that houses one of the less (if not the least) influential legislatures of Western Europe.

11 In some cases, even in single-member-district electoral systems, it is the political parties that assume the responsibility for facilitating these activities. However, the implicit cost is a decrease in the autonomy of the legislator who becomes dependent on her political party for support.

¹² The Congressional Budget Office (CBO) of the American Congress is an example of an extremely important staff resource that permits the legislature to effectively negotiate with the executive branch over the details of the annual national budget.

¹³ This dichotomy ignores the existence of hybrid systems such as the French semi-presidential model. The rationale for this is twofold. First, true hybrid systems are comparatively rare, despite an upswing in numbers following the fall of the former Soviet Union. Second, hybrid systems are functionally more accurately described as alternating systems. That is, in most cases the systems operate as either a fused-powers system or a separation-of-powers system, depending on the partisan identity of the two aspects of the executive branch. Returning to the French Fifth Republic, this suggests that it would be more accurate to describe the general political system as one of fused powers when the party or coalition of the directly elected president and the majority in the legislature are the same and a separation-of-powers system during periods of 'cohabitation'.

¹⁴ In fact, on the American system there is a stream of research that suggests that the legislative process actually works better when the ideological orientations of the two branches are **not** aligned. See Fiorina (1996) among others.

¹⁵ Even in the case of a venal pursuit of power, within a democratic system policy outcomes will become important to the extent that they influence the probability of re-election, thus the two goals are inextricably linked.

Chapter 8

I am grateful to Michael Becher, Michael Danzer, and Ignazio De Ferrari for their help in preparing the tables.

¹ Another meaning of 'government' refers to the political science subdiscipline that takes its name from the subject of its study, i.e. government in its broadest meaning. This chapter thus is a contribution to 'Comparative government'.

Chapter 9

¹ Some social scientists adopt a narrow perspective: any rule that binds actors into a stable system of cooperation with one another, and thus enables them to achieve joint gains and purposes, should be considered 'constitutional'. Thus, the rule of reciprocity in a trade regime is a constitutional rule (Hermann-Pillath 2006), and so might be 'thou shalt not lie to or cheat on your neighbors', in a community without a formal state or law (see, generally, Taylor 1982). Consider the 'constituting' role of the Ten Commandments of the Old Testament. I am generally sympathetic to this idea (see Stone Sweet 1999), but will not explore it further here.

² In my view, all stable systems of community, not just states, are likely to possess meta-norms.

³ *Marbury* v. *Madison*, 5 US 137 (1803).

⁴ A 'complete' contract 'would specify precisely what each party is to do in every possible circumstance and arrange the distribution of realized costs and benefits in each contingency so that each party individually finds it optimal to abide by the contract's terms' (Milgrom and Roberts 1992: 127).

⁵ In the past, the legislator and the judge were often one and the same, as when the king or feudal lord or corporate body both made law and resolved disputes.

⁶ In this chapter, I do not discuss the extent to which appointment procedures, the partisan affiliation of judges, have influenced the development of constitutional law around the world. These factors have surely mattered, but how much remains a mystery. To date, no sophisticated comparative work on the topic has been produced.

⁷ Civil Rights Cases, 109 US 3 (1883); *Plessy* v. *Ferguson*, 163 US 537 (1896).

⁸ The dataset was compiled by Christina Andersen and Alec myself. It includes 196 states, but we were unable to find adequate information on two (Brunei and the Central African Republic), so we do not count them here.

Chapter 10

¹ One complication about secession or sovereignty referenda, though, is that a decision needs to be taken as to who may vote: whether the people of the larger unit should also have a say in whether a new member may join, or an existing province may secede.

Chapter 11

¹ Only the three micro-states of Andorra, Monaco, and San Marino have not signed it and France has signed but not ratified it.

Chapter 12

¹ The importance of the referendum is one of the factors underlying the Swiss practice of entrusting executive power to an apparently permanent coalition of *all* the major parties. As Lehner and Homann (1987) explain, given the threat that any parliamentary decision can be overturned by referendum, the ruling parties are at pains to assemble overwhelming majorities in the hope of deterring any referendum in the first place (see also Ch. 10).

² To date, the only women's party that had any lasting success was the Icelandic Kvinnalistinn (Women's List), which existed from 1983 to 1999, and at the height of its success (1987) won more than 10% of the national vote, and 6 of 63 seats in parliament. In 1999, the Women's List merged into a more general left-wing alliance.

³ The term 'genetic myth' is used here in the same sense that the term 'stylized' is often used in rational choice theory to suggest the essence of a story without claiming that it fits the details of any particular case.

⁴ Or with different terms, but equivalent meaning, they might define the interest of their particular class **to be** the national interest.

⁵ There is no inherent reason why a cadre party must be on the right, but as history developed they generally were parties of the propertied classes—who were the only ones who could vote under the *régimes censitaires*.

⁶ It should be noted that these regulations apply only to federal parties, which are organizationally distinct from provincial parties, even when they apparently have the same name. For example, the Liberal Party of Quebec has not been affiliated with the Liberal Party of Canada since 1955, and indeed when Jean Charest resigned the leadership of the federal Progressive Conservative Party in 1998, it was to become leader of the Quebec Liberal Party.

⁷ 527s are tax-exempt organizations created under section 527 of the Internal Revenue Code (see Ch. 14). While they engage in political advocacy, so long as they do not directly advocate the election or defeat of a named candidate for federal office, they are not subject to the spending limits imposed on ordinary Political Action Committees. They can, however, engage in issue advocacy, and they can praise or attack a named candidate so long as they do not link this to an overt exhortation to vote for or against that candidate.

⁸ Exceptions include some schemes for media access (as well as the British free mailing of electoral addresses) that allocate resources equally among parties or candidates without regard to prior electoral success, schemes that base support at least in part on numbers of members rather than voters, and schemes of (partial) public matching of privately raised contributions.

⁹ Women were not seen as the basis for a potential cleavage, notwithstanding that they are more than half of the population and in many countries they remained without the vote into the 1940s.

¹⁰ As Lynn and Jay (1988: 134) put it, in the modern world apparently the only people who care about preserving the countryside are those who do not have to live in it.

Chapter 13

¹ In the US two-party systems exist largely due to rules to form a party making it difficult for third parties to present candidates. For this reason there is no high disproportionality between votes and seats in Table 13.3 (LSq index).

² The literature on the positive sides of multi-party systems insists on a different decision-making mode based on consensus. This literature includes Rustow (1955), Daalder (1966a and 1966b), Lorwin (1966), Lijphart (1968b), McRae (1974), and Steiner (1974), all stressing accommodation, agreement, and compromise.

³ In the Federal Republic of Germany a rule of the Constitutional Court banned both Communist and Nazi parties.

⁴ 1958 marks the beginning of the Fifth Republic in France with the new 'Gaullist' constitution and a two-ballot majority system in single-member constituencies.

⁵ If the effective number of parties is calculated on votes this is usually referred to as 'effective number of elective parties' (ENEP), whereas if it is calculated on seats it is called 'effective number of parliamentary parties' (ENPP).

⁶ Additional causes of distortion between votes and seats are the rules to form a party and present candidates, the size of parliamentary groups, the threshold of representation and the number of tiers (i.e. various levels of constituencies for the allocation of seats).

⁷ A further assumption is that if a voter prefers the ideological position 60 over 70, then the voter will also prefer 60 over 80, 90, etc. (transitivity). This is an assumption of single-peakedness of voter preferences, i.e. if a voter prefers 60 then the further away from 60 the less the position is liked.

⁸ Such a modification of the left–right distribution through new voters is unique. Later 'waves' of enfranchisement did not have by far a similar effect—namely, when women and younger generations were enfranchised with the lowering of the voting age.

⁹ As a response to the criticism about full information, rational choice theorists argue that it is not rational to spend a lot of time gathering political information (the costs outweigh benefits). This is a free-rider attitude.

Chapter 18

¹ Of course, a case can be made that these voluntary, spontaneous modes of social coordination in many instances cannot be sustained unless they operate under the shadow of state coercive authority that ultimately enforces voluntary agreements, such as contractual relations.

² We cannot delve into the complications of the interaction between voluntary decentralized coordination and central political authority in human cooperation. Encompassing systems of voluntary exchange organized as markets do not evolve spontaneously, but presuppose some coercive political authority to protect property rights and guarantee the voluntary, non-violent character of contractual relations.

³ With regard to late democratizers in the 1970s and 1980s, such as Greece, Portugal, Spain, and South Korea, of course, the impact of lower affluence and recent authoritarianism depressing political participation cannot be easily sorted out.

⁴ For a summary evaluation of research on political opportunity structures in democracies and political participation, see McAdam (1996) and Tarrow (1996) as well as Goodwin (2001). See also Ch. 16.

⁵ Trail-blazing contributions were Powell (1986) and Jackman (1987) as well as the meticulous study by Franklin (2004). For a comprehensive meta-analysis on which we rely here see now Geys (2006).

⁶ For a sophisticated effort to disentangle these causal linkages with Bayesian statistical estimations and qualitative, comparative-historical priors, see Western (1997), esp. chs. 6 and 7.

⁷ On the difference between the organizational requisites and strategic dilemmas of monological and dialogical interest association, see Offe and Wiesenthal (1980).

⁸ Examples would be the French Ecologistes of the 1970s or 1980s or the Swedish Miljöpartiet in the early 1990s. Both efforts failed, but not because of electoral system (institutions) or strategic configuration (no established party had fully occupied the potential 'place' of Greens. In the case of the unsuccessful British Green Party, its failure may be overdetermined by the single-member-district electoral system.

⁹ For this section, see esp. Brady et al. (1995) and Verba et al. (1995). For an overview, see Schlozman (2002).

¹⁰ Again, no factor alone will be sufficient to explain political participation. Below, we will show e.g. that the impact of education on participation varies by context.

¹¹ Time sovereignty refers to the capacity to determine when and where to work, not the absolute amount of free time beyond one's professional life. Highly educated people may have more time sovereignty, but less free time, than people with less education.

¹² Just consider the example of the incoming Speaker of the US House of Representatives, Nancy Pelosi, in 2006, who as the youngest child of a then Baltimore mayor, had to keep her father's ledger on 'favours done and favours owed' to politicians in the city, when she was a teenager.

13 Basically, we use both rounds of the Comparative Study of Electoral Systems (CSES; see web links at the end of the chapter) and fit a probit model for each country-election observation. We fit the following model: Turnout = level of education + age + income + gender. Figure 18.2 reports marginal effects of the coefficient on education for each country-election observation on the Y-axis (actual percentages of turnout at the country-level are on the X-axis). Loosely speaking, these marginal effects indicate by how much the probability of an individual to vote changes when education is changed by one step (say, from 4 to 5).

Chapter 19

1 While the invention of the WWW predates the release of Mosaic (Tim Berners-Lee having published the blueprint proposal for it in 1990 and released the first version of a web browser in 1991), this browser (developed by Marc Andressen at the National Center for Supercomputing Applications) is considered to have launched the WWW into the public domain, integrating it for the first time with the Windows operating system, and thus bringing it to individuals' desk tops.

2 Usenet and listservs are asynchronous interactive forums where individuals exchange views via postings on particular topics (generally subject to moderator approval). While Usenet relies on users visiting the central location or 'bulletin board' to post and read messages, listservs deliver postings 'en masse' to users who have subscribed. Both predate the Web, the Usenet system first emerging in 1979 at Duke University in the US (Davis 2005: 8).

3 See the latest UN Global E-government Readiness Report 2005. Available at http://unpan1.un.org/intradoc/groups/public/documents/un/unpan021888.pdf (New York: UN, accessed 22 Nov. 2006).

4 Source: 'Internet Strukturdaten, Repräsentative Unfrage—IV. Quartal 2005' Forschungsgruppe Wahlen. Available at www.forschungsgruppe.de/Ergebnisse/Internet-Strukturdaten/web_IV_05.pdf.

5 For discussions of Web 2.0 origins and meaning see Tim O'Reilly, 'What is Web 2.0: Design Patterns and Business Models for the Next Generation of Software', 30 Sept. 2005: www.oreillynet.com/pub/a/oreilly/tim/news/2005/09/30/what-is-web-20.html (accessed 21 July 2006); 'Web 2.0' Wikipedia http:en.wikipedia.org/wiki/Web_2 (accessed 21 July 2006).

6 Blogs constitute perhaps the best known form of Web 2.0 software. Although variously defined, key components include a website containing dated entries, presented in reverse chronological order and some element of individual control/ownership (Pacquet 2003). A wiki (meaning 'super fast' in Hawaiian) refers to a hyper-text-based collaborative software that enables documents to be authored collectively using a web browser (Cunningham and Leuf 2001). Tagging is a mode of classifying an online resource (picture, article, or video clip) whereby keywords are assigned informally and personally by the author/creator of the item, leading to a flexible and dynamic user-based system of taxonomy and cross-referencing (see entry on Wikipedia http://en.wikipedia.org/wiki/Tag_%28metadata%29).

7 Source: L. Raine (2005) 'The State of Blogging', Pew Internet and American Life Project Report, available at www.pewinternet.org/pdfs/PIP_blogging_data.pdf.

Chapter 20

1 Dyson's (1980) proposition about the strength of a state is about how power is exercised. The strong state is characterized by an authoritative way of exercising power, while the weak state displays strong elements of pluralism, representation, and a debating culture.

2 A similar observation is also made by van Thiel (2006). In her study on the differences in the creation of quasi-autonomous organizations in the Netherlands, she finds support for her hypothesis that sectors have a dominant style of reform. Nonetheless, her analysis does not involve cross-country comparison so that we cannot say anything about national policy styles as compared to sector-specific ones.

Chapter 22

1 This idea of openness was later challenged by Cusack and Iversen (2000) who argued that deindustrialization is the decisive variable.

2 This was avoided in a few countries where demand-stimulating policies were combined with unusually tight incomes policies (e.g. in Austria, see Scharpf 1987; Hemerijck *et al.* 2000).

3 Esping-Andersen (1990) originally spoke of 'welfare **state** regimes' but because of increasing emphasis on the relationship between the state and the family in provision of care, this was later substituted by welfare regimes (Esping-Andersen 1999).

4 As pointed out by Korpi (2005), there are many other problems. The first generation of studies often failed to take account of initial settings (and thereby misinterpreted catching up effects). Such problems have increasingly been overcome, and complex multivariate techniques have made it possible to make more refined analyses. The analyses typically used in such studies are increasingly pooled time-series and cross-sectional analyses. Still, no sophisticated technique can solve the problem that the underlying data are often quite unreliable—even historical GDP data are continually revised (Korpi 2005).

5 Note that this discussion is about what gives meaning to policy elites—about the 'puzzling' of governments, experts, politicians etc.—not about discourses that give meaning to mass publics. Such discourses may be highly important in persuading voters/citizens to accept otherwise unpopular retrenchment policies (e.g. Cox 2001; Schmidt 2001, 2002), but this is not so much a matter of policy impact, but more a question of political communication.

Chapter 24

1 I have discussed the subject in two books (Sørensen 2001, 2004). Some formulations in this chapter draw on those works.

References

Aberbach, J. D., and Rockman, B. A. (2000) *In the Web of Politics: Three Decades of the US Federal Executive* (Washington, DC: Brookings Institution Press).

—— Putnam, R. D., and Rockman, B. A. (1981) *Bureaucrats and Politicians in Western Democracies* (Cambridge, Mass.: Harvard University Press).

Aboura, S. (2005) 'French Media Bias and the Vote on the European Constitution', *European Journal of Political Economy*, 21(4): 1093–8.

Acemoglou, D., and Robinson, J. A. (2006) *Economic Origins of Dictatorship and Democracy* (Cambridge: Cambridge University Press).

Adcock, R., and Collier, D. (2001) 'Measurement Validity: A Common Standard for Quantitative and Qualitative Research', *American Political Science Review*, 95: 529–46.

Adema, W. (1999) *Net Social Expenditure*, Labour Market and Social Policy Occasional Paper, 39 (Paris: OECD).

—— and Ladaique, M. (2005) *Net Social Expenditure*. Social, Employment and Migration Paper, 29 (Paris: OECD).

Aja, E. (2004) 'Spain: Nation, Nationalities, and Regions', in Loughlin *et al.* 2004.

Akdeniz, Y. (2000) 'Policing the Internet: Regulation and Censorship', in R. Gibson and S. Ward (eds.), *Reinvigorating Democracy? British Politics and the Internet* (Aldershot: Ashgate), 169–88.

Alber, J. (1982) *Vom Armenhaus zum Wohlfahrtsstaat. Analysen zur Entwicklung der Sozialversicherung in Westeuropa* (Frankfurt am Main: Campus).

Albrow, M. (1996) *The Global Age: State and Society Beyond Modernity* (Oxford and Cambridge: Polity Press).

Aldrich, J. H. (1993) 'Rational Choice and Turnout', *American Journal of Political Science*, 37(1): 246–78.

—— (1995) *Why Parties? The Origin and Transformation of Political Parties in America* (Chicago: University of Chicago Press).

Alexander, G. (2002) *The Sources of Democratic Consolidation* (Ithaca, NY: Cornell University Press).

Allan, J., and Scruggs, L. (2006) 'The Material Consequences of Welfare States: Benefit Generosity and Absolute Poverty in 16 OECD Countries', *Comparative Political Studies*, 39(7): 880–904.

Allison, G. T. (1971) *Essence of Decision* (Boston: Little, Brown).

Almond, G. A. (1966) 'Comparative Political Systems', *Journal of Politics*, 18(3): 391–409.

—— (1966) 'Political Theory and Political Science', *American Political Science Review*, 60: 869–79.

—— (1988) 'The Return to the State', *American Political Science Review*, 82(3): 853–74.

—— (1990) *A Discipline Divided: Schools and Sects in Political Science* (London: Sage).

—— (1996) *Political Science: The History of the Discipline*, in Goodin and Klingemann 1996: 50–96.

—— and Powell, G. B., Jr. (1967) *Comparative Politics: A Developmental Approach* (Boston: Little, Brown).

—— —— and Mundt, R. J. (1993) *Comparative Politics: A Theoretical Framework* (New York: Harper Collins College Publishers).

—— —— Strøm, K., and Dalton, R. J. (2004) *Comparative Politics Today: A World View* (New York: Pearson Longman, 8th edn).

—— and Verba, S. (1963) *The Civic Culture: Political Attitudes and Democracy in Five Nations* (Princeton: Princeton University Press).

—— and —— (eds) (1980) *The Civic Culture Revisited* (Boston: Little, Brown).

Alter, P. (1994) *Nationalism* (London: Edward Arnold, 2nd edn).

Alvarez, R. M., Garrett, G., and Lange, P. (1991) 'Government Partisanship, Labor Organization, and Macroeconomic Performance', *American Political Science Review*, 85(2): 539–56.

Amadae, S. M., and Bueno de Mesquita, B. (1999) 'The Rochester School: The Origins of Positive Political Economy', *Annual Review of Political Science*, 2: 269–95.

Amalrik, A. A. (1970) *Kann die Sowjetunion das Jahr 1984 erleben?* (Zurich: Diogenes).

Amenta, E. (2003) 'What we Know about the Development of Social Policy: Comparative and Historical Research in Comparative and Historical Perspective', in J. Mahoney and D. Rueschemeyer (eds.), *Comparative Historical Analysis in the Social Sciences* (Cambridge: Cambridge University Press), 91–130.

Ames, B. (2002) *The Deadlock of Democracy in Brazil* (Michigan: Michigan University Press).

Amin, A. (1999) 'An Institutionalist Perspective on Regional Economic Development', *International Journal of Urban and Regional Research*, 23(2): 365–78.

Andersen, J. G. (2002) 'Work and Citizenship: Unemployment and Unemployment Policies in Denmark, 1980–2000', in J. G. Andersen and P. H. Jensen (eds.), *Changing Labour Markets, Welfare Policies and Citizenship* (Bristol: Policy Press), 59–84.

—— (2007) 'The Danish Welfare State as "Politics for Markets": Combining Equality and Competitiveness in a Global Economy', *New Political Economy*, 12(1): 71–8.

—— and Christiansen, P. M. (1991) *Skatter uden velfærd* (Taxes without welfare)(Copenhagen: Jurist- og Økonomforbundets Forlag).

Andersen, L. (2006) 'Veje til flere i arbejde' (Ways to increase employment), in J. H. Petersen and K. Petersen (eds.), *13 Løsninger for den danske velfærdsstat* (13 solutions for the

Danish welfare state) (Odense: Southern Denmark University Press), 65–76.

Anderson, B. (1983) *Imagined Communities: Reflections on the Origin and Spread of Nationalism* (London: Verso, rev. edns. in 1991 and 2006).

Anderson, C. (1998) 'When in Doubt, Use Proxies: Attitudes towards Domestic Politics and Support for European Integration', *Comparative Political Studies*, 31(5): 569–601.

Anderson, C. J., and Beramendi, P. (2008) 'Income Inequality and Electoral Participation', in P. Bezamendi and C. J. Anderson (eds.), *Democracy, Inequality and Representation* (New York: Russell Sage Foundation).

Anderson, H. D., and Davidson, P. E. (1943) *Ballots and the Democratic Class Struggle: A Study in the Background of Political Education* (Stanford, Calif.: Stanford University Press).

Anderson, J. E. (2003) *Public Policymaking* (Boston: Houghton Mifflin Co.).

Anderson, L. (1991) 'Absolutism and the Resilience of Monarchy in the Middle East', *Political Science Quarterly*, 106(1): 1–15.

Anderson, P. (2007) 'Russia's Managed Democracy', *London Review of Books*, 29(2).

Andeweg, R. (1997) 'Collegiality and Collectivity: Cabinets, Cabinet Committees and Cabinet Ministers', in P. Weller, H. Bakevits, and R. A. W. Rhodes (eds.), *The Hollow Crown: Countervailing Trends in Core Executives* (London: Macmillan).

—— (2000) 'Ministers as Double Agents? The Delegation Process between Cabinet and Ministers', *European Journal of Political Research*, 37: 377–95.

—— (2005) 'The Netherlands: The Sanctity of Proportionality', in Gallagher and Mitchell 2005: 491–510.

Ansolabehere, S., de Figueiredo, J. M., and Snyder, J. M. (2003) 'Why is there so Little Money in US Politics?', *Journal of Economic Perspectives*, 17(1): 105–30.

—— Snyder, J. M., and Ueda, M. (2004) 'Did Firms Profit from Soft Money?', *Election Law Journal*, 3(2): 193–8.

Arentsen, M. J. (2003) 'The Invisible Problem and How to Deal with it: National Policy Styles in Radiation Protection Policy in the Netherlands, England and Belgium', in M.-L. Bemelmans-Videc, R. C. Rist, and E. Vedung (eds.), *Carrots, Sticks and Sermons: Policy Instruments and their Evaluation* (New Brunswick, NJ and London: Transaction Publishers), 211–30.

Armingeon, K., and Beyeler, M. (eds.) (2004) *The OECD and European Welfare States* (Cheltenham: Edward Elgar).

Arts, W., and Gelissen, J. (2002) 'Three Worlds of Welfare Capitalism or More? A State-of-the-Art Report', *Journal of European Social Policy*, 12(2): 137–58.

Asher, H. B. (2001) *American Labor Unions in the Electoral Arena* (Lanham, Md.: Rowman & Littlefield).

Ashford, D. (1977) 'Political Science and Policy Studies: Toward a Structural Solution', *Policy Studies Journal*, 5: 570–83.

Åslund, A., and McFaul, M. (eds.) (2006) *Revolution in Orange* (Washington, DC: Carnegie Endowment for International Peace).

Atkinson, A. B. (1999) *The Economic Consequences of Rolling back the Welfare State* (Cambridge, Mass.: MIT Press).

Auer, A. (2001) 'General Conclusion', in Auer and Bützer 2001: 345–55.

—— and Bützer, M. (eds.) (2001) *Direct Democracy: The Eastern and Central European Experience* (Aldershot: Ashgate).

Auer, P. (2000) *Employment Revival in Europe: Labour Market Success in Austria, Denmark, Ireland and the Netherlands* (Geneva: ILO).

Austen-Smith, D., and Wright, J. R. (1994) 'Counteractive Lobbying', *American Journal of Political Science*, 38(1): 25–44.

—— and —— (1996) 'Theory and Evidence for Counteractive Lobbying', *American Journal of Political Science*, 40(2): 543–64.

Axelrod, R. (1984) *The Evolution of Cooperation* (New York: Basic Books).

Aya, R. (1990) *Rethinking Revolutions and Collective Violence: Studies on Concept, Theory and Method* (Amsterdam: Het Spinhuis).

Ayoob, M. (1995) *The Third World Security Predicament* (Boulder, Colo.: Lynne Rienner).

Bache, I., and Flinders, M. (2004) *Multi-Level Governance* (Oxford: Oxford University Press).

Bachrach, P., and Baratz, M. S. (1962) 'Two Faces of Power', *American Political Science Review*, 56: 947–52.

Badie, B., and Birnbaum, P. (1983 [1979]) *The Sociology of the State* (Chicago: University of Chicago Press).

Bagehot, W. (1889) *The Works of Walter Bagehot* (Hartford, Conn.: Travelers Insurance Companies).

Bairoch, P. (1985) *De Jéricho à Mexico: Villes et économie dans l'histoire* (Paris: Gallimard).

Balassa, B. (1961) *The Theory of Economic Integration* (Homewood, Ill.: Richard D. Irwin).

Baldersheim, H., and Ståhlberg, K. (eds.) (1994) *Towards the Self-Regulating Municipality: Free Communes and Administrative Modernization in Scandinavia* (Aldershot: Ashgate).

Baldwin, P. (1990) *The Politics of Social Solidarity: Class Bases of the European Welfare State 1875–1975* (Cambridge: Cambridge University Press).

Balkin, J. (2005) 'Wrong the Day it was Decided: Lochner and Constitutional Historicism', *Boston University Law Review*, 85: 677–725.

Banaszak, L. A. (1996) *Why Movements Succeed or Fail: Opportunity, Culture and the Struggle for Women's Suffrage* (Princeton: Princeton University Press).

Banfield, E. (1958) *The Moral Basis of a Backward Society* (New York: Free Press).

Bannerji, H. (2000) *The Dark Side of Nation: Essays on Multiculturalism and Gender* (Toronto: Canadian Scholar's Press).

Barber, J. D. (1992) *Presidential Character: Predicting Performance in the White House* (Englewood Cliffs, NJ: Prentice-Hall, 4th edn).

Bardach, E. (1976) 'Policy Termination as a Political Process', *Policy Sciences*, 7: 123–31.

—— (1977) *The Implementation Game: What Happens After a Bill Becomes a Law* (Cambridge: MIT Press).

Barnes, S. H., and Kaase, M. (1979) *Political Action: Mass Participation in Five Western Democracies* (London: Sage Publications).

Barros, R. (2002) *Constitutionalism and Dictatorship: Pinochet, the Junta, and the 1980 Constitution* (Cambridge: Cambridge University Press).

Barry, B. (2000) *Culture and Equality: An Egalitarian Critique of Multiculturalism* (Cambridge: Polity Press).

Bartolini, S. (1993) 'On Time and Comparative Research', *Journal of Theoretical Politics*, 5(2): 131–67.

—— (2000) *The Political Mobilization of the European Left, 1860–1980: The Class Cleavage* (Cambridge: Cambridge University Press).

—— and Mair, P. (1990) *Identity, Competition and Electoral Availability: The Stabilisation of European Electorates 1885–1985* (Cambridge: Cambridge University Press).

—— Caramani, D., and Hug, S. (1998) *Parties and Party Systems: A Bibliographical Guide to the Literature on Parties and Party Systems in Europe since 1945* (London: Sage).

Bastian, S., and Luckham, R. (eds.) (2003) *Can Democracy be Designed? The Politics of Institutional Choice in Conflict-Torn Societies* (London: Zed Books).

Bates, R. H. (1981) *Markets and States in Tropical Africa: The Political Basis of Agricultural Policies* (Berkeley, Calif.: University of California Press).

Bates, R., Greif, A., Levi, M., Rosenthal, J.-L., and Weingast, B. (2002) *Analytic Narratives* (Princeton: Princeton University Press).

Bauer, M. W. (2006) 'Politikbeendigung als policyanalytisches Konzept', *Politische Vierteljahresschrift*, 47(2): 147–68.

Bauer, R. A., and Bauer, A. H. (1960) 'America, Mass Society and Mass Media', *Journal of Social Issues*, 10(3): 3–66.

—— Sola Pool., I. de, and Dexter, L. A. (1963) *American Business and Public Policy: The Politics of Foreign Trade* (New York: Atherton Press).

Baumgartner, F. R. (1994) 'Attention, Boundary Effects, and Large-Scale Policy Change in Air Transportation Policy', in D. A. Rochefort and R. W. Cobb (eds.), *The Politics of Problem Definition: Shaping the Policy Agenda* (Lawrence, Kan.: University of Kansas Press), 50–66.

—— and Jones, B. D. (1991) 'Agenda Dynamics and Policy Subsystems', *Journal of Politics*, 53(4): 1044–74.

—— and —— (1993) *Agendas and Instability in American Politics* (Chicago: University of Chicago Press).

—— and Leech, B. L. (1996a) 'The Multiple Ambiguities of "Counteractive Lobbying"', *American Journal of Political Science*, 40(2): 521–42.

—— and —— (1996b) 'Good Theories Deserve Good Data', *American Journal of Political Science*, 40(2): 565–9.

—— and —— (1998) *Basic Interests: The Importance of Groups in Politics and in Political Science* (Princeton: Princeton University Press).

—— and —— (2001) 'Interest Niches and Policy Bandwagons: Patterns of Interest Group Involvement in National Politics', *Journal of Politics*, 63(4): 1191–213.

Baylis, J., and Smith, S. (2005) *The Globalization of World Politics* (Oxford: Oxford University Press, 3rd edn).

Beck, N. (2001) 'Time-Series Cross-Section Data: What have we Learned in the Past Few Years?', *Annual Review of Political Science*, 4: 271–93.

Beer, S. H. (1965) *British Politics in the Collectivist Age* (New York: Knopf).

—— and Ulam, A. B. (eds.) (1958) *Patterns of Government: The Major Political Systems of Europe* (New York: Random House).

Behn, R. D. (2001) *Rethinking Democratic Accountability* (Washington, DC: Brookings Institution Press).

Béland, D. (2006) 'The Politics of Social Learning: Finance, Institutions, and Pensions Reform in the United State and Canada', *Governance*, 19(4): 559–83.

Bell, D. (1965) *The End of Ideology: On the Exhaustion of Political Ideas in the Fifties* (Glencoe, Ill.: Free Press).

—— (1973) *The Coming of Post-Industrial Society* (New York: Basic Books).

Bell, D. A. (ed.) (2004) *Race, Racism and American Law* (New York: Aspen Publishers).

Bendix, R. (1960) *Max Weber: An Intellectual Portrait* (Garden City, NY: Doubleday).

Benedetto, G., and Hix, S. (2007) 'The Rejected, the Dejected and the Ejected: Explaining Government Rebels in the 2001–05 British House of Commons', *Comparative Political Studies*, 40: 755–81.

Bennett, C. (1991) 'What is Policy Convergence and What Causes it?', *British Journal of Political Science*, 21: 215–33.

Bennett, C. J., and Howlett, M. (1992) 'The Lessons of Learning: Reconciling Theories of Policy Learning and Policy Change', *Policy Sciences*, 25(3): 275–94.

Benoit, K. (2005) 'Hungary: Holding Back the Tiers', in Gallagher and Mitchell 2005: 231–52.

—— (2006a) 'Duverger's Law and the Study of Electoral Systems', *French Politics*, 4(1): 69–83.

—— (2006b) 'Electoral Laws as Political Consequences: Explaining the Origins and Change of Electoral Institutions', *Annual Review of Political Science*, 10: 101–36.

—— and Laver, M. (2006) *Party Policy in Modern Democracies* (London: Routledge).

Bentley, A. F. (1908) *The Process of Government: A Study of Social Pressures* (Chicago: University of Chicago Press).

—— (1949) *The Process of Government: A Study of Social Pressures* (Evanston, Ill.: Principia Press of Illinois).

Berglund, S., and Thomsen, S. (eds.) (1990) *Modern Political Ecological Analysis* (Åbo: Åbo Akademis Förlag).

Berg-Schlosser, D. (ed.) (2004) *Democratization: The State of the Art* (Wiesbaden: VS Verlag für Sozialwissenschaften).

—— and Meur, G. de (1996) 'Conditions of Authoritarianism, Fascism, and Democracy in Interwar Europe: Systematic Matching and Contrasting of Cases for "Small N" Analysis', *Comparative Political Studies*, 29(4): 423–68.

Berman, L. (2006) *The Art of Political Leadership: Essays in Honor of Fred I. Greenstein* (Lanham, Md.: Rowman & Littlefield).

Bernstein, S., and Cashore, B. (2000) 'Internationalization and Domestic Policy Change: The Case of Eco-forestry Policy Change in British Columbia, Canada', *Canadian Journal of Political Science*, 33(1): 67–99.

Berry, F. S., and Berry, W. D. (1990) 'State Lottery Adoptions as Policy Innovations: An Event History Analysis', *American Political Science Review*, 84(2): 395–415.

Berry, J. M. (1977) *Lobbying for the People: The Political Behavior of Public Interest Groups* (Princeton: Princeton University Press).

—— (1997) *The Interest Group Society* (New York: Longman, 3rd edn).

—— (1999) *The New Liberalism: The Rising Power of Citizen Groups* (Washington, DC: Brookings Institution Press).

Bertola, G., Boeri, T., and Cazes, S. (1999) *Employment Protection and Labour Market Adjustments in OECD Countries: Evolving Institutions and Variable Enforcement*, Employment and Training Papers, 48 (Geneva: Employment and Training Department, ILO).

Bertrand, J. (2004) *Nationalism and Ethnic Conflict in Indonesia* (Cambridge: Cambridge University Press).

Betz, H.-G. (1994) *Radical Right-Wing Populist in Western Europe* (New York: St Martin's Press).

Beyme, K. von (1988) *Der Vergleich in der Politikwissenschaft* (Munich: Piper).

—— (1998) *The Legislator: German Parliament as a Centre of Political Decision-Making* (Aldershot: Ashgate).

Bickerton, J. (1990) *Nova Scotia, Ottawa, and the Politics of Regional Development* (Toronto: University of Toronto Press).

—— (1999) 'Regionalism in Canada', in J. Bickerton and A.-G. Gagnon (eds.), *Canadian Politics* (Peterborough, Ont.: Broadview Press, 3rd edn), 209–38.

—— (2007) 'Between Integration and Fragmentation: Political Parties and the Representation of Regions', in A.-G. Gagnon and B. Tanguay (eds.), *Canadian Parties in Transition* (Peterborough, Ont.: Broadview Press, 3rd edn), 411–35.

—— Gagnon, A.-G., and Smith, P. (1999) *Ties that Bind: Parties and Voters in Canada* (Toronto: Oxford University Press).

Biezen, I. van (2003) *Political Parties in New Democracies: Party Organization in Southern and East-Central Europe* (Basingstoke: Palgrave).

—— and Caramani, D. (2006) '(Non)Comparative Politics in Britain', *Politics*, 26: 29–37.

Biller, R. P. (1976) 'On Tolerating Policy and Organization: Some Design Considerations', *Policy Sciences*, 7: 133–49.

Bimber, B. (1998) 'The Internet and Political Transformation: Populism, Community, and Accelerated Pluralism', *Polity*, 31(1): 133–60.

—— (2001) 'Information and Political Engagement in America: The Search for Effects of Information Technology at the Individual Level', *Political Research Quarterly*, 54(1): 53–67.

—— (2003) *Information and American Democracy: Technology in the Evolution of Political Power* (New York: Cambridge University Press).

—— and Davis, R. (2003) *Campaigning Online* (New York: Oxford University Press).

Binder, S. H. (2003) *Stalemate* (Washington, DC: Brookings Institution Press).

Birch, A. H. (1967) *Representative and Responsible Government* (London: Allen & Unwin).

Birkland, T. A. (2001) *An Introduction to the Policy Process: Theories, Concepts, and Model of Public Policy Making* (Armonk, NY: M. E. Sharpe).

Björn, L. (1979) 'Labor Parties, Economic Growth, and Redistribution in Five Capitalist Countries', *Comparative Social Research*, 2: 93–128.

Black, D. (1948) 'On the Rationale of Group Decision-Making', *Journal of Political Economy*, 56: 23–34.

Blais, A. (2006) 'What Affects Voter Turnout?', *Annual Review of Political Science*, 9(1): 111–25.

—— and Dion, S. (eds.) (1991) *The Budget-Maximizing Bureaucrat: Appraisals and Evidence* (Pittsburgh: University of Pittsburgh Press).

—— and Dobrzynska, A. (1998) 'Turnout in Electoral Democracies', *European Journal of Political Research*, 33: 239–56.

—— Gidengil, E., Nevitte, N., and Nadeau, R. (2004) 'Where does Turnout Decline Come from?', *European Journal of Political Research*, 43: 221–49.

—— Massicotte, L., and Dobrzynska, A. (1997) 'Direct Presidential Elections: A World Summary', *Electoral Studies*, 16(4): 441–55.

Blanchard, O., and Katz, L. F. (1996) 'What we know and do not know about the natural rate of unemployment', *Journal of Economic Perspectives*, 11(1): 51–72.

—— and Summers, L. H. (1986) 'Hysteresis and the European Unemployment Problem', in S. Fischer (ed.), *NBER Macroeconomics Annual*, 1 (Fall): 15–78.

Blondel, J. (1970) 'Legislative Behaviour: Some Steps toward a Cross-National Measurement', *Government and Opposition*, 5(1): 67–85.

—— (1988) 'Introduction: Western European Cabinets in Comparative Perspective', in J. Blondel and F. Müller-Rommel (eds.), *Cabinets in Western Europe* (London: Macmillan).

—— and Cotta, M. (eds.) (1996) *Party and Government* (London: Macmillan).

—— and —— (eds.) (2000) *The Nature of Party Government* (Houndmills: Palgrave).

—— and Müller-Rommel, F. (eds.) (1993) *Governing Together* (London: Macmillan).

—— and —— (eds.) (1997) *Cabinets in Western Europe* (London: Macmillan, 2nd edn).

Blumer, H. (1933) *Movies and Conduct* (New York: Macmillan).

—— and Hauser, P. (1933) *Movies, Delinquency and Crime* (New York: Macmillan).

Blumler, J. G., and McQuail, D. (1968) *Television in Politics: Its Use and Influence* (London: Faber).

Blyth, M. (2002) *Great Transformations: Economic and Institutional Change in the Twentieth Century* (Cambridge: Cambridge University Press).

Boccalini, T. (1614) *Ragguagli di Parnaso: Centuria Prima* (Milan: Battista Bidelli).

Bogaards, M. (2000) 'The Uneasy Relationship between Empirical and Normative Types in Consociational Theory', *European Journal of Political Research*, 12: 395–423.

—— (2008) 'Measuring Democracy through Election Outcomes: A Critique with African Data', *Comparative Political Studies* (forthcoming).

Bogdani, M., and Loughlin, J. (2007) *Albania and the European Union: The Tumultuous Journey towards Integration and Accession* (London: Tauris).

Boix, C. (1999) 'Setting the Rules of the Game: The Choice of Electoral Systems in Advanced Democracies', *American Political Science Review*, 93(3): 609–24.

Bolingbroke, H. St John, Viscount (1841) *The Works of Lord Bolingbroke* (Philadelphia: Carey & Hart).

Bonchek, M. (1995) 'Grassroots in Cyberspace', paper presented at 53rd Annual Meeting of the Midwest Political Science Association, 6 April, Chicago.

Bonoli, G. (2000) *The Politics of Pension Reform* (Cambridge: Cambridge University Press).

—— (2001) 'Political Institutions, Veto Points, and the Process of Welfare State Adaptation', in Pierson 2001: 238–64.

Borre, O., and Scarbrough, E. (1995) *The Scope of Government* (Oxford: Oxford University Press).

Bosso, C. J. (1987) *Pesticides and Politics: The Life Cycle of a Public Issue* (Pittsburgh: University of Pittsburgh Press).

Botero, G. (1589) *Della Ragion di Stato* (Turin: UTET, 1948 repr.).

Bourdieu, P. (1986) 'The Forms of Capital', in J. G. Richardson (ed.), *Handbook of Theory and Research for the Sociology of Education* (New York: Greenwood Press), 241–58.

—— and Wacquant, L. J. D. (1992) *An Invitation to Reflexive Sociology* (Cambridge: Polity Press).

Bovens, M., t'Hart, P. and Peters, B. G. (eds.) (2001) *Success and Failure in Public Governance* (Cheltenham: Edgar Elgar).

Bowler, S., and Donovan, T. (1998) *Demanding Choices: Opinion, Voting, and Direct Democracy* (Ann Arbor, Mich.: University of Michigan Press).

—— and Farrell, D. M. (eds.) (1992) *Electoral Strategies and Political Marketing* (Houndmills: Macmillan).

—— —— and Katz, R. S. (eds.) (1999) *Party Discipline and Parliamentary Government* (Columbus: Ohio State University Press).

—— —— and Pettit, R. T. (2005*b*) 'Expert Opinion on Electoral Systems: So Which Electoral System is "Best"?', *Journal of Elections, Public Opinion, and Parties*, 15(1): 3–19.

—— —— and Tolbert, C. J. (eds.) (1998) *Citizens as Legislators: Direct Democracy in the United States* (Columbus: Ohio State University Press).

—— —— and Van Heerde, J. (2005*a*) 'The United States of America: Perpetual Campaigning in the Absence of Competition', in Gallagher and Mitchell 2005: 185–205.

Brady, D. (2005) 'The Welfare State and Relative Poverty in Rich Western Democracies, 1967–1997', *Social Forces*, 83(4): 1329–64.

—— Beckfield, J. and Stephens, J. D. (2004) 'The Comparative Welfare States Data Set, Update', www.lisproject.org/publications/welfaredata/welfareaccess.htm.

Brady, H. D., and Collier, D. (eds.) (2004) *Rethinking Social Enquiry: Diverse Tools, Shared Standards* (Lanham, Md.: Rowman & Littlefield).

Brady, H. E., Verba, K., and Schlozman, L. (1995) 'Beyond SES: A Resource Model of Political Participation', *American Political Science Review*, 89: 271–94.

Braun, D., and Busch, A. (1999) *Public Policy and Political Ideas* (Cheltenham: Edward Elgar).

—— and Gilardi, F. (2006) Taking Galton's Problem Seriously: Towards a Theory of Policy Diffusion', *Journal of Theoretical Politics*, 18(3): 298–322.

Bräuninger, T., and Debus, M. (2007) *Legislative Agenda-Setting in Parliamentary Democracies*, Working Paper (Konstanz: University of Konstanz).

—— and König, T. (1999) 'The Checks and Balances of Party Federalism: German Federal Government in a Divided Legislature', *European Journal of Political Research*, 36(6): 207–34.

—— and —— (2001) *Indices of Power: IOP 2.0* [computer program] (www.uni-konstanz.de/FuF/Verwiss/koenig/IOP.html) (Konstanz: University of Konstanz).

Bredgaard, T., Larsen, F., and Madsen, P. K. (2005) *The Flexible Danish Labour Market: A Review*, CARMA Research Papers, 1 (Aalborg: Aalborg University).

Brehm, J., and Gates, S. (1997) *Working, Shirking, and Sabotage* (Ann Arbor, Mich.: University of Michigan Press).

Brenner, N. (eds.) (2003) *State/Space: A Reader* (Oxford: Basil Blackwell).

Brenner, R. (1977) 'The Origin of Capitalist Development: A Critique of Neo-Smithian Marxism', *New Left Review*, 104 (July–Aug.): 25–92.

Brooker, P. (1995) *Twentieth-Century Dictatorships* (Basingstoke: Macmillan).

—— (1997) *Defiant Dictatorships: Communist and Middle-Eastern Dictatorships in a Democratic Age* (Basingstoke: Macmillan).

—— (2000) *Non-Democratic Regimes: Theory, Government and Politics* (Basingstoke: Macmillan).

Brooks, S. M. (2005) 'Interdependent and Domestic Foundations of Policy Change: The Diffusion of Pension Privatization around the World', *International Studies Quarterly*, 49(2): 273–94.

Brouillaud, C. (2005) 'La Ligue du Nord et les politiques publiques italiennes: Influence, instrumentalisation et échecs (1991–2004)', in *Les partis régionalistes en Europe: Des acteurs en développement?* (Brussels: Éditions de l'Université de Bruxelles), 119–46.

Browne, W. P. (1998) 'Exchange Theory and the Institutional Impetus for Interest Group Formation', in A. J. Cigler and B. A. Loomis (eds.) *Interest Group Politics* (Washington, DC: Congressional Quarterly Press, 6th edn).

Brusis, M. (2002) 'Between EU Requirements, Competitive Politics and National Traditions: Recreating Regions in the Accession Countries of Central and Eastern Europe', *Governance: An International Journal of Policy, Administration and Institutions*, 15(4): 531–59.

Brym, R. (ed.) (1986) *Regionalism in Canada* (Richmond Hill, Ont: Irwin).

Buchanan, J. M. (1977) 'Why does Government Grow?', in T. Borcherding (ed.), *Budgets and Bureaucrats: The Sources of Government Growth* (Durham, NC: Duke University Press), 3–18.

Buchanan, J. M. and Tullock, G. (1962) *The Calculus of Consent: Logical Foundations of Constitutional Democracy* (Ann Arbor, Mich.: University of Michigan Press).

Budge, I. (2000) 'Deliberative Democracy versus Direct Democracy—Plus Political Parties!', in M. Saward (ed.) *Democratic Innovation* (London: Routledge).

—— (2001) 'Political Parties in Direct Democracy', in Mendelsohn and Parkin 2001: 67–87.

—— and Farlie, D. (1977) *Voting and Party Competition* (London: Wiley).

—— and Klingemann, H.-D. (2001) 'Finally! Comparative Over-Time Mapping of Party Policy Movement', in I. Budge, H.-D. Klingemann, A. Volkens, J. Bara, and E. Tanenbaum (eds.), *Mapping Policy Preferences: Estimates for Parties, Electors and Governments 1945–1998* (Oxford: Oxford University Press), 75–90.

—— Crewe, I., and Farlie, D. (eds.) (1976) *Party Identification and Beyond: Representations of Voting and Party Competition* (London: Wiley).

Buechler, S. M. (2004) 'The Strange Career of Strain and Breakdown Theories of Collective Action', in Snow, Soule, and Kriesi 2004: 47–66.

Burgess, K., and Levitsky, S. (2003) 'Explaining Populist Party Adaptation in Latin America: Environmental and Organizational Determinants of Party Change in Argentina, Mexico, Peru, and Venezuela', *Comparative Political Studies*, 36(8): 881–911.

Burgess, M. (ed.) (1986) *Federalism and Federation in Western Europe* (London: Croom Helm).

—— and Gagnon, A.-G. (eds.) (1993) *Comparative Federalism and Federation: Competing Traditions and Future Directions* (New York and London: Harvester Wheatsheaf).

Burke, E. (1770) 'Thoughts on the Present Discontents', in *The Works of the Right Honourable Edmund Burke* (Boston: Little, Brown, 9th edn 1889), 433–551.

Burnell, P. (ed.) (2000) *Democracy Assistance: International Co-operation for Democratization* (London: Frank Cass).

—— (2005) 'Political Strategies of External Support for Democratization', *Foreign Policy Analysis*, 1(3): 361–84.

—— (2006a) 'Autocratic Opening to Democracy: Why Legitimacy Matters', *Third World Quarterly*, 27(4): 545–62.

—— (ed.) (2006b) *Globalizing Democracy: Party Politics in Emerging Democracies* (London: Routledge).

—— (2007) 'From Assessing Democracy Assistance to Appraising Democracy Promotion', *Political Studies* (forthcoming).

Burnham, P., Gilland, K., Grant, W., and Layton-Henry, Z. (2004) *Research Methods in Politics* (Basingstoke: Palgrave Macmillan).

Burns, N., Schlozman, K. L., and Verba, S. (2001) *The Private Roots of Public Action: Gender, Equality, and Political Participation* (Cambridge, Mass.: Harvard University Press).

Burstein, P. (1998) 'Interest Organizations, Political Parties, and the Study of Democratic Politics', in A. N. Costain and A. S. McFarland (eds.), *Social Movements and American Political Institutions: People, Passions, and Power* (Lanham, Md.: Rowman & Littlefield), 39–56.

Bussemaker, J., and Kersbergen, K. van (1994) 'Gender and Welfare States: Some Theoretical Reflections', in Sainsbury 1994: 8–25.

Butler, D., and Ranney, A. (1994a) 'Practice', in Butler and Ranney 1994b: 1–10.

—— and —— (eds.) (1994b) *Referendums around the World: The Growing Use of Direct Democracy* (Basingstoke: Macmillan).

Buzan, B. (1991) *People, States and Fear* (Hemel Hempstead: Harvester Wheatsheaf, 2nd edn).

Caenegem, R. C. (1995) *An Historical Introduction to Western Constitutional Law* (Cambridge: Cambridge University Press).

Caillaud, B., and Tirole, J. (2006) 'Consensus Building: How to Persuade a Group', unpublished.

Cairns, A. (1968) 'The Electoral System and the Party System in Canada, 1921–1965', *Canadian Journal of Political Science*, 1(1): 55–80.

—— (2004) 'First Nations and the Canadian Nation: Colonization and Constitutional Alienation', in J. Bickerton and A.-G. Gagnon (eds.), *Canadian Politics* (Peterborough, Ont.: Broadview Press, 4th edn), 349–67.

Caldeira, G., and Wright, J. R. (1988) 'Organized Interests and Agenda Setting in the US Supreme Court', *American Political Science Review*, 82(4): 1109–27.

—— and —— (1998) 'Lobbying for Justice: Organized Interests Supreme Court Nominations, and United States Senate', *American Journal of Political Science*, 42(2): 499–523.

—— *et al.* (1995) 'The Visibility of the Court of Justice in the European Union', paper for the 1995 APSA Meeting, Chicago.

Calmfors, L., and Driffill, J. (1988) 'Bargaining Structure, Corporatism and Macroeconomic Performance', *Economic Policy*, 6(1): 12–61.

—— and Holmlund, B. (2000) 'Den euroeiska arbetslösheten', *NOU* (Oslo): 21, appendix 4.

Cameron, A., and Palan, R. (2004) *The Imagined Economies of Globalization* (London: Sage).

Cameron, D. R. (1978) 'The Expansion of the Public Economy: A Comparative Analysis', *American Political Science Review*, 72(4): 1243–61.

—— (1984) 'Social Democracy, Corporatism, Labor Quiescence and the Representation of Economic Interests in Advanced Capitalist Society', in J. H. Goldthorpe (ed.), *Order and Conflict in Contemporary Capitalism* (Oxford: Oxford University Press), 143–78.

Cammack, P. (1997) 'Globalisation and Liberal Democracy', *European Review*, 6(2): 249–63.

Campbell, J. L. (1998) 'Institutional Analysis and the Role of Ideas in Political Economy', *Theory and Society*, 27: 377–409.

—— (2004) *Institutional Change and Globalization* (Princeton: Princeton University Press).

—— and Hall, J. A. (2006) 'Introduction: The State of Denmark', in J. L. Campbell, J. A. Hall, and O. K. Pedersen (eds.), *National Identity and the Varieties of Capitalism: The Danish Experience* (Copenhagen: DJØF Publishing), 1–49.

Capling, A., and Nossal, K. (2001) 'Death of Distance or Tyranny of Distance? The Internet, Deterritorialization, and the Anti-Globalization Movement in Australia', *Pacific Review*, 14(3): 443–65.

Capoccia, G. (2002) 'Anti-System Parties: A Conceptual Reassessment', *Journal of Theoretical Politics*, 14(1): 9–35.

—— (2005) *Defending Democracy: Reactions to Extremism in Interwar Europe* (Baltimore, Md.: Johns Hopkins University Press).

Caramani, D. (2000) *Elections in Western Europe since 1815: Electoral Results by Constituencies* (supplemented with CD-ROM) (London and New York: Palgrave).

—— (2004) *The Nationalization of Politics: The Formation of National Electorates and Party Systems in Western Europe* (Cambridge: Cambridge University Press).

—— (2008) *Introduction to the Comparative Method with Boolean Algebra* (Beverly Hills, Calif: Sage, 'Quantitative Applications in the Social Science').

Carey, J. M., and Shugart, M. S. (eds.) (1998) *Executive Decree Authority* (Cambridge: Cambridge University Press).

Carling, K., Holmlund, B., and Vejsiu, A. (2001) 'Do Benefits Cuts Boost Jobs Findings?', *Economic Journal*, 111: 766–90.

Carney, J. (1980) 'Regions in Crisis: Accumulation, Regional Problems and Crisis Formation', in J. Carney, R. Hudson, and J. Lewis (eds.), *Regions in Crisis: New Perspectives in European Regional Theory* (London: Croom Helm), 28–59.

Carothers, T. (2004) *Critical Mission: Essays on Democracy Promotion* (Washington, DC: Carnegie Endowment for International Peace).

—— (2006) 'The Backlash Against Democracy Promotion', *Foreign Affairs*, 85(1): 55–68.

Carter, N. (2003) 'Political Identity, Territory, and Institutional Change: The Case of Belgium', *Mobilization: An International Journal*, 8(2): 205–20.

Castells, M. (1998) *The Power of Identity* (Oxford: Blackwell).

Castles, F. G. (1978) *The Social Democratic Image of Society: A Study of the Achievements and Origins of Scandinavian Social Democracy in Comparative Perspective* (London: Routledge & Kegan Paul).

—— (1985) *The Working Class and Welfare: Reflections on the Political Development of the Welfare State in Australia and New Zealand, 1890–1980* (London: Allen & Unwin).

—— (1987) 'Comparative Public Policy Analysis: Problems, Progress and Prospects', in F. G. Castles, F. Lehner, and M. G. Schmidt (eds.), *Managing Mixed Economies* (Berlin and New York: Walter de Gruyter), 197–224.

—— (1989) 'Social Protection by Other Means: Australia's Strategy of Coping with External Vulnerability', in idem (ed.) *The Comparative History of Public Policy* (Cambridge: Polity Press), 16–55.

—— (ed.) (1993) *Families of Nations: Patterns of Public Policy in Western Democracy* (Aldershot: Dartmouth).

—— (1996) 'Needs-Based Strategies of Social Protection in Australia and New Zealand', in G. Esping-Andersen (ed.), *Welfare States in Transition: National Adaptations in Global Economies* (London: Sage), 88–115.

—— (1998) *Comparative Public Policy: Patterns of Post-War Transformation* (Cheltenham: Edgar Elgar).

—— and Mitchell, D. (1992) 'Identifying Welfare State Regimes: The Links between Politics, Instruments and Outcomes', *Governance*, 5(1): 1–26.

—— and Wildenmann, R. (1986) *Visions and Realities of Party Government* (Berlin: de Gruyter).

Caulfield, J. (2000) 'Local Government Finance in OECD Countries', paper presented to 'Local Government at the Millenium' International Seminar, 19 Feb., University of New South Wales.

Cavalli-Sforza, L. L. (2001) *Genes, Peoples and Languages* (London: Penguin).

Chadwick, A. (2006) *Internet Politics: States, Citizens, and New Communication Technologies* (New York: Oxford University Press).

—— and May, C. (2003) 'Interaction between States and Citizens in the Age of the Internet: "E-government" in the United States, Britain and the European Union', *Governance*, 16(2): 271–300.

Chambers, W. N. (1967) *The American Party Systems: Stages of Political Development* (New York: Oxford University Press).

Chang, W. H., Park, J.-J., and Shim, S. W. (1998) 'Effectiveness of Negative Political Advertising', *Web Journal of Mass Communication Research*, 2(1); available at www.scripps.ohiou.edu/wjmcr/vol02/2-1a-B.htm.

Chapman, K., and Walker, D. F. (1991) *Industrial Location: Principles and Policies* (Oxford: Blackwell, 2nd edn).

Chehabi, H. E., and Linz, J. J. (1998) *Sultanistic Regimes* (New York: Johns Hopkins University Press), chs. 1 and 2.

Cheibub, J. A. (2007) *Presidentialism, Parliamentarism, and Democracy* (Cambridge: Cambridge University Press).

—— Przeworski, A., and Saiegh, S. M. (2004) 'Government Coalitions and Legislative Success under Presidentialism and Parliamentarism', *British Journal of Political Science*, 34: 565–87.

Chhibber, P., and Kollman, K. (2004) *The Formation of National Party Systems: Federalism and Party Competition in Canada, Great Britain, India, and the United States* (Princeton: Princeton University Press).

Chilcote, R. H. (1994) *Theories of Comparative Politics: The Search for a Paradigm Reconsidered* (Boulder, Colo.: Westview Press, 2nd edn).

Chong, D. (1991) *Collective Action and the Civil Rights Movement* (Chicago: University of Chicago Press).

Chua, A. (2003) *World on Fire: How Exporting Free Market Democracy Breeds Ethnic Hatred and Global Instability* (New York: Doubleday).

Chwe, M. S.-Y. (2001) *Rational Ritual: Culture, Coordination, and Common Knowledge* (Princeton: Princeton University Press).

Clark, G. (1980) 'Capitalism and Regional Disparities', *Annals of the American Association of Geographers*, 70(2): 521–32.

Clayton, R., and Pontusson, J. (1998) 'Welfare-State Retrenchment Revisited: Entitlement Cuts, Public Sector Restructuring, and Inegalitarian Trends in Advanced Capitalist Societies', *World Politics*, 51(1): 67–98.

Clement, S. A., and Andersen, J. G. (2007) *Unemployment and Incentives: What do we Know? Micro-Level Evidence from Scandinavian Surveys*, CCWS Working Papers (forthcoming).

Cobb, R. W., and Elder, C. D. (1972) *Participation in American Politics: The Dynamics of Agenda-Building* (Baltimore, Md.: Johns Hopkins University Press).

Cobb, R. W., and Elder, C. D. (1983) *Participation in American Politics: The Dynamics of Agenda Building* (Baltimore, Md.: Johns Hopkins University Press, 2nd edn).

—— Ross, J.-K., and Ross, M.-K. (1976) 'Agenda Building as a Comparative Political Process', *American Political Science Review*, 70: 26–138.

Coen, D. (2007) *Lobbying the European Union: Institutions, Actors and Policy* (Oxford: Oxford University Press).

Cohen, M., March, J., and Olsen, J. (1972) 'A Garbage Can Model of Organizational Choice', *Administrative Science Quarterly*, 17(1): 1–25.

Coleman, J. S. (1990) *Foundations of Social Theory* (Cambridge, Mass.: Belknap Press of Harvard University Press).

Colley, L. (1992) *Britons: Forging the Nation, 1707–1837* (New Haven: Yale University Press).

Collier, D. (1991) 'New Perspectives on the Comparative Method', in D. A. Rustow and K. P. Ericksen (eds.), *Comparative Political Dynamics: Global Research Perspectives* (New York: Harper & Collins), 7–31.

—— (1993) 'The Comparative Method', in A. W. Finifter (ed.), *Political Science: The State of the Discipline II* (Washington, DC: APSA), 105–19.

—— and Adcock, R. (1999) 'Democracy and Dichotomies: A Pragmatic Approach to Choices about Concepts', *Annual Review of Political Science*, 2: 537–65.

—— and Levitsky, S. P. (1997) 'Democracy with Adjectives', *World Politics*, 49(3): 430–51.

—— and Mahon, J. E. Jr. (1993) 'Conceptual Stretching Revisited: Adapting Categories in Comparative Analysis', *American Political Science Review*, 87(4): 845–55.

Collier, R. B. (1999) *Paths toward Democracy: The Working Class and Elites in Western Europe and South America* (Cambridge: Cambridge University Press).

—— and Collier, D. (1991) *Shaping the Political Agenda: Critical Junctures, the Labor Movement and Regime Dynamics in Latin America* (Notre Dame, Ind.: University of Notre Dame Press).

Colomer, J. (ed.) (2004a) *Handbook of Electoral System Choice* (Basingstoke: Palgrave Macmillan).

—— (2004b) 'The Strategy and History of Electoral System Choice', in Colomer 2004a: 3–78.

—— (2005) 'It's Parties that Choose Electoral Systems (or, Duverger's Laws Upside Down)', *Political Studies*, 53(1): 1–21.

—— and Negretto, G. L. (2005) 'Can Presidentialism Work like Parliamentarianism?', *Government and Opposition*, 41.

Considine, M. (2005) *Making Public Policy: Institutions, Actors, Strategies* (Cambridge and Malden: Polity Press).

Copeland, G., and Patterson, S. (1994) *Parliaments in the Modern World* (Ann Arbor, Mich.: University of Michigan Press).

Coppedge, M., and Reinicke, W. H. (1990) 'Measuring Polyarchy', *Studies in Comparative International Development*, 25: 51–72.

Cortell, A. P., and Peterson, S. (1999) 'Altered States: Explaining Domestic Institutional Change', *British Journal of Political Science*, 29: 177–203.

Council of Europe (1985) *The European Charter of Local Self-Government* (http://conventions.coe.int/Treaty/EN/Reports/HTML/122.htm).

—— (2000) 'The Financial Resources of Local Authorities in Relation to their Responsibilities: A Litmus Test for Subsidiarity', 4th General Report on Political Monitoring of the Implementation of the European Charter of Local Self-Government, rapporteur Jean-Claude Frécon, Strasbourg, 20 Apr.

Cox, G. (1997) *Making Votes Count: Strategic Coordination in the World's Electoral Systems* (Cambridge: Cambridge University Press).

—— and Morgenstern, S. (2002) 'Epilogue: Latin America's Reactive Assemblies and Proactive Presidents', in Morgenstern and Nacif 2002.

Cox, R. H. (2001) 'The Social Construction of an Imperative: Why Welfare Reform Happened in Denmark and the Netherlands But Not in Germany', *World Politics*, 53(3): 463–98.

Crafts, N., and Toniolo, G. (1996) 'Postwar Growth: An Overview', in idem (eds.), *Economic Growth in Europe since 1945* (Cambridge: Cambridge University Press), 1–37.

Crawford, G. (2001) *Foreign Aid and Political Reform* (Basingstoke: Palgrave).

Crombez, C. (1997) 'Policy Making and Commission Appointment in the European Union', *Aussenwirtschaft*, 52(1–2): 63–82.

Crossman, R. H. S. (1963) 'Introduction', in W. Bagehot, *The English Constitution* (Glasgow: Collins).

—— (1972) *The Myths of Cabinet Government* (Cambridge, Mass.: Harvard University Press).

Cunningham, W., and Leuf, B. (2001) *The Wiki Way: Collaboration and Sharing on the Internet* (Boston, Mass.: Addison-Wesley Professional).

Curtis, J. E., Grabb, E. G., and Baer, D. E. (1992) 'Voluntary Association Membership in Fifteen Countries: A Comparative Analysis', *American Sociological Review*, 57(2): 139–52.

Cutright, P. (1965) 'Political Structure, Economic Development and National Social Security Programs', *American Journal of Sociology*, 70(5): 537–50.

Daalder, H. (1966) 'The Netherlands: Opposition in a Segmented Society', in R. Dahl 1966: 188–236.

—— (1991) *Paths towards State Formation in Europe: Democratization, Bureaucratization and Politicization*, Working paper 1991/20 (Madrid Instituto Juan March de Estudios e Investigaciones).

—— (ed.) (1997) *Comparative European Politics: The Story of a Profession* (London: Pinter).

—— (2002) 'The Development of the Study of Comparative Politics', in Keman 2002a: 16–31.

Dahl, R. A. (1956) *A Preface to Democratic Theory* (Chicago: University of Chicago Press).

—— (1961) *Who Governs?* (New Haven, Conn.: Yale University Press).

—— (ed.) (1966) *Political Oppositions in Western Democracies* (New Haven, Conn.: Yale University Press).

—— (1971) *Polyarchy* (New Haven, Conn.: Yale University Press).

—— (1989) *Democracy and its Critics* (New Haven, Conn.: Yale University Press).

—— (2000) 'A Democratic Paradox?', *Political Science Quarterly*, 115(1): 35–40.

—— (2002) *How Democratic is the American Constitution?* (New Haven, Conn.: Yale University Press).

D'Alessio, D. W. (1997) 'Use of the Web in the 1996 US Election', *Electoral Studies*, 16(4): 489–501.

D'Alimonte, R. (2005) 'Italy: A Case of Fragmented Bipolarism', in Gallagher and Mitchell 2005: 253–76.

Dalton, R. J. (1991) 'Comparative Politics of the Industrial Democracies: From the Golden Age to Island Hopping', in W. Crotty (ed.), *Political Science* (Evanston, Ill.: Northwestern University Press), 15–43.

—— (1996) 'Comparative Politics: Micro-Behavioral Perspectives' in Goodin and Klingemann 1966: 336–52.

—— (2002) *Citizen Politics: Public Opinion and Political Parties in Advanced Industrial Democracies* (Chatham, NJ: Chatham House Publishers/Seven Bridges Press, 3rd edn).

—— (ed.) (2004) *Democratic Challenges, Democratic Choices: The Erosion of Political Support in Advanced Industrial Democracies* (Oxford: Oxford University Press).

—— and Weldon, S. A. (2005) 'Public Images of Political Parties: A Necessary Evil?', *West European Politics*, 28(5): 931–51.

—— Flanagan, S., and Beck, P. A. (1985) *Electoral Change in Advanced Industrial Democracies: Realignment or Dealignment?* (Princeton: Princeton University Press).

Danzer, M. (2007) 'Regime Characteristics, and Government Attributes as Causes of Government Stability in Central Eastern Europe', unpublished manuscript, University of Mannheim.

Darcy, R., and Laver, M. (1990) 'Referendum Dynamics and the Irish Divorce Amendment', *Public Opinion Quarterly*, 54(1): 1–20.

Davieri, F., and Tabellini, G. (2000) 'Unemployment, Growth and Taxation in Industrial Countries', *Economic Policy*, 30(1): 49–90.

Davis, M. (1986) *Prisoners of the American Dream: Politics and Economy in the History of the US Working Class* (London: Verso).

Davis, R. (2005) *Politics Online: Blogs, Chatrooms, and Discussion Groups in American Democracy* (New York: Routledge).

Debus, M. (2007) *Pre-Electoral Alliances, Coalition Rejections, and Multiparty Governments* (Baden-Baden: Nomos).

De la Porte, C., Pochet, P., and Room, G. (2001) 'Social Benchmarking, Policy Making and the Instruments of New Governance', *Journal of European Social Policy*, 11(4): 291–307.

Delcamp, A., and Loughlin, J. (eds.) (2003) *La Decentralisation dans les États de l'Union européenne* (Paris: La Documentation Française).

DeLeon, P. (1978) 'A Theory of Policy Termination', in J. May and A. Wildavsky (eds.), *The Policy Cycle* (Beverly Hills, Calif.: Sage), 279–300.

Della Porta, D., and Diani, M. (1999) *Social Movements: An Introduction* (Oxford and Malden, Mass.: Blackwell).

—— Kriesi, H., and Rucht, D. (eds.) (1999) *Social Movements in a Globalizing World* (London: Macmillan).

Delwitt, P. (2005) 'Les Partis régionalistes, des acteurs politico-électoraux en essor? Performances électorales et participations gouvernementales', in *Les Partis régionalistes en Europe: Des Acteurs en Développement?* (Brussels: Éditions de l'Université de Bruxelles), 51–84.

Deng, Y. (1998) 'The Chinese Conception of National Interests in International Relations', *China Quarterly*, 154: 308–29.

Denver, D., and Hands, G. (2000) ' "Post-Fordism" in the Constitutencies: The Continuing Development of Constituency Campaigning in Britain', in D. Farrell and R. Schmitt-Beck (eds.), *Do Political Campaigns Matter?* (London: Routledge).

Deszõ, M. (2001) 'Plebiscites and Referendums', in Auer and Bützer 2001: 264–70.

Deudney, D., and Ikenberry, G. J. (1999) 'The Nature and Sources of Liberal International Order', *Review of International Studies*, 25(2): 179–96.

Deutsch, K. (1966a) *Nationalism and Social Communication: An Inquiry into the Foundations of Nationality* (Cambridge, Mass.: MIT Press).

—— (1966b) *The Nerves of Government: Models of Political Communication and Control* (New York: Free Press).

—— Lasswell, H. D., Merritt, R. L., and Russett, B. M. (1966) 'The Yale Political Data Program', in Merritt and Rokkan 1966: 81–94.

De Vreese, C. H. (2006) 'Political Parties in Dire Straits? Consequences of National Referendums for Political Parties', *Party Politics*, 12(5): 581–98.

—— and Semetko, H. A. (2004) *Political Campaigning in Referendums: Framing the Referendum Issue* (Abingdon: Routledge).

De Winter, L. (2005) 'Belgium: Empowering Voters or Party Elites?', in Gallagher and Mitchell 2005: 417–32.

De Zeeuw, J., and Kumar, K. (eds.) (2006) *Promoting Democracy in Post-Conflict Societies* (Boulder, Colo.: Lynne Rienner).

Diamond, L. (1999) *Developing Democracy* (Baltimore, Md.: Johns Hopkins University Press).

—— (2005) *Squandered Victory: The American Occupation and the Bungled Effort to Bring Democracy to Iraq* (New York: Henry Holt & Co.).

—— and Morlino, L. (eds.) (2005) *Assessing the Quality of Democracy* (Baltimore, Md.: Johns Hopkins University Press).

Diani, M., and Bison, I. (2004) 'Organizations, Coalitions, and Movements', *Theory and Society*, 3: 281–309.

Dicken, P. (1998) *Global Shift: Transforming the World Economy* (London: Paul Chapman).

DiMaggio, P. J., and Powell, W. W. (1991) 'The Iron Cage Revisited: Institutionalised Isomorphism and Collective Rationality in Organizational Fields', in idem (eds.), *The New Institutionalism in Organizational Analysis* (Chicago: Chicago University Press), 63–82.

Dippel, H. (2005) 'Modern Constitutionalism: A History in the Need of Writing', *Legal History Review*, 73(1–2): 153–70.

Disney, R. (2000) *Fiscal Policy and Employment*, i. *A Survey of Macroeconomic Models, Methods and Findings* (Washington, DC: IMF).

Dobbin, F. (1994) *Forging Industrial Policy: The United States, Britain, and France in the Railway Age* (Cambridge: Cambridge University Press).

Dogan, M. (1975) *The Mandarins of Western Europe: The Political Roles of Top Civil Servants* (London: Sage).

—— and Pelassy, D. (1990) *How to Compare Nations: Strategies in Comparative Politics* (Chatham, NJ: Chatham House, 2nd edn.).

—— and Rokkan, S. (eds.) (1969) *Quantitative Ecological Analysis in the Social Sciences* (Cambridge, Mass.: MIT Press).

Dolowitz, D. (1997) 'British Employment Policy in the 1980s: Learning from the American Experience', *Governance*, 10(1): 23–42.

—— (2000) 'Learning from Abroad: The Role of Policy Transfer in Contemporary Policy Making', *Governance*, 13: 5–24.

—— and Marsh, D. (1996) 'Who Learns What from Whom: A Review of the Policy Transfer Literature', *Political Studies*, 44: 343–57.

Donovan, T., and Bowler, S. (1998) 'Responsive or Responsible Government?', in Bowler *et al.* 1998: 249–73.

—— and Karp, J. A. (2006) 'Popular Support for Direct Democracy', *Party Politics*, 12(5): 671–88.

Doorenspleet, R. (2000) 'Reassessing the Three Waves of Democratization', *World Politics*, 52(3): 384–406.

—— (2005) *Democratic Transitions: Exploring the Structural Sources of the Fourth Wave* (Boulder, Colo.: Lynne Rienner).

Döring, H. (ed.) (1995) *Parliaments and Majority Rule in Western Europe* (Frankfurt and New York: Campus).

—— (2001) 'Parliamentary Agenda Control and Legislative Outcomes in Western Europe', *Legislative Studies Quarterly*, 26: 145–66.

—— and Hallerberg, M. (2004) *Patterns of Parliamentary Behavior: Passage of Legislation across Western Europe* (Burlington, Vt.: Ashgate).

Douglas, M. (1978) *Cultural Bias* (London: Royal Anthropological Institute).

Downs, A. (1957) *An Economic Theory of Democracy* (New York: Harper & Row).

—— (1967) *Inside Bureaucracy* (Boston: Little, Brown & Co.).

Drezner, D. W. (2001) 'Globalization and Policy Convergence', *International Studies Review*, 3: 53–78.

Droysen, J. G. (1858) *Historik* (Darmstadt: Wissenschaftliche Buchgesellschaft, 1969 repr.).

Druckman, J. N., and Roberts, A. (2007) 'Communist Successor Parties and Coalition Formation in Eastern Europe', *Legislative Studies Quarterly*, 32: 5–31.

Dunleavy, P. (1991) *Democracy, Bureaucracy and Public Choice* (New York: Harvester Wheatsheaf).

—— and Bastow, S. (2001) 'Modelling Coalitions that Cannot Coalesce: A Critique of the Laver-Shepsle Approach', *West European Politics*, 24: 1–26.

—— and Rhodes, R. A. W. (1990) 'Core Executive Studies in Britain', *Public Administration*, 68: 3–28.

Dunn, W. N. (1999) *Public Policy Analysis* (Englewood Cliffs, NJ: Prentice-Hall).

Dunning, J. (2000) 'The New Geography of Foreign Direct Investment', in N. Woods (ed.), *The Political Economy of Globalisation* (London: Macmillan), 20–54.

Durkheim, É. (1950) *Les Règles de la Méthode Sociologique* (Paris: PUF, 11th edn.).

—— (1964) *The Division of Labor in Society* (New York: Free Press, 1st publ. 1893).

Duverger, M. (1954) *Political Parties* (New York: John Wiley).

—— (ed.) (1988) *Les Régimes Sémi-Présidentiels* (Paris : PUF).

Dye, T. R. (1966) *Politics, Economics, and the Public: Policy Outcomes in the American States* (Chicago: Rand McNally).

—— (2005) *Understanding Public Policy* (Upper Saddle River, NJ: Pearson/Prentice-Hall).

Dyson, E. (1998) *Release 2: A Design for Living in the Digital Age* (New York: Broadway Books).

Dyson, K. (1980). *The State Tradition in Western Europe: A Study of an Idea and Institution* (Oxford: Martin Robertson).

Easton, D. (1953) *The Political System: An Inquiry into the State of Political Science* (New York: Knopf).

—— (1957) 'An Approach to the Study of Political Systems', *World Politics*, 9(5): 383–400.

—— (1965a) *A Framework for Political Analysis* (Englewood Cliffs, NJ: Prentice-Hall).

—— (1965b) *A Systems Analysis of Political Life* (New York: Wiley).

Ebbinghaus, B. (2005) 'When Less is More: Selection Problems in Large-N and Small-N Cross-National Comparisons', *International Sociology*, 20(2): 133–52.

—— and Manow P. (eds.) (2001) *Comparing Welfare Capitalism: Social Policy and Political Economy in Europe, Japan and the USA* (London: Routledge).

Eisinger, P. K. (1973) 'The Conditions of Protest Behavior in American Cities', *American Political Science Review*, 67: 11–28.

Ekiert, G., Kubik J., and Vachudova, M. A. (2007) 'Democracy in the Post-Communist World: An Unending Quest?', *East European Politics and Societies*, 21(1): 7–30.

Elazar, D. J. (1966) *American Federalism: A View from the States* (New York: Thomas Y. Crowell).

—— (ed.) (1991) *Federal Systems of the World: A Handbook of Federal, Confederal and Autonomy Arrangements* (Harlow: Longman Current Affairs).

—— (1995) *Federalism: An Overview* (Pretoria: HSRC Publishers).

Elgie, R. (1998) 'The Classification of Democratic Regime Types: Conceptual Ambiguity and Contestable Assumptions', *European Journal of Political Research*, 33(2): 219–38.

—— (ed.) (1999) *Semi-Presidentialism in Europe* (Oxford: Oxford University Press).

—— (ed.) (2001) *Divided Government in Comparative Perspective* (Oxford: Oxford University Press).

—— (2005) 'France: Stacking the Deck', in Gallagher and Mitchell 2005: 119–36.

Elkins, D., and Simeon, R. (1974) 'Regional Political Cultures in Canada', *Canadian Journal of Political Science*, 6(3): 397–437.

—— and —— (1979) 'A Cause in Search of an Effect: Or What does Political Culture Explain?', *Comparative Politics*, 11: 127–45.

—— and —— (eds.) (1980) *Small Worlds: Provinces and Parties in Canadian Political Life* (Agincourt, Ontario: Methuen).

Elkins, Z., and Simmons, B. (2005) 'On Waves, Clusters and Diffusions: A Conceptual Framework', in J. Jordana and D. Levi-Faur (eds.), *The Rise of Regulatory Capitalism: The Global Diffusion of a New Order* (Special Issue: The Annals of the American Academy of Political and Social Science, 598; Thousand Oaks, Calif.: Sage), 33–51.

Elklit, J. (2005) 'Denmark: Simplicity Embedded in Complexity (or is it the Other Way Round?)', in Gallagher and Mitchell 2005: 453–72.

Ellis, R., and Wildavsky, A. (1987) *Dilemmas of Presidential Leadership: From Washington through Lincoln* (Somerset, NJ: Transaction).

Elmeskov, J., and MacFarland, M. (1993) 'Unemployment Persistence', OECD Economic Studies, 21 (Paris: OECD), 59–88.

—— Martin, J., and Scarpetta S. (1998) 'Key Lessons for Labour Market Reforms: Evidence from OECD Countries' Experiences', *Swedish Economic Policy Review*, 5(2): 205–52.

Encarnación, O. G. (2001) 'Civil Society and the Consolidation of Democracy in Spain', *Political Science Quarterly*, 116(1): 53–79.

Enyedi, Z. (2006) 'Party Politics in Post-Communist Transition', in R. S. Katz and W. Crotty (eds.), *Handbook of Party Politics* (London: Sage), 228–38.

Epp, C. (1998) *The Rights Revolution: Lawyers, Activists, and Supreme Courts in Comparative Perspective* (Chicago: University of Chicago Press).

Epstein, L. D. (1967) *Political Parties in Western Democracies* (New York: Praeger).

—— (1986) *Political Parties in the American Mold* (Madison, Wis.: University of Wisconsin Press).

Esping-Andersen, G. (1985a) *Politics Against Markets: The Social Democratic Road to Power* (Princeton: Princeton University Press).

—— (1985b) 'Power and Distributional Regimes', *Politics and Society*, 14: 223–56.

—— (1990) *The Three Worlds of Welfare Capitalism* (Cambridge: Polity Press).

—— (1996) 'After the Golden Age? Welfare State Dilemmas in a Global Economy', in G. Esping-Andersen (ed.), *Welfare States in Transition. National Adaptations in Global Economies* (London: Sage), 1–31.

—— (1999) *Social Foundations of Post-Industrial Economies* (Oxford: Oxford University Press).

—— (2000) 'Who is Harmed by Labour Market Regulations?', in G. Esping-Andersen and M. Regini (eds.), *Why Deregulate Labour Markets?* (Oxford: Oxford University Press), 66–98.

—— (ed.) (2002) *Why We Need a New Welfare State* (Oxford: Oxford University Press).

Estevez-Abe, M., Iversen T., and Soskice D. (2001) 'Social Protection and the Formation of Skills: A Reinterpretation of the Welfare State', in Hall and Soskice 2001b: 145–83.

Etzioni, A. (1990) *The Moral Dimension: Toward a New Economics* (New York: Free Press).

European Commission (2006) *Allocation of 2005 EU Expenditure by Member State* (Brussels: European Commission).

Evans, P. B. (1995) *Embedded Autonomy: States and Industrial Transformation* (Princeton: Princeton University Press).

Fabbrini, S., and Donà, A. (2003) 'Europeanisation as Strengthening of Domestic Executive Power? The Italian Experience and the Case of "Legge Comunitaria"', *Journal of European Integration*, 25(1): 31–50.

Fallows, D. (2003) 'Spam: How it is Hurting Email and Degrading Life on the Internet', Pew Internet and American Life Project, Washington DC. Available at www.pewinternet.org/pdfs/PIP_Spam_Report.pdf.

Falter, J., and Klingemann H.-D. (1998) 'Die deutsche Politikwissenschaft im Urteil der Fachvertreter', in M. T. Greven (ed.), *Demokratie eine Kultur des Westens?* (Wiesbaden: Westdeutscher Verlag), 306–41.

Fanon, F. (1966) *The Wretched of the Earth* (New York: Grove Press).

Farnsworth, S. J., and Owen, D. (2004) 'Internet Use and the 2000 Presidential Election', *Electoral Studies*, 23(3): 415–29.

Farrell, B. (1971) *Chairman or Chief? The Role of the Taoiseach in Irish Government* (Dublin: Gill & Macmillan).

Farrell, D. M. (2001) *Electoral Systems: An Introduction* (Basingstoke: Palgrave).

—— (2006) 'Political Parties in a Changing Campaign Environment', in R. Katz and W. Crotty (eds.), *Handbook of Party Politics* (London: Sage), 122–33.

—— and Webb, P. (2000) 'Political Parties as Campaign Organizations', in R. Dalton and M. Wattenberg (eds.), *Comparing Democracies: Elections and Voting in Global Perspective* (Thousand Oaks, Calif.: Sage).

—— and McAllister, I. (2005) 'Australia: The Alternative Vote in a Compliant Political Culture', in Gallagher and Mitchell 2005.

—— and Schmitt-Beck, R. (eds.) (2002) *Do Campaigns Matter?* (London: Routledge).

Fauré, M. (1994) 'Methodological Problems in Comparative Politics', *Journal of Theoretical Politics*, 6(3): 307–22.

Fearon, J. D., and Laitin, D. D. (1996) 'Explaining Interethnic Cooperation', *American Political Science Review*, 90(4): 715–35.

Feick, J., and Jann, W. (1988) ' "Nations Matter": Vom Eklektizismus zur Integration in der vergleichenden Policy-Forschung?', in M. G. Schmidt (ed.), *Staatstätigkeit Special Issue Politische Vierteljahresschrift*, 19 (Opladen: Leske & Budrich), 196–220.

Ferrara, F., Herron E. S., and Nishikawa, M. (2005) *Mixed Electoral Systems: Contamination and its Consequences* (Basingstoke: Palgrave Macmillan).

Ferree, M. M., and McClurg Mueller, C. (2004) 'Feminism and the Women's Movement: A Global Perspective', in Snow, Soule, and Kriesi 2004: 576–607.

Ferree, M. M., Gamson, W. A., Gerhards J., and Rucht, D. (2002) *Shaping Abortion Discourse: Democracy and the Public Sphere in Germany and the United States* (Cambridge: Cambridge University Press).

Ferrera, M. (1996) 'The "Southern Model" of Welfare in Social Europe', *Journal of European Social Policy*, 6(1): 17–37.

—— (1997) 'Introduction Génerale', *MIRE: Comparer les Systèmes de Protection Sociale en Europe du Sud* (Paris: Ministère Affaire Sociales), 15–26.

—— (2005) *The Boundaries of Welfare: European Integration and the New Spatial Politics of Social Protection* (Oxford: Oxford University Press).

Finer, H. (1932) *The Theory and Practice of Modern Government* (London: Methuen).

Finer, S. E. (1958) *Anonymous Empire: A Study of the Lobby in Great Britain* (London: Pall Mall Press).

—— (1970) *Comparative Government* (London: Allen Lane).

—— (1976) *The Man on Horseback: The Role of the Military in Politics* (Harmondsworth: Penguin, 1st publ. 1962).

—— (1997) *The History of Government*, 3 vols (Oxford: Oxford University Press).

Finkel, S. E., Pérez-Liñán, A., Seligson, M. A., with Azpuru D. (2006) *Effects of US Foreign Assistance on Democracy Building: Results of a Cross-National Quantitative Study*, Final Report (www.usaid.gov).

Finnemore, M., and Sikkink, K. (2001) 'Taking Stock: The Constructivist Research Program in International Relations and Comparative Politics', *Annual Review of Political Science*, 4: 391–416.

Fiorina, M. (1996) *Divided Government* (Boston: Allyn & Bacon, 2nd edn)

Fischer, F. (2003) *Reframing Public Policy: Discursive Politics and Deliberative Practices* (Oxford: Oxford University Press).

Flora, P. (1974) *Modernisierungsforschung: Zur empirischen Analyse der gesellschaftlichen Entwicklung* (Opladen: Westdeutscher Verlag).

—— (1977) *Quantitative Historical Sociology: A Trend Report and Bibliography* (The Hague and Paris: Mouton).

—— (ed.) (1986) *Growth to Limits: The Western European Welfare States since World War II*, 4 vols. (Berlin: de Gruyter).

—— and Alber, J. (1981) 'Modernization, Democratization, and the Development of Welfare States in Western Europe', in P. Flora and A. J. Heidenheimer (eds.), *The Development of Welfare States in Europe and America* (New Brunswick, NJ, and London: Transaction Books), 37–80.

—— and Heidenheimer, A. J. (1981) 'Introduction', in idem (eds.), *The Development of Welfare States in Europe and America* (New Brunswick, NJ, and London: Transaction Books), 17–34.

Florida, R. (2003) *The Rise of the Creative Class* (New York: Basic Books).

Foley, M. (1993) *The Rise of the British Presidency* (Manchester: Manchester University Press).

—— (2000) *The British Presidency: Tony Blair and the Politics of Public Leadership* (Manchester: Manchester University Press).

Føllesdal, A., and Hix, S. (2006) 'Why there is a Democratic Deficit in the EU: A Response to Majone and Moravcsik', *Journal of Common Market Studies*, 44(3): 533–62.

Foot, K. A., and Schneider, S. M. (2002) 'Online Action in Campaign 2000: An Exploratory Analysis of the US Political Web Sphere', *Journal of Broadcast and Electronic Media*, 46(2): 222–44.

—— and —— (2006), *Web Campaigning* (Cambridge, Mass.: MIT Press).

Forbes, E. (1979) *The Maritime Rights Movement, 1919–1927: A Study in Canadian Regionalism* (Montreal: McGill-Queen's University Press).

Förster, M., and d'Ercole, M. M. (2005) *Income Distribution and Poverty in OECD Countries in the Second Half of the 1990s*, OECD Social, Employment and Migration Working Papers, 22 (Paris: OECD).

Forsyth, M. (1981) *Union of States: The Theory and Practice of Confederation* (Leicester: Leicester University Press).

Foucault, M. (1969) *L'Archéologie du savoir* (Paris: Gallimard).

Franklin, B. (1995) 'Packaging Politics: Causes and Consequences for Britain's Media Democracy', in J. Lovenduski and J. Stanyer (eds.), *Contemporary Political Studies 1995: Proceedings of the Annual Conference of the Political Studies Association of the UK* (Belfast: Political Studies Association of the UK), 582–92.

Franklin, M. N. (1992) 'The Decline of Cleavage Politics', in M. N. Franklin, T. Mackie, and H. Valen (eds.), *Electoral Change: Responses to Evolving Social and Attitudinal Structures in Western Countries* (Cambridge: Cambridge University Press), 383–405.

—— (1999) 'Electoral Engineering and Cross-National Turnout Differences: What Role for Compulsory Voting?', *British Journal of Political Science*, 29(1): 205–16.

—— (2002) 'Learning from the Danish Case: A Comment on Palle Svensson's Critique of the Franklin Thesis', *European Journal of Political Research*, 41(5): 751–7.

—— (2004) *Voter Turnout and the Dynamics of Electoral Competition in Established Democracies since 1945* (Cambridge: Cambridge University Press).

—— Lyons, P., and Marsh, M. (2004) 'Generational Basis of Turnout Decline in Established Democracies', *Acta Politica*, 39: 115–51.

Franz, M. M. (2005) 'Choices and Changes: Interest Groups and the Electoral Process', Ph.D. thesis, University of Wisconsin, Madison.

Freeman, G. P. (1985) 'National Styles and Policy Sectors: Explaining Structured Variation', *Journal of Public Policy*, 5(4): 467–96.

Freud, S., and Bullitt, W. C. (1967) *Thomas Woodrow Wilson: A Psychological Portrait* (Boston: Houghton Mifflin).

Fried, R. (1966) *Comparative Political Institutions* (New York: Macmillan).

Friedrich, C. J. (1950) *Constitutional Government and Democracy: Theory and Practice in Europe and America* (Boston: Ginn).

—— (1963) *Man and His Government* (New York: McGraw-Hill).

Fukuyama, F. (1992) *The End of History and the Last Man* (New York: Free Press).

—— (1995) *Trust: The Social Virtues and the Creation of Prosperity* (London: Hamish Hamilton).

Gabel, M. J. (1998) *Interests and Integration: Market Liberalization, Public Opinion, and European Union* (Ann Arbor, Mich.: University of Michigan Press).

Gagnon, A.-G., and Hérivault, J. (2007) 'The Bloc Québécois: Charting New Territories?', in Gagnon and Tanguay (eds.) (2007) *Canadian Parties in Transition* (Peterborough, Ont.: Broadview Press), 111–36.

——and Iacovino, R. (2007) *Federalism, Citizenship and Quebec: Debating Multinationalism* (Toronto: University of Toronto Press).

——and Lachapelle, G. (1996) 'Québec Confronts Canada: Two Competing Projects Searching for Legitimacy', *Publius*, 26/3: 177–91.

——and Tully, J. (eds.) (2001) *Multinational Democracies* (Cambridge: Cambridge University Press).

Galbraith, J. K., Conceicao, P., and Ferreira, P. (1999) 'Inequality and Unemployment in Europe: The American Cure', *New Left Review*, 237 (Sept.–Oct.): 28–51.

Gallagher, M. (1991) 'Proportionality, Disproportionality, and Electoral Systems', *Electoral Studies*, 10(1): 33–51.

——(1996) 'Conclusion', in Gallagher and Uleri 1996: 226–52.

——(2005a) 'Conclusion', in Gallagher and Mitchell 2005: 535–78.

——(2005b) 'Ireland: The Discreet Charm of PR-STV', in Gallagher and Mitchell 2005: 511–32.

——and Mitchell, P. (eds.) (2005) *The Politics of Electoral Systems* (Oxford: Oxford University Press).

——and Uleri, P. V. (eds.) (1996) *The Referendum Experience in Europe* (Basingstoke: Macmillan).

——Laver, M., and Mair, P. (2005) *Representative Government in Modern Europe* (New York: McGraw-Hill, 4th edn)

Gallie, D. (1983) *Social Inequality and Class Radicalism in France and Britain* (Cambridge: Cambridge University Press).

——and Paugam, S. (eds.) (2000a) *Welfare Regimes and the Experience of Unemployment in Europe* (Oxford: Oxford University Press).

——and ——(2000b) 'The Experience of Unemployment in Europe: The Debate', in D. Gallie and S. Paugam (eds.), *Welfare Regimes and the Experience of Unemployment in Europe* (Oxford: Oxford University Press), 1–24.

Gambetta, D. (1993) *The Sicilian Mafia: The Business of Private Protection* (Cambridge, Mass.: Harvard University Press).

——(2005) *Making Sense of Suicide Missions* (Oxford: Oxford University Press).

Gamson, W. (1968) *Power and Discontent* (Homewood, Ill.: Dorsey Press).

——(1975) *The Strategy of Social Protest* (Homewood, Ill: Dorsey).

——and Meyer, D. S. (1996) 'Framing Political Opportunity', in McAdam, McCarthy, and Zald 1996: 275–90.

——Croteau, D., Hoynes, W., and Sasson, T. (1992) 'Media Images and the Social Construction of Reality', *Annual Review of Sociology*, 18: 373–93.

Ganz, M. (2000) 'Resources and Resourcefulness: Strategic Capacity in the Unionization of California Agriculture, 1959–1966', *American Journal of Sociology*, 105(4): 1003–62.

Gardbaum, S. (2001) 'The New Commonwealth Model of Constitutionalism', *American Journal of Comparative Law*, 49(4): 707–61.

Garon, S. (1987) *The State and Labor in Modern Japan* (Berkeley, Calif.: University of California Press).

Garrett, B. (2001) 'China Faces, Debates, the Contradictions of Globalization', *Asian Survey*, 41(3): 409–27.

Garrett, G. (1998) *Partisan Politics in the Global Economy* (Cambridge: Cambridge University Press).

——and Mitchell, D. (2001) 'Globalization, Government Spending and Taxation in the OECD', *European Journal of Political Research*, 39(2): 145–77.

——and Nickerson, D. (2005) 'Globalization, Democratization, and Government Spending in Middle-Income Countries', in Glatzer and Rueschemeyer 2005: 23–48.

Garry, J., Marsh, M., and Sinnott, R. (2005) ' "Second-Order" Versus "Issue-Voting" Effects in EU Referendums: Evidence from the Irish Nice Treaty Referendums', *European Union Politics*, 6(2): 201–21.

Geertz, C. (1973) *The Interpretation of Cultures: Selected Essays* (New York: Basic Books).

Gerring, J., and Baresi, P. A. (2003) 'Putting Ordinary Language to Work: A Min-Max Strategy of Concept Formation in the Social Sciences', *Journal of Theoretical Politics*, 15: 201–32.

——Thacker, S. C., and Moreno, C. (2005) 'Centripetal Democratic Governance: A Theory and Global Inquiry', *American Political Science Review*, 99(4): 567–81.

Gershman, C., and Allen, M. (2006) 'The Assault on Democracy Assistance', *Journal of Democracy*, 17(2): 36–51.

Gerston, L. N. (2004) *Public Policy Making: Process and Principles* (Armonk, NY: M. E. Sharpe).

Geva-May, I. (2004) 'Riding the Wave Opportunity: Termination in Public Policy', *Journal of Public Administration Research and Theory*, 14: 309–33.

Geys, B. (2006) 'Explaining Voter Turnout: A Review of Aggregate-Level Research', *Electoral Studies*, 25(4): 637–63.

Gibbins, R. (1980) *Prairie Politics and Society: Regionalism in Decline* (Toronto: Butterworths).

——(2004a) 'Constitutional Politics', in J. Bickerton and A.-G. Gagnon (eds.), *Canadian Politics* (Peterborough, Ont.: Broadview Press, 4th edn), 127–44.

——(2004b) 'Regional Integration and National Contexts: Constraints and Opportunities', in S. Tomblin and C. Colgan (eds.), *Regionalism in a Global Society: Persistence and Change in Atlantic Canada and New England* (Peterborough, Ont.: Broadview Press), 37–56.

——(2005) 'Early Warning, No Response: Alan Cairns and Electoral Reform', in G. Kernerman and P. Resnick (eds.), *Insiders and Outsiders: Alan Cairns and the Reshaping of Canadian Citizenship* (Vancouver: University of British Columbia Press), 39–50.

——and Berdahl, L., (2003) *Western Visions, Western Futures: Perspectives on the West in Canada* (Peterborough: Broadview Press, 2nd edn).

Gibson, R. K. (2004) 'Web Campaigning from a Global Perspective', *Asia Pacific Review*, 11(1): 95–126.

——and McAllister, I. (2006) 'Does Cybercampaigning Win Votes? Online Political Communication in the 2004 Australian Election', *Journal of Elections Public Opinion and Parties*, 16(3): 243–64.

Gibson, R. K. and Römmele, A. (2001) 'A Party-Centered Theory of Professionalized Campaigning', *Harvard International Journal of Press/Politics*, 6(4): 31–44.

—— and Ward, S. (1998) 'UK Political Parties and the Internet: Politics as Usual in the New Media?', *Harvard International Journal of Press/Politics*, 3(3): 14–38.

—— and —— (2000) 'A Proposed Methodology for Measuring the Function and Effectiveness of Party and Candidate Websites', *Social Science Computer Review*, 18(3): 301–19.

—— and —— (2002) 'Virtual Campaigning: Australian Parties and the Internet', *Australian Journal of Political Science*, 35(1): 99–122.

—— Margolis, M., Resnick, D., and Ward, S. (2003a) 'Election Campaigning on the WWW in the US and the UK: A Comparative Analysis', *Party Politics*, 9(1): 47–76.

—— Römmele, A., and Ward, S. (2003b) 'German Parties and Internet Campaigning in the 2002 Federal Election', *German Politics*, 12(1): 79–108.

——, Ward, S., and Lusoli, W. (2003) 'The Internet and Political Campaigning: The New Medium Comes of Age?', *Representation*, 39(3): 166–80.

—— —— and —— (2005) 'Online Participation in the UK: Testing a Contextualised Model of Internet Effects', *British Journal of Politics and International Relations*, 7(4): 561–83.

Giddens, A. (1990) *The Consequences of Modernity* (Cambridge: Polity Press).

—— (1994) *Beyond Left and Right: The Future of Radical Politics* (Stanford, Calif.: Stanford University Press).

—— (2000) *Runaway World* (London: Profile Books).

Ginsburg, T. (2003), *Judicial Review in New Democracies: Constitutional Courts in Asian Cases* (Cambridge: Cambridge University Press).

Gilardi, F., Jordana, J., and Levi-Faur, D. (2006) *Regulation in the Age of Globalization: The Diffusion of Regulatory Agencies across Europe and Latin America*, Working Paper (Barcelona: IBEI).

Gilbert, N. (2002) *Transformation of the Welfare State: The Silent Surrender of Public Responsibility* (Oxford: Oxford University Press).

Gilpin, R. (2002) 'The Nation-State in the Global Economy', in D. Held and A. McGrew (eds.), *The Global Transformations Reader* (Cambridge: Polity Press), 349–58.

Gitlin, T. (1980) *The Whole World is Watching: Mass Media in the Making and Unmaking of the New Left* (Berkeley, Calif.: University of California Press).

Giugni, M. G. (1998) 'Was it Worth the Effort? The Outcomes and Consequences of Social Movements', *Annual Review of Sociology*, 98: 171–93.

—— McAdam, D., and Tilly, C. (eds.) (1999) *How Social Movements Matter* (Minneapolis: University of Minnesota Press).

Glatzer, M., and Rueschemeyer, D. (eds.) (2005) *Globalization and the Future of the Welfare State* (Pittsburgh: University of Pittsburgh Press).

Godwin, R. K., and Sheldon, B. J. (1998) 'What Corporations Really Want from Government: The Public Provision of Private Goods', in A. J. Cigler and B. A. Loomis (eds.), *Interest Group Politics* (Washington, DC: Congressional Quarterly Press, 6th edn).

Goldstein, K. M. (1999) *Interest Groups, Lobbying, and Participation in America* (New York: Cambridge University Press).

Goldthorpe, J. (2000) *On Sociology: Numbers, Narratives, and the Integration of Research and Theory* (Oxford: Oxford University Press).

Goodin, R. E., and Klingemann, H.-D. (eds.) (1996) *A New Handbook of Political Science* (Oxford: Oxford University Press).

—— and LeGrand, J. (1987) *Not Only the Poor: The Middle Classes and the Welfare State* (London: Allen & Unwin).

—— Headey, B., Muffels, R., and Dirven, H.-J. (1999) *The Real Worlds of Welfare Capitalism* (Cambridge: Cambridge University Press).

Goodwin, J. (2001) *No Other Way Out: States and Revolutionary Movements, 1945–1991* (Cambridge, Mass.: Cambridge University Press).

—— and Jasper, J. M. (1999) 'Caught in a Winding, Snarling Vine: The Structural Bias of Political Process Theory', *Sociological Forum*, 14(1): 27–92.

Grant, W. (2000) *Pressure Groups and British Politics* (New York: St Martin's Press).

Gray, V. (1973) 'Innovation in the States: A Diffusion Study', *American Political Science Review*, 67: 1174–85.

Green, A., and Kohl, R. (2007) 'Challenges of Evaluating Democracy Assistance: Perspectives from the Donor Side', *Democratization*, 14(1): 151–65.

Green, D., and Shapiro, I. (1994) *Pathologies of Rational Choice: A Critique of Applications in Political Science* (New Haven, Conn.: Yale University Press).

Green-Pedersen, C. (2001) 'Welfare-State Retrenchment in Denmark and the Netherlands, 1982–1998: The Role of Party Competition and Party Consensus', *Comparative Political Studies*, 34(9): 963–85.

—— (2004) 'The Dependent Variable Problem within the Study of Welfare-State Retrenchment: Defining the Problem and Looking for Solutions', *Journal of Comparative Policy Analysis*, 6(1): 3–14.

—— (2007) 'The Conflict of Conflicts in Comparative Perspective: Euthanasia as a Political Issue in Denmark, Belgium, and the Netherlands', *Comparative Politics*, 39(3): 273–91.

—— and Haverland, M. (2002) 'The New Politics and Scholarscip of the Welfare State', *Journal of European Social Policy*, 12(1): 43–51.

Greenwood, J. (2003) *Interest Representation in the European Union* (Basingstoke: Palgrave).

Greider, W. (1977) *One World Ready or Not: The Manic Logic of Global Capitalism* (New York: Simon & Schuster).

Grier, K. B., and Munger, M. C. (1993) 'Comparing Interest Group PAC Contributions to House and Senate Incumbents, 1980–1986', *Journal of Politics*, 55(3): 615–43.

Griffin, L. J., O'Connell, P. J., and McCammon, H. J. (1989) 'National Variation in the Context of Struggle: Postwar Class Conflict and Market Distribution in the Capitalist Democracies', *Canadian Review of Sociology and Anthropology*, 26: 37–68.

Gros, J.-G. (1996) 'Towards a Taxonomy of Failed States in the New World Order', *Third World Quarterly*, 17(3): 455–71.

Grossman, L. K. (1995) *The Electronic Republic: Reshaping Democracy in the Information Age* (New York: Viking).

Grossman, S. J., and Hart, O. D. (1983) 'An Analysis of the Principal–Agent Problem', *Econometrica*, 51(1): 7–46.

Grzymala-Busse, A. (2006) 'The Discreet Charm of Formal Institutions: Postcommunist Party Competition and State Oversight', *Comparative Political Studies*, 39(3): 271–300.

Guéhenno, J.-M. (1995) *The End of the Nation-State* (Minneapolis and London: University of Minnesota Press).

Guibernau, M. (1996) *Nationalisms: The Nation-State and Nationalism in the Twentieth Century* (Cambridge: Polity).

—— (2006) 'National Identity, Devolution and Secession in Canada, Britain and Spain', *Nations and Nationalism*, 12(1): 51–76.

Guler, I., Guillen, M. F., and Macpherson, J. M. (2002)' Global Competition, Institutions, and the Diffusion of Organizational Practices: The International Spread of ISO 9000 Quality Certificates', *Administrative Science Quarterly*, 47(2): 207–32.

Gunther, R., Sani, G., and Shabad, G. (1986) 'Micronationalism and the Regional Party Systems of Euskadi, Catalunya, and Galicia', in idem, *Spain After Franco: The Making of a Competitive Party System* (Berkeley and Los Angeles, Calif.: University of California Press).

Gupta, A., and Kapur, V. (eds.) (2000) *Microsimulation in Government Policy and Forecasting* (Amsterdam: North-Holland).

Gurr, T. (1970) *Why Men Rebel* (Princeton: Princeton University Press).

Guttmann, A., and Thompson, D. (2004) *Why Deliberative Democracy?* (Princeton: Princeton University Press).

Haarmann, H. (2002) *Sprachenalmanach* (Frankfurt: Campus).

Haas, E. B. (1958) *The Uniting of Europe: Political, Social and Economic Forces 1950–1957* (London: Stevens & Sons).

—— (1961) 'International Integration: The European and the Universal Process', *International Organization*, 15(3): 366–92.

Haas, P. M. (1992) 'Introduction: Epistemic Communities and International Policy Coordination', *International Organization*, 46(1): 1–37.

Habermas, J. (1999) 'The European Nation-State and the Pressures of Globalization', *New Left Review*, 235: 46–59.

Hacker, J. S. (2002) *The Divided Welfare State: The Battle over Public and Private Social Benefits in the United States* (New York: Cambridge University Press).

Hage, J., Hanneman, R., and Gargan, E. T. (1989) *State Responsiveness and State Activism: An Examination of the Social Forces and State Strategies that Explain the Rise in Social Expenditure in Britain, France, Germany and Italy 1870–1968* (London: Unwin Hyman).

Hahn, R. W. (1990) 'The Political Economy of Environmental Regulation: Towards a Unifying Framework', *Public Choice*, 65(1): 21–47.

Hainsworth, P. (2006) 'France Says No: The 29 May 2005 Referendum on the European Constitution', *Parliamentary Affairs*, 59(1): 98–117.

Hall, P. A. (1989) *The Political Power of Economic Ideas* (Princeton: Princeton University Press).

—— (1993) 'Policy Paradigms, Social Learning and the State', *Comparative Politics*, 25(3): 275–96.

—— (2004) 'Beyond the Comparative Method', *APSA-Comparative Politics Newsletter*, 15(2): 1–4.

—— (2006) 'Systematic Process Analysis: When and How to Use it', *European Management Review*, 24–31.

—— and Soskice, D. (2001) 'An Introduction to Varieties of Capitalism', in idem 2001*b*: 1–70.

—— and —— (2001*b*) *Varieties of Capitalism: The Institutional Foundations of Comparative Advantage* (New York and Oxford: Oxford University Press).

—— and Taylor, R. (1996) 'Political Science and the Three New Institutionalisms', *Political Studies*, 44(5): 936–57.

Hallin, D. C., and Mancini, P. (2004) *Comparing Media Systems: Three Models of Media and Politics* (Cambridge: Cambridge University Press).

Hammond, T. H. (1986) 'Agenda Control, Organizational Structure, and Bureaucratic Politics', *American Journal of Political Science*, 30: 379–420.

—— and Knott, J. (1996) 'Who Controls the Bureaucracy? Presidential Power, Congressional Dominance, Legal Constraints, and Bureaucratic Autonomy in a Model of Multi-Institutional Policy-Making', *Journal of Law, Economics, and Organization*, 12: 119–66.

Hancock, M. D. (1983) 'Comparative Public Policy', in A. Finifter (ed.), *Political Science: The State of the Discipline* (Washington, DC: American Political Science Association), 283–308.

Hansard Society (2002) *Technology: Enhancing Representative Democracy in the UK?* (London: Hansard Society).

Hardin, R. (1982) *Collective Action* (Balitmore, Md.: Johns Hopkins University Press).

—— (1995) *One for All: The Logic of Group Conflict* (Princeton: Princeton University Press).

—— (2006) *Trust* (Cambridge: Polity).

Harper, D. (2001) *The Online Etymology Dictionary* (www.etymonline.com/).

Harrop, M., and Miller, W. L. (1987) *Elections and Voters: A Comparative Introduiiton* (Basingstoke: Macmillan Education).

Hartz, L. (1955) *The Liberal Tradition in America* (New York: Harcourt, Brace & World).

—— (ed.) (1964) *The Founding of New Societies* (New York: Harcourt, Brace & World).

Hayes, M. (2001) *The Limits of Policy Change: Incrementalism, Worldview, and the Rule of Law* (Washington, DC: Georgetown University Press).

Hayes-Renshaw, F., and Wallace, H. (2006) *The Council of Ministers* (Basingstoke: Palgrave, 2nd edn).

Hayward, J. E. S. (1983) *Governing France: The One and Indivisible Republic* (London: Weidenfeld & Nicolson, 2nd edn).

Heath, A., Glouharova, S., and Heath, O. (2005) 'India: Two-Party Contests within a Multiparty System', in Gallagher and Mitchell 2005: 137–56.

Hechter, M. (1975) *Internal Colonialism: The Celtic Fringe in British National Development, 1536–1966* (Berkeley, Calif.: University of California Press).

Heclo, H. (1975) *Modern Social Policy in Britain and Sweden: From Relief to Income Maintenance* (New Haven, Conn.: Yale University Press).

—— (1977) *A Government of Strangers* (Washington, DC: Brookings Institution Press).

—— (1978) 'Issue Networks and the Executive Establishment', in A. King (ed.), *The New American Political System* (Washington, DC: American Enterprise Institute Press, 1st edn).

—— and Madsen, H. J. (1986) *Policy and Politics in Sweden* (Philadelphia: Temple University Press).

Heichel, S., Pape, J., and Sommerer, T. (2005) 'Is there Convergence in Convergence Research? An Overview of Empirical Studies on Policy Convergence', *Journal of European Public Policy*, 12(5): 817–40.

Heidenheimer, A. J., Heclo, H., and Adams, C. T. (1975) *Comparative Public Policy: The Politics of Social Choice in Europe and America* (New York: St Martin's Press).

Heinz, J. P., Laumann, E. O., Nelson, R. L., and Salisbury, R. H. (1993) *The Hollow Core: Private Interests in National Policy Making* (Cambridge, Mass.: Harvard University Press).

Held, D., and McGrew, A. (2002) *Globalization/Anti-Globalization* (Cambridge: Polity).

—— —— Goldblatt, D., and Perraton, J. (1999) *Global Transformations: Politics, Economics and Culture* (Cambridge: Cambridge University Press).

Hemerijck, A. C., and Schludi, M. (2000) 'Sequences of Policy Failures and Effective Policy Responses', in Scharpf and Schmidt 2000: 125–228.

—— Unger, B., and Visser, J. (2000) 'How Small Countries Negotiate Change: Twenty-Five Years of Policy Adjustment in Austria, the Netherlands, and Belgium', in Scharpf and Schmidt 2000: 175–263.

Herb, M. (1999) *All in the Family: Absolutism, Revolution, and Democratic Prospects in the Middle Eastern Monarchies* (Albany, NY: State University of New York Press).

Herman, E. S. (1999) 'The Threat of Globalization', *New Politics*, 7(2): 1–4.

Hermens, F. A. (1941) *Democracy or Anarchy? A Study of Proportional Representation* (Bloomington, Ind.: Indiana University Press).

Hesse, J. J., and Sharpe, L. J. (1991) 'Local Government in International Perspective: Some Comparative Perspectives', in J. J. Hesse (ed.), *Local Government and Urban Affairs in International Perspective: Analyses of 20 Western Industrialised Countries* (Baden-Baden: Nomos Verlagsgesellschaft).

Hettne, B. (2003) 'The New Regionalism Revisited', in F. Söderbaum and T. Shaw (eds.), *Theories of New Regionalism: A Palgrave Reader* (New York: Palgrave Macmillan), 22–42.

Hewitt, C. (1977) 'The Effect of Political Democracy and Social Democracy on Equality in Industrial Societies: A Cross-National Comparison', *American Sociological Review*, 42(1): 450–64.

Hibbing, J., and Theiss-Morse, E. (2002) *Stealth Democracy: Americans' Beliefs about How Government should Work* (Cambridge: Cambridge University Press).

Hicks, A. M. (1999) *Social Democracy and Welfare Capitalism: A Century of Income Security Politics* (Ithaca, NY: Cornell University Press).

—— and Swank, D. H. (1984) 'On the Political Economy of Welfare Expansion: A Comparative Analysis of 18 Advanced Capitalist Democracies, 1960–1971', *Comparative Political Studies*, 17(1): 81–119.

—— —— and Ambuhl, M. (1989) 'Welfare Expansion Revisited: Policy Routines and their Mediation by Party, Class and Crisis, 1957–1982', *European Journal of Political Research*, 17(4): 401–30.

Higgins, W., and Apple, N. (1981) *Class Mobilization and Economic Policy: Struggles over Full Employment in Britain and Sweden* (Stockholm: Arbetslivcentrum).

Hill, L. (2006) 'Low Voter Turnout in the United States: is Compulsory Voting a Viable Solution?', *Journal of Theoretical Politics*, 18(2): 207–32.

Hill, M. (2005) *The Public Policy Process* (Harlow: Pearson/Longman).

—— (2006) *Social Policy in the Modern World* (Malden, Mass.: Blackwell Publishing).

—— and Hupe, P. (2005) *Implementing Public Policy* (London: Sage).

—— and —— (2006) 'Models of the Policy Process', in B. G. Peters and J. Pierre (eds.), *Handbook of Public Policy* (London: Sage).

Hindman, M., Tsioutsiouliklis, K., and Johnson, J. (2003) '"Googlearchy": How a Few Heavily-Linked Sites Dominate Politics on the Web'. Available at www.cs.princeton.edu/~kt/mpsa03.pdf.

Hinnebusch, R. (1994) 'Liberalization in Syria: The Struggle of Economic and Political Rationality', in E. Kienle (ed.), *Contemporary Syria* (London: Academic Press).

Hirschl, R. (2001) 'The Political Origins of Judicial Empowerment through Constitutionalization: Lessons from Israel's Constitutional Revolution', *Comparative Politics*, 33(3): 315–36.

Hirschman, A. O. (1970) *Exit, Voice, and Loyalty: Responses to Decline in Firms, Organizations, and States* (Cambridge, Mass. Harvard University Press).

—— (1982) *Shifting Involvements: Private Interest and Public Action* (Princeton: Princeton University Press).

Hirst, P. (1990) *Representative Democracy and its Limits* (Cambridge: Polity Press).

—— and Thompson, G. (1996) *Globalization in Question* (Oxford: Polity Press).

—— and —— (2000) *Globalization in Question* (Cambridge: Polity Press, 2nd edn).

Hix, S. (2002) 'Constitutional Agenda-Setting through Discretion in Rule Interpretation: Why the European Parliament Won at Amsterdam', *British Journal of Political Science*, 32(2): 259–80.

—— (2005) *The Political System of the European Union* (Basingstoke: Palgrave, 2nd edn).

—— and Marsh, M. (2007) 'Punishment or Protest? Understanding European Parliament Elections', *Journal of Politics* (forthcoming).

—— Noury, A., and Roland, G. (2007) *Democratic Politics in the European Parliament* (Cambridge: Cambridge University Press).

Hoberg, G. (2001) 'Globalization and Policy Convergence: Symposium Overview', *Journal of Comparative Policy Analysis: Research and Practice*, 3: 127–32.

Hobolt, S. B. (2006) 'Direct Democracy and European Integration', *Journal of European Public Policy*, 13(1): 153–66.

Hobsbawm, E. (1977) 'Some Reflections on "The Breakup of Britain"', *New Left Review*, 105: 3–23.

Hoffmann, S. (1966) 'Obstinate or Obsolete? The Fate of the Nation State and the Case of Western Europe', *Daedalus*, 95(4): 862–915.

—— (1982) 'Reflections on the Nation-State in Western Europe Today', *Journal of Common Market Studies*, 21(1–2): 21–37.

Hofstede, G. (2001) *Culture's Consequences: Comparing Values, Behaviors Institutions and Organizations* (Thousand Oaks, Calif.: Sage).

Holm, H. H., and Sørensen, G. (eds.) (1995) *Whose World Order? Uneven Globalization and the End of the Cold War* (Boulder, Colo.: Westview).

Holmes, L. (1986) *Politics in the Communist World* (Oxford: Oxford University Press).

Holmes Cooper, A. (2002) 'Media Framing and Social Movement Mobilization: German Peace Protest Against INF Missiles, the Gulf War, and NATO Peace Enforcement in Bosnia', *European Journal of Political Research*, 41: 37–80.

Holmlund, B. (1998) 'Unemployment Insurance in Theory and Practice', *Scandinavian Journal of Economics*, 100: 113–41.

Holsti, K. J. (1991) *Peace and War: Armed Conflicts and International Order, 1649–1989* (Cambridge: Cambridge University Press).

Holzinger, K. (2002) 'The Provision of Transnational Common Goods: Regulatory Competition for Environmental Standards', in A. Héritier (ed.), *Common Goods: Reinventing European and International Governance* (Lanham, Md.: Rowman & Littlefield), 59–82.

—— (2003) 'Common Goods, Matrix Games, and Institutional Solutions', *European Journal of International Relations*, 9: 173–212.

—— and Knill, C. (2005) 'Causes and Conditions of Cross-National Policyconvergence', *Journal of European Public Policy*, 12(5): 775–96.

—— —— and Sommerer, T. (2008) 'The Pair Approach: What Causes Convergence of Environmental Policies?', in K. Holzinger, C. Knill, and B. Arts (eds.), *Environmental Policy Convergence in Europe? The Impact of International Institutions and Trade* (Cambridge: Cambridge University Press).

Hood, C. (2000) *The Art of the State: Culture, Rhetoric and Public Management* (Oxford: Oxford University Press).

Hooghe, L. (ed.) (1996) *Cohesion Policy and European Integration: Building Multi-Level Governance* (Oxford: Oxford University Press).

—— (2001) *The European Commission and the Integration of Europe: Images of Governance* (Cambridge: Cambridge University Press).

—— and Marks, G. (2001) *Multi-Level Governance and European Integration* (Lanhan, Md.: Rowman & Littlefield).

Hoogvelt, A. (2001) *Globalization and the Postcolonial World* (Basingstoke: Palgrave Macmillan).

Hopkin, J. (2005) 'Spain: Proportional Representation with Majoritarian Outcomes', in Gallagher and Mitchell 2005: 375–94.

Hopkin, J., and Paolucci, C. (1999) 'New Parties and the Business Firm Model of Party Organization: Cases from Spain and Italy', *European Journal of Political Research*, 35(3): 307–39.

Horowitz, D. L. (1985) *Ethnic Groups in Conflict* (Berkeley, Calif.: University of California Press).

Hotteling, H. (1929) 'Stability in Competition', *Economic Journal*, 29(1): 41–57.

Hough, J. (1977) *The Soviet Union and Social Science Theory* (Cambridge, Mass: Harvard University Press).

Hovland, C., Lumsdaine, A., and Sheffield, F. (1949) *Experiments on Mass Communications* (Princeton: Princeton University Press).

—— Janis, I., and Kelley, H. (1953) *Communication and Persuasion* (New Haven, Conn.: Yale University Press).

Howard, C. (1993) 'The Hidden Side of the American Welfare State', *Political Science Quarterly*, 108(3): 403–36.

Howard, P. (2006) *New Media Campaigns and the Managed Citizen* (New York: Cambridge University Press).

Howlett, M. (1991) 'Policy Instruments, Policy Styles and Policy Implementation', *Policy Studies Journal*, 19(2): 1–21.

—— and Ramesh, M. (2003) *Studying Public Policy: Policy Cycles and Policy Subsystems* (Oxford: Oxford University Press).

Hsing, Y., and Smyth, D. J. (1995) 'In Search of an Optimal Debt Ratio for Economic Growth', *Contemporary Economic Policy*, 13(4): 51–9.

Huber, E., (2001) *Development and Crisis of the Welfare State: Parties and Politics in Global Markets* (Chicago and London: University of Chicago Press).

—— and Stephens, J. D. (2000) 'Partisan Governance, Women's Employment, and the Social Democratic Service State', *American Sociological Review*, 65(3): 323–42.

Huber, J. D. (1996) *Rationalizing Parliament* (Cambridge: Cambridge University Press).

Huckshorn, R. (1984) *Political Parties in America* (Monterey, Calif.: Brooks/Cole).

Hueglin, T. (1979) 'Johannes Althusius: Medieval Constitutionalist or Modern Federalist?', *Publius*, 9(4): 9–41.

—— (2003) 'Federalism at the Crossroads: Old Meanings, New Significance', *Canadian Journal of Political Science/Revue Canadienne de Science Politique*, 36(2): 275–94.

Hug, S. (2003) 'Endogenous Preferences and Delegation in the European Union', *Comparative Political Studies*, 36(1–2): 41–74.

Hulme, R. (2005) 'Policy Transfer and the Internationalisation of Social Policy', *Social Policy and Society*, 4: 417–25.

Hume, D. (1741) *Essays, Literary, Moral, and Political* (Edinburgh: Kincaid).

Huntington, S. P. (1968) *Political Order in Changing Societies* (New Haven, Conn.: Yale University Press).

—— (1991) *The Third Wave: Democratization in the Late Twentieth Century* (Norman, Okla.: University of Oklahoma Press).

—— (1996) *The Clash of Civilizations and the Remaking of World Order* (New York: Simon & Schuster).

—— (2000) 'Culture Counts', in L. E. Harrison and S. P. Huntington (eds.), *Culture Matters: How Values Shape Human Progress* (New York: Basic Books), xiii–xvi.

Huntington, S. P. (2005) *Who Are We: America's Great Debate* (New York: Free Press).

—— and Nelson, J. M. (1976) *No Easy Choice: Political Participation in Developing Countries* (Cambridge, Mass.: Harvard University Press).

Husa, J. (2000) 'Guarding the Constitutionality of Laws in the Nordic Countries: A Comparative Perspective', *American Journal of Comparative Law*, 48(3): 345–81.

Hwang, J.-Y. (2006) *Direct Democracy in Asia: A Reference Guide to the Legislations and Practices* (Taipei: Taiwan Foundation for Democracy).

Immervoll, H., Kleven, H. J., Kreiner, C. T., and Saez, E. (2007) 'Welfare Reform in European Countries: A Microsimulation Analysis', *Economic Journal*, 117(516): 1–44.

Inglehart, R. (1977) *The Silent Revolution: Changing Values and Political Styles among Western Publics* (Princeton: Princeton University Press).

—— (1990) *Culture Shift* (Princeton: Princeton University Press).

—— (1997) *Modernization and Postmodernization: Cultural, Economic and Political Change in 43 Societies* (Princeton: Princeton University Press).

—— and Baker, W. E. (2000) 'Modernization, Cultural Change, and the Persistence of Traditional Values', *American Sociological Review*, 65: 19–51.

—— and Norris, P. (2003) *Rising Tide: Gender Equality and Cultural Change around the World* (Cambridge: Cambridge University Press).

—— and Welzel, C. (2005) *Modernization, Cultural Change, and Democracy: The Human Development Sequence* (Cambridge: Cambridge University Press).

—— *et al.* (2000) 'World Values Surveys and European Values Surveys, 1981–1984, 1990–1993, and 1995–1997' (computer file), ICPSR version (Ann Arbor, Mich.: Inter-university Consortium for Political and Social Research [distributor]).

—— *et al.* (2004) European Values Study Group and World Values Survey Association, 'European and World Values Surveys Integrated Data File, 1999–2002, Release I' (Computer file), 2nd ICPSR version (Ann Arbor, Mich.: Inter-university Consortium for Political and Social Research [distributors]).

Ivaldi, G. (2006) 'Beyond France's 2005 Referendum on the European Constitutional Treaty: Second-Order Model, Anti-Establishment Attitudes and the End of the Alternative European Utopia', *West European Politics*, 29(1): 47–69.

Iversen, T. (2005) *Capitalism, Democracy and Welfare* (Cambridge: Cambridge University Press).

—— (2006) 'Capitalism and Democracy', in D. Wittman and B. R. Weingast (eds.), *Oxford Handbook of Political Economy* (New York: Oxford University Press), 601–23.

—— and Cusack, T. R. (2000) 'The Causes of Welfare State Expansion: Deindustralization or Globalization?', *World Politics*, 52(3): 313–49.

—— and Soskice, D. (2001) 'An Asset Theory of Social Policy Preferences', *American Political Science Review*, 95(4): 875–93.

—— and —— (2006) 'Electoral Institutions and the Politics of Coalitions: Why Some Democracies Redistribute More than

Others', *American Political Science Review*, 100(2): 165–81.

—— and Wren, A. (1998) 'Equality, Employment, and Budgetary Restraint: The Trilemma of the Service Economy', *World Politics*, 50(4): 507–46.

Jackman, R. (1998) 'European Unemployment: Why is it so High and What should be Done about it?', in G. Debelle and J. Borland (eds.), *Unemployment and the Australian Labour Market* (Sydney: Reserve Bank of Australia), 39–63.

—— Layard, R., and Nickell, S. (1996) 'Combating Unemployment: Is Flexibility Enough?', paper presented at OECD Conference on Interactions between Structural Reform, Macroeconomic Policies and Economic Performance (London: LSE).

Jackman, R. W. (1975) *Politics and Social Equality: A Comparative Analysis* (New York: Wiley).

—— (1986) 'Elections and the Democratic Class Struggle', *World Politics*, 39(1): 123–46.

—— (1987) 'Political Institutions and Voter Turnout in the Industrial Democracies', *American Political Science Review*, 81(2): 405–24.

—— and Miller, R. A. (1995) 'Voter Turnout in the Industrial Democracies during the 1980s', *Comparative Political Studies*, 27: 467–92.

—— and —— (1998) 'Social Capital and Politics', *Annual Review of Political Science*, 1: 47–73.

—— and —— (2004) *Before Norms: Institutions and Civic Culture* (Ann Arbor, Mich.: University of Michigan Press).

Jackson, R. (1990) *Quasi-States: Sovereignty, International Relations and the Third World* (Cambridge: Cambridge University Press).

—— and Rosberg, C. G. (1982) *Personal Rule in Black Africa: Prince, Autocrat, Prophet, Tyrant* (Berkeley, Calif.: University of California Press).

Jahn, D. (2006) 'Globalization as Galton's Problem: The Missing Link in the Analysis of Diffusion Patterns in Welfare State Development', *International Organization*, 60(2): 401–31.

Jagger, K., and Gurr, T. (1995) 'Tracking Democracy's Third Wave with the Polity III Data', *Journal of Peace Research*, 32(4): 469–82.

Jakee, K., and Sun, G. Z. (2006) 'Is Compulsory Voting More Democratic?', *Public Choice*, 129(1–2): 61–75.

James, A. (1999) 'The Practice of Sovereign Statehood in Contemporary International Society', *Political Studies*, 47(3): 457–74.

James, S. (1999) *British Cabinet Government* (London: Routledge, 2nd edn).

Jamison, A., and Baark, E. (1999) 'National Shades of Green: Comparing the Swedish and Danish Styles in Ecological Modernisation', *Environmental Values*, 8(2): 199–218.

Janda, K. (1980) *Political Parties: A Cross-National Survey* (New York: Free Press).

Janis, I. L. (1972) *Victims of Groupthink* (Boston: Houghton Mifflin).

Jann, W., and Wegrich, K. (2006) 'Theories of the Policy Cycle', in F. Fischer, G. Miller, and M. Sidney (eds.), *Handbook of Public Policy Analysis: Theory, Politics, and Methods* (Boca Raton: CRC Press), 43–62.

Janoski, T., and Hicks, A. M. (1994) *The Comparative Political Economy of the Welfare State* (Cambridge: Cambridge University Press).

Jeffery, C. (ed.) (1997) *The Regional Dimension of the European Union: Towards a Third Level in Europe?* (London: Frank Cass).

Jennings, M. K. (1990) *Continuities in Political Action: A Longitudinal Study of Political Orientations in Three Western Democracies* (Berlin: de Gruyter).

Jessop, B. (2002) *The Future of the Capitalist State* (Cambridge: Polity).

Jobert, B., and Muller, P. (1987) *L'État en Action* (Paris: PUF).

John, P. (2006) 'The Policy Agenda Project: A Review', *Journal of European Public Policy*, 13(7): 975–86.

John, P. (2001) *Local Governance in Western Europe* (London: Sage).

Johnson, C. (1982) *MITI and the Japanese Miracle: The Growth of Industrial Policy, 1925–1975* (Stanford, Calif.: Stanford University Press).

Johnson-Cartee, K. S., and Copeland, G. A. (1997) *Inside Political Campaigns: Theory and Practice* (Westport, Conn.: Praeger).

Jones, B. D., and Baumgartner, F. R. (2004) 'Representation and Agenda-Setting', *Policy Studies Journal*, 32(1): 1–24.

—— and —— (2005) 'A Model of Choice for Public Policy', *Journal of Public Administration Research and Theory*, 15(3): 325–51.

Jones, E. L. (1981) *The European Miracle: Environments, Economies, and Geopolitics in the History of Europe and Asia* (Cambridge: Cambridge University Press).

Jones, M., and Mainwaring, S. (2003) 'The Nationalization of Parties and Party Systems: An Empirical Measure and an Application to the Americas', *Party Politics*, 9(2): 139–66.

Jones, T., and Newburn, T. (2002) 'Learning from Uncle Sam? Exploring US Influences on British Crime Control Policy', *Governance*, 15(1): 97–119.

Jordan, A., and Liefferink, D. (2004) *Environmental Policy in Europe: The Europeanisation of National Environmental Policy* (London: Routledge).

Jordana, J., and Levi-Faur, D. (2005) 'The Diffusion of Regulatory Capitalism in Latin America: Sectoral and National Channels in the Making of a New Order', in idem (eds.), *The Rise of Regulatory Capitalism: The Global Diffusion of a New Order*, Special Issue: The Annals of the American Academy of Political and Social Science, 598 (Thousand Oaks, Calif.: Sage), 102–24.

Jowett, K. (1992) *New World Disorder: The Leninist Extinction* (Berkeley, Calif.: University of California Press).

Julius, D. (1997) 'Globalization and Stakeholder Conflicts: A Corporate Perspective', *International Affairs*, 73(3): 453–69.

Kaase, M., and Newton, K. (1995) *Beliefs in Government* (Oxford: Oxford University Press).

Kahler, M., and Lake, D. A. (2003) 'Globalization and Changing Patterns of Political Authority', in idem (eds.), *Governance in a Global Economy* (Princeton: Princeton University Press).

Kalyvas, S. N. (1996) *The Rise of Christian Democracy in Europe* (Ithaca, NY: Cornell University Press).

Kamens, D. H. (1986) 'The Importance of Historical Sequencing: Party Legitimacy in the United States and Europe', *Comparative Social Research*, 9: 331–45.

Kangas, O. (1991) *The Politics of Social Rights: Studies on the Dimensions of Sickness Insurance in OECD Countries* (Stockholm: Swedish Institute for Social Research).

Kanter, R. M. (1995) *World Class: Thriving Locally in the Global Economy* (New York: Simon & Schuster).

Kapstein, E. B. (1993) 'Territoriality and Who is "US"', *International Organization*, 47: 501–3.

Karmis, D., and Norman, W. (2005) 'The Revival of Federalism', in idem (eds.), *Theories of Federalism: A Reader* (Basingstoke and New York: Palgrave Macmillan).

Katz, R. S. (1986) 'Party Government: A Rationalistic Conception', in Castles and Wildenmann 1986.

—— (1987) 'Party Government and its Alternatives', in idem, *Party Governments: European and American Experiences* (Berlin: de Gruyter), 1–26.

—— (1990) 'Party as Linkage: A Vestigial Function?', *European Journal of Political Research*, 18: 143–61.

—— (1997) *Democracy and Elections* (Oxford: Oxford University Press).

—— (2003) 'Europeanization and the Decline of Partisan Political Activity', prepared for the 2003 General Conference of the European Consortium for Political Research, Marburg, Germany.

—— and Mair, P. (1995) 'Changing Models of Party Organization and Party Democracy: The Emergence of the Cartel Party', *Party Politics*, 1 (Jan.): 5–28.

Katzenstein, P. J. (1985) *Small States in World Markets: Industrial Policy in Europe* (Ithaca, NY: Cornell University Press).

Kaufmann, D., Kraay, A., and Mastruzzi, M. (2006) *Governance Matters*, v. *Aggregate and Individual Governance Indicators for 1996–2005*, World Bank Policy Research Working Paper, 4012, (Washington, DC: World Bank).

Keating, M. (1997) 'The Political Economy of Regionalism', in Keating and Loughlin 1997: 17–40.

—— (1998a) 'Is there a Regional Level of Government in Europe?', in P. LeGalès and C. Lequesne (eds.), *Regions in Europe* (London and New York: Routledge), 11–29.

—— (1998b) *The New Regionalism in Western Europe: Territorial Restructuring and Political Change* (Cheltenham: Edward Elgar).

—— (1999) 'Asymmetrical Governments: Multinational States in an Integrating Europe', *Publius: The Journal of Federalism*, 29(1): 71–86.

—— (2001) 'Rethinking the Region: Culture, Institutions and Economic Development in Catalonia and Galicia', *European Urban and Regional Studies*, 8(3): 217–34.

—— (2004) 'Introduction', in idem (ed.), *Regions and Regionalism in Europe* (Cheltenham: Edward Elgar), xi–xv.

—— and Loughlin, J. (eds.) (1997) *The Political Economy of Regionalism* (London: Routledge).

Keck, M. E., and Sikkink, K. (1998a) *Articles beyond Border: Networks in International Politics* (Ithaca, NY: Cornell University Press).

—— and —— (1998b) 'Transnational Advocacy Networks in the Movement Society', in Meyer and Tarrow 1998a: 217–38.

Kelley, J. (2006) 'New Wine in Old Wineskins: Promoting Political Reforms through the New European Neighbourhood Policy', *Journal of Common Market Studies*, 44(1): 29–55.

Keman, H. (1988) *The Development Toward Surplus Welfare: Social Democratic Politics and Policies in Advanced Capitalist Democracies (1965–1984)* (Amsterdam: CT Press).

—— (1990) 'Social Democracy and the Politics of Welfare Statism', *Netherlands' Journal of Social Sciences*, 26(1): 17–34.

—— (1993a) 'Comparative Politics: A Distinctive Approach to Political Science?', in idem 1993b : 31–57.

—— (ed.) (1993b) *Comparative Politics: New Directions in Theory and Method* (Amsterdam: VU Press).

—— (ed.) (2002a) *Comparative Democratic Politics: A Guide to Contemporary Theory and Research* (London: Sage).

—— (2002b) 'Comparing Democracies: Theory and Evidence', in idem 2002a: 32–61.

—— (2002c) 'Policy-Making Capacities of European Party Government', in K. R. Luther and F. Müller-Rommel (eds.), *Political Parties in the New Europe* (Oxford: Oxford University Press), 207–45.

—— (2007) 'Experts and Manifestos: Different Sources—Same Results for Comparative Research?', Special Issue of *Electoral Politics*, 26(1): 1–14.

—— and Pennings, P. (1995) 'Managing Political and Societal Conflict in Democracies: Do consensus and corporatism matter?', *British Journal of Political Science*, 25(2): 271–81.

Kenworthy, L. (1999) 'Do Social-Welfare Policies Reduce Poverty? A Cross-National Assessment', *Social Forces*, 77(3): 1119–40.

—— (2001) 'Wage-Setting Measures: A Survey and Assessment', *World Politics*, 54(1): 57–98.

—— (2004) *Egalitarian Capitalism: Jobs, Incomes and Growth in Affluent Countries* (New York: Russell Sage Foundation).

Kern, K. (2000) *Die Diffusion von Politikinnovationen: Umweltpolitische Innovationen im Mehrebenensystem der USA* (Opladen: Leske & Budrich).

—— Jörgens, H., and Jänicke, M. (2000) 'Die Diffusion umweltpolitischer Innovationen: Ein Beitrag zur Globalisierung von Umweltpolitik', *Zeitschrift für Umweltpolitik*, 23: 507–46.

Kerr, C., Dunlop, J. T., Harbison, F. H., and Myers, C. A. (1973) *Industrialism and Industrial Man* (London: Penguin).

Key, V. O., Jr. (1964) *Politics, Parties, and Pressure Groups* (New York: Thomas Y. Crowell).

King, A. (1973) 'Ideas, Institutions, and the Policies of Government: A Comparative Analysis', *British Journal of Political Science*, 3: 291–313.

—— (1975) 'Executives', in F. I. Greenstein and N. W. Polsby (eds.), *Handbook of Political Science*, v. *Governmental Institutions and Processes* (Reading, Mass.: Addision-Wesley).

—— (1981) 'How to Strengthen Legislature: Assuming that is What we Want to Do', in N. J. Ornstein (ed.), *The Role of the Legislature in Western Democracies* (Washington, DC: American Enterprise Institute), ch. 6.

King, D. C., and Walker, J. L., Jr. (1992) 'The Provisions of Benefits by Interest Groups in the United States', *Journal of Politics*, 54(2): 394–426.

King, G. (1997) *A Solution to the Ecological Inference Problem* (Princeton: Princeton University Press).

—— Keohane, R. D., and Verba, S. (1994) *Designing Social Inquiry* (Princeton: Princeton University Press).

—— Rosen, O., and Tanner, M. A. (2004) *Ecological Inference: New Methodological Strategies* (Cambridge: Cambridge University Press).

King, P. (1982) *Federalism and Federation* (London: Croom Helm).

Kingdon, J. W. (1984) *Agendas, Alternatives, and Public Policies* (Boston: Little, Brown).

—— (1995) *Agenda, Alternatives, and Public Policies* (New York: HarperCollins).

Kirchheimer, O. (1966) 'The Transformation of West European Party Systems', in J. LaPalombara and M. Weiner (eds.), *Political Parties and Political Development* (Princeton: Princeton University Press).

Kitschelt, H. (1986) 'Political Opportunity Structures and Political Protest: Anti-Nuclear Movements in Four Democracies', *British Journal of Political Science*, 16: 57–85.

—— (1992) *Political Regime Change: Structure and Process-Driven Explanations* (New Haven, Conn.: Yale University Press).

—— (ed.) (1994) *The Transformation of European Social Democracy* (Cambridge: Cambridge University Press).

—— (1995) *The Radical Right in Western Europe* (Ann Arbor, Mich.: University of Michigan Press).

—— (2001) 'Partisan Competition and Welfare State Retrenchment: When Do Politicians Choose Unpopular Policies?', in Pierson 2001: 265–302.

—— and Wilkinson, S. (2006) 'Citizen-Politician Linkages: An Introduction', in idem (eds.), *Patrons, Clients and Policies* (Cambridge, Mass.: Cambridge University Press), 1–49.

—— Marks, G., Lange, P., and Stephens, J. D. (eds.) (1999) *Continuity and Change in Contemporary Capitalism* (Cambridge: Cambridge University Press).

Kittel, B. (1999) 'Sense and Sensitivity in Pooled Analysis of Political Data', *European Journal of Political Research*, 35: 225–53.

—— (2006) 'A Crazy Methodology? On the Limits of Macro-Quantitative Social Science Research', *International Sociology*, 21(5): 647–77.

Klapper, J. (1960) *The Effects of Mass Communication* (New York: Free Press).

Klein, E. (1971) *A Comprehensive Etymological Dictionary of the English Language* (Amsterdam: Elsevier Scientific Publishing Co.).

Kleinman, M. (2002) *A European Welfare State? European Union Social Policy in Context* (London: Palgrave).

Klingemann, H.-D., and Fuchs, D. (1995) *Citizens and the State* (Oxford: Oxford University Press).

Klotz, R. (1997) 'Positive Spin: Senate Campaigning on the Web', *PS: Political Science and Politics*, 30(3): 482–6.

Klug, H. (2000) *Constituting Democracy: Law, Globalism, and South Africa's Political Reconstruction* (New York: Cambridge University Press).

Knack, S. (2002) 'Social Capital and the Quality of Government: Evidence from the States', *American Journal of Political Science*, 46: 772–85.

Knill, C. (1998) 'European Policies: The Impact of National Administrative Traditions', *Journal of Public Policy*, 18(1): 1–28.

—— (2001) *The Europeanisation of National Administration: Patterns of Institutional Change and Persistence* (Cambridge: Cambridge University Press).

—— (2005) 'Introduction: Cross-National Policy Convergence: Concepts, Approaches and Explanatory Factors', *Journal of European Public Policy*, 12(5): 764–74.

—— (2006) 'Implementation', in J. Richardson (ed.), *European Union: Power and Policy-Making* (Abingdon and New York: Routledge), 351–75.

Kobach, K. W. (2001) 'Lessons Learned in the Participation Game', in Auer and Bützer 2001: 292–309.

Kooiman, J. (2003) *Governing as Governance* (London: Sage).

Koopmans, R. (1992) *Democracy from Below: New Social Movements and the Political System in West Germany* (Boulder, Colo.: Westview).

—— (1995) 'The Dynamics of Protest Waves', in Kriesi, Koopmans, Duyvendak, and Giugni 1995: 111–42.

—— (2001) 'Better off by Doing Good: Why Antiracism Must Mean Different Things to Different Groups', in M. Giugni and F. Passy (eds.), *Political Altruism? Solidarity Movements in International Perspective* (Lanham, Md.: Rowman & Littlefield), 111–32.

—— and Statham, P. (1999) 'Ethnic and Civic Conceptions of Nationhood and the Differential Success of the Extreme Right in Germany and Italy', in Giugni, McAdam, and Tilly 1999: 225–52.

Koppenjan, J., and Klijn, E.-H. (2005) *Managing Uncertainties in Networks* (London: Routledge).

Korn, J. (1996) *The Power of Separation: American Constitutionalism and the Myth of the Legislative Veto* (Princeton: Princeton University Press).

Kornhauser, W. (1959) *The Politics of Mass Society* (Glencoe, Ill.: Free Press).

Korpi, W. (1983) *The Democratic Class Struggle* (London: Routledge & Kegan Paul).

—— (1985) 'Economic Growth and the Welfare State: Leaky Bucket or Irrigation System?', *European Sociological Review*, 1(2): 97–118.

—— (1989) 'Power, Politics, and State Autonomy in the Development of Social Citizenship: Social Rights during Sickness in Eighteen OECD Countries since 1930', *American Sociological Review* 54(3): 309–28.

—— (2002) 'The Great Through in Unemployment: A Long-Term View of Unemployment, Strikes, and the Profit/Wage Ratio', *Politics and Society*, 30(3): 365–426.

—— (2005) 'Does the Welfare State Harm Economic Growth? Sweden as a Strategic Test Case', in O. Kangas and J. Palme (eds.), *Social Policy and Economic Development in the Nordic Countries* (Houndsmills: Palgrave Macmillan), 186–209.

—— (2006) 'Power Resources and Employer-Centered Approaches in Explanations of Welfare States and Varieties of Capitalism', *World Politics*, 58(2): 167–206.

—— and Palme, J. (1998) 'The Paradox of Redistribution and Strategies of Equality: Welfare State Institutions, Inequality, and Poverty in Western Countries', *American Sociological Review*, 63(5): 661–87.

—— and —— (2003) 'New Politics and Class Politics in the Context of Austerity and Globalization: Welfare State Regress in Eighteen Countries, 1975–1995', *American Political Science Review*, 97(3): 425–46.

Kostadinova, T. (2003) 'Voter Turnout Dynamics in Post-Communist Europe', *European Journal of Political Research*, 42: 741–59.

Koven, S. G., and Mausloff, C. (2002) 'The Influence of Political Culture on State Budgets: Another Look at Elazar's Formulation', *American Review of Public Administration*, 32: 66–77.

Krasner, S. D. (1999) *Sovereignty: Organized Hypocrisy* (Princeton: Princeton University Press).

Kreppel, A. (2001) *The Development of the European Parliament and Supranational Party System* (Cambridge: Cambridge University Press).

Kriesi, H. (1995) 'The Political Opportunity Structure of New Social Movements: Its Impact on their Mobilization', in J. C. Jenkins and B. Klandermans (eds.), *The Politics of Social Protest: Comparative Perspectives on States and Social Movements* (Minneapolis: University of Minnesota Press), 167–98.

—— (1998) 'The Transformation of Cleavage Politics', *European Journal of Political Research*, 33(1): 165–85.

—— (2004) 'Political Context and Political Opportunity', in Snow, Soule, and Kriesi 1998: 67–90.

—— Koopmans, R., Duyvendak, J. W., and Giugni, M. G. (eds.) (1995) *New Social Movements in Western Europe: A Comparative Analysis* (Minneapolis: University of Minnesota Press).

Kroeber, A. L., and Kluckhohn, C. (1963) *Culture: A Critical Review of Concepts and Definitions* (New York: Vintage).

Krouwel, A. (2006) 'Party Models', in R. S. Katz and W. Crotty (eds.), *Handbook of Party Politics* (London: Sage), 249–69.

Krueger, B. (2002) 'Assessing the Potential of Internet Political Participation in the United States: A Resource Approach', *American Politics Research*, 30(5): 476–98.

Krugman, P. (1990) 'Policy Problems of a Monetary Union', in P. de Grauwe and L. Papademos (eds.), *The European Monetary System in the 1990s* (London: Longman).

Küchenhoff, E. (1967) *Möglichkeiten und Grenzen begrifflicher Klarheit in der Staatsformenlehre* (Berlin: Duncker & Humblot).

Kuhn, T. S. (1962) *The Structure of Scientific Revolutions* (Chicago: University of Chicago Press).

Kühner. S. (2007) 'Country-Level Comparisons of Welfare State Change Measures: Another Facet of the Dependent Variable Problem within the Comparative Analysis of the Welfare State?', *Journal of European Social Policy*, 17(1): 5–18.

Kuhnle, S. (ed.) (2000) *Survival of the European Welfare State* (London and New York: Routledge).

Kuran, T. (1991) 'The East European Revolution of 1989: Is It Surprising That We Were Surprised?', *American Economic Review*, 81(2): 121–5.

Kurian, G., Longley, T. L. D., and Melia, T. O. (1998) *World Encyclopedia of Parliaments and Legislatures* (Washington, DC: Congressional Quarterly).

Kvist, J. (1999) 'Welfare State Reform in the Nordic Countries in the 1990s: Using Fuzzy-Set Theory to Assess Conformity to Ideal Types', *Journal of European Social Policy*, 9(3): 231–52.

Kymlicka, W., (1999) *Finding our Way: Rethinking Ethnocultural Dimensions in Canada* (Toronto: Oxford University Press).

Laakso, M., and Taagepera, R. (1979) 'Effective Number of Parties: A Measure with Application to West Europe', *Comparative Political Studies*, 12: 3–27.

Lancaster, T., and Lewis-Beck, M. (1989) 'Regional Vote Support: The Spanish Case', *International Studies Quarterly*, 33(1): 29–43.

Landman, T. (2003) *Issues and Methods in Comparative Politics: An Introduction* (London: Routledge).

Lane, J.-E., and Ersson, S. O. (1994) *Comparative Politics: An Introduction and New Approach* (Oxford: Polity).

—— and —— (1997) *Comparative Political Economy: A Developmental Approach* (London and Washington, DC: Pinter).

—— and —— (2005) *Culture and Politics* (Aldershot: Ashgate).

Lang, G., and Lang, K. (1981) 'Mass Communication and Public Opinion: Strategies for Research', in M. Rosenberg and R. Turner (eds.), *Social Psychology, Sociological Perspectives* (New York: Basic), 653–82.

Larsen, C. A. (2002) 'Policy Paradigms and Cross-National Policy (Mis-) Learning from the Danish Employment Miracle', *Journal of European Public Policy*, 9(5): 715–35.

—— (2006) *Social Capital and Welfare Regimes: The Impact of Institution Dependent Living Conditions and Perceptions of Poor and Unemployed*, CCWS Working Papers, 38 (Aalborg University).

—— and Andersen, J. G. (2007) *Social Democracy and the Development of the Danish Multipillar Pension System: Ambivalent Preferences, Incremental Change and Mechanisms of Path Dependency* (Department of Economics, Politics and Public Administration Working Papers, Aalborg University).

Lasswell, H. D. (1936) *Politics: Who Gets What, When, How* (New York: McGraw-Hill).

—— (1960) *Psychopathology and Politics: A New Edition with Afterthoughts by the Author* (New York: Viking Press.).

—— (1968) 'The Future of the Comparative Method', *Comparative Politics* 1: 3–18.

Latham, E. (1952) 'The Group Basis of Politics: Notes for a Theory', *American Political Science Review*, 46(2): 376–97.

—— (1965) *The Group Basis of Politics: A Study in Basing-Point Legislation* (New York: Octagon Books).

Lavenex, S. (2002) 'EU Enlargement and the Challenge of Policy Transfer', *Journal of Ethnic and Migration Studies*, 28(4): 701–21.

Laver, M. (ed.) (2001) *Estimating the Policy Positions of Political Actors* (London: Routledge).

—— and Hunt, W. B. (1992) *Policy and Party Competition* (New York and London: Routledge).

—— and Schofield, N. (1990) *Multiparty Government* (Oxford: Oxford University Press).

—— and Shepsle, K. A. (1990) 'Coalitions and Cabinet Government', *American Political Science Review*, 84: 873–90.

—— and —— (1991) 'Divided Government: America is Not Exceptional', *Governance*, 4: 250–69.

—— and —— (eds.) (1994) *Cabinet Ministers and Parliamentary Government* (Cambridge: Cambridge University Press).

—— and —— (1996) *Making and Breaking Governments: Cabinets and Legislatures in Parliamentary Democracies* (Cambridge: Cambridge University Press).

—— Benoit, K., and Garry, J. (2003) 'Extracting Policy Positions from Political Texts Using Words as Data', *American Political Science Review*, 97(2): 311–31.

Lazarsfeld, P., Berelson, B., and Gaudet, H. (1944) *The People's Choice: How the Voter Makes up his Mind in a Presidential Campaign* (New York: Columbia University Press).

Lecours, A. (2005) 'New Institutionalism: Issues and Questions', in idem (ed.), *New Institutionalism: Theory and Analysis* (Toronto: University of Toronto Press), 3–26.

—— and Moreno, L. (2003) 'Paradiplomacy: A Nation Building Strategy? A Reference to the Basque Country', in A.-G. Gagnon, M. Guibernau, and F. Rocher (eds.), *The Conditions of Diversity in Multinational Democracies* (Montreal: IRPP/McGill-Queen's University Press).

LeDuc, L. (2003) *The Politics of Direct Democracy: Referendums in Global Perspective* (Peterborough, Ontario: Broadview Press).

—— Niemi, R. G., and Norris, P. (eds.) (2002) *Comparing Democracies 2* (London: Sage).

Lee, C. (2007) 'We Are All Comparativists Now: Why and How Single Country Scholarship Must Adapt and Incorporate the Comparative Politics Approach', *Comparative Political Studies*, 39: 1084–108.

Leeke, M., Sear, C., and Gay, O. (2003) *An Introduction to Devolution in the UK*, Research Paper, 03/84 (London: Parliament and Constitution Centre, House of Commons Library).

LeGrand, J. (1982) *The Strategy of Equality* (London: Allen & Unwin).

Lehmbruch, G. (1967) *Proporzdemokratie* (Tübingen: Mohr).

Lehner, F., and Homann, B. (1987) 'Consociational Decision-Making and Party Government in Switzerland', in Richard S. Katz (ed.), *Party Governments: European and American Experiences* (Berlin: de Gruyter), 243–69.

Lenaerts, K. (1990) 'Constitutionalism and the Many Faces of Federalism', *American Journal of Comparative Law*, 38: 205–63.

Lenschow, A., Liefferink, D., and Veenman, S. (2005) 'When Birds Sing: A Framework for Analysing Domestic Factors Behind Policy Convergence', *Journal of European Public Policy*, 12(5): 764–74.

Levitsky, S., and Way, L. (2005) 'International Linkage and Democratization', *Journal of Democracy*, 16(3): 20–34.

Levy, J. D. (1999) 'Vice into Virtue? Progressive Politics and Welfare Reform in Continental Europe', *Politics and Society* 27(2): 239–74.

Lewis, J. (1992) 'Gender and the Development of Welfare Regimes', *Journal of European Social Policy*, 2(3): 159–73.

Lichbach, M. I. (1995) *The Rebel's Dilemma, Economics, Cognition, and Society* (Ann Arbor, Mich.: University of Michigan Press).

—— and Zuckermann, A. (eds.) (1997) *Comparative Politics: Rationality, Culture and Structure* (Cambridge: Cambridge University Press).

Leibfried, S., and Pierson, P. (1995) 'Semisovereign Welfare States: Social Policy in a Multitiered Europe', in idem (eds.), *European Social Policy: Between Fragmentation and Integration* (Washington, DC: Brookings Institution).

Light, P. C. (1995) *Thickening Government: Federal Hierarchy and the Diffusion of Accountability* (Washington, DC: Brookings Institution).

Lijphart, A. (1968a) *The Politics of Accommodation: Pluralism and Democracy in the Netherlands* (Berkeley, Calif.: University of California Press).

—— (1968b) 'Typologies of Democratic Systems', *Comparative Political Studies*, 1(1): 3–44.

—— (1971) 'Comparative Politics and Comparative Method', *American Political Science Review*, 65: 682–93.

—— (1975) 'The Comparable-Cases Strategy in Comparative Research', *Comparative Political Studies*, 8: 158–77.

—— (1977) *Democracy in Plural Societies: A Comparative Exploration* (New Haven, Conn. and London: Yale University Press).

—— (1979a) 'Religious vs. Linguistic vs. Class Voting: The "Crucial Experiment" of Comparing Belgium, Canada, South Africa, and Switzerland', *American Political Science Review*, 73: 442–58.

—— (1979b) 'Still Muddling, Not Yet Through', *Public Administration Review* 39(6): 517–26.

—— (1984) *Democracies: Patterns of Majoritarian and Consensus Government in Twenty-One Countries* (New Haven, Conn.: Yale University Press).

Lijphart, A. (ed.) (1992) *Parliamentary versus Presidential Government* (Oxford: Oxford University Press).

—— (1994) *Electoral Systems and Party Systems: A Study of Twenty-Seven Democracies, 1945–1990* (Oxford: Oxford University Press).

—— (1996) 'The Puzzle of Indian Democracy: A Consociational Interpretation', *American Political Science Review*, 90: 258–68.

—— (1997) 'Unequal Participation: Democracy's Unresolved Dilemma', *American Political Science Review*, 91(1–14): 1.

—— (1999) *Patterns of Democracy: Government Forms and Performance in Thirty-Six Countries* (New Haven, Conn.: Yale University Press).

—— (2000) 'Varieties of Nonmajoritarian Democracy', in M. M. L. Crepaz, T. A. Koelble, and D. Wilsford (eds.), *Democracy and Institutions: The Life Work of Arend Lijphart* (Ann Arbor, Mich.: University of Michigan Press).

—— and Waisman, C. (eds.) (1996) *Institutional Design in New Democracies* (Boulder, Colo.: Westview Press).

Lin, W.-Y., and Dutton, W. H. (2003) 'The "Net" Effect in Politics: The "Stop the Overlay" Campaign in Los Angeles', *Party Politics*, 9(1): 124–36.

Lindbeck, A., and Snower, D. (1988) *The Insider–Outsider Theory of Unemployment* (Cambridge, Mass.: MIT Press).

Lindberg, L. N. (1963) *The Political Dynamics of Economic Integration* (Oxford: Oxford University Press).

Lindblom, C. E. (1959) 'The Science of Muddling Through', *Public Administration Review*, 19(2): 79–88.

—— (1977) *Politics and Markets: The World's Political-Economic Systems* (New York: Basic Books).

Lindert, P. H. (2004a) *Growing Public: Social Spending and Economic Growth since the Eighteenth Century*, i. *The Story* (Cambridge: Cambridge University Press).

—— (2004b) *Growing Public. Social Spending and Economic Growth since the Eighteenth Century: Further Evidence* (Cambridge: Cambridge University Press).

Linz, J. (1970) 'An Authoritarian Regime: Spain', in E. Allardt and S. Rokkan (eds.) *Mass Politics* (New York: Free Press; 1st publ. 1964).

—— (1975) 'Totalitarian and Authoritarian Regimes', in F. Greenstein and N. Polsby (eds.), *Handbook of Political Science*, iii. *Macropolitical Theory* (Reading, Mass.: Addison-Wesley).

—— (1978) *The Breakdown of Democratic Regimes: Crisis, Breakdown and Equilibration* (Baltimore, Md.: Johns Hopkins University Press).

—— (1990a) 'The Perils of Presidentialism', *Journal of Democracy*, 2: 131–45.

—— (1990b) 'Transitions to Democracy', *Washington Quarterly*, 13(3): 143–64.

—— (1992) 'Change and Continuity in the Nature of Contemporary Democracies', in G. Marks and L. Diamond (eds.), *Reexamining Democracy: Essays in honor of Seymour Martin Lipset* (Beverly Hills, Calif.: Sage).

—— (1994) 'Presidential or Parliamentary Democracy: Does it Make a Difference?', in Linz and Valenzuela 1994.

—— and Stepan, A. (1996) *Problems of Democratic Transition and Consolidation: Southern Europe, South America, and Post-Communist Europe* (Baltimore, Md.: Johns Hopkins University Press).

—— and Valenzuela, A. (eds.) (1994) *The Failure of Presidential Democracies*, i. *Comparative Perspectives* (Baltimore, Md.: Johns Hopkins University Press).

Lipmann, W. (1997) *Public Opinion* (New York: Free Press, 1st publ. 1922).

Lipow, A., and Seyd, P. (1995) 'The Politics of Anti-Partyism', *Parliamentary Affairs*, 49(2): 273–84.

Lipset, S. M. (1959) 'Some Social Requisites of Democracy: Economic Development and Political Legitimacy', *American Political Science Review*, 53(1): 69–105.

—— (1960) *Political Man: The Social Bases of Politics* (Garden City, NY: Doubleday).

—— (1968) *Agrarian Socialism: The Cooperative Commonwealth Federation of Saskatchewanm: A Study in Political Sociology* (Garden City, NY: Doubleday, 1st publ. 1950).

—— (1990) *Continental Divide: The Values and Institutions of the United States and Canada* (New York: Routledge).

—— and Rokkan, S. (1967) 'Cleavage Structures, Party Systems, and Voter Alignments: An Introduction', in idem (eds.), *Party Systems and Voter Alignments* (New York: Free Press), 1–64.

Lipsky, M. (1971) 'Street Level Bureaucracy and the Analysis of Urban Reform', *Urban Affairs Quarterly*, 6: 391–409.

—— (1980) *Street-Level Bureaucracy: The Dilemmas of Individuals in the Public Service* (New York: Russell Sage Foundation).

Ljungkvist, L., and Sargent, T. J. (1998) 'The European Employment Dilemma', *Journal of Political Economy*, 106(3): 514–50.

Lohmann, S. (1994) 'The Dynamics of Informational Cascades: The Monday Demonstrations in Leipzig, East Germany, 1989–91', *World Politics*, 47(1): 42–101.

Lorwin, V. (1966a) 'Belgium: Religion, Class, and Language in National Politics', in R. Dahl 1966: 147–87.

—— (1966b) 'Segmented Pluralism, Ideological Cleavages and Political Cohesion in the Smaller European Democracies', *Comparative Politics*, 3: 141–75

Loughlin, J. (1986) 'Regionalist and Federalist Movements in Contemporary France', in M. Burgess (ed.), *Comparative Federalism and Federation* (London: Croom Helm), 76–98.

—— (1989) *Regionalism and Ethnic Nationalism in France: A Case Study of Corsica* (Florence: European University Institute).

—— (1996) 'Europe of the Regions and the Federalization of Europe', *Publius: The Journal of Federalism*, 26(4): 141–62.

—— (2004a) 'Greece: Between "Henosis" and Decentralization', in Loughlin *et al.* 2004: 271–88.

—— (2004b) 'The "Transformation" of Governance: New Directions in Policy and Politics', *Australian Journal of Politics and History*, 50(1): 8–22.

—— (2007a) 'Les Nationalismes Britannique et Français Face aux Défis de l'Européanisation et de la Mondialisation', in A.-G. Gagnon, A. Lecours, and G. Nootens (eds.), *Les Nationalismes Majoritaires Contemporains: Identité, Mémoire et Pouvoir* (Montréal: Québec Amérique), 193–215.

—— (2007b) *Subnational Government: The French Experience* (Basingstoke: Palgrave Macmillan).

—— and Martin, S. (2003) *International Lesson on Balance of Funding Issues: Initial Paper* (London: Office of the Deputy Prime Minister).

—— and Mazey, S. (eds.) (1995) *The End of the French Unitary State? Ten Years of Regionalization in France* (London: Frank Cass).

—— and Peters, B. G. (1997) 'State Traditions, Administrative Reform and Regionalization', in Keating and Loughlin (eds.) 1997: 41–62.

—— *et al.* (2004) *Subnational Democracy in the European Union: Challenges and Opportunties* (Oxford: Oxford University Press).

—— Lidstrom, A., and Hudson, C. (2005) 'The Politics of Local Taxation in Sweden: Reform and Continuity', *Local Government Studies*, 31(3): 334–68.

Lowi, T. (1964) 'American Business, Public Policy, Case Studies, and Political Theory', *World Politics*, 16: 677–715.

—— (1969) *The End of Liberalism: Ideology, Policy and the Crisis of Public Authority* (New York: Norton).

—— (1972) 'Four Systems of Policy, Politics, and Choice', *Public Administration Review*, 32(4): 298–310.

Lucas, R. E. (1972) 'Expectations and Neutrality of Money', *Journal of Economic Theory*, 4(2): 103–24.

—— (1973) 'Some International Evidence on Output-Inflation Tradeoffs', *American Economic Review*, 63(3): 326–34.

Luhmann, N. (1970) *Soziologische Aufklärung* (Cologne: Westdeutscher Verlag).

—— (1985) *A Sociological Theory of Law* (London: Routledge & Kegan Paul).

Lukes, S. (1974) *Power: A Radical View* (London: Macmillan).

Lunaria (2006) *Come si Vive in Italia? Indice di Qualità Regionale dello Sviluppo (QUARS) 2006* (Rome: Lunaria).

Lupia, A., and Johnston, R. (2001) 'Are Voters to Blame? Voter Competence and Elite Maneuvers in Referendums', in Mendelsohn and Parkin 2001: 191–210.

Lynn, J., and Jay, A. (1988) *The Complete Yes Minister* (London: BBC Books).

McAdam, D. (1982) *Political Process and the Development of Black Insurgency, 1930–1970* (Chicago: University of Chicago Press).

—— (1996) 'Conceptual Origins, Current Problems, Future Directions', in McAdam, McCarthy, and Zald 1996: 23–40.

—— (1999) *Political Process and the Development of Black Insurgency, 1930–1970* (Chicago: University of Chicago Press, 2nd edn).

—— McCarthy, J. D., and Zald, M. N. (1996) *Comparative Perspectives on Social Movements: Political Opportunities, Mobilizing Structures, and Cultural Framings* (Cambridge: Cambridge University Press).

—— Tarrow, S., and Tilly, C. (2001) *Dynamics of Contention* (Cambridge: Cambridge University Press).

McCarthy, J. D., and Zald, M. N. (1977) 'Resource Mobilization and Social Movements: A Partial Theory', *American Journal of Sociology*, 82(6): 1212–41.

McCombs, M. E. (2004) *Setting the Agenda: The Mass Media and Public Opinion* (Cambridge: Polity Press).

—— and Shaw, D. L. (1972) 'The Agenda-Setting Function of Mass Media', *Public Opinion Quarterly*, 36: 176–87.

McConnell, G. (1966) *Private Power and American Democracy* (New York: Knopf).

McDonald, M. D., and Budge, I. (2005) *Elections, Parties, Democracy* (Oxford: Oxford University Press).

McElroy, G., and Benoit, K. (2005) *Party Groups and Policy Positions in the European Parliament*, IIS Discussion Paper, 101 (Dublin: Trinity College).

McEwen, N., and Moreno, L. (eds.) (2005) *The Territorial Politics of Welfare* (Abingdon: Routledge).

McFaul, M. (2004) 'Democracy Promotion as a World Value', *Washington Quarterly*, 28(1): 147–63.

McKay, D. (1996) *Rush to Union: Understanding the European Federal Bargain* (Oxford: Clarendon).

Mackie, T. T., and Rose, R. (1991) *The International Almanac of Electoral History* (London: Macmillan).

Mackintosh, J. P. (1977) *The British Cabinet* (London: Stevens & Sons).

McMillan, J. (1991) *Napoleon III* (Harlow: Longman).

Macpherson, C. (1953) *Democracy in Alberta: The Theory and Practice of a Quasi-Party System* (Toronto: University of Toronto Press).

McQuail, D. (2005) *Mass Communication Theory* (London: Sage, 5th edn).

McRae, K. (1964) 'The Structure of Canadian History', in Hartz 1964.

—— (1974) *Consociational Democracy: Political Accommodation in Segmented Societies* (London: McClelland & Stewart).

Macridis, R. (1955) *The Study of Comparative Government* (New York: Random House).

Maddison, A. (1995) *Monitoring the World Economy: 1820–1992* (Paris: OECD).

—— (2001) *The World Economy: A Millennial Perspective* (Paris: OECD).

Madsen, P. K. (2002) 'The Danish Model of Flexicurity: A Paradise—With Some Snakes', in H. Sarfati and G. Bonoli (eds.), *Labour Market and Social Protection Reforms in International Perspective: Parallel or Converging Tracks?* (London: Ashgate), 243–65.

Magleby, D. B. (1994) 'Direct Legislation in the American States', in Butler and Ranney 1994: 218–57.

Mahler, G. (1998) 'Israel', in G. Kurian (ed.), *World Encyclopedia of Parliaments and Legislatures* (Washington, DC: Congressional Quarterly Press), 352–359.

Mainwaring, S., and Shugart, M. S. (eds.) (1997) *Presidentialism and Democracy in Latin America* (Cambridge: Cambridge University Press).

Mair, P. (1995) 'Political Parties, Popular Legitimacy and Public Privilege', *West European Politics*, 18(3): 40–57.

—— (1996) 'Comparative Politics: An Overview', in Goodin and Klingemann 1996: 309–35.

—— (2002) 'Populist Democracy *vs.* Party Democracy', in Yves Mény and Yves Surel (eds.), *Democracies and the Populist Challenge* (Basingstoke: Palgrave), 81–98.

—— (2006*a*) 'Party System Change', in R. S. Katz and W. J. Crotty (eds.), *Handbook of Political Parties* (London: Sage), 63–73.

—— (2006*b*) 'Sistemi Partitici e Alternanza al Governo, 1950–1999', in L. Bardi (ed.), *Partiti e Sistemi di Partito* (Bologna: Il Mulino), 245–64.

—— (2006*c*) 'Ruling the Void: The Hollowing of Western Democracy', *New Left Review*, 42: 25–51.

—— (2007) 'Political Opposition and the European Union', *Government and Opposition*, 42(1): 1–17.

—— and Biezen, I. van (2001) 'Party Membership in Twenty European Democracies, 1980–2000', *Party Politics*, 7(1): 5–21.

Majone, G. (1993) 'The European Community between Social Policy and Social Regulation', *Journal of Common Market Studies*, 31(2): 153–70.

—— (1996) *Regulating Europe* (London: Routledge).

Malinowski, B. (1931) 'Culture', in E. R. A. Seligman and A. Johnson (eds.), *Encyclopaedia of the Social Sciences* (New York: Macmillan), iv. 621–46.

Manin, B. (1997) *The Principles of Representative Government* (Cambridge: Cambridge University Press).

Manners, I. (2002) 'Normative Power Europe: A Contradiction in Terms?', *Journal of Common Market Studies*, 40(2): 235–58.

Manow, P. (2004) *The Good, the Bad, and the Ugly: Esping-Andersen's Regime Typology and the Religious Roots of the Western Welfare State*, MPIfG Working Paper, 3 (Bonn).

March, J. G., and Olsen, J. P. (1984) 'The New Institutionalism: Organizational Factors in the Political Life', *American Political Science Review*, 78(3): 734–49.

—— and —— (1989) *Rediscovering Institutions* (New York: Free Press).

Margetts, H. (2006) 'Cyber Parties', in R. S. Katz and W. Crotty (eds.), *Handbook of Party Politics* (London: Sage), 528–35.

Margolis, M., and Resnick, D. (2000) *Politics as Usual: The Cyberspace 'Revolution'* (London: Sage).

—— —— and Tu, C. (1997) 'Campaigning on the Internet: Parties and Candidates on the World Wide Web in the 1996 Primary Season', *Harvard International Journal of Press Politics*, 2(1): 59–78.

—— —— and Wolfe, J. (1999) 'Party Competition on the Internet in the United States and Britain', *Harvard International Journal of Press Politics*, 4(4): 24–7

Marin, B., and Mayntz, R. (eds.) (1991) *Policy Networks: Empirical Evidence and Theoretical Considerations* (Frankfurt am Main: Campus).

Marks, G. (1992) 'Rational Sources of Chaos in Democratic Transition', *American Behavioral Scientist*, 35: 397–421.

—— Hooghe, L., and Blank, K. (1996) 'European Integration from the 1980s: State-Centric v. Multi-Level Governance', *Journal of Common Market Studies*, 34(3): 341–78.

Markusen, A. (1987) *Regions: The Economics and Politics of Territory* (Totowa, NJ: Rowman & Littlefield).

Marmor, T. L., Mashaw, J. L., and Harvey, P. L. (1990) *America's Misunderstood Welfare State: Persistent Myth, Enduring Realities* (New York: Basic Books).

Marsh, A. (1990) *Political Action in Europe and the USA* (Basingstoke: Macmillan).

Marshall, T. H. (1949) *The Marshall Lectures* (Cambridge: Cambridge University Press).

—— (1950) *Citizenship and Social Class, and Other Essays* (Cambridge: Cambridge University Press).

—— (1965) *Class, Citizenship and Social Development* (New York: Anchor).

Marthaler, S. (2005) 'The French Referendum on Ratification of the EU Constitutional Treaty, 29 May 2005', *Representation*, 41(3): 230–9.

Martin, B., and Richards, E. (1995) 'Scientific Knowledge, Controversy, and Public Decision-Making', in S. Jasanoff, G. E. Markle, J. C. Petersen, and T. Pinch (eds.), *Handbook of Science and Technology Studies* (Newbury Park, Calif.: Sage), 506–26.

Martin, J. P. (2000) *What Works among Active Labour Market Policies: Evidence from OECD Countries' Experiences*, OECD Economic Studies, 30 (Paris: OECD).

Martin, L., and Simmons, B. (1998) 'Theories and Empirical Studies of International Institutions', *International Organization*, 52: 729–57.

Martin, L. W., and Vanberg, G. (2004) 'Policing the Bargain: Coalition Government and Parliamentary Scrutiny', *American Journal of Political Science*, 48: 13–27.

Mattson, I. (1995), 'Private Members Initiatives and Amendments', in Döring 1995: 448–87.

Massey, D. (1978) 'Regionalism: Some Current Issues', *Capital and Class*, 6: 106–25.

Massicotte, L. (2005) 'Canada: Sticking to First-Past-the-Post, for the Time Being', in Gallagher and Mitchell 2005: 99–118.

Mattila, M. (2004) 'Contested Decisions: Empirical Analysis of Voting in the European Union Council of Ministers', *European Journal of Political Research*, 43(1): 29–50.

Mavrogordatos, G. T. (1996) 'Duverger and the Jacobins', *European Journal of Political Research*, 30(1): 1–17.

Mayer, L. R. (1989) *Redefining Comparative Politics: Promise versus Performance* (Beverly Hills, Calif. and London: Sage).

Mayhew, D. R. (1991) *Divided we Govern* (New Haven, Conn.: Yale University Press).

Mayntz, R. (1977) 'Die Implementation politischer Programme: Theoretische Überlegungen zu einem neuen Forschungsgebiet', *Die Verwaltung*, 10: 51–66.

—— (1979) 'Public Bureaucracies and Policy Implementation', *International Social Science Journal*, 31(4): 633–45.

Mazey, S., and Richardson, J. (1996) 'EU Policy Making: A Garbage Can or Anticipatory Policy Style?', in Y. Mény, P. Muller, and J.-L. Quermonne (eds.), *Adjusting to Europe: The Impact of the European Union on National Institutions and Policies* (London: Routledge), 41–58.

—— and —— (eds.) (2001) *European Union: Power and Policy-Making* (London: Routledge).

Mazmanian, D., and Sabatier, P. (1983) *Implementation and Public Policy* (Glenview: Scott).

Mead, M. (1951) 'The Study of National Character', in D. Lerner and H. D. Lasswell (eds.), *The Policy Sciences* (Stanford, Calif.: Stanford University Press), 70–85.

Meier, K. J. (2000) *Politics and the Bureaucracy: Policymaking in the Fourth Branch of Government* (New York: Harcourt College).

—— and Bohte, J. (2001) 'Structure and Discretion: The Missing Link in Representative Bureaucracy', *Journal of Public Administration Research and Theory*, 11: 455–70.

Meikle, G. (2002) *Future Active: Media Activism and the Internet* (New York: Routledge).

Melia, T. (2006) 'Toolbox: The Democracy Bureaucracy', *American Interest*, 1(4): 122–30.

Meltzer, A. H., and Richard, S. F. (1981) 'A Rational Theory of the Size of Government', *Journal of Political Economy*, 89(5): 914–27.

Mendelsohn, M., and Parkin, A. (eds.) (2001) *Referendum Democracy: Citizens, Elites and Deliberation in Referendum Campaigns* (Basingstoke: Palgrave).

Mény, Y., and Surel, Y. (eds.) (2002) *Democracies and the Populist Challenge* (Basingstoke: Palgrave).

Merkel, W. *et al.* (2003) *Defekte Demokratie* (Opladen: Leske & Budrich).

Merrit, S. (1984) 'Negative Political Advertising: Some Empirical Findings', *Journal of Advertising*, 13: 27–38.

Merritt, R., and Rokkan, S. (eds.) (1966) *Comparing Nations* (New Haven, Conn.: Yale University Press).

Meseguer Yebra, C. (2003) *Learning and Economic Policy Choices: A Bayesian Approach*, EUI Working Paper RSC, 2003/5 (San Domenico: European University Institute).

—— (2006) 'Rational Learning and Bounded Learning in the Diffusion of Policy Innovations', *Rationality and Society*, 18(1): 35–66.

Meyer, D. S., and Tarrow, S. (1998*a*) 'A Movement Society: Contentious Politics for a New Century', in idem 1998*b*: 1–28.

—— and —— (eds.) (1998*b*) *The Social Movement Society: Contentious Politics for a New Century* (Lanham, Md., and Boulder, Colo.: Rowman & Littlefield).

Meyers, P., and Vorsanges, J. (2005) 'Street Level Bureaucracy', in B. G. Peters and J. Pierre (ed.), *Handbook of Public Administration* (London: Sage).

Mezey, M. (1979) *Comparative Legislatures* (Durham, NC: Duke University Press).

Michalopoulos, C. *et al.* (2002) *Making Work Pay: Final Report on the Self-Sufficiency Project for Long-Term Welfare Recipients*, SRDC Working Paper Series (Ottawa: Social Research and Demonstration Corporation).

Michels, R. (1915) *Political Parties: A Sociological Study of the Oligarchical Tendencies of Modern Democracy* (London: Jarrold & Sons).

Milgrom, P., and Roberts, J. (1992) *Economics, Organization and Management* (Englewood Cliffs, NJ: Prentice-Hall International).

Mill, J. S. (1843) *A System of Logic* (London: Longman, 1959 repr.; also in *John Stuart Mill on Politics and Society* (London: Fontana, 1976)), 55–89.

—— (1859) 'M. de Tocqueville and Democracy in America', in *Dissertations and Discussions* (London: John W. Parker).

Miller, D. (1997) *On Nationality* (Oxford: Oxford University Press).

Miller, E. A., and Banaszak-Holl, J. (2005) 'Cognitive and Normative Determinants of State Policymaking Behavior: Lessons from the Sociological Institutionalism', *Publius*, 35(2): 191–216.

Mills, C. W. (1956) *The Power Elite* (New York: Oxford University Press).

Milner, H. (1989) *Sweden: Social Democracy in Practice* (Oxford: Oxford University Press).

Milward, A. S. (2000) *The European Rescue of the Nation-State* (London: Routledge, 2nd edn).

Minns, J. (2006) *The Politics of Developmentalism: The Midas States of Mexico, South Korea and Taiwan* (Basingstoke: Palgrave).

Mitchell, D. (1990) 'Income Transfer Systems: A Comparative Study Using Microdata', Ph.D. thesis, Australian National University.

Mitchell, P. (2005) 'United Kingdom: Plurality Rule under Siege', in Gallagher and Mitchell 2005: 157–84.

Møller, J. (2007) 'The Gap between Electoral and Liberal Democracy Revisited: Some Conceptual and Empirical Qualifications', *Acta Politica* (forthcoming).

Montesquieu (1721) *Persian Letters* (Harmondsworth: Penguin, 1973).

Moore, B. (1966) *Social Origins of Dictatorship and Democracy: Lord and Peasant in the Making of the Modern World* (Boston: Beacon Press).

Moravcsik, A. (1991) 'Negotiating the Single European Act: National Interests and Conventional Statecraft in the European Community', *International Organization*, 45(1): 19–56.

—— (1993) 'Preferences and Power in the European Community: A Liberal Intergovernmentalist Approach', *Journal of Common Market Studies*, 31(4): 473–524.

—— (1998) *The Choice for Europe: Social Purpose and State Power from Messina to Maastricht* (Ithaca, NY: Cornell University Press).

—— (2002) 'In Defense of the "Democratic Deficit": Reassessing the Legitimacy of the European Union', *Journal of Common Market Studies*, 40(4): 603–34.

Moreno, L. (2001) *The Federalization of Spain* (London: Routledge).

Morgan, K. J. (2002) 'Forging the Frontiers between State, Church and Family: Religious Cleavages and the Origins of Early Childhood Education in France, Sweden, and Germany', *Politics and Society*, 30(1): 113–48.

—— (2003) 'The Politics of Mothers' Employment', *World Politics*, 55(2): 259–89.

—— (2006) *Working Mothers and the Welfare State: Religion and the Politics of Work–Family Policies in Western Europe and the States* (Stanford, Calif.: Stanford University Press).

Morgenstern, S., and Nacif, B. (eds.) (2002) *Legislative Politics in Latin America* (Cambridge: Cambridge University Press).

Mortensen, D. T. (1977) 'Unemployment Insurance and Job Search Decisions', *Industrial and Labor Relations Review*, 30: 505–17.

Moustafa, T. (2007) *The Struggle for Constitutional Power: Law, Politics, and Economic Development in Egypt* (Cambridge: Cambridge University Press).

Mozzafer, S. (2006) 'Party, Ethnicity and Democratization in Africa', in R. S. Katz and W. Crotty (eds.), *Handbook of Party Politics* (London: Sage), 239–47.

Mudde, C. (2004) 'The Populist *Zeitgeist*', *Government and Opposition*, 39(3): 541–63.

Mueller, D. C. (2003) *Public Choice III* (Cambridge: Cambridge University Press).

Mueller, W., and Strom, K. (2000) *Coalition Governments in Western Europe* (Oxford: Oxford University Press).

Muller, E. N. (1989) 'Distribution of Income in Advanced Capitalist States: Political Parties, Labour Unions, and the International Economy', *European Journal of Political Research*, 17(4): 367–400.

Müller, W. C. (1994) 'Models of Goverment and the Austrian Cabinet', in Laver and Shepsle 1994.

—— and —— (eds.) (2000) *Coalition Governments in Western Europe* (Oxford: Oxford University Press).

Müller-Rommel, F., and Poguntke, T. (eds.) (2002) *Green Parties in National Governments* (London: Frank Cass).

—— Fettelschloss, K., and Harfst, P. (2004) 'Party Government in Central Eastern European Democracies: A Data Collection (1990–2003)', *European Journal of Political Research*, 43: 869–93.

Munck, G. L. (2001) 'Game Theory and Comparative Politics: New Perspectives and Old Concerns', *World Politics*, 53(2): 173–204.

—— and Verkuilen, J. (2002) 'Conceptualizing and Measuring Democracy', *Comparative Political Studies*, 35(1): 5–34.

Mundell, R. (1961) 'A Theory of Optimal Currency Areas', *American Economic Review*, 51: 657–65.

Munger, M. C. (2000) *Analyzing Policy: Choices, Conflicts, and Practices* (New York: W. W. Norton & Co.).

Mungiu-Pippidi, A. (2005) 'The Unbearable Lightness of Democracy: Is Good Quality Democracy Possible in a Post-Communist Environment?', in Diamond and Morlino 2005.

Murphy, D. (2006) *The Structure of Regulatory Competition: Corporations and Public Policies in a Global Economy* (Oxford: Oxford University Press).

Murray, C. (1984) *Losing Ground: American Social Policy 1950–1980* (New York: Basic Books).

Musso, J., Weare, C., and Hale, M. (2000) 'Designing Web Technologies for Local Governance Reform: Good Management or Good Democracy?', *Political Communication*, 17(1): 1–19.

Myles, J. (1989) *Old Age in the Welfare State: The Political Economy of Public Pensions* (Lawrence, Kan.: University Press of Kansas, rev. edn).

—— and Pierson, P. (2001) 'The Comparative Political Economy of Pension Reform', in Pierson 2001: 305–33.

—— and Quadagno, J. (2002) 'Political Theories and the Welfare State', *Social Service Review*, 76(1): 34–57.

Myrdal, G. (1957) *Economic Theory and Underdeveloped Regions* (London: Gerald Duckworth).

Nairn, T. (1977) *The Break-up of Britain: Crisis and Neo-nationalism* (London: New Left Books).

Naisbitt, J. (1994) *The Global Paradox* (New York: Avon).

Naroll, R. (1961) 'Two Solutions to Galton's Problem', *Philosophy of Science*, 28: 16–39.

Narud, H. M., and Valen, H. (2007) 'Coalition Membership and Electoral Performance', in Strøm, Müller, and Bergman 2007.

Ndegwa, S. N. (1997) 'Citizenship and Ethnicity: An Examination of Two Transition Moments in Kenyan Politics', *American Political Science Review*, 91(3): 599–617.

Needham, C. (2003) 'The Citizen as Consumer: E-Government in the United Kingdom and the United States', in Gibson, Ward, and Römmele 2003b: 43–69.

Negrine, R., and Papathanassopoulos, S. (1996) 'The "Americanization" of Political Communication: A Critique', *Harvard Journal of Press/Politics*, 1: 45–62.

Negroponte, N. (1995) *Being Digital* (London: Hodder & Stoughton).

Neidhardt, F. (1994) 'Öffentlichkeit, öffentliche Meinung, soziale Bewegungen', in idem (ed.), *Öffentlichkeit, öffentliche Meinung, soziale Bewegungen*, Kölner Zeitschrift Sonderheft, 34 (Opladen: Westdeutscher Verlag), 7–41.

Newell, J. L. (2001) 'Italian Political Parties on the Web', *Harvard International Journal of Press Politics*, 6: 60–87.

Newman, E., and Rich, R. (eds.) (2004) *The UN Role in Promoting Democracy: Between Ideals and Reality* (Tokyo and New York: United Nations University Press).

Newton, K. (1997) 'Social Capital and Democracy', *American Behavioral Scientist*, 50: 575–86.

—— (2004) 'Social Trust: Individual and Cross-National Approaches', *Portuguese Journal of Social Sciences*, 3: 15–35.

—— and van Deth, J. W. (2005) *Foundations of Comparative Politics* (Cambridge: Cambridge University Press).

Nickell, S. '(1997) 'Unemployment and Labor Market Rigidities: Europe versus North America', *Journal of Economic Perspectives*, 11(3): 55–74.

—— and Layard, R. (1999) 'Labour Market Institutions and Economic Performance', in O. Ashenfelter and D. Card (eds.), *Handbook of Labour Economics* (Amsterdam: North Holland), iii. 3029–84.

—— Nunziata, L., and Ochel, W. (2004) 'Unemployment in the OECD since the 1960s: What do we Know?', *Economic Journal*, 115(1): 1–27.

Nie, N. H., and Verba, S. (1975) 'Political Participation', in F. I. Greenstein and N. W. Polsby (eds.), *Handbook of Political Science*, iv. *Nongovernmental Politics* (Reading, Mass.: Addison-Wesley).

Nijeboer, A. (2005) 'The Dutch Referendum', *European Constitutional Law Review*, 1(3): 393–405.

Nikolenyi, C. (2004) 'Cabinet Stability in Post-Communist Cnetral Europe', *Party Politics*, 10: 123–50.

Niskanen, W. A. (1971) *Bureaucracy and Representative Government* (Chicago: Aldine Atherton).

Noel, S. (2005) *From Power-Sharing to Democracy: Post-Conflict Institutions in Ethnically Divided Societies* (Montreal: McGill-Queens University Press).

Noelle-Neumann, E. (1973) 'Return to the Concept of Powerful Media', *Studies of Broadcasting*, 9: 66–112.

Nordlinger, E. A. (1977) *Soldiers in Politics: Military Coups and Governments* (Englewood Cliffs, NJ: Prentice-Hall).

Norris, P. (1999) 'Introduction: The Growth of Critical Citizens', in idem (ed.), *Critical Citizens: Global Support for Democratic Government* (Oxford: Oxford University Press), 1–27.

—— (2000) *A Virtuous Circle: Political Communications in Postindustrial Societies* (Cambridge: Cambridge University Press).

—— (2003) 'Revolution, What Revolution? The Internet and US Elections, 1992–2000', in E. C. Kamarck and J. S. Nye (eds.), *Governance.com: Democracy in the Information Age* (Washington, DC: Brookings Institution).

—— (2004) *Electoral Engineering: Voting Rules and Political Behaviour* (Cambridge: Cambridge University Press).

—— and Inglehart, R. (2004) *Sacred and Secular: Religion and Politics Worldwide* (Cambridge: Cambridge University Press).

Nownes, A. J. (1995) 'The Other Exchange: Public Interest Groups, Patrons, and Benefits', *Social Science Quarterly*, 76(2): 381–401.

—— and Cigler, A. (1995) 'Public Interest Groups and the Road to Survival', *Polity*, 27(3): 379–404.

Nye, J. S. (2001). 'Globalizations's Democratic Deficit', *Foreign Affairs*, 80: 2–6.

—— (2002) *The Paradox of American Power* (Oxford: Oxford University Press).

Nye, J., Jr. (2005), *Soft Power: The Means to Success in World Politics* (New York: Public Affairs).

Oberschall, A. (1973) *Social Conflict and Social Movements* (Englewood Cliffs, NJ: Prentice-Hall).

Oberthür, S., and Tänzler, D. (2002) 'International Regimes as a Trigger of Policy Diffusion: The Development of Climate Policies in the European Union', in F. Biermann, R. Brohm, and K. Dingwerth (eds.), *Proceedings of the 2001 Berlin Conference on the Human Dimensions of Global Environmental Change 'Global Change and the Nation State'* (Potsdam: Potsdam Institute for Climate Change Impact Research), 317–28.

O'Connor, J. (1973) *The Fiscal Crisis of the State* (New York: St Martin's Press).

—— Orloff, A., and Shaver, S. (1999) *States, Markets, and Families: Gender, Liberalism and Social Policy in Australia, Canada, Great Britain and the United States* (New York: Cambridge University Press).

O'Donnell, G. (1973) *Modernization and Bureaucratic Authoritarianism: Studies in South American Politics* (Berkeley, Calif.: Institute of International Studies/University of California, repr. 1979).

—— (1994) 'Delegative Democracy', *Journal of Democracy*, 5(1): 55–69.

—— (1996) 'Illusions about Democracy', *Journal of Democracy*, 7(2): 34–51.

—— and Schmitter, P. (1986) *Transitions from Authoritarian Rule: Tentative Conclusions about Uncertain Democracies* (Baltimore, Md.: Johns Hopkins University Press).

O'Dwyer, C. (2006) *Runaway State-Building: Patronage Politics and Democratic Development* (Baltimore, Md.: Johns Hopkins University Press).

OECD (1994) *The OECD Jobs Study: Evidence and Explanations. Part I: Labour Market Trends and Underlying Forces of Change; Part II: The Adjustment Potential of the Labour Market* (Paris: OECD).

—— (1997) *The OECD Jobs Strategy: Implementing the OECD Jobs Strategy. Member Countries' Experiences. and Making Work Pay: Taxation, Benefit, Employment and Unemployment* (Paris: OECD).

—— (2004) *Employment Outlook* (Paris: OECD).

—— (2006) *OECD Employment Outlook: Boosting Jobs and Incomes* (Paris: OECD).

—— (2007) *OECD Social Expenditure Database* (Paris: OECD, Feb.).

Offe, C., and Wiesenthal, H. (1980) 'Two Logics of Collective Action', *Political Power and Social Theory*, 1: 67–115.

Ohmae, K. (1993) 'The Rise of the Region State', *Foreign Affairs*, 72(2): 78–87.

—— (1995) *End of the Nation State: The Rise of Regional Economies* (London: HarperCollins).

Ohnet, J.-M. (1996) *Histoire de la Décentralisation Française* (Paris: Livre de poche).

Okun, A. M. (1975) *Equality and Efficiency: The Big Tradeoff* (Washington, DC: Brookings Institution Press).

Olson, D. (1980) *The Legislative Process: A Comparative Approach* (New York: Harper & Row Publishers).

Olson, M. (1965) *The Logic of Collective Action* (Cambridge, Mass.: Harvard University Press).

—— (1982) *The Rise and Decline of Nations: Economic Growth, Stagflation, and Social Rigidities* (New Haven, Conn.: Yale University Press).

Orloff, A. (1993) 'Gender and the Social Rights of Citizenship', *American Sociological Review*, 58(3): 303–28.

Ostrom, E. (1990) *Governing the Commons: The Evolution of Institutions of Collective Action* (Cambridge: Cambridge University Press).

—— (2007) 'Institutional Rational Choice: An Assessment of the Institutional Analysis and Development Framework', in P. A. Sabatier (ed.), *Theories of the Policy Process* (Boulder, Colo.: Westview Press, 2nd edn), 21–64.

Oversloot, H., and Verheul, R. (2006) 'Managing Democracy: Political Parties and the State in Russia', *Journal of Communist Studies and Transition Politics*, 22(3): 383–405.

Owen, D. (2006) 'The Internet and Youth Civic Engagement in the United States', in S. Oates, D. Owen, and R. Gibson (eds.), *The Internet and Politics: Citizens, Voters and Activists* (Abingdon: Routledge).

Pacquet, S., 'Personal Knowledge Publishing and its Uses in Research'. Available at http://radio.weblogs.com/0110772/stories/2002/10/03/personalKnowledge-PublishingAnd Its UsesInResearch.html.

Page, E., and Goldsmith, M. (eds.) (1987) *Central and Local Government Relations: A Comparative Analysis of West European Unitary States* (London and Beverly Hills, Calif.: Sage).

—— and Wright, V. (eds.) (1999) *Bureaucratic Élites in Western European States* (Oxford: Oxford University Press).

—— and —— (eds.) (2007) *From the Active to the Enabling State* (Houndmills: Palgrave Macmillan).

Painter, A., and Wardle, B. (eds.) (2001) *Viral Politics: Communication in the New Media Era* (London: Politico).

Palme, J. (1990) *Pension Rights in Welfare Capitalism: The Development of Old-Age Pensions in Eighteen OECD Countries, 1930 to 1985* (Stockholm: Swedish Institute for Social Research).

Panebianco, A. (1988) *Political Parties: Organization and Power* (Cambridge: Cambridge University Press).

Paquin, S. (2003) 'Paradiplomatie Identitaire et Diplomatie en Belgique Fédérale: Le Cas de la Flandre', *Revue Canadienne de Science Politique*, 36(3): 621–42.

Parekh, B. (2000) *Rethiniking Multiculturalism: Cultural Diversity and Political Theory* (Basingstoke: Macmillan).

Parkinson, C. N. (1958) *Parkinson's Law: The Pursuit of Progress* (London: John Murray).

Parsons, T. (1968) *The Structure of Social Action* (New York: Free Press, 2nd edn).

Patterson, T. E., and McClure, R. D. (1976) *The Unseeing Eye: The Myth of Television Power in National Elections* (New York: Putnam).

Paxton, P. (2002) 'Social Capital and Democracy: An Interdependent Relationship', *American Sociological Review*, 67: 254–77.

Pedersen, S. (1990) 'Gender, Welfare, and Citizenship in Britain during the Great War', *American Historical Review*, 95(4): 983–1006.

—— (1993) *Family Dependence and the Origin of the Welfare State, Britain and France, 1914–1945* (Cambridge: Cambridge University Press).

Peeters, P. (2007) 'Multinational Federations: Reflections on the Belgian State', in M. Burgess and J. Pinder (eds.), *Multinational Federations* (London: Routledge), 31–49.

Pei, M., and Kasper, S. (2003) *Lessons from the Past: The American Record on Nation Building*, Policy Brief, 24 (Washington, DC: Carnegie Endowment for International Peace).

Pempel, T. J. (1998) *Regime Shift: Comparative Dynamics of the Japanese Political Economy* (Ithaca, NY: Cornell University Press).

Penner, E., Blidook, K., and Soroka, S. (2006) 'Legislative Priorities and Public Opinion: Representation of Partisan Agendas in the Canadian House of Commons', *Journal of European Public Policy*, 13(7): 1006–20.

Pennings, P., Keman, H., and Kleinnijenhuis, J. (2006) *Doing Research in Political Science: An Introduction to Comparative Methods and Statistics* (London: Sage, 2nd edn).

Perroux, F. (1950) 'Economic Space: Theory and Applications', *Quarterly Journal of Economics*, 64: 89–104.

Perse, E. M. (2001) *Media Effects and Society* (Mahwah, NJ: Erlbaum).

Peters, B. G. (1998) *Comparative Politics: Theory and Methods* (Basingstoke: Macmillan).

—— (2000) *Institutional Theory in Political Science: The New Institutionalism* (London: Continuum).

—— (2006) 'Consociationalism, Corruption and Chocolate: Belgian Exceptionalism', *West European Politics*, 29: 129–45.

—— and Pierre, J. (eds.) (2001) *Politicians, Bureaucrats, and Administrative Reform* (London: Routledge).

Peterson, M. (1992) 'The Presidency and Organized Interests: White House Patterns of Interest Group Liaison', *American Political Science Review*, 86(3): 612–25.

Pew Report (2003) 'Cable and Internet Loom Large in Fragmented Internet Universe.' Available at www.pewinternet.org/pdfs/PIP_Political_Info_Jan04.pdf, released 11 Jan. (Washington, DC: Pew Research Center for People and the Press).

Piccone, T., and Youngs, R. (eds.) (2006) *Strategies for Democratic Change* (Washington, DC and Madrid: Democracy Coalition Project and Fundación para las Relaciones Internacionales y el Diálogo Exterior).

Pickerill, J. (2003) *Cyberprotest: Environmental Action On-Line* (Manchester: Manchester University Press).

Pierre, J., and Peters, B. G. (2000) *Governance, Politics and the State* (Basingstoke: Palgrave).

Pierson, C. (2003) 'Learning from Labor? Welfare Policy Transfer between Australia and Britain', *Commonwealth and Comparative Politics*, 41(1): 77–100.

Pierson, P. (1994) *Dismantling the Welfare State? Reagan, Thatcher, and the Politics of Retrenchment* (New York: Cambridge University Press).

—— (1996) 'The Path to European Integration: A Historical Institutionalist Analysis', *Comparative Political Studies*, 29(2): 123–63.

—— (1998) 'Irresistible Forces, Immovable Objects: Post-Industrial Welfare States Confront Permanent Austerity', *Journal of European Public Policy*, 5(4): 539–60.

—— (2000) 'Increasing Returns, Path Dependence, and the Study of Politics', *American Political Science Review*, 94(2): 251–67.

Pierson, P. (2001*a*) 'Coping with Permanent Austerity: Welfare State Restructuring in Affluent Democracies', in idem 2001*b*: 411–56.

—— (2001*b*) *The New Politics of the Welfare State* (Oxford: Oxford University Press).

—— and Skocpol, T. (2002) 'Historical Institutionalism in Contemporary Political Science', in I. Katznelson and H. V. Milner (eds.), *Political Science: The State of the Discipline* (New York and Washington, DC: Norton and American Political Science Association), 693–721.

Piore, M. J., and Sabel, C. F. (1984) *The Second Industrial Divide: Possibilities for Prosperity* (New York: Basic Books).

Pitkin, H. (1967) *The Concept of Representation* (Berkeley, Calif.: University of California Press).

Piven, F. F., and Cloward, R. A. (1977) *Poor People's Movements: Why they Succeed, How they Fail* (New York: Vintage Books).

Plasser, F. (2000) 'American Campaign Techniques Worldwide', *Harvard International Journal of Press/Politics*, 5: 33–54.

—— and Plasser, G. (2002) *Global Political Campaigning: A Worldwide Analysis of Campaign Professionals and their Practice* (Westport, Conn.: Praeger).

Poggi, G. (1999) *The State: Its Nature, Development and Prospects* (Cambridge: Polity Press).

Poguntke, T., and Webb, P. (eds.) (2005) *The Presidentialization of Politics* (Oxford: Oxford University Press).

Pollack, M. A. (1997) 'Delegation, Agency and Agenda Setting in the European Community', *International Organization*, 51(1): 99–134.

—— (2003) *The Engines of European Integration: Delegation, Agency, and Agenda Setting in the EU* (Oxford: Oxford University Press).

Polsby, N. W. (1960) *Community Power and Political Theory* (New Haven, Conn.: Yale University Press).

—— (1975) 'Legislatures', in F. I. Greenstein and N. Polsby (eds.), *Handbook of Political Science* (Reading, Mass.: Addison-Wesley Press).

Pontusson, J. (1995) 'From Comparative Public Policy to Political Economy: Putting Institutions in their Place', *Comparative Political Studies*, 27: 117–47.

—— (2005) *Inequality and Prosperity: Social Europe vs. Liberal America* (Ithaca, NY: Cornell University Press).

Popitz, H. (1992) *Phänomene der Macht* (Tübingen: Mohr, 2nd edn).

Popkin, S. L. (1979) *The Rational Peasant: The Political Economy of Rural Society in Vietnam* (Berkeley, Calif.: University of California Press).

—— (1991) *The Reasoning Voter: Communication and Persuasion in Presidential Campaigns* (Chicago: University of Chicago Press).

Porter, B. D. (1994) *War and Rise of the State: The Military Foundations of Modern Politics* (New York: Free Press).

Porter, M. E. (1990) *The Comparative Advantages of Nations* (New York: Free Press).

Post, R. (2000) *Democratic Constitutionalism and Cultural Heterogeneity*, Working Paper, 2000-8 (Berkeley, Calif.: UC Berkeley, Institute of Governmental Studies).

Powell, G. B., Jr. (1982) *Contemporary Democracies: Participation, Stability and Violence* (Cambridge, Mass.: Harvard University Press).

—— (1986) 'American Voter Turnout in Comparative Perspective', *American Political Science Review*, 80(1): 17–43.

Powell, W. W. (1991) 'Expanding the Scope of Institutional Analysis', in W. W. Powell and P. J. DiMaggio (eds.), *The New Institutionalism in Organizational Analysis* (Chicago: University of Chicago Press), 183–203.

Pralle, S. (2006) 'Timing and Sequence in Agenda-Setting and Policy Change: A Comparative Study of Lawn Care Pesticide Politics in Canada and the US', *Journal of European Public Policy*, 13(7): 987–1005.

Pressman, J. L., and Wildavsky, A. (1973) *Implementation: How Great Expectations in Washington are Dashed in Oakland* (Berkeley, Calif.: University of California Press).

Preuß, U. (1996) 'The Political Meaning of Constitutionalism', in R. Bellamy (ed.), *Constitutionalism, Democracy, and Sovereignty* (Aldershot: Avebury Press).

Pridham, G. (2005) *Designing Democracy: EU Enlargement and Regime Change in Post-Communist Europe* (Basingstoke: Palgrave).

Przeworski, A. (1985) *Capitalism and Social Democracy* (New York: Cambridge University Press).

—— (1987) 'Methods of Cross-National Research 1970–1983', in M. Dierkes, H. Weiler, and A. B. Antal (eds.), *Comparative Policy Research: Learning from Experience* (Aldershot: Gower), 25–57.

—— (1991) *Democracy and the Market: Political and Economic Reforms in Eastern Europe and Latin America* (Cambridge: Cambridge University Press).

—— (2004) 'Institutions Matter?', *Government and Opposition*, 39(4): 527-40.

—— and Sprague, J. D. (1986) *Paper Stones: A History of Electoral Socialism* (Chicago: University of Chicago Press).

—— and Teune, H. (1970) *The Logic of Comparative Social Inquiry* (New York: Wiley Interscience).

Pryce, S. (1997) *Presidentializing the Premiership* (Houndmills: Macmillan).

Pryor, F. L. (1968) *Public Expenditure in Communist and Capitalist Countries* (London: Allen & Unwin).

Pülzl, H., and Treib, O. (2006) 'Policy Implementation', in F. Fischer, G. Miller, and M. Sidney (eds.), *Handbook of Public Policy Analysis: Theory, Politics, and Methods* (Boca Raton: CRC Press), 89–107.

Putnam, R. D. (1976) *The Comparative Study of Political Elites* (Englewood Cliffs, NJ: Prentice-Hall).

—— (1993) *Making Democracy Work: Civic Traditions in Modern Italy* (Princeton: Princeton University Press).

—— (1995) 'Tuning in, Tuning out: The Strange Disappearance of Social Capital in America', *PS: Political Science and Politics*, 28(4): 664–83.

—— (2000) *Bowling Alone: The Collapse and Revival of American Community* (New York: Simon & Schuster).

—— Leonardi, R., and Nanetti, R. Y. (1993) *Making Democracy Work: Civic Traditions in Modern Italy* (Princeton: Princeton University Press).

Pye, L. (1968) 'Introduction', in idem (ed.), *Political Culture and Political Development* (Princeton: Princeton University Press).

—— and Verba, S. (eds.) (1969) *Political Culture and Political Development* (Princeton: Princeton University Press, 1st publ. 1965)

Qvortrup, M. (2005) *A Comparative Study of Referendums: Government by the People* (Manchester: Manchester University Press, 2nd edn).

Radaelli, C. (2000) 'Policy Transfer in the European Union: Institutional Isomorphism as a Source of Legitimacy', *Governance*, 13: 25–43.

—— (2005) 'Diffusion Without Convergence: How Political Context Shapes the Adoption of Regulatory Impact Assessment', *Journal of European Public Policy*, 12(5): 924–43.

Radcliff, B., and Davis, P. (2000) 'Labor Organization and Electoral Participation in Industrial Democracies', *American Journal of Political Science*, 44: 132.

Rae, D. W. (1971) *The Political Consequences of Electoral Laws* (New Haven, Conn.: Yale University Press, 2nd edn).

Ragin, C. (1987) *The Comparative Method: Moving Beyond Qualitative and Quantitative Strategies* (Berkeley, Calif.: University of California Press).

—— (ed.) (1991) *Issues and Alternatives in Comparative Social Research* (Leiden: Brill).

—— (2000) *Fuzzy-Set Social Science* (Chicago: University of Chicago Press).

Rahat, G., and Hazan, R. Y. (2005) 'Israel: The Politics of an Extreme Electoral System', in Gallagher and Mitchell 2005: 333–52.

Rainie, L., Cornfield, M., and Horrigan, J. (2005) 'The Internet and Campaign 2004', 6 Mar. Pew Research Center. Available at www.pewinternet.org/pdfs/PIP_2004_macrosgt-Campaign.pdf.

Rakove, J. N. (1996) *Original Meanings: Politics and Ideas in the Making of the Constitution* (New York: Knopf).

Ranney, A. (1962) *The Doctrine of Responsible Party Government* (Urbana, Ill.: University of Illinois Press).

—— (1981) 'The Working Conditions of Members of Parliament and Congress: Changing the Tools of the Job', in N. J. Ornstein (ed.), *The Role of the Legislature in Western Democracies* (Washington, DC: American Enterprise Institute), ch. 5.

Rapoport, A., and Chammah, A. M. (1966) 'The Game of Chicken', *American Behavioral Scientist*, 10: 23–8.

Rasporich, B. (1997) 'Regional Identities: Introduction', in D. Taras and B. Rasporich (eds.), *A Passion for Identity: An Introduction to Canadian Studies* (Toronto: Nelson, 3rd edn).

Raunio, T. (2005) 'Finland: One Hundred Years of Quietude', in Gallagher and Mitchell 2005: 473–90.

Rawlings, R. (2001) 'Law, Territory and Integration: A View from the Atlantic Shore', *International Review of Administrative Sciences*, 67(3): 479–504.

Reed, S. R. (2005) 'Japan: Haltingly toward a Two-Party System', in Gallagher and Mitchell 2005: 277–94.

Requejo, F. (2005) *Multinational Federalism and Value Pluralism: The Spanish Case* (London: Routledge).

Reynolds, A. (2002) *The Architecture of Democracy: Constitutional Design, Conflict Management and Democracy* (Oxford: Oxford University Press).

—— Reilly, B., and Ellis, A. (2005) *Electoral System Design: The New International IDEA Handbook* (Stockholm: International IDEA).

Rheingold, H. (1995) *The Virtual Community: Homesteading on the Electronic Frontier* (London: Minerva).

Rhodes, R. A. W. (1995) 'From Prime Ministerial Power to Core Executive', in Rhodes and Dunleavy 1995.

—— (1997) *Understanding Governance: Policy Networks, Governance, Reflexivity and Accountability* (Buckingham: Open University Press).

—— and Dunleavy, P. (eds.) (1995) *Prime Minister, Cabinet and Core Executive* (London: Macmillan).

—— and Marsh, D. (1992) 'New Directions in the Study of Policy Networks', *European Journal of Political Research*, 21(1–2): 181–205.

Richardson, J. (ed.) (1982) *Policy Styles in Western Europe* (London: Allen & Unwin).

Rieger, E., and Leibfried, S. (1998) 'Welfare State Limits to Globalization', *Politics and Society*, 26(3): 363–90.

—— and —— (2001) *Welfare State Mercantilism: The Relations between Democratic Social Policy and the World Market Order* (Frankfurt a.M.: Suhrkamp).

Riggs, F. W. (1994) 'Thoughts about Neoidealism vs. Realism: Reflections on Charles Kegley's ISA Presidential Address', *International Studies Notes*, 19 (Winter): 1–6.

Riker, W. H. (1962) *The Theory of Political Coalitions* (New Haven, Conn.: Yale University Press).

—— (1982) *Liberalism against Populism* (San Francisco: Freeman).

—— (1990) 'Political Science and Rational Choice', in J. E. Alt and K. A. Shepsle (eds.), *Perspectives on Positive Political Economy* (Cambridge: Cambridge University Press), 163-81.

Rimlinger, G. V. (1971) *Welfare Policy and Industrialization in Europe, America and Russia* (New York: Wiley).

Ringen, S. (2006) *The Possibility of Politics: A Study in the Political Economy of the Welfare State* (New Brunswick, NJ: Transaction Publishers).

Risse-Kappen, T. (1995) 'Bringing Transnational Relations Back In: Introduction', in idem (ed.), *Bringing Transnational Relations back in: Non-State Actors, Domestic Structures, and International Institutions* (Cambridge: Cambridge University Press), 3–33.

Robertson, D. (1976) *A Theory of Party Competition* (London: Wiley).

Robinson, W. (1950) 'Ecological Correlations and the Behavior of Individuals', *American Sociological Review*, 15: 351-7.

Robinson, W. I. (1996) *Promoting Polyarchy: Globalization, US Intervention and Hegemony* (Cambridge: Cambridge University Press).

Rochon, T. R. (1990) 'The West European Peace Movement and the Theory of New Social Movements', in R. J. Dalton and M. Kuechler (eds.), *Challenging the Political Order* (Cambridge: Polity Press), 105–21.

Rodrik, D. (1996) *Why do More Open Economies have Bigger Governments?*, Nber Working Paper Series, 5537 (Cambridge: NBER).

Rogers, E. M. (1995) *Diffusion of Innovations* (New York: Free Press).

Rogowski, R. (1989) *Commerce and Coalitions: How Trade Affects Domestic Political Alignments* (Princeton: Princeton University Press).

Rohrschneider, R. (2002) 'The Democratic Deficit and Mass Support for an EU-Wide Government', *American Journal of Political Science*, 46(2): 463–75.

Rokkan, S. (1966) 'Norway: Numerical Democracy and Corporate Pluralism', in Dahl 1966: 70–115.

—— (1968) 'The Growth and Structuring of Mass Politics in the Smaller European Democracies', *Comparative Studies in Society and History*, 10: 173–210.

—— (1970) *Citizens, Elections, Parties* (Oslo: Universitetsforlaget).

—— (1980) 'Territories, Centres and Peripheries: Toward a Geoethnic, Geoeconomic, Geopolitical Model of Differentiation within Western Europe', in J. Gottman (ed.), *Centre and Periphery: Spatial Variation in Politics* (Beverly Hills, Calif. and London: Sage), 163–204.

—— and Urwin, D. (eds.) (1982) 'Introduction: Centres and Peripheries in Western Europe', in idem (eds.), *The Politics of Territorial Identity: Studies in European Regionalism* (London: Sage), 1–17.

Romano, S. (1947) *Principii di Diritto Costituzionale Generale* (Milan: Giuffè).

Römmele, A. (2005) *Direkte Kommunikation zwischen Parteien und Wählern* (Wiesbaden: Verlag für Sozialwissenschaften, 2nd edn).

Roper, J. (1999) 'New Zealand Political Parties Online: The World Wide Web as a Tool for Democratization or Political Marketing', in C. Toulouse and T. Luke (eds.), *The Politics of Cyberspace* (London: Routledge), 69–83.

Rose, R. (1969) 'The Variability of Party Government: A Theoretical and Empirical Critique', *Political Studies*, 17: 413–45.

—— (1974) *The Problem of Party Government* (New York: Macmillan).

—— (1991) 'What is Lesson-Drawing?', *Journal of Public Policy*, 11: 3–30.

—— (1993) *Lesson Drawing in Public Policy: A Guide to Learning Across Time and Space* (Chatham, NJ: Chatham House).

—— and Urwin, D. W. (1970) 'Persistence and Change in Western Party Systems since 1945', *Political Studies*, 18: 287–319.

Rosenau, J. N. (1993) 'Citizenship in a Changing Global Order', in J. N. Rosenau, and E.-O. Czempiel (eds.), *Governance without Government: Order and Change in World Politics* (Cambridge: Cambridge University Press), 272–95.

Rosenberg, J. (2005) 'Globalization Theory: A Post-Mortem', *International Politics*, 42: 2–74.

Rosenfeld, M. (ed.) (1994) *Constitutionalism, Identity, Difference, and Legitimacy: Theoretical Perspectives* (Durham, NC: Duke University Press).

Rosenstone, S. J., and Hansen, J. M. (1993) *Mobilization, Participation, and Democracy in America* (Boston: Allyn & Bacon).

Ross, F. (2000) ' "Beyond Left and Right": The New Partisan Politics of Welfare', *Governance*, 13(2): 155–83.

Rossi, P. H., Lipsey, M. W., and Freeman, H. E. (2004) *Evaluation: A Systematic Approach.* (Thousand Oaks, Calif.: Sage).

Rothstein, B. (1998) *Just Institutions Matter: The Moral and Political Logic of the Universal Welfare State* (Cambridge: Cambridge University Press).

Rueschemeyer, D., Huber, E., and Stephens, J. D. (1992) *Capitalist Development and Democracy* (Cambridge: Polity Press).

Russett, B., Alker, H. R., Deutsch, K. W., and Lasswell, H. D. (1964) *World Handbook of Political and Social Indicators* (New Haven, Conn.: Yale University Press, 1st edn).

Russett, B. M. (1993) *Grasping the Democratic Peace* (Princeton: Princeton University Press).

Rustow, D. (1955) *The Politics of Compromise: A Study of Parties and Cabinet Government in Sweden* (Princeton: Princeton University Press).

Saalfeld, T. (2005) 'Germany: Stability and Strategy in a Mixed-Member Proportional System', in Gallagher and Mitchell 2005: 209–30.

Sabatier, P. A. (1988) 'An Advocacy-Coalition Framework of Policy Change and the Role of Policy-Oriented Learning Therein', *Policy Sciences*, 21: 129–68.

—— (1998) 'The Advocacy Coalition Framework: Revisions and Relevance for Europe', *Journal of European Public Policy*, 5(1): 98–130.

—— and Jenkins-Smith, H. (eds.) (1993) *Policy Change and Learning* (Boulder, Colo.: Westview Press).

Sabatini, F. (2006) *Social Capital, Public Spending and the Quality of Economic Development: The Case of Italy* (Milan: Fondazione Eni Enrico Mattei).

Sabato, L. (1981) *The Rise of Political Consultants: New Way of Winning Elections* (New York: Basic Books).

Sabel, C. F. (1982) *Work and Politics: The Division of Labor in Industry, Cambridge Studies in Modern Political Economies* (Cambridge: Cambridge University Press).

Sadurski, W. (2005) *Rights Before Courts: A Study of Constitutional Courts in Postcommunist States of Central and Eastern Europe* (Dordrecht: Kluwer Academic Publishers).

Said, E. W. (1978) *Orientalism* (New York: Pantheon).

Sainsbury, D. (ed.) (1994) *Gendering Welfare States* (London: Sage).

—— (ed.) (1996) *Gender and Welfare State Regimes* (Oxford: Oxford University Press).

Salisbury, R. H. (1984) 'Interest Representation: The Dominance of Institutions', *American Political Science Review*, 78(1): 64–76.

Salvaggio, J. L. (ed.) (1989) *The Information Society: Economic, Social, and Structural Issues* (Hillsdale, NJ: Erlbaum).

Samuels, R. (1987) *The Business of the Japanese State: Energy Markets in Comparative and Historical Perspective* (Ithaca, NY: Cornell University Press).

Sanderson, I. (2002) 'Evaluation, Policy Learning and Evidence-Based Policy Making', *Public Administration*, 80(1): 1–22.

Sandholtz, W., and Stone Sweet, A. (eds.) (1998) *European Integration and Supranational Governance* (Oxford: Oxford University Press).

—— and Zysman J. (1989) '1992: Recasting the European Bargain', *World Politics*, 42(1): 95–128.

Sandmo, A. (1991) 'Presidential Address: Economists and the Welfare State', *European Economic Review*, 35(2–3): 213–39.

Sarcinelli, U. (1998) 'Parteien und Politikvermittlung: Von der Parteien- zur Mediendemokratie', in idem (ed.), *Politikvermittlung und Demokratie in der Mediengesellschaft* (Bonn: Bundeszentrale fr Politische Bildung), 273–96.

Sartori, G. (1962) *Democratic Theory* (Detroit: Wayne State University Press).

—— (1970) 'Concept Misformation in Comparative Politics', *American Political Science Review*, 65: 1033–53.

—— (1976) *Parties and Party Systems: A Framework for Analysis* (Cambridge: Cambridge University Press).

—— (1986) 'The Influence of Electoral Systems: Faulty Laws or Faulty Method?', in B. Grofman and A. Lijphart (eds.), *Electoral Laws and their Political Consequences* (New York: Agathon Press), 43–68.

—— (1987) *The Theory of Democracy Revisited* (Chatham, NJ: Chatham House).

—— (1991) 'Comparing and Miscomparing', *Journal of Theoretical Politics*, 3: 243–57.

—— (1994) *Comparative Constitutional Engineering: An Inquiry into Structures, Incentives and Outcomes* (New York and London: New York University Press and Macmillan).

Savoie, D. (1986) *Regional Economic Development; Canada's Search for Solutions* (Toronto: University of Toronto Press).

Sbragia, A. M. (ed.) (1992) *Euro-Politics: Institutions and Policymaking in the 'New' European Community* (Washington, DC: Brookings Institution).

Scammell, M. (1997) 'The Wisdom of the War Room: US Campaigning and Americanization', *Media, Culture and Society*, 20(3): 146–70.

Scarbrough, E. (2000) 'West European Welfare States: The Old Politics of Retrenchment', *European Journal of Political Research*, 38(2): 225–59.

Scarpetta, S. (1996) 'Assessing the Role of Labour Market Policies and Institutional Settings on Unemployment: A Cross-Country Study', *OECD Economic Studies*, 26: 43–98.

Scarrow, S. E. (2003) 'Making Elections More Direct? Reducing the Role of Parties in Elections', in B. E. Cain, R. J. Dalton, and S. E. Scarrow (eds.), *Democracy Transformed? Expanding Political Opportunities in Advanced Industrial Democracies* (Oxford: Oxford University Press, 2003), 44–58.

Schain, M., and Menon, A. (2007) *Comparative Federalism* (Oxford: Oxford University Press).

Schapiro, L. (1972) *Totalitarianism* (London: Pall Mall).

Scharpf, F. W. (1984) 'Economic and Institutional Constraints of Full Employment Strategies: Sweden, Austria and Germany, 1973–1982', in J. H. Goldthorpe (ed.), *Order and Conflict in Contemporary Capitalism* (Oxford: Clarendon), 275–90.

—— (1987) *Sozialdemokratische Krisenpolitik in Europa* (Frankfurt: Campus).

—— (1988) 'The Joint-Decision Trap: Lessons from German Federalism and European Integration', *Public Administration*, 66(3): 277–304.

—— (1997a) 'Economic Integration, Democracy and the Welfare State', *Journal of European Public Policy*, 4(1): 18–36.

—— (1997b) *Employment and the Welfare State: A Continental Dilemma*, MPIfG Working Paper, 97/7 (Bonn).

—— (1997c) *Games Real Actors Play: Actor-Centered Institutionalism in Policy Research* (Boulder, Colo.: Westview).

—— (1997d) 'Introduction: The Problem-Solving Capacity of Multi-level Governance', *Journal of European Public Policy*, 4: 520–38.

—— (2000) 'Economic Changes, Vulnerabilities, and Institutional Capabilities', in Scharpf and Schmidt 2000:i., 21–124.

—— (2001) 'Politisches Einflusspotential von Regierungsbürokratien in OECD-Ländern', *Aus Politik und Zeitgeschichte*, B 05/2001: 14–24.

—— and Schmidt, V. A. (eds.) (2000) *Welfare and Work in the Open Economy*, i. *From Vulnerability to Competitiveness*; ii. *Diverse Responses to Common Challenges* (Oxford: Oxford University Press).

Schattschneider, E. E. (1942) *Party Government* (New York: Holt, Rinehart & Winston).

—— (1988) *The Semi-Sovereign People: A Realist's View of Democracy in America* (London and New York: Wadsworth and Holt, Rinehart & Winston, 1st publ. 1960).

Scheinin, M. (ed.) (2001) *Welfare State and Constitutionalism: Nordic Perspectives* (Copenhagen: Nordic Council of Ministers).

Scheppele, K. L. (2005) 'Democracy by Judiciary (or Why Courts can Sometimes be More Democratic than Parliaments)', in W. Sadurski, M. Krygier, and A. Csarnota (eds.), *Rethinking the Rule of Law in Post Communist Europe: Past Legacies, Institutional Innovations, and Constitutional Discourses* (Budapest: CEU Press).

Schifferes, S. (2006) 'Downloading Democracy: Politics and the Internet', paper presented at the Oxford Internet Institute, Oxford University, 19 October.

Schimmelfennig, F., and Sedelmeier, U. (2005) *Europeanization of Central and Eastern Europe* (Ithaca, NY: Cornell University Press).

Schlesinger, J. (1991) *Political Parties and the Winning of Office* (Ann Arbor, Mich.: University of Michigan Press).

Schlozman, K. L. (1984) 'What Accent the Heavenly Chorus? Political Equality and the American Pressure System', *Journal of Politics*, 46(4): 1006–32.

—— (2002) 'Citizen Participation in America: What do we Know? Why do We Care?', in I. Katznelson and H. V. Milner (eds.), *Political Science: The State of the Discipline* (New York: Norton and American Political Science Association).

—— and Tierney, J. T. (1986) *Organized Interests and American Democracy* (New York: Harper & Row).

Schmidt, M. G. (1982) *Wohlfahrtsstaatliche Politik unter bürgerlichen und sozialdemokratischen Regierungen* (Frankfurt and New York: Campus).

Schmidt, M. G. (1983) 'The Welfare State and the Economy in Periods of Economic Crisis', *European Journal of Political Research*, 11(1): 1–26.

—— (1998) *Sozialpolitik in Deutschland Historische Entwicklung und internationaler Vergleich* (Opladen: Leske & Budrich).

—— (2002) 'The Impact of Parties, Constitutional Structures and Veto Players on Public Policy', in H. Keman (ed.) *Comparative Democratic Politics. A Guide to Contemporary Theory and Research* (London: Sage Publications).

Schmidt, V. A. (1990) *Democratizing France: The Political and Administrative History of Decentralization* (Cambridge: Cambridge University Press).

—— (2001) 'The Politics of Economic Adjustment in France and Britain: When does Discourse Matter?', *Journal of European Public Policy*, 8(2): 247–64.

—— (2002a) 'Does Discourse Matter in the Politics of Welfare State Adjustment?', *Comparative Political Studies*, 35(2): 168–93.

—— (2002b) *The Futures of European Capitalism* (Oxford: Oxford University Press).

Schmitter, P. C. (1974) 'Still the Century of Corporatism?', *Review of Politics*, 36: 85–131.

—— (1985) 'Neo-Corporatism and the State', in W. Grant (ed.), *The Political Economy of Corporatism* (London: Macmillan).

—— (1989) 'Corporatism is Dead! Long Live Corporatism', *Government and Opposition*, 24: 131–57.

—— (1993) 'Comparative Politics', in J. Krieger (ed.), *The Oxford Companion to Politics of the World* (Oxford: Oxford University Press), 171–7.

—— (2000) 'Neo-Corporatism and the Consolidation of Neo-Democracy', in S. U. Larsen (ed.), *The Challenges of Theories on Democracy* (New York: Columbia University Press).

—— and Karl, T. (1991) 'What Democracy is . . . and is Not', *Journal of Democracy*, 2(3): 75–88.

—— and Lembruch, G. (1979) *Trends toward Corporatist Intermediation* (London: Sage).

—— and —— (eds.) (1982) *Trends Towards Corporatist Intermediation* (London: Sage).

—— and Trechsel, A. H. (eds.) (2004) *The Future of Democracy in Europe: Trends, Analyses and Reforms* (Strasbourg: Council of Europe).

Schnapp, K.-U. (2000) *Ministerial Bureaucracies as Stand-in Agenda Setters? A Comparative Description*, Discussion Paper FS III 00–204 (Berlin: WZB).

—— (2001) 'Politisches Einflusspotential von Regierungsbürokratien in OECD-Länderen', *Aus Politik und Zeitgeschichte*, B(05): 14–24.

Schneider, S. M., and Foot, K. A. (2004) 'The Web as an Object of Study', *New Media and Society*, 6(1): 114–22.

Scholte, J. A. (2005) *Globalization: A Critical Introduction* (Basingstoke: Palgrave Macmillan, 2nd edn).

Schumpeter, J. A. (1943) *Capitalism, Socialism and Democracy* (New York: Harper & Row).

—— (1947) *Capitalism, Socialism, and Democracy* (New York: Harper & Brothers, 2nd edn).

—— (1962) *Capitalism, Socialism and Democracy* (New York: Harper & Row).

Schwartz, H. (2001) 'Round Up the Usual Suspects! Globalization, Domestic Politics, and Welfare State Change', in P. Pierson (ed.), *The New Politics of the Welfare State* (Oxford: Oxford University Press), 17–44.

Scully, T. (1995) 'Reconstituting Party Politics in Chile', in S. Mainwaring and T. Scully (eds.), *Building Democratic Institutions: Party Systems in Latin America* (Stanford, Calif.: Stanford University Press).

Scruggs, L., and Allan, J. (2006a) 'The Material Consequences of Welfare States: Benefit Generosity and Absolute Poverty in Sixteen OECD Countries', *Comparative Political Studies*, 39(7): 880–904.

—— and —— (2006b) 'Welfare State Decommodification in Eighteen OECD Countries: A Replication and Revision', *Journal of European Social Policy*, 16(1): 55–72.

Seeliger, R. (1996) 'Conceptualizing and Researching Policy Convergence', *Policy Studies Journal*, 24: 153–72.

Seldon, S. C. (1997) *The Promise of Representative Bureaucracy* (Armonk, NY; M. E. Sharpe).

Selznick, P. (1952) *The Organizational Weapon; a Study of Bolshevik Strategy and Tactics* (New York: Rand Corp.).

Semetko, H., and Krasnoboka, N. (2003) 'The Political Role of the Internet in Societies in Transition: Russia and Ukraine Compared', *Party Politics*, 9(1): 77–104.

Sen, A. (1999) 'Democracy as a Universal Value', *Journal of Democracy*, 10(3): 3–17.

Setälä, M. (1999) *Referendums and Democratic Government: Normative Theory and the Analysis of Institutions* (Basingstoke: Macmillan).

Shalev, M. (1983) 'The Social Democratic Model and Beyond: Two Generations of Comparative Research on the Welfare State', *Comparative Social Research*, 6: 315–51.

Shapiro, M. (1964) *Law and Politics in the Supreme Court: Studies in Political Jurisprudence* (Glencoe, Ill.: Free Press).

—— and Stone, A. (1994) 'The New Constitutional Politics of Europe', *Comparative Political Studies*, 26: 397–420.

Sharkansky, Ira (1969) 'The Utility of Elazart's Political Culture', *Polity*, 2: 66–83.

Sharpe, L. (1993a) 'The European Meso: An Appraisal', in idem (ed.), 1993b: 1–39.

—— (1993b) *The Rise of Meso Government in Europe* (London: Sage).

Shaw, J. (1999) 'Post-National Constitutionalism in the EU', *Journal of European Public Policy*, 6(4): 579–97.

Sheffer, G. (2003) *Diaspora Politics: At Home Abroad* (Cambridge: Cambridge University Press).

Shepsle, K. A. (1989) 'Studying Institutions: Lessons from the Rational Choice Approach', *Journal of Theoretical Politics*, 1: 131–47.

—— (2006) 'Rational Choice Institutionalism', in R. A. W. Rhodes *et al.* (eds.), *Political Institutions* (Oxford: Oxford University Press), 23–38.

—— and Weingast, B. (1987) 'The Institutional Foundations of Committee Power', *American Political Science Review*, 81(1): 85–104.

——and Bonchek, M. S. (1997) *Analyzing Politics* (New York and London: W. W. Norton).

Shils, E. (1975) *Center and Periphery: Essays in Macrosociology* (Chicago: University of Chicago Press).

Shiratori, H. (2004) 'Changing Japanese Style Democracy: Party System Change: Dealignment and Realignment', *Shakaishirin*, 50: 79–143.

Shugart, M. S. (2005) 'Comparative Electoral Systems Research: The Maturation of a Field and New Challenges Ahead', in Gallagher and Mitchell 2005: 25–56.

——and Carey, J. M. (1992) *Presidents and Assemblies* (Cambridge: Cambridge University Press).

——and Wattenberg, M. P. (eds.) (2003) *Mixed-Member Electoral Systems: The Best of Both Worlds?* (Oxford: Oxford University Press).

——Valdini, M. E., and Suominen, K. (2005) 'Looking for Locals: Voter Information Demands and Personal Vote-Earning Attributes of Legislators under Proportional Representation', *American Journal of Political Science*, 49(2): 437–49.

Siaroff, A. (1999) 'Corporatism in Twenty-four Industrial Democracies: Meaning and Measurement', *European Journal of Political Research*, 36: 175–205.

Siavelis, P. M. (2005) 'Chile: The Unexpected (and Expected) Consequences of Electoral Engineering', in Gallagher and Mitchell 2005: 433–52.

Sieder, R., Schjolden, L., and Angell, A. (2005), *The Judicialization of Politics in Latin America* (New York: Palgrave Macmillan).

Silverstein, M. (1994) *Judicious Choices: The New Politics of Supreme Court Confirmations* (New York: W. W. Norton).

Simeon, R. (1977) 'Regionalism and Canadian Political Institutions', in J. Meekison (ed.), *Canadian Federalism: Myth or Reality?* (Toronto: Methuen), 293.

Simmons, B. A., and Elkins, Z. (2004) 'The Globalization of Liberalization: Policy Diffusion in the International Political Economy', *American Political Science Review*, 98: 171–89.

Simon, H. A. (1955) 'A Behavioral Model of Rational Choice', *Quarterly Journal of Economics*, 69(1): 99–118.

——(ed.) (1957) *Models of Man: Social and Rational* (New York: Wiley).

Simonton, D. K. (1993) 'Putting the Best Leaders in the White House: Personality, Policy and Performance', *Political Psychology*, 14: 537–48.

Singh, N., and Srinivasan, T. N. (2003) 'Can India Survive Globalization?', *Project Syndicate* (www.project-syndicate.org/commentary/nsingh1).

Sinnott, R. (2005) 'The Rules of the Electoral Game', in J. Coakley and M. Gallagher (eds.), *Politics in the Republic of Ireland* (Abingdon: Routledge and PSAI Press, 4th edn), 105–34.

Sitkoff, R. H. (2003) 'Politics and the Business Corporation', *Regulation*, 26(4): 30–6.

Skocpol, T. (1979) *States and Social Revolution: A Comparative Analysis of France, Russia and China* (Cambridge: Cambridge University Press).

——(ed.) (1984) *Visions and Methods in Historical Sociology* (Cambridge: Cambridge University Press).

——(1985) 'Bringing the State Back In: Strategies of Analysis in Current Research', in P. Evans, D. Rueschenmeyer, and T. Skocpol (eds.), *Bringing the State Back In* (Cambridge: Cambridge University Press), 3–37.

——(1992) *Protecting Soldiers and Mothers: The Political Origins of Social Policy in the United States* (Cambridge, Mass.: Belknap Press).

——(1996) *Boomerang: Clinton's Health Security Effort and the Turn against Government in US Politics* (New York: W. W. Norton).

——(2003) *Diminished Democracy: From Membership to Management in American Civic Life* (Norman, Okla.: University of Oklahoma Press).

——and Amenta, E. (1986) 'States and Social Policies', *Annual Review of Sociology*, 12: 131–57.

——and Orloff, A. S. (1986) 'Explaining the Origins of Welfare States: A Comparison of Britain and the United States, 1880s–1920s', in S. Lindenberg, J. S. Coleman, and S. Nowak (eds.), *Approaches to Social Theory: Proceedings of the W. I. Thomas and Florian Znaniecki Memorial Conference on Social Theory, Held Nov. 9–12 at the University of Chicago* (New York: Russell Sage Foundation), 229–54.

——and Somers, M. (1980) 'The Use of Comparative History in Macrosocial Inquiry', *Comparative Studies of Society and History*, 22: 174–97.

Slaughter, A.-M. (1997). 'The Real New World Order', *Foreign Affairs*, 76: 183–97.

Smeeding, T. M. (2005) 'Public Policy, Economic Inequality, and Poverty: The United States in Comparative Perspective', *Social Science Quarterly* (suppl. to vol.), 86: 955–83.

——and Gottschalk, P. (1999) 'Cross-National Income Inequality: How Great is it and What can we Learn from it?', *International Journal of Health Services*, 29(4): 733–41.

——O'Higgins, M., and Rainwater, L. (1990) *Poverty, Inequality and Income Distribution in Comparative Perspective: The Luxembourg Income Study (LIS)* (New York: Harvester Wheatsheaf).

Smelser, N. J. (1962) *Theory of Collective Behavior* (New York: Free Press).

——(1966) 'Mechanisms of Change and Adjustment to Change', in J. Finkle and R. Gable (eds.), *Political Development and Social Change* (New York: Wiley).

Smith, A. (1998) *Nationalism and Modernism* (London: Routledge).

——(2004) *The Antiquity of Nations* (Cambridge: Polity Press).

Smith, D. (1985) 'Party Government, Representation and National Integration in Canada', in P. Aucoin (ed.), *Party Government and Regional Representation in Canada* (Toronto: University of Toronto Press), 1–68.

Smith, D. A. (1998) *Tax Crusaders and the Politics of Direct Democracy* (London: Routledge).

Smith, M. J. (1999) *The Core Executive in Britain* (Houndmills: Macmillan).

Smithies, A. (1941) 'Optimum Location in Spatial Competition', *Journal of Political Economy*, 49: 423–39.

Snow, D. A., and Benford, R. D. (1988) 'Ideology, Frame Resonance, and Participant Mobilization', *International Social Movement Research*, 1: 197–217.

Snow, D. A., Rochford, R. B., Jr., Worden, S. K., and Benford, R. D. (1986) 'Frame Alignment Processes, Micromobilization, and Movement Participation', *American Sociological Review*, 51: 464–81.

—— Soule, S. A., and Kriesi, H. (2004) *The Blackwell Companion to Social Movements*, Blackwell Companions to Sociology (Malden, Mass.: Blackwell).

Söderbaum, F. (2003) 'Introduction: Theories of New Regionalism', in F. Söderbaum and T. Shaw (eds.), *Theories of New Regionalism: A Palgrave Reader* (New York: Palgrave Macmillan), 1–21.

Soja, E. (1989) *Postmodern Geographies: The Reassertion of Space in Critical Social Theory* (New York: Verso).

Somit, A., and Tanenhaus, A. (1964) *American Political Science: A Profile of a Discipline* (New York : Atherton).

Sørenson, E., and Torfing, J. (2007) *Theories of Democratic Network Governance* (Basingstoke: Palgrave).

Sørensen, G. (2001) *Changes in Statehood: The Transformation of International Relations* (Basingstoke: Palgrave Macmillan).

—— (2004) *The Transformation of the State: Beyond the Myth of Retreat* (Basingstoke: Palgrave Macmillan).

Soysal, Y. N. (1994) *Limits of Citizenship: Migrants and Postnational Membership in Europe* (Chicago: University of Chicago Press).

Spruyt, H. (1994) *The Sovereign State and its Competitor: An Analysis of Systems Change* (Princeton: Princeton University Press).

Stanley J., and Weare, C. (2004) 'The Effects of Internet Use on Political Participation: Evidence From an Agency Online Discussion Forum', *Administration and Society*, 36(5): 503–27.

Starke, P. (2006) 'The Politics of Welfare State Retrenchment: A Literature Review', *Social Policy and Administration*, 40(1): 104–20.

Steiner, J. (1974) *Amicable Agreement versus Majority Rule: Conflict Resolution in Switzerland* (Chapel Hill, NC: University of North Carolina Press).

Steinmo, S. (1993) *Taxation and Democracy: Swedish, British and American Approaches to Financing the Modern State* (New Haven, Conn.: Yale University Press).

—— and Thelen, K. (1992) 'Historical Institutionalism in Comparative Politics', in Steinmo, Thelen, and Longstreth 1992: 1–32.

—— —— and Longstreth, F. (eds.) (1992) *Structuring Politics: Historical Institutionalism in Comparative Analysis* (Cambridge: Cambridge University Press).

Stepan, A. (1971) *The Military in Politics: Changing Patterns in Brazil* (Princeton: Princeton University Press).

—— and Skach, C. (1994) 'Presidentialism and Parliamentarism in Comparative Perspective,' in Linz and Valenzuela 1994.

Stephens, J. D. (1979) *The Transition from Capitalism to Socialism* (Urbana, Ill. and Chicago: University of Illinois Press).

—— (2005) 'Economic Internationalization and Domestic Compensation: Northwestern Europe in Comparative Perspective', in Glatzer and Rueschemeyer 2005: 49–74.

Stevenson, G. (1980) 'Canadian Regionalism in Continental Perspective', *Journal of Canadian Studies*, 15(2): 16–27.

Stohr, W. (ed.) (1990) *Global Challenge and Local Response: Initiatives for Economic Regeneration in Contemporary Europe* (London and New York: United Nations University and Mansell Publishing).

Stolleis, M. (2003) 'Judicial Review, Administrative Review, and Constitutional Review in the Weimar Republic', *Ratio Juris*, 16(2): 266–80.

Stone, A. (1990) *The Birth of Judicial Politics in France: The Constitutional Council in Comparative Perspective* (Oxford: Oxford University Press).

Stone, D. (2005) *Capturing the Political Imagination: Think Tanks and the Policy Process* (London: Frank Cass).

Stone Sweet, A. (2000) *Governing with Judges: Constitutional Politics in Europe* (Oxford: Oxford University Press).

—— (2002), 'Constitutional Courts and Parliamentary Democracy', *West European Politics*, 25: 77–100.

—— and Thatcher, M. (2002) 'The Politics of Delegation: Non-Majoritarian Institutions in Europe', special issue of *West European Politics*, 25(1): 1–22.

Storper, M. (1995) 'The Resurgence of Regional Economies, Ten Years Later: The Region as a Nexus of Untraded Interdependencies', *European Urban and Regional Studies*, 2(3): 191–221.

Strang, D., and Meyer, J. (1993) 'Institutional Conditions for Diffusion', *Theory and Society*, 22: 487–511.

—— and Soule, S. A. (1998) 'Diffusion in Organizations and Social Movements: From Hybrid Corn to Poison Pills', *Annual Review of Sociology*, 24: 265–90.

Strange, S. (1996) *The Retreat of the State: The Diffusion of Power in the World Economy* (Cambridge: Cambridge University Press).

Streeck, W. (1996) 'Neo-Voluntarism: A European Social Policy Regime?', in G. Marks, F. W. Scharpf, P. C. Schmitter, and W. Streeck (eds.), *Governance in the European Union* (London: Sage).

—— and Schmitter, P. C. (1991) 'From National Corporatism to Transnational Pluralism: Organized Interests in the Single European Market', *Politics and Society*, 19(2): 133–64.

—— and Thelen, K. (2005) 'Introduction: Institutional Change in Advanced Political Economies', in idem (eds.), *Beyond Continuity: Institutional Change in Advanced Political Economies* (Oxford: Oxford University Press), 1–39.

Strøm, K. (1990) *Minority Government and Majority Rule* (Cambridge: Cambridge University Press).

—— and Swindle, S. M. (2002) 'Strategic Parliamentary Dissolution', *American Political Science Review*, 96: 575–91.

—— Müller, W. C., and Bergman, T. (eds.) (2003) *Delegation and Accountability in Parliamentary Democracies* (Oxford: Oxford University Press).

—— —— and —— (eds.) (2007) *Cabinets and Coalition Bargaining: The Democratic Life Cycle in Western Europe* (Oxford: Oxford University Press).

Suleiman, E. N. (2003) *Dismantling Democratic States* (Princeton: Princeton University Press).

Sundberg, J. (1987) 'Exploring the Basis of Declining Party Membership in Denmark: A Scandinavian Comparison', *Scandinavian Political Studies*, 10.

Surel, Y. (2000) 'The Role of Cognitive and Normative Frames in Policy-Making', *Journal of European Public Policy*, 7(4): 495–512.

Svensson, P. (2002) 'Five Danish Referendums on the European Community and European Union: A Critical Assessment of the Franklin Thesis', *European Journal of Political Research*, 41(5): 733–50.

Swank, D. (2001) 'Political Institutions and Welfare State Restructuring: The Impact of Institutions on Social Policy Change in Developed Democracies', in Pierson 2001*b*: 197–237.

Swank, D. (2002) *Global Capital, Political Institutions, and Policy Change in Developed Welfare States* (Cambridge: Cambridge University Press).

—— and Steinmo, S. (2002). 'The New Political Economy of Taxation in Advanced Capitalist Democracies', *American Journal of Political Science*, 46(3): 477–89.

—— and Hicks, A. (1985) 'The Determinants and Redistributive Impacts of State Welfare Spending in the Advanced Capitalist Democracies, 1960–1980', in N. J. Vig and S. E. Schier (eds.), *Political Economy in Western Democracies* (New York: Holmes & Meier), 115–39.

Swann, A. de (1973) *Coalition Theories and Cabinet Formations* (Amsterdam: Elsevier).

Swanson, D. L., and Mancini, P. (eds.) (1966) *Politics, Media and Modern Democracy* (Westport, Conn.: Praeger).

Swenson, P. (1989) *Fair Shares: Unions, Pay, and Politics in Sweden and West Germany* (Ithaca, NY: Cornell University Press).

—— (2002) *Employers Against Markets* (Cambridge: Cambridge University Press).

Taagapera, R., and Shugart, M. (1989) *Seats and Votes: The Effects and Determinants of Electoral Systems* (New Haven, Conn.: Yale University Press).

Tallberg, J. (2006) *Leadership and Negotiation in the European Union* (Cambridge: Cambridge University Press).

Tarrow, S. (1977) *Between Center and Periphery: Grassroots Politicians in Italy and France* (New York: Yale University Press).

—— (1988) 'Old Movements in New Cycles of Protest: The Career of an Italian Religious Movement', *International Social Movement Research*, 1: 281–304.

—— (1994) *Power in Movement: Social Movements, Collective Action and Politics* (Cambridge: Cambridge University Press).

—— (1996) 'States and Opportunities: The Political Structuring of Social Movements', in McAdam, McCarthy, and Zald 1996: 41–61.

—— (2005) *The New Transnational Activism* (New York: Cambridge University Press).

Taylor, C. L., and Hudson, M. C. (1972) *World Handbook of Political and Social Indicators* (New Haven, Conn.: Yale University Press, 2nd edn).

—— and Jodice, D. A. (1983) *World Handbook of Political and Social Indicators* (New Haven, Conn.: Yale University Press, 3rd edn).

Taylor, M. (1987) *The Possibility of Cooperation: Studies in Rationality and Social Change* (Cambridge: Cambridge University Press).

Taylor, P. (1982) 'Intergovernmentalism in the European Communities in the 1970s: Patterns and Perspectives', *International Organization*, 36(4): 741–66.

Tepe, S. (2006) 'When and How does Electoral Competition Moderate Religious Parties?', paper presented at the 2006 Annual Meeting of the American Political Science Association, Philadelphia.

Tews, K. (2002) *Der Diffusionsansatz für die vergleichende Politikanalyse: Wurzeln und Potenziale eines Konzepts—Eine Literaturstudie*, FU-Report 2002-02 (Berlin: Environmental Policy Research Centre).

—— Busch, P.-O., and Jörgens, H. (2003) 'The Diffusion of New Environmental Policy Instruments', *European Journal of Political Research*, 42(2): 569–600.

Thames, F. C., and Edwards, M. S. (2006) 'Differentiating Mixed-Member Electoral Systems: Mixed-Member Majoritarian and Mixed-Member Proportional Systems and Government Expenditures', *Comparative Political Studies*, 39(7): 905–27.

't Hart, P. (1990) *Groupthink in Government* (Amsterdam: Swets & Teitlinger).

Thatcher, M., and Stone Sweet, A. (eds.) (2002) *The Politics of Delegation: Non-Majoritarian Institutions in Europe*, special issue of *West European Politics*, 25(1): 1–219.

Thelen, K. A. (1999) 'Historical Institutionalism in Comparative Politics', *Annual Review of Political Science*, 2: 369–404.

—— and Steinmo, S. (1992) 'Historical Institutionalism in Comparative Politics', in Steinmo, Thelen, and Longstreth 1992: 1–32.

Theobald, H. (2007) *Care Arrangements and Social Integration*, CCWS Working Papers, 48 (University of Aarhus).

Therborn, G. (1977) 'The Rule of Capital and the Rise of Democracy', *New Left Review*, 103: 3–42.

—— (1989) ' "Pillarization" and "Popular Movements": Two Variants of Welfare State Capitalism: The Netherlands and Sweden', in F. G. Castles (ed.), *The Comparative History of Public Policy* (Cambridge: Polity), 192–241.

Thies, M. F. (2001) 'Keeping Tabs on Partners: The Logic of Delegation in Coalition Governments', *American Journal of Political Science*, 45: 580–98.

Thomas, C. S. (ed.) (1993) *First World Interest Groups: A Comparative Perspective* (Westport, Conn.: Greenwood Press).

Thompson, M., Ellis, R., and Wildavsky, A. (1990) *Cultural Theory* (Boulder, Colo.: Westview Press).

Tilly, C. (1978) *From Modernization to Revolution* (New York: Random House).

—— (1984*a*) *Big Structures, Large Processes, Huge Comparisons* (New York: Russell Sage Foundation).

—— (1984*b*) 'Social Movements and National Politics', in C. Bright and S. Harding (eds.), *Statemaking and Social Movements* (Ann Arbor, Mich.: University of Michigan Press), 297–317.

—— (1990) *Coercion, Capital, and European States AD 990–1990* (Oxford: Blackwell).

—— (1995) *Popular Contention in Great Britain: 1758–1834* (Cambridge, Mass.: Harvard University Press).

Tilly, C., and Tarrow, S. (2007) *Contentious Politics* (London: Paradigm Publishers).

—— Tilly, L., and Tilly, R. (1975) *The Rebellious Century, 1830–1930* (Cambridge, Mass.: Harvard University Press).

Timmermans, A. I. (2003) *High Politics in the Low Countries* (Aldershot: Ashgate).

—— (2006) 'Standing Apart and Sitting Together: Enforcing Coalition Agreements in Multiparty Systems', *European Journal of Political Research*, 45: 263–83.

—— and Scholten, P. (2006) 'The Political Flow of Wisdom: Science Institutions as Policy Venues in the Netherlands', *Journal of European Public Policy*, 13(7): 1104–18.

Titmuss, R. (1958) *Essays on the Welfare State* (London: Allen & Unwin).

—— (1974) *Social Policy: An Introduction* (New York: Pantheon Books).

Tocqueville, A. de (1961) *De la démocratie en Amérique Œuvres complètes*, 1/1 (Paris: Gallimard; originally publ. 1835).

Todd, E. (1983) *La Troisième Planète: Structures Familiales et Systèmes Idéologiques* (Paris: Seuil).

Tolbert, C. J., Lowenstein, D. H., and Donovan, T. (1998) 'Election Law and Rules for Using Initiatives', in Bowler *et al.* 1998: 27–54.

Tönnies, F. (2001) *Community and Civil Society* (Cambridge: Cambridge University Press).

Trenaman, J. S. M., and McQuail, D. (1961) *Television and the Political Image* (London: Methuen).

Trigilia, C. (1991) 'The Paradox of the Region: Economic Regulation and the Representation of Interests', *Economy and Society*, 20(3): 306–27.

Troeltsch, E. (1922) *Der Historismus und seine Probleme* (Aalen: Scientia).

Truman, D. B. (1951) *The Governmental Process: Political Interests and Public Opinion* (New York: Knopf).

Tsebelis, G. (1990) *Nested Games: Rational Choice in Comparative Politics* (Berkeley, Calif.: University of California Press).

—— (1994) 'The Power of the European Parliament as a Conditional Agenda-Setter', *American Political Science Review*, 88(1): 128–42.

—— (1995) 'Decision Making in Political Systems: Veto Players in Presidentialism, Parliamentarism, Multicameralism and Multipartism', *British Journal of Political Science*, 25: 289–325.

—— (2000) 'Veto Players and Institutional Analysis', *Governance*, 13: 441–74.

—— (2002) *Veto Players: How Political Institutions Work* (Princeton: Princeton University Press).

—— and Money, J. (1997) *Bicameralism* (Cambridge: Cambridge University Press).

Turan, Y., İba, Ş., and Zarakol, A. (2005) 'Inter-Party Mobility in the Turkish Grand National Assembly: Curse or Blessing?', *European Journal of Turkish Studies*, thematic issue 3: electronic publication.

Turner, F. (1894) 'The Significance of the Frontier in American History', in American Historical Association, *Annual Report for 1893* (Washington, DC), 199–277.

Turner, R. A., and Killian, L. (1987) *Collective Behavior* (Englewood Cliffs, NJ: Prentice-Hall, 3rd edn).

Uhlaner, C. J. (2001) 'Political Participation', in N. J. Smelser and P. B. Baltes (eds.), *International Encyclopedia of the Social Behavioral Sciences* (Amsterdam: Elsevier).

Uleri, P. V. (1996a) 'Introduction', in Gallagher and Uleri 1996: 1–19.

—— (1996b) 'Italy: Referendums and Initiatives from the Origins to the Crisis of a Democratic Regime', in Gallagher and Uleri 1996: 106–25.

—— (2003) *Referendum e Democrazia: Una Prospettiva Comparata* (Bologna: Il Mulino).

UN (United Nations) (1997) *World Investment Report 1997* (New York: United Nations).

UNCTAD (United Nations Conference on Trade and Development) (1993) *World Investment Report 1993: Transnational Corporations and Integrated International Production* (New York: United Nations).

UNDP (United Nations Development Programme) (1996) *Human Development Report 1996* (New York: Oxford University Press).

—— (2005) *Human Development Report 2005* (New York: Oxford University Press).

Urwin, D. (1998) 'Modern Democratic Experiences of Territorial Management: Single Houses, But Many Mansions', *Regional and Federal Studies*, 8(2): 81–110.

Uslaner, E. M. (1999) 'Democracy and Social Capital', in M. E. Warren (ed.), *Democracy and Trust* (Cambridge: Cambridge University Press), 121–50.

Vachudova, M. (2005) *Europe Undivided: Democracy, Leverage and Integration after Communism* (Oxford: Oxford University Press).

Van der Eijk, C., and Franklin, M. (eds.) (1996) *Choosing Europe? The European Electorate and National Politics in the Face of Union* (Ann Arbor, Mich.: University of Michigan Press).

Van Deth, J. W. (ed.) (1998) *Comparative Politics: The Problem of Equivalence* (London and New York: Routledge).

—— and Scarbrough, E. (1995) *The Impact of Values* (Oxford: Oxford University Press).

Van Gunsteren, H. R. (1998) *A Theory of Citizenship: Organizing Plurality in Contemporary Democracies* (Boulder, Colo.: Westview Press).

Van Kersbergen, K. (1995) *Social Capitalism: A Study of Christian Democracy and the Welfare State* (London: Routledge).

—— (2002) 'The Politics of Welfare State Reform', *Swiss Political Science Review*, 8(2): 1–19.

Van Thiel, S. (2006) 'Styles of Reform: Differences in Quango Creation between Policy Sectors in the Netherlands', *Journal of Public Policy*, 26(2): 115–39.

Van Waarden, F. (1995) 'Persistence of National Policy Styles', in B. Unger and F. van Waarden (eds.), *Convergence or Diversity?* (Avebury: Aldershot), 333–72.

Van Wersch, J., and de Zeeuw, J. (2005) *Mapping European Assistance*, Working Paper, 36 (The Hague: Netherlands Institute of International Relations).

Verba, S. (1969) 'Comparative Political Culture', in Pye and Verba 1969: 512–60.

—— (1985) 'Comparative Politics: Where Have We Been, Where are we Going?', in H. J. Wiarda (ed.), *New Directions in Comparative Politics* (Boulder, Colo.: Westview Press), 26–38.

—— and Nie, N. H. (1972) *Participation in America* (New York: Harper & Row).

—— Schlozman, K. L., and Brady, H. (1995) *Voice and Equality: Civic Voluntarism in American Politics* (Cambridge, Mass.: Cambridge University Press).

—— Nie, N. H., and Kim, J.-O. (1978) *Participation and Political Equality: A Seven-Nation Comparison* (Cambridge, Mass.: Cambridge University Press).

Verma, S. K., and Kumar, K. (eds.) (2003) *Fifty Years of The Supreme Court of India: Its Grasp and Reach* (New Delhi: Oxford University Press).

Vilar, P. (1977) *Catalunya en la Espana moderna* (Barcelona: Editorial Critica).

Vile, M. J. C. (1967) *Constitutionalism and the Separation of Powers* (Oxford: Oxford University Press).

Vis, B., and van Kersbergen, K. (2007) 'Why and How do Political Actors Pursue Risky Reforms?', *Journal of Theoretical Politics*, 19(2): 153–72.

—— Woldendorp, J., and Keman, H. (2007) 'Do Miracles Exist? Economic Performance of Nineteen OECD Democracies 1975–1999', *Journal of Business Research*, 60: 531–8.

Visser, J., and Hemerijck, A. (1997) *'A Dutch Miracle': Job Growth, Welfare Reform and Corporatism in the Netherlands* (Amsterdam: Amsterdam University Press).

Voerman, G. (1999) 'Distributing Electronic Folders: The Digital Electoral Campaign of 1998 in the Netherlands', Documentatie-centrum Nederlandse Politieke Partijen, University of Groningen.

Vogel, D. J. (1995) *Trading up: Consumer and Environmental Regulation in a Global Economy* (Cambridge, Mass.: Harvard University Press).

—— (2006) 'The Private Regulation of Global Corporate Conduct', paper presented at the annual meeting of the American Political Science Association, Philadelphia, 30 Aug.–3 Sept.

Volcansek, M. (ed.) (1997) *Law Above Nations: Supranational Courts and the Legalization of Politics* (Gainesville, Fla.: University of Florida Press).

Voltmer, K. (ed.) (2004) *Mass Media and Political Communication in New Democracies* (London: Routledge).

Vowles, J. (2005), 'New Zealand: The Consolidation of Reform?', in Gallagher and Mitchell 2005: 295–312.

Wagschal, U. (2000) 'Besonderheiten der gezügelten Sozialstaaten', in U. Wagschal and H. Obinger (eds.), *Der gezügelte Wohlfahrtsstaat. Sozialpolitik in reichen Industrienationen* (Frankfurt am Main: Campus), 37–72.

Walgrave, S., Varone, F., and Dumont, P. (2006) 'Policy with or without Parties? A Comparative Analysis of Policy Priorities and Policy Change in Belgium, 1991 to 2000', *Journal of European Public Policy*, 13(7): 1021–38.

Walker, J. L., Jr. (1983) 'The Origins and Maintenance of Interest Groups in America', *American Political Science Review*, 77(2): 390–406.

—— (1991) *Mobilizing Interest Groups in America* (Ann Arbor, Mich.: University of Michigan Press).

Walker, N. (1996) 'European Constitutionalism and European Integration', *Public Law* (Summer): 266.

Wallerstein, I. (1979) *The Capitalist World Economy* (Cambridge: Cambridge University Press).

Waltz, K. N. (1999) 'Globalization and Governance', *PS: Political Science and Politics*: 693–700.

Wannop, U. (1997) 'Regional Planning and Urban Governance in Europe and the USA', in Keating and Loughlin 1997: 139–70.

Ward, S., and Lusoli, W. (2005) 'Logging on or Switching off: The Public and the Internet at the 2005 General Election', in S. Coleman and S. Ward (eds.), *Spinning the Web* (London: Hansard Society).

Warshaw, S. A. (1996) *Powersharing: White House Cabinet Relations in the Modern Presidency* (Albany, NY: State University of New York Press).

Watson, A. (1992) *The Evolution of International Society* (London: Routledge).

Watts, R. (1996) *Comparing Federal Systems in the 1990s* (Kingston, Ont.: Institute of Intergovernmental Relations, Queen's University).

—— (1999) *Comparing Federal Systems* (Kingston, Ont.: Institute of Intergovernmental Relations, 2nd edn).

Weaver, R. K., and Rockman, B. A. (1993*a*) 'Assessing the Effects of Institutions', in idem 1993*b*: 1–41.

—— and —— (eds.) (1993*b*) *Do Institutions Matter? Government Capabilities in the United States and Abroad* (Washington, DC: Brookings Institution).

Weber, E. (1976) *Peasants into Frenchmen: The Modernization of Rural France, 1870–1914* (Stanford, Calif.: Stanford University Press).

Weber, M. (1920) *Gesammelte Aufsätze zur Religionssoziologie* (Tübingen: J. C. B. Mohr).

—— (1947) *The Theory of Social and Economic Organization* (New York: Free Press).

—— (1963) *The Sociology of Religion* (Boston: Beacon Press).

—— (1965) *Politics as a Vocation* (Facet Books, Social Ethics Series, 3; New York: Fortress Press).

—— (1978) *Economy and Society: An Outline of Interpretative Sociology* (Berkeley, Calif.: University of California Press, 1st publ. 1922).

Wedeen, L. (2002) 'Conceptualizing Culture: Options for Political Science', *American Political Science Review*, 96: 713–28.

Weiler, J. H. H. (1991) 'The Transformation of Europe', *Yale Law Journal*, 100: 2403–83.

Weingast, B. R. (2002) 'Rational Choice Institutionalism', in I. Katznelson and H. V. Milner (eds.), *The State of the Discipline* (New York and Washington, DC: Norton and American Political Science Association), 660–92.

—— Shepsle, K. A., and Johnsen, C. (1981) 'The Political Economy of Benefits and Costs: A Neoclassical Approach to

Distributive Politics', *Journal of Political Economy*, 89(4): 642–64.

Weiss, L. (1998) *The Myth of the Powerless State* (New York: Cornell University Press).

Wen, D. (2005) *China Copes with Globalization* (San Francisco: International Forum on Globalization).

West, D. M. (2005) *Digital Government: Technology and Public Sector Performance* (Princeton: Princeton University Press).

—— (2006) 'Global E-government 2006', a report produced for Inside Politics.org. Available at www.insidepolitics.org/egovt06int.pdf. Accessed 22 Nov. 2006.

Western, B. (1997) *Between Class and Market: Postwar Unionization in the Capitalist Democracies* (Princeton: Princeton University Press).

Weyland, K. (2004) 'Learning from Foreign Models in Latin American Policy Reform: An Introduction', in idem (ed.), *Learning from Foreign Models in Latin American Policy Reform* (Washington, DC and Baltimore, Md.: Woodrow Wilson Center and Johns Hopkins University Press), 1–34.

—— (2005) 'Theories of Policy Diffusion: Lessons from Latin American Pension Reform', *World Politics*, 57(2): 262–95.

Wheare, K. (1963) *Federal Government* (Oxford: Oxford University Press, 4th edn).

White, S. (2005) 'Russia: The Authoritarian Adaptation of an Electoral System', in Gallagher and Mitchell 2005: 313–30.

Wildavsky, A. (1964) *The Politics of the Budgetary Process* (Boston: Little, Brown).

—— (1997) *But Is It True? Citizen's Guide to Environmental Health and Safety Issues* (Cambridge, Mass.: Harvard University Press).

—— (2004) *Cultural Analysis: Politics, Public Law and Administration* (Somerset, NJ: Transaction Publishers).

Wilensky, H. L. (1975) *The Welfare State and Equality: Structural and Ideological Roots of Public Expenditures* (Berkeley, Calif.: University of California Press).

—— (1981) 'Leftism, Catholicism, and Democratic Corporatism: The Role of Political Parties in Recent Welfare State Development', in P. Flora and A. J. Heidenheimer (eds.), *The Development of Welfare States in Europe and America* (New Brunswick, NJ and London: Transaction), 345–82.

—— and Lebeaux, C. N. (1965) *Industrial Society and Social Welfare: The Impact of Industrialization on the Supply and Organization of Social Welfare Services in the United States* (New York and London: Free Press and Macmillan).

Wilson, G. K. (1979) *Unions in American National Politics* (New York: Macmillan).

—— (1985) *The Politics of Safety and Health: Occupational Safety and Health in the United States and Britain* (New York: Oxford University Press).

—— (1990) *Interest Groups* (Cambridge, Mass.: Blackwell).

Wilson, J. (1983) 'On the Dangers of Bickering in a Federal State: Some Reflections on the Failure of the National Party System', in A. Kornberg and H. Clarke (eds.), *Political Support in Canada: The Crisis Years* (Durham, NC: Duke University Press), 171–222.

Wilson, J. Q. (1973) *Political Organizations* (Beverly Hills, Calif.: Sage).

—— (1974) *Political Organizations* (New York: Basic Books).

—— (1980) *The Politics of Rgulation* (New York: Basic Books).

—— (1989) *Bureaucracy* (New York: Basic Books).

—— (1995) *Political Organizations* (Princeton: Princeton University Press).

Wilthagen, T. (1998) *Flexicurity: A New Paradigm for Labour Market Policy Reform?*, WZB Discussion Paper (Berlin: FSI).

—— Tros, F., and van Lishout, H. (2003) 'Towards "Flexicurity": Balancing Flexicurity and Security in EU Member States', invited paper for the 13th World Congress of IIRA, Berlin, Sept.

Windhoff-Héritier, A. (1980) *Politikimplementation: Ziel und Wirklichkeit politischer Entscheidungen* (Königstein: Anton Hain).

Wiseman, N. (1981) 'The Pattern of Prairie Politics', *Queen's Quarterly*, 88: 298–315.

Woldendorp, J. (2005) *The Poldermodel: From Disease to Miracle?* (Amsterdam: VU Press).

Wolfsfeld, G. (1997) *Media and Political Conflict: News from the Middle East* (Cambridge: Cambridge University Press).

Wolin, S. S. (1989) *The Presence of the Past: Essays on the State and the Constitution* (Baltimore, Md.: Johns Hopkins University Press).

World Bank (2006) *World Development Report 2006* (New York: Oxford University Press).

Wright, J. (1985) 'PACs, Contributions, and Roll Call: An Organizational Perspective', *American Political Science Review*, 79(2): 400–14.

—— (1996) *Interest Groups and Congress: Lobbying, Contributions, and Influence* (Boston: Allyn & Bacon).

Wriston, W. B. (1992) *The Twilight of Sovereignty: How the Information Revolution is Transforming our World* (New York: Charles Scribner's Sons).

Young, L., and Archer, K. (eds.) (2002) *Regionalism and Party Politics in Canada* (Don Mills, Ont.: Oxford University Press).

Youngs, R. (2006) *Survey of European Democracy Promotion Policies 2000–2006* (Madrid: Fundación par alas Relaciones Internacionales y el Diálogo Exterior).

Zacher, M. V. (1992) 'The Decaying Pillars of the Westphalian Temple: Implications for International Order and Governance', in J. N. Rosenau and E.-O. Czempiel (eds.), *Governance without Government: Order and Change in World Politics* (Cambridge: Cambridge University Press), 58–102.

Zakaria, F. (1997) 'The Rise of Illiberal Democracy', *Foreign Affairs*, 76(6): 22–43.

Zartman, W. I. (ed.) (1995) *Collapsed States: The Disintegration and Restauration of Legitimate Authority* (Boulder, Colo.: Lynne Rienner), 1–15.

Zittel, T., and Gschwend, T. (2007) 'Individualisierte Wahlkämpfe im Wahlkreis: Eine Analyse am Beispiel des Bundestagswahlkampfes von 2005', *Politische Vierteljahresschrift*, 48(2): 293–321.

Zürn, M. (1998) *Regieren jenseits des Nationalstaates: Globalisierung und Denationalisierung als Chance* (Frankfurt am Main: Suhrkamp).

——and Leibfried, S. (2005) 'A New Perspective on the State: Reconfiguring the National Constellation', *European Review*, 13(supp. 1): 1–36.

Other Sources

The German Marshall Fund of the US (2005) *Transatlantic Trends 2005*. Available at http://gmfus.org, accessed 3 April 2006.

Afrobarometer (2002) Afrobarometer data, round 1 (see web links).

ANES (2004) American National Election Study 2004 (see web links).

CAWP (2006) Center for American Women and Politics (see web links).

CSES (2006) Comparative Study of Electoral Systems (see web links).

Comparative Study of Electoral Systems, 'CSES Module 2: 2001–2006', www.cses.org, 2005.

Comparative Study of Electoral Systems, 'CSES Module 1: 1996–2001', www.cses.org, 2001.

European Values Study Group and World Values Survey Association, 'European and World Values Surveys Four-Wave Integrated Data File, 1981–2004 (V.20060423)', www.worldvaluessurvey.org, 2006.

Elections in Euskadi (2006) (see the Online Resource Centre).

EUSTAT (2006) Instituto Vasco de Estadística (see web links).

Foreign Policy and Kearney, A. T. (2006) 'The Globalization Index', *Foreign Policy*, November/December: 26–36.

Freedom House (2006) *Freedom in the World 2006: The Annual Survey of Political Rights and Civil Liberties* (Lanham, Md.: Rowman & Littlefield).

Huber, E., Ragin, C., and Stephens, J. D. 'The Comparative Welfare States Data Set', www.lisproject.org/publications/welfaredata/welfareaccess.htm, 1997.

IDEA, International Institute for Democracy and Electoral Assistance, 'Voter Turnout', http://www.idea.int/vt/, 2006.

ILO, 'Statistics of Trade Union Membership: Data for 47 Countries Taken Mainly from National Statistical Publications', 2006.

Inter-Parliamentary Union (2006) 'Women in National Parliaments', (see web links).

NILT (2004) Northern Ireland Life and Times Survey 2004 (see web links).

Index

D

U